CURRENT LAW STATUTES ANNOTATED
1991

VOLUME THREE

AUSTRALIA
The Law Book Company
Sydney

CANADA
The Carswell Company
Toronto, Ontario

INDIA
N. M. Tripathi (Private) Ltd.
Bombay
and
Eastern Law House (Private) Ltd.
Calcutta

M.P.P. House
Bangalore

Universal Book Traders
Delhi

ISRAEL
Steimatzky's Agency Ltd.
Tel Aviv

PAKISTAN
Pakistan Law House
Karachi

CURRENT LAW
STATUTES
ANNOTATED
1991

VOLUME THREE

SWEET & MAXWELL EDITORIAL TEAM
SARAH ANDREWS
CAROLINE EADIE
BARBARA GRANDAGE
PHILIPPA JOHNSON
KATE NICOL
BETHAN OWEN
ROSANNA ROTHERY
ALAN THOMPSON
CLARE TURNER

W. GREEN EDITORIAL TEAM
ELANOR BOWER
ALISON GAY
PETER NICHOLSON
JACQUELINE NORRIE
IAN YOUNG

LONDON

SWEET & MAXWELL

EDINBURGH

W. GREEN

1991

Published by
SWEET & MAXWELL LIMITED
of South Quay Plaza, 183 Marsh Wall, London,
and W. GREEN LIMITED
of 21 Alva Street, Edinburgh,
and printed in Great Britain
by The Bath Press,
Bath, Avon.

ISBN This Volume only : 0 421 46350 3
As a set : 0 421 46370 8

CONTENTS

CHRONOLOGICAL TABLE

VOLUME THREE

VOLUME ONE

c.1. Development Board for Rural Wales Act 1991
2. Caravans (Standard Community Charge and Rating) Act 1991
3. Statutory Sick Pay Act 1991
4. Namibia Act 1991
5. Ministerial and Other Pensions and Salaries Act 1991
6. Census (Confidentiality) Act 1991
7. Consolidated Fund Act 1991
8. Community Charges (Substitute Setting) Act 1991
9. Community Charges (General Reduction) Act 1991
10. Consolidated Fund (No. 2) Act 1991
11. Representation of the People Act 1991
12. Civil Jurisdiction and Judgments Act 1991
13. War Crimes Act 1991
14. Motor Vehicles (Safety Equipment for Children) Act 1991
15. Local Government Finance (Publicity for Auditors' Reports) Act 1991
16. Oversea Superannuation Act 1991
17. Maintenance Enforcement Act 1991
18. Crofter Forestry (Scotland) Act 1991
19. Football (Offences) Act 1991
20. Registered Homes (Amendment) Act 1991
21. Disability Living Allowance and Disability Working Allowance Act 1991
22. New Roads and Street Works Act 1991
23. Children and Young Persons (Protection from Tobacco) Act 1991
24. Northern Ireland (Emergency Provisions) Act 1991
25. Criminal Procedure (Insanity and Unfitness to Plead) Act 1991
26. Road Traffic (Temporary Restrictions) Act 1991
27. Radioactive Material (Road Transport) Act 1991
28. Natural Heritage (Scotland) Act 1991
29. Property Misdescriptions Act 1991
30. Welfare of Animals at Slaughter Act 1991

VOLUME TWO

VOLUME THREE

Contents

MEASURES

INDEX OF SHORT TITLES

STATUTES 1991

(References are to chapter numbers of 1991)

CRIMINAL JUSTICE ACT 1991*

(1991 c. 53)

ARRANGEMENT OF SECTIONS

PART I

POWERS OF COURTS TO DEAL WITH OFFENDERS

Custodial sentences

PART II

EARLY RELEASE OF PRISONERS

Preliminary

---

* Annotations by Rudi Fletcher Fortson, LL.B. (Lond.) of the Middle Temple, Barrister.

PART III

CHILDREN AND YOUNG PERSONS

An Act to make further provision with respect to the treatment of offenders and the position of children and young persons and persons having responsibility for them; to make provision with respect to certain services provided or proposed to be provided for purposes connected with the administration of justice or the treatment of offenders; to make financial and other provision with respect to that administration; and for connected purposes.   [25th July 1991]

PARLIAMENTARY DEBATES
Hansard, H.C. Vol. 181, col. 139; Vol. 183, col. 22; Vol. 186, cols. 287, 678; Vol. 193, 866; Vol. 195, col. 309; H.L. Vol. 527, cols. 73, 848, 960, 988, 1030, 1053, 1349, 1427, 1563, 1617; Vol. 528, cols. 11, 32, 75, 109, 142, 162, 223, 1480, 1564; Vol. 529, cols. 9, 59, 189, 219, 543; Vol. 530, col. 989; Vol. 531, col. 647.
The Bill was considered in Standing Committee A from November 29, 1990 to February 7, 1991.

INTRODUCTION AND GENERAL NOTE

Part I
Described by Earl Ferrers as "one of the most important criminal justice measures of our time" (*Hansard*, Vol. 527, col. 73), the Act endeavours to give legislative force to the Government's proposals set out both in the Green Paper, *Punishment, Custody and the Community* (1988) and in the White Paper *Crime, Justice and Protecting the Public* (Cm. 965). At the heart of these proposals is the Government's stated aim to ensure that convicted criminals "get their just deserts" (para. 2.1), based, in part, on a statutory framework for sentencing intended to achieve a more coherent and comprehensive approach so that sentences are commensurate with the seriousness of the offence. The Act has also been claimed to be a "signal attempt" not at "trying to bolt the door after the penal or criminal horse has escaped but at trying to deal with issues at the root" (*per* John Patten, *Hansard*, H.C. Vol. 186, col. 749). The emphasis has therefore been placed on keeping people out of penal institutions and getting them to operate usefully within the community (*per* Alun Michael, *Official Report*, Standing Committee A, December 11, 1990).
Part I concerns itself with the powers of the courts to deal with offenders. Restrictions are placed on the court's power to impose custodial sentences but Parliament has increased and strengthened the powers of the courts to impose "community sentences" on offenders. The system for early release of prisoners is reformed in Pt. II to ensure that those who are sent to prison will ordinarily spend more of their sentence in custody than at present, and will be supervised on release subject to serving the remainder of their sentence in full if they commit an offence punishable with imprisonment. The way child witnesses and their evidence are to be treated by the courts is dealt with in Pt. III and the Government has also taken the opportunity to enact a framework which may allow the private sector to become involved in the provision of certain services (Pt. IV).

Lord Hutchinson of Lullington has remarked that "it is of overwhelming importance that the philosophy behind the Bill should be observed by the courts. . . . Deciding whether the person should go to prison . . . is not the way from now on that the courts will look upon matters. There are serious ways of dealing with serious offences . . . which have nothing to do with prison" (*Hansard*, H.L. Vol. 528, col. 1499). Thus, if a custodial sentence is imposed, it is to be "commensurate with the seriousness of the offence", with longer sentences reserved in cases of violent or certain sexual offences where there is a need to protect the public from serious harm from the offender (ss.1 and 2). A significant theme of Pt. I of the Act is that the court must focus on the seriousness of the charge before it and not sentence offenders on their criminal past: see the debates in *Hansard*, H.L. Vol. 528, cols. 1480–1504. Accordingly, by s.29 of the Act, an offence shall not be regarded as more serious by reason of any previous convictions of an offender or any failure of his to respond to previous sentences. As will be seen, the rationale of s.29 is that the mere repetition of minor offences by an offender should not ordinarily warrant a custodial sentence because the sentence should be appropriate for the offence before the court. This is not inconsistent with the view of the Court of Appeal: see *R.* v. *Queen* (1981) 3 Cr.App.R.(S) 245; *R.* v. *Thompson* (1989) 4 Cr.App.R. 245; *R.* v. *Davidson* (1989) 11 Cr.App.R. 570. However, the combined effect of s.29, s.31(2) and ss.1 and 2 may lead to conclusions that affront common sense, particularly in relation to multiple offences: see *Hansard*, H.L. Vol. 528, cols. 1492–1504: see also *R.* v. *Howard* (August 24, 1990, unreported) and read the commentary to ss.1, 2 and 29 of the 1991 Act.

Magistrates must also review the way they approach committals for sentence to the Crown Court. Section 38 of the Magistrates' Courts Act 1980 (which gives the power to commit for sentence) originally included the words ". . . if, on obtaining information about his character and antecedents. . . ." Those words have disappeared. Section 38 has been substantially amended to bring the basis for a committal for sentence into line with the thinking of the Act: see s.25.

If Lord Hutchinson is right, and the underlying philosophy of the Act is that the seriousness of the offence is to be determined not by reference to whether a custodial sentence can, or should, be imposed, but by reference to the non-custodial options open to the court, then it is perhaps unfortunate that the Act neither expressly declares that philosophy nor manifestly implies it, in the presentation of statutory provisions within Pt. I. By contrast, in the U.S.A., s.212 of the United States Sentencing Reform Act 1984 specifies "factors to be considered in imposing a sentence" (see also N. Kittrie and E. Zenoff, *Sanctions, Sentencing and Corrections* (1981) Foundation Press, and *Stockdale and Devlin on Sentencing*, Waterlow). This model has not been followed in the 1991 Act. There exists no concise declaration of philsophy, objectives or principles in this Act and suggestions made, in both Houses, for the creation of a Sentencing Council to develop guidance on sentencing have not become a statutory reality (*Hansard*, H.L. Vol. 527, col. 79). Under Pt. I the court is not directed to follow a logical progression of statutory steps from non-custodial options to custody (if appropriate) culminating in a decision. The Act opens with a mandatory provision that the court shall not pass a custodial sentence unless certain statutory criteria are fulfilled. Next, by s.6, a court shall not pass on an offender a "community sentence", *e.g.* a probation order and/or community service order, unless the statutory criteria are fulfilled. Financial penalties are dealt with in ss.17–24 inclusive (see also Sched. 4) and important amendments have been made to the Powers of the Criminal Courts Act 1973 in relation to absolute and conditional discharges (Sched. 1). Partly suspended sentences and extended sentences are abolished: s.5(2).

After an initial reading of Pt. I the reader might be forgiven for wondering to what extent the sentencing policy of the courts will change in the light of these provisions. One explanation for Parliament's approach to Pt. I is to be found in Chapter 2 of the *White Paper*, where it is stated that "No government should try to influence the decisions of the courts in individual cases" and that the "independence of the judiciary is rightly regarded as a cornerstone of our liberties" (para. 2.1). The independence of the judiciary from the executive has often been stressed by the courts to be a matter of considerable constitutional importance (see *British Airways Board* v. *Laker Airways* [1984] Q.B. 142) but the limited basis upon which Parliament has offered guidance on sentencing in previous enactments (see the Powers of the Criminal Courts Act 1973 and the Criminal Justice Acts 1982 and 1988) has probably more to do with disagreement as to the ultimate purpose of a system of sentencing than with a desire to preserve the constitutional concept of the separation of powers: see *Penal Policy-Making in England*, Cambridge Institute of Criminology, and A. Ashworth (NACRO), *A Prison System for the 80s and Beyond*; but see also the *Fifteen Report from the Expenditure Committee* (1978) HMSO, which did endorse the constitutional position. See also the *Reduction of Pressure on the Prison System: Observations* (1980) HMSO (Cm. 7948).

The 1991 Act does go considerably further than previous enactments in offering sentencing guidance but it is questionable to what extent the 1991 Act alters (still less overrules) the guidance offered by the Court of Appeal to sentencers in a series of sentencing decisions, all of which not only considered when custody was appropriate but also suggested the appropriate tariff, *e.g. R.* v. *Bibi* [1980] 1 W.L.R. 1193; *R.* v. *Aramah* (1982) 4 Cr.App.R.(S) 407; *R.* v. *Billam* [1986] 1 W.L.R. 349; *R.* v. *Barrick* (1985) 81 Cr.App.R. 78. Traditionally, Parliament's views on the seriousness of a statutory offence is loosely marked by the "maximum penalty" specified in the enactment but in practice such maxima often afford little or no guidance to the sentencer. Thus, by s.7 of the Theft Act 1968 the maximum sentence for theft was 10 years' imprisonment. It is difficult to envisage a case which would ever attract such a long sentence. Parliament has realistically reduced the maximum to seven years: see s.26(1); see also *R.* v. *Farrugia, Borg, Aguis and Gauchi* (1979) 69 Cr.App.R. 1018. The 1991 Act does not offer any guidance as to how maximum penalties should be viewed.

However, Pt. I of the Act may have indicated a philosophical view in connection with the theory of deterrent sentencing. The Government in their *White Paper* recognised deterrence as having "immediate appeal" but thought it "unrealistic to construct sentencing arrangements on the assumption that most offenders will . . . base their conduct on rational calculation": (para. 2.8). The Court of Appeal has also questioned the value of deterrent sentences: see *R.* v. *Sargeant (James Henry)* (1974) 60 Cr.App.R. 74; *R.* v. *Storey* (1984) 6 Cr.App.R.(S) 104; but see, *contra, R.* v. *Aramah* (1982) 4 Cr.App.R.(S) 407 and *R.* v. *Bilinski* (1987) 86 Cr.App.R. 146. When one looks at the wording of ss.1, 2, 29 and 31(2) (in the context of the remaining provisions of Pt. I) it is difficult to see how the theory of deterrent sentencing has any place within Pt. I, and this seems to accord with the views expressed in the White Paper. Even s.2(2)(b) is intended to do no more than protect the public from serious harm "from the offender". See the notes to s.2(2)(a) below.

As originally drafted, the Bill did not extend the provisions which restrict the imposition of custodial sentences, to persons convicted of offences triable only on indictment and in respect of whom a sentence of imprisonment had previously been passed. This was rectified by the House of Lords so that the provisions apply to all offenders, including those convicted of serious offences who have received a prison sentence in the past. This approach is consistent with the policy of the Act that an offender should not be prejudiced by his antecedent history: see *Hansard*, H.L. Vol. 528, col. 1480.

How, then, is a court to approach a given case? It is submitted that broadly speaking the position is as follows. First, one considers whether the offence can properly be dealt with by way of an absolute or conditional discharge (Sched. 1). If the answer is "no", then one goes on to consider whether it would be appropriate to impose a financial penalty (subject to the provisions affecting magistrates' courts under ss.17–24 inclusive). At this stage one might also need to consider whether the offence is "serious enough" to warrant a "community sentence". Only if the court feels that the offence is "so serious" that "only" a custodial sentence can be justified does the court move on to see if the procedural requirements under ss.1–5 inclusive are fulfilled. If the answer is "no", then the court can only impose non-custodial options.

Life Sentences

Despite the powerfully persuasive and eloquent arguments advanced in the House of Lords to introduce, by amendment, discretionary life sentences in cases of murder (formerly clause 24 of the Bill) the amendment was rejected by the Commons for reasons which many commentators may consider intellectually unconvincing: see *Hansard*, H.L. Vol. 527, col. 1563 and Vol. 527, col. 93; H.C. Vol. 193, col. 866. The debates are significant because the House of Lords attempted to amend the Bill to take account of the findings and recommendations of the *House of Lords Select Committee on Murder and Life Imprisonment* (1989) and the judgment of the European Court on Human Rights in *Thynne, Wilson and Gunnell* v. *U.K., The Independent*, November 2, 1990, E.C.H.R. The Lords amendments would have resulted in a far more radical system for early release in the case of offenders sentenced to life imprisonment than has in fact occurred: see the introductory note to Pt. II of the Act.

Part II

A separate introductory note appears under Part II below. Part II of the Act gives effect to many of the conclusions expressed in the Report of the Review Committee, under the chairmanship of the Rt. Hon. The Lord Carlisle of Bucklow, Q.C., entitled *The Parole System in England and Wales* (1988, Cm. 532). One object of the reforms is to make custodial sentences mean what they say. A selective parole system will operate in cases where the offender has been sentenced to four years' imprisonment or more so that parole eligibility commences at one-half of sentence rather than one-third at present (s.35). All offenders sentenced to less than four years should be required to serve half the sentence in custody (s.33). The Parole Board continues to exist (s.32). Young offenders sentenced under s.53(2) of the Children and Young Persons Act 1933 are effectively brought within the same release and supervision schemes as all other young offenders (s.43).

Part III

Various aspects of the Pigot Report have been given statutory force, including (1) the taking and showing of video recordings of testimony from child witnesses; (2) conditions for admissibility of such recordings; and (3) cross-examination of child witnesses by an advocate (and not by an accused in person: s.55(7) amending s.34 of the Criminal Justice Act 1988). The evidence of children is to be given unsworn (s.52).

Part III also compels the attendance of parents or guardians at court in certain cases (s.56) and increases the incidence of responsibility of parents or guardians in respect of financial penalties (s.57), with further power of the court to bind over a parent or guardian (s.58).

Complaints concerning the remand of children and young persons in unsuitable accommodation have been tackled to some degree in ss.59–62 inclusive.

Parts IV, V and VI

These are set out separately.

PART I

POWERS OF COURTS TO DEAL WITH OFFENDERS

Custodial sentences

Restrictions on imposing custodial sentences

1.—(1) This section applies where a person is convicted of an offence punishable with a custodial sentence other than one fixed by law.

(2) Subject to subsection (3) below, the court shall not pass a custodial sentence on the offender unless it is of the opinion—

(a) that the offence, or the combination of the offence and one other offence associated with it, was so serious that only such a sentence can be justified for the offence; or

(b) where the offence is a violent or sexual offence, that only such a sentence would be adequate to protect the public from serious harm from him.

(3) Nothing in subsection (2) above shall prevent the court from passing a custodial sentence on the offender if he refuses to give his consent to a community sentence which is proposed by the court and requires that consent.

(4) Where a court passes a custodial sentence, it shall be its duty—

(a) in a case not falling within subsection (3) above, to state in open court that it is of the opinion that either or both of paragraphs (a) and (b) of subsection (2) above apply and why it is of that opinion; and

(b) in any case, to explain to the offender in open court and in ordinary language why it is passing a custodial sentence on him.

(5) A magistrates' court shall cause a reason stated by it under subsection (4) above to be specified in the warrant of commitment and to be entered in the register.

DEFINITIONS

"community sentence": s.31(1).
"custodial sentence": s.31(1).
"offence associated with it": s.31(2).
"protect the public from serious harm": s.31(3).
"serious offence": s.29.
"sexual offence": s.31(1).
"violent offence": s.31(1).

GENERAL NOTE

Sections 1, 2, 3, 4, 29, 31(1), 31(2) and 31(3) should be studied together. The aims of these provisions appear to be as follows. First, the court should not pass a custodial sentence on an offender except where such a sentence can be justified. Secondly, the court should focus on the offence before it. Thirdly, an offender should not ordinarily be sentenced on the basis of his antecedent record. Fourthly, sentences imposed which are longer than the term commensurate with the seriousness of the offence (or offences) are to be limited to violent or certain sexual offences where it is necessary to protect the public from serious harm from the offender. Fifthly, the court must ensure that it has sufficient information before it to form any of the opinions as is mentioned in ss.1(2) and 2(2). Sixth, the court must pay further regard to mentally disordered offenders and the likely effect of a custodial sentence on their condition.

Subs. (1)

Section 1 will not apply where the offender is convicted of murder, treason or any other offence where the sentence is fixed by law. The offence may be indictable, summary or triable either way.

Subs. (2)(a)

No court exercising criminal jurisdiction may pass a custodial sentence unless it forms one of two opinions set out in subs. 2(a) or (b). Whereas the court's attention is focused on the *seriousness* of the offence in subs. (2)(a), it would seem that a court is entitled, under subs. (2)(b), to take the view that even if the violent or sexual offence is not particularly serious in itself, nevertheless only a custodial sentence would be adequate "to protect the public from serious harm" from the offender.

Subs. (2)(a) and (4) impose an obligation on the sentencer to give reasons in open court to "justify" a custodial sentence on grounds relating to the seriousness of the offence. If the words "or the combination of the offence and one other offence associated with it" had not been included in s.1(2)(a) then it would have been plain that seriousness was related solely to the offence before the court. This would clearly reflect the Government's view that "people who commit minor offences, even if committed in considerable numbers, should not necessarily be sent to prison": *per* Earl Ferrers, *Hansard*, H.L. Vol. 528, col. 1501; see also *R.* v. *Roberts* (1987) 9 Cr.App.R.(S.) 152. The problem of multiple offences raises difficult issues. As Lord Ackner has pointed out (*Hansard*, H.L. Vol. 528, col. 1492), if D steals £100 per week from his employers and thereby acquires £10,000, is the court constrained to look at the one or two specimen counts alleging the theft of £200 and to form an opinion under s.1(2)(a) on that narrow basis? Technical rules prevent counts being drafted on an indictment which are either duplicitous, rolled-up or too numerous. Yet if the court goes on to consider the length of a custodial sentence, then, by s.2(2)(a), the sentencer may impose a length commensurate with "the offence" and "other offences" (not just one) associated with the offence. Is Parliament applying a double standard as between s.1(2)(a) and s.2(2)(a)? The Parliamentary thinking behind s.1(2)(a) would seem to be that it is for the indictment to contain appropriate counts to reflect the seriousness of the offence and that s.1 raises merely a *preliminary question* as to whether a custodial sentence is appropriate. Section 31(2) defines an offence "associated with another" to include cases where the offender admits the commission of another offence which he wishes to be taken into consideration. However, s.31(2) presupposes either the existence of a conviction (s.32(2)(a)), or a formal admission of guilt which may not be forthcoming (s.32(2)(b)). Earl Ferrers explained the Government's reasons for including the words "and one other offence" by reference to s.1 of the Criminal Justice Act 1982 as amended by s.123 of the Criminal Justice Act 1988, which prevented a court from passing a custodial sentence on a young offender where the "offence of which he has been convicted . . . was so serious that a non-custodial sentence for it cannot be justified." Earl Ferrers stated (*Hansard*, H.L. Vol. 528, col. 1501) that "there are bound to be borderline cases. That is what the reference to 'one other offence' is meant to address . . . the two offences concerned would have to be relatively serious individually before, taken together, they would justify a custodial sentence. . . . The provision therefore allows a second offence to tip the balance between a custodial sentence and a community penalty in a borderline case . . . ". A little later Earl Ferrers cited what is now s.3(3)(a) (circumstances of the offence to be taken into account) and said "Those may well include the fact that the offences were planned, were persistent, and were committed in breach of trust" (*Hansard*, H.L. Vol. 528, col. 1502).

It is submitted that reference to the "combination of the offence and one other offence" is an unhelpful if not irrelevant concept if it was designed to do no more than tip the balance in borderline cases. As worded it does not address the problem of multiple offences as analysed by Lord Ackner and other members of the House of Lords. It is also debatable whether s.3(3)(a) can be construed so as to include "persistent offending"—as suggested by Earl Ferrers— particularly where guilt (in respect of other offences) has not either been proved in respect of counts on the indictment, or formally admitted (*e.g.* by way of offences to be taken into consideration); and see *R.* v. *Howard* (August 24, 1990, unreported), cited by Lord Ackner (*Hansard*, H.L. Vol. 528, col. 1503; see also s.29(2) of the 1991 Act, and consider the approach taken in *R.* v. *Bragson* [1988] Crim.L.R. 778; *R.* v. *Nicholson* [1990] Crim.L.R. 530; *R.* v. *Saunders* (1991) 92 Cr.App.R. 6; *Reeves (R.J.)* (1983) 5 Cr.App.R.(S.) 292.

Offence . . . so serious. These words have already been considered by the courts in relation to the provisions under the Criminal Justice Act 1982 as amended by s.123 of the 1988 Act. In *R.* v. *Bradbourn* (1985) 7 Cr.App.R.(S.) 180 the Court of Appeal described "so serious" as being referable to the sort of case in which right-thinking members of the public knowing all the facts would feel that justice had not been done by the passing of any sentence other than a custodial one: see also *R.* v. *Howard, ante*; *R.* v. *Munday* (1985) 7 Cr.App.R.(S.) 216; and *R.* v. *Fleming and Dodge* (1985) 6 Cr.App.R.(S.) 222. See also the remarks of Lord Lane C.J. in *R.* v. *Scott* (*Tracey*) (1990) 12 Cr.App.R.(S.).

Under the 1991 Act, Parliament offers no real guidance as to the meaning of the word "serious" except that an offence is not to be regarded as "more serious" by reason of any previous convictions of the offender or any failure of his to respond to previous sentences (s.29(1)). This conflicts to some extent with sentiments expressed by Parliament in earlier enactments: see s.1(4A) of the 1982 Act (as amended by s.123 of the 1988 Act). By s.29(2) of the 1991 Act, the court is entitled to take into account "aggravating factors of an offence disclosed by the circumstances of other offences committed by the offender . . .". Presumably these could include persistent use of a weapon for systematic attacks on people and/or property and so on. Reconciling the ambit of s.29((1) and (2) is not straightforward.

Subs. (4)
It is rare indeed for a judge of the Crown Court not to give reasons when sentencing but there is a trend towards requiring magistrates to give their reasons. Nothing in the 1991 Act suggests that a sentence will be invalidated merely because the court fails to give any (or adequate) reasons, presumably because the remedy of the accused is to appeal (*R.* v. *Chesterfield Justices*, ex p. *Hewitt* [1973] Crim.L.R. 181).

Length of custodial sentences

2.—(1) This section applies where a court passes a custodial sentence other than one fixed by law.

(2) The custodial sentence shall be—

(a) for such term (not exceeding the permitted maximum) as in the opinion of the court is commensurate with the seriousness of the offence, or the combination of the offence and other offences associated with it; or

(b) where the offence is a violent or sexual offence, for such longer term (not exceeding that maximum) as in the opinion of the court is necessary to protect the public from serious harm from the offender.

(3) Where the court passes a custodial sentence for a term longer than is commensurate with the seriousness of the offence, or the combination of the offence and other offences associated with it, the court shall—

(a) state in open court that it is of the opinion that subsection (2)(b) above applies and why it is of that opinion; and

(b) explain to the offender in open court and in ordinary language why the sentence is for such a term.

(4) A custodial sentence for an indeterminate period shall be regarded for the purposes of subsections (2) and (3) above as a custodial sentence for a term longer than any actual term.

DEFINITIONS
"custodial sentence": s.31(1).
"offence associated with it": s.31(2).
"protect the public from serious harm": s.31(3).
"serious offence": s.29.
"sexual offence": s.31(1).
"violent offence": s.31(1).

Subs. (1)
Again, s.2 applies to offences other than murder, treason or any other offence when a custodial sentence is fixed by law.

Subs. (2)(a)
Section 2 should be read in conjunction with ss.1, 3, 4, 29 and 31(1), (2) and (3). Once the

court forms one of two opinions mentioned in s.1(2) it must then go on to consider the length of sentence, subject to the restrictions set out in s.2(2)(a).

The overriding principle in s.2(2) is that the length should be no more than is necessary to mark the gravity (or seriousness) of the offence. Whereas, in s.1(2), the court is constrained to form an opinion based on "the offence" and only *one* other offence "associated with it" the court is entitled under s.2(2)(a) to take a global view. Why the court cannot take a global view in relation to s.1(2) is difficult to understand. In so far as it is relevant to look at the combination of the offence, and associated offences, the language of s.2(2)(a) makes it plain that the court's attention must remain focused on the offence before it. Significantly, s.2(2)(a) opens with a mandatory requirement, *i.e.* that the custodial sentence *shall be* commensurate with the seriousness of the offence. On one extreme interpretation those words might be thought to restrict the court's ability to take into account factors which had previously been regarded as good mitigation. Thus, if 10 years' imprisonment is commensurate with the seriousness of a particular armed robbery, is a court entitled to pass a sentence of only five years on the basis of assistance given by the offender to the police?

Section 28 makes it plain that the court may take into account all matters relevant in mitigation of sentence and that the court may have regard to the totality of sentences. Accordingly, although the court must begin by determining the length which is "commensurate with the seriousness" of the offence it is obvious that the sentence actually passed may seem to a lay person to fall short of that objective.

Seriousness of the offence. The Government's White Paper *Crime, Justice and Protecting the Public* (Cm. 965) states that convicted criminals are to get "their just deserts" (para. 2.1). The 1991 Act does not offer statutory guidance at all as to how this "concept" is to be approached. Section 29 states that an offence shall not be regarded as more serious by reason of any previous convictions of an offender, but circumstances of previous offences may be taken into account if they disclose aggravating features in the offence to be dealt with (s.29(2)).

Para 2.4 in the White Paper suggests that "Punishment can effectively denounce criminal behaviour and exact retribution for it . . . if the punishment is just, and in proportion to the seriousness of the offence . . . there will be no desire for further retaliation or private revenge". The Government thought it "unrealistic to construct sentencing arrangements" based on the deterrence principle (para. 2.8) and considered that the "first objective for all sentences is denunciation of and retribution for the crime" (para. 2.9). "The Government will look to the Judicial Studies Board to make arrangements for training sentencers to give effect to the new sentencing policies, and the more detailed interpretation of the legislation, by the Court of Appeal" (para. 2.20).

It is questionable whether s.2(2)(a) legislates any philosophy of punishment at all. It may embrace the nebulous *theory of retribution,* whether in the guise of vengeance or reprobation (read *Sentences of Imprisonment: A Review of Maximum Penalties* (1978) HMSO; *Do Sentences Affect Public Disapproval?:* British Journal of Criminology, Walker and Marsh, Vol. 24, p. 27; and read the speech of the Lord Bishop of Liverpool (*Hansard,* H.L. Vol. 527, col. 91; see also *R.* v. *Sargeant* (1974) 60 Cr.App.R. 74). In any event, the courts already do mark the nature and gravity of the offence and public disapprobation of the offence: *R.* v. *Jacob* (1981) 3 Cr.App.R.(S.) 298.

Arguably, the theory of deterrent sentencing is not compatible with the wording of s.2(2)(a) in that if a given offence has its "worth" then a sentence of imprisonment cannot be "commensurate" with that value if a longer sentence is imposed to deter others. In that eventuality the offender gets not just *his* deserts but also someone else's. Sentences imposed on drug traffickers often have a deterrent element to them: see the sentencing guidelines given in *R.* v. *Aramah* (1982) 4 Cr.App.R.(S.) 407; *R.* v. *Bilinski* (1988) 86 Cr.App.R. 146. Can these cases now stand with the "spirit" of the 1991 Act?

What is plain, from the juxtaposition of s.2(2)(a) and (b), is that the only basis for imposing a term longer than would otherwise be commensurate with the offence is the protection of the public from serious harm from the offender in cases of violence or certain sexual offences. To impose a longer sentence merely because the offender is a persistent "social nuisance" is not permitted under the 1991 Act. In any event, as Lawton L.J. remarked in *R.* v. *King and Simpkins* (1973) 57 Cr.App.R. 696, "the Court has to bear in mind that in our system of jurisprudence there is no offence known as being an enemy of society".

Commensurate . . . with the offence. Nothing in the 1991 Act changes the principle that an accused is entitled to be sentenced on the basis of what is proved or formally admitted: *R.* v. *Wishart* (1979) 1 Cr.App.R.(S.) 322; *R.* v. *Mitchell* (1982) 4 Cr.App.R.(S.) 277; *R.* v. *Lawless* [1981] Crim.L.R. 845; *R.* v. *Lawrence* (1981) 3 Cr.App.R.(S.) 49; *R.* v. *Ayensu and Ayensu* (1982) 4 Cr.App.R.(S.) 248; *R.* v. *O'Conner* (1981) 3 Cr.App.R.(S.) 225. The trial judge may still determine questions of fact relevant to mitigation in accordance with the principle in *R.* v. *Newton* (1983) Cr.App.R. 13, and see s.29 of the Act; see also *R.* v. *Boyer* (1981) 3 Cr.App.R. (S.) 35; *R.* v. *Bragson* [1988] Crim.L.R. 778; *R.* v. *Nicholson* [1990] Crim.L.R. 530;

R. v. *Reeves (R.J.)* (1983) 5 Cr.App.R.(S.) 292; *R.* v. *Fisher* (1981) 3 Cr.App.R.(S.) 313.

The judge is still also entitled to differentiate between the rôles played by two or more defendants: *R.* v. *Michaels and Skoblo* (1981) 3 Cr.App.R.(S.) 188.

Regard must also be had to the totality of the sentences imposed: see s.28(2)(b) and *R.* v. *French* (1982) 4 Cr.App.R.(S.) 57.

However, difficulties may arise where the prosecution choose to bring specimen counts: see notes to s.1 above; but see also *D.P.P.* v. *Anderson* [1978] A.C. 964; *R.* v. *Price* (1978) 68 Cr.App.R.154; *R.* v. *McKenzie* (D.A.) (1984) 6 Cr.App.R.(S.) 99; *R.* v. *Burfoot* (1990) 12 Cr.App.R.(S.) 252.

Subs. (2)(b)

The basis for imposing a custodial sentence in this category relates, it would seem, not necessarily to the seriousness of the offence itself but to the magnitude of risk of serious harm to the public from the offender. "Violent offence" is defined by s.31(1) to include arson (whether or not with intent to endanger life) and may, perhaps, be construed as embracing the administering of a noxious substance or (arguably) the unlawful supplying of heroin or LSD to another. The relevant sexual offences are restricted to the offences set out in s.31(12) and the section meets many of the complaints raised by homosexuals during the course of the Parliamentary Debates in respect of what was then known as "Clause 25".

"Protecting the public from serious harm from the offender" is defined by s.31(3). Why the phrase "members of the public" was adopted in favour of "any person" is unclear. One hopes that the courts will not be asked to construe "members of the public" as excluding any other group of persons who might be affected by the acts of the offender.

One complaint levelled against this provision is that it contains a highly subjective and speculative element: namely that a decision is based "not on what the offender has done, but on the judge's guess as to what he might do in the future" (NACRO, and see *Hansard*, H.L. Vol. 527, col. 81), see also *R.* v. *Parsley* (1990) 12 Cr.App.R.(S.).

Note the requirements of ss.3 and 4.

Note too that ss.20 and 20A of the Powers of the Criminal Courts Act 1973 are repealed by s.101(2) and Sched. 13.

Procedural requirements for custodial sentences

3.—(1) Subject to subsection (2) below, a court shall obtain and consider a pre-sentence report before forming any such opinion as is mentioned in subsection (2) of section 1 or 2 above.

(2) Where the offence or any other offence associated with it is triable only on indictment, subsection (1) above does not apply if, in the circumstances of the case, the court is of the opinion that it is unnecessary to obtain a pre-sentence report.

(3) In forming any such opinion as is mentioned in subsection (2) of section 1 or 2 above a court—

  (a) shall take into account all such information about the circumstances of the offence (including any aggravating or mitigating factors) as is available to it; and

  (b) in the case of any such opinion as is mentioned in paragraph (b) of that subsection, may take into account any information about the offender which is before it.

(4) No custodial sentence which is passed in a case to which subsection (1) above applies shall be invalidated by the failure of a court to comply with that subsection but any court on an appeal against such a sentence—

  (a) shall obtain a pre-sentence report if none was obtained by the court below; and

  (b) shall consider any such report obtained by it or by that court.

(5) In this Part "pre-sentence report" means a report in writing which—

  (a) with a view to assisting the court in determining the most suitable method of dealing with an offender, is made or submitted by a probation officer or by a social worker of a local authority social services department; and

  (b) contains information as to such matters, presented in such manner, as may be prescribed by rules made by the Secretary of State.

DEFINITIONS
"offence associated with it: s.31(2).
"pre-sentence report": subs. (5) and s.31(1).

GENERAL NOTE
As a matter of common sense, if a court is to form a proper opinion or conclusion in respect of matters mentioned in ss.1(2) and 2(2), it needs as much information as necessary about the offence and the offender. Certain offences, triable only on indictment, may be so patently serious that the court has ample information to proceed to sentence without wasting time and resources obtaining a pre-sentence report. Where there is evidence that the offender appears to be mentally disordered then the court must comply with s.4.

Additional requirements in the case of mentally disordered offenders

4.—(1) Subject to subsection (2) below, in any case where section 3(1) above applies and the offender is or appears to be mentally disordered, the court shall obtain and consider a medical report before passing a custodial sentence other than one fixed by law.

(2) Subsection (1) above does not apply if, in the circumstances of the case, the court is of the opinion that it is unnecessary to obtain a medical report.

(3) Before passing a custodial sentence other than one fixed by law on an offender who is or appears to be mentally disordered, a court shall consider—

(a) any information before it which relates to his mental condition (whether given in a medical report, a pre-sentence report or otherwise); and

(b) the likely effect of such a sentence on that condition and on any treatment which may be available for it.

(4) No custodial sentence which is passed in a case to which subsection (1) above applies shall be invalidated by the failure of a court to comply with that subsection, but any court on an appeal against such a sentence—

(a) shall obtain a medical report if none was obtained by the court below; and

(b) shall consider any such report obtained by it or by that court.

(5) In this section—

"duly approved," in relation to a registered medical practitioner, means approved for the purposes of section 12 of the Mental Health Act 1983 ("the 1983 Act") by the Secretary of State as having special experience in the diagnosis or treatment of mental disorder;

"medical report" means a report as to the offenders' mental condition made or submitted orally or in writing by a registered medical practitioner who is duly approved.

(6) Nothing in this section shall be taken as prejudicing the generality of section 3 above.

DEFINITIONS
"custodial sentence": s.31(1).
"medical report": subs. (5).
"mentally disordered": s.31(1).
"pre-sentence report": s.31(1).

GENERAL NOTE
Section 4 should be read in conjunction with ss.27 and 28(4). These sections are the product of amendments introduced in the House of Lords during the Committee stage and the Third Reading of the Bill (see *Hansard*, H.L. Vol. 527, col. 1053; Vol. 529, cols. 566, 572 and 576; see also Second List of Amendments, April 12, 1991, Nos. 23, 24, 25 and 26).

The provisions are designed to go some way towards ensuring that people who ought to be receiving health or social services treatment do not find themselves in prison. Several members of the House of Lords favoured a prescriptive approach imposing a mandatory obligation on the court not to pass a custodial sentence on an offender suffering from mental illness (see

Amendment 23). The Government's priority, however, has been to establish a practical framework to give legislative encouragement to the number of steps already being taken to improve the position of mentally disordered offenders. The legislature's hope is that it will be possible to develop a national scheme by which duty psychiatrists are available to attend court and give an oral report without the need for remand in custody (*per* Earl Ferrers, *Hansard,* H.L. Vol. 527, col. 1053; and see Home Office Circular 66/90). Sections 4, 27 and 28 have been enacted prior to the findings of a Review Committee, examining health and social services for mentally disordered offenders, and due to report in 1992.

The medical report must be made by a suitably qualified practitioner (s.4(5)) and should not form part of the pre-sentence report, since a pre-sentence report can only be made in writing.

The exception provided in s.4(2) seems primarily intended to cover cases where there is sufficient information before the court about the offender's mental state.

The new s.39A of the Mental Health Act 1983 (see s.27) is intended to enable the courts to acquire better information about the facilities available for guardianship of hospital treatment and to facilitate the tightening-up of the time limits for the admission to hospital of mentally disordered offenders.

Despite the provisions of ss.1 and 2, Parliament, by s.28(4), expressly provides that a court is not required to pass a custodial sentence, or any particular custodial sentence, on a mentally disordered offender because prison may not be suitable for such cases. The court is obliged under s.4(3)(b) to consider the effect a custodial sentence would have on the offender. Note the advice recently given in the Home Office Circular 66/90, and see *Hansard,* H.L. Vol. 527, col. 1350.

Suspended and extended sentences of imprisonment 1973 c.62

5.—(1) For subsection (2) of section 22 (suspended sentences of imprisonment) of the Powers of Criminal Courts Act 1973 ("the 1973 Act") there shall be substituted the following subsections—

"(2) A court shall not deal with an offender by means of a suspended sentence unless it is of the opinion—

    (a) that the case is one in which a sentence of imprisonment would have been appropriate even without the power to suspend the sentence; and

    (b) that the exercise of that power can be justified by the exceptional circumstances of that case.

(2A) A court which passes a suspended sentence on any person for an offence shall consider whether the circumstances of the case are such as to warrant in addition the imposition of a fine or the making of a compensation order."

(2) The following shall cease to have effect, namely—

    (a) sections 28 and 29 of the 1973 Act (extended sentences of imprisonment for persistent offenders); and

    (b) section 47 of the Criminal Law Act 1977 (sentence of imprisonment partly served and partly suspended).

GENERAL NOTE

Subs. (1)

The power to suspend a sentence of imprisonment was given by s.22(1) of the Powers of Criminal Court Act 1973. Such a sentence was to be treated as a sentence of imprisonment by s.22(2) of the 1973 Act. However, since the Criminal Justice Act 1982 the court has had no power to suspend a custodial sentence on offenders under 21. Research suggests that this change has undermined the value of this option and that the sentence was not always appropriately deployed: see *The Parole System in England and Wales* 1988; (Cm. 531). In the White Paper the Government took the view that the suspended sentence does not fit easily into the proposed new sentencing arrangements but recognised its value (para. 3.21). Whereas the suspended term was originally seen as an effective method of preventing the offender from re-offending, it now seems (by s.5(2)(a)) that the court must not only justify its imposition, but also do so only where the circumstances are "exceptional". It may be that Parliament hopes that the courts will thus be encouraged to impose a community sentence on an offender rather than a suspended sentence which the public may see as a "let off" (see para. 3.22 of the White Paper). If this was the intended message, then the phrase "exceptional circumstances" is unhelpful, if not meaningless. Many mitigating factors give rise to exceptional circumstances on the facts of a particular case. How can it be ensured that the courts will approach this provision consistently? Once the court forms the opinion that a custodial sentence is justified, it will be difficult for the court to reach the seemingly contradictory decision that the term can in fact be suspended, or even abandoned, in favour of a non-custodial sentence. An amendment moved in the House of Lords, in favour of the abolition of the suspended sentence, was withdrawn: *Hansard,* H.L. Vol. 527, cols. 1367–1377.

Subs. (2)
Extended and partly suspended sentences have been abolished following the reasoning and recommendations of the Review Committee (*The Parole System in England and Wales,* 1988, Cm. 532).

Community sentences

Restrictions on imposing community sentences

6.—(1) A court shall not pass on an offender a community sentence, that is to say, a sentence which consists of or includes one or more community orders, unless it is of the opinion that the offence, or the combination of the offence and one other offence associated with it, was serious enough to warrant such a sentence.

(2) Subject to subsection (3) below, where a court passes a community sentence—

    (a) the particular order or orders comprising or forming part of the sentence shall be such as in the opinion of the court is, or taken together are, the most suitable for the offender; and

    (b) the restrictions on liberty imposed by the order or orders shall be such as in the opinion of the court are commensurate with the seriousness of the offence, or the combination of the offence and other offences associated with it.

(3) In consequence of the provision made by section 11 below with respect to combination orders, a community sentence shall not consist of or include both a probation order and a community service order.

(4) In this Part "community order" means any of the following orders, namely—

    (a) a probation order;

    (b) a community service order;

    (c) a combination order;

    (d) a curfew order;

    (e) a supervision order; and

    (f) an attendance centre order.

DEFINITIONS
    "commensurate": see notes to s.2 above.
    "community orders": s.6(4); 31(1).
    "community sentence": s.31(1).
    "curfew order": s.31(1).
    "other offence associated with it": s.31(2).
    "supervision order": s.3(1).

GENERAL NOTE
    Parliament's clear view is that more offenders should be punished in the community and that custody should not be seen as the only "real" punishment—a view reinforced by the cliché "alternatives to custody" (see para. 4.1 of *Crime, Justice and Protecting the Public,* 1990, Cm. 965). The "community sentence" may (subject to ss.6(3) and 11) be comprised of one or more "community orders", the effect of which places restrictions on an offender's liberty and requires a commitment, backed up by sanctions (see s.14(1) and Sched. 2) and covering what may be a lengthy period. By combining "community orders", Parliament believes that the courts will have at their disposal a range of sentences to "reflect the concept of graduated restrictions on liberty" (para. 4.7, *ibid.*) and thus enable offenders to get their "just deserts".
    The court is required to go through two broad stages. First, to determine whether the offence is "serious enough" (s.6(1)) to warrant a community sentence, or whether the offence is "so serious" (s.1(2)(a)) that only a custodial sentence can be justified. Secondly, if an opinion is formed under s.6(1), the court must pass such a sentence, which not only reflects the serious-

ness of the offence (s.6(2)(b)) but which is also the most suitable sentence for the offender: s.6(2)(a). The court will therefore need to consider the offender; the victim; the nature of the offence (s.7); the totality of the punishment (s.28(2)); mitigating (s.7 and 28) as well as aggravating factors (ss.7 and 29(2)) but the offender should not, in the ordinary way, be sentenced on the basis of his previous convictions (s.29(1) but *cf.* s.29(2)).

In addition to the imposition of a "community sentence", the court may also impose financial penalties, award compenstion or forfeit or confiscate property by virtue of any enactment.

Although a probation order and a community service order are both "community orders", they cannot be combined or form part of a community sentence; s.6(3). This is because s.11, by virtue of a separate order, empowers a court to direct that an offender (of or over 16 years of age) must perform unpaid work and be supervised by a probation officer in cases where the offender needs to be rehabilitated (s.11(2)(a)) or where the public need to be protected from harm from him or to prevent the commission by him of further offences: s.11(2)(b).

By s.8(1), s.2 of the Powers of Criminal Courts Act 1973 is amended so that a probation order is now a sentence. The terms of such an order can now be considerably strengthened to deal with persistent, as well as first-time offenders: see Sched. 1, Pt. II.

Day centres will now be called "probation centres": para. 3(7)(a) of Sched. 1 to the 1991 Act.

Procedural requirements for community sentences

7.—(1) In forming any such opinion as is mentioned in subsection (1) or (2)(b) of section 6 above, a court shall take into account all such information about the circumstances of the offence (including any aggravating or mitigating factors) as is available to it.

(2) In forming any such opinion as is mentioned in subsection (2)(a) of that section, a court may take into account any information about the offender which is before it.

(3) A court shall obtain and consider a pre-sentence report before forming an opinion as to the suitability for the offender of one or more of the following orders, namely—

(a) a probation order which includes additional requirements authorised by Schedule 1A to the 1973 Act;

(b) a community service order;

(c) a combination order; and

(d) a supervision order which includes requirements imposed under section 12, 12A, 12AA, 12B or 12C of the Children and Young Persons Act 1969 ("the 1969 Act").

(4) No community sentence which consists of or includes such an order as is mentioned in subsection (3) above shall be invalidated by the failure of a court to comply with that subsection, but any court on an appeal against such a sentence—

(a) shall obtain a pre-sentence report if none was obtained by the court below; and

(b) shall consider any such report obtained by it or by that court.

DEFINITIONS
   "combination order": s.11; s.31(1).
   "community sentence": s.6(1); s.31(1).
   "community service order": s.10.
   "pre-sentence report": s.3(5); s.31(1).
   "probation order": s.8.

Probation and community service orders

Probation orders

8.—(1) For section 2 of the 1973 Act there shall be substituted the following section—

"Probation

Probation orders

2.—(1) Where a court by or before which a person of or over the age of sixteen years is convicted of an offence (not being an offence for which the sentence is fixed by law) is of the opinion that the supervision of the offender by a probation officer is desirable in the interests of—

    (a) securing the rehabilitation of the offender; or

    (b) protecting the public from harm from him or preventing the commission by him of further offences,

the court may make a probation order, that is to say, an order requiring him to be under the supervision of a probation officer for a period specified in the order of not less than six months nor more than three years.

For the purposes of this subsection the age of a person shall be deemed to be that which it appears to the court to be after considering any available evidence.

(2) A probation order shall specify the petty sessions area in which the offender resides or will reside; and the offender shall, subject to paragraph 12 of Schedule 2 to the Criminal Justice Act 1991 (offenders who change their residence), be required to be under the supervision of a probation officer appointed for or assigned to that area.

(3) Before making a probation order, the court shall explain to the offender in ordinary language—

    (a) the effect of the order (including any additional requirements proposed to be included in the order in accordance with section 3 below);

    (b) the consequences which may follow under Schedule 2 to the Criminal Justice Act 1991 if he fails to comply with any of the requirements of the order; and

    (c) that the court has under that Schedule power to review the order on the application either of the offender or of the supervising officer,

and the court shall not make the order unless he expresses his willingness to comply with its requirements.

(4) The court by which a probation order is made shall forthwith give copies of the order to a probation officer assigned to the court, and he shall give a copy—

    (a) to the offender;

    (b) to the probation officer responsible for the offender's supervision; and

    (c) to the person in charge of any institution in which the offender is required by the order to reside.

(5) The court by which such an order is made shall also, except where it itself acts for the petty sessions area specified in the order, send to the clerk to the justices for that area—

    (a) a copy of the order; and

    (b) such documents and information relating to the case as it considers likely to be of assistance to a court acting for that area in the exercise of its functions in relation to the order.

(6) An offender in respect of whom a probation order is made shall keep in touch with the probation officer responsible for his supervision in accordance with such instructions as he may from time to time be given by that officer and shall notify him of any change of address.

(7) The Secretary of State may by order direct that subsection (1) above shall be amended by substituting, for the minimum or maximum period specified in that subsection as originally enacted or as previously amended under this subsection, such period as may be specified in the order.

(8) An order under subsection (7) above may make in paragraph 12(2)(a)(i) of Schedule 2 to the Criminal Justice Act 1990 any amend-

ment which the Secretary of State thinks necessary in consequence of any substitution made by the order."

(2) Section 13 of that Act (effect of probation and discharge) shall cease to have effect so far as relating to offenders placed on probation.

(3) For the purpose of rearranging Part I of that Act in consequence of the amendments made by subsections (1) and (2) above, that Part shall have effect subject to the following amendments, namely—

(a) after section 1 there shall be inserted as sections 1A to 1C the provisions set out in Part I of Schedule 1 to this Act;

(b) sections 7 and 9 (which are re-enacted with minor modifications by sections 1A and 1B) shall cease to have effect;

(c) sections 8 and 13 (which, so far as relating to discharged offenders, are re-enacted with minor modifications by sections 1B and 1C) shall cease to have effect so far as so relating; and

(d) immediately before section 11 there shall be inserted the following cross heading—

"Probation and discharge"

GENERAL NOTE

The *Report of the Departmental Committee on the Probation Service*, 1962, HMSO (Cm. 1650) expressed the traditional view that probation both minimised the restrictions placed upon the offender while offering him the help of society in adjusting his conduct to its demands. Accordingly, a probation order was not to be seen as a sentence of the court: ss.2 and 13 of the Powers of the Criminal Courts Act 1973. Requirements made of an offender could not be punitive in nature (s.2(3) of the 1973 Act) or be oppressive (see also *Cullen* v. *Rogers* [1982] 1 W.L.R. 729). The court could impose requirements which it considered necessary for securing the good conduct of the offender or for preventing the repetition by him of the same offence or the commission of other offences (s.2(3) of the 1973 Act). Accordingly, courts could require an offender to participate in certain activities or to refrain from various activities: see s.4(A) of the 1973 Act.

Although probation has often been viewed as being ideally suited to the first-time offender (because the prospects of rehabilitation are then most favourable) the courts have increasingly used probation orders in the case of recidivists at the right psychological moment: *R.* v. *Weston* [1967] Crim.L.R. 377, or where the offender may respond to, and benefit from, assistance and supervision: *R.* v. *Heather* (1979) 1 Cr.App.R.(S.) 189; see also *R.* v. *Bradley* (1983) 5 Cr.App.R.(S.) 363.

The Government, in *Crime, Justice and Protecting the Public*, 1990, Cm. 965, considered that the probation order could be employed as a penalty making significant demands on the offender (para. 4.10). By ss.8, 9, 11 of and Sched. 1 to the 1991 Act, Parliament has considerably revised the nature of the probation order so that it is now a sentence which may be combined with financial penalties. The court's powers, in terms both of imposing conditions and of monitoring/ enforcing probation orders, have been significantly clarified and strengthened. No order may be made without the offender's consent (s.2(3) of the 1973 Act). The commission of a further offence will not be a breach of the order but a separate matter: Sched. 2, para. 8.

See also H.C. Standing Committee A, December 13, 1990 (a.m.) pp. 205–229 (*Hansard*, H.L. Vol. 527, cols. 1403–1414).

Section 2(1) of the 1973 Act

The requisite age is now 16 years (formerly 17). The stated aim in subs. (1) is no longer merely rehabilitation but includes protecting the public from the persistent offender. The relevant statutory period (six months to three years) may be amended by the Secretary of State: s.2(7) of the 1973 Act.

Section 2(2) of the 1973 Act

The petty sessions area where the offender resides is relevant for two reasons. First, the offender will be under the supervision of a probation order appointed for that area: s.2(2). Secondly, it is the magistrates' court for that area which will monitor/enforce the order. Accordingly, where the offender changes address, the magistrates' court *may* (or, on application by the responsible officer, *shall*) amend the order by substituting the appropriate petty sessions area: Sched. 2, para. 12(2); this is another reason why the offender must notify the probation officer of his change of address (s.2(6) of the 1973 Act). A copy of the order and other relevant information should be sent to the appropriate clerk to the justices for that area: s.2(5) of the 1973 Act.

Section 2(3) of the 1973 Act

A similar provision was formerly found in s.2(6) of the 1973 Act as originally drafted.

The consequences flowing from a breach or failure to comply with the order are considered in s.14 of and Sched. 2 to the 1991 Act (see also the notes to s.12, below).

A probation order cannot be made without the offender expressing the willingness to consent to the order. In reality, the offender who refuses to give his consent exposes himself to the danger of receiving a custodial sentence for the reasons set out in s.1(3) of the 1991 Act (note also *R.* v. *Marquis* [1974] 1 W.L.R. 1087). If, having given his consent, the offender wilfully and persistently fails to comply with the requirements of the order, the court *may* assume that he has "refused to give his consent to a community sentence" and deal with him accordingly: see Sched. 2, paras. 3(2)(b) and 4(2)(b) of the 1991 Act and note the significance of such an assumption in terms of the application s.1(3).

Additional requirements which may be included in such orders

9.—(1) For sections 3 to 4B of the 1973 Act there shall be substituted the following section—

> **"Additional requirements which may be included in such orders**
> **3.**—(1) Subject to subsection (2) below, a probation order may in addition require the offender to comply during the whole or any part of the probation period with such requirements as the court, having regard to the circumstances of the case, considers desirable in the interest of—
> > (a) securing the rehabilitation of the offender; or
> > (b) protecting the public from harm from him or preventing the commission by him of further offences.
>
> (2) Without prejudice to the power of the court under section 35 of this Act to make a compensation order, the payment of sums by way of damages for injury or compensation for loss shall not be included among the additional requirements of a probation order.
>
> (3) Without prejudice to the generality of subsection (1) above, the additional requirements which may be included in a probation order shall include the requirements which are authorised by Schedule 1A to this Act."

(2) After Schedule 1 to that Act there shall be inserted as Schedule 1A the provisions set out in Part II of Schedule 1 to this Act.

GENERAL NOTE

By virtue of s.2(6) of the 1973 Act (see s.8(1)) an offender is required to keep in touch with the probation officer and to notify him of any change of address. By s.9(1), ss.3–48 of the 1973 Act are repealed, and a new s.3 is substituted, so as to enable a court to impose other requirements which may be included in a probation order. These may be formulated on the basis of (and subject to) any of the detailed provisions in Pt. II of Sched. 2 to the 1991 Act or they may be requirements formulated by the court itself: see s.3(1) of the 1973 Act. In any event, the requirement must fulfil the criteria set out in either s.3(1)(a) or (b).

Residence: Sched. 1, para. 1

A condition of residence (formerly imposed under s.2(5) of the 1973 Act) may be required but the court must now consider the home surroundings of the offender: Sched. 1, para. 1(2).

Activities

After a court has consulted a probation officer and satisfied itself that compliance is feasible (Sched. 1, para. 2(2)) it may require the offender to participate, or refrain from participating, in activities specified in the order (para. 2(1)(b)), but a requirement to *participate* in activities shall not endure for more than 60 days in aggregate (para. 2(6)) except that in respect of certain cases involving a sexual offender, a greater number of days may be specified (para. 4(1)).

Attendance at Probation Centres

"Day centres" (see s.4B(6) of the 1973 Act) are renamed "probation centres" (Sched. 1, para. 3(7)(a)). Attendance at a probation centre may be required after the court has consulted a probation officer and after the criterion in para. 3(2) is satisfied.

Treatment
Where an offender has a mental condition susceptible to treatment and not such as to warrant the making of a hospital order (para. 5) or where the offender is dependent on drugs or alcohol and which dependency caused or contributed to the offence (para. 6(1)), the probation order may include a requirement that the offender shall submit to treatment as prescribed by Sched. 1A to the 1973 Act (see Sched. 1, paras. 5 and 6, of the 1991 Act).

Community service orders

10.—(1) In subsection (1) of section 14 of the 1973 Act (community service orders in respect of offenders), the words "instead of dealing with him in any other way" shall cease to have effect.

(2) In subsection (1A) of that section, for paragraph (b) there shall be substituted the following paragraph—
      "(b) not more than 240."
(3) For subsections (2) and (2A) of that section there shall be substituted the following subsections—
      "(2) A court shall not make a community service order in respect of any offender unless the offender consents and the court, after hearing (if the court thinks it necessary) a probation officer or social worker of a local authority social services department, is satisfied that the offender is a suitable person to perform work under such an order.
      (2A) Subject to paragraphs 3 and 4 of Schedule 3 to the Criminal Justice Act 1991 (reciprocal enforcement of certain orders) a court shall not make a community service order in respect of an offender unless it is satisfied that provision for him to perform work under such an order can be made under the arrangements for persons to perform work under such orders which exist in the petty sessions area in which he resides or will reside."
(4) In section 15(1) of that Act (obligations of persons subject to community service orders), for paragraph (a) there shall be substituted the following paragraph—
      "(a) keep in touch with the relevant officer in accordance with such instructions as he may from time to time be given by that officer and notify him of any change of address;".

GENERAL NOTE

Subs. (1)
The Community Service Order tends to be seen as an alternative to custody but it is also a sentence in its own right: see *R.* v. *Lawrence* (1982) 4 Cr.App.R.(S.) 69. The "alternative" aspect of this order stems from the words "instead of dealing with him in any other way" as they originally appeared in s.14(1) of the 1973 Act. However, by s.6 of the 1991 Act, Parliament's intention is that community service should be capable of being combined with other "community orders" (save probation: s.6(3); see also s.11). Accordingly, s.10(1) removes the words mentioned therein from s.14(1) of the 1973 Act.

Subs. (2)
Formerly, offenders aged 16 could be ordered to serve no more than 120 hours' community service (s.14(1A)(b)(i) of the 1973 Act). Section 10(2) of the 1991 Act imposes a maximum of 240 hours on all offenders over 16 years.

Subs. (3)
Section 14(2) of the 1973 Act imposed an obligation on the court to obtain and to consider a report by a probation officer, or by a social worker of a local authority social services department, about the offender and his circumstances, before making a community service order. That particular provision in s.14(2) of that Act is no longer required in view of the court's obligations under s.7 of the 1991 Act to obtain and consider a "pre-sentence" report.

Subs. (4)
To ensure the offender's compliance with the order and to ensure that he may be adequately advised and reminded of his obligations (as well as the consequences of failure to comply), s.10(4) enables the relevant officer to require that the offender reports to him at any stage during the order: (see para. 4.15) of *Crime, Justice, and Protecting the Public*, 1990, Cm. 965).

Orders combining probation and community service

11.—(1) Where a court by or before which a person of or over the age of sixteen years is convicted of an offence punishable with imprisonment (not being an offence for which the sentence is fixed by law) is of the opinion mentioned in subsection (2) below, the court may make a combination order, that is to say, an order requiring him both—

(a) to be under the supervision of a probation officer for a period specified in the order, being not less than twelve months nor more than three years; and

(b) to perform unpaid work for a number of hours so specified, being in the aggregate not less than 40 nor more than 100.

(2) The opinion referred to in subsection (1) above is that the making of a combination order is desirable in the interests of—

(a) securing the rehabilitation of the offender; or

(b) protecting the public from harm from him or preventing the commission by him of further offences.

(3) Subject to subsection (1) above, Part I of the 1973 Act shall apply in relation to combination orders—

(a) in so far as they impose such a requirement as is mentioned in paragraph (a) of that subsection, as if they were probation orders; and

(b) in so far as they impose such a requirement as is mentioned in paragraph (b) of that subsection, as if they were community service orders.

DEFINITIONS
"combination order": s.31(1).

GENERAL NOTE
Following the Scottish model, Parliament has empowered the courts in England and Wales to impose on an offender a "combination order", which incorporates features of probation and community service so that the sentence incorporates an element of reparation coupled with supervision and counselling, *i.e.* probation. The Goverment hopes that the order will be particularly suitable for some persistent property offenders: see para. 4.16, *Crime, Justice and Protecting the Public, ante,* and hence the significance of subs. (2)(b) above.

The Secretary of State may make Regulations in respect of Combination Orders: see ss.15 and 15(4) of the Act.

Curfew orders

Curfew orders

12.—(1) Where a person of or over the age of sixteen years is convicted of an offence (not being an offence for which the sentence is fixed by law), the court by or before which he is convicted may make a curfew order, that is to say, an order requiring him to remain, for periods specified in the order, at a place so specified.

(2) A curfew order may specify different places or different periods for different days, but shall not specify—

(a) periods which fall outside the period of six months beginning with the day on which it is made; or

(b) periods which amount to less than 2 hours or more than 12 hours in any one day.

(3) The requirements of a curfew order shall, as far as practicable, be such as to avoid—

(a) any conflict with the offender's religious beliefs or with the requirements of any other community order to which he may be subject; and

(b) any interference with the times, if any, at which he normally works or attends school or other educational establishment.

(4) A curfew order shall include provision for making a person responsible for monitoring the offender's whereabouts during the curfew periods spec-

ified in the order; and a person who is made so responsible shall be of a description specified in an order made by the Secretary of State.

(5) Before making a curfew order, the court shall explain to the offender in ordinary language—

(a) the effect of the order (including any additional requirements proposed to be included in the order in accordance with section 13 below);

(b) the consequences which may follow under Schedule 2 to this Act if he fails to comply with any of the requirements of the order; and

(c) that the court has under that Schedule power to review the order on the application either of the offender or of the supervising officer,

and the court shall not make the order unless he expresses his willingness to comply with its requirements.

(6) Before making a curfew order, the court shall obtain and consider information about the place proposed to be specified in the order (including information as to the attitude of persons likely to be affected by the enforced presence there of the offender).

(7) The Secretary of State may by order direct—

(a) that subsection (2) above shall have effect with the substitution, for any period there specified, of such period as may be specified in the order; or

(b) that subsection (3) above shall have effect with such additional restrictions as may be so specified.

DEFINITIONS
"curfew order": s.31(1).

GENERAL NOTE
Confining certain people to their homes at certain times of the day or night was considered in the Green Paper *"Punishment, Custody and the Community"* and again in the White Paper, *Crime, Justice and Protecting the Public.* The Government clearly believes that such orders may be used effectively in keeping offenders away from places where they may tend to associate and commit offences: (para. 4.20; see also *Hansard,* H.L. Vol. 527, col. 145). By s.12 of the Children and Young Persons Act 1969 (as amended by the Criminal Justice Act 1982), a juvenile may be required to live with a particular person (s.12(1) of the 1969 Act). The court could also impose a *night restriction order* upon a juvenile for up to 30 nights (not exceeding 10 hours per night) to remain at a place or places specified in the order (s.12(3C)(b)) and to refrain from participating in certain activities: s.12(3C)(c) of the 1969 Act. Not many night restriction orders have been made but the Government hopes that the courts will be creative in their sentencing: see the *Official Report,* Standing Committee A, December 18, 1990 (a.m.), cols. 272 and 273.

The curfew order may be used by itself, but it is more likely that such orders will be used to support other community orders. A curfew order has a penal element in that the liberty and free movement of the offender are restricted but the court must endeavour to ensure, so far as practicable, that the order does not conflict with the offender's religious beliefs (s.12(3)(a)) or interfere with his hours of work or education (s.12(3)(b)).

The curfew order "has a strong element of protecting the public and, in the first instance, it is not about rehabilitation" (*per* John Patten, the Minister of State, Home Office *Official Report,* Standing Committee A, December 18, 1990, col. 258). The enforced presence of an offender at a particular place for a given period is likely to affect the interests of innocent third parties, including the offender's family, causing difficulties and tensions within. Accordingly, the court, before making an order, must take their views and difficulties into account: s.12(6) (see also *Hansard,* H.L. Vol. 528, col. 1583).

By s.12(4) every curfew order must make someone (approved by the Secretary of State) responsible for monitoring the offender's movements. Electronic "tagging" may be employed to assist in this respect (s.13), following the Nottingham experiment: *Hansard,* H.C. Vol. 181, col. 145; White Paper, Cm. 965, para. 4.21 and the Home Office Research Study No. 120). The intention seems to be that agencies, approved by the Secretary of State, and separate from the probation service, would enforce the orders and report infringements to the police (para. 4.24 of the White Paper).

Because the curfew order is a community sentence it is for the court to determine whether the order is suitable and "commensurate with the seriousness of the offence" (s.6; see also the *Official Report,* Standing Committee A, December 18, 1990 (a.m.), col. 260).

Subject to any order which the Secretary of State may make (s.12(7), a Curfew Order shall endure between two and 12 hours in any one day, for a period of up to six months: s.12(2).

Electronic monitoring of curfew orders

13.—(1) Subject to subsection (2) below, a curfew order may in addition include requirements for securing the electronic monitoring of the offender's whereabouts during the curfew periods specified in the order.

(2) A court shall not make a curfew order which includes such requirements unless the court—

(a) has been notified by the Secretary of State that electronic monitoring arrangements are available in the area in which the place proposed to be specified in the order is situated; and

(b) is satisfied that the necessary provisions can be made under those arrangements.

(3) Electronic monitoring arrangements made by the Secretary of State under this section may include entering into contracts with other persons for the electronic monitoring by them of offenders' whereabouts.

DEFINITIONS
"curfew order": s.31(1).

GENERAL NOTE
See the notes to s.12 above. The concept of electronic monitoring is controversial, not least because of its implications for civil liberties and its uncertain success-rate. For debates, see the *Official Report,* Standing Committee A, December 18, 1990 (a.m.), cols. 273–288.

Orders: supplemental

Enforcement etc. of community orders

14.—(1) Schedule 2 to this Act (which makes provision for dealing with failures to comply with the requirements of certain community orders, for amending such orders and for revoking them with or without the substitution of other sentences) shall have effect.

(2) Sections 5, 6, 16 and 17 of, and Schedule 1 to, the 1973 Act (which are superseded by Schedule 2 to this Act) shall cease to have effect.

GENERAL NOTE
Enforcement of Community Orders is set out in Sched. 2 to the 1991 Act.

Where an offender fails to comply with any *requirement* of an order, he may be brought before a magistrates' court by way of summons, or by warrant for his arrest (Sched. 2, para. 2) and, in the absence of any reasonable excuse, dealt with by way of a fine not exceeding £1,000 (paras. 3(1)(a) and 4(1)(a)) or in any one of the ways set out in paras. 3 or 4 of Sched. 2.

The commission of a further offence during the period of the order is not a breach for the purposes of paras. 3 or 4, but it does fall to be dealt with separately as if it were a separate offence: paras. 5 and 8.

Persistent and wilful failure to comply with an order may be *assumed* to be a refusal by the offender to give his consent to the order in question (paras. 3(2)(b) and 4(2)(b)) and thereby exposes the offender to the risk of a custodial sentence for the purposes of ss.1 and 2 (see s.1(3)).

Revocation
An order may be revoked, because, *inter alia,* the offender has made good progress and responded well to supervision (Sched. 2, para. 7(3)); or where he has committed a further offence (para. 8) or where he has received a custodial sentence imposed by another court (para. 9(2)).

Regulation of community orders

15.—(1) The Secretary of State may make rules for regulating—

(a) the supervision of persons who are subject to probation orders;

(b) the arrangements to be made under Schedule 3 to the 1973 Act for persons who are subject to community service orders to perform work under those orders and the performance by such persons of such work;

(c) the monitoring of the whereabouts of persons who are subject to curfew orders (including electronic monitoring in cases where arrangements for such monitoring are available); and

(d) without prejudice to the generality of paragraphs (a) to (c) above, the functions of the responsible officers of such persons as are mentioned in those paragraphs.

(2) Rules under subsection (1)(b) above may in particular—

(a) limit the number of hours of work to be done by a person on any one day;

(b) make provision as to the reckoning of hours worked and the keeping of work records; and

(c) make provision for the payment of travelling and other expenses in connection with the performance of work.

(3) In this Part "responsible officer" means—

(a) in relation to an offender who is subject to a probation order, the probation officer responsible for his supervision;

(b) in relation to an offender who is subject to a community service order, the relevant officer within the meaning of section 14(4) of the 1973 Act; and

(c) in relation to an offender who is subject to a curfew order, the person responsible for monitoring his whereabouts during the curfew periods specified in the order.

(4) This section shall apply in relation to combination orders—

(a) in so far as they impose such a requirement as is mentioned in paragraph (a) of subsection (1) of section 11 above, as if they were probation orders; and

(b) in so far as they impose such a requirement as is mentioned in paragraph (b) of that subsection, as if they were community service orders.

DEFINITIONS
  "combination order": s.31(1).
  "curfew order": s.31(1).
  "responsible officer": ss.15(3) and 31(1).

Reciprocal enforcement of certain orders

16. Schedule 3 to this Act shall have effect for making provision for and in connection with—

(a) the making and amendment in England and Wales of community orders relating to persons residing in Scotland or Northern Ireland; and

(b) the making and amendment in Scotland or Northern Ireland of corresponding orders relating to persons residing in England and Wales.

Financial penalties

Increase of certain maxima

17.—(1) In section 37 (standard scale of fines) of the Criminal Justice Act 1982 ("the 1982 Act") and section 289G of the Criminal Procedure (Scotland) Act 1975 (corresponding Scottish provision), for subsection (2) there shall be substituted the following subsection—

"(2) The standard scale is shown below—

Level on the scale	Amount of fine
1	£200
2	£500
3	£1,000
4	£2,500
5	£5,000".

(2) Part I of the Magistrates' Courts Act 1980 ("the 1980 Act") shall be amended as follows—

(a) in section 24(3) and (4) (maximum fine on summary conviction of young person for indictable offence) and section 36(1) and (2) (maximum fine on conviction of young person by magistrates' court), for "£400" there shall be substituted "£1,000";

(b) in section 24(4) (maximum fine on summary conviction of child for indictable offence) and section 36(2) (maximum fine on conviction of child by magistrates' court), for "£100" there shall be substituted "£250"; and

(c) in section 32(9) (maximum fine on summary conviction of offence triable either way), for "£2,000" there shall be substituted "£5,000"; and in section 289B(6) of the Criminal Procedure (Scotland) Act 1975 (interpretation), in the definition of "prescribed sum," for "£2,000" there shall be substituted "£5,000."

(3) Schedule 4 to this Act shall have effect as follows—

(a) in each of the provisions mentioned in column 1 of Part I (the general description of which is given in column 2), for the amount specified in column 3 there shall be substituted the amount specified in column 4;

(b) in each of the provisions mentioned in column 1 of Part II (the general description of which is given in column 2), for the amount specified in column 3 there shall be substituted the level on the standard scale specified in column 4;

(c) in each of the provisions mentioned in column 1 of Part III (the general description of which is given in column 2), for the amount specified in column 3 there shall be substituted a reference to the statutory maximum;

(d) the provisions set out in Part IV shall be substituted for Schedule 6A to the 1980 Act (fines that may be altered under section 143); and

(e) the provisions mentioned in Part V shall have effect subject to the amendments specified in that Part, being amendments for treating certain failures as if they were summary offences punishable by fines not exceeding levels on the standard scale.

GENERAL NOTE

Section 17 increases the maxima for a large range of offences set out in s.17 and Sched. 4. The maximum amount for a combination order (see s.40(1) of the Magistrates' Court Act 1980) is now £5,000.

Fixing of certain fines by reference to units

18.—(1) This section applies where a magistrates' court imposes a fine on an individual—

(a) for a summary offence which is punishable by a fine not exceeding a level on the standard scale; or

(b) for a statutory maximum offence, that is to say, an offence which is triable either way and which, on summary conviction, is punishable by a fine not exceeding the statutory maximum.

(2) Subject to the following provisions of this section, the amount of the fine shall be the product of—

(a) the number of units which is determined by the court to be commensurate with the seriousness of the offence, or the combination of the offence and other offences associated with it; and

(b) the value to be given to each of those units, that is to say, the amount which, at the same or any later time, is determined by the court in accordance with rules made by the Lord Chancellor to be the offender's disposable weekly income.

(3) In making any such determination as is mentioned in subsection (2)(a) above, a court shall take into account all such information about the circumstances of the offence (including any aggravating or mitigating factors) as is available to it.

(4) The number of units determined under subsection (2)(a) above shall not exceed—

(a) 2 units in the case of a level 1 offence;
(b) 5 units in the case of a level 2 offence;
(c) 10 units in the case of a level 3 offence;
(d) 25 units in the case of a level 4 offence; and
(e) 50 units in the case of a level 5 offence or a statutory maximum offence;

and in this subsection "level 1 offence" means a summary offence which is punishable by a fine not exceeding level 1 on the standard scale, and corresponding expressions shall be construed accordingly.

(5) Subject to subsection (6) below, the amount determined under subsection (2)(b) above in the case of any offender shall not be—

(a) less than 1/50th of level 1 on the standard scale (£4 at the commencement of section 17 above); or
(b) more than 1/50th of level 5 on that scale (£100 at that commencement).

(6) Where the fine is payable by a person who is under the age of 18 years, subsection (5) above shall have effect as if for any reference to a fraction or amount there were substituted—

(a) a reference to 1/20th of that fraction or amount in the case of a fine payable by a person who is under the age of 14 years; and
(b) a reference to 1/5th of that fraction or amount in the case of a fine payable by a person who has attained that age.

(7) Nothing in subsection (2) above shall prevent any of the following, namely—

(a) in the case of an offence in relation to which a compensation order is made, the reduction of the amount of the fine in pursuance of section 35(4A) of the 1973 Act;
(b) in the case of a fixed penalty offence (within the meaning of Part III of the Road Traffic Offenders Act 1988), the increase of the amount of the fine to the level of the fixed penalty; and
(c) in the case of an offence of installing or using any apparatus for wireless telegraphy except under a licence granted under section 1 of the Wireless Telegraphy Act 1949, the increase of the amount of the fine by an amount not exceeding the sum which would have been payable on the issue of such a licence.

(8) Where the offender—

(a) has been convicted in his absence in pursuance of section 11 or 12 of the 1980 Act (non-appearance of accused); or
(b) has failed to comply with an order under section 20(1) below,

and (in either case) the court has insufficient information to make a proper determination under subsection (2)(b) above, it may, within the limits set by subsection (5) above, make such determination as it thinks fit.

(9) In section 41 of the Criminal Justice Act 1988 ("the 1988 Act"), subsection (7) (Crown Court sentencing powers in relation to summary offence dealt with together with either way offence) shall have effect as if this section had not been enacted.

DEFINITIONS
"offence associated with it": s.31(2).
"statutory maximum offence": s.18(1)(b).

GENERAL NOTE
The Government in *Crime, Justice and Protecting the Public* (Cm. 965) expressed their belief

that "there are substantial benefits to be gained from maximising the effectiveness of fines" (para. 5.1). Some 80 per cent. of offenders were punished by way of financial penalties in 1989 (*per* David Waddington, *Hansard*, H.C. Vol. 181, col. 146). The White Paper highlights three limitations of the fine: (a) it is not regarded as suitable for very serious offences; (b) the offender must have financial resources; and (c) the level of the fine can seem derisory where the offender is wealthy (para. 5.1). However, substantial fines have been imposed upon offenders convicted of fraud, *e.g.* in the "Guinness Fraud" case. Indeed, there is no limit on the fine which may be imposed where the offender is convicted in the Crown Court or where he has been committed for sentence under s.38 of the Magistrates' Courts Act 1980 (s.32(1) of the Criminal Law Act 1977: see also s.42(1) of the Power of Criminal Courts Act 1973). In determining the amount of the fine, the court assesses a figure which is commensurate with the seriousness of the offence and adjusts that figure in accordance wih the means of the offender. Current sentencing practice is to reduce the amount of the fine where the offender's means are inadequate but not to increase the amount of the fine where the offender is well off: *R.* v. *Messane* (1981) 3 Cr.App.R.(S.) 88. The provisions in ss.18, 21 and 22 of the 1991 Act endeavour to change that practice, as far as certain magistrates' court cases are concerned, so that the gravity of the offence is marked by reference to the "number of units" assessed (s.18(4)) which is then used as the multiplier to the value of the offender's "disposable weekly income" (s.18(2)(b)). Thus, if the offence is sufficiently serious to represent two units, then D will be fined £20 if his disposable weekly income is £10, but E will pay £100 if his disposable weekly income is £50 (see s.18(2)).

Each level of offence (1 to 5) has a corresponding maximum (see s.17(1)), *e.g.* level 1 has a maximum of £200. The maximum number of "units" which can be determined for a level 1 offence is "two" (see s.18(4) and note s.28(3)). Thus, the maximum value for each unit is £100 at the commencement of the Act. Indeed, it will be seen that the maximum value of each unit is the same at each level on the scale, *i.e.* £100 (comparing s.17(1) and s.18(4)). No fine can, of course, exceed the maximum amount stated in s.17(1).

The large number of unpaid fines and the significant number of defaulters serving sentences of imprisonment in default of payment have resulted in changes to the law, both in terms of method of collecting fines and in sentencing defaulters (see s.24, and ss.22 and 23).

Subss. (2) and (3)

The court is required to focus its attention on the offence before it, but the court may take a fuller view where other offences are admitted or proved (see the notes to ss.1, 2 and 3 above; and note the definition of "offences associated with it" in s.31(2)). The court must have regard to aggravating as well as mitigating factors (see s.18(3), and s.28(1) and (2), and note s.28(3)). The offender is not to be sentenced on his record (s.29(1)) save in so far as aggravating factors are disclosed by the circumstances of other offences committed by him (s.29(2)).

Section 18(2)(b) must be read together with s.18(5), and with s.21 well in mind. The effect of s.18(5)(b) is to impose a ceiling on the value of a unit which is consistent with the maxima specified in s.17(1). Thus, at the commencement of s.17, each unit cannot exceed £100; see the general notes above.

By s.18(5) the minimum value payable is £4, but there may well be cases where the offender's disposable income is so low that it would be unjust to compel him to pay the minimum figure referred to in s.28(5)(a). In these circumstances the magistrates have power, under s.21, to remit the fine to a lesser amount, having regard to the offender's means and within the terms of s.21(2) (see *Hansard*, H.L. Vol. 529, col. 573).

Subs. (6)

In the case of an offender who is under the age of 14, the minimum value per unit is 20 pence (£4 ÷ 20) and the maximum is £5 (£100 ÷ 20): s.28(6)(a).

In the case of offenders aged between 14 and 18 years the minimum amount is 80 pence (£4 ÷ 5) and the maximum is £20 (£100 ÷ 5): s.18(6)(b).

Fixing of fines in other cases

19.—(1) In fixing the amount of a fine (other than one the amount of which falls to be fixed under section 18 above), a court shall take into account among other things the means of the offender so far as they appear or are known to the court.

(2) Subsection (1) above applies whether taking into account the means of the offender has the effect of increasing or reducing the amount of the fine.

Statements as to offenders' means

20.—(1) Where a person has been convicted of an offence by a magistrates' court, the court may, before sentencing him, order him to furnish to the court within a period specified in the order such a statement of his means as the court may require.

(2) A person who without reasonable excuse fails to comply with an order under subsection (1) above shall be liable on summary conviction to a fine not exceeding level 3 on the standard scale.

(3) If a person in furnishing any statement in pursuance of an order under subsection (1) above—

  (a) makes a statement which he knows to be false in a material particular;
  (b) recklessly furnishes a statement which is false in a material particular; or
  (c) knowingly fails to disclose any material fact,

he shall be liable on summary conviction to imprisonment for a term not exceeding three months or a fine not exceeding level 4 on the standard scale or both.

(4) Proceedings in respect of an offence under subsection (3) above may, notwithstanding anything in section 127(1) of the 1980 Act (limitation of time), be commenced at any time within two years from the date of the commission of the offence or within six months from its first discovery by the prosecutor, whichever period expires the earlier.

(5) Without prejudice to the generality of subsection (1) of—

  (a) section 84 of the Supreme Court Act 1981; and
  (b) section 144 of the 1980 Act,

the power to make rules under each of those sections shall include power to prescribe the form in which statements are to be furnished in pursuance of orders under subsection (1) above; and rules made by virtue of this subsection may make different provision for different cases or classes of case.

GENERAL NOTE

By virtue of both ss.18(2) and 19(1) the court is required to enquire into the means of the offender. Under s.18(2)(b), the court must comply with the rules made by the Lord Chancellor, but there seems to be no reason in principle why the court cannot require a statement of means pursuant to s.20. The statement must be obtained before the offender is sentenced and therefore s.20 has no application in respect of remission of fines under s.21(2).

Section 20(1) makes it plain that it is for the court to determine how much information it requires (if any) as to means, although it is likely that the majority of cases will be met by issuing forms prescribed under rules made pursuant to s.84 of the Supreme Court Act 1981 and s.144 of the Magistrates' Courts Act 1980: see s.20(5).

Financial penalties: supplemental

Remission of fines fixed under section 18

21.—(1) This section applies where, in the case of a fine the amount of which has been fixed by a magistrates' court under section 18 above, the determination of the offender's disposable weekly income—

  (a) would have been of a lesser amount but for subsection (5)(a) of that section; or
  (b) was made by virtue of subsection (8) of that section.

(2) In a case falling within subsection (1)(a) above, the court may, on inquiring into the offender's means or at a hearing under section 82(5) of the 1980 Act (issue of warrant of commitment for default), remit the whole or any part of the fine if the court considers that its payment by the offender within twelve months of the imposition of the fine would cause the offender undue hardship.

(3) In a case falling within subsection (1)(b) above, the court may, on inquiring into the offender's disposable weekly income or at such a hearing as is mentioned in subsection (2) above, remit the whole or any part of the fine if the court thinks it just to do so having regard—

  (a) to the amount of that income as determined by the court under this subsection in accordance with rules made by the Lord Chancellor; and

(b) if applicable, to the provisions of subsection (2) above.

(4) Where the court remits the whole or part of a fine under subsection (2) or (3) above after a term of imprisonment has been fixed under the said section 82(5), it shall also reduce the term by an amount which bears the same proportion to the whole term as the amount remitted bears to the whole fine or, as the case may be, shall remit the whole term.

(5) In calculating the reduction in a term of imprisonment required by subsection (4) above, any fraction of a day shall be left out of account.

GENERAL NOTE

Where the disposable weekly income falls below the sum prescribed in s.18(5)(a), being the least amount determinable under s.18(2)(b) (*i.e.* £4 at the commencement of s.17), then the court may alleviate the harshness of that determination by remitting the fine in accordance with the provisions of s.21(2).

The court may similarly remit a fine determined under s.18(8) of the 1991 Act.

Default in paying fines fixed under that section

22.—(1) Where default is made in paying a fine the amount of which has been fixed under section 18 above without applying paragraph (b) or (c) of subsection (7) of that section, this section shall have effect, in place of Schedule 4 to the 1980 Act, in relation to any committal of the defaulter to prison.

(2) Subject to subsection (3) below, the maximum period of imprisonment applicable in the case of a fine fixed on the basis of a number of units specified in the first column of the following Table shall be the period set out opposite to it in the second column of that Table.

TABLE

Not more than 2 units	7 days
More than 2 units but not more than 5 units	14 days
More than 5 units but not more than 10 units	28 days
More than 10 units but not more than 25 units	45 days
More than 25 units	3 months

(3) Where the amount of a fine due at the time the imprisonment is imposed is so much of the fine as remains due after part payment, then, subject to subsection (4) below, the maximum period given by subsection (2) above shall be reduced by such number of days as bears to the total number of days in it the same proportion as the part of the fine paid bears to the whole fine.

(4) In calculating the reduction required under subsection (3) above, any fraction of a day shall be left out of account and the maximum period shall not be reduced to less than 7 days.

(5) In this section "prison" includes a young offender institution and "imprisonment" includes detention in such an institution.

GENERAL NOTE

Subs. (1)

Schedule 4 to the Magistrates' Courts Act 1980 continues to apply where default is made in paying a fine which has not been fixed under s.18.

Subss. (2), (3) and (4)

The period in default is set not by the amount of the fine actually imposed (as computed under s.18), but by reference to the number of units determined by the court to be commensurate with the seriousness of the offence. However, where there has only been part payment, the number of days' imprisonment which the defaulter shall have imposed upon him is calculated proportionately. For example: D is fined £70, of which only £10 has been paid, and where the court has determined the number of units to be three. Thus the term of imprisonment will be reduced by two days (*i.e.* 14 days ÷ ⅐).

By s.22(3) any fraction of a day shall be "left out of account". For example: D is fined £200; three units, £40 only, has been paid. Therefore 14 days ÷ 40/200 = 2·8 days. The fraction shall be left out of account and therefore the offender's term is reduced by two days only.

Default in other cases

23.—(1) In the Tables in section 31(3A) of the 1973 Act and paragraph 1 of Schedule 4 to the 1980 Act (maximum periods of imprisonment for default in paying fines etc.), for the entries relating to amounts not exceeding £5,000 there shall be substituted the following entries—

"An amount not exceeding £200	7 days
An amount exceeding £200 but not exceeding £500	14 days
An amount exceeding £500 but not exceeding £1,000	28 days
An amount exceeding £1,000 but not exceeding £2,500	45 days
An amount exceeding £2,500 but not exceeding £5,000	3 months".

(2) For the Table in section 407(1A) of the Criminal Procedure (Scotland) Act 1975 (maximum period of imprisonment for failure to pay fine or find caution) there shall be substituted the following Table—

"Amount of fine or caution	*Maximum period of imprisonment*
An amount not exceeding £200	7 days
An amount exceeding £200 but not exceeding £500	14 days
An amount exceeding £500 but not exceeding £1,000	28 days
An amount exceeding £1,000 but not exceeding £2,500	45 days
An amount exceeding £2,500 but not exceeding £5,000	3 months
An amount exceeding £5,000 but not exceeding £10,000	6 months
An amount exceeding £10,000 but not exceeding £20,000	12 months
An amount exceeding £20,000 but not exceeding £50,000	18 months
An amount exceeding £50,000 but not exceeding £100,000	2 years
An amount exceeding £100,000 but not exceeding £250,000	3 years
An amount exceeding £250,000 but not exceeding £1 million	5 years
An amount exceeding £1 million	10 years."

(3) In Schedule 16 (repeals) to the 1988 Act, the entry relating to subsection (8) of section 41 of the Administration of Justice Act 1970 shall cease to have effect; and that subsection (discretion of Crown Court to specify extended period of imprisonment in default of payment of compensation) shall have effect as if that entry had not been enacted.

Recovery of fines etc. by deductions from income support

24.—(1) The Secretary of State may be regulations provide that where a fine has been imposed on an offender by a magistrates' court, or a sum is required to be paid by a compensation order which has been made against an

offender by such a court, and (in either case) the offender is entitled to income support—
  (a) the court may apply to the Secretary of State asking him to deduct sums from any amounts payable to the offender by way of income support, in order to secure the payment of any sum which is or forms part of the fine or compensation; and
  (b) the Secretary of State may deduct sums from any such amounts and pay them to the court towards satisfaction of any such sum.
(2) The regulations may include—
  (a) provision that, before making an application, the court shall make an enquiry as to the offender's means;
  (b) provision allowing or requiring adjudication as regards an application, and provision as to appeals and reviews;
  (c) provision as to the circumstances and manner in which and the times at which sums are to be deducted and paid;
  (d) provision as to the calculation of such sums (which may include provision to secure that amounts payable to the offender by way of income support do not fall below prescribed figures);
  (e) provision as to the circumstances in which the Secretary of State is to cease making deductions;
  (f) provision requiring the Secretary of State to notify the offender, in a prescribed manner and at any prescribed time, of the total amount of sums deducted up to the time of notification; and
  (g) provision that, where the whole amount to which the application relates has been paid, the court shall give notice of that fact to the Secretary of State.
(3) In subsection (1) above—
  (a) the reference to a fine having been imposed by a magistrates' court includes a reference to a fine being treated, by virtue of section 32 of the 1973 Act, as having been so imposed; and
  (b) the reference to a sum being required to be paid by a compensation order which has been made by a magistrates' court includes a reference to a sum which is required to be paid by such an order being treated, by virtue of section 41 of the Administration of Justice Act 1970, as having been adjudged to be paid on conviction by such a court.
(4) In this section—
  "fine" includes—
        (a) a penalty imposed under section 8(1) or 18(4) of the Vehicles (Excise) Act 1971 or section 102(3)(aa) of the Customs and Excise Management Act 1979 (penalties imposed for certain offences in relation to vehicle excise licences);
        (b) an amount ordered to be paid, in addition to any penalty so imposed, under section 9, 18A or 26A of the said Act of 1971 (liability to additional duty);
        (c) an amount ordered to be paid by way of costs which is, by virtue of section 41 of the Administration of Justice Act 1970, treated as having been adjudged to be paid on a conviction by a magistrates' court;
  "income support" means income support within the meaning of the Social Security Act 1986, either alone or together with any unemployment, sickness or invalidity benefit, retirement pension or severe disablement allowance which is paid by means of the same instrument of payment;
  "prescribed" means prescribed by regulations made by the Secretary of State.
(5) In the application of this section to Scotland—
  (a) references in subsections (1) and (2) above to a magistrates' court shall be construed as references to a court; and

(b) in subsection (3) above, for paragraphs (a) and (b) there shall be substituted the following paragraphs—

"(a) the reference to a fine having been imposed by a court includes a reference to a fine being treated, by virtue of section 196(2) of the Criminal Procedure (Scotland) Act 1975, as having been so imposed; and

(b) the reference to a compensation order having been made by a court includes a reference to such an order being treated, by virtue of section 66 of the Criminal Justice (Scotland) Act 1980, as having been so made."

DEFINITIONS
"fine": s.24(4).
"income support": s.24(4).
"prescribed": s.24(4).

GENERAL NOTE
The Government's White Paper *Crime, Justice and Protecting the Public*, Cm. 965, shows that in 1988 fewer people were sent into custody for fine default than in 1987 and 1982 but that the number of defaulters is still considerable: see para. 5.4. The Government hopes that the new measures in ss.17–24 will reduce the numbers still further (*Hansard*, H.C. Vol. 181, col. 146). Section 24 (subject to regulations being introduced) would enable the court to apply to the Secretary of State asking him to deduct sums payable to offenders by way of income support. The danger is that if income is so reduced for an offender already in need of state assistance, he may be encouraged to commit offences in order to "recover his losses". No doubt it is with this fear in mind that regulations may be introduced to reflect the matters set out in s.24(2).

Miscellaneous

Committals for sentence

25.—(1) For section 38 of the 1980 Act there shall be substituted the following section—

"Committal for sentence on summary trial of offence triable either way
38.—(1) This section applies where on the summary trial of an offence triable either way (not being an offence as regards which this section is excluded by section 33 above) a person who is not less than 18 years old is convicted of the offence.
(2) If the court is of opinion—
(a) that the offence or the combination of the offence and other offences associated with it was so serious that greater punishment should be inflicted for the offence than the court has the power to impose; or
(b) in the case of a violent or sexual offence committed by a person who is not less than 21 years old, that a sentence of imprisonment for a term longer than the court has power to impose is necessary to protect the public from serious harm from him,
the court may, in accordance with section 56 of the Criminal Justice Act 1967, commit the offender in custody or on bail to the Crown Court for sentence in accordance with the provisions of section 42 of the Powers of Criminal Courts Act 1973.
(3) Paragraphs (a) and (b) of subsections (2) above shall be construed as if they were contained in Part I of the Criminal Justice Act 1991.
(4) The preceding provisions of this section shall apply in relation to a corporation as if—
(a) the corporation were an individual who is not less than 18 years old; and

    (b) in subsection (2) above, paragraph (b) and the words 'in cus-
        tody or on bail' were omitted."
  (2) In Schedule 3 to the 1980 Act, paragraph 5 (provisions relating to
committal to Crown Court for sentence not to apply to a corporation) shall
cease to have effect.

DEFINITIONS
  "offences associated with it": s.31(1).
  "protect the public from serious harm from him": s.31(1).
  "sentence of imprisonment": s.31(1).
  "sexual offence": s.31(1).
  "violent offence": s.31(1).

GENERAL NOTE
  Section 25 amends s.38 of the Magistrates' Courts Act 1980 to bring committals for sentence
to the Crown Court into line with the framework of Pt. I of the Act. Whereas s.38 of the 1980
Act formerly empowered a magistrates' court to take into account information concerning the
offender's "character and antecedents", the effect of s.29(1) (subject to s.29(2)) means that the
court is no longer entitled to commit the offender on the basis of his record, but must focus its
attention on the seriousness of the offence within the meaning of s.38(2)(a) (as substituted) or
having regard to the nature of the offence within the context of s.38(2)(b).

Alteration of certain penalties

  26.—(1) In section 7 of the Theft Act 1968 (theft), for the words "ten
years" there shall be substituted the words "seven years."
  (2) For subsections (3) and (4) of section 9 of that Act (burglary) there
shall be substituted the following subsections—
    "(3) A person guilty of burglary shall on conviction on indictment
  be liable to imprisonment for a term not exceeding—
    (a) where the offence was committed in respect of a building or
        part of a building which is a dwelling, fourteen years;
    (b) in any other case, ten years.
    (4) References in subsections (1) and (2) above to a building, and
  the reference in subsection (3) above to a building which is a dwelling, shall apply also to an inhabited vehicle or vessel, and shall apply
  to any such vehicle or vessel at times when the person having a
  habitation in it is not there as well as at times when he is."
  (3) In section 10(2) of the Badgers Act 1973 (enforcement, penalties etc.),
for the words preceding the proviso there shall be substituted the
following—
    "(2) Any person guilty of an offence under this Act shall be liable
  on summary conviction—
    (a) in the case of an offence under section 1 or 2, to a fine not
        exceeding level 5 on the standard scale or to imprisonment for
        a term not exceeding six months or to both;
    (b) in the case of an offence under section 3 or 4, to a fine not
        exceeding that level; and
    (c) in the case of an offence under section 5, to a fine not exceed-
        ing level 3 on that scale";
and in the proviso for the words "paragraph (b)" there shall be substituted
the words "paragraph (a) or (b)."
  (4) In section 51(4) of the Criminal Law Act 1977 (penalties for bomb
hoaxes)—
    (a) in paragraph (a), for the words "three months" there shall be sub-
        stituted the words "six months"; and
    (b) in paragraph (b), for the words "five years" there shall be substituted
        the words "seven years."
  (5) The power saved by subsection (1) of section 70 of the 1982 Act
(vagrancy offences) shall not include, in the case of an offence mentioned in

paragraph (b)(i) of that subsection (sleeping rough), power to impose a fine which exceeds level 1 on the standard scale.

GENERAL NOTE
As has been pointed out by the learned authors of *Stockdale and Devlin on Sentencing,* Waterlow, a maximum sentence fixed by Parliament often has little relevance. The maximum may be set too high and therefore offers no practical benefit or, it may be set too low, so that sentencers "bump" against it; see also *R. v. Cade* (1984) 6 Cr.App.R.(S.) 28. A popular example in the former category was theft. Parliament has now, sensibly, reduced the maximum to seven years, which is far more realistic.

However, less convincing is Parliament's maximum sentence for burglary. The distinction drawn between dwellings and non-dwellings reflects the current attitude of the courts and public alike to offences falling within each category; see *R. v. McCann* (1980) 2 Cr.App.R.(S.) 189; *R. v. Murdoch* (1981) 3 Cr.App.R.(S.) 142; *R. v. Harvey* (1980) 12 Cr.App.R.(S.) 165.

The high maximum specified in s.9(3) of the Theft Act 1968 (as substituted) is undoubtedly a clear expression of society's strong condemnation of offences of burglary but, in reality, it is difficult to envisage a case which would attract 10 years' imprisonment, let alone 14 years, even where a large number of offences had been committed.

Subs. (4)
In the early part of 1991 a spate of serious and well-publicised bomb hoaxes (mainly of the copy-cat variety) prompted the Government to increase the maximum sentences of imprisonment under s.51(4) of the Criminal Law Act 1977 (see also *Hansard,* H.C. Vol. 193, col. 923).

Treatment of offenders under 1983 Act

27.—(1) After section 39 of the 1983 Act there shall be inserted the following section—

"Information to facilitate guardianship orders

39A. Where a court is minded to make a guardianship order in respect of any offender, it may request the local social services authority for the area in which the offender resides or last resided, or any other local social services authority that appears to the court to be appropriate—

    (a) to inform the court whether it or any other person approved by it is willing to receive the offender into guardianship; and

    (b) if so, to give such information as it reasonably can about how it or the other person could be expected to exercise in relation to the offender the powers conferred by section 40(2) below;

and that authority shall comply with any such request."

(2) After section 54 of that Act there shall be inserted the following section—

"Reduction of period for making hospital orders

54A.—(1) The Secretary of State may by order reduce the length of the periods mentioned in sections 37(4) and (5) and 38(4) above.

(2) An order under subsection (1) above may make such consequential amendments of sections 40(1) and 44(3) above as appear to the Secretary of State to be necessary or expedient."

(3) In section 143(2) of that Act (general provisions as to regulations, orders and rules), after the words "this Act" there shall be inserted the words "or any order made under section 54A above."

GENERAL NOTE
See the notes to s.4 above.

Supplemental

Savings for mitigation and mentally disordered offenders

28.—(1) Nothing in this Part shall prevent a court from mitigating an offender's sentence by taking into account such matters as, in the opinion of the court, are relevant in mitigation of sentence.

(2) Without prejudice to the generality of subsection (1) above, nothing in this Part shall prevent a court—

(a) from mitigating any penalty included in an offender's sentence by taking into account any other penalty included in that sentence; or

(b) in a case of an offender who is convicted of one or more other offences, from mitigating his sentence by applying any rule of law as to the totality of sentences.

(3) Any mitigation of a fine the amount of which falls to be fixed under section 18 above shall be effected by determining under subsection (2)(a) of that section a smaller number of units than would otherwise have been determined.

(4) Nothing in this Part shall be taken—

(a) as requiring a court to pass a custodial sentence, or any particular custodial sentence, on a mentally disordered offender; or

(b) as restricting any power (whether under the 1983 Act or otherwise) which enables a court to deal with such an offender in the manner it considers to be most appropriate in all the circumstances.

GENERAL NOTE

See the notes to ss.1, 2 and 3 above. Section 28 was inserted by way of an amendment (No. 71) in the House of Lords: see *Hansard,* H.L. Vol. 527, cols. 1030 and 1620.

Factors relevant to mitigation prior to the commencement of s.28 will continue to be relevant. The Legislature declined to specify some mitigating factors lest the courts conclude that Parliament intended to exclude others.

Effect of previous convictions etc.

29.—(1) An offence shall not be regarded as more serious for the purposes of any provision of this Part by reason of any previous convictions of the offender or any failure of his to respond to previous sentences.

(2) Where any aggravating factors of an offence are disclosed by the circumstances of other offences committed by the offender, nothing in this Part shall prevent the court from taking those factors into account for the purpose of forming an opinion as to the seriousness of the offence.

GENERAL NOTE

Section 29 is likely to present itself as yet another statutory conundrum, for, on its face, subss. (1) and (2) seem to be in conflict, or at least subss. (2) is ambiguous as to its scope. The present wording of s.29 was introduced by Amendment No. 14, in the House of Lords on Third Reading, in substitution for clause 28 of the Bill, which itself gave rise to problems of construction (see *Hansard,* H.L. Vol. 527, col. 1620; Vol. 529, cols. 557 and 580–586).

Parliament's aims are threefold. First, that the courts should not aggregate large numbers of very minor offences to justify a custodial sentence. "Our view is that people who commit minor offences, even if committed in considerable numbers, should not necessarily be sent to prison" (*per* Earl Ferrers, *Hansard,* H.L. Vol. 528, col. 1501; see also *Hansard,* H.L. Vol. 259, col. 582; and see *R.* v. *Roberts* (1987) 9 Cr.App.R.(S.) 152). Secondly, s.29 is intended to discourage "sentencing on record", but where "other offences committed by the offender" show a pattern of offending (*e.g.* a series of racial attacks or persistent fraud) then such factors should be capable of being taken into account when assessing the seriousness of the offence before the court (*Hansard,* H.L. Vol. 529, col. 557). "As a general rule the sentence for each offence should be that which is commensurate with its seriousness" (*per* Earl Ferrers, *Hansard,* H.L. Vol. 529, col. 582). Thirdly, an offence is not to be regarded as more serious by reason of any failure of the offender to respond to previous sentences. This is on the basis that the sentence should be commensurate with the seriousness of the offence and not based on the offender's previous response to sentencing: see *Hansard,* H.L. Vol. 529, col. 583.

These aims have been attacked (principally by Lord Ackner) as imposing upon the courts a "blinkered approach" to sentencing: see *Hansard,* H.L. Vol. 527, col. 1621; Vol. 528, cols. 1492 and 1502; Vol. 529, cols. 547 and 584–585. There is, with respect, much force in the arguments and observations of Lord Ackner, which should not be lightly ignored. The position might be more satisfactory if s.29 had never been enacted.

There is already clear authority for the proposition that an offender is not to be sentenced for the previous offences which he has committed and in respect of which he has already been punished: *R.* v. *Queen* (1981) 3 Cr.App.R.(S.) 245. The sentence is to be "appropriate for the offence for which the prisoner is before the court" (*per* Kenneth Jones J., *ibid.*); see also *R.* v. *Biggs* (1990) 12 Cr.App.R.(S.) 341, and *R.* v. *Galloway* (1979) 1 Cr.App.R.(S.) 311. Previous convictions may disclose mitigation (*e.g.* the "cry for help") or aggravating factors (frequent use of a knife). The courts will take such factors into account and this practice does not seem to be inconsistent with Parliament's own views (see *Hansard,* H.L. Vol. 529, col. 582). However, problems may arise where, for example, an offender has several previous convictions for obtaining money by deception by the dishonest presentation of stolen cheques. He is subsequently charged with five counts, alleging that he obtained £250 in this way (£50 per cheque) and he asks for 100 offences to be taken into consideration (totalling £5,000). Each offence— taken by itself—may be viewed as being relatively minor and (by itself) would not warrant a custodial sentence. Parliament recognises that "systematic and persistent fraud" may be an "aggravating factor", but the significance of such a conclusion fits uncomfortably against Parliament's first aim (stated above). The upshot is that the courts must perform odd-looking feats of gymnastics in order to satisfy the requirements of the Act. Thus, the court may only look to "the offence" and "*one* other offence associated with it" for the purposes of s.1 (in this example two offences totalling only £100) but it may look at *all* offences associated with it for the purposes of determining the length of any custodial sentence (s.2) (£5,250), but it shall ignore previous convictions unless "other offences committed by the offender" disclose an aggravating factor in the offence charged, *e.g.* persistent fraud, and it shall ignore the offender's failure to respond to previous sentences when assessing the seriousness of the offence for the purposes of the Act.

Failure to respond

In the case of young offenders, Parliament, in the Criminal Justice Act 1988, s.123(3), provided that an offender qualified for a custodial sentence if he had a history of failure to respond to non-custodial sentences. In s.29 of the 1991 Act, Parliament has changed course 180 degrees and s.123(2) and (3) is repealed. A court (whether the offender is an adult or not) is no longer entitled to regard the offence as more serious by his failure to respond to previous sentence (nor may it be seen as an "aggravating factor") but any consequent offending which is systematic, persistent and wilful can, it seems, be an aggravating factor within the meaning of s.29(2): see also *Hansard,* H.L. Vol. 527, col. 1621, and the notes to s.1 above.

Subs. (2)

Section 29(1) imposes a clear and unequivocal embargo. However, s.29(1) will be in conflict with s.29(2) if the words "other offences committed by the offender" are construed as including not only offences committed contemporaneously with the charge before the court (*e.g.* offences to be taken into consideration) but also previous convictions. This aspect was considered by the House of Lords during the Third Reading of the Bill, but, with respect, the issue was not unequivocally resolved during the debate: see *Hansard,* H.L. Vol. 529, col. 585. The Minister of State for the Home Office, Earl Ferrers, stated: "I do not believe that the mere fact of the offender having previous convictions should lead necessarily to a heavier sentence. The circumstances of previous offences may point to aggravating factors and Clause 28 (now s.29) now makes it quite clear how these are to be dealt with" (*Hansard,* H.L. Vol. 529, col. 582). A little later Earl Ferrers said "Lord Campbell of Alloway . . . was concerned about whether [subs. (2)] allows the court to have regard to previous offences as aggravating factors. My noble friend was quite right. The circumstances of other offences can be taken into account as aggravating factors. I can confirm that this also applies to . . . TICs" (*Hansard,* H.L. Vol. 529, col. 582).

Unfortunately, the phrase "previous offence" and "other offences" seem, occasionally, to have been used interchangeably during the debates. Subs. (1) does refer to "convictions", whereas subs. (2) does not. The question is whether the words "other offences committed by the offender" are sufficiently wide to include previous offences, *i.e.* convictions. If the answer is in the affirmative then it is submitted that (in so far as previous convictions are concerned) subs. (2) runs into conflict with subs. (1) and a distinction between the fact of conviction and the circumstances of the offence itself is artificial. By its very definition, every safe "conviction" is the product of the pertinent circumstances relating to it. Earlier in the debate Earl Ferrers said: "If we asked the courts to ignore completely the offender's past conduct . . . this would quite artificially prevent them from considering information which can in some cases be highly relevant to the judgment about the seriousness of the offence for which sentence is now being given" (*Hansard,* H.L. Vol. 529, col. 557). See also the speech of Lord Ackner, *Hansard,* H.L. Vol. 529, col. 585; and see the opening General Note to s.29 (above) and the remarks of Lord Lane C.J. in *R.* v. *Scott* (*Tracey*) (1990) 12 Cr.App.R.(S.) 23.

Rules, regulations and orders

30.—(1) Any power of the Secretary of State or the Lord Chancellor to make rules, regulations or orders under this Part—
(a) shall be exercisable by statutory instrument; and
(b) shall include power to make different provision for different cases or classes of case.

(2) A statutory instrument containing any rules, regulations or order under this Part (other than an order under section 12(4) above) shall be subject to annulment in pursuance of a resolution of either House of Parliament.

Interpretation of Part I

31.—(1) In this Part—
"attendance centre order" means an order under section 17 of the 1982 Act;
"combination order" means an order under section 11 above;
"community order" has the meaning given by section 6(4) above;
"community sentence" has the meaning given by section 6(1) above;
"curfew order" means an order under section 12 above;
"custodial sentence" means—
> (a) in relation to an offender of or over the age of twenty-one years, a sentence of imprisonment; and
> (b) in relation to an offender under that age, a sentence of detention in a young offender institution or under section 53 of the Children and Young Persons Act 1933 ("the 1933 Act"), or a sentence of custody for life under section 8(2) of the 1982 Act;

"mentally disordered," in relation to any person, means suffering from a mental disorder within the meaning of the 1983 Act;
"pre-sentence report" has the meaning given by section 3(5) above;
"responsible officer" has the meaning given by section 15(3) above;
"sentence of imprisonment" does not include a committal or attachment for contempt of court;
"sexual offence" means an offence under the Sexual Offences Act 1956, the Indecency with Children Act 1960, the Sexual Offences Act 1967, section 54 of the Criminal Law Act 1977 or the Protection of Children Act 1978, other than—
> (a) an offence under section 12 or 13 of the Sexual Offences Act 1956 which would not be an offence but for section 2 of the Sexual Offences Act 1967;
> (b) an offence under section 30, 31 or 33 to 36 of the said Act of 1956; and
> (c) an offence under section 4 or 5 of the said Act of 1967;

"supervision order" means a supervision order under the 1969 Act;
"violent offence" means an offence which leads, or is intended or likely to lead, to a person's death or to physical injury to a person, and includes an offence which is required to be charged as arson (whether or not it would otherwise fall within this definition).

(2) For the purposes of this Part, an offence is associated with another if—
(a) the offender is convicted of it in the proceedings in which he is convicted of the other offence, or (although convicted of it in earlier proceedings) is sentenced for it at the same time as he is sentenced for than offence; or
(b) the offender admits the commission of it in the proceedings in which he is sentenced for the other offence and requests the court to take it into consideration in sentencing him for that offence.

(3) In this Part any reference, in relation to an offender convicted of a violent or sexual offence, to protecting the public from serious harm from

him shall be construed as a reference to protecting members of the public from death or serious injury, whether physical or psychological, occasioned by further such offences committed by him.

PART II

EARLY RELEASE OF PRISONERS

INTRODUCTION AND GENERAL NOTE

The Government's primary aim, as stated in the White Paper, *Crime, Justice and Protecting the Public* (1990) (Cm. 965), is to ensure that convicted criminals are punished according to the seriousness of the offence; in other words "that they get their just deserts" (para. 2.1). A system of early release for prisoners might be said to conflict with that aim but the White Paper states that "a policy of just deserts need not be operated in ways which provide no incentive to offenders to turn away from crime" (para. 6.7). In any event, the concept of "early release" has a long history, dating back to the Royal Prerogative and "tickets of leave" (see Pt. I of the Carlisle Committee Report). Since 1948 all but a small core of prisoners became eligible for release after serving two-thirds of their sentence without being subject to licence or recall to prison. In 1987 remission was increased to 50 per cent. for those serving sentences of 12 months or less. "Parole", on the other hand, is largely a creature of the Criminal Justice Act 1967. By 1985, life-sentence prisoners could on average expect to be released (upon review) after about nine years (para. 19 of the Carlisle Report). Accordingly lifers were often in a better position than prisoners serving determinate sentences in excess of 15 years. The 1967 Act empowered the Home Secretary to release on licence prisoners serving long determinate sentences after serving a minimum period. In its administration, "parole" has three key features (i) selective early release on licence; (2) the criteria for eligibility; and (3) the person, or body of persons, who takes the decision to release. In the ordinary way a prisoner was eligible for parole once he had served one-third of his total sentence (including time spent on remand) or six months, whichever term expired later (see para. 110; Criminal Justice Act 1967 (as amended); Eligibility for Release on Licence Order 1983, S.I. 1983 No. 1959). The licence endured until the day he would ordinarily have been released, *i.e.* after serving two-thirds of the sentence. Thus the Minimum Qualifying Period (MQP) which the prisoner had to serve was six months before he could be *released* on parole even if he was *eligible* for parole after serving one-third (the remand time did not count towards the MQP). This produced a common eligibility date for parole even where offenders were serving sentences of different lengths (see para. 189).

Between 1967 and 1991 the interaction between parole and remission produced many anomalies—some created by ministerial intervention: see, for example, *Findlay* v. *Secretary of State* (1984) 3 All E.R. 801. General criticisms of the system included the following: (a) that distinctions between certain sentences became nugatory (para. 36 of the Report); (b) the interaction of the minimum qualifying period for parole and remission could lead to prisoners who had been given different sentences of imprisonment being released at the same time, *e.g.* prisoners sentenced to 12, 15 and 18 months' imprisonment could all be released after six months (see *Hansard*, H.C. Vol. 181, col. 147); (c) parole under s.60 of the Criminal Justice Act 1967 and under s.33 of the Criminal Justice Act 1982 were approached differently by the probation service (para. 40(d)); (d) selective parole for short sentences was unworkable (para. 186); (e) the restricted policy introduced for those sentenced to five years or more for certain offences was flawed (para. 190); (f) the parole system was excessively secretive (para. 193); (g) the tripartite structure of Home Secretary, Parole Board and Local Review Committee was inappropriate (para. 302); (h) the decision to release on parole should be taken away from the Home Secretary (paras. 305–313); and (i) some meaning should be restored to the sentence actually passed by the court (paras. 240–243).

Under the 1991 Act the Parole Board continues to exist (s.32); prisoners sentenced to less than four years' imprisonment shall be released unconditionally or on licence after serving half their sentence (s.33); prisoners serving four years or more shall be released on licence after serving two-thirds of their sentence (s.33(2)) and *may* be released on licence after serving one-half, upon the recommendation of the Board (s.35); prisoners sentenced to life for a violent or sexual offence may be released on licence if certain requirements are met (s.34).

The Act gives effect to the recommendation of the Carlisle Committee that the Minimum Qualifying Period should be scrapped and replaced by a minimum qualifying *sentence* for parole (para. 266) on the basis that a four-year sentence provides the most appropriate threshold beyond which a selective parole system can operate (para. 268). The Carlisle Committee took the view that it was not realistic to "regard the deterrent and retributive purpose of their sentence as having been met" until the offender has served half of the sentence in custody (para. 272). This view accords with the "just deserts" aspect of sentencing expressed in the White Paper *Crime, Justice and Protecting the Public* (Cm. 965).

Early Release for Prisoners Sentenced to Life

Although the reforms in the 1991 Act are significant, the provisions are nowhere near as reformative as they might have been had the amendments introduced in the House of Lords been accepted by the House of Commons. The Amendments centred around proposed reforms in sentencing for murder and release decisions recommended by the *House of Lords Select Committee on Murder and Life Imprisonment, 1989.* The main proposal was that the sentence for murder should be at the discretion of the court, so that the court could determine the circumstances of the offence and impose a sentence commensurate with the nature and gravity of the offence. This measure (formerly Clause 24) was well argued and compelling, but it did not find favour in the House of Commons: (see *Hansard*, H.L. Vol. 527, cols. 99–128, and 1563–1606; Vol. 529, col. 60, and *Hansard*, H.C. Vol. 193, col. 866).

At the heart of the debate was the issue whether murder can be properly described as an exceptional crime which therefore requires an exceptional penalty to be administered in an exceptional fashion. In *R*. v. *Howe*; *R*. v. *Bannister* (*J.D.*); *R*. v. *Burke* (*C.J.*); *R*. v. *Clarkson* [1987] A.C. 417, Lord Hailsham observed that murder "consists in a whole bundle of offences of vastly differing degree of culpability ranging from brutal . . . to the . . . mercy killing of a beloved partner" (and see the opinions delivered in *R*. v. *Hyam* [1975] A.C. 55). Those remarks reflected the attitude of the House of Lords. By contrast, in the House of Commons, murder was described as a "crime of dreadful finality" (*per* Kenneth Baker, Secretary of State for the Home Department) yet "where there are powerful extenuating circumstances and where there is no continuing danger to the public . . . the person might be released after a short period": *Hansard*, H.C. Vol. 193, cols. 866–868. The question then arises whether it should be for the judiciary or the executive to take responsibility for releasing (on licence or unconditionally) a lifer. The Carlisle Committee considered, but rejected, a judicial system involving either the courts or tribunals for taking the responsibility for granting or refusing parole (paras. 311 and 312). However, in the House of Lords their Lordships considered that a shift of responsibility away from the Home Secretary to an independent tribunal with the characteristics of a court was desirable and practical (*Hansard*, H.L. Vol. 529, col. 61; see also the decision of *Thynne, Wilson and Gunnell* v. *U.K.*, *The Independent*, November 2, 1990, E.C.H.R.). Clause 31 of the Bill (as amended in Report) proposed the creation of the "Life Sentences Review Tribunal" to which the case of every life prisoner would have been referred for review not later than two years before the expiry of a so-called "penal term" fixed by the court (clause 32). These proposals were also rejected by the House of Commons. It will be seen that under the 1991 Act the Secretary of State continues to play a powerful rôle in the decision-making process.

The debates in the House of Lords and in Committee (see the debates of Standing Committee A, January 15, 1991) reflected public anxiety that the system for early release was executive meddling with the decisions of the courts and that the system not only produced seemingly artificial results but also operated in an unduly secretive way. The Carlisle Committee described the pre-1991 arrangements as "cumbersome and conducive to delay. They work in a way which ensures that the inmate is kept in the dark for the longest possible period" (para. 306). Although the Committee recognised that certain matters must remain confidential, their firm view was that the "advantages of open reporting far outweigh any disadvantages" (para. 331). However, there was one aspect of the secretive nature of the decision-making process in respect of lifers which did not prompt widespread debate until the decision of the European Court on Human Rights in *Thynne, Wilson and Gunnell* v. *U.K.*, *The Independent*, November 2, 1990, E.C.H.R. Following the abolition of the death penalty and the introduction of a *mandatory* sentence of life imprisonment for murder (see s.1 of the Murder (Abolition of Death Penalty) Act 1965, and *R*. v. *Fleming* [1973] 2 All E.R. 401, C.A.) the trial judge may (by s.1(2) of the 1965 Act) recommend to the Home Secretary the minimum number of years which the judge considered the offender should serve before being released on licence. Such a declaration would be made in open court. However, even in the absence of such a recommendation, the Home Office would ask the judge to recommend how long a lifer should spend in custody in the interests of retribution and deterrence (the so-called tariff or "penal term"). A measure of consistency was sought by asking the Lord Chief Justice to add his own recommendation on what the tariff should be (*per* Lord Windlesham, *Hansard*, H.L. Vol. 529, col. 61). In practice these judicial recommendations were adjusted by a junior Minister and thus Ministers could reflect their own views of the gravity of the crime. This procedure (carried out in secret) applied even in cases where discretionary life sentences were imposed (*i.e.* in cases other than murder). In respect of discretionary life sentencers the procedure was held to be unlawful by the European Court on Human Rights in *Thynne, Wilson and Gunnell* v. *U.K.* The Court considered that the release of discretionary lifers ought to be determined by a body having the status of a court. Lord Waddington indicated that the Government considered that the Parole Board, operating under special procedure, and chaired by a judicial member of the Board, might be appropriate. This seems to be what has occurred (see s.32 and s.32(5) and note Sched. 5). The Carlisle Committee remarked that the "Home Secretary may wish to continue to exercise his traditional responsibility" in lifer cases. However, that committee, which reported in 1988, was mindful that the *House of Lords Select Committee on Murder and Life Imprisonment* had only then been set up and had yet to report and the case of *Thynne, Wilson and Gunnell* v. *U.K.* had not been decided.

The Significance of the Thynne Case
The way Parliament (or more precisely the House of Commons) has interpreted the case of *Thynne, Wilson and Gunnell* v. *U.K.* has had a major impact on the shape of Pt. II of the 1991 Act.

In *Thynne*, the E.C.H.R. said that the "discretionary life sentence had clearly developed in English law as a measure to deal with mentally unstable and dangerous offenders. Such sentences were composed of both a punitive and security element, the latter being designed to confer on the Secretary of State the responsibility for determining when the public interest permitted the prisoner's release". The court added that the "factors of mental instability and dangerousness were susceptible to change over the passage of time and new issues of lawfulness could arise". Discretionary lifers were therefore entitled under Art. 5.4 of the European Convention on Human Rights to "take proceedings to have the lawfulness of their continued detention decided by a court at reasonable intervals . . .". The Government's view was that the European Court in that case drew a "clear distinction" between discretionary and mandatory sentences of life imprisonment (*Hansard*, H.L. Vol. 530, col. 1007; Vol. 531, col. 649; H.C. Vol. 193, col. 902; Vol. 195, col. 311). Accordingly, the Government argued that (a) murder is an offence of exceptional gravity; (b) the mandatory sentence is therefore different in that the element of risk is not the decisive factor in passing a life sentence (*Hansard*, H.C. Vol. 195, col. 311); (c) the Home Secretary is accountable to Parliament and he must take into account, *inter alia*, how society would view the prisoner's release *(Hansard*, H.L. Vol. 531, col. 650); and, therefore, (d) the distinction between mandatory and discretionary life sentences permits a different method of approach to early release.

Although the Home Secretary is accountable to Parliament, the criticism advanced is that the powers have been exercised by him in secret (*Hansard*, H.L. Vol. 531, col. 655) and that, logically, there is no justification for distinguishing between the procedure for mandatory and discretionary life sentences (see the speech of Lord Ackner, *Hansard*, H.L. Vol. 530, col. 1017) or even with long-term prisoners (*per* Lord Campbell and Alloway, *Hansard*, H.L. Vol. 529, col. 69).

Accordingly, under the 1991 Act, the Parole Board may now form certain functions in a court-like fashion, chaired by a judicial member of the Board (Sched. 5) and in accordance with rules made by the Secretary of State (s.32(5)), and subject to the matter mentioned in s.32(6) and s.34(4).

Approach to Sentencing
There is clear authority that judges should pass what they consider to be the appropriate sentence and not to concern themselves with dates of release or remission: *R.* v. *Maguire; R.* v. *Enos* (1956) 40 Crim.App.R. 92; *R.* v. *Ouless and Ouless* (1986) 8 Crim.App.R.(S.) 124.

Summary

Short-Term Prisoners (less than four years)
(1)   They must be released *unconditionally* if the term imposed was less than 12 months and half the sentence is served: s.33(1)(a) (or *on licence* if the term is 12 months or more: s.33(1)(b)).
(2)   A prisoner may be released on licence on compassionate grounds at any time. The Board need not be consulted by the Secretary of State: s.36(1) and (2).
(3)   Any short-term prisoner may be returned to prison if he commits any offence punishable with imprisonment before the date on which he would have served his sentence in full: s.40.
(4)   The licence shall remain in force until the date on which he would have served three-quarters of his sentence (but for his release): s.37(1).
(5)   If a short-term prisoner fails to comply with conditions specified in the licence he shall be guilty of an offence (s.38(1)) and punished by a fine. He may also be recalled to prison for up to six months (s.38(2)) but shall in any event be released unconditionally after he has served three-quarters of the sentence originally imposed: s.33(3), unless the offence is of a sexual nature and s.44 applies (s.44).
(6)   Additional days may be added for disciplinary offences committed in prison: s.42.
(7)   Special provisions apply to young offenders: s.43, and fine defaulters and contemnors: s.45.

Long-Term Prisoners (four years or more)
(1)   A long-term prisoner must be released on licence after he has served two-thirds of his sentence: s.33(2).

(2) He may be released at any time by the Secretary of State on compassionate grounds after consultation with the Parole Board: s.36.
(3) He may be released on licence by the Secretary of State, upon the recommendation of the Board, upon half the sentence being served: s.35(1).
(4) The licence shall remain in force until the date on which he would (but for his release) have served three-quarters of his sentence: s.37(1).
(5) A long-term prisoner may be recalled by the Secretary of State either upon the recommendation of the Board (s.39(1)) or without their recommendation if the conditions in s.39(2) are met.
(6) If recalled under s.39(1) the prisoner must, in any event, be released unconditionally after he would have served three-quarters of his sentence but for his release (s.33(3)), unless the offence is of a sexual nature, to which s.44 applies.
(7) He may be returned to prison if he commits an offence punishable with imprisonment before the date on which he would have served his sentence in full: s.40(1).
(8) Additional days may be added for disciplinary offences: s.42.

Discretionary Life Prisoners
(1) They may be released on licence at any time on compassionate grounds, by the Secretary of State, after consultation with the Board if practicable: s.36(1).
(2) They may be released on licence following the procedure laid down in ss.32 and 34.

Other Persons Sentenced to Life
(1) They may be released at any time by the Secretary of State on compassionate grounds in consultation with the Board if practicable: s.36(1).
(2) They may be released on licence by the Secretary of State upon the recommendation of the Board and after consultation with the Lord Chief Justice, the trial judge if available, and after receiving advice from the Board: s.35.
(3) The licence remains in force until death or until revoked: s.37(3).
(4) A life prisoner may be recalled by the Secretary of State upon the recommendation of the Board (s.39(1)) or without their recommendation if the conditions of s.39(1) are met.

Preliminary

The Parole Board

32.—(1) There shall continue to be a body to be known as the Parole Board ("the Board") which shall discharge the functions conferred on it by this Part.

(2) It shall be the duty of the Board to advise the Secretary of State with respect to any matter referred to it by him which is connected with the early release or recall of prisoners.

(3) The Board shall deal with cases as respects which it makes recommendations under this Part on consideration of—

(a) any documents given to it by the Secretary of State; and
(b) any other oral or written information obtained by it,

and if in any particular case the Board thinks it necessary to interview the person to whom the case relates before reaching a decision, the Board may authorise one of its members to interview him and shall consider the report of the interview made by that member.

(4) The Board shall deal with cases as respects which it gives directions under this Part on consideration of all such evidence as may be adduced before it.

(5) Without prejudice to subsections (3) and (4) above, the Secretary of State may make rules with respect to the proceedings of the Board, including provision authorising cases to be dealt with by a prescribed number of its members or requiring cases to be dealt with at prescribed times.

(6) The Secretary of State may also give to the Board directions as to the matters to be taken into account by it in discharging any functions under this Part; and in giving any such directions the Secretary of State shall in particular have regard to—

(a) the need to protect the public from serious harm from offenders; and

(b) the desirability of preventing the commission by them of further offences and of securing their rehabilitation.

(7) Schedule 5) to this Act shall have effect with respect to the Board.

GENERAL NOTE
See the Introduction and General Note above. The Board may now sit so as to have the status of a court to determine the release of "discretionary life prisoners" within the meaning of s.34 of the Act and in accordance with the procedure laid down by rules made by the Secretary of State. Section 32 has been enacted with the case of *Thynne, Wilson and Gunnell* v. *U.K.*, *The Independent*, November 2, 1990, E.C.H.R., in mind. The Secretary of State continues to play an active rôle in the process for the early release of prisoners (consider the effect of ss.32(6), 34(4)(a), 36, 39(2) and 51(3). The Local Review Committee will no longer be needed: *per* the *White Paper*, para. 6.18.

New arrangements for early release

Duty to release short-term and long-term prisoners

33.—(1) As soon as a short-term prisoner has served one-half of his sentence, it shall be the duty of the Secretary of State—
(a) to release him unconditionally if that sentence is for a term of less than twelve months; and
(b) to release him on licence if that sentence is for a term of twelve months or more.

(2) As soon as a long-term prisoner has served two-thirds of his sentence, it shall be the duty of the Secretary of State to release him on licence.

(3) As soon as a short-term or long-term prisoner who—
(a) has been released on licence under subsection (1)(b) or (2) above or section 35 or 36(1) below; and
(b) has been recalled to prison under section 38(2) or 39(1) below,
would (but for his release) have served three-quarters of his sentence, it shall be the duty of the Secretary of State to release him unconditionally.

(4) Where a prisoner whose sentence is for a term of less than twelve months has been released on licence under section 36(1) below and recalled to prison under section 38(2) below, subsection (3) above shall have effect as if for the reference to three-quarters of his sentence there were substituted a reference to one-half of that sentence.

(5) In this Part—
"long-term prisoner" means a person serving a sentence of imprisonment for a term of four years or more;
"short-term prisoner" means a person serving a sentence of imprisonment for a term of less than four years.

DEFINITIONS
"long-term prisoner": ss.33(5), 43(1), 45(1), 51.
"short-term prisoner": ss.33(5), 43(1), 45(1), 51.

GENERAL NOTE
See summary of ss.32–45 above.

Duty to release discretionary life prisoners

34.—(1) A life prisoner is a discretionary life prisoner for the purposes of this Part if—
(a) his sentence was imposed for a violent or sexual offence the sentence for which is not fixed by law; and
(b) the court by which he was sentenced for that offence ordered that this section should apply to him as soon as he had served a part of his sentence specified in the order.

(2) A part of a sentence so specified shall be such part as the court considers appropriate taking into account—

(a) the seriousness of the offence, or the combination of the offence and other offences associated with it; and

(b) the provisions of this section as compared with those of section 33(2) above and section 35(1) below.

(3) As soon as, in the case of a discretionary life prisoner—

(a) he has served the part of his sentence specified in the order ("the relevant part"); and

(b) the Board has directed his release under this section,

it shall be the duty of the Secretary of State to release him on licence.

(4) The Board shall not give a direction under subsection (3) above with respect to a discretionary life prisoner unless—

(a) the Secretary of State has referred the prisoner's case to the Board; and

(b) the Board is satisfied that it is no longer necessary for the protection of the public that the prisoner should be confined.

(5) A discretionary life prisoner may require the Secretary of State to refer his case to the Board at any time—

(a) after he has served the relevant part of his sentence; and

(b) where there has been a previous reference of his case to the Board, after the end of the period of two years beginning with the disposal of that reference; and

(c) where he is also serving a sentence of imprisonment for a term, after he has served one-half of that sentence;

and in this subsection "previous reference" means a reference under subsection (4) above or section 39(4) below made after the prisoner had served the relevant part of his sentence.

(6) In determining for the purpose of subsection (3) or (5) above whether a discretionary life prisoner has served the relevant part of his sentence, no account shall be taken of any time during which he was unlawfully at large within the meaning of section 49 of the Prison Act 1952 ("the 1952 Act").

(7) In this Part "life prisoner" means a person serving one or more sentences of life imprisonment; but—

(a) a person serving two or more such sentences shall not be treated as a discretionary life prisoner for the purpose of this Part unless the requirements of subsection (1) above are satisfied as respects each of those sentences; and

(b) subsections (3) and (5) above shall not apply in relation to such a person until after he has served the relevant part of each of those sentences.

DEFINITIONS
"the Board": s.32(1).
"discretionary life prisoner": ss.34, 43(2), 51(1).
"life prisoner": ss.34(7), 51.
"other offences associated with it": s.31(2).
"previous reference": s.34(5).
"sexual offence": ss.31(1), 51(1).
"violent offence": ss.31(1), 51(1).

GENERAL NOTE
  See the notes introducing Pt. II of the Act. Where the offence is a "violent" or "sexual" offence, then the judge may state in open court the term, within the life sentence imposed, which in his judgment (and subject to s.34(2)) marks the seriousness of the offence, *i.e.* the punitive element of the sentence. If no term is indicated then the Secretary of State may take that to be an indication that life is justified, irrespective of the risk to the public (see *Hansard*, H.C. Vol. 193, col. 903). The sentence does not therefore fall to be considered under s.34. Where the term has been announced, then, upon the prisoner serving that term (the "relevant part": s.34(3)), the Secretary of State is empowered to refer the prisoner's case to the Board (s.34(4)(a)) for their consideration. If the Board is satisfied that the prisoner need no longer be detained "for the protection of the public" (sometimes referred to as the "security element" of

the sentence: see *Thynne, Wilson and Gunnell* v. *U.K., The Independent,* November 2, 1990, E.C.H.R.), then the Board may direct his release under s.34, whereupon the Secretary of State shall release him: s.34(3).

Power to release long-term and life prisoners

35.—(1) After a long-term prisoner has served one-half of his sentence, the Secretary of State may, if recommended to do so by the Board, release him on licence.

(2) If recommended to do so by the Board, the Secretary of State may, after consultation with the Lord Chief Justice together with the trial judge if available, release on licence a life prisoner who is not a discretionary life prisoner.

(3) The Board shall not make a recommendation under subsection (2) above unless the Secretary of State has referred the particular case, or the class of case to which that case belongs, to the Board for its advice.

DEFINITIONS
  "the Board": s.32(1).
  "life prisoner": s.34(7).
  "long-term prisoner": s.33(5).

Power to release prisoners on compassionate grounds

36.—(1) The Secretary of State may at any time release a prisoner on licence if he is satisfied that exceptional circumstances exist which justify the prisoner's release on compassionate grounds.

(2) Before releasing a long-term or life prisoner under subsection (1) above, the Secretary of State shall consult the Board, unless the circumstances are such as to render such consultation impracticable.

DEFINITIONS
  "life prisoner": s.34(7).
  "long-term prisoner": s.33(5).

Duration and conditions of licences

37.—(1) Subject to subsection (2) below, where a short-term or long-term prisoner is released on licence, the licence shall, subject to any suspension under section 38(2) below or, as the case may be, any revocation under section 39(1) or (2) below, remain in force until the date on which we would (but for his release) have served three-quarters of his sentence.

(2) Where a prisoner whose sentence is for a term of less than twelve months is released on licence under section 36(1) above, subsection (1) above shall have effect as if for the reference to three-quarters of his sentence there were substituted a reference to one-half of that sentence.

(3) Where a life prisoner is released on licence, the licence shall, unless previously revoked under section 39(1) or (2) below, remain in force until his death.

(4) A person subject to a licence shall comply with such conditions (which shall include on his release conditions as to his supervision by a probation officer) as may for the time being be specified in the licence; and the Secretary of State may make rules for regulating the supervision of any description of such persons.

(5) The Secretary of State shall not include on release, or subsequently insert, a condition in the licence of a long-term or life prisoner, or vary or cancel any such condition, except—

(a) in the case of the inclusion of a condition in the licence of a discretionary life prisoner, in accordance with recommendations of the Board; and

(b) in any other case, after consultation with the Board.

(6) For the purposes of subsection (5) above, the Secretary of State shall be treated as having consulted the Board about a proposal to include, insert, vary or cancel a condition in any case if he has consulted the Board about the implementation of proposals of that description generally or in that class of case.

(7) The power to make rules under this section shall be exercisable by statutory instrument which shall be subject to annulment in pursuance of a resolution of either House of Parliament.

DEFINITIONS
"life prisoner": s.34(7).
"long-term prisoner": s.33(5).
"short-term prisoner": s.33(5).

GENERAL NOTE
Section 37(7) allows the Secretary of State to make rules regulating the supervision of offenders released on licence. It would appear that the Home Secretary will issue to the Probation Service a set of national standards for the supervision of offenders before and after their release from custody. The aim is to incorporate special conditions if they are needed, *e.g.* to attend a drug abuse clinic: see *Official Report,* Standing Committee A, January 17, 1991; see also *Crime, Justice and Protecting the Public* (1990) Cm. 965, Chapter 7.

Misbehaviour after release

Breach of licence conditions by short-term prisoners

38.—(1) A short-term prisoner—
(a) who is released on licence under this Part; and
(b) who fails to comply with such conditions as may for the time being be specified in the licence,
shall be liable on summary conviction to a fine not exceeding level 3 on the standard scale.

(2) The magistrates' court by which a person is convicted of an offence under subsection (1) above may, whether or not it passes any other sentence on him—
(a) suspend the licence for a period not exceeding six months; and
(b) order him to be recalled to prison for the period during which the licence is suspended.

(3) On the suspension of the licence of any person under this section, he shall be liable to be detained in pursuance of his sentence and, if at large, shall be deemed to be unlawfully at large.

DEFINITIONS
"short-term prisoner": s.33(5).

GENERAL NOTE
See summary of ss.32–45 above.

Recall of long-term and life prisoners while on licence

39.—(1) If recommended to do so by the Board in the case of a long-term or life prisoner who has been released on licence under this Part, the Secretary of State may revoke his licence and recall him to prison.

(2) The Secretary of State may revoke the licence of any such person and recall him to prison without a recommendation by the Board, where it appears to him that it is expedient in the public interest to recall that person before such a recommendation is practicable.

(3) A person recalled to prison under subsection (1) or (2) above—
(a) may make representations in writing with respect to his recall; and
(b) on his return to prison, shall be informed of the reasons for his recall and of his right to make representations.

(4) The Secretary of State shall refer to the Board—
(a) the case of a person recalled under subsection (1) above who makes representations under subsection (3) above; and
(b) the case of a person recalled under subsection (2) above.
(5) Where on a reference under subsection (4) above the Board—
(a) directs in the case of a discretionary life prisoner; or
(b) recommends in the case of any other person,
his immediate release on licence under this section, the Secretary of State shall give effect to the direction or recommendation.
(6) On the revocation of the licence of any person under this section, he shall be liable to be detained in pursuance of his sentence and, if at large, shall be deemed to be unlawfully at large.

DEFINITIONS
"the Board": s.32(1).
"life prisoner": ss.33(5), 43(2), 51.
"long-term prisoner": ss.33(5), 51.

Convictions during currency of original sentences

40.—(1) This section applies to a short-term or long-term prisoner who is released under this Part if—
(a) before the date on which he would (but for his release) have served his sentence in full, he commits an offence punishable with imprisonment; and
(b) whether before or after that date, he is convicted of that offence ("the new offence").
(2) Subject to subsection (3) below, the court by or before which a person to whom this section applies is convicted of the new offence may, whether or not it passes any other sentence on him, order him to be returned to prison for the whole or any part of the period which—
(a) begins with the date of the order; and
(b) is equal in length to the period between the date on which the new offence was committed and the date mentioned in subsection (1) above.
(3) A magistrates' court—
(a) shall not have power to order a person to whom this section applies to be returned to prison for a period of more than six months; but
(b) may commit him in custody or on bail to the Crown Court for sentence in accordance with section 42 of the 1973 Act (power of Crown Court to sentence persons convicted by magistrates' courts of indictable offences).
(4) The period for which a person to whom this section applies is ordered under subsection (2) above to be returned to prison—
(a) shall be taken to be a sentence of imprisonment for the purposes of this Part;
(b) shall, as the court may direct, either be served before and be followed by, or be served concurrently with, the sentence imposed for the new offence; and
(c) in either case, shall be disregarded in determining the appropriate length of that sentence.

DEFINITIONS
"long-term prisoner": ss.33(5), 51.
"short-term prisoner": ss.33(5), 51.

Remand time and additional days

Remand time to count towards time served

41.—(1) This section applies to any person whose sentence falls to be reduced under section 67 of the Criminal Justice Act 1967 ("the 1967 Act") by any relevant period within the meaning of that section ("the relevant period").

(2) For the purpose of determining for the purposes of this Part—

(a) whether a person to whom this section applies has served one-half or two-thirds of his sentence; or

(b) whether such a person would (but for his release) have served three-quarters of that sentence,

the relevant period shall, subject to subsection (3) below, be treated as having been served by him as part of that sentence.

(3) Nothing in subsection (2) above shall have the effect of reducing the period for which a licence granted under this Part to a short-term or long-term prisoner remains in force to a period which is less than—

(a) one-quarter of his sentence in the case of a short-term prisoner; or

(b) one-twelfth of his sentence in the case of a long-term prisoner.

DEFINITIONS
"long-term prisoner": ss.33(5), 51.
"short-term prisoner": ss.33(5), 51.

Additional days for disciplinary offences

42.—(1) Prison rules, that is to say, rules made under section 47 of the 1952 Act, may include provision for the award of additional days—

(a) to short-term or long-term prisoners; or

(b) conditionally on their subsequently becoming such prisoners, to persons on remand,

who (in either case) are guilty of disciplinary offences.

(2) Where additional days are awarded to a short-term or long-term prisoner, or to a person on remand who subsequently becomes such a prisoner, and are not remitted in accordance with prison rules—

(a) any period which he must serve before becoming entitled to or eligible for release under this Part; and

(b) any period for which a licence granted to him under this Part remains in force,

shall be extended by the aggregate of those additional days.

DEFINITIONS
"long-term prisoner": ss.33(5), 51.
"short-term prisoner": ss.33(5), 51.

Special cases

Young offenders

43.—(1) Subject to subsections (4) and (5) below, this Part applies to persons serving sentences of detention in a young offender institution, or determinate sentences of detention under section 53 of the 1933 Act, as it applies to persons serving equivalent sentences of imprisonment.

(2) Subject to subsection (5) below, this Part applies to persons serving—

(a) sentences of detention during Her Majesty's pleasure or for life under section 53 of the 1933 Act; or

(b) sentences of custody for life under section 8 of the 1982 Act,

as it applies to persons serving sentences of imprisonment for life.

(3) References in this Part to prisoners (whether short-term, long-term or life prisoners), or to prison or imprisonment, shall be construed in accordance with subsections (1) and (2) above.

(4) In relation to a short-term prisoner under the age of 18 years to whom subsection (1) of section 33 above applies, that subsection shall have effect as if it required the Secretary of State—

(a) to release him unconditionally if his sentence is for a term of twelve months or less; and

(b) to release him on licence if that sentence is for a term of more than twelve months.

(5) In relation to a person under the age of 22 years who is released on licence under this Part, section 37(4) above shall have effect as if the reference to supervision by a probation officer included a reference to supervision by a social worker of a local authority social services department.

DEFINITIONS
"life prisoners": ss.34(7), 43(2), 51.
"long-term prisoner": ss.33(5), 51(1).
"short-term prisoner": ss.33(5), 51(1).

Sexual offenders

44. Where, in the case of a long-term or short-term prisoner—

(a) the whole or any part of his sentence was imposed for a sexual offence; and

(b) the court by which he was sentenced for that offence, having had regard to the matters mentioned in section 32(6)(a) and (b) above, ordered that this section should apply,

sections 33(3) and 37(1) above shall each have effect as if for the reference to three-quarters of his sentence there were substituted a reference to the whole of that sentence.

DEFINITIONS
"long-term prisoner": ss.33(5), 51(1).
"short-term prisoner": ss.33(5), 51(1).

Fine defaulters and contemnors

45.—(1) Subject to subsection (2) below, this Part (except sections 35 and 40 above) applies to persons committed to prison or to be detained under section 9 of the 1982 Act—

(a) in default of payment of a sum adjudged to be paid by a conviction; or

(b) for contempt of court or any kindred offence,

as it applies to persons serving equivalent sentences of imprisonment; and references in this Part to short-term or long-term prisoners, or to prison or imprisonment, shall be construed accordingly.

(2) In relation to persons committed as mentioned in subsection (1) above, the provisions specified in subsections (3) and (4) below shall have effect subject to the modifications so specified.

(3) In section 33 above, for subsections (1) to (4) there shall be substituted the following subsections—

"(1) As soon as a person committed as mentioned in section 45(1) below has served the appropriate proportion of his term, that is to say—

(a) one-half, in the case of a person committed for a term of less than twelve months;

(b) two-thirds, in the case of a person committed for a term of twelve months or more,

it shall be the duty of the Secretary of State to release him unconditionally.

(2) As soon as a person so committed who—

(a) has been released on licence under section 36(1) below; and

(b) has been recalled under section 38(2) or 39(1) below,

would (but for his release) have served the appropriate proportion of his term, it shall be the duty of the Secretary of State to release him unconditionally."

(4) In section 37 above, for subsections (1) to (3) there shall be substituted the following subsection—

"(1) Where a person committed as mentioned in section 45(1) below is released on licence under section 36(1) above, the licence shall, subject to—

(a) any suspension under section 38(2) below; or
(b) any revocation under section 39(1) below,

continue in force until the date on which he would (but for his release) have served the appropriate proportion of his term; and in this subsection 'appropriate portion' has the meaning given by section 33(1) above."

Persons liable to removal from the United Kingdom

46.—(1) In relation to a long-term prisoner who is liable to removal from the United Kingdom, section 35 above shall have effect as if the words "if recommended to do so by the Board" were omitted.

(2) In relation to a person who is liable to removal from the United Kingdom, section 37(4) above shall have effect as if the words in parentheses were omitted.

(3) A person is liable to removal from the United Kingdom for the purposes of this section if—

(a) he is liable to deportation under section 3(5) of the Immigration Act 1971 and has been notified of a decision to make a deportation order against him;
(b) he is liable to deportation under section 3(6) of that Act;
(c) he has been notified of a decision to refuse him leave to enter the United Kingdom; or
(d) he is an illegal entrant within the meaning of section 33(1) of that Act.

Persons extradited to the United Kingdom

47.—(1) A short-term or long-term prisoner is an extradited prisoner for the purposes of this section if—

(a) he was tried for the offence in respect of which his sentence was imposed—
    (i) after having been extradited to the United Kingdom; and
    (ii) without having first been restored or had an opportunity of leaving the United Kingdom; and
(b) he was for any period kept in custody while awaiting his extradition to the United Kingdom as mentioned in paragraph (a) above.

(2) If, in the case of an extradited prisoner, the court by which he was sentenced so ordered, section 67 of the 1967 Act (computation of sentences of imprisonment) shall have effect in relation to him as if a period specified in the order were a relevant period for the purposes of that section.

(3) The period that may be so specified is such period as in the opinion of the court is just in all the circumstances and does not exceed the period of custody mentioned in subsection (1)(b) above.

(4) In this section—

"extradited to the United Kingdom" means returned to the United Kingdom—
    (i) in pursuance of extradition arrangements;
    (ii) under any law of a designated Commonwealth country corresponding to the Extradition Act 1989;
    (iii) under that Act as extended to a colony or under any corresponding law of a colony; or

(iv) in pursuance of a warrant of arrest endorsed in the Republic of Ireland under the law of that country corresponding to the Backing of Warrants (Republic of Ireland) Act 1965;
"extradition arrangements" has the meaning given by section 3 of the Extradition Act 1989;
"designated Commonwealth country" has the meaning given by section 5(1) of that Act.

Life prisoners transferred to England and Wales

48.—(1) This section applies where, in the case of a transferred life prisoner, the Secretary of State, after consultation with the Lord Chief Justice, certifies his opinion that, if—
(a) he had been sentenced for his offence in England and Wales after the commencement of section 34 above; and
(b) the reference in subsection (1)(a) of that section to a violent or sexual offence the sentence for which is not fixed by law were a reference to any offence the sentence for which is not so fixed,
the court by which he was so sentenced would have ordered that that section should apply to him as soon as he had served a part of his sentence specified in the certificate.

(2) In a case to which this section applies, this Part except section 35(2) above shall apply as if—
(a) the transferred life prisoner were a discretionary life prisoner for the purposes of this Part; and
(b) the relevant part of his sentence within the meaning of section 34 of this Act were the part specified in the certificate.

(3) In this section "transferred life prisoner" means a person—
(a) on whom a court in a country or territory outside England and Wales has imposed one or more sentences of imprisonment or detention for an indeterminate period; and
(b) who has been transferred to England and Wales, in pursuance of—
(i) an order made by the Secretary of State under section 26 of the Criminal Justice Act 1961 or section 2 of the Colonial Prisoners Removal Act 1884; or
(ii) a warrant issued by the Secretary of State under the Repatriation of Prisoners Act 1984,
there to serve his sentence or sentences or the remainder of his sentence or sentences.

(4) A person who is required so to serve the whole or part of two or more such sentences shall not be treated as a discretionary life prisoner for the purposes of this Part unless the requirements of subsection (1) above are satisfied as respects each of those sentences; and subsections (3) and (5) of section 34 above shall not apply in relation to such a person until after he has served the relevant part of each of those sentences.

Supplemental

Alteration by order of relevant proportions of sentences

49.—(1) The Secretary of State may by order made by statutory instrument provide—
(a) that the references in section 33(5) above to four years shall be construed as references to such other period as may be specified in the order;
(b) that any reference in this Part to a particular proportion of a prisoner's sentence shall be construed as a reference to such other proportion of a prisoner's sentence as may be so specified.

(2) An order under this section may make such transitional provisions as appear to the Secretary of State necessary or expedient in connection with any provisions made by the order.

(3) No order shall be made under this section unless a draft of the order has been laid before and approved by resolution of each House of Parliament.

Transfer by order of certain functions to Board

50.—(1) The Secretary of State, after consultation with the Board, may by order made by statutory instrument provide that, in relation to such class of case as may be specified in the order, the provisions of this Part specified in subsections (2) to (4) below shall have effect subject to the modifications so specified.

(2) In section 35 above, in subsection (1) for the word "may" there shall be substituted the word "shall"; but nothing in this subsection shall affect the operation of that subsection as it has effect in relation to a long-term prisoner who is liable to removal from the United Kingdom (within the meaning of section 46 above).

(3) In section 37 above, in subsection (5)(a) after the words "in the case of" there shall be inserted the words "the licence of a long-term prisoner or," and subsection (6) shall be omitted.

(4) In section 39 above, in subsection (1) for the word "may" there shall be substituted the word "shall," and subsection (2) shall be omitted.

(5) No order shall be made under this section unless a draft of the order has been laid before and approved by resolution of each House of Parliament.

Interpretation of Part II

51.—(1) In this Part—
"the Board" means the Parole Board;
"discretionary life prisoner" has the meaning given by section 34 above (as extended by section 43(2) above);
"life prisoner" has the meaning given by section 34(7) above (as extended by section 43(2) above);
"long-term prisoner" and "short-term prisoner" have the meanings given by section 33(5) above (as extended by sections 43(1) and 45(1) above);
"sentence of imprisonment" does not include a committal in default of payment of any sum of money, or for want of sufficient distress to satisfy any sum of money, or for failure to do or abstain from doing anything required to be done or left undone.
"sexual offence" and "violent offence" have the same meanings as in Part I of this Act.

(2) For the purposes of any reference in this Part, however expressed, to the term of imprisonment to which a person has been sentenced or which, or part of which, he has served, consecutive terms and terms which are wholly or partly concurrent shall be treated as a single term.

(3) Nothing in this Part shall require the Secretary of State to release a person who is serving—
(a) a sentence of imprisonment for a term; and
(b) one or more sentences of imprisonment for life,
unless and until he is entitled under this Part to be released in respect of each of those sentences.

(4) Subsections (2) and (3) of section 31 above shall apply for the purposes of this Part as they apply for the purposes of Part I of this Act.

Part III

Children and Young Persons

Children's evidence

General Note

The Government's White Paper *Crime, Justice and Protecting the Public* (1990) Cm. 965 devoted an entire chapter to Young Offenders (Chap. 8), but the Bill from a very early stage went very much further and included provisions to enact various recommendations of the "Pigot Report" (*The Report of the Advisory Committee on Video Evidence*). The way children, and the evidence that they intend to give, are handled by the courts has received much public attention in recent years. A significant step forward was made in 1988 when Parliament introduced the Criminal Justice Act 1988. By s.32 of that Act a child is now entitled to give admissible evidence, with the leave of the court, through a live television link in the Crown Court, or the Court of Appeal, where the accused was charged with offences specified in s.32(2) of that Act. By intelligent deployment of cameras and equipment, the child witness need not see the accused or anyone other than the person whom the child is addressing. However, Parliament's response to the way evidence of children should be dealt with during committal proceedings before a magistrates' court was unsatisfactory. By s.33 of the 1988 Act, Parliament amended s.103 of the Magistrates' Courts Act 1980 so that a child shall not be called as a witness for the prosecution in respect of any of the offences (mentioned above) but any statement made by the child shall be admissible in evidence except, *inter alia*, where the defence objected to its admission (formerly s.103(3)(a) of the 1980 Act). This exception was capable of being abused by an unscrupulous accused who wished to test the resolve of the child to attend court and give oral evidence which could not be presented through a live television link. This exception has been removed: s.55(1) of the 1991 Act. Furthermore, the 1988 Act did little to prevent or reduce the ordeal the child would encounter if the ordinary rules of criminal procedure were allowed to take their course. The Pigot Report has addressed these issues.

The 1991 Act makes a number of radical changes. By s.52 it removes the competency test imposed by s.38(1) of the Children and Young Persons Act 1933 so that all children of tender years may now give unsworn evidence subject to the common law rules of competency affecting all witnesses (see *Toohey* v. *Metropolitan Police Commissioner* [1965] A.C. 595). The rule that unsworn evidence under s.38(1) of the 1933 Act had to be corroborated was abolished by s.34 of the 1988 Act. When a child may be said to be of "tender years" is left to the good sense of the court: *R.* v. *Campbell* [1956] 2 Q.B. 432.

By s.53 of the 1991 Act, the Director of Public Prosecutions may now, in appropriate cases, by-pass committal proceedings in the magistrates' court subject to the safeguards and procedures set out in Sched. 6 to the 1991 Act.

The circumstances in which video recordings of the testimony of children may be admitted in evidence appear in s.54 and restrictions have been imposed on the extent to which child witnesses shall be examined-in-chief in respect of matters covered by the video evidence (s.54(5)(b)). Significantly, an accused is absolutely debarred from carrying out cross-examination himself in the circumstances specified in the new s.34(A) to the 1991 Act. This is to protect the child witness from defendants who deliberately or otherwise subject such witnesses to an ordeal which may not only flout the rules of evidence and procedure, but which the trial judge himself may find difficult to control or stop. Where such conduct results in a re-trial (for whatever reason) the ordeal is protracted.

Competence of children as witnesses

52.—(1) After section 33 of the 1988 Act there shall be inserted the following section—

> **"Evidence given by children**
> 33A.—(1) A child's evidence in criminal proceedings shall be given unsworn.
> (2) A deposition of a child's unsworn evidence may be taken for the purposes of criminal proceedings as if that evidence had been given on oath.
> (3) In this section 'child' means a person under fourteen years of age."

(2) Subsection (1) of section 38 of the 1933 Act (evidence of child of tender years to be given on oath or in certain circumstances unsworn) shall cease to

have effect; and accordingly the power of the court in any criminal proceedings to determine that a particular person is not competent to give evidence shall apply to children of tender years as it applies to other persons.

DEFINITIONS
"child": s.52(3).

GENERAL NOTE

Subs. (1)
The new s.33(A)(1) to the 1988 Act provides that *all* children shall give their evidence unsworn in criminal proceedings. The object is to establish one class of child witness "undifferentiated in the eyes of the jury" (see John Patten, Minister of State, Home Office, *Official Report*, Standing Committee A, January 22, 1991, col. 380). This marks a significant change in attitude towards the effect of sworn and unsworn testimony. Historically, the evidence of a witness in a criminal trial was not admissible unless he had sworn (or affirmed) to speak the truth: see *R.* v. *Kelly* (1948) 3 Cox 75, and the Oaths Act 1978 (repealing the Acts of 1838, 1888, 1909 and 1961). The swearing of an oath or the making of a "solemn affirmation" is seen as a powerful if not compelling force put upon the witness to tell the whole truth. The significance of the oath or affirmation is lost if the witness does not understand the nature of the oath in the context of the solemnity of the occasion: see *R.* v. *Khan* (1981) 73 Cr.App.R. 190. Accordingly, the courts have never objected to children being sworn—however old they are—provided that they understand the nature of the oath. Competency is not seen as a matter of age but of understanding: *Young* v. *Slaughterford* (1709) 11 Mod. Rep. 228; *R.* v. *Brassier* (1779) 1 East P.C. 443; *R.* v. *Perkins* (1840) 9 C. & P. 395; *R.* v. *Williams* (1835) 7 C. & P. 320 and *R.* v. *Campbell* [1983] Crim.L.R. 174.
An exception to this high standard was made in s.38(1) of the 1933 Act, in respect of children of tender years whose evidence could be received unsworn if (in the opinion of the court) the child possessed sufficient intelligence to justify the reception of the evidence and understood the duty to speak the truth. As a safeguard the unsworn evidence of a child required corroboration: s.38(1). This last requirement disappeared with s.34(1) of the Criminal Justice Act 1988 and the judge is no longer obliged to warn the jury about the dangers of convicting the accused on the uncorroborated evidence of a child (s.34(2) of the 1988 Act). By s.34(3) of the 1988 Act, the unsworn evidence admitted by virtue of s.38 of the 1933 Act may indeed corroborate evidence given by any other person: s.34(3) of the 1988 Act. However, s.38(1) of the 1933 Act is now repealed, as is s.34(1) of the 1988 Act. S.34(3) of the 1988 Act is amended by Sched. 11, para. 37 of the 1991 Act and indicates Parliament's view that the unsworn evidence of a child should not be belittled merely because the evidence is unsworn and comes from a child of whatever age—on the contrary.

Subs. (2)
Section 38(1) of the 1933 Act and s.34(1) of the 1988 Act are repealed. The object of subs. (2) is to prevent the court from embarking on an enquiry which it was permitted to do under s.38(1) of the 1933 Act. The aim is to put the evidence of children on the same footing as any other witness so far as competence is concerned. The judge has an inherent power to decide on the competency of any witness at any stage of his evidence and upon proof of facts affecting the capacity of the witness, and the judge may direct the jury to consider the case upon other evidence: *Whitehead* (1866) L.R. 1 C.C.R. 33; see also para. 5.13 of the Pigot Report.

Notices of transfer in certain cases involving children

53.—(1) If a person has been charged with an offence to which section 32(2) of the 1988 Act applies (sexual offences and offences involving violence or cruelty) and the Director of Public Prosecutions is of the opinion—
  (a) that the evidence of the offence would be sufficient for the person charged to be committed for trial;
  (b) that a child who is alleged—
     (i) to be a person against whom the offence was committed; or
     (ii) to have witnessed the commission of the offence,
  will be called as a witness at the trial; and
  (c) that, for the purpose of avoiding any prejudice to the welfare of the child, the case should be taken over and proceeded with without delay by the Crown Court,

a notice ("notice of transfer") certifying that opinion may be served by or on behalf of the Director on the magistrates' court in whose jurisdiction the offence has been charged.

(2) A notice of transfer shall be served before the magistrates' court begins to inquire into the case as examining justices.

(3) On the service of a notice of transfer the functions of the magistrates' court shall cease in relation to the case except as provided by paragraphs 2 and 3 of Schedule 6 to this Act or by section 20(4) of the Legal Aid Act 1988.

(4) The decision to serve a notice of transfer shall not be subject to appeal or liable to be questioned in any court.

(5) Schedule 6 to this Act (which makes further provisions in relation to notices of transfer) shall have effect.

(6) In this section "child" means a person who—

(a) in the case of an offence falling within section 32(2)(a) or (b) of the 1988 Act, is under fourteen years of age or, if he was under that age when any such video recording as is mentioned in section 32A(2) of that Act was made in respect of him, is under fifteen years of age; or

(b) in the case of an offence falling within section 32(2)(c) of that Act, is under seventeen years of age or, if he was under that age when any such video recording was made in respect of him, is under eighteen years of age.

(7) Any reference in subsection (6) above to an offence falling within paragraph (a), (b) or (c) of section 32(2) of that Act includes a reference to an offence which consists of attempting or conspiring to commit, or of aiding, abetting, counselling, procuring or inciting the commission of, an offence falling within that paragraph.

DEFINITIONS
"child": s.53(6).

GENERAL NOTE
The new procedure affords protection to both child victim and child witness alike; see also the transfer provisions in Sched. 6 to the 1991 Act. Parliament's aim has been to spare the child the stress of court appearances when possible and to get the case tried expeditiously. An application may be made by an accused to a judge of the Crown Court for the case to be dismissed (para. 5 of Sched. 6) but para. 5(5) prevents the court from giving leave, under subpara. (4), for oral evidence of the child to be given in support of the application for dismissal (see *Hansard*, H.L. Vol. 529, col. 122 and see also H.L. Vol. 528, col. 32).

Video recordings of testimony from child witnesses

54. After section 32 of the 1988 Act (evidence through television links) there shall be inserted the following section—

"Video recordings of testimony from child witnesses
32A.—(1) This section applies in relation to the following proceedings, namely—

(a) trials on indictment for any offence to which section 32(2) above applies;

(b) appeals to the criminal division of the Court of Appeal and hearings of references under section 17 of the Criminal Appeal Act 1968 in respect of any such offence; and

(c) proceedings in youth courts for any such offence and appeals to the Crown Court arising out of such proceedings.

(2) In any such proceedings a video recording of an interview which—

(a) is conducted between an adult and a child who is not the accused or one of the accused ('the child witness'); and

(b) relates to any matter in issue in the proceedings,

may, with the leave of the court, be given in evidence in so far as it is not excluded by the court under subsection (3) below.

(3) Where a video recording is tendered in evidence under this section, the court shall (subject to the exercise of any power of the court to exclude evidence which is otherwise admissible) give leave under subsection (2) above unless—

(a) it appears that the child witness will not be available for cross-examination;

(b) any rules of court requiring disclosure of the circumstances in which the recording was made have not been complied with to the satisfaction of the court; or

(c) the court is of the opinion, having regard to all the circumstances of the case, that in the interests of justice the recording ought not to be admitted;

and where the court gives such leave it may, if it is of the opinion that in the interests of justice any part of the recording ought not to be admitted, direct that that part shall be excluded.

(4) In considering whether any part of a recording ought to be excluded under subsection (3) above, the court shall consider whether any prejudice to the accused, or one of the accused, which might result from the admission of that part is outweighed by the desirability of showing the whole, or substantially the whole, of the recorded interview.

(5) Where a video recording is admitted under this section—

(a) the child witness shall be called by the party who tendered it in evidence;

(b) that witness shall not be examined in chief on any matter which, in the opinion of the court, has been dealt with in his recorded testimony.

(6) Where a video recording is given in evidence under this section, any statement made by the child witness which is disclosed by the recording shall be treated as if given by that witness in direct oral testimony; and accordingly—

(a) any such statement shall be admissible evidence of any fact of which such testimony from him would be admissible;

(b) no such statement shall be capable of corroborating any other evidence given by him;

and in estimating the weight, if any, to be attached to such a statement, regard shall be had to all the circumstances from which any inference can reasonably be drawn (as to its accuracy or otherwise).

(7) In this section 'child' means a person who—

(a) in the case of an offence falling within section 32(2)(a) or (b) above, is under fourteen years of age or, if he was under that age when the video recording was made, is under fifteen years of age; or

(b) in the case of an offence falling within section 32(2)(c) above, is under seventeen years of age or, if he was under that age when the video recording was made, is under eighteen years of age.

(8) Any reference in subsection (7) above to an offence falling within paragraph (a), (b) or (c) of section 32(2) above includes a reference to an offence which consists of attempting or conspiring to commit, or of aiding, abetting, counselling, procuring or inciting the commission of, an offence falling within that paragraph.

(9) In this section—

'statement' includes any representation of fact, whether made in words or otherwise;

'video recording' means any recording, on any medium, from which a moving image may by any means be produced and includes the accompanying sound-track.

(10) A magistrates' court inquiring into an offence as examining justices under section 6 of the Magistrates' Courts Act 1980 may consider any video recording as respects which leave under subsection (2) above is to be sought at the trial, notwithstanding that the child witness is not called at the committal proceedings.

(11) Without prejudice to the generality of any enactment conferring power to make rules of court, such rules may make such provision as appears to the authority making them to be necessary or expedient for the purposes of this section.

(12) Nothing in this section shall prejudice the admissibility of any video recording which would be admissible apart from this section."

DEFINITIONS
"child": s.54(7).
"statement": s.54(9).
"video recording": s.54(9).
"youth courts": s.70(1).

GENERAL NOTE

Subs. (1)
Juvenile courts are to be renamed "youth courts" and s.32 of the 1988 Act now applies as much to these courts (but not to magistrates' courts) as to any other.

Concern has been expressed as to the resources needed to give effect to these provisions. Not only do youth courts not have, at present, the necessary equipment, but some court houses lack the necessary facilities. One solution is for the youth court to sit at a location where the necessary facilities do exist. However, without statutory intervention, this could present practical difficulties of jurisdiction if the appropriate place fell outside the petty sessions area for which the youth court was appointed. Accordingly, s.55(4) of the 1991 Act was introduced to meet this particular problem (see *Hansard*, H.L. Vol. 529, col. 147).

It is not entirely clear why magistrates' courts have not been included in the new s.32(A)(1) of the 1988 Act.

Section 32(A)(2), (3) and (4)
Criticisms that the adversarial system was both "frightening and formal" (*per* Ann Winterton, *Official Report*, Standing Committee A, January 22, 1991 (p.m.), col. 410) have been met, in part, by relaxing rules of evidence and court procedure, to spare the child *examination-in-chief* if his or her testimony in chief can be recorded pre-trial in an informal setting and then showed to the court. This accords with the recommendations of the Pigot Report. However, as the Lord Chancellor pointed out during Report (*Hansard*, H.L. 529, col. 137) the procedure is not without its difficulties, not least because the result may be a series of lengthy interviews and not just one concise, relevant account.

An important safeguard is afforded to an accused by subs. (3)(a) so that leave will not be given if it appears that the child witness will not be available for cross-examination. Where the child is available, and the recording admitted, then the child shall be simply "tendered" for cross-examination (subs. (5)). This procedure, of course, continues to expose the child to the "agony of being cross-examined in open court" (see speech of Ms. Golding, *Official Report*, Standing Committee A, January 22, 1991 (p.m.), col. 406). The Pigot Report recommended that child witnesses "ought never to be required to appear in public as witnesses in the Crown Court" and suggested that the prosecution should be able to apply, as of right, for a child witness to be examined and cross-examined at a pre-trial out-of-court hearing which would be video-recorded and shown to the court. An amendment was introduced by the House of Lords in an attempt to give effect to these recommendations (amendment No. 82) but was subsequently withdrawn (*Hansard*, H.L. Vol. 528, col. 35). One month later Lord Mottistone moved a similar amendment (then No. 78B) which was resolved in the negative (*Hansard*, H.L. Vol. 529, col. 123). Although the Council of Her Majesty's Circuit Judges supported such a scheme (*Hansard*, H.L. Vol. 528, col. 45), it does not seem to have represented the majority view of "judicial interests", and at least two presiding judges warned that pre-trial cross-examination could end up duplicating the trial (*Hansard*, H.L. Vol. 528, col. 53). The Criminal Bar Association appears to have supported the scheme (*Hansard*, H.L. Vol. 529, cols. 127–128). The thrust of the objection to the scheme was twofold. First, preparing and conducting cross-examination long before the trial, adequately and without the need for re-calling the child witness if new material came to light, was impractical and unrealistic. Secondly, given that recall for cross-examination was foreseeable and could happen at any time during the trial proper, the scheme might be in danger of causing more stress to the child rather than less (*Hansard*, H.L. Vol. 528, col. 51).

The upshot is a compromise. The child may still be cross-examined, but not by the accused acting in person (see s.55(7) of the 1991 Act). However, the child's evidence may be given relatively informally through the live television link procedure introduced under the Criminal Justice Act 1988.

Further amendments of enactments relating to children's evidence

55.—(1) In section 103 of the 1980 Act (evidence of children in committal proceedings) subsection (3)(a) shall cease to have effect and for subsection (5) there shall be substituted the following subsection—

"(5) In this section 'child' has the same meaning as in section 53 of the Criminal Justice Act 1991."

(2) In subsection (1) of section 32 of the 1988 Act (evidence through television links)—

(a) for the words from "on a trial" to "1968" there shall be substituted the words "in proceedings to which subsection (1A) below applies"; and

(b) for paragraph (b) there shall be substituted the following paragraph—

"(b) the witness is a child, or is to be cross-examined following the admission under section 32A below of a video recording of testimony from him, and the offence is one to which subsection (2) below applies,".

(3) After that subsection there shall be inserted the following subsection—

"(1A) This subsection applies—

(a) to trials on indictment, appeals to the criminal division of the Court of Appeal and hearings of references under section 17 of the Criminal Appeal Act 1968; and

(b) to proceedings in youth courts and appeals to the Crown Court arising out of such proceedings.

(4) After subsection (3) of that section there shall be inserted the following subsections—

"(3A) Where, in the case of any proceedings before a youth court—

(a) leave is given by virtue of subsection (1)(b) above for evidence to be given through a television link; and

(b) suitable facilities for receiving such evidence are not available at any petty-sessional court-house in which the court can (apart from this subsection) lawfully sit,

the court may sit for the purposes of the whole or any part of those proceedings at any place at which such facilities are available and which has been appointed for the purposes of this subsection by the justices acting for the petty sessions area for which the court acts.

(3B) A place appointed under subsection (3) above may be outside the petty sessions area for which it is appointed; but it shall be deemed to be in that area for the purpose of the jurisdiction of the justices acting for that area."

(5) In subsection (5) of that section, for paragraphs (a) and (b) there shall be substituted the words "Magistrates' Courts Rules, Crown Court Rules and Criminal Appeal Rules."

(6) After subsection (5) of that section there shall be inserted the following subsection—

"(6) Subsection (7) of section 32A below shall apply for the purposes of this section as it applies for the purposes of that section, but with the omission of the references to a person being, in the cases there mentioned, under the age of fifteen years or under the age of eighteen years."

(7) After section 34 of the 1988 Act there shall be inserted the following section—

"Cross-examination of alleged child victims

34A.—(1) No person who is charged with an offence to which section 32(2) above applies shall cross-examine in person any witness who—

(a) is alleged—

(i) to be a person against whom the offence was committed; or

(ii) to have witnessed the commission of the offence; and

(b) is a child, or is to be cross-examined following the admission under section 32A above of a video recording of testimony from him.

(2) Subsection (7) of section 32A above shall apply for the purposes of this section as it applies for the purposes of that section, but with the omission of the references to a person being, in the cases there mentioned, under the age of fifteen years or under the age of eighteen years."

DEFINITIONS

"youth court": s.70(1).

GENERAL NOTE

Subs. (7)

See the notes to s.54. It will be of interest to see how the courts deal with the problem of the accused acting in person who flatly refuses to be legally represented. If counsel is nominated by the court to conduct that part of the proceedings to which s.34A relates, but the accused refuses to give him instructions, then it seems that the accused faces the stark alternative of being unable to challenge the evidence of the child at all. Some truculent defendants may see that prohibition as a frustrating inconvenience, but not an overriding obstacle, and save the "attack" until he gives evidence and/or makes his own final speech.

Responsibilities of parent or guardian

Attendance at court of parent or guardian

56. Subsection (1) of section 34 (attendance at court of parent or guardian) of the 1933 Act shall cease to have effect and after that section there shall be inserted the following section—

"Attendance at court of parent or guardian

34A.—(1) Where a child or young person is charged with an offence or is for any other reason brought before a court, the court—

(a) may in any case; and

(b) shall in the case of a child or a young person who is under the age of sixteen years,

require a person who is a parent or guardian of his to attend at the court during all the stages of the proceedings, unless and to the extent that the court is satisfied that it would be unreasonable to require such attendance, having regard to the circumstances of the case.

(2) In relation to a child or young person for whom a local authority have parental responsibility and who—

(a) is in their care; or

(b) is provided with accommodation by them in the exercise of any functions (in particular those under the Children Act 1989) which stand referred to their social services committee under the Local Authority Social Services Act 1970,

the reference in subsection (1) above to a person who is a parent or guardian of his shall be construed as a reference to that authority or, where he is allowed to live with such a person, as including such a reference.

In this subsection 'local authority' and 'parental responsibility' have the same meanings as in the Children Act 1989.''

DEFINITIONS
"local authority": Children Act 1989.
"parental responsibility": Children Act 1989.

GENERAL NOTE
Section 34(1) of the 1933 Act, as originally drafted, did not impose a mandatory obligation on parents or guardians to attend court unless the court thought it "desirable" that they should. The new s.34(A)(1) removes the "desirability" test and imposes a mandatory obligation to attend in cases where the child is under 16 years, subject to the proviso which, it is submitted, excuses parents or guardians whose attendance is unnecessary "in the circumstances".

Responsibility of parent or guardian for financial penalties

57.—(1) After subsection (1A) of section 55 of the 1933 Act (power to order parent or guardian to pay fine etc. instead of child or young person) there shall be inserted the following subsection—

"(1B) In the case of a young person who has attained the age of sixteen years, subsections (1) and (1A) above shall have effect as if, instead of imposing a duty, they conferred a power to make such an order as is mentioned in those subsections."

(2) After subsection (4) of that section there shall be inserted the following subsection—

"(5) In relation to a child or young person for whom a local authority have parental responsibility and who—
(a) is in their care; or
(b) is provided with accommodation by them in the exercise of any functions (in particular those under the Children Act 1989) which stand referred to their social services committee under the Local Authority Social Services Act 1970,
references in this section to his parent or guardian shall be construed as references to that authority.

In this subsection 'local authority' and 'parental responsibility' have the same meanings as in the Children Act 1989."

(3) For the purposes of any order under that section made against the parent or guardian of a child or young person, such of the following as is applicable, namely—
(a) section 18(2) above;
(b) section 19 above; and
(c) section 35(4)(a) of the 1973 Act (fixing amount of compensation order),
shall have effect as if any reference to the disposable weekly income or means of the offender, or the means of the person against whom the compensation order is made, were a reference to the disposable weekly income or, as the case may be, means of the parent or guardian.

(4) For the purposes of any such order made against a local authority—
(a) section 18(2) above shall, where applicable, have effect as if the reference in paragraph (b) to the disposable weekly income of the offender were a reference to the maximum amount which could be determined under that paragraph in relation to a person of the same age as the offender; but
(b) neither section 19 above nor section 35(4)(a) of the 1973 Act shall apply;
and in this subsection "local authority" has the same meaning as in the Children Act 1989.

DEFINITIONS
"local authority": Children Act 1989.

GENERAL NOTE
    Section 55 of the Children and Young Persons Act 1933 imposes a duty on the court to order a
parent or guardian to pay the financial penalties imposed on a child or young person unless it is
unreasonable to expect the parent or guardian to pay or if he or she cannot be found. The
purpose of s.55 of the 1933 Act is to express Parliament's view that parents should take their
duties seriously but it is not to hold them vicariously liable: *Lenihan* v. *Yorkshire Metropolitan
Police* (1981) 3 Cr.App.R.(S.) 42 D.C.
    The new s.55(1B) gives the court a power but not a duty in respect of s.55(1) where the young
person has attained the age of 16.
    Note that these provisions must now take account of the "unit fine" system enacted in ss.18
and 19 of the 1991 Act; and note s.35(4)(a) of the Powers of Criminal Courts Act 1973.

Binding over of parent or guardian

58.—(1) Where a child or young person ("the relevant minor") is convicted of an offence, the powers conferred by this section shall be exercisable
by the court by which he is sentenced for that offence; and it shall be the duty
of the court, in a case where the relevant minor has not attained the age of 16
years—
  (a) to exercise those powers if it is satisfied, having regard to the circum-
      stances of the case, that their exercise would be desirable in the
      interests of preventing the commission by him of further offences;
      and
  (b) where it does not exercise them, to state in open court that it is not
      satisfied as mentioned in paragraph (a) above and why it is not so
      satisfied.
(2) The powers conferred by this section are as follows—
  (a) with the consent of the relevant minor's parent or guardian, to order
      the parent or guardian to enter into a recognisance to take proper care
      of him and exercise proper control over him; and
  (b) if the parent or guardian refuses consent and the court considers the
      refusal unreasonable, to order the parent or guardian to pay a fine not
      exceeding £1,000.
(3) An order under this section shall not require the parent or guardian to
enter into a recognisance—
  (a) for an amount exceeding £1,000; or
  (b) for a period exceeding three years or, where the relevant minor will
      attain the age of 18 years in a period shorter than three years, for a
      period exceeding that shorter period;
and section 120 of the 1980 Act (which relates to the forfeiture of recogni-
sances) shall apply in relation to a recognisance entered into in pursuance of
such an order as it applies to a recognisance to keep the peace.
(4) Section 18 above shall apply for the purposes of subsection (2)(b)
above as if the refusal to enter into a recognisance were a summary offence
punishable by a fine not exceeding level 3 on the standard scale; and a fine
imposed under that subsection shall be deemed for the purposes of any
enactment to be a sum adjudged to be paid by a conviction.
(5) In fixing the amount of a recognisance under this section, the court
shall take into account among other things the means of the parent or
guardian so far as they appear or are known to the court; and this subsection
applies whether taking into account the means of the parent or guardian has
the effect of increasing or reducing the amount of the recognisance.
(6) A parent or guardian may appeal to the Crown Court against an order
under this section made by a magistrates' court.
(7) A parent or guardian may appeal to the Court of Appeal against an
order under this section made by the Crown Court, as if he had been
convicted on indictment and the order were a sentence passed on his
conviction.

(8) A court may vary or revoke an order made by it under this section if, on the application of the parent or guardian, it appears to the court, having regard to any change in the circumstances since the order was made, to be in the interests of justice to do so.

DEFINITIONS
    "relevant minor": s.58(1).

GENERAL NOTE
    Section 58 applies where the offender is 15 years of age or less. The age level was determined on the basis that many 16- and 17-year-old youths are sufficiently grown up to take responsibility (*per* John Patten, *Official Report* Standing Committee A, January 24, 1991 (a.m.), col. 463).
    The proposals have been opposed on the basis that where parents refuse to give their consent the hearing is likely to be protracted and so lead to more contested juvenile cases being heard (*ibid.* col. 466).
    Fines must be determined in accordance with the "unit fine" scheme of s.18 of the 1991 Act.

Detention etc. pending trial

Detention at a police station

59. In section 38 of the Police and Criminal Evidence Act 1984 (duties of custody officer after charge), for subsections (6) and (6A) there shall be substituted the following subsections—
    "(6) Where a custody officer authorises an arrested juvenile to be kept in police detention under subsection (1) above, the custody officer shall, unless he certifies—
        (a) that, by reason of such circumstances as are specified in the certificate, it is impracticable for him to do so; or
        (b) in the case of an arrested juvenile who has attained the age of 15 years, that no secure accommodation is available and that keeping him in other local authority accommodation would not be adequate to protect the public from serious harm from him,
secure that the arrested juvenile is moved to local authority accommodation.
    (6A) In this section—
        'local authority accommodation' means accommodation provided by or on behalf of a local authority (within the meaning of the Children Act 1989);
        'secure accommodation' means accommodation provided for the purpose of restricting liberty;
        'sexual offence' and 'violent offence' have the same meanings as in Part I of the Criminal Justice Act 1991;
and any reference, in relation to an arrested juvenile charged with a violent or sexual offence, to protecting the public from serious harm from him shall be construed as a reference to protecting members of the public from death or serious personal injury, whether physical or psychological, occasioned by further such offences committed by him."

DEFINITIONS
    "local authority accommodation": s.59.
    "secure accommodation": s.59.
    "sexual offence": s.31(1).
    "violent offence": s.31(1).

GENERAL NOTE
    Section 38(6) of the Police and Criminal Evidence Act 1984 is the successor to s.29(3) of the Children and Young Persons Act 1969. Section 38(6) should be read with Code C, para. 16.6 and note 16B of the Codes of Practice Revised Edition 1991 in mind.

Section 38(6) of the 1984 Act caused confusion as to what was meant by "impracticable" and there were some differences in practice by the police as to how the sections should be applied (and see *R.* v. *Chief Constable of the Cambridgeshire Constabulary*, ex p. *M.* [1991] 2 All E.R. 777).

By way of the new s.38(6)(a) of the 1984 Act, the young person *must* be transferred to local authority accommodation unless there are practical circumstances which make that impractical, *e.g.* bad weather, or where the conditions set out in s.38(6)(b) apply. There is some difficulty, however, as to how the interaction of these two exceptions will operate in practice in the light of *R.* v. *Chief Constable of Cambridgeshire Constabulary*, ex p. *M. M.*, aged 16, was in voluntary care and was arrested by police for theft. He was detained in custody and the custody officer refused to release him into the care of the local authority because the hostel proposed was insecure and he would be able to commit further offences. By s.38(6) of the 1984 Act, as formerly drafted, the circumstances of detention were not entirely a matter for the local authority and accordingly the Divisional Court held that the custody officer was entitled to act as he did. So far as the new s.38(6)(a) is concerned, it is submitted that the facts of *R.* v. *Chief Constable of Cambridgeshire*, ex p. *M.* fall outside that exception but the wording of s.38(6)(b) makes it plain that the circumstances of detention are *not* exclusively a matter for the local authority in cases where the arrested juvenile has attained the age of 15 years, in circumstances where there is no secure accommodation available *and* where keeping him in other local authority accommodation would not be adequate to "protect the public from serious harm from him". Where a 15- or 16-year-old is accused of a "violent" or "sexual" offence then the words "serious harm" are clarified in s.38(6A) of the 1984 Act, but what does "serious harm" mean where the accused juvenile (aged 15 or 16) is charged with a series of domestic burglaries and the police fear he will offend again without secure accommodation? Earl Ferrers, in supporting the new s.38(6)(b), clearly did not think that domestic burglaries, frequently committed by the accused juvenile, would necessarily be excluded from s.38(6)(b) (see *Hansard*, H.L. Vol. 529, col. 169).

Remands and committals to local authority accommodation

60.—(1) For section 23 of the 1969 Act there shall be substituted the following section—

> **"Remands and committals to local authority accommodation**
> 23.—(1) Where—
> (a) a court remands a child or young person charged with or convicted of one or more offences or commits him for trial or sentence; and
> (b) he is not released on bail,
> the remand or committal shall be to local authority accommodation; and in the following provisions of this section, any reference (however expressed) to a remand shall be construed as including a reference to a committal.
>
> (2) A court remanding a person to local authority accommodation shall designate the local authority who are to receive him; and that authority shall be—
> (a) in the case of a person who is being looked after by a local authority, that authority; and
> (b) in any other case, the local authority in whose area it appears to the court that he resides or the offence or one of the offences was committed.
>
> (3) Where a person is remanded to local authority accommodation, it shall be lawful for any person acting on behalf of the designated authority to detain him.
>
> (4) Subject to subsection (5) below, a court remanding a person to local authority accommodation may, after consultation with the designated authority, require that authority to comply with a security requirement, that is to say, a requirement that the person in question be placed and kept in secure accommodation.
>
> (5) A court shall not impose a security requirement except in respect of a young person who has attained the age of fifteen, and then only if—

(a) he is charged with or has been convicted of a violent or sexual offence, or an offence punishable in the case of an adult with imprisonment for a term of fourteen years or more; or

(b) he has a recent history of absconding while remanded to local authority accommodation, and is charged with or has been convicted of an imprisonable offence alleged or found to have been committed while he was so remanded,

and (in either case) the court is of opinion that only such a requirement would be adequate to protect the public from serious harm from him.

(6) Where a court imposes a security requirement in respect of a person, it shall be its duty—

(a) to state in open court that it is of such opinion as is mentioned in subsection (5) above; and

(b) to explain to him in open court and in ordinary language why it is of that opinion;

and a magistrates' court shall cause a reason stated by it under paragraph (b) above to be specified in the warrant of commitment and to be entered in the register.

(7) A court remanding a person to local authority accommodation without imposing a security requirement may, after consultation with the designated authority, require that person to comply with any such conditions as could be imposed under section 3(6) of the Bail Act 1976 if he were then being granted bail.

(8) Where a court imposes on a person any such conditions as are mentioned in subsection (7) above, it shall be its duty to explain to him in open court and in ordinary language why it is imposing those conditions; and a magistrates' court shall cause a reason stated by it under this subsection to be specified in the warrant of commitment and to be entered in the register.

(9) A court remanding a person to local authority accommodation without imposing a security requirement may, after consultation with the designated authority, impose on that authority requirements—

(a) for securing compliance with any conditions imposed on that person under subsection (7) above; or

(b) stipulating that he shall not be placed with a named person.

(10) Where a person is remanded to local authority accommodation, a relevant court—

(a) may, on the application of the designated authority, impose on that person any such conditions as could be imposed under subsection (7) above if the court were then remanding him to such accommodation; and

(b) where it does so, may impose on that authority any requirements for securing compliance with the conditions so imposed.

(11) Where a person is remanded to local authority accommodation, a relevant court may, on the application of the designated authority or that person, vary or revoke any conditions or requirements imposed under subsection (7), (9) or (10) above.

(12) In this section—

'court' and 'magistrates' court' include a justice;

'imprisonable offence' means an offence punishable in the case of an adult with imprisonment;

'relevant court', in relation to a person remanded to local authority accommodation, means the court by which he was so remanded, or any magistrates' court having jurisdiction in the place where he is for the time being;

'secure accommodation' means accommodation which is provided in a community home for the purpose of restricting liberty, and is approved for that purpose by the Secretary of State;

'sexual offence' and 'violent offence' have the same meanings as in Part I of the Criminal Justice Act 1991;

'young person' means a person who has attained the age of fourteen years and is under the age of seventeen years.

(13) In this section—

(a) any reference to a person who is being looked after by a local authority shall be construed in accordance with section 22 of the Children Act 1989;

(b) any reference to consultation shall be construed as a reference to such consultation (if any) as is reasonably practicable in all the circumstances of the case; and

(c) any reference, in relation to a person charged with or convicted of a violent or sexual offence, to protecting the public from serious harm from him shall be construed as a reference to protecting members of the public from death or serious personal injury, whether physical or psychological, occasioned by further such offences committed by him.

(14) This section has effect subject to—

(a) section 37 of the Magistrates' Courts Act 1980 (committal to the Crown Court with a view to a sentence of detention in a young offender institution); and

(b) section 128(7) of that Act (remands to the custody of a constable for periods of not more than three days),

but section 128(7) shall have effect in relation to a child or young person as if for the reference to three clear days there were substituted a reference to 24 hours."

(2) In Section 37 of the 1980 Act (committal of young person to Crown Court for sentence)—

(a) in subsection (1), for the words "17 years old" there shall be substituted the words "18 years old";

(b) in subsection (2), for the words "A person committed in custody under subsection (1) above" there shall be substituted the words "Where a person committed in custody under subsection (1) above is not less than 17 years old, he"; and

(c) after that subsection there shall be inserted the following subsection—

"(3) Where a person committed in custody under subsection (1) above is less than 17 years old—

(a) he shall be committed to accommodation provided by or on behalf of a local authority (within the meaning of the Children Act 1989) and

(b) the court by which he is so committed shall impose a security requirement within the meaning of section 23 of the Children and Young Persons Act 1969."

(3) In the case of a child or young person who has been remanded or committed to local authority accommodation by a youth court or a magistrates' court other than a youth court, any application under section 25 of the Children Act 1989 (use of accommodation for restricting liberty) shall, notwithstanding anything in section 92(2) of that Act or section 65 of the 1980 Act, be made to that court.

DEFINITIONS
  "court": subs. (12).
  "imprisonable offence": subs. (12).
  "relevant court": subs. (12).
  "secure accommodation": subs. (12).

"sexual offence": s.31(1).
"violent offence": s.31(1).
"young person": subs. (12).

GENERAL NOTE
The aim of these provisions is to follow the findings and proposals in the Home Office
consultative paper *The Remand of Alleged Juvenile Offenders* and to end, in so far as it is
practicable, prison remands for juvenile defendants (see debates at *Hansard*, H.L. Vol. 528,
col. 123).

Provision by local authorities of secure accommodation

61.—(1) It shall be the duty of every local authority to secure that they are
in a position to comply with any security requirement which may be imposed
on them under—
   (a) section 23(4) of the 1969 Act (remands and committals to local
       authority accommodation); or
   (b) section 37(3) of the 1980 Act (committal of young person to Crown
       Court for sentence).
(2) A local authority may discharge their duty under subsection (1) above
either by providing secure accommodation themselves or by making
arrangements with other local authorities for the provision by them of such
accommodation.
(3) The Secretary of State may by regulations make provision as to the
co-operation required of local authorities in the provision of secure
accommodation.
(4) The power to make regulations under this section shall be exercisable
by statutory instrument which shall be subject to annulment in pursuance of
a resolution of either House of Parliament.
(5) In this section expressions used in section 23 of the 1969 Act have the
same meanings as in that section.

Transitory provisions pending provision of secure accommodation

62.—(1) In relation to any time before such day as the Secretary of State
may by order made by statutory instrument appoint, section 23 of the 1969
Act as substituted by section 60(1) above shall have effect with the following
modifications.
(2) In subsection (1), immediately before the words "the remand" there
shall be inserted the words "then, unless he is declared by the court, after
consultation with a probation officer or a social worker of a local authority
social services department, to be a person to whom subsection (5) below
applies."
(3) For subsections (4) and (5) there shall be substituted the following
subsections—
   "(4) Where a court declares a person to be one to whom subsection
   (5) below applies, it shall remand him—
      (a) to a remand centre, if it has been notified that such a centre is
          available for the reception from the court of such persons; and
      (b) to a prison, if it has not been so notified.
   (4A) A court shall not declare a person who is not legally represented in the court to whom subsection (5) below applies unless—
      (a) he applied for legal aid and the application was refused on the
          ground that it did not appear his means were such that he
          required assistance; or
      (b) having been informed of his right to apply for legal aid and had
          the opportunity to do so, he refused or failed to apply.
   (5) This subsection applies to a young person who is male and has
   attained the age of fifteen, but only if—
      (a) he is charged with or has been convicted of a violent or sexual

offence, or an offence punishable in the case of an adult with imprisonment for a term of fourteen years or more; or

(b) he has a recent history of absconding while remanded to local authority accommodation, and is charged with or has been convicted of an imprisonable offence alleged or found to have been committed while he was so remanded,

and (in either case) the court is of opinion that only remanding him to a remand centre or prison would be adequate to protect the public from serious harm from him."

(4) In subsection (6)—

(a) for the words "imposes a security requirement in respect of a young person" there shall be substituted the words "declares a person to be one to whom subsection (5) above applies"; and

(b) for the words "subsection (5) above" there shall be substituted the words "that subsection."

(5) In subsections (7) and (9) the words "without imposing a security requirement" shall be omitted.

(6) After subsection (9) there shall be inserted the following subsection—

"(9A) Where a person is remanded to local authority accommodation, a relevant court may, on the application of the designated authority, declare him to be a person to whom subsection (5) above applies; and on its doing so, he shall cease to be remanded to local authority accommodation and subsection (4) above shall apply."

(7) In subsection (12), the definition of "secure accommodation" shall be omitted.

Young offenders

INTRODUCTION AND GENERAL NOTE

The thinking behind the legislation is revealed in the Green Paper *Punishment Custody and the Community* and in the White Paper *Crime, Justice and Protecting the Public* (1990) Cm. 965. One objective has been to bring 17-year-old youths into the juvenile courts but such a description would no longer be apt and therefore by s.70 of the 1991 Act these courts are renamed "youth courts".

Custodial sentences under 1982 Act

63.—(1) Part I of the 1982 (Act) treatment of young offenders) shall be amended as follows.

(2) In section 1A (detention in a young offender institution)—

(a) in subsection (1), for the words "a male offender under 21 but not less than 14 years of age or a female offender under 21 but not less than 15 years of age" there shall be substituted the words "an offender under 21 but not less than 15 years of age";

(b) in subsection (2), for the words "section 1B(1) and (2)" there shall be substituted the words "section 1B(2)";

(c) in subsection (3), the words "section 1B(3) below" shall cease to have effect and for the words "21 days" there shall be substituted the words "the minimum period applicable to the offender under subsection (4A) below";

(d) in subsection (4), for the words "21 days" there shall be substituted the words "the minimum period applicable"; and

(e) after subsection (4) there shall be inserted the following subsection—

"(4A) For the purposes of subsections (3) and (4) above, the minimum period of detention applicable to an offender is—

(a) in the case of an offender under 21 but not less than 18 years of age, the period of 21 days; and

(b) in the case of an offender under 18 years of age, the period of two months."

(3) In section 1B (special provision for offenders under 17)—
(a) subsections (1) and (3) shall cease to have effect;
(b) in subsection (2), for the words "aged 15 or 16" there shall be substituted the words "aged 15, 16 or 17"; and
(c) for subsections (4) and (5) there shall be substituted the following subsections—

"(4) A court shall not pass on an offender aged 15, 16 or 17 a sentence of detention in a young offender institution whose effect would be that the offender would be sentenced to a total term which exceeds 12 months.

(5) Where the total term of detention in a young offender institution to which an offender aged 15, 16 or 17 is sentenced exceeds 12 months, so much of the term as exceeds 12 months shall be treated as remitted."

(4) In section 1C (accommodation of offenders in a young offender institution), for the words "under 17" there shall be substituted the words "under 18."

(5) In section 8 (custody for life) and section 9 (detention of persons aged 17 to 20 for default or contempt), the words "17 years" there shall be substituted the words "18 years."

Custodial sentences under 1933 Act

64. Section 53(2) of the 1933 Act (punishment of certain grave crimes) shall have effect, in relation to a person who has attained the age of 16, as if the reference to any offence punishable in the case of an adult with imprisonment for 14 years or more, not being an offence the sentence for which is fixed by law, included a reference to an offence under section 14 of the Sexual Offences Act 1956 (indecent assault on a woman).

Supervision of young offenders after release

65.—(1) Where a person under the age of 22 years ("the offender") is released from a term of detention in a young offender institution or under section 53 of the 1933 Act, he shall be under the supervision of a probation officer or a social worker of a local authority social services department.

(2) The supervision period ends on the offender's 22nd birthday if it has not ended before.

(3) Subject to subsection (2) above, where the offender is released otherwise than on licence under Part II of this Act, the supervision period begins on his release and ends three months from his release.

(4) Subject to subsection (2) above, where the offender is released on licence under Part II of this Act and the licence expires less than three months from his release, the supervision period begins on the expiry of the licence and ends three months from his release.

(5) Where a person is under supervision under this section, he shall comply with such requirements, if any, as may for the time being be specified in a notice from the Secretary of State.

(6) A person who without reasonable excuse fails to comply with a requirement imposed under section 5 above shall be liable on summary conviction—
(a) to a fine not exceeding level 3 on the standard scale; or
(b) to an appropriate custodial sentence for a period not exceeding 30 days,
but not liable to be dealt with in any other way.

(7) In subsection (6) above "appropriate custodial sentence" means—
(a) a sentence of imprisonment, if the offender has attained the age of 21 years when he is sentenced; and

(b) a sentence of detention in a young offender institution, if he has not attained that age.

(8) A person released from a custodial sentence passed under subsection (6) above shall not be liable to a period of supervision in consequence of his conviction under the subsection, but his conviction shall not prejudice any liability to supervision to which he was previously subject, and that liability shall accordingly continue until the end of the supervision period.

Supervision orders

66. For section 15 of the 1969 Act (variation and discharge of supervision orders) there shall be substituted the provisions set out in Schedule 7 to this Act.

Attendance centre orders

67.—(1) In section 17 of the 1982 Act (maximum number of hours at attendance centre for persons of different age)—
   (a) subsection (3) shall cease to have effect; and
   (b) in subsection (5), for the words "17 years," in both places where they occur, there shall be substituted the words "16 years."

(2) In section 18 of that Act (discharge and variation of attendance centre orders), after subsection (4) there shall be inserted the following subsection—

> "(4A) The power to discharge an attendance centre order includes power to deal with the offender, for the offence in respect of which the order was made, in any manner in which he could have been dealt with for that offence by the court which made the order if the order had not been made."

(3) In subsection (6)(b) of that section, the words " if the court is satisfied that the offender proposes to change or has changed his residence" shall cease to have effect.

(4) In subsection (3) of section 19 of that Act (breaches of attendance centre orders or attendance centre rules) after the words "that court" there shall be inserted the words "may, without prejudice to the continuation of the order, impose on him a fine not exceeding £1,000 or."

(5) After that subsection there shall be inserted the following subsection—

> "(3A) Section 18 of the Criminal Justice Act 1991 (fixing of certain fines by reference to units) shall apply for the purposes of subsection (3) above as if the failure to attend or the breach of the rules were a summary offence punishable by a fine not exceeding level 3 on the standard scale; and a fine imposed under that subsection shall be deemed for the purposes of any enactment to be a sum adjudged to be paid by a conviction."

(6) After subsection (5) of that section there shall be inserted the following subsection—

> "(5A) In dealing with an offender under subsection (3)(a) or (5) above, the court concerned—
>   (a) shall take into account the extent to which the offender has complied with the requirements of the attendance centre order; and
>   (b) may assume, in the case of an offender who has wilfully and persistently failed to comply with those requirements, that he has refused to give his consent to a community sentence which has been proposed by the court and requires that consent."

Miscellaneous

Persons aged 17 to be treated as young persons for certain purposes

68. The following enactments, namely—
(a) the Children and Young Persons Acts 1933 to 1969;
(b) section 43(3) of the 1952 Act (remand centres, young offender institutions etc.);
(c) section 5(2) of the Rehabilitation of Offenders Act 1974 (which provides for rehabilitation periods to be reduced by half for young offenders); and
(d) the 1980 Act,
shall have effect subject to the amendments specified in Schedule 8 to this Act, being amendments which, for certain purposes of those enactments, have the effect of substituting the age of 18 years for the age of 17 years.

Non-appearance of persons aged 16 and 17: plea of guilty

69. In section 12 of the 1980 Act (non-appearance of accused: plea of guilty), after subsection (1) there shall be inserted the following subsection—
　　　"(1A) The reference in subsection (1) above to the issue of a summons requiring a person to appear before a magistrates' court other than a youth court includes a reference to the issue of a summons requiring a person who has attained the age of 16 at the time when it is issued to appear before a youth court."

Renaming of juvenile courts etc.

70.—(1) Juvenile courts shall be renamed youth courts and juvenile court panels shall be renamed youth court panels.
(2) Any reference to juvenile courts or juvenile court panels in any enactment passed or instrument made before the commencement of this section shall be construed in accordance with subsection (1) above.

Amendments to service law

71. The enactments mentioned in Schedule 9 to this Act shall have effect subject to the amendments there specified (being amendments to service law corresponding to certain provisions of this Act).

Repeal of certain provisions not brought in force

72. The following provisions (none of which has been brought into force), namely—
　　　section 4 of the 1969 Act (prohibition of criminal proceedings for offences by children);
　　　in section 5 of that Act (restrictions on criminal proceedings for offences by young persons), subsections (1) to (7) and, in subsection (9), the definitions of "qualified informant" and "designated";
　　　section 8 of that Act (fingerprinting of suspected young persons); and
　　　in section 37 of the Police and Criminal Evidence Act 1984, subsections (11) to (14) (duties of custody officer as respects young persons),
shall cease to have effect.

Part IV

Provision of Services

Probation services

Inspectors of probation

73.—(1) The Secretary of State may appoint such number of inspectors of probation (to be known collectively as "Her Majesty's Inspectorate of Probation") as he may with the approval of the Treasury determine.

(2) The Secretary of State shall appoint one of the persons so appointed to be Her Majesty's Chief Inspector of Probation.

(3) It shall be the duty of inspectors of probation—

(a) to inspect and report to the Secretary of State on the probation service for each probation area, and the activities carried out by or on behalf of that service; and

(b) to discharge such other functions in connection with the provision of probation or related services (whether or not provided by or on behalf of the probation service for any area) as the Secretary of State may from time to time direct.

(4) The Secretary of State shall make to or in respect of inspectors of probation such payments by way of remuneration, allowances or otherwise as he may with the approval of the Treasury determine.

Default power where probation committee fails to discharge statutory duty

74.—(1) The Secretary of State may make an order under this section if he is of the opinion that, without reasonable excuse, a probation committee—

(a) is failing properly to discharge any duty imposed on it by or under any enactment; or

(b) has so failed and is likely to do so again.

(2) An order under this section shall—

(a) state that the Secretary of State is of the said opinion; and

(b) make such provision as he considers requisite for the purpose of securing that duty is properly discharged by the committee.

(3) Where an order is made under this section, it shall be the duty of the committee to comply with the provision made by the order.

The inner London probation area

75.—(1) Schedule 3 to the 1973 Act (the probation service and its functions) shall be amended as follows.

(2) In paragraph 1 (probation areas), for sub-paragraphs (3) and (4) there shall be substituted the following sub-paragraph—

"(3) The Secretary of State—

(a) shall make provision by an order under sub-paragraph (1) above for combining in one probation area (in this Schedule referred to as 'the inner London probation area') all of the petty sessions divisions of the inner London area; and

(b) may make provision by such an order for including in that probation area one or more other petty sessions areas."

(3) In paragraphs 2(3), 4, 5, 6(3), 13(3) and 18(3), for the words "inner London area," in each place where they occur, there shall be substituted the words "inner London probation area."

(4) In paragraph 2(3), for paragraph (b) there shall be substituted the following paragraph—

"(b) of such number as may be so specified of justices of the peace for the petty sessions areas of the inner London probation area who are not metropolitan stipendiary magistrates, chosen in such manner as may be so specified by the justices for those areas who are not such magistrates;".

(5) For paragraph 16 there shall be substituted the following paragraph—

"16.—(1) Paragraph 15 above shall not apply in relation to expenses incurred by the probation committee for the inner London probation area, but such sums as the Secretary of State may direct to meet the expenses and contributions which, in the case of any other probation area, would be payable by virtue of that paragraph by the local authority—

(a) shall be paid out of the metropolitan police fund; or

(b) where the inner London probation area includes one or more petty sessions areas outside the inner London area, shall be partly paid out of that fund and partly defrayed by the local authority or authorities concerned.

(2) Where paragraph (b) of sub-paragraph (1) above applies, the proportions to be paid or defrayed under that paragraph shall be such as may be agreed between the Receiver for the metropolitan police district and the local authority or authorities concerned or, in default of agreement, as may be determined by the Secretary of State.

(3) In this paragraph 'the local authority or authorities concerned' means the local authority or authorities in whose area or areas the petty sessions area or areas outside the inner London area is or are situated."

(6) In paragraph 17 (provision of accommodation by local authorities for the probation service)—

(a) in sub-paragraph (1), after the words "paragraph 15(1) or (3)" there shall be inserted the words "or 16(1) or (2)"; and

(b) after sub-paragraph (3) there shall be inserted the following sub-paragraph—

"(4) The foregoing provisions of this paragraph shall apply as if the Receiver for the metropolitan police district were a local authority and any sums required to be paid out of the metropolitan police fund were required to be defrayed by him; and any contribution received by him under sub-paragraph (3) above shall be paid into that fund."

(7) At the end of paragraph 19(1), there shall be added the words "and 'inner London probation area' has the meaning given by paragraph 1(3) above."

Court security

Provision of court security officers

76.—(1) In relation to each petty sessions area, the committee shall from time to time determine—

(a) whether court security officers should be provided, that is to say, persons whose duty it is to maintain order in any court-house to which they are for the time being assigned by the committee; and

(b) if so, how many such officers should be provided, and whether they should be provided by the committee or by the responsible authority.

(2) As soon as practicable after the making of a determination under subsection (1)(b) above, the committee or, as the case may be, the responsible authority shall provide the required number of court security officers, on such terms and conditions as they may determine—

(a) by employing persons to act as court security officers; or

(b) by entering into a contract with another person for the employment by him of persons to act as such officers.

(3) Before making any determination under subsection (1) or (2) above in relation to a petty sessions area which does not consist of or form part of the

inner London area, the committee shall consult with the responsible authority.

(4) Where, in relation to a petty sessions area which does not consist of or form part of the inner London area, the responsible authority is aggrieved by any determination made by the committee under subsection (1) or (2) above, the authority may, within one month from the receipt by the authority of written notice of the determination, appeal to the Secretary of State, whose decision shall be binding on the committee and the authority.

(5) Any determination which, in relation to a petty session area which consists of or forms part of the inner London area, is made by the committee under subsection (1) or (2) above, other than a determination that court security officers should not be provided for that area, shall not have effect unless it is confirmed, with or without modifications, by the Secretary of State.

(6) In this section—

"the committee" means—

(a) in relation to a petty sessions area which consists of or forms part of a non-metropolitan county, a metropolitan district, an outer London borough, the City of London or a joint committee area, the magistrates' courts committee for that county, district, borough, City or area; and

(b) in relation to a petty sessions area which consists of or forms part of the inner London area, the committee of magistrates;

"the responsible authority" means—

(a) in relation to a petty sessions area which consists of or forms part of a non-metropolitan county, a metropolitan district, an outer London borough or the City of London, the council of that county, district or borough or, as the case may be, the Common Council of that City; and

(b) in relation to a petty sessions area which consists of or forms part of the inner London area, the Receiver.

DEFINITIONS
"the committee": subs. (6).
"the responsible authority": subs. (6).

Powers and duties of court security officers

77.—(1) A court security officer acting in the execution of his duty shall have the following powers, namely—

(a) to search any person who is in or is seeking to enter the court-house, and any article in the possession of such a person;

(b) to exclude or remove from the court-house any person who refuses to permit such a search as is mentioned in paragraph (a) above, or refuses to surrender any article in his possession which the officer reasonably believes may jeopardise the maintenance of order in the court-house;

(c) to exclude or remove any person from the court-house, or restrain any person in the court-house, where (in either case) it is reasonably necessary to do so in order—

(i) to maintain order in the court-house;

(ii) to enable court business to be carried on without interference or delay; or

(iii) to secure his or any other person's safety.

(2) The powers conferred by subsection (1)(a) above to search a person shall not be construed as authorising a court security officer to require a person to remove any of his clothing other than an outer coat, jacket or gloves.

(3) The powers conferred by subsection 1(b) and (c) above shall include power to use reasonable force, where necessary.

(4) In the execution of his duty, a court security officer shall act in accordance with any general or specific instructions which have been given to him (whether orally or in writing) by a person in authority.

(5) In subsection (4) above "person in authority," in relation to any court-house, means—
  (a) a justice of the peace, chief clerk or justices' clerk who is exercising any functions in the court-house; and
  (b) any officer or staff employed to assist such a clerk and authorised by him for the purpose.

(6) For the purposes of this section and section 78 below, a court security officer shall not be regarded as acting in the execution of his duty at any time when he is not readily identifiable as such an officer (whether by means of a uniform or badge which he is wearing or otherwise).

DEFINITIONS
"person in authority": subs. (5).

Protection of court security officers

78.—(1) Any person who assaults a court security officer acting in the execution of his duty shall be liable on summary conviction to a fine not exceeding level 5 on the standard scale or to imprisonment for a term not exceeding six months or to both.

(2) Any person who resists or wilfully obstructs a court security officer acting in the execution of his duty shall be liable on summary conviction to a fine not exceeding level 3 on the standard scale.

Duties of responsible authorities

79.—(1) In section 55(2) (duties of local authorities outside Greater London) of the Justices of the Peace Act 1979 ("the 1979 Act"), for paragraph (b) there shall be substituted the following paragraphs—
  "(b) the sums payable under Part II of this Act on account of a person's salary or expenses as justices' clerk for the non-metropolitan county or metropolitan district or any part thereof, the remuneration of any staff employed by the magistrates' courts committee to assist him and the remuneration of any court security officers employed (whether by that committee or the council) under section 76(2)(a) of the Criminal Justice Act 1991, together with—
      (i) secondary Class I contributions payable in respect of any such person, staff or officers under Part I of the Social Security Act 1975, and
      (ii) state scheme premiums so payable under Part III of the Social Security Pensions Act 1975;
  (bb) the sums payable under any contract entered into (whether by the magistrates' courts committee or the council) under section 76(2)(b) of the Criminal Justice Act 1991;".

(2) In section 58(2) of that Act (corresponding arrangements in the inner London area), for paragraph (b) there shall be substituted the following paragraphs—
  "(b) the sums payable by way of salary or expenses to justices' clerks and other officers employed by the committee of magistrates and the remuneration of any court security officers employed (whether by that committee or the Receiver) under section 76(2)(a) of the Criminal Justice Act 1991, together with—
      (i) secondary Class I contributions payable in respect of

any such officers under Part I of the Social Security Act 1975, and

      (ii) state scheme premiums so payable under Part III of the Social Security Pensions Act 1975;

  (bb) the sums payable under any contract entered into (whether by the committee of magistrates or the Receiver) under section 76(2)(b) of the Criminal Justice Act 1991;".

Prisoner escorts

Arrangements for the provision of prisoner escorts

80.—(1) The Secretary of State may make arrangements for any of the following functions, namely—

  (a) the delivery of prisoners to court premises;
  (b) the custody of prisoners held on such premises (whether or not they would otherwise be in the custody of the court) and their production before the court;
  (c) the delivery of prisoners so held to a prison or police station;
  (d) the delivery of prisoners from one prison to another; and
  (e) the custody of prisoners while they are outside a prison for temporary purposes,

to be performed in such cases as may be determined by or under the arrangements by prisoner custody officers who are authorised to perform such functions.

(2) Arrangements made by the Secretary of State under this section ("prisoner escort arrangements") may include entering into contracts with other persons for the provision by them of prisoner custody officers.

(3) Any person who, under a warrant of commitment, is responsible for the performance of any such function as is mentioned in subsection (1) above shall be deemed to have complied with that warrant if he does all that he reasonably can to secure that the function is performed by a prisoner custody officer acting in pursuance of prisoner escort arrangements.

Monitoring etc. of prisoner escort arrangements

81.—(1) Prisoner escort arrangements shall include the appointment of—

  (a) a prisoner escort monitor, that is to say, a Crown servant whose duty it shall be to keep the arrangements under review and to report on them to the Secretary of State; and
  (b) a panel of lay observers whose duty it shall be to inspect the conditions in which prisoners are transported or held in pursuance of the arrangements and to make recommendations to the Secretary of State.

(2) It shall also be the duty of a prisoner escort monitor to investigate and report to the Secretary of State on—

  (a) any allegations made against prisoner custody officers acting in pursuance of prisoner escort arrangements; and
  (b) any alleged breaches of discipline on the part of prisoners for whose delivery or custody such officers so acting are responsible.

(3) Any expenses incurred by members of lay panels may be defrayed by the Secretary of State to such extent as he may with the approval of the Treasury determine.

Powers and duties of prisoner custody officers acting in pursuance of such arrangements

82.—(1) A prisoner custody officer acting in pursuance of prisoner escort arrangements shall have the following powers, namely—

  (a) to search in accordance with rules made by the Secretary of State any prisoner for whose delivery or custody he is responsible in pursuance of the arrangements; and

(b) to search any other person who is in or is seeking to enter any place where any such prisoner is or is to be held, and any article in the possession of such a person.

(2) The powers conferred by subsection (1)(b) above to search a person shall not be construed as authorising a prisoner custody officer to require a person to remove any of his clothing other than an outer coat, jacket or gloves.

(3) A prisoner custody officer shall have the following duties as respects prisoners for whose delivery or custody he is responsible in pursuance of prisoner escort arrangements, namely—

(a) to prevent their escape from lawful custody;
(b) to prevent, or detect and report on, the commission or attempted commission by them of other unlawful acts;
(c) to ensure good order and discipline on their part;
(d) to attend to their wellbeing; and
(e) to give effect to any directions as to their treatment which are given by a court,

and the Secretary of State may make rules with respect to the performance by prisoner custody officers of their duty under paragraph (d) above.

(4) It shall also be the duty of a prisoner custody officer who is on any premises in which the Crown Court is sitting to give effect to any order of that Court made under section 34A of the 1973 Act (power of Court to order search of persons before it).

(5) The powers conferred by subsection (1) above, and the powers arising by virtue of subsection (3) and (4) above, shall include power to use reasonable force where necessary.

(6) The power to make rules under this section shall be exercisable by statutory instrument which shall be subject to annulment in pursuance of a resolution of either House of Parliament.

Breaches of discipline by prisoners

83.—(1) Where a prisoner for whose delivery or custody a prisoner custody officer has been responsible in pursuance of prisoner escort arrangements is delivered to a prison, he shall be deemed, for the purposes of such prison rules as relate to disciplinary offences, to have been—

(a) in the custody of the governor of the prison; or
(b) in the case of a contracted out prison, in the custody of its director,

at all times while that officer was so responsible.

(2) Nothing in subsection (1) above shall enable a prisoner to be punished under prison rules for any act or omission of his for which he has already been punished by a court.

Contracted out prisons

Contracting out of certain prisons

84.—(1) The Secretary of State may enter into a contract with another person for the running by him of any prison which—

(a) is established after the commencement of this section; and
(b) is for the confinement of remand prisoners, that is to say, persons charged with offences who are remanded in or committed to custody pending their trial, or persons committed to custody on their conviction who have not been sentenced for their offences;

and while such a contract is in force, the prison to which it relates shall be run subject to and in accordance with sections 85 and 86 below, the 1952 Act (as modified by section 87 below) and prison rules.

(2) In this Part—

"contracted out prison" means a prison as respects which such a contract is for the time being in force;

"the contractor," in relation to such a prison, means the person who has contracted to run it.

(3) The Secretary of State may by order made by statutory instrument provide that this section shall have effect as if there were omitted from subsection (1) above either—

(a) paragraph (a) and the word "and" immediately following that paragraph; or

(b) paragraph (b) and the said word "and"; or

(c) the words from "which," in the first place where it occurs, to the end of paragraph (b).

(4) An order under subsection (3)(b) or (c) above shall provide that section 87 below shall have effect as if subsection (5) were omitted.

(5) No order shall be made under subsection (3) above unless a draft of the order has been laid before and approved by resolution of each House of Parliament.

DEFINITIONS
"contracted-out prison": subs. (2).
"the contractor": subs. (2).

Officers of contracted out prisons

85.—(1) Instead of a governor, every contracted out prison shall have—

(a) a director, who shall be a prisoner custody officer appointed by the contractor and specially approved for the purposes of this section by the Secretary of State; and

(b) a controller, who shall be a Crown servant appointed by the Secretary of State;

and every officer of such a prison who performs custodial duties shall be a prisoner custody officer who is authorised to perform such duties.

(2) Subject to subsection (3) below, the director shall have such functions as are conferred on him by the 1952 Act (as modified by section 87 below) or as may be conferred on him by prison rules.

(3) The director shall not—

(a) inquire into a disciplinary charge laid against a prisoner, conduct the hearing of such a charge or make, remit or mitigate an award in respect of such a charge; or

(b) except in cases of urgency, order the removal of a prisoner from association with other prisoners, the temporary confinement of a prisoner in a special cell or the application to a prisoner of any other special control or restraint.

(4) The controller shall have such functions as may be conferred on him by prison rules and shall be under a duty—

(a) to keep under review, and report to the Secretary of State on, the running of the prison by or on behalf of the director; and

(b) to investigate, and report to the Secretary of State on, any allegations made against prisoner custody officers performing custodial duties at the prison.

(5) The contractor shall be under a duty to do all that he reasonably can (whether by giving directions to the officers of the prison or otherwise) to facilitate the exercise by the controller of all such functions as are mentioned in or conferred by subsection (4) above.

Powers and duties of prisoner custody officers employed at contracted out prisons

86.—(1) A prisoner custody officer performing custodial duties at a contracted out prison shall have the following powers, namely—

(a) to search in accordance with prison rules any prisoner who is confined in the prison; and

(b) to search any other person who is in or is seeking to enter the prison, and any article in the possession of such a person.

(2) The powers conferred by subsection (1)(b) above to search a person shall not be construed as authorising a prisoner custody officer to require a person to remove any of his clothing other than an outer coat, jacket or gloves.

(3) A prisoner custody officer performing custodial duties at a contracted out prison shall have the following duties as respects prisoners confined in the prison, namely—

(a) to prevent their escape from lawful custody;

(b) to prevent, or detect and report on, the commission or attempted commission by them of other unlawful acts;

(c) to ensure good order and discipline on their part; and

(d) to attend to their wellbeing.

(4) The powers conferred by subsection (1) above, and the powers arising by virtue of subsection (3) above, shall include power to use reasonable force where necessary.

Consequential modifications of 1952 Act

87.—(1) In relation to a contracted out prison, the provisions of the 1952 Act specified in subsections (2) to (8) below shall have effect subject to the modifications so specified.

(2) In section 7(1) (prison officers), the reference to a governor shall be construed as a reference to a director and a controller.

(3) Section 8 (powers of prison officers) and section 11 (ejectment of prison officers and their families refusing to quit) shall not apply.

(4) In sections 10(5), 12(3), 13(1) and 19(1) and (3) (various functions of the governor of a prison), references to the governor shall be construed as references to the director.

(5) In section 12(1) and (2) (place of confinement of prisoners), any reference to a prisoner or prisoners shall be construed as a reference to a remand prisoner or prisoners.

(6) In section 13(2) (legal custody of prisoners), the reference to an officer of the prison shall be construed as a reference to a prisoner custody officer performing custodial duties at the prison.

(7) In section 14(2) (cells), the reference to a prison officer shall be construed as a reference to a prisoner custody officer performing custodial duties at the prison.

(8) Section 35 (vesting of prison property in the Secretary of State) shall have effect subject to the provisions of the contract entered into under section 84(1) above.

Intervention by the Secretary of State

88.—(1) This section applies where, in the case of a contracted out prison, it appears to the Secretary of State—

(a) that the director has lost, or is likely to lose, effective control of the prison or any part of it; and

(b) that the making of an appointment under subsection (2) below is necessary in the interests of preserving the safety of any person, or of preventing serious damage to any property.

(2) The Secretary of State may appoint a Crown servant to act as governor of the prison for the period—

(a) beginning with the time specified in the appointment; and

(b) ending with the time specified in the notice of termination under subsection (4) below.

(3) During that period—

(a) all the functions which would otherwise be exercisable by the director or the controller shall be exercisable by the governor;

(b) the contractor shall do all that he reasonably can to facilitate the exercise by the governor of those functions; and

(c) the officers of the prison shall comply with any directions given by the governor of those functions.

(4) Where the Secretary of State is satisfied—

(a) that the governor has secured effective control of the prison or, as the case may be, the relevant part of it; and

(b) that the governor's appointment is no longer necessary as mentioned in subsection (1)(b) above,

he shall, by a notice to the governor, terminate the appointment at a time specified in the notice.

(5) As soon as practicable after making or terminating an appointment under this section, the Secretary of State shall give a notice of the appointment, or a copy of the notice of termination, to the contractor, the director and the controller.

Supplemental

Certification of prisoner custody officers

89.—(1) In this Part "prisoner custody officer" means a person in respect of whom a certificate is for the time being in force certifying—

(a) that he has been approved by the Secretary of State for the purpose of performing escort functions or custodial duties or both; and

(b) that he is accordingly authorised to perform them.

(2) The provisions of Schedule 10 to this Act shall have effect with respect to the certification of prisoner custody officers.

(3) In this section and Schedule 10 to this Act—

"custodial duties" means custodial duties at a contracted out prison;

"escort functions" means the functions specified in section 80(1) above.

DEFINITIONS
"custodial duties": subs. (3).
"escort functions": subs. (3).

Protection of prisoner custody officers

90.—(1) Any person who assaults a prisoner custody officer acting in pursuance of prisoner escort arrangements, or performing custodial duties at a contracted out prison, shall be liable on summary conviction to fine not exceeding level 5 on the standard scale or to imprisonment for a term not exceeding six months or to both.

(2) Section 17(2) of the Firearms Act 1968 (additional penalty for possession of firearms when committing certain offences) shall apply to offences under subsection (1) above.

(3) Any person who resists or wilfully obstructs a prisoner custody officer acting in pursuance of prisoner escort arrangements, or performing custodial duties at a contracted out prison, shall be liable on summary conviction to a fine not exceeding level 3 on the standard scale.

(4) For the purposes of this section, a prisoner custody officer shall not be regarded as acting in pursuance of prisoner escort arrangements at any time when he is not readily identifiable as such an officer (whether by means of a uniform or badge which he is wearing or otherwise).

Wrongful disclosure of information

91.—(1) A person who is or has been employed (whether as a prisoner custody officer or otherwise) in pursuance of prisoner escort arrangements, or at a contracted out prison, shall be guilty of an offence if he discloses, otherwise than in the course of his duty or as authorised by the Secretary of State, any information which he acquired in the course of his employment and which relates to a particular prisoner.

(2) A person guilty of an offence under subsection (1) above shall be liable—

(a) on conviction of indictment, to imprisonment for a term not exceeding two years or a fine or both;

(b) on summary conviction, to imprisonment for a term not exceeding six months or a fine not exceeding the statutory maximum or both.

Interpretation of Part IV

92.—(1) In this Part—

"contracted out prison" and "the contractor" have the meanings given by section 84(2) above;

"court-house" means a petty sessional court-house within the meaning of the 1980 Act or an occasional court-house appointed under section 147 of that Act;

"court security officer" has the meaning given by section 76(1) above;

"prison" includes a young offender institution or remand centre;

"prisoner" means any person who—

(a) is held in custody in a prison;

(b) is kept in police detention after being charged with an offence;

(c) has been committed to detention at a police station under section 128(7) of the 1980 Act; or

(d) is in the custody of a court;

"prisoner custody officer" has the meaning given by section 89(1) above;

"prisoner escort arrangements" has the meaning given by section 80(2) above.

(2) Unless the contrary intention appears, expressions used in sections 76 to 79 above which are also used in the 1979 Act have the same meanings as in that Act.

(3) Section 80, 81(1) and (2)(a), 82 and 89 to 91 above, subsection (1) above and Schedule 10 to this Act shall have effect as if—

(a) any reference in section 80(1), 81(1), 82 or 91 above to prisoners included a reference to persons kept in secure accommodation by virtue of a security requirement imposed under section 23(4) of the 1969 Act (remands and committals to local authority accommodation; and

(b) any reference in section 80(1)(c) to (e) above to a prison included a reference to such accommodation.

PART V

FINANCIAL AND OTHER PROVISIONS

Cash limits

Cash limits for magistrates' courts

93.—(1) In section 55 of the 1979 Act (duties of local authorities outside Greater London), after subsection (2) there shall be inserted the following subsection—

"(2A) Nothing in subsection (1) or (2) above shall require a council to incur any expenditure or make any payment which would—

(a) cause the net cost to it in any year of the matters mentioned in subsection (1) of section 59 of this Act to exceed the amount which, in relation to the council and that year, is for the time being determined by the Secretary of State under subsection (3)(b) of that section; or

  (b) cause its capital expenditure in any year in pursuance of functions under this Part of this Act to exceed the amount which, in relation to the council and that year, is for the time being determined by the Secretary of State under subsection (4)(b) of that section;

and in determining any such net cost as is mentioned in paragraph (a) above there shall be disregarded any such capital expenditure as is mentioned in paragraph (b) above."

(2) In section 58 of that Act (corresponding arrangements in inner London area), after subsection (2) there shall be inserted the following subsection—

  "(2A) Nothing in subsection (1) or (2) above shall require the Receiver to incur any expenditure or make any payment which would—

  (a) cause the net cost to him in any year of the matters mentioned in subsection (1) of section 59 of this Act to exceed the amount which, in relation to the Receiver and that year, is for the time being determined by the Secretary of State under subsection (3)(b) of that section; or

  (b) cause his capital expenditure in any year in pursuance of functions under this Part of this Act to exceed the amount which, in relation to the Receiver and that year, is for the time being determined by the Secretary of State under subsection (4)(b) of that section;

and in determining any such net cost as is mentioned in paragraph (a) above there shall be disregarded any such capital expenditure as is mentioned in paragraph (b) above."

(3) For section 59 of that Act there shall be substituted the following section—

"Grants by Secretary of State to responsible authorities

59.—(1) The Secretary of State may out of money provided by Parliament pay to the responsible authorities grants towards the net cost to them in any year—

  (a) of their functions under this Part or Part II of this Act;

  (b) of their functions under any regulations made, or having effect as if made, under section 7 of the Superannuation Act 1972 with respect to court staff or, in the case of the Receiver, his corresponding functions; and

  (c) of making payments under section 12 or 53 of this Act;

and in determining any such net cost as is mentioned above there shall be disregarded any such capital expenditure as is mentioned in subsection (2) below.

(2) The Secretary of State may also out of money provided by Parliament pay to the responsible authorities grants towards their capital expenditure in any year in pursuance of their functions under this Part of this Act.

(3) The amount of any grant under subsection (1) above towards the net cost to a responsible authority in any year of the matters mentioned in that subsection shall not exceed 80 per cent. of whichever of the following is the less, namely—

  (a) that net cost; and

  (b) the amount which, in relation to the authority and that year, is for the time being determined by the Secretary of State.

(4) The amount of any grant under subsection (2) above towards the capital expenditure in any year of a responsible authority in pursuance of its functions under this Part of this Act shall not exceed 80 per cent. of whichever of the following is the less, namely—
  (a) that capital expenditure; and
  (b) the amount which, in relation to the authority and that year, is for the time being determined by the Secretary of State.

(5) The Secretary of State, with the concurrence of the Treasury, may by statutory instrument make regulations as to the manner in which—
  (a) income and expenditure of responsible authorities are to be taken into account in determining the net cost to them in any year of the matters mentioned in subsection (1) above; or
  (b) expenditure of such authorities is to be taken into account in determining their capital expenditure in any year in pursuance of their functions under this Part of this Act;

and for the purposes of this section any question as to that net cost or that capital expenditure shall (subject to the regulations) be determined by the Secretary of State.

(6) The Secretary of State may direct that, in determining—
  (a) the net cost to a responsible authority in any year of the matters mentioned in subsection (1) above; or
  (b) the capital expenditure of such an authority in any year in pursuance of its functions under this Part of this Act,

there shall be taken into account or disregarded, to such extent as may be specified in the direction, such items as may be so specified.

(7) Grants under this section shall be paid at such times, in such manner and subject to such conditions as the Secretary of State may with the approval of the Treasury determine.

(8) In this section—
  'court staff' means persons appointed or deemed to have been appointed as justices' clerks, or employed by a magistrates' courts committee to assist a justices' clerk, under Part III of the Justices of the Peace Act 1949 or Part II of this Act.
  'responsible authority' means any of the following, namely, the council of a non-metropolitan county, metropolitan district or outer London borough, the Common Council of the City of London and the Receiver."

(4) In section 70 of that Act (interpretation), before the definition of "commission area" there shall be inserted the following definition—
  " 'capital expenditure' means expenditure for capital purposes (construed in accordance with section 40 of the Local Government and Housing Act 1989);".

Cash limits for probation services

94.—(1) After subsection (3) of section 51 of the 1973 Act (expenses and grants payable out of money provided by Parliament) there shall be inserted the following subsection—
  "(3A) The amount of any payments under subsection (3) above towards any person's expenditure, or towards any expenditure out of the metropolitan police fund, in any year shall not exceed the appropriate percentage of whichever of the following is the less, namely—
  (a) that expenditure; and
  (b) the amount which, in relation to that expenditure and that year, is for the time being determined by the Secretary of State;

and in this subsection 'the appropriate percentage', in relation to expenditure of any description, means the percentage which in relation to expenditure of that description is for the time being determined by the Secretary of State."

(2) In paragraph 3 of Schedule 3 to the 1973 Act (the probation service and its functions)—

(a) for paragraph (a) of sub-paragraph (1) there shall be substituted the following paragraph—

"(a) to appoint such number of probation officers—
(i) as may be determined by them without objection by the responsible authority; or
(ii) where objection is made, as any be agreed between them and that authority,
to be a sufficient number of such officers for their probation area, subject, in the case of such classes or descriptions of officers as may be prescribed, to the approval of the appointment by the Secretary of State;";

(b) at the end of that sub-paragraph there shall be inserted the words "and any question as to number arising under paragraph (a) above shall, in default of agreement, be determined by the Secretary of State"; and

(c) for sub-paragraph (5) there shall be substituted the following sub-paragraph—

"(5) In this paragraph 'the responsible authority'—
(a) in relation to a probation area other than the inner London probation area, means the local authority in whose area that probation area is situated; and
(b) in relation to the inner London probation area, means—
(i) the Receiver for the metropolitan police district; and
(ii) where that area includes one or more petty sessions areas outside the inner London area, the local authority or authorities in whose area or areas that petty sessions area or those petty sessions areas is or are situated;
and 'supervision order' and 'supervisor' have the meanings assigned to them by section 11 of the Children and Young Persons Act 1969."

(3) After paragraph 16 of that Schedule there shall be inserted the following paragraph—

"*Limits on sums payable under paragraphs 15 and 16*

"16A.—(1) Nothing in paragraph 15 or 16 above shall require a local authority to defray any sums which would cause its expenditure in any year to exceed the amount which, in relation to that expenditure and that year, is for the time being determined by the Secretary of State under section 51(3A)(b) of this Act.

(2) Nothing in paragraph 16 above shall require there to be paid out of the metropolitan police fund any sums which would cause the expenditure out of that fund in any year to exceed the amount which, in relation to that expenditure and that year, is for the time being so determined.

(3) In this paragraph 'expenditure' means expenditure under this Schedule."

Miscellaneous

Information for financial and other purposes

95.—(1) The Secretary of State shall in each year publish such information as he considers expedient for the purpose of—

(a) enabling persons engaged in the administration of criminal justice to become aware of the financial implications of their decisions; or

(b) facilitating the performance by such persons of their duty to avoid discriminating against any persons on the ground of race or sex or any other improper ground.

(2) Publication under subsection (1) above shall be effected in such manner as the Secretary of State considers appropriate for the purpose of bringing the information to the attention of the persons concerned.

Grants out of money provided by Parliament

96. In section 51(3) of the 1973 Act (grants payable out of money provided by Parliament), after paragraph (c) there shall be inserted the following paragraph—

"(cc) towards the expenditure of any society or individual engaged in supervising or assisting persons on bail;".

Grants by probation committees

97. In Schedule 3 to the 1973 Act (the probation service and its functions), after paragraph 12 there shall be inserted the following paragraph—

"Payment of grants in prescribed cases

12A. A probation committee may, in prescribed cases, make such payments and to such persons as may be prescribed."

PART VI

SUPPLEMENTAL

Expenses etc. under Act

98. There shall be paid out of money provided by Parliament—

(a) any sums required by the Secretary of State for making payments under contracts entered into under section 12, 80 or 84 above, or payments to or in respect of inspectors of probation appointed under section 73 above;

(b) any sums so required for defraying the expenses of the Parole Board, or any expenses incurred by members of lay panels appointed under section 81 above;

(c) any administrative expenses incurred by the Secretary of State under this Act; and

(d) any increase attributable to this Act in the sums payable out of money so provided under any other Act.

General interpretation

99.—(1) In this Act—

"the 1933 Act" means the Children and Young Persons Act 1933;

"the 1952 Act" means the Prison Act 1952;

"the 1967 Act" means the Criminal Justice Act 1867;

"the 1969 Act" means the Children and Young Persons Act 1969;

"the 1973 Act" means the Powers of Criminal Courts Act 1973;

"the 1979 Act" means the Justices of the Peace Act 1979;

"the 1980 Act" means the Magistrates' Court Act 1980;

"the 1982 Act" means the Criminal Justice Act 1982;

"the 1983 Act" means the Mental Health Act 1983;

"the 1988 Act" means the Criminal Justice Act 1988;

"child," unless the contrary intention appears, means a person under the age of fourteen years;

"prison rules" means rules made under section 47 of the 1952 Act;
"young person" means a person who has attained the age of fourteen
years and is under the age of eighteen years.

(2) For the purposes of any provision of this Act which requires the
determination of the age of a person by the court or the Secretary of State,
his age shall be deemed to be that which it appears to the court or the
Secretary of State to be after considering any available evidence.

Minor and consequential amendments

100. The enactments mentioned in Schedule 11 to this Act shall have
effect subject to the amendments there specified (being minor amendments
and amendments consequential on the preceding provisions of this Act).

Transitional provisions, savings and repeals

101.—(1) The transitional provisions and savings contained in Schedule
12 to this Act shall have effect; but nothing in this subsection shall be taken
as prejudicing the operation of sections 16 and 17 of the Interpretation Act
1978 (which relate to the effect of repeals).

(2) The enactments mentioned in Schedule 13 to this Act (which includes
some that are spent or no longer of practical utility) are hereby repealed to
the extent specified in the third column of that Schedule.

Short title, commencement and extent

102.—(1) This Act may be cited as the Criminal Justice Act 1991.

(2) This Act shall come into force on such day as the Secretary of State
may by order made by statutory instrument appoint, and different days may
be appointed for different provisions or for different purposes.

(3) Without prejudice to the provisions of Schedule 12 to this Act, an
order under subsection (2) above may make such transitional provisions and
savings as appear to the Secretary of State necessary or expedient in connection with any provision brought into force by the order.

(4) Subject to subsections (5) to (8) below, this Act extends to England
and Wales only.

(5) The following provisions of this Act, namely—

(a) this section;

(b) sections 16, 17(1) and (2), 24 and 26(3) and (4); and

(c) Schedule 3, paragraph 6 of Schedule 6, paragraph 5 of Schedule 8,
paragraph 15 of Schedule 11 to this Act and, so far as relating to the
Social Work (Scotland) Act 1968, Schedule 13,

also extend to Scotland; and section 23(2) above and, in so far as relating to
the Criminal Procedure (Scotland) Act 1975, Schedule 13 to this Act extent
to Scotland only.

(6) This section, section 16 above, Schedule 3 to this Act, paragraph 16 of
Schedule 11 to this Act and, so far as relating to the Social Work (Scotland)
Act 1968, Schedule 13 to this Act also extend to Northern Ireland.

(7) An Order in Council under section 81(11) of the 1982 Act may direct
that both or either of—

(a) section 37 of that Act as amended by section 17(1) above; and

(b) section 32 of the 1980 Act as amended by section 17(2) above,

shall extend, subject to such modifications as may be specified in the Order,
to the Isle of Man or any of the Channel Islands.

(8) Nothing in subsection (4) above affects the extent of this Act in so far
as it amends or repeals any provision of the Army Act 1955, the Air Force
Act 1955, the Naval Discipline Act 1957 or the Armed Forces Act 1991.

SCHEDULES

       SCHEDULE 1

AMENDMENTS OF 1973 ACT

PART I

PROVISIONS INSERTED AS SECTIONS 1A TO 1C

"Discharge

Absolute and conditional discharge

1A.—(1) Where a court by or before which a person is convicted of an offence (not being an offence the sentence for which is fixed by law) is of opinion, having regard to the circumstances including the nature of the offence and the character of the offender, that it is inexpedient to inflict punishment, the court may make an order either—

    (a) discharging him absolutely; or

    (b) if the court thinks fit, discharging him subject to the condition that he commits no offence during such period, not exceeding three years from the date of the order, as may be specified in the order.

(2) An order discharging a person subject to such a condition is in this Act referred to as 'an order for conditional discharge', and the period specified in any such order as 'the period of conditional discharge'.

(3) Before making an order for conditional discharge the court shall explain to the offender in ordinary language that if he commits another offence during the period of conditional discharge he will be liable to be sentenced for the original offence.

(4) Where, under the following provisions of this Part of this Act, a person conditionally discharged under this section is sentenced for the offence in respect of which the order for conditional discharge was made, that order shall cease to have effect.

(5) The Secretary of State may by order direct that subsection (1) above shall be amended by substituting, for the maximum period specified in that subsection as originally enacted or as previously amended under this subsection, such period as may be specified in the order.

Commission of further offence by person conditionally discharged

1B.—(1) If it appears to the Crown Court, where that court has jurisdiction in accordance with subsection (2) below, or to a justice of the peace having jurisdiction in accordance with that subsection, that a person in whose case an order for conditional discharge has been made—

    (a) has been convicted by a court in any part of Great Britain of an offence committed during the period of conditional discharge; and

    (b) has been dealt with in respect of that offence,

that court or justice may, subject to subsection (3) below, issue a summons requiring that person to appear at the place and time specified therein or a warrant for his arrest.

(2) Jurisdiction for the purposes of subsection (1) above may be exercised—

    (a) if the order for conditional discharge was made by the Crown Court, by that court;

    (b) if the order was made by a magistrates' court, by a justice acting for the petty sessions area for which that court acts.

(3) A justice of the peace shall not issue a summons under this section except on information and shall not issue a warrant under this section except on information in writing and on oath.

(4) A summons or warrant issued under this section shall direct the person to whom it relates to appear or to be brought before the court by which the order for conditional discharge was made.

(5) If a person in whose case an order for conditional discharge has been made by the Crown Court is convicted by a magistrates' court of an offence committed during the period of conditional discharge, the magistrates' court—

    (a) may commit him to custody or release him on bail until he can be brought or appear before the Crown Court; and

    (b) if it does so, shall send to the Crown Court a copy of the minute or memorandum of the conviction entered in the register, signed by the clerk of the court by whom the register is kept.

(6) Where it is proved to the satisfaction of the court by which an order for conditional discharge was made that the person in whose case the order was made has been convicted of an offence committed during the period of conditional discharge, the court may deal with him, for the offence for which the order was made, in any manner in which it could deal with him if he had just been convicted by or before that court of that offence.

(7) If a person in whose case an order for conditional discharge has been made by a magistrates' court—

(a) is convicted before the Crown Court of an offence committed during the period of conditional discharge; or

(b) is dealt with by the Crown Court for any such offence in respect of which he was committed for sentence to the Crown Court,

the Crown Court may deal with him, for the offence for which the order was made, in any manner in which the magistrates' court could deal with him if it had just convicted him of that offence.

(8) If a person in whose case an order for conditional discharge has been made by a magistrates' court is convicted by another magistrates' court of any offence committed during the period of conditional discharge, that other court may, with the consent of the court which made the order, deal with him, for the offence for which the order was made, in any manner in which the court could deal with him if it had just convicted him of that offence.

(9) Where an order for conditional discharge has been made by a magistrates' court in the case of an offender under eighteen years of age in respect of an offence triable only on indictment in the case of an adult, any powers exercisable under subsection (6), (7) or (8) above by that or any other court in respect of the offender after he has attained the age of eighteen years shall be those which would be exercisable if that offence were an offence triable either way and had been tried summarily.

(10) For the purposes of this section the age of an offender at a particular time shall be deemed to be or to have been that which appears to the court after considering any available evidence to be or to have been his age at that time.

Effect of discharge

1C.—(1) Subject to subsection (2) below and to section 50(1A) of the Criminal Appeal Act 1968 and section 108(1A) of the Magistrates' Courts Act 1980, a conviction of an offence for which an order is made under this Part of this Act discharging the offender absolutely or conditionally shall be deemed not to be a conviction for any purpose other than—

(a) the purposes of the proceedings in which the order is made and of any subsequent proceedings which may be taken against the offender under the following provisions of this Act; and

(b) the purposes of section 1(2)(bb) of the Children and Young Persons Act 1969.

(2) Where the offender was of or over eighteen years of age at the time of his conviction of the offence in question and is subsequently sentenced under this Part of this Act for that offence, subsection (1) above shall cease to apply to the conviction.

(3) Without prejudice to the preceding provisions of this section, the conviction of an offender who is discharged absolutely or conditionally under this Part of this Act shall in any event be disregarded for the purposes of any enactment or instrument which—

(a) imposes any disqualification or disability upon convicted persons; or

(b) authorises or requires the imposition of any such disqualification or disability.

(4) The preceding provisions of this section shall not affect—

(a) any right of any offender discharged absolutely or conditionally under this Part of this Act to rely on his conviction in bar of any subsequent proceedings for the same offence; or

(b) the restoration of any property in consequence of the conviction of any such offender; or

(c) the operation, in relation to any such offender, of any enactment or instrument in force at the commencement of this Act which is expressed to extend to persons dealt with under section 1(1) of the Probation Offenders Act 1907 as well as to convicted persons.

(5) In this section 'enactment' includes and enactment contained in a local Act and 'instrument' means an instrument having effect by virtue of an Act."

Part II

Provisions Inserted as Schedule 1A

"Schedule 1A

Additional Requirements in Probation Orders

Requirements as to residence

1.—(1) Subject to sub-paragraphs (2) and (3) below, a probation order may include requirements as to the residence of the offender.

(2) Before making a probation order containing any such requirement, the court shall consider the home surroundings of the offender.

(3) Where a probation order requires the offender to reside in an approved hostel or any other institution, the period for which he is so required to reside shall be specified in the order.

Requirements as to activities etc.

2.—(1) Subject to the provisions of this paragraph, a probation order may require the offender—
  (a) to present himself to a person or persons specified in the order at a place or places so specified;
  (b) to participate or refrain from participating in activities specified in the order—
      (i) on a day or days so specified; or
      (ii) during the probation period or such portion of it as may be so specified.

(2) A court shall not include in a probation order a requirement such as is mentioned in sub-paragraph (1) above unless—
  (a) it has consulted a probation officer; and
  (b) it is satisfied that it is feasible to secure compliance with the requirement.

(3) A court shall not include a requirement such as is mentioned in sub-paragraph (1)(a) above or a requirement to participate in activities if it would involve the co-operation of a person other than the offender and the probation officer responsible for his supervision, unless that other person consents to its inclusion.

(4) A requirement such as is mentioned in sub-paragraph (1)(a) above shall operate to require the offender—
  (a) in accordance with instructions given by the probation officer responsible for his supervision, to present himself at a place or places for not more than 60 days in the aggregate; and
  (b) while at any place, to comply with instructions given by, or under the authority of, the person in charge of that place.

(5) A place specified in an order shall have been approved by the probation committee for the area in which the premises are situated as providing facilities suitable for persons subject to probation orders.

(6) A requirement to participate in activities shall operate to require the offender—
  (a) in accordance with instructions given by the probation officer responsible for his supervision, to participate in activities for not more than 60 days in the aggregate; and
  (b) while participating, to comply with instructions given by, or under the authority of, the person in charge of the activities.

(7) Instructions given by a probation officer under sub-paragraph (4) or (6) above shall, as far as practicable, be such as to avoid any interference with the times, if any, at which the offender normally works or attends a school or other educational establishment.

Requirements as to attendance at probation centre

3.—(1) Subject to the provisions of this paragraph, a probation order may require the offender during the probation period to attend at a probation centre specified in the order.

(2) A court shall not include such a requirement in a probation order unless—
  (a) it has consulted a probation officer; and
  (b) it is satisfied—
      (i) that arrangements can be made for the offender's attendance at a centre; and
      (ii) that the person in charge of the centre consents to the inclusion of the requirement.

(3) A requirement under sub-paragraph (1) above shall operate to require the offender—
  (a) in accordance with instructions given by the probation officer responsible for his supervision, to attend on not more than 60 days at the centre specified in the order; and

(b) while attending there to comply with instructions given by, or under the authority of, the person in charge of the centre.

(4) Instructions given by a probation officer under sub-paragraph (3) above shall, so far as is practicable, be such as to avoid any interference with the times, if any, at which the offender normally works or attends a school or other educational establishment.

(5) Reference in this paragraph to attendance at a probation centre include reference to attendance elsewhere than at the centre for the purpose of participating in activities in accordance with instructions given by, or under the authority of, the person in charge of the centre.

(6) The Secretary of State may make rules for regulating the provision and carrying on of probation centres and the attendance at such centres of persons subject to probation orders; and such rules may in particular include provision with respect to hours of attendance, the reckoning of days of attendance and the keeping of attendance records.

(7) In this paragraph 'probation centre' means premises—

(a) at which non-residential facilities are provided for use in connection with the rehabilitation of offenders; and

(b) which are for the time being approved by the Secretary of State as providing facilities suitable for persons subject to probation orders.

Extension of requirements for sexual offenders

4.—(1) If the court so directs in the case of an offender who has been convicted of a sexual offence—

(a) sub-paragraphs (4) and (6) of paragraph 2 above; and

(b) sub-paragraph (3) of paragraph 3 above,

shall each have effect as if for the reference to 60 days there were substituted a reference to such greater number of days as may be specified in the direction.

(2) In this paragraph 'sexual offence' has the same meaning as in Part I of the Criminal Justice Act 1991.

Requirements as to treatment for mental condition etc.

5.—(1) This paragraph applies where a court proposing to make a probation order is satisfied, on the evidence of a duly qualified medical practitioner approved for the purposes of section 12 of the Mental Health Act 1983, that the mental condition of the offender—

(a) is such as requires and may be susceptible to treatment; but

(b) is not such as to warrant the making of a hospital order or guardianship order within the meaning of that Act.

(2) The probation order may include a requirement that the offender shall submit, during the whole of the probation period or during such part of that period as may be specified in the order, to treatment by or under the direction of a duly qualified medical practitioner with a view to the improvement of the offender's mental condition.

(3) The treatment required by any such order shall be such one of the following kinds of treatment as may be specified in the order, that is to say—

(a) treatment as a resident patient in a mental hospital;

(b) treatment as a non-resident patient at such institution or place as may be specified in the order; and

(c) treatment by or under the direction of such duly qualified medical practitioner as may be so specified;

but the nature of the treatment shall not be specified in the order except as mentioned in paragraph (a), (b) or (c) above.

(4) A court shall not by virtue of this paragraph include in a probation order a requirement that the offender shall submit to treatment for his mental condition unless it is satisfied that arrangements have been made for the treatment intended to be specified in the order (including arrangements for the reception of the offender where he is to be required to submit to treatment as a resident patient).

(5) While the offender is under treatment as a resident patient in pursuance of a requirement of the probation order, the probation officer responsible for his supervision shall carry out the supervision to such extent only as may be necessary for the purpose of the revocation or amendment of the order.

(6) Where the medical practitioner by whom or under whose direction an offender is being treated for his mental condition in pursuance of a probation order is of the opinion that part of the treatment can be better or more conveniently given in or at an institution or place which—

(a) is not specified in the order; and

(b) is one in or at which the treatment of the offender will be given by or under the direction of a duly qualified medical practitioner, he may, with the consent of the offender, make arrangements for him to be treated accordingly.

(7) Such arrangements as are mentioned in sub-paragraph (6) above may provide for the offender to receive part of his treatment as a resident patient in an institution or place notwithstanding that the institution or place is not one which could have been specified for that purpose in the probation order.

(8) Where any such arrangements as are mentioned in sub-paragraph (6) above are made for the treatment of an offender—

    (a) the medical practitioner by whom the arrangements are made shall give notice in writing to the probation officer responsible for the supervision of the offender, specifying the institution or place in or at which the treatment is to be carried out; and

    (b) the treatment provided for by the arrangements shall be deemed to be treatment to which he is required to submit in pursuance of the probation order.

(9) Subsections (2) and (3) of section 54 of the Mental Health Act 1983 shall have effect with respect to proof for the purposes of sub-paragraph (1) above of an offender's mental condition as they have effect with respect to proof of an offender's mental condition for the purposes of section 37(2)(a) of that Act.

(10) In this paragraph "mental hospital" means a hospital within the meaning of the Mental Health Act 1983 or mental nursing home within the meaning of the Registered Homes Act 1984, not being a special hospital within the meaning of the National Health Service Act 1977.

Requirements as to treatment for drug or alcohol dependency

6.—(1) This paragraph applies where a court proposing to make a probation order is satisfied—

    (a) that the offender is dependent on drugs or alcohol;

    (b) that his dependency caused or contributed to the offence in respect of which the order is proposed to be made; and

    (c) that his dependency is such as requires and may be susceptible to treatment.

(2) The probation order may include a requirement that the offender shall submit, during the whole of the probation period or during such part of that period as may be specified in the order, to treatment by or under the direction of a person having the necessary qualifications or experience with a view to the reduction or elimination of the offender's dependency on drugs or alcohol.

(3) The treatment required by any such order shall be such one of the following kinds of treatment as may be specified in the order, that is to say—

    (a) treatment as a resident in such institution or place as may be specified in the order;

    (b) treatment as a non-resident in or at such institution or place as may be so specified; and

    (c) treatment by or under the direction of such person having the necessary qualifications or experience as may be so specified;

but the nature of the treatment shall not be specified in the order except as mentioned in paragraph (a), (b) or (c) above.

(4) A court shall not by virtue of this paragraph include in a probation order a requirement that the offender shall submit to treatment for his dependency on drugs or alcohol unless it is satisfied that arrangements have been made for the treatment intended to be specified in the order (including arrangements for the reception of the offender where he is to be required to submit to treatment as a resident).

(5) While the offender is under treatment as a resident in pursuance of a requirement of the probation order, the probation officer responsible for his supervision shall carry out the supervision to such extent only as may be necessary for the purpose of the revocation or amendment of the order.

(6) Where the person by whom or under whose direction an offender is being treated for dependency on drugs or alcohol in pursuance of a probation order is of the opinion that part of the treatment can be better or more conveniently given in or at an institution or place which—

    (a) is not specified in the order; and

    (b) is one in or at which the treatment of the offender will be given by or under the direction of a person having the necessary qualifications or experience,

he may, with the consent of the offender, make arrangements for him to be treated accordingly.

(7) Such arrangements as are mentioned in sub-paragraph (6) above may provide for the offender to receive part of his treatment as a resident in an institution or place notwithstanding that the institution or place is not one which could have been specified for that purpose in the probation order.

(8) Where any such arrangements as are mentioned in sub-paragraph (6) above are made for the treatment of an offender—

    (a) the person by whom the arrangements are made shall give notice in writing to the probation officer responsible for the supervision of the offender, specifying the institution or place in or at which the treatment is to be carried out; and

(b) the treatment provided for by the arrangements shall be deemed to be treatment to which he is required to submit in pursuance of the probation order.

(9) In this paragraph the reference to the offender being dependent on drugs or alcohol includes a reference to his having a propensity towards the misuse of drugs or alcohol, and reference to his dependency on drugs or alcohol shall be construed accordingly."

Section 14(1)   SCHEDULE 2

ENFORCEMENT ETC. OF COMMUNITY ORDERS

PART I

PRELIMINARY

1.—(1) In this Schedule "relevant order" means any of the following orders, namely, a probation order, a community service order and a curfew order; and "the petty sessions area concerned" means—

(a) in relation to probation or community service order, the petty sessions area for the time being specified in the order; and

(b) in relation to a curfew order, the petty sessions area in which the place for the time being specified in the order is situated.

(2) Subject to sub-paragraph (3) below, this Schedule shall apply in relation to combination orders—

(a) in so far as they impose such a requirement as is mentioned in paragraph (a) of subsection (1) of section 11 of this Act, as if they were probation orders, and

(b) in so far as they impose such a requirement as is mentioned in paragraph (b) of that subsection, as if they were community service orders.

(3) In its application to combination orders, paragraph 6(3) below shall have effect as if the reference to section 14(1A) of the 1973 Act were a reference to section 11(1) of this Act.

PART II

BREACH OF REQUIREMENT OF ORDER

Issue of summons or warrant

2.—(1) If at any time while a relevant order is in force in respect of an offender it appears on information to a justice of the peace acting for the petty sessions area concerned that the offender has failed to comply with any of the requirements of the order, the justice may—

(a) issue a summons requiring the offender to appear at the place and time specified in it; or

(b) if the information is in writing and on oath, issue a warrant for his arrest.

(2) Any summons or warrant issued under this paragraph shall direct the offender to appear or be brought before a magistrates' court acting for the petty sessions area concerned.

Powers of magistrates' court

3.—(1) If it is proved to the satisfaction of the magistrates' court before which an offender appears or is brought under paragraph 2 above that he has failed without reasonable excuse to comply with any of the requirements of the relevant order, the court may deal with him in respect of the failure in any one of the following ways, namely—

(a) it may impose on him a fine not exceeding £1,000;

(b) subject to paragraph 6(3) to (5) below, it may make a community service order in respect of him;

(c) where the relevant order is a probation order and the case is one to which section 17 of the 1982 Act applies, it may make an order under that section requiring him to attend at an attendance centre; or

(d) where the relevant order was made by a magistrates' court, it may revoke the order and deal with him, for the offence in respect of which the order was made, in any manner in which it could deal with him if he had just been convicted by the court of the offence.

(2) In dealing with an offender under sub-paragraph (1)(d) above, a magistrates' court—

(a) shall take into account the extent to which the offender has complied with the requirements of the relevant order; and

(b) may assume, in the case of an offender who has wilfully and persistently failed to comply with those requirements, that he has refused to give his consent to a community sentence which has been proposed by the court and requires that consent.

(3) Where a relevant order was made by the Crown Court and magistrates' court has power to deal with the offender under sub-paragraph (1)(a), (b) or (c) above, it may instead commit him to custody or release him on bail until he can be brought or appear before the Crown Court.

(4) A magistrates' court which deals with an offender's case under sub-paragraph (3) above shall send to the Crown Court—

    (a) a certificate signed by a justice of the peace certifying that the offender has failed to comply with the requirements of the relevant order in the respect specified in the certificate; and

    (b) such other particulars of the case as may be desirable;

and a certificate purporting to be so signed shall be admissible as evidence of the failure before the Crown Court.

(5) A person sentenced under sub-paragraph (1)(d) above for an offence may appeal to the Crown Court against the sentence.

Powers of Crown Court

4.—(1) Where by virtue of paragraph 3(3) above an offender is brought or appears before the Crown Court and it is proved to the satisfaction of the court that he has failed to comply with any of the requirements of the relevant order, that court may deal with him in respect of the failure in any one of the following ways, namely—

    (a) it may impose on him a fine not exceeding £1,000;

    (b) subject to paragraph 6(3) to (5) below, it may make a community service order in respect of him;

    (c) where the relevant order is a probation order and the case is one to which section 17 of the 1982 Act applies, it may make an order under that section requiring him to attend at an attendance centre; or

    (d) it may revoke the order and deal with him, for the offence in respect of which the order was made, in any manner in which it could deal with him if he had just been convicted by or before the court of the offence.

(2) In dealing with an offender under sub-paragraph (1)(d) above, the Crown Court—

    (a) shall take into account the extent to which the offender has complied with the requirements of the relevant order; and

    (b) may assume, in the case of an offender who has wilfully and persistently failed to comply with those requirements, that he has refused to give his consent to a community sentence which has been proposed by the court and requires that consent.

(3) In proceedings before the Crown Court under this paragraph any question whether the offender has failed to comply with the requirements of the relevant order shall be determined by the court and not by the verdict of a jury.

Exclusions

5.—(1) Without prejudice to paragraphs 7 and 8 below, an offender who is convicted of a further offence while a relevant order is in force in respect of him shall not on that account be liable to be dealt with under paragraph 3 or 4 above in respect of a failure to comply with any requirement of the order.

(2) An offender who is required by a probation order to submit to treatment for his mental condition, or his dependency on drugs or alcohol, shall not be treated for the purposes of paragraph 3 or 4 above as having failed to comply with that requirement on the ground only that he has refused to undergo any surgical, electrical or other treatment if, in the opinion of the court, his refusal was reasonable having regard to all the circumstances.

Supplemental

6.—(1) Any exercise by a court of its powers under paragraph 3(1)(a), (b) or (c) or 4(1)(a) or (b) above shall be without prejudice to the continuance of the relevant order.

(2) Section 18 of this Act shall apply for the purposes of paragraph 3(1)(a) above as if the failure to comply with the requirement were a summary offence punishable by a fine not exceeding level 3 on the standard scale; and a fine imposed under that paragraph or paragraph 4(1)(a) above shall be deemed for the purposes of any enactment to be a sum adjudged to be paid by a conviction.

(3) The number of hours which an offender may be required to work under a community service order made under paragraph 3(1)(b) or 4(1)(b) above—

    (a) shall be specified in the order and shall not exceed 60 in the aggregate; and

    (b) where the relevant order is a community service order, shall not be such that the total number of hours under both orders exceeds the maximum specified in section 14(1A) of the 1973 Act.

(4) Section 14(2) of the 1973 Act and, so far as applicable—

(a) the following provisions of that Act relating to community service orders; and

(b) the provisions of this Schedule so far as so relating,

shall have effect in relation to a community service order under paragraph 3(1)(b) or 4(1)(b) above as they have effect in relation to a community service order in respect of an offender.

(5) Where the provisions of this Schedule have effect as mentioned in sub-paragraph (4) above, the powers conferred by those provisions to deal with the offender for the offence in respect of which the community service order was made shall be construed as powers to deal with the offender for the failure to comply with the requirements of the relevant order in respect of which the community service order was made.

PART III

REVOCATION OF ORDER

Revocation of order with or without re-sentencing

7.—(1) This paragraph applies where a relevant order is in force in respect of any offender and, on the application of the offender or the responsible officer, it appears to a magistrates' court acting for the petty sessions area concerned that, having regard to circumstances which have arisen since the order was made, it would be in the interests of justice—

(a) that the order should be revoked; or

(b) that the offender should be dealt with in some other manner for the offence in respect of which the order was made.

(2) The court may—

(a) if the order was made by a magistrates' court—

(i) revoke the order; or

(ii) revoke the order and deal with the offender, for the offence in respect of which the order was made, in any manner in which it could deal with him if he had just been convicted by the court of the offence; or

(b) if the order was made by the Crown Court, commit him to custody or release him on bail until he can be brought or appear before the Crown Court.

(3) The circumstances in which a probation order may be revoked under sub-paragraph (2)(a)(i) above shall include the offender's making good progress or his responding satisfactorily to supervision.

(4) In dealing with an offender under sub-paragraph (2)(a)(ii) above, a magistrates' court shall take into account the extent to which the offender has complied with the requirements of the relevant order.

(5) An offender sentenced under sub-paragraph (2)(a)(ii) above may appeal to the Crown Court against the sentence.

(6) Where the court deals with an offender's case under sub-paragraph (2)(b) above, it shall send to the Crown Court such particulars of the case as may be desirable.

(7) Where a magistrates' court proposes to exercise its powers under this paragraph otherwise than on the application of the offender it shall summon him to appear before the court and, if he does not appear in answer to the summons, may issue a warrant for his arrest.

(8) No application may be made by the offender under sub-paragraph (1) above while an appeal against the relevant order is pending.

8.—(1) This paragraph applies where an offender in respect of whom a relevant order is in force—

(a) is convicted of an offence before the Crown Court; or

(b) is committed by a magistrates' court to the Crown Court for sentence and is brought or appears before the Crown Court; or

(c) by virtue of paragraph 7(2)(b) above is brought or appears before the Crown Court.

(2) If it appears to the Crown Court to be in the interests of justice to do so, having regard to circumstances which have arisen since the order was made, the Crown Court may—

(a) revoke the order; or

(b) revoke the order and deal with the offender, for the offence in respect of which the order was made, in any manner in which it could deal with him if he had just been convicted by or before the court of the offence.

(3) The circumstances in which a probation order may be revoked under sub-paragraph (2)(a) above shall include the offender's making good progress or his responding satisfactorily to supervision.

(4) In dealing with an offender under sub-paragraph (2)(b) above, the Crown Court shall take into account the extent to which the offender has complied with the requirements of the relevant order.

53–91

Revocation of order following custodial sentence

9.—(1) This paragraph applies where—

(a) an offender in respect of whom a relevant order is in force is convicted of an offence before a magistrates' court other than a magistrates' court acting for the petty sessions area concerned; and

(b) the court imposes a custodial sentence on the offender.

(2) If it appears to the court, on the application of the offender or the responsible officer, that it would be in the interests of justice to do so having regard to circumstances which have arisen since the order was made, the court may—

(a) if the order was made by a magistrates' court, revoke it; and

(b) if the order was made by the Crown Court, commit the offender in custody or release him on bail until he can be brought or appear before the Crown Court.

(3) Where the court deals with an offender's case under sub-paragraph (2)(b) above, it shall send to the Crown Court such particulars of the case as may be desirable.

10. Where by virtue of paragraph 9(2)(b) above an offender is brought or appears before the Crown Court and it appears to the Crown Court to be in the interests of justice to do so, having regard to circumstances which have arisen since the relevant order was made, the Crown Court may revoke the order.

Supplemental

11.—(1) On the making under this Part of this Schedule of an order revoking a relevant order, the clerk to the court shall forthwith give copies of the revoking order to the responsible officer.

(2) A responsible officer to whom in accordance with sub-paragraph (1) above copies of a revoking order are given shall give a copy to the offender and to the person in charge of any institution in which the offender was required by the order to reside.

PART IV

AMENDMENT OF ORDER

Amendment by reason of change of residence

12.—(1) This paragraph applies where, at any time while a relevant order is in force in respect of an offender, a magistrates' court acting for the petty sessions area concerned is satisfied that the offender proposes to change, or has changed, his residence from that petty sessions area to another petty sessions area.

(2) Subject to sub-paragraphs (3) and (4) below, the court may, and on the application of the responsible officer shall, amend the relevant order by substituting the other petty sessions area for the area specified in the order or, in the case of a curfew order, a place in that other area for the place so specified.

(3) The court shall not amend under this paragraph a probation or curfew order which contains requirements which, in the opinion of the court, cannot be complied with unless the offender continues to reside in the petty sessions area concerned unless, in accordance with paragraph 13 below, it either—

(a) cancels those requirements; or

(b) substitutes for those requirements other requirements which can be complied with if the offender ceases to reside in that area.

(4) The court shall not amend a community service order under this paragraph unless it appears to the court that provision can be made for the offender to perform work under the order under the arrangements which exist for persons who reside in the other petty sessions area to perform work under such orders.

Amendment of requirements of probation or curfew order

13.—(1) Without prejudice to the provisions of paragraph 12 above, but subject to sub-paragraph (2) below, a magistrates' court for the petty sessions area concerned may, on the application of the offender or the responsible officer, by order amend a probation or curfew order—

(a) by cancelling any of the requirements of the order; or

(b) by inserting in the order (either in addition to or in substitution for any such requirement) any requirement which the court could include if if were then making the order.

(2) The power of a magistrates' court under sub-paragraph (1) above shall be subject to the following restrictions, namely—

(a) the court shall not amend a probation order—
    (i) by reducing the probation period, or by extending that period beyond the end of three years from the date of the original order; or
    (ii) by inserting in it a requirement that the offender shall submit to treatment for his mental condition, or his dependency on drugs or alcohol, unless the amending order is made within three months after the date of the original order; and

(b) the court shall not amend a curfew order by extending the curfew periods beyond the end of six months from the date of the original order.

(3) In this paragraph and paragraph 14 below, references to the offender's dependency on drugs or alcohol include references to his propensity towards the misuse of drugs or alcohol.

Amendment of certain requirements of probation order

14.—(1) Where the medical practitioner or other person by whom or under whose direction an offender is being treated for his mental condition, or his dependency on drugs or alcohol, in pursuance of any requirement of a probation order—

(a) is of the opinion mentioned in sub-paragraph (2) below; or

(b) is for any reason unwilling to continue to treat or direct the treatment of the offender,

he shall make a report in writing to that effect to the responsible officer and that officer shall apply under paragraph 13 above to a magistrates' court for the petty sessions area concerned for the variation or cancellation of the requirement.

(2) The opinion referred to in sub-paragraph (1) above is—

(a) that the treatment of the offender should be continued beyond the period specified in that behalf in the order;

(b) that the offender needs different treatment, being treatment of a kind to which he could be required to submit in pursuance of a probation order;

(c) that the offender is not susceptible to treatment; or

(d) that the offender does not require further treatment.

Extension of community service order

15. Where—

(a) a community service order is in force in respect of any offender; and

(b) on the application of the offender or the responsible officer, it appears to a magistrates' court acting for the petty sessions area concerned that it would be in the interests of justice to do so having regard to circumstances which have arisen since the order was made,

the court may, in relation to the order, extend the period of twelve months specified in section 15(2) of the 1973 Act.

Supplemental

16. No order may be made under paragraph 12 above, and no application may be made under paragraph 13 or 15 above, while an appeal against the relevant order is pending.

17.—(1) Subject to sub-paragraph (2) below, where a court proposes to exercise its powers under this Part of this Schedule, otherwise than on the application of the offender, the court—

(a) shall summon him to appear before the court; and

(b) if he does not appear in answer to the summons, may issue a warrant for his arrest;

and the court shall not amend a relevant order under this Part of this Schedule unless the offender expresses his willingness to comply with the requirements of the order as amended.

(2) This paragraph shall not apply to an order cancelling a requirement of a relevant order or reducing the period of any requirement, or substituting a new petty sessions area or a new place for the one specified in a relevant order.

18.—(1) On the making under this Part of this Schedule of an order amending a relevant order, the clerk to the court shall forthwith—

(a) if the order amends the relevant order otherwise than by substituting a new petty sessions area or a new place for the one specified in the relevant order, give copies of the amending order to the responsible officer;

(b) if the order amends the relevant order in the manner excepted by paragraph (a) above, sent to the clerk to the justices for the new petty sessions area or, as the case may be, for the petty sessions area in which the new place is situated—
    (i) copies of the amending order; and
    (ii) such documents and information relating to the case as he considers likely to be of assistance to a court acting for that area in exercising its functions in relation to the order;

and in a case falling within paragraph (b) above the clerk to the justices for that area shall give copies of the amending order to the responsible officer.

(2) A responsible officer to whom in accordance with sub-paragraph (1) above copies of an order are given shall give a copy to the offender and to the person in charge of any institution in which the offender is or was required by the order to reside.

Section 16   SCHEDULE 3

RECIPROCAL ENFORCEMENT OF CERTAIN ORDERS

PART I

TRANSFER OF COMMUNITY ORDERS TO SCOTLAND OR NORTHERN IRELAND

Probation orders: Scotland

1.—(1) Where a court considering the making of a probation order is satisfied that the offender resides in Scotland, or will be residing there when the order comes into force, section 2 of the 1973 Act (probation orders) shall have effect as if after subsection (1) there were inserted the following subsection—

"(1A) A court shall not make a probation order in respect of any offender unless it is satisfied that suitable arrangements for his supervision can be made by the regional or islands council in whose area he resides, or will be residing when the order comes into force."

(2) Where a probation order has been made and—

(a) a magistrates' court acting for the petty sessions area specified in the order is satisfied that the offender proposes to reside or is residing in Scotland; and

(b) it appears to the court that suitable arrangements for his supervision can be made by the regional or islands council in whose area he proposes to reside or is residing,

the power of the court to amend the order under Part IV of Schedule 2 to this Act shall include power to amend it by requiring him to be supervised in accordance with arrangements so made.

(3) Where a court is considering the making or amendment of a probation order in accordance with this paragraph, Schedule 1A to the 1973 Act (additional requirements in probation orders) shall have effect as if—

(a) any reference to a probation officer were a reference to an officer of the regional or islands council in whose area the offender resides or will be residing when the order or amendment comes into force;

(b) the reference in paragraph 2(5) to the probation committee for the area in which the premises are situated were a reference to the regional or islands council for that area;

(c) paragraph 3 (requirements as to attendance at probation centre) were omitted; and

(d) the reference in paragraph 5(3) to a mental hospital were a reference to a hospital within the meaning of the Mental Health (Scotland) Act 1984, not being a State hospital within the meaning of that Act.

(4) A probation order made or amended in accordance with this paragraph shall—

(a) specify the locality in Scotland in which the offender resides or will be residing when the order or amendment comes into force; and

(b) specify as the appropriate court for the purposes of subsection (2) of section 183 or 384 of the Criminal Procedure (Scotland) Act 1975 a court of summary jurisdiction (which, in the case of an offender convicted on indictment, shall be the sheriff court) having jurisdiction in the locality specified under paragraph (a) above.

Probation orders: Northern Ireland

2.—(1) Where a court considering the making of a probation order is satisfied that the offender resides in Northern Ireland, or will be residing there when the order comes into force, section 2 of the 1973 Act shall have effect as if after subsection (1) there were inserted the following subsection—

"(1A) A court shall not make a probation order in respect of any offender unless it is satisfied that suitable arrangements for his supervision can be made by the Probation Board for Northern Ireland."

(2) Where a probation order has been made and—

(a) a magistrates' court acting for the petty sessions area specified in the order is satisfied that the offender proposes to reside or is residing in Northern Ireland; and

(b) it appears to the court that suitable arrangements for his supervision can be made by the Probation Board for Northern Ireland,

the power of the court to amend the order under Part IV of Schedule 2 to this Act shall include power to amend it by requiring him to be supervised in accordance with arrangements so made.

(3) Where a court is considering the making or amendment of a probation order in accordance with this paragraph, Schedule 1A to the 1973 Act shall have effect as if—

(a) any reference to a probation officer were a reference to a probation officer assigned to the petty sessions district in Northern Ireland in which the offender resides or will be residing when the order or amendment comes into force;

(b) the reference in paragraph 2(5) to the probation committee for the area in which the premises are situated were a reference to the Probation Board for Northern Ireland;

(c) references in paragraph 3 to a probation centre were references to a day centre within the meaning of section 2B of the Probation Act (Northern Ireland) 1950; and

(d) the reference in paragraph 5(3) to treatment as a resident patient in a mental hospital were a reference to treatment (whether as an in-patient or an out-patient) at such hospital as may be specified in the order, being a hospital within the meaning of the Health and Personal Social Services (Northern Ireland) Order 1972, approved by the Department of Health and Social Services for Northern Ireland for the purposes of section 2 of the Probation Act (Northern Ireland) 1950.

(4) A probation order made or amended in accordance with this paragraph shall specify the petty sessions district in Northern Ireland in which the offender resides or will be residing when the order or amendment comes into force.

Community service orders: Scotland

3.—(1) Where a court considering the making of a community service order is satisfied that the offender resides in Scotland, or will be residing there when the order comes into force, section 14 of the 1973 Act shall have effect as if for subsection (2A) there were substituted the following subsection—

"(2A) A court shall not make a community service order in respect of any offender unless—

(a) the court has been notified by the Secretary of State that arrangements exist for persons who reside in the locality in Scotland in which the offender resides, or will be residing when the order comes into force, to perform work under community service orders made under section 1 of the Community Service by Offenders (Scotland) Act 1978; and

(b) it appears to the court that provision can be made for him to perform work under those arrangements."

(2) Where a community service order has been made and—

(a) a magistrates' court acting for a petty sessions area for the time being specified in it is satisfied that the offender proposes to reside or is residing in Scotland;

(b) the court has been notified by the Secretary of State that arrangements exist for persons who reside in the locality in Scotland in which the offender proposes to reside or is residing to perform work under community service orders made under section 1 of the Community Service by Offenders (Scotland) Act 1978; and

(c) it appears to the court that provision can be made for him to perform work under the community service order under those arrangements,

it may amend the order by specifying that the unpaid work required to be performed by the order be so performed.

(3) A community service order made or amended in accordance with this paragraph shall—

(a) specify the locality in Scotland in which the offender resides or will be residing when the order or amendment comes into force; and

(b) require the regional or islands council in whose area the locality specified under paragraph (a) above is situated to appoint or assign an officer who will discharge in respect of the order the functions in respect of community service orders conferred on the local authority officer by the Community Service by Offenders (Scotland) Act 1978.

Community service orders: Northern Ireland

4.—(1) Where a court considering the making of a community service order is satisfied that the offender resides in Northern Ireland, or will be residing there when the order comes into force, section 14 of the 1973 Act shall have effect—

(a) in the case of an offender aged sixteen, as if the reference in subsection (1A) to 240 hours were a reference to 120 hours; and

(b) in any case, as if for subsection (2A) there were substituted the following subsection—

"(2A) A court shall not make a community service order in respect of any offender unless it appears to the court that provision can be made by the Probation Board for Northern Ireland for him to perform work under the order."

(2) Where a community service order has been made and—

(a) a magistrates' court acting for a petty sessions area for the time being specified in it is satisfied that the offender proposes to reside or is residing in Northern Ireland; and

(b) it appears to the court that provision can be made by the Probation Board for Northern Ireland for him to perform work under the order,

it may amend the order by specifying that the unpaid work required to be performed by the order be so performed and, where the offender is aged sixteen, by making any such reduction in the aggregate number of hours specified in the order as is required by sub-paragraph (1)(a) above.

(3) A community service order made or amended in accordance with this paragraph shall—

(a) specify the petty sessions district in Northern Ireland in which the offender resides or will be residing when the order or amendment comes into force; and

(b) require the Probation Board for Northern Ireland to select an officer who will discharge in respect of the order the functions in respect of community service orders conferred on the relevant officer by the Treatment of Offenders (Northern Ireland) Order 1976.

Combination orders: Scotland

5. Paragraphs 1 and 3 above shall apply in relation to combination orders—

(a) in so far as they impose such a requirement as is mentioned in paragraph (a) of subsection (1) of section 11 of this Act, as if they were probation orders; and

(b) in so far as they impose such a requirement as is mentioned in paragraph (b) of that subsection, as if they were community service orders.

General

6.—(1) Where a community order is made or amended in any of the circumstances specified in this Schedule, the court which makes or amends the order shall send three copies of it as made or amended to the home court, together with such documents and information relating to the case as it considers likely to be of assistant to that court.

(2) Where a community order is made or amended in any of the circumstances specified in this Schedule, then, subject to the following provisions of this paragraph—

(a) the order shall be treated as if it were a corresponding order made in the part of the United Kingdom in which the offender resides, or will be residing at the relevant time; and

(b) the legislation relating to such orders which has effect in that part of the United Kingdom shall apply accordingly.

(3) Before making or amending a community order in those circumstances the court shall explain to the offender in ordinary language—

(a) the requirements of the legislation relating to corresponding orders which has effect in the part of the United Kingdom in which he resides or will be residing at the relevant time;

(b) the powers of the home court under the legislation, as modified by this paragraph; and

(c) its own powers under this paragraph,

and an explanation given in accordance with this sub-paragraph shall be sufficient without the addition of an explanation under section 2(3) or 14(5) of the 1973 Act.

(4) The home court may exercise in relation to the community order any power which it could exercise in relation to a corresponding order made by a court in the part of the United Kingdom in which the home court exercises jurisdiction, by virtue of the legislation relating to such orders which has effect in that part, except the following, namely—

(a) in the case of a probation order or a combination order, a power conferred by section 186(2)(b), 187, 387(2)(b) or 388 of, or paragraph 1 of Schedule 5 to, the Criminal Procedure (Scotland) Act 1975;

(b) in the case of a probation order, a power conferred by section 4(3)(d) or (4B)(d) or 6 of, or paragraph 1 of Schedule 2 to, the Probation Act (Northern Ireland) 1950; and

(c) in the case of a community service order—

(i) a power conferred by section 4(2)(b) or 5(1)(c) or (d) of the Community Service by Offenders (Scotland) Act 1978;

(ii) a power conferred by Article 9(3)(a) or (b) or (5)(b) or 10 of the Treatment of Offenders (Northern Ireland) Order 1976; or

(iii) a power to vary the order by substituting for the number of hours of work specified in it any greater number than the court which made the order could have specified.

(5) If at any time while legislation relating to corresponding orders which has effect in Scotland or Northern Ireland applies by virtue of sub-paragraph (2) above to a community order made in England and Wales—

(a) it appears to the home court—

(i) if that court is in Scotland, on evidence on oath from the local authority officer concerned; and

(ii) If it is in Northern Ireland, upon a complaint being made to a justice of the peace acting for the petty sessions district for the time being specified in the order,

that the offender has failed to comply with any of the requirements of the legislation applicable to the order; or

(b) it appears to the home court on the application of the offender or—

(i) if that court is in Scotland, of the local authority officer concerned; and

(ii) if it is in Northern Ireland, of the probation officer concerned,

that it would be in the interests of justice for a power conferred by paragraph 7 or 8 of Schedule 2 to this Act to be exercised,

the home court may require the offender to appear before the court which made the order.

(6) Where an offender is required by virtue of sub-paragraph (5) above to appear before the court which made the community order, that court—

(a) may issue a warrant for his arrest; and

(b) may exercise any power which it could exercise in respect of the community order if the offender resided in England and Wales,

and any enactment relating to the exercise of such powers shall have effect accordingly, and with any reference to the responsible officer being construed as a reference to the local authority or probation officer concerned.

(7) Where an offender is required by virtue of paragraph (a) of sub-paragraph (5) above to appear before the court which made the community order—

(a) the home court shall send to that court a certificate certifying that the offender has failed to comply with such of the requirements of the order as may be specified in the certificate, together with such other particulars of the case as may be desirable; and

(b) a certificate purporting to be signed by the clerk of the home court shall be admissible as evidence of the failure before the court which made the order.

(8) In this paragraph—

"corresponding order," in relation to a combination order, means a probation order including such a requirement as is mentioned in subsection (5A) of section 183 or 384 of the Criminal Procedure (Scotland) Act 1975;

"home court" means—

(a) if the offender resides in Scotland, or will be residing there at the relevant time, the sheriff court having jurisdiction in the locality in which he resides or proposes to reside; and

(b) if he resides in Northern Ireland, or will be residing there at the relevant time, the court of summary jurisdiction acting for the petty sessions district in which he resides or proposes to reside;

"the local authority officer concerned," in relation to an offender, means the officer of a regional or islands council responsible for his supervision or, as the case may be, discharging in relation to him the functions assigned by the Community Service by Offenders (Scotland) Act 1978;

"the probation officer concerned," in relation to an offender, means the probation officer responsible for his supervision or, as the case may be, discharging in relation to him the functions conferred by Part III of the Treatment of Offenders (Northern Ireland) Order 1976;

"the relevant time" means the time when the order or the amendment to it comes into force.

Part II

Transfer of Corresponding Orders from Scotland

Probation orders

7.—(1) The Criminal Procedure (Scotland) Act 1975 shall be amended as follows.

(2) In each of sections 183 and 384 (which provide, respectively, for probation orders in solemn and in summary proceedings), in subsection (1A) for the words "by the local authority in whose area he resides or is to reside" there shall be substituted the following paragraphs—

"(a) in a case other than that mentioned in paragraph (b) below, by the local authority in whose area he resides or is to reside; or

(b) in a case where, by virtue of section 188(1) of this Act, subsection (2) of this section would not apply, by the probation committee for the area which contains the petty sessions area which would be named in the order."

(3) In each of sections 188 and 389 (which provide, respectively, for probation orders relating to persons residing in England being made in solemn and in summary proceedings)—
   (a) in subsection (1)—
        (i) for the words "that the offender shall perform unpaid work" there shall be substituted the words "which, while corresponding to a requirement mentioned in paragraph 2 or 3 of Schedule 1A to the Powers of Criminal Courts Act 1973, would if included in a probation order made under that Act fail to accord with a restriction as to days of presentation, participation or attendance mentioned in paragraph 2(4)(a) or (6)(a), or as the case may be 3(3)(a), of that Schedule;
        (ii) for the word "17" there shall be substituted the word "16"
        (iii) the word "and," where it secondly occurs, shall cease to have effect; and
        (iv) at the end there shall be added the words "; and where the order includes a requirement that the probationer perform unpaid work for a number of hours, the number specified shall not exceed one hundred.";
   (b) in subsection (2)—
        (i) for the words "that the probationer has attained the age of 17 years and proposes to reside in or is residing in England" there shall be substituted the following paragraphs—
      "(a) that the probationer has attained the age of 16 years;
      (b) that he proposes to reside, or is residing, in England; and
      (c) that suitable arrangements for his supervision can be made by the probation committee for the area which contains the petty sessions area in which he resides or will reside"; and
        (ii) after the word "section," where it secondly occurs, there shall be inserted the words "or to vary any requirement for performance of unpaid work so that such hours as remain to be worked to not exceed one hundred";
   (c) in subsection (3)—
        (i) in paragraph (a), for the words "section 3(2) of" and "section 3 of" there shall be substituted, respectively, the words "paragraph 5(3) of Schedule 1A to" and "paragraph 5 of Schedule 1A to"; and
        (ii) in paragraph (b), for the words "subsections (4) to (6) of section 3 of" there shall be substituted the words "sub-paragraphs (5) to (7) of paragraph 5 of Schedule 1A to";
   (d) in subsection (4), for the words from "the Powers" to the end of the proviso there shall be substituted the words "Schedule 2 to the Criminal Justice Act 1991 shall apply to the order—
      (a) except in the case mentioned in paragraph (b) below, as if that order were a probation order made under section 2 of the Powers of Criminal Courts Act 1973; and
      (b) in the case of an order which contains a requirement such as is mentioned in subsection (5A) of section 183 or 384 of this Act, as if it were a combination order made under section 11 of the said Act of 1991:
      Provided that Part III of that Schedule shall not so apply; and sub-paragraphs (3) and (4) of paragraph 3 of that Schedule shall so apply as if for the first reference in the said sub-paragraph (3) to the Crown Court there were substituted a reference to a court in Scotland and for the other references in those sub-paragraphs to the Crown Court there were substituted references to the court in Scotland."; and
   (e) in subsection (5), for the words from "for which" to "this section" there shall be substituted the words "named in a probation order made or amended under this section that the person to whom the order relates."
(4) Sections 189 and 390 (which make further provision as to probation orders in, respectively, solemn and summary proceedings) shall cease to have effect.

Community service orders

8. Section 6 of the Community Service by Offenders (Scotland) Act 1978 (community service orders relating to persons residing in England and Wales) shall be amended as follows—
   (a) in subsection (1)(a), for the words from "for paragraphs" to the end of paragraph (b) as substituted in section 1(2) of that Act there shall be substituted the words ", in subsection (2), paragraph (b) were omitted and for paragraph (d) there were substituted the following paragraph—";
and
   (b) in subsection (2), paragraph (b) shall cease to have effect.

Supervision requirements

9. Section 72 of the Social Work (Scotland) Act 1968 (supervision of children moving to England and Wales or to Northern Ireland) shall be amended as follows—

(a) in subsection (1)(b), for the words "to a juvenile court acting for the petty sessions area" there shall be substituted the following sub-paragraphs—

"(i) in the case of residence in England and Wales, to a youth court acting for the petty sessions area (within the meaning of the Children and Young Persons Act 1969);

(ii) in the case of residence in Northern Ireland, to a juvenile court acting for the petty sessions district (within the meaning of Part III of the Magistrates' Courts (Northern Ireland) Order 1981).";

(b) in subsection (1A)—

(i) for the words "The juvenile court in England or Wales" there shall be substituted the words "A youth court";

(ii) after the word "12" there shall be inserted the words ", 122A, 12AA, 12B or 12C"; and

(iii) paragraph (a), and the word "and" immediately following that paragraph, shall cease to have effect;

(c) in subsection (2), for the words "The juvenile court in Northern Ireland" there shall be substituted the words "A juvenile court";

(d) in subsection (3), after the words "by a" there shall be inserted the words "youth court or as the case may be; and

(e) subsection (4) shall cease to have effect.

PART III

TRANSFER OF PROBATION ORDERS FROM NORTHERN IRELAND

10.—(1) Where, in the case of an offender of or over the age of 16 years, a court in Northern Ireland considering the making of a probation order is satisfied that the offender resides in England and Wales, or will be residing there when the order comes into force, section 1 of the Probation Act (Northern Ireland) 1950 (probation orders) shall have effect as if after sub-section (1) there were inserted the following subsection—

"(1A) A court shall not make a probation order in respect of any offender unless it is satisfied that suitable arrangements for his supervision can be made by the probation committee for the area which contains the petty sessions area in which he resides or will reside."

(2) Where a probation order has been made by a court in Northern Ireland and—

(a) a court of summary jurisdiction acting for the petty sessions district in Northern Ireland for the time being specified in the order is satisfied that the offender has attained the age of 16 years and proposes to reside or is residing in England and Wales; and

(b) it appears to the court that suitable arrangements for his supervision can be made by the probation committee for the area which contains the petty sessions area in which he resides or will reside,

the power of the court to amend the order under Schedule 2 to the Probation Act (Northern Ireland) 1950 shall include power to amend it by requiring him to be supervised in accordance with arrangements so made.

(3) Where a court is considering the making or amendment of a probation order in accordance with this paragraph, sections 2, 2A and 2B of the Probation Act (Northern Ireland) 1950 shall have effect as if—

(a) any reference to a probation officer were a reference to a probation officer assigned to the petty sessions area in England and Wales in which the offender resides or will be residing when the order or amendment comes into force;

(b) the reference in section 2(2) to treatment (whether as an in-patient or an out-patient) at such hospital as may be specified in the order, being a hospital within the meaning of the Health and Personal Social Services (Northern Ireland) Order 1972, approved by the Department of Health and Social Services for Northern Ireland for the purposes of that section were a reference to treatment as a resident patient in a mental hospital within the meaning of paragraph 5 of Schedule 1A to the 1973 Act;

(c) the reference in section 2A(5) to the Probation Board for Northern Ireland were a reference to the probation committee for the area in which the premises are situated; and

(d) references in section 2B to a day centre were references to a probation centre within the meaning of paragraph 3 of Schedule 1A to the 1973 Act.

(4) A probation order made or amended in accordance with this paragraph shall specify the petty sessions area in England and Wales in which the offender resides or will be residing when the order or amendment comes into force.

11.—(1) Where a probation order is made or amended in any of the circumstances specified in paragraph 10 above, the court which makes or amends the order shall send three copies of it as made or amended to the home court, together with such documents and information relating to the case as it considers likely to be of assistance to that court.

(2) Where a probation order is made or amended in any of the circumstances specified in paragraph 10 above, then, subject to the following provisions of this paragraph—

(a) the order shall be treated as if it were a probation order made in England and Wales; and

(b) the provisions relating to such orders of the 1973 Act and Schedule 2 to this Act (except paragraphs 9 and 10) shall apply accordingly.

(3) Before making or amending a probation order in the circumstances specified in paragraph 10 above the court shall explain to the offender in ordinary language—

(a) the requirements of the 1973 Act relating to probation orders;

(b) the powers of the home court under that Act and Schedule 2 to this Act, as modified by this paragraph; and

(c) its own powers under this paragraph,

and an explanation given in accordance with this sub-paragraph shall be sufficient without the addition of an explanation under section 1(5) of the Probation Act (Northern Ireland) 1950.

(4) The home court may exercise in relation to the probation order any power which it could exercise in relation to a probation order made by a court in England and Wales by virtue of the 1973 Act, except a power conferred by paragraph 3(1)(d), 4(1)(d), 7(2) or 8(2) of Schedule 2 to this Act.

(5) If at any time while the 1973 Act applies by virtue of sub-paragraph (2) above to a probation order made in Northern Ireland it appears to the home court—

(a) on information to a justice of the peace acting for the petty sessions area for the time being specified in the order, that the offender has failed to comply with any of the requirements of the 1973 Act applicable to the order; or

(b) on the application of the offender or the probation officer, that it would be in the interests of justice for the power conferred by paragraph 1 of Schedule 2 to the Probation Act (Northern Ireland) 1950 to be exercised,

the home court may require the offender to appear before the court which made the order.

(6) Where an offender is required by virtue of sub-paragraph (5) above to appear before the court which made the probation order, that court—

(a) may issue a warrant for his arrest; and

(b) may exercise any power which it could exercise in respect of the probation order if the offender resided in Northern Ireland,

and section 4(2) to (7) of the Probation Act (Northern Ireland) 1959 shall have effect accordingly.

(7) Where an offender is required by virtue of paragraph (a) of sub-paragraph (5) above to appear before the court which made the probation order—

(a) the home court shall send to that court a certificate certifying that the offender has failed to comply with such of the requirements of the order as may be specified in the certificate, together with such other particulars of the case as may be desirable; and

(b) a certificate purporting to be signed by the clerk of the home court shall be admissable as evidence of the failure before the court which made the order.

(8) In this paragraph "home court" means, if the offender resides in England and Wales, or will be residing there at the time when the order or the amendment to it comes into force, the court of summary jurisdiction acting for the petty sessions area in which he resides or proposes to reside.

Section 17(3)   SCHEDULE 4

INCREASE OF CERTAIN MAXIMA

PART I

SUBSTITUTION OF OTHER AMOUNTS

(1) Provision	(2) General description	(3) Present amount	(4) New amount
In Schedule 5a to the Army Act 1955 and the Air Force Act 1955, paragraph 11(2).	Maximum amount of compensation order.	£2,000	£5,000

(1) Provision	(2) General description	(3) Present amount	(4) New amount
Section 23(3) of the Attachment of Earnings Act 1971.	Maximum judge's fine in High Court or county court.	£100	£250
Section 27(3) of the 1973 Act.	Maximum fine for failure to comply with suspended sentence supervision order.	£400	£1,000
Section 8(1) of the Armed Forces Act 1976.	Maximum fine awarded by Standing Civilian Courts.	£2,000	£5,000
Section 40(1) of the 1980 Act.	Maximum amount of compensation order.	£2,000	£5,000
Section 63(3)(a) of that Act.	Maximum fine for disobedience of order other than for payment of money.	£2,000	£5,000
Section 97(4) of that Act.	Maximum fine for refusal to give evidence.	£1,000	£2,500
Section 12(2) of the Contempt of Court Act 1981.	Maximum fine for contempt in face of magistrates' court.	£1,000	£2,500
Section 14(2) of that Act.	Maximum fine for contempt in an inferior court.	£1,000	£2.500
Section 55(2) of the County Courts Act 1984.	Maximum fine for neglecting witness summons.	400	£1,000
Section 118(1) of that Act.	Maximum fine for contempt of court.	£1,000	£2,500
Section 10(1) and (2) and 21(5) of the Coroners Act 1988.	Maximum coroner's fine for refusal to give evidence etc.	£400	£1,000

PART II

SUBSTITUTION OF LEVELS ON STANDARD SCALE

(1) Provision	(2) General description	(3) Present amount	(4) Level on standard scale
Section 33(1)(a) of the 1980 Act.	Maximum fine on summary conviction of offence tried in pursuance of section 22 of that Act (certain offences triable either way to be tried summarily if value involved is small).	£1,000	Level 4
Section 34(3)(b) of that Act.	Maximum fine on summary conviction where statute provides no express power to fine.	£400	Level 3

PART III

SUBSTITUTION OF STATUTORY MAXIMUM

(1) Provision	(2) General description	(3) Present amount
Section 6(8) of the Whaling Industry (Regulation) Act 1934.	Maximum fine on summary conviction for failure to to keep or falsify records.	£1,000
Section 9(1) of that Act.	Maximum fine on summary conviction for forgery of certain documents.	£1,000
Section 11(1)(c) of the Sea Fisheries (Conservation) Act 1967.	Maximum fine on summary conviction for an offence under section 1, 2, 4(7) or (7A), 4A(7) or (8), 6(5) or (5A)(b) or 7(3) of that Act.	£1,000
Section 16(1A) of that Act.	Maximum fine on summary conviction for assaulting or obstructing officer exercising enforcement powers.	£1,000
Section 5(4) of the Sea Fisheries Act 1968.	Maximum fine on summary conviction for contravening order regulating fishing operations.	£1,000

PART IV

PROVISIONS SUBSTITUTED FOR SCHEDULE 6A TO 1980 ACT

"SCHEDULE 6A

FINES THAT MAY BE ALTERED UNDER SECTION 143

Enactment	Maximum fine
CHILDREN AND YOUNG PERSONS ACT 1969 (c. 54)	
Section 15(3)(a) (failure to comply with supervision order)	£1,000
Section 15(5)(b) and (c) (failure to comply with supervision order)	£5,000
ATTACHMENT OF EARNINGS ACT 1971 (c. 32)	
Section 23(3) (judge's fine)	£250
POWERS OF CRIMINAL COURTS ACT 1973 (c. 62)	
Section 27(3) (failure to comply with suspended sentence supervision order)	£1,000
MAGISTRATES' COURTS ACT 1980 (c. 43)	
Section 63(3)(a) (disobedience of orders other than payment of money)	£5,000
Section 97(4) (refusal to give evidence etc.)	£2,500
CONTEMPT OF COURT ACT 1981 (c. 49)	
Section 12(2) (contempt in face of magistrates' court)	£2,500
Section 14(2) (contempt in an inferior court)	£2,500
CRIMINAL JUSTICE ACT 1982 (c. 48)	
Section 19(3) (failure to comply with attendance centre order or attendance centre rules)	£1,000
COUNTY COURTS ACT 1984 (c. 28)	
Section 55(2) (neglect or refusal to give evidence)	£1,000
Section 118(1) (contempt in face of court)	£2,500
CORONERS ACT 1988 (c. 13)	
Sections 10(1) and (2) and 21(5) (refusal to give evidence etc.)	£1,000
CRIMINAL JUSTICE ACT 1991 (c. 53)	
In Schedule 2, paragraphs 3(1) and 4(1) (failure to comply with probation, community service, curfew or combination order)	£1,000".

PART V

OTHER AMENDMENTS

1. In section 27 of the 1973 Act (breach of requirement of suspended sentence supervision order), for subsection (4) there shall be substituted the following subsection—
"(4) Section 18 of the Criminal Justice Act 1991 (fixing of certain fines by reference to units) shall apply for the purposes of subsection (3) above as if the failure to comply with the requirement were a summary offence punishable by a fine not exceeding level 3 on the standard scale; and a fine imposed under that subsection shall be deemed for the purposes of any enactment to be a sum adjudged to be paid by a conviction."
2. In section 97 of the 1980 Act (maximum fine for refusal to give evidence), after subsection (4) there shall be inserted the following subsection—
"(5) Section 18 of the Criminal Justice Act 1991 (fixing of certain fines by reference to units) shall apply for the purposes of subsection (4) above as if the failure to attend before the magistrates' court were a summary offence punishable by a fine not exceeding level 4 on the standard scale; and a fine imposed under that subsection shall be deemed for the purposes of any enactment to be a sum adjudged to be paid by a conviction."
3. In section 12 of the Contempt of Court Act 1981 (maximum fine for contempt in face of magistrates' court), after subsection (2) there shall be inserted the following subsection—
"(2A) Section 18 of the Criminal Justice Act 1991 (fixing of certain fines by reference to units) shall apply for the purposes of subsection (2) above as if the failure to attend before the magistrates' court were a summary offence punishable by a fine not exceeding level 4 on the standard scale; and a fine imposed under that subsection shall be deemed for the purposes of any enactment to be a sum adjudged to be paid by a conviction."
4. In section 14 of that Act (maximum fine for contempt in an inferior court), after subsection (2) there shall be inserted the following subsection—
"(2A) Section 18 of the Criminal Justice Act 1991 (fixing of certain fines by reference to units) shall apply for the purposes of subsection (2) above as if the failure to attend before the magistrates' court were a summary offence punishable by a fine not exceeding level 4 on the standard scale; and a fine imposed under that subsection shall be deemed for the purposes of any enactment to be a sum adjudged to be paid by a conviction."

Section 32(7)   SCHEDULE 5

THE PAROLE BOARD

Membership

1. The Board shall consist of a chairman and not less than four other members appointed by the Secretary of State.
2. The Board shall include among its members—
(a) a person who holds or has held judicial office;
(b) a registered medical practitioner who is a psychiatrist;
(c) a person appearing to the Secretary of State to have knowledge and experience of the supervision or after-care of discharged prisoners; and
(d) a person appearing to the Secretary of State to have made a study of the causes of delinquency or the treatment of offenders.
3. A member of the Board—
(a) shall hold and vacate office in accordance with the terms of his appointment;
(b) may resign his office by notice in writing addressed to the Secretary of State;
and a person who ceases to hold office as a member of the Board shall be eligible for reappointment.

Remuneration and allowances

4. There shall be paid to the members of Board such remuneration and allowances as the Secretary of State may with the consent of the Treasury determine.
5. The expenses of the Board under paragraph 4 above and any other expenses incurred by the Board in discharging its functions under Part II of this Act shall be defrayed by the Secretary of State.

Reports

6. The Board shall as soon as practicable after the end of each year make to the Secretary of State a report on the performance of its functions during that year; and the Secretary of State shall lay a copy of the report before Parliament.

Section 53(5) SCHEDULE 6

NOTICES OF TRANSFER: PROCEDURE IN LIEU OF COMMITTAL

Contents of notice of transfer

1.—(1) A notice of transfer shall specify the proposed place of trial; and in selecting that place the Director of Public Prosecutions shall have regard to the considerations to which a magistrates' court committing a person for trial is required by section 7 of the 1980 Act to have regard when selecting the place at which he is to be tried.

(2) A notice of transfer shall specify the charge or charges to which it relates and include or be accompanied by such additional material as regulations under paragraph 4 below may require.

Remand

2.—(1) If a magistrates' court has remanded in custody a person to whom a notice of transfer relates, it shall have power, subject to section 4 of the Bail Act 1976 and regulations under section 22 of the Prosecution of Offences Act 1985—

(a) to order that he shall be safely kept in custody until delivered in due course of law; or

(b) to release him on bail in accordance with the Bail Act 1976, that is to say, by directing him to appear before the Crown Court for trial.

(2) Where—

(a) a person's release on bail under paragraph (b) of sub-paragraph (1) above is conditional on his providing one or more sureties; and

(b) in accordance with subsection (3) of section 8 of the Bail Act 1976, the court fixes the amount in which a surety is to be bound with a view to his entering into his recognisance subsequently in accordance with subsections (4) and (5) or (6) of that section,

the court shall in the meantime make an order such as is mentioned in paragraph (a) of that sub-paragraph.

(3) If the conditions specified in sub-paragraph (4) below are satisfied, a court may exercise the powers conferred by sub-paragraph (1) above in relation to a person charged without his being brought before it in any case in which by virtue of subsection (3A) of section 128 of the 1980 Act it would have the power further to remand him on an adjournment such as is mentioned in that subsection.

(4) The conditions referred to in sub-paragraph (3) above are—

(a) that the person in question has given his written consent to the powers conferred by sub-paragraph (1) above being exercised without his being brought before the court; and

(b) that the court is satisfied that, when he gave his consent, he knew that the notice of transfer had been issued.

(5) Where a notice of transfer is given after a person to whom it relates has been remanded on bail to appear before a magistrates' court on an appointed day, the requirement that he shall so appear shall cease on the giving of the notice unless the notice states that it is to continue.

(6) Where that requirement ceases by virtue of sub-paragraph (5) above, it shall be the duty of the person in question to appear before the Crown Court at the place specified by the notice of transfer as the proposed place of trial or at any place substituted for it by a direction under section 76 of the Supreme Court Act 1981.

(7) If, in a case where the notice states that the requirement mentioned in sub-paragraph (5) above is to continue, a person to whom the notice relates appears before the magistrates' court, the court shall have—

(a) the powers and duties conferred on a magistrates' court by sub-paragraph (1) above but subject as there provided; and

(b) power to enlarge, in the surety's absence, a recognisance conditioned in accordance with section 128(4)(a) of the 1980 Act so that the surety is bound to secure that the person charged appears also before the Crown Court.

Witnesses

3. For the purposes of the Criminal Procedure (Attendance of Witnesses) Act 1965—

(a) any magistrates' court for the petty sessions area for which the court from which a case was transferred sits shall be treated as examining magistrates; and

(b) a person indicated in the notice of transfer as a proposed witness shall be treated as a person who has been examined by the court.

Regulations

4.—(1) The Attorney General—
(a) shall by regulations make provision requiring a copy of a notice of transfer, together with a statement of the evidence on which any charge to which it relates is based, to be given—
    (i) to any person to whom the notice of transfer relates; and
    (ii) to the Crown Court sitting at the place specified by the notice of transfer as the proposed place of trial; and
(b) may by regulations make such further provision in relation to notices of transfer, including provision as to the duties of the Director of Public Prosecutions in relation to such notices, as appears to him to be appropriate.
(2) The power to make regulations under this paragraph shall be exercisable by a statutory instrument subject to annulment in pursuance of a resolution of either House of Parliament.

Applications for dismissal

5.—(1) Where a notice of transfer has been given, any person to whom the notice relates may, at any time before he is arraigned (and whether or not an indictment has been preferred against him), apply orally or in writing to the Crown Court sitting at the place specified by the notice of transfer as the proposed place of trial for the charge, or any of the charges, in the case to be dismissed.
(2) The judge shall dismiss a charge (and accordingly quash a count relating to it in any indictment preferred against the applicant) which is the subject of any such application if it appears to him that the evidence against the applicant would not be sufficient for a jury properly to convict him.
(3) No oral application may be made under sub-paragraph (1) above unless the applicant has given the Crown Court mentioned in that sub-paragraph written notice of his intention to make the application.
(4) Oral evidence may be given on such an application only with the leave of the judge or by his order; and the judge shall give leave or make an order only if it appears to him, having regard to any matters stated in the application for leave, that the interests of justice require him to do so.
(5) No leave or order under sub-paragraph (4) above shall be given or made in relation to oral evidence from a child (within the meaning of section 53 of this Act) who is alleged—
(a) to be a person against whom an offence to which the notice of transfer relates was committed; or
(b) to have witnessed the commission of such an offence.
(6) If the judge gives leave permitting, or makes an order requiring, a person to give oral evidence, but that person does not do so, the judge may disregard any document indicating the evidence that he might have given.
(7) Dismissal of the charge, or all the charges, against the applicant shall have the same effect as a refusal by examining magistrates to commit for trial, except that no further proceedings may be brought on a dismissed charge except by means of the preferment of a voluntary bill of indictment.
(8) Crown Court Rules may make provision for the purposes of this paragraph and, without prejudice to the generality of this sub-paragraph, may make provision—
(a) as to the time or stage in the proceedings at which anything required to be done is to be done (unless the court grants leave to do it at some other time or stage);
(b) as to the contents and form of notices or other documents;
(c) as to the manner in which evidence is to be submitted; and
(d) as to persons to be served with notices or other material.

Reporting restrictions

6.—(1) Except as provided by this paragraph, it shall not be lawful—
(a) to publish in Great Britain a written report of an application under paragraph 5(1) above; or
(b) to include in a relevant programme for reception in Great Britain a report of such an application,
if (in either case) the report contains any matter other than that permitted by this paragraph.
(2) An order that sub-paragraph (1) above shall not apply to reports of an application under paragraph 5(1) above may be made by the judge dealing with the application.

(3) Where in the case of two or more accused one of them objects to the making of an order under sub-paragraph (2) above, the judge shall make the order if, and only if, he is satisfied, after hearing the representations of the accused, that it is in the interests of justice to do so.

(4) An order under sub-paragraph (2) above shall not apply to reports of proceedings under sub-paragraph (3) above, but any decision of the court or make or not to make such an order may be contained in reports published or included in a relevant programme before the time authorised by sub-paragraph (5) below.

(5) It shall not be unlawful under this paragraph to publish or include in a relevant programme a report of an application under paragraph 5(1) above containing any matter other than that permitted by sub-paragraph (8) below where the application is successful.

(6) Where—

(a) two or more persons were jointly charged; and

(b) applications under paragraph 5(1) above are made by more than one of them, sub-paragraph (5) above shall have effect as if for the words "the application is" there were substituted the words "all the applications are."

(7) It shall not be unlawful under this paragraph to publish or include in a relevant programme a report of an unsuccessful application at the conclusion of the trial of the person charged, or of the last of the persons charged to be tried.

(8) The following matters may be contained in a report published or included in a relevant programme without an order under sub-paragraph (2) above before the time authorised by sub-paragraphs (5) and (6) above, that is to say—

(a) the identity of the court and the name of the judge;

(b) the names, ages, home addresses and occupations of the accused and witnesses;

(c) the offence or offences, or a summary of them, with which the accused is or are charged;

(d) the names of counsel and solicitors engaged in the proceedings;

(e) where the proceedings are adjourned, the date and place to which they are adjourned;

(f) the arrangements as to bail;

(g) whether legal aid was granted to the accused or any of the accused.

(9) The addresses that may be published or included in a relevant programme under sub-paragraph (8) above are addresses—

(a) at any relevant time; and

(b) at the time of their publication or inclusion in a relevant programme.

(10) If a report is published or included in a relevant programme in contravention of this paragraph, the following persons, that is to say—

(a) in the case of a publication of a written report as part of a newspaper or periodical, any proprietor, editor or publisher of the newspaper or periodical;

(b) in the case of a publication of a written report otherwise than as part of a newspaper or periodical, the person who publishes it;

(c) in the case of the inclusion of a report in a relevant programme, any body corporate which is engaged in providing the service in which the programme is included and any person having functions in relation to the programme corresponding to those of the editor of a newspaper;

shall be liable on summary conviction to a fine not exceeding level 5 on the standard scale.

(11) Proceedings for an offence under this paragraph shall not, in England and Wales, be instituted otherwise than by or with the consent of the Attorney General.

(12) Sub-paragraph (1) above shall be in addition to, and not in derogation from, the provisions of any other enactment with respect to the publication of reports of court proceedings.

(13) In this paragraph—

"publish," in relation to a report, means publish the report, either by itself or as part of a newspaper or periodical, for distribution to the public;

"relevant programme" means a programme included in a programme service (within the meaning of the Broadcasting Act 1990);

"relevant time" means a time when events giving rise to the charges to which the proceedings relate occurred.

Avoidance of delay

7.—(1) Where a notice of transfer has been given in relation to any case—

(a) the Crown Court before which the case is to be tried; and

(b) any magistrates' court which exercises any functions under paragraph 2 or 3 above or section 20(4) of the Legal Aid Act 1988 in relation to the case,

shall, in exercising any of its powers in relation to the case, have regard to the desirability of avoiding prejudice to welfare of any relevant child witness that may be occasioned by unnecessary delay in bringing the case to trial.

(2) In this paragraph "child" has the same meaning as in section 53 of this Act and "relevant child witness" means a child who will be called as a witness at the trial and who is alleged—
  (a) to be a person against whom an offence to which the notice of transfer relates was committed; or
  (b) to have witnessed the commission of such an offence.

Procedures for indictment of offenders

8.—(1) In subsection (2) of section 2 of the Administration of Justice (Miscellaneous Provisions) Act 1933 (procedures for indictment of offenders), after paragraph (aa), there shall be inserted the following paragraph—
  "(ab) the offence is specified in a notice of transfer under section 53 of the Criminal Justice Act 1991 (violent or sexual offences against children); or."
(2) In paragraph (iA) of the proviso to that subsection—
  (a) after the words "paragraph (aa)" there shall be inserted the words "or (ab)"; and
  (b) for the words "regulations under section 5(9) of the Criminal Justice Act 1987" there shall be substituted the words "regulations under the relevant provision."
(3) At the end of that proviso there shall be inserted the words "and in paragraph (iA) above 'the relevant provision' means section 5(9) of the Criminal Justice Act 1987 in a case to which paragraph (aa) above applies, and paragraph 4 of Schedule 6 to the Criminal Justice Act 1991 in a case to which paragraph (ab) above applies."

Legal aid

9. In section 20(4) of the Legal Aid Act 1988 (power of magistrates' court to grant legal aid for Crown Court proceedings), in paragraph (b), after the word "cases)" there shall be inserted the words "or section 53 of the Criminal Justice Act 1991 (transfer of certain cases involving children)."

Section 66   SCHEDULE 7

PROVISIONS SUBSTITUTED FOR SECTION 15 OF 1969 ACT

"Variation and discharge of supervision orders

15.—(1) While a supervision order is in force in respect of a supervised person it appears to a relevant court, on the application of the supervisor or the supervised person, that it is appropriate to make an order under this subsection, the court may make an order discharging the supervision order or varying it—
  (a) by cancelling any requirement included in it in pursuance of section 12, 12A, 12AA, 12B, 12C or 18(2)(b) of this Act; or
  (b) by inserting in it (either in addition to or in substitution for any of its provisions) any provision which could have been included in the order if the court had then had power to make it and were exercising the power.
(2) The powers of variation conferred by subsection (1) above do not include power—
  (a) to insert in the supervision order, after the expiration of three months beginning with the date when the order was originally made, a requirement in pursuance of section 12B(1) of this Act, unless it is in substitution for such a requirement already included in the order; or
  (b) to insert in the supervision order a requirement in pursuance of section 12A(3)(b) of this Act in respect of any day which falls outside the period of three months beginning with the date when the order was originally made.
(3) If while a supervision order made under section 7(7) of this Act is in force in respect of a person it is proved to the satisfaction of a relevant court, on the application of the supervisor, that the supervised person has failed to comply with any requirement included in the supervision order in pursuance of section 12, 12A, 12AA, 12C or 18(2)(b) of this Act, the court—
  (a) whether or not it also makes an order under subsection (1) above, may order him to pay a fine of an amount not exceeding £1,000 or, subject to section 16A(1) of this Act, may make an attendance centre order in respect of him; or
  (b) in the case of a person who has attained the age of eighteen, may (if it also discharges the supervision order) make an order imposing on him any punishment, other than a sentence of detention in a young offender institution, which it could have imposed on him if it—
    (i) had then had power to try him for the offence in consequence of which the supervision order was made; and
    (ii) had convicted him in the exercise of that power.

(4) If while a supervision order is in force in respect of a person it is proved to the court under subsection (3) above that the supervised person has failed to comply with any requirement included in the supervision order in pursuance of section 12A(3)(a) of this Act directing the supervised person to participate in specified activities, the court may, if it also discharges the supervision order, make an order imposing on him any sentence which it could have imposed on him if it—

(a) had then had power to try him for the offence in consequence of which the supervision order was made; and

(b) had convicted him in the exercise of that power.

(5) In a case falling within subsection (3)(b) or (4) above where the offence in question is of a kind which the court has no power to try, or has no power to try without appropriate consents, the sentence imposed by virtue of that provision—

(a) shall not exceed that which any court having power to try such an offence could have imposed in respect of it; and

(b) where the case falls within subsection (3)(b) above and the sentence is a fine, shall not in any event exceed £5,000; and

(c) where the case falls within subsection (4) above, shall not in any event exceed a custodial sentence for a term of six months and a fine of £5,000.

(6) A court may not make an order by virtue of subsection (4) above unless the court which made the supervision order made a statement under subsection (1) of section 12D of this Act; and for the purposes of this subsection a certificate under that section shall be evidence of the making of the statement to which it relates.

(7) Section 18 of the Criminal Justice Act 1991 (fixing of certain fines by reference to units) shall apply—

(a) for the purposes of subsection (3)(a) above as if the failure to comply with the requirement were a summary offence punishable by a fine not exceeding level 3 on the standard scale; and

(b) for the purposes of subsections (3)(b) and (4) above as if the failure to comply with the requirement were a summary offence punishable by a fine not exceeding level 5 on that scale;

and a fine imposed under any of those provisions shall be deemed for the purposes of any enactment to be a sum adjudged to be paid by a conviction.

(8) In dealing with a supervised person under subsection (3) or (4) above, the court shall take into account the extent to which that person has complied with the requirements of the supervision order.

(9) If a medical practitioner by whom or under whose direction a supervised person is being treated for his mental condition in pursuance of a requirement included in a supervision order by virtue of section 12B(1) of this Act is unwilling to continue to treat or direct the treatment of the supervised person or is of opinion—

(a) that the treatment should be continued beyond the period specified in that behalf in the order; or

(b) that the supervised person needs different treatment; or

(c) that he is not susceptible to treatment; or

(d) that he does not require further treatment,

the practitioner shall make a report in writing to that effect to the supervisor.

(10) On receiving a report under subsection (9) above, the supervisor shall refer it to a relevant court; and on such a reference, the court may make an order cancelling or varying the requirement.

(11) In this section 'relevant court' means—

(a) in the case of a supervised person who has not attained the age of eighteen, a youth court;

(b) in the case of a supervised person who has attained that age, a magistrates' court other than a youth court.

(12) The provisions of this section shall have effect subject to the provisions of section 16 of this Act."

Section 68   SCHEDULE 8

AMENDMENTS FOR TREATING PERSONS AGED 17 AS YOUNG PERSONS

Children and Young Persons Act 1933 (c. 12)

1.—(1) Section 31 of the 1933 Act shall be renumbered as subsection (1) of that section and after that provision as so renumbered there shall be inserted the following subsection—

"(2) In this section and section 34 of this Act, 'young person' means a person who has attained the age of fourteen and is under the age of seventeen years."

(2) In sections 46(1) and (1A), 48(2) and 99(1) of that Act, for the words "the age of seventeen" there shall be substituted the words "the age of eighteen."

(3) In section 107(1) of that Act, for the definition of "young person" there shall be substituted the following definition—

"'young person' means a person who has attained the age of fourteen and is under the age of eighteen years."

Prison Act 1952 (c. 52)

2. In section 43(3) of the 1952 Act (remand centres, young offender institutions, etc.), for the words "aged 17 years" there shall be substituted the words "aged 18 years."

Children and Young Persons Act 1963 (c. 37)

3. In section 29(1) of the Children and Young Persons Act 1963, for the words "the age of seventeen" there shall be substituted the words "the age of eighteen."

Children and Young Persons Act 1969 (c. 54)

4.—(1) Section 29 of the 1969 Act shall be renumbered as subsection (1) of that section and after that provision as so renumbered there shall be inserted the following subsection—

"(2) In this section 'young person' means a person who has attained the age of fourteen and is under the age of seventeen years."

(2) In section 70(1) of that Act, for the definition of "young person" there shall be substituted the following definition—

"'young person' means a person who has attained the age of fourteen and is under the age of eighteen years;".

Rehabilitation of Offenders Act 1974 (c. 53)

5. In section 5(2) of the Rehabilitation of Offenders Act 1974 (which provides for rehabilitation periods to be reduced by half for young offenders)—

(a) in paragraph (a), for the words "seventeen years of age" there shall be substituted the words "eighteen years of age"; and

(b) in the heading to Table A, for the words "under 17" there shall be substituted the words "under 18."

Magistrates' Courts Act 1980 (c. 43)

6.—(1) Part I of the 1980 Act (criminal jurisdiction and procedure) shall be amended as follows—

(a) for the words "the age of 17," in each place where they occur, there shall be substituted the words "the age of 18 years";

(b) in section 22(9), for the words "under 17" there shall be substituted the words "under 18";

(c) in section 36(1), for the words "17 years of age" there shall be substituted the words "18 years of age"; and

(d) in section 38 for the words "17 years old" there shall be substituted the words "18 years old."

(2) In section 81(1), (3) and (8) of that Act, for the words "the age of 17" there shall be substituted the words "the age of 18."

(3) In sections 96A, 135(3) and 136(4) of that Act, for the words "aged 17" there shall be substituted the words "aged 18."

Section 71   SCHEDULE 9

AMENDMENTS TO SERVICE LAW

Army Act 1955 (c. 18) and Air Force Act 1955 (c. 19)

1. In section 71A of the Army Act 1955 and the Air Force Act 1955 (life custody for young offenders), in subsections (1B) and (4)(a), for the words "17 years" there shall be substituted the words "18 years."

2. In section 71AA of those Acts (young service offenders; custodial orders)—

(a) in subsection (1), for the words "not exceeding" there shall be substituted the words "which—
    (a) shall not be less than the appropriate minimum period, that is to say—
        (i) in the case of an offender who has attained eighteen years of age, the period of 21 days; or
        (ii) in the case of an offender who is under that age, the period of two months; and
    (b) shall not exceed";
(b) subsection (1A) and, in subsection (1), the words "subject to subsection (1A) below" shall cease to have effect;
(c) before subsection (1B) there shall be inserted the following subsection—
    "(1AA) The court shall not make a custodial order committing an offender aged 17 to be detained for a period exceeding twelve months or for a period such that the continuous period for which he is committed to be detained under that order and any one or more other custodial orders exceeds twelve months."; and
(d) in subsection (6A), for the words "Section 15 of the Criminal Justice Act 1982" there shall be substituted the words "Section 65 of the Criminal Justice Act 1991."
3. For subsection (2) of section 93 of those Acts (evidence on oath in court-martial) there shall be substituted the following subsections—
    "(1B) A witness before a court-martial—
    (a) shall be examined on oath if he has attained the age of fourteen; and
    (b) shall give evidence unsworn if he is under that age.
    (2) Unsworn evidence admitted by virtue of subsection (1B)(b) above may corroborate evidence (sworn or unsworn) given by any other person."
4. In paragraph 10 of Schedule 5A to those Acts (civilian offenders: custodial orders)—
(a) in sub-paragraph (1), for the words from "detained" to "and in this sub-paragraph" there shall be substituted the words "detained for a period, to be specified in the order, which—
    (a) shall not be less than the appropriate minimum period, that is to say—
        (i) in the case of an offender who has attained the age of 18, the period of 21 days; or
        (ii) in the case of an offender who is under 18 years of age, the period of two months;
    (b) shall not exceed the maximum period for which he could have been sentenced to imprisonment if he had attained the age of 21; and
    (c) if the order is made by a Standing Civilian Court, shall not exceed six months. and in this sub-paragraph."
(b) in sub-paragraph (1A), for the words "17 years" there shall be substituted the words "18 years"; and
(c) in sub-paragraph (6A), for the words "Section 15 of the Criminal Justice Act 1982" there shall be substituted the words "Section 65 of the Criminal Justice Act 1991."

Naval Discipline Act 1957 (c. 53)

5. In section 43A of the Naval Discipline Act 1957 (life custody for young offenders), in subsections (1B) and (4)(a), for the words "17 years" there shall be substituted the words "18 years."
6. In section 43AA of that Act (young service offenders: custodial orders)—
(a) in subsection (1), for the words "not exceeding" there shall be substituted the words "which—
    (a) shall be not less than the appropriate minimum period, that is to say—
        (i) in the case of an offender who has attained eighteen years of age, the period of 21 days; or
        (ii) in the case of an offender who is under that age, the period of two months; and
    (b) shall not exceed";
(b) subsection (1A) and, in subsection (1), the words "subject to subsection (1A) below," shall cease to have effect; and
(c) before subsection (1B) there shall be inserted the following subsection—
    "(1AA) The court shall not make a custodial order committing an offender aged 17 to be detained for a period exceeding twelve months or for a period such that the continuous period for which he is committed to be detained under that order and any one or more other custodial orders exceeds twelve months."; and
(d) in subsection (6A), for the words "Section 15 of the Criminal Justice Act 1982" there shall be substituted the words "Section 65 of the Criminal Justice Act 1991."

7. For subsections (2) and (3) of section 60 of that Act (evidence on oath in court-martial) there shall be substituted the following subsections—
"(2) A witness before a court-martial—
(a) shall be examined on oath if he has attained the age of fourteen; and
(b) shall give evidence unsworn if he is under that age.
(3) Unsworn evidence admitted by virtue of subsection (2)(b) above may corroborate evidence (sworn or unsworn) given by any other person."
8. In paragraph 10 of Schedule 4A to that Act (civilian offenders: custodial orders)—
(a) in sub-paragraph (1), for the words from "detained" to "and in this sub-paragraph" there shall be substituted the words "detained for a period, to be specified in the order, which—
(a) shall be not less than the appropriate minimum period, that is to say—
(i) in the case of an offender who has attained the age of 18, the period of 21 days; or
(ii) in the case of an offender who is under 18 years of age, the period of two months; and
(b) shall not exceed the maximum period for which he could have been sentenced to imprisonment if he had attained the age of 21;
and in this sub-paragraph";
(b) in sub-paragraph (1A), for the words "17 years" there shall be substituted the words "18 years"; and
(c) in sub-paragraph (6A), for the words "Section 15 of the Criminal Justice Act 1982" there shall be substituted the words "Section 65 of the Criminal Justice Act 1991".

Section 89   SCHEDULE 10

CERTIFICATION OF PRISONER CUSTODY OFFICERS

Preliminary

1. In this Schedule—
"certificate" means a certificate under section 89 of this Act;
"the relevant functions", in relation to a certificate, means the escort functions or custodial duties authorised by the certificate.

Issue of certificates

2.—(1) Any person may apply to the Secretary of State for the issue of a certificate in respect of him.
(2) The Secretary of State shall not issue a certificate on any such application unless he is satisfied that the applicant—
(a) is a fit and proper person to perform the relevant functions; and
(b) has received training to such standard as he may consider appropriate for the performance of those functions.
(3) Where the Secretary of State issues a certificate, then, subject to any suspension under paragraph 3 or revocation under paragraph 4 below, it shall continue in force until such date or the occurrence of such event as may be specified in the certificate.
(4) A certificate authorising the performance of both escort functions and custodial duties may specify different dates or events as respects those functions and duties respectively.

Suspension of certificate

3.—(1) This paragraph applies where at any time it appears—
(a) in the case of a prisoner custody officer acting in pursuance of prisoner escort arrangements, to the prisoner escort monitor for the area concerned; or
(b) in the case of such an officer performing custodial duties at a contracted out prison, to the controller of that prison,
that the officer is not a fit and proper person to perform the escort functions or, as the case may be, custodial duties.
(2) The prisoner escort monitor or controller may—
(a) refer the matter to the Secretary of State for a decision under paragraph 4 below; and
(b) in such circumstances as may be prescribed by regulations made by the Secretary of State, suspend the officer's certificate so far as it authorises the performance of escort functions or, as the case may be, custodial duties pending that decision.
(3) The power to make regulations under this paragraph shall be exercisable by statutory instrument which shall be subject to annulment in pursuance of a resolution of either House of Parliament.

Revocation of certificate

4. Where at any time it appears to the Secretary of State that a prisoner custody officer is not a fit and proper person to perform escort functions or custodial duties, he may revoke that officer's certificate so far as it authorises the performance of those functions or duties.

False statements

5. If any person, for the purpose of obtaining a certificate for himself or for any other person—
(a) makes a statement which he knows to be false in a material particular, or
(b) recklessly makes a statement which is false in a material particular,
he shall be liable on summary conviction to a fine not exceeding level 4 on the standard scale.

Section 100   SCHEDULE 11

MINOR AND CONSEQUENTIAL AMENDMENTS

Children and Young Persons Act 1933 (c. 12)

1. In section 38(2) of the 1933 Act (false evidence by child) for the words "as aforesaid" there shall be substituted the words "unsworn in any proceedings for an offence by virtue of section 52 of the Criminal Justice Act 1991".

Criminal Justice Act 1967 (c. 80)

2.—(1) Section 67 of the 1967 Act (remand time to be taken into account in computing sentences) shall be amended as follows.
(2) In subsection (1A)(c)—
(a) after the word "remanded" there shall be inserted the words "or committed"; and
(b) after the words "section 23 of the Children and Young Persons Act 1969" there shall be inserted the words "or section 37 of the Magistrates' Courts Act 1980".
(3) For subsection (5) there shall be substituted the following subsection—
    "(5) This section applies—
      (a) to sentences of detention in a young offender institution; and
      (b) to determinate sentences of detention passed under section 53(2) of the Children and Young Persons Act 1933 (sentences for serious indictable offences),
   as it applies to sentences of imprisonment."
(4) In subsection (6)—
(a) after the word "being", in the second place where it occurs, there shall be inserted the words "remanded or";
(b) for the words "committed to the care of a local authority" there shall be substituted the words "remanded or committed to local authority accommodation"; and
(c) after the words "the said section 23" there shall be inserted the words "or 37".

Criminal Appeal Act 1968 (c. 19)

3. In section 10(2) of the Criminal Appeal Act 1968 (appeal against sentence in other cases dealt with by Crown Court), for paragraph (b) there shall be substituted the following paragraph—
    "(b) having been made the subject of an order for conditional discharge or a community order within the meaning of Part I of the Criminal Justice Act 1991 (other than a supervision order within the meaning of that Part) or given a suspended sentence, appears or is brought before the Crown Court to be further dealt with for his offence."
4. In section 50(1A) of that Act (right of appeal of probationer, etc.), for the words "Section 13" there shall be substituted the words "Section 1C" and the words "a probation order or" shall cease to have effect.

Civil Evidence Act 1968 (c. 64)

5. In section 11(5)(a) of the Civil Evidence Act 1968 (convictions as evidence in civil proceedings), for the words "section 13" there shall be substituted the words "section 1C" and the words "probation or" shall cease to have effect.

Children and Young Persons Act 1969 (c. 54)

6.—(1) In subsection (1) of section 12D of the 1969 (duty of court to state in certain cases that requirement is in place of custodial sentence), in paragraph (ii), for sub-paragraphs (a) to (c) there shall be substituted the following sub-paragraphs—

"(a) the offence of which he has been convicted, or the combination of that offence and one other offence associated with it, was so serious that only a supervision order containing such a requirement or a custodial sentence can be justified for that offence; or

(b) that offence was a violent or sexual offence and only a supervision order containing such a requirement or such a sentence would be adequate to protect the public from serious harm from him."

(2) After that subsection there shall be inserted the following subsection—

"(1A) Sub-paragraphs (a) and (b) of subsection (1)(ii) above shall be construed as if they were contained in Part I of the Criminal Justice Act 1991."

7.—(1) In subsection (4) of section 16 of that Act (provisions supplementary to section 15), for the words "a court" there shall be substituted the words "a youth court".

(2) In subsection (6)(b) of that section, for the words "subsection (5)" there shall be substituted the words "subsection (10)".

(3) In subsection (10) of that section for the words "paragraph (b) of subsection (2A) and paragraph (a) of subsection (4)" there shall be substituted the words "paragraph (a) of subsection (3)".

8.—(1) In subsection (1) of section 16A of that Act (application of sections 17 to 19 of the 1982 Act), for the words "section 15(2A)(b) and (4)(a)" there shall be substituted the words "section 15(3)(a)."

(2) In subsection (2) of that section, for the words "each of those paragraphs" there shall be substituted the words "section 15(3)(a) of this Act."

Vehicles (Excise) Act 1971 (c. 10)

9. In section 9(5) of the Vehicles (Excise) Act 1971 (additional liability for keeping unlicensed vehicle), for the words "Part I of the Criminal Justice Act 1948" there shall be substituted the words "section 1C of the Powers of Criminal Courts Act 1973" and the words "placing him on probation or" shall cease to have effect.

Powers of Criminal Courts Act 1973 (c. 62)

10. In section 11(2) of the 1973 Act (substitution of conditional discharge for probation) for the words "section 8 of this Act" there shall be substituted the words "paragraph 7 of Schedule 2 to the Criminal Justice Act 1991."

11. In section 12 of that Act (supplementary provisions as to probation and discharge)—

(a) in subsection (2), for the words "section 2(7) and paragraph 1 of Schedule 1" there shall be substituted the words "section 2(4)";

(b) in subsection (4), for the words "section 2 or 7" there shall be substituted the words "section 1A or 2."

12. In section 14 of that Act (community service orders)—

(a) in subsection (4), for the words "section 17(5) of this Act" there shall be substituted the words "Part IV of Schedule 2 to the Criminal Justice Act 1991";

(b) in subsection (5)(b), for the words "section 16" there shall be substituted the words "Part II of Schedule 2 to the Criminal Justice Act 1991"; and

(c) in subsection (5)(c), for the words "section 17" there shall be substituted the words "Parts III and IV of that Schedule."

13. In section 15(2) of that Act (obligations of person subject to community service order), for the words "section 17(1) of this Act" there shall be substituted the words "paragraph 15 of Schedule 2 to the Criminal Justice Act 1991."

14. In section 31(3C) of that Act (maximum periods of imprisonment in default of payment of Crown Court fine), for the words "five days" there shall be substituted the word "seven days."

15. In section 58 of that Act (application to Scotland), for the words "sections 8(4), 10, 13, 17C, 25(3), 29(7)" there shall be substituted the words "sections 1C, 25(3) and 29(7)."

16. In section 59 of that Act (application to Northern Ireland), for the words "Sections 17C and 29(7)" there shall be substituted the words "Section 29(7)."

17.—(1) In paragraph 2(2)(a) of Schedule 3 of that Act (the probation service and its functions), the word "several" shall cease to have effect.

(2) In paragraph 8(1) of that Schedule, after the words "any person" there shall be inserted the words "and to make reports on such matters."

Juries Act 1974 (c. 23)

18.—(1) In Schedule 1 to the Juries Act 1974, Group B (which disqualifies from jury service persons concerned with the administration of justice) shall be amended as follows.

(2) After the entry relating to a shorthandwriter in any court, there shall be inserted the following entry—

"A court security officer within the meaning of Part IV of the Criminal Justice Act 1991."

(3) After the entry relating to governors, chaplains, medical officers and other officers of penal establishments and members of boards of visitors for such establishments, there shall be inserted the following entry—

"Prisoner custody officers within the meaning of Part IV of the Criminal Justice Act 1991."

Solicitors Act 1974 (c. 47)

19. In section 43(7) of the Solicitors Act 1974 (control of employment of certain clerks), for the words "placing a person on probation or discharging him" there shall be substituted the words "discharging a person" and for the words "section 13" there shall be substituted the words "section 1C."

Rehabilitation of Offenders Act 1974 (c. 53)

20. In section 1(4) of the Rehabilitation of Offenders Act 1974 (rehabilitated persons and spent convictions)—

(a) for the words "section 13" there shall be substituted the words "section 1C";
(b) the words "put on probation or" shall cease to have effect; and
(c) for the words "placing the person concerned on probation or discharging him" there shall be substituted the words "discharging the person concerned."

Bail Act 1976 (c. 63)

21. In section 4(3) of the Bail Act 1976 (general right to bail of accused persons and others), for the words "section 6 or section 16 of the Powers of Criminal Courts Act 1973 (breach of requirement of probation or community service order)" there shall be substituted the words "Part II of Schedule 2 to the Criminal Justice Act 1991 (breach of requirement of probation, community service, combination or curfew order)."

22.—(1) Paragraph 8 of Schedule 1 to that Act (restrictions on the imposition of bail conditions) shall be amended as follows.

(2) In sub-paragraph (1), after the words "(4) to (7)" there shall be inserted the words "(except subsection (6)(d)" and the words from "or, in the case" to the end shall cease to have effect.

(3) After sub-paragraph (1) there shall be inserted the following sub-paragraph—

"(1A) No condition shall be imposed under section 3(6)(d) of this Act unless it appears to be necessary to do so for the purpose of enabling inquiries or a report to be made."

(4) In sub-paragraph (2) for the words "Sub-paragraph (1) above also applies," there shall be substituted the words "Sub-paragraphs (1) and (1A) above also apply."

(5) In sub-paragraph (3), for the words "sub-paragraph (1)" there shall be substituted the words "sub-paragraph (1A)."

Licensed Premises (Exclusion of Certain Persons) Act 1980 (c. 32)

23. In section 1(2) of the Licensed Premises (Exclusion of Certain Persons) Act 1980 (exclusion orders), for paragraph (b) there shall be substituted the following paragraph—

"(b) where the offence was committed in England and Wales notwithstanding the provisions of sections 1A and 1C of the Power of Criminal Courts Act 1973 (cases in which absolute and conditional discharges may be made, and their effect), in addition to an order discharging him absolutely or conditionally;".

Magistrates' Courts Act 1980 (c. 43)

24. In section 12(1)(a) of the 1980 Act (non-appearance of accused: plea of guilty), after the words "this section" there shall be inserted the words "and section 18 of the Criminal Justice Act 1991 (unit fines)."

25. In section 20(2)(b) of that Act (procedure where summary trial appears more suitable), for the words from "on obtaining information" to the end there shall be substituted the words "is of such opinion as mentioned in subsection (2) of that section."

26. In section 81(3)(a) of that Act (enforcement of fines imposed on young offenders), for the words "section 19(1) of the Criminal Justice Act 1948" there shall be substituted the words "section 17(1) of the Criminal Justice Act 1982."

27.—(1) In subsection (2) of section 143 of that Act (power to alter sums specified in certain provisions), paragraph (i) shall cease to have effect and after paragraph (o) there shall be inserted the following paragraph—

"(p) section 58(2) and (3) of the Criminal Justice Act 1991 (recognisance from parents or guardians);".

(2) For subsection (3) of that section there shall be inserted the following subsection—

"(3) In subsection (1) above the 'relevant date' means—

(a) the date of the coming into force of section 17 of the Criminal Justice Act 1991 (increase of certain maxima); or

(b) where the sums specified in a provision mentioned in subsection (2) above have been substituted by an order under subsection (1) above, the date of that order."

28. In paragraph 2(2) of Schedule 4 to that Act (maximum periods of imprisonment in default of payment of magistrates' court fine), for the words "five days" there shall be substituted the words "seven days."

Contempt of Court Act 1981 (c. 49)

29.—(1) Section 12(2) of the Contempt of Court Act 1981 (offences of contempt of magistrates' court) shall have effect as if the reference to any officer of the court included a reference to any court security officer assigned to the court-house in which the court is sitting.

(2) In this paragraph "court security officer" and "court-house" have the meanings given by section 92(1) of this Act.

Criminal Justice Act 1982 (c. 48)

30. For subsection (5) of section 1 of the 1982 Act (general restrictions on custodial sentences) there shall be substituted the following subsections —

"(5) No court shall commit a person under 21 years of age to be detained under section 9 below unless it is of the opinion that no other method of dealing with him is appropriate; and in forming any such opinion, the court—

(a) shall take into account all such information about the circumstances of the default or contempt (including any aggravating or mitigating factors) as is available to it; and

(b) may take into account any information about that person which is before it.

(5A) Where a magistrates' court commits a person under 21 years of age to be detained under section 9 below, it shall—

(a) state in open court the reason for its opinion that no other method of dealing with him is appropriate; and

(b) cause that reason to be specified in the warrant of commitment and to be entered on the register."

31.—(1) In subsection (1) of section 1A of that Act (detention in a young offender institution), for paragraph (b) there shall be substituted the following paragraph—

"(b) the court is of the opinion that either or both of paragraphs (a) and (b) of subsection (2) of section 1 of the Criminal Justice Act 1991 apply or the case falls within subsection (3) of that section,".

(2) In subsection (4) of that section, for the words "section 15(11) below" there shall be substituted the words "section 65(6) of the Criminal Justice Act 1991."

32. In section 3(1) of that Act (restrictions on imposing custodial sentences on persons under 21 not legally represented), for paragraphs (a) and (b) there shall be substituted the following paragraph—

"(a) pass a sentence of detention in a young offender institution under section 1A above."

33. In section 13 of that Act (conversion of sentence of detention in a young offender institution to imprisonment), after subsection (5) there shall be inserted the following subsection—

"(6) This section applies to a person who is serving a sentence of custody for life under section 8(2) above, or is detained under section 53 of the Children and Young Persons Act 1933, as it applies to a person serving a sentence of detention in a young offender institution."

34. In section 17(1) of that Act (attendance centre orders), for the words "section 6 of the Powers of Criminal Courts Act 1973" there shall be substituted the words "Part II of Schedule 2 to the Criminal Justice Act 1991."

Repatriation of Prisoners Act 1984 (c. 47)

35.—(1) In section 2 of the Repatriation of Prisoners Act 1984 (transfer of prisoners out of

United Kingdom) in subsection (4)(b), for sub-paragraph (i) there shall be substituted the following sub-paragraph—
> "(i) released on licence under section 33(1)(b) or (2), 34(3) or 35(1) or (2) of the Criminal Justice Act 1991;".

(2) In section 3 of that Act (transfer of prisoners into United Kingdom), after subsection (8) there shall be inserted the following subsection—
> "(9) The provisions contained by virtue of subsection (1)(c) above in a warrant under this Act shall, in the case of a prisoner to whom section 48 of the Criminal Justice Act 1991 (discretionary life prisoners transferred to England and Wales) applies, include provision specifying the relevant part of his sentence within the meaning of section 34 of that Act (duty of Secretary of State to release discretionary life prisoners)."

(3) In paragraph 2 of the Schedule to that Act (operation of certain enactments in relation to prisoners transferred into United Kingdom)—
  (a) in sub-paragraph (1), for the words from "section 60" to "of that section" there shall be substituted the words "section 33(1)(b) or (2), 34(3) or (5) or 35(1) of the Criminal Justice Act 1991 whether the prisoner has at any time served a particular proportion or part of his sentence specified in that provision,"; and
  (b) in sub-paragraph (2), for the words "one third" there shall be substituted the words "any particular proportion or part."

(4) In paragraph 3 of that Schedule, for the words "section 61 of the Criminal Justice Act 1967" there shall be substituted the words "section 35(2) of the Criminal Justice Act 1991."

Prosecution of Offences Act 1985 (c. 23)

36. In section 22(11) of the Prosecution of Offences Act 1985 (time limits in relation to preliminary stages of criminal proceedings), after the definition of "appropriate court" there shall be inserted the following definition—
> " 'custody' includes local authority accommodation to which a person is remanded or committed by virtue of section 23 of the Children and Young Persons Act 1969, and references to a person being committed to custody shall be construed accordingly;".

Criminal Justice Act 1988 (c. 33)

37. In section 34 of the Criminal Justice Act 1988 (abolition of requirement of corroboration for unsworn evidence of children), subsection (1) shall cease to have effect and, in subsection (3), for the words "section 38 of the Children and Young Persons Act 1933" there shall be substituted the words "section 52 of the Criminal Justice Act 1991."

Road Traffic Offenders Act 1988 (c. 53)

38.—(1) In subsection (1) of section 46 of the Road Traffic Offenders Act 1988 (combination of disqualification and endorsement with probation orders and orders for discharge), for the words "section 13(3)" there shall be substituted the words "section 1C(3)" and the words "placed on probation or" shall cease to have effect.

(2) In subsection (2) of that section, for the words "section 13(1)" there shall be substituted the words "section 1C(1)" and the words "placed on probation or" shall cease to have effect.

Extradition Act 1989 (c. 33)

39. In section 20(2)(b)(i) of the Extradition Act 1989 (restoration of persons not tried or acquitted), for the words "section 7(1)" there shall be substituted the words "section 1A(1)."

References to juvenile courts

40.—(1) Without prejudice to the generality of section 70(2) of this Act, in the enactments specified in sub-paragraph (2) below, for the words "juvenile court" or "juvenile courts," in each place where they occur, there shall be substituted the words "youth court" or, as the case may require, "youth courts."

(2) The enactments referred to in sub-paragraph (1) above are as follows—
  (a) in the 1933 Act, sections 45 to 49, 56 and 108(4) and Schedule 2;
  (b) in the Education Act 1944, section 40;
  (c) in the Children Act 1948, section 4B;
  (d) in the Adoption Act 1958, sections 43, 47 and 48;
  (e) in the Children and Young Persons Act 1963, sections 3, 18, 23, 26, 28, 29 and 57;
  (f) in the Administration of Justice Act 1964, section 12;
  (g) in the 1969 Act, sections 1 to 3, 7, 10, 15, 16, 20A to 22 and 70(1) and Schedule 4;
  (h) in the Criminal Justice Act 1972, section 51(1);

  (i) in the 1973 Act, section 46;

  (j) in the Adoption Act 1976, sections 34 and 37;

  (k) in the 1979 Act, sections 35(3), 37(1), 38(2) and 58(1) and (5);

  (l) in the Child Care Act 1980, sections 5 to 7, 12C to 12E, 21A, 67 and 79(2);

  (m) in the Foster Children Act 1980, sections 11(1), 12(1) and 14;

  (n) in the 1980 Act, sections 12(1), 29, 104 and 146;

  (o) in the 1982 Act, section 16(2) and in Schedule 3, the entry relating to section 49(2) of the 1933 Act;

  (p) in the Administration of Justice Act 1985, section 61;

  (q) in the Legal Aid Act 1988, sections 3(4), 19(3) and (5), 27(3) and (4), 28(3) and (7), 30(2) and in Schedule 3, paragraphs 9 and 10; and

  (r) in the Children Act 1989, section 90(1) and Schedule 14.

References to juvenile court panels

41.—(1) Without prejudice to the generality of section 70(2) of this Act, in the enactments specified in sub-paragraph (2) below, for the words "juvenile court panel" or "juvenile court panels," in each place where they occur, there shall be substituted the words "youth court panel" or, as the case may require, "youth court panels."

(2) The enactments referred to in sub-paragraph (1) above are as follows—

  (a) in the 1933 Act, Schedule 2;

  (b) in the 1973 Act, in Schedule 3, paragraph 2(3);

  (c) in the 1979 Act, section 35(3);

  (d) in the Child Care Act 1980, section 12E(5); and

  (e) in the 1980 Act, section 146.

Section 101(1)   SCHEDULE 12

Transitional Provisions and Savings

Custodial and community sentences

1. Each of sections 1 to 13 of this Act shall apply in relation to offenders convicted (but not sentenced) before the commencement of that section as it applies in relation to offenders convicted after that commencement.

2. Neither subsection (2) of section 8 of this Act, nor the repeal by this Act of section 13 of the 1973 Act, shall affect the operation of section 13 in relation to persons placed on probation before the commencement of that subsection or, as the case may be, that repeal.

3. An establishment which immediately before the commencement of Part II of Schedule 1 to this Act is a day centre within the meaning of section 4B of the 1973 Act shall be treated as if, immediately after that commencement it had been approved by the Secretary of State as a probation centre within the meaning of paragraph 3(7) of Schedule 1A to that Act.

4. Paragraph 6 of Schedule 11 to this Act shall apply in relation to offenders convicted (but not sentenced) before the commencement of that paragraph as it applies to offenders convicted after that commencement.

Community orders: supplemental

5.—(1) Paragraphs 3 and 4 of Schedule 2 to this Act shall apply in relation to pre-existing failures to comply with the requirements of probation orders or community service orders as if, in sub-paragraph (1)(a), for "£1,000" there were substituted "£400."

(2) In this paragraph "pre-existing," in relation to either of those paragraphs, means occurring before the commencement of that paragraph.

Financial penalties

6. None of sections 17 to 20 of this Act shall apply in relation to offences committed before the commencement of that section.

Increase of certain penalties

7. Neither of subsections (3) and (4) of section 26 of this Act shall apply in relation to offences committed before the commencement of that subsection.

Early release: general

8.—(1) In this paragraph and paragraphs 9 to 11 below—

"existing licensee" means any person who, before the commencement of Part II of this Act, has been released on licence under section 60 of the 1967 Act and whose licence under that section is in force at that commencement;

"existing prisoner" means any person who, at that commencement, is serving a custodial sentence;

and sub-paragraphs (2) to (7) below shall have effect subject to those paragraphs.

(2) Subject to sub-paragraphs (3) to (7) below, Part II of this Act shall apply in relation to an existing licensee as it applies in relation to a person who is released on licence under that Part; and in its application to an existing prisoner, or to an existing licensee who is recalled under section 39 of this Act, that Part shall apply with the modifications made by those sub-paragraphs.

(3) Section 40 of this Act shall not apply in relation to an existing prisoner or licensee.

(4) In relation to an existing prisoner whose sentence is for a term of twelve months, section 33(1) of this Act shall apply as if that sentence were for a term of less than twelve months.

(5) In relation to an existing prisoner or licensee whose sentence is for a term of—

(a) more than twelve months; and

(b) less than four years or, as the case may require, such other period as may for the time being be referred to in section 33(5) of this Act,

Part II of this Act shall apply as if he were or had been a long-term rather than a short-term prisoner.

(6) In relation to an existing prisoner or licensee whose sentence is for a term of more than twelve months—

(a) section 35(1) of this Act shall apply as if the reference to one half of his sentence were a reference to one-third of that sentence or six months, whichever is the longer; and

(b) sections 33(3) and 37(1) of this Act shall apply as if the reference to three-quarters of his sentence were a reference to two-thirds of that sentence.

(7) In relation to an existing prisoner or licensee—

(a) whose sentence is for a term of more than twelve months; and

(b) whose case falls within such class of cases as the Secretary of State may determine after consultation with the Parole Board,

section 35(1) of this Act shall apply as if the reference to a recommendation by the Board included a reference to a recommendation by a local review committee established under section 59(6) of the 1967 Act.

(8) In this paragraph "custodial sentence" means—

(a) a sentence of imprisonment;

(b) a sentence of detention in a young offender institution;

(c) a sentence of detention (whether during Her Majesty's pleasure, for life or for a determinate term) under section 53 of the 1933 Act; or

(d) a sentence of custody for life under section 8 of the 1982 Act.

9.—(1) This paragraph applies where, in the case of an existing life prisoner, the Secretary of State certifies his opinion that, if—

(a) section 34 of this Act had been in force at the time when he was sentenced; and

(b) the reference in subsection (1)(a) of that section to a violent or sexual offence the sentence for which is not fixed by law were a reference to any offence the sentence for which is not so fixed,

the court by which he was sentenced would have ordered that that section should apply to him as soon as he had served a part of his sentence specified in the certificate.

(2) In a case to which this paragraph applies, Part II of this Act except section 35(2) shall apply as if—

(a) the existing life prisoner were a discretionary life prisoner for the purposes of that Part; and

(b) the relevant part of his sentence within the meaning of section 34 of this Act were the part specified in the certificate.

(3) In this paragraph "existing life prisoner" means a person who, at the commencement of Part II of this Act, is serving one or more of the following sentences, namely—

(a) a sentence of life imprisonment;

(b) a sentence of detention during her Majesty's pleasure or for life under section 53 of the 1933 Act; or

(c) a sentence of custody for life under section 8 of the 1982 Act.

(4) A person serving two or more such sentences shall not be treated as a discretionary life prisoner for the purposes of Part II of this Act unless the requirements of sub-paragraph (1) above are satisfied as respects each of those sentences; and subsections (3) and (5) of section 34 of this Act shall not apply in relation to such a person until after he has served the relevant part of each of those sentences.

10. Prison rules made by virtue of section 42 of this Act, in relation to any existing prisoner or licensee who has forfeited any remission of his sentence, as if he had been awarded such number of additional days as may be determined by or under the rules.

Early release of young persons detained under 1933 Act

11. In relation to an existing prisoner or licensee whose sentence is a determinate sentence of detention under section 53 of the 1933 Act—
   (a) Part II of this Act shall apply as if he were or had been a life rather than a long-term or short-term prisoner;
   (b) section 35(2) of this Act shall apply as if the requirement as to consultation were omitted; and
   (c) section 37(3) of this Act shall apply as if the reference to his death were a reference to the date on which he would (but for his release) have served the whole of his sentence.

Early release of prisoners serving extended sentences

12.—(1) In relation to an existing prisoner or licensee on the passing of whose sentence an extended sentence certificate was issued—
   (a) section 33(3) of this Act shall apply as if the duty to release him unconditionally were a duty to release him on licence; and
   (b) section 37(1) of this Act shall apply as if the reference to three-quarters of his sentence were a reference to the whole of that sentence.

(2) In this paragraph "extended sentence certificate" means a certificate issued under section 28 of the 1973 Act stating that an extended term of imprisonment was imposed on an offender under that section.

Early release of fine defaulters and contemnors

13. Part II of this Act shall apply in relation to any person who, before the commencement of that Part, has been committed to prison or to be detained under section 9 of the 1982 Act—
   (a) in default of payment of a sum adjudged to be paid by a conviction; or
   (b) for contempt of court or any kindred offence,
as it applies in relation to any person who is so committed after that commencement.

Responsibilities of parent or guardian

14. None of sections 56 to 58 of this Act shall apply in relation to offences committed before the commencement of that section; and the repeals of subsections (7)(c), (7B) and (7C) of section 7 of the 1969 Act shall not apply in relation to offences committed before the commencement of those repeals.

Remands and committals of children and young persons

15.—(1) In this paragraph—
   "section 23" means section 23 of the 1969 Act as substituted by section 60(1) of this Act;
   "the modifications" means the modifications of section 23 set out in section 62 of this Act;
   "remand or committal" means a remand of a child or young person charged with or convicted of one or more offences, or a committal of a child or young person for trial or sentence.

(2) Section 23 as it has effect with the modifications shall not apply in relation to any remand or committal which is in force immediately before the commencement of sections 60 and 62 of this Act.

(3) Subject to sub-paragraphs (4) and (5) below, section 23 as it has effect without the modifications shall not apply in relation to any remand or committal which is in force immediately before the day appointed under section 62(1) of this Act.

(4) Any person who, in pursuance of any such remand or committal, is held in a remand centre or prison shall be brought before the court which remanded or committed him before the end of the period of 8 days beginning with the day so appointed.

(5) Where any person is brought before a court under sub-paragraph (4) above, section 23 as it has effect without the modifications shall apply as if the court were just remanding or committing him as mentioned in subsection (1)(a) of that section.

16.—(1) Subsection (2)(a) of section 60 of this Act shall not apply in any case where proceedings for the offence in question have begun before the commencement of that section.

(2) Subject to sub-paragraphs (3) and (4) below, subsection (2)(b) and (c) of that section shall not apply in relation to any committal under section 37 of the 1980 Act which is in force immediately before that commencement.

(3) Any person less than 17 years old who, in pursuance of any such committal, is held in a remand centre or prison shall be brought before the court which committed him before the end of the period of 8 days beginning with that commencement.

(4) Where any person is brought before a court under sub-paragraph (3) above, section 37 of the 1980 Act shall apply as if the court were just committing him under that section.

Custodial sentences for young offenders

17.—(1) Subject to sub-paragraph (2) below, section 63 of this Act shall apply in relation to young offenders convicted (but not sentenced) before the commencement of that section as it applies in relation to young offenders convicted after that commencement.

(2) Subsections (2), (3) and (5) of that section shall not apply in any case where proceedings for the offence in question have begun before that commencement and the offender is aged 17 at the date of his conviction.

(3) For the purposes of the provisions substituted by subsection (3)(c) of that section, any sentence of detention in a young offender institution which, at that commencement, is being served by an offender aged 17 shall be disregarded.

18. Section 64 of this Act shall not apply in any case where the offence in question was committed before the commencement of that section and the offender is aged 16 at the date of his conviction.

Supervision of young offenders after release

19. Section 65 of this Act shall not apply in relation to any person under the age of 22 years who, before the commencement of that section, is released from a term of detention in a young offender institution or under section 53 of the 1933 Act; and the repeal by this Act of section 15 of the 1982 Act shall not affect the operation of that section in relation to any such person who is so released.

Supervision orders

20.—(1) In relation to pre-existing failures to comply with the requirements of supervision orders, section 15 of the 1969 Act as substituted by Schedule 7 to this Act shall apply as if—
    (a) in subsection (3)(a), for "£1,000" there were substituted "£100";
    (b) in subsection (5)(b), for "£5,000" there were substituted "£2,000"; and
    (c) in subsection (5)(c), for "£5,000" there were substituted the words "£2,000 in the case of a person who has attained the age of 18 years and £400 in the case of a person who has not attained that age."

(2) In this paragraph "pre-existing" means occurring before the commencement of section 66 of this Act and that Schedule.

Attendance centre orders

21.—(1) Subsection (2) of section 67 of this Act shall not apply in relation to attendance centre orders made before the commencement of that section.

(2) Subsection (4) of that section shall not apply in relation to pre-existing failures to attend in accordance with an attendance centre order or pre-existing breaches of rules made under section 16(3) of the 1982 Act.

(3) In this paragraph "pre-existing" means occurring or committed before that commencement.

Provisions for treating persons age 17 as young persons

22.—(1) Paragraphs 1, 3, 4 and 6 of Schedule 8 shall not apply in any case where proceedings for the offence in question have begun before the commencement of that Schedule.

(2) Paragraph 5 of that Schedule shall apply in relation to any sentence imposed on any person who was convicted before that commencement and was aged 17 at the date of his conviction.

Renaming of juvenile courts, etc.

23. In relation to any time before the commencement of section 70 of this Act, references in any other provision of this Act, or in any enactment amended by this Act, to youth courts shall be construed as references to juvenile courts.

Supplemental

24. For the purposes of this Schedule proceedings for an offence shall be regarded as having begun as follows—

(a) in the case of an offence triable only summarily, when a plea is entered;
(b) in the case of an offence triable only on indictment, when the magistrates' court begins to inquire into the offence as examining magistrates;
(c) in the case of an offence triable either way, when the magistrates' court determines to proceed with the summary trial of the offence or, as the case may be, to proceed to inquire into the offence as examining justices.

Section 101(2)   SCHEDULE 13

REPEALS

Chapter	Short title	Extent of repeal
2 & 3 Vict. c. 47.	The Metropolitan Police Act 1839.	Section 11.
23 & 24 Geo. 5 c. 12.	The Children and Young Persons Act 1933.	Section 34(1). Section 38(1).
15 & 16 Geo. 6 & 1 Eliz. 2 c. 52.	The Prison Act 1952.	Section 25.
3 & 4 Eliz. 2 c. 18.	The Army Act 1955.	In section 71AA(1), the words "subject to subsection (1A) below" and "being not less than 21 days and". Section 71AA(1A). Section 93(2A).
3 & 4 Eliz. 2 c. 19.	The Air Force Act 1955.	In section 71AA(1), the words "subject to subsection (1A) below" and "being not less than 21 days and". Section 71AA(1A). Section 93(2A).
5 & 6 Eliz. 2 c. 53.	The Naval Discipline Act 1957.	In section 43AA(1), the words "subject to subsection (1A) below" and "being not less than 21 days and". Section 43AA(1A). Section 60(3A).
1967 c. 80.	The Criminal Justice Act 1967.	Sections 59 to 64. In section 67(6), the words "remanded or", in the first place where they occur, and the words "section 23 of the Children and Young Persons Act 1969 or". Schedule 2.
1968 c. 19	The Criminal Appeal Act 1968.	In section 50(1A), the words "a probation order or".
1968 c. 49.	The Social Work (Scotland) Act 1968.	In section 72, in subsection (1A), paragraph (a) and the word "and" immediately following that paragraph, and subsection (4).
1968 c. 64.	The Civil Evidence Act 1968.	In section 11(5)(a), the words "probation or".
1969 c. 54.	The Children and Young Persons Act 1969.	In section 3, the words "disregarding section 4 of this Act", in each place where they occur. Section 4. In section 5, subsections (1) to (7) and, in subsection (9), the definitions of "qualified informant" and "designated". In section 7, in subsection (7), the words "is found guilty of homicide" and paragraph (c), and subsections (7B) and (7C). Section 8. Section 10(1)(a). In section 12AA, subsections (7), (8) and (12). In section 34(1), in paragraph (a), the word "4," and paragraph (b). In Schedule 4, paragraphs 2 and 3.

Chapter	Short title	Extent of repeal
1971 c. 10.	The Vehicles (Excise) Act 1971.	In section 9(5), the words "placing him on probation or".
1971 c. 23.	The Courts Act 1971.	In Schedule 8, in paragraph 57(1)(a), the reference to subsection (2) of section 10.
1972 c. 19.	The Criminal Justice Act 1972.	Section 35.
1973 c. 62.	The Powers of Criminal Courts Act 1973.	Sections 5 to 10. Section 13. In section 14, in subsection (1), the words "instead of dealing with him in any other way" and, in subsection (3), the words "(i) or (ii)". Sections 16 to 17C. Sections 20 and 20A. Sections 28 and 29. In section 30(1), the words "(such as the power to make a probation order)". In section 42(2)(a), the words from "subject to" to "twelve months)". Section 45. Section 48. In section 57(1), the definition of "supervising court". Schedule 1. In Schedule 3, in paragraph 2(2)(a), the word "several".
1974 c. 53.	The Rehabilitation of Offenders Act 1974.	In section 1(4), the words "put on probation or".
1975 c. 21.	The Criminal Procedure (Scotland) Act 1975.	In section 403, the proviso to subsection (4) and, in subsection (6), the words "the proviso to subsection (4) of this section shall not apply, but". In Schedule 9, paragraph 50.
1976 c. 63.	The Bail Act 1976.	In Schedule 1, in paragraph 8(1), the words from "or, in the case" to the end.
1977 c. 45.	The Criminal Law Act 1977.	Section 47. In Schedule 12, in the entry relating to the Children and Young Persons Act 1969, paragraph 3.
1980 c. 43.	The Magistrates' Courts Act 1980.	In section 24(4), the words from "but this subsection" to the end. Section 35. In section 36(2), the words from "but this subsection" to the end. Section 103(3)(a). Section 37(1A). In section 108(1A), the words "a probation order or". Section 143(2)(i). In Schedule 3, paragraph 5.
1982 c. 48.	The Criminal Justice Act 1982.	In section 1, subsections (3) to (4A). In section 1A(3), the words "and section 1B(3) below". In section 1B, subsections (1) and (3). Section 2. Section 15. Section 17(3). In section 18(6)(b), the words from the beginning to "residence". Section 33. In section 48, subsections (1)(c) and (2). Section 62. Schedule 5. In Schedule 11, paragraph 6(a)(v).

Chapter	Short title	Extent of repeal
		In Schedule 13, Part I.
		In Schedule 14, paragraphs 23(a), 25 and 32.
1983 c. 20.	The Mental Health Act 1983.	In section 50(3), the words from "and that period" to the end.
1984 c. 60.	The Police and Criminal Evidence Act 1984.	In section 37, subsections (11) to (14).
1988 c. 33.	The Criminal Justice Act 1988.	Section 34(1).
		In section 123, subsections (2) and (3).
		Section 131(2).
		In Schedule 8, in paragraph 3(1)(c), the words "1(3) and".
		In Schedule 10, in Part II, the words "section 15(1)", "section 15(1) and (5) and" and "section 15(1)(a) and", and Part III.
		In Schedule 15, paragraph 22(1).
		In Schedule 16, the entry relating to section 41(8) of the Administration of Justice Act 1970.
1988 c. 38.	The Legal Aid Act 1988.	In section 20(4), the word "or" immediately following paragraph (b).
1988 c. 53.	The Road Traffic Offenders Act 1988.	In section 46, in subsections (1) and (2), the words "placed on probation or".
1989 c. 41.	The Children Act 1989.	In Schedule 12, paragraphs 21 and 24.
		In Schedule 13, paragraph 53(1).
1989 c. 42.	The Local Government and Housing Act 1989.	Section 189.
1991 c. 62.	The Armed Forces Act 1991.	In section 3(1), the words from "and after the words" to the end.
		In section 5, subsections (2)(b) and (9).
		In Schedule 2, paragraph 3.

INDEX

References are to section and Schedule numbers

DEER ACT 1991

(1991 c. 54)

[A table showing the derivation of the provisions of this consolidation Act will be found at the end of the Act. The table has no official status.]

ARRANGEMENT OF SECTIONS

Offences relating to deer

An Act to consolidate certain enactments relating to deer with amendments to give effect to recommendations of the Law Commission.

[25th July 1991]

PARLIAMENTARY DEBATES
    Hansard, H.L. Vol. 527, col. 1261; Vol. 528, col. 1863.

INTRODUCTION

    This Act consolidates a number of other enactments in relation to offences concerning deer, covering poaching, taking or killing deer at night and taking or killing Red Deer, Fallow Deer, Roe Deer or Sika Deer in close season. Enforcement measures are contained in the statute giving powers of search, arrest and seizure to the police if it is suspected that a person had committed or is committing an offence under the Act.

Offences relating to deer

Poaching of deer

    1.—(1) Subject to subsection (3) below, if any person enters any land without the consent of the owner or occupier or other lawful authority in search or pursuit of any deer with the intention of taking, killing or injuring it, he shall be guilty of an offence.

(2) Subject to subsection (3) below, if any person while on any land—

(a) intentionally takes, kills or injures, or attempts to take, kill or injure, any deer,

(b) searches for or pursues any deer with the intention of taking, killing or injuring it, or

(c) removes the carcase of any deer,

without the consent of the owner or occupier of the land or other lawful authority, he shall be guilty of an offence.

(3) A person shall not be guilty of an offence under subsection (1) or subsection (2) above by reason of anything done in the belief that—

(a) he would have the consent of the owner or occupier of the land if the owner or occupier knew of his doing it and the circumstances of it; or

(b) he has other lawful authority to do it.

(4) If any authorised person suspects with reasonable cause that any person is committing or has committed an offence under subsection (1) or subsection (2) above on any land, he may require that person—

(a) to give his full name and address; and

(b) to quit that land forthwith;

and any person who fails to comply with a requirement under this subsection shall be guilty of an offence.

(5) In subsection (4) above "authorised person", in relation to any land, means the owner or occupier of the land or any person authorised by the owner or occupier, and includes any person having the right to take or kill deer on the land.

Taking or killing of certain deer in close season

2.—(1) Subject to sections 6 to 8 below and to subsection (3) below, if any person takes or intentionally kills any deer of a species and description mentioned in Schedule 1 to this Act during the prescribed close season, he shall be guilty of an offence.

(2) The prescribed close season, in relation to a particular deer, is the close season prescribed by Schedule 1 to this Act in relation to deer of that species and description.

(3) Where—

(a) any person, by way of business, keeps deer on land enclosed by a deer-proof barrier for the production of meat or other foodstuffs or skins or other by-products, or as breeding stock, and

(b) those deer are conspicuously marked in such a way as to identify them as deer kept by that person as mentioned in the preceding paragraph,

the killing of any of those deer by that person, or by any servant or agent of that person authorised by him for the purpose, shall not constitute an offence under this section.

(4) The Secretary of State may by order amend Schedule 1 to this Act by the addition of any species not mentioned in that Schedule and of a close season for any description of deer of that species, or by varying or deleting any such addition.

(5) Before making any order under subsection (4) above the Secretary of State shall consult any organisations that appear to him to represent persons likely to be interested in or affected by the order.

Taking or killing of deer at night

3. Subject to sections 6 and 8 below, if any person takes or intentionally kills any deer between the expiry of the first hour after sunset and the beginning of the last hour before sunrise, he shall be guilty of an offence.

Use of prohibited weapons and other articles

4.—(1) Subject to sections 6 and 8 below, if any person—

(a) sets in position any article which is a trap, snare, or poisoned or stupefying bait and is of such a nature and so placed as to be calculated to cause bodily injury to any deer coming in contact with it, or

(b) uses for the purpose of taking or killing any deer any trap, snare or poisoned or stupefying bait, or any net,

he shall be guilty of an offence.

(2) Subject to sections 6 to 8 below, if any person uses for the purpose of taking or killing or injuring any deer—

(a) any firearm or ammunition mentioned in Schedule 2 to this Act,

(b) any arrow, spear or similar missile, or

(c) any missile, whether discharged from a firearm or otherwise, carrying or containing any poison, stupefying drug or muscle-relaxing agent,

he shall be guilty of an offence.

(3) The Secretary of State may by order amend Schedule 2 to this Act by adding any firearm or ammunition or by altering the description of, or deleting, any firearm or ammunition for the time being mentioned in that Schedule.

(4) Subject to subsection (5) below, if any person—

(a) discharges any firearm, or projects any missile, from any mechanically propelled vehicle at any deer, or

(b) uses any mechanically propelled vehicle for the purpose of driving deer,

he shall be guilty of an offence.

(5) An act which, apart from this subsection, would constitute an offence under subsection (4) above shall not constitute such an offence if it is done—

(a) by, or with the written authority of, the occupier of any enclosed land where deer are usually kept; and

(b) in relation to any deer on that land.

Attempts to commit certain offences, etc.

5.—(1) Any person who attempts to commit an offence under any of sections 2 to 4 above shall be guilty of an offence.

(2) If any person, for the purpose of committing an offence under any of sections 2 to 4 above, has in his possession—

(a) any article the use of which is prohibited by section 4(1)(b), section 4(2)(b) or section 4(2)(c) above, or

(b) any firearm or ammunition,

he shall be guilty of an offence.

General exceptions to certain provisions of this Act

6.—(1) Nothing in section 2 or section 3 above shall make unlawful anything done in pursuance of a requirement by the Minister of Agriculture, Fisheries and Food under section 98 of the Agriculture Act 1947.

(2) A person shall not be guilty of an offence under section 2 or section 3 above by reason of any act done for the purpose of preventing the suffering of an injured or diseased deer.

(3) A person shall not be guilty of an offence under section 4(1)(a) or section 4(1)(b) above by reason of setting in position, or using, any trap or net for the purpose of preventing the suffering of an injured or diseased deer.

(4) A person shall not be guilty of an offence under section 4(2)(a) above by reason of the use of any smooth-bore gun for the purpose of killing any deer if he shows that the deer had been so seriously injured otherwise than by his unlawful act, or was in such a condition, that to kill it was an act of mercy.

(5) A person shall not be guilty of an offence under section 4(2)(a) above by reason of the use as a slaughtering instrument, for the purpose of killing any deer, of a smooth-bore gun which—
  (a) is of not less gauge than 12 bore;
  (b) has a barrel less than 24 inches (609.6 millimetres) in length; and
  (c) is loaded with a cartridge purporting to contain shot none of which is less than .203 inches (5.16 millimetres) in diameter (that is to say, size AAA or any larger size).

Exceptions for occupiers etc. of land where deer are

7.—(1) Subject to subsection (3) below, a person to whom this section applies shall not be guilty of an offence under section 2 above by reason of—
  (a) the taking or killing of any deer by means of shooting, or
  (b) the injuring of any deer by means of shooting in an attempt to take or kill it,
on any cultivated land, pasture or enclosed woodland.
  (2) Subject to subsection (3) below, a person to whom this section applies shall not be guilty of an offence under section 4(2)(a) above by reason of the use, for the purpose of taking or killing any deer on any land, of any smooth-bore gun of not less gauge than 12 bore which is loaded with—
  (a) a cartridge containing a single non-spherical projectile weighing not less than 22.68 grammes (350 grains); or
  (b) a cartridge purporting to contain shot each of which is .203 inches (5.16 millimetres) in diameter (that is to say, size AAA).
  (3) A person to whom this section applies shall not be entitled to rely on the defence provided by subsection (1) or subsection (2) above as respects anything done in relation to any deer on any land unless he shows that—
  (a) he had reasonable grounds for believing that deer of the same species were causing, or had caused, damage to crops, vegetables, fruit, growing timber or any other form of property on the land;
  (b) it was likely that further damage would be so caused and any such damage was likely to be serious; and
  (c) his action was necessary for the purpose of preventing any such damage.
  (4) The persons to whom this section applies are—
  (a) the occupier of the land on which the action is taken;
  (b) any member of the occupier's household normally resident on the occupier's land, acting with the written authority of the occupier;
  (c) any person in the ordinary service of the occupier on the occupier's land, acting with the written authority of the occupier; and
  (d) any person having the right to take or kill deer on the land on which the action is taken or any person acting with the written authority of a person having that right.
  (5) The Secretary of State and the agriculture Minister acting jointly may by order, either generally or in relation to any area or any species and description of deer specified in the order,—
  (a) repeal subsection (2) above or amend it by adding any firearm or ammunition or by altering the description of, or deleting, any firearm or ammunition for the time being mentioned in it;
  (b) amend subsection (3) above by adding any further conditions which must be satisfied or by varying or deleting any conditions so added.
  (6) Before making any order under subsection (5) above the Secretary of State and the agriculture Minister shall consult organisations that appear to them to represent persons likely to be interested in or affected by the order.
  (7) In this section "agriculture Minister" means—
  (a) in relation to England, the Minister of Agriculture, Fisheries and Food; and

(b) in relation to Wales, the Secretary of State.

Exceptions for persons licensed by the Nature Conservancy Council for England or the Countryside Council for Wales

8.—(1) A licence may be granted to any person by the Nature Conservancy Council for England exempting that person, and any persons acting with his written authority, from sections 2 to 4 above in respect of any of the acts specified in subsection (3) below which are done in England for the purpose of removing deer from one area to another or of taking deer alive for scientific or educational purposes.

(2) A licence may be granted to any person by the Countryside Council for Wales exempting that person, and any persons acting with his written authority, from sections 2 to 4 above in respect of any of the acts specified in subsection (3) below which are done in Wales for the purpose of removing deer from one area to another or of taking deer alive for scientific or educational purposes.

(3) The acts referred to in subsections (1) and (2) above are—
(a) using any net, trap, stupefying drug or muscle-relaxing agent of a type authorised by the licence;
(b) using any missile carrying or containing such stupefying drug or muscle-relaxing agent and discharging any such missile by any means authorised by the licence.

(4) A licence granted under subsection (1) above may be revoked at any time by the Nature Conservancy Council for England and a licence granted under subsection (2) above may be revoked at any time by the Countryside Council for Wales; and a licence granted under either of those subsections may be granted subject to conditions.

(5) Without prejudice to any other liability to a penalty which he may have incurred under this or any other Act, any person who contravenes or fails to comply with any condition imposed on the grant of a licence under subsection (1) or subsection (2) above shall be guilty of an offence.

Penalties for offences relating to deer

9.—(1) Subject to subsection (2) below, a person guilty of an offence under any of the preceding provisions of this Act shall be liable on summary conviction to a fine not exceeding level 4 on the standard scale or to imprisonment for a term not exceeding three months or to both.

(2) Where an offence under any of the preceding provisions of this Act was committed in respect of more than one deer the maximum fine which may be imposed under subsection (1) above shall be determined as if the person convicted had been convicted of a separate offence in respect of each deer.

Offences relating to venison etc.

Offences relating to sale and purchase etc. of venison

10.—(1) If any person who is not a licensed game dealer—
(a) at any time during the prohibited period sells or offers or exposes for sale, or has in his possession for sale, any venison to which this paragraph applies, or
(b) at any time sells or offers or exposes for sale any venison otherwise than to a licensed game dealer,
he shall be guilty of an offence and liable on summary conviction to a fine not exceeding level 3 on the standard scale.

(2) Paragraph (a) of subsection (1) above applies to any venison which comes from a deer of a species and description in relation to which a close season is prescribed by Schedule 1 to this Act; and the prohibited period, in

relation to any such venison, is the period beginning with the expiry of the tenth day, and ending with the expiry of the last day, of that close season.

(3) If any person—

(a) sells or offers or exposes for sale, or has in his possession for sale, or

(b) purchases or offers to purchase or receives,

any venison which comes from a deer to which this subsection applies, he shall be guilty of an offence and liable on summary conviction to a fine not exceeding level 4 on the standard scale or to imprisonment for a term not exceeding three months or to both.

(4) Subsection (3) above applies to any deer—

(a) which has been taken or killed in circumstances which constitute an offence under any of the preceding provisions of this Act; and

(b) which the person concerned knows or has reasons to believe has been so taken or killed.

(5) In this section—

"licensed game dealer" means a person licensed to deal in game under the Game Act 1831 and the Game Licences Act 1860, and includes a servant of such a person; and

"sale" includes barter and exchange, and "sell" and "purchase" shall be construed accordingly.

Licensed game dealers to keep records

11.—(1) Every licensed game dealer who sells or offers or exposes for sale, or has possession for sale, any venison shall—

(a) in accordance with the provisions of this section keep or cause to be kept a book containing records (in this section referred to as a "record book"); and

(b) subject to subsection (3) below, enter or cause to be entered in his record book forthwith full particulars of all his purchases and receipts of venison;

and, subject to subsection (2) below, those records shall be in the form set out in Schedule 3 to this Act or a form substantially to the same effect.

(2) The Secretary of State may by order vary the form in which records are required to be kept under this section.

(3) Where a licensed game dealer has purchased or received venison from another licensed game dealer, or from a venison dealer licensed under Part IIIA of the Deer (Scotland) Act 1959, he need record in his record book only—

(a) that the venison was so purchased or received;

(b) the name and address of the other licensed game dealer or the venison dealer so licensed;

(c) the date when the venison was so purchased or received; and

(d) the total weight of the venison.

(4) Any authorised officer, on producing, if so required, his written authority, and any constable, may inspect—

(a) the record book of a licensed game dealer,

(b) any venison in the licensed game dealer's possession or under his control, or on premises or in vehicles under his control, and

(c) any invoices, consignment notes, receipts and other documents which relate to entries in the record book (including, where the originals are not available, copies),

and may take copies of, or extracts from, the record book and any such documents.

(5) A record book shall be kept until the end of the period of three years beginning with the day on which the last entry was made in the book, and any such documents as are mentioned in subsection (4)(c) above shall be kept

until the end of the period of three years beginning with the date of the entry to which they relate.

(6) Any licensed game dealer who, without reasonable excuse, fails to comply with the provisions of this section shall be guilty of an offence.

(7) If any person—

(a) intentionally obstructs any authorised officer or constable making an inspection under this section, or

(b) knowingly or recklessly makes or causes to be made in a record book any entry which is false or misleading in a material particular,

he shall be guilty of an offence.

(8) A person guilty of an offence under this section shall be liable on summary conviction to a fine not exceeding level 2 on the standard scale.

(9) In this section—

"authorised officer" means any officer of the council of a district or London borough, or of the Common Council of the City of London, who is authorised by them in writing to exercise the powers conferred by this section;

"licensed game dealer" has the same meaning as in section 10 above; and

"sale" has the same meaning as in that section, and "sell" and "purchase" shall be construed accordingly.

Enforcement etc.

Powers of search, arrest and seizure

12.—(1) If a constable suspects with reasonable cause that any person is committing or has committed an offence under this Act, the constable may without warrant—

(a) stop and search that person if the constable suspects with reasonable cause that evidence of the commission of the offence is to be found on that person;

(b) search or examine any vehicle, animal, weapon or other thing which that person may then be using if the constable suspects with reasonable cause that evidence of the commission of the offence is to be found on that vehicle, animal, weapon or other thing;

(c) seize and detain for the purposes of proceedings under this Act anything which is evidence of the commission of the offence and any deer, venison, vehicle, animal, weapon or other thing which is liable to be forfeited under section 13 below.

(2) For the purposes of—

(a) exercising the powers conferred by subsection (1) above, or

(b) arresting a person, in accordance with section 25 of the Police and Criminal Evidence Act 1984 (general arrest conditions), for an offence under this Act,

a constable may enter any land other than a dwelling-house.

(3) A constable may sell any deer or venison seized under this section and the net proceeds of the sale shall be liable to be detained and forfeited in the same manner as the deer or venison sold; but he shall not be subject to any liability on account of his neglect or failure to exercise the powers conferred on him by this subsection.

Forfeitures and disqualifications

13.—(1) The court by which a person is convicted of any offence under this Act may order the forfeiture of—

(a) any deer or venison in respect of which the offence was committed or which was found in that person's possession;

(b) any vehicle, animal, weapon or other thing which was used to commit the offence or which was capable of being used to take, kill or injure deer and was found in his possession.

(2) Where the offence of which the person is convicted is an offence under any of sections 1, 10 and 11 above or under subsection (3)(c) below, the court (without prejudice to its powers under subsection (1) above)—

(a) may disqualify that person for holding or obtaining a licence to deal in game for such period as the court thinks fit; and

(b) may cancel any firearm or shotgun certificate held by him.

(3) Where the court cancels a firearm or shotgun certificate under subsection (2)(b) above—

(a) the court shall cause notice in writing of that fact to be sent to the chief officer of police by whom the certificate was granted; and

(b) the chief officer of police shall by notice in writing require the holder of the certificate to surrender it; and

(c) if the holder fails to surrender the certificate within twenty-one days from the date of that requirement, he shall be guilty of an offence and liable on summary conviction to a fine not exceeding level 2 on the standard scale.

Offences by bodies corporate

14.—(1) Where an offence under any of sections 1, 10 and 11 above which has been committed by a body corporate is proved to have been committed with the consent or connivance of, or to be attributable to any neglect on the part of, any director, manager, secretary or other similar officer of the body corporate or any person who was purporting to act in any such capacity, he as well as the body corporate shall be guilty of that offence and be liable to be proceeded against and punished accordingly.

(2) Where the affairs of a body corporate are managed by its members, subsection (1) above shall apply in relation to the acts and defaults of a member in connection with his functions of management as if he were a director of the body corporate.

Supplementary

Orders

15.—(1) Any power to make orders under this Act shall be exercisable by statutory instrument.

(2) A statutory instrument containing an order made under any of sections 2(4), 4(3) and 11(2) above shall be subject to annulment in pursuance of a resolution of either House of Parliament.

(3) No order shall be made under section 7(5) above unless a draft of the order has been laid before and approved by a resolution of each House of Parliament.

Interpretation

16. In this Act, unless the context otherwise requires,—

"ammunition" and "firearms" have the same meaning as in the Firearms Act 1968;

"deer" means deer of any species and includes the carcase of any deer or any part thereof;

"vehicle" includes an aircraft, hovercraft or boat; and

"venison" includes imported venison and means—

(a) any carcase of a deer, or

(b) any edible part of the carcase of a deer,

which has not been cooked or canned.

Transitional provisions, consequential amendment and repeals

17.—(1) Anything done under any provision of the Deer Act 1963 or the Deer Act 1980 shall have effect as if it had been done under the corresponding provision of this Act.

(2) Without prejudice to the generality of subsection (1) above, a licence granted by the Nature Conservancy Council under section 11 of the Deer Act 1963 which, by virtue of paragraph 8 of Schedule 11 to the Environmental Protection Act 1990, has effect as if granted by the Nature Conservancy Council for England or the Countryside Council for Wales, shall be treated as if it had been granted under subsection (1) or, as the case may be, subsection (2) of section 8 above.

(3) Where a licence granted under section 11 of the Deer Act 1963 contains a reference to an enactment repealed by this Act, the licence shall be construed as referring, or, as the context requires, as including a reference to, the corresponding provision of this Act.

(4) Where a period of time specified in an enactment repealed by this Act is current at the commencement of this Act, this Act shall have effect as if the corresponding provision thereof had been in force when that period began to run.

(5) In section 25C of the Deer (Scotland) Act 1959 for the words "section 2(4) of the Deer Act 1980" there shall be substituted "section 10(5) of the Deer Act 1991".

(6) The enactments specified in Schedule 4 to this Act are hereby repealed to the extent specified in the third column of that Schedule.

Short title, extent and commencement

18.—(1) This Act may be cited as the Deer Act 1991.

(2) With the exception of section 17(5) above, which extends to Scotland only, this Act extends to England and Wales only.

(3) This Act shall come into force at the end of the period of three months beginning with the day on which it is passed.

SCHEDULES

Section 2   SCHEDULE 1

CLOSE SEASONS

RED DEER [Cervus elaphus]

Stags...............................	1st May to 31st July inclusive.
Hinds	1st March to 31st October inclusive.

FALLOW DEER [Dama dama]

Buck...............................	1st May to 31st July inclusive.
Doe................................	1st March to 31st October inclusive.

ROE DEER [Capreolus capreolus]

Buck...............................	1st November to 31st March inclusive.
Doe................................	1st March to 31st October inclusive.

SIKA DEER [Cervus nippon]

Stags...............................	1st May to 31st July inclusive.
Hinds	1st March to 31st October inclusive.

        SCHEDULE 2

PROHIBITED FIREARMS AND AMMUNITION

Firearms

1. Any smooth-bore gun.
2. Any rifle having a calibre of less than .240 inches or a muzzle energy of less than 2,305 joules (1,700 foot pounds).
3. Any air gun, air rifle or air pistol.

Ammunition

4. Any cartridge for use in a smooth-bore gun.
5. Any bullet for use in a rifle other than a soft-nosed or hollow-nosed bullet.

Section 11

SCHEDULE 3

FORM OF RECORD TO BE KEPT BY LICENSED GAME DEALERS

Date of purchase or receipt*	Species	Means by which the deer was killed†	Particulars of carcases purchased or received						Particulars of parts of carcases purchased or received			Particulars of seller, or in the case of a receipt the source‡ from which receipt obtained, and registration number of vehicle delivering venison
			Male		Female		Total		Number (of parts)	Description (of parts)	Weight	
			No.	Weight	No.	Weight	No.	Weight				

* Where the venison comes from deer killed by the dealer, enter date of killing.
† If killed by rifle or smooth-bore gun, enter "rifle" or "smooth-bore gun".
‡ Where the venison comes from deer killed by the dealer, enter name of premises or place in which killed.

Deer Act 1991

SCHEDULE 4

ENACTMENTS REPEALED

Chapter	Short title	Extent of repeal
1963 c. 36.	The Deer Act 1963.	The whole Act.
1973 c. 54.	The Nature Conservancy Council Act 1973.	In Schedule 1, paragraph 5.
1977 c. 4.	The Roe Deer (Close Seasons) Act 1977.	The whole Act.
1980 c. 49.	The Deer Act 1980.	The whole Act.
1981 c. 69.	The Wildlife and Countryside Act 1981.	In Schedule 7, paragraphs 4 to 6.
1982 c. 19.	The Deer (Amendment) (Scotland) Act 1982.	In Schedule 2, paragraph 4.
1984 c. 60.	The Police and Criminal Evidence Act 1984.	In Schedule 6, paragraphs 13 and 23.
1987 c. 28.	The Deer Act 1987.	The whole Act.
1990 c. 43.	The Environmental Protection Act 1990.	In Schedule 9, paragraph 3.

TABLE OF DERIVATIONS

Note:

The following abbreviations are used in this Table:—

1963	= The Deer Act 1963
1973	= The Nature Conservancy Council Act 1973
1977	= The Roe Deer (Close Seasons) Act 1977
1978	= The Interpretation Act 1978
1980	= The Deer Act 1980
1981	= The Wildlife and Countryside Act 1981
1982 c. 19	= The Deer (Amendment) (Scotland) Act 1982
1982 c. 48	= The Criminal Justice Act 1982
1984	= The Police and Criminal Evidence Act 1984
1987	= The Deer Act 1987
1990	= The Environmental Protection Act 1990
R (followed by a number)	= The recommendation set out in the paragraph of that number in the Appendix to the Report of the Law Commission on the consolidation (Cm. 1476).

Provision	Derivation
1(1)–(4)	1980 s.1(1)–(4).
(5)	1980 s.1(7).
2(1), (2)	1963 s.1(1), (4); 1981 Sched. 7, para. 5(2); R.1.
(3)	1963 s.10(2A); 1987 s.1.
(4)	1963 s.1(2), s.12(2).
(5)	1963 s.1(3).
3	1963 s.2; R.1.
4(1), (2)	1963 s.3(1); 1981 Sched. 7, para. 5(2).
(3)	1963 s.3(4).
(4), (5)	1963 s.3(2), (3).
5	1963 s.4; R.2.
6(1)	1963 s.10(2).
(2), (3)	1963 s.10(1).
(4), (5)	1963 s.10(3), (4); 1981 Sched. 7, para. 4.
7(1)–(3)	1963 s.10A(1)–(3); 1981 Sched. 7, para. 5(1); R.3.
(4)	1963 s.10A(6) (part); 1981 Sched. 7, para. 5(1).
(5)	1963 s.10A(4), s.12(2); 1981 Sched. 7, para. 5(1); R.4.
(6)	1963 s.10A(5); 1981 Sched. 7, para. 5(1).
(7)	1963 s.10A(6) (part); 1981 Sched. 7, para. 5(1).

Provision	Derivation
8(1)–(3)	1963 s.11(1), (3); 1973 Sched. 1, para. 5; 1990 Sched. 9, para. 3.
(4), (5)	1963 s.11(2), (3); 1973 Sched. 1, para. 5; 1990 Sched. 9, para. 3.
9(1)	1963 s.6(1); 1980 s.1(5), Sched. 2; 1982 c. 48 s.46.
(2)	1963 s.6(2); 1980 s.1(6), Sched. 2.
10(1)	1980 s.2(1); 1982 c. 48 s.46.
(2)	1980 s.2(3).
(3), (4)	1980 s.2(2); 1982 c. 48 s.46.
(5)	1980 s.2(4).
11(1)	1980 s.3(1).
(2)	1980 s.3(2) (part).
(3)	1980 s.3(3); 1982 c. 19 Sched. 2, para. 4; R.5.
(4)–(7)	1980 s.3(4)–(7); R.1.
(8)	1980 s.3(8); 1982 c. 48 s.46.
(9)	1980 s.3(9), s.2(4).
12(1)	1963 s.5(1); 1980 s.4(1), Sched. 2; 1984 Sched. 7, Part I.
(2)	1963 s.5(2); 1980 s.4(2), Sched. 2; 1984 Sched. 6, paras. 13, 23.
(3)	1963 s.5(3); 1980 s.4(3), Sched. 2.
13(1)	1963 s.6(3); 1980 s.5(1)(a), (b), Sched. 2.
(2)	1980 s.5(1)(c), (d).
(3)	1980 s.5(2); 1982 c. 48 s.46.
14	1980 s.6; R.6.
15(1), (2)	1963 s.12(1), (1A); 1980 s.3(2) (part); 1981 Sched. 7, para. 5(3).
(3)	1963 s.12(1B); 1981 Sched. 7, para. 5(3).
16	1963 s.9; 1978 s.17(2)(a); 1980 s.8; R.7.
17	—
18(1)	—
(2)	1963 s.13(2), 1980 s.9(3), 1987 s.2(3).
(3)	—
Sched. 1	1963 Sched. 1; 1977 s.1.
Sched. 2	1963 Sched. 2; 1981 Sched. 17, Part II; R.3.
Sched. 3	1980 Sched. 1.
Sched. 4	—

INDEX

References are to sections

AGRICULTURAL HOLDINGS (SCOTLAND) ACT 1991*

(1991 c. 55)

[A table showing the derivation of the provisions of this Consolidation Act will be found at the end of the Act. The table has no official status.]

ARRANGEMENT OF SECTIONS

PART I

AGRICULTURAL HOLDINGS

PART II

TERMS OF LEASES AND VARIATIONS THEREOF

Variation of rent

Termination of tenancy

PART III

NOTICE TO QUIT AND NOTICE OF INTENTION TO QUIT

PART IV

COMPENSATION FOR IMPROVEMENTS

---

* Annotations by A.G.M. Duncan, M.A., LL.B., W.S.

An Act to consolidate the Agricultural Holdings (Scotland) Act 1949 and other enactments relating to agricultural holdings in Scotland.

[25th July 1991]

PARLIAMENTARY DEBATES
Hansard, H.L. Vol. 527, col. 296; Vol. 528, col. 1357; Vol. 529, col. 111; H.C. Vol. 195, col. 1115.

INTRODUCTION AND GENERAL NOTE

The Agricultural Holdings (Scotland) Act 1949 consolidated the statutory provisions affecting agricultural tenancies (other than those of crofts and smallholdings) as contained in the Agriculture (Scotland) Act 1948 and earlier Acts. In the period of more than 40 years which has elapsed since that consolidation there have been a number of significant developments requiring radical amendment of the 1949 provisions. It appears that there are prospects of further changes involving a greater measure of freedom of contract in the landlord-tenant relationship. It is, however, appropriate that any such developments there may be should have been preceded by a much-needed consolidation of the statutory provisions in force, which provisions may be expected to continue to apply to tenancy contracts entered into before further changes are enacted.

The 1948 provisions, as re-enacted in the 1949 Act, may be said to have represented a high-water mark in the protection of tenants' interests. Subsequent legislation has maintained a somewhat fluctuating balance as between the respective interests of landlord and tenant. The Agricultural Act of 1958 struck a blow for landlords in enabling them, by taking action within time limits prescribed, to enforce compliance with a Notice to Quit given to a successor of a deceased tenant without having to seek consent from the appropriate authority. The same Act effected a transfer of certain quasi-judicial functions, including the granting of consent for the operation of Notices to Quit, from the Secretary of State to the Scottish Land Court. It also contained provisions making clear that an open market basis was to be the sole criterion in the review of rents under the statutory machinery. The Succession (Scotland) Act 1964 assimilating succession rights in heritage and moveables itself contains certain provisions referring to agricultural holdings as well as amending the provisions of the 1949 Act to take account of the replacement of the tenant's heir at law by an acquirer from his executor. A more significant change affecting the succession to tenancies is, however, contained in the Agriculture (Miscellaneous Provisions) Act 1968, which makes a distinction between near relative successors (*i.e.* spouses and children of a deceased tenant) and other successors testate or intestate. Reversing to this extent the effect of the 1958 Act, the 1968 Act gave the near relative successor a continuation of the security of tenure of his predecessor subject only to the right of the landlord, if taking action within time limits prescribed, to invoke any one of certain special grounds in applying for consent to the operation of the notice to quit. The 1968 Act also created what is known as reorganisation compensation, being additional payments due to tenant farmers by landlords, who without being able to establish personal hardship, are recovering possession in order to use the land for a non-agricultural purpose. The same Act entitles tenants who have part of their holdings resumed on short notice to compensation for loss of profits. Again, important amendments to the 1949 provisions were made by the Agricultural Holdings (Amendment) (Scotland) Act 1983. This Act extended and amended for tenancies originating from 1984 onwards the special grounds for Land Court consent to a Notice to Quit given to a near relative successor. The Act's most significant effect was, however, its modification of the statutory directions for review of rents as contained in the 1949 Act as amended by the 1958 Act. A lack of comparable lettings of farms had made it difficult in many cases to apply the open market basis. Where this situation arises the arbiter or the Land Court is permitted to take into account a number of external factors instead of proceeding on the basis of a market distorted by the element of scarcity. The 1983 Act also created for the Land Court a special appellate jurisdiction applicable to rent reviews carried out by arbiters officially appointed and reduces from five to three years the minimum period between rent reviews.

The present Act incorporates in ss.68–72 and Scheds. 9 and 10 the provisions for valuation of bound sheep stocks previously dealt with in other legislation. However, for the rules of good husbandry and good estate management, matters central to the landlord and tenant relationship, we have still to refer to the Agriculture (Scotland) Act 1948, of which only a few provisions of significance now remain in force. Among provisions of the 1949 Act which have been omitted from the present Act as being unnecessary or spent is s.100. It provided that apart from express provision nothing in the 1949 Act should prejudicially affect any power, right or remedy of a landlord, tenant or other person derived from any other Act or law or any custom of the country or otherwise. The corresponding provision continues to appear in English legislation (see the Agricultural Holdings Act 1986, s.97) and references in Scottish text books indicate that the section was not without potential significance (see Gill, *The Law of Agricultural Holdings in Scotland* (2nd ed.), paras. 10, 177, 439 and 554 and Connell, *The Agricultural Holdings (Scotland) Acts* (6th ed.), pp. 206/7). Accordingly its omission seems surprising with the saving provisions in s.87 of and Sched. 12 to this Act applying only to rights of statutory origin.

While this Act has been described in Parliament as being pure consolidation, it contains much redrafting and rearrangement of the existing legislation. Instances of this are referred to in the annotations which follow. It would appear that certain drafting errors might have been avoided by closer adherence to the wording of the existing provisions (see ss.46(3) and 56(2)).

For the most part the content of provisos as appearing in the 1949 Act has been reproduced in separate subsections. With the possible exception of s.55(7), as commented on in the relative annotation, this change does not appear to have altered the meaning or effect of the proviso.

In some respects, however, the rearrangement of sections within this Act seems unfortunate. For example, certain matters which the 1949 Act conveniently dealt with together and in sequence in ss.4, 5 and 6 are now distributed between ss.4, 5, 14 and 46, with s.46(3) apparently ignoring the fact that s.6(2) of the 1949 Act has been treated as spent. Again we have the complex and interrelated provisions of ss.13 and 14 of the Agriculture (Miscellaneous Provisions) Act 1976 dealing with demands on tenants to remedy defects in fixed equipment and Notices to Quit following thereon, covered in reverse order by ss.32 and 66 of this Act.

It appears that consideration was given to the omission of the provisions for compensation for old improvements which in practice are not often invoked. The possibility had, however, to be envisaged of claims for long-standing improvements of the more permanent type arising, particularly in cases of tenancies passing by succession. The 1949 Act contained separate provisions for old and new improvements. The form of the relative Schedules has been retained but Pt. IV of this Act consists of sections dealing with both categories of improvements. The 1949 arrangement, although involving some repetition, had the advantage of ready reference to the rules applicable in a particular case.

In the annotation of each section the sections of the 1949 Act or other Acts from which it is derived are noted. References have also been made to the appropriate paragraphs in Gill, *Law of Agricultural Holdings in Scotland* (2nd ed. 1990), which forms an up-to-date and definitive treatment of the law as it stood prior to the present consolidation. Again, there have been inserted, so far as possible, references to the corresponding statutory provisions as operating in England. The interpretation of these provisions by the English courts can be helpful in resolving some problems of construction on which Scottish authority may be lacking. The significance of English decisions is exemplified by the frequent references made in Scotland to the ruling of the House of Lords in *Johnson* v. *Moreton* [1980] A.C. 87, demonstrating the public interest aspect of the agricultural holdings legislation as affecting attempts to circumvent or contract out of its effects.

ABBREVIATIONS

    1886 Act: Removal Terms (Scotland) Act 1886
    1907 Act: Sheriff Courts (Scotland) Act 1907
    1923 Act: Agricultural Holdings (Scotland) Act 1923
    1931 Act: Small Landholders and Agricultural Holdings (Scotland) Act 1931
    1937 Act: Sheep Stocks Valuation (Scotland) Act 1937
    1946 Act: Hill Farming Act 1946
    1948 Act: Agriculture (Scotland) Act 1948
    1949 Act: Agricultural Holdings (Scotland) Act 1949
    1958 Act: Agriculture Act 1958
    1963 Act: Agriculture (Miscellaneous Provisions) Act 1963
    1964 Act: Succession (Scotland) Act 1964
    1968 Act: Agriculture (Miscellaneous Provisions) Act 1968
    1973 Act: Local Government (Scotland) Act 1973

1976 Act: Agriculture (Miscellaneous Provisions) Act 1976
1983 Act: Agricultural Holdings (Amendment) (Scotland) Act 1983
1986 Act: The Agriculture Act 1986
Connell: The Agricultural Holdings (Scotland) Acts (6th ed.)
Gill: The Law of Agricultural Holdings in Scotland (2nd ed.)

PART I

AGRICULTURAL HOLDINGS

Meaning of "agricultural holding" and "agricultural land"

1.—(1) In this Act (except sections 68 to 72) "agricultural holding" means the aggregate of the agricultural land comprised in a lease, not being a lease under which the land is let to the tenant during his continuance in any office, appointment or employment held under the landlord.

(2) In this section and in section 2 of this Act, "agricultural land" means land used for agriculture for the purposes of a trade or business, and includes any other land which, by virtue of a designation of the Secretary of State under section 86(1) of the Agriculture (Scotland) Act 1948, is agricultural land within the meaning of that Act.

DEFINITIONS
"agriculture": s.85(1).
"landlord": s.85(1).
"lease": s.85(1).
"tenant": s.85(1).

DERIVATIONS
Agriculture Act 1958, s.9(1).
Agricultural Holdings (Scotland) Act 1949, s.1.

GENERAL NOTE
See Gill, Chap. 2. (For the corresponding English provision see the Agricultural Holdings Act 1986, s.1).

Subs. (1)
Sections 68 to 72 relating to valuation of sheep stocks are excepted because their application is restricted to holdings wholly or partially pastoral (see s.72(a)). "The aggregate of agricultural land" has reference to the wide variety of activities coming within the definition of "agriculture" contained in s.85(1). There is no minimum size for the agricultural holding (see *Stevens* v. *Sedgeman* [1951] 2 K.B. 434 and *Malcolm* v. *Dougall* [1916] S.C. 283). Corresponding provisions at one time operative in England have been held to result that a dwelling-house or building, if used for agriculture, may itself constitute agricultural land (see *Blackmore* v. *Butler* [1954] 2 Q.B. 171).
The exception of a let to the tenant during employment with the landlord may be taken as relating to what is known as a service occupancy rather than a tenancy in the proper sense. The status of the tenant or occupier in any particular case will be a matter of proof (see, *e.g.* *Dunbar's Trustees* v. *Bruce* [1900] 3F 137 and *McGregor* v. *Dunnett* [1949] S.C. 510).

Subs. (2)
It is a question of fact whether land is being used for trade or business (see *Blackmore* v. *Butler* [1954] 2 Q.B. 171, at pp. 175 and 181). The use must be a lawful one permitted by the lease, but it has been held that the trade or business need not be an agricultural one (*Rutherford* v. *Maurer* [1962] 1 Q.B. 16 and *Crawford* v. *Dun*, 1981 S.L.T. (Sh. Ct.) 66 and see notes on s.85(1)(b). In cases of mixed agricultural and non-agricultural use the predominant use will determine whether or not the tenancy as a whole constitutes an agricultural holding. A decision of the Land Court in *McGhie* v. *Lang*, 1953 S.L.C.R. 22 that the non-agricultural part of a mixed holding should be excised, leaving the remainder as the agricultural holding, is unlikely to be followed (see Gill, paras. 17–19 and the case of *Cameron* v. *Duke of Argyll's Trustees*, 1981 S.L.T. (Land Ct.) 2 at p. 7). However, in terms of s.49(3)(4), where the non-agricultural element in a holding predominates, the agricultural element is treated for compensation purposes as a separate agricultural holding, unless the parties agree otherwise. The power of

the Secretary of State under s.86(1) of the Agriculture (Scotland) Act 1948 to designate land as agricultural land has for long been unused.

Leases for less then year to year

2.—(1) Subject to subsection (2) below, where, under a lease entered into on or after November 1, 1948, land is let for use as agricultural land for a shorter period than from year to year, and the circumstances are such that if the lease were from year to year the land would be an agricultural holding, then, unless the letting was approved by the Secretary of State before the lease was entered into, the lease shall take effect, with the necessary modifications, as if it were a lease of the land from year to year.

(2) Subsection (1) above shall not apply to—

(a) a lease entered into (whether or not the lease expressly so provides) in contemplation of the use of the land only for grazing or mowing during some specified period of the year;

(b) a lease granted by a person whose interest in the land is that of a tenant under a lease for a shorter period than from year to year which has not by virtue of that subsection taken effect as a lease from year to year.

(3) Any question arising as to the operation of this section in relation to any lease shall be determined by arbitration.

DEFINITIONS
"agricultural holding": s.1(1).
"agricultural land": s.1(2).
"lease": s.85(1).
"tenant": s.85(1).

DERIVATION
Agricultural Holdings (Scotland) Act 1949, s.2.

GENERAL NOTE
See Gill, pp. 62–83. (For the corresponding English provision see the Agricultural Holdings Act 1986, s.2).

Subs. (1)
This is a vitally important provision preventing the avoidance of security of tenure by the use of short-term lets, whether for one period or for successive periods (*Rutherford* v. *Maurer* [1962] 1 Q.B. 16). By making such lets operative as year-to-year tenancies it brings them within the definition of a lease in s.85(1) and makes them subject to tacit relocation in terms of s.3. The rule has been held to apply to a lease for a fixed term of one year as being less then from year to year (*Bernays* v. *Prosser* [1963] 2 Q.B. 592).

The phrase "with the necessary modifications" covers only modifications consistent with the terms of the lease, which must remain "recognisably the same agreement" in contrast with "a transformation. . .into something radically different" (see *Harrison-Broadley* v. *Smith* [1964] 1 W.L.R. 456 at p. 467) and *Bahamas International Trust Co.* v. *Threadgold* [1974] 1 W.L.R. 1514, C.A.).

For the Secretary of State's approval to a short-term lease to be obtained, the Department of Agriculture, to whom there must be submitted a plan of the ground with duration and dates of the short-term let and the reasons for proposing it, has to be satisfied that the granting of a normal agricultural tenancy is unreasonable or impracticable, *e.g.* because proposed developments will take the land out of agricultural use in the fairly near future. (Other examples of special circumstances in which consent has been given are to be found in Gill, para. 64.) The Secretary of State is not concerned with the terms of the proposed let but has to decide whether in principle the land should be let on a short-term basis. To be effective, the approval must precede the lease, but the lease must be entered into before the duration of the approval expires (*Secretary of State for Social Services* v. *Beavington* (1982) 262 E.G. 551). Again the approval must apply to the whole subjects of let (*NCB* v. *Drysdale*, 1989 S.L.T. 825) but it appears to be undecided whether the lease must be of an area which has been the subject of specific prior approval or whether it is sufficient that it relates to part of a larger area covered by a prior approval (see *NCB* v. *Drysdale* (above) and Gill, para. 65).

Subs. (2)(a)

To be excepted from the application of security of tenure, both the duration of the lease and the parties' contemplation of the use of the subjects must comply with the statutory requirements. In the case of verbal lets, as often occurring with seasonal or short-term tenancies, it may be difficult to establish the purpose of the tenancy as contemplated by the parties at its commencement. Again, if there is a formal lease not containing express provisions as regards purpose and/or duration, there may be doubts as to whether extrinsic evidence on these matters is admissible. The tenant's facilities should be confined to grazing animals or mowing grass. Any form of cultivation or cropping during the seasonal let will normally involve security of tenure for the tenant but in one unusual case the tenant's ploughing operations were treated as ancillary to his use of the grassland (*Sanson* v. *Chalmers*, 1965 S.L.C.R., p. 135). An obligation on the tenant to maintain fixed equipment and grassland is not inconsistent with a grazing let (*Mackenzie* v. *Laird* (1959) S.C. 266).

The "period of the year" does not need to be defined by specific dates but can be described in general terms such as "grazing season" or "growing season," the meaning of which, as sometimes varying according to district, will be known to parties likely to be concerned (*Mackenzie* v. *Laird*; *Gairneybridge Farm* v. *King*, 1974 S.L.T. (Land Ct.) 8). The period may be as long as 364 days (*Reid* v. *Dawson* [1955] 1 Q.B. 214). A single contract for a succession of seasonal grazing lets over a period of years, which may be indefinite, is within the terms of this subsection (*Mackenzie* v. *Laird*). Successive periods of let involving continuous occupation for a year or more can however, give rise to difficulty, and the safe course is for the landlord to insist on a temporary removal of the stock, even though the subjects are being relet to the existing tenant (see *Rutherford* v. *Maurer* [1962] 1 Q.B. 16 and *per contra Scene Estate* v. *Amos* [1957] 2 Q.B. 205).

For the significance of grazing lets under s.2(2)(a) in transactions in milk quotas, see Gill, para. 73.

Subs. (2)(b)

As a sub-tenant can have no better right than the tenant as his author, the sub-tenant in a tenancy within the terms of subs. (2)(a) has himself no security of tenure. In any event, sub-letting in such seasonal tenancies, as in agricultural tenancies generally, is not permissible without the landlord's consent.

Subs. (3)

Arbitration is here being applied to the operation of the section as opposed to its application. In the past, however, the effect of the distinction, as interpreted by the courts, has not been entirely clear or consistent (for a full discussion of the matter see Gill, paras. 76–83).

The Scottish Courts have taken the view that the question of whether the approval of the Secretary of State has been given as provided for in subs. (1) is a matter for arbitration (*NCB* v. *Drysdale*, 1989 S.L.T. 825) but under the corresponding provision in the English legislation the matter has been treated as within the jurisdiction of the courts (see, for example, *Epsom and Ewell Borough Council* v. *Bell (C.) (Tadworth)* [1983] 1 W.L.R. 379). In both countries, however, it appears to be accepted that if the question is whether there was agreement between the parties or whether such agreement could take effect as a year-to-year let under subs. (1) it is a matter for the courts. In England it also appears to be accepted that any question as to whether a particular contract falls within the equivalent of subs. (2) is one for the courts (*Goldsack* v. *Shore* [1950] 1 K.B. 708), but Scottish decisions on this matter give conflicting views (*Love* v. *Montgomerie & Logan*, 1982 S.L.T. Sh. Ct. 60) following the English view but earlier decisions such as *Gairneybridge Farm* v. *King*, 1974 S.L.T. (Land Ct.) 8 and *Maclean* v. *Galloway*, 1979 S.L.T. (Sh. Ct.) 32 being to the opposite effect.

In consistency with the reference in this subsection to the operation of the section, the better view would appear to be that the only function of arbitration in such cases should be to determine the consequential modifications of a lease which the court has decided should be enlarged from a short-term tenancy to a year-to-year tenancy.

Leases to be continued by tacit relocation

3. Notwithstanding any agreement or any provision in the lease to the contrary, the tenancy of an agricultural holding shall not come to an end on the termination of the stipulated endurance of the lease, but shall be continued in force by tacit relocation for another year and thereafter from year to year, unless notice to quit has been given by the landlord or notice of intention to quit has been given by the tenant.

DEFINITIONS
  "agricultural holding": s.1(1).
  "landlord": s.85(1).
  "notice of intention to quit": s.21(2).
  "notice to quit": s.21(2).
  "tenant": s.85(1).
  "termination": s.85(1).

DERIVATIONS
  Agricultural Holdings (Scotland) Act 1949, ss.3, 24(1).

GENERAL NOTE
  See Gill, Chap. 5. (For the corresponding English provision see the Agricultural Holdings
Act 1986, s.3).
  The section, which should be read along with s.21 applies the common-law rule of tacit
relocation, subject only to the modification that to prevent the tenancy continuing after the
expiry of its duration, notice of not less than one year nor more than two years must be given by
one party to the other, these being the maximum and minimum periods prescribed by s.21(3).
The opening words of the section make it clear that contracting out is prohibited. As to the
meaning of "agreement" in this context, see the note to s.21(1).
  The section applies to leases generally and so in terms of s.85(1) includes a lease for a term of
years. A lease for 18 months is in that category and thus would not escape security of tenure as it
did in the English case of *Gladstone* v. *Bower* [1960] 2 Q.B. 384, C.A., decided under reference
to a statutory provision for prolongation of a tenancy applying only to tenancies of two years or
more. The section does not apply to seasonal lets, which are unaffected by the doctrine of tacit
relocation (see Rankine, *Leases* (3rd ed.), p. 599; *Secretary of State for Air* v. *Davidson* (1950)
66 Sh.Ct.Rep. 59).

PART II

TERMS OF LEASES AND VARIATIONS THEREOF

Written leases and the revision of certain leases

4.—(1) Where in respect of the tenancy of an agricultural holding—
(a) there is not in force a lease in writing; or
(b) there is in force a lease in writing, being either—
        (i) a lease entered into on or after November 1, 1948, or
        (ii) a lease entered into before that date, the stipulated period of
    which has expired and which is being continued in force by tacit
    relocation,
    but such lease contains no provision for one or more of the matters
    specified in Schedule 1 to this Act or contains a provision inconsistent
    with that Schedule or with section 5 of this Act,
either party may give notice in writing to the other requesting him to enter
into a lease in writing containing, as the case may be, provision for all of the
matters specified in Schedule 1 to this Act, or a provision which is consistent
with that Schedule or with section 5 of this Act; and if within the period of 6
months after the giving of such notice no such lease has been concluded, the
terms of the tenancy shall be referred to arbitration.
  (2) On a reference under subsection (1) above, the arbiter shall by his
award specify the terms of the existing tenancy and, in so far as these terms
do not make provision for all the matters specified in Schedule 1 to this Act
or make provision inconsistent with that Schedule or with section 5 of this
Act, make such provision for those matters as appears to the arbiter to be
reasonable.
  (3) On a reference under subsection (1) above, the arbiter may include in
his award any further provisions relating to the tenancy which may be agreed
between the landlord and the tenant, and which are not inconsistent with
this Act.
  (4) The award of an arbiter under this section or section 5 of this Act shall
have effect as if the terms and provisions specified and made therein were

contained in an agreement in writing between the landlord and the tenant, having effect as from the making of the award or from such later date as the award may specify.

DEFINITIONS
"agricultural holding": s.1(1).
"landlord": s.85(1).
"lease": s.85(1).
"tenant": s.1(1).

DERIVATIONS
Agricultural Holdings (Scotland) Act 1949, ss.4, 6(4).

GENERAL NOTE
See Gill, paras. 89–92.

Subs. (1)
This provision confers on a party to a tenancy the right to have a written lease in terms conforming to the statutory requirements as prescribed in Sched. 1 and s.5. Even if no formal lease exists, there may be informal writings meeting the requirements and binding on the parties by reason of their actings, in which case para. (a) of this subsection will not apply (*Grieve v. Barr*, 1954 S.L.T. 261). In practice, however, it is unlikely that the statutory requirements will be met except in a formal lease. The effect of para. (b) is that all current leases must conform to Sched. 1 but s.5 (see subs. (6)) applies only to leases entered into on or after November 1, 1948.

Subss. (2) and (3)
In the absence of agreement the arbiter cannot introduce in the lease any provision outwith the scope of the first Schedule.

Subs. (4)
Deferment of the effective date of the award is left entirely to the arbiter's discretion. The arbiter's power to vary the rent in respect of any provision in his award is dealt with in s.14, while s.46 deals with claims by a landlord or tenant for default in maintenance or repair of fixed equipment prior to transfer of liabilities in terms of the arbiter's award.

Fixed equipment and insurance premiums

5.—(1) When a lease of an agricultural holding to which this section applies is entered into, a record of the condition of the fixed equipment on the holding shall be made forthwith, and on being so made shall be deemed to form part of the lease; and section 8 of this Act shall apply to the making of such a record and to the cost thereof as it applies to a record made under that section.

(2) There shall be deemed to be incorporated in every lease of an agricultural holding to which this section applies—
   (a) an undertaking by the landlord that, at the commencement of the tenancy or as soon as is reasonably practicable thereafter, he will put the fixed equipment on the holding into a thorough state of repair, and will provide such buildings and other fixed equipment as will enable an occupier reasonably skilled in husbandry to maintain efficient production as respects both—
      (i) the kind of produce specified in the lease, or (failing such specification) in use to be produced on the holding, and
      (ii) the quality and quantity thereof,
   and that he will during the tenancy effect such replacement or renewal of the buildings or other fixed equipment as may be rendered necessary by natural decay or by fair wear and tear; and
   (b) a provision that the liability of the tenant in relation to the maintenance of fixed equipment shall extend only to a liability to maintain the fixed equipment on the holding in as good a state of repair (natural decay and fair wear and tear excepted) as it was in—

(i) immediately after it was put in repair as aforesaid, or

(ii) in the case of equipment provided, improved, replaced or renewed during the tenancy, immediately after it was so provided, improved, replaced or renewed.

(3) Nothing in subsection (2) above shall prohibit any agreement made between the landlord and the tenant after the lease has been entered into whereby one party undertakes to execute on behalf of the other, whether wholly at his own expense or wholly or partly at the expense of the other, any work which the other party is required to execute in order to fulfil his obligations under the lease.

(4) Any provision in a lease to which this section applies requiring the tenant to pay the whole or any part of the premium due under a fire insurance policy over any fixed equipment on the holding shall be null and void.

(5) Any question arising as to the liability of a landlord or tenant under this section shall be determined by arbitration.

(6) This section applies to any lease of an agricultural holding entered into on or after November 1, 1948.

DEFINITIONS
"agricultural holding": s.1(1).
"fixed equipment": s.85(1).
"landlord": s.85(1).
"lease": s.85(1).
"produce": s.85(1).
"tenant": s.85(1).

DERIVATIONS
Agricultural Holdings (Scotland) Act 1949, s.5.

GENERAL NOTE
See Gill, paras. 119–129, 136.

Subs. (1)
The expense of making a record, along with the absence of a penalty for failure to comply with this requirement, has had the result that the requirement is rarely met, although the existence of a record can be important in relation to the undertakings as to the condition of fixed equipment implied in all leases entered into after November 1, 1948 in terms of subs. (2). Where the record is being made, the provisions of s.8(3)(4)(6)–(9) will apply.

Subs. (2)(a)
These provisions impose on the landlord contractual obligations *ad factum praestandum*, breach of which will render him liable to the tenant in damages. *Mora* may not be fatal to a tenant's claim (see *Secretary of State for Scotland* v. *Sinclair*, 1960 S.L.C.R. 10) but it may be affected by negative prescription. The obligation arising at the commencement of the tenancy must be complied with as soon thereafter as circumstances, including the existing state of the fixed equipment, permit. "A thorough state of repair" would seem to imply a higher standard than the phrase "good and sufficient tenantable order" or words to that effect as sometimes used in leases and other contexts. The obligation for repair or renewal is a continuing one subsisting throughout the period of the lease and any extension thereof by tacit relocation. "Fair wear and tear" is construed in accordance with established common-law principles. The landlord's obligations are, however, limited to what is required for the purposes of the lease and the type of farming for which it was granted (*Taylor* v. *Burnett's Trustees*, 1966 S.L.C.R., p. 139. See also *Spencer-Nairn* v. *I.R.C.*, 1985 S.L.T. (Lands Ct.) 46). Again, it is requirements of a hypothetical occupier as a reasonably competent farmer which have to be fulfilled and not those of the particular tenant in possession.

The non-application of these provisions to pre-1948 leases (see subs. (6)) means that under these leases, unless they provide otherwise, the landlord cannot be forced to undertake renewal or replacement of fixed equipment worn out by natural decay or fair wear and tear. In such cases the rules of the common law determine the extent of the landlord's obligation.

Subs. (2)(b)
These provisions, unlike those affecting the landlord, do not depart from the rules of the

common law. As the counterpart of the landlord's obligations as regards the fixed equipment the tenant's obligations will not be enforceable while the landlord is in default (*Austin* v. *Gibson*, 1979 S.L.T. (Land Ct.) 12). Prima facie the landlord's claim for a breach by the tenant will be the cost of restoring the items affected to the required condition (*Duke of Portland* v. *Wood's Trustees*, 1927 S.C.(H.L.)1).

Subs. (3)
This is the authority for the post-lease agreement very frequently adopted in the creation of a new tenancy to overcome the incompetence of contracting out of the section's provisions and impose on the tenant a full repairing liability. It is important to ensure that the lease has been executed by both parties before they sign the post-lease agreement. Execution of the two documents on the same day may make the effectiveness of the post-lease agreement a matter of proof, should its effectiveness be called into question.

Subs. (4)
This subsection prohibits a practice whereby landlords in pre-1948 leases required their tenants to insure or pay the insurance premiums in respect of the fixed equipment. It would appear that this prohibition cannot be overcome by a provision in a post-lease agreement under subs. (3). Section 6 deals with the case of a pre-1948 lease with such a provision.

Subs. (5)
The arbiter's power to vary the rent in respect of any provision in his award is dealt with in s.14.

Subs. (6)
Among the important effects of the rules regulating leases which came into force on November 1, 1948 are matters mentioned in respect of subss. (2) and (4).
Note: In terms of s.25(4) of the Agriculture (Safety, Health and Welfare Provisions) Act 1956 as amended in terms of Sched. 11, para. 8, subss. (2), (3) and (5) of s.5 apply where a notice under s.3 of that Act requires any works in the nature of fixed equipment to be executed on an agricultural holding.

Sums recovered under fire insurance policy

6. Where the tenant of an agricultural holding is responsible for payment of the whole or part of the premium due under a fire insurance policy in the name of the landlord over any buildings or other subjects included in the lease of the holding and the landlord recovers any sum under such policy in respect of the destruction of, or damage to, the buildings or other subjects by fire, the landlord shall be bound, unless the tenant otherwise agrees, to expend such sum on the rebuilding, repair, or restoration of the buildings or subjects so destroyed or damaged in such manner as may be agreed or, failing agreement, as may be determined by the Secretary of State.

DEFINITIONS
"agricultural holdings": s.1(1).
"building": s.85(1).
"landlord": s.85(1).
"lease": s.85(1).
"tenant": s.85(1).

DERIVATION
Agricultural Holdings (Scotland) Act 1949, s.23.

GENERAL NOTE
See Gill, paras. 128 and 675.
See note to s.5(4). This matter comes within the administrative jurisdiction of the Secretary of State and so is outwith the scope of arbitration.

Freedom of cropping and disposal of produce

7.—(1) Subject to subsections (2) and (5) below, the tenant of an agricultural holding shall, notwithstanding any custom of the country or the provisions of any lease or of any agreement respecting the disposal of crops or the

method of cropping of arable lands, have full right, without incurring any penalty, forfeiture or liability,—
   (a) to dispose of the produce of the holding, other than manure produced thereon;
   (b) to practise any system of cropping of the arable land on the holding.
   (2) Subsection (1) above shall not have effect unless, before exercising his rights thereunder or as soon as is practicable after exercising them, the tenant makes suitable and adequate provision—
   (a) in the case of an exercise of the right to dispose of crops, to return to the holding the full equivalent manurial value to the holding of all crops sold off or removed from the holding in contravention of any such custom, lease or agreement; and
   (b) in the case of an exercise of the right to practise any system of cropping, to protect the holding from injury or deterioration.
   (3) If the tenant of an agricultural holding exercises his rights under subsection (1) above so as to injure or deteriorate, or to be likely to injure or deteriorate, the holding, the landlord shall have the following remedies, but no other—
   (a) should the case so require, he shall be entitled to obtain an interdict restraining the exercise of the tenant's rights under that subsection in that manner;
   (b) in any case, on the tenant quitting the holding on the termination of the tenancy the landlord shall be entitled to recover damages for any injury to or deterioration of the holding attributable to the exercise by the tenant of his rights under that subsection.
   (4) For the purposes of any proceedings for an interdict brought under subsection (3)(a) above, the question whether a tenant is exercising, or has exercised, his rights under subsection (1) above in such a manner as to injure or deteriorate, or to be likely to injure or deteriorate the holding, shall be determined by arbitration; and a certificate of the arbiter as to his determination of any such question shall, for the purposes of any proceedings (including an arbitration) brought under this section, be conclusive proof of the facts stated in the certificate.
   (5) Subsection (1) above shall not apply—
   (a) in the case of a tenancy from year to year, as respects the year before the tenant quits the holding or any period after he has received notice to quit or given notice of intention to quit which results in his quitting the holding; or
   (b) in any other case, as respects the year before the expiry of the lease.
   (6)—
   (a) In this section "arable land" does not include land in grass which, by the terms of a lease, is to be retained in the same condition throughout the tenancy;
   (b) the reference in paragraph (a) above to the terms of a lease shall, where the Secretary of State has directed under section 9 of the 1949 Act or an arbiter has directed under that section or under section 9 of this Act that the lease shall have effect subject to modifications, be construed as a reference to the terms of the lease as so modified.

DEFINITIONS
  "agricultural holding": s.1(1).
  "landlord": s.85(1).
  "lease": s.85(1).
  "produce": s.85(1).
  "tenant": s.85(1).
  "termination": s.85(1).

DERIVATION
  Agricultural Holdings (Scotland) Act 1949, s.12.
  Agriculture Act 1958, Sched. 1, Pt. II, para. 23.

GENERAL NOTE

See Gill, pp. 152–161. (For the corresponding English provision see the Agricultural Holdings Act 1986, s.15).

Subs. (1)

This provision contains the basic right of the agricultural tenant to act as he sees fit in the disposal of the produce of the holding (other than manure) and the cropping of the arable land (defined in subs. (6) as excluding land required by the lease to remain in grass). These rights are unaffected by any provisions in the lease or any custom which would prevent or restrict their exercise. The statutory provision, however, does not make such provision in leases illegal or inoperative but merely absolves the tenant, in certain defined circumstances and subject to certain safeguards, from complying with provisions inconsistent with his rights (see *Gore-Brown Henderson's Trustees* v. *Grenfell*, 1968 S.L.T. 237).

Subs. (2)

The pre-conditions prescribed for the tenant's exercise of his rights under subs. (1) are that he return to the holding the full manurial value of crops sold off in contravention of his lease or local custom and that in practising any system of cropping he take steps to protect the holding from injury or deterioration.

Subs. (3)

The landlord's remedies, should the tenant exercise his rights disregarding the requirements of subs. (2), are (a) interdict and (b) damages exigible when the tenant leaves. It is doubtful if the award of damages in this case is within the jurisdiction of an arbiter (see Gill, para. 161 and authorities there cited).

Subs. (4)

Interdict proceedings have to be taken in the court but the question of whether the tenant's actions are injuring or liable to injure or deteriorate the holding has to be determined by arbitration, the arbiter's certificate being conclusive for the purposes of the interdict proceedings or the damages claim.

Subs. (5)

While it is considered desirable that a farm tenant should have freedom of action in the matters referred to during the currency of his tenancy, it is right that a landlord should be able to prescribe the condition in which he will recover the holding on the tenant's departure. Hence it is provided that the tenant's freedoms under subs. (1) are not to apply during the final year of the tenancy in the case of a lease running on tacit relocation and during any period after the issue of notice to quit in any other case. It is suggested by Gill (para. 156) that it is now unnecessary legislatively to distinguish between the two cases with the same minimum period of notice of termination applying in all tenancies.

Subs. (6)

Para. (b) should be read along with s.9, under which the terms of a lease as regards land to be retained in grass may be varied in the manner thus prescribed.

Record of condition, etc., of holding

8.—(1) The landlord or the tenant of an agricultural holding may, at any time during the tenancy, require the making of a record of the condition of the fixed equipment on, and of the cultivation of, the holding.

(2) The tenant may, at any time during the tenancy, require the making of a record of—

(a) existing improvements carried out by him or in respect of the carrying out of which he has, with the consent in writing of his landlord, paid compensation to an outgoing tenant;

(b) any fixtures or buildings which, under section 18 of this Act, he is entitled to remove.

(3) A record under this section shall be made by a person to be appointed by the Secretary of State, and shall be in such form as may be prescribed.

(4) A record made under this section shall show any consideration or allowances which have been given by either party to the other.

(5) Subject to section 5 of this Act, a record may, if the landlord or the tenant so requires, be made under this section relating to a part only of the holding or to the fixed equipment only.

(6) Any question or difference between the landlord and the tenant arising out of the making of a record under this section shall, on the application of the landlord or the tenant, be referred to the Land Court for determination by them.

(7) The cost of making a record under this section shall, in default of agreement between the landlord and the tenant, be borne by them in equal shares.

(8) The remuneration of the person appointed by the Secretary of State to make a record under this section shall be such amount as the Secretary of State may fix, and any other expenses of and incidental to the making of the record shall be subject to taxation by the auditor of the sheriff court, and that taxation shall be subject to review by the sheriff.

(9) The remuneration of the person appointed by the Secretary of State to make a record under this section shall be recoverable by that person from either the landlord or the tenant, but any amount paid by either of those parties in respect of—

(a) that remuneration, or

(b) any other expenses of and incidental to the making of the record,

in excess of the share payable by him under subsection (7) above of the cost of making the record, shall be recoverable by him from the other party.

DEFINITIONS
   "agricultural holdings": s.1(1).
   "buildings": s.85(1).
   "fixed equipment": s.85(1).
   "landlord": s.85(1).
   "prescribed": s.85(1).
   "tenant": s.85(1).

DERIVATIONS
   Agricultural Holdings (Scotland) Act 1949, s.17.

GENERAL NOTE
   See Gill, pp. 132–139. (For the corresponding English provision see the Agricultural Holdings Act 1986, s.22).

Subs. (1)
   This provision is wider than s.5(1) in so far as it results that a Record can be called for at any time under any lease irrespective of its date and may cover the state of cultivation as well as that of the fixed equipment. But a record made during the currency of a lease does not, like a record made in compliance with s.5(1), form part of the lease.

Subs. (2)
   Para. (a). For the payment of compensation by an incoming tenant, see s.35.

Subs. (3)
   The recorder is not functioning as an arbiter and need not be a member of the panel of arbiters. For the form of record see the Agriculture Records (Scotland) Regulations 1948 (S.I. 1948 No. 2817) as amended by the Agriculture Records (Scotland) Amendment Regulations 1979 (S.I. 1979 No. 799).

Subs. (4)
   This provision would apply where, for example, the landlord had supplied materials for repair work the tenant was obliged to carry out or had paid for some part of an improvement effected by the tenant.

Subs. (5)
   A record made in compliance with s.5(1) must deal with all fixed equipment on the holding.

Subs. (6)
Disputes in this matter are referred to the Land Court and not to an arbiter.

Subss. (6)–(9)
These administrative provisions, like the provisions of subss. (3) and (4), apply also to records made in compliance with s.5(1).

Arbitration as to permanent pasture

9.—(1) Where under the lease of an agricultural holding, whether entered into before or after the commencement of this Act, provision is made for the maintenance of specified land, or a specified proportion of the holding, as permanent pasture, the landlord or the tenant may, by notice in writing served on the other party, demand a reference to arbitration under this Act of the question whether it is expedient in order to secure the full and efficient farming of the holding that the amount of land required to be maintained as permanent pasture should be reduced.

(2) On a reference under subsection (1) above the arbiter may by his award direct that the lease shall have effect subject to such modifications of its provisions as to land which is to be maintained as permanent pasture or is to be treated as arable land, and as to cropping, as may be specified in the direction.

(3) If the arbiter gives a direction under subsection (2) above reducing the area of land which is to be maintained as permanent pasture, he may also by his award direct that the lease shall have effect as if it provided that on quitting the holding on the termination of the tenancy the tenant should leave—

(a) as permanent pasture, or

(b) as temporary pasture sown with seeds mixture of such kind as may be specified in that direction,

(in addition to the area of land required by the lease, as modified by the direction, to be maintained as permanent pasture) a specified area of land not exceeding the area by which the land required to be maintained as permanent pasture has been reduced by the direction under subsection (2) above.

DEFINITIONS
"agricultural holding": s.1(1).
"landlord": s.85(1).
"lease": s.85(1).
"tenant": s.85(1).
"termination of tenancy": s.85(1).

DERIVATIONS
Agricultural Holdings (Scotland) Act 1949, s.9.

GENERAL NOTE
See Gill, pp. 163–164. (For the corresponding English provision see the Agricultural Holdings Act 1986, s.14).

Subs. (1)
While these provisions apply to leases irrespective of their date, the requirement to maintain an area of permanent pasture has now become uncommon in leases. The jurisdiction in the matter formerly belonged to the Secretary of State but since 1958 it has come under arbitration.

In the case of *Secretary of State* v. *Maclean*, 1950 S.L.C.R. 33 the phrase "full and efficient use for agriculture" occurring in s.57 of the Agriculture (Scotland) Act 1948 (concerning compulsory acquisition to secure full and efficient use of land) was interpreted as meaning "use of land as a commercial unit, *i.e.* use of land in the normal course of good farming by an active intelligent farmer."

There are no statutory definitions of "pasture" or "permanent pasture." The statement in s.93(1) of the 1949 Act that "pasture includes meadow" has not been included in the interpretation provisions of s.85(1) of this Act.

These provisions fall to be read along with the provisions of ss.51 and 53(2). As shown by s.53(2), the parties may achieve the result of an arbitration under s.9 by agreement in writing and exclude compensation for improvements, just as it is excluded by s.51 for anything done under the arbiter's direction under s.9.

Power of landlord to enter on holding

10. The landlord of an agricultural holding or any person authorised by him may at all reasonable times enter on the holding for any of the following purposes—

(a) viewing the state of the holding;

(b) fulfilling the landlord's responsibilities to manage the holding in accordance with the rules of good estate management;

(c) providing, improving, replacing or renewing fixed equipment on the holding otherwise than in fulfilment of such responsibilities.

DEFINITIONS
"agricultural holdings": s.1(1).
"fixed equipment": s.85(1).
"good estate management": s.85(2) and Sched. 5 to the Agriculture (Scotland) Act 1948.
"landlord": s.85(1).

DERIVATIONS
Agricultural Holdings (Scotland) Act 1949, s.18.

GENERAL NOTE
See Gill, pp. 143–144. (For the corresponding English provision see the Agricultural Holdings Act 1986, s.23).

It appears that the landlord may have a common-law right to enter the holding and again the lease may contain provisions for entry, but this provision puts the matter beyond doubt.

Para. (c) covers work for which the landlord is responsible at common law where his obligation has not been written into the lease (s.4 and para. 5 of Sched. 1) or work for which he is responsible in terms of special provisions in a lease, or again work which he is doing in making an improvement within the terms of s.15(1).

It is doubtful if a landlord entering the holding under these provisions is entitled to handle the tenant's livestock (see *Luss Estates Co.* v. *Firkin Farm Co.*, 1985 S.L.T. (Land Ct.) 17).

Bequest of lease

11.—(1) Subject to subsections (2) to (8) below, the tenant of an agricultural holding may, by will or other testamentary writing, bequeath his lease of the holding to his son-in-law or daughter-in-law or to any one of the persons who would be, or would in any circumstances have been, entitled to succeed to the estate on intestacy by virtue of the Succession (Scotland) Act 1964.

(2) A person to whom the lease of a holding is so bequeathed (in this section referred to as "the legatee") shall, if he accepts the bequest, give notice of the bequest to the landlord of the holding within 21 days after the death of the tenant, or, if he is prevented by some unavoidable cause from giving such notice within that period, as soon as practicable thereafter.

(3) The giving of a notice under subsection (2) above shall import acceptance of the lease and, unless the landlord gives a counter-notice under subsection (4) below, the lease shall be binding on the landlord and on the legatee, as landlord and tenant respectively, as from the date of the death of the deceased tenant.

(4) Where notice has been given under subsection (2) above, the landlord may within one month thereafter give to the legatee a counter-notice intimating that he objects to receiving him as tenant under the lease.

(5) If the landlord gives a counter-notice under subsection (4) above, the legatee may make application to the Land Court for an order declaring him

to be tenant under the lease as from the date of the death of the deceased tenant.

(6) If, on the hearing of such an application, any reasonable ground of objection stated by the landlord is established to the satisfaction of the Land Court, they shall declare the bequest to be null and void, but in any other case they shall make an order in terms of the application.

(7) Pending any proceedings under this section, the legatee, with the consent of the executor in whom the lease is vested under section 14 of the Succession (Scotland) Act 1964, shall, unless the Land Court on cause shown otherwise direct, have possession of the holding.

(8) If the legatee does not accept the bequest, or if the bequest is declared null and void under subsection (6) above, the right to the lease shall be treated as intestate estate of the deceased tenant in accordance with Part I of the Succession (Scotland) Act 1964.

DEFINITIONS
  "lease": s.85(1).
  "landlord": s.85(1).
  "tenant": s.85(1).

DERIVATIONS
  Agricultural Holdings (Scotland) Act 1949, s.20.
  Succession (Scotland) Act 1964, s.31(1), Sched. 2, paras. 19, 20, 21.

GENERAL NOTE
  See Gill, paras. 570–583.

Subs. (1)
  It appears that a bequest in terms of this provision should be to a single individual (*Kennedy* v. *Johnstone*, 1956 S.C. 39) and again that a general bequest of estate or residue as opposed to specific bequest of the lease may not be an effective exercise of the statutory power of bequest (*Reid's Trustees* v. *Macpherson*, 1975 S.L.T. 101 at 109).

  The category of possible legatees as here prescribed is wider than that of the persons to whom, on the tenant's intestacy *quoad* his lease, the executor may make over the lease under s.16 of the 1964 Act. But in practice this difference is of limited importance. In a tenancy constituted by a formal lease there will usually be an express exclusion of assignees resulting that the tenant has contracted out of his right to bequeath the tenancy (see *Kennedy* v. *Johnstone*, above) thus making a bequest ineffective unless the landlord has agreed to it in the tenant's lifetime or accepts the legatee after his death. Again, even if the power of bequest is exercisable, s.25 results that on the succession to the lease of anyone other than a near relative of the tenant (defined in Sched. 2, Pt. 3, para. 1 as his or her spouse or child, natural or adopted) the tenancy can be terminated by an incontestable notice to quit taking effect at the appropriate term. Such a successor does not have the extended security of tenure enjoyed by his predecessor in the tenancy.

  The case of *Kennedy* v. *Johnstone* (above) which establishes that a tenant can contract out of his power of bequest of his tenancy has also been regarded as giving some support to the view that the transmissibility of the tenancy can be wholly renounced by the inclusion in the lease of an express exclusion of all successors. Such a provision, if effective, renders inapplicable, in the particular case, the provisions of s.12 *infra* and the various related provisions of the 1964 Act (see Gill Chaps. 4 and 5 and para. 585 and the article "Agricultural Tenancies; the Exclusion of Successors": 1988 33 J.L.S. 384).

Subs. (2)
  Written notice is not specified and in one instance verbal notice by telephone was conceded by the landlord to be effective (*Irving* v. *Church of Scotland General Trustees*, 1960 S.L.C.R. 16). In practice, however, written notice by recorded delivery should be given to the person or persons ascertained to be the present owners of the property. There are reports of Land Court rulings on the question of "unavoidable course" as a reason for failure to give notice timeously (see *Mackinnon* v. *Martin*, 1958 S.L.C.R. 19 where the plea succeeded and *Wright* v. *Marquis of Lothian's Trustees*, 1952 S.L.C.R. 25 and *Thomson* v. *Lyall*, 1966 S.L.C.R. at p. 136 being cases in which it failed). It may be noted that "practicable" has been substituted for "possible" in the concluding phrase of this subsection but presumably it is considered that this variation in wording in a consolidating act leaves the meaning and effect of the provision unchanged. With

the Court of Session decision in *Garvie's Trustees* v. *Still*, 1972 S.L.T. 29 emphasising the limits of the Land Court's jurisdiction as resting entirely on statutory provision, it must now be accepted that the only functions of the Land Court under this section are to determine whether in terms of subs. (6) a reasonable ground of objection to the legatee as tenant has been stated by the landlord and to deal with the matter of interim possession under subs. (7). Neither the validity of the bequest nor the effectiveness of the notification to the landlord is within its jurisdiction (see Gill, paras. 605 and 667).

Subs. (3)

If notice to the landlord is duly given and not met by counter-notice under subs. (4) the legatee becomes tenant as from the date of the late tenant's death. If a legatee gives notice late and cannot show unavoidable cause for the delay he loses the right to the tenancy in a question with the landlord. But as the notice, although given late, implies his acceptance of the lease the tenancy interest comes to an end instead of becoming intestate estate available for transfer by the executor in terms of s.16 of the 1964 Act as referred to in s.12(1) (*Coats* v. *Logan*, 1985 S.L.T. 221, O.H.T.). As the terms of s.16(2) of the 1964 Act stand, this result cannot be avoided by the legatee's subsequently renouncing the tenancy.

Subs. (4)

While written counter-notice is not specified, counter-notice in writing should in practice be given by recorded delivery.

Subs. (5)

No time limit is prescribed for the tenant making application to the Land Court. It has been suggested that should the tenant's application be long delayed the landlord may take the initiative in bringing the matter before the court. There being, however, no statutory warrant for this course, any action by the landlord should be taken in the Sheriff Court. Pending the Land Court's decision whether the landlord has reasonable ground of objection to the legatee, the tenancy interest remains vested in the tenant's executor by Confirmation in terms of s.14(1) of the 1964 Act. If, however, the landlord's objection is rejected, the legatee becomes tenant as from the date of the tenant's death.

Subs. (6)

The grounds of objection must be personal to the legatee, the landlord not being entitled to found on considerations such as his need for vacant possession of the land or his ability to improve its standard of husbandry (*Fraser* v. *Murray's Trustees*, 1954 S.L.C.R. 10). On the other hand, it has been recognised that the landlord is entitled to have a tenant of reputable character with the necessary agricultural knowledge or skill and adequate financial resources to farm the particular holding. Alcoholism or convictions for serious crimes but not conviction for some minor offence would be regarded as a reasonable objection (*Luss Estate Co.* v. *Campbell*, 1973 S.L.C.R. App. 96). Again youth or inexperience will not disqualify a legatee who is in a position to get the necessary advice and assistance (see *Macrae* v. *Macdonald*, 1986 S.L.C.R. 69 (D.C.) and *Dunsinnon Estate Trustees* v. *Alexander*, 1978 S.L.C.R. App. 146). However, his performance in farming elsewhere, or on the farm itself, if he has had interim possession under subs. (7), will be relevant (see *Dunsinnon Estate Trustees* v. *Alexander*). His financial resources will not be regarded as inadequate because they are derived, in part, at least, from bank loans or similar sources (*Reid* v. *Duffus Estate*, 1955 S.L.C.R. 13).

Subs. (7)

The vesting of the lease in the executor, whose consent to interim possession is required, assumes that the executor has confirmed to the tenancy interest as part of the late tenant's estate. While the executor's consent would not normally be withheld, the landlord may be able to show cause why interim possession should be refused (see Gill, para. 579).

Subs. (8)

The provisions of the 1964 Act directly relevant are those of s.16 under which the executor, except with the landlord's consent, can dispose of the lease only to someone entitled to succeed to the late tenant's estate or part thereof or to claim legal rights or prior rights, therefrom. This represents a more limited class than that of the parties qualified to receive a bequest of the lease where that is permissible. Again, however, it is important from the point of view of security of tenure that the beneficiary selected to acquire the lease should if possible be a near relative as mentioned in connection with subs. (1).

It should be noted here that s.16(8) of the 1964 Act, as amended in terms of para. 24(c) of Sched. 11, makes it clear that when there is a valid bequest of a lease, vesting in the executor under s.14 of that Act, does not prevent the operation, in relation to the legatee, of subss. (2)–(8) of this section.

Right of landlord to object to acquirer of lease

12.—(1) A person to whom the lease of an agricultural holding is transferred under section 16 of the Succession (Scotland) Act 1964 (referred to in this section as "the acquirer") shall give notice of the acquisition to the landlord of the holding within 21 days after the date of the acquisition, or, if he is prevented by some unavoidable cause from giving such notice within that period, as soon as is practicable thereafter and, unless the landlord gives a counter-notice under subsection (2) below, the lease shall be binding on the landlord and on the acquirer, as landlord and tenant respectively, as from the date of the acquisition.

(2) Within one month after receipt of a notice given under subsection (1) above the landlord may give a counter-notice to the acquirer intimating that the landlord objects to receive him as tenant under the lease; and not before the expiry of one month from the giving of the counter-notice the landlord may make application to the Land Court for an order terminating the lease.

(3) On an application under subsection (2) above, the Land Court shall, if they are satisfied that the landlord has established a reasonable ground of objection, make an order terminating the lease, to take effect as from such term of Whitsunday or Martinmas as they may specify.

(4) Pending any proceedings under this section, the acquirer, with the consent of the executor in whom the lease is vested under section 14 of the Succession (Scotland) Act 1964 shall, unless the Land Court on cause shown otherwise direct, have possession of the holding.

(5) Termination of the lease under this section shall be treated, for the purposes of Parts IV and V of this Act (compensation), as termination of the acquirer's tenancy of the holding; but nothing in this section shall entitle him to compensation for disturbance.

DEFINITIONS
   "agricultural holdings": s.1(1).
   "landlord": s.85(1).
   "lease": s.85(1).
   "tenant": s.85(1).
   "termination of tenancy": s.85(1).

DERIVATIONS
   Agricultural Holdings (Scotland) Act 1949, s.21.
   Successions Act (Scotland) Act 1964, Sched. 2, para. 22.

GENERAL NOTE
   See Gill, Chap. 34.

Subss. (1) and (2)
   The substantive provisions of the 1964 Act concerning intestate succession to a tenancy interest are fully explained in the text referred to. This subsection, proceeding on the same lines as the corresponding provisions in s.11, prescribes the steps to be taken by the acquirer, as the intestate successor is called, to intimate his claim to the lease to the landlord and, subject to the landlord's right of objection, to become tenant as from the date of his acquisition.
   It should be noted that in contrast with the situation where the lease is effectively bequeathed, the successor's tenure of the tenancy runs not from the date of the late tenant's death but from the date of the successor's acquisition. Again the acquisition will have to be effected by some document of transfer from an executor who has confirmed to the tenant interest. There is no automatic divestiture of the executor such as takes place in the case of a bequest. It is doubtful whether the provisions of s.15(2) of the 1964 Act for the transfer of heritable property to a successor by docket on the confirmation or certificate of confirmation apply to leases but the terms of Sched. 1 to that Act could readily be adapted to provide a simple form of transfer. Differing from the position where a legatee is subject to objection by the

landlord, the landlord objecting to an acquirer is authorised, not less than a month after giving counter-notice, to apply to the Land Court for an order terminating the lease.

Subs. (3)

The same considerations as apply under s.11(6) will influence the court in deciding whether or not the landlord has a reasonable ground of objection to the acquirer. A decision in the affirmative, however, results in an order terminating the tenancy, the executor having no further power of disposal. The Term and Quarter Days (Scotland) Act 1990, s.1(1)(a) and (2)(a), now defines "Whitsunday" and "Martinmas" as meaning May 28 and November 28 respectively for the purposes of any enactment or rule of law. Normally the court's order will take effect at the next term day but there would appear to be a discretion to defer its effect to a later term if circumstances justify this course.

Subs. (4)

This provides (as does s.11(7) in the case of a legatee) for interim possession by the acquirer pending proceedings. The reference to the lease as being vested in the executor seems at first sight, at least, inconsistent with the fact that a transfer of the lease to the acquirer will have been granted by the executor and intimated to the landlord, whose objection, if successful, has the result that the executor has no further concern with or interest in the tenancy. It appears, however, that the transfer to the acquirer must be regarded as subject to a suspensive condition, purified only if the landlord fails timeously to object to the acquirer as tenant, or having objected, is unsuccessful in the Land Court proceedings.

Subs. (5)

While the acquirer to whom the landlord successfully objects never attains the status of tenant, he is treated for certain purposes, such as compensation for improvements, as a tenant going out on the termination of the lease. (As to the different position of an unsuccessful legatee see Gill, para. 604.) The acquirer, however, is not entitled to compensation for disturbance, which, as a general rule, is payable only when a holding is vacated in compliance with a notice to quit from the landlord (see s.43).

Variation of rent

Variation of rent

13.—(1) Subject to subsection (8) below, the landlord or the tenant of an agricultural holding may, whether the tenancy was created before or after the commencement of this Act, by notice in writing served on the other party, demand a reference to arbitration of the question what rent should be payable in respect of the holding as from the next day after the date of the notice on which the tenancy could have been terminated by notice to quit (or notice of intention to quit) given on that date, and the matter shall be referred accordingly.

(2) On a reference under subsection (1) above, the arbiter shall determine, in accordance with subsections (3) to (7) below the rent properly payable in respect of the holding as from the "next day" mentioned in subsection (1) above.

(3) For the purposes of this section the rent properly payable in respect of a holding shall normally be the rent at which, having regard to the terms of the tenancy (other than those relating to rent), the holding might reasonably be expected to be let in the open market by a willing landlord to a willing tenant, there being disregarded (in addition to the matters referred to in subsection (5) below) any effect on rent of the fact that the tenant is in occupation of the holding.

(4) Where the evidence available to the arbiter is in his opinion insufficient to enable him to determine the rent properly payable or he is of the view that the open market for rents of comparable subjects in the surrounding area is distorted by scarcity of lets or by other factors, the rent properly payable for the purposes of this section shall be the rent which he would expect to be paid, in a market which was not affected by such distortion, having particular regard to the following—

  (a) information about open market rents of comparable subjects outside the surrounding area;

  (b) the entire range of offers made as regards any lease of subjects which are comparable after regard is had to the terms of that lease;

  (c) sitting tenants' rents fixed by agreement for subjects in the surrounding area which are comparable after regard is had to any element attributable to goodwill between landlord and tenant or to similar considerations; and

  (d) the current economic conditions in the relevant sector of agriculture.

(5) The arbiter shall not take into account any increase in the rental value of the holding which is due to improvements—

  (a) so far as—

      (i) they have been executed wholly or partly at the expense of the tenant (whether or not that expense has been or will be reimbursed by a grant out of moneys provided by Parliament) without equivalent allowance or benefit having been made or given by the landlord in consideration of their execution; and

      (ii) they have not been executed under an obligation imposed on the tenant by the terms of his lease;

  (b) which have been executed by the landlord, in so far as the landlord has received or will receive grants out of moneys provided by Parliament in respect of the execution thereof,

nor fix the rent at a higher amount than would have been properly payable if those improvements had not been so executed.

(6) The continuous adoption by the tenant of a standard of farming or a system of farming more beneficial to the holding than the standard or system required by the lease or, in so far as no system of farming is so required, than the system of farming normally practised on comparable holdings in the district, shall be deemed, for the purposes of subsection (5) above, to be an improvement executed at his expense.

(7) The arbiter shall not fix the rent at a lower amount by reason of any dilapidation or deterioration of, or damage to, fixed equipment or land caused or permitted by the tenant.

(8) Subject to subsection (9) below, a reference to arbitration under subsection (1) above shall not be demanded in circumstances which are such that any increase or reduction of rent made in consequence thereof would take effect as from a date earlier than the expiry of 3 years from the latest in time of the following—

  (a) the commencement of the tenancy;

  (b) the date as from which there took effect a previous variation of rent (under this section or otherwise);

  (c) the date as from which there took effect a previous direction under this section that the rent should continue unchanged.

(9) There shall be disregarded for the purposes of subsection (8) above—

  (a) a variation of rent under section 14 of this Act;

  (b) an increase of rent under section 15(1) of this Act;

  (c) a reduction of rent under section 31 of this Act.

DEFINITIONS
"agricultural holdings": s.1(1).
"improvement": s.85(1).
"landlord": s.85(1).
"lease": s.85(1).
"notice of intention to quit": s.21(2).
"notice to quit": s.21(2).
"tenant": s.85(1).

DERIVATIONS
Agricultural Holdings (Amendment) (Scotland) Act 1983, s.2.
Agricultural Holdings (Scotland) Act 1949, s.7.

GENERAL NOTE
See Gill, paras. 198–220a. (For the corresponding English provision see the Agricultural Holdings Act 1986, s.12 and Sched. 2).

Subss. (1) and (2)
Security of tenure for the tenant resulting in a tenancy's being able to continue indefinitely beyond its prescribed duration arrangements are necessary to keep rents in line with changing conditions. This is achieved by enabling either party to serve notice on the other, demanding arbitration as to the rent which should be payable as from the next day after the date on which the tenancy could have been terminated on due notice being given. In effect, therefore, a rent review is obtainable on the same period of notice as is required in terms of s.21(3) for termination of the tenancy, *i.e.* not less than one year and not more than two years. It follows that unless there is provision in the lease for a break, the rent cannot be varied during the prescribed duration of the tenancy, but only as from its expiry or subsequently as from the appropriate term where the tenancy is continuing on tacit relocation. While the matter is dealt with in subs. (8), it may be noted here that the rent of a holding cannot be reviewed under the provisions of this section more frequently than at intervals of three years.

Subs. (3)
This subsection contains the basic directions for the determination of the rent by the arbiter. Under the 1949 Act as originally framed the arbiter had a wide discretion and could take into account such considerations as the "sitting tenant" factor or the tenant's personal circumstances (see, *e.g. Guthe* v. *Broatch*, 1956 S.C. 132). The basis of assessment was more akin to a fair rent as applying under crofting legislation than to the market rent as introduced by amendments made by the 1958 Act. An exposition of the operation of the open market basis for determining a rent is to be found in certain decisions of the Land Court functioning in place of the arbiter under provisions now contained in s.60(2) (see *Secretary of State* v. *Young*, 1960 S.L.C.R. 31 and *Crown Estate Commissioners* v. *Gunn*, 1961 S.L.C.R. 173). As this subsection indicates, account has to be taken of the terms of the lease other than rent. Features such as a full repairing obligation on the tenant, a requirement to reside on the holding, a prohibition on letting grazings or a requirement to maintain a bound sheep stock could affect the rent a hypothetical tenant would be prepared to pay (see, *e.g. Secretary of State* v. *Davidson*, 1969 S.L.T. (Land Ct.) 7, *Strathclyde R.C.* v. *Arneil*, 1987 S.L.C.R. 44 and *British Alcan Aluminium Co.* v. *Shaw*, 1987 S.L.C.R. 1). Difficulty, however, has in many cases been experienced in arriving at the rent appropriate for a particular holding, there being in some districts at least few lets of comparable farms being negotiated and increasing competition for any available tenancies. Thus rents tended to be fixed on the basis of a hypothetical open market unfairly distorted in favour of the landlords (see *Kilmarnock Estates* v. *Tenants*, 1977 S.L.C.R. App. 141 and *Witham* v. *Stockdale*, 1981 S.L.T. (Land Ct.) 27). To remedy, or at least improve, the situation in this respect, the 1983 Act introduced the provisions now contained in subs. (4).
In a recent case the Land Court decided that parties to an agricultural lease cannot contract out of the statutory provisions for review of rent which are based on the open market criterion discounted for scarcity and intended to achieve a degree of consistency in farm renting. Accordingly they held to be invalid and ineffective a post-lease agreement requiring the rent of the holding to be reviewed annually by reference to the retail price index (*Moll* v. *Macgregor*, 1990 S.L.T. (Land Ct.) 59: also reported *sub nom. Wallace* v. *Moll*, 1989 S.L.C.R. 21.) In that case the lease was running on tacit relocation. In an earlier case of *Duncan* v. *Anderson*, 1985 S.L.C.R. 1 it was indicated, at p. 14, that provisions superseding the statutory provisions could be enforceable during the currency of the lease. There are, however, indications in the court's decision in the case of *Moll* (see p. 66 of the S.L.T. Report) that that view is no longer held.

Subs. (4)
This provision applies where the arbiter considers he has insufficient evidence to determine a rent or that the open market for rents of comparable subjects in the district on which he would normally base his decision is distorted by scarcity of lets or other factors. The arbiter is directed in such circumstances to fix a rent which he would expect to be paid in a market unaffected by distortion having regard to certain factors listed. Of these factors the first, being information about open market rents of comparable subjects in other districts, is useful where local conditions are not too dissimilar. Secondly, where there is evidence of a recent let of a comparable subject, the arbiter should consider not merely the rent offered by the successful applicant for the tenancy but also the whole range of offers, as the successful offer may involve an element of premium which should be disregarded. The terms of the respective leases must of

course be kept in view. Thirdly, transactions with sitting tenants are to be relevant provided that special factors such as mutual goodwill can be eliminated. In practice there are likely to be more of these transactions taking place than there will be new lets. Finally, the current economic condition in the relevant section of agriculture should be considered. The matters referred to in the subsection are, of course, not exhaustive of the factors or elements which may enter into the arbiter's determination of an appropriate rent for a holding. By way of precedents in law, and in some cases also as comparables in relation to the holding under consideration, arbiters will find guidance in the reports of Land Court decisions. Some of these will have arisen under the court's appellate jurisdiction in rent cases introduced by the 1983 Act and now provided for by s.61(2) and Sched. 7, para. 22. In other cases, particularly those decided before the 1983 Provisions took effect, the court will have been functioning as tribunal of first instance where parties have invoked the provisions of s.60(2) to refer their dispute to the Land Court instead of to an arbiter. Among recent Land Court cases which illustrate the application and working of the provisions of this subsection and related provisions are the following: *Earl of Seafield* v. *Stewart*, 1985 S.L.T. (Land Ct.) 35; *Kinnaird Trust* v. *Boyne*, 1985 S.L.C.R. 19; *Aberdeen Endowments Trust* v. *Will*, 1985 S.L.T. (Land Ct.) 23; *Buccleuch Estates* v. *Kennedy*, 1986 S.L.C.R. App. 1; *British Alcan Aluminium Co.* v. *Shaw*, 1987 S.L.C.R. 1; *Shand* v. *Christie's Trs.*, 1987 S.L.C.R. 29; *Towns* v. *Anderson*, 1989 S.L.T. (Land Ct.) 17.

Where the rent review has been undertaken by an arbiter appointed by the Secretary of State as opposed to one nominated by agreement of the parties (see Sched. 7, para. 1) the arbiter's award, which must disclose his findings in fact and the reasons for his decision, has, since the passing of the 1983 Act, been required to be made available to the Secretary of State as well as to the parties (see Sched. 7, para. 10) and a register of such awards can be seen at the Scottish Record Office. This arrangement was introduced with a view to achieving greater consistency in awards in rent arbitrations and must, as time goes on, provide an increasingly valuable source of information and guidance for arbiters undertaking rent reviews as well as for parties and their advisers involved in review proceedings.

Subs. (5)

While the application of this provision is not restricted to improvements for which the tenant on his outgoing can claim compensation under Pt. IV of this Act (*Towns* v. *Anderson*, 1989 S.L.T. (Land Ct.) 17), it does not apply to improvements made by the tenant or his predecessor under a previous lease (*Kilmarnock Estates* v. *Barr*, 1969 S.L.T. (Land Ct.) 10).

Where a rent is being reviewed on a holding where there are improvements affected by these provisions, the approved course appears to be to assess the rental value on the assumption that none of these improvements existed (*Mackenzie* v. *Bocardo S.A.*, 1986 S.L.C.R. 53, p. 64).

There are certain provisions in other Acts about matters which the arbiter is to disregard in assessing the rent of a holding. Under s.16 of the Agriculture Act 1986, as amended in terms of para. 44 of Sched. 11, the tenant is protected from being rented on a milk quota which he himself had transferred on to the holding (for an explanation of the arrangements applying according to circumstances see Gill, para. 207).

Under the Housing (Scotland) Act 1987, ss.246 and 256(4), an assessment of the rent during the period in which grant conditions apply should disregard so much of the value of the house or of any improvement works as is attributable to the grant. Again, the arbiter is directed by s.14A(1) of the Open Cast Coal Act 1958, as amended in terms of para. 11 of Sched. 11, to disregard any increase or diminution of rental value attributable to occupation of the holding or any part of it by the British Coal Corporation.

Subs. (6)

The tenant's claim for what is popularly known as High Farming is dealt with in s.44. It is not often that the conditions of that section are met but when this happens it is appropriate that the resulting improvement for which the tenant is responsible should not be reflected in his liability for rent.

Subs. (7)

Where the tenant has held successive leases the only dilapidations, *etc.* relevant to this provision will be those occurring during the current lease (*Kilmarnock Estates* v. *Barr*, 1969 S.L.T. (Land Ct.) 10), which the arbiter should ignore in assessing the rental value of the holding.

Subs. (8)

Before the passing of the 1983 Act the application of the statutory machinery for rent reviews was on a quinquennial basis. The 1983 Act introduced a triennial basis, which should result in rents being kept more closely in line with varying market trends and make it easier for an arbiter to arrive, as he should endeavour to do, at a rent which reflects the fact that it is to remain in force till the time for another review arrives.

As regards para. (a), the better view appears to be that the reference is to the commencement of the current lease and not to that of any previous lease between the same parties.

One effect of para. (b) is that if parties agree a revision of a rent without resorting to arbitration, the statutory machinery cannot be invoked so as to take effect less than three years after the agreed rent became operative.

Para. (c) shows that an unsuccessful attempt to have the rent varied by the statutory machinery has the result that three years must elapse before a variation can be effected in that way. It is perhaps not clear whether an agreement by the parties that the rent should remain unchanged would have the same effect. It had been indicated that the availability of the statutory machinery at intervals, as prescribed, does not prevent parties agreeing to an earlier review of the rent (*Boyd* v. *MacDonald*, 1958 S.L.C.R. 10 at p. 12) but in *Moll* v. *Macgregor* (*above*) at p. 66, the Land Court appears to have taken the view that an agreement in the lease or other document to vary the frequency of rent reviews would be unenforceable. In the past the general practice in lets for a term of years has been to make provision for breaks coinciding with the quinquennial, or as it is now, triennial availability of the statutory machinery.

Subs. (9)

In each of the cases referred to, what is taking place is not a review of the rent as a whole, which occurs when the statutory machinery is invoked, but an adjustment to take account of some change affecting the holding or the terms on which it is let.

Arbitrations under sections 4 and 5

14. Where it appears to an arbiter—

(a) on a reference under section 4 of this Act that, by reason of any provision which he is required by that section to include in his award, or

(b) on a reference under section 5 of this Act that, by reason of any provision included in his award,

it is equitable that the rent of the holding should be varied, he may vary the rent accordingly.

DEFINITIONS
    "holding": s.1(1).

DERIVATIONS
    Agricultural Holdings (Scotland) Act 1949, s.6(3).

GENERAL NOTE
    See Gill, paras. 127 and 221. (For the corresponding English provision see the Agricultural Holdings Act 1986, s.8(4)).

Para. (a)

It would appear that it is only a provision which the arbiter is required to include in his award that can justify a variation and that a variation in respect of some other provision included with the agreement of the parties in terms of s.4(3) is not competent.

Increase of rent for certain improvements by landlord

15.—(1) Where the landlord of an agricultural holding has, whether before or after the commencement of this Act, carried out on the holding an improvement (whether or not one for the carrying out of which compensation is provided for under Part IV of this Act)—

(a) at the request of, or in agreement with, the tenant,

(b) in pursuance of an undertaking given by the landlord under section 39(3) of this Act, or

(c) in compliance with a direction given by the Secretary of State under powers conferred on him by or under any enactment,

subject to subsections (2) and (3) below, the rent of the holding shall, if the landlord by notice in writing served on the tenant within 6 months from the completion of the improvement so requires, be increased as from the completion of the improvement by an amount equal to the increase in the rental value of the holding attributable to the carrying out of the improvement.

(2) Where any grant has been made to the landlord out of moneys provided by Parliament, in respect of an improvement to which subsection (1) above applies, the increase in rent provided for by that subsection shall be reduced proportionately.

(3) Any question arising between the landlord and the tenant in the application of this section shall be determined by arbitration.

DEFINITIONS
"agricultural holdings": s.1(1).
"improvements": s.85(1).
"landlord": s.85(1).
"tenant": s.85(1).

DERIVATIONS
Agricultural Holdings (Scotland) Act 1949, s.13.

GENERAL NOTE
See Gill, paras. 224–227. (For the corresponding English provision see the Agricultural Holdings Act 1986, s.13).

Subs. (1)
The improvements covered by this provision are not restricted to improvements for which, if the tenant had made them, he could claim compensation at his outgoing. At least where there is agreement between the parties as contemplated in para. (a), anything enhancing the rental value of the holding will qualify for a rent increase.

In terms of s.25(5) of the Agriculture (Safety, Health and Welfare Provisions) Act 1956, works executed in compliance with that Act are deemed landlord's improvements for this purpose.

Para. (b) refers to the situation provided for in s.39 where the landlord elects to carry out himself an improvement which the tenant was proposing to make.

Subs. (2)
Another ground for reduction or abatement of the increase of rent can arise where the improvement takes the form of a livestock-rearing land improvement scheme under the Hill Farming Act 1946 as amended by the 1949 Act. In terms of s.7(3) of the 1946 Act the Secretary of State, if reducing the grant on the ground that the work has been badly done, may direct that the increase of rent be restricted accordingly, with retrospective effect if an increase in rent has already taken effect.

In terms of the Open Cast Coal Act 1958, s.14A(1) and (9), as amended in terms of the Housing and Planning Act 1986, Sched. A, para. 5 and in terms of para. 12 of Sched. 11, the landlord's right to claim an increase in rent in respect of an improvement is not to be prejudiced by the effect of any open-cast coal operations taking place.

Termination of tenancy

Leases not terminated by variation of terms, etc.

16. The lease of an agricultural holding shall not be brought to an end, and accordingly neither party shall be entitled to bring proceedings to terminate the lease or, except with the consent of the other party, to treat it as at an end, by reason only that any new term has been added to the lease or that any terms of the lease (including the rent payable) have been varied or revised in pursuance of this Act.

DEFINITIONS
"agricultural holding": s.1(1).
"lease": s.85(1).

DERIVATIONS
Agricultural Holdings (Scotland) Act 1949, s.10.

GENERAL NOTE
See Gill, paras. 99–101.

At common law the terms of a lease may be so altered by agreement of the parties that a new tenancy contract is regarded as having been created, a result which can be significant in relation to statutory provisions the application of which is dependent on the date when a lease was entered into (see, *e.g.* s.5 and ss.68–70). Cases illustrating the point are *Tufnell* v. *Nether Whitehaugh Co.*, 1977 S.L.T. (Land Ct.) 14 and *Mackie* v. *Gardner*, 1973 S.L.T. (Land Ct.) 11. The intention of the section appears to be to make it clear that variation in the terms of leases made in pursuance of provisions of the Act does not result in the creation of a new tenancy contract.

Differing from s.10 of the 1949 Act which it replaces, the section refers to variation or revision "in pursuance of this Act" as contrasted with "in pursuance of any of the foregoing provisions of this Act in that behalf," as the 1949 provision was worded. It would appear, however, that this difference has no practical significance, the only relevant provisions being in ss.2(1), 4, 5(2) and (3), 9, 13, 14 and 15, all of which replace provisions contained within the first nine sections of the 1949 Act.

Prohibition of removal of manure, etc., after notice to quit, etc.

17. Where, in respect of an agricultural holding, notice to quit is given by the landlord or notice of intention to quit is given by the tenant, the tenant shall not, subject to any agreement to the contrary, at any time after the date of the notice, sell or remove from the holding any manure or compost, or any hay, straw or roots grown in the last year of the tenancy, unless and until he has given the landlord or the incoming tenant a reasonable opportunity of agreeing to purchase them on the termination of the tenancy at their fair market value, or at such other value as is provided by the lease.

DEFINITIONS
"agricultural holding": s.1(1).
"landlord": s.85(1).
"notice of intention to quit": s.85(1).
"notice to quit": s.85(1).
"tenant": s.85(1).
"termination of tenancy": s.85(1).

DERIVATIONS
Agricultural Holdings (Scotland) Act 1949, s.13.

GENERAL NOTE
See Gill, paras. 440–445.

As the wording of the section shows, contracting out is permissible, with the result that the terms of the lease may supersede those of the section. It is suggested by Gill (*cf.* Connell's *Agricultural Holdings (Scotland) Acts* (6th ed.) p. 122) that the words "the last year" be interpreted to mean the last calendar year of the tenant's agricultural operations, being the only basis on which, in the case of a Whitsunday outgoing, the separation of the tenant's last crop could be covered. On what constitutes "a reasonable opportunity," see *Barbour* v. *McDowall*, 1914 S.C. 844. The opportunity may be given either to the landlord or to the incoming tenant; it is not necessary that both should have it.

If the lease makes no provision for the value at which the items specified in the section are to be taken over, then, failing agreement, the matter will have to be dealt with by an arbitration under the Act if it is the landlord who is taking over. If, however, an incoming tenant is acquiring the goods, the arbitration provisions of the Act do not apply and any dispute as to value will have to be settled by a private remit to a valuer if it is not to involve litigation. The fair market value, being what the tenant could obtain for the items in question were he free to remove them, may be greater than their value for consumption on the holding (see *Williamson* v. *Stewart*, 1912 S.C. 235). If the lease provides for a take-over at valuation the arbitration will be a non-statutory one even if the landlord is the party taking over (s.61(7)).

Tenant's right to remove fixtures and buildings

18.—(1) Subject to subsections (2) to (4) below, and to section 40(4)(a) of this Act—

  (a) any engine, machinery, fencing or other fixture affixed to an agricultural holding by the tenant thereof; and

  (b) any building (other than one in respect of which the tenant is entitled to compensation under this Act or otherwise) erected by him on the holding,

not being a fixture affixed or a building erected in pursuance of some obligation in that behalf, or instead of some fixture or building belonging to the landlord, shall be removable by the tenant at any time during the continuance of the tenancy or before the expiry of 6 months, or such longer period as may be agreed, after the termination of the tenancy and shall remain his property so long as he may remove it by virtue of this subsection.

  (2) The right conferred by subsection (1) above shall not be exercisable in relation to a fixture or building unless the tenant—

  (a) has paid all rent owing by him and has performed or satisfied all his other obligations to the landlord in respect of the holding; and

  (b) has, at least one month before whichever is the earlier of the exercise of the right and the termination of the tenancy, given to the landlord notice in writing of his intention to remove the fixture or building.

  (3) If, before the expiry of the period of notice specified in subsection (2)(b) above, the landlord gives to the tenant a counter-notice in writing electing to purchase a fixture or building comprised in the notice, subsection (1) above shall cease to apply to that fixture or building, but the landlord shall be liable to pay to the tenant the fair value thereof to an incoming tenant of the holding.

  (4) In the removal of a fixture or building by virtue of subsection (1) above, the tenant shall not do to any other building or other part of the holding any avoidable damage, and immediately after the removal shall make good all damage so occasioned.

DEFINITIONS

  "agricultural holdings": s.1(1).
  "building": s.85(1).
  "landlord": s.85(1).
  "tenant": s.85(1).
  "termination of tenancy": s.85(1).

DERIVATIONS

  Agricultural Holdings (Scotland) Act 1949, s.14.

GENERAL NOTE

  See Gill, Chap. 9. (For the corresponding English provision see the Agricultural Holdings Act 1986, s.10).

Subs. (1)

  Contracting out of these provisions is permissible (see *Premier Dairies* v. *Garlick* [1920] 2 Ch. 17), but, when operative, the provisions supersede the rules of common law applying to a tenant's trade fixtures. The fixtures or buildings which the tenant is given a statutory right to remove must be additional to anything provided by the landlord at the start of the tenancy and must be affixed or erected by the tenant without obligation. The term "building" appears to be used in a wide general sense and "fixtures" is not restricted to those having an agricultural purpose. The tenant's right of removal does not apply to any building for which he will be entitled to compensation at his outgoing. It could, however, apply if the tenant has carried out during the tenancy an improvement in the form of a building without giving the landlord due notice and so is not entitled to compensation (see s.38).

Subs. (2), para. (b)

  This provision takes account of the fact that the right of removal is exercisable at any time during the tenancy and not merely at or after its termination.

Subs. (3)

  The fair value to an incoming tenant, who may be hypothetical, may be less than the outgoing tenant could obtain for the items if free to remove them. Failing agreement, the value will fall to be determined by arbitration under the Act.

Subs. (4)
At common law the prospect of damage to the heritable property being caused by the removal of a fixture could exclude the tenant's right of removal, but this provision contemplates damage being done and made good.

Payment for implements, etc., sold on quitting holding

19.—(1) Where a tenant of an agricultural holding has entered into an agreement or it is a term of the lease of the holding that the tenant will on quitting the holding, sell to the landlord or to the incoming tenant any implements of husbandry, fixtures, farm produce or farm stock on or used in connection with the holding, notwithstanding anything in the agreement or lease to the contrary, it shall be deemed to be a term of the agreement or of the lease, as the case may be, that the property in the goods shall not pass to the buyer until the price is paid and that payment of the price shall be made within one month after the tenant has quitted the holding or, if the price of the goods is to be ascertained by a valuation, within one month after the delivery of the award in the valuation.

(2) Where payment of the price is not made within one month as aforesaid the outgoing tenant shall be entitled to sell or remove the goods and to receive from the landlord or the incoming tenant, as the case may be, by whom the price was payable, compensation of an amount equal to any loss or expense unavoidably incurred by the outgoing tenant upon or in connec-tion with such sale or removal, together with any expenses reasonably incurred by him in the preparation of his claim for compensation.

(3) Any question arising as to the amount of compensation payable under subsection (2) above shall be determined by arbitration.

DEFINITIONS
 "landlord": s.85(1).
 "lease": s.85(1).
 "produce": s.85(1).
 "tenant": s.85(1).

DERIVATIONS
 Agricultural Holdings (Scotland) Act 1949, s.22.

GENERAL NOTE
 See Gill, paras. 445 and 470.

Subs. (1)
 Contracting out is prohibited. The lease or agreement will usually specify whether the sale is to be to the landlord or to the incoming tenant. In the absence of such specification the outgoing tenant has the choice and may elect to deal with the landlord as the party with the more permanent interest.

Subs. (2)
 It is indicated in Connell (*op.cit.* p. 133) that there are difficulties in applying this provision in the case of sheep stocks bound to the ground.

Subs. (3)
 Arbitration under this Act will apply if the landlord is involved but otherwise it would appear that the arbitration will be at common law.

Removal, of tenant for non-payment of rent

20.—(1) When 6 months' rent of an agricultural holding is due and unpaid, the landlord shall be entitled to raise an action of removing in the sheriff court against the tenant, concluding for his removal from the holding at the term of Whitsunday or Martinmas next ensuing after the action is raised.

(2) In an action raised under subsection (1) above, the sheriff may, unless the arrears of rent then due are paid or caution is found to his satisfaction for them, and for one year's rent further, decern the tenant to remove, and may eject him at the said term in like manner as if the lease were determined and the tenant had been legally warned to remove.

(3) A tenant of a holding removed under this section shall have the rights of an outgoing tenant to which he would have been entitled if his tenancy had terminated by operation of notice to quit or notice of intention to quit at the term when he is removed.

(4) Section 5 of chapter XV of Book L of the Codifying Act of Sederunt of June 14, 1913, anent removings, shall not apply in any case where the procedure under this section is competent.

DEFINITIONS
"agricultural holdings": s.1(1).
"landlord": s.85(1).
"notice of intention to quit": s.21(2).
"notice to quit": s.21(2).
"tenant": s.85(1).

DERIVATIONS
Agricultural Holdings (Scotland) Act 1949, s.19.

GENERAL NOTE
See Gill, paras. 272–273.

Subs. (1)
Under the Term and Quarter Days (Scotland) Act 1990, s.1(1)(a), (2)(a) the terms Whitsunday and Martinmas signify May 28 and November 28 respectively. If, as the wording of this subsection appears to indicate, a decree, when granted, must specify removal at the term specified in the crave, there may be practical difficulties if that term is reached before decree is granted.

Subs. (2)
The fact that the tenant can retain possession by paying or finding caution for the arrears at any time up to the granting of decree (see *Fletcher* v. *Fletcher*, 1932 S.L.T. (Sh. Ct.) 10 and *Westwood* v. *Keay* (1950) 66 Sh.Ct.Rep. 147) has the result that in practice the legal irritancy represented by this section is not often invoked. Where there is a lease it will usually contain a conventional irritancy which cannot be purged, or, again, the date on which the tenancy can be terminated by notice to quit may make it convenient for the landlord to proceed under s.22(2)(d).

Subs. (3)
It appears that the tenant removed under this section will be entitled to make his common-law waygoing claims as implied or expressed in the terms of the lease including compensation for improvements, provided that the statutory requirements are fulfilled. Gill (para. 272) indicates that compensation for disturbance will not be payable looking to the wording of the relevant section, now s.43(1). That view is expressed with reference to s.19 of the 1949 Act, which speaks of the tenancy terminating naturally at the appropriate term. As now worded, the subsection envisages the tenancy as terminating by the operation of notice to quit *or* notice of intention to quit. Compensation for disturbance would not be payable in the case of termination by notice of intention to quit but under s.43 is normally due where the tenant goes out in compliance with a notice to quit. Again, entitlement to compensation for disturbance may entail entitlement to an additional payment in terms of s.54.

Subs. (4)
The statutory provision now in force has superseded, in relation to rent arrears, a legal irritancy under the Act of Sederunt referred to. This applies where the tenant under an agricultural lease is one year in arrear with his rent or has deserted the holding, but is never used in present day practice.

PART III

NOTICE TO QUIT AND NOTICE OF INTENTION TO QUIT

Notice to quit and notice of intention to quit

21.—(1) Subject to section 20 of this Act and to subsections (6) and (7) below a tenancy of an agricultural holding shall not come to an end except by operation of a notice which complies with this subsection notwithstanding any agreement or any provision in the lease to the contrary.

(2) In this Act, a notice which complies with subsection (1) above is referred to as a "notice to quit" if it is given by the landlord to the tenant and as a "notice of intention to quit" if it is given by the tenant to the landlord.

(3) A notice complies with subsection (1) above if—

(a) it is in writing;

(b) it is a notice of intention to bring the tenancy to an end;

(c) where the notice is to take effect at the termination of the stipulated endurance of the lease, it is given not less than one year nor more than 2 years before that date;

(d) in the case of a lease continued in force by tacit relocation, it gives not less than one year nor more than 2 years' notice.

(4) The provisions of the Sheriff Courts (Scotland) Act 1907 relating to removings shall, in the case of an agricultural holding, have effect subject to this section.

(5) Notice to quit shall be given either—

(a) in the same manner as notice of removal under section 6 of the Removal Terms (Scotland) Act 1886; or

(b) in the form and manner prescribed by the Sheriff Courts (Scotland) Act 1907,

and such notice shall come in place of the notice required by the said Act of 1907.

(6) Nothing in this section shall affect the right of the landlord of an agricultural holding to remove a tenant whose estate has been sequestrated under the Bankruptcy (Scotland) Act 1985 or the Bankruptcy (Scotland) Act 1913, or who by failure to pay rent or otherwise has incurred irritancy of his lease or other liability to be removed.

(7) This section shall not apply—

(a) to a notice given in pursuance of a stipulation in a lease entitling the landlord to resume land for building, planting, feuing or other purposes (not being agricultural purposes); or

(b) in relation to subjects let under a lease for any period less than a year, not being a lease which by virtue of section 2 of this Act takes effect as a lease from year to year.

DEFINITIONS

"agricultural holding": s.1(1).
"agriculture": s.85(1).
"landlord": s.85(1).
"lease": s.85(1).
"tenant": s.85(1).

DERIVATIONS

Agricultural Holdings (Scotland) Act 1949, s.24.
Agriculture Act 1958, Sched. 1, Pt. II, para. 34.

GENERAL NOTE

See Gill, paras. 234–241 (resumption), 271 and 274–282 (irritancy), 283–306. (For the corresponding English provision see the Agricultural Holdings Act 1986, s.25).

Subs. (1)

This provision should be read along with s.3 concerning the continuation of leases by tacit relocation. The concluding words of this subsection make it clear that contracting out of its provisions is not permissible. "Agreement" as used in the corresponding provision, s.24(1) of the 1949 Act, has been construed as applying not only to an agreement made before the lease was entered into and to any agreement incorporated in the lease, but also to any agreement the parties may make during the currency of the tenancy. Thus in *Morrison's Executors* v. *Rendall*, 1986 S.L.T. 227 it was held that an agreement to terminate a lease otherwise than by statutory notice was invalid irrespective of when it was made as being an attempt to contract out of s.24(1) of the 1949 Act. It appears, however, that unilateral renunciation by the tenant may be effective to terminate a tenancy without statutory notice being given (see Gill, para. 250).

Subs. (2)

While in terms of subs. (5) notice to quit must conform to certain requirements in the matter of content and service, these do not apply to a notice of intention to quit. Any document making clear the tenant's intention to terminate the tenancy giving the requisite period of notice and served in conformity with the provisions of s.84 will suffice as a notice of intention to quit. The term "notice of intention to quit" appears to be an innovation in terminology but is more appropriate than the term "notice to quit" where the tenant is the party terminating the tenancy.

Subs. (3)

Notice must be given not less than one year and not more than two years before its effective date, being the date at which the contractual duration of the lease expires or at which there operates a provision for a break or an anniversary of the expiry date where tacit relocation is operating. Notice cannot be given before the commencement of the tenancy, *i.e.* before the contractual relationship of landlord and tenant has taken effect (*Lower* v. *Sorrell* [1963] 1 Q.B. 959).

Subs. (4)

The effect of this subsection is to amend, as regards the period of notice, the relevant provisions of the 1907 Act, being ss.34–38 and r.103 of the first Schedule as imported by s.39. In the case of *Milne* v. *The Earl of Seafield*, 1981 S.L.T. (Sh. Ct.) 37 a problem arose with the lease specifying a series of hand-over dates for different parts of the holding at the end of the tenancy. It was held that s.24(3) of the 1949 Act (which this subsection replaces) substituted the provisions of the 1949 Act for those of the 1907 Act not only in regard to the period of notice but also in regard to the terminus which the notice must specify, that being the termination of the lease and not, as under r.110 of the 1907 Act, the term of removal first in date if different from the date of termination.

Subs. (5)

Dealing with notices to quit, this subsection refers alternatively to s.6 of the Removal Terms (Scotland) Act 1886 and to the Sheriff Courts (Scotland) Act 1907. Section 6 of the 1886 Act provides for transmission by registered post of a notice of removal, the terms of which it does not specify. The first Schedule to the 1907 Act has been replaced by the Act of Sederunt (Ordinary Cause Rules Sheriff Court) 1983 (S.I. 1983 No. 747) as amended by the Act of Sederunt (Ordinary Cause Rules Amendment) 1983 (S.I. 1983 No. 1546). Rule 106 of the Schedule permits notice to be given by Messenger at Arms or Sheriff Officer or by registered letter. The Recorded Delivery Service Act 1962 makes recorded delivery equivalent to registered post. It has been held that any other method of giving notice to quit is ineffective even if receipt is acknowledged or could be proved. That was the view taken in the case of the *Department of Agriculture* v. *Goodfellow*, 1931 S.C. 556 where ordinary post had been used but that case was decided when the Agricultural Holdings (Scotland) Act 1923 which did not contain provisions for the service of notices, etc. as included in s.90(1) of the 1949 Act and now in s.84(1) was in force. Whatever method of service is adopted, the notice must as required by Rule 104 conform as nearly as possible to Form L (formerly H), in the Schedule. Form L has three essential elements; the subjects let, the lease or other tenancy contract, and the date of ish. The omission of any of these is fatal. Any description sufficient to identify the subjects and not in any way misleading will suffice (*Scott* v. *Livingstone*, 1919 S.C. 1). The lease must be referred to in terms which will identify it (*Rae* v. *Davidson*, 1954 S.C. 361, *Taylor* v. *Brick*, 1982 S.L.T. 25) and this may present difficulties in verbal or informal lettings where no formal lease has been entered into. The lease has to be specified as "the warrant upon which the notice is based" (*Watters* v. *Hunter*, 1927 S.C. 310 at p. 315). Where no lease exists, however, some indication of the basis of the tenancy may suffice (see *Watters* v. *Hunter*, above and *Gemmell* v. *Andrew*, 1975 S.L.T. (Land Ct.) 5). Finally, the notice must specify the ish, which, as explained with reference to subs. (3), is the date of termination of the lease and not any other date on which part of the subjects has to be vacated. Again, there may be difficulty if there is no formal lease or only some tenancy document not specifying the duration of the let. If a date of entry is specified, an ish on the anniversary of that date may be inferred (see *Morrison's Executors* v. *Rendall*, 1989 S.L.T. (Land Ct.) 89) but if neither entry nor ish is specified the date of the latter will be a matter of proof. (For a discussion of these questions with full citation of authorities see Gill (paras. 300–305)).

Subs. (6)
   This subsection preserves for the landlord, as an exception to the requirements for a notice to quit, the right to operate a conventional irritancy contained in the lease in the event of a breach by the tenant of a condition to which the irritancy applies. It is pointed out by Gill, para. 271 that in referring to the tenant's bankruptcy in this context the Act is amplifying the common law under which sequestration alone is not a ground of legal irritancy and can justify removal of the tenant only if it is the subject of a conventional irritancy. In practice, irritancy clauses tend to be framed in broad general terms covering any form of default by the tenant and in many cases listing his bankruptcy as a ground for irritancy. The significant difference between the conventional irritancy and the legal irritancy as provided for in s.20 is that the conventional irritancy, once incurred, cannot be purged (*McDouall's Trs.* v. *McLeod*, 1949 S.C. 593 and *Dorchester Studios (Glasgow)* v. *Stone*, 1975 S.C. (H.L.) 56). This, however, applies only to irritancies which are in their terms materially different from the legal irritancy which would operate by implication (*British Rail Pension Trustee Co.* v. *Wilson*, 1989 S.L.T. 340 (O.H.)). A conventional irritancy will normally provide for the lease terminating and the tenant vacating the holding immediately on its occurrence. This does not, however, permit the landlord to reclaim possession of the holding *brevi manu*. If the tenant remains in possession after being notified that an irritancy has been incurred there will need to be an action of declarator of the irritancy with a conclusion for the tenant's removal and a defence by the tenant will usually result in the action being sisted for the issues to be examined in a statutory arbitration. Unless his right to do so is excluded in terms of the lease, the tenant, on the principle of mutuality, may base a defence on some failure by the landlord to fulfil his obligations under the lease (*MacNab* v. *Willison*, 1960 S.L.T. (Notes) 25). A tenant going out in terms of a conventional irritancy will forfeit all his statutory waygoing claims and, if the terms of the lease so provide, will even be deprived of the right to reap a crop which is growing when he leaves (*Chalmers Tr.* v. *Dick's Tr.*, 1909 S.C. 761).

Subs. (7)
   Para. (a). Most formal leases give the landlord power to resume parts of the holding for purposes such as building and feuing. Provided that the resumption is not for an agricultural purpose it is exempted from the requirements of a notice to quit. While some leases purport to sanction resumption without any prior notice, it appears to be established that sufficient notice must be given to enable the tenant to make, in respect of the land resumed, such outgoing claims as have to be notified to the landlord before the land is vacated. This applies to claims arising under ss.18 (removal of fixtures and buildings), 43(4)(b) (compensation for disturbance), and 44 (High Farming), where in each case a month's notice has to be given. To allow time for preparation of the claim it is considered that the landlord should be required to give at least two months' notice of the intended resumption and although Scottish authority on the matter is lacking it appears that any provision in the lease for a period of notice insufficient to enable the tenant, if so advised, to make these claims is invalid (*Disraeli's Agreement* [1939] Ch. 382; *Coates* v. *Diment* [1957] 1 All E.R. 890). As the wording of the subsections shows, the resumption, to qualify for exemption from the notice to quit requirements, must be for a non-agricultural purpose and in the event of dispute on this point a proof will be necessary (see *Sykes* v. *Edgar*, 1974 S.L.T. (Land Ct.) 4). It is of course essential that the resumption proposed falls within the terms of the relevant clause in the lease but in any event resumption will not be permitted if it appears contrary to good faith, or, as it is sometimes put, constitutes a fraud on the lease, *e.g.* in leaving the tenant with a holding which is not a viable agricultural unit (see *Trotter* v. *Torrance*, 1891 18R 848; *Admiralty* v. *Burns*, 1910 S.C. 531; *Turner* v. *Wilson*, 1954 S.C. 296; *Glencruilten Trs.* v. *Love*, 1966 S.L.T. (Land Ct.) 5; *Fotheringham* v. *Fotheringham*, 1987 S.L.T. (Land Ct.) 10; *Thomson* v. *Murray*, 1990 S.L.T. (Land Ct.) 45).
   It has been held that the principle of mutuality in a lease does not prevent a landlord exercising a right of resumption because he is in default in his obligations under the lease (*Edmonstone* v. *Lamont*, 1975 S.L.T. (Sh. Ct.) 57).
   The compensation and other rights of a tenant part of whose holding is resumed are dealt with in ss.49(1)(b) and (2), 54(1) and (2) and 58.

Para. (*b*). This exempts from the requirements of notices to quit and notices of intention to quit short lets sanctioned by the Secretary of State and the two categories of short-term lets covered by s.2(2).

Restrictions on operation of notices to quit

22.—(1) Where not later than one month from the giving of a notice to quit an agricultural holding (or, in a case where section 23(3) of this Act applies, within the extended period therein mentioned) the tenant serves on the landlord a counter-notice in writing requiring that this subsection shall apply to the notice to quit, subject to subsection (2) below and to section 25 of this Act, the notice to quit shall not have effect unless the Land Court consent to the operation thereof.

(2) Subsection (1) above shall not apply where—

(a) the notice to quit relates to land being permanent pasture which the landlord has been in the habit of letting annually for seasonal grazing or of keeping in his own occupation and which has been let to the tenant for a definite and limited period for cultivation as arable land on the condition that he shall, along with the last or waygoing crop, sow permanent grass seeds;

(b) the notice to quit is given on the ground that the land is required for use, other than agriculture, for which permission has been granted on an application made under the enactments relating to town and country planning, or for which (otherwise than by virtue of any provision of those enactments) such permission is not required;

(c) the Land Court, on an application in that behalf made not more than 9 months before the giving of the notice to quit, were satisfied that the tenant was not fulfilling his responsibilities to farm the holding in accordance with the rules of good husbandry, and certified that they were so satisfied;

(d) at the date of the giving of the notice to quit the tenant had failed to comply with a demand in writing served on him by the landlord requiring him within 2 months from the service thereof to pay any rent due in respect of the holding, or within a reasonable time to remedy any breach by the tenant, which was capable of being remedied, of any term or condition of his tenancy which was not inconsistent with the fulfilment of his responsibilities to farm in accordance with the rules of good husbandry;

(e) at the date of the giving of the notice to quit the interest of the landlord in the holding had been materially prejudiced by a breach by the tenant, which was not capable of being remedied in reasonable time and at economic cost, of any term or condition of the tenancy which was not inconsistent with the fulfilment by the tenant of his responsibilities to farm in accordance with the rules of good husbandry;

(f) at the date of the giving of the notice to quit the tenant's apparent insolvency had been constituted in accordance with section 7 of the Bankruptcy (Scotland) Act 1985;

(g) section 25(1) of this Act applies, and the relevant notice complies with section 25(2)(a), (b) and (d) of this Act;

and, where any of paragraphs (a) to (f) above applies, the ground under the appropriate paragraph on which the notice to quit proceeds is stated in the notice.

Definitions
 "agricultural holding": s.1(1).
 "agriculture": s.85(1).
 "landlord": s.85(1).
 "notice to quit": s.21(2).
 "rules of good husbandry": s.85(2); Agriculture (Scotland) Act 1948, Sched. 6.
 "tenant": s.85(1).

DERIVATIONS
Agricultural Holdings (Scotland) Act 1949, s.25.
Agriculture Act 1958, s.3(1)(3), Sched. 1, Pt. II, para. 35.

GENERAL NOTE
See Gill, paras. 327–341, 354–357, 366–369. (For the corresponding English provision see the Agricultural Holdings Act 1986, s.26 and Sched. 3, amended in respect of Case B by the Agricultural Holdings (Amendment) Act 1990).

Subs. (1)
There is no prescribed form of counter-notice, but the notice given should disclose that this subsection is being invoked (*Luss Estate Co.* v. *Colquhoun*, 1982 S.L.C.R. 1). Examples of documents held ineffective as counter-notices are to be found in *Secretary of State* v. *Fraser*, 1954 S.L.C.R. 24; *Mountford* v. *Hodkinson* [1956] 1 W.L.R. 422 and *Taylor* v. *Brick*, 1990 S.L.T. 25. Service within the time allowed is essential (*Luss Estates Co.* v. *Colquhoun*, above).

Subs. (2)
Listed here are the various circumstances in which the consent of the Land Court to the operation of a notice to quit is not required.

Para. (*a*). The land must be permanent pasture which the landlord has been letting as such for seasonal grazing or retaining for his own use. The requirement of "a definite and limited period" means that a lease from year to year does not qualify but there is no maximum period (see *Roberts* v. *Simpson* (1954) 70 Sh.Ct.Rep. 159 and *Stirrat* v. *Whyte*, 1968 S.L.T. 157, *per* Lord Cameron at p. 163). The statutory wording should be closely followed in drafting the lease. If the lease is allowed to continue on tacit relocation the landlord cannot invoke this provision to enable him to operate a notice to quit without Land Court consent.

Para. (*b*). The land must be required at the date of the notice (*Paddock Investments* v. *Long* [1975] 236 E.G. 803; *Jones* v. *Gates* [1954] 1 W.L.R. 222) but not necessarily by the landlord (*Rugby Joint Water Board* v. *Shaw Fox*; *Rugby Joint Water Board* v. *Foottit* [1973] A.C. 202). Planning permission for a non-agricultural use must already have been applied for and granted unless the proposed use is permissible irrespective of the Planning Acts, *e.g.* where it is not a development or is to be undertaken by the Crown. Where the authority for the proposed use is a development order, special or general, an application for Land Court consent founding on s.24(1)(e) will be the appropriate course. While an outline planning permission is sufficient for the purposes of this paragraph (*Paddock Investments* v. *Lang*, above; *Dow Agrochemicals* v. *Lane (E.A.) (North Lynn)* [1965] 192 E.G. 737) it appears to depend on the circumstances whether permission not covering the entire holding will suffice. As to specialities in applications for planning consent affecting agricultural holdings, see Gill, paras. 332–333).

Para. (*c*). Section 26 contains the procedure for obtaining a Certificate of Bad Husbandry from the Land Court. This paragraph enables the landlord to use the Certificate as a means of operating a notice to quit without Land Court consent. The notice to quit has to be served not later than nine months after the application for the Certificate is made but cannot be served before the Certificate is obtained. As to the reasoning underlying the timing of these steps, see *Macnabb* v. *A. J. Anderson*, 1955 S.C. 38, *per* Lord Patrick at p. 44.

Para. (*d*). The rent demand must be explicit and must be accurate as regards the parties and the amount of the rent which must be already due. As a result of the Term and Quarter Days (Scotland) Act 1990, s.(1), rents payable half-yearly or quarterly will in future fall due on the 28th of the respective months unless the lease specifies otherwise. On the expiry of the two-month period (but not earlier), the landlord may issue a notice to quit founding on the paragraph (*Macnabb* v. *A. J. Anderson* above, at p. 45). Payment of the rent after the expiry of the two-month period, whether before or after the issue of the notice to quit, is of no effect. (*Stoneman* v. *Brown* [1973] 1 W.L.R. 459; *Price* v. *Romilly* [1960] 1 W.L.R. 1360 at p. 1361). If the rent demand is invalid in any respect the notice to quit will be ineffective, provided that the tenant has demanded arbitration in accordance with s.23(2).

The demand to remedy can apply to a breach of any of the conditions of tenancy implied in the case of an oral or informal let or expressed in a formal lease, always provided that the condition in question is consistent with the rules of good husbandry as statutorily defined. The demand must be in clear and unambiguous terms for it to form the ground of a notice to quit. It does not, like a demand for rent, have to specify a time for compliance, but any time limit it prescribes must be reasonable for the action required to be taken and where no time is specified in the demand the question of fact will be whether the interval between the demand and the notice to quit has been in the circumstances reasonable (see *Pentland* v. *Hart*, 1967 S.L.T.

(Land Ct.) 2 and *Nicholls Trs.* v. *Maclarty*, 1971 S.L.C.R. 85. The breach must be one which is capable of being remedied, in contrast with the situation provided for in para. (e) dealing with an irremediable breach.

It appears that default in payment of rent or in remedying a breach as contemplated in this paragraph cannot, like an irritancy legal or conventional, be met with the plea that the landlord is in default in some obligation affecting him (*Wilson Clarke* v. *Graham*, 1963 S.L.T. (Sh. Ct.) 2) except where, in the case of a demand to remedy, the landlord's default is in some way preventing the tenant from taking the necessary action (*Shepherd* v. *Lomas* [1963] 1 W.L.R. 962).

Demands to remedy relating to the maintenance and repair of fixed equipment are the subject of special provisions contained in ss.32 and 66.

Para. (e). Examples of irremediable breaches as referred to in this paragraph are felling of timber contrary to the terms of the lease and without the landlord's consent or the neglect to maintain buildings or other structures, so that they collapse or disintegrate. As under para. (d), the condition breached must be consistent with the rules of good husbandry.

While paras. (d) and (e) are mutually exclusive, instances of both categories of breach may be present at the same time on a holding, in which case the landlord, after the expiry of his demand to remedy the remediable breaches, may serve a notice to quit founded on both categories of breach, provided that it discriminates in its terms between the breaches coming under the respective paragraphs and contains the necessary statement in each case (*MacNab* v. *Anderson*, 1957 S.C. 213).

In a case coming under para. (e) (but not in one coming under para. (d)) the Succession (Scotland) Act 1964, s.16(6)(b) as amended in terms of Sched. 11, para. 24(b), gives the arbiter a discretion as regards making an order in favour of the landlord where the tenancy interest is held by an executor.

Para. (f). Under s.7 of the 1985 Act, apparent insolvency is constituted in various ways, are being the granting of a trust deed for creditors, but in cases falling within s.7(1)(c) of that Act the debtor can disprove his apparent insolvency by showing that at the material time he was able and willing to pay his debts as they fell due (*cf. Murray* v. *Nisbet*, 1967 S.L.T. (Land Ct.) 14, a case dealt with under s.5 of the now-repealed Bankruptcy (Scotland) Act 1913). Para. (f) applies even if the tenant was apparently insolvent when the tenancy commenced (*cf. Hart* v. *Cameron* (1935) 51 Sh.Ct.Rep. 166).

It may be noted here that the section concludes with a statement that where any of the paras. (a) to (f) applies, the ground under the appropriate paragraph on which the notice to quit proceeds is to be stated in the notice. This requirement should be complied with in explicit terms, reproducing, or at least closely following, the wording of the relevant paragraph.

Para. (g). This relates to a notice to quit complying with the basic requirement of such a notice (see s.25(2)(a), referring to s.21) given to a tenant who is a legatee or intestate successor of a former tenant (see s.25(1)) and specifying an effective date complying with s.25(2)(b), the successor tenant not being a near relative of his predecessor and having acquired right to the lease after August 1, 1958.

Since the coming into force of s.6 of the Agriculture Act 1958 on August 1, 1958, the security of tenure given to agricultural tenants has not extended to their successors other than those who qualify as near relatives under provisions introduced in 1968. Provided that a notice to quit is issued to a successor other than a near relative of the late tenant, having its effective date within the time limits prescribed in s.25(2)(b), Land Court consent to its operation is not required.

Under s.6(3) of the 1958 Act the notice to quit had to contain a statement that it was given under that subsection. This requirement was not included when the 1958 provision was replaced by the Agricultural Holdings (Amendment) (Scotland) Act 1983 and does not appear in the present Act. The omission seems unfortunate, but it is apparently assumed that a successor tenant, other than a near relative, who receives a notice to quit should appreciate from the timing of its effective date that it is being given by virtue of para. (g) of this section. See also Gill, 360.

Consent by Land Court or arbitration on notices to quit

23.—(1) An application by a landlord for the consent of the Land Court under section 22 of this Act to the operation of a notice to quit shall be made within one month after service on the landlord by the tenant of a counter-notice requiring that subsection (1) of that section shall apply to the notice to quit.

(2) A tenant who has been given a notice to quit in connection with which any question arises under section 22(2) of this Act shall, if he requires such question to be determined by arbitration under this Act, give notice to the

landlord to that effect within one month after the notice to quit has been served on him.

(3) Where the award of the arbiter in an arbitration required under subsection (2) above is such that section 22(1) of this Act would have applied to the notice to quit if a counter-notice had been served within the period provided for in that subsection, that period shall be extended up to the expiry of one month from the issue of the arbiter's award.

(4) Where such an arbitration as is referred to in subsection (2) above has been required by the tenant, or where an application has been made to the Land Court for their consent to the operation of a notice to quit, the operation of the notice to quit shall be suspended until the issue of the arbiter's award or of the decision of the Land Court, as the case may be.

(5) Where the decision of the Land Court giving their consent to the operation of a notice to quit, or the award of the arbiter in such an arbitration as is referred to in subsection (2) above, is issued at a date later than 6 months before the date on which the notice to quit is expressed to take effect, the Land Court, on application made to them in that behalf at any time not later than one month after the issue of the decision or award aforesaid, may postpone the operation of the notice to quit for a period not exceeding 12 months.

(6) If the tenant of an agricultural holding receives from the landlord notice to quit the holding or a part thereof and in consequence thereof gives to a sub-tenant notice to quit that holding or part, section 22(1) of this Act shall not apply to the notice given to the sub-tenant; but if the notice to quit given to the tenant by the landlord does not have effect, then the notice to quit given by the tenant to the sub-tenant shall not have effect.

(7) For the purposes of subsection (6) above, a notice to quit part of the holding which under section 30 of this Act is accepted by the tenant as notice to quit the entire holding shall be treated as a notice to quit the holding.

(8) Where notice is served on the tenant of an agricultural holding to quit the holding or a part thereof, being a holding or part which is subject to a sub-tenancy, and the tenant serves on the landlord a counter-notice in accordance with section 22(1) of this Act, the tenant shall also serve on the sub-tenant notice in writing that he has served such counter-notice on the landlord and the sub-tenant shall be entitled to be a party to any proceedings before the Land Court for their consent to the notice to quit.

DEFINITIONS
 "agricultural holdings": s.1(1).
 "landlord": s.85(1).
 "lease": s.85(1).
 "notice to quit": s.85(1).
 "tenant": s.85(1).

DERIVATIONS
 Agricultural Holdings (Scotland) Act 1949, s.27.
 Agriculture Act 1958, Sched. 1, Pt. II, para. 37.

GENERAL NOTE
 See Gill, paras. 49–52 (Sub-tenants), 320–326 (Tenants' response to quit notice), 362–365, 370–374 (Landlord's application to Land Court) and 410 (Postponement of operation of notice to quit).

Subs. (1)
 The time limit is strictly enforced and cannot be extended (*Still* v. *Reid*, 1957 S.L.C.R. 16; *Gemmell* v. *Hodge*, 1974 S.L.T. (Land Ct.) 2). The application is made on a form provided by the Land Court.

Subs. (2)
 When notice to quit is given on any of the grounds provided in paras. (a) to (f) of s.22(2) the

ground will be stated in the notice and the tenant, if disputing the relevant facts, must call for arbitration within a month of receiving the notice.

Subs. (3)

A counter-notice is incompetent and of no effect as an initial response to a s.22(2) notice to quit, but if the arbitration called for by the tenant results in a decision in his favour the notice becomes one to which s.22(1) applies. Accordingly the tenant is given a month from the arbiter's decision to serve a counter-notice. There has been some question as to whether a landlord can proceed on a notice referring to s.22(2) on the basis that s.22(1) applies to the notice without the notice having indicated that he is to claim that right should the arbiter decide against him, but the better view appears to be that he can do so (see Gill, para. 364). Accordingly, the tenant who has succeeded in an arbitration on a s.22(2) notice should exercise his right to serve a counter-notice unless he is satisfied that the landlord is not to proceed further on the notice to quit.

Subss. (4) and (5)

These subsections make provision for delay taking place in the issue of the Land Court decision or the arbiter's award. Initially the operation of the notice to quit is suspended pending the issue of the decision so that the tenant may have a fair opportunity to adjust his farming activities but the Land Court is given a discretion where the award or decision is issued less than six months before the effective date of the notice to quit to postpone the operation of the notice for not more than 12 months. The application for postponement must be made not later than a month after the issue of the decision or award but may be made before its issue (*Moffat* v. *Young*, 1975 S.L.C.R. App. 98) and the postponement may be granted after the operative date of the notice has passed (*Allan-Fraser's Trs.* v. *Macpherson* 1981 S.L.T. (Land Ct.) 17).

Subs. (6)

Only a limited measure of protection is given by the Act to sub-tenants, even where, contrary to the legal implication in agricultural tenancies, sub-letting is permitted by the lease or authorised by the landlord. This subsection has the result that if the tenant, having received a notice to quit from the landlord, gives notice to quit to the sub-tenant, the latter must comply with that notice, but if for any reason the landlord's notice does not take effect the sub-tenant can ignore the notice he received from the tenant. The vulnerability of the sub-tenant has sometimes been used in a device to avoid the tenant's security of tenure, a nominee of the landlord taking the tenancy and sub-letting to the party who is to farm the holding. Since the decision of the Court of Appeal in *Gisbourne* v. *Burton* [1988] 3 W.L.R. 921, treating the occupant of the farm, who was a sub-tenant of the landlord's wife, as the true tenant, this device seems likely to fall out of use.

Subs. (7)

This refers to the option given by s.30 to a tenant who has to comply with a notice to quit covering part only of the holding, to treat the notice as affecting the whole holding. If this option is exercised any sub-lets there may be are terminated.

Subs. (8)

It is clear that sub-tenants have a concern with any action the tenant may take to prevent the operation of a notice to quit issued by the landlord. Accordingly, sub-tenants have to be notified that a counter-notice has been served and they are entitled to be parties to the ensuing proceedings in the Land Court.

Consents for purposes of section 22

24.—(1) Subject to subsection (2) below and to section 25(3) of this Act, the Land Court shall consent under section 22 of this Act to the operation of a notice to quit an agricultural holding or part of an agricultural holding if, but only if, they are satisfied as to one or more of the following matters, being a matter or matters specified by the landlord in his application for their consent—

    (a) that the carrying out of the purpose for which the landlord proposes to terminate the tenancy is desirable in the interests of good husbandry as respects the land to which the notice relates, treated as a separate unit;

    (b) that the carrying out thereof is desirable in the interests of sound management of the estate of which that land consists or forms part;

(c) that the carrying out thereof is desirable for the purposes of agricultural research, education, experiment or demonstration, or for the purposes of the enactments relating to allotments, smallholdings or such holdings as are referred to in section 64 of the Agriculture (Scotland) Act 1948;

(d) that greater hardship would be caused by withholding than by giving consent to the operation of the notice;

(e) that the landlord proposes to terminate the tenancy for the purpose of the land being used for a use, other than for agriculture, not falling within section 22(2)(b) of this Act.

(2) Notwithstanding that they are satisfied as aforesaid, the Land Court shall withhold consent to the operation of the notice to quit if in all the circumstances it appears to them that a fair and reasonable landlord would not insist on possession.

(3) Where the Land Court consent to the operation of a notice to quit they may (subject to section 25(4) of this Act) impose such conditions as appear to them requisite for securing that the land to which the notice relates will be used for the purpose for which the landlord proposes to terminate the tenancy.

(4) Where, on an application by the landlord in that behalf the Land Court are satisfied that by reason of any change of circumstances or otherwise any condition imposed under subsection (3) above ought to be varied or revoked, they shall vary or revoke the condition accordingly.

DEFINITIONS

"agricultural holding": s.1(1).
"agriculture": s.85(1).
"good estate management": s.85(2); Agriculture (Scotland) Act 1948, Sched. 5.
"good husbandry": s.85(2); Agriculture (Scotland) Act 1948, Sched. 6.
"landlord": s.85(1).
"notice to quit": s.21(2).
"tenant": s.85(1).

DERIVATIONS

Agricultural Holdings (Scotland) Act 1949, s.26.
Agricultural Holdings (Amendment) (Scotland) Act 1983, s.4(1).
Agriculture Act 1958, s.3(2)(3) and Sched. 1, Pt. II, para. 36.

GENERAL NOTE

See Gill, paras. 375–390. (For the corresponding English provision see the Agricultural Holding Act 1986, s.27).

Subs. (1)

This subsection sets out the five grounds on any one of which the Land Court may consent to the operation of a notice to quit. The ground or grounds on which the landlord is to found have to be specified in the application made by him under s.23(1) but in many cases the ground will already have been disclosed in the notice to quit in compliance with s.55 in order to obtain exemption from the additional payment to which outgoing tenants may be entitled in terms of s.54. The onus is, of course, on the landlord to satisfy the court on at least one ground.

Para. (a). Here the landlord must demonstrate that he has proposals for the use of the holding as an agricultural unit by himself, or by a tenant of his selection, which will represent a material improvement on the management of the holding as farmed by the tenant, particularly in such respects as productive capacity or future fertility (*Clark* v. *Smith*, 1981 S.L.C.R. 84; *Prior* v. *J. & A. Henderson*, 1984 S.L.T. (Land Ct.) 51). He is not required to prove that the tenant is inefficient or has been guilty of bad husbandry but what he must show is that under his proposed régime there will be a material improvement in the farming of the holding. In support of the case he may adduce evidence of his own, or his prospective tenants, standard of farming on some other farm.

The concluding words of the paragraph, however, make it clear that in arriving at their decision the court must consider the issue of good husbandry in relation to the holding itself treated as a separate unit (*Clark* v. *Smith*, above) and not, as the landlord may envisage it, as part of some larger unit produced by amalgamation (*Clark* v. *Smith*, above; *Austin* v. *Gibson*, 1979 S.L.T. (Land Ct.) 12).

Para. (*b*). It seems to be open to question whether there is any significant difference between sound estate management as referred to in this paragraph and the landlord's duty of good estate management as described in the Schedule to the 1948 Act. It appears that management in this context is referred to in a physical rather than in a financial sense (*National Coal Board* v. *Naylor* [1972] 1 W.L.R. 908). The important difference from the ground for consent in para. (*a*) is that this paragraph involves consideration of the management situation in relation to the rest of the landlord's estate where such exists (*Peace* v. *Peace*, 1984 S.L.T. (Land Ct.) 6 at p. 7; *cf. Leask* v. *Gairns*, 1981 S.L.T. (Land Ct.) 11) although the paragraph is capable of application where the estate comprises the holding alone (*National Coal Board* v. *Naylor*, above).

Para. (*c*). There appears to be no recent instance of this ground for consent being invoked. The report in the case of *Edinburgh University* v. *Craik*, 1954 S.C. 190 involving an application for consent under the corresponding provision in the 1949 Act deals only with questions of procedure arising under the statutory provisions then in force. The paragraph seems to envisage a consideration by the court of the relative desirability in the public interest of the use of the holding for agriculture on the one hand and its use for one or more of the purposes indicated on the other.

Para. (*d*). As the copious citation of authorities in Gill (paras. 384–389) indicates, hardship is the most frequently invoked ground of consent and indeed is often invoked by landlords, along with one or more of the other grounds listed. Here it is possible to mention only some of the main conclusions which can be drawn from the decided cases. The onus is, of course, on the landlord to demonstrate that he will suffer greater hardship than the tenant from an adverse decision. In most cases there will be elements of hardship on both sides and it is for the Land Court to decide whether the landlord has demonstrated the greater hardship. Two cases which were concerned not with the consent to operation of a notice to quit but with the intimation of hardship to be given in that notice to avoid the landlord's being liable to the tenant for reorganisation compensation in accordance with provisions now contained in ss.54 and 55, must be taken as confirming that the mere fact of being unable to recover possession does not constitute hardship to the landlord (see *Graham* v. *Lamont*, 1971 S.C. 170 and *Copeland* v. *McQuaker*, 1973 S.L.T. 186, particularly the opinion of Sheriff Principal Maxwell, Q.C. (whose decision was sustained on appeal) at p. 190). While hardship is normally related to individuals, it may be pled by a company, a firm or a body of trustees who are in the position of landlords. Again, while hardship is normally personal to the parties involved in the proceedings, the effect of the decision on other parties such as employees, if not too remotely related to the tenancy, may be taken into consideration. A landlord's hardship may be minimised by balancing considerations such as the financial liabilities he would incur on the termination of the tenancy in payment of outgoing claims or the taking over of a bound sheep stock, or again by the fact he has purchased the farm with a tenant in possession, of whose security of tenure he must be regarded as having been aware, or, again, if he has acquired a tenanted farm gratuitously as opposed to purchasing it on the market. Also, in some cases the landlord's plea of hardship may fail because he has means of mitigating it otherwise than by terminating the tenancy.

Para. (*e*). It is necessary to appreciate the distinction between this provision and the provision contained in s.22(2)(b). That provision applies where planning permission for a non-agricultural use has already been granted or is not required otherwise than by virtue of any provision in the Planning Act. This provision applies when the proposed non-agricultural use is one for which permission is not required by reason of a particular provision in the Planning Act, an example being afforestation (see the Town and Country Planning (Scotland) Act 1972, s.19(2)(e), and *Carnegie* v. *Davidson*, 1966 S.L.T. (Land Ct.) 3). The tenant receiving and desiring to resist a notice to quit given in terms of s.22(2)(b) must call for arbitration on the statement in the notice. On the other hand, when a landlord invokes s.24(1)(e) and receives counter-notice from the tenant, the Land Court's consent to the operation of the notice to quit is required although with the merits and practicability of the landlord's proposals not being relevant, defence by the tenant will be difficult unless based on subs. (2) (*Carnegie* v. *Davidson*, above). As will be seen from the provisions of s.55, this ground of consent differs from the other grounds of consent in s.24 in relation to the tenant's entitlement to the additional payment for which s.54 provides.

Subs. (2)

This subsection takes the place of a proviso in identical terms which qualified s.26(1) of the 1949 Act. While a tenant must give notice in his pleadings if he is found on this provision, the plea is frequently taken either along with another defence by the tenant or by itself. The number of reported instances of it succeeding is, however, limited. It would seem to be difficult to envisage it doing so where the court has found in the landlord's favour on hardship. Even a fair and reasonable landlord could hardly be expected to insist on possession when he had satisfied the court that he would have sustained the greater hardship from an adverse decision. There are, however, cases of the plea succeeding against landlords seeking the court's consent on grounds other than hardship, the court's discretion in the matter being unlimited and enabling it to consider hardship although that had not been in issue as a ground of the landlord's application. In *Carnegie* v. *Davidson*, above, where consent was sought for afforestation under the equivalent of s.24(1)(e), the court, holding that the success of the landlord's scheme was "problematic" and that the landlord had another area equally suitable for the purpose, applied the proviso, as it then was, in favour of the tenant who was farming efficiently. Again in *Altyre Estate Trs.* v. *McLay*, 1975 S.L.T. (Land Ct.) 12, where the landlord was held to have succeeded under the equivalent of s.24(1)(b) *i.e.* on grounds of sound estate management, the tenant, an efficient farmer who would have suffered substantial loss if dispossessed and who was willing to take on the other farm with which amalgamation was proposed, invoked the plea successfully. More recently, the plea succeeded in the case of *Trustees of the Main Calthorpe Settlement* v. *Calder*, 1988 S.L.T. (Land Ct.) 30, a case of a near relative successor tenant occupying other agricultural land, involving the equivalent of Case 3 of Sched. 2 as the ground for consent in terms of s.25. The tenancy had been in the family and the holding efficiently farmed for many years and its addition as proposed to the landlord's other land was considered likely to make only a marginal addition to the efficiency of the unit.

Subs. (3)
   This provision, which entitles the Land Court to attach conditions to its consent so as to ensure that the landlord uses the holding for the purposes stated in his application, may be regarded as a means of testing the good faith and veracity of the landlord in seeking consent to the operation of his notice to quit. The qualification referring to s.25(4) takes account of the fact that in certain amalgamation proposals affecting successor tenants, attachment of conditions to the consent is mandatory. A question may be said to arise whether the power is confined to cases of consent given in respect of applications under paras. (a), (b), (c) or (e) of subs. (1) and does not apply where hardship is the ground on which consent is given. Hardship applications, however, will nearly always disclose the landlord's proposals for the holding and in a number of instances conditions have been attached to the consent accordingly (see, *e.g. Robertson* v. *Lindsay*, 1957 S.L.C.R. 3; *Shaw-Mackenzie* v. *Forbes* 1957 S.L.C.R. 34; *Graham* v. *Lamont*, 1970 S.L.T. (Land Ct.) 100). The sanction for breach of conditions imposed under this section is to be found in s.27.

Subs. (4)
   This takes account of the fact that conditions as attached to consent may subsist for a substantial period, during which there may be a significant change in circumstances.

Termination of tenancies acquired by succession

   25.—(1) This section applies where notice to quit is duly given to the tenant of an agricultural holding who acquired right to the lease of the holding—
   (a) under section 16 of the Succession (Scotland) Act 1964; or
   (b) as a legatee, under section 11 of this Act.
   (2) Notice to quit is duly given to a tenant to whom this section applies if—
   (a) it complies with section 21 of this Act; and
   (b) it specifies as its effective date—
         (i) where, when he acquired right to the lease, the unexpired period of the lease exceeded 2 years, the term of outgo stipulated in the lease;
         (ii) where, when he acquired right to the lease, the unexpired period was 2 years or less, the term of outgo stipulated in the lease or the corresponding date in any subsequent year, being a date not less than one nor more than 3 years after the said acquisition;
   (c) where he was a near relative of the deceased tenant from whom he acquired right, it specifies the Case set out in Schedule 2 to this Act under which it is given; and
   (d) where he was not a near relative of the deceased tenant from whom he acquired right, he acquired right to the lease after August 1, 1958.

(3) Section 22(1) of this Act shall apply and section 24 of this Act shall not apply where subsection (2)(c) above applies and notice to quit is duly given in accordance with subsection (2)(a) to (c) above; and in such a case the Land Court shall consent to the operation of a notice duly given—
(a) where the holding was let before January 1, 1984, if they are satisfied that the circumstances are as specified in any Case set out in Part I of Schedule 2 to this Act;
(b) where the holding was let on or after that date and the notice specifies any of Cases 4, 5 or 7 in that Schedule, unless the tenant satisfies them that the circumstances are not as specified in that Case (provided that, for the purposes of Case 7, the tenant shall not be required to prove that he is not the owner of any land);
(c) where the holding was let on or after that date, if they are satisfied that the circumstances are as specified in Case 6 in that Schedule;
except that where any of Cases 1, 2, 3, 6 or 7 in that Schedule is specified, the Court shall withhold consent on that ground if it appears to them that a fair and reasonable landlord would not insist on possession.
(4) Where consent is given because the circumstances are as specified in Case 2 or 6 in Schedule 2 to this Act, the Land Court shall impose such conditions as appear to them necessary to secure that the holding to which the notice relates will, within 2 years after the termination of the tenancy, be amalgamated with the land specified in the notice; and section 27 of this Act shall, with any necessary modifications, apply to a condition imposed under this subsection as that section applies to a condition imposed under section 24 of this Act.
(5) Part III of Schedule 2 to this Act shall have effect for the purposes of interpretation of this section and that Schedule.

DEFINITIONS
"agricultural holding": s.1(1).
"amalgamation": Sched. 2, Pt. III.
"landlord": s.85(1).
"lease": s.85(1).
"near relative": Sched. 2, Pt. III.
"notice to quit": s.21(2).
"tenant": s.85(1).

DERIVATIONS
Agricultural Holdings (Scotland) Act 1949, s.26A.
Agricultural Holdings (Amendment) (Scotland) Act 1983, ss.3, 4(2).

GENERAL NOTE
See Gill, paras. 358–361, 363.

Subs. (1)
Section 22(2)(g) excludes from the requirement of Land Court consent to its operation a notice to quit to which this section applies, *i.e.* a notice given to a successor, testate or intestate, of a former tenant, which complies with the conditions of subs. (2)(a)(b) and (d).

Subs. (2)
Firstly, under para. (a) the notice to quit must comply with the requirements of s.21.
Secondly, under para. (b) the notice has to be given for an effective date within the time limits prescribed. Under the 1949 Act as it originally stood, a successor, testate or intestate, had the same security of tenure as his predecessor. The 1958 Act changed the position in this respect by permitting the landlord to terminate the tenancy of a successor provided that he did so within certain time limits, disregard of which put the successor in the same position as his predecessor. These time limits run from the successor's acquisition of the tenancy which for the legatee or testate successor will normally be the date of the former tenant's death but in the case of the intestate successor that of his acquisition from the executor. If the lease when acquired by the successor tenant has more than two years to run, it must be terminated at the date of its expiry. Where the unexpired period is shorter, termination may be at the date of expiry or the

corresponding date in any subsequent year not less than one nor more than three years after the acquisition.

Consistently with these requirements, the notice may be given for a break in the lease occurring not less than a year after the acquisition.

Thirdly, under para. (d) the recipient of the notice must have acquired a right to the lease after August 1, 1958, when the 1958 Act took effect, and must not be within the category of near relatives of the former tenant as defined for purposes of the Act in Sched. 2, Pt. III, para. 1. The remaining subsections are concerned with the position of the near relative successor who since the passing of the 1968 Act has had security of tenure like his predecessor, but subject to the qualification that his tenancy may be terminated on any one of a number of special grounds now set out in Sched. 2 to this Act, provided that the necessary action is taken by the landlord within the time limits specified in subs. (2)(b).

Subs. (3)

This prescribes the procedure applicable where notice to quit is given to a successor within the statutory category of a near relative of the late tenant. Differing in this respect from a notice to quit given to a successor outwith that category, this notice is affected by s.22(1) and so requires Land Court consent for its operation if counter-notice is served. Provided, however, that he complies with the time limits prescribed in subs. (2)(b), the grounds on which a landlord may apply for consent are not restricted to those specified in s.24(1) but include the additional grounds contained in Sched. 2 which apply only to tenancies held by near relative successors. To found on any of these grounds the landlord must give a notice to quit complying with s.25(2)(a) to (c), *i.e.* fulfilling (1) the basic requirements of s.21 for all notices to quit; (2) the requirements of s.25(2)(b) as regards its effective date; and (3) the requirement of s.25(2)(c) by specifying the Case set out in Sched. 2 under which it is given. Sched. 2 distinguishes between holdings according to whether they were or were not let before January 1, 1984, the 1983 Act having made changes effective from that date. The three Cases in Pt. I of the Schedule apply to pre-1984 tenancies and in these cases the onus of satisfying the court is on the landlord. The four Cases in Pt. II of the Schedule apply to tenancies originating from 1984 onwards. In Case 6 the onus rests on the landlord in the usual way. In Cases 4, 5 or 7, however, it is for the tenant to satisfy the court that the circumstances are not as specified in the Case founded on, but where Case 7 is invoked the tenant is not to be required to prove that he is not the owner of any land. Except where consent is sought under Case 4 or Case 5, it is in the court's discretion to withhold consent on the fair and reasonable landlord plea.

For details of the Cases and comments thereon, reference should be made to Sched. 2 and the annotations thereto.

Subs. (4)

Cases 2 and 6 in the Schedule each involve a proposal by the landlord to use the holding for amalgamation with certain other land within two years of the tenancy ending. In these cases it has been considered appropriate to make mandatory the attachment to the Land Court's consent of conditions which will secure that the amalgamation, as projected, takes place within that period.

Subs. (5)

Part III of Sched. 2 contains, *inter alia*, the definition of "near relative" as meaning a surviving spouse or child, natural or adopted, of the deceased tenant.

Certificates of bad husbandry

26.—(1) For the purposes of section 22(2)(c) of this Act, the landlord of an agricultural holding may apply to the Land Court for a certificate that the tenant is not fulfilling his responsibilities to farm in accordance with the rules of good husbandry, and the Land Court, if satisfied that the tenant is not fulfilling his said responsibilities, shall grant such a certificate.

(2) In determining whether to grant a certificate under this section, the Land Court shall disregard any practice adopted by the tenant in compliance with any obligation imposed on him by or accepted by him under section 31B of the Control of Pollution Act 1974.

DEFINITIONS
"agricultural holding": s.1(1).
"landlord": s.85(1).
"rules of good husbandry": s.85(2); Agriculture (Scotland) Act 1948, Sched. 6.
"tenant": s.85(1).

DERIVATIONS
Agricultural Holdings (Scotland) Act 1949, s.28.
Agriculture Act 1958, Sched. 1, Pt. II, para. 38.
Water Act 1989, Sched. 25, para. 12.

GENERAL NOTE
See Gill, paras. 107–114 and 169. (For the corresponding English provision see the Agricultural Holdings Act 1986, Sched. 3, Pt. II, para. 9).

Subs. (1)
The Certificate, if obtained, enables the landlord, in accordance with s.22(2)(c), to serve within the prescribed time limit of nine months a notice to quit for the operation of which Land Court consent is not required. In making his application for a Certificate, the landlord must specify the husbandry rules on the breach of which he is to found and he must adduce convincing evidence to discharge the onus of proof (see, *e.g. McGill* v. *Bichan*, 1982 S.L.C.R. 33 and *Austin* v. *Gibson*, 1977 S.L.T. (Land Ct.) 12). A proof is required even if the application is unopposed (*Buchanan* v. *Buchanan*, 1983 S.L.T. (Land Ct.) 31) and the court's inspection of the holding, which may have to take place more than once, is a crucial element (*Rae* v. *Pringle*, 1990 Borders R.N. 27). In a recently reported case (*Cambusmore Estate Trs.* v. *Little*, 1991 S.L.T. (Land Ct.) 33), the court, having found that a definite breach of r. 1 of the Rules of Good Husbandry (which requires, *inter alia*, a reasonable standard of efficient production to be maintained with the unit kept in a condition to enable such a standard to be attained in future) had occurred, granted the Certificate, holding that the words "other relevant circumstances" as used in that rule were restricted to circumstances relating to the unit itself and its production and did not include mitigating factors relating to the tenant's personal circumstances. A tenant's breach may, however, be excused if it has been materially contributed to by the landlord's breach of the rules of good estate management as contained in Sched. 5 to the 1948 Act (*Austin* v. *Gibson* and *Buchanan* v. *Buchanan*, above) but the fact that the landlord is entitled to remedy the tenant's breach of the lease at his own hand does not debar him from claiming a Certificate based on such a breach (*Halliday* v. *Ferguson*, 1961 S.C. 24).

Subs. (2)
This replaces the proviso added to s.28 of the 1949 Act by the Water Act 1989, s.190, and Sched. 25, para. 12. Section 31(B) of the Control of Pollution Act 1974, as amended in terms of Sched. 11, para. 39, contains special provisions operative in an area designated as a nitrate-sensitive area (see Gill, para. 169).

Penalty for breach of condition

27.—(1) Where, on giving consent under section 22 of this Act to the operation of a notice to quit an agricultural holding or part of an agricultural holding, the Land Court imposes a condition under section 24(3) of this Act, and it is proved, on an application to the Land Court on behalf of the Crown that the landlord—

(a) has failed to comply with the condition within the period allowed, or
(b) has acted in breach of the condition,

the Land Court may impose on the landlord a penalty of an amount not exceeding 2 years' rent of the holding at the rate at which rent was payable immediately before the termination of the tenancy, or, where the notice to quit related to a part only of the holding, of an amount not exceeding the proportion of the said 2 years' rent which it appears to the Land Court is attributable to that part.

(2) A penalty imposed under this section shall be a debt due to the Crown and shall, when recovered, be paid into the Consolidated Fund.

DEFINITIONS
"agricultural holdings": s.1(1).
"landlord": s.85(1).
"notice to quit": s.21(2).
"termination of tenancy": s.85(1).

DERIVATIONS
Agricultural Holdings (Scotland) Act 1989, s.30.
Agriculture Act 1958, Sched. 1, Pt. II, para. 40.

GENERAL NOTE
See Gill, para. 411. (For the corresponding English provision see the Agricultural Holdings
Act 1986, s.27 (6)–(9)).

Subs. (1)
This enables the Land Court, on an application on behalf of the Crown, to impose a penalty
for breach by a landlord of conditions attached by the court in giving consent to a notice to quit
in exercise of the power given them by s.24(3) or in compliance with the direction in s.25(4).

Subs. (2)
The penalty, which will be recoverable by civil diligence, belongs to the Crown and it is not
available to compensate the tenant who may be deprived of his tenancy unjustly. It may be
questionable if, in practice, the maximum penalty of two years' rent represents a sufficient
deterrent. Before its amendment in 1958, s.30 of the 1949 Act empowered the Secretary of
State to take possession of the land affected by a breach.

Effect on notice to quit of sale of holding

28.—(1) This section shall apply where a contract for the sale of the
landlord's interest in land which comprises or forms part of an agricultural
holding is made after the giving of a notice to quit and before its expiry.

(2) Unless, within the period of 3 months ending with the date on which a
contract to which this section applies is made, the landlord and the tenant
have agreed in writing whether or not the notice to quit shall continue to
have effect—
  (a) the landlord shall—
          (i) within 14 days after the making of the contract; or
          (ii) before the expiry of the notice to quit,
      whichever is the earlier, give notice to the tenant of the making of the
      contract; and
  (b) the tenant may, before the expiry of the notice to quit and not later
      than one month after he has received notice under paragraph (a)
      above, give notice in writing to the landlord that he elects that the
      notice to quit shall continue to have effect.

(3) Where this section applies, unless—
  (a) the landlord and tenant have agreed that the notice to quit shall
      continue to have effect;
  (b) the tenant has so elected, under subsection (2)(b) above; or
  (c) the landlord having failed to give notice of the making of the contract
      in accordance with subsection (2)(a) above, the tenant quits the
      holding in consequence of the notice to quit,
the notice to quit shall cease to have effect.

(4) Where this section applies and there is an agreement between the
landlord and the tenant that the notice to quit shall continue to have effect,
the notice shall not be invalid by reason only that the agreement is
conditional.

DEFINITIONS
"agricultural holdings": s.1(1).
"landlord": s.85(1).
"notice to quit": s.21(2).
"tenant": s.85(1).

DERIVATIONS
Agricultural Holdings (Scotland) Act 1949, s.31.

GENERAL NOTE
See Gill, paras. 414–416.

Subs. (1)

As is indicated here, the section is concerned with the situation in which a landlord is seeking to sell the holding with entry and vacant possession at or after the termination of the current tenancy. The section originated in the Act of 1923 under which tenants had no security of tenure beyond the endurance of their leases, the intention apparently being to dissuade the landlord from terminating tenancies solely for the purpose of selling with vacant possession. With the security of tenure now enjoyed by tenants the provision would appear to be unnecessary. Its counterpart in England, s.30 of the Agricultural Holdings Act 1948, is no longer in force. Its continued existence in Scottish legislation, however, may be said to represent a trap for the unwary as it means that even when a notice to quit has been served and became unconditional as a result of the tenant not taking timeous action to oppose it, or again where his opposition has failed, the landlord cannot conclude an effective contract of sale till the operative date of the notice to quit arrives.

Subss. (2) and (3)

Subs. (2) indicates the action to be taken in the situation envisaged in subs. (1) and the way in which the difficulty can be overcome by agreement between the parties or by the tenant's election to let the notice to quit remain in force after receiving from the landlord the appropriate notice of the contract of sale. Subs. (3)(c) covers the situation where, with the landlord having failed to give notice to the tenant in accordance with subs. (2)(a), the tenant has gone out in compliance with the notice to quit. In these circumstances the notice to quit is to be regarded as effective, with the result that the tenant will be entitled to make the usual outgoing claims.

Subs. (4)

This provision enables a landlord to arrange with his tenant that the notice to quit will be effective if, but only if, the landlord is able, during the currency of the notice, to find a purchaser for the property. In accordance with subs. (2), however, the contract with the purchaser will have to be concluded not later than three months after the agreement between landlord and tenant.

Notice to quit part of holding to be valid in certain cases

29.—(1) A notice to quit part of an agricultural holding held on a tenancy from year to year shall not be invalid on the ground that it relates to part only of the holding if it is given—

    (a) for the purpose of adjusting the boundaries between agricultural units or of amalgamating agricultural units or parts thereof, or

    (b) with a view to the use of the land to which the notice relates for any of the purposes mentioned in subsection (2) below,

and the notice states that it is given for that purpose or with a view to such use, as the case may be.

(2) The purposes referred to in subsection (1)(b) above are—

    (a) the erection of farm labourers' cottages or other houses with or without gardens;

    (b) the provision of gardens for farm labourers' cottages or other houses;

    (c) the provision of allotments;

    (d) the provision of small holdings under the Small Landholders (Scotland) Acts 1886 to 1931, or of such holdings as are referred to in section 64 of the Agriculture (Scotland) Act 1948;

    (e) the planting of trees;

    (f) the opening or working of coal, ironstone, limestone, brickearth, or other minerals, or of a stone quarry, clay, sand, or gravel pit, or the construction of works or buildings to be used in connection therewith;

    (g) the making of a watercourse or reservoir;

    (h) the making of a road, railway, tramroad, siding, canal or basin, wharf, or pier, or work connected therewith.

DEFINITIONS
   "agricultural holding": s.1(1).
   "agricultural unit": s.85(1).
   "notice to quit": s.21(2).

DERIVATIONS
    Agricultural Holdings (Scotland) Act 1949, s.32.

GENERAL NOTE
    See Gill, Chap. 20. (For the corresponding English provision see the Agricultural Holdings
Act 1986, s.31).

Subs. (1)
    A notice to quit part of the subjects of let is at common law invalid and but for some enabling
provision would be invalid under the Act as not relating to the whole subjects of let.
    The facilities given by the section are restricted to yearly lets, including lets running on tacit
relocation. They do not enable a tenancy to be broken during its currency. They are made
available in general terms for adjustments of boundaries and amalgamations affecting agricultural units and also for certain specific purposes as listed in subs. (2). The notice to quit must
state the purpose or intended use for which it is given.

Subs. (2)
    There is some doubt as to whether "other houses" in paras. (a) and (b) is restricted to houses
for purposes connected with agriculture. On the basis of an English decision in the case of
Paddock Investments v. *Lorg* [1975] 236 E.G. 803, Gill (at para. 418) considers that the
restriction applies. The opposite view, as taken in Connell's *Agricultural Holdings (Scotland)*
Act (6th ed.), p. 148), would make the section applicable to housing development generally and
might be expected to be used by landlords such as local authorities seeking building ground. In
practice, however, it appears that the section is not often invoked. While resumption clauses as
usually found in agricultural leases cannot be used for agricultural purposes, their use for any
other purpose has the advantage that the tenant cannot, as he can do under s.29, invoke the
procedure for contesting the operation of a notice to quit.
    In the case of *Hamilton* v. *Lorimer*, 1959 S.L.C.R. 7 the tenant appealed successfully to the
Land Court against sanction being given by the Secretary of State for the operation of a notice
to quit under s.32 of the 1949 Act.

Tenant's right to treat notice to quit part as notice to quit entire holding

30. Where a notice to quit part of an agricultural holding is given to a
tenant, being a notice which is rendered valid by section 29 of this Act, and
the tenant within 28 days after—
    (a) the giving of the notice, or
    (b) where the operation of the notice depends on any proceedings under
        the foregoing provisions of this Act, the time when it is determined
        that the notice has effect,
whichever is later, gives to the landlord a counter-notice in writing that he
accepts the notice as a notice to quit the entire holding, to take effect at the
same time as the original notice, the notice to quit shall have effect
accordingly.

DEFINITIONS
    "agricultural holdings": s.1(1).
    "landlord": s.85(1).
    "notice to quit": s.21(2).
    "tenant": s.85(1).

DERIVATION
    Agricultural Holdings (Scotland) Act 1949, s.33.

GENERAL NOTE
    See Gill, para. 421. (For the corresponding English provision see the Agricultural Holdings
Act 1986, s.32).
    If the tenant who is to lose part of his holding by the operation of s.29 does not wish to
continue the tenancy of the holding as thus reduced, he can terminate the tenancy at the date at
which the notice to quit takes effect by serving a counter-notice on the landlord within 28 days
after he received notice to quit under s.29, or, if he has contested that notice, 28 days after the
Land Court's decision against him.
    For the effect of such action on the tenant's claim for compensation for disturbance, see
s.43(7).

Reduction of rent where tenant dispossessed of part of holding

31.—(1) Where—

(a) the tenancy of part of an agricultural holding terminates by reason of a notice to quit which is rendered valid by section 29 of this Act; or

(b) the landlord of an agricultural holding resumes possession of part of the holding in pursuance of a provision in that behalf contained in the lease,

the tenant shall be entitled to a reduction of rent of an amount, to be determined by arbitration, proportionate to that part of the holding, together with an amount in respect of any depreciation of the value to him of the residue of the holding caused by the severance or by the use to be made of the part severed.

(2) Where subsection (1)(b) above applies, the arbiter, in determining the amount of the reduction, shall take into account any benefit or relief allowed to the tenant under the lease in respect of the part whose possession is being resumed.

DEFINITIONS
   "agricultural holding": s.1(1).
   "landlord": s.85(1).
   "lease": s.85(1).
   "notice to quit": s.21(2).
   "tenant": s.85(1).

DERIVATIONS
   Agricultural Holdings (Scotland) Act 1949, s.34.

GENERAL NOTE
   See Gill, paras. 228–233. (For the corresponding English provision see the Agricultural Holdings Act 1986, s.33).

Subs. (1)
   When the size of the holding is reduced as a result of the operation of a notice to quit affecting part of the holding or the exercise of a power of resumption in the lease, the tenant is entitled to have the rent reduced. Three elements enter into the arbiter's calculation of this reduction. Firstly, the rental value of the land of which the tenant is dispossessed forms the basis of assessment of the reduction of rent proportionate to the part of the holding taken back, the basis of assessment being the rental value of the area of which the tenant is dispossessed rather than the average rental per hectare of the holding (*Hoile* v. *Sheriffs*, 1948 S.L.C.R. 24; *cf.* s.43(7)). Secondly, there is the severance element, which should be assessed on the lines applied in compensation for compulsory acquisition. Finally, there is the injurious affection element which will be assessed, as in a compulsory acquisition, reflecting any prejudice to the land retained in the holding likely to be caused by the intended use of the land taken back by the landlord.

Subs. (2)
   If, as sometimes happens, the lease makes provision for compensation for the tenant's loss of part of the holding as a result of the exercise of a power of assumption and this provision is more favourable to the tenant than the provision in this section, the tenant is entitled to disregard the statutory provision and base his claim on the lease alone. The same applies to the tenant's outgoing claims under s.49.

Further restrictions on operation of certain notices to quit

32.—(1) Subsections (2) to (5) below shall apply where—

(a) notice to quit an agricultural holding or part of an agricultural holding is given to a tenant; and

(b) the notice includes a statement in accordance with section 22(2) of this Act and paragraph (d) thereof to the effect that it is given by reason of the tenant's failure to remedy a breach of a kind referred to in section 66(1) of this Act.

(2) If not later than one month from the giving of the notice to quit the tenant serves on the landlord a counter-notice in writing requiring that this subsection shall apply to the notice to quit, subject to subsection (3) below, the notice to quit shall not have effect (whether as a notice to which section 22(1) of this Act does or does not apply) unless the Land Court consent to the operation thereof.

(3) A counter-notice under subsection (2) above shall be of no effect if within one month after the giving of the notice to quit the tenant serves on the landlord an effective notice under section 23(2) of this Act requiring the validity of the reason stated in the notice to quit to be determined by arbitration.

(4) Where—

(a) the tenant has served on the landlord a notice of the kind referred to in subsection (3) above;

(b) the notice to quit would, apart from this subsection, have effect in consequence of the arbitration; and

(c) not later than one month from the date on which the arbiter's award is delivered to the tenant the tenant serves on the landlord a counter-notice in writing requiring that this subsection shall apply to the notice to quit;

the notice to quit shall not have effect (whether as a notice to which section 22(1) of this Act does or does not apply) unless the Land Court consent to the operation thereof.

(5) On an application made in that behalf by the landlord, the Land Court shall consent under subsection (2) or (4) above or (6) below to the operation of the notice to quit unless in all the circumstances it appears to them that a fair and reasonable landlord would not insist on possession.

(6) Where a notice to quit is given in accordance with section 66(3) of this Act in a case where the arbitration under that section followed an earlier notice to quit to which subsection (1) above applied, if the tenant serves on the landlord a counter-notice in writing within one month after the giving of the subsequent notice to quit (or, if the date specified in that notice for the termination of the tenancy is earlier, before that date), the notice to quit given under section 66(3) of this Act shall not have effect unless the Land Court consent to the operation thereof.

DEFINITIONS
    "agricultural holding": s.1(1).
    "landlord": s.85(1).
    "notice to quit": s.21(2).
    "tenant": s.85(1).
    "termination of tenancy": s.85(1).

DERIVATIONS
    Agriculture (Miscellaneous Provisions) Act 1976, s.14.

GENERAL NOTE
    See Gill, paras. 342–353. (For the corresponding English provision see the Agricultural Holdings Act 1986, s.28).

Subs. (1)
    As disclosed here the operative provisions of the section apply where a notice to quit in terms of s.22(2)(d) is given founding on the tenant's failure to comply with a demand to remedy a breach of a condition of his tenancy by doing any work of provision, repair, maintenance or replacement of fixed equipment, that being the kind of breach referred to in s.66(1).

Subs. (2)
    Normally a notice to quit given in terms of s.22(2) does not require Land Court consent for its operation and so cannot be met with a counter-notice, but in the particular circumstances referred to in subs. (1), the tenant is empowered, by serving a counter-notice, to make Land Court consent necessary.

Subs. (3)

The counter-notice is, however, rendered ineffective if within the month following the service of the notice to quit the tenant takes the course open to him with any s.22(2) notice to quit by calling for arbitration on the reasons stated therein.

Subs. (4)

When the tenant, having duly called for arbitration, receives an adverse decision from the arbiter, he has a month to serve a counter-notice applying this subsection to the notice to quit and making the notice ineffective except with Land Court consent.

Subs. (5)

This subsection has the result, however, that the only ground on which the Land Court can refuse their consent is that in their view a fair and reasonable landlord would not insist on possession. Again, as pointed out by Gill (para. 349), the wording of this provision is significantly different from that of the proviso to s.26 of the 1949 Act (now replaced by s.24(2) of this Act), the use of the words "shall consent...unless" putting the onus on the tenant to demonstrate circumstances justifying the refusal of consent.

Subs. (6)

One of the possible consequences of the power conferred on arbiters by s.66 is that a landlord may have to serve a second notice to quit, the first one having been rendered inoperative by the time allowed by the arbiter for the tenant to comply with the demand to remedy. In these circumstances the Land Court, on application to them being made, will fix a new date for termination of the tenancy and the landlord can serve a second notice to quit in conformity with the provisions of s.66(3). The subsection under discussion here enables the tenant by counter-notice to make the operation of the second notice to quit subject to Land Court consent.

Part IV

Compensation for Improvements

Improvements

33. In this Part the following are referred to as "improvements"—
> "1923 Act improvement" means an improvement carried out on an agricultural holding, being an improvement specified in Schedule 3 to this Act, and begun before July 31, 1931;
> "1931 Act improvement" means an improvement so carried out, being an improvement specified in Schedule 4 to this Act and begun on or after July 31, 1931 and before November 1, 1948;
> "old improvement" means a 1923 Act improvement or a 1931 Act improvement;
> "new improvement" means an improvement carried out on an agricultural holding, being an improvement specified in Schedule 5 to this Act begun on or after November 1, 1948.

DEFINITIONS

"agricultural holding": s.1(1).

DERIVATIONS

Agricultural Holdings (Scotland) Act 1949, ss.36, 47.

GENERAL NOTE

See Gill, para. 473.

This classification of improvements is based on the principle that a tenant's rights to compensation for improvements depends on the law as it stood when he made the improvements and is unaffected by any changes in the law which may have taken place subsequently but before his outgoing. While claims for old improvements in the 1923 Act category must now be rare, the right to make such claims does not begin to prescribe until they are exigible. Thus, for example, the successor of the tenant who made the improvement may still be occupying a holding where there is an improvement of a lasting nature such as a building for which compensation on the basis of the 1923 Act will be payable at his outgoing.

Right to compensation for improvements

34.—(1) Subject to subsections (2) to (4), (7) and (8) below, and to sections 36 and 39 to 42 of this Act, a tenant of an agricultural holding shall be entitled, on quitting the holding at the termination of the tenancy, to compensation from the landlord in respect of improvements carried out by the tenant.

(2) A tenant whose lease was entered into before January 1, 1921 shall not be entitled to compensation under this section for an improvement which he was required to carry out by the terms of his tenancy.

(3) A tenant shall not be entitled to compensation under this section for an old improvement carried out on land which, at the time the improvement was begun, was not a holding within the meaning of the Agricultural Holdings (Scotland) Act 1923 as originally enacted, or land to which provisions of that Act relating to compensation for improvements and disturbance were applied by section 33 of that Act.

(4) Nothing in this section shall prejudice the right of a tenant to any compensation to which he is entitled—

(a) in the case of an old improvement, under custom, agreement or otherwise;

(b) in the case of a new improvement, under an agreement in writing between the landlord and the tenant;

in lieu of any compensation provided by this section.

(5) Where a tenant has remained in an agricultural holding during two or more tenancies, he shall not be deprived of his right to compensation under subsection (1) above by reason only that the improvements were not carried out during the tenancy on the termination of which he quits the holding.

(6) Subject to section 36(4) of this Act, a tenant shall be entitled to compensation under this section in respect of the 1931 Act improvement specified in paragraph 28 of Schedule 4 to this Act, or the new improvement specified in paragraph 32 of Schedule 5 to this Act (laying down of temporary pasture), notwithstanding that the laying down or the leaving at the termination of the tenancy of temporary pasture was in contravention of the terms of the lease or of any agreement made by the tenant respecting the method of cropping the arable lands; but, in ascertaining the amount of the compensation, the arbiter shall take into account any injury to or deterioration of the holding due to the contravention (except insofar as the landlord may have recovered damages therefor).

(7) Where under an agreement in writing entered into before January 1, 1921 a tenant is entitled to compensation which is fair and reasonable having regard to the circumstances existing at the time of the making of the agreement, for an old improvement specified in Part III of Schedule 3 to this Act or in Part III of Schedule 4 to this Act, such compensation shall, as respects that improvement, be substituted for compensation under subsection (1) above.

(8) Compensation shall not be payable under this Part of this Act in respect of repairs of the kind specified in paragraph 29 of Schedule 3 to this Act or in paragraph 29 of Schedule 4 to this Act unless, before beginning to execute any such repairs, the tenant gave to the landlord notice in writing under paragraph (29) of Schedule 1 to the Agricultural Holdings (Scotland) Act 1923, or under paragraph (30) of Schedule 1 to the Small Landholders and Agricultural Holdings (Scotland) Act 1931, of his intention to execute the repairs, together with particulars thereof, and the landlord failed to exercise the right conferred on him by the said paragraph (29) or, as the case may be, the said paragraph (30) to execute the repairs himself within a reasonable time after receiving the notice.

DEFINITIONS
  "agricultural holding": s.1(1).

"landlord": s.85(1).
"new improvement": s.33.
"old improvement": s.33.
"tenant": s.85(1).
"termination of tenancy": s.85(1).

DERIVATIONS
Agricultural Holdings (Scotland) Act 1949, ss.37, 41, 42, 43, 44(4), 45, 53, 54.

GENERAL NOTE
See Gill, paras. 471–496. (For the corresponding English provision see the Agricultural Holdings Act 1986, s.64 and Scheds. 7–9).

Subs. (1)
The scheme of this Part of the Act being to deal together with old and new improvements, this subsection replaces ss.37(1) and 48(1) of the 1949 Act. The tenant is entitled to compensation for improvements on quitting at the termination of the tenancy as defined in s.85(1) whether or not he leaves as a consequence of a notice to quit which under s.43 is normally essential for compensation for disturbance to be due.

Subs. (2)
The exclusion, as previously contained in provisos to ss.37(1) and 48(1) of the 1949 Act, applies irrespective of when the improvement has been carried out.

Subs. (3)
This replaces s.44(4) of the 1949 Act dealing with old improvements. As to rights of compensation in relation to non-statutory land, see Gill, para. 20.

Subs. (4)
This replaces s.37(2) of the 1949 Act for old improvements and s.48(2) for new improvements, being provisions for what is known as "substituted compensation," *i.e.* compensation for improvements claimed on a basis other than that of the relevant provisions of the Act. In the case of new improvements, para. (b) makes the only alternative basis agreement in writing between the parties but such an agreement need not be in probative form (see s.78). By contrast, para. (a), dealing with old improvements, contains a much wider basis for substituted compensation, referring as it does to "custom, agreement or otherwise." The last two words would seem to imply that verbal agreement, proved in any way, would suffice. As regards customary compensation, it may be noted here that there have not been included in this Act the provisions of s.100 of the 1949 Act, which in broad general terms preserved any rights derived from, *inter alia*, "any custom of the country." Section 85(4), however, replacing s.93(5) of the 1949 Act, provides for custom (apparently local or general) being taken into account in relation to the terms and provisions of leases or agreements relating to agricultural holdings. Customary compensation as arising under s.37(2) of the 1949 Act, is discussed in Connell (*op. cit.*, p. 156, note 6).
As noted under the reference to subs. (7), the general rule is that substituted compensation does not apply to improvements listed in Pt. III of the statutory Schedules.

Subs. (5)
This replaces ss.45 and 54 of the 1949 Act, which made identical provisions for old and new improvements. It is implied that the tenancies must have been continuous.

Subs. (6)
This replaces s.43 of the 1949 Act (old improvements) and s.53 (new improvements). The tenant's right to compensation for temporary pasture, even if laid down in contravention of the lease, is a consequence of his freedom of cropping in terms of s.7. In contrast with the laying down of permanent pasture, it does not require the prior consent of the landlord to qualify for compensation. Where there is injury or deterioration of the holding by reason of the contravention of the lease, the landlord may have recovered damages under s.7(3)(b).

Subs. (7)
This replaces s.42 of the 1949 Act. There must now be very few cases in which its provisions will apply, particularly as it relates only to the improvements of a temporary nature as appearing in Pt. III of the statutory Schedules. A commentary on certain aspects of the 1949 section is to be found in Connell (*op. cit.*, pp. 160/161).

It should be noted here that it is only in the circumstances of this subsection and in the special case of market gardens (see s.41(1)) that substituted compensation can apply to Pt. III improvements.

Subs. (8)
This replaces s.41 of the 1949 Act, excluding compensation for repairs to buildings as old improvements unless prior notice in writing was given to the landlord to conform to the provisions of the 1923 Act or those of the 1931 Act, as the case might be, and he failed to exercise, within a reasonable time, his right to execute the repairs himself.

Payment of compensation by incoming tenant

35.—(1) This section applies to compensation which is payable or has been paid to an outgoing tenant of an agricultural holding by the landlord under or in pursuance of this Act or the Agricultural Holdings (Scotland) Act 1923, the Small Landholders and Agricultural Holdings (Scotland) Act 1931, the Agriculture (Scotland) Act 1948 or the 1949 Act.

(2) Subject to subsection (3) below, any agreement made after November 1, 1948 between an incoming tenant and his landlord whereby the tenant undertakes to pay to the outgoing tenant or to refund to the landlord any compensation to which this section applies shall be null and void.

(3) Subsection (2) above shall not apply in the case of an improvement of a kind referred to in Part III of Schedule 5 to this Act, where the agreement is in writing and states a maximum amount which may be payable thereunder by the incoming tenant.

(4) Where, on entering into occupation of an agricultural holding, a tenant, with the consent in writing of the landlord pays to the outgoing tenant compensation to which this section applies—

(a) in respect of an old improvement, in pursuance of an agreement in writing made before November 1, 1948; or

(b) where subsection (3) above applies,

the incoming tenant shall be entitled, on quitting the holding, to claim compensation for the improvement or part in like manner, if at all, as the outgoing tenant would have been entitled if the outgoing tenant had remained tenant of the holding and quitted it at the time at which the tenant quits it.

(5) Where, in a case not falling within subsection (2) or (3) above, a tenant, on entering into occupation of an agricultural holding, paid to his landlord any amount in respect of the whole or part of a new improvement, he shall, subject to any agreement in writing between the landlord and the tenant, be entitled on quitting the holding to claim compensation in respect of the improvement or part in like manner, if at all, as he would have been entitled if he had been tenant of the holding at the time when the improvement was carried out and the improvement or part thereof had been carried out by him.

DEFINITIONS
"agricultural holding": s.1(1).
"improvement": ss.33, 85(1).
"landlord": s.85(1).
"new improvement": ss.33, 85(1).
"old improvement": ss.33, 85(1).
"tenant": s.85(1).

DERIVATIONS
Agricultural Holdings (Scotland) Act 1949, ss.11, 46, 55.

GENERAL NOTE
See Gill, paras. 475, 491. (For the corresponding English provision see the Agricultural Holding Act 1986, s.69(2)(3)).

Subs. (1)

The terms of this subsection indicate that the section is to apply to payment of compensation to an outgoing tenant, whether for new improvements or for 1923 or 1931 old improvements.

Subss. (2) and (3)

Subs. (2) replaces s.11(1) and (2) of the 1949 Act. It will be noted that the exception made by subs. (3) is restricted to new improvements of a temporary nature. It is, however, only agreements between landlords and incoming tenants which are affected by these provisions. They do not affect any agreements which may be made between incoming and outgoing tenants.

Subs. (4)

Subs. (4) replaces s.46 of the 1949 Act. Head (a) covers the first part of the 1949 section and deals with the case of a pre-November 1948 agreement for payment for an old improvement; head (b) covers the latter part of s.46 along with s.55(1) of the 1949 Act and thus applies to agreements entered into after November 1, 1948 for payment for old improvements or new improvements within the category of temporary improvements covered by the current or post-1948 Schedule. It will be noted that this Schedule is being applied here even although the improvements in question may be old improvements made before it came into force. This is the effect of the reference in s.46 of the 1949 Act to "an old improvement of the kind specified in Pt. III of the First Schedule to this Act": *cf.* subs. (3), referring to Pt. III of Sched. 5 to this Act. The practical effect as regards an agreement enfranchised by these provisions is that the tenant who has made payment for his predecessor's improvements will have a claim for these improvements in so far as they still have value at his outgoing.

Subs. (5)

This replaces s.55(2) of the 1949 Act, covering cases of agreement not within subss. (2) or (3) of the section. These subsections concern agreements involving an incoming tenant, a landlord and an outgoing tenant. There may, however, be no outgoing tenant, in which case the incoming tenant will simply be paying the landlord for a new improvement. Again, the improvement may be one outwith the category of temporary improvements referred to in subs. (3). In such cases, in the absence of agreement to the contrary, the tenant, having paid for the improvement, is entitled to claim for it at his outgoing in so far as it still has value.

Amount of compensation under this Part

36.—(1) Subject to subsections (2) to (4) below, the amount of any compensation payable to a tenant under this Part of this Act shall be such sum as fairly represents the value of the improvement to an incoming tenant.

(2) In the ascertainment of the amount of compensation payable in respect of an old improvement, there shall be taken into account any benefit which the landlord has given or allowed to the tenant (under the lease or otherwise) in consideration of the tenant carrying out the improvement.

(3) In the ascertainment of the amount of compensation payable under this section for a new improvement, there shall be taken into account—

(a) any benefit which the landlord has agreed in writing to give the tenant in consideration of the tenant carrying out the improvement; and

(b) any grant out of moneys provided by Parliament which has been or will be made to the tenant in respect of the improvement.

(4) In ascertaining the amount of any compensation payable under section 34(6) of this Act, the arbiter shall take into account any injury to or deterioration of the holding due to the contravention of the lease or agreement referred to in that subsection, except in so far as the landlord has recovered damages in respect of such injury or deterioration.

DEFINITIONS
"landlord": s.85(1).
"lease": s.85(1).
"new improvement": s.33.
"old improvement": s.33.
"tenant": s.85(1).

DERIVATIONS
Agricultural Holding (Scotland) Act 1949, ss.38, 43, 44(1), 49, 53.

GENERAL NOTE
See Gill, paras. 478, 479, 490. (For the corresponding English provision see the Agricultural Holdings Act 1986, s.66).

Subs. (1)
This replaces ss.38 (old improvements) and 49(1) (new improvements) of the 1949 Act, the same basis of valuation applying in both cases. This basis applies whether or not there is an incoming tenant and in any event falls to be applied disregarding any special needs of an incoming tenant, should there be one, the true criterion being the value to a hypothetical tenant continuing to use the holding as has been done. The value of the improvement should be assessed as the addition it makes to the value of the holding as a whole (*Mackenzie* v. *McGillivray*, 1921 S.C. 722). While the cost to the outgoing tenant of making the improvement is of doubtful relevance, an appropriate basis of assessment may be the current or present-day cost of providing the improvement, less some allowance for the age and condition of the item in question.

Subs. (2)
This deals with old improvements and replaces s.44(1)(a) of the 1949 Act. Differing in this respect from the corresponding provision for new improvements (see subs. (3)) the benefit for which deduction is to be made does not require to be documented in any way. It must, however, be given voluntarily and not under obligation by the landlord. It will often have taken the form of provision of material for work or a pecuniary contribution to its cost. In the absence of express evidence it is for the landlord to prove its causal connection with the execution of the improvement (*McQuater* v. *Ferguson*, 1911 S.C. 640; *Earl of Galloway* v. *McLelland*, 1915 S.C. 1062; *Muckenzie* v. *McGillivray*, above).
The provisions of subs. (1)(b)(2)(3) and (5) of s.44 of the 1949 Act dealing with deductions for manure sold off the holding, and Government grants for liming or for drainage works carried out to implement Defence regulations, being apparently regarded as spent, have been omitted.

Subs. (3)
This deals with new improvements and replaces s.49(2) of the 1949 Act.
Para. (a). The requirement of a written agreement would seem to eliminate some, at least, of the questions which could arise in connection with an old improvement. Problems of valuation, however, can arise in either case and it is suggested by Gill (para. 478) that the proportion of the original cost represented by the benefit should be ascertained and that proportion of the current value of the improvement should be deducted to arrive at the amount of compensation due.
Para. (b). In the case of improvement grants for the provision or repair of housing accommodation, deduction will be required only so long as the grant conditions remain in force (see Housing (Scotland) Act 1987, ss.246 and 256 (as amended in terms of Sched. 11, para. 54)).

Subs. (4)
See note to s.34(6), the content of which subsection, so far as replacing ss.43 and 53 of the 1949 Act, is being reported in this subsection.

Consents necessary for compensation for some improvements

37.—(1) Compensation under this Part of this Act shall not be payable for—
  (a) a 1923 Act improvement specified in Part I of Schedule 3 to this Act;
  (b) a 1931 Act improvement specified in Part I of Schedule 4 to this Act; or
  (c) a new improvement specified in Part I of Schedule 5 to this Act;
unless, before the improvement was carried out, the landlord consented to it in writing (whether unconditionally or upon terms as to compensation or otherwise agreed on between the parties).
  (2) Where such consent was given on terms agreed as to compensation, the compensation payable under the agreement shall be substituted for compensation under section 34 of this Act.

DEFINITIONS
"1923 Act improvement": s.33.
"1931 Act improvement": s.33.
"landlord": s.85(1).
"new improvement": s.33.

DERIVATIONS
Agricultural Holdings (Scotland) Act 1949, ss.39, 50.

GENERAL NOTE
See Gill, paras. 474, 481, 492. (For the corresponding English provision see the Agricultural Holding Act 1986, s.67).

Subs. (1)
This replaces ss.39(1) (old improvements) and 50(1) (new improvements) of the 1949 Act, stating the rule that for permanent or major improvements listed in the first part of the Schedules the landlord's prior written consent is necessary if the improvement is to qualify for compensation at the tenant's outgoing. The terms on which consent is given, which can vary widely, are exemplified by Gill (para. 481). It appears that an agreement excluding compensation is valid (*Turnbull* v. *Millar*, 1942 S.C. 521).

Subs. (2)
This replaces ss.39(2) (old improvements) and 50(2) (new improvements) of the 1949 Act. When substituted compensation has been agreed in this way, an arbiter will, in accordance with Sched. 7, para. 13, make an award in terms of the agreement.

Notice required of certain improvements

38.—(1) Subject to subsections (2) to (6) below, compensation under this Act shall not be payable for—
   (a) a 1923 Act improvement specified in Part II of Schedule 3 to this Act;
   (b) a 1931 Act improvement specified in Part II of Schedule 4 to this Act;
   (c) a new improvement specified in Part II of Schedule 5 to this Act;
unless the tenant gave notice to the landlord in accordance with subsection (3) below of his intention to carry it out and of the manner in which he proposed to do so.

   (2) Subsection (1) above shall not apply in the case of an improvement mentioned in subsection (1)(a) or (b) above, if the parties agreed by the lease or otherwise to dispense with the requirement for notice under subsection (3).

   (3) Notice shall be in accordance with this subsection if it is in writing and—
   (a) in the case of an improvement mentioned in subsection (1)(a) above, it was notice under section 3 of the Agricultural Holdings (Scotland) Act 1923, given not more than 3 nor less than 2 months,
   (b) in the case of an improvement mentioned in subsection (1)(b) above, it was notice under the said section 3, given not more than 6 nor less than 3 months,
   (c) in the case of an improvement mentioned in subsection (1)(c) above, it was given not less than 3 months,
before the tenant began to carry out the improvement.

   (4) In the case of an improvement mentioned in subsection (1)(a) or (b) above, compensation shall not be payable unless—
   (a) the parties agreed on the terms as to compensation or otherwise on which the improvement was to be carried out;
   (b) where no such agreement was made and the tenant did not withdraw the notice, the landlord failed to exercise his right under the said section 3 to carry out the improvement himself within a reasonable time; or
   (c) in the case of an improvement mentioned in subsection (1)(b) above, where the landlord gave notice of objection and the matter was

referred under section 28(2) of the Small Landholders and Agricultural Holdings (Scotland) Act 1931 for determination by the appropriate authority, that authority was satisfied that the improvement should be carried out and the improvement was carried out in accordance with any directions given by that authority as to the manner of so doing.

(5) If the parties agreed (either after notice was given under this section or by an agreement to dispense with it) on terms as to compensation, the compensation payable under the agreement shall be substituted for compensation under this Part of this Act.

(6) In subsection (4) above, "the appropriate authority" means—

(a) in relation to the period before September 4, 1939, the Department of Agriculture for Scotland;

(b) in relation to the period starting on that day, the Secretary of State.

DEFINITIONS
"1923 Act improvement": s.33.
"1931 Act improvement": s.33.
"improvement": s.85(1).
"landlord": s.85(1).
"lease": s.85(1).
"new improvement": s.85(1).
"tenant": s.85(1).

DERIVATIONS
Agricultural Holdings (Scotland) Act 1949, ss.40, 51.

GENERAL NOTE
See Gill, paras. 482–485, 494, 495. (For the corresponding English provision see the Agricultural Holdings Act 1986, s.68).

Subs. (1)
This replaces ss.40(1)(2) (old improvements) and 51(1) (new improvements) of the 1949 Act and applies the requirement of notice to the landlord before execution to all improvements appearing in Pt. II of the statutory schedules. The only 1923 Act improvement affected falls under the heading of Drainage (Sched. 3, para. 19).

Subs. (2)
This replaces the provisos to ss.40(1) (1923 Act improvements) and 40(2) (1931 Act improvements) of the 1949 Act whereby the parties may, by agreement, have dispensed with notice.

Subs. (3)
This provides for notice being given in writing and specifies the period applying in respect of each category of improvement as previously prescribed in ss.40(1)(2) and 51(1) of the 1949 Act.

Subs. (4)
This deals in paras. (a) and (b) with old improvements in both categories and replaces s.40(1)(b) and (2)(b) of the 1949 Act, restricting compensation to cases where, notice having been given and not withdrawn, the landlord failed to exercise his statutory right to carry out the improvements himself. Para. (c), replacing s.40(2)(c) of the 1949 Act dealing with 1931 Act improvements, refers to certain special provisions of that Act whereby objection by the landlord led to an appropriate authority (as now defined in subs. (6)) determining whether an improvement should be carried out and, if considered necessary, supervising its execution.

Subs. (5)
This replaces ss.40(3) (old improvements) and 51(2)(3) (new improvements) of the 1949 Act, enabling the parties, either after notice has been given or by an agreement dispensing with notice, to agree on "substituted compensation". It is not, however, clear that the right to compensation can be wholly eliminated, as appears to be the case with improvements requiring the landlord's consent in terms of s.37.

Subs. (6)
This defines "appropriate authority" for the purposes of subs. (4), taking account of a departmental reorganisation in 1939.

Compensation for Sch. 5, Pt. II, improvements conditional on approval of Land Court in certain cases

39.—(1) Subject to subsections (2) to (4) below, compensation under this Part of this Act shall not be payable in respect of a new improvement specified in Part II of Schedule 5 to this Act if, within one month after receiving notice under section 38(3) of this Act from the tenant of his intention to carry out the improvement, the landlord gives notice in writing to the tenant that he objects to the carrying out of the improvement or to the manner in which the tenant proposes to carry it out.

(2) Where notice of objection has been given under subsection (1) above, the tenant may apply to the Land Court for approval of the carrying out of the improvement, and on such application the Land Court may approve the carrying out of the improvement either—

(a) unconditionally, or

(b) upon such terms, as to reduction of the compensation which would otherwise be payable or as to other matters, as appears to them to be just,

or may withhold their approval.

(3) If, on an application under subsection (2) above, the Land Court grant their approval, the landlord may, within one month after receiving notice of the decision of the Land Court, serve notice in writing on the tenant undertaking to carry out the improvement himself.

(4) Where, on an application under subsection (2) above the Land Court grant their approval, then if either—

(a) no notice is served by the landlord under subsection (3) above, or

(b) such a notice is served but, on an application made by the tenant in that behalf, the Land Court determines that the landlord has failed to carry out the improvement within a reasonable time,

the tenant may carry out the improvement and shall be entitled to compensation under this Part of this Act in respect thereof as if notice of objection had not been given by the landlord, and any terms subject to which the approval was given shall have effect as if they were contained in an agreement in writing between the landlord and the tenant.

DEFINITIONS

"improvement": s.85(1).
"landlord": s.85(1).
"tenant": s.85(1).

DERIVATION

Agricultural Holdings (Scotland) Act 1949, s.52.
Agriculture Act 1958, Sched. 1, Pt. II, para. 41.

GENERAL NOTE

See Gill, paras. 485–487.

Subs. (1)

Section 38(4) having dealt under reference to earlier legislation with the landlord's right to object to old improvements in Pt. II of the statutory schedules and so prevent them qualifying for compensation at the tenant's outgoing, this section provides the landlord with similar rights in respect of new improvements.

Subs. (2)

Whereas with old improvements an objection maintained by the landlord resulted in a reference to a Government department or Minister, the Land Court has the jurisdiction when there is an objection to a proposed new improvement. While subs. (1) gives the landlord a month from receiving the tenant's notice to give notice of objection, no time limit is prescribed for the tenant's application to the court. The test to be applied by the court is whether the proposed improvement is reasonable and desirable on agricultural grounds for the efficient management of the holding. A landlord is not to have imposed on him a contingent liability to pay compensation for an improvement which is inconsistent with the type of farming prescribed by the lease or is to be executed in a manner injurious to or out of keeping with other parts of the holding. The following cases, some of them involving the attachment of conditions to the approval, exemplify the Land Court's exercise of this jurisdiction: *Taylor* v. *Burnett's Trs.*, 1966 S.L.C.R. 139; *Fotheringham* v. *Fotheringham*, 1978 S.L.C.R. 144; *Hutchison* v. *Wolfe Murray*, 1980 S.L.C.R. 112; *Renwick* v. *Rodger*, 1988 S.L.T. (Land Ct.) 23; *Mackinnon* v. *Arran Estate Trust*, 1988 S.L.C.R. 32.

Subs. (3)
It will be to the landlord's advantage to carry out the improvement himself if he can do so at less cost than the tenant's proposal would entail. In so doing he will not only be extinguishing a contingent liability for outgoing compensation but also becoming entitled to claim an increase of rent under the provisions of s.15.

Subs. (4)
What is a reasonable time for the landlord to carry out the improvement must depend on the circumstances. It should be noted that where a landlord defaults and the tenant himself proceeds with the improvement, he will do so subject to any conditions the Land Court may have imposed in giving their approval.

PART V

OTHER PROVISIONS REGARDING COMPENSATION

Market gardens

Market gardens

40.—(1) This section applies to any agricultural holding which, by virtue of an agreement in writing made on or after January 1, 1898, is let or is to be treated as a market garden.
(2) This section also applies where—
(a) a holding was, on January 1, 1898 under a lease then current, in use or cultivation as a market garden with the knowledge of the landlord; and
(b) an improvement of a kind specified in Schedule 6 to this Act (other than such an alteration of a building as did not constitute an enlargement thereof) has been carried out on the holding; and
(c) the landlord did not, before the improvement was carried out, serve on the tenant a written notice dissenting from the carrying out of the improvement;
in relation to improvements whether carried out before or after January 1, 1898.
(3) In the application of Part IV of this Act to an agricultural holding to which this section applies, subject to subsections (5) and (7) below, the improvements specified in Schedule 6 to this Act shall be included in the improvements specified in Part III of each of Schedules 3, 4 and 5 to this Act.
(4) In the case of an agricultural holding to which this section applies—
(a) section 18 of this Act shall apply to every fixture or building affixed or erected by the tenant to or upon the holding or acquired by him since December 31, 1900 for the purposes of his trade or business as a market gardener;
(b) it shall be lawful for the tenant to remove all fruit trees and fruit bushes planted by him on the holding and not permanently set out, but if the tenant does not remove such fruit trees and fruit bushes before the termination of his tenancy they shall remain the property of the landlord and the tenant shall not be entitled to any compensation in respect thereof; and
(c) the right of an incoming tenant to claim compensation in respect of the whole or part of an improvement which he has purchased may be

exercised although the landlord has not consented in writing to the purchase.

(5) Where a tenancy of a kind described in subsection (2) above was a tenancy from year to year, the compensation payable in respect of an improvement of a kind referred to in that subsection shall be such (if any) as could have been claimed if the 1949 Act had not been passed.

(6) Where the land to which this section applies consists of part only of an agricultural holding this section shall apply as if that part were a separate holding.

(7) Nothing in this section shall confer a right to compensation for the alteration of a building (not being an alteration constituting an enlargement of the building) where the alteration was begun before November 1, 1948.

DEFINITIONS
"agricultural holding": s.1(1).
"building": s.85(1).
"improvement": s.85(1).
"landlord": s.85(1).
"lease": s.85(1).
"market garden": s.85(1).
"tenant": s.85(1).

DERIVATIONS
Agricultural Holdings (Scotland) Act 1949, s.65

GENERAL NOTE
See Gill, paras. 541–548. (For the corresponding English provision see the Agricultural Holdings Act 1986, s.79 and Sched. 10).

Subs. (1)
A market garden is defined in s.85(1) as a holding cultivated wholly or mainly for the purpose of the trade or business of market gardening. That trade or business has been judicially described as one producing the class of goods characteristic of a greengrocer's shop which in ordinary course would reach the shop via the early morning market where such goods are disposed of wholesale (*Watters* v. *Hunter*, 1927 S.C. 310, *per* Lord President Clyde at p. 317). In a very recent case concerning rating, a market garden was described as supplying a market for buying and selling produce for consumption (*Twygen* v. *Assessor for Tayside*, 1991 4 G.W.D. 226. Questions have arisen as to whether a particular holding, *e.g.* one used wholly or mainly for growing flowers, constituted a market garden (see Gill, para. 542, and authorities there cited).
Special compensation provisions favouring the tenants of market gardens originated in the Market Gardeners Compensation (Scotland) Act 1897, coming into force on January 1, 1898.
For an agricultural holding to be used as and constitute a market garden there must be agreement in the lease or some other document, or a direction by the Land Court under s.41.

Subs. (2)
These provisions as appearing in the 1949 Acts and earlier legislation for holdings being used as market gardens when the 1897 Act as above mentioned took effect, are discussed in some detail in Connell (*op. cit.* pp. 179/180) but seem unlikely to be of practical significance now.

Subs. (3)
The effect of the inclusion of the market garden improvements listed in Sched. 6 in the improvements specified in Pt. III of the schedules of old and new improvements is that market garden improvements can be carried out and qualify for outgoing compensation without the consent of or notification to the landlord being required.

Subs. (4)
This covers certain privileges enjoyed by the market garden tenant. Firstly, his right of removal of fixtures and buildings under s.18 extends to every fixture or building provided by him for the purposes of his trade or business at any time since December 31, 1900, including buildings for which he could have claimed compensation. Secondly, he is entitled to remove fruit trees and fruit bushes planted by him but not permanently set out. It has been suggested that he may in any case have this right by implication at common law (see Connell, *op. cit.* p. 179). In any event, he is not entitled to compensation if and in so far as he does not exercise it.

Finally, he can claim compensation for an improvement purchased from the outgoing tenant without the consent of the landlord, which consent under s.35(4) is normally required for a tenant to make such a claim.

Subs. (5)

This, like subs. (2), concerns holdings leased as market gardens on January 1, 1898. As to the position with year-to-year tenancies of such holdings, see Connell, *op. cit.*, p. 180.

Subs. (6)

This provides for the situation in which the parties have agreed that part of an agricultural holding shall be a market garden for the purposes of the Act. The location of the ground allocated to market gardening may, by agreement, be varied during the course of the tenancy, but the tenant's right of freedom of cropping under s.7 does not apply to the market gardening ground (*Taylor* v. *Steel Maitland*, 1913 S.C. 562).

Subs. (7)

Item 4 of Sched. 6 covers the erection, alteration or enlargement of buildings. For the landlord, this can represent a substantial potential liability. A farm tenant, if intending to claim outgoing compensation, would need to have notified his landlord before proceeding. The potential liability of the landlord in a market garden tenancy is limited by this subsection but only as regards an old improvement to a building.

Recent cases illustrating the liabilities incurred by landlords for Sched. 6 market gardening improvements are *Macdonald's Trs.* v. *Taylor*, 1983 S.L.C.R. 9, and *Ritson* v. *McIntyre*, 1982 S.L.C.R. 13.

Direction by Land Court that holding be treated as market garden

41.—(1) Where—
  (a) the tenant of an agricultural holding intimates to the landlord in writing his desire to carry out on the holding or any part thereof an improvement specified in Schedule 6 to this Act;
  (b) the landlord refuses, or within a reasonable time fails, to agree in writing that the holding, or that part thereof, shall be treated as a market garden;
  (c) the tenant applies to the Land Court for a direction under this subsection; and
  (d) the Land Court is satisfied that the holding or that part thereof is suitable for the purposes of market gardening;
the Land Court may direct that section 40 of this Act shall apply to the holding or, as the case may be, part of a holding, either—
  (i) in respect of all the improvements specified in Schedule 6 to this Act, or
  (ii) in respect of some only of those improvements,
and that section shall apply accordingly as respects any improvement carried out after the date on which the direction is given.

(2) A direction under subsection (1) above may be given subject to such conditions, if any, for the protection of the landlord as the Land Court may think fit and, in particular, where the direction relates to part only of the holding, the direction may, on the application of the landlord, be given subject to the condition that the tenant shall consent to the division of the holding into two parts (one such part being the part to which the direction relates) to be held at rents agreed by the landlord and tenant or in default of agreement determined by arbitration, but otherwise on the same terms and conditions (so far as applicable) as those on which the holding is held.

(3) Where a direction is given under subsection (1) above, if the tenancy is terminated—
  (a) by notice of intention to quit given by the tenant, or
  (b) by reason of the tenant's apparent insolvency being constituted under section 7 of the Bankruptcy (Scotland) Act 1985,
the tenant shall not be entitled to compensation in respect of improvements specified in the direction unless he produces an offer which complies with

subsection (4) below and the landlord fails to accept the offer within 3 months after the production thereof.

(4) An offer complies with this subsection if—

(a) it is in writing;

(b) it is made by a substantial and otherwise suitable person;

(c) it is produced by the tenant to the landlord not later than one month after the date of the notice of intention to quit or constitution of apparent insolvency as the case may be, or at such later date as may be agreed;

(d) it is an offer to accept a tenancy of the holding from the termination of the existing tenancy on the terms and conditions of the existing tenancy so far as applicable;

(e) it includes an offer, subject to subsection (5) below, to pay to the outgoing tenant all compensation payable under this Act or under the lease;

(f) it is open for acceptance for a period of 3 months from the date on which it is produced.

(5) If the landlord accepts an offer which complies with subsection (4) above the incoming tenant shall pay to the landlord on demand all sums payable to him by the outgoing tenant on the termination of the tenancy in respect of rent or breach of contract or otherwise in respect of the holding.

(6) Any amount paid by the incoming tenant under subsection (5) above may, subject to any agreement between the outgoing tenant and incoming tenant, be deducted by the incoming tenant from any compensation payable by him to the outgoing tenant.

(7) A tenancy created by the acceptance of an offer which complies with subsection (4) above shall be deemed for the purposes of section 13 of this Act not to be a new tenancy.

DEFINITIONS

    "agricultural holding": s.1(1).

    "improvement": s.85(1).

    "landlord": s.85(1).

    "lease": s.85(1).

    "market garden": s.85(1).

    "notice of intention to quit": s.21(2).

    "tenant": s.85(1).

    "termination of tenancy": s.85(1).

DERIVATIONS

    Agricultural Holdings (Scotland) Act 1949, s.66.

    Agriculture Act 1958, Sched. 1, Pt. II, para. 43.

GENERAL NOTE

    See Gill, paras. 549, 552. (For the corresponding English provision see the Agricultural Holdings Act 1986, s.80).

Subs. (1)

    The onus is on the tenant who wishes to carry on market gardening but has been unable to obtain the agreement of his landlord to satisfy the Land Court that the holding or part of it is suitable for market gardening. A direction by the Court applies only to market garden improvements subsequently carried out.

Subs. (2)

    Connell (*op. cit.*, p. 182) suggests that the only obvious way of protecting the landlord's interest would be to require an increase in rent. Where the holding is divided as provided for in this subsection the aggregate rental may well be greater than the rent of the original holding.

Subs. (3)

    This gives effect to what is known as the Evesham Custom, whereby, when the use of the holding for market garden purposes depends on a direction of the Land Court, the tenant, if responsible for the tenancy terminating, is not to be entitled to compensation for his market garden improvements unless he can produce an offer from a third party to take on the tenancy and pay to the outgoing tenant all compensation due to him under this Act or the lease.

Subs. (4)

This prescribes certain requirements for such an offer. Connell (*op. cit.* p. 181–2), referring to the words "substantial and otherwise suitable person" (para. (b)) suggests that the offer must come from someone having sufficient capital resources and being otherwise capable, from experience and character, of undertaking the obligations of tenant. He indicates that objections similar to those which can be stated against a legatee or intestate successor under ss.11 and 12 could apply here. Should the landlord not, within the period prescribed, accept an offer complying with these requirements, the outgoing tenant will be entitled to compensation for his Sched. 6 improvements as well as his other outgoing claims.

Subss. (5) and (6)

This has the result that if the landlord accepts an offer complying with the requirements of subs. (4), the incoming tenant is in effect substituted for the outgoing tenant in respect of the latter's liability of any kind to the landlord at the termination of the tenancy. However, the incoming tenant can set off this liability against his liability to the outgoing tenant whose claims he will have undertaken to meet.

Subs. (7)

But for this provision, a new tenancy having been created by the change of tenant, the three-year period for review of the rent under s.13 would have started at the incoming tenant's entry. This subsection has the result that the three-year period is counted as if the original tenant had remained under tacit relocation.

Agreements as to compensation relating to market gardens

42.—(1) Where under an agreement in writing a tenant of an agricultural holding is entitled to compensation which is fair and reasonable having regard to the circumstances existing at the time of making the agreement, for an improvement for which compensation is payable by virtue of section 40 of this Act, such compensation shall, as respects that improvement, be substituted for compensation under this Act.

(2) The landlord and the tenant of an agricultural holding who have agreed that the holding shall be let or treated as a market garden may by agreement in writing substitute, for the provisions as to compensation which would otherwise be applicable to the holding, the provisions as to compensation in section 41(3) to (6) of this Act.

DEFINITIONS
"agricultural holding": s.1(1).
"improvement": s.85(1).
"landlord": s.85(1).
"market garden": s.85(1).
"tenant": s.85(1).

DERIVATIONS
Agricultural Holdings (Scotland) Act 1949, s.67.

GENERAL NOTE
See Gill, para. 553. (For the corresponding English provision see the Agricultural Holdings Act 1986, s.81).

Subs. (1)

This authorises the adoption of substituted compensation in respect of market garden improvements, although substituted compensation is inapplicable to other improvements in Pt. III of the Schedules unless the lease was entered into before January 1, 1921.

Subs. (2)

This results that where a holding is created as a market garden by agreement as opposed to Land Court direction, the parties can agree for substituted compensation on the basis of the Evesham Custom as embodied in s.41.

Miscellaneous

Compensation for disturbance

43.—(1) Where the tenancy of an agricultural holding terminates by reason of—
   (a) a notice to quit given by the landlord; or
   (b) a counter-notice given by the tenant under section 30 of this Act,
and in consequence the tenant quits the holding, subject to subsections (2) to (8) below, compensation for the disturbance shall be payable by the landlord to the tenant.

(2) Compensation shall not be payable under this section where the application of section 22(1) of this Act to the notice to quit is excluded by any of paragraphs (a) or (c) to (f) of subsection (2) of that section.

(3) Subject to subsection (4) below, the amount of the compensation payable under this section shall be the amount of the loss or expense directly attributable to the quitting of the holding which is unavoidably incurred by the tenant upon or in connection with the sale or removal of his household goods, implements of husbandry, fixtures, farm produce or farm stock on or used in connection with the holding, and shall include any expenses reasonably incurred by him in the preparation of his claim for compensation (not being expenses of an arbitration to determine any question arising under this section).

(4) Where compensation is payable under this section—
   (a) the compensation shall be an amount equal to one year's rent of the holding at the rate at which rent was payable immediately before the termination of the tenancy without proof by the tenant of any such loss or expense as aforesaid;
   (b) the tenant shall not be entitled to claim any greater amount than one year's rent of the holding unless he has given to the landlord not less than one month's notice of the sale of any such goods, implements, fixtures, produce or stock as aforesaid and has afforded him a reasonable opportunity of making a valuation thereof;
   (c) the tenant shall not in any case be entitled to compensation in excess of 2 years' rent of the holding.

(5) In subsection (4) above "rent" means the rent after deduction of such an amount as, failing agreement, the arbiter finds to be the amount payable by the landlord in respect of the holding for the year in which the tenancy was terminated by way of any public rates, taxes or assessments or other public burdens, the charging of which on the landlord would entitle him to relief in respect of tax under Part II of the Income and Corporation Taxes Act 1988.

(6) Where the tenant of an agricultural holding has lawfully sub-let the whole or part of the holding, and in consequence of a notice to quit given by his landlord becomes liable to pay compensation under this section to the sub-tenant, the tenant shall not be debarred from recovering compensation under this section by reason only that, owing to not being in occupation of the holding or part of the holding, on the termination of his tenancy he does not quit the holding or that part.

(7) Where the tenancy of an agricultural holding terminates by virtue of a counter-notice given by the tenant under section 30 of this Act and—
   (a) the part of the holding affected by the notice to quit given by the landlord, together with any part of the holding affected by any previous notice to quit given by the landlord which is rendered valid by section 29 of this Act, is either less than a quarter of the area of the original holding or of a rental value less than one quarter of the rental value of the original holding, and

   (b) the holding as proposed to be diminished is reasonably capable of being farmed as a separate holding,

compensation shall not be payable under this section except in respect of the part of the holding to which the notice to quit relates.

   (8) Compensation under this section shall be in addition to any compensation to which the tenant may be entitled apart from this section.

DEFINITIONS
   "agricultural holdings": s.1(1).
   "landlord": s.85(1).
   "notice to quit": s.21(2).
   "produce": s.85(1).
   "tenant": s.85(1).
   "termination of tenancy": s.85(1).

DERIVATIONS
   Agricultural Holdings (Scotland) Act 1949, s.35.

GENERAL NOTE
   See Gill, paras. 502–508. (For the corresponding English provision see the Agricultural Holdings Act 1986, ss.60, 61, 63).

Subs. (1)
   It appears that a defective notice to quit, if acted upon by the tenant, entitles him to compensation for disturbance (*Kestell* v. *Longmaid* [1950] 1 K.B. 233), the contrary view being, however, taken in two Sheriff Court Cases: *Forbes* v. *Pratt*, 1923 S.L.T. (Sh. Ct.) 91 and *Earl of Galloway* v. *Elliot*, 1926 S.L.T. (Sh. Ct.) 123. The tenant retains his claim to compensation for disturbance, although his waygoing is delayed as a result of his serving a counter-notice or demanding arbitration as the case may be (see s.23(3)(4)). Again, the better view appears to be that the unsuccessful defence of the action of removing does not deprive the tenant of his claim (*Preston* v. *Norfolk County Council* [1947] K.B. 775).
   In addition to the two instances mentioned in this subsection, compensation for disturbance is payable (a) when the tenant has lawfully sublet and becomes liable to compensate his sub-tenant in consequence of a notice to quit issued by the landlord (see subs. (6)); and (b) in terms of s.49(1)(a) where the tenancy is terminated *quoad* part of the holding under s.29; and (c) in terms of s.49(1)(b) where part of the holding is resumed in exercise of a power of resumption in the lease.

Subs. (2)
   In a case coming under para. (a) of s.22(2) the temporary nature of the let makes compensation for its termination unjustifiable. Again, in the cases covered by paras. (c) to (f) of s.22(2), the tenant's default as a result of which the tenancy is being terminated justifies the exclusion of this compensation. On the other hand, the compensation will be payable under para. (b) of that subsection where termination is taking place at the instigation of the landlord to make the holding or part of it available for non-agricultural use.
   Other cases in which compensation for disturbance is not payable are termination of the tenancy by the tenant's notice of intention to quit, termination by notice served on an executor under s.16 of the Succession (Scotland) Act 1964 and again termination by conventional irritancy. As to terination by legal irritancy see note to s.20.

Subs. (3)
   For reasons referred to below it is not often that a tenant will submit a detailed claim in terms of this provision. As to matters arising, where this is to be done see Connell (*op. cit.* pp. 153–154).

Subs. (4)
   Compensation of a year's rent as provided for in para. (a) is usually accepted particularly as the maximum that can be recovered by making a detailed claim is two years' rent. When a detailed claim is made, however, it is a question of fact whether the landlord has had a reasonable opportunity of valuing the items included (*Barbour* v. *McDonall*, 1914 S.C. 844).

Subs. (5)
   With owner's rates abolished in 1956 and agricultural land and farm buildings exempt from

rates since then, it seems unlikely that the rent forming the measure of compensation will require to be abated as provided for in this subsection. It appears that the rent payable for the last year of the tenancy should always form the criterion for compensation, disregarding any variation there may have been in earlier years.

Subs. (6)
The effect of this provision is to protect the position of the tenant who has lawfully sublet the holding wholly or partially and having received notice to quit from his landlord has required to give notice to quit to his sub-tenant, making him liable to the latter for compensation for disturbance. The tenant's own claim for compensation is preserved although he will not himself be quitting the holding or the part of it sub-let.

Subs. (7)
This gives significant relief to the landlord where, in response to a notice to quit a limited part of the holding, given under s.29, the tenant serves counter-notice in terms of s.30. The effect of this provision is that compensation for disturbance will be restricted to the rental value of the part of the holding affected by the notice to quit unless that part and any other part of the holding previously repossessed by the landlord under s.29 amounts to not less than a quarter of the holding in area or rental value and the holding as it remains is not reasonably capable of being worked as a separate unit.

Subs. (8)
This confirms the existence of compensation for disturbance as a separate claim which will be unaffected by any arrangements landlord and tenant may have made in respect of any other waygoing claims.

Compensation for continuous adoption of special standard of farming

44.—(1) Where the tenant of an agricultural holding proves that the value of the holding to an incoming tenant has been increased during the tenancy by the continuous adoption of a standard of farming or a system of farming which has been more beneficial to the holding than—
  (a) the standard or system required by the lease, or
  (b) in so far as no system of farming is so required, the system of farming normally practised on comparable holdings in the district,
the tenant shall be entitled, on quitting the holding, to obtain from the landlord such compensation as represents the value to an incoming tenant of the adoption of that more beneficial standard or system.

(2) Compensation shall not be recoverable under subsection (1) above unless—
  (a) the tenant has, not later than one month before the termination of the tenancy, given to the landlord notice in writing of his intention to claim such compensation; and
  (b) a record of the condition of the fixed equipment on, and the cultivation of, the holding has been made under section 8 of this Act;
and shall not be so recoverable in respect of any matter arising before the date of the record so made or, where more than one such record has been made during the tenancy, before the date of the first such record.

(3) In assessing the compensation to be paid under subsection (1) above, due allowance shall be made for any compensation agreed or awarded to be paid to the tenant under Part IV of this Act for any improvement which has caused or contributed to the benefit.

(4) Nothing in this section shall entitle a tenant to recover, in respect of any improvement, any compensation which he would not be entitled to recover apart from this section.

DEFINITIONS
  "agricultural holding": s.1(1).
  "improvement": s.85(1).
  "landlord": s.85(1).
  "lease": s.85(1).
  "tenant": s.85(1).

DERIVATIONS
    Agricultural Holdings (Scotland) Act 1949, s.56.

GENERAL NOTE
    See Gill, paras. 497–501. (For the corresponding English provision see the Agricultural Holdings Act 1986, s.70).

Subs. (1)
    While this subsection speaks of the continuous adoption of a standard or system of farming, it would appear that the tenant's claim will not be excluded because he has needed, in compliance with his lease, to depart from the system in the last year of his tenancy when his freedom of cropping and disposal of produce, as derived from s.7, does not apply. In practice, however, the possibility of a claim for what is termed "high farming" will often be excluded by requirements of the lease going beyond the normal standards of good husbandry. "High farming" as an independent statutory qualification for compensation was introduced by the 1923 Act. For the purpose of rent review s.13(6) directs that it be treated as a tenant's improvement but it does not fall within the category of improvements generally. Thus a tenant who has had successive tenancies of a holding does not have the benefit of s.34(5) as regards a high farming claim. Such a claim has to be as at the conclusion of the tenancy during which it has been earned. As with improvements generally, the criterion of assessment is the value to an incoming tenant assumed to be farming the holding on the same lines as his predecessor.

Subs. (2)
    While outgoing claims generally have to be intimated within two months of the tenant's waygoing, this is a claim of which intimation prior to waygoing is required. Again, a record of the state of cultivation prior to the application of the special standard or system is essential for the assessment of the claim.

Subs. (3)
    This is required to prevent duplication as between the allowance to be made for "high farming" and any amounts allowed for items of improvement which have contributed to the benefit derived from the tenant's operations.

Subs. (4)
    This is intended to obviate the possibility of a "high farming" claim enabling a tenant to recover compensation for some improvement which does not qualify for compensation, *e.g.* because it does not have the required consent of the landlord or because it had not been notified to him in conformity with the relevant statutory provision.

Compensation to landlord for deterioration etc. of holding

45.—(1) The landlord of an agricultural holding shall be entitled to recover from the tenant, on his quitting the holding on termination of the land tenancy compensation—
  (a) where the landlord shows that the value of the holding has been reduced by dilapidation, deterioration or damage caused by;
  (b) where dilapidation, deterioration or damage has been caused to any part of the holding or to anything in or on the holding by;
non-fulfilment by the tenant of his responsibilities to farm in accordance with the rules of good husbandry.
  (2) The amount of compensation payable under subsection (1) above shall be—
  (a) where paragraph (a) of that subsection applies, (insofar as the landlord is not compensated for the dilapidation, deterioration or damage under paragraph (b) thereof) an amount equal to the reduction in the value of the holding;
  (b) when paragraph (b) of that subsection applies, the cost, as at the date of the tenant's quitting the holding, of making good the dilapidation, deterioration or damage.
  (3) Notwithstanding anything in this Act, the landlord may, in lieu of claiming compensation under subsection (1)(b) above, claim compensation in respect of matters specified therein, under and in accordance with a lease in writing, so however that—

(a) compensation shall be so claimed only on the tenant's quitting the holding on the termination of the tenancy;

(b) subject to section 46(4) of this Act compensation shall not be claimed in respect of any one holding both under such a lease and under subsection (1) above;

and compensation under this subsection shall be treated, for the purposes of subsection (2)(a) above and of section 46 (2) of this Act as compensation under subsection (1)(b) above.

DEFINITIONS
"agricultural holding": s.1(1).
"landlord": s.85(1).
"lease" s.85(1).
"rules of good husbandry": s.85(1); Agriculture (Scotland) Act 1948, Sched. 6.
"tenant": s.85(1).
"termination of tenancy": s.85(1).

DERIVATIONS
Agricultural Holdings (Scotland) Act 1949, ss.57, 58.

GENERAL NOTE
See Gill, paras. 555–557. (For the corresponding English provision see the Agricultural Holdings Act 1986, ss.71, 72).

Subs. (1)
The section replaces s.58 of the 1949 Act, covering general depreciation of the holding and s.57 of the 1949 Act, covering dilapidation or deterioration of, or damage to, particular parts of the holding or anything thereon, the two matters being dealt with in paras. (a) and (b) respectively of this subsection.

There are no statutory definitions of the terms "dilapidation" and "deterioration" but in Scammell and Densham, *The Law of Agricultural Holdings* (7th ed.), pp. 34 *et seq.*, where the matter is discussed at some length, it is indicated that "dilapidation" arises from a failure to repair items such as gates, fences or drains while "deterioration" applies to conditions not readily curable such as the loss of soil fertility resulting from lack of fertilisation or other forms of neglect.

Subs. (2)
For general depreciation, the measure of compensation is the decrease in value of the holding for which the tenant has been responsible in so far as not covered by compensation due for specific instances of dilapidation, etc.

Subs. (3)
Subsections (1) and (2) having dealt with the landlord's statutory claims for dilapidation, etc., this subsection preserves his right to claim in terms of a written lease where there is one, the measure of damages being that specified in the lease or applying by legal implication. Like the statutory claim, however, the claim under the lease as authorised by this subsection can be brought only on the tenant quitting the holding. The view has been expressed that the claim for compensation under s.57 of the 1949 Act did not prevent the landlord from proceeding against the tenant at any time during the currency of the tenancy for breaches of the lease (Gill, para. 554) but s.100 of the 1949 Act, which is referred to in support of that view, has not been reproduced in this Act.

The landlord cannot adopt the statutory basis for some items of a claim and the contractual basis for others, but it appears that he may present his claim in alternative terms and subsequently elect on which basis he is to pursue it (*Boyd* v. *Wilton* [1957] 2 Q.B. 277). In this connection a claim under s.46 is regarded as a separate matter. The concluding words of this subsection appear to be intended to make it clear that compensation recovered on a contractual basis for specific items is to be set against any statutory claim for general depreciation of the holding, it being permissible to present the respective claims on different grounds.

Compensation for failure to repair or maintain fixed equipment

46.—(1) This section applies where, by virtue of section 4 of this Act, the liability for the maintenance or repair of an item of fixed equipment is transferred from the tenant to the landlord.

(2) Where this section applies, the landlord may within the period of one month beginning with the date on which the transfer takes effect require that there shall be determined by arbitration, and paid by the tenant, the amount of any compensation which would have been payable under section 45(1)(b) of this Act in respect of any previous failure by the tenant to discharge the said liability, if the tenant had quitted the holding on the termination of his tenancy at the date on which the transfer takes effect.

(3) Where this section applies, any claim by the tenant in respect of any previous failure by the landlord to discharge the said liability shall, if the tenant within the period of one month referred to in subsection (2) above so requires, be determined by arbitration, and any amount directed by the award to be paid by the landlord shall be paid by him to the tenant.

(4) For the purposes of section 45(3)(b) of this Act any compensation under this section shall be disregarded.

DEFINITIONS
  "fixed equipment": s.85(1).
  "landlord": s.85(1).
  "tenant": s.85(1).
  "termination": s.85(1).

DERIVATIONS
  Agricultural Holdings (Scotland) Act 1949, ss.6(1)(2), 57(3).
  Agriculture Holdings (Scotland) Regulations 1950 (S.I. 1950 No. 1553).

GENERAL NOTE
  See Gill, para. 96. (For the corresponding English provision see the Agricultural Holdings Act 1986, s.9).

Subs. (1)
  This relates to the application of this section to the provisions of s.4 for the revision of written leases which may involve a transfer of liability for the repair and maintenance of items of fixed equipment from tenant to landlord.

Subs. (2)
  This proceeds on the basis that where a transfer of liabilities takes place, the tenant, having been previously liable, should make good any default by paying forthwith to the landlord compensation computed as it would be at the tenant's outgoing.

Subs. (3)
  Subsections (1) and (2) having dealt with the case of a transfer of liability from tenant to landlord as provided for in s.6(1) of the 1949 Act, this subsection could have been expected to deal with the transfer of liability from landlord to tenant as provided for in s.6(2) of the 1949 Act. It appears, however, that s.6(2) has been treated as spent, having been regarded as misconceived and unnecessary in respect of the fact that s.5 (in this Act and in the 1949 Act) determines the tenant's liability for the maintenance of fixed equipment, making an arbitration on that matter unnecessary and inappropriate. Whether or not that view is justified even in the case of leases to which s.5 applies it is clear that without the transfer provisions of s.6(2) of the 1949 Act, this subsection is meaningless and ineffective.

Subs. (4)
  The effect of this provision is that a landlord who has proceeded either on the basis of the lease or under the Act in making a claim under this section is to be entitled, if he chooses, to make his claim for dilapidations, etc. at the tenant's outgoing on the other basis.

Provisions supplementary to ss.45 and 46

47.—(1) Compensation shall not be recoverable under section 45 of this Act, unless the landlord has, not later than 3 months before the termination of the tenancy, given notice in writing to the tenant of his intention to claim compensation thereunder.

(2) Subsection (3) below shall apply to compensation—

(a) under section 45 of this Act, where the lease was entered into after July 31, 1931; or

(b) where the lease was entered into on or after November 1, 1948.

(3) When this subsection applies, no compensation shall be recoverable—

(a) unless during the occupancy of the tenant a record of the condition of the fixed equipment on, and cultivation of, the holding has been made under section 8 of this Act;

(b) in respect of any matter arising before the date of the record referred to in paragraph (a) above; or

(c) where more than one such record has been made during the tenant's occupancy, in respect of any matter arising before the date of the first such record.

(4) If the landlord and the tenant so agree in writing a record of the condition of the holding shall, notwithstanding that it was made during the occupancy of a previous tenant, be deemed, for the purposes of subsection (3) above, to have been made during the occupancy of the tenant and on such date as may be specified in the agreement and shall have effect subject to such modifications (if any) as may be so specified.

(5) Where the tenant has remained in his holding during 2 or more tenancies, his landlord shall not be deprived of his right to compensation under section 45 of this Act in respect of any dilapidation, deterioration or damage by reason only that the tenancy during which the relevant act or omission occurred was a tenancy other than the tenancy at the termination of which the tenant quit the holding.

DEFINITIONS
"landlord": s.85(1).
"lease": s.85(1).
"tenant": s.85(1).
"termination": s.85(1).

DERIVATIONS
Agricultural Holdings (Scotland) Act 1949, s.59.

GENERAL NOTE
See Gill, paras. 558–560.

Subs. (1)
In contrast with claims by the tenant, whether on a statutory or contractual basis, and claims by the landlord on a contractual basis, which in terms of s.62(2) can be intimated at any time not later than two months after the termination of the tenancy, claims by the landlord under the Act have to be intimated at least three months before the termination. This has the result that in practice a landlord may be unable to make a statutory claim for dilapidation, deterioration or damage emerging during the last three months of the tenancy.

Subss. (2) and (3)
These relate to the existence of a record as a condition of the landlord's right to make outgoing claims. A record is required for a claim under the Act if the lease was entered into after July 31, 1931, when the 1931 Act took effect, and for a claim under any lease entered into after November 1, 1948, when the 1948 Act took effect. Since the provisions of s.5(1) for the making of a record of fixed equipment at the commencement of the tenancy tend, in practice, to be disregarded, a landlord, if he is to be in a position to make claims at the tenant's outgoing, will have to ensure that at some time during the course of the tenancy the provisions of s.8(1) are invoked by him or his tenant. Subs. (3) of this section has the result that a record made at a late stage in the tenancy may be of little or no value for this purpose.

Subs. (4)
This appears to recognise that the making of a record can entail considerable expense which can be minimised by the parties agreeing to adapt, as necessary, and accept a record made during the occupancy of a previous tenant.

Subs. (5)
This may be compared with s.34(5) in extending the scope of outgoing claims to events or happenings taking place during a previous tenancy of the outgoing tenant.

Landlord not to have right to penal rent or liquidated damages

48. Notwithstanding any provision to the contrary in a lease of an agricultural holding, the landlord shall not be entitled to recover any sum, by way of higher rent, liquidated damages or otherwise, in consequence of any breach or non-fulfilment of a term or condition of the lease, which is in excess of the damage actually suffered by him in consequence of the breach or non-fulfilment.

DEFINITIONS
"agricultural holding": s.1(1).
"landlord": s.85(1).
"lease": s.85(1).

DERIVATIONS
Agricultural Holdings (Scotland) Act 1949, s.16.

GENERAL NOTE
See Gill, paras. 2 and 145, Connell (*op. cit.* p. 127). (For the corresponding English provision see the Agricultural Holdings Act 1986, s.24).
This section strikes at penalty clauses in leases such as those exacting inflated amounts for breach of conditions affecting cultivation or cropping. The English case of *Wilson* v. *Love* [1896] 1 Q.B. 626 exemplifies the limitation of damages for such a breach to the loss actually incurred.

Compensation provisions to apply to parts of holdings in certain cases

49.—(1) Where—
  (a) the tenancy of part of an agricultural holding terminates by reason of a notice to quit which is rendered valid by section 29 of this Act; or
  (b) the landlord of an agricultural holding resumes possession of part of the holding in pursuance of a provision in that behalf contained in the lease;
the provisions of this Act with respect to compensation shall apply as if that part of the holding were a separate holding which the tenant had quitted in consequence of a notice to quit.

(2) In a case falling within subsection (1)(b) above, the arbiter, in assessing the amount of compensation payable to the tenant, shall take into account any benefit or relief allowed to the tenant under the lease in respect of the land possession of which is resumed by the landlord.

(3) Where any land comprised in a lease is not an agricultural holding within the meaning of this Act by reason only that the land so comprised includes land to which subsection (4) below applies, the provisions of this Act with respect to compensation for improvements and for disturbance shall, unless it is otherwise agreed in writing, apply to the part of the land exclusive of the land to which subsection (4) below applies as if that part were a separate agricultural holding.

(4) This subsection applies to land which, owing to the nature of the building thereon or the use to which it is put, would not, if it had been separately let, be an agricultural holding.

DEFINITIONS
"agricultural holding": s.1(1).
"improvements": s.85(1).
"landlord": s.85(1).
"lease": s.85(1).
"tenant": s.85(1).

DERIVATIONS
Agricultural Holdings (Scotland) Act 1949, s.60.

GENERAL NOTE
See Gill, paras. 233, 244–247, 422, 507, 508.

Subs. (1)
This provides for the payment of compensation in the same two situations in which s.31
provides for reduction of rent, namely the landlord's repossession of part of the holding as a
result of a notice to quit affecting that part or his exercise of a power of resumption. The
compensation will include the value of any improvements qualifying for compensation on the
area repossessed, as well as compensation for disturbance under s.43, and reorganisation
compensation under s.54, both based on the rental value of the area vacated. In the case of a
resumption, the tenant will also be entitled to compensation in terms of s.58.

Subs. (2)
As in the case of s.31(2), the practical effect of this provision is that where, as often happens,
the lease contains provisions for compensation payable to the tenant on resumption, the tenant
has the option of accepting these provisions or claiming his statutory rights, whichever is the
more advantageous course for him.

Subss. (3) and (4)
These deal with the special case where a tenancy which is predominantly non-agricultural,
and consequently does not comprise an agricultural holding within the meaning of this Act,
includes land used for agricultural purposes. Such land is to be treated for purposes of
compensation for improvements and for disturbance (and reorganisation compensation if
applicable) as a separate agricultural holding. The situation is one not often occurring in
practice, subs. (3) permitting the parties to contract out of the operation of the statutory
provisions.

Determination of claims for compensation where holding is divided

50. Where the interest of the landlord in an agricultural holding has
become vested in several parts in more than one person and the rent payable
by the tenant of the holding has not been apportioned with his consent or
under any statute, the tenant shall be entitled to require that any compensation payable to him under this Act shall be determined as if the holding had
not been divided; and the arbiter shall, where necessary, apportion the
amount awarded between the persons who for the purposes of this Act
together constitute the landlord of the holding, and any additional expenses
of the award caused by the apportionment shall be directed by the arbiter to
be paid by those persons in such proportions as he shall determine.

DEFINITIONS
"agricultural holding": s.1(1).
"landlord": s.85(1).
"tenant": s.85(1).

DERIVATIONS
Agricultural Holdings (Scotland) Act 1949, s.61.

GENERAL NOTE
See Gill, para. 437. (For the corresponding English provision see the Agricultural Holdings
Act 1986, s.75).
In addition to affecting the settlement of compensation for improvements and compensation
for disturbance, this provision applies under s.55(5) to reorganisation compensation and under
the Agriculture Act 1986, Sched. 2, para. 11(5) (as amended in terms of Sched. 11, para. 52(c))
to a claim for compensation for milk quota. On the rent being apportioned as directed the
tenant's claim will be payable by each proprietor in proportion to the rent payable for his
property.

Compensation not to be payable for things done in compliance with this Act

51.—(1) Notwithstanding anything in the foregoing provisions of this Act
or any custom or agreement—

(a) no compensation shall be payable to the tenant of an agricultural holding in respect of anything done in pursuance of a direction under section 9(2) of this Act;

(b) in assessing compensation to an outgoing tenant of an agricultural holding where land has been ploughed up in pursuance of a direction under section 9(2) of this Act, the value per hectare of any tenant's pasture comprised in the holding shall be taken not to exceed the average value per hectare of the whole of the tenant's pasture comprised in the holding on the termination of the tenancy.

(2) In subsection (1)(b) above "tenant's pasture" means pasture laid down at the expense of the tenant or paid for by the tenant on entering the holding.

(3) The tenant of an agricultural holding shall not be entitled to compensation for an improvement specified in Part III of any of Schedules 3 to 5 to this Act, being an improvement carried out for the purposes of—

(a) the proviso to section 35(1) of the Agricultural Holdings (Scotland) Act 1923;

(b) the proviso to section 12(1) of the 1949 Act; or

(c) section 9 of this Act.

DEFINITIONS
"agricultural holding": s.1(1).
"tenant": s.85(1).
"termination of tenancy": s.85(1).

DERIVATIONS
Agricultural Holdings (Scotland) Act 1949, s.63.
Agriculture (Adaptation of Enactments) (Scotland) Regulations 1977 (S.I. 1977 No. 2007).
Agriculture (Scotland) Act 1948, Sched. 1, Pt. II, para. 42.

GENERAL NOTE
See Gill, paras. 164 (subs. (1)), 476 (subs. (2)). (For the corresponding English provision see the Agricultural Holdings Act 1986, s.76).

Subss. (1) and (2)
Where land which the lease provided should remain as permanent pasture has been ploughed up in pursuance of an order under s.9 the order may require that a specified area in addition to the reduced area of permanent pasture should be left at the tenant's waygoing as permanent pasture or temporary pasture sown with a specified mixture of seeds. Such restoration of pasture does not qualify for compensation and the intention of subs. (1)(b) is to prevent a tenant who has a claim for pasture other than that left in accordance with the order nominating his inferior pasture as that laid down in terms of the order and claiming compensation for better pasture.

Subs. (3)
The provisos referred to in paras. (a) and (b) concern the tenant's obligation to restore fertility in cases where he has exercised his statutory rights of freedom of cropping and disposal of produce. Para. (c) is referring to action taken by a tenant in accordance with an order authorising the reduction of the area prescribed by the lease to be retained as permanent pasture. The effect of this subsection is that the tenant is not entitled to compensation for an improvement old or new in the part of the respective Schedules listing improvements for which no consent or notice is required if carried out for the purposes of any of the provisions listed. Section 9 having already been referred to in subs. (1), its inclusion here is perhaps *ob majorem cautelam*. Only the provisos referred to in paras. (a) and (b) appeared in the corresponding provision, being s.63(2) of the 1949 Act.

Compensation for damage by game

52.—(1) Subject to subsection (2) below, where the tenant of an agricultural holding has sustained damage to his crops from game, the right to kill and take which is vested neither in him nor in anyone claiming under him other than the landlord, and which the tenant has not permission in writing to kill, he shall be entitled to compensation from his landlord for the damage if it exceeds in amount the sum of 12 pence per hectare of the area over which it extends.

(2) Compensation shall not be recoverable under subsection (1) above, unless—

    (a) notice in writing is given to the landlord as soon as is practicable after the damage was first observed by the tenant, and a reasonable opportunity is given to the landlord to inspect the damage—

        (i) in the case of damage to a growing crop, before the crop is begun to be reaped, raised or consumed;

        (ii) in the case of damage to a crop reaped or raised, before the crop is begun to be removed from the land; and

    (b) notice in writing of the claim, together with the particulars thereof, is given to the landlord within one month after the expiry of the calendar year, or such other period of 12 months as by agreement between the landlord and the tenant may be substituted therefor, in respect of which the claim is made.

(3) The amount of compensation payable under subsection (1) above shall, in default of agreement made after the damage has been suffered, be determined by arbitration.

(4) Where the right to kill and take the game is vested in some person other than the landlord, the landlord shall be entitled to be indemnified by that other person against all claims for compensation under this section; and any question arising under this subsection shall be determined by arbitration.

(5) In this section "game" means deer, pheasants, partridges, grouse and black game.

DEFINITIONS
    "agricultural holding": s.1(1).
    "landlord": s.1(1).
    "tenant": s.1(1).

DERIVATIONS
    Agricultural Holdings (Scotland) Act 1949, s.15.
    Agriculture (Adaptation of Enactments) (Scotland) Regulations 1977 (S.I. 1977 No. 2007).

GENERAL NOTE
    See Gill, paras. 189–197. (For the corresponding English provision see the Agricultural Holdings Act 1986, s.20).

Subs. (1)
    The wording "damage from game the right to kill and take which is vested neither in him (the tenant) nor in anyone claiming under him other than the landlord" is intended to defeat a device whereby the landlord, to avoid liability, would, instead of reserving the shooting rights, require the tenant to sub-let the shootings to him.
    To exclude his claim the tenant must have express and unqualified written permission to kill the type of game causing the damage. A limited statutory right to kill deer, as conferred by the now-repealed provisions of s.43(1) of the 1948 Act, was held not to exclude the claim for damage done by deer (*Lady Auckland* v. *Dowie*, 1965 S.L.T. 76). A landlord may, however, restrict the tenant's right to kill game to certain species of game, in which case a claim for damage by that species, but not by any other form of game, will be excluded. The tenant was held to have a claim even where the game causing the damage came from an adjacent estate and that during the close season for shooting the type of game in question (*Thomson* v. *Earl of Galloway*, 1919 S.C. 611). While the damage for which a claim can be made has to exceed the minimum stated it appears that where this is so the whole amount and not merely the excess is payable (Connell, *op. cit.* p. 126).

Subs. (2)
    A tenant intending to make a claim must give the landlord two notices in writing, the first being a notice of damage and the second a notice of claim. The notice of damage has to be given "as soon as is practicable" after the tenant's first observance of the damage. In the correspond-

ing provision of the 1949 Act (s.15(1), proviso (a)) the words used are "as soon as may be" but the difference would appear to be insignificant. As regards the reasonable opportunity to be given for the landlord to inspect the damage, a distinction is made between the growing crop and a crop which has been reaped or raised but is still on the ground. Connell (*op. cit.* p. 126) recommends that if harvesting is imminent the landlord should be so advised and that the reference to crop in this context should be regarded as meaning the whole crop, including any part of it undamaged. As regards the notice of claim, it is convenient and customary for the lease to relate its terms to the rental year rather than to the calendar year, as the latter may result in the claim being received some considerable time after the tenant's outgoing. Specimen forms of notice of damage and notice of claim will be found in Connell (*op. cit.* pp. 239–240). The claim may be lodged during the currency of the yearly or rental period but it is doubtful if more than one claim can be lodged in respect of any one period (*Earl of Morton's Trs.* v. *Macdougall*, 1944 S.C. 410).

Subss. (3) and (4)
Here we have the statutory arbitration procedure applying not only as between landlord and tenant but also in a matter involving a third party. Provision is made for the situation in which the landlord has let the shooting rights to someone other than the agricultural tenant. In the absence of contracting out, which could appear to be permissible, the sporting tenant will carry the responsibility for damage by game to the agricultural tenant's crops and, although not a party to the agricultural tenancy, will have his liability determined, if necessary, by arbitration under this Act.

Subs. (5)
The basic principle being that the tenant is able to take action to prevent damage to his crops by any species of game which he is entitled to kill (*Ross* v. *Watson*, 1943 S.C. 406 at p. 419), ground game, comprising hares and rabbits, are excluded from the definition of game for the purposes of this section because of the tenant's rights under the Ground Game Act of 1880 and at common law.

Extent to which compensation recoverable under agreements

53.—(1) Unless this Act makes express provision to the contrary, where provision is made in this Act for compensation to be paid to a landlord or tenant—
  (a) he shall be so entitled notwithstanding any agreement, and
  (b) he shall not be entitled to compensation except under that provision.
  (2) Where the landlord and the tenant of an agricultural holding enter into an agreement in writing for such a variation of the terms of the lease as could be made by direction under section 9 of this Act, the agreement may provide for the exclusion of compensation in the same manner as under section 51(1) of this Act.
  (3) A claim for compensation by a landlord or tenant of an agricultural holding in a case for which this Act does not provide for compensation shall not be enforceable except under an agreement in writing.

DEFINITIONS
  "agricultural holding": s.1(1).
  "landlord": s.85(1).
  "tenant": s.85(1).

DERIVATIONS
  Agricultural Holdings (Scotland) Act 1949, s.64.

GENERAL NOTE
  See Gill, paras. 164 (subs. (2)), 438 (subss. (1)(3)). (For the corresponding English provision see the Agricultural Holdings Act 1986, s.78).

Subs. (1)
  "Express provision to the contrary" is to be found, *e.g.* in ss.34(4)(7), 37(2), 38(5), 42 and 45(3), each providing for substituted compensation. The general prohibition of contracting out is exemplified in the case of *Coates* v. *Diment* [1951] 1 All E.R. 890, where a limitation in a lease of the right to compensation for disturbance was held void.

Subs. (2)
This adds another exception to the general rule formulated in subs. (1) by enabling compensation for restriction of permanent pasture to be excluded where the parties to a lease have agreed on a reduction of the prescribed area of permanent pasture instead of having the matter referred to arbitration under the provisions of s.9.

Subs. (3)
It is not necessary that the agreement be a probative document—see s.78.

PART VI

ADDITIONAL PAYMENTS

Additional payments to tenants quitting holdings

54.—(1) Where compensation for disturbance in respect of an agricultural holding or part of such a holding becomes payable—
(a) to a tenant, under this Act; or
(b) to a statutory small tenant, under section 13 of the 1931 Act;
subject to this Part of this Act, there shall be payable by the landlord to the tenant, in addition to the compensation, a sum to assist in the reorganisation of the tenant's affairs of the amount referred to in subsection (2) below.
(2) The sum payable under subsection (1) above shall be equal to 4 times the annual rent of the holding or, in the case of part of a holding, times the appropriate portion of that rent, at the rate at which the rent was payable immediately before the termination of the tenancy.

DEFINITIONS
"agricultural holding": s.1(1).
"landlord": s.85(1)
"statutory small tenant": s.59.
"tenant": s.85(1).
"termination of tenancy": s.85(1).

DERIVATIONS
Agriculture (Miscellaneous Provisions) Act 1968, ss.9, 16, Sched. 5, para. 1.

GENERAL NOTE
See Gill, para. 509. (For the corresponding English provision see the Agricultural Holdings Act 1986, ss.60, 61).

Subs. (1)
Compensation for disturbance is regulated by s.43. While compensation under this provision is intended "to assist in the reorganisation of the tenant's affairs," it is payable without proof of loss in all cases where it applies (*Copeland* v. *McQuaker*, 1973 S.L.T. 186 at p. 191).
The statutory small tenant is a person who would have been a landholder with the security of tenure and other rights provided by crofting legislation but for the fact that the whole or greater part of the buildings and permanent improvements on his holding were not provided by him or by any predecessor in the same family. On being dispossessed by his landlord he has the same rights of compensation, including compensation for disturbance, as would be payable under the Agricultural Holdings legislation.

Subs. (2)
The rent payable immediately before termination is the criterion irrespective of any variation or abatement affecting earlier rents.

Provisions supplementary to s.54

55.—(1) Subject to subsection (2) below no sum shall be payable under section 54 of this Act in consequence of the termination of the tenancy of an agricultural holding or part of such a holding by virtue of a notice to quit where—
(a) the notice contains a statement that the carrying out of the purpose for which the landlord proposes to terminate the tenancy is desirable

on any grounds referred to in section 24(1)(a) to (c) of this Act and, if an application for consent in respect of the notice is made to the Land Court in pursuance of section 22(1) of this Act, the Court consent to its operation and state in the reasons for their decision that they are satisfied that termination of the tenancy is desirable on that ground;

(b) the notice contains a statement that the landlord will suffer hardship unless the notice has effect and, if an application for consent in respect of the notice is made to the Land Court in pursuance of section 22(1) of this Act, the Court consent to its operation and state in the reasons for their decision that they are satisfied that greater hardship would be caused by withholding consent than by giving it;

(c) the notice is one to which section 22(1) of this Act applies by virtue of section 25(3) of this Act and the Land Court consent to its operation and specify in the reasons for their decision the Case in Schedule 2 to this Act as regards which they are satisfied; or

(d) section 22(1) of this Act does not apply to the notice by virtue of section 29(4) of the Agriculture Act 1967 (which relates to notices to quit given by the Secretary of State or a Rural Development Board with a view to boundary adjustments or an amalgamation).

(2) Subsection (1) above shall not apply in relation to a notice to quit where—

(a) the reasons given by the Land Court for their decision to consent to the operation of the notice include the reason that they are satisfied as to the matter referred to in section 24(1)(e) of this Act; or

(b) the reasons so given include the reason that the Court are satisfied as to the matter referred to in section 24(1)(b) of this Act or, where the tenant has succeeded to the tenancy as the near relative of a deceased tenant, as to the matter referred to in any of Cases 1, 3, 5 and 7 in Schedule 2 to this Act; but the Court state in their decision that they would have been satisfied also as to the matter referred to in section 24(1)(e) of this Act if it had been specified in the application for consent.

(3) In assessing the compensation payable to the tenant of an agricultural holding in consequence of the compulsory acquisition of his interest in the holding or part of it or the compulsory taking of possession of the holding or part of it, no account shall be taken of any benefit which might accrue to the tenant by virtue of section 54 of this Act.

(4) Any sum payable in pursuance of section 54 of this Act shall be so payable notwithstanding any agreement to the contrary.

(5) The following provisions of this Act shall apply to sums claimed or payable in pursuance of section 54 of this Act as they apply to compensation claimed or payable under section 43 of this Act—

sections 43(6);
section 50;
section 74;

(6) No sum shall be payable in pursuance of section 54 of this Act in consequence of the termination of the tenancy of an agricultural holding or part of such a holding by virtue of a notice to quit where—

(a) the relevant notice is given in pursuance of section 25(2)(a), (b) and (d) of this Act;

(b) the landlord is terminating the tenancy for the purpose of using the land for agriculture only; and

(c) the notice contains a statement that the tenancy is being terminated for the said purpose.

(7) If any question arises between the landlord and the tenant as to the purpose for which a tenancy is being terminated, the tenant shall, notwithstanding section 61(1) of this Act, refer the question to the Land Court for determination.

(8) In this section—

(a) references to section 54 of this Act do not include references to it as applied by section 56 of this Act; and

(b) for the purposes of subsection (1)(a) above, the reference in section 24(1)(c) of this Act to the purposes of the enactments relating to allotments shall be ignored.

DEFINITIONS

"agricultural holding": s.1(1).

"agriculture": s.85(1).

"landlord": s.85(1).

"near relative": Sched. 2, Pt. III, para. 1.

"notice to quit": s.21(2).

"tenant": s.85(1).

"termination of tenancy": s.85(1).

DERIVATIONS

Agriculture (Miscellaneous Provisions) Act 1968, s.11.

GENERAL NOTE

See Gill, paras. 509–511. (For the corresponding English provision see the Agricultural Holdings Act 1986, s.61).

Note: the replacement of s.11 of the 1968 Act by this section would appear to have removed the problems referred to in Gill, para. 5.10 caused by s.11 remaining unamended after the repeal of s.18 of the 1968 Act.

Subs. (1)

Section 54 having linked the payment of reorganisation compensation with compensation for disturbance, this subsection deals with cases in which, although compensation for disturbance is payable, liability for reorganisation compensation can be avoided. Basically this applies where the landlord is obtaining possession of the land to use it for an agricultural purpose or where he establishes a case of hardship. Apart from the provisions made here a landlord does not have to disclose the ground on which he is to seek the Land Court's consent to the operation of a Notice to Quit until, having received counter-notice from the tenant, he applies for consent. If, however, a landlord, on obtaining possession is to avoid liability for reorganisation compensation, his notice to quit must disclose grounds which, if accepted by the Court in the event of the tenant contesting possession, will give him exemption. The tenant, when receiving notice to quit and deciding whether or not to contest possession, is to be made aware of whether or not he will be entitled to reorganisation compensation on quitting the holding.

Paras. (a) and (b) each provide for the landlord's statement of grounds for seeking possession being contained in the notice to quit. In a decision which has been the subject of some criticism, however, the Court of Session, overruling the Land Court's decision, held that the statement, which they regarded as constituting intimation of the plea of hardship, could be contained in a letter accompanying the notice to quit (*Graham* v. *Lamont*, 1971 S.L.T. 341; see also Gill, para. 309 and Articles 1972 S.L.T. (News) 129 and 1973 S.L.T. (News) 141).

In terms of para. (a), the grounds qualifying for exemption are to be taken from the alternatives specified in subs. (1)(a)–(c) of s.24, *i.e.* that interests of good husbandry or sound estate management or the desirability of use for agricultural purposes such as research.

Para. (b) deals with hardship as a ground for exemption. The nature of hardship in its statutory sense and the considerations making for a successful plea have been discussed under reference to s.24. A question has arisen as to what other than a specific reference to hardship in the notice constitutes adequate notice that the plea is to be taken. In *Graham* v. *Lamont* the Court of Session, again overruling the Land Court, accepted as sufficient the reference in the letter accompanying the notice to quit to an agreement made by the tenant when he obtained the tenancy to give it up if the landlord or a member of his family wished to farm the holding, coupled with a statement that the landlord's son, having completed a training in agriculture, wanted to take over the farm. On the other hand, in *Copeland* v. *McQuaker*, 1973 S.L.T. 186, a letter stating that the landlords had purchased the holding after the tenant had declined to exercise an option to purchase it and now required it for their own use was held not to constitute intimation of the hardship plea. A fuller discussion of this matter will be formed in the Articles referred to above and in Gill, paras. 384–385.

Para. (c) deals with the case of a notice to quit served on a near relative successor of a deceased tenant as referred to in s.25(2)(c). As to the procedure to be followed in such cases, see s.25(3) and the note thereon. With s.25(3) applying s.22(1), such a successor is entitled to serve a counter-notice. If, however, the notice to quit specifies a case taken from Sched. 2 (which Schedule lists the various special grounds on which consent to the operation of a notice to quit served on a near relative successor may be given), exemption from reorganisation compensation may, subject to subs. (2), be obtained.

Para. (d) deals with the special case for exemption arising under s.29(4) of the Agriculture Act 1967 where the tenancy being terminated is one granted on a terminable basis by the Secretary of State. In such cases no statement is required in the notice to quit and counter-notice is not competent.

Subs. (2)

This makes important restrictions on the scope of exemptions available under subs. (1).

Para. (a) excludes the case where the Land Court's reasons for consenting to the operation of a notice to quit include their being satisfied on the landlord's proposal to use the land for a non-agricultural purpose as referred to in s.24(1)(e).

Para. (b) excludes the case where the reasons for the court's consent include satisfaction on the matter of sound estate management, as referred to in s.24(1)(b), or, again, in a case involving a near relative successor, include his inadequate training or experience in agriculture (Case 1 or 3 of Sched. 2), or his occupancy of other agricultural land (Case 5 or 7 of Sched. 2), but in any of these cases the court, as stated in their decision, would also have been satisfied on the desirability of non-agricultural use as referred to in s.24(1)(e), had it been specified in the landlord's application.

Subs. (3)

Provisions for the payment of reorganisation compensation in cases of compulsory acquisition are contained in s.56.

Subs. (4)

As with the tenant's other outgoing claims, including compensation for disturbance, contracting-out is made incompetent.

Subs. (5)

This applies the rules applicable to payment of compensation for disturbance to reorganisation compensation payable in respect of holdings affected by sub-letting (s.43(6)), holdings where there has been division of ownership (s.50) and holdings where limited owners are in the position of landlords (s.74).

Subs. (6)

Subs. (1)(c) having dealt with the case of the near relative successor, this subsection is concerned with that of the successor who is not a near relative of the deceased tenant. Provided that notice to quit is given in conformity with the timing requirements of s.25(2) (*q.v.* with note thereon), counter-notice cannot be given. However, to secure exemption from liability for reorganisation compensation, the notice to quit must state that the tenancy is being terminated for the purpose of using the land for agriculture only.

Subs. (7)

The content of this subsection appeared in the 1968 Act as a proviso to subs. (7) of s.11, the subsection replaced by subs. (6). This restricted its effect in referring questions as to the purpose for which a tenancy is being terminated to the Land Court instead of to an arbitrator, to cases arising under the subsection of which it formed part. As a separate subsection, however, the provision may have a wider application. While it is not necessary for it to be invoked to give the Land Court jurisdiction in cases arising under subss. (1) and (2) of this section in which Land Court decisions follow upon counter-notices served by tenants, it could be significant in relation to what Gill, para. 510, describes as a lacuna in the 1968 Act not expressly remedied by this Act. This lacuna, which is discussed in the Article in 1973 S.L.T. (News) 41 referred to above, is represented by the absence of provisions enabling a tenant who is not seeking to retain possession to dispute the landlord's intentions as stated in the notice to quit, with a view to maintaining a claim for reorganisation compensation. If one can assume that a tenant can take this course although not serving a counter-notice, this subsection would seem to have the result that the dispute will be resolved by the Land Court and not referred to arbitration.

Subs. (8)

In s.56, s.54 is applied in relation to the compulsory acquisition of the tenant's interest.

The law relative to allotments is contained in the Allotment (Scotland) Acts 1892–1950, but the facilities for the creation of allotments are now seldom used.

Additional payments in consequence of compulsory acquisition etc. of agricultural holdings

56.—(1) This section applies where, in pursuance of any enactment providing for the acquisition or taking of possession of land compulsorily, any person (referred to in this section and in sections 57 and 58 of and Schedule 8 to this Act as "an acquiring authority") acquires the interest of the tenant in, or takes possession of, an agricultural holding or any part of an agricultural holding or the holding of a statutory small tenant.

(2) Subject to subsection (3) below and sections 57 and 58 of this Act, where this section applies section 54 of this Act shall apply as if the acquiring authority were the landlord of the holding and compensation for disturbance in respect of the holding or part in question had become payable to the tenant on the date of the acquisition or taking of possession.

(3) No compensation shall be payable by virtue of this section in respect of an agricultural holding held under a tenancy for a term of 2 years or more unless the amount of such compensation is less than the aggregate of the amounts which would have been payable by virtue of this section if the tenancy had been from year to year: and in such a case the amount of compensation payable by virtue of this section shall (subject to section 57(4) of this Act) be equal to the difference.

DEFINITIONS
"acquisition": s.59.
"agricultural holding": s.1(1).
"landlord": s.85(1).
"tenant": s.85(1).

DERIVATIONS
Agriculture (Miscellaneous Provisions) Act 1968, ss.12, 16.

GENERAL NOTE
See Gill, paras. 562 and 563. (For the corresponding English provision see the Agricultural Holdings Act 1986, s.12).

Subs. (1)
This defines the application of the section as relating to a compulsory acquisition of an agricultural tenancy interest or all interests in land subject to an agricultural tenancy.

Subs. (2)
This gives the tenant thus dispossessed a claim against the acquiring authority for reorganisation compensation as payable under s.54.
In the case of a compulsory acquisition this claim, like the dispossessed tenant's other claims against the acquiring authority, is tax free in the hands of the tenant.

Subs. (3)
This restricts the scope of the tenant's claim by excluding it if the duration of the tenancy is two years or more, unless the tenant would otherwise receive less than a tenant from year to year. It is assumed that with the tenancy of longer duration the compensation payable by the acquiring authority other than reorganisation compensation will adequately compensate the tenant dispossessed. That will not be so in the case of a year-to-year tenancy but if the exclusion of reorganisation compensation in the case of a longer tenancy is to have the result that the tenant receives less compensation than he would have received in aggregate as a yearly tenant, he will be entitled to receive reorganisation compensation to the extent of the difference.
The foregoing is thought to represent the intended meaning of the subsection. Its effect, however, would seem to have been rendered at least doubtful by a drafting error involving the omission in line 4, after the word "payable," of the words "by way of compensation and." Without these words, which appeared in s.12(2) of the 1949 Act, which this subsection replaces, the term "aggregate," as used in this subsection, would seem to be inapplicable.

Provisions supplementary to s.56

57.—(1) For the purposes of section 56 of this Act, a tenant of an agricultural holding shall be deemed not to be a tenant of it in so far as, immediately before the acquiring of the interest or taking of possession referred to in that section, he was neither in possession, nor entitled to take possession, of any land comprised in the holding: and in determining, for those purposes, whether a tenant was so entitled, any lease relating to the land of a kind referred to in section 2(1) of this Act which has not taken effect as a lease of the land from year to year shall be ignored.

(2) Section 56(1) of this Act shall not apply—

(a) where the acquiring authority require the land comprised in the holding or part in question for the purposes of agricultural research or experiment or of demonstrating agricultural methods or for the purposes of the enactments relating to smallholdings;

(b) where the Secretary of State acquires the land under section 57(1)(c) or 64 of the Agricultural (Scotland) Act 1948.

(3) Where an acquiring authority exercise, in relation to any land, power to acquire or take possession of land compulsorily which is conferred on the authority by virtue of section 102 or 110 of the Town and Country Planning (Scotland) Act 1972 or section 7 of the New Towns (Scotland) Act 1968, the authority shall be deemed for the purposes of subsection (2) above not to require the land for any of the purposes mentioned in that subsection.

(4) Schedule 8 to this Act shall have effect in relation to payments under section 56 of this Act.

DEFINITIONS
"acquiring authority": ss.56(1); 59.
"agricultural holding": s.1(1).
"tenant": s.85(1).

DERIVATIONS
Agriculture (Miscellaneous Provisions) (Scotland) Act 1968, s.14.
Town and Country Planning (Scotland) Act 1972, Sched. 21, Pt. II.

GENERAL NOTE
See Gill, paras. 562–563.

Subs. (1)
This excludes the right to compensation under s.56 where the tenant is neither in possession nor entitled to take possession of any land comprised in the holding. "Possession" is apparently intended to mean "actual possession." This was made clear in an interpretation provision (see s.17 of the 1968 Act) but it is not referred to in s.59, the interpretation section for this part of this Act. The particular situation contemplated appears to be one where the tenant has sublet but not where the sub-let is for less than from year to year and has not taken effect as a lease from year to year under s.2(1).

Subs. (2)
This excludes the right to compensation when the land is required for such purposes as agricultural research or the creation of smallholdings (*cf.* ss.24(1)(c) and 55(1)(a)) and again when the Secretary of State is acquiring land affected by severance in order to secure its full and efficient use (s.57(1)(c) of the 1948 Act) or land to be used for providing agricultural holdings of limited size (s.64 of the 1948 Act).

Subs. (3)
This limits the operation of subs. (2) by excluding from the acquiring authority's exemption from reorganisation compensation certain cases of acquisition for development purposes by local authorities or development corporations as authorised by the Secretary of State.

Subs. (4)
The assessment and payment of claims arising under s.56 is dealt with in Sched. 8 (*q.v.*), the claims being determined by the Lands Tribunal for Scotland.

Effect of early resumption clauses on compensation

58.—(1) Where—

(a) the landlord of an agricultural holding resumes land under a provision in the lease entitling him to resume land for building, planting, feuing or other purposes (not being agricultural purposes); or

(b) the landlord of the holding of a statutory small tenant resumes the holding or part thereof on being authorised to do so by the Land Court under section 32(15) of the 1911 Act; and

(c) in either case, the tenant has not elected that section 55(2) of the Land Compensation (Scotland) Act 1973 (right to opt for notice of entry compensation) should apply to the notice;

compensation shall be payable by the landlord to the tenant (in addition to any other compensation so payable apart from this subsection) in respect of the land.

(2) The amount of compensation payable under subsection (1) above shall be equal to the value of the additional benefit (if any) which would have accrued to the tenant if the land had, instead of being resumed at the date of resumption, been resumed at the expiry of 12 months from the end of the current year of the tenancy.

(3) Section 55(4) and (5) of this Act shall apply to compensation claimed or payable under subsection (1) above with the substitution for references to section 54 of this Act of references to this section.

(4) In the assessment of the compensation payable by an acquiring authority to a statutory small tenant in the circumstances referred to in section 56(1) of this Act, any authorisation of resumption of the holding or part thereof by the Land Court under section 32(15) of the 1911 Act for any purpose (not being an agricultural purpose) specified therein shall—

(a) in the case of an acquisition, be treated as if it became operative only on the expiry of 12 months from the end of the year of the tenancy current when notice to treat in respect of the acquisition was served or treated as served on the tenant; and

(b) in the case of a taking of possession, be disregarded;

unless compensation assessed in accordance with paragraph (a) or (b) above would be less than would be payable but for this subsection.

(5) For the purposes of subsection (1) above, the current year of a tenancy for a term of 2 years or more is the year beginning with such day in the period of 12 months ending with a date 2 months before the resumption mentioned in that subsection as corresponds to the day on which the term would expire by the effluxion of time.

DEFINITIONS
   "acquiring authority": s.59.
   "acquisition": s.59.
   "agricultural": s.85(1).
   "landlord": s.85(1).
   "lease": s.85(1).
   "statutory small tenant": s.59.
   "tenant": s.85(1).

DERIVATIONS
   Agriculture (Miscellaneous Provisions) Act 1968, ss.15, 14, Sched. 5, para. 5.

GENERAL NOTE
   See Gill, paras. 562–569, particularly paras. 563 and 566. (For the corresponding English provision see the Agricultural Holdings Act 1986, s.62).

Subs. (1)
   This shows that the section applies to resumption in respect of agricultural holdings under the provisions of leases as referred to in s.21(7)(a) and resumptions affecting statutory small tenants made with the authority of the Land Court under the relevant statutory provisions. In either case, however, the tenant's right to compensation under this section does not apply if the tenant is being dispossessed as a result of a notice to quit or notice of resumption under s.55(8)

of the Land Compensation (Scotland) Act 1973, given by the landlord by reason of a compulsory acquisition scheme and the tenant has opted under s.55(2)(b) of that Act (as amended in terms of Sched. 11, para. 2(c)) for the wider measure of compensation available to him under the compulsory purchase code.

Subs. (2)
Compensation under this section is in effect being given for dispossession without the normal period of notice and so is based on the additional benefit (if any) which the tenant would have obtained from the land affected had he been vacating it on the normal period of notice. The subsection postulates the land being due to be vacated on the expiry of twelve months from the end of the year of the tenancy current at a date two months before the date of resumption. The two-month period appears to be prescribed on the basis of the rules established in England as regards the minimum notice for resumption—see notes to s.21(7). It is necessary to read, along with this subsection, subs. (5), which defines the current year in the case of a tenancy of two years or more. The practical effect of these provisions is exemplified in Connell (*op. cit.* p. 29) the period covered by the claim varying according to the point within the tenancy year at which resumption takes effect. Failing agreement, the tenant's claim will go to statutory arbitration. In the case of arable land the arbiter will estimate the value of the crop or other produce of the land and make deduction for such disbursements as rent and expense of cultivation to arrive at the amount due. Where the land is in grass its potential letting value as grazings, less rent and expenses, will usually form the basis of assessment.

Subs. (3)
This renders contracting out incompetent and applies the provisions of the Act as regards divided holdings, holdings affected by sub-letting and holdings with limited owners in the position of landlords.

Subs. (4)
This puts resumption affecting statutory small tenancies in a similar position to resumption affecting agricultural holdings, which under s.44 of the Land Compensation (Scotland) Act 1973 (as amended in terms of Sched. 11, para. 34) are disregarded in assessing the compensation payable by an acquiring authority (see Gill, para. 564) except in the special circumstances specified.

Subs. (5)
See notes to subs. (2).

Interpretation etc. of Part VI

59. In sections 54 to 58 of and Schedule 8 to this Act—
"acquiring authority" has the meaning assigned to it by section 56(1) of this Act;
"statutory small tenant" and "holding" in relation to a statutory small tenant have the meanings given in section 32(1) of the 1911 Act; and
references to the acquisition of any property are references to the vesting of the property in the person acquiring it.

DERIVATIONS
Agriculture (Miscellaneous Provisions) Act 1968, ss.16, 17.

GENERAL NOTE
With regard to statutory small tenants, see note to s.54(1).
"Acquisition" applies to the transfer of ownership to the acquiring authority as contrasted with the "taking of possession," signifying a temporary requisition.

PART VII

ARBITRATION AND OTHER PROCEEDINGS

Questions between landlord and tenant

60.—(1) Subject to subsection (2) below and except where this Act makes express provision to the contrary, any question or difference between the landlord and the tenant of an agricultural holding arising out of the tenancy or in connection with the holding (not being a question or difference as to liability for rent) shall, whether such question or difference arises during the currency or on the termination of the tenancy, be determined by arbitration.

(2) Any question or difference between the landlord and the tenant of an agricultural holding which by or under this Act or under the lease is required to be determined by arbitration may, if the landlord and the tenant so agree, in lieu of being determined by arbitration be determined by the Land Court, and the Land Court shall, on the joint application of the landlord and the tenant, determine such question or difference accordingly.

DEFINITIONS
"agricultural holding": s.1(1).
"landlord": s.85(1).
"tenant": s.85(1).
"termination of tenancy": s.85(1).

DERIVATIONS
Agricultural Holdings (Scotland) Act 1949, ss.74, 78.

GENERAL NOTE
See Gill, paras. 606–610, 613, 662.

Subs. (1)
This provision, as previously embodied in s.74 of the 1949 Act, has a wide scope, being excluded only where the Act otherwise "expressly" provides (for instances of its exclusion such as existing under ss.20, 22 and 39 and 41, see Gill, para. 613). While the provision covers all questions arising during or at the termination of a tenancy it does not apply to questions concerning the creation or existence of a landlord-tenant relationship in an agricultural tenancy (*Houison Cranfords Trs.* v. *Davies*, 1951 S.C. 1; *Brodie* v. *Kerr*: *McCallum* v. *McNair*, 1952 S.C. 216, *Cormack* v. *McIldowie's Executor*, 1974 S.L.T. 178 (O.H.), *Craig and Another*, 1981 S.L.T. (Land Ct.) 12). For its application there must be a subsisting relationship of landlord and tenant between the parties. Thus it does not affect questions between incoming and outgoing tenants.

Where the statutory arbitration applies, the jurisdiction of the court cannot be expressly prorogated nor can it be impliedly prorogated by the failure of a defender in a court action to plead the provision (*Craig and Another*, above; see also *Taylor* v. *Brick*, 1982 S.L.T. 25). Thus any action of removing, whether based on irritancy, resumption or notice to quit if defended on the merits, must be sisted for the statutory arbitration. In other processes a defender seeking to invoke this subsection must aver specifically and relevantly that a question or difference falling within the subsection exists (*Brodie* v. *Kerr*, *supra*, at p. 227).

It appears, however, that a claim of damages arising *ex delicto* but involving the parties to a tenancy is not a matter for the statutory arbitration (*McDiarmid* v. *Secretary of State*, 1971 S.L.T. (Land Ct.) 4).

The wording "question or difference" involves that except in relation to waygoing claims covered by s.61(7) there is no distinction to be made between matters of arbitration and matters of valuation. The exclusion, however, of any "question or difference as to liability of rent" places a certain limitation on the scope of the statutory arbitration, but this is restricted to cases where the liability to pay the rent sued for is disputed upon grounds which, if sustained, would extinguish that liability. Hence it does not apply where the tenant claims to be entitled to withhold payment in respect of some default in performance of the landlord's obligations under the lease (*Brodie* v. *Kerr* (*supra*, at p. 226)). Again, a rent review under s.13 does not involve a question of difference as to liability for rent (*Boyd* v. *Macdonald*, 1958 S.L.C.R. 10).

Subs. (2)
The subsection does not extend the scope of the statutory arbitration (*Craig and Another*), but the practical advantages of the facility as compared with the statutory arbitration procedure are brought out in Gill, para. 662. To what is said there may be added the comment that the Fee Fund or court fees paid in the Land Court will normally be much less than the cost of an arbitration: again, the fact that the facility exists, even although it is not as widely used as it might be, has resulted in there being available reports of important cases, which would not have been published in any way had they been dealt with by arbitration.

Arbitrations

61.—(1) Any matter which by or under this Act, or by regulations made thereunder, or under the lease of an agricultural holding is required to be determined by arbitration shall, whether the matter arose before or after the passing of this Act, be determined, notwithstanding any agreement under the lease or otherwise providing for a different method of arbitration, by a single arbiter in accordance with the provisions of Schedule 7 to this Act, and the Arbitration (Scotland) Act 1894 shall not apply to any such arbitration.

(2) An appeal by application to the Land Court by any party to an aribitration under section 13(1) of this Act (variation of rent) against the award of an arbiter appointed by the Secretary of State or the Land Court on any question of law or fact (including the amount of the award) shall be competent.

(3) An appeal under subsection (2) above must be brought within 2 months of the date of issue of the award.

(4) The Secretary of State may by regulations made by statutory instrument subject to annulment in pursuance of a resolution of either House of Parliament make such provision as he thinks desirable for expediting, or reducing the expenses of, proceedings on arbitrations under this Act.

(5) The Secretary of State shall not make regulations under subsection (4) above which are inconsistent with the provisions of Schedule 7 to this Act.

(6) Section 62 of this Act shall apply to the determination by arbitration of any claims which arise—

(a) under this Act or any custom or agreement, and

(b) on or out of the termination of the tenancy of an agricultural holding or part thereof.

(7) This section and section 60 of this Act shall not apply to valuations of sheep stocks, dung, fallow, straw, crops, fences and other specific things the property of an outgoing tenant, agreed under a lease to be taken over from him at the termination of a tenancy by the landlord or the incoming tenant, or to any questions which it may be necessary to determine in order to ascertain the sum to be paid in pursuance of such an agreement, whether such valuations and questions are referred to arbitration under the lease or not.

(8) Any valuation or question mentioned in subsection (7) above falling to be decided by reference to a date after May 16, 1975, which would, if it had fallen to be decided by reference to a date immediately before that day, have been decided by reference to fiars prices, shall be decided in such manner as the parties may by agreement determine or, failing such agreement, shall, notwithstanding the provisions of that subsection, be decided by arbitration under this Act.

DEFINITIONS
  "agricultural holding": s.1(1).
  "landlord": s.85(1).
  "lease": s.85(1).
  "tenant": s.85(1).
  "termination of tenancy": s.85(1).

DERIVATIONS
  Agricultural Holdings (Scotland) Act 1949, ss.68, 75.
  Local Government (Scotland) Act 1973, s.228(5).
  Agricultural Holdings (Scotland) Act 1983, s.5(1).

GENERAL NOTE
  See Gill, paras. 219, 448, 611, 612, 614. (For the corresponding English provision see the Agricultural Holdings Act 1986, s.84 and Sched. 11).

Subs. (1)
  This establishes the form of the statutory arbitration involving a reference to a single arbiter

applying to all questions or disputes between landlord and tenant apart from the matters referred to in subs. (7). When subs. (1) operates, a reference to two arbiters and an oversman, as sometimes prescribed in leases or agreements, is incompetent. The same rule has been applied to arbitrations on milk quota compensation (Agriculture Act 1986, Sched. 2, paras. 10(1) and 11(4) as amended in terms of Sched. 11, paras. 51 and 52).

Subss. (2) and (3)
This right of appeal, restricted to arbitrations for variation of rent, and available within two months of the issue of the arbiter's award, was introduced by the 1983 Act. Certain procedural matters arising in connection with these appeals are discussed in Gill, para. 219. It should be noted that if the court sustains the appeal it must make its own determination of the question at issue, a remit to the arbiter, who is by then *functus*, not being competent.

Subss. (4) and (5)
The Secretary of State's power, which has not yet been exercised, has been extended to arbitrations under the Opencast Coal Act 1958 (Sched. 7, paras. 4(4) and 25, as amended in terms of Sched. 11, para. 21), the Agriculture Act 1967 (Sched. 3, para. 7(5) as amended in terms of Sched. 11, para. 31 on breach of conditions applying to amalgamated agricultural units), and the Agriculture Act 1986 (Sched. 2, paras. 10(1) and 11(4) as amended in terms of Sched. 11, paras. 51, 52 dealing with milk quota compensation). Any regulations made under these powers must not be inconsistent with the code of rules for arbitration procedure contained in Sched. 7 to this Act.

Subs. (6)
The substantive content of this provision is repeated in s.62(1) (*q.v.*).

Subs. (7)
The exclusion of the statutory arbitration procedure applies only where the items in question belong to an outgoing tenant. It does not apply to transactions between an incoming tenant and a landlord who has been in possession (*Methven* v. *Burn*, 1923 S.L.T. (Sh. Ct.) 25) nor to the valuation of milk quota compensation (Agriculture Act 1986, Sched. 2, para. 11(4) as amended *ut sup.*). The excluded transactions may be referred to a single arbiter along with the statutory claims, but in the past, at least, it has been customary for the quantification and valuation of such items, as dung or crops for which an outgoing tenant is entitled to payment, to be covered by a reference to two arbiters and an oversman. These are common law arbitrations but are subject, where applicable, to provisions of the Arbitration (Scotland) Act 1894 and the Administration of Justice (Scotland) Act 1972 (see Gill, para. 615).

Subs. (8)
In the past Fiars Prices of grain, as fixed annually at the Fiars Court for determination of minister's stipends where there had not been created standard charges under the legislation of 1925, were sometimes prescribed as a measure of value in the claims of outgoing tenants for crops. The Local Government (Scotland) Act 1973, in abolishing Fiars Prices, provided by s.228(4) that any valuation or question which would have been decided on the basis of Fiars Prices should in future be decided, failing agreement on some other method, by a statutory arbitration.

Claims on termination of tenancy

62.—(1) Without prejudice to any other provision of this Act, any claim by a tenant of an agricultural holding against his landlord or by a landlord of an agricultural holding against his tenant, being a claim which arises, under this Act or under any custom or agreement, on or out of the termination of the tenancy (or of part thereof shall, subject to subsections (2) to (5) below, be determined by arbitration.

(2) Without prejudice to any other provision of this Act, no claim to which this section applies shall be enforceable unless before the expiry of 2 months after the termination of the tenancy the claimant has given notice in writing to his landlord or his tenant, as the case may be, of his intention to make the claim.

(3) A notice under subsection (2) above shall specify the nature of the claim, and it shall be a sufficient specification thereof if the notice refers to the statutory provision, custom, or term of an agreement under which the claim is made.

(4) The landlord and the tenant may within 4 months after the termination of the tenancy by agreement in writing settle any such claim and the Secretary of State may upon the application of the landlord or the tenant made within that period extend the said period by 2 months and, on a second such application made during these 2 months, by a further 2 months.

(5) Where before the expiry of the period referred to in subsection (4) above and any extension thereof under that subsection any such claim has not been settled, the claim shall cease to be enforceable unless before the expiry of one month after the end of the said period and any such extension, or such longer time as the Secretary of State may in special circumstances allow, an arbiter has been appointed by agreement between the landlord and the tenant under this Act or an application for the appointment of an arbiter under those provisions has been made by the landlord or the tenant.

(6) Where a tenant lawfully remains in occupation of part of an agricultural holding after the termination of a tenancy, references in subsections (2) and (4) above to the termination of the tenancy thereof shall be construed as references to the termination of the occupation.

DEFINITIONS
"agricultural holding": s.1(1).
"landlord": s.85(1).
"tenant": s.85(1).
"termination of tenancy": s.85(1).

DERIVATIONS
Agricultural Holdings (Scotland) Act 1949, s.68.

GENERAL NOTE
See Gill, paras. 429–436. (For the corresponding English provision see the Agricultural Holdings Act 1986, s.83).

Subs. (1)
Despite the comprehensive terms of s.60 it has been considered necessary to include in earlier legislation specific provision for arbitration as applying to certain matters. Here we have it applied to outgoing claims generally. As to the application of custom, see s.85(4), and as to "termination" of the tenancy s.85(1).

Subs. (2)
Two months from the termination of the tenancy (modified by subs. (6) if applicable) is the basic period for intimation of outgoing claims, but exceptions involving requirements of earlier notice exist under s.44(2) ("high farming") and s.47(1) (landlord's claims for dilapidation or deterioration). On the wording of this provision there would appear to be no reason why notice should not be given before the termination of the tenancy. Again it would appear that where in one of the exceptional cases notice as required has been given before the termination of the tenancy, further notice within the supervening period should not be required.

Subs. (3)
In contrast with the requirements applying after an arbiter has been appointed (see Sched. 7, para. 5), notice given at this stage does not require to be in detailed terms, nor need it quantify the claim.

Subs. (4)
The negotiating period, like the period for intimation of claims, runs from the termination of the tenancy. Hence if intimation of the claim has been delayed as long as permissible, the negotiating period may be only two months or slightly more. Any application for extension or further extension of that period must be made before expiry of the period or the initial extension.

Subs. (5)
Where claims are not settled within the negotiating period extended, as the case may be, a further month is allowed for the appointment of an arbiter by agreement (an agreement to appoint an arbiter not being sufficient; see *Chalmers Property Investment Co.* v. *MacCall*, 1951

S.C. 24) or for an application to the Secretary of State to be made for an appointment. That is the alternative available in terms of para. 1 of Sched. 7. The Secretary of State is, however, given a discretion enabling him, in special circumstances, to extend this period of one month. The only reported case bearing on the exercise of this discretion, as contained in previous legislation, appears to be *Crawford's Trs.* v. *Smith*, 1952 S.L.T. (Notes) 5.

Subs. (6)

The statutory interpretation of "termination" of the tenancy (s.85(1)) has been taken to mean the date when the contractual relationship ends rather than the date of complete vacation of the holding or cessation of the tenant's possession. As contained in s.68(5) of the 1949 Act, the provisions of this subsection have been held as not applying where the lease provides for vacation of part of the holding being deferred to enable a crop to be ingathered by the outgoing tenant, but only where a new agreement affecting part of the holding is concluded after the termination of the lease (*Coutts* v. *Barclay Harvey*, 1956 S.L.T. (Sh. Ct.) 54 following decisions of the English courts in *Swinburne* v. *Andrews* [1923] 2 K.B. 483 at p. 487 and *Arden* v. *Rutter* [1923] 2 K.B. 865). This subsection could not be invoked by a tenant unsuccessfully challenging or refusing to obtemper a notice to quit, his occupation beyond the ish not being "lawful" (see *Hendry* v. *Walker*, 1927 S.L.T. 333).

Panel of arbiters, and remuneration of arbiter

63.—(1) Such number of persons as may be appointed by the Lord President of the Court of Session, after consultation with the Secretary of State, shall form a panel of persons from whom any arbiter appointed, otherwise than by agreement, for the purposes of this Act shall be selected.

(2) The panel of arbiters constituted under subsection (1) above shall be subject to revision by the Lord President of the Court of Session, after consultation with the Secretary of State, at such intervals not exceeding 5 years, as the Lord President and the Secretary of State may from time to time agree.

(3)—

(a) the remuneration of an arbiter appointed by the Secretary of State under Schedule 7 to this Act shall be such amount as is fixed by the Secretary of State;

(b) the remuneration of an arbiter appointed by the parties to an arbitration under this Act shall, in default of agreement between those parties and the arbiter, be such amount as, on the application of the arbiter or of either of the parties, is fixed by the auditor of the sheriff court, subject to appeal to the sheriff;

(c) the remuneration of an arbiter, when agreed or fixed under this subsection, shall be recoverable by the arbiter as a debt due from either of the parties;

(d) any amount paid in respect of the remuneration of the arbiter by either of the parties in excess of the amount (if any) directed by the award to be paid by that party in respect of the expenses of the award shall be recoverable from the other party.

DERIVATIONS

Agricultural Holdings (Scotland) Act 1949, s.76.
Sheriffs Courts (Scotland) Act 1971, s.4.

GENERAL NOTE

With reference to subs. (3) it is pointed out by Connell (*op. cit.* p. 188) that it is for the arbiter to apply to the Secretary of State to fix his fee which is over and above his out-of-pocket expenses and that his application should give details of work done and time occupied, the process in the arbitration being submitted for reference in important or complex cases.

Appointment of arbiter in cases where Secretary of State is a party

64. Where the Secretary of State is a party to any question or difference which under this Act is to be determined by arbitration or by an arbiter appointed in accordance with this Act, the arbiter shall, in lieu of being appointed by the Secretary of State, be appointed by the Land Court, and the remuneration of the arbiter so appointed shall be such amount as may be fixed by the Land Court.

DERIVATIONS
Agricultural Holdings (Scotland) Act 1949, ss.77, 87(2).
Agriculture (Miscellaneous Provisions) Act 1968, s.17(3).

GENERAL NOTE
With the Secretary of State, through the Department of Agriculture, being a party to many tenancy contracts of agricultural land, a provision avoiding a situation of *auctor in rem suam* is appropriate and indeed necessary. This section is confined in its application to the appointment and remuneration of an arbiter but the position of the Secretary of State as landlord or tenant is dealt with on a more general basis by s.80.

Recovery of compensation and other sums due

65. Any award or agreement under this Act as to compensation, expenses or otherwise may, if any sum payable thereunder is not paid within one month after the date on which it becomes payable, be recorded for execution in the Books of Council and Session or in the sheriff court books, and shall be enforceable in like manner as a recorded decree arbitral.

DERIVATIONS
Agricultural Holdings (Scotland) Act 1949, s.69

GENERAL NOTE
See Gill, para. 438.
It is suggested by Connell (*op. cit.* p. 185) that the submission or award would not require to contain a warrant of registration for execution. It would seem, however, to be advisable that any agreement intended to be enforceable under this provision should contain a consent to registration for execution. The provisions of this section apply to compensation for milk quotas in terms of the Agriculture Act 1986, Sched. 2, para. 2 as amended in terms of para. 53 of Sched. 11 to this Act.

Power to enable demand to remedy a breach to be modified on arbitration

66.—(1) Where a question or difference required by section 60 of this Act to be determined by arbitration relates to a demand in writing served on a tenant by a landlord requiring the tenant to remedy a breach of any term or condition of his tenancy by the doing of any work of provision, repair, maintenance or replacement of fixed equipment, the arbiter may—
(a) in relation to all or any of the items specified in the demand, whether or not any period is specified as the period within which the breach should be remedied, specify such period for that purpose as appears in all the circumstances to the arbiter to be reasonable;
(b) delete from the demand any item or part of an item which, having due regard to the interests of good husbandry as respects the holding and of sound-management of the estate of which the holding forms part or which the holding constitutes, the arbiter is satisfied is unnecessary or unjustified;
(c) substitute, in the case of any item or part of an item specified in the demand, a different method or material for the method or material which the demand would otherwise require to be followed or used where, having regard to the purpose which that item or part is intended to achieve, the arbiter is satisfied that—
(i) the latter method or material would involve undue difficulty or expense,
(ii) the first-mentioned method or material would be substantially as effective for the purpose, and
(iii) in all the circumstances the substitution is justified.

(2) Where under subsection (1)(a) above an arbiter specifies a period within which a breach should be remedied or the period for remedying a breach is extended by virtue of subsection (4) below, the Land Court may, on the application of the arbiter or the landlord, specify a date for the termination of the tenancy by notice to quit in the event of the tenant's failure to remedy the breach within that period, being a date not earlier than whichever of the two following dates is the later, that is to say—

(a) the date on which the tenancy could have been terminated by notice to quit served on the expiry of the period originally specified in the demand, or if no such period is so specified, on the date of the giving of the demand, or

(b) 6 months after the expiry of the period specified by the arbiter or, as the case may be, of the extended period.

(3) A notice to quit on a date specified in accordance with subsection (2) above shall be served on the tenant within one month after the expiry of the period specified by the arbiter or the extended time, and shall be valid notwithstanding that it is served less than 12 months before the date on which the tenancy is to be terminated or that that date is not the end of a year of the tenancy.

(4) Where—

(a) notice to quit to which 22(2)(d) of this Act applies is stated to be given by reason of the tenant's failure to remedy within the period specified in the demand a breach of any term or condition of his tenancy by the doing of any work of provision, repair, maintenance or replacement of fixed equipment, or within that period as extended by the landlord or the arbiter; and

(b) it appears to the arbiter on an arbitration required by notice under section 23(2) of this Act that, notwithstanding that the period originally specified or extended was reasonable, it would, in consequence of any happening before the expiry of that period, have been unreasonable to require the tenant to remedy the breach within that period;

the arbiter may treat the period as having been extended or further extended and make his award as if the period had not expired; and where the breach has not been remedied at the date of the award, the arbiter may extend the period as he considers reasonable, having regard to the length of period which has elapsed since the service of the demand.

DEFINITIONS
    "fixed equipment": s.85(1).
    "good husbandry": s.85(1).
    "landlord": s.85(1).
    "notice to quit": s.21(2).
    "sound estate management": s.85(1).
    "tenant": s.85(1).
    "termination of tenancy": s.85(1).

DERIVATIONS
    Agriculture (Miscellaneous Provisions) Act 1976, s.13.

GENERAL NOTE
    See Gill, paras. 342–353.

Subs. (1)
    This subsection, like the remainder of the section, should be read along with the provisions of s.32. It discloses that the breach of the kind inferred to in s.32(1)(b) is one requiring to be remedied by work of provision, repair maintenance or replacement of fixed equipment and results that an arbiter called upon to consider a demand to remedy such a breach has a wide discretion in modifying or altering its content and specifying or extending the time allowed for compliance. From the tenant's point of view the importance of this provision is that whereas

before its introduction in the Act of 1976 he took the risk of losing his tenancy if he did not comply with such a demand to remedy, no modification of the demand nor extension of time allowed being then within the arbiter's powers, he can now invoke the arbiter's discretion on receiving the demand and base his response to it on the resultant ruling.

Subs. (2)

The specification or extension by the arbiter of a period for compliance with the demand to remedy may have the result that even if the tenant defaults in complying with the demand to remedy as modified or amended, the landlord will not be able to serve a notice to quit for the term for which it could otherwise have been served. To prevent a defaulting tenant in this way obtaining an extra year's possession of the holding, provision is made for the Land Court, on the application of the arbiter or the landlord, to specify a date for termination of the tenancy by notice to quit, which date must, however, be not earlier than the later of (a) the date on which the tenancy could have been terminated by notice to quit served on the expiry of the period specified in the demand or the date of the demand when no period is specified; or (b) six months after the expiry of the period specified or extended by the arbiter. The application in practice of this and the following subsections is exemplified in Gill, paras. 351–352.

Subs. (3)

This provides for the situation in which a second notice to quit has to be served. It requires service within a month of the expiry of the period specified or extended by the arbiter but enables a notice to be effective although served less than twelve months before its effective date and/or for a date other than the termination of the tenancy. Section 32(6), however, enables the tenant by serving counter-notice to make the operation of such second notice to quit subject to Land Court consent.

Subs. (4)

This deals with the situation in which the tenant's failure to obtemper timeously a demand to remedy can be attributed to something happening before the period for remedial action has expired which would make it unreasonable to require the breach to be remedied within that period. Although the nature of the occurrence is not specified, the subsection would appear to be referring to some personal disaster affecting the tenant or again to some external factor such as failure of contractors, industrial disputes or exceptional weather conditions. When notice to quit founding on the failure to remedy is served and the tenant calls for arbitration, the arbiter, if the demand has been fulfilled late, may make an award in the tenant's favour by treating the time limit for compliance as having been extended retrospectively. Again, if the breach remains unremedied he can extend the time for compliance to the extent he considers reasonable, having regard to the time which has already passed since the service of the demand.

In either case the notice to quit, as a notice under s.22(2)(d) enforceable without Land Court consent, will be invalidated, but in the latter case the landlord will be able to serve a second notice to quit based on the demand to remedy should the tenant fail to obtemper the demand within the extended period allowed by the arbiter.

Prohibition of appeal to sheriff principal

67. Where jurisdiction is conferred by this Act on the sheriff, there shall be no appeal to the sheriff principal.

DERIVATIONS

Agricultural Holdings (Scotland) Act 1949, s.91.
Sheriffs Courts (Scotland) Act 1971, s.4.

GENERAL NOTE

See Gill, para. 674.

The terms "Sheriff" and "Sheriff Substitute" now fall to be interpreted in accordance with s.49 of the Sheriff Courts (Scotland) Act 1971 and the Interpretation Act 1978, Sched. 1. Either the Sheriff or the Sheriff Substitute is entitled to execute jurisdiction. The section applies only to jurisdiction conferred by this Act and not to any proceedings falling within the Sheriff's normal jurisdiction under the Sheriff Courts (Scotland) Acts 1907 and 1971 (*Cameron* v. *Ferrier* (1912) 28 Sh.Ct.Rep. 220).

Sheep stock valuation

68.—(1) This section and sections 69 to 72 of this Act shall apply where under a lease of an agricultural holding, the tenant is required at the termination of the tenancy to leave the stock of sheep on the holding to be taken over by the landlord or by the incoming tenant at a price or valuation to be fixed by arbitration, referred to in this section and sections 69 to 72 of this Act as a "sheep stock valuation."

(2) In a sheep stock valuation where the lease was entered into before or on November 6, 1946, the arbiter shall in his award show the basis of valuation of each class of stock and state separately any amounts included in respect of acclimatisation or hefting or of any other consideration or factor for which he has made special allowance.

(3) In a sheep stock valuation where the lease was entered into after November 6, 1946, the arbiter shall fix the value of the sheep stock in accordance—

(a) in the case of a valuation made in respect of a tenancy terminating at Whitsunday in any year, with Part I of Schedule 9 to this Act if the lease was entered into before December 1, 1986, otherwise with Part I of Schedule 10 to this Act; or

(b) in the case of a valuation made in respect of a tenancy terminating at Martinmas in any year, with the provisions of Part II of Schedule 9 to this Act, if the lease was entered into before December 1, 1986, otherwise with Part II of Schedule 10 to this Act,

and subsection (2) above shall apply in such a case as if for the words from "show the basis" to the end of the subsection there were substituted the words "state separately the particulars set forth in Part III of Schedule 9 (or, as the case may be, Schedule 10) to this Act."

(4) Where an arbiter fails to comply with any requirement of subsection (2) or (3) above, his award may be set aside by the sheriff.

(5) The Secretary of State may, by order made by statutory instrument subject to annulment in pursuance of a resolution of either House of Parliament, vary the provisions of Schedule 10 to this Act, in relation to sheep stock valuations under leases entered into on or after the date of commencement of the order.

DEFINITIONS
"agricultural holding": s.72.
"arbiter": s.72.
"landlord": s.85(1).
"lease": s.85(1).
"tenant": s.85(1).
"termination of tenancy": s.85(1).

DERIVATIONS
Sheep Stocks Valuation (Scotland) Act 1937, s.1.
Hill Farming Act 1946, s.28.
Hill Farming Act 1946 (Variation of Second Schedule) (Scotland) Order 1986 (S.I. 1986 No. 1823).
Law Reform (Miscellaneous Provisions) (Scotland) Act 1985, s.32.

GENERAL NOTE
See Gill, paras. 454–470 and paras. 659–660.

Subs. (1)
The group of sections of which this is the first has the effect of embodying in this Act the statutory provisions previously existing outwith the agricultural holdings legislation, for the valuation of what are generally referred to as bound sheep stocks. This subsection prescribes the basic conditions for the application of these provisions. When the lease requires the outgoing tenant to leave a sheep stock to be taken over by the landlord or incoming tenant the sheep are said to be bound to the ground. The lease may specify the price at which the sheep are to be taken over but such an arrangement, which can operate inequitably with changes in value taking place during a tenancy of even moderate duration, is now uncommon in practice. The usual course is for the lease to provide for the price of the stock to be fixed by arbitration at the

tenant's waygoing and it is to such an arrangement that the legislation first introduced in 1937 has applied. The statutory provisions do not apply unless the outgoing tenant is obliged by the lease to leave the sheep stock. Otherwise any arrangement with the landlord or incoming tenant for the stock to be taken over at valuation will be implemented by a common law arbitration unaffected by these provisions (*Bell* v. *Simpson*, 1965 S.L.T. (Sh. Ct.) 9; see also *Toms* and *Parnell*, 1948 S.L.C.R. 8). Again, arrangements between a landlord who has been in occupation and an incoming tenant for the taking over by the latter of the sheep stock are unaffected, although the parties may agree to have the statutory basis operate at the tenant's entry as it will at his waygoing (*Secretary of State and White*, 1967 S.L.C.R. App. 133).

Subs. (2)
  With the exception of the basic provisions of the 1937 Act the legislation on sheep stock valuation has not operated retrospectively. November 6, 1946 is the date on which the Hill Farming Act of 1946 came into force. Section 28 of that Act amended the directions for valuation of sheep stock as contained in s.1(1) of the 1937 Act. These provisions, however, remain unaltered as applying to the terms of leases entered into not later than that date. They require firstly that the arbiter's award disclose the basis of valuation of each class of stock. (The various grades and classes of stock are now conveniently set out in Sched. 2 to the 1946 Act). Secondly, they require that there be stated separately any allowance made for acclimatisation or hefting or other special factors. By acclimatisation is meant the immunity which sheep reared and kept on certain ground acquire to diseases or infections prevalent there. Hefting signifies the tendency of sheep to remain on ground on which they have been reared and kept, thus reducing the costs of fencing and herding. While it was considered that these requirements for specification should counteract a tendency for arbiters to make over-generous awards, particularly for items such as hefting and acclimatisation, these provisions did nothing to limit the arbiter's unrestricted discretion in fixing the value of stock.

Subs. (3)
  In the case of a lease to which it applies, the 1946 Act severcly restricted the arbiter's discretion in the matters referred to above, conformity with the statutory schedule involving that he base his valuation of female stock and lambs on records of sales off the hill by auction during certain past years. This, however, was found to be an unsatisfactory basis of valuation, inconsistent as it is with the modern practice whereby only the cast ewes are normally disposed of by auction. This practice renders it difficult, if not impossible, to carry out a valuation on the prescribed basis and results that such a valuation may produce unjustified and unfair results. The difficulties experienced by the Land Court in making such valuations are exemplified in *Potts J.F.* v. *Johnston*, 1952 S.L.C.R. 22 and *Garrow and Another*, 1958 S.L.C.R. 13. An example of a result grossly unfair to the tenant is to be found in the case of *Tufnell and Nether Whitehaugh Co.* 1977 S.L.T. (Land Ct.) 14 (see also the article "Valuation of Bound Sheep Stocks," 1978 S.L.T. (News) 37). To resolve, so far as possible, the problems thus arising, the Secretary of State, in exercise of his powers under the equivalent of subs. (5) (*i.e.* s.28(1A) and (1B) of the 1946 Act) by S.I. 1986 No. 1823 provided, in relation to leases entered into on or after December 1, 1986, for a new method of determining basic ewe value, and extended certain limits within which under the 1946 provisions prices for animals in a particular stock could be adjusted. Where this amendment applies the basic ewe value is derived from sales evidence relating to "regular cast ewes" sold off the hill. For regular cast ewes as the term is applied in the locality where the stock is maintained, a true market exists. As introduced in the 1946 Act, the statutory schedule for valuations had to distinguish between and make separate provisions for Whitsunday outgoings in which a lamb crop is involved and Martinmas outgoings where that is not so. As a result of the 1983 S.I. we now have two Schedules, Scheds. 9 and 10, applying respectively to leases entered into before December 1, 1986 and other leases, each Schedule containing provision for a Whitsunday outgoing in Pt. I and a Martinmas outgoing in Pt. II. For fuller details of the valuation process as now operating, reference must be made to these Schedules.

Subs. (4)
  As an example of the operation of this provision as contained in s.1(2) of the 1937 Act, see *Dunlop* v. *Mundell*, 1943 S.L.T. 286.

Subs. (5)
  As mentioned in relation to subs. (3), the corresponding powers as contained in the previous legislation have been exercised to alter the rules for valuation as contained in the relative schedules.

Submission of questions of law for decision of sheriff

69.—(1) In a sheep stock valuation where the lease was entered into after June 10, 1937 the arbiter may, at any stage of the proceedings, and shall, if so directed by the sheriff (which direction may be given on the application of either party) submit, in the form of a stated case for the decision of the sheriff, any question of law arising in the course of the arbitration.

(2) The decision of the sheriff on questions submitted under subsection (1) above shall be final unless, within such time and in accordance with such conditions as may be prescribed by Act of Sederunt, either party appeals to the Court of Session, from whose decision no appeal shall lie.

(3) Where a question is submitted under subsection (1) above for the decision of the sheriff, and the arbiter is satisfied that, whatever the decision on the question may be, the sum ultimately to be found due will be not less than a particular amount, it shall be lawful for the arbiter, pending the decision of such question, to make an order directing payment to the outgoing tenant of such sum, not exceeding that amount, as the arbiter may think fit, to account of the sum that may ultimately be awarded.

DEFINITIONS
    "arbiter": s.72.
    "lease": s.85(1).
    "sheep stock valuation": ss.68(1) and 72.

DERIVATIONS
    Sheep Stocks Valuation (Scotland) Act 1937.

GENERAL NOTE
    See Gill, para. 659.

Subs. (1)
    June 10, 1937 is the date of passing of the 1937 Act which introduced this form of appeal but did not make it available under existing leases.

Subs. (2)
    As in the case of statutory arbitrations concerning matters other than sheep stock valuation, there is, under the Stated Case procedure, no right of appeal to the House of Lords (*cf.* Sched. 7, para. 21).

Subs. (3)
    As the preparation and hearing of a Stated Case may take some considerable time, this provision for an interim payment may be useful in preventing hardship to the tenant resulting from the delay.

Determination by Land Court of questions as to value of sheep stock

70.—(1) Any question which would fall to be decided by a sheep stock valuation—
    (a) where the lease was entered into before or on November 6, 1946 may, on the joint application of the parties; and
    (b) where the lease was entered into after that date shall, on the application of either party,
in lieu of being determined in the manner provided in the lease, be determined by the Land Court.

(2) The Land Court shall determine any question or difference which they are required to determine, in a case where subsection (1)(b) above applies, in accordance with the appropriate provisions—
    (a) where the lease was entered into before December 1, 1986, of Schedule 9 to this Act;
    (b) where the lease was entered into on or after that date, of Schedule 10 to this Act.

DERIVATIONS
    Sheep Stock Valuation (Scotland) Act 1937, s.3.
    Hill Farming Act 1946, s.29.
    Hill Farming Act 1946 (Variation of Second Schedule) (Scotland) Order 1986 (S.I. 1986 No. 1823)

GENERAL NOTE
    See Gill, paras. 663 and 467.

Subs. (1)
    Prior to the passing of the 1946 Act the position as regards referring sheep stock valuations to the Land Court instead of to arbitration was the same as that existing in respect of matters coming under the general statutory arbitration, *i.e.*, it required a joint application of the parties (*cf.* s.60(2)). In the case of leases entered into after its passing, however, the 1946 Act made the application of either party sufficient for this purpose.

Subs. (2)
    This contains provisions confirming that in exercising their jurisdiction in the case of a lease entered into after the passing of the 1946 Act, the Land Court are to proceed under the provisions of the appropriate Schedule according to whether the lease was entered into before or after December 1, 1986, when the rules for valuation were amended by statutory instrument.

Statement of sales of stock

71.—(1) Where any question as to the value of any sheep stock has been submitted for determination to the Land Court or to an arbiter, the outgoing tenant shall, not less than 28 days before the determination of the question, submit to the Court or to the arbiter, as the case may be—
    (a) a statement of the sales of sheep from such stock—
        (i) in the case of a valuation made in respect of a tenancy terminating at Whitsunday during the preceding three years; or
        (ii) in the case of a valuation made in respect of a tenancy terminating at Martinmas during the current year and in each of the two preceding years; and
    (b) such sale-notes and other evidence as may be required by the Court or the arbiter to vouch the accuracy of such statement.
    (2) Any document submitted by the outgoing tenant in pursuance of this section shall be open to inspection by the other party to the valuation proceedings.

DEFINITIONS
    "arbiter": s.72.
    "tenant": s.85(1).

DERIVATIONS
    Hill Farming Act 1946, s.30.

GENERAL NOTE
    See Gill, para. 468.

Subs. (1)
    This concerns the documents submission of which by the tenant is regarded as necessary to enable the arbiter or Land Court to value the sheep stock on the basis introduced by the 1946 Act.

Subs. (2)
    The documents submitted in compliance with subs. (1) being in effect productions in the valuation procedure, it is appropriate that they be open to inspection by the other party.

Interpretation of sections 68 to 71

72. In sections 68 to 71 of this Act—

(a) "agricultural holding" means a piece of land held by a tenant which is wholly or in part pastoral, and which is not let to the tenant during and in connection with his continuance in any office, appointment, or employment held under the landlord;

(b) "arbiter" includes an oversman and any person required to determine the value or price of sheep stock in pursuance of any provision in the lease of an agricultural holding, and "arbitration" shall be construed accordingly; and

(c) "sheep stock valuation" shall be construed in accordance with section 68(1) of this Act.

DERIVATIONS
Sheep Stocks Valuation (Scotland) Act 1937, s.4.

GENERAL NOTE
See Gill, para. 11.
Agricultural holding. The definition in s.1(1) requires modification as there cannot be a bound sheep stock on a holding which is wholly arable.
Arbiter. In terms of s.61(7) the provisions of s.61 making reference to a single arbiter mandatory in the case of a statutory arbitration under s.60 do not apply to sheep stock valuations, which in practice are frequently carried out by two arbiters with an oversman.
Sheep stock valuation. See s.68(1) and note thereon.

PART VIII

MISCELLANEOUS

Power of Secretary of State to vary Schedules 5 and 6

73.—(1) The Secretary of State may, after consultation with persons appearing to him to represent the interests of landlords and tenants of agricultural holdings, by order vary the provisions of Schedules 5 and 6 to this Act.

(2) An order under this section may make such provision as to the operation of this Act in relation to tenancies current when the order takes effect as appears to the Secretary of State to be just having regard to the variation of the said Schedules effected by the order.

(3) Nothing in any order made under this section shall affect the right of a tenant to claim, in respect of an improvement made or begun before the date on which such order comes into force, any compensation to which, but for the making of the order, he would have been entitled.

(4) Orders under this section shall be made by statutory instrument which shall be of no effect unless approved by resolution of each House of Parliament.

DEFINITIONS
"agricultural holding": s.1(1).
"improvement": s.85(1).
"landlord": s.85(1).
"tenant": s.85(1).

DERIVATIONS
Agricultural Holdings (Scotland) Act 1949, s.79.

GENERAL NOTE
See also the corresponding English provision: Agricultural Holdings Act 1986, s.91.
The Schedules referred to list respectively new improvements as defined in s.33(1) and market garden improvements as referred to in s.40(3). Under s.69 of the 1949 Act, which this section replaces, variations of the Schedule of new improvements which are incorporated in

Sched. 5 were made by the Agricultural Holdings (Scotland) Act 1949 (Variation of First Schedule) Order 1978 (S.I. 1978 No. 798).

Power of limited owners to give consents, etc.

74. The landlord of an agricultural holding, whatever may be his estate or interest in the holding, may for the purposes of this Act give any consent, make any agreement, or do or have done to him any act which he might give or make or do or have done to him if he were the owner of the dominium utile of the holding.

DEFINITIONS
"agricultural holding": s.1(1).
"landlord": s.85(1).

DERIVATIONS
Agricultural Holdings (Scotland) Act 1949, s.80.

GENERAL NOTE
See Gill, paras. 32 and 36. (For the corresponding English provision see the Agricultural Holdings Act 1986, s.88).
This provision is consistent with the definition of "landlord" in s.85(1) which includes a number of parties other than absolute owners. Among these are liferenters, who, while they may act as owners in many respects, would appear to be precluded from granting a lease of agricultural holding since by reason of the tenant's security of tenure it could extend beyond the life of the grantor.
As to "owner of the *dominium utile*" replacing "absolute owner", see notes on s.75. This section does not appear to contemplate the case where the landlord's title takes the form of a registered lease, although that possibility is provided for in s.75.

Power of tenant and landlord to obtain charge on holding

75.—(1) Where any sum has become payable to the tenant of an agricultural holding in respect of compensation by the landlord and the landlord has failed to discharge his liability therefor within one month after the date on which the sum became payable, the Secretary of State may, on the application of the tenant and after giving not less than 14 days' notice of his intention so to do to the landlord, create, where the landlord is the owner of the dominium utile of the holding, a charge on the holding, or where the landlord is the lessee of the holding under a lease recorded under the Registration of Leases (Scotland) Act 1857 a charge on the lease for the payment of the sum due.

(2) For the purpose of creating a charge of a kind referred to in subsection (1) above, the Secretary of State may make in favour of the tenant a charging order charging and burdening the holding or the lease, as the case may be, with an annuity to repay the sum due together with the expenses of obtaining the charging order and recording it in the General Register of Sasines or registering it in the Land Register of Scotland.

(3) Where the landlord of an agricultural holding, not being the owner of the dominium utile of the holding, has paid to the tenant of the holding the amount due to him under this Act, or under custom or agreement, or otherwise, in respect of compensation for an improvement or in respect of compensation for disturbance, or has himself defrayed the cost of an improvement proposed to be executed by the tenant, the Secretary of State may, on the application of the landlord and after giving not less than 14 days notice to the absolute owner of the holding, make in favour of the landlord a charging order charging and burdening the holding with an annuity to repay the amount of the compensation or of the cost of the improvement, as the case may be, together with the expenses of obtaining the charging order and recording it in the General Register of Sasines or registering it in the Land Register of Scotland.

(4) Section 65(2), (4) and (6) to (10) of the Water (Scotland) Act 1980 shall, with the following and any other necessary modifications, apply to any such charging order as is mentioned in subsection (2) or (3) above, that is to say—

(a) for any reference to an islands or district council there shall be substituted a reference to the Secretary of State;

(b) for any reference to the period of 30 years there shall be substituted—
    (i) where subsection (1) above applies, a reference to such period (not exceeding 30 years) as the Secretary of State may determine;
    (ii) in the case of a charging order made in respect of compensation for, or of the cost of, an improvement, a reference to the period within which the improvement will, in the opinion of the Secretary of State, have become exhausted;

(c) for references to Part V of the said Act of 1980 there shall be substituted references to this Act.

(5) Where subsection (3) above applies, an annuity constituted a charge by a charging order recorded in the General Register of Sasines or registered in the Land Register of Scotland shall be a charge on the holding specified in the order and shall rank after all prior charges heritably secured thereon.

(6) The creation of a charge on a holding under this section shall not be deemed to be a contravention of any prohibition against charging or burdening contained in the deed or instrument under which the holding is held.

DEFINITIONS
    "compensation for disturbance": s.43(1).
    "improvement": s.85(1).
    "landlord": s.85(1).
    "lease": s.85(1).
    "tenant": s.85(1).

DERIVATIONS
    Agricultural Holdings (Scotland) Act 1949, ss.70, 82.
    Water (Scotland) Act 1980, Sched. 10.

GENERAL NOTE
    See Gill, paras. 437, 438. (For the corresponding English provision see the Agricultural Holdings Act 1986, ss.86, 87).

Subss. (1) and (2)
    These provisions give the outgoing tenant to whom the landlord is due money by way of compensation in any form, a remedy additional to that available to him under s.65. They are extended to apply to compensation due for milk quota under para. 12 of Sched. 2 to the 1986 Act, as amended in terms of para. 53 of Sched. 11. While in practice this remedy is seldom used by an outgoing tenant, its existence has the result that where a purchaser is taking over a holding at the tenant's outgoing, although the outgoing claims will be the responsibility of the selling proprietor, the purchaser should be satisfied that these have been settled and so could not be made the subject of a charge in favour of the outgoing tenant.

Subs. (3)
    This will apply, for example, where a liferenter exercising the power which he will normally have under s.74, settles an outgoing tenant's claims. The wording of this provision differs from s.82(1) of the 1949 Act, which it replaces, in referring to the limited owner as not being owner of the *dominium utile* of the holding, whereas the 1949 Act used the words "not being absolute owner of the holding." "Absolute owner" is defined by s.93(1) of the 1949 Act as meaning "the owner or person capable of disposing by disposition or otherwise of the fee simple or the *dominium utile* of the whole interest of or in land, although the land or his interest therein is burdened charged or encumbered." It has not, however, been considered necessary to amplify on these lines the wording adopted in this subsection. That wording has been adopted in place of the reference to the absolute owner in the amendment of s.18 of the 1986 Act (concerning restrictions on agricultural use in environmentally sensitive areas) in terms of para. 45 of Sched. 11. The wording could conceivably cause difficulty in the rare case where the land in question is held otherwise than on feudal or leasehold tenure, *e.g.* on udal tenure or as allodial property.

This possibility was apparently envisaged in a now-repealed provision, s.38(1) of the 1948 Act, defining "owner" as "the person who is for the time being proprietor of the *dominium utile* or, in the case of land other than feudal land, is the owner thereof".

Subs. (4)

While the Secretary of State is empowered in terms of para. (b)(i) and (ii) to reduce the basic annuity period of 30 years, the method of repayment over a substantial period makes the arrangement unattractive, particularly to an outgoing tenant, and as a result such charges on agricultural land are seldom encountered in practice.

Subs. (5)

This has the result that the charge in favour of the limited owner will rank after such charges as feuduty or ground annual (if not redeemed) and heritable securities previously recorded.

Subs. (6)

Such prohibitions are not often included in modern deeds but will be found in Deeds of Entail as formerly in use. It has apparently been considered unnecessary to include in this Act the special provisions of s.81 of the 1949 Act, enabling an heir of entail to apply the proceeds of sales of entailed estate in reimbursement of expenditure incurred in settling outgoing tenants' claims.

Power of land improvement companies to advance money

76. Any company incorporated by Parliament or incorporated under the Companies Act 1985 or under the former Companies Acts within the meaning of that Act and having power to advance money for the improvement of land, or for the cultivation and farming of land, may make an advance of money upon a charging order duly made and recorded or registered under this Act, on such terms and conditions as may be agreed upon between the company and the person entitled to the order.

DEFINITIONS
"farming of land": s.85(3).

DERIVATIONS
Agricultural Holdings (Scotland) Act 1949, s.13.

GENERAL NOTE
For the corresponding English provision see the Agricultural Holdings Act 1986, s.87(7).
Charges of this kind are not common in practice, advances made by bodies such as the Scottish Agricultural Securities Corporation or by lenders such as banks being normally secured by Standard Security in terms of the Conveyancing and Feudal Reform (Scotland) Act 1970 granted by the proprietor of the security subjects.

Appointment of guardian to landlord or tenant

77. Where the landlord or the tenant of an agricultural holding is a pupil or a minor or is of unsound mind, not having a tutor, curator or other guardian, the sheriff, on the application of any person interested, may appoint to him, for the purposes of this Act, a tutor or a curator, and may recall the appointment and appoint another tutor or curator if and as occasion requires.

DEFINITIONS
"agricultural holding": s.1(1).
"landlord": s.85(1).
"tenant": s.85(1).

DERIVATIONS
Agricultural Holdings (Scotland) Act 1949, s.84.

GENERAL NOTE
The tutor, curator or other person appointed in terms of these provisions falls within the

statutory definitions of "landlord" or "tenant" as the case may be and, in the case of a landlord, will have the powers provided for in s.74.

Validity of consents, etc.

78. It shall be no objection to any consent in writing or agreement in writing under this Act signed by the parties thereto or by any persons authorised by them that the consent or agreement has not been executed in accordance with the enactments regulating the execution of deeds in Scotland.

DERIVATIONS
Agricultural Holdings (Scotland) Act 1949, s.85.

GENERAL NOTE
See Gill, para. 679.
This section has the result that any provision of the Act requiring agreement or consent in writing can be implemented by a document not fulfilling the requirements of probativity by being attested or adopted as holograph. Connell (*op. cit.* p. 192) suggests that this in effect places such documentation in the category of privileged writs such as these *in re mercatoria* on account of the rapidity with which they may have to be prepared.

PART IX

SUPPLEMENTARY

Crown and Secretary of State

Application to Crown land

79.—(1) This Act shall apply to land belonging to Her Majesty in right of the Crown, with such modifications as may be prescribed; and for the purposes of this Act the Crown Estate Commissioners or other proper officer or body having charge of the land for the time being, or if there is no such officer or body, such person as Her Majesty may appoint in writing under the Royal Sign Manual, shall represent Her Majesty and shall be deemed to be the landlord.

(2) This Act shall apply to land notwithstanding that the interest of the landlord or the tenant thereof belongs to a government department or is held on behalf of Her Majesty for the purposes of any government department with such modifications as may be prescribed.

DEFINITIONS
"landlord": s.85(1).
"prescribed": s.85(1).
"tenant": s.85(1).

DERIVATIONS
Agricultural Holdings (Scotland) Act 1949, s.86.
Agriculture (Miscellaneous Provisions) Act 1968, s.17(3).

GENERAL NOTE
See Gill, para. 29. (For the corresponding English provision see the Agricultural Holdings Act 1986, s.95).
These provisions are extended by s.16(7) of the Agriculture Act 1986 (as amended in terms of Sched. 11, para. 44(b)) to apply to rent arbitrations where milk quota is involved.
The power of the Secretary of State to prescribe modifications has not yet been exercised.

Determination of matters where Secretary of State is landlord or tenant

80.—(1) This section applies where the Secretary of State is the landlord or the tenant of an agricultural holding.

(2) Where this section applies, any provision of this Act—
(a) under which any matter relating to the holding is referred to the decision of the Secretary of State; or
(b) relating to an arbitration concerning the holding,
shall have effect with the substitution for every reference to "the Secretary of State" of a reference to "the Land Court," and any provision referred to in paragraph (a) above which provides for an appeal to an arbiter from the decision of the Secretary of State shall not apply.

DEFINITIONS
   "agricultural holding": s.1(1).
   "landlord": s.85(1).
   "tenant": s.85(1).

DERIVATIONS
Agricultural Holdings (Scotland) Act 1949, s.87(1).

GENERAL NOTE
   See Gill, para. 666(h).

Subs. (1)
   Like s.64 this section is directed to dealing but on a broader basis, with the problem of *auctor in rem suam* as it could arise where the Secretary of State as representing the Department of Agriculture is involved in the letting of holdings to farm tenants. The holding of tenancies departmentally is less common although not unknown. The Land Court's jurisdiction as derived from this section is extended to milk quota arbitrations in terms of paras. 10 and 11 of Sched. 2 to the Agriculture Act 1986 as amended to conform to paras. 51 and 52 of Sched. 11.

Subs. (2)
   Examples of cases to which these provisions will apply are to be found in ss.62(4)(5) and 75(1)(2)(3)(4). For a full list of functions of the Secretary of State which may be affected by these provisions, see Gill, para. 675.

Expenses and receipts

81.—(1) All expenses incurred by the Secretary of State under this Act shall be paid out of moneys provided by Parliament.
   (2) All sums received by the Secretary of State under this Act shall be paid into the Consolidated Fund.

DERIVATIONS
   Agricultural Holdings (Scotland) Act 1949, s.88.

Powers of entry and inspection

82.—(1) Any person authorised by the Secretary of State in that behalf shall have power at all reasonable times to enter on and inspect any land for the purpose of determining whether, and if so in what manner, any of the powers conferred on the Secretary of State by this Act are to be exercised in relation to the land, or whether, and if so in what manner, any direction given under any such power has been complied with.
   (2) Any person authorised by the Secretary of State who proposes to exercise any power of entry or inspection conferred by this Act shall, if so required, produce some duly authenticated document showing his authority to exercise the power.
   (3) Admission to any land used for residential purposes shall not be demanded as of right in the exercise of any such power unless 24 hours notice of the intended entry has been given to the occupier of the land.
   (4) Save as provided by subsection (3) above, admission to any land shall not be demanded as of right in the exercise of any such power unless notice has been given to the occupier of the land that it is proposed to enter during a period, specified in the notice, not exceeding 14 days and beginning at least

24 hours after the giving of the notice and the entry is made on the land during the period specified in the notice.

(5) Any person who obstructs a person authorised by the Secretary of State exercising any such power shall be guilty of an offence and shall be liable on summary conviction to a fine not exceeding level 2 on the standard scale.

DERIVATIONS
  Agricultural Holdings (Scotland) Act 1949, s.89.
  Criminal Law Act 1977, s.31.
  Criminal Procedure (Scotland) Act 1975, s.289.

GENERAL NOTE
  The provisions of this section may be compared with these of s.10 giving the landlord power of entry to the holding. These provisions for official inspection are more specific as regards the required notice of entry and the period during which access facilities are to operate. Their terms are virtually identical with those of s.82 of the 1948 Act. The powers concerning the exercise of which access may be required under this Act would appear to include the approval of an alternative provision made by landlord or tenant in lieu of his insurance obligation under paras. 5 and 6 of Sched. 1 or the making of charging orders in favour of outgoing tenants or limited owners in terms of s.75.

Land Court

Proceedings of the Land Court

83. The provisions of the Small Landholders (Scotland) Acts 1886 to 1931 relating to the Land Court shall apply, with any necessary modifications, for the purposes of the determination by the Land Court of any matter referred to them under this Act, as they apply for the purposes of the determination of matters referred to them under those Acts.

DERIVATIONS
  Agricultural Holdings (Scotland) Act 1949, s.73.
  Agriculture (Miscellaneous Provisions) Act 1976, s.14(6).
  Crofting Reform (Scotland) Act 1976, Sched. 2, para. 25.

GENERAL NOTE
  See Gill, paras. 668–671.
  The general effect of this section is to import into cases in the Land Court concerning agricultural holdings the Rules of the Court made under the Small Landholders Acts, small-holdings and crofts having been the court's original fields of jurisdiction. In addition to making detailed provision as to pleadings and procedure, the Rules, which are reproduced in the Parliament House Book and in Gill, pp. 717 *et seq.*, provide for an appeal by way of special care, on questions of law, from the Land Court to the Court of Session.

Service of notices

Service of notices, etc.

84.—(1) Any notice or other document required or authorised by or under this Act to be given to or served on any person shall be duly given or served if it is delivered to him, or left at his proper address, or sent to him by registered post or recorded delivery.

(2) Any such document required or authorised to be given to or served on an incorporated company or body shall be duly given or served if it is delivered to or sent by registered post or recorded delivery to the registered office of the company or body.

(3) For the purposes of this section and of section 7 of the Interpretation Act 1978, the proper address of any person to or on whom any such document as aforesaid is to be given or served shall, in the case of the secretary or clerk of any incorporated company or body, be that of the registered or principal office of the company or body, and in any other case be the last known address of the person in question.

(4) Unless or until the tenant of an agricultural holding shall have received notice that the person previously entitled to receive the rents and profits of the holding (hereinafter referred to as "the original landlord") has ceased to be so entitled, and also notice of the name and address of the person who has become so entitled, any notice or other document served on or delivered to the original landlord by the tenant shall be deemed to have been served on or delivered to the landlord of the holding.

DEFINITIONS
"agricultural holding": s.1(1).
"landlord": s.85(1).
"tenant": s.85(1).

DERIVATIONS
Agricultural Holdings (Scotland) Act 1949, s.90.
Companies Act 1985, s.725(1).

GENERAL NOTE
See Gill, para. 574 (relating to subs. (41)) and para. 678. (For the corresponding English provision see the Agricultural Holdings Act 1986, s.93).

Subss. (1)–(3)
These contain standard provisions for service of notices as required or authorised by statute. While these apply to notices generally, they would appear to be overridden in the case of notices to quit served by landlords which in terms of s.21(5) require registered post or recorded delivery (see Gill, para. 288).

Subs. (4)
This applies only where the party giving the notice holds the position of tenant. Accordingly, a legatee of a deceased tenant giving notice under s.11(2) or a successor on intestacy given notice under s.12(1), not yet having become tenant, will have to satisfy himself as to the identity and whereabouts of the present owner of the holding if there has been any change of ownership since the commencement of the tenancy.

Interpretation

Interpretation

85.—(1) In this Act, unless the context otherwise requires—
"the 1911 Act" means the Small Landholders (Scotland) Act 1911;
"the 1949 Act" means the Agricultural Holdings (Scotland) Act 1949;
"agricultural holding" (except in sections 68 to 72 of this Act) and "agricultural land" have the meanings assigned to them by section 1 of this Act;
"agricultural unit" means land which is an agricultural unit for the purposes of the Agriculture (Scotland) Act 1948;
"agriculture" includes horticulture, fruit growing; seed growing; dairy farming; livestock breeding and keeping; the use of land as grazing land, meadow land, osier land, market gardens and nursery grounds; and the use of land for woodlands where that use is ancillary to the farming of land for other agricultural purposes: and "agricultural" shall be construed accordingly;
"building" includes any part of a building;
"fixed equipment" includes any building or structure affixed to land and any works on, in, over or under land, and also includes anything grown on land for a purpose other than use after severance from the land, consumption of the thing grown or of produce thereof, or amenity, and, without prejudice to the foregoing generality, includes the following things, that is to say—
(a) all permanent buildings, including farm houses and farm cottages, necessary for the proper conduct of the agricultural holding;

(b) all permanent fences, including hedges, stone dykes, gate posts and gates;

(c) all ditches, open drains and tile drains, conduits and culverts, ponds, sluices, flood banks and main water courses;

(d) stells, fanks, folds, dippers, pens and bughts necessary for the proper conduct of the holding;

(e) farm access or service roads, bridges and fords;

(f) water and sewerage systems;

(g) electrical installations including generating plant, fixed motors, wiring systems, switches and plug sockets;

(h) shelter belts,

and references to fixed equipment on land shall be construed accordingly;

"improvement" shall be construed in accordance with section 33 of this Act, and "new improvement," "old improvement," "1923 Act improvement" and "1931 Act improvement" have the meanings there assigned to them;

"Land Court" means the Scottish Land Court;

"Lands Tribunal" means the Lands Tribunal for Scotland;

"landlord" means any person for the time being entitled to receive the rents and profits or to take possession of an agricultural holding, and includes the executor, assignee, legatee, disponee, guardian, curator bonis, tutor, or permanent or interim trustee (within the meaning of the Bankruptcy (Scotland) Act 1985), of a landlord;

"lease" means a letting of land for a term of years, or for lives, or for lives and years, or from year to year;

"livestock" includes any creature kept for the production of food, wool, skins or fur, or for the purpose of its use in the farming of land;

"market garden" means a holding, cultivated, wholly or mainly, for the purpose of the trade or business of market gardening;

"prescribed" means prescribed by the Secretary of State by regulations made by statutory instrument which shall be subject to annulment in pursuance of a resolution of either House of Parliament;

"produce" includes anything (whether live or dead) produced in the course of agriculture;

"tenant" means the holder of land under a lease of an agricultural holding and includes the executor, assignee, legatee, disponee, guardian, tutor, curator bonis, or permanent or interim trustee (within the meaning of the Bankruptcy (Scotland) Act 1985), of a tenant;

"termination," in relation to a tenancy, means the termination of the lease by reason of effluxion of time or from any other cause;

(2) Schedules 5 and 6 to the Agriculture (Scotland) Act 1948, (which have effect respectively for the purpose of determining for the purposes of that Act whether the owner of agricultural land is fulfilling his responsibilities to manage it in accordance with the rules of good estate management and whether the occupier of such land is fulfilling his responsibilities to farm it in accordance with the rules of good husbandry) shall have effect for the purposes of this Act as they have effect for the purposes of that Act.

(3) References in this Act to the farming of land include references to the carrying on in relation to the land of any agricultural activity.

(4) References to the terms, conditions, or requirements of a lease of or of an agreement relating to, an agricultural holding shall be construed as including references to any obligations, conditions or liabilities implied by the custom of the country in respect of the holding.

(5) Anything which by or under this Act is required or authorised to be done by, to or in respect of the landlord or the tenant of an agricultural holding may be done by, to or in respect of any agent of the landlord or of the tenant.

DERIVATIONS
Agricultural Holdings (Scotland) Act 1949, s.93.

GENERAL NOTE
See Gill, para. 574 (relating to subs. (4)) and para. 678. (For the corresponding English provision see the Agricultural Holdings Act 1986, s.96).

Subs. (1)
This forms the main or general interpretation provision in the Act. The following comments relate to the particular items specified.

Agricultural unit. This is defined in s.86(2) of the 1948 Act (*q.v.*) as land which is occupied as a unit for agricultural purposes. In *Jenners Princes Street Edinburgh* v. *Howe*, 1990 S.L.T. (Land Ct.) 26 it was held that the unit included any land actually occupied for agricultural purposes as a single unit whether formally or informally.

Agriculture. See Gill, paras. 23–25. This definition should be read with the definition of "agricultural land" for the purpose of ss.1 and 2. In the English case of *Rutherford* v. *Maurer* [1962] 1 Q.B. 16 the Court of Appeal held that the use of land let for grazing of horses belonging to a riding school constituted use for agriculture and being related to a business made the land agricultural although the business itself was not of an agricultural nature. That decision, which has been criticised in England (see *Howkins* v. *Jardine* [1951] 1 K.B. 614, *per* Jenkins L.J. at p. 629), has been followed in Scotland in *Crawford* v. *Dun*, 1981 S.L.T. (Sh. Ct.) 66. The definition of "livestock," as appearing later in this subsection, has the result that "livestock breeding and keeping" as a form of agriculture is not confined to ordinary farm animals such as horses, cattle, sheep and poultry. Modern livestock rearing includes activities such as deer farming and the definition refers not only to the production of food but also to that of wool, skins or fur. Where, however, the primary purpose of breeding or keeping certain types of livestock is unconnected with the commercial operation of farming, *e.g.* breeding for sport or for scientific research, it will not come within the statutory definitions of "livestock breeding and keeping" and "agriculture."

Fixed equipment. It should be noted that the items specified include "shelter belts," the creation of which results from "the use of land for woodlands as ancillary to the farming of land or other agriculture purpose" as referred to in the definition of "agriculture."

Lands Tribunal. The Lands Tribunal for Scotland established under the Lands Tribunal Act 1949 has sole jurisdiction in questions of compensation under the Land Compensation (Scotland) Act 1973 as affecting agricultural holdings and likewise under the provisions of this Act so far as relating to their compulsory purchase, *viz.* ss.56 and 57 and Sched. 8.

Landlord. See Gill, paras. 30–36. The term is widely defined so as to cover not only absolute beneficial owners but also limited owners such as liferenters or parties in right in administrative or fiduciary capacities. In all cases it is essential that the party who is to be regarded as holding the position of landlord should be entitled either to take possession of the property or to draw the rents due in respect of it. Steps to recover possession from a tenant may be initiated by a holder of the landlord's interest on an incomplete or unfeudalised title but the title must be completed before decree can be obtained (*Walker* v. *Hendry*, 1925 S.C. 855). A purchaser under Missives is not regarded as a landlord and cannot even initiate proceedings for recovery of possession (*Grandison* v. *Mackay*, 1919 1 S.L.T.). The appointment of a guardian such as tutor may be made under s.77 or under other statutory or common law authority. Liferenters will generally be regarded as landlords *pro tem.*, although it would be inconsistent with the limitation of their interest for them to grant an agricultural lease which by reason of security of tenure could endure beyond the expiry of a liferent.

Where the ownership of the holding is divided, the several proprietors together constitute the landlord and all must concur in any action relating to the tenancy such as proceedings for recovery of rent or steps taken to terminate the lease. A similar position exists in the case of *pro indiviso* ownership.

Lease. See Gill, paras. 57–61. Like other definitions in this subsection, the definition of "lease" which originated in an Act of 1883 applies "unless the context otherwise requires." It does so in the case of a lease of the kind referred to in s.2(1). Even where it applies, however, the definition excludes certain leases which would be valid at common law. A lease for a rotation of cropping but subject to termination in the event of a sale was held invalid (*Stirrat* v. *Whyte*, 1968 S.L.T. 157), while on the other hand a let for four years for cropping in each year (*McKenzie* v. *Buchan* (1889) 5 Sh.Ct.Rep. 40) and a lease for "four years and crops" as from its date (*Stonehaven* v. *Adam*, 1970 S.L.T. (Sh. Ct.) 43) were both held to be within the statutory category. Again, however, the wording "for lives or for lives and years" would seem to exclude a lease for the single life of the tenant. A year-to-year lease as referred to in the definition exists by inference where the tenant enters into possession without any ish being specified (*Gray* v. *Edinburgh University*, 1962 S.C. 157).

Livestock. The definition clearly includes farm animals such as working horses and sheep-dogs. As to its other content see under "agriculture," *supra*.

Market garden. For amplification of this definition see note to s.40(1).

Produce. The wide terms of the definition are consistent with the tenant's freedom of cropping and disposal of produce in terms of s.7. Manure produced on the holding, not being disposable by the tenant, is not covered by this definition.

Tenant. See Gill, para. 38 *et seq*. Like *landlord*, *supra*, this term is widely defined but while parties such as curators or guardians have the same position as they would have in relation to the landlord's interest, the rights of executors, even if duly confirmed in respect of the tenancy interest, are limited by the rules requiring them, within the time prescribed, to divest themselves in favour of a successor of the late tenant who does not himself become a tenant unless due intimation has been made to the landlord whose objections, if any, have failed (see s.12). Again, where the tenant has been entitled to and has bequeathed his lease, the legatee does not attain the status of tenant until due intimation has been made to the landlord whose objections, if any, have failed (see s.11). In *inter vivos* transmission the assignee or disponee of an agriculture tenant is by implication, even if not expressly, excluded unless the landlord chooses to accept him. The common law position of the trustee in bankruptcy is the same in relation to a tenancy interest as it is in relation to a right of ownership. Thus a lease is not automatically annulled by the tenant's sequestration but the provisions of s.21(6) or of s.22(2)(f) are likely to result in the trustee's tenure of the lease being of limited duration.

Where there are joint tenants all tenants come within the statutory definition and must as a general rule be parties to any action affecting the tenancy, such as notices and counter-notices given to or received from the landlord.

It may be noted that the definitions of "Whitsunday" and "Martinmas," as contained in s.93(1) of the 1949 Act, have been omitted here, this matter now being regulated by the Term and Quarter Days (Scotland) Act 1990 which, *inter alia*, confirms the meaning of these terms as the 28th day of the month in each case.

Subs. (2)

It may be thought surprising that the Schedules to the 1948 Act have not been incorporated in the consolidation but theoretically at least they may still have significance for certain powers of the authorities based on provisions of the 1948 Act such as s.35 which remain in force.

Subs. (3)

Such references are to be found, *e.g.* in ss.44 and 76.

Subs. (4)

See Gill, paras. 102 and 103.

Custom cannot override the express terms of the lease or agreement but evidence of custom may be invoked to determine the rights and duties of the parties so far as not specifically defined in the relevant documents. The application of the principles of good husbandry will be determined in each case by reference to the situation and character of the holding and the custom of the district (see *Mackenzie* v. *McGillivray*, 1921 S.C. 722, *per* Lord President Clyde at p. 731).

Subs. (5)

This has the effect that any notices may be served by or on the agents of the parties. It is advisable, although perhaps not essential, that the agency should be disclosed in a notice given by an agent (see Gill, paras. 290 and 306).

Construction of references in other Acts to holdings as defined by earlier Acts

86. References, in whatever terms, in any enactment, other than an enactment contained in—
>   this Act,
>   the Agricultural Holdings (Scotland) Acts 1923 and 1931, or,
>   Part I of the Agriculture (Scotland) Act 1948

to a holding within the meaning of the Agricultural Holdings (Scotland) Act 1923 or of the Agricultural Holdings (Scotland) Acts 1923 to 1948 shall be construed as references to an agricultural holding within the meaning of this Act.

DEFINITIONS

"agricultural holding": s.1(1).

DERIVATIONS
    Agricultural Holdings (Scotland) Act 1949, s.95.

Savings

87. Schedule 12 to this Act, which exempts from the operation of this Act certain cases current at the commencement of this Act and contains other transitional provisions and savings shall have effect.

DERIVATIONS
    Agricultural Holdings (Scotland) Act 1949, s.99.

Consequential amendments and repeals

Consequential amendments and repeals

88.—(1) The enactments specified in Schedule 11 to this Act shall be amended in accordance with that Schedule.

(2) The enactments specified in Schedule 13 to this Act are repealed to the extent there specified.

DERIVATIONS
    Agricultural Holdings (Scotland) Act 1949, s.97.

Citation, commencement and extent

Citation, commencement and extent

89.—(1) This Act may be cited as the Agricultural Holdings (Scotland) Act 1991.

(2) This Act shall come into force at the end of the period of 2 months beginning with the date on which it is passed.

(3) This Act shall extend to Scotland only, except for those provisions in Schedule 11 which amend enactments which extend to England and Wales or to Northern Ireland.

DERIVATIONS
    Agricultural Holdings (Scotland) Act 1949, s.101.

GENERAL NOTE
    The Act received Royal Assent on July 25, 1991.

SCHEDULES

Section 4   SCHEDULE 1

PROVISIONS REQUIRED IN LEASES

1. The names of the parties.
2. Particulars of the holding with sufficient description, by reference to a map or plan, of the fields and other parcels of land comprised therein to identify the extent of the holding.
3. The term or terms for which the holding or different parts thereof is or are agreed to be let.
4. The rent and the dates on which it is payable.
5. An undertaking by the landlord in the event of damage by fire to any building comprised in the holding to reinstate or replace the building if its reinstatement or replacement is required for the fulfilment of his responsibilities to manage the holding in accordance with the rules of good estate management, and (except where the interest of the landlord is held for the purposes of a government department or a person representing Her Majesty under section 79 of this Act is deemed to be the landlord, or where the landlord has made provision approved by the Secretary of State for defraying the cost of any such reinstatement or replacement) an undertaking by the landlord to insure to their full value all such buildings against damage by fire.
6. An undertaking by the tenant, in the event of the destruction by fire of harvested crops grown on the holding for consumption thereon, to return to the holding the full equivalent

manurial value of the crops destroyed, in so far as the return thereof is required for the fulfilment of his responsibilities to farm in accordance with the rules of good husbandry, and (except where the interest of the tenant is held for the purposes of a government department or where the tenant has made provision approved by the Secretary of State in lieu of such insurance) an undertaking by the tenant to insure to their full value all dead stock on the holding and all such harvested crops against damage by fire.

DEFINITIONS
"landlord": s.85(1).
"rules of good estate management": s.85(2); Agriculture (Scotland) Act 1948, Scheds. 5, 6.
"rules of good husbandry": s.85(2); Agriculture (Scotland) Act 1948, Scheds. 5, 6.

DERIVATIONS
Agricultural Holdings (Scotland) Act 1949, Sched. 5.

GENERAL NOTE
See Gill, paras. 93–95. (For the corresponding English provision see the Agricultural Holdings Act 1986, Sched. 1).
Reference should be made to s.4 and the notes on that section. The following notes refer to the paragraphs of the Schedule indicated by their numbers.

Para. 2
This requirement can be and often is conveniently met by using as the plan the appropriate sheet or sheets of a large-scale Ordnance Survey Map on which the fields or enclosures comprised in the farm will be identified by numbers and their areas indicated.

Paras. 5 and 6
It is practically unknown for a landlord or tenant to make provision approved by the Secretary of State in lieu of insurance.

Para. 6
The terms of this paragraph are consistent with those of s.7 under which the tenant's right to dispose of the produce of the holding is qualified by an undertaking to return to the holding the manurial value of crops sold off the holding. There is no statutory definition of "dead stock" but in relation to a farm the term is generally regarded as covering such items belonging to the tenant as stored materials, farming implements, machinery and vehicles.

Section 25   SCHEDULE 2

GROUNDS FOR CONSENT TO OPERATION OF NOTICES TO QUIT A TENANCY WHERE SECTION 25(3) APPLIES

PART I

GROUNDS FOR CONSENT TO OPERATION OF NOTICE TO QUIT A TENANCY LET BEFORE JANUARY 1, 1984

Case 1

The tenant has neither sufficient training in agriculture nor sufficient experience in the farming of land to enable him to farm the holding with reasonable efficiency.

Case 2

(a) The holding or any agricultural unit of which it forms part is not a two-man unit;
(b) the landlord intends to use the holding for the purpose of effecting an amalgamation within 2 years after the termination of the tenancy; and
(c) the notice specifies the land with which the holding is to be amalgamated.

Case 3

The tenant is the occupier (either as owner or tenant) of agricultural land which—
(a) is a two-man unit;
(b) is distinct from the holding and from any agricultural unit of which the holding forms part; and
(c) has been occupied by him since before the death of the person from whom he acquired right to the lease of the holding;
and the notice specifies the agricultural land.

Part II

Grounds for Consent to Operation of Notice to Quit a Tenancy Let on or After January 1, 1984

Case 4

The tenant does not have sufficient financial resources to enable him to farm the holding with reasonable efficiency.

Case 5

The tenant has neither sufficient training in agriculture nor sufficient experience in the farming of land to enable him to farm the holding with reasonable efficiency:

Provided that this Case shall not apply where the tenant has been engaged, throughout the period from the date of death of the person from whom he acquired right to the lease, in a course of relevant training in agriculture which he is expected to complete satisfactorily within 4 years from the said date, and has made arrangements to secure that the holding will be farmed with reasonable efficiency until he completes that course.

Case 6

(a) The holding or any agricultural unit of which it forms part is not a two-man unit;

(b) the landlord intends to use the holding for the purpose of effecting an amalgamation within 2 years after the termination of the tenancy; and

(c) the notice specifies the land with which the holding is to be amalgamated.

Case 7

The tenant is the occupier (either as owner or tenant) of agricultural land which—

(a) is a two-man unit;

(b) is distinct from the holding; and

(c) has been occupied by him throughout the period from the date of giving of the notice; and the notice specifies the land.

Part III

Supplementary

1. For the purposes of section 25 of this Act and this Schedule—

"amalgamation" means a transaction for securing that agricultural land which is comprised in a holding to which a notice to quit relates and which together with other agricultural land could form an agricultural unit, shall be owned and occupied in conjunction with that other land (and cognate expressions shall be construed accordingly);

"near relative" in relation to a deceased tenant of an agricultural holding means a surviving spouse or child of that tenant, including a child adopted by him in pursuance of an adoption order (as defined in section 23(5) of the Succession (Scotland) Act 1964); and

"two-man unit" means an agricultural unit which in the opinion of the Land Court is capable of providing full-time employment for an individual occupying it and at least one other man.

2. For the purposes of determining whether land is a two-man unit, in assessing the capability of the unit of providing employment it shall be assumed that the unit is farmed under reasonably skilled management, that a system of husbandry suitable for the district is followed and that the greater part of the feeding stuffs required by any livestock kept on the unit is grown there.

3. For the purposes of Case 7 of this Schedule, occupation of agricultural land—

(a) by a company which is controlled by the tenant shall be treated as occupation by the tenant; and

(b) by a Scottish partnership shall, notwithstanding section 4(2) of the Partnership Act 1890, be treated as occupation by each of its partners.

Definitions
"agricultural land": s.1(2).
"agricultural unit": s.85(1).
"agriculture": s.85(1).

"farming of land": s.85(3).
"landlord": s.85(1).
"tenant": s.85(1).

DERIVATIONS
Agricultural Holdings (Amendment) (Scotland) Act 1983, Sched. 1.

GENERAL NOTE
Part I of the Schedule, containing Cases 1–3, originates in the 1968 Act and applies to tenancies let before the 1983 Act came into force on January 1, 1984. Part II, containing cases 4–7 as introduced by that Act, applies to tenancies let on or after that date. The following comments applying to the particular cases should be read along with s.25 and the notes thereon.

Case 1
The landlord must prove the tenant's inadequacy in both respects but it is the tenant's personal capacity which will be in issue and he will not be entitled to plead that he has access to skilled advice or has available the service of a competent manager, as has sometimes been permitted in the case of objections to a successor under the provisions now contained in ss.11 and 12. Here the only issue is the tenant's own personal training and experience. Training in agriculture envisages a formal course of instruction, but in its absence adequate farming experience may suffice (see on this matter generally *Macdonald* v. *Macrae*, 1987 S.L.C.R. 72). In opposing an application for consent involving this Case the tenant may invoke the "fair and reasonable landlord" plea (see s.25(3)) but the prospects of its success would seem to be at best doubtful.

Case 2
To succeed under this Case the landlord must discharge the onus of proving that the holding or any agricultural unit of which it forms part is not a two-man unit. In *Jenners Princes Street Edinburgh* v. *Howe*, 1990 S.L.T. (Land Ct.) 26 it was held that any land actually occupied for agricultural purposes by the tenant, whether formally or informally, as a single unit was included in the agricultural unit, the wording in this Case being significantly different from that of Case 3, which requires that the tenant be occupier ("either as owner or tenant") of the land comprising the unit in question. The landlord must also show that he has a genuine proposal for the amalgamation of the holding with specific land, to take place within two years of the termination of the tenancy. The cases of *Mackenzie* v. *Lyon*, 1984 S.L.T. (Land Ct.) 30 and *Earl of Seafield* v. *Currie*, 1980 S.L.T. (Land Ct.) 10 illustrate the problems of proof which may arise under this Case.
"Two-man unit" and "amalgamation," as referred to here and in other parts of this Schedule, are defined in Pt. III of the Schedule (see below). In terms of s.25(3) the "fair and reasonable landlord" plea is available to the tenant in this case. It was successfully invoked, although in somewhat special circumstances, in *Altyre Estates* v. *McLay*, 1975 S.L.T. (Land Ct.) 12) and the Land Court in *Earl of Seafield* v. *Currie* (above) indicated that they would have sustained the plea as taken by the tenant, had the landlord satisfied them on the grounds of his application for consent.

Case 3
The two-man unit must be distinct from the holding and from any agricultural unit of which the holding forms part. The latter requirement is dispensed with in Case 7, which applies to tenancies originating on or after January 1, 1984. Actual occupation by the tenant of the land in question must be proved. Ownership of tenanted subjects will not suffice. Again, the occupation must be as owner or tenant. Informal occupation, as meeting the requirements of Case 2, is not sufficient for the land in question to be regarded as existing or alternative source of livelihood for the tenant (see *Jenners Princes Street Edinburgh* v. *Howe*, above, p. 28).
In terms of this case, as appearing in the 1968 Act, it has been held that occupation of the other land by a firm of which the tenant is a partner is not relevant (*Haddo House Estate Trs.* v. *Davidson*, 1982 S.L.T. (Land Ct.) 14), but in this respect again the position is changed in Case 7. Similar provisions in force in England were held by the House of Lords not to require sole occupancy of the other ground (see *Jackson* v. *Hall*; *Williamson* v. *Thompson* [1980] A.C. 854 concerning a provision now represented by the 1986 Act, s.36(3)(b)), a ruling which would seem to be unfair if joint occupancy is not providing the tenant with a livelihood.
Two questions not resolved by the wording of Case 3 or of Case 7 or by any reported case are raised by Gill (para. 395). Firstly, must the other agricultural land in the tenant's occupation be in Scotland? This is an important question in border districts where farming enterprises may embrace land in both countries. It is suggested that no such limitation should be regarded as

implied. Secondly, does the tenant's occupation of the land in question have to be as a tenant with security of tenure under the Act if not as owner? Here again it is suggested that no such restriction can be inferred, although this seems inconsistent with the apparent intention of the legislation that the tenant should have secure possession of the land in question, making retention of the holding to which he has succeeded unnecessary for his livelihood.

The requirement that the other agricultural land should have been occupied by the successor tenant since before the late tenant's death can be unfair to the landlord in certain circumstances, *e.g.* where the death results in the tenant inheriting land owned by the late tenant. Again Case 7 contains an alteration in this respect. Section 25(3) makes the "fair and reasonable landlord" plea available to the tenant under Case 3, and, while there are no reported instances of its being invoked, it would appear that in certain circumstances it might succeed.

Case 4

This ground of consent was introduced by the 1983 Act. While there is as yet no reported instance of the Case being invoked the question of a successor tenant's financial standing has on occasion arisen under the provisions now contained in ss.11 and 12. In *Reid* v. *Duffus Estates*, 1953 S.L.C.R. 13, an objection to a legatee as tenant because he required a bank overdraft to provide necessary working capital was unsuccessful, the Land Court taking the view that a guarantee of solvency could not be required of a tenant. The onus there was on the landlord to substantiate his objection but here the position is reversed in terms of s.25(3), requiring the tenant to satisfy the court that the circumstances are not as specified in this case. Section 25(3) also means that the "fair and reasonable landlord" plea is not available to the tenant.

Case 5

See note to Case 1, the requirement of this case being basically the same but in terms of s.25(3) the onus is on the tenant and the "fair and reasonable landlord" plea does not apply. A proviso, however, gives the youthful successor or novice a chance to meet the charge of inadequate training or experience by having been from the date of the late tenant's death engaged in a suitable course of training which he is expected to complete satisfactorily within four years of that date and having made arrangements for the efficient farming of the holding till completion of the course. It should be noted that the proviso will not benefit a tenant who takes up a course of training after his acquisition of the tenancy, which acquisition may, under the provisions of s.16 of the 1964 Act, take place a considerable time after the late tenant's death.

Case 6

The terms of this case are identical with those of Case 2. As under that Case, s.25(3) has the result that the onus is on the landlord, and the "fair and reasonable landlord" plea is available to the tenant.

Case 7

Basically, this involves the same requirements as Case 3, with the "fair and reasonable landlord" plea available to the tenant in terms of s.25(3). There are, however, significant differences. In the first place, the onus in terms of s.25(3) is on the tenant, although he is not to be required to prove that he is not the owner of any land. Secondly, while the other agricultural land occupied by the tenant must be distinct from the holding, it need not be outwith any agricultural unit of which the holding forms part. Again, occupation of the other agricultural land from the date of giving of the notice to quit is substituted for occupation since before the late tenant's death as required in Case 3. This results that where after succeeding to a tenancy a party obtains occupation of other agricultural land the landlord in the tenancy to which he has succeeded may be able to serve a notice to quit based on this case, complying with the requirement of s.25(2)(b) as regards its effective date. Other provisions affecting Case 7 but not Case 3 are contained in para. 3 of Pt. III of the Schedule.

Para. 1

As to the nature of amalgamation, see *Mackenzie* v. *Lyon*, 1984 S.L.T. (Land Ct.) 30. The ownership and occupation of the resulting agricultural unit need not coincide. The landlord's intention may be to let the unit to a tenant. It is, however, necessary that the landlord own the land with which the holding is to be amalgamated and that the resulting unit is to be in single occupation (*Mackenzie* v. *Lyon*).

Reference has been made to the definition of a near relative in connection with s.25.

Paragraph 2 should be read along with the definition of a two-man unit as referred to in Cases 2, 3, 6 and 7. That paragraph specifies certain assumptions which the Land Court are to make in deciding whether or not they are dealing with a "two-man" unit. They involve that the matter be dealt with on an objective basis irrespective of the standard of farming achieved by the tenant, normal commercial criteria applying to the results of the farming operations. The Land Court have considered this matter in the cases of *Poett* v. *Henderson*, 1979 Central RN 11 and *Earl of Seafield* v. *Currie*, 1980 S.L.T. (Land Ct.) 10, and more recently in *Jenners Princes Street Edinburgh* v. *Howe*, 1990 S.L.T. (Land Ct.) 26, at pp. 28–29, where it was remarked that "full-time" employment must be taken to mean what it says and cannot be applied to casual workers such as raspberry pickers.

Para. (3)

It would seem to be right that in the matter of occupation of other agricultural land under Case 7 the successor tenant should be identified with a company in which he has a controlling interest. A question might be said to arise as to the fairness of this ruling in the case of companies in which the proprietor of the ground as landlord is empowered by liquidating the company or by other means to bring the tenancy to an end. Such arrangements for the avoidance of the agricultural tenant's security of tenure are, however, uncommon now, the lease to a limited partnership involving tenant and landlord or tenant and landlord's nominee having become the standard format.

In discarding for the purposes of Case 7 the rule confirmed by statute that a Scottish firm is a legal person as distinct from its partners, this paragraph not only reverses the ruling of the Land Court in *Haddo House Estate Trust* v. *Davidson*, in which a firm, of which the successor tenant was a member, owned and occupied a number of agricultural units. It also has the result, unfortunately perhaps, that a successor tenant will be treated as occupying other agricultural land let to a partnership (probably in limited form) between himself and the landlord or his nominee, where security of tenure is conditional on the continued existence of the firm.

Section 33   SCHEDULE 3

1923 ACT IMPROVEMENTS FOR WHICH COMPENSATION MAY BE PAYABLE

PART I

IMPROVEMENTS FOR WHICH CONSENTS REQUIRED

1. Erection, alteration, or enlargement of buildings.
2. Formation of silos.
3. Laying down of permanent pasture.
4. Making and planting of osier beds.
5. Making of water meadows or works of irrigation.
6. Making of gardens.
7. Making or improvement of roads or bridges.
8. Making or improvement of watercourses, ponds, wells, or reservoirs, or of works for the application of water power or for supply of water for agricultural or domestic purposes.
9. Making or removal of permanent fences.
10. Planting of hops.
11. Planting of orchards or fruit bushes.
12. Protecting young fruit trees.
13. Reclaiming of waste land.
14. Warping or weiring of land.
15. Embankments and sluices against floods.
16. Erection of wirework in hop gardens.
17. Provision of permanent sheep dipping accommodation.
18. In the case of arable land, the removal of bracken, gorse, tree roots, boulders, or other like obstructions to cultivation.

PART II

IMPROVEMENTS FOR WHICH NOTICE REQUIRED

19. Drainage.

PART III

IMPROVEMENTS FOR WHICH NO CONSENTS OR NOTICE REQUIRED

20. Chalking of land.

21. Clay-burning.

22. Claying of land or spreading blaes upon land.

23. Liming of land.

24. Marling of land.

25. Application to land of purchased artificial or other manure.

26. Consumption on the holding by cattle, sheep, or pigs, or by horses other than those regularly employed on the holding, of corn, cake, or other feeding stuff not produced on the holding.

27. Consumption on the holding by cattle, sheep, or pigs, or by horses other than those regularly employed on the holding, of corn proved by satisfactory evidence to have been produced and consumed on the holding.

28. Laying down temporary pasture with clover, grass, lucerne, sainfoin, or other seeds, sown more than 2 years prior to the termination of the tenancy, in so far as the value of the temporary pasture on the holding at the time of quitting exceeds the value of the temporary pasture on the holding at the commencement of the tenancy for which the tenant did not pay compensation.

29. Repairs to buildings, being buildings necessary for the proper cultivation or working of the holding, other than repairs which the tenant is himself under an obligation to execute.

DERIVATIONS

Agricultural Holdings (Scotland) Act 1949, Sched. 2. This Schedule lists old improvements in the 1923 category for which compensation may be claimed. The relevant provisions of the Act are to be found in ss.33, 34, 36, 38, 40, 51 and 79.

GENERAL NOTE

For the corresponding English provision see the Agricultural Holdings Act 1986, Sched. 9, Pt. II, applying to this Schedule and Sched. 4.

Section 33   SCHEDULE 4

1931 ACT IMPROVEMENTS FOR WHICH COMPENSATION MAY BE PAYABLE

PART I

IMPROVEMENTS FOR WHICH CONSENT REQUIRED

1. Erection, alteration, or enlargement of buildings.

2. Laying down of permanent pasture.

3. Making and planting of osier beds.

4. Making of water meadows or works of irrigation.

5. Making of gardens.

6. Planting of orchards or fruit bushes.

7. Protecting young fruit trees.

8. Warping or weiring of land.

9. Making of embankments and sluices against floods.

PART II

IMPROVEMENTS OF WHICH NOTICE REQUIRED

10. Drainage.

11. Formation of silos.

12. Making or improvement of roads or bridges.

13. Making or improvement of watercourses, ponds or wells, or of works for the application of water power or for the supply of water for agricultural or domestic purposes.

14. Making or removal of permanent fences.

15. Reclaiming of waste land.

16. Repairing or renewal of embankments and sluices against floods.

17. Provision of sheep dipping accommodation.

18. Provision of electrical equipment other than moveable fittings and appliances.

PART III

IMPROVEMENTS FOR WHICH NO CONSENT OR NOTICE REQUIRED

19. Chalking of land.

20. Clay-burning.
21. Claying of land or spreading blaes upon land.
22. Liming of land.
23. Marling of land.
24. Eradication of bracken, whins, or gorse growing on the holding at the commencement of a tenancy and in the case of arable land the removal of tree roots, boulders, stones or other like obstacles to cultivation.
25. Application to land of purchased artificial or other manure.
26. Consumption on the holding by cattle, sheep, or pigs, or by horses other than those regularly employed on the holding, of corn, cake, or other feeding stuff not produced on the holding.
27. Consumption on the holding by cattle, sheep, or pigs, or by horses other than those regularly employed on the holding, of corn proved by satisfactory evidence to have been produced and consumed on the holding.
28. Laying down temporary pasture with clover, grass, lucerne, sainfoin, or other seeds, sown more than 2 years prior to the termination of the tenancy, in so far as the value of the temporary pasture on the holding at the time of quitting exceeds the value of the temporary pasture on the holding at the commencement of the tenancy for which the tenant did not pay compensation.
29. Repairs to buildings, being buildings necessary for the proper cultivation or working of the holding, other than repairs which the tenant is himself under an obligation to execute.

DERIVATIONS
Agricultural Holdings (Scotland) Act 1949, Sched. 3.
This schedule lists old improvements in the 1931 category for which compensation may be claimed. The relevant provisions of the Act are to be found in ss.33, 34, 36, 38, 40, 51 and 79.

Section 33   SCHEDULE 5

NEW IMPROVEMENTS FOR WHICH COMPENSATION MAY BE PAYABLE

PART I

IMPROVEMENTS FOR WHICH CONSENT IS REQUIRED

1. Laying down of permanent pasture.
2. Making of water-meadows or works of irrigation.
3. Making of gardens.
4. Planting of orchards or fruit bushes.
5. Warping or weiring of land.
6. Making of embankments and sluices against floods.
7. Making or planting of osier beds.
8. Haulage or other work done by the tenant in aid of the carrying out of any improvement made by the landlord for which the tenant is liable to pay increased rent.

PART II

IMPROVEMENTS FOR WHICH NOTICE IS REQUIRED

9. Land drainage.
10. Construction of silos.
11. Making or improvement of farm access or service roads, bridges and fords.
12. Making or improvement of watercourses, ponds or wells, or of works for the application of water power for agricultural or domestic purposes or for the supply of water for such purposes.
13. Making or removal of permanent fences, including hedges, stone dykes and gates.
14. Reclaiming of waste land.
15. Renewal of embankments and sluices against floods.
16. Provision of stells, fanks, folds, dippers, pens and bughts necessary for the proper conduct of the holding.
17. Provision or laying on of electric light or power, including the provision of generating plant, fixed motors, wiring systems, switches and plug sockets.
18. Erection, alteration or enlargement of buildings, making or improvement of permanent yards, loading banks and stocks and works of a kind referred to in paragraph 13(2) of Schedule 8 to the Housing (Scotland) Act 1987 (subject to the restrictions mentioned in that subsection).

19. Erection of hay or sheaf sheds, sheaf or grain drying racks, and implement sheds.

20. Provision of fixed threshing mills, barn machinery and fixed dairying plant.

21. Improvement of permanent pasture by cultivation and re-seeding.

22. Provision of means of sewage disposal.

23. Repairs to fixed equipment, being equipment reasonably required for the efficient farming of the holding, other than repairs which the tenant is under an obligation to carry out.

PART III

IMPROVEMENTS FOR WHICH NO CONSENT OR NOTICE REQUIRED

24. Protecting fruit trees against animals.

25. Clay burning.

26. Claying of land.

27. Liming (including chalking) of land.

28. Marling of land.

29. Eradication of bracken, whins or broom growing on the holding at the commencement of the tenancy and, in the case of arable land, removal of tree roots, boulders, stones or other like obstacles to cultivation.

30. Application to land of purchased manure and fertiliser, whether organic or inorganic.

31. Consumption on the holding of corn (whether produced on the holding or not) or of cake or other feeding stuff not produced on the holding by horses, cattle, sheep, pigs or poultry.

32. Laying down temporary pasture with clover, grass, lucerne, sainfoin, or other seeds, sown more than 2 years prior to the termination of the tenancy, in so far as the value of the temporary pasture on the holding at the time of quitting exceeds the value of the temporary pasture on the holding at the commencement of the tenancy for which the tenant did not pay compensation.

DERIVATIONS

Agricultural Holdings (Scotland) Act 1949, Sched. 1.

GENERAL NOTE

See Gill, para. 569. (For the corresponding English provision see the Agricultural Holdings Act 1986, Scheds. 7 and 8, Pt. I).

This Schedule lists new improvements for which compensation can be claimed. The relevant provisions of the Act are to be found in ss.33–40, 51, 73, 75 and 79.

Section 40   SCHEDULE 6

MARKET GARDEN IMPROVEMENTS

1. Planting of fruit trees or bushes permanently set out.

2. Planting of strawberry plants.

3. Planting of asparagus, rhubarb, and other vegetable crops which continue productive for 2 or more years.

4. Erection, alteration or enlargement of buildings for the purpose of the trade or business of a market gardener.

DERIVATIONS

Agricultural Holdings (Scotland) Act 1949, Sched. 4.

GENERAL NOTE

See Gill, para. 548. (For the corresponding English provision see the Agricultural Holdings Act 1986, Sched. 10).

The Schedule lists market garden improvements for which compensation may be claimed. The relevant provisions of the Act are to be found in ss.40, 41, 73 and 79.

Section 61   SCHEDULE 7

ARBITRATIONS

APPOINTMENT OF ARBITERS

1. A person agreed upon between the parties or, in default of agreement, appointed on the

application in writing of either of the parties by the Secretary of State from among the members of the panel constituted under this Act for the purpose, shall be appointed arbiter.

2. If a person appointed arbiter dies, or is incapable of acting, or for 7 days after notice from either party requiring him to act fails to act, a new arbiter may be appointed as if no arbiter had been appointed.

3. Neither party shall have the power to revoke the appointment of the arbiter without the consent of the other party.

4. An appointment, notice, revocation and consent of a kind referred to in any of paragraphs 1 to 3 of this Schedule must be in writing.

PARTICULARS OF CLAIM

5. Each of the parties to the arbitration shall, within 28 days from the appointment of the arbiter, deliver to him a statement of that party's case with all necessary particulars; and—
   (a) no amendment or addition to the statement or particulars delivered shall be allowed after the expiration of the said 28 days except with the consent of the arbiter;
   (b) a party to the arbitration shall be confined at the hearing to the matters alleged in the statement and particulars so delivered and any amendment thereof or addition thereto duly made.

EVIDENCE

6. The parties to the arbitration, and all persons claiming through them respectively, shall, subject to any legal objection—
   (a) submit to be examined by the arbiter on oath or affirmation in relation to the matters in dispute; and
   (b) produce before the arbiter;
all samples, books, deeds, papers, accounts, writings, and documents, within their possession or power respectively which may be required or called for, and do all other things which during the proceedings the arbiter may require.

7. The arbiter shall have power to administer oaths, and to take the affirmation of parties and witnesses appearing, and witnesses shall, if the arbiter thinks fit, be examined on oath or affirmation.

AWARD

8. The arbiter shall make and sign his award within 3 months of his appointment or within such longer period as may, either before or after the expiry of the aforesaid period be agreed to in writing by the parties, or be fixed by the Secretary of State.

9. The arbiter may, if he thinks fit, make an interim award for the payment of any sum on account of the sum to be finally awarded.

10. An arbiter appointed by the Secretary of State or the Land Court in an arbitration under section 13(1) of this Act shall, in making his award, state in writing his findings of fact and the reasons for his decision and shall make that statement available to the Secretary of State and to the parties.

11. The award and any statement made under paragraph 10 of this Schedule shall be in such form as may be specified by statutory instrument made by the Secretary of State.

12. The arbiter shall—
   (a) state separately in his award the amounts awarded in respect of the several claims referred to him; and
   (b) on the application of either party, specify the amount awarded in respect of any particular improvement or any particular matter which is the subject of the award.

13. Where by virtue of this Act compensation under an agreement is to be substituted for compensation under this Act for improvements, the arbiter shall award compensation in accordance with the agreement instead of in accordance with this Act.

14. The award shall fix a day not later than one month after delivery of the award for the payment of the money awarded as compensation, expenses or otherwise.

15. Subject to section 61(2) of this Act, the award shall be final and binding on the parties and the persons claiming under them respectively.

16. The arbiter may correct in an award any clerical mistake or error arising from any accidental slip or omission.

EXPENSES

17. The expenses of and incidental to the arbitration and award shall be in the discretion of the arbiter, who may direct to and by whom and in what manner those expenses or any part

thereof are to be paid, and the expenses shall be subject to taxation by the auditor of the sheriff court on the application of either party, but that taxation shall be subject to review by the sheriff.

18. The arbiter shall, in awarding expenses, take into consideration the reasonableness or unreasonableness of the claim of either party whether in respect of amount or otherwise, and any unreasonable demand for particulars or refusal to supply particulars, and generally all the circumstances of the case, and may disallow the expenses of any witness whom he considers to have been called unnecessarily and any other expenses which he considers to have been incurred unnecessarily.

19. It shall not be lawful to include in the expenses of and incidental to the arbitration and award, or to charge against any of the parties, any sum payable in respect of remuneration or expenses to any person appointed by the arbiter to act as clerk or otherwise to assist him in the arbitration unless such appointment was made after submission of the claim and answers to the arbiter and with either the consent of the parties to the arbitration or the sanction of the sheriff.

STATEMENT OF CASE

20. Subject to paragraph 22 of this Schedule, the arbiter may at any stage of the proceedings, and shall, if so directed by the sheriff (which direction may be given on the application of either party), state a case for the opinion of the sheriff on any question of law arising in the course of the arbitration.

21. Subject to paragraph 22 of this Schedule, the opinion of the sheriff on any case stated under the last foregoing paragraph shall be final unless, within such time and in accordance with such conditions as may be specified by act of sederunt, either party appeals to the Court of Session, from whose decision no appeal shall lie.

22. Where the arbiter in any arbitration under section 13(1) of this Act has been appointed by the Secretary of State or by the Land Court, paragraphs 20 and 21 of this Schedule shall not apply, and instead the arbiter may at any stage of the proceedings state a case (whether at the request of either party or on his own initiative) on any question of law arising in the course of the arbitration, for the opinion of the Land Court, whose decision shall be final.

REMOVAL OF ARBITER AND SETTING ASIDE OF AWARD

23. Where an arbiter has misconducted himself the sheriff may remove him.

24. When an arbiter has misconducted himself, or an arbitration or award has been improperly procured, the sheriff may set the award aside.

FORMS

25. Any forms for proceedings in arbitrations under this Act which may be specified by statutory instrument made by the Secretary of State shall, if used, be sufficient.

DERIVATIONS
   Agricultural Holdings (Scotland) Act 1949, Sched. 6.
   Agriculture Holdings (Amendment) (Scotland) Act 1983, s.5(2).

GENERAL NOTE
   See Gill, paras. 617–657. (For the corresponding English provision see the Agricultural Holdings Act 1986, s.5(2)).
   Reference should be made to s.61 and the notes on that section. The following notes refer to the paragraphs of the Schedule indicated by their numbers.

Para. 1
   This provides the parties with the alternative of an arbiter whom they agree to nominate and an arbiter appointed by the Secretary of State. Gill (paras. 619–620) explains the various points of distinction between the private arbiter, as the appointee of the parties is sometimes called, and the statutory arbiter. The latter, but not the former, requires to be a member of the official panel of arbiters (see s.63(1)(2)) and is affected by the provisions of the Tribunals and Inquiries Act 1971.
   The appointment of a private arbiter will normally be effected by a joint document of submission on the lines exemplified in Connell (*op. cit.* pp. 253–254). To have a statutory arbiter appointed, application requires to be made to the Secretary of State in a form prescribed in Sched. 2 to the Agricultural Holdings (Specification of Forms) (Scotland) Order 1983 (S.I. 1983 No. 1073), in which Form A applies to cases other than rent variations and Form B to rent variations. The document of submission to a private arbiter will make clear the nature and scope of the reference. In making application to the Secretary of State for an appointment, the

questions or differences at issue should be precisely stated, as the content of the application in this respect will be reproduced verbatim in the instrument of appointment. While either party to a dispute can submit the application, it is appropriate that the application should be a joint one if each of the parties has claims against the other, *e.g.* landlord and outgoing tenant, it not being competent to present a counterclaim in the arbitration proceedings (see *Chalmers Property Investment Co.* v. *Bowman*, 1953 S.L.T. (Sh. Ct.) 38 and Gill, para. 623).

Para. 2
   The words "incapable of acting" cover incapacity from any cause, including removal from office under para. 23 (*Dundee Corporation* v. *Guthrie*, 1969 S.L.T. 93).

Para. 3
   It appears that an appointment by the Secretary of State may be revoked by consent (*Dundee Corporation* v. *Guthrie*, above, at p. 98).

Para. 5
   The date of appointment of the arbiter, from which date the period of 28 days runs, is, in the case of a private arbiter, the date of the submission and not that of the arbiter's acceptance. In a statutory arbitration it is the date of the instrument of appointment (see Gill, para. 622). The arbiter cannot extend this time limit (*Stewart* v. *Brims*, 1969 S.L.T. (Sh. Ct.) 2) but may allow late delivery of the party's statement of case if the other party consents (*Suggett* v. *Shaw*, 1987 S.L.T. (Land Ct.) 5). As to the result of a party's failure to lodge a statement of case, see Gill, para. 628 and the cases of *Jamieson* v. *Clark* (1951) 67 Sh.Ct.Rep. 17 and *Collett* v. *Deeley*, 1949 100 L.J. 108. Briefly stated, he is precluded from setting up a case and leading evidence at the hearing, so that if he is a respondent he is limited to attacking his opponent's case by cross-examination of witnesses and if he is a claimant carrying the onus of proof he will have his claim rejected *de plano*. It appears that the statement of case and particulars may, if desired, be contained in one document. Whatever form they take, they must give fair notice of the basis or nature of the claim, quantifying it if it is a pecuniary one. It will be appreciated that, as affecting matters such as outgoing claims, much more detail and precision is required here than under the provisions of s.62(2)(3).
   Sub-para. (a) has the result that some amendment or adjustment of the parties' statement of case may be allowed, this being desirable as neither party has the right to see its opponent's statement of case before it is lodged with the arbiter. In this way an "amendment or addition" to a party's statement of case as referred to in sub-para. (b) may be allowed, but if the document originally lodged by a party does not constitute a statement of case, the defect cannot be cured in this way (*Robertson Trs.* v. *Cunningham*, 1951 S.L.T. (Sh. Ct.) 89). Sub-para. (b) has been held to be peremptory in effect and incapable of being waived, even of consent (*Stewart* v. *Brims*, 1969 S.L.T. (Sh. Ct.) 2 at pp. 6–7).

Para. 6
   The duties incumbent on the parties will include giving access facilities in any case where an inspection by an arbiter is required. Legal objections such as confidentiality may, however, be invoked as regards the giving of evidence or production of documents. In practice, parties will usually be required by the arbiter to lodge any documents on which they are founding, including of course any written lease there may be, by a date some time before the hearing.

Para. 7
   In general, the arbiter has a wide discretion in the conduct of proceedings in which there may be a degree of informality which would not be acceptable in court (*Paterson* v. *Glasgow Corporation*, 1901 3F H.L. 34, *per* Lord Robertson at p. 40). For the basic principles applicable and the practice in the arbitration procedure, see Gill, paras. 631–636).

Para. 8
   Gill (para. 637) explains the practice of issuing proposed findings before the issue of an award. The three-month time limit for issue of the award running from the date of appointment as explained in respect of para. 5 is peremptory, disregard of it constituting misconduct on the part of the arbiter (*Halliday* v. *Semple*, 1960 S.L.T. (Sh. Ct.) 11). There are, however, provisions for extension of the time limit which is often found necessary in the more difficult cases. The agreement of the parties to an extension must be in written form delivered to the arbiter. An application to the Secretary of State for extension can be made even after the expiry of the statutory time limit (*Dundee Corporation* v. *Guthrie*, above). It should conform to Form C in Sched. 2 to the Agricultural Holdings (Specification of Forms) (Scotland) Order 1983 (S.I. 1983 No. 1073).

Para. 9
   Cf. s.69(3), which provides for interim awards in sheep stock valuation cases but only where the outcome of an appeal to the Sheriff by way of stated case is awaited.

Para. 10
   This provision, applying only to rent arbitrations, was introduced by the 1983 Act, along with the directions to arbiters now incorporated in s.13(4). In other arbitrations a private arbiter cannot be required to give reasons for his decision but a statutory arbiter must do so at the request of either party, the statement of reasons forming part of his decision and being incorporated in his award (Tribunals and Inquiries Act 1971, s.12).
   In accordance with s.64, the appointment of the arbiter will be made by the Land Court in cases where the Secretary of State, through the appropriate department, is in the position of landlord or tenant. Where the appointment has been made by the Secretary of State, by whom the arbiter's remuneration will fall to be fixed in terms of s.63(3)(a), it may be found convenient to submit to the Department, along with the application to have the arbiter's remuneration fixed, the findings in fact and statement of reasons.

Para. 11
   The prescribed form is in Sched. 1 to the 1983 Order, referred to under para. 8. It requires to be attested.

Para. 12
   Adherence to the form provided should in most cases result in these requirements being met (see under para. 24).

Para. 13
   This accords with provisions of the Act such as s.37 dealing with substituted compensation.

Para. 14
   In arbitrations on milk quota compensation the period is three months after delivery of the award (1986 Act, Sched. 2, para. 11(4), as amended in terms of Sched. 11, para. 2(b)).

Para. 15
   The exception occurs in rent arbitrations where in terms of s.61(2)(3) an appeal to the Land Court against the award of a statutory arbiter on any question of law or fact (including the amount of the award) may be brought within two months of the date of issue of the award.

Para. 16
   The correction may be made at any time after the delivery of the award.

Para. 17
   The rule generally applied in the courts whereby expenses follow success is applicable to arbitrations but in rent arbitrations or other arbitrations concerning matters of valuation it is usual for each party to be required to bear his own expenses.
   Where there is an appeal from the arbiter to the Land Court the arbiter's ruling on expenses is unlikely to be altered (*MacGregor* v. *Glencruitten Trust*, 1985 S.L.C.R. 77).
   As mentioned in connection with s.61(4) the power given to the Secretary of State by that subsection to make regulations for expediting or reducing the expense of proceedings on arbitrations under this Act has not yet been exercised.

Para. 18
   In complying with this paragraph the arbiter will again be following the usual practice of the courts.

Para. 19
   As to the appointment and functions of a clerk, usually a legally qualified person, see Gill (626). In arbitrations of any size or complexity, appointment of consent is normal.

Paras. 20 and 21
   Paragraph 22 deals with appeals in rent arbitrations. In all other arbitrations under the Act the appeal procedure is by Stated Case, the content of these paras. 20 and 21 covering the whole course of procedure (*Forsyth Grant* v. *Salmon*, 1961 S.C. 54, *per* Lord Mackintosh at p. 58). The case can be stated at any time before the issue of the final award and is dealt with by the Sheriff in whose jurisdiction the holding lies. It has been held that the expenses of the States

Case in the Sheriff Court fall to be determined by the Sheriff and not by the arbiter (*Thomson* v. *Earl of Galloway*, 1919 S.C. 611; *Jamieson* v. *Clark* (1951) 67 Sh.Ct.Rep. 17 at p. 21), although the arbiter deals with the expenses of preparation of the Stated Case. (As to procedure and practice in this matter see Gill, 649 and 650.) An appeal from the Sheriff to the Court of Session, the decision of which is final, can be taken following the procedure prescribed in paras. 262–263 of the Court of Session Rules of Court. While the case is said to be stated "for the opinion" of the Sheriff, his ruling, or that of the Court of Session on appeal, is binding on and must be implemented by the arbiter (*Mitchell Gill* v. *Buchan*, 1921 S.C. 390).

Para. 22

This paragraph prescribes the procedure for appeal by Stated Case in rent arbitrations conducted by a statutory arbiter, these being excluded from the application of paras. 20 and 21. The appeal here, which is on any question of law arising, is to the Land Court, the decision of which is final, but there is no provision as there is in para. 20 for the arbiter being directed to state a case. It should be noted that this right of appeal is distinct from and in addition to the appeal to the Land Court on any question of law or fact against the decision of a statutory arbiter under s.61(2)(3).

Para. 23

"Misconduct" in this context can signify any fault or mistake by the arbiter in the conduct of the arbitration (*Paterson* v. *Glasgow Corporation*, 1901 3F H.L. 34, *per* Lord Chancellor Halsbury at p. 38). Thus it will include not only failures to comply with the directions of this Schedule, *e.g.* by issuing an award out of time (*Halliday* v. *Semple*, 1960 S.L.T. (Sh. Ct.) 11) but also anything inconsistent with justice having been done (see *Mitchell Gill* v. *Buchan*, above). But it need not involve any impropriety, nor any wilful or malicious conduct by the arbiter (*Mitchell Gill* v. *Buchan*). Specific averments are required from a party seeking to have an arbiter removed for misconduct (*MacLean* v. *Chalmers Property Investment Co.*, 1951 S.L.T. (Sh. Ct.) 71). The objection to the arbiter's action should be taken when it occurs but failure to do so then does not validate the objectionable action (*MacLean*, at p. 72).

On removal of the arbiter and reduction of any award he has made, a new arbiter may be appointed (*Dundee Corporation* v. *Guthrie*, 1969 S.L.T. 93).

Para. 24

It appears that the aggrieved party may have the alternative of reduction proceedings in the Court of Session (see *Dunlop* v. *Mundell*, 1943 S.L.T. 286—a decision on the similar wording in s.1(2) of the Sheep Stocks Valuation (Scotland) Act 1937).

Para. 25

As to forms in use under the Agricultural Holdings (Specification of Forms) (Scotland) Order 1983 (S.I. 1983 No. 1073) see under paras. 8 and 11.

Section 57   SCHEDULE 8

SUPPLEMENTARY PROVISIONS WITH RESPECT TO PAYMENTS UNDER SECTION 56

1. Subject to paragraph 4 of this Schedule, any dispute with respect to any sum which may be or become payable by virtue of section 56(1) of this Act shall be referred to and determined by the Lands Tribunal for Scotland.

2. If in any case the sum to be paid by virtue of the said section 56(1) to the tenant of an agricultural holding or to a statutory small tenant by an acquiring authority would, apart from this paragraph and paragraph 3 of this Schedule, fall to be ascertained in pursuance of section 54(2) of this Act by reference to the rent of the holding at a rate which was not—

    (a) determined by arbitration under section 13 or 15 of this Act;

    (b) determined by the Land Court in pursuance of section 61(2) of this Act; or

    (c) in the case of a statutory small tenant, fixed by the Scottish Land Court in pursuance of section 32(7) and (8) of the 1911 Act;

and which the authority consider is unduly high, the authority may make an application to the Lands Tribunal for Scotland for the rent to be considered by the tribunal;

3. Where, on an application under paragraph 2 above, the tribunal are satisfied that—

    (a) the rent to which the application relates is not substantially higher than the rent which in their opinion would be determined for the holding in question on a reference to arbitration duly made in pursuance of—

       (i) section 13 of this Act; or

       (ii) in the case of a statutory small tenancy, the equitable rent which in their opinion would be fixed by the Land Court under section 32(7) and (8) of the 1911 Act;

(hereafter in this paragraph referred to as "the appropriate rent"); or
  (b) the rent to which the application relates is substantially higher than the appropriate rent but was not fixed by the parties to the relevant lease with a view to increasing the amount of any compensation payable, or of any sum to be paid by virtue of section 56(1) of this Act, in consequence of the compulsory acquisition or taking of possession of any land included in the holding,

they shall dismiss the application; and if the tribunal do not dismiss the application in pursuance of the foregoing provisions of this paragraph they shall determine that, in the case to which the application relates, the sum to be paid by virtue of section 56(1) of this Act shall be ascertained in pursuance of the said section 13 by reference to the appropriate rent instead of by reference to the rent to which the application relates.

4. For the purposes of paragraph 3(a) above, section 13(1) of this Act shall have effect as if for the reference therein to the next ensuing day there were substituted a reference to the date of the application referred to in paragraph 3(a) above.

5. The enactments mentioned in paragraph 6 of this Schedule shall, subject to any necessary modifications, have effect in their application to such an acquiring of an interest or taking of possession as is referred in section 56(1) of this Act (hereafter in this paragraph referred to as "the relevant event")—
  (a) in so far as those enactments make provision for the doing, before the relevant event, of any thing connected with compensation (including in particular provision for determining the amount of the liability to pay compensation or for the deposit of it in a Scottish bank or otherwise), as if references to compensation, except compensation for damage or injurious affection, included references to any sum which will become payable by virtue of section 56 of this Act in consequence of the relevant event; and
  (b) subject to sub-paragraph (a) above, as if references to compensation (except compensation for damage or injurious affection) included references to sums payable or, as the context may require, to sums paid by virtue of section 56 of this Act in the consequence of the relevant event.

6. The enactments aforesaid are—
  (a) sections 56 to 60, 62, 63 to 65, 67 to 70, 72, 74 to 79, 83 to 87, 114, 115 and 117 of the Lands Clauses (Scotland) Act 1845;
  (b) paragraph 3 of Schedule 2 to the Acquisition of Land (Authorisation Procedure) (Scotland) Act 1947;
  (c) Parts I and II and section 40 of the Land Compensation (Scotland) Act 1963;
  (d) paragraph 4 of Schedule 6 to the New Towns (Scotland) Act 1968;
  (e) any provision in any local or private Act, in any instrument having effect by virtue of an enactment, or in any order or scheme confirmed by Parliament or brought into operation in accordance with special parliamentary procedure, corresponding to a provision mentioned in sub-paragraph (a), (b) or (d) above.

DEFINITIONS
  "agricultural holding": s.1(1).
  "statutory small tenant": s.54(1).

DERIVATIONS
  Agriculture (Miscellaneous Provisions) Act 1968, Scheds. 4 and 5, paras. 6 and 7.

GENERAL NOTE
  For the corresponding English provision see the Agriculture (Miscellaneous Provisions) Act 1968, Sched. 3.
  The provisions of this Schedule are intended to prevent excessive amounts being claimed from the acquiring authority under s.56 by tenants of subjects which are being acquired compulsorily. Claims for additional payments under s.56 being based on the rental of the subjects acquired, a collusive arrangement between landlord and tenant could result in an unduly high rent being payable at the relevant time. This possibility does not exist if the rent payable has been determined by arbitration or by the Land Court under the relevant statutory provisions, but where that is not so the acquiring authority is empowered to have the rent reviewed by the Lands Tribunal for Scotland as the tribunal dealing with questions of compensation in compulsory acquisition. The Tribunal has a discretion to substitute "an appropriate rent" for the rent payable as the measure of the acquiring authority's liability. They are not to do so, however, if they consider that the rent payable is not substantially higher than the appropriate rent, *i.e.* the rent which could be expected to be determined by an arbiter or by the Land Court under the relevant statutory provisions or if in the Tribunal's view the rent, even although substantially higher than such appropriate rent, has not been fixed by the parties with a view to increasing the compensation payable.

SCHEDULE 9

VALUATION OF SHEEP STOCK IN SCOTLAND IN RESPECT OF OLD LEASES

PART I

VALUATION MADE IN RESPECT OF A TENANCY TERMINATING AT WHITSUNDAY

1. The Land Court or the arbiter (in Part I and Part II of this Schedule referred to as "the valuer") shall ascertain the number of, and the prices realised for, the ewes and the lambs sold off the hill from the stock under valuation at the autumn sales in each of the 3 preceding years, and shall determine by inspection the number of shotts present in the stock at that time of the valuation.

2. The valuer shall calculate an average price per ewe, and an average price per lamb, for the ewes and lambs sold as aforesaid for each of the 3 preceding years. In calculating the average price for any year the valuer shall disregard such number of ewes and lambs so sold in that year, being the ewes or lambs sold at the lowest prices, as bears the same proportion to the total number of ewes or lambs so sold in that year as the number of shotts as determined bears to the total number of ewes or lambs in the stock under valuation.

3. The valuer shall then ascertain the mean of the average prices so calculated for the 3 preceding years for ewes and for lambs, respectively. The figures so ascertained or ascertained, in a case to which paragraph 4 below applies, in accordance with that paragraph, are in this Part of this Schedule referred to as the "3-year average price for ewes" and the "3-year average price for lambs."

4. In the case of any sheep stock in which the number of ewes or the number of lambs sold off the hill at the autumn sales during the preceding 3 years has been less than half the total number of ewes or of lambs sold, the 3-year average price for ewes or the 3-year average price for lambs, as the case may be, shall, in lieu of being ascertained by the valuer as aforesaid, be determined by the Land Court on the application of the parties; and the Land Court shall determine such prices by reference to the prices realised at such sales for ewes and for lambs respectively from similar stocks kept in the same district and under similar conditions.

5. The 3-year average price for ewes shall be subject to adjustment by the valuer within the limits of 20 per cent. (in the case of leases entered into before May 15, 1963, 50 pence) upwards or downwards as he may think proper having regard to the general condition of the stock under valuation and to the profit which the purchaser may reasonably expect it to earn. The resultant figure shall be the basis of the valuation of the ewes, and is in this Part of this Schedule referred to as the "basic ewe value."

The valuer shall similarly adjust the 3 year average price for lambs, and the resultant figure shall be the basis for the valuation of the lambs and is in this Part of this Schedule referred to as the "basic lamb value."

6. In making his award the valuer shall value the respective classes of stock in accordance with the following rules, that is to say—
   (a) ewes of all ages (including gimmers) shall be valued at the basic ewe value with the addition of 30 per cent. (in the case of leases entered into before May 15, 1963, 75 pence) of such value per head;
   (b) lambs shall be valued at the basic lamb value; so however that twin lambs shall be valued at such price as the valuer thinks proper;
   (c) ewe hoggs shall be valued at two-thirds of the combined basic values of a ewe and a lamb subject to adjustment by the valuer within the limits of 10 per cent. (in the case of leases entered into before May 15, 1963, 25 pence) per head upwards or downwards as he may think proper, having regard to their quality and condition;
   (d) tups shall be valued at such price as in the opinion of the valuer represents their value on the farm having regard to acclimatisation or any other factor for which he thinks it proper to make allowance;
   (e) eild sheep shall be valued at the value put upon the ewes subject to such adjustment as the valuer may think proper having regard to their quality and condition; and
   (f) shotts shall be valued at such value not exceeding two-thirds of the value put upon good sheep of the like age and class on the farm as the valuer may think proper.

PART II

VALUATION MADE IN RESPECT OF A TENANCY TERMINATING AT MARTINMAS

7. The valuer shall ascertain the number of, and the prices realised for, the ewes sold off the hill from the stock under valuation at the autumn sales in the current year and in each of the 2 preceding years, and shall calculate an average price per ewe so sold for each of the said years. In calculating the average price for any year the valuer shall disregard one-tenth of the total number of ewes so sold in that year being the ewes sold at the lowest price.

8. The mean of the average prices so calculated shall be subject to adjustment by the valuer within the limits of 10 per cent. (in the case of leases entered into before May 15, 1963, 25 pence) upward or downwards as he may think proper having regard to the general condition of the stock under valuation and to the profit which the purchaser may reasonably expect it to earn. The resultant figure shall be the basis of the valuation of the ewes and is in this Part of this Schedule referred to as the "basic ewe value."

9. In making his award the valuer shall assess the respective classes of stock in accordance with the following rules, that is to say—

   (a) ewes of all ages (including gimmers) shall be valued at the basic ewe value with the addition of 30 per cent. (in the case of leases entered into before May 15, 1963, 75 pence) of such value per head;

   (b) ewe lambs shall be valued at the basic ewe value subject to adjustment by the valuer within the limits of 10 per cent. (in the case of leases entered into before May 15, 1963, 25 pence) per head upwards or downwards as he may think proper having regard to their quality and condition; and

   (c) tups shall be valued at such price as in the opinion of the valuer represents their value on the farm having regard to acclimatisation or any other factor for which he thinks it proper to make allowance.

PART III

PARTICULARS TO BE SHOWN IN AN ARBITER'S AWARD

10. The 3-year average price for ewes and the 3-year average price for lambs ascertained under Part I, or the mean of the average prices calculated under Part II, of this Schedule, as the case may be.

11. Any amount added or taken away by way of adjustment for the purpose of fixing the basic ewe value or the basic lamb value, and the grounds on which such adjustment was made.

12. The number of each class of stock valued (ewes and gimmers of all ages with lambs being taken as one class, and eild ewes and eild gimmers being taken as separate classes at a Whitsunday valuation, and ewes and gimmers of all ages being taken as one class at a Martinmas valuation) and the value placed on each class.

13. Any amount added to or taken away by way of adjustment in fixing the value of ewe hoggs at a Whitsunday valuation, or the value of ewe lambs at a Martinmas valuation, and the grounds on which such adjustment was made.

PART IV

INTERPRETATION

14. In this Schedule the expressions "ewe," "gimmer," "eild ewe," "eild gimmer," "lamb," "ewe hogg," "eild sheep" and "tup" shall be construed as meaning respectively sheep of the classes customarily known by those designations in the locality in which the flock under valuation is maintained.

DERIVATION
Hill Farming Act 1946, Sched. 2.
Agriculture (Miscellaneous Provisions) Act 1963, s.21.

GENERAL NOTE
This Schedule contains the directions for valuations of sheep stocks by an arbiter or by the Land Court. These are based on average prices obtained at the autumn sales for ewes and lambs sold off the hill in the case of a Whitsunday outgoing in each of the three preceding years and in the case of a Martinmas outgoing for ewes sold in the current and each of the two preceding years. These directions apply to tenancies under what are termed old leases, *i.e.* leases entered into after November 6, 1946, but before December 1, 1986. Within its terms, however, the

Schedule distinguishes between leases entered into before May 15, 1963 and leases entered into on or after that date, certain additions permitted to be made to basic prices of stock being limited to fixed cash amounts in the former case but based on percentages of the prices in the latter. The resulting difference can be substantial. See also s.68 and notes thereon.

Section 70   SCHEDULE 10

VALUATION OF SHEEP STOCK IN SCOTLAND IN RESPECT OF LEASES ENTERED INTO AFTER DECEMBER 1, 1986

PART I

VALUATION MADE IN RESPECT OF A TENANCY TERMINATING AT WHITSUNDAY

1. The Land Court or the arbiter (in Part I and Part II of this Schedule referred to as "the valuer") shall ascertain the number of, and the prices realised for, the regular cast ewes and the lambs sold off the hill from the stock under valuation at the autumn sales in each of the 3 preceding years, and shall determine by inspection the number of shotts present in the stock at that time of the valuation.

2. The valuer shall calculate an average price per ewe, and an average price per lamb, for the regular cast ewes and lambs sold as aforesaid for each of the 3 preceding years. In calculating the average price for any year the valuer shall disregard such number of regular cast ewes and lambs so sold in that year, being the ewes or lambs sold at the lowest prices, as bears the same proportion to the total number of regular cast ewes or lambs so sold in that year as the number of shotts as determined bears to the total number of ewes or lambs in the stock under valuation.

3. The valuer shall then ascertain the mean of the average prices so calculated for the 3 preceding years for regular cast ewes and for lambs, respectively. The figures so ascertained or ascertained, in a case to which paragraph 4 below applies, in accordance with that paragraph, are in this Part of this Schedule referred to as the "3-year average price for regular cast ewes" and the "3-year average price for lambs."

4. In the case of any sheep stock in which the number of regular cast ewes or the number of lambs sold off the hill at the autumn sales during the preceding 3 years has been less than half the total number of regular cast ewes or of lambs sold, the 3-year average price for regular cast ewes or the 3-year average price for lambs, as the case may be shall, in lieu of being ascertained by the valuer as aforesaid, be determined by the Land Court on the application of the parties; and the Land Court shall determine such prices by reference to the prices realised at such sales for regular cast ewes and for lambs respectively from similar stocks kept in the same district and under similar conditions.

5. The 3-year average price for regular cast ewes shall be subject to adjustment by the valuer within the limits of 30 per cent. upwards or downwards as he may think proper having regard to the general condition of the stock under valuation and to the profit which the purchaser may reasonably expect it to earn. The resultant figure shall be the basis of the valuation of the ewes, and is in this Part of this Schedule referred to as the "basic ewe value."

The valuer shall adjust the 3 year average price for lambs within the limits of 20 per cent. upwards or downwards as he may think proper having regard to their quality and condition. The resultant figure shall be the basis for the valuation of the lambs and is in this Part of this Schedule referred to as the "basic lamb value."

6. In making his award the valuer shall value the respective classes of stock in accordance with the following rules, that is to say—

(a) ewes of all ages (including gimmers) shall be valued at the basic ewe value with the addition of 30 per cent. of such value per head;

(b) lambs shall be valued at the basic lamb value but twin lambs shall be valued at such price as the valuer thinks proper;

(c) ewe hoggs shall be valued at three quarters of the combined basic values of a ewe and a lamb subject to adjustment by the valuer within the limits of 25 per cent. per head upwards or downwards as he may think proper, having regard to their quality and condition;

(d) tups shall be valued at such price as in the opinion of the valuer represents their value on the farm having regard to acclimatisation or any other factor for which he thinks it proper to make allowance;

(e) eild sheep shall be valued at the value put upon the ewes subject to such adjustment as the valuer may think proper having regard to their quality and condition; and

(f) shotts shall be valued at such value not exceeding two-thirds of the value put upon good sheep of the like age and class on the farm as the valuer may think proper.

PART II

VALUATION MADE IN RESPECT OF A TENANCY TERMINATING AT MARTINMAS

7. The valuer shall ascertain the number of, and the prices realised for, the regular cast ewes sold off the hill from the stock under valuation at the autumn sales in the current year and in each of the 2 preceding years, and shall calculate an average price per ewe so sold for each of the said years. In calculating the average price for any year the valuer shall disregard one-fifth of the total number of regular cast ewes so sold in that year being the ewes sold at the lowest price.

8. The mean of the average prices so calculated shall be subject to adjustment by the valuer within the limits of 30 per cent. upward or downwards as he may think proper having regard to the general condition of the stock under valuation and to the profit which the purchaser may reasonably expect it to earn. The resultant figure shall be the basis of the valuation of the ewes and is in this Part of this Schedule referred to as the "basic ewe value."

9. In making his award the valuer shall assess the respective classes of stock in accordance with the following rules, that is to say—

(a) ewes of all ages (including gimmers) shall be valued at the basic ewe value with the addition of 30 per cent. of such value per head;

(b) ewe lambs shall be valued at the basic ewe value subject to adjustment by the valuer within the limits of 20 per cent. per head upwards or downwards as he may think proper having regard to their quality and condition; and

(c) tups shall be valued at such price as in the opinion of the valuer represents their value on the farm having regard to acclimatisation or any other factor for which he thinks it proper to make allowance.

PART III

PARTICULARS TO BE SHOWN IN AN ARBITER'S AWARD

10. The 3-year average price for regular cast ewes and the 3-year average price for lambs ascertained under Part I, or the mean of the average prices calculated under Part II, of this Schedule, as the case may be.

11. Any amount added or taken away by way of adjustment for the purpose of fixing the basic ewe value or the basic lamb value, and the grounds on which such adjustment was made.

12. The number of each class of stock valued (ewes and gimmers of all ages with lambs being taken as one class, and eild ewes and eild gimmers being taken as separate classes at a Whitsunday valuation, and ewes and gimmers of all ages being taken as one class at a Martinmas valuation) and the value placed on each class.

13. Any amount added to or taken away by way of adjustment in fixing the value of ewe hoggs at a Whitsunday valuation, or the value of ewe lambs at a Martinmas valuation, and the grounds on which such adjustment was made.

PART IV

INTERPRETATION

14. In this Schedule the expressions "regular cast ewes," "ewe," "gimmer," "eild ewe," "eild gimmer," "lamb," "ewe hogg," "eild sheep" and "tup" shall be construed as meaning respectively sheep of the classes customarily known by those designations in the locality in which the flock under valuation is maintained.

DERIVATIONS

Hill Farming Act 1946, Sched. 2.

Hill Farming Act 1946 (Variation of Second Schedule) (Scotland) Order 1986 (S.I. 1986 No. 1823).

GENERAL NOTE

This Schedule, applying to tenancies under leases entered into on or after December 1, 1986, contains directions for the valuation of sheep stocks by an arbiter or by the Land Court based on average prices obtained in the case of a Whitsunday outgoing, for regular cast ewes and lambs sold off the hill at the Autumn Sales of the three preceding years and in the case of a Martinmas outgoing for regular case ewes sold off the hill at the Autumn Sales of the current year and the two preceding years.

In general, the terms of the Schedule reproduce those of Sched. 9 but are adjusted to incorporate the changes made by the Statutory Instrument of 1986.

See also s.68 and notes thereon.

CONSEQUENTIAL AMENDMENTS OF ENACTMENTS

Hill Farming Act 1946 (c. 73)

1. In section 9, as substituted by the Seventh Schedule to the 1949 Act,—
(a) in subsection (1), for "Agricultural Holdings (Scotland) Act 1949" substitute "Agricultural Holdings (Scotland) Act 1991, referred to in subsections (2) and (4) below as "the 1991 Act";
(b) in subsections (2) and (4), for "the said Act of 1949" substitute "the 1991 Act";
(c) in subsection (2)—
(i) for "Part I or Part II of the First Schedule" substitute "Part I or II of Schedule 5,";
(ii) in paragraph (a), for "section fifty of that Act" substitute "section 37 of the 1991 Act";
(iii) in paragraph (b), for "section fifty-one of that Act" substitute "section 38 of the 1991 Act";
(iv) in paragraph (b), for "section fifty-two of that Act" substitute "section 39 of the 1991 Act,";
(v) for "the said section fifty or the said fifty-one" substitute "section 37 or 38 of the 1991 Act";
(d) in subsection (3), for "section eight of the Agricultural Holdings (Scotland) Act 1949" substitute "section 15 of the 1991 Act."

Reserve and Auxiliary forces (Protection of Civil Interests) Act 1951 (c. 65)

2. In section 21—
(a) in subsection (2) for "Subsection (1) of section twenty-five of the Agricultural Holdings (Scotland) Act 1949" substitute "section 22 of the Agricultural Holdings (Scotland) Act 1991," and for "section twenty-six of that Act" substitute "section 24 of that Act,";
(b) in subsection (3) for "section twenty-five" in both places where it occurs substitute "section 22," and for "section twenty-six" substitute "section 24";
(c) in subsection (8) for "the said Act of 1949" substitute "the Agricultural Holdings (Scotland) Act 1991."
3. In section 22(4)(a), for "subsection (1) of section twenty five of the Agricultural Holdings (Scotland) Act 1949" substitute "section 22(1) of the Agricultural Holdings (Scotland) Act 1991."
4. In section 38(6)(a)(i), for "Agricultural Holdings (Scotland) Act 1949" substitute "Agricultural Holdings (Scotland) Act 1991."

Crofters (Scotland) Act 1955 (c. 21)

5. In section 14(10), for "Agricultural Holdings (Scotland) Act 1949" substitute "Agricultural Holdings (Scotland) Act 1991."
6. In section 37(1), in the definition of "fixed equipment," for "Agricultural Holdings (Scotland) Act 1949" substitute "Agricultural Holdings (Scotland) Act 1991."
7. In Schedule 2, paragraph 10, for "section 15 of the Agricultural Holdings (Scotland) Act 1949" substitute "section 52 of the Agricultural Holdings (Scotland) Act 1991."

Agriculture (Safety, Health and Welfare Provisions) Act 1956 (c. 49)

8. In section 25(4), for the words from "the provisions" to "section eighteen" substitute "section 5(2), (3) and (5) of the Agricultural Holdings (Scotland) Act 1991 (liabilities of landlord and tenant of agricultural holding regarding fixed equipment) and section 10."
9. In section 25(5), for "section eight of the Agricultural Holdings (Scotland) Act 1949" substitute "section 15 of the Agricultural Holdings (Scotland) Act 1991."
10. In section 25(10), in the definition of "agricultural holding," "fixed equipment" and "landlord," for "the Agricultural Holdings (Scotland) Act, 1949" substitute "the Agricultural Holdings (Scotland) Act 1991."

Coal Mining (Subsidence) Act 1957 (c. 59)

11. In section 10(1)(a), for "Agricultural Holdings (Scotland) Act 1949" substitute "Agricultural Holdings (Scotland) Act 1991."

Opencast Coal Act 1958 (c. 69)

12. In section 14A—

(a) in subsection (3), for the words "Agricultural Holdings (Scotland) Act 1949 in this Act referred to as the Scottish Act of 1949" substitute "the Scottish Act of 1991,";

(b) in subsection (4), for "the Scottish Act of 1949" substitute "the Scottish Act of 1991";

(c) in subsection (5), for "the Scottish Act of 1949" substitute "the Scottish Act of 1991";

(d) in subsection (6)—

(i) for "section 25(2) of the Scottish Act of 1949" substitute "section 22(2) of the Scottish Act of 1991"; and

(ii) for "(c)" substitute "(b)";

(e) in subsection (7), for the words from "For the purposes" to "paragraph (e) of subsection (1)" substitute "The condition specified in section 24(1)(e) of the Scottish Act of 1991 (consent of Land Court to notice to quit where land to be used for purposes other than agriculture)";

(f) in subsection (8), for "section 7 of the Scottish Act of 1949" substitute "section 13 of the Scottish Act of 1991";

(g) in subsection (9), for "section 8 of the Scottish Act of 1949" substitute "section 15 of the Scottish Act of 1991."

13. For section 24(10) substitute—

"(10) In the application of this section to Scotland, for references—

(a) to the Act of 1986 and to sections 70 and 83(4) of that Act there shall be substituted respectively references to the Scottish Act of 1991 and to sections 44 and 62(3) of that Act;

(b) to subsections (1), (2) and (3) of section 69 of the Act of 1986 there shall be substituted respectively references to sections 34(5) and 35(4) and (5) of the Scottish Act of 1991 (as they apply to new improvements);

(c) to Parts I and II of Schedule 7 to the Act of 1986 and to the first day of March 1948 there shall be substituted respectively references to Parts I and II of Schedule 5 to the Scottish Act of 1991 and to the first day of November 1948; and

(d) to sub-paragraphs (1) and (2) of paragraph 5 of Part I of Schedule 9 to the 1986 Act there shall be substituted respectively references to sections 34(5) and 35(4) of the Scottish Act of 1991 (as they apply to old improvements).".

14. For section 25(3) substitute—

"(3) In the application of this section to Scotland, for paragraphs (a) and (b) of subsection (1) above there shall be substituted the words "under section 45 of the Scottish Act of 1991 (which relates to compensation for deterioration of a holding or part thereof for which a tenant is responsible).".

15. In section 26(6) after "Scotland" insert "(a)" and for the words from "in subsection (3)" to the end substitute—

"(b) in subsection (3) of this section for the reference to the Act of 1986 there shall be substituted a reference to the Scottish Act of 1991; and

(c) in subsection (5) of this section there shall be substituted—

(i) for the reference to section 91 of the Act of 1986 a reference to section 73 of the Scottish Act of 1991;

(ii) for the reference to Schedule 8 to the Act of 1986 a reference to Part III of Schedule 5 to the Scottish Act of 1991;

(iii) for the reference to Parts I, II and III of the Fourth Schedule to this Act a reference to Parts IV and V of that Schedule.".

16. In section 27(4), for "section fourteen of the Scottish Act of 1949" substitute "section 18 of the Scottish Act of 1991."

17. In section 28(6)—

(a) for "to section sixty-five of the Scottish Act of 1949 and to paragraph (b) of subsection (1) of that section" substitute "section 40 of the Scottish Act of 1991 and to subsection (4)(a) of that section";

(b) for "to subsection (1) of section sixty-six of the Scottish Act of 1949 and to section 14 of that Act" substitute "to section 41(1) and to section 18 of the Scottish Act of 1991";

(c) for "to section seventy-nine of the Scottish Act of 1949 and to the Fourth Schedule to that Act" substitute "to section 73 of the Scottish Act of 1991 and to Schedule 6 thereto."

18. In section 52(2)—

(a) in the definition of "agricultural holding," for "1949" substitute "1991";
(b) for the definition of "the Scottish Act of 1949" substitute " "the Scottish Act of 1991" means the Agricultural Holdings (Scotland) Act 1991;".
19. In section 52(5)(a)—
(a) for "the Scottish Act of 1949" where it first occurs substitute "the Scottish Act of 1991"; and
(b) for "sections fifty-seven and fifty-eight of the Scottish Act of 1949" substitute "section 45 of the Scottish Act of 1991."
20. In Schedule 6, paragraph 31, for "section 2(1) of the Scottish Act of 1949" substitute "section 2 of the Scottish Act of 1991."
21. For Schedule 7, paragraph 25(a) substitute—
"(a) for references—
            (i) to the Act of 1986 and to sections 12, 13, 23 and 84 of that Act there shall be substituted respectively references to the Scottish Act of 1991 and to sections 13, 15, 10 and 61 of that Act;
            (ii) to section 10 of the Act of 1986 and to subsections (3) and (4) of that section there shall be substituted respectively references to section 18 of the Scottish Act of 1991 and to subsections (2) and (3) of that section; and
            (iii) to subsection (3) of section 79 of the Act of 1986 there shall be substituted references to section 40(4)(a) of the Scottish Act of 1991.".

Horticulture Act 1960 (c. 22)

22. In section 1(1)(b), for "Agricultural Holdings (Scotland) Act 1949" substitute "Agricultural Holdings (Scotland) Act 1991."

Crofters (Scotland) Act 1961 (c. 58)

23. In section 13(1), for "the Agricultural Holdings (Scotland) Act 1949" substitute "the Agricultural Holdings (Scotland) Act 1991."

Succession (Scotland) Act 1964 (c. 41)

24. In section 16—
(a) in subsections (2)(c) and (3)(b)(i), for "section 20 of the Act of 1949" substitute "section 11 of the 1991 Act";
(b) in subsection (6)(b), for "section 27(2) of the Act of 1949" substitute "section 23(2) and (3) of the 1991 Act" and for "section 25(2)(f)" substitute "section 22(2)(e)";
(c) in subsection (8), for "subsections (2) to (7) of section 20 of the Act of 1949" substitute "section 11(2) to (8) of the 1991 Act";
(d) in subsection 9—
            (i) in the definition of "agricultural lease," for "the Act of 1949" substitute "the 1991 Act";
            (ii) for the definition of "the Act of 1949" substitute "the 1991 Act" means the Agricultural Holdings (Scotland) Act 1991;".
25. In section 29(2), for "section 20 of the Agricultural Holdings (Scotland) Act 1949" substitute "section 11 of the Agricultural Holdings (Scotland) Act 1991."

Agriculture Act 1967 (c. 22)

26. In section 26(1), for "the Agricultural Holdings (Scotland) Act 1949" substitute "the Agricultural Holdings (Scotland) Act 1991."
27. In section 27(5B), for "the Agricultural Holdings (Scotland) Act 1949" substitute "the Agricultural Holdings (Scotland) Act 1991."
28. In section 28(1)(a), for "section 35 of the Agricultural Holdings (Scotland) Act 1949" substitute "section 43 of the Agricultural Holdings (Scotland) Act 1991."
29. In section 29—
(a) in subsection (3)(a), for "section 35 of the Agricultural Holdings (Scotland) Act 1949" substitute "section 43 of the Agricultural Holdings (Scotland) Act 1991"; and
(b) in subsection (4), for "section 25(1) of the Agricultural Holdings (Scotland) Act 1949" substitute "section 22(1) of the Agricultural Holdings (Scotland) Act 1991."
30. In section 48(2)(a), for "section 35 of the Agricultural Holdings (Scotland) Act 1949" substitute "section 43 of the Agricultural Holdings (Scotland) Act 1991."
31. In Schedule 3, paragraph 7(5)—
(a) for "sections 75 and 77 of the Agricultural Holdings (Scotland) Act 1949" substitute "sections 61 and 64 of the Agricultural Holdings (Scotland) Act 1991"; and
(b) for "sections 78 and 87(2)" substitute "sections 60(2) and 80(2)."

Conveyancing and Feudal Reform (Scotland) Act 1970 (c. 35)

32. In Schedule 1 in paragraph 5(a), for "Agricultural Holdings (Scotland) Act 1949" substitute "Agricultural Holdings (Scotland) Act 1991."

Land Compensation (Scotland) Act 1973 (c. 56)

33. In section 31(3)(c) for "Agricultural Holdings (Scotland) Act 1949" substitute "Agricultural Holdings (Scotland) Act 1991."

34. In section 44—
(a) in subsection (2)(a)(i) for "section 25(2)(c) of the Agricultural Holdings (Scotland) Act 1949" substitute "section 22(2)(b) of the Agricultural Holdings (Scotland) Act 1991";
(b) in subsection (2)(a)(ii)—
   (i) for "section 26(1)(e)" substitute "section 24(1)(e)"; and
   (ii) for "section 25(2)(c)" substitute "section 22(2)(b)";
(c) in subsection (3)(a) for "sections 25(2)(c) and 26(1)(e)" substitute "sections 22(2)(b) and 24(1)(e)";
(d) in subsection (4), for "section 12 of the Agricultural (Miscellaneous Provisions) Act 1968" substitute "section 56 of the Agricultural Holdings (Scotland) Act 1991."

35. In section 52—
(a) in subsection (3)(d) for "Agricultural Holdings (Scotland) Act 1949" substitute "Agricultural Holdings (Scotland) Act 1991"; and
(b) in subsection (4) for "section 59(1) of the Agricultural Holdings (Scotland) Act 1949" substitute "section 47(1) of the Agricultural Holdings (Scotland) Act 1991" and for "the said section 59(1)" substitute "the said section 47(1)."

36. In section 55—
(a) for subsection (1)(b) substitute—
   "(b) either—
        (i) section 22(1) of the Agricultural Holdings (Scotland) Act 1991 does not apply by virtue of subsection (2)(b) of that section; or
        (ii) the Scottish Land Court have consented to the notice on the ground set out in section 24(1)(e) of that Act.";
(b) in subsection (2)(a), for "section 12 of the Agriculture (Miscellaneous Provisions) Act 1968" substitute "section 56 of the Agricultural Holdings (Scotland) Act 1991";
(c) in subsection (2)(b) for "Agricultural Holdings (Scotland) Act 1949" substitute "Agricultural Holdings (Scotland) Act 1991," and for "sections 9 and 15(3) of the Agriculture (Miscellaneous Provisions) Act 1968" substitute "sections 54 and 58(1) and (2) of that Act";
(d) in subsection (6) for "section 33 of the Agricultural Holdings (Scotland) Act 1949" substitute "section 30 of the Agricultural Holdings (Scotland) Act 1991."

37. In section 80(1), in the definitions of "agricultural holding" and "holding" for "Agricultural Holdings (Scotland) Act 1949" substitute "Agricultural Holdings (Scotland) Act 1991."

Land Tenure Reform (Scotland) Act 1974 (c. 38)

38. In section 8(5)(a), for "Agricultural Holdings (Scotland) Act 1949" substitute "Agricultural Holdings (Scotland) Act 1991."

Control of Pollution Act 1974 (c. 40)

39. In section 31(B)(2)(a), for the words "an absolute owner (within the meaning of section 93 of the Agricultural Holdings (Scotland) Act 1949)" substitute "the owner of the dominium utile."

Matrimonial Homes (Family Protection) (Scotland) Act 1981 (c. 59)

40. In section 13(8), in the definition of "agricultural holding," for "Agricultural Holdings (Scotland) Act 1949" substitute "Agricultural Holdings (Scotland) Act 1991."

Rent (Scotland) Act 1984 (c. 58)

41. For section 25(1)(iii) substitute—
   "(iii) the Agricultural Holdings (Scotland) Act 1991."

Law Reform (Miscellaneous Provisions) (Scotland) Act 1985 (c. 73)

42. In section 7(2), in the definition of "agricultural holding," for "section 1 of the Agricultural Holdings (Scotland) Act 1949" substitute "the Agricultural Holdings (Scotland) Act 1991."

Agriculture Act 1986 (c. 49)

43. In section 14(a) for "the Agricultural Holdings (Scotland) Act 1949" substitute "the 1991 Act."

44. In section 16—

(a) in subsection (2), for "section 7 of the 1949 Act" substitute "section 13 of the 1991 Act"; and

(b) in subsection (7), for "section 86 of the 1949 Act" substitute "section 79 of the 1991 Act."

45. In section 18(6) for the words from "the absolute owner" to "1949" substitute "the owner of the dominium utile."

46. In section 19(4) for "the Crofters (Scotland) Act 1955" substitute "the 1955 Act."

47. After section 23 insert—

"23A. In this Act—

"the 1886 Act" means the Crofters Holdings (Scotland) Act 1886;

"the 1911 Act" means the Small Landholders (Scotland) Act 1911;

"the 1955 Act" means the Crofters (Scotland) Act 1955; and

"the 1991 Act" means the Agricultural Holdings (Scotland) Act 1991."

48. In Schedule 2, paragraph 1(1)—

(a) in the definition of "landlord"—

      (i) in sub-paragraph (a), for "the 1949 Act" substitute "the 1991 Act" and for "section 93(1)" substitute "section 85(1)"; and

      (ii) in sub-paragraph (c), for "the 1949 Act" substitute "the 1991 Act";

(b) in the definition of "tenancy," for "the 1949 Act" substitute "the 1991 Act"; and

(c) in the definition of "tenant"—

      (i) in sub-paragraph (a), for "the 1949 Act" substitute "the 1991 Act" and for "section 93(1)" substitute "section 85(1)"; and

      (ii) in sub-paragraph (c), for "the 1949 Act" substitute "the 1991 Act."

49. In Schedule 2, paragraph 3(1)(b), for "section 20 of the 1949 Act" substitute "section 11 of the 1991 Act."

50. In Schedule 2, paragraph 7—

(a) in sub-paragraph (2), for "the 1949 Act" where it first occurs substitute "the 1991 Act" and for "section 7 of the 1949 Act" substitute "section 13 of the 1991 Act"; and

(b) in sub-paragraph (4)—

      (i) in sub-paragraph (a)(i), for "section 93 of the 1949 Act" substitute "section 85 of the 1991 Act";

      (ii) in sub-paragraph (a)(iii), for "the 1949 Act" substitute "the 1991 Act" and

      (iii) in sub-paragraph (b), for "section 93 of the 1949 Act" substitute "section 85 of the 1991 Act."

51. In Schedule 2, paragraph 10(1)—

(a) in sub-paragraph (a), for "the 1949 Act" substitute "the 1991 Act" and for "section 78" substitute "section 60(2)"; and

(b) for "section 75 (or, where the circumstances require, sections 77 and 87) of the 1949 Act" substitute "section 60(1) (or, where the circumstances require, sections 64 and 80) of the 1991 Act."

52. In Schedule 2, paragraph 11—

(a) in sub-paragraph (1)(a), for "the 1949 Act" substitute "the 1991 Act" and for "section 78" substitute "section 60(2)";

(b) in sub-paragraph (4)—

      (i) for "section 75 (or, where the circumstances require, sections 77 and 87) of the 1949 Act" substitute "section 60(1) (or, where the circumstances require, sections 64 and 80) of the 1991 Act"; and

      (ii) for "paragraph 13 of the Sixth Schedule" substitute "paragraph 14 of Schedule 7"; and

(c) in sub-paragraph (5), for "section 61 of the 1949 Act" substitute "section 50 of the 1991 Act."

53. In Schedule 2, for paragraph 12 substitute—

"Sections 65 and 75(1), (2), (4) and (6) of the 1991 Act (recovery of sums due and power of tenant to obtain charge on holding) shall apply in relation to any sum payable to the tenant under this Schedule as they apply to sums payable under that section.".

Housing (Scotland) Act 1987 (c. 26)

54. In section 256(1) and (3) for "Agricultural Holdings (Scotland) Act 1949" substitute "Agricultural Holdings (Scotland) Act 1991."

55. In section 338(1), in the definition of "agricultural holding," for "Agricultural Holdings (Scotland) Act 1949" substitute "Agricultural Holdings (Scotland) Act 1991."

56. In Schedule 8, Part IV, paragraph 13—

(a) in sub-paragraph (1)—

    (i) for "Section 8 of the Agricultural Holdings (Scotland) Act 1949" substitute "Section 15 of the Agricultural Holdings (Scotland) Act 1991;

    (ii) for "the said section 8" substitute "the said section 15";

(b) in sub-paragraph (2)—

    (i) for "paragraph 18 of Schedule 1 to the said Act of 1949" substitute "paragraph 18 of Schedule 5 to the Agricultural Holdings (Scotland) Act 1991";

    (ii) for "section 79" substitute "section 73";

    (iii) for "the said Schedule 1" substitute "the said Schedule 5";

    (iv) for "sections 51 and 52" substitute "sections 38 and 39";

    (v) for "section 49 of the said Act of 1949" substitute "section 36 of that Act."

Housing (Scotland) Act 1988 (c. 43)

57. In Schedule 4 in paragraph 6(a), for "Agricultural Holdings (Scotland) Act 1949" substitute "Agricultural Holdings (Scotland) Act 1991."

Section 87   SCHEDULE 12

TRANSITIONALS AND SAVINGS

Continuation of savings

1. The repeal by this Act of an enactment which repealed a previous enactment subject to a saving shall not affect the continued operation of that saving.

Construction of references to old and new law

2.—(1) Where an enactment contained in this Act repeals and re-enacts an earlier enactment—

(a) for the purpose of giving effect to any instrument or other document it shall be competent, so far as the context permits, to construe a reference to either enactment as a reference to the other;

(b) anything done or required to be done for the purposes of either enactment may, so far as the context permits, be treated as having been done or as something required to be done for the purposes of the other.

(2) In this paragraph, a reference to an enactment reenacted in this Act includes a reference to any such enactment repealed by the Agricultural Holdings Act 1923, the 1949 Act or the Agricultural Holdings (Amendment) (Scotland) Act 1983.

Savings for specific enactments

3. Nothing in this Act shall affect any provision of the Allotments (Scotland) Act 1922.

4. Section 21 of the Reserve and Auxiliary Forces (Protection of Civil Interests) Act 1951 (as read with section 24 of that Act) shall continue to have effect—

(a) in subsections (2) and (3) with the substitution for references to the Secretary of State of references to the Land Court; and

(b) with the reference in subsection (6) to section 27 of the 1949 Act being construed as a reference to that section as originally enacted.

Compensation

5. Notwithstanding section 16 of the Interpretation Act 1978, rights to compensation conferred by this Act shall be in lieu of rights to compensation conferred by any enactment repealed by this Act.

SCHEDULE 13

REPEALS AND REVOCATIONS

PART I

REPEALS

Chapter	Short title	Extent of repeal
1 Edw. 8 & 1 Geo. 6. c. 34.	Sheep Stocks Valuation (Scotland) Act 1937.	The whole Act.
9 & 10 Geo. 6. c. 73.	Hill Farming Act 1946.	Sections 28 to 31. Second Schedule.
11 & 12 Geo. 6. c. 45.	Agriculture (Scotland) Act 1948.	Section 52. In section 54, the definitions of "deer", "occupier of an agricultural holding" and "woodlands".
12, 13 and 14 Geo. 6. c. 75.	Agricultural Holdings (Scotland) Act 1949.	The whole Act.
14 & 15 Geo. 6. c. 18.	Livestock Rearing Act 1951.	In section 1(2)(b) the words "in paragraph (d) of subsection (1) of section 8 of the Agricultural Holdings (Scotland) Act 1949".
14 & 15 Geo. 6. c. 65.	Reserve and Auxiliary Forces (Protection of Civil Interests) Act 1951.	In section 24(b), the words from "for references" to "twenty-seven thereof".
6 & 7 Eliz. 2 c. 71.	Agriculture Act 1958.	Section 3. Schedule 1.
1963 c. 11.	Agriculture (Miscellaneous Provisions) Act 1963.	Section 21
1964 c. 41.	Succession (Scotland) Act 1964.	In Schedule 2, paragraphs 19 to 23.
1968 c. 34.	Agriculture (Miscellaneous Provisions) Act 1968.	Part II. Schedules 4 and 5.
1973 c. 65.	Local Government (Scotland) Act 1973.	Section 228(5).
1976 c. 21.	Crofting Reform (Scotland) Act 1976.	Schedule 2, para. 25.
1976 c. 55.	Agriculture (Miscellaneous Provisions) Act 1976.	Section 13 and 14.
1980 c. 45.	Water (Scotland) Act 1980.	In Schedule 10, Part II, the entry relating to the 1949 Act.
1983 c. 46.	Agricultural Holdings (Amendment) (Scotland) Act 1983.	The whole Act.
1985 c. 73.	Law Reform (Miscellaneous Provisions) (Scotland) Act 1985.	Section 32.
1986 c. 5.	Agricultural Holdings Act 1986.	In Schedule 14, paras. 25(8), 26(11) and 33(8).
1986 c. 49.	Agriculture Act 1986.	In Schedule 2, para. 1, the definitions of "the 1986 Act", "the 1911 Act", "the 1949 Act" and "the 1955 Act".

PART II

REVOCATIONS OF SUBORDINATE LEGISLATION

Number	Citation	Extent of revocation
S.I. 1950/1553.	The Agricultural Holdings (Scotland) Regulations 1950.	The whole Instrument.

Number	Citation	Extent of revocation
S.I. 1978/798.	The Agricultural Holdings (Scotland) Act 1949 (Variation of First Schedule) Order 1978.	The whole Order.
S.I. 1986/1823.	The Hill Farming Act 1946 (Variation of Second Schedule) (Scotland) Order 1986.	The whole Order.

TABLE OF DERIVATIONS

Notes: The following abbreviations are used in this Table—

1937	=	The Sheep Stocks Valuation (Scotland) Act 1937 (1 Edw. 8 & 1 Geo. 6. c. 34).
1946	=	The Hill Farming Act 1946 (9 & 10 Geo. 6. c. 73).
1948	=	The Agriculture (Scotland) Act 1948 (11 & 12 Geo. 6. c. 45).
1949	=	The Agricultural Holdings (Scotland) Act 1949 (12, 13 & 14 Geo. 6. c. 75).
1958	=	The Agriculture Act 1958 (c. 71).
1963	=	The Agriculture (Miscellaneous Provisions) Act 1963 (c. 11).
1964	=	The Succession (Scotland) Act 1964 (c. 41).
1968	=	The Agriculture (Miscellaneous Provisions) Act 1968 (c. 34).
1973	=	The Local Government (Scotland) Act 1973 (c. 65).
1976	=	The Agriculture (Miscellaneous Provisions) Act 1976 (c. 55).
1983	=	The Agriculture Holdings (Amendment) (Scotland) Act 1983 (c. 46).
1986	=	The Agriculture Holdings Act 1986 (c. 5).
S.I. 1950/1553	=	The Agriculture Holdings (Scotland) Regulations 1950 (S.I. 1950/1553).
S.I. 1978/798	=	The Agricultural Holdings (Scotland) Act 1949 (Variation of First Schedule) Order 1978 (c.I. 1978/798).
S.I. 1986/1823	=	The Hill Farming Act 1946 (Variation of Second Schedule) (Scotland) Order 1986.

Provision of Act	Derivation
1	1949 s.1; 1958 s.9(1).
2	1949 s.2.
3	1949 s.3; 1949 s.24(1).
4	1949 s.4, s.6(4).
5	1949 s.5.
6	1949 s.23.
7	1949 s.12; 1958 Sch. 1, Pt.II, para. 33.
8	1949 s.17.
9	1949 s.9; 1958 Sch. 1, Pt.II, para. 32.
10	1949 s.18.
11	1949 s.20; 1964 s.34(1), Sch. 2, paras. 19, 20 and 21.
12	1949 s.21; 1964 s.34(1), Sch. 2, para. 22.
13	1949 s.7; 1983 s.2.
14	1949 s.6(3).
15	1949 s.8.
16	1949 s.10.
17	1949 s.13.
18	1949 s.14.
19	1949 s.22.
20	1949 s.19.
21	1949 s.24; 1958 Sch. 1, Pt. II, para. 34.
22	1949 s.25; 1958 s.3(1), (3), Sch. 1, Pt. II, para. 35.
23	1949 s.27; 1958 Sch. 1, Pt. II, para. 37.
24	1949 s.26; 1958 s.3(2), (3), Sch. 1, Pt. II, para. 36; 1983 s.4(1).
25	1949 s.26A; 1983 s.3, s.4(2).

Provision of Act	Derivation
26	1949 s.28; 1958 Sch. 1, Pt. II, para. 38; 1989 (c. 15) Sch. 25, para. 12.
27	1949 s.30; 1958 Sch. 1, Pt. II, para. 40.
28	1949 s.31.
29	1949 s.32.
30	1949 s.33.
31	1949 s.34.
32	1976 s.14.
33	1949 s.36; s.47.
34	1949 s.37, s.41, s.42, s.43, s.44(4), s.45, s.48, s.53, s.54.
35	1949 s.11, s.46, s.55
36	1949 s.38, s.43, s.44(1), s.49, s.53.
37	1949 s.39, s.50.
38	1949 s.40, s.51.
39	1949 s.52; 1958 Sch. 1, Pt. II, para. 41.
40	1949 s.65.
41	1949 s.66; 1958 Sch. 1, Pt. II, para. 43.
42	1949 s.67.
43	1949 s.35.
44	1949 s.56.
45	1949 s.57, s.58.
46	1949 s.6(1), (2); s.57(3); S.I. 1950/1553.
47	1949 s.59.
48	1949 s.16.
49	1949 s.60.
50	1949 s.61.
51	1949 s.63; 1958 Sch. 1, Pt.II, para. 42; S.I. 1977/2007.
52	1949 s.15; S.I. 1977/2007.
53	1949 s.64.
54	1968 s.9, s.16, Sch. 5, para. 1.
55	1968 s.11.
56	1968 s.12, s.16.
57	1968 s.14; 1972 (c. 52) Sch. 21, Pt.II.
58	1968 s.15, s.16, Sch. 5, para. 5.
59	1968 s.16, s.17.
60	1949 s.74, s.78.
61	1949 s.68, s.75; 1973 s.228(5); 1983 s.5(1).
62	1949 s.68.
63	1949 s.76; 1971 c. 58 s.4.
64	1949 s.77, s.87(2); 1986 s.17(3).
65	1949 s.69.
66	1976 s.13.
67	1949 s.91; 1971 c. 58 s.4.
68	1937 s.1; 1946 s.28; 1985 c. 73 s.32; S.I. 1986/1823.
69	1937 s.2.
70	1937 s.3; 1946 s.29; S.I. 1986/1823.
71	1946 s.30.
72	1937 s.4.
73	1949 s.79.
74	1949 s.80.
75	1949 s.70, s.82; 1980 (c. 45) Sch. 10.
76	1949 s.83.
77	1949 s.84.
78	1949 s.85.
79	1949 s.86; 1968 s.17(3).
80	1949 s.87(1).
81	1949 s.88.
82	1949 s.89; 1975 c. 21 s.289; 1977 c. 45 s.31.
83	1949 s.73; 1976 s.14(6); 1976 (c. 21) Sch. 2, para. 25.
84	1949 s.90; 1985 c. 6 s.725(1).
85	1949 s.93.
86	1949 s.95.
87	1949 s.99(2).

Provision of Act	Derivation
88	1949 s.97.
89	1949 s.101.
Schedule 1	1949 Sch. 5.
Schedule 2	1983 Sch. 1.
Schedule 3	1949 Sch. 2.
Schedule 4	1949 Sch. 3.
Schedule 5	1949 Sch. 1; S.I. 1978/798.
Schedule 6	1949 Sch. 4.
Schedule 7	1949 Sch. 6; 1983 s.5(2).
Scheduie 8	1968 Sch. 4, Sch. 5, para. 6, para. 7.
Schedule 9	1946 Sch. 2; 1963 s.21.
Schedule 10	1946 Sch. 2; 1963; s.21.

INDEX

References are to sections and Schedules

55–137

WATER INDUSTRY ACT 1991*

(1991 c. 56)

[A table showing the derivation of the provisions of this Consolidation Act will be found at the end of the Act. The table has no official status.]

---

* Annotations by Neil Stanley, LL.B, Solicitor, Research Associate with Hammond Suddards Research Limited, Saltaire, Bradford. The Annotator gratefully acknowledges the work of Professor Richard Macrory, M.A., Barrister, Imperial College London, the annotator of the Water Act 1989.

CHAPTER III

QUALITY AND SUFFICIENCY OF SUPPLIES

Standards of wholesomeness

General obligations of undertakers

Waste, contamination, misuse etc.

Local authority functions

Assessors for the enforcement of water quality

An Act to consolidate enactments relating to the supply of water and the provision of sewerage services, with amendments to give effect to recommendations of the Law Commission. [25th July 1991]

PARLIAMENTARY DEBATES
Hansard, H.L. Vol. 528, cols. 482, 1738; Vol. 529, cols. 745, 1006; H.C. Vol. 195, col. 1110.

INTRODUCTION
The Water Industry Act 1991, together with the Water Resources Act 1991, the Statutory Water Companies Act 1991, the Land Drainage Act 1991 and the Water Consolidation (Consequential Provisions) Act 1991, comprise the newly consolidated legislation relating to water. Although principally a consolidating act, the Water Industry Act 1991 gives effect to the recommendations of the Law Commission comprised in its Report No. 198, "*Report on the Consolidation of the Legislation Relating To Water*", Cmnd. 1483.

The Act provides the detailed legislation relating to the functions of water supply undertakers, sewerage undertakers and the remit of the Director General of Water Services. The key provisions of the Act are derived principally from the Water Act 1989, which enacted the privatisation and restructuring of the water industry in England and Wales.

The legislative background
Legislation relating to the water industry in England and Wales has undergone substantial change in the last two decades. The basic structure of the water industry during this period was established by the Water Act 1973. The Water Act 1973 introduced the water industry to the concept of public authorities with dual utility and regulatory functions. This was followed in 1986 by the White Paper "*Privatisation of the Water Authorities in England and Wales*" (Cmnd. 9734, February 1986). The White Paper put forward the proposal to privatise the integrated system of water management established by the Water Act 1973 by transferring Water Authorities to the private sector, inclusive of all their functions, except land drainage. A detailed policy framework was proposed in the consultation paper "*The Water Environment: the next steps*" (DOE/WO Consultation Paper, April 1986). That proposal proved to be politically unacceptable and as a result the privatisation of the water industry was delayed until after the 1987 General Election. This was followed by a further consultation paper entitled "*The National Rivers Authority: the Government's proposals for a public regulatory body in a privatised water industry*" (DOE/Ministry of Agriculture, Fisheries and Food and Welsh Office, July 1987). The consultation paper considered the establishment of a new public body, the National Rivers Authority, which was designed to inherit the regulatory and water management functions of water authorities, leaving water supply and sewerage services of water authorities to be privatised.

The Public Utility Transfers and Water Charges Act 1988 further prepared the way for privatisation by allowing water authorities to divide themselves into utility and regulatory divisions.

The Water Act 1989
The Water Act 1989 divided the property, rights and liabilities of the 10 former water authorities between a newly established public body, the National Rivers Authority, and the

successor companies to the water authorities. The National Rivers Authority inherited the main regulatory and water management functions of water authorities, leaving the utility rôles of water supply and sewerage services for privatisation.

The legislation provided that the successor companies would initially belong to nominated holding companies which were in turn owned by the Crown, pending flotation. The Water Act 1989 enabled the successor companies to be nominated as water undertakers and sewerage undertakers, thereby succeeding to the utility functions of the former water authorities. Detailed conditions governing each water undertaker and sewerage undertaker were set out in the relevant instruments of appointment. A Water Services Office was created by the Water Act 1989, controlled by a Director General of Water Services whose responsibilities were concentrated upon the conditions of appointment of undertakers and thereafter regulating the economic performance and consumer service aspects of each undertaker's functions.

Existing statutory water companies were appointed water undertakers for their existing areas and were given the option to convert themselves into public limited companies should the majority of their shareholders so desire.

The post Water Act 1989 Regulatory Régime
   The Water Act 1989 fundamentally altered the structure of the water and sewerage industry in England and Wales. Privatisation altered the legal and economic basis on which the industry functioned. As privatised public limited companies the water companies have freedom to pay dividends, determine salaries and raise capital without the need for prior Government approval. Similarly, they now operate their services subject to price constraints and performance standards regulated by the Director General of Water Services. The Director General has a dual rôle in protecting the interests of the consumer whilst ensuring that the undertakers of water and sewerage services are properly financed to enable them to carry out their functions. The Water Act 1989 also contained more detailed environmental and public health standards which are no longer enforceable solely by self-regulation. The water and sewerage undertakers are now of course subject to identical controls both in terms of company law and stock exchange requirements as are other public limited companies.

In the interests of protecting the consumer, water and sewerage undertakers are not allowed to commence a voluntary winding-up and in addition proposed mergers will be viewed strictly from a public interest viewpoint, paying particular attention to the desirability of competition. The Water Act 1989 was important in establishing the division between the core functions of a water or sewerage undertaker on the one hand and non-core activity related to other business ventures on the other. The question of what is and what is not a non-core activity is likely to pose difficult questions for the water industry.

The régime established by the Water Act 1989 relies in a large part on control of water and sewerage undertakers by regulations. The conditions of appointment of each undertaker contain key regulatory requirements concerning prices, performance standards and other aspects of the relationship of undertakers with their customers. The conditions of appointment contained in each instrument of appointment provide a significant parallel set of regulatory requirements which will supplement those originally contained in the Water Act 1989 and which are now contained in this Act.

Consolidation
   The Water Act 1989 by no means provided a complete picture of the legislation relating to water supply and sewerage services and reference at that time still had to be made to many other pieces of legislation. In addition, the arrangement of the Water Act 1989 necessitated a large amount of cross-referencing, plus reference to the 27 Schedules to the Act which contained not simply elaborative or supplementary provisions but in effect amounted to substantive primary law. It is perhaps no surprise therefore that within two years of the implementation of the Water Act 1989 the legislation relating to the water industry has now been consolidated. The Water Industry Act 1991 is part of the present consolidation which is designed to rationalise the legislation relating to the water industry whilst making only drafting amendments and no substantive changes, save for the technical changes introduced by the Law Commission's "*Report on the Consolidation of the Legislation Relating to Water*" (Cmnd. 1483, April 1991).

Arrangement of the Act
   The Act is divided into eight Parts and 15 Schedules. All parts, save for Pts. I, VII and VIII, are sub-divided into separate chapters.

Part I
   Sections 1–5 are concerned with the functions of the office of the Director General of Water Services—the regulatory body of the water industry. The fundamental general duties of the

Director General relating to the water industry, environment and recreation are set out together with the more specific environmental duties.

Part II

Sections 6–36 deal with the appointment and regulation of the industry's water and sewerage undertakers.

Chapter I (ss.6–17) provides for the appointment of water and sewerage undertakers, the conditions upon which those undertakers will carry out their functions and procedures for modifying the conditions of appointment.

Chapter II (ss.18–26) contains the enforcement provisions which detail how compliance with relevant conditions and duties is to be effected. In the event of insolvency or serious default by an undertaker, provision is made for the appointment of a special administrator.

Chapter III (ss.27–35) is concerned with the protection of customers' interests. It details the duties of the Director General regarding the monitoring of the activities of the industry and complaints. It provides for the establishment and functions of customer service committees. There are additional provisions relating to competition which address considerations relevant to any merger proposal.

Chapter IV (s.36) relates to the interpretation of this part of the Act.

Part III

Sections 37–93 deal with the water supply functions of water undertakers.

Chapter I (ss.37–39) details the general duty to develop and maintain an efficient and economical water supply system, performance standards and regulations.

Chapter II (ss.40–66) contains provisions relating to bulk supplies of water by one undertaker to another, the provision of water supplies for both domestic and non-domestic purposes, disconnection and the maintenance and constancy of such supplies.

Chapter III (ss.67–86) is concerned with the quality and sufficiency of water supplies. Included within this chapter are provisions detailing standards of water quality, associated regulations and an offence of supplying water unfit for human consumption. Additional offences relate to waste, contamination and misuse of water resources with associated preventive regulations. The chapter also deals with local authority functions and powers relating to water quality and supplies. Provision is also made for the appointment of assessors for the enforcement of water quality.

Chapter IV (ss.87–91) contains provisions relating to the fluoridation of water supplies.

Chapter V (ss.92–93) contains supplemental information to Pt. II of the Act.

Part IV

Sections 94–141 contain detailed provisions relating to sewerage services, and provide a control régime relating to the discharge of trade effluent into sewerage systems.

Chapter I (ss.94–97) includes a general duty upon undertakers to provide a sewerage system and associated standards of performance and regulations. It also deals with the circumstances in which a sewerage undertaker's functions may be performed by a local authority.

Chapter II (ss.98–117) concerns the provision of sewerage services. Duties and conditions relating to the requisition of a public sewer are set out, as are provisions relating to the adoption of sewers and disposal works. Rights of communication relating both to drains and private sewers with the public sewerage system and connections between public sewers themselves are also contained within this chapter. In addition there are other provisions designed to safeguard the sewerage system.

Chapter III (ss.118–141) contains provisions controlling the disposal of trade effluent. A consent procedure authorising the discharge of trade effluent into a public sewer is the means whereby such control is effected.

Part V

Sections 142–154 detail the financial provisions relating to undertakers. These concern fixing charges for services and financial assistance to undertakers in appropriate circumstances.

Chapter I (ss.142–150) contains provisions detailing the manner in which undertakers may fix their charges, how these charges are restricted, metering charges and charges for services provided with the help of an undertaker.

Chapter II (ss.151–154) provides for financial assistance to undertakers in a limited number of instances, including the provision of services in rural areas, grants for national security purposes and in circumstances where a special administration order has been made.

Part VI

Sections 155–192 set out the range of an undertaker's powers.

Chapter I (ss.155–173) provides powers in relation to land, compulsory purchase, pipe-laying, the carrying out of a range of specified works, the discharge of water and rights of entry.

Chapter II (ss.174–178) concerns the protection of an undertaker's apparatus and meters. It also provides a remedy for anyone who wilfully obstructs sewerage works.

Chapter II (ss.180–192) details the supplemental provisions with respect to an undertaker's powers. These provisions include the vesting of works in an undertaker, compensation for damage caused by an undertaker's operations, codes of practice relating to work on private land, alteration of public sewers, the moving of pipes and mineral rights.

Part VII

Sections 193–207 are concerned with the provision of information. Such provision includes the making of reports by both the Director General and customer services committees, the compilation of a series of registers and maps, and powers to acquire and duties to provide relevant information.

Part VIII

Sections 208–223 contain miscellaneous and supplementary provisions.

Commencement

The Act came into force on December 1, 1991 by virtue of s.223.

PART I

PRELIMINARY

The Director General of Water Services

The Director General of Water Services

1.—(1) There shall continue to be an officer known as the Director General of Water Services (in this Act referred to as "the Director") for the purpose of carrying out the functions of that Director under this Act.

(2) Appointment of any person to hold office as the Director shall be made by the Secretary of State.

(3) An appointment of a person to hold office as the Director shall be for a term not exceeding five years; but previous appointment to that office shall not affect eligibility for re-appointment.

(4) The Director may at any time resign his office as the Director by notice addressed to the Secretary of State; and the Secretary of State may remove any person from that office on the ground of incapacity or misbehaviour.

(5) Subject to the preceding provisions of this section, the Director shall hold and vacate office as such in accordance with the terms of his appointment.

(6) The provisions of Schedule 1 to this Act shall have effect with respect to the Director.

GENERAL NOTE

This section and Sched. 1 of the Act provide for the continuation in office of the present Director General of Water Services and for the subsequent appointment of his successor. The Director is in charge of the water services office which regulates the activities of the water and sewerage undertakers. The costs of the water services office are met from appointment fees paid by water and sewerage undertakers under s.11(1)(c).

The Director's main responsibility relates to the supervision and regulation of the undertakers' core activities. He will pay particular attention to the conditions upon which an undertaker was appointed under its instrument of appointment. One interesting aspect of the Act, derived from the provisions of the Water Act 1989, is the extent to which the Director's remit has been left for subsequent determination by the Secretary of State. For example, the Director's involvement in a number of significant areas is dependent on receiving a general authorisation from the Secretary of State. The authorisation process is applicable to the appointment of undertakers in s.6, enforcement of s.19(1)(b), compliance with undertakings by companies (s.19(2)(b)), and enforcement of general water supply and general sewerage services duties (ss.37 and 94).

The office of water services is a non-ministerial Government department. The Director has a significant degree of independence from the Secretary of State but the Secretary of State may circumscribe the activities of the Director by prohibiting any proposed modification to the conditions of an instrument of appointment (s.13(4)), give general directions concerning matters to be kept under review by the Director (s.27(3)), and require the Director to exclude matters from the published report of the Monopolies Commission (s.15(6)).

General duties

General duties with respect to water industry

2.—(1) This section shall have effect for imposing duties on the Secretary of State and on the Director as to when and how they should exercise and perform the following powers and duties, that is to say—
- (a) in the case of the Secretary of State, the powers and duties conferred or imposed on him by virtue of the provisions of this Act relating to the regulation of relevant undertakers; and
- (b) in the case of the Director, the powers and duties conferred or imposed on him by virtue of any of those provisions, by the provisions relating to the financial conditions of requisitions or by the provisions relating to the movement of certain pipes.

(2) The Secretary of State or, as the case may be, the Director shall exercise and perform the powers and duties mentioned in subsection (1) above in the manner that he considers is best calculated—
- (a) to secure that the functions of a water undertaker and of a sewerage undertaker are properly carried out as respects every area of England and Wales; and
- (b) without prejudice to the generality of paragraph (a) above, to secure that companies holding appointments under Chapter I of Part II of this Act as relevant undertakers are able (in particular, by securing reasonable returns on their capital) to finance the proper carrying out of the functions of such undertakers.

(3) Subject to subsection (2) above, the Secretary of State or, as the case may be, the Director shall exercise and perform the powers and duties mentioned in subsection (1) above in the manner that he considers is best calculated—
- (a) to ensure that the interests of every person who is a customer or potential customer of a company which has been or may be appointed under Chapter I of Part II of this Act to be a relevant undertaker are protected as respects the fixing and recovery by that company of water and drainage charges and, in particular—
  - (i) that the interests of customers and potential customers in rural areas are so protected; and
  - (ii) that no undue preference is shown, and that there is no undue discrimination, in the fixing of those charges;
- (b) to ensure that the interests of every such person are also protected as respects the other terms on which any services are provided by that company in the course of the carrying out of the functions of a relevant undertaker and as respects the quality of those services;
- (c) to ensure that the interests of every such person are further protected as respects benefits that could be secured for them by the application in a particular manner of any of the proceeds of any disposal (including a disposal before the Secretary of State and the Director became subject to the duties imposed by virtue of this paragraph) of any of that company's protected land or of any interest or right in or over any of that land;
- (d) to promote economy and efficiency on the part of any such company in the carrying out of the functions of a relevant undertaker; and
- (e) to facilitate effective competition, with respect to such matters as he

considers appropriate, between persons holding or seeking appointments under that Chapter.

(4) In performing his duty under subsection (3) above, so far as it requires him to do anything in the manner which he considers is best calculated to ensure that the interests of the customers and potential customers of any company are protected as respects the quality of any services provided by that company in the course of the carrying out of the functions of a relevant undertaker, the Secretary of State or, as the case may be, the Director shall take into account, in particular, the interests of those who are disabled or of pensionable age.

(5) In this section the references to water and drainage charges are references to—

(a) any charges in respect of any services provided in the course of the carrying out of the functions of a relevant undertaker; and

(b) amounts of any other description which such an undertaker is authorised by or under any enactment to require any of its customers or potential customers to pay.

(6) For the purposes of this section—

(a) the reference in subsection (1) above to the provisions of this Act relating to the regulation of relevant undertakers is a reference to the provisions contained in Part II of this Act (except section 28 and Schedule 4), or in any of sections 38, 39, 95, 96, 153, 181, 182, 193 to 195 and 201 to 203 below;

(b) the reference in that subsection to the provisions relating to the financial conditions of requisitions is a reference to the provisions contained in sections 42, 43, 48, 99 and 100 below; and

(c) the reference in that subsection to the provisions relating to the movement of certain pipes is a reference to the provisions of section 185 below.

DEFINITIONS
"functions": ss.217 and 219(1).
"protected land": s.219(1).
"relevant undertaker": s.219(1).

GENERAL NOTE
This section is fundamental to the regulatory framework detailed in the Act. It lays down primary and secondary considerations that govern the relationship of the Secretary of State and the Director with water and sewerage undertakers.

Provisions subject to s.2 duties
The general primary duties under this section apply to the powers and duties of the Secretary of State and the Director contained in ss.6–36, and include the appointment and replacement of undertakers, competition provisions, modification of appointment conditions and the exercise of enforcement powers under s.18 (applicable to both the conditions of appointment and the primary duties of water and sewerage undertakers).

The s.2 duties apply to the Secretary of State's power to prescribe performance standards in respect of an undertaker's general duties relating to water supply and sewerage services (ss.38(2) and 95(2)) and his power to approve a statutory code of practice regarding the powers of undertakers to lay pipes, etc. on private land (s.182(2)). The s.2 duties also apply to the Director in respect of his power to fix interest rates regarding requisitioning provisions (ss.42(4) and 99(4)) and security deposits for moving pipes (s.185(6)).

Primary duties
The two primary duties of the Secretary of State and the Director are to secure that the functions of water and sewerage undertakers are properly carried out throughout England and Wales (subs. (2)(a)) and that water and sewerage undertakers are able to finance the proper carrying out of their functions (subs. (2)(b)).

The inclusion of the phrase in subs. (2)(b) "without prejudice to the generality of paragraph (a)" implies that greater weight will be given to the duty comprised in subs. (2)(a).

Section 2 of the Act is derived from s.7 of the Water Act 1989. In the Parliamentary discussions which preceded implementation of s.7 of the Water Act 1989 there was some discussion on the use of the word "able" which now appears in subs. (2)(b) of this Act. It was suggested that the use of the word "able" did not necessarily imply that undertakers were bound to earn a reasonable return on capital. The Secretary of State and the Director were to exercise their functions to enable them to do so but whether they actually did so would depend on other factors, for example each undertaker's overall efficiency.

Secondary Duties
Subsections (3) and (4) set out a range of secondary duties, none of which is expressed to have priority over another. General principles of statutory interpretation confirm this view. Attempts during the committee stage of the Water Act 1989 to impose a ranking order of the secondary duties were rejected by Michael Howard (Standing Committee D, col. 575; January 26, 1989). The Secretary of State and the Director are involved in a balancing exercise and must attempt to reconcile the factors "in the manner he considers best", should there be a conflict of interest.

Legal significance of s.2 duties
From an administrative point of view the duties contained in s.2 of the Act provide the policy priorities and justifications for decision-making. Should any decision of the Director or Secretary of State be challenged, for example, by an application to the High Court for judicial review (an application may be made to the High Court under s.21 of the Act to challenge the validity of a s.18 enforcement order), then the s.2 duties are likely to be considered by the courts in determining the policy and objectives of the Act (*Bromley London Borough Council* v. *Greater London Council* [1983] A.C. 768, *Padfield* v. *Minister of Agriculture, Fisheries and Food* [1968] A.C. 997).

Subs. (3)(a)
This subsection refers to the need to protect the interests of customers and potential customers in rural areas. It relates to the general power of water and sewerage undertakers under s.142 to fix charges. Subsection (3)(a) is designed to avoid unacceptable distortion between rural and non-rural areas.

Subs. (3)(c)
This relates to disposals of land by undertakers pursuant to s.156 and is designed to ensure that customers as well as shareholders benefit from the proceeds of such disposals. Conditions within each Instrument of Appointment translate these aims into practice.

General environmental and recreational duties

3.—(1) It shall be the duty of each of the following, that is to say—
(a) the Secretary of State;
(b) the Minister of Agriculture, Fisheries and Food;
(c) the Director; and
(d) every company holding an appointment as a relevant undertaker,
in formulating or considering any proposals relating to any functions of a relevant undertaker (including, in the case of such a company, any functions which, by virtue of that appointment, are functions of the company itself) to comply with the requirements imposed in relation to the proposals by subsections (2) and (3) below.
(2) The requirements imposed by this subsection in relation to any such proposals as are mentioned in subsection (1) above are—
(a) a requirement, so far as may be consistent—
(i) with the purposes of any enactment relating to the functions of the undertaker; and
(ii) in the case of the Secretary of State and the Director, with their duties under section 2 above,
so to exercise any power conferred with respect to the proposals on the person subject to the requirement as to further the conservation and enhancement of natural beauty and the conservation of flora, fauna and geological or physiographical features of special interest;
(b) a requirement to have regard to the desirability of protecting and conserving buildings, sites and objects of archaeological, architectural or historic interest; and

(c) a requirement to take into account any effect which the proposals would have on the beauty or amenity of any rural or urban area or on any such flora, fauna, features, buildings, sites or objects.

(3) The requirements imposed by this subsection in relation to any such proposals as are mentioned in subsection (1) above are, subject to the requirements imposed by subsection (2) above—

(a) a requirement to have regard to the desirability of preserving for the public any freedom of access to areas of woodland, mountains, moor, heath, down, cliff or foreshore and other places of natural beauty;

(b) a requirement to have regard to the desirability of maintaining the availability to the public of any facility for visiting or inspecting any building, site or object of archaeological, architectural or historic interest; and

(c) a requirement to take into account any effect which the proposals would have on any such freedom of access or on the availability of any such facility.

(4) Subsections (1) to (3) above shall apply so as to impose duties on the Director and any company holding an appointment as a relevant undertaker in relation to any proposal relating to—

(a) the functions of the NRA; or

(b) the functions of an internal drainage board,

as they apply in relation to any proposals relating to the functions of such an undertaker; and for the purposes of this subsection the reference in subsection (2)(a) above to the functions of the undertaker shall have effect as a reference to the functions of the NRA or, as the case may be, of the internal drainage board in question.

(5) Subject to obtaining the consent of any navigation authority, harbour authority or conservancy authority before doing anything which causes navigation which is subject to the control of that authority to be obstructed or otherwise interfered with, it shall be the duty of every company holding an appointment as a relevant undertaker to take such steps as are—

(a) reasonably practicable; and

(b) consistent with the purposes of the enactments relating to the functions of the undertaker in question,

for securing, so long as that company has rights to the use of water or land associated with water, that those rights are exercised so as to ensure that the water or land is made available for recreational purposes and is so made available in the best manner.

(6) It shall be the duty of a company holding an appointment as a relevant undertaker, in determining what steps to take in performance of any duty imposed by virtue of subsection (5) above, to take into account the needs of persons who are chronically sick or disabled.

(7) The obligations under this section of a company holding an appointment as a relevant undertaker shall be enforceable under section 18 below by the Secretary of State.

(8) Nothing in this section or the following provisions of this Act shall require recreational facilities made available by a relevant undertaker to be made available free of charge.

(9) References in this section to the functions of a relevant undertaker shall be construed, without prejudice to section 156(7) below, as if those functions included the management, by a company holding an appointment as such an undertaker, of any land for the time being held by that company for any purpose whatever (whether or not connected with the carrying out of the functions of a relevant undertaker).

(10) In this section "building" includes structure.

DEFINITIONS
"building": subs. (10).

"conservancy authority": s.219(1).
"enactment": s.219(1).
"functions of a relevant undertaker": subs. (9).
"harbour authority": s.219(1).
"navigation authority": s.219(1).
"relevant undertaker": s.219(1).

GENERAL NOTE

This section imposes general environmental duties on the Secretary of State, the Minister of Agriculture, Fisheries and Food, the Director and each water and sewerage undertaker. Reference should also be made to the more specific provisions in ss.4, 5 and 156.

These environmental duties relate to the core functions of undertakers relating to water supply and sewerage services. The duties do not apply to non-core activities save that the term "functions" in s.3(1) receives an extended definition under s.217 so that the management of land, whether for functional or non-functional purposes, is included in s.3(9). In addition, special controls exist in respect of disposals of land designated as being of high environmental quality (s.156).

It should be noted that the s.2 duties applicable to the Director and Secretary of State override the environmental duties contained in s.3. It is clear that the duty to provide essential water and sewerage services override any duty to further the interests of conservation. Similarly, the duty to supply wholesome water or effectively to sewer an area could override the environmental duties (see *Hansard*, H.L. Vol. 507, col. 433).

The final important distinction between the s.2 general primary duties and those contained in s.3 concerns enforcement of the s.3 duties. These are enforceable against water and sewerage undertakers by the Secretary of State via a s.18 enforcement order (s.3(7)). Whilst the use of s.18 orders to enforce s.3 obligations may be rare, their availability is important as a deterrent. Contravention of codes of practice made under s.5 are to be taken into account in determining whether there has been a breach of the environmental duties contained in s.3. It should be noted that none of the environmental duties has priority over another.

Subs. (2)(b)

In the context of the desirability of protecting and conserving the built environment, note the decisions in *Bath Society* v. *Secretary of State for the Environment and Hammercrest Developments* [1991] J.P.L. 663, and *South Lakeland District Council* v. *Secretary of State for the Environment and Carlisle Parsonages Board, The Times*, February 3, 1992, H.L.

Subs. (8)

This provision is to be read in conjunction with the duty under subs. (3)(c). The subs. (3)(c) requirement does not provide a guarantee that existing freedom of access to land belonging to relevant undertakers is to be preserved; however, it does go some way towards restricting the imposition of charges.

Subs. (9)

The environmental duties contained in s.3 apply to land managed by undertakers for both core business and non-core business activities. The provision applies only to the management of land, but the environmental duties under this section also extend to proposals for the disposal of protected land in national parks, the Broads, areas of outstanding natural beauty, or sites of special scientific interest (s.156(7)).

Environmental duties with respect to sites of special interest

4.—(1) Where the Nature Conservancy Council for England or the Countryside Council for Wales are of the opinion that any area of land in England or, as the case may be, in Wales—
   (a) is of special interest by reason of its flora, fauna or geological or physiographical features; and
   (b) may at any time be affected by schemes, works, operations or activities of a relevant undertaker,
that Council shall notify the fact that the land is of special interest for that reason to every relevant undertaker whose works, operations or activities may affect the land.
   (2) Where a National Park authority or the Broads Authority is of the opinion that any area of land in a National Park or in the Broads—

(a) is land in relation to which the matters for the purposes of which section 3 above has effect are of particular importance; and

(b) may at any time be affected by schemes, works, operations or activities of a relevant undertaker,

the National Park authority or Broads Authority shall notify the fact that the land is such land, and the reasons why those matters are of particular importance in relation to the land, to every relevant undertaker whose works, operations or activities may affect the land.

(3) Where a relevant undertaker has received a notification under subsection (1) or (2) above with respect to any land, that undertaker shall consult the notifying body before carrying out any works, operations or activities which appear to that undertaker to be likely—

(a) to destroy or damage any of the flora, fauna, or geological or physiographical features by reason of which the land is of special interest; or

(b) significantly to prejudice anything the importance of which is one of the reasons why the matters mentioned in subsection (2) above are of particular importance in relation to that land.

(4) Subsection (3) above shall not apply in relation to anything done in an emergency where particulars of what is done and of the emergency are notified to the Nature Conservancy Council for England, the Countryside Council for Wales, the National Park authority in question or, as the case may be, the Broads Authority as soon as practicable after that thing is done.

(5) The obligations under this section of a relevant undertaker shall be enforceable under section 18 below by the Secretary of State.

(6) In this section—

"the Broads" has the same meaning as in the Norfolk and Suffolk Broads Act 1988; and

"National Park authority" means a National Park Committee or a joint or special planning board for a National Park;

and section 3(9) above shall apply, as it applies in relation to that section, for construing (in accordance with section 6 below) any references in this section to a relevant undertaker.

DEFINITIONS

"Broads Authority": subs. (6).
"National Park authority": subs. (6).

GENERAL NOTE

This section is concerned with the more specific environmental duties relating to sites of special interest. Section 4 requires undertakers to consult with the Nature Conservancy Council for England, the Countryside Council for Wales, the Broads Authority, or a National Park authority prior to undertaking potentially damaging operations or works. These requirements are not restricted to the core activities of water or sewerage undertakers and are enforceable by the Secretary of State by means of s.18 enforcement orders (subs. (5)).

The Nature Conservancy Council for England or the Countryside Council for Wales are not constrained to include in a s.4 notification only those sites which are of special scientific interest under s.28 of the Wildlife and Countryside Act 1981. This is in contrast to the specific reference to such sites in s.156(8). Under this section the burden is on the Nature Conservancy Council for England or the Countryside Council for Wales to identify those works and operations which may destroy or damage features of the site. Where a relevant undertaker has received a notice from the relevant council, consultations must take place (subs. (3)(a)) before works are commenced.

The provisions in subs. (2) concern National Parks authorities and the Broads Authority, who are required to notify undertakers of land within their jurisdiction which is of "particular importance" in relation to the environmental duties contained in s.3. In contrast to the Nature Conservancy Council for England and Countryside Council for Wales, notifications to undertakers by a National Park authority or the Broads Authority must be accompanied by reasons. The requirement to give reasons refers to subs. (3)(b), requiring undertakers to consult before carrying out works and operations which may "prejudice" the considerations which gave the land its particular importance. The responsibility to identify the works and operations that fall within this category is that of the relevant undertaker.

Codes of practice with respect to environmental and recreational duties

5.—(1) The Secretary of State may by order approve any code of practice issued (whether by him or by another person) for the purpose of—

(a) giving practical guidance to relevant undertakers with respect to any of the matters for the purposes of which sections 3 and 4 above have effect; and

(b) promoting what appear to him to be desirable practices by such undertakers with respect to those matters,

and may at any time by such an order approve a modification of such a code or withdraw his approval of such a code or modification.

(2) A contravention of a code of practice as for the time being approved under this section shall not of itself constitute a contravention of any requirement imposed by section 3 or 4 above or give rise to any criminal or civil liability; but the Secretary of State and the Minister of Agriculture, Fisheries and Food shall each be under a duty to take into account whether there has been or is likely to be any such contravention in determining when and how he should exercise his powers in relation to any relevant undertaker by virtue of this Act, any of the other consolidation Acts or the Water Act 1989.

(3) The power of the Secretary of State to make an order under this section shall be exercisable by statutory instrument subject to annulment in pursuance of a resolution of either House of Parliament.

(4) The Secretary of State shall not make an order under this section unless he has first consulted—

(a) the NRA;

(b) the Countryside Commission, the Nature Conservancy Council for England and the Countryside Council for Wales;

(c) the Historic Buildings and Monuments Commission for England;

(d) the Sports Council and the Sports Council for Wales; and

(e) such relevant undertakers and other persons as he considers it appropriate to consult.

(5) In this section "the other consolidation Acts" means the Water Resources Act 1991, the Statutory Water Companies Act 1991, the Land Drainage Act 1991 and the Water Consolidation (Consequential Provisions) Act 1991.

DEFINITIONS

"modification": s.219(1).

"NRA": s.219(1).

"the other consolidation Acts": subs. (5).

GENERAL NOTE

Codes of practice under this section provide a mechanism for translating the s.3 general environmental duties into specific requirements and facilitate the use of s.18 enforcement orders.

The Secretary of State may approve a code of practice, whether or not issued by himself, which is designed to give practical guidance to undertakers with regard to environmental duties and also in respect of the promotion of best practice. In addition, the Secretary of State can at any time either modify or cancel his approval in respect of any code.

Contravention of any code approved under s.5 does not automatically constitute a contravention of ss.3 or 4 or give rise to any criminal or civil liability. Prior to making, modifying or withdrawing his approval of any code the Secretary of State must consult with the NRA, the Countryside Commission, the Nature Conservancy Council for England, the Countryside Council for Wales, the Historic Buildings and Monuments Commission for England, the Sports Council, the Sports Council for Wales, and relevant undertakers and other persons he considers it appropriate to consult.

PART II

APPOINTMENT AND REGULATION OF UNDERTAKERS

CHAPTER I

APPOINTMENTS

Making of appointments

Appointment of relevant undertakers

6.—(1) Subject to the following provisions of this Chapter, a company may be appointed—
(a) by the Secretary of State; or
(b) with the consent of or in accordance with a general authorisation given by the Secretary of State, by the Director,
to be the water undertaker or sewerage undertaker for any area of England and Wales.

(2) Without prejudice to the obligation of a company holding an appointment under this Chapter to comply with the conditions of its appointment, the appointment of a company to be the water undertaker or sewerage undertaker for any area shall have the effect, while the appointment remains in force—
(a) of requiring the company to perform any duty imposed by or under any enactment on an undertaker of the relevant description (that is to say, a water undertaker or, as the case may be, sewerage undertaker);
(b) of authorising the company, for the purposes of, or in connection with, the carrying out of any of the functions of an undertaker of the relevant description, to exercise any power conferred by or under any enactment on an undertaker of that description;
(c) of requiring enactments and subordinate legislation authorising or requiring anything to be done in relation to an undertaker of the relevant description to be construed as authorising or requiring that thing to be done in relation to that company; and
(d) of requiring other references in any enactment or subordinate legislation to an undertaker of the relevant description, or to the area of that undertaker, to be construed, so far as necessary for the purposes of, or in connection with, the carrying out by that company of the functions of an undertaker of that description, as references to that company or, as the case may be, to that area.

(3) The appointment of a company to be a relevant undertaker shall be by service on the company of an instrument in writing containing the appointment and describing the area for which it is made.

(4) A single instrument may contain the appointment of a company to be the sewerage undertaker for an area and the appointment of the same company to be the water undertaker for the whole or any part of that area or for an area which includes the whole or any part of that area.

(5) A company shall not be appointed to be a water undertaker unless it is a limited company or a statutory water company and shall not be appointed to be a sewerage undertaker unless it is a limited company.

(6) As soon as practicable after making an appointment under this Chapter, the Secretary of State shall send a copy of the appointment to the Director.

DEFINITIONS
  "enactment": s.219(1).
  "functions": ss.219(1) and 217.
  "limited company": s.219(1).

GENERAL NOTE

Sections 6–13 relate to the appointment and replacement of undertakers, provisions relating to conditions of appointment and their subsequent variation.

Unlike previous arrangements under the Water Act 1973, areas served by water and sewerage undertakers need not be co-extensive. Appointments of undertakers may be made by the Director under general authorisation or by the Secretary of State. It is intended that the responsibility for appointment and variation should primarily rest with the Director. (See *Hansard*, H.L. Vol. 508, col. 1045). The Secretary of State and the Director under the general authorisation procedure both have powers to terminate the appointments of undertakers (s.7(2)) but this is subject to the existence of replacement appointees (s.7(3)) and the provisions of s.11 (conditions regarding a proposed appointment or variation).

Continuity of appointments, replacement appointments etc.

7.—(1) It shall be the duty of the Secretary of State to secure that such appointments are made under this Chapter as will ensure that for every area of England and Wales there is at all times both—

(a) a company holding an appointment under this Chapter as water undertaker; and

(b) whether or not the same company in relation to the whole or any part of that area, a company holding an appointment as sewerage undertaker.

(2) Subject to the following provisions of this section—

(a) the Secretary of State; and

(b) with the consent of or in accordance with a general authorisation given by the Secretary of State, the Director,

shall have power, by notice to a company holding an appointment under this Chapter, to terminate the appointment or to vary the area to which it relates.

(3) The appointment of a company to be a water undertaker or sewerage undertaker shall not be terminated or otherwise cease to relate to or to any part of any area except with effect from the coming into force of such appointments and variations replacing that company as a relevant undertaker as secure either—

(a) that another company becomes the water undertaker or, as the case may be, sewerage undertaker for that area or part or for an area that includes that area or part; or

(b) that two or more companies each become the water undertaker or, as the case may be, sewerage undertaker for one of a number of different areas that together constitute or include that area or part.

(4) An appointment or variation replacing a company as a relevant undertaker shall not be made in relation to the whole or any part of the area to which that company's appointment as water undertaker or, as the case may be, sewerage undertaker relates except where—

(a) that company consents to the appointment or variation;

(b) the appointment or variation relates only to parts of that area none of the premises in which is served by that company; or

(c) the appointment or variation is made in such circumstances as may be set out for the purposes of this paragraph in the conditions of that company's appointment.

GENERAL NOTE

This section is concerned with the continuity and replacement of appointed undertakers and variations in areas served by appointed undertakers which have the effect of reducing the areas of other appointed undertakers. The section envisages that the areas served by water and sewerage undertakers no longer need be co-extensive.

Subsection (4) specifies the three instances in which the powers of appointment and variation may be exercised by the Secretary of State or the Director under the general authorisation procedure. In subs. (4)(a) an appointment or variation replacing a company as a relevant undertaker may be made if that company consents to the appointment or variation. One effect of this provision would be to allow a special administrator appointed under s.24 in cases of defaulting undertakers to consent to the appointment of a replacement undertaker. Secondly, in subs. (4)(b) the appointment or variation relates to areas, *i.e.* premises not served by existing undertakers. This is a significant power and in exercising this the Director acting under a general authorisation under s.7(2)(b) will be guided by his general duties under s.2, especially those under s.2(3)(e) requiring him to facilitate effective competition between undertakers holding or seeking appointments. Existing undertakers who have already made arrangements or who have committed expenditure towards connecting premises to the existing water supply and sewerage systems will have some protection, since the Director is required to have regard to such expenditure before exercising his power under s.9(3). Finally, an appointment or variation can be made under s.7(4)(c) in accordance with the conditions of appointment of the undertaker set out in the instrument of appointment. Under condition O of the model instrument of appointment a minimum of 10 years' notice must be given, expiring not earlier than 25 years after September 1, 1989.

Procedure with respect to appointments and variations

8.—(1) An application for an appointment or variation replacing a company as a relevant undertaker shall be made in such manner as may be prescribed.

(2) Within fourteen days after making an application under this section, the applicant shall—

(a) serve notice of the application on the existing appointee and on every local authority whose area includes the whole or any part of the area to which the application relates; and

(b) publish a copy of the notice in such manner as may be prescribed.

(3) Before making an appointment or variation replacing a company as a relevant undertaker, the Secretary of State or the Director shall give notice—

(a) stating that he proposes to make the appointment or variation;

(b) stating the reasons why he proposes to make the appointment or variation; and

(c) specifying the period (not being less than twenty-eight days from the date of publication of the notice) within which representations or objections with respect to the proposed appointment or variation may be made.

(4) A notice under subsection (3) above shall be given—

(a) by publishing the notice in such manner as the Secretary of State or, as the case may be, the Director considers appropriate for bringing it to the attention of persons likely to be affected by the making of the proposed appointment or variation; and

(b) by serving a copy of the notice on the existing appointee and on every local authority whose area includes the whole or any part of the area to which the proposed appointment or variation relates.

(5) As soon as practicable after making an appointment or variation replacing a company as a relevant undertaker, the Secretary of State or the Director shall—

(a) serve a copy of the appointment or variation on the existing appointee; and

(b) serve notice of the making of the appointment or variation on every local authority whose area includes the whole or any part of the area to which the appointment or variation relates,

and as soon as practicable after exercising any power to vary the area to which an appointment under this Chapter relates, the Secretary of State shall send a copy of the variation to the Director.

(6) In this section "the existing appointee," in relation to an appointment or variation replacing a company as a relevant undertaker, means the company which is replaced in relation to the whole or any part of the area to which the appointment or variation relates or, where there is more than one such company, each of them.

DEFINITIONS
"local authority": s.219(1).

"notice": s.219(1).
"prescribed": s.219(1).
"relevant undertaker": s.219(1).
"the existing appointee": subs. (6).

General Note
This section contains the procedural requirements for the making of replacement appointments or variations under s.7. Schedule 2 to the Act provides for transitional arrangements between existing and replacement appointees, including the requirement for a transfer scheme of properties, rights and liabilities to be approved by the Secretary of State or the Director.
Subsection (3) provides that the Secretary of State or the Director shall state the reasons why he proposes to make the appointment or variation. The subsection also provides a mechanism for lodging representations or objections.

Duties affecting making of appointments and variations

9.—(1) Before making an appointment or variation replacing a company as a relevant undertaker, the Secretary of State or the Director shall consider any representations or objections which have been duly made in pursuance of the notice under section 8(3) above and have not been withdrawn.

(2) Before making an appointment or variation replacing a company as a relevant undertaker, the Secretary of State shall consult the Director.

(3) In determining whether to make an appointment or variation by virtue of section 7(4)(b) above in relation to any part of an area, the Secretary of State or, as the case may be, the Director shall have regard, in particular, to any arrangements made or expenditure incurred by the existing appointee for the purpose of enabling premises in that part of that area to be served by that appointee.

(4) It shall be the duty of the Secretary of State or, as the case may be, of the Director—

(a) in making an appointment or variation replacing a company as a relevant undertaker; and

(b) where he makes such an appointment or variation, in determining what provision is to be made with respect to the fixing by the new appointee of any water or drainage charges,

to ensure, so far as may be consistent with his duties under Part I of this Act, that the interests of the members and creditors of the existing appointee are not unfairly prejudiced as respects the terms on which the new appointee could accept transfers of property, rights and liabilities from the existing appointee.

(5) In this section—

"existing appointee," in relation to an appointment or variation replacing a company as a relevant undertaker in relation to any area or part of an area, means the company which is replaced by that appointment or variation;

"new appointee," in relation to such an appointment or variation, means the company which by virtue of the appointment or variation becomes a relevant undertaker for the area or part of an area in question;

"water or drainage charges" means—

(a) charges in respect of any services provided in the course of the carrying out of the functions of a water undertaker or sewerage undertaker; or

(b) amounts of any other description which such an undertaker is authorised by or under any enactment to require any person to pay.

Definitions
"existing appointees": subs. (5).

"new appointee": subs. (5).
"water or drainage charges": subs. (5).

GENERAL NOTE
This section makes provision for the Secretary of State or the Director to consider any representations or objections which have been made in pursuance of a s.8(3) notice which have not been withdrawn. The section provides that consultation shall take place between the Secretary of State and the Director prior to the making of any appointment or variation.

The danger of existing appointees being unfairly prejudiced by new appointees offering lower service charges and squeezing down the transfer costs of any property transferred to the new appointee is recognised in the duties of both the Secretary of State and Director in subs. (4) to ensure that the interests of the members and creditors of the existing appointee are not unfairly prejudiced in respect of the terms on which the new appointee could accept transfers of property, rights and liabilities from the existing appointee.

Transitional provision with respect to replacement appointments

10. Schedule 2 to this Act shall have effect for enabling provision to be made with respect to cases in which a company is replaced by another as a relevant undertaker by an appointment or variation under this Chapter.

GENERAL NOTE
This section refers to the transitional provision with respect to replacement appointments which are to be found in Sched. 2 to the Act.

Conditions of appointments

Power to impose conditions

11.—(1) An appointment under this Chapter may include—
(a) such conditions as appear to the Secretary of State or, as the case may be, the Director to be requisite or expedient having regard to the duties imposed on him by Part I of this Act;
(b) conditions for the purposes of section 7(4)(c) above; and
(c) conditions requiring the rendering to the Secretary of State of a payment on the making of an appointment, or payments while such an appointment is in force, or both, of such amount or amounts as may be determined by or under the conditions.

(2) Conditions may be included by virtue of subsection (1)(a) above in an appointment under this Chapter whether or not they are connected with the supply of water, the provision of sewerage services or the exercise or performance of any power or duty conferred or imposed by or under any enactment on water undertakers or sewerage undertakers.

(3) Conditions included in an appointment under this Chapter may contain provision for the conditions to cease to have effect or be modified at such times, in such manner and in such circumstances as may be specified in or determined by or under the conditions.

(4) Any provision included by virtue of subsection (3) above in an appointment under this Chapter shall have effect in addition to the provision made by this Chapter with respect to the modification of the conditions of an appointment.

(5) For the purposes of this Act where the same instrument contains an appointment of the same company to be both a water undertaker and a sewerage undertaker (whether or not for the same area), all the conditions included in that instrument by virtue of this section shall have effect, irrespective of their subject-matter, as conditions of both appointments.

(6) Where an instrument of appointment has been served under subsection (3) of section 6 above on any company, the coming into force of the appointment for the purposes specified in subsection (2) of that section shall not be affected by any contravention of the requirements of this Act with respect to the provision contained by way of conditions of appointment in that instrument.

(7) If the Secretary of State considers it appropriate to do so in consequence of any legal proceedings with respect to any such provision as is mentioned in subsection (6) above, he may by order made by statutory instrument direct that such conditions as may be specified in the order are to be treated as included in the appointment in question until there is an opportunity for the provision to which the proceedings relate to be replaced by virtue of any of the other provisions of this Chapter.

(8) Any sums received by the Secretary of State in consequence of the provisions of any condition of an appointment under this Chapter shall be paid into the Consolidated Fund.

GENERAL NOTE

This section is concerned with the Secretary of State or Director's powers to make conditions on the appointment of a water or sewerage undertaker. Such conditions would appear in the instrument of appointment and would effectively form a parallel system of control to the statutory provisions in the Act itself. The main emphasis of the conditions which are imposed relate to the economic regulation of pricing structures but a number of important aspects of an undertaker's service obligations are also reflected in the conditions, especially where, as in the case of undue preference or discrimination in charges, and disconnection procedures, the conditions convert what are discretionary powers in the Act to appointment obligations. The conditions of each undertaker's appointment are contained in the Director's public register which is compiled pursuant to s.195. Conditions may be enforced by s.18 enforcement orders (s.18(1)(a)) and ultimately by the making of special administration orders (s.24) which lead to loss of the appointment itself.

Subsection (2) is an important provision empowering the Secretary of State or, as the case may be, the Director to make conditions concerning non-core business activities of water and sewerage undertakers, where these are felt to impinge on the general considerations in Pt. 1 of the Act, especially with regard to the s.2 duties. Such conditions could be used to prevent or restrict undercharging of services provided by the appointee to associated companies in the same group.

Subsection (3) makes provision for the inclusion of "self-modifying" conditions which would avoid the need for the implementation of the modification procedures under ss.13–17 which in cases of dispute would involve a reference to the Monopolies and Mergers Commission. Subsections (6) and (7) are transitional and take into account the possibility that appointment conditions regarding appointments taking effect under the Water Act 1989 might be incomplete.

Determination under conditions of appointment

12.—(1) Without prejudice to the generality of paragraph (a) of section 11(1) above, conditions included in an appointment by virtue of that paragraph may—

   (a) require the appointed company to comply with any direction given by the Director as to such matters as are specified in the appointment or are of a description so specified; and

   (b) require the appointed company, except in so far as the Director consents to the company's doing or not doing them, not to do or to do such things as are specified in the appointment or are of a description so specified.

(2) Without prejudice as aforesaid, such conditions may provide for the reference to and determination by—

   (a) the Secretary of State or the Director; or

   (b) on a reference by the Director, the Monopolies and Mergers Commission (in this Act referred to as "the Monopolies Commission"),

of such questions arising under the appointment and of such other matters, including (in the case of references to the Commission) disputes as to determinations by the Director, as are specified in the appointment or are of a description so specified.

(3) Where any question or other matter falls to be determined by the Monopolies Commission in pursuance of a provision contained in an appointment under this Chapter—

(a) it shall be the duty of the Director, on being required to do so by the company holding that appointment, to refer that question or matter to that Commission; and

(b) it shall be the duty of that Commission to determine any question or other matter referred by virtue of paragraph (a) above in accordance with—

    (i) any regulations under subsection (4) below; and

    (ii) the principles which apply, by virtue of Part I of this Act, in relation to determinations under this Chapter by the Director.

(4) The Secretary of State may by regulations make such provision as he considers appropriate for regulating the procedure to be followed with respect to the reference of any question or other matter to the Monopolies Commission in pursuance of provision contained in an appointment under this Chapter.

(5) Without prejudice to the generality of the power conferred by subsection (4) above, regulations under that subsection may, in relation to any such reference as is mentioned in that subsection, apply (with or without modifications) the provisions of any enactment relating to references to the Monopolies Commission under the following provisions of this Act, the 1973 Act or the 1980 Act.

DEFINITIONS
"enactment": s.219(1).
"Monopolies Commission": s.219(1).

GENERAL NOTE
This section enables conditions to be included in an appointment requiring the appointed company to comply with or refrain from doing matters which are specified in the appointment. The conditions for appointment may specify that the Secretary of State, the Director or the Monopolies and Mergers Commission determine questions which may arise under the conditions of appointment.

The Director is under a duty (subs. (3)) to refer matters to the Monopolies Commission which are within the Commission's remit provided that a request is made by the company holding the appointment.

Subsection (4) provides a power for the Secretary of State to make regulations in respect of the procedure to be followed regarding a reference under this section to the Monopolies Commission.

Modification of appointment conditions

Modification by agreement

13.—(1) Subject to the following provisions of this section, the Director may modify the conditions of a company's appointment under this Chapter if the company consents to the modifications.

(2) Before making modifications under this section, the Director shall give notice—

(a) stating that he proposes to make the modifications and setting out their effect;

(b) stating the reasons why he proposes to make the modifications; and

(c) specifying the period (not being less than 28 days from the date of publication of the notice) within which representations or objections with respect to the proposed modifications may be made,

and shall consider any representations or objections which are duly made and not withdrawn.

(3) A notice under subsection (2) above shall be given—

(a) by publishing the notice in such manner as the Director considers appropriate for the purpose of bringing the notice to the attention of persons likely to be affected by the making of the modifications; and

(b) by serving a copy of the notice on the company and on the Secretary of State.

(4) The Director shall not under this section make any modifications which the Secretary of State has, within the time specified in the notice under subsection (2) above, directed the Director not to make.

(5) The Secretary of State shall not give a direction under subsection (4) above in relation to any modification unless—

(a) the modification is a modification of provision contained in the appointment for the purposes of section 7(4)(c) above;

(b) the modification is a modification of a provision of the appointment which relates to the disposal of, or of interests or rights in or over, a company's protected land and is stated in the appointment to be a provision which cannot be modified; or

(c) it appears to the Secretary of State that the modification should be made, if at all, under section 16 below.

DEFINITIONS
"modifications": s.219(1).
"notice": s.219(1).
"protected land": s.219(1).

GENERAL NOTE
This section makes provision for the modification of appointment conditions, provided that the company concerned consents to the proposed modifications. Before making any proposed modifications under s.13 the Director must publish a notice detailing the proposed modifications and their effect and allow a 28-day period for representations or objections (subs. (2)). No specific statutory consultees, for example a local authority, are prescribed, although publication of the notice must be in a manner which the Director considers appropriate for bringing the notice to the attention of persons likely to be affected by the modifications.

The Secretary of State has no power to modify conditions of appointment himself under the Act, but may do so under other legislation. However, under subs. (4) the Secretary of State may direct the Director not to make modifications. The three cases where the Secretary of State may prevent modification are set out in subs. (5). The Director may be prevented from making modifications by the Secretary of State if the proposed modification relates to conditions affecting termination or variation of the appointment, conditions relating to the disposal of protected land (see s.156) and in circumstances where the Secretary of State considers that the modification should be made only after a reference to the Monopolies and Mergers Commission in accordance with s.16.

Modification references to Monopolies Commission

14.—(1) The Director may make to the Monopolies Commission a reference which is so framed as to require the Commission to investigate and report on the questions—

(a) whether any matters which—

    (i) relate to the carrying out of any function which is a function of any company by virtue of an appointment of that company under this Chapter; and

    (ii) are specified in the reference,

operate, or may be expected to operate, against the public interest; and

(b) if so, whether the effects adverse to the public interest which those matters have or may be expected to have could be remedied or prevented by modifications of the conditions of the company's appointment.

(2) The Director may, at any time, by notice given to the Monopolies Commission vary a reference under this section by—

(a) adding to the matters specified in the reference; or

(b) excluding from the reference some or all of the matters so specified; and on receipt of any such notice the Commission shall give effect to the variation.

(3) The Director may specify in a reference under this section, or a variation of such a reference, for the purpose of assisting the Monopolies Commission in carrying out the investigation on the reference—

(a) any effects adverse to the public interest which, in his opinion, the matters specified in the reference or variation have or may be expected to have; and

(b) any modifications of the conditions of any appointment mentioned in the reference or variation by which, in his opinion, those effects could be remedied or prevented.

(4) As soon as practicable after making a reference under this section or a variation of such a reference, the Director shall—

(a) serve a copy of the reference or variation on the company whose appointment is mentioned in the reference or variation; and

(b) publish particulars of the reference or variation in such manner as he considers appropriate for the purpose of bringing the reference or variation to the attention of persons likely to be affected by it.

(5) It shall be the duty of the Director, for the purpose of assisting the Monopolies Commission in carrying out an investigation on a reference under this section, to give to the Commission—

(a) any information in his possession which relates to matters falling within the scope of the investigation, and which is either—

(i) requested by the Commission for that purpose; or

(ii) information which, in his opinion, it would be appropriate for that purpose to give to the Commission without any such request; and

(b) any other assistance which the Commission may require, and which it is within his power to give, in relation to any such matters;

and the Commission, for the purpose of carrying out any such investigation, shall take account of any information given to them for that purpose under this subsection.

(6) In determining for the purposes of this section whether any particular matter operates, or may be expected to operate, against the public interest, the Monopolies Commission shall have regard to the matters as respects which duties are imposed on the Secretary of State and the Director by Part I of this Act.

(7) Sections 70 (time limit for report on merger reference), 81 (procedure in carrying out investigations) and 85 (attendance of witnesses and production of documents) of the 1973 Act, Part II of Schedule 3 to that Act (performance of functions of the Monopolies Commission) and section 24 of the 1980 Act (modifications of provisions about performance of such functions) shall apply in relation to references under this section as if—

(a) the functions of the Commission in relation to those references were functions under the 1973 Act;

(b) the expression "merger reference" included a reference under this section;

(c) in the said section 70, references to the Secretary of State were references to the Director and the reference to three months were a reference to six months;

(d) in paragraph 11 of the said Schedule 3, the reference to section 71 of the 1973 Act were a reference to subsection (2) above; and

(e) paragraph 16(2) of that Schedule were omitted.

(8) For the purposes of references under this section, there shall be not less than eight additional members of the Monopolies Commission appointed from time to time by the Secretary of State; and, if any functions of that Commission in relation to any such reference are performed through a group—

(a) the chairman of that Commission shall select one or more of those additional members to be members of the group; and

(b) the number of regular members to be selected by him under paragraph 10 of Schedule 3 to the 1973 Act shall be reduced by the number of additional members selected.

DEFINITIONS
"modifications": s.219(1).
"notice": s.219(1).
"the Monopolies Commission": s.219(1).

GENERAL NOTE
This section empowers the Director to make a reference to the Monopolies Commission in respect of a proposed modification to an undertaker's conditions of appointment. The Monopolies Commission does not have power itself to review any proposed modification falling to be determined under this section, but must depend upon a referral by the Director (subs. (1)). The Commission does not possess executive powers in respect of any proposed modifications and its remit is confined to investigations and reporting to the Director, who retains executive powers (s.16).

Referrals to the Monopolies Commission under s.14 will occur when the undertaker does not consent to a proposed modification, thereby preventing the utilisation of s.13. The section may also be appropriate where the Secretary of State requires a reference to be made to the Monopolies Commission, even though the undertaker consents to the modification (s.13(5) (c)). The Director has power to refer proposed modifications to the Monopolies Commission where he requires an independent assessment by the Commission of the effects of the proposed modification. The Director's discretion to request a report encompasses any function of an undertaker which may be expected to operate against the public interest (subs. (1)).

Once a reference has been made by the Director to the Monopolies Commission of any matter falling within s.14, then the Director must publish details of the reference "as soon as practicable" in order to bring the details of the reference to the Monopolies Commission to the attention of "persons likely to be affected by it".

Under subs. (5) the Director has a duty to assist the Monopolies Commission by supplying information, whether or not requested by the Commission, and other assistance which the Commission may require. Should the Director not exercise his power under s.14 to make a reference to the Monopolies Commission in circumstances where the proposed modification may work against the public interest, the Secretary of State has an overriding power under s.13(5) to ensure that a reference is made to the Monopolies Commission.

Subsection (6) is an important provision which specifies the matters to which the Monopolies Commission must have regard when deciding whether the issue referred to them operates against the public interest. In place of the criteria specified in s.84 of the Fair Trading Act 1973, the Monopolies Commission must have regard to the more extensive range of considerations covered by the duties of the Secretary of State and the Director under Pt. 1 of the Act. This primarily refers back to the s.2 duties.

Subsection (8) enables the Monopolies Commission to appoint extra members of the Commission with particular expertise in the water and sewerage industries.

Reports on modification references

15.—(1) In making a report on a reference under section 14 above, the Monopolies Commission—
(a) shall include in the report definite conclusions on the questions comprised in the reference together with such an account of their reasons for those conclusions as, in their opinion, is expedient for facilitating a proper understanding of those questions and of their conclusions;
(b) where they conclude that any of the matters specified in the reference operate, or may be expected to operate, against the public interest, shall specify in the report the effects adverse to the public interest which those matters have or may be expected to have; and
(c) where they conclude that any adverse effects so specified could be remedied or prevented by modifications of the conditions of a company's appointment under this Chapter, shall specify in the report modifications by which those effects could be remedied or prevented.
(2) Where, on a reference under section 14 above, the Monopolies Commission conclude that a company holding an appointment under this Chapter is a party to an agreement to which the Restrictive Trade Practices Act

1976 applies, the Commission, in making their report on that reference, shall exclude from their consideration the question whether the provisions of that agreement, in so far as they are provisions by virtue of which it is an agreement to which that Act applies, operate, or may be expected to operate, against the public interest; and paragraph (b) of subsection (1) above shall have effect subject to the provisions of this subsection.

(3) Section 82 of the 1973 Act (general provisions as to reports) shall apply in relation to reports of the Monopolies Commission on references under section 14 above as it applies to reports of the Commission under that Act.

(4) A report of the Monopolies Commission on a reference under section 14 above shall be made to the Director.

(5) Subject to subsection (6) below, the Director—

(a) shall, on receiving such a report, send a copy of it to the company to whose appointment under this Chapter the report relates and to the Secretary of State; and

(b) shall, not less than fourteen days after that copy is received by the Secretary of State, publish another copy of that report in such manner as he considers appropriate for bringing the report to the attention of persons likely to be affected by it.

(6) If it appears to the Secretary of State that the publication of any matter in such a report would be against the public interest or the commercial interests of any person, he may, before the end of the period of fourteen days mentioned in paragraph (b) of subsection (5) above, direct the Director to exclude that matter from every copy of the report to be published by virtue of that paragraph; and the Director shall comply with any such direction.

DEFINITIONS
"modifications": s.219(1).
"Monopolies Commission": s.219(1).

GENERAL NOTE
This section is concerned with the contents of the Monopolies Commission report in respect of a reference under s.14 to the Monopolies Commission of any proposed modifications to an undertaker's conditions of appointment. The report must provide definite conclusions on the questions contained in the s.14 reference and the reasons for the Monopolies Commission's conclusions. Where the report contains a conclusion that any proposed modification will be against the public interest, the Monopolies Commission is required to specify in its report what the adverse effects are and, if appropriate, how those adverse effects may be remedied or prevented by modifications of the conditions of appointment.

On receipt of the report of the Monopolies Commission the Director must send a copy to the Secretary of State and the relevant undertaker. In addition, the Director must within 14 days after receipt by the Secretary of State of a copy of the report publish another copy in such manner as the Director considers appropriate for bringing the report to the attention of persons likely to be affected by it. The Secretary of State has a power under subs. (6) to make a direction compelling the Director to exclude any matter from every copy of the report to be published if in the Secretary of State's opinion it operates against the public interest or the commercial interests of any person.

Subsection (2) is a non-duplicative provision preserving the jurisdiction of the Restrictive Practices Court and parallels an equivalent restriction in s.10 of the Fair Trading Act 1973.

Modification following report

16.—(1) Where a report of the Monopolies Commission on a reference under section 14 above—

(a) includes conclusions to the effect that any of the matters specified in the reference operate, or may be expected to operate, against the public interest;

(b) specifies effects adverse to the public interest which those matters have or may be expected to have;

(c) includes conclusions to the effect that those effects could be remedied

or prevented by modifications of the conditions of a company's appointment under this Chapter; and
  (d) specifies modifications by which those effects could be remedied or prevented,
the Director shall, subject to the following provisions of this section, make such modifications of the conditions of that appointment as appear to him requisite for the purpose of remedying or preventing the adverse effects specified in the report.

(2) Before making modifications under this section, the Director shall have regard to the modifications specified in the report.

(3) Before making modifications under this section, the Director shall give notice—
  (a) stating that he proposes to make the modifications and setting out their effect;
  (b) stating the reasons why he proposes to make the modifications; and
  (c) specifying the period (not being less than 28 days from the date of publication of the notice) within which representations or objections with respect to the proposed modifications may be made,
and shall consider any representations or objections which are duly made and not withdrawn.

(4) A notice under subsection (3) above shall be given—
  (a) by publishing the notice in such manner as the Director considers appropriate for the purpose of bringing the matters to which the notice relates to the attention of persons likely to be affected by the making of the modifications; and
  (b) by serving a copy of the notice on the company whose appointment it is proposed to modify.

(5) The Director shall not under this section make any modification of any provisions of a company's appointment under this Chapter which—
  (a) are contained in that appointment for the purposes of section 7(4)(c) above; or
  (b) being provisions relating to the disposal of, or of interests or rights in or over, a company's protected land, are stated in the appointment to be provisions which cannot be modified.

DEFINITIONS
  "modifications": s.219(1).
  "notice": s.219(1).
  "protected land": s.219(1).

GENERAL NOTE
  This provision is concerned with modification of appointment conditions following receipt by the Director of a report of the Monopolies and Mergers Commission on a reference under s.14. If the Monopolies Commission makes positive recommendations, the Director is required to make modifications to remedy the adverse effects specified in the report, but he is not obliged to adopt the precise modifications suggested by the Commission, since the Director may make such modifications as he considers "requisite" for the purpose of remedying or preventing the adverse effects (subs. (1)). The Director is prevented from allowing any modification to conditions which relate to the termination or variation of the undertaker's appointment or to the disposal of protected land (subs. (5)).

Modification by order under other enactments

17.—(1) Subject to subsection (3) below, where in the circumstances mentioned in subsection (2) below the Secretary of State by order exercises any of the powers specified in—
  (a) Parts I and II of Schedule 8 to the 1973 Act; or
  (b) section 10(2)(a) of the 1980 Act,
the order may also provide for the modification of the conditions of a company's appointment under this Chapter to such extent as may appear to

him to be requisite or expedient for the purpose of giving effect to, or taking account of, any provision made by the order.

(2) Subsection (1) above shall have effect where—

(a) the circumstances are as mentioned in section 56(1) of the 1973 Act (order on report on monopoly reference) and the monopoly situation exists in relation to the carrying out of any of the functions of a relevant undertaker;

(b) the circumstances are as mentioned in section 73(1) of that Act (order on report on merger reference) and the two or more enterprises which ceased to be distinct enterprises were both engaged in carrying out functions of a relevant undertaker; or

(c) the circumstances are as mentioned in section 10(1) of the 1980 Act (order on report on competition reference) and the anti-competitive practice relates to the carrying out of any of the functions of a relevant undertaker.

(3) No modification shall be made by virtue of this section of any provisions of a company's appointment under this Chapter which—

(a) are contained in that appointment for the purposes of section 7(4)(c) above; or

(b) being provisions relating to the disposal of, or of interests or rights in or over, a company's protected land, are stated in the appointment to be provisions which cannot be modified.

(4) Expressions used in this section and in the 1973 Act or the 1980 Act have the same meanings in this section as in that Act.

DEFINITIONS
"functions": ss.217 and 219(1).
"modification": s.219(1).
"protected land": s.219(1).

GENERAL NOTE
This section provides the Secretary of State with a direct power to modify conditions of appointment where these relate to proposed modifications in reports on either a monopoly reference, merger reference or competition reference (see s.17(2)). No modification may be made relating to termination or variation of the appointment or to the disposal of protected land (s.17(3)).

Note the provisions with respect to competition contained in ss.31–35. The Secretary of State is under a duty to make a merger reference to the Monopolies Commission in the circumstances specified in s.32.

CHAPTER II

ENFORCEMENT AND INSOLVENCY

Enforcement orders

Orders for securing compliance with certain provisions

18.—(1) Subject to subsection (2) and sections 19 and 20 below, where in the case of any company holding an appointment under Chapter I of this Part the Secretary of State or the Director is satisfied—

(a) that that company is contravening—

(i) any condition of the company's appointment in relation to which he is the enforcement authority; or

(ii) any statutory or other requirement which is enforceable under this section and in relation to which he is the enforcement authority;

or

(b) that that company has contravened any such condition or requirement and is likely to do so again, he shall by a final enforcement order make such provision as is requisite for the purpose of securing compliance with that condition or requirement.

(2) Subject to section 19 below, where in the case of any company holding an appointment under Chapter I of this Part—

(a) it appears to the Secretary of State or the Director as mentioned in paragraph (a) or (b) of subsection (1) above; and

(b) it appears to him that it is requisite that a provisional enforcement order be made,

he may (instead of taking steps towards the making of a final order) by a provisional enforcement order make such provision as appears to him requisite for the purpose of securing compliance with the condition or requirement in question.

(3) In determining for the purposes of subsection (2)(b) above whether it is requisite that a provisional enforcement order be made, the Secretary of State or, as the case may be, the Director shall have regard, in particular, to the extent to which any person is likely to sustain loss or damage in consequence of anything which, in contravention of any condition or of any statutory or other requirement enforceable under this section, is likely to be done, or omitted to be done, before a final enforcement order may be made.

(4) Subject to sections 19 and 20 below, where the Secretary of State or the Director has made a provisional enforcement order, he shall confirm it, with or without modifications, if—

(a) he is satisfied that the company to which the order relates—

(i) is contravening any condition or statutory or other requirement in relation to which he is the enforcement authority; or

(ii) has contravened any such condition or requirement and is likely to do so again;

and

(b) the provision made by the order (with any modifications) is requisite for the purpose of securing compliance with that condition or requirement.

(5) An enforcement order—

(a) shall require the company to which it relates (according to the circumstances of the case) to do, or not to do, such things as are specified in the order or are of a description so specified;

(b) shall take effect at such time, being the earliest practicable time, as is determined by or under the order; and

(c) may be revoked at any time by the enforcement authority who made it.

(6) For the purposes of this section and the following provisions of this Act—

(a) the statutory and other requirements which shall be enforceable under this section in relation to a company holding an appointment under Chapter I of this Part shall be such of the requirements of any enactment or of any subordinate legislation as—

(i) are imposed in consequence of that appointment; and

(ii) are made so enforceable by that enactment or subordinate legislation;

(b) the Director shall be the enforcement authority in relation to the conditions of an appointment under Chapter I of this Part; and

(c) the enforcement authority in relation to each of the statutory and other requirements enforceable under this section shall be the Secretary of State, the Director or either of them, according to whatever provision is made by the enactment or subordinate legislation by which the requirement is made so enforceable.

(7) In this section and the following provisions of this Chapter—

"enforcement order" means a final enforcement order or a provisional enforcement order;

"final enforcement order" means an order under this section other than a provisional enforcement order;

"provisional enforcement order" means an order under this section which, if not previously confirmed in accordance with subsection (4) above, will cease to have effect at the end of such period (not exceeding three months) as is determined by or under the order.

(8) Where any act or omission constitutes a contravention of a condition of an appointment under Chapter I of this Part or of a statutory or other requirement enforceable under this section, the only remedies for that contravention, apart from those available by virtue of this section, shall be those for which express provision is made by or under any enactment and those that are available in respect of that act or omission otherwise than by virtue of its constituting such a contravention.

DEFINITIONS
"enforcement order": subs. (7).
"final enforcement order": subs. (7).
"provisional enforcement order": subs. (7).

GENERAL NOTE
Sections 18–22 provide the procedural framework for the making of final or provisional enforcement orders by the Secretary of State or the Director. Enforcement orders, together with special administration orders (see s.23–26), provide the mechanisms to secure undertakers' compliance with conditions of appointment and their statutory duties under the Act.

Exclusive effect of enforcement orders and judicial review
The use of s.18 enforcement orders is declared to be an exclusive remedy, in the absence of any other express provision (subs. (8)). This apparently accords with case law where the courts have been reluctant to intervene where a statute provides a specific method of enforcement: see *Passmore* v. *Oswaldtwistle Urban District Council* [1898] A.C. 387, *R*. v. *Kensington London Borough Council*, ex p. *Birdwood* [1976] 74 L.G.R. 424 and *R*. v. *Wessex Water Authority*, ex p. *Cutts* (March 18, 1988, unreported). The implications are that the duties on undertakers to which enforcement orders apply are not generally amenable to judicial review by third parties, although this restrictive effect is countered by the fact that the enforcement procedure is now applicable to a number of duties expressed in terms that are so general that they would otherwise probably be unenforceable by ordinary legal remedies. The exclusiveness of the remedies would not necessarily preclude a civil action based on breach of statutory duty. Breach of an enforcement order leading to loss or damage is expressly declared to be actionable, although subject to special defences (s.22(2) and (3)). Water and sewerage undertakers have the right to challenge enforcement orders made by the Secretary of State or the Director on the grounds of *ultra vires* or failure to comply with procedural requirements (s.21(1)). It is unclear whether third parties could challenge a decision not to make an enforcement order. Once the Secretary of State or the Director is satisfied that there has been a contravention to which the enforcement procedure is applicable, he has no choice but to make the order (s.18(1)), but this does not necessarily imply that lack of action by the Secretary of State or the Director would be subject to judicial review. With regard to the more general duties contained in ss.3, 37 and 94 there must be doubt, in the light of recent trends in case law, whether an ordinary citizen would be considered to have sufficient standing: see *I.R.C.* ex p. *National Federation of Self-Employed and Small Businesses* [1982] A.C. 617 and *R*. v. *Secretary of State for the Environment*, ex p. *Rose Theatre Trust Company* [1990] C.O.D. 47. In the *Rose Theatre* case, which concerned the discretionary power of the Secretary of State to schedule a monument of national importance under the Ancient Monuments and Archaeological Areas Act 1979, Schiemann J. explained the approach of the courts towards standing:

"The Court would look at the matter to which the application related and the statute under which the decision was taken and decide whether that statute gave that individual expressly or impliedly a greater right than any other citizen to have that decision taken lawfully. We all expect our decisionmakers to act lawfully. We were not all given the right to apply for judicial review."

Duties to which enforcement orders apply
The duties which are enforceable by means of s.18 orders are scattered throughout the Act. Most are exclusively enforceable either by the Secretary of State or the Director, but in the case of the general powers under s.37 (general duty to maintain water system) and s.94 (general duty

to maintain public sewerage system) those duties are enforceable either by the Secretary of State or the Director, although the Director's power to use the s.18 enforcement procedures will require the authorisation of the Secretary of State.

Section 213(2) empowers the Secretary of State to include in any regulations made under the Act provision for duties or requirements to be enforceable by him, or the Director, or by either of them under s.18. Again, the utilisation of the s.18 procedure in this case by the Director is subject to the authorisation of the Secretary of State.

Enforcement discretion

The Secretary of State's and Director's duty to serve enforcement orders (subs. (1)) is qualified in three instances by s.19(1); however, the three qualifications referred to in s.19(1) do not preclude the making of the order where the Secretary of State or the Director is satisfied that the provisions are applicable. The effect of s.19(1) is to convert the statutory duty in subs. (1) into a discretion. The exceptions to the duty to enforce contained in s.19(1) are discussed below.

(1) *Trivial contraventions* (s.19(1)(a))

The Act does not provide any further guidance on the meaning of the phrase "trivial contraventions". During the Committee stage of the passage of the Water Act 1989, the Minister stated that "it is very unlikely that circumstances giving rise to a danger to health could properly be regarded as trivial" (Michael Howard, Standing Committee D, col. 923; February 9, 1989).

(2) *Undertaking given by companies to secure compliance* (s.19(1)(b))

This provision allows the Secretary of State or Director to accept a compliance programme for meeting the contravention in lieu of serving a s.18 enforcement order. The use of the word "undertaking" is significant in that the exception to the s.18 enforcement duty will only apply as long as the undertaker complies with the undertaking. Failure to comply with an undertaking will result in enforcement action (s.19(2)). The underlying aim of the provision is to take account of the large-scale investment programmes which may be needed to secure compliance with duties imposed on undertakers, especially those relating to drinking water standards (s.68). It is arguable that the provision is superfluous since a compliance programme could be incorporated within the terms of a s.18 order itself. An order may include specified requirements and can take effect at "the earliest practicable time" as determined in the order (s.18(5)(b)). The distinguishing feature of subs. (1)(b) and perhaps the main rationale for including it here is that the burden is placed explicitly on the undertaker to draw up the necessary programme to justify the exception's application. A copy of the relevant undertaking is required to be placed on the Director's public register (s.195(2)(d)). A copy of any undertaking accepted by the Secretary of State under this provision is required to be served on the Director (s.19(3)(c)).

(3) *Overriding duties under Part I of the Act precluding the making of an enforcement order* (s.19(1)(c))

When considering whether to exercise the enforcement provisions under s.18 the Secretary of State or the Director, as the case may be, is required to consider the general duties under Pt. I of the Act, especially s.2, which includes the overriding requirement to ensure that the undertaker's functions are properly carried out and that undertakers are able adequately to finance their functions. The secondary considerations in subss. (3) and (4) of s.2 and the environmental duties in s.3 are also relevant in determining whether to utilise the enforcement provisions. Where these considerations prevail, s.19(1)(c) contains a discretion not to make an enforcement order.

Distinction between final and provisional enforcement orders

Both final and provisional orders may be made under s.18. A provisional order is appropriate for serious contraventions where loss or damage is likely to occur before the procedures for making a final order would be complete (s.18(3)). Provisional orders can take immediate effect and have a maximum duration of three months (s.18(7)) unless confirmed in accordance with the requirements set out in s.18(4). Final enforcement orders do not take effect unless the procedural requirements specified in s.20 have been complied with.

Procedure for the implementation of enforcement orders and publicity

Section 203 empowers the Secretary of State and the Director to obtain information from any undertaker. These powers are qualified by the requirement in s.203(1) that it must appear to the Secretary of State or the Director that an undertaker may have contravened an appointment condition or a statutory or other requirement enforceable under s.18 before information can be requested from an undertaker.

Before making a final order or confirming a provisional order (which has the effect of removing its temporary status), notice must be served on the undertaker (s.20(1)(b)). The notice must also be placed on the Director's public register (s.195(2)(c)) and published in a manner appropriate to bring it to the attention of persons likely to be affected by the matters to which it relates (s.20(2)(a)). There is no requirement to notify statutory bodies such as the National Rivers Authority and local authorities where the relevant contravention is of concern to them. The notice must specify a minimum period of 28 days in which representations or objections may be made (s.20(1)(c)). Proposed modifications must also be notified to the relevant undertaker and a further minimum period of 28 days allowed for representations, but there is no equivalent requirement to give wider publicity of modifications (s.20(4)). Further notification requirements are necessary in respect of the making or confirmation of an order (subs. (5)) and where the order is proposed to be revoked (subss. (6) and (7)). All orders, once made or confirmed, whether by the Director or Secretary of State, are required to be placed on the Director's public register (s.195(2)(c)).

Challenging the validity of orders

If a company to which an enforcement order relates is aggrieved it may challenge its validity in the High Court within 42 days (s.21). A provisional order will have taken effect before confirmation (s.18(2)) and an application to the court will therefore not suspend its operation. The Act does not contain any express provision regarding the effect of an application in relation to a final order and it would seem that the order therefore remains valid until held otherwise by a court: see *Hoffman-La Roche & Co.* v. *Secretary of State for Trade and Industry* [1975] A.C. 295.

An enforcement order may be challenged on the following grounds: that the order was not within the powers of s.18 or that the procedural requirements under s.20 have been followed.

An applicant who challenges the validity of an order on the basis of *ultra vires*, *i.e.* not within the powers of s.18, will have greater difficulty in challenging an unconfirmed provisional order than in challenging a final order or confirmed provisional order. In making a provisional order the Secretary of State or the Director may make such provision "as appears to him requisite for the purpose of securing compliance with the condition or requirement in question" (subs. (2)), implying a *Wednesbury* test for review. In contrast, for final orders or confirmed provisional orders, an objective test is appropriate, since the phrase "as appears to him" is omitted, and the provisions must simply be "requisite" for securing compliance (subss. (1) and (4)(b)).

Sanctions for non-compliance with enforcement orders

There are three forms of sanction: first, the Secretary of State or the Director may bring civil proceedings for an injunction or other relief in the case of contravention or apprehended contravention (s.22(4)). Relief can be sought for contravention of provisional orders before their confirmation. Secondly, contravention or likely contravention of a final order or confirmed provisional order is one of the grounds for applying for a special administration order under s.24 although this is a sanction of last resort. Thirdly, anyone affected by contravention of an order may bring a civil action in respect of resulting loss and damage (s.22(4)). If such proceedings are instituted an undertaker may utilise the special defence of taking all reasonable steps and exercising all due diligence to avoid contravention (s.22(3)).

Exceptions to duty to enforce

19.—(1) Neither the Secretary of State nor the Director shall be required to make an enforcement order in relation to any company, or to confirm a provisional enforcement order so made, if he is satisfied—

(a) that the contraventions were, or the apprehended contraventions are, of a trivial nature;

(b) that the company has given, and is complying with, an undertaking to take all such steps as it appears to him for the time being to be appropriate for the company to take for the purpose of securing or facilitating compliance with the condition or requirement in question; or

(c) that the duties imposed on him by Part I of this Act preclude the making or, as the case may be, the confirmation of the order.

(2) The requirement to comply with an undertaking given for the purposes of subsection (1)(b) above shall be treated as a statutory requirement enforceable under section 18 above—
(a) by the Secretary of State; or
(b) with the consent of or in accordance with a general authorisation given by the Secretary of State, by the Director.

(3) Where the Secretary of State or the Director, having notified a company that he is considering the making in relation to the company of an enforcement order or the confirmation of a provisional enforcement order so made, is satisfied as mentioned in paragraph (a), (b) or (c) of subsection (1) above, he shall—
(a) serve notice that he is so satisfied on the company;
(b) publish a copy of the notice in such manner as he considers appropriate for the purpose of bringing the matters to which the notice relates to the attention of persons likely to be affected by them; and
(c) in a case where the Secretary of State is satisfied as mentioned in the said paragraph (b), serve a copy of the notice and of the undertaking given for the purposes of that paragraph on the Director.

(4) The requirements of subsection (3) above shall not apply, in the case of any proposed order or confirmation in respect of a direction under section 208 below, to the extent that the Secretary of State directs that they should not be complied with in the interests of national security.

DEFINITIONS
"enforcement order": s.18(7).
"provisional enforcement order": s.18(7).
"notice": s.219(1).

GENERAL NOTE
See the General Note to s.18, especially the discussion relating to s.19(1) regarding exceptions to the s.18(1) duty to make an enforcement order.
Subsection (4) refers to directions made by the Secretary of State concerning matters of national security or civil emergencies (s.208).

Procedure for enforcement orders

20.—(1) Before making a final enforcement order or confirming a provisional enforcement order, the Secretary of State or the Director shall give notice—
(a) stating that he proposes to make or confirm the order and setting out the effect of the order;
(b) setting out—
(i) the condition or requirement for the purpose of securing compliance with which the order is to be made or confirmed;
(ii) the acts or omissions which, in his opinion, constitute or would constitute contraventions of that condition or requirement; and
(iii) the other facts which, in his opinion, justify the making or confirmation of the order; and
(c) specifying the period (not being less than 28 days from the date of publication of the notice) within which representations or objections with respect to the proposed order or proposed confirmation may be made,
and shall consider any representations or objections which are duly made and not withdrawn.
(2) A notice under subsection (1) above shall be given—
(a) by publishing the notice in such manner as the Secretary of State or, as the case may be, the Director considers appropriate for the purpose

of bringing the matters to which the notice relates to the attention of persons likely to be affected by them; and

(b) by serving a copy of the notice, and a copy of the proposed order or of the order proposed to be confirmed, on the company to which the order relates and, where the notice is given by the Secretary of State, on the Director.

(3) Neither the Secretary of State nor the Director shall make a final enforcement order with modifications, or confirm a provisional enforcement order with modifications, except—

(a) with the consent to the modifications of the company to which the order relates; or

(b) after complying with the requirements of subsection (4) below.

(4) The requirements mentioned in subsection (3) above are that the Secretary of State or, as the case may be, the Director shall—

(a) serve on the company to which the order relates such notice as appears to him to be requisite of his proposal to make or confirm the order with modifications;

(b) in that notice specify the period (not being less than 28 days from the date of the service of the notice) within which representations or objections with respect to the proposed modifications may be made; and

(c) consider any representations or objections which are duly made and not withdrawn.

(5) As soon as practicable after making an enforcement order or confirming a provisional enforcement order, the Secretary of State or, as the case may be, the Director shall—

(a) serve a copy of the order on the company to which the order relates and, where this subsection applies in the case of an order made or confirmed by Secretary of State, on the Director; and

(b) publish such a copy in such manner as he considers appropriate for the purpose of bringing the order to the attention of persons likely to be affected by it.

(6) Before revoking an enforcement order, other than an unconfirmed provisional order, the Secretary of State or the Director shall give notice—

(a) stating that he proposes to revoke the order and setting out its effect; and

(b) specifying the period (not being less than 28 days from the date of publication of the notice) within which representations or objections with respect to the proposed revocation may be made,

and shall consider any representations or objections which are duly made and not withdrawn.

(7) If, after giving a notice under subsection (6) above, the Secretary of State or the Director decides not to revoke the order to which the notice relates, he shall give notice of that decision.

(8) A notice under subsection (6) or (7) above shall be given—

(a) by publishing the notice in such manner as the Secretary of State or, as the case may be, the Director considers appropriate for the purpose of bringing the matters to which the notice relates to the attention of persons likely to be affected by them; and

(b) by serving a copy of the notice on the company to which the order relates and, where the notice is given by the Secretary of State, on the Director.

(9) The requirements of the preceding provisions of this section shall not apply, in the case of any order in respect of a contravention of a direction under section 208 below, to the extent that the Secretary of State directs that they should not be complied with in the interests of national security.

DEFINITIONS
"final enforcement order": s.18(7).

"modifications": s.219(1).
"notice": s.219(1).
"provisional enforcement order": s.18(7).

GENERAL NOTE
See General Note to s.18.

Validity of enforcement orders

21.—(1) If the company to which an enforcement order relates is aggrieved by the order and desires to question its validity on the ground—

(a) that its making or confirmation was not within the powers of section 18 above; or

(b) that any of the requirements of section 20 above have not been complied with in relation to it,

the company may, within 42 days from the date of service on it of a copy of the order, make an application to the High Court under this section.

(2) On any such application the High Court may, if satisfied that the making or confirmation of the order was not within those powers or that the interests of the company have been substantially prejudiced by a failure to comply with those requirements, quash the order or any provision of the order.

(3) Except as provided by this section, the validity of an enforcement order shall not be questioned in any legal proceedings whatsoever.

DEFINITIONS
"enforcement order": s.18(7).

GENERAL NOTE
See General Note to s.18.

Effect of enforcement order

22.—(1) The obligation to comply with an enforcement order shall be a duty owed to any person who may be affected by a contravention of the order.

(2) Where a duty is owed by virtue of subsection (1) above to any person, any breach of the duty which causes that person to sustain loss or damage shall be actionable at the suit of that person.

(3) In any proceedings brought against any company in pursuance of subsection (2) above, other than proceedings in respect of so much of a contravention of any order as consists in a breach of the duty imposed by virtue of section 68(1)(a) below, it shall be a defence for the company to show that it took all reasonable steps and exercised all due diligence to avoid contravening the order.

(4) Without prejudice to any right which any person may have by virtue of subsection (1) above to bring civil proceedings in respect of any contravention or apprehended contravention of an enforcement order, compliance with any such order shall be enforceable by civil proceedings by the relevant enforcement authority for an injunction or for any other appropriate relief.

(5) In subsection (4) above "the relevant enforcement authority," in relation to any enforcement order, means the Secretary of State or the Director or either of them according to who is the enforcement authority in relation to the condition or requirement compliance with which was to be secured by the order.

DEFINITIONS
"damage": s.219(1).
"enforcement order": s.18(7)
"relevant enforcement authority": subs. (5).

GENERAL NOTE
See General Note to s.18.

Special administration orders

Meaning and effect of special administration order

23.—(1) A special administration order is an order of the High Court made in accordance with section 24 or 25 below in relation to a company holding an appointment under Chapter I of this Part and directing that during the period for which the order is in force, the affairs, business and property of the company shall be managed, by a person appointed by the High Court—

(a) for the achievement of the purposes of such an order; and

(b) in a manner which protects the respective interests of the members and creditors of the company.

(2) The purposes of a special administration order made in relation to any company shall be—

(a) the transfer to another company, or (as respects different parts of the area to which the company's appointment relates, or different parts of its undertaking) to two or more different companies, as a going concern, of so much of the company's undertaking as it is necessary to transfer in order to ensure that the functions which have been vested in the company by virtue of its appointment may be properly carried out; and

(b) the carrying out of those functions pending the making of the transfer and the vesting of those functions in the other company or companies (whether by virtue of the transfer or of an appointment or variation which replaces the former company as a relevant undertaker).

(3) Schedule 3 to this Act shall have effect for applying provisions of the Insolvency Act 1986 where a special administration order is made.

(4) Schedule 2 to this Act shall have effect for enabling provision to be made with respect to cases in which a company is replaced by another as a relevant undertaker, without an appointment or variation under Chapter I of this Part, in pursuance of a special administration order.

(5) In this section "business" and "property" have the same meanings as in the Insolvency Act 1986.

DEFINITIONS
"business": subs. (5).
"functions": s.219(1).
"property": subs. (5).

GENERAL NOTE

Special administration orders
  Sections 23–25 detail the meaning and effect of a special administration order, how such orders are implemented, and their effect. Section 24 empowers the Secretary of State or the Director to apply to the High Court for a special administration order directing that the court appoint an administrator to take over the running of the undertaker's business. The main object of the exercise is to transfer sufficient of the undertaking as a going concern to a replacement appointee or appointees to enable them to carry on the undertaker's functions. In the meantime, the business is to be carried on by the special administrator, with the injection of Government grants or loans if necessary under s.153, reflecting the need to ensure continuity of water and sewerage supplies. Sections 23–25 are supplemented by s.26, which prohibits the winding-up of companies as long as they hold an appointment.
  In this context, condition K of the model instrument of appointment ("Ring Fencing") is significant in that it aims to prevent undertakers diverting their assets elsewhere by requiring them to have sufficient rights and assets (other than financial resources) to enable a special administrator to manage its business were he to be appointed. This obligation is enforceable by s.18 enforcement orders and ultimately a court injunction if necessary under s.22(4).
  There are five grounds specified in s.24(2) for making a special administration order:
  (1) There has been or is likely to be a contravention of the undertaker's principal duty with respect to water supply (s.37) or sewerage services (s.94). Although these duties are

enforceable by means of the s.18 enforcement procedures, this section allows an application to be made for a special administration order without first going through the process of making a s.18 order.

(2) For other duties under the Act, which are enforceable by s.18 orders, there has been or is likely to be a contravention of a final or confirmed provisional order which is serious enough to warrant the undertaker losing its appointment.

(3) The undertaker is or is likely to be unable to pay its debts.

(4) It would have been appropriate to wind up the undertaker's business under s.440 of the Companies Act 1985 following an inspector's report had s.26 of this Act prevented such action.

(5) The undertaker is unable or unwilling to participate in arrangements for termination certified as necessary by the Secretary of State or Director following notice of termination in accordance with its appointment conditions (s.7(4)(c)). See condition O of the model instrument of appointment which requires at least ten years' notice.

In addition, any court is empowered to make a special administration order in circumstances where an application is made for the winding-up of an undertaker, which it would have granted but for the restrictions in s.26 (s.25).

Schedule 3 modifies provisions of the Insolvency Act 1986 to apply to special administration orders. Following the making of an order and the identification of a replacement appointee, Sched. 2 provides for transitional arrangements, including schemes for transferring property, rights and liabilities to the new company to be approved by the Secretary of State or the Director (Sched. 2, para. 2(2)). Schemes may include provision for consideration to be paid by the new appointee (Sched. 2, para. 3(3)).

Creditors and special administration orders

The provisions for special administration orders are a substitute for winding-up procedures or administration orders under Pt. II of the Insolvency Act 1986 (see s.26) and as a result place creditors of an undertaker in a different position from those of an ordinary commercial enterprise. During the Committee stage in the House of Lords regarding s.23 of the Water Act 1989, from which s.23 of this Act is derived, the Government confirmed that a special administrator was empowered, as part of his management of the business, to pay both existing creditors (undertaker's creditors prior to the making of the order) and new creditors arising during the time the order was in force (*Hansard*, H.L. Vol. 507, col. 962). However, possible tensions may occur because whilst the administrator is running the company the purpose of the order is stated to be in subs. (2)(b), "the carrying out of those functions", whilst in subs. (1)(b) the company's affairs are to be managed "in a manner which protects the respective interests of the members and creditors of the company". The implication is that should there be a conflict of interest, then priority must be given to the carrying out of the functions of the undertaker rather than securing the assets of creditors and members. During the passage of the Water Act 1989 (s.23) the Government stated that the peculiar nature of the assets of a water or sewerage undertaker meant that creditors were best protected if the undertaker's business was sold as a going concern rather than split piecemeal. Nevertheless, "insolvency is a commercial risk that every trader is aware of and creditors of water authority successor companies should be fully aware of the special administration order when they commit themselves to business with those companies" (Lord Hesketh, *Hansard*, H.L. Vol. 507, col. 968).

Special administration orders made on special petitions

24.—(1) If, on an application made to the High Court by petition presented—

(a) by the Secretary of State; or

(b) with the consent of the Secretary of State, by the Director,

that Court is satisfied in relation to any company which holds an appointment under Chapter I of this Part that any one or more of the grounds specified in subsection (2) below is satisfied in relation to that company, that Court may make a special administration order in relation to that company.

(2) The grounds mentioned in subsection (1) above are, in relation to any company—

(a) that there has been, is or is likely to be such a contravention by the company of any principal duty, not being a contravention in respect of which a notice has been served under subsection (3) of section 19 above, as is serious enough to make it inappropriate for the company to continue to hold its appointment;

(b) that there has been, is or is likely to be such a contravention by the company of the provisions of any enforcement order which—
    (i) is not for the time being the subject-matter of proceedings brought by virtue of section 21(1) above; and
    (ii) if it is a provisional enforcement order, has been confirmed, as is serious enough to make it inappropriate for the company to continue to hold its appointment;
(c) that the company is or is likely to be unable to pay its debts;
(d) that, in a case in which the Secretary of State has certified that it would be appropriate, but for section 25 below, for him to petition for the winding-up of the company under section 440 of the Companies Act 1985 (petition by the Secretary of State following inspectors' report etc.), it would be just and equitable, as mentioned in that section, for the company to be wound up if it did not hold an appointment under Chapter I of this Part; or
(e) that the company is unable or unwilling adequately to participate in arrangements certified by the Secretary of State or the Director to be necessary by reason of, or in connection with, a proposal for the making by virtue of section 7(4)(c) above of any appointment or variation replacing a company as a relevant undertaker.

(3) Notice of any petition under this section for a special administration order shall be given forthwith to such persons and in such manner as may be prescribed by rules made under section 411 of the Insolvency Act 1986 ("the 1986 Act"); and no such petition shall be withdrawn except with the leave of the High Court.

(4) Subsections (4) and (5) of section 9 of the 1986 Act (powers on application for administration order) shall apply on the hearing of the petition for a special administration order in relation to any company as they apply on the hearing of a petition for an administration order.

(5) Subsections (1), (2) and (4) of section 10 of the 1986 Act (effect of petition) shall apply in the case of a petition for a special administration order in relation to any company as if—
(a) the reference in subsection (1) to an administration order were a reference to a special administration order;
(b) paragraph (b) of that subsection did require the leave of the court for the taking of any of the steps mentioned in paragraphs (b) and (c) of subsection (2) (appointment of, and exercise of functions by, administrative receiver); and
(c) the reference in paragraph (c) of subsection (1) to proceedings included a reference to any proceedings under or for the purposes of section 18 above.

(6) For the purposes of this section a company is unable to pay its debts if—
(a) it is a limited company which is deemed to be so unable under section 123 of the 1986 Act (definition of inability to pay debts); or
(b) it is an unregistered company which is deemed, by virtue of any of sections 222 to 224 of that Act, to be so unable for the purposes of section 221 of that Act (winding-up of unregistered companies).

(7) In this section "principal duty," in relation to a company, means a requirement imposed on the company by section 37 or 94 below.

DEFINITIONS
"enforcement order": s.18(7).
"principal duty": subs. (7).
"provisional enforcement order": s.18(7).
"special administration order": ss.23 and 219(1).
"unable to pay its debts": subs. (6).

GENERAL NOTE
See General Note to s.23.

Power to make special administration order on winding-up petition

25. On an application made to any court for the winding-up of a company which holds an appointment under Chapter I of this Part—
(a) the court shall not make a winding-up order in relation to the company; but
(b) if the court is satisfied that it would be appropriate to make such an order if the company were not a company holding such an appointment, it shall, instead, make a special administration order in relation to the company.

<small>DEFINITIONS</small>
"special administration order": ss.23 and 219(1).

<small>GENERAL NOTE</small>
See General Note to s.23.

Restrictions on voluntary winding-up and insolvency proceedings

Restrictions on voluntary winding-up and insolvency proceedings

26.—(1) Where a company holds an appointment under Chapter I of this Part—
(a) the company shall not be wound up voluntarily;
(b) no administration order shall be made in relation to the company under Part II of the Insolvency Act 1986; and
(c) no step shall be taken by any person to enforce any security over the company's property except where that person has served fourteen days' notice of his intention to take that step on the Secretary of State and on the Director.
(2) In this section "security" and "property" have the same meanings in Parts I to VII of the Insolvency Act 1986.

<small>DEFINITIONS</small>
"property": subs. (2).
"security": subs. (2).

<small>GENERAL NOTE</small>
This section effectively prohibits the winding-up of a company as long as it holds an appointment in order to ensure that there is no disruption in the supply of water or sewerage services. The requirement of a notice of intention to enforce security under subs. (1)(c) gives the Secretary of State or the Director the opportunity to apply for a special administration order under s.24.

CHAPTER III

PROTECTION OF CUSTOMERS ETC.

General provisions

General duty of Director to keep matters under review

27.—(1) It shall be the duty of the Director, so far as it appears to him practicable from time to time to do so, to keep under review the carrying on both in England and Wales and elsewhere of activities connected with the matters in relation to which water undertakers or sewerage undertakers carry out functions.
(2) It shall also be the duty of the Director, so far as it appears to him practicable from time to time to do so, to collect information with respect to—
(a) the carrying out by companies appointed under Chapter I of this Part of the functions of relevant undertakers; or

(b) any such company,
with a view to his becoming aware of, and ascertaining the circumstances relating to, matters with respect to which any power or duty is conferred or imposed on him by or under any enactment.

(3) The Secretary of State may give general directions indicating—

(a) considerations to which the Director should have particular regard in determining the order of priority in which matters are to be brought under review in performing his duty under subsection (1) or (2) above; and

(b) considerations to which, in cases where it appears to the Director that any of his powers under Parts II to V and VII of this Act are exercisable, he should have particular regard in determining whether to exercise those powers;

and it shall be the duty of the Director to comply with any such directions.

(4) It shall be the duty of the Director, where either he considers it expedient or he is requested by the Secretary of State or the Director General of Fair Trading to do so, to give information, advice and assistance to the Secretary of State or that Director with respect to any matter relating to—

(a) the functions of either description of relevant undertaker; or

(b) the carrying out of any such functions by a company holding an appointment under Chapter I of this Part.

DEFINITIONS
"enactment": s.219(1).
"functions": ss.217 and 219(1).

GENERAL NOTE

It is the Director's duty under s.27 to keep under review the activities of water and sewerage undertakers and to collect information regarding the discharge of their functions. The model instrument of appointment contains a number of conditions requiring undertakers to supply information to the Director and s.203 provides the Director with wide powers to obtain information from undertakers with regard to enforcement orders under s.18.

Subsection (3) provides the Secretary of State with a power to give directions to the Director. Subsection (3)(a) enables the Secretary of State to determine which considerations the Director should have particular regard to in determining the order of priority relating to his duties of review and collection of information. The power of the Secretary of State to give directions under subs. (3) is confined to s.27 alone and is not applicable to the other investigatory powers, *e.g.* those contained in s.203. Subsection (3)(b), in contrast, applies to other sections of this Part of the Act but is confined to the Director's *powers*. By way of example, the Secretary of State could not indicate particular considerations the Directors should bear in mind when deciding to make a final enforcement order under s.18, but could do so in respect of his power to make provisional orders under s.18(2).

The rationale behind the drafting of subs. (3) (s.26(3) of the Water Act 1989 from which subs. (3) is derived) was explained during the Committee stage of the Water Act 1989 in the House of Lords when the Earl of Arran stated:

"This would be relevant if an issue arose to which the Secretary of State considered particular attention should be paid, *e.g.* a matter of national or social or economic importance. This subsection would allow the Secretary of State to draw such matters to the attention of the Director and the Director would have a duty to have regard to those directions but he would not be barred from taking into account other relevant considerations. I can assure the Committee that the Secretary of State's power in no way dilutes the Director's obligation under the clause" (*Hansard*, H.L. Vol. 507, cols. 972–3).

Any directions made by the Secretary of State under this section must be set out in the Director's annual report (s.193(2)(b)).

Customer service committees

28.—(1) Every company holding an appointment under Chapter I of this Part shall be allocated by the Director to a committee established and maintained by him for the purpose, in relation to such companies as may be allocated to it, of carrying out—

(a) the functions assigned by this Act to such a committee; and

(b) such other functions as the committees maintained under this section may be required to carry out by the Director.

(2) The committees maintained under this section shall be known as customer service committees.

(3) There shall not at any time be more than ten customer service committees, but it shall be the duty of the Director so to exercise his powers under this section to establish and maintain customer service committees and to allocate companies to those committees as to secure that at all times—

(a) such customer service committees are maintained; and

(b) such allocations under subsection (1) above are in force,

as he considers appropriate for ensuring that the interests of the customers and potential customers of the companies for the time being holding appointments under Chapter I of this Part are effectively represented.

(4) A customer service committee shall consist of—

(a) a chairman appointed by the Director after consultation with the Secretary of State; and

(b) such number (not less than ten nor more than twenty) of other members appointed by the Director as the Director may determine.

(5) In appointing persons to be members of a customer service committee the Director shall have regard to—

(a) the desirability of the persons appointed being persons who have experience of, and have shown capacity in, some matter relevant to—

(i) the functions of a water undertaker or sewerage undertaker; or

(ii) the carrying out of those functions in relation to any area by a company which the Director has allocated, or is proposing to allocate, to that committee; and

(b) the desirability of—

(i) the committee including one or more persons with experience of work among, and the special needs of, disabled persons; and

(ii) persons appointed by virtue of this paragraph including disabled persons.

(6) An appointment of a person to hold office as the chairman of a customer service committee shall be for a term not exceeding four years.

(7) Subject to subsection (6) above, the chairman and other members of a customer service committee shall hold and vacate office in accordance with the terms of their appointments and, notwithstanding that subsection, shall on ceasing to hold office be eligible for re-appointment.

(8) The provisions of Schedule 4 to this Act shall have effect with respect to customer service committees.

DEFINITIONS
　"functions": ss.217 and 219(1).

GENERAL NOTE
　The provisions of s.28 of and Sched. 4 to the Act provide for the establishment of customer service committees. These replace the former consumer consultative committees set up under s.24(a) of the Water Act 1973. The new-style customer service committees were established under s.6 of the Water Act 1989 and are distinguished from the old-style consumer consultative committees in that local authorities lose their automatic right of representation and arrangements to maintain customer service committees are no longer a matter purely for the undertaker companies. Subsection (3) provides that there should be a maximum of 10 customer service committees. However, this does not prevent the establishment of local and other sub-committees being formed with the approval of the Director under Sched. 4(1). Such committees are subject to the Public Bodies (Admission to Meetings) Act 1960.
　Subsection (4) provides that a customer service committee shall consist of a chairman appointed by the Director, after consultation with the Secretary of State, and not less than 10 and no more than 20 persons appointed by the Director.

Subsection (5) provides the Director with a wide discretion as to whom he should appoint to the customer service committees. The Director must have regard to the experience of prospective committee members relating to the functions of the water and sewerage undertakers and the desirability that at least one person has experience of work in respect of the special needs of disabled persons. During the Committee stage of the Water Act 1989 the makeup of customer service committees was considered and Colin Moynihan stated:

> "We envisage that the customer service committees will have broadly the same balance of consumer interests as the present consumer consultative committees. In other words, there will be a three-way balance between industrial, commercial and farming consumers, domestic consumers and local authorities. The arrangements for determining how that balance is to be achieved and who the consumer representatives shall be are matters for the Director General. It is clear that he will need to ensure that there is effective consumer representation if he is to obtain the advice that he requires from customer service committees for the proper protection of customers" (Standing Committee D, col. 511, 1989).

Duties of customer service committees

29.—(1) It shall be the duty of a customer service committee—
(a) to keep under review all matters appearing to the committee to affect the interests of the persons who are customers or potential customers of the companies allocated to the committee;
(b) to consult each company so allocated about such of those matters as appear to affect the interests of the customers or potential customers of that company; and
(c) to make to a company so allocated all such representations about any such matter as the committee considers appropriate.
(2) Subject to subsection (3) below, it shall be the duty of a customer service committee to investigate any complaint which—
(a) is made to the committee by any person who is a customer or potential customer of a company allocated to the committee or is referred to the committee by the Director under section 30 below;
(b) does not appear to the committee to be vexatious or frivolous; and
(c) relates to the carrying out by that company of any of the functions of a relevant undertaker.
(3) It shall be the duty of a customer service committee to refer to the Director every complaint which is made to the committee by any person in relation to a company allocated to the committee and consists in or amounts to—
(a) an assertion that the company is contravening or has contravened any condition of the company's appointment under Chapter I of this Part or any statutory or other requirement enforceable under section 18 above; or
(b) a complaint which the Director would be required to investigate under section 181 below.
(4) It shall be the duty of a customer service committee, where the committee considers it appropriate to do so in connection with any such complaint as is mentioned in subsection (2) above, to make representations on behalf of the complainant to the company in question about any matter—
(a) to which the complaint relates; or
(b) which appears to the committee to be relevant to the subject-matter of the complaint;
and it shall be the duty of a customer service committee to refer to the Director or, as the case may be, back to the Director any such complaint as is so mentioned which the committee is unable to resolve.
(5) The only remedy for a breach by a customer service committee of a duty imposed on it by this section shall be the making of such a complaint to the Director as the Director is required to consider under section 30(3)(c) below.

(6) It shall be the duty of the Director to make such arrangements as he considers appropriate for facilitating the provision by one customer service committee to another of any such information as that other committee may require for any purpose relating to the carrying out of its functions.

DEFINITIONS
"customer or potential customer": s.219(1).
"functions": ss.217 and 219(1).

GENERAL NOTE
This section sets out the duties of customer service committees. Arrangements for investigating complaints and reviewing matters affecting the interests of customers or potential customers of water and sewerage undertakers are now more formalised than the provision made in the Water Act 1983, which made no express reference to the existence of customer service committees but simply required water authorities to prepare a report for the Secretary of State on the arrangements for the representation of consumer interests in accordance with Government guidelines. The new arrangements are especially significant because undertakers will no longer fall under the remit of the Local Government Ombudsman, and s.29 in effect provides a substitute for the investigation of maladministration by undertakers.

Investigations and referrals by customer service committees
Subsection (2) imposes a duty on customer service committees to investigate any complaint by a customer or potential customer relating to the functions of a water or sewerage undertaker unless such complaints appear to the committee to be vexatious or frivolous (subs. (2)(b)) or the complaint is of a type which must be referred to the Director. Complaints which must be referred to the Director concern contravention of appointment conditions or duties enforceable under s.18 (subs. (3)(a)). Customer service committees must also refer to the Director complaints which relate to the exercise of an undertaker's right to lay pipes and other works on private land under s.159, which must be investigated by the Director under s.181 (subs. (3)(6)). The Director is not required to investigate every complaint concerning the right to lay pipes, and the drafting of the section implies that the customer service committee may consider whether the exclusions in s.181(2) are applicable and would warrant non-referral. A customer's remedy for breach of the duties of the customer service committee is to make a complaint to the Director (subs. (5)).

Customer service committees are given no special statutory powers to assist their investigations, but conditions in the model instrument of appointment place important requirements on undertakers relating to such investigations, including a requirement to meet customer service committees at least once a year and at other times as reasonably required by the committee (condition G), to consult with committees on their codes of practice concerning disconnections, to provide statistical information on disconnections (condition H), and to consult with the committees on codes of practice concerning the liability of metered customers for leakages (condition I).

Duties of Director with respect to complaints

30.—(1) Where a complaint is made to the Director by a customer or potential customer of a company allocated to a customer service committee and the complaint does not consist in or amount to—
 (a) an assertion that the company is contravening or has contravened any condition of the company's appointment under Chapter I of this Part or any statutory or other requirement enforceable under section 18 above; or
 (b) a complaint which the Director is required to investigate under section 181 below,
it shall be the duty of the Director to consider whether the complaint should be referred to that committee, instead of being dealt with by the Director himself.

(2) Where a complaint which does consist in or amount to such an assertion as is mentioned in subsection (2)(a) above—
 (a) is made to the Director by a customer or potential customer of any company allocated to a customer service committee; or
 (b) is referred to him by such a committee,

it shall be the duty of the Director to consider whether the complaint should be referred by him to the Secretary of State.

(3) It shall be the duty of the Director to consider the following complaints, that is to say—

(a) any complaint to which the duty imposed by subsection (2) above applies and which is not referred by the Director to the Secretary of State;

(b) any complaint which is referred to the Director under section 29(4) above; and

(c) any complaint made to the Director by a customer or potential customer of a company allocated to a customer service committee that the committee has failed to perform any duty imposed on it by section 29(1) to (4) above.

(4) It shall be the duty of the Director to take such steps in consequence of his consideration of any matter in pursuance of this section (including, in a case falling within subsection (3)(b) or (c) above, any step which could have been taken by the committee itself) as he considers appropriate.

DEFINITIONS
"customer or potential customer": s.219(1).

GENERAL NOTE
This section is concerned with the duties of the Director regarding complaints made to him by customers or potential customers. Where such a complaint is made which is not a complaint concerning alleged contravention of appointment conditions or duties enforceable under s.18 and is not a complaint which the Director is required to investigate under s.181, then the Director has a duty to consider whether the complaint should be referred to the consumer service committee. In contrast to customer service committees, the Director is not under an express duty to *investigate* complaints, but must "consider" them and the various possible options specified in subs. (3). When considering such complaints the Director will have in mind his primary duties under s.2. Apart from his specific statutory powers to obtain information in connection with enforcement action under s.203, the model instrument of appointment contains a general condition requiring undertakers to furnish the Director with information he may reasonably require for the carrying out of his functions.

Provisions with respect to competition

Functions of Director with respect to competition

31.—(1) If and to the extent that he is requested by the Director General of Fair Trading to do so, it shall be the duty of the Director to exercise the functions of that Director under Part III of the 1973 Act so far as relating to courses of conduct which are or may be detrimental to the interests of persons who are consumers in relation to—

(a) the supply of water by water undertakers; or

(b) the provision of sewerage services by sewerage undertakers;

and this duty shall apply whether those interests are economic or interests in respect of health, safety or other matters.

(2) The Director shall continue to be entitled, concurrently with the Director General of Fair Trading, to exercise—

(a) the functions of that Director under sections 44 and 45 of the 1973 Act; and

(b) the functions of that Director under sections 50, 52, 53, 86 and 88 of that Act,

so far as relating to monopoly situations which exist or may exist in relation to commercial activities connected with the supply of water or the provision of sewerage services.

(3) The Director shall continue to be entitled, concurrently with the Director General of Fair Trading, to exercise the functions of that Director under sections 2 to 10 and 16 of the 1980 Act so far as relating to courses of

conduct which have or are intended to have or are likely to have the effect of restricting, distorting, or preventing competition in connection with the supply of water or securing a supply of water or with the provision or securing of sewerage services.

(4) So far as necessary for the purposes of or in connection with the provisions of subsections (1) to (3) above, the references to the Director General of Fair Trading in—

(a) Parts III and IV of the 1973 Act;
(b) sections 86, 88 and 133 of the 1973 Act; and
(c) sections 2 to 10, 16 and 19 of the 1980 Act,

shall be construed as if they were or, as the case may require, as if they included references to the Director.

(5) Before either Director first exercises in relation to any matter functions mentioned in paragraph (a) or in paragraph (b) of subsection (2) above or in subsection (3) above, he shall consult the other Director.

(6) Neither Director shall exercise in relation to any matter any functions mentioned in paragraph (a) or in paragraph (b) of subsection (2) above or in subsection (3) above if any of the functions mentioned in that paragraph or, as the case may be, in subsection (3) above have already been exercised in relation to that matter by the other Director.

(7) It shall be the duty of the Director, for the purpose of assisting the Monopolies Commission in carrying out an investigation on a reference made to them by the Director by virtue of subsection (2) or (3) above, to give to the Commission—

(a) any information which is in his possession and which relates to matters falling within the scope of the investigation, and which is either requested by the Commission for that purpose or is information which in his opinion it would be appropriate for that purpose to give to the Commission without any such request; and
(b) any other assistance which the Commission may require, and which it is within his power to give, in relation to any such matters;

and the Commission shall, for the purposes of carrying out any such investigation, take into account any information given to them for that purpose under this subsection.

(8) If any question arises as to whether subsection (2) or (3) above applies to any particular case, that question shall be referred to and determined by the Secretary of State; and no objection shall be taken to anything done under—

(a) Part IV or section 86 or 88 of the 1973 Act; or
(b) sections 2 to 10 of the 1980 Act,

by or in relation to the Director on the ground that it should have been done by or in relation to the Director General of Fair Trading.

(9) Expressions used in the 1973 Act or the 1980 Act and in this section have the same meanings in this section as in that Act.

GENERAL NOTE

This section is concerned with the functions of the Director regarding competition and allows the Director to exercise concurrently with the Director General of Fair Trading some of his functions under the Fair Trading Act 1973 and the Competition Act 1980 regarding the activities of water and sewerage undertakers. The provisions provide the Director with an important extra layer of regulatory powers in his relationship with undertakers, over and above his supervision of appointment conditions and those duties under the Act which he may enforce by means of s.18 orders. Each Director is required to consult the other before exercising the powers contained in this section (subs. (5)) and resolution of disputes between them can be determined by the Secretary of State (subs. (8)).

The functions specified in this section relate to:

(1) *Courses of conduct detrimental to the interests of consumers under Pt. III of the Fair Trading Act 1973 (subs. (1))*

In this context the interests are not confined to economic considerations, and may include health, safety and other matters but the conduct must be in relation to the provision of water or sewerage services (subs. (1)). The Director may only take action under this heading when requested to do so by the Director General of Fair Trading, but once engaged he has the power to exercise all the functions of the Director General of Fair Trading under Pt. III of the 1973 Act. This will include a duty to use his best endeavours to obtain a written assurance from the undertaker concerned to refrain from the practice identified, and the power to obtain a court order if the assurance is subsequently broken.

(2) *Monopoly references under the Fair Trading Act 1973 (subs. (2))*
The Director is given powers to require undertakers to provide him with information necessary to establish whether a monopoly exists (subs. (2)(a)) and to make a reference to the Monopolies and Mergers Commission himself under s.50 of the 1973 Act (subs. (2)(b)). In this context, both the Director General of Water Services and the Director General of Fair Trading are given the power to make references, a change to the original provisions of the Fair Trading Act which committed only the Secretary of State to make references in respect of water services (see Sched. 7(4) to the Fair Trading Act 1973, repealed by Sched. 25(45) to the Water Act 1989).

(3) *Anti-competitive practices under the Competition Act 1980 (subs. (3))*
The functions that the Director may exercise under this Act include preliminary investigations of possible anti-competitive practices, making competition references to the Monopolies and Mergers Commission and obtaining undertakings to render such references unnecessary. This provision ties in with the Director General's duties under s.2(3)(e) to facilitate effective competition between existing undertakers and potential undertakers.

Duty to refer merger of water or sewerage undertakings

32.—(1) Subject to the following provisions of this section and to section 33 below, it shall be the duty of the Secretary of State to make a merger reference to the Monopolies Commission if it appears to him that it is or may be the fact—
  (a) that arrangements are in progress which, if carried into effect, will result in a merger of any two or more water enterprises; or
  (b) that such a merger has taken place otherwise than as a result of the carrying into effect of arrangements that have been the subject of a reference by virtue of paragraph (a) above.

(2) The Secretary of State shall not make a merger reference under this section in respect of any actual or prospective merger of two or more water enterprises if it appears to him that the take over from which the merger has resulted or, as the case may be, would result was initiated before 9 a.m. on January 11, 1989.

(3) For the purposes of subsection (2) above a merger of two or more enterprises results from a take over initiated before 9 a.m. on January 11, 1989 if—
  (a) the Secretary of State or the Director General of Fair Trading was given notice before that time on that date of the material facts about the proposed arrangements or transactions resulting in the merger; or
  (b) the merger results exclusively from the acceptance of offers to acquire shares in a body corporate and those offers—
    (i) were all made before that time on that date; or
    (ii) in so far as they were not so made, consist in offers made, by the same person and in respect of the same shares, in substitution for offers made before that time on that date.

DEFINITIONS
"Monopolies Commission": s.219(1).
"water enterprises": s.35(1).

GENERAL NOTE

The water merger control régime s.32–35

Section 32 is concerned with the Secretary of State's duty to make a merger reference to the Monopolies Commission in respect of any actual or prospective merger of two or more water enterprises. Section 33 excludes proposed small mergers from the Secretary of State's duty to make a merger reference under s.32. Section 34 provides the key test with regard to merger references relating to proposed or actual water enterprise mergers, and, finally, s.35 is concerned with the construction of merger proposals.

Section 34(3) provides the key test for the Monopolies and Mergers Commission in determining whether a merger or proposed merger which has been referred to it under s.32 is against the "public interest", and it introduces the concept of what has been termed "comparative competition". Given that water and sewerage undertakers are in effect monopolies in relation to their principal functions of supplying water and sewerage services, the concept of "comparative competition" is fundamental to the effectiveness of the Director's regulatory functions under the Act.

The Government's position concerning the need to preserve an adequate number of independent undertakers after privatisation can be seen from the comments of Lord Hesketh during the committee stage in the House of Lords of the Water Act 1989:

"Privatisation will create a market for corporate control of water companies in which less efficient managements can be replaced by more efficient ones. The Government sees this corporate rivalry as a key advantage in the privatisation of the water industry. In general, therefore, we wish to minimise obstacles to take-over.

The pressure towards corporate efficiency is relevant also to the rôle of the Director General as regulator of the privatised water industry. He will need to be in a position to make comparisons between the performance of competing managements in assessing their relative efficiency, for example in carrying out his price-setting functions. But the Director General, in making his comparisons, will need to distinguish between factors outside management's control, such as those inherent in geographical variations and those, such as managing capital inputs economically, which are within their control. Against this background, there needs to be a cross-section of observations provided by independent water interests across England and Wales to allow an objective assessment of variations in performance to be made. Undue concentration of ownership in the industry will have a detrimental effect on the ability of the Director General to make yardstick comparisons. If a significant proportion of the industry were to come under the control of a few dominant owners who adopted common management practices, the true scope for efficiency improvements throughout the industry would be concealed" (*Hansard*, H.L. Vol. 507, col. 984).

The Government's concern is reflected in s.34(3).

Threshold tests

The duty of the Secretary of State to make a merger reference under s.32 encompasses mergers between water and sewerage undertakers and mergers of the predecessor companies (including statutory water companies) initiated on or after January 11, 1989 (subs. (2)). The merger is covered by the s.32 provisions and a threshold test is contained within s.33, which excludes mergers where the assets of the target company do not exceed £30m (s.31(1)(a)) or the person making the take-over owns no other water enterprises with assets less than £30m (s.31(1)(b)). The £30m figure, derived from s.64 of the Fair Trading Act 1973, may be altered by regulations made by the Secretary of State (s.33(4)), allowing the threshold test under this section to be detached from whatever figure is prevailing in the Fair Trading Act. These regulations could alter both the amount and the test of asset values, introducing criteria based on turnover, if that were considered to be more appropriate to the conditions prevailing in the industry.

Exclusion of small mergers from duty to make merger reference

33.—(1) The Secretary of State shall not make a merger reference under section 32 above in respect of any actual or prospective merger of two or more water enterprises if it appears to him—

(a) that the value of the assets taken over does not exceed or, as the case may be, would not exceed the amount for the time being specified in section 64(1)(b) of the 1973 Act (condition of merger reference relating to amount of assets taken over); or

(b) that the only water enterprises already belonging to the person making the take over are enterprises each of which has assets the value of which does not exceed or, as the case may be, would not exceed that amount.

(2) In relation to a merger of two or more water enterprises—

(a) the value of the assets taken over shall, for the purposes of subsection (1) above, be determined in accordance with section 67 of the 1973 Act by reference only to assets employed in or appropriated to a water enterprise; and

(b) the value of the assets of a water enterprise belonging to the person making the take over shall be taken for those purposes to be the value of such assets employed in or appropriated to that enterprise as by virtue of the exceptions in paragraph (a) of subsection (2) of that section are disregarded in determining the value of the assets taken over;

and paragraph (b) of that subsection shall apply for determining the value of the assets referred to in paragraph (b) above as it applies in relation to the assets taken over.

(3) For the purposes of this section and of any determination in accordance with this section—

(a) the assets treated as employed in or appropriated to a water enterprise carried on by a company holding an appointment under Chapter I of this Part shall include all the assets for the time being of that company;

(b) every water enterprise any of whose assets fall to be disregarded as mentioned in subsection (2)(b) above shall be treated as belonging to the person making the take over;

(c) the enterprises mentioned in paragraph (b) above shall be treated as separate enterprises in so far as they are carried on by different companies holding appointments under Chapter I of this Part; and

(d) subsections (3) and (4) of section 67 of the 1973 Act (assets treated as appropriated to an enterprise and mergers over a period) shall apply as they apply for the purposes of, and of any determination in accordance with, subsection (2) of that section.

(4) If the Secretary of State considers that it is appropriate—

(a) for subsection (1) above to have effect with a reference in paragraph (a) to a different amount; or

(b) for the condition set out in that paragraph to be modified in any other respect,

he may, in relation to mergers after the coming into force of the regulations, by regulations make such modifications of that paragraph and, for that purpose, of the other provisions of this section as may be prescribed.

DEFINITIONS
　"water enterprise": s.35(1).

GENERAL NOTE
　See General Note to s.32.

References with respect to water enterprise mergers

34.—(1) Subject to subsections (2) to (4) below, the 1973 Act shall have effect in relation to any reference under section 32 above as if—

(a) any such merger of two or more water enterprises as is required to be the subject of such a reference were a merger situation qualifying for investigation; and

(b) a reference under that section were made under section 64 of that Act or, as the case may be, under section 75 of that Act (references in anticipation of a merger).

(2) Nothing in subsection (1) above shall have the effect in relation to any reference under section 32 above of applying—

(a) so much of Part V of the 1973 Act as requires the Monopolies Commission to consider any of the matters set out in subsection (1) of section 64 of that Act; or

(b) the provisions of sections 69(2) to (4) and 75(3) of that Act (power to restrict matters referred).

(3) In determining on a reference under section 32 above whether any matter operates, or may be expected to operate, against the public interest the Monopolies Commission—

(a) shall have regard to the desirability of giving effect to the principle that the number of water enterprises which are under independent control should not be reduced so as to prejudice the Director's ability, in carrying out his functions by virtue of this Act, to make comparisons between different such water enterprises; and

(b) shall have regard to the desirability of achieving any other purpose so far only as they are satisfied—

(i) that that other purpose can be achieved in a manner that does not conflict with that principle; or

(ii) that the achievement of that other purpose is of substantially greater significance in relation to the public interest than that principle and cannot be brought about except in a manner that conflicts with that principle.

(4) No order shall be made under Part V of the 1973 Act in consequence of any merger reference made under section 32 above in respect of an actual merger unless the reference was made within the period of six months beginning with whichever is the later of—

(a) the day on which the merger took place; and

(b) the day on which the material facts about the transactions which resulted in the merger first came to the notice of the Secretary of State or the Director General of Fair Trading or were made public within the meaning of section 64 of the 1973 Act;

and if on such a reference the Monopolies Commission are satisfied that the reference was not made within that period their report on the reference shall state that fact and nothing else.

DEFINITIONS
"Monopolies Commission": s.219(1).
"water enterprise": s.35(1).

GENERAL NOTE
Subsection (3) contains the key provision regarding whether a merger reference under s.32 operates or may be expected to operate against the public interest. The Monopolies Commission must have regard to the desirability of maintaining the number of independently controlled water enterprises at a level which would not prejudice the Director's ability to make comparisons between such enterprises. See also the General Note to s.32.

Construction of merger provisions

35.—(1) In this Chapter—

"enterprise" has the meaning given for the purposes of sections 64 to 77 of the 1973 Act by section 63(2) of that Act; and

"water enterprise" means an enterprise carried on by a relevant undertaker.

(2) References in this Chapter, in relation to any two or more enterprises, to the merger of those enterprises are references to those enterprises ceasing, within the meaning of Part V of the 1973 Act, to be distinct enterprises; and sections 66 and 66A of that Act (time at which enterprises cease to be distinct) shall have effect for the purposes of this Chapter as they have effect for the purposes of that Part.

(3) The reference in section 34(3) above to the number of water enterprises under independent control is a reference to the number of water enterprises there would be if two or more water enterprises counted as one enterprise wherever they would be treated for the purposes of Part V of the 1973 Act as having ceased to be distinct enterprises.

(4) Nothing in sections 32 to 34 above shall prejudice any power of the Secretary of State, in a case in which he is not required to make a reference under section 32 above, to make a merger reference under Part V of the 1973 Act in respect of any actual or prospective merger of two or more water enterprises.

DEFINITIONS
"enterprise": subs. (1).
"water enterprise": subs. (1).

GENERAL NOTE
See discussion in s.32 regarding merger references to the Monopolies Commission.

CHAPTER IV

INTERPRETATION OF PART II

Interpretation of Part II

36.—(1) In this Part—
"the 1973 Act" means the Fair Trading Act 1973; and
"the 1980 Act" means the Competition Act 1980.

(2) References in this Part to an appointment or variation replacing a company as a relevant undertaker are references to the following, that is to say—

(a) the appointment of a company to be the water undertaker or sewerage undertaker for any area which is or includes the whole or any part of any area for which another company already holds an appointment as water undertaker or, as the case may be, sewerage undertaker; or

(b) a variation by virtue of which the area for which a company holds an appointment under Chapter I of this Part is modified so as to include the whole or any part of an area for which another company already holds an appointment as water undertaker or, as the case may be, sewerage undertaker.

(3) For the purposes of this Part premises in a part of an area are served by a company holding an appointment under Chapter I of this Part—

(a) in relation to an appointment or variation by virtue of which that company would be replaced as the water undertaker for that part of that area, if those premises—
(i) are supplied with water by means of a connection with a distribution main of that company; or
(ii) consist in a building or part of a building which is situated within thirty metres of such a main;
and

(b) in relation to an appointment or variation by virtue of which that company would be replaced as the sewerage undertaker for that part of that area, if those premises—
(i) are drained by means of a relevant sewer; or
(ii) consist in a building or part of a building which is situated within thirty metres of such a sewer, not being a storm-water overflow sewer.

(4) In this section—

"distribution main" means a water main that is not a trunk main; and
"relevant sewer," in relation to any appointment or variation which
would replace a company as a sewerage undertaker, means any of
the following, that is to say—
    (a) a public sewer vested in that company;
    (b) a sewer in relation to which that company has made a
declaration of vesting under section 102 below which has not yet
taken effect;
    (c) a drain or sewer in relation to which that company has
entered into an agreement under section 104 below.

GENERAL NOTE
  Section 36 concerns itself with the interpretation of a number of terms and references within
Pt. II of the Act.

PART III

WATER SUPPLY

GENERAL NOTE
  Sections 37–66 contain key duties and powers relating to the provision of water supply
services. There are two underlying themes to the legislation. The new régime relating to water
supply concentrates upon the application of rule-based standards. Matters which formerly
would have been left to the discretionary interpretation of water authorities or informal
guidance by central Government are now translated into detailed legal requirements, generally
in the form of regulations made by the Secretary of State. This shift from a reliance on legal
duties to a rule-based régime can be seen as a political response to both public concern and EEC
pressure demanding more explicit and formalised standards. The process of privatisation has
made the shift to a rule-based régime inevitable.
  The second underlying theme is the availability of the s.18 enforcement order which applies
to many of the important requirements contained in this and subsequent chapters of the Act.
Section 18 enforcement orders apply to the general duties under this section relating to water
supply, under s.68 regarding provision of wholesome water and under s.94, which deals with the
provision of a public sewerage system. The s.18 enforcement procedure places the legal
responsibility for enforcement of the various duties contained within the Act exclusively in the
hands of central administration, *i.e.* the Secretary of State or the Director, depending upon the
particular duty concerned.

Provision of water supply services
  Chapters 1 and 2 of Pt. III of the Act contain a mixture of general duties derived from
previous legislation relating to water authorities supplemented by regulations detailing the
performance standards required to meet those duties, *e.g.* s.38(1). Regulations may be made
governing day-to-day relations with individual customers, and should the relevant water
undertaker fail to meet the prescribed standard detailed in the regulations made by the
Secretary of State the undertaker is required to compensate the customer concerned (s.38(3)).
  The requisitioning procedures for water mains contained in ss.41–44 are derived from earlier
legislation, though with a new formula designed to improve the undertaker's opportunity to
recover the full extra costs from the requisitioner (s.42). These provisions are important in the
context of new developments where the persons benefiting from the extension of the water
supply to the new development are required to bear the costs of connection rather than the
burden falling upon existing customers.
  Existing arrangements in respect of bulk water transfer schemes are preserved but in s.40 the
Director is given power to order undertakers to make bulk transfers of water and to impose
terms and conditions.
  Disconnection powers for non-payment of charges are continued, but the circumstances in
which the power may be exercised are restricted (see ss.60–63). Coupled with further conditions in the instrument of appointment, the undertaker is now obliged in nearly every case to
obtain a court order for arrears of debt before proceeding to disconnection.

CHAPTER I

GENERAL DUTIES OF WATER UNDERTAKERS

General duty to maintain water supply system etc.

37.—(1) It shall be the duty of every water undertaker to develop and maintain an efficient and economical system of water supply within its area and to ensure that all such arrangements have been made—
   (a) for providing supplies of water to premises in that area and for making such supplies available to persons who demand them; and
   (b) for maintaining, improving and extending the water undertaker's water mains and other pipes,
as are necessary for securing that the undertaker is and continues to be able to meet its obligations under this Part.
   (2) The duty of a water undertaker under this section shall be enforceable under section 18 above—
   (a) by the Secretary of State; or
   (b) with the consent of or in accordance with a general authorisation given by the Secretary of State, by the Director.
   (3) The obligations imposed on a water undertaker by the following Chapters of this Part, and the remedies available in respect of contraventions of those obligations, shall be in addition to any duty imposed or remedy available by virtue of any provision of this section or section 38 below and shall not be in any way qualified by any such provision.

GENERAL NOTE

The duty to maintain water supply systems is one of the three key general duties imposed on undertakers and is important in respect of the operational and policy decisions taken by undertakers in relation to their water supply functions. An undertaker's duty to provide supplies of water to premises in its area and to maintain, improve and extend those supplies must be read in conjunction with the other obligations imposed on a water undertaker by the following chapters of this part of the Act (subs. (3)). In particular, regard should be had to ss.38 and 39, which provide the mechanism to establish regulations which will link breaches of the obligations contained in Pt. III of the Act with a potential breach of the general duty contained in s.37.

The duty is drafted in broad terms and is not susceptible to judicial review since subs. (2) provides that it should be enforceable by means of s.18 orders made by the Secretary of State or the Director under a general authorisation. The general duty in s.37 is significant in that it is only one of the two duties under the Act where a special administration order under s.24 can be obtained against a defaulting company without the need for first using the enforcement order procedure.

Standards of performance in connection with water supply

38.—(1) For the purpose—
   (a) of facilitating the determination of the extent to which breaches of the obligations imposed by the following provisions of this Part are to amount to breaches of the duty imposed by section 37 above; or
   (b) of supplementing that duty by establishing overall standards of performance in relation to that duty,
the Secretary of State may, in accordance with section 39 below, by regulations provide for contraventions of such requirements as may be prescribed to be treated for the purposes of this Act as breaches of that duty.
   (2) The Secretary of State may, in accordance with section 39 below, by regulations prescribe such standards of performance in connection with the provision of supplies of water as, in his opinion, ought to be achieved in individual cases.
   (3) Regulations under subsection (2) above may provide that if a water undertaker fails to meet a prescribed standard it shall pay such amount as

may be prescribed to any person who is affected by the failure and is of a prescribed description.

(4) Without prejudice to the generality of the power conferred by subsection (2) above, regulations under that subsection may—

(a) include in a standard of performance a requirement for a water undertaker, in prescribed circumstances, to inform a person of his rights by virtue of any such regulations;

(b) provide for any dispute under the regulations to be referred by either party to the dispute to the Director;

(c) make provision for the procedure to be followed in connection with any such reference and for the Director's determination on such a reference to be enforceable in such manner as may be prescribed;

(d) prescribe circumstances in which a water undertaker is to be exempted from requirements of the regulations.

DEFINITIONS
"prescribed": s.219(1).

GENERAL NOTE
This is an important enabling section which empowers the Secretary of State to make two types of regulations relating to performance standards for water supply and is matched by equivalent powers under s.94 concerning sewerage services. The Secretary of State's power under subs. (1) may help relate breaches of subsequent obligations under this Part of the Act to the breach of the general duty under s.37 or supplement that duty by adding overall standards of performance.

Regulations under subs. (2) can establish performance standards relating to individual consumers, including, as an economic sanction, automatic financial payments to be made to the consumer for failure to comply with the standards. This is a new mechanism which aims to put pressure on undertakers to improve their relationship with customers, and it explicitly recognises that a dissatisfied customer has no realistic option but to continue receiving supplies from the undertaker, unless he moves into another undertaker's area.

The Water Supply and Sewerage Services (Customer Service Standards) Regulations 1989 (S.I. 1989 No. 1147) and the Water Supply and Sewerage Services (Customer Service Standards) (Amendment) Regulations 1989 (S.I. 1989 No. 1383) have been made under subs. (2) and apply to domestic consumers only. The Regulations include provisions for automatic daily payments or credits of £5 for failure by the undertaker to keep a domestic appointment, failure to respond to account queries within specified time limits, and similar matters. Water undertakers are obliged to supply customers with a detailed statement of their rights under the Regulations. Payments under the scheme are expressly stated in the Regulations not to affect any other liability that the undertaker may owe to the customer.

Procedure for regulations under section 38

39.—(1) The Secretary of State shall not make any regulations under section 38 above unless—

(a) the Director has made to the Secretary of State a written application complying with subsection (2) below;

(b) the Secretary of State is satisfied that a copy of the application has been served by the Director on every water undertaker specified in the application;

(c) such period as the Secretary of State considers appropriate has been allowed for the making—
(i) by the Director; and
(ii) by any affected water undertaker,
of representations or objections with respect to the Director's proposals and any modifications proposed by the Secretary of State; and

(d) the Secretary of State has considered both the Director's reasons for his proposals and every representation or objection which has been duly made with respect to those proposals, or any proposed modifications of those proposals, and has not been withdrawn.

(2) An application made by the Director to the Secretary of State complies with this subsection if it—
 (a) sets out draft provisions proposed by the Director for inclusion in regulations under section 38 above;
 (b) specifies the water undertaker or undertakers in relation to which it is proposed those provisions should apply; and
 (c) summarises the Director's reasons for his proposals.
(3) The Secretary of State shall not make any regulations under section 38 above except where—
 (a) the only provisions of the regulations are the provisions proposed by the Director in his application or those provisions with such modifications as the Secretary of State considers appropriate; and
 (b) each of the modifications (if any) of the Director's proposals to which effect is given by the regulations is a modification the proposal to make which has been notified—
  (i) to the Director; and
  (ii) to any water undertaker appearing to the Secretary of State to be likely to be affected by the modifications.

DEFINITIONS
 "modifications": s.219(1).

GENERAL NOTE
 This section is concerned with the procedure for making regulations pursuant to s.38. Although the Secretary of State is responsible for making the regulations the responsibility for initiating the procedure rests with the Director General and his powers under this section interlock with his powers under the instrument of appointment to obtain information from the undertaker about its overall quality of service, and his general duties under s.2.

CHAPTER II

SUPPLY DUTIES

Major supplies

Bulk supplies
 40.—(1) Where, on the application of a water undertaker—
 (a) it appears to the Director that it is necessary or expedient for the purposes of this Part that another water undertaker should give a supply of water in bulk to the applicant; and
 (b) he is satisfied that the giving and taking of such a supply cannot be secured by agreement,
the Director may by order require the undertakers to give and to take such a supply for such period and on such terms and conditions as may be provided in the order.
 (2) An order under this section shall have effect as an agreement between the water undertakers in question but may be varied or revoked by a subsequent order made by the Director on the application of either of those undertakers, as well as by agreement between the undertakers.
 (3) The Director shall not make an order under this section which he considers affects the carrying out by the NRA of any of its functions unless he has first consulted the NRA.
 (4) In determining what provision to make by an order under this section in respect of the giving of any supply by a water undertaker the Director shall have regard to the desirability of the undertaker's recovering the expenses of complying with its obligations under this section and of securing a reasonable return on its capital.

DEFINITIONS
 "functions": ss.217 and 219(1).
 "supply of water in bulk": s.219(1).

General Note

   This provision has significant economic implications for future resource planning by water undertakers. Where undertakers are unable to reach agreement regarding the terms on which bulk transfers of water between them are to take place, the Director is empowered to order the transfer and to determine the terms under which this will take place. The Director's decision is final, and subs. (4) provides only the broadest of criteria that he must apply. Guidance on the Government's thinking on this issue was given in 1986 in a response to a Parliamentary question regarding the effect of privatisation on the Welsh Water Authority's current bulk transfer agreement. Mark Robinson, the Junior Welsh Office Minister, stated:

   "The water services Plcs will be free to negotiate for bulk supplies at a commercial rate. While having regard to the general principle that charges should be cost-related and should not be discriminatory, undertakers who are unable to agree terms will have the right to appeal to the Director General of Water Services and, in determining such appeals, the Director General will take account of all relevant factors. The Government would expect the Director General to allow Welsh Water, like any other exporting water company, to earn a reasonable profit from the sale of bulk supplies. Equally, the Director General would be expected to ensure that monopoly situations are not abused" (*Hansard*, H.C. Vol. 97, col. 111).

   Under subs. (3) the Director shall not make a bulk transfer order under s.40 which he considers may affect the carrying out by the National Rivers Authority of its functions. In that case he must first consult the National Rivers Authority.

Duty to comply with water main requisition

   41.—(1) It shall be the duty of a water undertaker (in accordance with section 44 below) to provide a water main to be used for providing such supplies of water to premises in a particular locality in its area as (so far as those premises are concerned) are sufficient for domestic purposes, if—
   (a) the undertaker is required to provide the main by a notice served on the undertaker by one or more of the persons who under subsection (2) below are entitled to require the provision of the main for that locality;
   (b) the premises in that locality to which those supplies would be provided by means of that main are—
         (i) premises consisting in buildings or parts of buildings; or
         (ii) premises which will so consist when proposals made by any person for the erection of buildings or parts of buildings are carried out;
      and
   (c) the conditions specified in section 42 below are satisfied in relation to that requirement.
   (2) Each of the following persons shall be entitled to require the provision of a water main for any locality, that is to say—
   (a) the owner of any premises in that locality;
   (b) the occupier of any premises in that locality;
   (c) any local authority within whose area the whole or any part of that locality is situated;
   (d) where the whole or any part of that locality is situated in a new town, within the meaning of the New Towns Act 1981—
         (i) the Commission for the New Towns; and
         (ii) the Development Board for Rural Wales or the development corporation for the new town, according to whether or not the new town is situated within the area for which that Board is for the time being responsible;
      and
   (e) where the whole or any part of that locality is situated within an area designated as an urban development area under Part XVI of the Local Government, Planning and Land Act 1980, the urban development corporation.

(3) The duty of a water undertaker under this section to provide a water main shall be owed to the person who requires the provision of the main or, as the case may be, to each of the persons who joins in doing so.

(4) Where a duty is owed by virtue of subsection (3) above to any person, any breach of that duty which causes that person to sustain loss or damage shall be actionable at the suit of that person; but, in any proceedings brought against a water undertaker in pursuance of this subsection, it shall be a defence for the undertaker to show that it took all reasonable steps and exercised all due diligence to avoid the breach.

(5) In this section "local authority," in relation to the Inner Temple and the Middle Temple, includes, respectively, the Sub-Treasurer of the Inner Temple and the Under-Treasurer of the Middle Temple.

DEFINITIONS
"domestic purposes": ss.218 and 219(1).
"local authority": s.219(1) and subs. (5).
"notice": s.219(1).
"owner": s.219(1).

GENERAL NOTE
This section is concerned with the rights of owners, occupiers and local authorities to require a water undertaker to provide a water main for domestic purposes in a particular locality, even though this may be ahead of the undertaker's own infrastructure plans required to comply with its general duty under s.37 to develop the water supply system for its area. The undertaker's duty to comply with a water-main requisition is important for developers of housing estates and similar buildings as they guarantee that mains will be available in time and at a reasonably certain cost. In addition to local authorities, subs. (2) specifies the other public bodies which are entitled to require the provision of a water main. Subsection (4) provides that a breach of a water undertaker's duty to supply a water main is actionable but this is subject to the defence that an undertaker took all reasonable steps and exercised all due diligence to avoid the breach of duty.

Financial conditions of compliance

42.—(1) The conditions mentioned in section 41(1)(c) above are satisfied in relation to a requirement for the provision of a water main by a water undertaker if—
  (a) such undertakings as the undertaker may have reasonably required in accordance with subsection (2) below have been given by the person or persons who have required the provision of the main; and
  (b) such security as the undertaker may have reasonably required has been provided for the discharge of any obligations imposed by those undertakings on any person who, under subsection (3) below, may be required to secure his undertakings.

(2) The undertakings which a water undertaker may require for the purposes of subsection (1) above in respect of any water main are undertakings which—
  (a) bind the person or persons mentioned in that subsection to pay to the undertaker, in respect of each of the twelve years following the provision of the main, an amount not exceeding the relevant deficit (if any) for that year on that main; and
  (b) in the case of undertakings binding two or more persons, bind them either jointly and severally or with liability to pay apportioned in such manner as they may agree.

(3) For the purposes of subsection (1)(b) above a person may be required to secure his undertakings in relation to the provision of a water main if—
  (a) it was by virtue of section 41(2)(a) or (b) above that he required, or joined in requiring, the provision of the main; and
  (b) he is not a public authority.

(4) Where for the purposes of subsection (1)(b) above any sums have been deposited with a water undertaker by way of security for the discharge of any

obligation, the undertaker shall pay interest at such rate as may be determined either—

   (a) by the undertaker with the approval of the Director; or

   (b) in default of a determination under paragraph (a) above, by the Director,

on every sum of 50p so deposited for every three months during which it remains in the hands of the undertaker.

   (5) An approval or determination given or made by the Director for the purposes of subsection (4) above—

   (a) may be given or made in relation to the provision of a particular water main, in relation to the provision of mains of a particular description or in relation to the provision of water mains generally; and

   (b) may be revoked at any time.

   (6) Any dispute between a water undertaker and any other person as to—

   (a) the undertakings or security required by the undertaker for the purposes of this section; or

   (b) the amount required to be paid in pursuance of any such undertaking,

shall be referred to the arbitration of a single arbitrator appointed by agreement between the undertaker and that person or, in default of agreement, by the President of the Institution of Civil Engineers.

   (7) In this section "relevant deficit" has the meaning given by section 43 below.

Definitions
   "public authority": s.219(1).
   "relevant deficit": subs. (7) and s.43.
   "water main": s.219(1).

General Note
   An undertaker's duty to provide a water main does not arise unless the three conditions specified in s.41(1) are satisfied. The third condition, concerning financial conditions of compliance, is detailed in s.42. The section ensures that an undertaker receives the full extra costs incurred in complying with the requisition. Owners and occupiers, but not public authorities, may be required to provide such advance "security as the undertaker may have reasonably required" (subs. (1)(a), but with disputes referred to arbitration under subs. (6)). In all cases the person or persons making the requisition may be required to pay to the undertaker over the following 12 years an amount not exceeding "the relevant deficit" for that year on that main. This figure is calculated in accordance with the formula contained in s.43.

Calculation of "relevant deficit" for the purposes of section 42

   43.—(1) For the purposes of section 42 above the relevant deficit for any year on a water main is the amount (if any) by which the water charges payable for the use during that year of that main are exceeded by the annual borrowing costs of a loan of the amount required for the provision of that main.

   (2) The annual borrowing costs of a loan of the amount required for the provision of a water main is the aggregate amount which would fall to be paid in any year by way of payments of interest and repayments of capital if an amount equal to so much of the costs reasonably incurred in providing that main as were not incurred in the provision of additional capacity had been borrowed, by the water undertaker providing the main, on terms—

   (a) requiring interest to be paid and capital to be repaid in twelve equal annual instalments; and

   (b) providing for the amount of the interest to be calculated at such rate, and in accordance with such other provision, as may have been determined for the purposes of this subsection.

   (3) A determination for the purposes of subsection (2) above shall be made either—

   (a) by the undertaker with the approval of the Director; or

(b) in default of such a determination, by the Director.

(4) For the purposes of this section the costs reasonably incurred in providing a water main ("the new main") shall include—

    (a) the costs reasonably incurred in providing such other water mains and such tanks, service reservoirs and pumping stations as it is necessary to provide in consequence of the provision of the new main; and

    (b) such proportion (if any) as is reasonable of the costs reasonably incurred in providing any such additional capacity in an earlier main as falls to be used in consequence of the provision of the new main.

(5) In subsection (4) above the reference to an earlier main, in relation to the new main, is a reference to any water main which—

    (a) has been provided in the period of twelve years immediately before the provision of the new main; and

    (b) was so provided in pursuance of a water main requisition.

(6) Any reference in this section to the provision of additional capacity in a water main provided in pursuance of a requirement under any enactment is a reference to such works carried out or other things done in connection with the provision of that main as are carried out or done for the purpose of enabling that main to be used for purposes in addition to those for which it is necessary to provide the main in order to comply with the requirement.

(7) Any reference in this section to the water charges payable for the use during any year of any main provided by a water undertaker is a reference to so much of the aggregate of any charges payable to the water undertaker in respect of services provided in the course of that year as represents charges which—

    (a) have been imposed by the undertaker in relation to premises which are connected with that main; and

    (b) are reasonably attributable to the provision of a supply of water (whether or not for domestic purposes) to those premises by means of that main.

(8) An approval or determination given or made by the Director for the purposes of subsection (2) above—

    (a) may be given or made in relation to the provision of a particular water main, in relation to the provision of mains of a particular description or in relation to the provision of water mains generally; and

    (b) may be revoked at any time except in relation to a water main that has already been provided.

(9) In this section "water main requisition" means—

    (a) a requirement under section 41 above (including, by virtue of paragraph 1 of Schedule 2 to the Water Consolidation (Consequential Provisions) Act 1991, a requirement under section 40 of the Water Act 1989);

    (b) a requirement under the provisions of section 36 or 37 of the Water Act 1945 or of section 29 of Schedule 3 to that Act (water main requisitions); or

    (c) a requirement under any local statutory provision corresponding to section 41 above or to any of those provisions of that Act of 1945.

DEFINITIONS
"water main": s.219(1).
"water main requisition": subs. (9).

GENERAL NOTE
    This section is concerned with the formula for calculating the amount the person making the water-main requisition may be required to pay to the undertaker. The important element in the formula, the "annual borrowing costs of a loan" contained in subs. (2), provides the water undertakers with a degree of flexibility, with the approval of the Director, to fix the rate of interest to be paid as part of the formula. Thus the formula can be aligned to current interest rates, which will enable undertakers to recover the full cost of their investment. Once fixed for a

particular requisition, it appears that the rate cannot be subsequently revised after provision of the main because of the restriction on the Director's power to revoke his approval under subs. (8)(b).

Determination of completion date and route for requisitioned main

44.—(1) A water undertaker shall not be in breach of a duty imposed by section 41 above in relation to any locality unless—
  (a) the period of three months beginning with the relevant day has expired; and
  (b) the water undertaker has not, before the end of that period, so laid the water main to be provided as to enable service pipes to premises in that locality to connect with the main at the places determined under subsection (3) below.

(2) The period mentioned in subsection (1)(a) above may be extended in any case—
  (a) by agreement between the water undertaker and the person or persons who required the provision of the main; or
  (b) where there is a dispute as to whether the period should be extended, by an arbitrator on a reference under subsection (4) below.

(3) The places mentioned in subsection (1)(b) above shall be—
  (a) such places as are determined by agreement between the water undertaker and the person or persons who required the provision of the water main; or
  (b) in default of agreement, such places as are determined by an arbitrator, on a reference under subsection (4) below, to be the places at which it is reasonable, in all the circumstances, for service pipes to premises in the locality in question to connect with the water main.

(4) A reference for the purposes of subsection (2) or (3) above shall be to a single arbitrator appointed—
  (a) by agreement between the undertaker and the person or persons who required the provision of the water main; or
  (b) in default of agreement, by the President of the Institution of Civil Engineers.

(5) In this section "relevant day," in relation to a requirement to provide a water main for any locality, means the day after whichever is the later of the following, that is to say—
  (a) the day on which the conditions specified in section 42 above are satisfied in relation to the requirement; and
  (b) the day on which the places where service pipes to premises in that locality will connect with the main are determined under subsection (3) above.

DEFINITIONS
  "relevant day": s.5.
  "water main": s.219(1).

GENERAL NOTE
  This section is concerned with the time allocated to a water undertaker to complete the laying of any requisitioned water main and also the route of such a main.
  A water undertaker will be in breach of the duty in s.41 if it has not laid the main within three months of the "relevant day", as defined in subs. (5). The time for compliance with a mains requisition may be extended in accordance with the provisions of subs. (2). The locality of the water main provided will clearly affect the costs of subsequent service pipes. Statutory provisions prior to the Water Act 1989 used the term "necessary mains" and disputes about the precise discretion of the water authority to determine the location of a main produced a body of litigation including *Cherwell District Council (formerly Banbury Borough Council)* v. *Thames Water Authority (formerly Oxfordshire and District Water Board)* [1975] 1 W.L.R. 448 and *Royco Homes* v. *Southern Water Authority* [1979] 1 W.L.R. 1366. The route for a requisition main in subs. (3) is to be determined by agreement between the parties or, failing that, arbitration based on the more flexible formulation that the location of the main should enable

the service pipes to be connected "at the places at which it is reasonable in all the circumstances" for them to be connected.

Domestic connections

Duty to make connections with main

45.—(1) Subject to the following provisions of this section and to sections 46 and 47 below, it shall be the duty of a water undertaker (in accordance with section 51 below) to make a connection under this section where the owner or occupier of any premises in the undertaker's area which—

    (a) consist in the whole or any part of a building; or

    (b) are premises on which any person is proposing to erect any building or part of a building,

serves a notice on the undertaker requiring it, for the purpose of providing a supply of water for domestic purposes to that building or part of a building, to connect a service pipe to those premises with one of the undertaker's water mains.

(2) Where a notice has been served for the purposes of this section, the duty imposed by subsection (1) above shall be a duty, at the expense of the person serving the notice, to make the connection required by the notice if—

    (a) the main with which the service pipe is required to be connected is neither a trunk main nor a water main which is or is to be used solely for the purpose of supplying water otherwise than for domestic purposes; and

    (b) such conditions as the undertaker may have imposed under sections 47 to 50 below have been satisfied;

and, subject to section 51 below, that duty shall arise whether or not the service pipe to which the notice relates has been laid when the notice is served.

(3) A notice for the purposes of this section—

    (a) shall be accompanied or supplemented by all such information as the undertaker may reasonably require; and

    (b) if the notice has effect so that a requirement is imposed on the undertaker by virtue of section 46(4) below, shall set out the matters that have given rise to the imposition of that requirement;

but, subject to section 51(5) below and without prejudice to the effect (if any) of any other contravention of this subsection, a failure to provide information in pursuance of the obligation to supplement such a notice shall not invalidate that notice.

(4) The duty imposed on a water undertaker by this section shall be owed to the person who served the notice by virtue of which the duty arises.

(5) Where a duty is owed by virtue of subsection (4) above to any person, any breach of that duty which causes that person to sustain loss or damage shall be actionable at the suit of that person; but, in any proceedings brought against a water undertaker in pursuance of this subsection, it shall be a defence for the undertaker to show that it took all reasonable steps and exercised all due diligence to avoid the breach.

(6) Where a water undertaker carries out any works which it is its duty under this section to carry out at another person's expense, the undertaker shall be entitled to recover from that person an amount equal to the expenses reasonably incurred by the undertaker in carrying out the works.

(7) Nothing in this section or in sections 46 to 51 below shall impose any duty on a water undertaker to connect a service pipe to any premises with a service pipe to any other premises.

(8) In the following provisions of this Chapter a notice served for the purposes of this section is referred to as a connection notice.

DEFINITIONS
 "domestic purposes": ss.218 and 219(1).
 "notice": s.219(1).
 "owner": s.219(1).
 "service pipe": s.219(1).

GENERAL NOTE
 This section imposes a duty on undertakers to make connections from their water mains to premises for domestic purposes as defined in s.218 following the service of a notice by an owner or occupier. The owner or occupier must occupy premises which consist of the whole or any part of a building or are premises on which any person is proposing to erect any building or part of a building (subs. (1)). The section must be read in conjunction with ss.46, 47 and 51, which specify the conditions that an undertaker may impose and which relate to the enforcement of the duty contained in s.45. Section 45(6) entitles an undertaker to recover costs or works which the undertaker has carried out from the person who serves the connection notice.
 The duty imposed by subs. (1) applies where the connection of the service pipe is to be made with the main which is not either a trunk main or a water main, which is to be used for supplying water for non-domestic purposes (subs. (2)(a)). The connection notice shall be accompanied by such information as the undertaker may reasonably require but failure to provide such information does not invalidate the connection notice (subs. (3)). Breach of the connection duty entitles the person serving the connection notice to commence a civil action for loss or damage occurring as a result of the undertaker's failure to perform his duty to connect under subs. (1). The undertaker will have a good defence to any proceedings where he can show that he took all reasonable steps and exercised all due diligence to avoid the breach (subs. (5)). This defence would encompass unanticipated climatic conditions. A water undertaker's duty to make connections with the main relates to premises which in subs. (1)(a) "consist in the whole or any part of the building". The Act does not define either "premises" or "building". In *West Mersea Urban District Council* v. *Fraser* [1950] K.B. 119, it was held that "premises" referred to property with a sufficient degree of permanency on the site it occupies, and therefore could include a permanently moored houseboat. In *Slaughter* v. *Sunderland Corporation* (1891) 60 L.J.M.C. 91 it was suggested that "a building should normally be understood to signify a construction or erection capable of enclosing some area of ground".
 The duty is owed in respect of the supply to a building rather than land associated with the building. Concern was raised during the passage of the Water Act 1989 in respect of s.45 that this interpretation could result in an undertaker being in default of its duty where problems occurred on a section of the service pipe on the customer's land which was outside the undertaker's responsibility. In reply, the Government stated that in these circumstances an undertaker could be expected to rely upon the defence of all reasonable steps (*Hansard*, H.L. Vol. 509, cols. 632–633) (s.45(8) of the Water Act 1989, now superseded by s.54(2) of this Act).

Duty to carry out ancillary works for the purpose of making domestic connection

 46.—(1) Where a water undertaker is required to make a connection in pursuance of any connection notice, it shall also be the duty of the undertaker, at the expense of the person serving the notice, to carry out such of the works to which this section applies as need to be carried out before the connection can be made.
 (2) This section applies to the laying of so much of the service pipe to be connected with the water main as it is necessary, for the purpose of making that connection, to lay in a street.
 (3) In a case where—
 (a) the water main with which the service pipe is to be connected is situated in a street;
 (b) the premises consisting in the building or part of a building in question together with any land occupied with it abut on the part of the street where the main is situated; and
 (c) the service pipe to those premises will—
  (i) enter the premises otherwise than through an outer wall of a building abutting on the street; and
  (ii) have a stopcock fitted to it by the undertaker in the premises,

this section applies to the laying of so much of the service pipe as it is necessary, for the purpose of making the required connection, to lay in land between the boundary of the street and that stopcock.

(4) In a case where the connection notice is served in compliance with a requirement imposed by a notice by a local authority under section 80 below, this section applies to the laying of so much of the service pipe to be connected with a water main in pursuance of the connection notice as it is necessary, for the purpose of making the connection, to lay in land owned or occupied by a person who is certified by that authority—

(a) to have unreasonably refused his consent to the laying of the service pipe; or

(b) to have sought to make the giving of his consent subject to unreasonable conditions.

(5) Where a water main is alongside a street and within eighteen metres of the middle of that street, subsections (2) to (4) above shall have effect in relation to the laying, for the purpose of making a connection with that main, of a service pipe to any premises as if the street included so much of the land between the main and the boundary of the street as is not comprised in those premises or in any land occupied with those premises.

(6) It shall be the duty of any water undertaker making a connection in pursuance of a connection notice to ensure that a stopcock belonging to the undertaker is fitted to the service pipe which is connected.

(7) Subsections (4) to (6) of section 45 above shall have effect—

(a) in relation to any duties which, by virtue of a connection notice, are imposed on a water undertaker by this section; and

(b) in relation to any works which, by virtue of the service of such a notice, such an undertaker carries out under this section at another person's expense,

as they have effect by virtue of that notice in relation to the duty which arises under that section or, as the case may be, to works which the undertaker carries out under that section at another person's expense.

(8) Subject to subsection (9) below, a water undertaker may comply with any duty under this section to lay a service pipe by laying a water main instead; but nothing in section 45 above or this section shall impose any duty on a water undertaker to lay a water main where it has no power to lay a service pipe.

(9) Where a water undertaker exercises its power under subsection (8) above to lay a water main instead of a service pipe—

(a) paragraph (a) of section 51(1) below shall have effect as if any additional time reasonably required by reason of the laying of the main instead of the service pipe were included in the time allowed by that paragraph for the laying of the service pipe; but

(b) the expenses recoverable by virtue of section 45(6) and subsection (7) above shall not exceed such amount as it would have been reasonable for the undertaker to have incurred in laying a service pipe instead of the main.

DEFINITIONS
"connection notice": s.45(8).
"service pipe": s.219(1).
"stopcock": s.219(1).
"street": s.219(1).

GENERAL NOTE
This section provides for an undertaker's duty to carry out ancillary works for the purpose of making a domestic connection in accordance with a notice served under s.45(1).

The section applies to the laying so much of a service pipe which is to be connected to the water main as is necessary for the purpose of making the connection between the water main and the customer's premises (consisting of a building and land occupied with the building).

Subsection (4) is concerned with the service of a connection notice by a local authority under the provisions of s.80 where the owner or occupier of the premises has unreasonably refused to consent to the laying of a service pipe or seeks to make the laying of a service pipe subject to unreasonable conditions.

Subsection (6) is concerned with an undertaker's duty in pursuance of making a connection with the water main to fit a stopcock to the service pipe.

Subsection (8) enables a water undertaker to comply with the s.46 duty to lay a service pipe by laying a water main instead. The decision to lay a water main, rather than a service pipe, does not permit the undertaker to recover any extra expenses incurred, though the time for compliance with its duty to lay the service pipe and make connections will be extended and the expenses recoverable by virtue of s.45(6) and (7) shall not exceed the cost of an undertaker's laying a service pipe instead of a main (subs. (9)).

Conditions of connection with water main

47.—(1) Subject to subsection (3) and sections 48 to 50 below, where the owner or occupier of any premises ("the relevant premises") serves a connection notice on a water undertaker, the undertaker may make compliance with one or more of the requirements specified in subsection (2) below a condition of its complying with the duties to which it is subject by virtue of that notice.

(2) The requirements mentioned in subsection (1) above are—

(a) a requirement that such security as the undertaker may reasonably require has been provided for the discharge of any obligations imposed by virtue of section 45(6) or 46(7)(b) above on the person who served the connection notice;

(b) a requirement, in a case where the connection required by the connection notice is necessary as a consequence of a disconnection made by reason of any person's failure to pay any charges, that the person serving the connection notice has paid any amount owed by him to the undertaker—

(i) in respect of a supply of water to the relevant premises; or

(ii) in respect of expenses incurred in the making of the disconnection;

(c) a requirement that a meter for use in determining the amount of any charges which have been or may be fixed in relation to the relevant premises by reference to volume has been installed and connected either—

(i) by the undertaker; or

(ii) in accordance with specifications approved by the undertaker;

(d) a requirement that—

(i) so much of the service pipe to the relevant premises as does not belong to, or fall to be laid by, the undertaker; and

(ii) the plumbing of the premises,

comply with specifications approved by the undertaker for the purpose of ensuring that it will be reasonably practicable for such a meter as is mentioned in paragraph (c) above to be installed and connected as so mentioned;

(e) a requirement that a separate service pipe has been provided—

(i) to each house or building on the relevant premises; or

(ii) where different parts of a building on the relevant premises are separately occupied, to each of those parts or to any of them;

(f) a requirement, in relation to the relevant premises—

(i) that such a requirement as may be imposed under section 66 below has been complied with; or

(ii) in a case where such a requirement could be imposed but for there already being such a cistern as is mentioned in that section, that the cistern and its float-operated valve are in good repair;

    (g) a requirement that there is no contravention in relation to the water fittings used or to be used in connection with—
        (i) the supply of water to the relevant premises; or
        (ii) the use of water in those premises,
      of such of the requirements of regulations under section 74 below as are prescribed for the purposes of this paragraph; and
    (h) a requirement that every such step has been taken as has been specified in any notice served on any person under section 75 below in relation to the relevant premises.

(3) A condition shall not be imposed by a water undertaker under this section on a person who has served a connection notice except by a counter-notice served on that person before the end of the period of fourteen days beginning with the day after the service of the connection notice.

(4) This section shall be without prejudice to the provisions of sections 233 and 372 of the Insolvency Act 1986 (conditions of supply after insolvency).

DEFINITIONS
    "connection notice": s.45(8).
    "meter": s.219(1).
    "service pipe": s.219(1) and (2).

GENERAL NOTE
    This section specifies the conditions a water undertaker may impose before it complies with its duty to make a connection as a result of a connection notice served under s.45(1).
    Under subs. (2)(c) and (d) the undertaker may require as a condition of connection the installation of a water meter, or of plumbing to enable one to be fitted at a later date, even if the undertaker has no immediate intention of charging via this method (see s.49).
    The apparent intention is to facilitate a transition to metering should undertakers wish to adopt this as a basis for charging customers at some stage in the future.
    Compliance with the undertaker's connection duty may also be made subject to the provision of such security as the undertaker may reasonably require (subs. (2)(a)) and payment of any sum due to the undertaker where the service of a reconnection notice follows a disconnection made by reason of the customer's failure to pay outstanding charges (subs. (2)(b)).

Interest on sums deposited in pursuance of the deposit condition

48.—(1) Where for the purposes of subsection (2)(a) of section 47 above any sums have been deposited with a water undertaker by way of security for the discharge of any obligation, the undertaker shall pay interest at such rate as may be determined either—
    (a) by the undertaker with the approval of the Director; or
    (b) in default of a determination under paragraph (a) above, by the Director,
on every sum of 50p so deposited for every three months during which it remains in the hands of the undertaker.

(2) An approval or determination by the Director for the purposes of this section—
    (a) may be given or made in relation to a particular case or description of cases or generally; and
    (b) may be revoked at any time.

GENERAL NOTE
    This section makes provision for the payment of interest by undertakers on sums deposited with a water undertaker by virtue of s.47(2)(a).

Supplemental provisions with respect to the metering conditions

49.—(1) The power conferred on a water undertaker to impose conditions under section 47 above for the purposes of metering—
    (a) shall be exercisable in relation to any premises even if the undertaker has no immediate intention, when the power is exercised, of fixing charges in relation to those premises by reference to volume; but

(b) shall not be exercisable so as to require the alteration or removal of any pipe laid or plumbing installed before April 1, 1989.

(2) Specifications approved by any water undertaker for the purposes of subsection (2)(c) or (d) of section 47 above may be approved—
(a) in relation to particular premises; or
(b) by being published in such manner as the undertaker considers appropriate, in relation to premises generally or to any description of premises.

(3) Any dispute between a water undertaker and any other person as to the terms of any condition imposed under section 47 above for the purposes of metering shall be referred to the arbitration of a single arbitrator appointed—
(a) by agreement between the undertaker and that person; or
(b) in default of agreement, by the Secretary of State.

(4) References in this section to the imposition of a condition under section 47 above for the purposes of metering are references to the imposition of conditions by virtue of subsection (2)(c) or (d) of that section.

GENERAL NOTE
Section 49 deals with supplemental provisions following the exercise by a water undertaker of its power under s.47 to impose conditions in consequence of the service of a connection notice.

The power to impose a condition relating to the installation of a meter for use in determining the amount of any charges due from a customer is exercisable in relation to any premises under subs. (1)(a) even if the undertaker has no immediate intention, when the power is exercised, of fixing charges in relation to those premises by reference to volume. The use of this power is restricted so that a water undertaker cannot require the alteration or removal of any pipe laid or plumbing installed before April 1, 1989 (s.49(1)). Any dispute between a water undertaker and customer regarding metering conditions may be referred to arbitration (subs. (3)).

Restriction on imposition of condition requiring separate service pipes

50.—(1) This section applies where the effect of a connection notice served in respect of any house is to require a service pipe to that house to be connected with a water main with which it has previously been connected.

(2) Where this section applies, the water undertaker on which the connection notice is served shall not be entitled to make the reconnection subject to any such condition as, apart from this section, may be imposed by virtue of section 47(2)(e) above unless the undertaker would have been entitled under section 64 below to require the provision of a separate service pipe if the reconnection had already been made.

DEFINITIONS
"connection notice": s.45(8).
"house": s.219(1).
"service pipe": s.219(1) and (2).
"water main": s.219(1) and (2).

GENERAL NOTE
This section restricts undertakers imposing conditions in relation to a connection notice requiring the provision of separate service pipes under s.47(2)(e). A water undertaker's requirement to impose a s.47(2)(e) notice shall not have effect unless the undertaker would have been entitled under s.64 to require the provision of a separate service pipe.

Time for performance of connection, etc. duties

51.—(1) A water undertaker shall not be in breach of a duty imposed by virtue of the service of a connection notice unless—
(a) in the case of a duty to lay any service pipe or to connect any service pipe to which such a duty relates, it has failed to lay that pipe or to make that connection as soon as reasonably practicable after the relevant day;

(b) in the case of a duty to connect a service pipe the whole of which has already been laid when the notice is served on the undertaker, it has failed to make the connection before the end of the period of fourteen days beginning with the relevant day.

(2) In any case in which a water undertaker is subject to any such duty as is mentioned in subsection (1)(a) above, it shall be presumed, unless the contrary is shown in relation to that case, that the period of 21 days beginning with the relevant day is the period within which it is reasonably practicable for a water undertaker—

(a) to lay so much of any service pipe; and

(b) to fit such stopcock,

as it is necessary to lay or fit in that case for connecting a water main in a street with a service pipe at the boundary of any premises which abut on the part of the street where the main is situated.

(3) Where—

(a) a connection notice is served in respect of any premises; and

(b) at the time when the notice is served, the customer's part of the service pipe to those premises has not been laid,

the duties of the undertaker under sections 45 and 46 above shall not arise by virtue of that notice until the person serving the notice, having obtained the necessary consents from the owners and occupiers of any affected land, has, at his own expense, laid so much of the service pipe as it is necessary, for the purpose of making the connection, to lay otherwise than in a street or in land mentioned in subsections (3) to (5) of section 46 above.

(4) In subsection (3) above the reference to the customer's part of the service pipe to any premises is a reference to so much of the service pipe to those premises as falls to be laid otherwise than by the water undertaker in pursuance of section 46 above.

(5) Where—

(a) a person who has served a connection notice on a water undertaker has failed to comply with his obligation under section 45(3)(a) above to supplement that notice with information required by the undertaker; and

(b) that requirement was made by the undertaker at such a time before the end of the period within which the undertaker is required to comply with the duties imposed by virtue of the notice as gave that person a reasonable opportunity to provide the required information within that period,

the undertaker may delay its compliance with those duties until a reasonable time after the required information is provided.

(6) In this section "the relevant day," in relation to a duty imposed on a water undertaker by virtue of a connection notice, means the day after whichever is the latest of the following days, that is to say—

(a) the day on which the notice was served on the undertaker;

(b) in a case where it is necessary for the person serving the notice to lay any service pipe after serving the notice, the day on which a notice stating that the pipe has been laid is served on the undertaker;

(c) the day on which all such conditions are satisfied as the undertaker has, under sections 47 to 50 above, made conditions of its compliance with that duty.

DEFINITIONS

"notice": s.219(1).

"relevant day": subs. (6).

"service pipe": s.219(1) and (2).

"stopcock": s.219(1).

"street": s.219(1).

"water main": s.219(1) and (2).

GENERAL NOTE
This section contains the detailed time limit in respect of performance of a water undertaker's connection duty contained in s.45. Note the defence in s.45(6) regarding the circumstances in which it can be shown that an undertaker took all reasonable steps and exercised all due diligence to avoid any breach of duty.

Subsection (1) specifies the circumstances in which an undertaker will be in breach of his duty to lay any service pipe (subs. (1)(a)), and his duty to connect a service pipe which has already been laid when the connection notice has been served upon the undertaker (subs. (1)(b)).

Subsection (2) establishes a presumption that it is reasonably practicable for an undertaker to lay or connect any service pipe and fit a stopcock to a water main within a period of 21 days beginning with the "relevant day" defined in subs. (6).

Subsection (3) makes provision that a water undertaker's duties under either s.45 or s.46 shall not arise in consequence of the service of a connection notice in circumstances where at the time of service of the notice the customer's part of the service pipe has not been laid.

Subsection (5) concerns extensions of time for performance of a water undertaker's duty in circumstances where information has not been supplied by a customer as required by s.45(3)(a).

Domestic supplies

The domestic supply duty

52.—(1) The domestic supply duty of a water undertaker in relation to any premises is a duty, until there is an interruption of that duty—
  (a) to provide to those premises such a supply of water as (so far as those premises are concerned) is sufficient for domestic purposes; and
  (b) to maintain the connection between the undertaker's water main and the service pipe by which that supply is provided to those premises.

(2) Subject to the following provisions of this section and to section 53 below, a water undertaker shall owe a domestic supply duty in relation to any premises to which this section applies and which are situated in the area of the undertaker if—
  (a) a demand for a supply of water for domestic purposes has been made, in accordance with subsection (5) below, to the undertaker in respect of those premises; or
  (b) those premises are premises to which this section applies by reason of a supply of water provided before September 1, 1989,
and there has been no interruption of the domestic supply duty in relation to those premises since that demand was made or, as the case may be, since the beginning of September 1, 1989.

(3) This section applies to any premises if—
  (a) they consist in the whole or any part of a building and are connected by means of a service pipe to a water main; and
  (b) the requirements of subsection (4) below are satisfied in relation to those premises.

(4) The requirements of this subsection are satisfied in relation to any premises if—
  (a) the pipe by means of which the premises are connected to the water main in question was first connected with that main in pursuance of a connection notice served in respect of those premises;
  (b) that pipe was the means by which a supply of water from that main was being supplied to those premises for domestic purposes immediately before September 1, 1989;
  (c) the condition specified in paragraph (b) above would be satisfied in relation to the premises if any service pipe to those premises had not been temporarily disconnected for the purposes of any necessary works which were being carried out immediately before September 1, 1989; or
  (d) the condition specified in any of the preceding paragraphs—

    (i) has been satisfied in relation to the premises at any time on or after September 1, 1989; and

    (ii) would continue to be satisfied in relation to the premises had not the whole or any part of a service pipe to those premises, or the main with which such a pipe had been connected, been renewed (on one or more previous occasions).

(5) For the purposes of this section a demand in respect of any premises is made in accordance with this subsection if it is made—

  (a) by the person who is the occupier of the premises at the time when the demand is made; or

  (b) by a person who is the owner of the premises at that time and agrees with the undertaker to pay all the undertaker's charges in respect of the supply demanded.

(6) For the purposes of this section—

  (a) there is an interruption of the domestic supply duty owed by a water undertaker in relation to any premises if that supply is cut off by anything done by the undertaker in exercise of any of its disconnection powers, other than a disconnection or cutting off for the purposes of the carrying out of any necessary works; and

  (b) a domestic supply duty owed in relation to any premises shall not be treated as interrupted by reason only of a change of the occupier or owner of the premises.

(7) Nothing in this section shall impose any duty on a water undertaker—

  (a) to provide a supply of water directly from, or maintain any connection with, a water main which is a trunk main or is or is to be used solely for the purpose of supplying water otherwise than for domestic purposes; or

  (b) to provide a supply of water to any premises, or maintain the connection between a water main and a service pipe to any premises, during any period during which it is reasonable—

    (i) for the supply of water to those premises to be cut off or reduced; or

    (ii) for the pipe to be disconnected,

for the purposes of the carrying out of any necessary works.

(8) In this section references to the disconnection powers of a water undertaker are references to the powers conferred on the undertaker by any of sections 60 to 62 and 75 below.

DEFINITIONS

   "connection notice": s.45(8).
   "domestic purposes": ss.218 and 219(1).
   "service pipe": s.219(1) and (2).
   "trunk main": s.219(1).
   "water main": s.219(1) and (2).

GENERAL NOTE

   This section lays down the general duty of each water undertaker to provide a "sufficient" supply of water to buildings for domestic purposes, and applies where a service pipe has been connected following the procedure detailed in ss.45–51 or where a service pipe was the means of supply immediately before September 1, 1989, even if temporarily disconnected for necessary works, or where any of these conditions exists after September 1, 1989. The duty is owed where the conditions in subs. (2) apply but is subject to the exceptions defined in subs. (6). Breach of the duty resulting in loss or damage to the consumer is actionable under s.54(2) but is subject to the defence of having taken all reasonable steps and having exercised all due care.

Conditions of compliance with domestic supply duty

   53.—(1) Where a demand for the purposes of section 52(2) above has been made to a water undertaker in respect of any premises ("the relevant premises"), the undertaker may make compliance with one or more of the requirements specified in subsection (2) below a condition of providing his first supply of water in compliance with that demand.

(2) The requirements mentioned in subsection (1) above are—

(a) a requirement, in a case where the demand is made as a consequence of a supply having been cut off by reason of any person's failure to pay any charges, that the person making the demand has paid any amount owed by him to the undertaker—

(i) in respect of a supply of water to the relevant premises; or

(ii) in respect of expenses incurred in cutting off any such supply;

(b) a requirement, in relation to the relevant premises

(i) that such a requirement as may be imposed under section 66 below has been complied with; or

(ii) in a case where such a requirement could be imposed but for there already being such a cistern as is mentioned in that section, that the cistern and its float-operated valve are in good repair;

(c) a requirement that there is no contravention in relation to the water fittings used or to be used in connection with—

(i) the supply of water to the relevant premises; or

(ii) the use of water in those premises,

of such of the requirements of regulations under section 74 below as are prescribed for the purposes of this subsection; and

(d) a requirement that every such step has been taken as has been specified in any notice served on any person under section 75 below in relation to the relevant premises.

(3) This section shall be without prejudice to the provisions of sections 233 and 372 of the Insolvency Act 1986 (conditions of supply after insolvency).

GENERAL NOTE

This section deals with the conditions which a water undertaker may impose following a demand made by a customer under s.52(2) and (5) for a domestic supply of water.

The conditions which an undertaker may impose relate firstly to payment of any amount owed to the undertaker as regards a domestic supply, arising out of a disconnection for non-payment of charges; secondly, to a power to require the installation of float-operated valve cisterns in certain cases; thirdly, to requirements relating to plumbing within the customer's premises; and, fourthly, to a requirement that steps have been taken to comply with a notice served pursuant to s.75. Section 75 provides a power for water undertakers to prevent damage and to take steps to prevent contamination and waste of water resources.

Enforcement of domestic supply duty

54.—(1) A duty imposed on a water undertaker under section 52 above—

(a) to provide a supply of water to any premises; or

(b) to maintain a connection between a water main and a service pipe by which such a supply is provided,

shall be owed to the consumer.

(2) Where a duty is owed by virtue of this section to any person, any breach of that duty which causes that person to sustain loss or damage shall be actionable at the suit of that person; but, in any proceedings brought against a water undertaker in pursuance of this subsection, it shall be a defence for the undertaker to show that it took all reasonable steps and exercised all due diligence to avoid the breach.

GENERAL NOTE

This section details how the domestic water supply duty may be enforced by the consumer.

Subsection (1) provides that the duty imposed on a water undertaker under s.52 to provide a domestic supply shall be owed to the customer.

Subsection (2) provides that breach of that s.52 duty shall be actionable in civil proceedings by the consumer, but this is subject to a water undertaker's defence that it took all reasonable steps and exercised all due care to avoid the breach of duty.

Other supplies

Supplies for non-domestic purposes

55.—(1) This section applies where the owner or occupier of any premises in the area of a water undertaker requests the undertaker to provide a supply of water to those premises and—

(a) the premises are premises which do not consist in the whole or any part of a building; or

(b) the requested supply is for purposes other than domestic purposes.

(2) Where this section applies, it shall be the duty of the water undertaker, in accordance with such terms and conditions as may be determined under section 56 below—

(a) to take any such steps as may be so determined in order to enable the undertaker to provide the requested supply; and

(b) having taken any such steps, to provide that supply.

(3) A water undertaker shall not be required by virtue of this section to provide a new supply to any premises, or to take any steps to enable it to provide such a supply, if the provision of that supply or the taking of those steps would—

(a) require the undertaker, in order to meet all its existing obligations to supply water for domestic or other purposes, together with its probable future obligations to supply buildings and parts of buildings with water for domestic purposes, to incur unreasonable expenditure in carrying out works; or

(b) otherwise put at risk the ability of the undertaker to meet any of the existing or probable future obligations mentioned in paragraph (a) above.

(4) A water undertaker shall not be required by virtue of this section to provide a new supply to any premises, or to take any steps to enable it to provide such a supply, if there is a contravention in relation to the water fittings used or to be used in connection with—

(a) the supply of water to those premises; or

(b) the use of water in those premises,

of such of the requirements of regulations under section 74 below as are prescribed for the purposes of this subsection.

(5) Where—

(a) a request has been made by any person to a water undertaker for the purposes of subsection (2) above; and

(b) the steps which the undertaker is required to take by virtue of that request include steps for the purpose of obtaining any necessary authority for, or agreement to, any exercise by the undertaker of any of its powers or the carrying out by the undertaker of any works,

the failure of the undertaker to acquire the necessary authority or agreement shall not affect any liability of that person, under any term or condition in accordance with which those steps are taken, to re-imburse the undertaker in respect of some or all of the expenses incurred by the undertaker in taking those steps.

(6) Nothing in this section shall impose any duty on a water undertaker to provide a supply of water to any premises during any period during which it is reasonable for the supply of water to those premises to be cut off or reduced for the purposes of the carrying out of any necessary works.

(7) The duty of a water undertaker to supply water under this section at the request of any person, and any terms and conditions determined under section 56 below in default of agreement between the undertaker and that person, shall have effect as if contained in such an agreement.

(8) Except so far as otherwise provided by the terms and conditions determined under section 56 below in relation to any supply, the duties of a

water undertaker under this section shall have effect subject to the provisions of sections 60 to 63 and 75 below.

DEFINITIONS
"domestic purposes": ss.218 and 219(1).
"prescribed": s.219(1).

GENERAL NOTE
This section is concerned with an undertaker's duty to supply water to consumers for non-domestic purposes.

Under s.55 a water undertaker is not obliged to provide a new non-domestic supply where this would involve the undertaker in unreasonable expenditure or put at risk its ability to meet its current and future obligations to supply water for domestic and non-domestic purposes. The limitations on the undertaker's obligations under subs. (3) relate to "new" supplies. This provision caused the House of Lords concern during the Committee stage of the Water Act 1989 (s.46 of the Water Act 1989), since it implied that existing non-domestic customers could demand as of right additional supplies even though this might cause operational difficulties for the undertaker. The Government acknowledged that few existing arrangements between non-domestic users and water undertakers contained quantity restrictions, and hinted that in future it would be a prudent precaution for water undertakers to include such provisions to avoid being obliged to provide increased supplies (*Hansard*, H.L. Vol. 508, cols. 1173–1176). A request from an existing customer for a substantially increased demand of water might amount to a "new" supply, thus bringing in the protection of subs. (3), but there is no statutory definition of "new", and this must ultimately be a question of fact and degree.

An undertaker will not be required to provide a new supply for non-domestic purposes where there is a contravention of any regulations prescribed under s.74 relating to water fittings within the premises to be supplied with water for non-domestic purposes (subs. (4)).

The failure of an undertaker to obtain authorities or agreements in pursuance of the undertaker's duty to supply water for non-domestic purposes will not prevent the undertaker from obtaining reimbursement of its expenses and taking steps to acquire the necessary authorities or agreements (subs. (5)).

An undertaker will not be in breach of its duty under s.55 where the supply of water is cut off or reduced to enable the undertaker to carry out any necessary works (subs. (6)).

Determinations on requests for non-domestic supplies

56.—(1) Subject to subsection (3) below, any terms or conditions or other matter which falls to be determined for the purposes of a request made by any person to a water undertaker for the purposes of section 55 above shall be determined—

(a) by agreement between that person and the water undertaker; or

(b) in default of agreement, by the Director according to what appears to him to be reasonable.

(2) Subject to subsection (3) below, the Director shall also determine any dispute arising between any person and a water undertaker by virtue of subsection (3) or (4) of section 55 above.

(3) The Director may, instead of himself making a determination under subsection (1) or (2) above, refer any matter submitted to him for determination under that subsection to the arbitration of such person as he may appoint.

(4) For the purposes of any determination under this section by the Director or any person appointed by him it shall be for a water undertaker to show that it should not be required to comply with a request made for the purposes of section 55 above.

(5) The charges in respect of a supply provided in compliance with any request made for the purposes of section 55 above—

(a) shall not be determined by the Director or a person appointed by him, except in so far as, at the time of the request, no provision is in force by virtue of a charges scheme under section 143 below in respect of supplies of the applicable description; and

(b) in so far they do fall to be determined, shall be so determined having regard to the desirability of the undertaker's—

(i) recovering the expenses of complying with its obligations under section 55 above; and

(ii) securing a reasonable return on its capital.

(6) To the extent that subsection (5)(a) above excludes any charges from a determination under this section, those charges shall be fixed from time to time by a charges scheme under section 143 below, but not otherwise.

(7) The determination of any matter under this section shall be without prejudice to the provisions of sections 233 and 372 of the Insolvency Act 1986 (conditions of supply after insolvency).

GENERAL NOTE

Where a request is made for a non-domestic supply under s.55 the provisions of s.56 are of relevance in determining the terms or conditions upon which such a supply will be made. In the first instance the customer and water undertaker shall agree terms, but in default of agreement the Director will impose such conditions as appear to him to be reasonable. The Director is empowered to determine any dispute arising between the customer and the water undertaker in relation to a non-domestic supply (subs. (2)).

Under subs. (3) the Director may refer any matter submitted to him under subss. (1) and (2) of this section to arbitration. The amount of any charges levied by a water undertaker in respect of a non-domestic supply of water are to be determined in accordance with the provisions of subs. (5), and subs. (6) enables, in certain circumstances, those charges to be fixed by means of a charges scheme under s.143.

Duty to provide a supply of water etc. for fire-fighting

57.—(1) It shall be the duty of a water undertaker to allow any person to take water for extinguishing fires from any of its water mains or other pipes on which a fire-hydrant is fixed.

(2) Every water undertaker shall, at the request of the fire authority concerned, fix fire-hydrants on its water mains (other than its trunk mains) at such places as may be most convenient for affording a supply of water for extinguishing any fire which may break out within the area of the undertaker.

(3) It shall be the duty of every water undertaker to keep every fire-hydrant fixed on any of its water mains or other pipes in good working order and, for that purpose, to replace any such hydrant when necessary.

(4) It shall be the duty of a water undertaker to ensure that a fire authority has been supplied by the undertaker with all such keys as the authority may require for the fire-hydrants fixed on the water mains or other pipes of the undertaker.

(5) Subject to section 58(3) below, the expenses incurred by a water undertaker in complying with its obligations under subsections (2) to (4) above shall be borne by the fire authority concerned.

(6) Nothing in this section shall require a water undertaker to do anything which it is unable to do by reason of the carrying out of any necessary works.

(7) The obligations of a water undertaker under this section shall be enforceable under section 18 above by the Secretary of State.

(8) In addition, where a water undertaker is in breach of its obligations under this section, the undertaker shall be guilty of an offence and liable—

(a) on summary conviction, to a fine not exceeding the statutory maximum;

(b) on conviction on indictment, to a fine.

(9) In any proceedings against any water undertaker for an offence under subsection (8) above it shall be a defence for that undertaker to show that it took all reasonable steps and exercised all due diligence to avoid the commission of the offence.

(10) In this section "fire authority" has the same meaning as in the Fire Services Act 1947.

"fire authority": subs. (10).
"trunk mains": s.219(1).
"water mains": s.219(1) and (2).

GENERAL NOTE
This section imposes a duty on water undertakers to allow *any* persons to use water from any of its mains or other pipes to which a fire hydrant is affixed for the purpose of extinguishing fires.

Under subs. (2), at the request of a fire authority a water undertaker must fix fire hydrants on to its water mains "at such places as may be most convenient" for extinguishing fires which may break out. A water undertaker has a duty under subs. (3) to keep fire hydrants in good repair. Subject to s.58(3), an undertaker's expenses incurred in supplying fire hydrants at the request of fire authorities under subs. (2) and providing fire hydrant keys under subs. (4) are borne by the fire authority.

A water undertaker's obligations under s.57 are enforceable by the Secretary of State using s.18 enforcement orders, and in addition subs. (8) provides criminal sanctions for breach of the water undertaker's obligations subject to the defence in subs. (9) that the water undertaker took all reasonable steps and exercised all due diligence to avoid the commission of the offence in subs. (8). The offence in s.73(1)(c) of misusing water for purposes other than that for which it was supplied does not apply where it was used for fire fighting purposes (s.73(2)).

Specially requested fire-hydrants

58.—(1) A water undertaker shall, at the request of the owner or occupier of any factory or place of business, fix a fire-hydrant, to be used for extinguishing fires and not other purposes, at such place on any suitable water main or other pipe of the undertaker as is as near as conveniently possible to that factory or place of business.

(2) For the purposes of subsection (1) above a water main or other pipe is suitable, in relation to a factory or place of business, if—

(a) it is situated in a street which is in or near to that factory or place of business; and

(b) it is of sufficient dimensions to carry a hydrant and is not a trunk main.

(3) Subsection (5) of section 57 above shall not apply in relation to expenses incurred in compliance, in relation to a specially requested fire-hydrant, with the obligations under subsections (3) and (4) of that section.

(4) Any expenses incurred by a water undertaker—

(a) in complying with its obligations under subsection (1) above; or

(b) in complying, in relation to a specially requested fire-hydrant, with its obligations under section 57(3) or (4) above,

shall be borne by the owner or occupier of the factory or place of business in question, according to whether the person who made the original request for the hydrant did so in his capacity as owner or occupier.

(5) Subsections (6) to (9) of section 57 above shall apply in relation to the obligations of a water undertaker under this section as they apply to the obligations of a water undertaker under that section.

(6) In this section—

"factory" has the same meaning as in the Factories Act 1961; and
"specially requested fire-hydrant" means a fire-hydrant which—

(a) is fixed on a water main or other pipe of a water under-taker; and

(b) was fixed on that main or pipe (whether before or after it became such a main or pipe under the Water Act 1989) in pursuance of a request made by the owner or occupier of a factory or place of business.

"factory": subs. (6).
"owner": s.219(1).
"specially requested fire hydrant": subs. (6).

"trunk main": s.219(1).
"water main": s.219(1) and (2).

GENERAL NOTE

This section is concerned with the obligation upon water undertakers to supply fire hydrants at the request of factory owners and owners of other similar premises. The costs of supplying such fire hydrants are borne by the owner or occupier of the relevant factory or place of business. Section 57(6)–(9) applies to the provision of specially requested fire hydrants.

Supplies for other public purposes

59.—(1) A water undertaker shall, at the request of a sewerage undertaker, highway authority or local authority, provide, from such of its pipes as are of an appropriate capacity, a supply of water for cleansing sewers and drains, for cleansing and watering highways or, as the case may be, for supplying any public pumps, baths or wash-houses.

(2) A supply of water provided by a water undertaker under this section shall be provided upon such terms and conditions as may be reasonable.

(3) A water main or other pipe of a water undertaker shall be treated as of an appropriate capacity for the purposes of this section if and only if it has a fire-hydrant fixed on it.

(4) Nothing in this section shall require a water undertaker to do anything which it is unable to do by reason of the carrying out of any necessary works.

(5) The obligations of a water undertaker under this section shall be enforceable under section 18 above by the Director.

DEFINITIONS

"drains": s.219(1) and (2).
"highway authority": s.219(1).
"local authority": s.219(1).
"sewers": s.219(1) and (2).
"water main": s.219(1).

GENERAL NOTE

This section is concerned with the provision of water supplies by water undertakers to sewerage undertakers, highway authorities and local authorities for public purposes such as cleansing sewers and drains, cleansing and watering highways and supplying water to any public pumps, baths or wash-houses (subs. (1)).

Under subs. (2) the supply of water for such purposes is provided "upon such terms and conditions as may be reasonable". No provision is made in this section for arbitration; however, subs. (5) provides that the obligations of a water undertaker under s.59 are enforceable under s.18 by the Director.

Disconnections

Disconnections for the carrying out of necessary works

60.—(1) Subject to the following provisions of this section, a water undertaker may—

(a) disconnect a service pipe which, for the purposes of providing a supply of water to any premises, is connected with any water main of that undertaker; or

(b) otherwise cut off a supply of water to any premises,

if it is reasonable for the disconnection to be made, or the supply to be cut off, for the purposes of the carrying out of any necessary works.

(2) The power of a water undertaker under this section to cut off a supply of water shall include power to reduce a supply of water.

(3) Except in an emergency or in the case of a reduction which is immaterial, the power of a water undertaker under this section to cut off or reduce a supply shall be exercisable in relation to any premises only after the undertaker has served reasonable notice on the consumer of the proposal for the carrying out of the necessary works.

(4) Where a water undertaker exercises its power under this section to make any disconnection or to cut off or reduce a supply of water to any premises for the purposes of the carrying out of any necessary works, it shall owe a duty to the consumer to secure—

(a) that those works are carried out with reasonable dispatch; and

(b) that any supply of water to those premises for domestic purposes is interrupted for more than 24 hours for the purposes of the carrying out of those works only if an emergency supply has been made available (whether or not in pipes) within a reasonable distance of the premises.

(5) Any breach by a water undertaker of the duty owed by virtue of subsection (4) above which causes any person to whom it is owed to sustain loss or damage shall be actionable at the suit of that person.

DEFINITIONS

"consumer": s.93(1).
"domestic purposes": ss.218 and 219(1).
"necessary works": s.93(1).
"service pipe": s.219(1) and (2).
"water main": s.219(1).

GENERAL NOTE

This section provides water undertakers with the power to make disconnections in order to carry out necessary works (as defined in s.93(1)). The power only applies if it is reasonable for the disconnection to be made, and the power to cut off a supply of water also extends to reducing the level of supply (subs. (2)).

An undertaker must give the consumer reasonable notice of the proposed disconnection except in circumstances where the disconnection has to be made in an emergency or the reduction in the level of supply is immaterial (subs. (3)).

Where a disconnection or reduction in the level of supply has been made, a water undertaker owes a duty to the consumer to secure that the necessary works are completed with reasonable despatch and where a domestic supply is interrupted for a period in excess of 24 hours an alternative emergency supply must be made available (subs. (4)). Any breach of the duty owed to the consumer under subs. (4) is actionable by the consumer (subs. (5)).

Disconnections for non-payment of charges

61.—(1) Subject to the following provisions of this section, a water undertaker may disconnect a service pipe which for the purposes of providing a supply of water to any premises is connected with any water main of that undertaker, or may otherwise cut off a supply of water to any premises, if the occupier of the premises—

(a) is liable (whether in his capacity as occupier or under any agreement with the undertaker) to pay charges due to the undertaker in respect of the supply of water to those premises; and

(b) has failed to do so before the end of the period of seven days beginning with the day after he is served with notice requiring him to do so.

(2) Where—

(a) a water undertaker has served a notice for the purposes of paragraph (b) of subsection (1) above on a person; and

(b) within the period of seven days mentioned in that paragraph, that person serves a counter-notice on the undertaker stating that he disputes his liability to pay the charges in question,

the undertaker shall not in respect of that notice exercise his power by virtue of that subsection in relation to any premises except at a time when that person is the occupier of the premises and those charges are enforceable against that person in a manner specified in subsection (3) below.

(3) For the purposes of subsection (2) above charges are enforceable in a manner specified in this subsection against a person if—

(a) the undertaker is able to enforce a judgment against that person for the payment of the charges; or

(b) that person is in breach of an agreement entered into, since the service of his counter-notice, for the purpose of avoiding or settling proceedings by the undertaker for the recovery of the charges.

(4) A water undertaker which exercises its power under this section to disconnect any pipe or otherwise to cut off any supply of water may recover, from the person in respect of whose liability the power is exercised, any expenses reasonably incurred by the undertaker in making the disconnection or in otherwise cutting off the supply.

(5) Where—

(a) a water undertaker has power under this section to disconnect any pipe to any premises, or otherwise to cut off any supply to any premises; and

(b) a supply of water is provided to those premises and to other premises wholly or partly by the same service pipe,

the undertaker may exercise that power so as to cut off the supply to those other premises if and only if the same person is the occupier of the premises in relation to which the charges are due and of the other premises.

DEFINITIONS

"notice": s.219(1).
"service pipe": s.219(1) and (2).
"water main": s.219(1) and (2).

GENERAL NOTE

This section empowers water undertakers to make disconnections in respect of non-payment of charges. Such a power to cut off an essential service, even for non-payment of bills, has always proved politically controversial, especially as it is the low-paid who are likely to be most affected. Several attempts were made during Parliamentary proceedings in relation to the Water Act 1989 to remove the power of undertakers (s.49 of the Water Act 1989) to disconnect in such circumstances, or to require court proceedings in all cases. These attempts were unsuccessful, but undertakers' powers are restricted in two ways. First, there is the statutory restriction in subss. (2) and (3), which provide that where the customer disputes liability the undertaker may not disconnect in the absence of a court judgment or broken settlement. Failure by the undertaker to comply with these provisions is a criminal offence under s.63. Secondly, the undertaker is bound by the conditions of its instrument of appointment relating to disconnection, which include provision of a code of practice to be approved by the Director (see condition H of the model instrument of appointment). This in essence requires the undertaker to obtain a court judgment for arrears of debt in all cases before exercising its powers in relation to disconnection, unless the occupier was already in breach of a previous court judgment for payment of water supply charges. These provisions are enforceable by the Director under a s.18 Enforcement Order, and allow the Director greater flexibility to revise and develop the code of practice at later stages. During the Committee stage (relating to s.49) of the Water Act 1989, Lord Hesketh summarised the main differences between the procedures under the previous law and those which were being introduced under the Water Act 1989:

"First, and most importantly, instead of the undertaker being able to disconnect a domestic water supply because of non-payment without going through the courts, it will now in virtually every case have to take such action. Secondly, it is the county court rather than the magistrates' court which is to consider these cases. Thirdly, where county court action is taken, the company cannot then proceed to disconnection unless the charges remain unpaid. Fourthly, even then the undertaker should make reasonable attempts to contact the customer with a view to agreeing a payment arrangement, failing which the undertaker would give due notice of disconnection. Fifthly, these principles are to be written, together with other customers safeguards, into the licence itself, and will be enforceable by the Director General" (*Hansard*, H.L. Vol. 507, cols. 1300–1301).

A water undertaker which exercises its powers to disconnect under s.61 may recover its reasonable expenses in making the disconnection (subs. (4)). Subsection (5) is concerned with disconnection in circumstances where more than one set of premises is provided with a supply of water via the same service pipe.

Disconnections at request of customer

62.—(1) Subject to the following provisions of this section, a water undertaker may—

   (a) disconnect a service pipe which for the purposes of providing a supply
      of water to any premises is connected with any water main of that
      undertaker; or
   (b) otherwise cut off a supply of water to any premises,
if notice specifying the time after which a supply of water to those premises
will no longer be required has been served on the undertaker by a consumer
and that time has passed.

(2) No person shall be liable to a water undertaker for any expenses
incurred by the undertaker in exercising the power conferred on the undertaker by this section.

DEFINITIONS
   "consumer": s.93(1).
   "service pipe": s.219(1) and (2).

GENERAL NOTE
   This section empowers a water undertaker to disconnect a water supply to any premises in
circumstances where the customer has served a notice on the water undertaker indicating the
date from which the premises will be uninhabited. In such circumstances the costs of any
disconnection are borne by the undertaker (subs. (2)).

General duties of undertakers with respect to disconnections

63.—(1) Where a water undertaker—
   (a) disconnects a service pipe to any inhabited house, or otherwise cuts
      off a supply of water to such a house; and
   (b) does so without restoring the supply to that house before the end of
      the period of 24 hours beginning with the time when it is cut off,
the undertaker shall, no later than 48 hours after that time, serve notice that
it has cut off that supply on the local authority in whose area the house is
situated.

(2) A water undertaker which fails, without reasonable excuse, to serve a
notice on a local authority as required by subsection (1) above shall be guilty
of an offence under this section.

(3) A water undertaker shall be guilty of an offence under this section if—
   (a) it disconnects a service pipe to any premises, or otherwise cuts off a
      supply of water to any premises, in a case in which it has no power to
      do so under sections 60 to 62 above, section 75 below or any other
      enactment; or
   (b) in disconnecting any such pipe or cutting off any such supply it fails,
      without reasonable excuse, to comply with any requirement of the
      provisions in pursuance of which it disconnects the pipe or cuts off the
      supply.

(4) A water undertaker which is guilty of an offence under this section
shall be liable, on summary conviction, to a fine not exceeding level 3 on the
standard scale.

DEFINITIONS
   "house": s.219(1).
   "local authority": s.219(1).
   "service pipe": s.219(1) and (2).

GENERAL NOTE
   This section details the general duties of undertakers regarding the disconnection of water
supplies to a house.
   Where a disconnection takes place and the supply is not restored within 24 hours, the
undertaker must serve a notice on the local authority in whose area the house is situated,
notifying the authority of disconnection no later than 48 hours after the time disconnection took
place. No other body has a similar statutory right of notification, but the Director has powers
under the instrument of appointment to require information both under the instrument of
appointment and under s.203. Customer service committees will also have the right to be kept

informed of the general situation since under condition H8 of the model instrument of appointment, the undertaker is required every six months to inform its customer service committees of the aggregate number of domestic disconnections for non-payment of charges, broken down into the undertaker's operating divisions.

A water undertaker who fails without reasonable excuse to serve a notice on the relevant local authority is guilty of an offence under s.63(2). A water undertaker also commits an offence if it disconnects any service pipe serving any premises where it has no power under ss.60, 61, 62, 75 and any other enactment to make the disconnection (subs. (3)).

Means of supply

Supply by means of separate service pipes

64.—(1) Subject to the following provisions of this section, a water undertaker may require the provision of a separate service pipe to any premises within its area which—

    (a) consist in a house or any other building or part of a building, being, in the case of a part of a building, a part which is separately occupied; and

    (b) are already supplied with water by the undertaker but do not have a separate service pipe.

(2) Where the supply of water to two or more houses was provided to those houses before April 15, 1981, wholly or partly by the same service pipe and continues to be so provided, the water undertaker shall not require the provision of separate service pipes to those houses until—

    (a) the service pipe, in so far as it belongs to a person other than the undertaker, becomes so defective as to require renewal or is no longer sufficient to meet the requirements of those houses;

    (b) a payment in respect of the supply of water to any of those houses remains unpaid after the end of the period for which it is due;

    (c) the houses are, by structural alterations to one or more of them, converted into a larger number of houses;

    (d) the owner or occupier of any of those houses has interfered with, or allowed another person to interfere with, the existing service pipe and thereby caused the supply of water to any house to be interfered with; or

    (e) the undertaker has reasonable grounds for believing that such interference as is mentioned in paragraph (d) above is likely to take place.

(3) If, in the case of any such premises as are described in subsection (1) above, the water undertaker which provides a supply of water to those premises serves notice on the consumer requiring the provision of a separate service pipe and setting out the power of the undertaker under subsection (4) below—

    (a) that consumer shall, within three months after the service of the notice, lay so much of the required pipe as the undertaker is not under a duty to lay by virtue of paragraph (b) below;

    (b) sections 45 to 51 above shall apply as if that consumer had by a connection notice required the undertaker to connect the separate service pipe to those premises with the undertaker's water main;

    (c) that consumer shall be presumed, without prejudice to his power to make further demands and requests—

        (i) in so far as those premises were provided before the service of the notice with a supply of water for domestic purposes, to have made a demand for the purposes of section 52 above that such a supply is provided by means of the separate service pipe; and

        (ii) in so far as those premises were provided before the service of the notice with a supply of water for other purposes, to have requested the undertaker to provide the same supply by means of that pipe as was provided before the service of the notice;

and

(d) on providing a supply of water to those premises by means of the separate service pipe, the undertaker may cut off any supply replaced by that supply and may make such disconnections of pipes by which the replaced supply was provided as it thinks fit.

(4) If a person upon whom a notice has been served for the purposes of subsection (3) above fails to comply with the notice, the water undertaker may—

(a) itself carry out the works which that person was required to carry out; and

(b) recover the expenses reasonably incurred by the undertaker in doing so from that person.

(5) Without prejudice—

(a) to the power of a water undertaker by virtue of paragraph (b) of subsection (3) above to impose conditions under section 47 above; or

(b) to the power conferred by virtue of paragraph (d) of that subsection, any works carried out by a water undertaker by virtue of the provisions of the said paragraph (b) or of subsection (4) above shall be necessary works for the purposes of this Chapter.

DEFINITIONS
   "connection notice": ss.45(8) and 93(1).
   "consumer": s.93(1).
   "domestic purposes"; s 218 and 219(1).
   "house": s.219(1).
   "notice": s.219(1).
   "owner": s.219(1).
   "service pipe": s.219(1) and (2).

GENERAL NOTE
   This section gives a water undertaker the power to require the provision of separate service pipes for a house or other building which is separately occupied. Where a reconnection to a main is being made under the provisions of subs. (2)(e), the undertaker cannot insist as a condition of reconnection on separate service pipes unless he would have been entitled to do so under s.50(2).
   Subsection (2) sets out the circumstances in which the water undertaker may require the provision of a separate service pipe. A water undertaker exercises its power to require the provision of a separate service pipe by serving a notice on the consumer (subs. (3)) and the consumer has a period of three months within which to lay so much of the pipe as the undertaker is not under a duty to lay by virtue of ss.45–51. Those sections of the Act apply as if the consumer had by connection notice required the water undertaker to connect the consumer's premises to the water main by means of a separate service pipe. Should the consumer fail to comply with the subs. (3) notice the undertaker can carry out the works and recover the costs from the consumer.

Duties of undertakers as respects constancy and pressure

65.—(1) Subject to the following provisions of this section, it shall be the duty of a water undertaker to cause the water in such of its water mains and other pipes as—

(a) are used for providing supplies of water for domestic purposes; or

(b) have fire-hydrants fixed on them,

to be laid on constantly and at such a pressure as will cause the water to reach to the top of the top-most storey of every building within the undertaker's area.

(2) Nothing in subsection (1) above shall require a water undertaker to provide a supply of water at a height greater than that to which it will flow by gravitation through its water mains from the service reservoir or tank from which that supply is taken.

(3) For the purposes of this section a water undertaker shall be entitled to choose the service reservoir or tank from which any supply is to be taken.

(4) Nothing in subsection (1) above shall impose any duty on a water undertaker to maintain the constancy or pressure of any supply of water during any period during which it is reasonable for that supply to be cut off or reduced for the purposes of the carrying out of any necessary works.

(5) The Secretary of State may by order modify the application of the preceding provisions of this section in relation to any water undertaker.

(6) The Secretary of State shall not make an order under subsection (5) above except—

(a) in accordance with Schedule 5 to this Act; and

(b) on an application made in accordance with that Schedule by the Director or by the water undertaker in relation to which the order is made.

(7) Subject to subsection (6) above, the power of the Secretary of State to make an order under subsection (5) above shall be exercisable by statutory instrument subject to annulment in pursuance of a resolution of either House of Parliament.

(8) An order under subsection (5) above may—

(a) require the payment of compensation by a water undertaker to persons affected by the order;

(b) make different provision for different cases, including different provision in relation to different persons, circumstances or localities; and

(c) contain such supplemental, consequential and transitional provision as the Secretary of State considers appropriate.

(9) The obligations of a water undertaker under this section shall be enforceable under section 18 above by the Secretary of State.

(10) In addition, where a water undertaker is in breach of a duty under this section, the undertaker shall be guilty of an offence and liable—

(a) on summary conviction, to a fine not exceeding the statutory maximum;

(b) on conviction on indictment, to a fine.

(11) In any proceedings against any water undertaker for an offence under subsection (10) above it shall be a defence for that undertaker to show that it took all reasonable steps and exercised all due diligence to avoid the commission of the offence.

DEFINITIONS
"domestic purposes": ss.218 and 219(1).
"necessary works": s.93(1).

GENERAL NOTE
This section is concerned with the duty of water undertakers to maintain the constancy and pressure of water for domestic purposes and firefighting supplies in respect of the provision of water for domestic purposes and the use of fire hydrants. See *Department of Transport* v. *North West Water Authority* [1984] A.C. 336 for the significance of this statutory duty in respect of an undertaker's liability in nuisance for a burst water main. The duty is enforceable by the Secretary of State using the s.18 enforcement procedure (subs. (9)). Breach of the statutory duty is made a criminal offence in subs. (10). *The consultation paper on water and sewerage law* (Department of the Environment, March 1986) reviewed the legal duties then applicable to the constancy and pressure of supply and recommended a number of changes, mainly on the grounds that the gravitational proviso was imprecise. The Act does not reflect these proposals; however, subs. (5) gives the Secretary of State power to modify the application of subs. (1)–(4), subject to the procedures in Sched. 5 to the Act. Thus the Secretary of State's power could be used to implement the type of changes discussed in the consultation paper.

In any proceedings brought against a water undertaker under subs. (10), it is a defence for an undertaker to show that it took all reasonable steps and exercised all due diligence to avoid the commission of the offence (subs. (11)). This provision is drafted in broad terms and possibly poses a heavier burden than the equivalent defence under the Water Act 1945. Where, for example, frost damage occurs, an undertaker could not rely upon this defence if it is judged that it should reasonably have laid the relevant pipes deep enough to be protected from adverse weather conditions. The Government considered that the provisions "strike the right balance between an undertaker's entitlement to a proper degree of protection against events outside its control and its obligations to consumers" (see Committee stage of the Water Act 1989, discussed in *Hansard*, H.L. Vol. 507, col. 1308).

Requirements by undertaker for maintaining pressure

66.—(1) A water undertaker may require that any premises consisting in—

(a) any building or part of a building the supply of water to which need not, in accordance with provision contained in or made under this Act, be constantly laid on under pressure; or

(b) any relevant house to which water is required to be delivered at a height greater than a point 10.5 metres below the draw-off level of the service reservoir or tank from which a supply of water is being provided by the undertaker to those premises,

shall be provided with a cistern which has a float-operated valve and is fitted on the pipe by means of which water is supplied to those premises.

(2) A water undertaker may, in the case of such a house as is mentioned in paragraph (b) of subsection (1) above, require that a cistern the provision of which is required under that subsection shall be capable of holding sufficient water to provide an adequate supply to the house for a period of 24 hours.

(3) If, where a water undertaker provides a supply of water to any premises, the consumer, after having been required to do so by notice served on him by the undertaker, fails before the end of the period specified in the notice—

(a) to provide a cistern in accordance with a requirement under this section; or

(b) to put any such cistern and its float-operated valve into good repair, the water undertaker may itself provide a cistern, or carry out any repairs necessary to prevent waste of water.

(4) The period specified for the purposes of subsection (3) above in a notice under this section shall be a period of not less than 28 days beginning with the day after the service of the notice.

(5) Where a water undertaker provides a cistern or carries out any repairs under subsection (3) above, it may recover the expenses reasonably incurred by it in doing so from the owner of the premises in question.

(6) In this section—

"pre-transfer supplier," in relation to a house, means the person who was supplying water to that house immediately before September 1, 1989; and

"relevant house" means any house other than a house in relation to which the following two conditions are satisfied, that is to say—

(i) the erection of the house was commenced before September 1, 1989; and

(ii) no such requirement as is mentioned in subsection (1) or (2) above could have been imposed in relation to the house under any enactment having effect immediately before that date in relation to the pre-transfer supplier.

DEFINITIONS
  "consumer": s.93(1).
  "notice": s.219(1).
  "pre-transfer supplier": subs. (6).
  "relevant house": subs. (6).

GENERAL NOTE
  This section provides a water undertaker with the power to require that premises consisting of either a building or a house are fitted with a cistern with a float-operated valve. The power contained in subs. (1) is designed to supplement the water undertaker's duties in respect of constancy and pressure of supply contained in s.65.

If a consumer has been served with a notice under subs. (3) requiring the provision of a cistern or the putting of an existing cistern into good repair, the water undertaker may itself provide a cistern or carry out any necessary repairs should the consumer fail to comply with the notice. In such circumstances the undertaker can recover its expenses (subs. (5)).

The provisions contained in s.66 do not apply to water mains and pipes belonging to water undertakers before September 1, 1989.

CHAPTER III

QUALITY AND SUFFICIENCY OF SUPPLIES

Standards of wholesomeness

Standards of wholesomeness

67.—(1) The Secretary of State may by regulations make provision that water that is supplied to any premises is or is not to be regarded as wholesome for the purposes of this Chapter if it satisfies or, as the case may be, fails to satisfy such requirements as may be prescribed.

(2) Without prejudice to the generality of subsection (1) above, regulations under this section may, for the purpose of determining the wholesomeness of any water—

(a) prescribe general requirements as to the purposes for which the water is to be suitable;

(b) prescribe specific requirements as to the substances that are to be present in or absent from the water and as to the concentrations of substances which are or are required to be present in the water;

(c) prescribe specific requirements as to other characteristics of the water;

(d) provide that the question whether prescribed requirements are satisfied may be determined by reference to such samples as may be prescribed;

(e) enable the Secretary of State to authorise such relaxations of and departures from the prescribed requirements (or from any of them) as may be prescribed, to make any such authorisation subject to such conditions as may be prescribed and to modify or revoke any such authorisation or condition; and

(f) enable the Secretary of State to authorise a local authority (either instead of the Secretary of State or concurrently with him) to exercise in relation to a private supply any power conferred on the Secretary of State by regulations made by virtue of paragraph (e) above.

DEFINITIONS
"local authority": s.219(1).
"prescribed": s.219(1).
"private supply": s.93(1) and (2).
"substances": s.219(1).
"wholesome": s.93(1).

GENERAL NOTE
This section provides a power for the Secretary of State to make regulations prescribing the technical standards and requirements to satisfy the test of "wholesomeness" in relation to the supply of water in England and Wales. This reflects the impact of European Commission legislation and in particular the 1980 E.C. Directive relating to the quality of water intended for human consumption (80/778/EEC), which prescribed over 60 mandatory standards and guidelines and which formed a backdrop to much of the Parliamentary debate on the subject of water quality prior to the implementation of the Water Act 1989. The directive was originally implemented in England and Wales by means of an administrative circular (Department of the Environment Circular 20/82), but this is a mechanism which is not favoured by the European Commission or the European Court of Justice (see *E.C. Commission* v. *Belgium* [1982] C.M.L.R. 627).

Regulations

The section enables the Secretary of State to make general regulations relating to the purposes for which water is to be suitable and also prescribe specific requirements relating to firstly the substances and concentrations of those substances which are to be present or absent from water, secondly requirements relating to other characteristics of water, for example, taste, and thirdly requirements which enable standards of wholesomeness to be determined by sample. The Secretary of State may also authorise relaxations from prescribed requirements and authorise local authorities to exercise in relation to private supplies the powers conferred on the Secretary of State by s.67(2)(e) and (f).

The Water Supply (Water Quality) Regulations 1989 (S.I. 1989 No. 1147) and the Water Supply (Water Quality) (Amendment) Regulations 1989 (S.I. 1989 No. 1383) have been made in part under s.65 of the Water Act 1989, which is replaced by s.67 of this Act. Part II of the Regulations prescribes standards relating to domestic water supplies for drinking, washing and cooking, whether supplied by undertakers or from private supplies, with mandatory values and concentrations contained in Regulation 3 and tables A to E of Sched. 2. These incorporate the EEC standards, but include further national standards, and are applicable to all samples of water. Under Pt. III, relaxations in certain circumstances, as authorised by the Directive, may be made by the Secretary of State in the case of water undertakers, and local authorities in respect of private water supplies. Monitoring and sampling requirements are specified in Pt. IV of the Regulations, and Pt. VIII imposes wide-ranging requirements on undertakers to make available to the public information on the subject and to publish an annual report covering specified matters.

The legal effect of compliance with the Regulations is contained in reg. 3(2), which prescribes that water supplies to which they apply are to be regarded as wholesome for the purposes of Pt. II of the Water Act 1989, now Pt. III of this Act, if they comply with the specified standards. The converse is not necessarily the case and the wording appears to leave open the possibility that water failing to comply with the standards could still be regarded as legally wholesome for the purposes of this Act. This interpretation is reinforced by the provision in Reg. 3(7) that water supplies containing an excess of prescribed concentrations of certain substances in table C of the Regulations are to be regarded as "unwholesome". This formulation is not applied to the remaining standards.

Enforcement

Enforcement of an undertaker's supply duties under Pt. III of this Act is the responsibility of the Secretary of State, using the s.18 enforcement procedure. Under s.19(1), the Secretary of State is not obliged to make a final or provisional s.18 order where he is satisfied with an undertaker's proposed programme for ensuring compliance. This mechanism will be important here because of investment and infrastructure requirements needed to meet all the standards. During the Committee stage of the Water Act 1989 in the House of Lords the Government was defeated when an amendment to s.38 of the Water Act 1989 (now ss.37–39 of this Act) was passed imposing on the face of the 1989 Act a requirement for performance regulations to include a specified deadline for meeting the standards in the E.C. Directive, but this was subsequently rejected in the Commons on the grounds that the 1989 Act contained other, more effective mechanisms for securing compliance. During consideration of the Lords' amendments, the Secretary of State provided further details on how the s.19(1) procedures would be employed:

> "The water undertakers must convince the Secretary of State that they are doing all they can to comply speedily with the drinking water directive, and the European Commission will want to see the programmes because it has a rôle in ensuring that European legislation is properly implemented. The undertakers' programmes are now being drawn up and will be made public later this year, as soon as we have them. The programmes will contain dates by which compliance with the remaining standards in the directive will be achieved. The details of these programmes will be set out in formal undertakings" (*Hansard*, H.C. Vol. 156, col. 91).

General obligations of undertakers

Duties of water undertakers with respect to water quality

68.—(1) It shall be the duty of a water undertaker—

(a) when supplying water to any premises for domestic or food production purposes to supply only water which is wholesome at the time of supply; and

(b) so far as reasonably practicable, to ensure, in relation to each source or combination of sources from which that undertaker supplies water to premises for domestic or food production purposes, that there is, in general, no deterioration in the quality of the water which is supplied from time to time from that source or combination of sources.

(2) For the purposes of this section and section 69 below and subject to subsection (3) below, water supplied by a water undertaker to any premises shall not be regarded as unwholesome at the time of supply where it has ceased to be wholesome only after leaving the undertaker's pipes.

(3) For the purposes of this section where water supplied by a water undertaker to any premises would not otherwise be regarded as unwholesome at the time of supply, that water shall be regarded as unwholesome at that time if—

(a) it has ceased to be wholesome after leaving the undertaker's pipes but while in a pipe which is subject to water pressure from a water main or which would be so subject but for the closing of some valve; and

(b) it has so ceased in consequence of the failure of the undertaker, before supplying the water, to take such steps as may be prescribed for the purpose of securing the elimination, or reduction to a minimum, of any prescribed risk that the water would cease to be wholesome after leaving the undertaker's pipes.

(4) The provisions of this section shall apply in relation to water which is supplied by a water undertaker whether or not the water is water which the undertaker is required to supply by virtue of any provision of this Act.

(5) The duties of a water undertaker under this section shall be enforceable under section 18 above by the Secretary of State.

DEFINITIONS
"domestic purposes": ss.218 and 219(1).
"food production purposes": s.93(1).
"water main": s.219(1).
"wholesome": s.93(1).

GENERAL NOTE
This section is concerned with the duties of water undertakers relating to water quality. Subsection (1) relates to water which is wholesome at the time for domestic food purposes. Where it is not practicable for the undertaker to supply water at reasonable cost then the procedures under s.79 apply, enabling the supply of water to be made other than in pipes. Reference in s.68(1)(b) to deterioration in the quality of water is a new duty on undertakers, designed to ensure that they maintain water quality and are deterred from bringing down standards of wholesomeness.

The water undertaker's duty to provide a supply of wholesome water in this section makes it clear that, in line with previous legislation, the statutory duty to supply wholesome water ends at the point where that water enters the consumer's own pipe. However, the E.C. directive on the subject (80/778/EEC) is ambiguous requiring monitoring to take place "at the point where it is made available to the consumer" (Art. 12), a phrase not defined and one which could be interpreted to mean either the tap or the connection to the consumer's service pipe. In any event, the statutory limitation under subs. (2) is now qualified by subs. (3), which states that water may still be regarded as unwholesome if it ceased to be wholesome because of the circumstances specified in paras. (a) and (b).

Part IV of the Water Supply (Water Quality) Regulations 1989 prescribes steps to be taken by the undertaker where there is a danger from contamination from copper, lead, or zinc, present in the consumer's pipes. Even where contamination occurs within the consumer's own pipes, and thus the statutory duty of wholesomeness is no longer applicable, it has been held that the undertaker may still be liable in negligence. See *Read* v. *Croydon Corporation* [1937] 37 L.G.R. 53, *Barnes* v. *Irwell Valley Water Board* [1939] 1 K.B. 21. Undertakers may also be strictly liable under the provisions of the Consumer Protection Act 1987 where injury or property damage has occurred.

Regulations for preserving water quality

69.—(1) The Secretary of State may by regulations require a water undertaker to take all such steps as may be prescribed for the purpose of securing compliance with section 68 above.

(2) Without prejudice to the generality of the power conferred by subsection (1) above, regulations under that subsection may impose an obligation on a water undertaker—

(a) to take all such steps as may be prescribed for monitoring and recording whether the water which that undertaker supplies to premises for domestic or food production purposes is wholesome at the time of supply;

(b) to take all such steps as may be prescribed for monitoring and recording the quality of the water from any source, or combination of sources, which that undertaker uses or is proposing to use for supplying water to any premises for domestic or food production purposes;

(c) to ensure that a source which that undertaker is using or proposing to use for supplying water for domestic or food production purposes is not so used until prescribed requirements for establishing the quality of water which may be supplied from that source have been complied with;

(d) to keep records of the localities within which all the premises supplied with water for domestic or food production purposes by that undertaker are normally supplied from the same source or combination of sources;

(e) to comply with prescribed requirements with respect to the analysis of water samples or with respect to internal reporting or organisational arrangements.

(3) Without prejudice to subsections (1) and (2) above, the Secretary of State may by regulations make provision with respect to the use by water undertakers, for the purposes of or in connection with the carrying out of their functions—

(a) of such processes and substances; and

(b) of products that contain or are made with such substances or materials,

as he considers might affect the quality of any water.

(4) Without prejudice to the generality of the power conferred by subsection (3) above, regulations under that subsection may—

(a) forbid the use by water undertakers of processes, substances and products which have not been approved under the regulations or which contravene the regulations;

(b) for the purposes of provision made by virtue of paragraph (a) above, require processes, substances and products used by water undertakers to conform to such standards as may be prescribed by or approved under the regulations;

(c) impose such other requirements as may be prescribed with respect to the use by water undertakers of prescribed processes, substances and products;

(d) provide for the giving, refusal and revocation, by prescribed persons, of approvals required for the purposes of the regulations, for such approvals to be capable of being made subject to such conditions as may be prescribed and for the modification and revocation of any such condition;

(e) impose obligations to furnish prescribed persons with information reasonably required by those persons for the purpose of carrying out functions under the regulations;

(f) provide for a contravention of the regulations to constitute—

(i) a summary offence punishable, on summary conviction, by a fine not exceeding level 5 on the standard scale or such smaller sum as may be prescribed; or

(ii) an offence triable either way and punishable, on summary

conviction, by a fine not exceeding the statutory maximum and, on conviction on indictment, by a fine;
and

(g) require prescribed charges to be paid to persons carrying out functions under the regulations.

(5) The Secretary of State may by regulations require a water undertaker—

(a) to publish information about the quality of water supplied for domestic or food production purposes to any premises by that undertaker; and

(b) to provide information to prescribed persons about the quality of water so supplied.

(6) Regulations under subsection (5) above—

(a) shall prescribe both the information which is to be published or provided in pursuance of the regulations and the manner and circumstances in which it is to be published or provided;

(b) may require the provision of information by a water undertaker to any person to be free of charge or may authorise it to be subject to the payment by that person to the undertaker of a prescribed charge; and

(c) may impose such other conditions on the provision of information by a water undertaker to any person as may be prescribed.

DEFINITIONS
"analysis": s.219(1).
"domestic purposes": ss.218 and 219(1).
"food production purposes": s.93(1).
"functions": ss.217 and 219(1).
"prescribed": s.219(1).
"wholesome": ss.80(7) and 93(1).

GENERAL NOTE
This section is an enabling power drawn in the widest possible terms, allowing the Secretary of State to specify in detail what is required of undertakers in respect of their general duty to supply wholesome water. This is in addition to the powers under s.68 to define what is meant by "wholesome". Since they relate to the duties under s.67, duties under the regulations would be enforceable by means of a s.18 enforcement order, but the regulations may also provide for criminal sanctions (subs. (4)(f)).

See also the Water Supply (Water Quality) Regulations 1989 (S.I. 1989 No. 1147) and the Water Supply (Water Quality) (Amendment) Regulations 1989 (S.I. 1989 No. 1384) for detailed requirements relating to the preservation of water quality. Part VII of those Regulations contains significant legal rights concerning public access to information concerning drinking water quality, including records of the results of sampling water taken in accordance with the regulations, together with information on progress towards compliance where standards are not met.

Offence of supplying water unfit for human consumption

70.—(1) Subject to subsection (3) below, where a water undertaker supplies water by means of pipes to any premises and that water is unfit for human consumption, the undertaker shall be guilty of an offence and liable—

(a) on summary conviction, to a fine not exceeding the statutory maximum;

(b) on conviction on indictment, to a fine.

(2) For the purposes of section 210 below and any other enactment under which an individual is guilty of an offence by virtue of subsection (1) above the penalty on conviction on indictment of an offence under this section shall be deemed to include imprisonment (in addition to or instead of a fine) for a term not exceeding two years.

(3) In any proceedings against any water undertaker for an offence under this section it shall be a defence for that undertaker to show that it—

(a) had no reasonable grounds for suspecting that the water would be used for human consumption; or

(b) took all reasonable steps and exercised all due diligence for securing that the water was fit for human consumption on leaving its pipes or was not used for human consumption.

(4) Proceedings for an offence under this section shall not be instituted except by the Secretary of State or the Director of Public Prosecutions.

GENERAL NOTE

This section replaces s.54 of the Water Act 1989, which provided a new offence where a water undertaker supplies water which is "unfit for human consumption". The offence is intended to deal with serious incidents where criminal prosecution is warranted rather than the s.18 enforcement procedure. The offence was principally introduced as a result of the major contamination of water supplies which occurred in Camelford, Cornwall, in 1988, when 20 tonnes of aluminium sulphate were pumped into water supplies. The phrase "unfit for human consumption" is not defined in the Act, and while the technical standards concerning "wholesomeness" made under s.67 may be of assistance in the interpretation of that phrase, they are not conclusive. A supply that is unwholesome for the purposes of the Act is not necessarily "unfit" under this section. At the other end of the scale, incidents may occur where water which is supplied to consumers may be discoloured or tainted by smells without giving rise to any health risk. The question of whether such an incident would make the supply "unfit" for the purposes of this section has not yet been the subject of judicial interpretation. It is possible that the offence would be made out if the contamination was sufficiently serious to deter a reasonable consumer from drinking the water. It seems likely that this may be an offence of absolute liability: see *Maidstone Borough Council* v. *Mortimer* [1985] 3 All E.R. 552.

Subsection (4) provides that proceedings under this section may only be instituted by the Secretary of State or the Director of Public Prosecutions.

Waste, contamination, misuse etc.

Waste from water sources

71.—(1) Subject to subsections (2) and (3) below, a person shall be guilty of an offence under this section if—

(a) he causes or allows any underground water to run to waste from any well, borehole or other work; or

(b) he abstracts from any well, borehole or other work water in excess of his reasonable requirements.

(2) A person shall not be guilty of an offence by virtue of subsection (1)(a) above in respect of anything done for the purpose—

(a) of testing the extent or quality of the supply; or

(b) of cleaning, sterilising, examining or repairing the well, borehole or other work in question.

(3) Where underground water interferes or threatens to interfere with the carrying out or operation of any underground works (whether waterworks or not), it shall not be an offence under this section, if no other method of disposing of the water is reasonably practicable, to cause or allow the water to run to waste so far as may be necessary for enabling the works to be carried out or operated.

(4) A person who is guilty of an offence under this section shall be liable, on summary conviction, to a fine not exceeding level 3 on the standard scale.

(5) On the conviction of a person under this section, the court may—

(a) order that the well, borehole or other work to which the offence relates shall be effectively sealed; or

(b) make such other order as appears to the court to be necessary to prevent waste of water.

(6) If any person fails to comply with an order under subsection (5) above, then, without prejudice to any penalty for contempt of court, the court may, on the application of the NRA, authorise the NRA to take such steps as may be necessary to execute the order; and any expenses incurred in taking any

such steps shall be recoverable summarily as a civil debt from the person convicted.

(7) Any person designated for the purpose by the NRA shall, on producing some duly authenticated document showing his authority, have a right at all reasonable times—

    (a) to enter any premises for the purpose of ascertaining whether there is, or has been, any contravention of the provisions of this section on or in connection with the premises;

    (b) to enter any premises for the purpose of executing any order of the court under this section which the NRA has been authorised to execute in those premises.

(8) Part I of Schedule 6 to this Act shall apply to the rights of entry conferred by subsection (7) above.

GENERAL NOTE

This section establishes the offence of causing or allowing any underground water to run to waste from any well or borehole and includes water which is abstracted in excess of the reasonable requirements of the person extracting the water supply (subs. (1)), but no offence is committed in respect of anything done for the purpose of examining the water supply or cleansing or maintaining of any well, borehole or other work (subs. (2)).

With regard to the abstraction of water in the circumstances specified in s.71(1)(b), abstractions which are within the limit set by an abstraction licence would no doubt be reasonable for the purposes of that subsection.

No offence is committed if underground water which interferes with underground works, or threatens to do so, is allowed to run to waste, provided that no other method of disposing of the water is reasonably practicable (subs. (3)). Any person authorised by the National Rivers Authority under the provisions of subs. (7) will, on production of his authority, have a right to enter any premises at a reasonable hour to ascertain whether any offence is being committed.

Upon a successful conviction under subs. (1) the court may make an order requiring the well, borehole or other waterworks to be sealed or alternatively requiring the person abstracting the water to take such steps as the court considers necessary to prevent waste of water (subs. (5)). In default of the court order the NRA may apply to the court for power to execute those works and to recover the expenses incurred from the defaulting consumer (subs. (6)).

Contamination of water sources

72.—(1) Subject to subsections (2) and (3) below, a person is guilty of an offence under this section if he is guilty of any act or neglect whereby the water in any waterworks which is used or likely to be used—

    (a) for human consumption or domestic purposes; or

    (b) for manufacturing food or drink for human consumption,

is polluted or likely to be polluted.

(2) Nothing in this section shall be construed as restricting or prohibiting any method of cultivation of land which is in accordance with the principles of good husbandry.

(3) Nothing in this section shall be construed as restricting or prohibiting the reasonable use of oil or tar on any highway maintainable at public expense so long as the highway authority take all reasonable steps for preventing—

    (a) the oil or tar; and

    (b) any liquid or matter resulting from the use of the oil or tar,

from polluting the water in any waterworks.

(4) A person who is guilty of an offence under this section shall be liable—

    (a) on summary conviction, to a fine not exceeding the statutory maximum and, in the case of a continuing offence, to a further fine not exceeding £50 for every day during which the offence is continued after conviction;

    (b) on conviction on indictment, to imprisonment for a term not exceeding two years or to a fine or to both.

(5) In this section "waterworks" includes—

    (a) any spring, well, adit, borehole, service reservoir or tank; and

(b) any main or other pipe or conduit of a water undertaker.

DEFINITIONS
"domestic purposes": ss.218 and 219(1).
"waterworks": subs. (5).

GENERAL NOTE
This section provides that a person shall be guilty of an offence if due to his act or neglect water is polluted or is likely to be polluted in any "waterworks" that is used or is likely to be used for domestic purposes or for manufacturing foods or drink for human consumption (subs. (1)). The term "waterworks" is defined in subs. (5) and includes any spring, well, adit, borehole or service reservoir or tank and also includes any main, pipe or conduit that is vested in a water undertaker.
    The offence under s.72 is not designed to prohibit or restrict any method of cultivation of land that is in accordance with the principles of good husbandry (subs. (2)), nor is it designed to affect the use of oil or tar in the construction and maintenance of public roads (subs. (3)). Subsection (4) concerns the penalties which may be imposed on a person found to be guilty of contaminating water supplies under s.72(1). Subsection (4)(a) provides for penalties of fines not exceeding £50 for every day during which the offence is continued after the date of conviction.
    This section implements the Law Commission's recommendation regarding the definition of "domestic purposes" (Law Commission *Report on the consolidation of the legislation relating to water*; Law Commission Report No. 198, Cmnd. 1483, p. 15 at para. 21). The definition of "domestic purposes" in s.189(2) and (3) of the Water Act 1989 included the provision of water for central heating purposes, whereas s.21 of the Water Act 1945 did not define "domestic purposes" for the purposes of s.21 of that Act in identical terms. Section 72 of this Act consolidates s.21 of the Water Act 1945 so that the reference to the use of water for domestic purposes in s.21 of the Water Act 1945 is capable of attracting the same definition of domestic purposes as that in s.189(2) and (3) of the Water Act 1989.

Offences of contaminating, wasting and misusing water etc.

73.—(1) If any person who is the owner or occupier of any premises to which a supply of water is provided by a water undertaker intentionally or negligently causes or suffers any water fitting for which he is responsible to be or remain so out of order, so in need of repair or so constructed or adapted, or to be so used—
    (a) that water in a water main or other pipe of a water undertaker, or in a pipe connected with such a water main or pipe, is or is likely to be contaminated by the return of any substance from those premises to that main or pipe;
    (b) that water that has been supplied by the undertaker to those premises is or is likely to be contaminated before it is used; or
    (c) that water so supplied is or is likely to be wasted or, having regard to the purposes for which it is supplied, misused or unduly consumed,
that person shall be guilty of an offence and liable, on summary conviction, to a fine not exceeding level 3 on the standard scale.
    (2) Any person who uses any water supplied to any premises by a water undertaker for a purpose other than one for which it is supplied to those premises shall, unless the other purpose is the extinguishment of a fire, be guilty of an offence and liable, on summary conviction, to a fine not exceeding level 3 on the standard scale.
    (3) Where a person has committed an offence under subsection (2) above, the water undertaker in question shall be entitled to recover from that person such amount as may be reasonable in respect of any water wasted, misused or improperly consumed in consequence of the commission of the offence.
    (4) For the purposes of this section the owner or occupier of any premises shall be regarded as responsible for every water fitting on the premises which is not a water fitting which a person other than the owner or, as the case may be, occupier is liable to maintain.

GENERAL NOTE
   This section is concerned with offences relating to the contamination, wasting and misuse of water. The offences under this section are committed where the owner or occupier of premises connected to water supplies provided by water undertakers intentionally or negligently causes or suffers any water fittings for which he is responsible to remain in a defective condition so that either the water in a water main or other pipe connected with the premises is likely to be contaminated by the return of any substance from those premises to the main or pipe (subs. (1)(a)), that water supplied by the undertaker to the premises is likely to be contaminated before use (subs. (1)(b)), that water supplied by the water undertaker is likely to be wasted, misused or unduly consumed (subs. (1)(c)).
   A person is also guilty of an offence if he uses water supplied to any premises by a water undertaker for a purpose other than that for which it was originally supplied except in the case of extinguishing fires (subs. (2)). For the purposes of s.73 a person will be regarded as being responsible for a water fitting if he is liable to maintain it (subs. (4)). Water undertakers are given powers under s.75 to take remedial action including disconnection in emergencies.

Regulations for preventing contamination, waste etc. and with respect to water fittings

74.—(1) The Secretary of State may by regulations make such provision as he considers appropriate for any of the following purposes, that is to say—
   (a) for securing—
      (i) that water in a water main or other pipe of a water undertaker is not contaminated; and
      (ii) that its quality and suitability for particular purposes is not prejudiced,
   by the return of any substance from any premises to that main or pipe;
   (b) for securing that water which is in any pipe connected with any such main or other pipe or which has been supplied to any premises by a water undertaker is not contaminated, and that its quality and suitability for particular purposes is not prejudiced, before it is used;
   (c) for preventing the waste, undue consumption and misuse of any water at any time after it has left the pipes of a water undertaker for the purpose of being supplied by that undertaker to any premises; and
   (d) for securing that water fittings installed and used by persons to whom water is or is to be supplied by a water undertaker are safe and do not cause or contribute to the erroneous measurement of any water or the reverberation of any pipes.
   (2) Without prejudice to the generality of subsection (1) above, regulations under this section may, for any of the purposes specified in that subsection, make provision in relation to such water fittings as may be prescribed—
   (a) for forbidding the installation, connection or use of the fittings if they have not been approved under the regulations or if they contravene the regulations;
   (b) for requiring the fittings, for the purposes of provision made by virtue of paragraph (a) above, to be of such a size, nature, strength or workmanship, to be made of such materials or in such a manner or to conform to such standards as may be prescribed by or approved under the regulations;
   (c) for imposing such other requirements as may be prescribed with respect to the installation, arrangement, connection, testing, disconnection, alteration and repair of the fittings and with respect to the materials used in their manufacture;
   (d) for the giving, refusal and revocation, by prescribed persons, of approvals required for the purposes of the regulations; and
   (e) for such approvals to be capable of being made subject to such conditions as may be prescribed and for the modification and revocation of any such condition.
   (3) Without prejudice as aforesaid, regulations under this section may—

(a) impose separate or concurrent duties with respect to the enforcement of the regulations on water undertakers, local authorities and such other persons as may be prescribed;

(b) confer powers on a water undertaker or local authority to carry out works and take other steps, in prescribed circumstances, for remedying any contravention of the regulations;

(c) provide for the recovery by a water undertaker or local authority of expenses reasonably incurred by the undertaker or authority in the exercise of any power conferred by virtue of paragraph (b) above;

(d) repeal or modify the provisions of section 73 above or section 75 below;

(e) provide for a contravention of the regulations to constitute a summary offence punishable, on summary conviction, by a fine not exceeding level 5 on the standard scale or such smaller sum as may be prescribed;

(f) require prescribed charges to be paid to persons carrying out functions under the regulations;

(g) enable the Secretary of State to authorise such relaxations of and departures from such of the requirements of the regulations as may be prescribed, to make any such authorisation subject to such conditions as may be prescribed and to modify or revoke any such authorisation or condition;

(h) enable the Secretary of State to authorise a water undertaker or local authority (either instead of the Secretary of State or concurrently with him) to exercise any power conferred on the Secretary of State by regulations made by virtue of paragraph (g) above; and

(i) require disputes arising under the regulations to be referred to arbitration and for determinations under the regulations to be subject to such rights of appeal as may be prescribed.

(4) Without prejudice to sections 84 and 170 below, any person designated in writing for the purposes of this subsection in such manner as may be prescribed may—

(a) enter any premises for the purpose of—

(i) ascertaining whether any provision contained in or made or having effect under this Act with respect to any water fittings or with respect to the waste or misuse of water is being or has been contravened;

(ii) determining whether, and if so in what manner, any power or duty conferred or imposed on any person by regulations under this section should be exercised or performed; or

(iii) exercising any such power or performing any such duty; or

(b) carry out such inspections, measurements and tests on premises entered by that person or on water fittings or other articles found on any such premises, and take away such samples of water or of any land and such water fittings and other articles, as that person has been authorised to carry out or take away in accordance with regulations under this section.

(5) Part II of Schedule 6 to this Act shall apply to the rights and powers conferred by subsection (4) above.

(6) The power of the Secretary of State under this section to make regulations with respect to the matters specified in the preceding provisions of this section shall include power, by regulations under this section—

(a) to modify the operation of Schedule 2 to the Water Consolidation (Consequential Provisions) Act 1991 in relation to any byelaws made under section 17 of the Water Act 1945 which have effect by virtue of paragraph 19 of Schedule 26 to the Water Act 1989 and that Schedule 2; and

(b) to revoke or amend any such byelaws;
but, so long as any such byelaws so have effect, the references in sections 47(2)(g), 53(2)(c) and 55(4) above to such regulations under this section as are prescribed shall have effect as including references to those byelaws.

(7) Any sums received by the Secretary of State in consequence of the provisions of any regulations under this section shall be paid into the Consolidated Fund.

(8) In this section "safe" has the same meaning as in Part II of the Consumer Protection Act 1987.

DEFINITIONS
"functions": ss.217 and 219(1).
"local authority": s.219(1).
"modification": s.219(1).
"prescribed": s.219(1).
"safe": subs. (8).
"substance": s.219(1).
"water fittings": s.93(1).
"water main": s.219(1) and (2).

GENERAL NOTE
This section provides the Secretary of State with a power to make regulations for preventing contamination, waste and misuse of water and also regulations relating to water fittings.

The power conferred on the Secretary of State to make such regulations can be seen as an important part of the new régime for the control of the use of water and water fittings established by the Water Act 1989 and now consolidated into this Act. The section ensures that the provisions contained in ss.73 and 75 are compatible with the detailed regulations outlined in s.74 by enabling the Secretary of State under subs. (3)(d) to repeal or modify ss.73 and 75. The installation and use of water fittings or the carrying out of other works may be subject to the approval of prescribed persons (subs. (2)) and such "prescribed persons" may be water undertakers, local authorities or other persons, whose powers may be exercised separately or concurrently as provided in subs. (3). Persons carrying out the functions prescribed by the regulations will be able to charge for their services under subs. (3)(f).

The regulations may be relaxed on the authorisation of the Secretary of State, or, with his consent, by a water undertaker or local authority (subs. (3)(g) and (h)). Disputes regarding the regulations are to be referred to arbitration (subs. (3)(i)). Subsections (4) and (5) are concerned with powers of entry. Breach of any of the regulations will constitute offences as provided in subs. (3)(e).

Power to prevent damage and to take steps to prevent contamination, waste etc.

75.—(1) Without prejudice to any power conferred on water undertakers by regulations under section 74 above, where a water undertaker which provides a supply of water to any premises has reason for believing—
  (a) that damage to persons or property is being or is likely to be caused by any damage to, or defect in, any water fitting used in connection with the supply of water to those premises which is not a service pipe belonging to the undertaker;
  (b) that water in a water main or other pipe of the undertaker is being or is likely to be contaminated by the return of any substance from those premises to that main or pipe;
  (c) that water which is in any pipe connected with any such main or other pipe or which has been supplied by the undertaker to those premises is being or is likely to be contaminated before it is used; or
  (d) that water which has been or is to be so supplied is being or is likely to be wasted or, having regard to the purposes for which it is supplied, misused or unduly consumed,
the undertaker may exercise the power conferred by subsection (2) below in relation to those premises.

(2) The power conferred by this subsection in relation to any premises is—

(a) where the case constitutes an emergency, power to disconnect the service pipe or otherwise to cut off the supply of water to those premises; and

(b) in any other case, power to serve notice on the consumer requiring him to take such steps as may be specified in the notice as necessary to secure that the damage, contamination, waste, misuse or undue consumption ceases or, as the case may be, does not occur.

(3) Where a water undertaker, in exercise of the power conferred by virtue of subsection (2)(a) above, disconnects a service pipe to any premises or otherwise cuts off any supply of water to any premises, the undertaker shall, as soon as reasonably practicable after the supply is disconnected or cut off, serve a notice on the consumer specifying the steps which that person is required to take before the undertaker will restore the supply.

(4) The steps specified in a notice under subsection (3) above shall be the steps necessary to secure that, as the case may be—

(a) the damage, contamination, waste, misuse or undue consumption; or

(b) the likelihood of damage, contamination, waste, misuse or undue consumption,

would not recur if the supply were restored.

(5) A water undertaker which fails, without reasonable excuse, to serve a notice in accordance with subsection (3) above shall be guilty of an offence and liable, on summary conviction, to a fine not exceeding level 3 on the standard scale.

(6) A notice served for the purposes of subsection (2)(b) above shall—

(a) specify the period, not being less than the period of seven days beginning with the day after the service of the notice, within which the steps specified in the notice are to be taken; and

(b) set out the powers of the undertaker under subsections (7) to (9) below.

(7) Where a water undertaker has served a notice for the purposes of subsection (2)(b) above in relation to any premises and—

(a) the case becomes an emergency; or

(b) the premises appear to be unoccupied and the steps specified in the notice are not taken before the end of the period so specified,

the undertaker may disconnect the service pipe to those premises or otherwise cut off the supply of water to those premises.

(8) Subsections (3) to (5) above shall apply where a water undertaker exercises its power under subsection (7) above as they apply where such an undertaker exercises its power by virtue of subsection (2)(a) above.

(9) Where, in a case not falling within subsection (7)(a) or (b) above, any steps specified in a notice served by a water undertaker for the purposes of subsection (2)(b) above have not been taken by the end of the period so specified, the water undertaker shall have power—

(a) to take those steps itself; and

(b) subject to subsection (10) below, to recover any expenses reasonably incurred by the undertaker in taking those steps from the person on whom the notice was served;

and any steps taken by a water undertaker by virtue of paragraph (a) above shall be necessary works for the purposes of Chapter II of this Part.

(10) Where any steps are taken by virtue of this section and it is shown that, in the circumstances of the case, those steps were not necessary as mentioned in subsection (2) or, as the case may be, (4) above, the water undertaker in question—

(a) shall not be entitled to recover any expenses incurred by it in taking those steps; and

(b) shall be liable to pay to any other person who took any of those steps an amount equal to any expenses reasonably incurred by that person in taking any of those steps.

DEFINITIONS
"consumer": s.93(1).
"damage": s.219(1).
"notice": s.219(1).
"service pipe": s.219(1) and (2).
"water fitting": s.93(1).
"water main": s.219(1) and (2).

GENERAL NOTE
In addition to any powers that may derive from the regulations under s.74, water undertakers are given powers by this section to take steps to prevent contamination or waste of water supplies in the circumstances specified in subs. (1). In an emergency the undertaker may disconnect without prior notice (subs. (2)(a)). In a non-emergency, a notice must first be served on the consumer specifying remedial steps to be taken within a period of not less than seven days and only in the case of a subsequent emergency may the undertaker disconnect within the specified period (subs. (7)(a)). Undertakers may also disconnect where the premises appear unoccupied and no steps are taken to comply with the notice served for the purposes of subs. (2)(b) (subs. (7)(b)).

Undertakers are given the power to take remedial steps specified in the notice in default of compliance with a notice and to recover expenses incurred (subs. (9)(b)), subject to limitations (subs. (10)). Where the powers to disconnect are exercised in an emergency or in relation to unoccupied premises, it seems that the undertaker has no powers to recover the disconnection expenses involved (should the occupier later reappear): contrast the express powers in s.61, where disconnection takes place for non-payment of charges.

Where disconnection takes place under the provisions of s.75, the general duty to supply water for domestic purposes is suspended (s.52(7)).

Temporary hosepipe bans

76.—(1) If a water undertaker is of the opinion that a serious deficiency of water available for distribution by that undertaker exists or is threatened, that undertaker may, for such period as it thinks necessary, prohibit or restrict, as respects the whole or any part of its area, the use for the purpose of—

(a) watering private gardens; or

(b) washing private motor cars,

of any water supplied by that undertaker and drawn through a hosepipe or similar apparatus.

(2) A water undertaker imposing a prohibition or restriction under this section shall, before it comes into force, give public notice of it, and of the date on which it will come into force, in two or more newspapers circulating in the locality affected by the prohibition or restriction.

(3) Any person who, at a time when a prohibition or restriction under this section is in force, contravenes its provisions shall be guilty of an offence and liable, on summary conviction, to a fine not exceeding level 3 on the standard scale.

(4) Where a prohibition or restriction is imposed by a water undertaker under this section, charges made by the undertaker for the use of a hosepipe or similar apparatus shall be subject to a reasonable reduction and, in the case of a charge paid in advance, the undertaker shall make any necessary repayment or adjustment.

(5) In this section "private motor car" means any mechanically propelled vehicle intended or adapted for use on roads other than—

(a) a public service vehicle, within the meaning of the Public Passenger Vehicles Act 1981; or

(b) a goods vehicle within the meaning of the Road Traffic Act 1988,

and includes any vehicle drawn by a private motor car.

DEFINITIONS
"private motor car": subs. (5).

GENERAL NOTE
This section is concerned with temporary hosepipe bans. If a water undertaker is of the

opinion that a serious deficiency exists or is threatened the undertaker may for such period as it considers necessary in respect of the whole or part of its area introduce a hosepipe ban. Such bans extend to watering private gardens and washing private motor cars using hosepipes or similar apparatus. Note the extended definition of private motor car in subs. (5).

Before a ban or restriction can come into force a water undertaker must publish notice of the ban in two or more newspapers circulating in the locality (subs. (2)). Contravention of a hosepipe ban is a criminal offence under subs. (3) and is punishable by a fine. Subsection (4) provides that where an undertaker makes a special charge to private consumers for the use of the hosepipe, that charge should be reduced if a ban or restriction is imposed by the undertaker.

Local authority functions

General functions of local authorities in relation to water quality

77.—(1) It shall be the duty of every local authority to take all such steps as they consider appropriate for keeping themselves informed about the wholesomeness and sufficiency of water supplies provided to premises in their area, including every private supply to any such premises.

(2) It shall be the duty of a local authority to comply with any direction given by the Secretary of State to that authority, to authorities of a description applicable to that authority or to local authorities generally as to—

(a) the cases and circumstances in which they are or are not to exercise any of the powers conferred on them by this Chapter in relation to private supplies; and

(b) the manner in which those powers are to be exercised.

(3) The Secretary of State may by regulations make such provision, supplementing the provisions of this section and of sections 78 and 79(2) below, as he considers appropriate for—

(a) imposing duties and conferring powers on local authorities with respect to the acquisition of information about the quality and sufficiency of water supplies provided to premises in their areas; and

(b) regulating the performance of any duty imposed by or under any of those provisions.

(4) Without prejudice to the generality of subsection (3) above, regulations under that subsection may—

(a) prescribe the matters to be taken into account by a local authority in determining, for the purposes of subsection (1) above, what is appropriate;

(b) provide, for the purposes of the exercise or performance of any power or duty conferred or imposed on a local authority by or under any of the provisions mentioned in subsection (3) above, for such samples of water to be taken and analysed at such times and in such manner as may be prescribed;

(c) authorise local authorities to exercise or perform any such power or duty through prescribed persons;

(d) provide for the recovery by a local authority from prescribed persons of such amounts as may be prescribed in respect of expenses reasonably incurred by the authority in the exercise of any such power or the performance of any such duty.

DEFINITIONS
    "local authority": s.219(1).
    "prescribed": s.219(1).
    "private supply": s.93(1).
    "wholesome": s.93(1).

GENERAL NOTE
    This section concerns the general functions of local authorities in relation to the quality of water supplies.
    Subsection (1) imposes a duty on every local authority to monitor the wholesomeness and sufficiency of water supplies provided to premises in its area, including every private supply.

This is a broad duty which will be implemented along with the more detailed regulatory framework created by the Secretary of State via regulations prescribing technical standards relating to "wholesomeness" (s.67), information which must be made available by water undertakers (s.69(5)), and regulations made under the provisions contained in subss. (3) and (4) of this section regarding the exercise by local authorities of the powers and duties contained in this section. See also Pt. VIII of the Water Supply (Water Quality) Regulations 1989 (S.I. 1989 No. 1147). Those Regulations require a water undertaker to inform the local authority and District Health Authority of any event which threatens water supplies by giving rise to a significant health risk (see reg. 30, subs. (6)).

Local authority functions in relation to undertakers' supplies

78.—(1) It shall be the duty of a local authority to notify any water undertaker of anything appearing to the authority to suggest—
- (a) that any supply by that undertaker of water for domestic or food production purposes to any premises in the area of that authority is, has been or is likely to become unwholesome or (so far as any such premises are concerned) insufficient for domestic purposes;
- (b) that the unwholesomeness or insufficiency of any such supply is, was or is likely to be such as to cause a danger to life or health; or
- (c) that the duty imposed on that undertaker by virtue of section 68(1)(b) above is being, has been or is likely to be so contravened as to affect any supply of water to premises in that area.

(2) Where a local authority have notified a water undertaker of any such matter as is mentioned in subsection (1) above, it shall be the duty of that authority, if they are not satisfied that all such remedial action as is appropriate will be taken by the undertaker, to inform the Secretary of State about the contents of the notification.

DEFINITIONS
"domestic purposes": ss.218 and 219(1).
"food production purposes": s.93(1).
"local authority": s.219(1).

GENERAL NOTE
Local authorities do not have direct powers of enforcement in respect of the unwholesome or insufficient nature of any supply of water where supplies are provided by water undertakers. However, under the provisions of s.78 a local authority has a duty to notify any water undertaker of the following matters relating to apprehended unwholesomeness or insufficiency of water supplies: (i) that supplies of water for domestic or food production purposes to any premises in the local authority's area are or are likely to become unwholesome or insufficient for domestic purposes; (ii) that such unwholesomeness or insufficiency is likely to cause a danger to life or health; (iii) alternatively, that the water undertaker's duty under s.68(1)(b) relating to maintaining the quality of the supply of water by a water undertaker is or is likely to be contravened. If a local authority is not satisfied that appropriate remedial action has been taken by the water undertaker concerned then the authority has a duty to inform the Secretary of State of the contents of the original notification to the water undertaker concerned.

Local authority functions where piped supplies insufficient or unwholesome

79.—(1) This section applies to a case in which it is not practicable at reasonable cost for a water undertaker, by supplying water in pipes, to provide or maintain such a supply of wholesome water to any particular premises in its area as (so far as those premises are concerned) is sufficient for domestic purposes.

(2) In any case to which this section applies, it shall be the duty of the local authority in whose area the premises in question are situated, if they are satisfied—
- (a) that the insufficiency or unwholesomeness of the supply of water for domestic purposes to those premises is such as to cause a danger to life or health; and
- (b) that it is practicable at reasonable cost for the water undertaker, by

providing it otherwise than in pipes, to provide to those premises such a supply of wholesome water as is sufficient for those purposes,
to require the undertaker, under subsection (3) below, to provide a supply of water to those premises otherwise than in pipes.

(3) Where, in a case to which this section applies—

(a) the insufficiency or unwholesomeness of the supply of water for domestic purposes to the premises in question is such as to cause a danger to life or health;

(b) it is practicable at reasonable cost for the water undertaker, by providing it otherwise than in pipes, to provide to those premises such a supply of wholesome water as (so far as those premises are concerned) is sufficient for domestic purposes; and

(c) the local authority in whose area those premises are situated notify the undertaker of the danger to life or health and require the undertaker to provide a supply otherwise than in pipes,

it shall be the duty of the undertaker, for such period as may be required by that local authority, to provide any supply to those premises which it is practicable at reasonable cost to provide otherwise than in pipes and which it is required to provide by that authority.

(4) Where under this section a local authority require the provision by a water undertaker of a supply of water to any premises, that authority—

(a) shall be liable to the undertaker for any charges payable by virtue of Chapter I of Part V of this Act in respect of the provision of that supply; but

(b) shall have power to recover the whole or any part of any charges paid by virtue of this subsection from the owner or occupier of the premises to which the supply is provided.

(5) In this section references to the provision of a supply of water to any premises otherwise than in pipes shall have effect, in a case in which it is practicable at reasonable cost to provide a supply (whether or not in pipes) to a place within a reasonable distance of those premises, as including references to the provision of a supply to that place.

(6) The duty of a water undertaker under subsection (3) above shall be enforceable under section 18 above by the Secretary of State.

DEFINITIONS
"domestic purposes": ss.218 and 219(1).
"local authority": s.219(1).
"wholesome": s.93(1).

GENERAL NOTE
This section details the responsibilities of local authorities in respect of piped water supplies which are insufficient or unwholesome. The section applies where it is not financially viable for a water undertaker to maintain a piped supply of wholesome water to any premises in the local authority's area sufficient for domestic purposes.

Under subs. (2) a local authority has a duty to require water undertakers to provide supplies for domestic purposes other than in pipes in circumstances where the existing supply for domestic purposes is likely to cause a danger to life or health and the water undertaker could at reasonable cost provide a wholesome supply of water by alternative means. Subsection (3) imposes a duty upon water undertakers in such circumstances to provide the alternative supply for such period as may be required by the relevant local authority.

Water undertakers may recover their costs in providing an alternative supply from local authorities under subs. (4) and in turn local authorities can recover their costs from the owner or occupier of premises to which alternative supplies have been provided. The water undertaker's duty under subs. (3) to provide alternative water supplies in such circumstances is enforceable by the Secretary of State using the s.18 enforcement procedure (subs. (6)).

Remedial powers of local authorities in relation to private supplies

80.—(1) Subject to the following provisions of this section, where a local authority are satisfied in relation to any premises in their area which are supplied with water for domestic or food production purposes by means of a private supply—

(a) that any water which is being, has been or is likely to be supplied for those purposes to those premises by means of that private supply is not, was not or, as the case may be, is likely not to be wholesome; or

(b) that that private supply is failing, has failed or is likely to fail to provide to any house on those premises such a supply of wholesome water as (so far as that house is concerned) is sufficient for domestic purposes,

the authority may serve a notice in relation to that private supply on one or more of the relevant persons.

(2) A notice under this section in relation to a private supply of water to any premises shall—

(a) give particulars of the matters mentioned in subsection (1) above in respect of which the notice is served;

(b) specify the steps which, in the opinion of the authority serving the notice, are required to be taken for ensuring that there is a supply of water to those premises which is both wholesome and (so far as any house on those premises is concerned) sufficient for domestic purposes;

(c) specify a period, ending not less than 28 days after the day on which the notice is served, within which any representations or objections with respect to the notice must be received by that authority; and

(d) state the effect in relation to that notice of section 81(2) and (3) below.

(3) Subject to sections 81 and 82 below, where a local authority serve a notice under this section on any relevant person they may do one or more of the following, that is to say—

(a) by that notice designate as steps to be taken by the authority themselves such of the steps specified in the notice as they consider it appropriate so to designate;

(b) by that notice require that person, within such reasonable period as may be specified in the notice, to take one or more of the steps so specified;

(c) by that notice require that person, at such times as may be determined in accordance with provision contained in the notice, to make to another relevant person or to that authority such payments as may be so determined in respect of expenses reasonably incurred by that other person or that authority in taking any step specified in the notice;

(d) by that notice undertake from time to time to make such payments to that person as may be so determined in respect of expenses reasonably incurred by that person in taking any step specified in the notice.

(4) The power of a local authority to serve a notice under this section specifying the steps which are required to be taken in relation to any source from which a private supply is provided both to premises in the area of that authority and to premises in the area of another local authority shall be exercisable only where—

(a) the other authority consent to the service of the notice; or

(b) the authorities act jointly in exercising their respective powers under this section in relation to that source.

(5) The powers conferred by this section and sections 81 and 82 below shall be so exercised in relation to a private supply of water to any premises where there is no house as to secure that no local authority are required to bear any of the expenses incurred (whether by the authority or by any other person) in taking any of the steps for ensuring that the supply is wholesome which are specified in a notice under this section.

(6) The steps that a relevant person may be required by a notice under this section to take in relation to any premises shall include—

(a) requiring a supply of water to be provided to those premises by a water undertaker or by any other person; and

(b) taking such steps for the purpose of securing that such a requirement is complied with, and of enabling such a supply to be so provided, as may be specified in the notice.

(7) For the purposes of this section and sections 81 to 83 below the relevant persons, in relation to a private supply of water to any premises in the area of a local authority, are—

(a) the owners and occupiers of those premises; and

(b) whether or not the source of the private supply is in that authority's area, the owners and occupiers of the premises where that source is situated and any other person who exercises powers of management or control in relation to that source;

and in sections 81 to 83 below a notice under this section is referred to as a private supply notice.

DEFINITIONS
"domestic purposes": ss.218 and 219(1).
"food production purposes": s.93(1).
"house": s.219(1).
"local authority": s.219(1).
"notice": s.219(1).
"owner": s.219(1).
"private supply": s.93(1) and (2).
"relevant persons": subs. (7).
"wholesome": s.93(1).

GENERAL NOTE
This section is concerned with the remedial powers of local authorities in relation to private water supplies.

Local authorities are given the main responsibility for regulating the quality of domestic private water supplies. A private supply is one which is provided other than by a water undertaker. This section gives local authorities enforcement powers to serve notices requiring remedial action in respect of substandard private supplies. See also the local authority's enforcement powers under s.82.

The general duty upon water undertakers to supply wholesome water (s.68) does not apply to private suppliers, but the effect of this section is to give local authorities the discretion to ensure that such supplies meet the standard required of supplies by undertakers. Technical standards defining wholesomeness are contained in the Water Supply (Water Quality) Regulations 1989 (S.I. 1989 No. 1147). Local authorities are given the power to authorise a relaxation of the standards in line with the permissible derogations under E.C. Directive 80/778/EEC relating to the quality of water intended for human consumption, provided that no threat to public health is involved, but must consult with the Secretary of State before doing so where the supply concerned serves or is to serve more than 500 people (Reg. 8).

The definition of "relevant persons" (under subs. (7)) who may be served with a notice includes both owners or occupiers of the premises supplied, owner or occupiers of the premises where the source of supply is situated, or any other person managing or controlling the source. Local authorities are therefore given a wide discretion in deciding who, they consider, should be responsible for taking remedial action. This section replaces s.57 of the Water Act 1989. During the passage of the Water Act 1989 concern was expressed during Committee stage at the possible implications of the new powers, and the Government acknowledged that local authorities would have to exercise their powers with care to avoid unfair results:

"We fully recognise that private supplies have very varied histories and circumstances and that it is not possible to draft legislation tailor-made for each circumstance. However, the clause has been drafted in a way which covers all those circumstances and allows the local authority to tailor its action under (the relevant) clause to the circumstances of the particular supply" (Lord Hesketh, *Hansard*, H.L. Vol. 507, col. 1353).

Confirmation of private supply notices

81.—(1) Subject to subsection (2) below, a private supply notice served by a local authority shall not take effect until the end of the period specified in the notice as the period within which representations or objections with respect to the notice must be received by that authority.

(2) Where any written representation or objection with respect to a private supply notice served by a local authority is received by the authority, before the end of the period specified in the notice, from a person on whom the notice was served, that notice shall not take effect unless—
  (a) the notice is submitted by the authority to the Secretary of State and is confirmed by him either with or without modifications; or
  (b) the representation or objection is withdrawn.

(3) If a local authority submit a private supply notice to the Secretary of State for confirmation, the Secretary of State—
  (a) shall consider whether the notice should be confirmed and whether, if it is confirmed, it should be confirmed with or without modifications;
  (b) may, with respect to the matters specified in the notice or any proposed modification of it, direct the local authority to serve a private supply notice, in such terms as may be specified in the direction, on any relevant person who has not previously been served with such a notice;
  (c) may, for the purposes of paragraph (a) or (b) above cause a local inquiry to be held or afford—
      (i) to the local authority; and
      (ii) to every person who has made representations or objections with respect to the notice or any proposed direction under paragraph (b) above,
    an opportunity of appearing before and being heard by a person appointed by the Secretary of State for the purpose; and
  (d) if he is satisfied that the person on whom any notice to be served in pursuance of a direction under paragraph (b) above has had a proper opportunity of having his representations or objections with respect to the proposal for the direction considered, may dispense, in relation to the notice so served, with the provisions of subsections (1) and (2) above and of section 80(2)(c) and (d) above.

(4) Where the Secretary of State confirms a private supply notice (whether with or without modifications)—
  (a) he, or if he so directs, the local authority concerned shall serve notice of that confirmation on every person originally served with the notice under section 80 above; and
  (b) that notice shall take effect, with any modifications made by the Secretary of State, at such time as may be specified in the notice served under this subsection.

DEFINITIONS
  "local authority": s.219(1).
  "modifications": s.219(1).
  "notice": s.219(1).
  "private supply notice": ss.80(7) and 93(1).

GENERAL NOTE
  This section details the procedures required to be followed regarding the service of a private supply notice under s.80, together with the effects of such a notice.
  Subsections (2), (3) and (4) provide for what is in effect an appeals system to the Secretary of State. Confirmation of private supply notices, which can under s.80(6) require water supplies to be provided to any premises by water undertakers, will not take effect until the end of the period specified in the notice, which must not be less than 28 days (s.80(2)(c)).
  There appears to be no restriction on who may make representations or objections under subs. (2). The requirement for the Secretary of State to confirm a notice under subss. (2), (3) or (4) only comes into play where the person served with a notice makes an unwithdrawn representation or objection.
  The Secretary of State has wide powers to confirm private supply notices with or without modifications and may (subs. (3)(c)) cause a local inquiry to be held to enable both the local authority and every person who has made representations or objections with respect of the private supply notice an opportunity of being heard at the local inquiry.

Enforcement and variation of private supply notice

82.—(1) Where any relevant person who is required by virtue of a private supply notice to take any step in relation to any premises fails to take that step within the period specified in the notice, the authority which served the notice may, in accordance with any applicable provision having effect by virtue of section 83 or 84 below, take that step themselves.

(2) Where any step is taken by a local authority in relation to any premises by virtue of subsection (1) above—

(a) the authority may recover from the person who failed to take that step within the specified period any expenses reasonably incurred by the authority in taking that step; and

(b) for the purposes of any requirement under which payments are required to be made to that person by any person other than the authority, sums paid by virtue of paragraph (a) above in respect of the taking of any step shall be deemed to be expenses incurred in the taking of that step by the person who failed to take it.

(3) Nothing in this Act shall confer any right of action on any person in respect of any loss or damage sustained by that person in consequence of the failure by any other person to take any step specified in a private supply notice.

(4) Any sum required to be paid to any person by virtue of any requirement or undertaking contained in a private supply notice shall be recoverable by that person from the person who is required to pay it.

(5) Any requirement which—

(a) is imposed by virtue of a private supply notice on the owner or occupier of any premises; and

(b) is expressed to bind those premises in relation to the owners or occupiers from time to time,

shall bind successive owners or, as the case may be, occupiers of those premises and shall be a local land charge.

(6) Subject to subsection (7) below, a local authority may by notice served on any person modify or revoke the effect in relation to that person of any private supply notice or notice under this subsection (including a notice which has been confirmed, with or without modifications, by the Secretary of State).

(7) Sections 80(2)(c) and (d) and 81 above shall apply, as they apply in relation to a private supply notice, in relation to any notice served by a local authority on any person under subsection (6) above except where the notice—

(a) extends the period within which any step is required to be taken by that person; or

(b) discharges, postpones or abates any obligation of that person to make a payment to the local authority.

DEFINITIONS
  "local authority": s.219(1).
  "notice": s.219(1).
  "private supply notice": s.93(1).
  "relevant person": s.80(7).

GENERAL NOTE
  Section 82 is concerned with the enforcement of the contents of private supply notices served under s.80. The section permits the local authority to take remedial action in default of compliance with the notice and to recover costs from the person served with the notice. The requirements of private supply notices may bind successive owners or occupiers if registered as a local land charge under subs. (5). Subsections (6) and (7) are concerned with the modification or revocation of the contents of a private supply notice.

Application of certain powers to local authorities in relation to private supplies

83.—(1) For the purposes of the taking of any steps falling to be taken by a local authority by virtue of a designation under subsection (3)(a) of section 80 above the provisions of Part VI of this Act shall have effect—

(a) as if the relevant works powers, so far as conferred on a water undertaker for the purpose of carrying out its functions, were also conferred on a local authority for the purpose of ensuring that a supply of water provided by means of a private supply to any premises in the authority's area is both wholesome and (so far as any house on those premises is concerned) sufficient for domestic purposes;

(b) as if any such power, so far as it is conferred on a water undertaker in relation to things belonging to or operated or used by the undertaker for the purposes of its functions, were conferred by virtue of paragraph (a) above on a local authority in relation to things belonging to or operated or used by that authority, or a relevant person, in connection with the provision of water by means of a private supply;

(c) as if references to a water undertaker in any provision of Part VI of this Act relating to a relevant works power, except the references in sections 181 and 182 below, included references to a local authority; and

(d) as if the making by any person in pursuance of a private supply notice of any payment in respect of sums incurred in the laying of any pipe entitled that person, for the purposes of section 179(1) below, to an interest in the pipe.

(2) Where by virtue of this Act a local authority have power under Part VII of the Local Government Act 1972 (miscellaneous powers of a local authority) to acquire (whether compulsorily or otherwise) any land or right over land for the purpose of ensuring that private supplies of water to premises in their area are both wholesome and (so far as houses on those premises are concerned) sufficient for domestic purposes, that power shall include power to acquire land or any interest or right in or over land in order, for that purpose, to dispose of the land or the interest or right to a person who is a relevant person in relation to such a private supply.

(3) In this section "relevant works powers" means the powers conferred on water undertakers by sections 158, 159, 161, 163 and 165 below.

DEFINITIONS
"domestic purposes": ss.218 and 219(1).
"functions": s.219(1).
"local authority": s.219(1).
"private supply": s.93(1) and (2).
"relevant person": s.80(7).
"relevant works powers": subs. (3).
"wholesome": s.93(1).

GENERAL NOTE
This section details the power of local authorities to take remedial action in respect of private water supplies under s.80. The section is designed to align a local authority's powers with those available to water undertakers regarding the laying of pipes and related matters. Where a local authority exercises the power to lay pipes on private land, the provisions in ss.181 and 182 concerning complaints to the Director with respect to the exercise of works powers on private land and the statutory code of practice relating to work on private land do not apply as they would do in the case of water undertakers (subs. (1)(c)). In such cases the appropriate course would be to lodge a complaint to a local government ombudsman under the Local Government Act 1974.

Local authority rights of entry etc.

84.—(1) Any person designated for the purpose by a local authority within whose area any waterworks are situated shall, on producing some duly authenticated document showing his authority, have a right at all reasonable hours to enter any premises for the purpose of ascertaining whether there is or has been any contravention of section 72 above in relation to those waterworks.

(2) Any person designated in writing for the purpose by a local authority may—

(a) enter any premises for the purpose of—

(i) ascertaining whether any provision contained in or made or having effect under this Act with respect to any water fittings, or with respect to the waste or misuse of water, is being or has been contravened;

(ii) determining whether, and if so in what manner, any power or duty conferred or imposed on any person by regulations under section 74 above should be exercised or performed; or

(iii) exercising any such power or performing any such duty; or

(b) carry out such inspections, measurements and tests on premises entered by that person or on water fittings or other articles found on any such premises, and take away such samples of water or of any land and such water fittings and other articles, as that person has been authorised to carry out or take away in accordance with regulations under that section.

(3) Any person designated in writing for the purpose by any local authority may—

(a) enter any premises for the purpose, in relation to any private supply, of—

(i) determining whether, and if so in what manner, any power or duty conferred or imposed on that authority by or under any of sections 77 to 82 above should be exercised or performed; or

(ii) exercising any such power or performing any such duty;

(b) enter any premises to which a supply of water is provided by a water undertaker for the purpose, in relation to a supply so provided of—

(i) determining whether, and if so in what manner, any such power should be exercised or any such duty performed; or

(ii) exercising any such power or performing any such duty; or

(c) carry out such inspections, measurements and tests on premises entered by that person or of articles found on any such premises, and take away such samples of water or of any land or articles, as the local authority—

(i) consider appropriate for the purposes of any such power or duty; and

(ii) have authorised that person to carry out or take away.

(4) Part I of Schedule 6 to this Act shall apply to the right of entry conferred by subsection (1) above; but nothing in that subsection or in that Part of that Schedule shall entitle any person designated for the purposes of that subsection by a local authority to have access to any waterworks belonging to a water undertaker.

(5) Part II of Schedule 6 to this Act shall apply to the rights and powers conferred by subsections (2) and (3) above.

(6) In subsection (1) above the reference to a local authority includes a reference to a county council and to the Sub-Treasurer of the Inner Temple and the Under-Treasurer of the Middle Temple; and any expenses incurred by the Common Council of the City of London in the exercise of their functions under that subsection shall be defrayed as part of their general expenses.

(7) In this section "waterworks" has the same meaning as in section 72 above.

DEFINITIONS
"local authority": s.219(1).
"private supply": s.93(1).
"water fittings": s.93(1).
"water works": subs. (7).

GENERAL NOTE
Section 84 makes provision for representatives of local authorities to have rights of entry for the following purposes:
   (i) to enter any premises (at all reasonable hours) for the purposes of ascertaining whether there has been any contravention of s.72 (contamination of water sources which are likely to be used for human consumption, domestic purposes or food or drink manufacture intended for human consumption);
   (ii) to ascertain whether any waste or misuse of water is occurring in respect of any water fittings. This right extends to determining how any power or duty imposed by regulations under s.74 should be exercised (subs. (2)(a)) and carrying out such inspections, measurements and tests on premises entered or in respect of water fittings found on any such premises (subs. (2)(b));
   (iii) to enter premises, in relation to private supplies, for the purpose of determining the manner in which the powers and duties under ss.77–82 should be exercised and to carry out any inspections, measurements and tests (subs. (3)).
Subsection (4) excludes certain persons designated by the local authorities, rights of access to any water works belonging to a water undertaker. Part I of Sched. 6 to the Act applies to the right of entry conferred by subs. (1). Part II of Sched. 6 applies to the rights and powers conferred on local authority representatives by subss. (2) and (3) of this section.

Local authority power to obtain information for the purposes of functions under Chapter III

85.—(1) Subject to subsection (2) below, a local authority may serve on any person a notice requiring him to furnish that authority, within a period or at times specified in the notice and in a form and manner so specified, with such information as is reasonably required by that authority for the purpose of exercising or performing any power or duty conferred or imposed on that authority by or under any of sections 77 to 82 above.

(2) The Secretary of State may by regulations make provision for restricting the information which may be required under subsection (1) above and for determining the form in which the information is to be so required.

(3) A person who fails without reasonable excuse to comply with the requirements of a notice served on him under subsection (1) above shall be guilty of an offence and liable, on summary conviction, to a fine not exceeding level 5 on the standard scale.

DEFINITIONS
"local authority": s.219(1).
"notice": s.219(1).

GENERAL NOTE
This section enables a local authority to serve on any person a notice requiring that person to furnish the authority within a specified period with such information as the authority reasonably requires for the purpose of exercising or performing any power or duty conferred by ss.77–82 (subs. (1)). This power is subject to the Secretary of State's power to make regulations which may include provisions restricting the information which a local authority may require (subs. (2)). Failure to comply with a notice served under s.85 will result in the commission of an offence (subs. (3)).

Assessors for the enforcement of water quality

Assessors for the enforcement of water quality

86.—(1) The Secretary of State may for the purposes of this section appoint persons to act on his behalf as technical assessors in relation to some or all of—

(a) the powers and duties conferred or imposed on him by or under sections 67 to 70 and 77 to 82 above; and

(b) such other powers and duties in relation to the quality and sufficiency of water supplied by a water undertaker as are conferred or imposed on him by or under any other enactments.

(2) A person appointed under this section shall—

(a) carry out such investigations as the Secretary of State may require him to carry out for the purpose of—

    (i) ascertaining whether any duty or other requirement imposed on that undertaker by or under any of sections 68 to 70 or section 79 above is being, has been or is likely to be contravened; or

    (ii) advising the Secretary of State as to whether, and if so in what manner, any of the powers of the Secretary of State in relation to such a contravention, or any of the powers (including the powers to make regulations) which are conferred on him by or under any of sections 67 to 70 and 77 to 82 above should be exercised; and

(b) make such reports to the Secretary of State with respect to any such investigation as the Secretary of State may require.

(3) Without prejudice to the powers conferred by subsection (4) below it shall be the duty of a water undertaker—

(a) to give a person appointed under this section all such assistance; and

(b) to provide a person so appointed with all such information,

as that person may reasonably require for the purpose of carrying out any such investigation as is mentioned in subsection (2) above.

(4) Any person appointed under this section who is designated in writing for the purpose by the Secretary of State may—

(a) enter any premises for the purpose of carrying out any such investigation as is mentioned in subsection (2) above;

(b) carry out such inspections, measurements and tests on premises entered by that person or of articles or records found on any such premises, and take away such samples of water or of any land or articles, as that person considers appropriate for the purpose of enabling him to carry out any such investigation; or

(c) at any reasonable time require any water undertaker to supply him with copies of, or of extracts from, the contents of any records kept for the purpose of complying with any duty or other requirement imposed on that undertaker by or under any of sections 68 to 70 or section 79 above.

(5) Part II of Schedule 6 to this Act shall apply to the rights and powers conferred by subsection (4) above.

(6) Any water undertaker which fails to comply with the duty imposed on it by virtue of subsection (3) above shall be guilty of an offence and liable, on summary conviction, to a fine not exceeding level 5 on the standard scale.

DEFINITIONS
    "enactments": s.219(1).
    "information": s.219(1).

GENERAL NOTE
    This section provides the Secretary of State with a power to appoint "technical assessors" regarding the provisions of ss.67–70 and 77–82 and such other powers and duties in relation to the quality and sufficiency of water supplied by an undertaker as are conferred or imposed on the Secretary of State by or under any other legislation.

    This section forms the basis for the appointment of the staff of the Drinking Water Inspectorate who monitor, investigate and report to the Secretary of State.

    Water undertakers have a duty under subs. (3) to provide such inspectors with both assistance and information to enable them to carry out their functions. Breach of this duty is a criminal offence (subs. (6)).

Subsection (1) refers to the appointment of "technical assessors". This term is not defined and does not restrict the Secretary of State to full-time civil servant appointments.

The section is derived from s.60 of the Water Act 1989. During the passage of the Water Act 1989, the Government provided information regarding the likely remit of the Drinking Water Inspectorate to be established within the Department of the Environment:

"The Inspector's main job will be to carry out a thorough technical audit of each undertakers' compliance with the water quality regulations. They will monitor the progress of improvement programmes. They will of course check for failures to comply with standards. They will also check for deterioration in quality. They will have to assess the adequacy of the undertakers' sampling and analysis arrangements and the quality of laboratory results. If they are not satisfied on any of these counts they will obviously need to discuss corrective action with that undertaker. They will advise the Secretary of State on the use of his enforcement and prosecution powers. They will also need to produce regular published reports on their assessments. Clearly a considerable amount of information will have to be assessed by the inspectors, for which computing and statistical expertise will be required" (Lord Hesketh, *Hansard*, H.L. Vol. 508, col. 1209).

CHAPTER IV

FLUORIDATION

Fluoridation of water supplies at request of health authorities

87.—(1) Where a District Health Authority have applied in writing to a water undertaker for the water supplied within an area specified in the application to be fluoridated, that undertaker may, while the application remains in force, increase the fluoride content of the water supplied by the undertaker within that area.

(2) For the purposes of subsection (1) above an application under this section shall remain in force until the Health Authority, after giving reasonable notice to the water undertaker, withdraw it.

(3) The area specified in an application under this section may be the whole, or any part of, the district of the authority making the application.

(4) Where in exercise of the power conferred by this section, the fluoride content of any water is increased, the increase may be effected only by the addition of one or more of the following compounds of fluorine, that is to say—

    hexafluorosilicic acid (H_2SiF_6);
    disodium hexafluorosilicate (Na_2SiF_6).

(5) Any District Health Authority making arrangements with a water undertaker in pursuance of an application under this section shall ensure that those arrangements include provisions designed to secure that the concentration of fluoride in the water supplied to consumers in the area in question is, so far as reasonably practicable, maintained at one milligram per litre.

(6) Water to which fluoride has been added by a water undertaker in exercise of the power conferred by this section (with a view to its supply in any area) may be supplied by that or any other undertaker to consumers in any other area if the undertaker or undertakers concerned consider that it is necessary to do so—

(a) for the purpose of dealing with any serious deficiency in supply; or

(b) in connection with the carrying out of any works (including cleaning and maintenance) by the undertaker concerned or, as the case may be, by any of the undertakers concerned.

(7) In subsection (6) above—

(a) the reference to water to which fluoride has been added by a water undertaker in exercise of the power conferred by this section includes a reference to water to which fluoride has been added by a water authority (within the meaning of the Water (Scotland) Act 1980) in exercise of the power conferred by section 1 of the Water (Fluoridation) Act 1985; and

(b) in relation to a supply of such water by a water undertaker, the reference to the water undertakers concerned shall have effect as references to the water undertaker and the water authority concerned.

(8) In this section "serious deficiency in supply" means any existing or threatened serious deficiency in the supply of water (whether in quantity or quality) caused by an exceptional lack of rain or by any accident or unforeseen circumstances.

(9) In this section and the following provisions of this Chapter references to a District Health Authority are references to any such authority within the meaning of the National Health Service Act 1977.

DEFINITIONS
"district health authority": subs. (9).
"serious deficiency in supply": subs. (8).

GENERAL NOTE
This section makes provision for the fluoridation of water supplies at the request of a district health authority to an undertaker (subs. (1)). The application for fluoridation remains in force until such time as the health authority gives reasonable notice to withdraw the application (subs. (2)). The whole or any part of the district health authority's area may be specified in the application (subs. (3)), and fluoridation may only be implemented using the chemicals specified in subs. (4).

Subsection (5) specifies the concentration of fluoride in water supplies which must be maintained by the water undertaker in exercise of the power conferred by subs. (1).

Fluoridated water may be supplied to consumers in any other area, *i.e.* outside the original area to which the application relates, provided that an undertaker considers that this is necessary for the purpose of dealing with any serious deficiency in supply or in connection with the carrying out of any works (subs. (6)).

Serious deficiency in supply. This is defined as any existing or threatened serious deficiency in the supply of water (whether in quantity or quality) caused by an exceptional lack of rain or by any accident or unforeseen circumstances.

Power to vary permitted fluoridation agents

88.—(1) The Secretary of State may by order amend section 87(4) above by—

(a) adding a reference to another compound of fluorine; or
(b) removing any reference to a compound of fluorine.

(2) The power of the Secretary of State to make orders under this section shall be exercisable by statutory instrument subject to annulment in pursuance of a resolution of either House of Parliament.

GENERAL NOTE
This section empowers the Secretary of State to amend s.87(4) by altering the chemical substances which may be added to the water supply to effect fluoridation.

Publicity and consultation

89.—(1) This section applies where a District Health Authority propose to make or withdraw an application under section 87 above.

(2) At least three months before implementing their proposal the District Health Authority shall—

(a) publish details of the proposal in one or more newspapers circulating within the area affected by the proposal; and
(b) give notice of the proposal to every local authority whose area falls wholly or partly within that area.

(3) Before implementing the proposal the District Health Authority shall consult each of the local authorities to which they are required, by virtue of subsection (2)(b) above, to give notice of the proposal.

(4) The District Health Authority shall, not earlier than seven days after publishing details of the proposal in the manner required by subsection (2)(a) above, republish them in that manner.

(5) Where a District Health Authority have complied with this section in relation to the proposal they shall, in determining whether or not to proceed, have such regard as they consider appropriate—

(a) to any representations which have been made to them with respect to it; and

(b) to any consultations under subsection (3) above.

(6) The Secretary of State may direct that this section shall not apply in relation to any proposal of a District Health Authority to withdraw an application under section 87 above.

(7) Where, at any meeting of a District Health Authority, consideration is given to the question whether the authority should make or withdraw an application under section 87 above, section 1(2) of the Public Bodies (Admission to Meetings) Act 1960 (which allows the exclusion of the public in certain circumstances) shall not apply to any proceedings on that question.

(8) In this section "local authority" includes a county council.

DEFINITIONS
"local authority": subs. (8); s.219(1).

GENERAL NOTE
This section makes provision for publicity and consultation procedures where a district health authority proposes to make or withdraw an application under s.87 for fluoridation. The district health authority must publish details of the proposal at least three months before the planned implementation under subs. (2). The district health authority must consult widely (subs. (3)) and in determining whether or not to proceed must have regard to any representations which have been made and any consultations carried out under the provisions of subs. (3). The definition of local authorities who must be consulted is extended to include county councils (subs. (8)). Community health councils must also be consulted by virtue of the Community Health Council Regulations 1985 (S.I. 1985 No. 304).

Where a district health authority proposes to withdraw a fluoridation application the Secretary of State may direct that the publicity and consultation provisions contained in this section should not apply (subs. (6)). The meeting at which the district health authority considers implementing or withdrawing a fluoridation application must be held in public (subs. (7)).

Indemnities in respect of fluoridation

90. The Secretary of State may, with the consent of the Treasury, agree to indemnify any water undertaker in respect of such of any of the following as he thinks fit, that is to say—

(a) liabilities incurred by the undertaker in connection with anything done by the undertaker for the purpose of increasing the fluoride content of any water supplied by the undertaker;

(b) costs or expenses which are incurred by the undertaker, or for which the undertaker is liable, in connection with any proceedings which have been or may be brought by any person with respect to—

(i) things done for the purpose of increasing the fluoride content of any water; or

(ii) a proposal to increase the fluoride content of any water;

(c) expenditure incurred by the undertaker in complying with an order made in any such proceedings;

(d) liabilities transferred to the undertaker in accordance with a scheme under Schedule 2 to the Water Act 1989 or Schedule 2 to this Act which, in relation to the person from whom they were transferred, were liabilities falling within paragraph (a) above or liabilities in respect of costs, expenses or other expenditure mentioned in subparagraph (b) or (c) above.

GENERAL NOTE
This section details the indemnities which may apply to a fluoridation application. The Secretary of State's power to indemnify any water undertaker under this section is subject to the consent of the Treasury and extends to the liabilities, costs and expenses specified in paras. (a) to (d) of this section.

Pre-1985 fluoridation schemes

91. Schedule 7 to this Act shall have effect with respect to fluoridation schemes made before the coming into force of the Water (Fluoridation) Act 1985.

GENERAL NOTE
This section introduces Sched. 7 to this Act which relates to pre-1985 fluoridation schemes.

CHAPTER V

SUPPLEMENTAL PROVISIONS OF PART III

Power to give effect to international obligations

92.—(1) Subject to subsection (2) below, the Secretary of State may by regulations provide that the provisions of Chapters I to III of this Part shall have effect with such modifications as may be prescribed for the purpose of enabling Her Majesty's Government in the United Kingdom to give effect—
  (a) to any Community obligations; or
  (b) to any international agreement to which the United Kingdom is for the time being a party.

(2) This section shall not authorise any modification of any of sections 71, 72 and 76 above or of any other provisions of this Part so far as they have effect for the purposes of or in relation to those sections.

GENERAL NOTE
This section provides the Secretary of State with a power to modify certain provisions of the Act by regulations in order to give effect to a Community obligation or an international agreement. The power under this section does not extend to modifications of ss.71, 72 and 76, which relate to waste, contamination and misuse of water supplies, or any other provisions of Pt. III of this Act so far as they have relevance to the operation of ss.71, 72 and 76.

These limitations are based on a presumption that Community or international obligations are unlikely to affect the structural arrangements, general duties and other areas of the Act. With respect to community obligations, these provisions appear to be superfluous, since s.2(2) of the European Communities Act 1972 already provides a broad general power to make regulations needed to implement any community obligations, and since by s.2(4) such regulations may include "any such provision (of any such extent) as might be made by Act of Parliament", they may amend or in other ways modify existing primary legislation. The powers, however, are not precisely co-extensive, since Sched. 2, para. 1(1) of the European Communities Act 1972 provides some limitation on the scope of limitations made under the Act which are not paralleled here.

Interpretation of Part III

93.—(1) In this Part—
  "connection notice" shall be construed in accordance with section 45(8) above;
  "consumer," in relation to a supply of water provided by a water undertaker to any premises, means (except in Chapter IV) a person who is for the time being the person on whom liability to pay charges to the undertaker in respect of that supply of water would fall;
  "food production purposes" means the manufacturing, processing, preserving or marketing purposes with respect to food or drink for which water supplied to food production premises may be used,

and for the purposes of this definition "food production premises" means premises used for the purposes of a business of preparing food or drink for consumption otherwise than on the premises;

"necessary works" includes works carried out, in exercise of any power conferred by or under any enactment, by a person other than a water undertaker;

"private supply" means, subject to subsection (2) below, a supply of water provided otherwise than by a water undertaker (including a supply provided for the purposes of the bottling of water), and cognate expressions shall be construed accordingly;

"private supply notice" shall be construed in accordance with section 80(7) above;

"water fittings" includes pipes (other than water mains), taps, cocks, valves, ferrules, meters, cisterns, baths, water closets, soil pans and other similar apparatus used in connection with the supply and use of water;

"wholesome" and cognate expressions shall be construed subject to the provisions of any regulations made under section 67 above.

(2) For the purposes of any reference in this Part to a private supply, or to supplying water by means of a private supply, water shall be treated as supplied to any premises not only where it is supplied from outside those premises, but also where it is abstracted, for the purpose of being used or consumed on those premises, from a source which is situated on the premises themselves; and for the purposes of this subsection water shall be treated as used on any premises where it is bottled on those premises for use or consumption elsewhere.

(3) For the purposes of this Part a service pipe shall be treated as connected with a water main other than a trunk main even if the connection is an indirect connection made by virtue of a connection with another service pipe.

(4) The rights conferred by virtue of this Part as against the owner or occupier of any premises shall be without prejudice to any rights and obligations, as between themselves, of the owner and occupier of the premises.

PART IV

SEWERAGE SERVICES

CHAPTER I

GENERAL FUNCTIONS OF SEWERAGE UNDERTAKERS

Principal duties and standards of performance

General duty to provide sewerage system

94.—(1) It shall be the duty of every sewerage undertaker—

(a) to provide, improve and extend such a system of public sewers (whether inside its area or elsewhere) and so to cleanse and maintain those sewers as to ensure that that area is and continues to be effectually drained; and

(b) to make provision for the emptying of those sewers and such further provision (whether inside its area or elsewhere) as is necessary from time to time for effectually dealing, by means of sewage disposal works or otherwise, with the contents of those sewers.

(2) It shall be the duty of a sewerage undertaker in performing its duty under subsection (1) above to have regard—

(a) to its existing and likely future obligations to allow for the discharge of trade effluent into its public sewers; and

(b) to the need to provide for the disposal of trade effluent which is so discharged.

(3) The duty of a sewerage undertaker under subsection (1) above shall be enforceable under section 18 above—

(a) by the Secretary of State; or

(b) with the consent of or in accordance with a general authorisation given by the Secretary of State, by the Director.

(4) The obligations imposed on a sewerage undertaker by the following Chapters of this Part, and the remedies available in respect of contraventions of those obligations, shall be in addition to any duty imposed or remedy available by virtue of any provision of this section or section 95 below and shall not be in any way qualified by any such provision.

(5) In this section "trade effluent" has the same meaning as in Chapter III of this Part.

DEFINITIONS
"sewers": s.219(1).
"trade effluent": subs. (5).

GENERAL NOTE
This section imposes a key general duty on sewerage undertakers, which matches the duty imposed on water undertakers by s.37. Compliance with the general duty to provide a sewerage system is enforced by means of a s.18 enforcement order. In addition, regulations under s.95 may prescribe standards of performance for the s.94 duty.

Subsection (1) is drafted to ensure that the sewerage undertaker's area "is and continues to be effectually drained". This duty is enforceable under s.18. The Act, however, contains no express provisions making an undertaker liable for loss or damage caused by sewer flooding. Any liability will normally require proof of some negligence on the part of the undertaker (see *Smeaton* v. *Ulford Corporation* [1954] Ch. 450) and for a recent review of the principles of the liability of undertakers performing a statutory duty see *Department of Transport* v. *North West Water Authority* [1983] 3 W.L.R. 707.

Subsection (2) imposes a duty upon undertakers to have regard to the discharge of trade effluent and its disposal when complying with the subs. (1) duty to provide a sewerage system. Schedule 8 to the Act is concerned with pre-1989 transitional authority for trade effluent discharges. The Schedule preserves the general right to discharge trade effluent into sewers subject to consents under the Public Health (Drainage of Premises) Act 1937, but with various amendments. Charge schemes in respect of trade effluent discharges may be made under s.143.

In carrying out their functions, undertakers are involved in drawing a fine balance between operating a commercial business and a system of environmental protection. Sewerage undertakers are now made responsible for granting consents, whilst appeals are made to the Director rather than the Secretary of State. There is no restriction on the right to prosecute for the offence of discharging trade effluent without a consent under s.118(5) and enforcement will therefore rest primarily with sewerage undertakers. Section 196 makes provision for public registers of consents and agreements relating to trade effluent discharges.

The general duty to provide, improve and extend a system of public sewers and to empty the system is enforceable by means of a s.18 enforcement order. A serious breach of this duty may result in an application by the Secretary of State or the Director to the High Court for a special administration order under s.24. Apart from s.37, this is the only duty under the Act where it is not first necessary to have made a s.18 order before making such an application.

The term "trade effluent" is defined in s.141(1), but see also *Thames Water Authority* v. *Blue and White Launderettes* [1980] 1 W.L.R. 700 regarding "trade premises".

Standards of performance in connection with provision of sewerage services

95.—(1) For the purpose—

(a) of facilitating the determination of the extent to which breaches of the obligations imposed by virtue of the following provisions of this Part are to amount to breaches of the duty imposed by section 94 above; or

(b) of supplementing that duty by establishing overall standards of performance in relation to the provision of sewerage services by any sewerage undertaker, the Secretary of State may, in accordance with section 96 below, by regulations provide for contraventions of such requirements as may be prescribed to be treated for the purposes of this Act as breaches of that duty.

(2) The Secretary of State may, in accordance with section 96 below, by regulations prescribe such standards of performance in connection with the provision of sewerage services as, in his opinion, ought to be achieved in individual cases.

(3) Regulations under subsection (2) above may provide that, if a sewerage undertaker fails to meet a prescribed standard, it shall pay such amount as may be prescribed to any person who is affected by the failure and is of a prescribed description.

(4) Without prejudice to the generality of the power conferred by subsection (2) above, regulations under that subsection may—

(a) include in a standard of performance a requirement for a sewerage undertaker, in prescribed circumstances, to inform a person of his rights by virtue of any such regulations;

(b) provide for any dispute under the regulations to be referred by either party to the dispute to the Director;

(c) make provision for the procedure to be followed in connection with any such reference and for the Director's determination on such a reference to be enforceable in such manner as may be prescribed;

(d) prescribe circumstances in which a sewerage undertaker is to be exempted from requirements of the regulations.

DEFINITIONS
"prescribed": s.219(1)

GENERAL NOTE
This section provides the Secretary of State with a power to make regulations relating to the standards of performance of sewerage services and match those relating to water supply in s.38.

Under subs. (1), regulations can be made by the Secretary of State only on the application of the Director under s.96. These regulations are intended to back up the Director's powers under the instrument of appointment to monitor an undertaker's target levels of service and progress on asset management. In addition to performance standards, under subs. (2) the Secretary of State may make regulations governing the day-to-day relations between an undertaker and its customers and such regulations may provide for financial penalties to be payable to individuals where the standards are not met. Such a scheme is contained in the Water Supply and Sewerage Services (Customer Service Standards) Regulations 1989 (S.I. 1989 No. 1159) and the Water Supply and Sewerage Services (Customer Service Standards) (Amendment) Regulations 1989 (S.I. 1989 No. 1383), providing for £5 payments or credits where various standards such as the keeping of appointments are not met.

Procedure for regulations under section 95

96.—(1) The Secretary of State shall not make any regulations under section 95 above unless—

(a) the Director has made to the Secretary of State a written application complying with subsection (2) below;

(b) the Secretary of State is satisfied that a copy of the application has been served by the Director on every sewerage undertaker specified in the application;

(c) such period as the Secretary of State considers appropriate has been allowed for the making—
(i) by the Director; and
(ii) by any affected sewerage undertaker,
of representations or objections with respect to the Director's proposals and any modifications proposed by the Secretary of State; and

(d) the Secretary of State has considered both the Director's reasons for his proposals and every representation or objection which has been duly made with respect to those proposals, or any proposed modifications of those proposals, and has not been withdrawn.

(2) An application made by the Director to the Secretary of State complies with this subsection if it—

(a) sets out draft provisions proposed by the Director for inclusion in regulations under section 95 above;

(b) specifies the sewerage undertaker or undertakers in relation to which it is proposed those provisions should apply; and

(c) summarises the Director's reasons for his proposals.

(3) The Secretary of State shall not make any regulations under section 95 above except where—

(a) the only provisions of the regulations are the provisions proposed by the Director in his application or those provisions with such modifications as the Secretary of State considers appropriate; and

(b) each of the modifications (if any) of the Director's proposals to which effect is given by the regulations is a modification the proposal to make which has been notified—

(i) to the Director; and

(ii) to any sewerage undertaker appearing to the Secretary of State to be likely to be affected by the modifications.

DEFINITIONS
"modifications": s.219(1).

GENERAL NOTE
This section details the procedure that is required to be followed before regulations can be implemented by the Secretary of State in relation to standards of performance in the provision of sewerage services.

Subsection (1) enables the Director to draw up proposals for regulations and for a copy of the draft regulations to be served upon the affected sewerage undertakers. The subsection also deals with the representations or objections which may be made and any modifications proposed by the Secretary of State. Regulations are only likely to be drawn up where the Director feels that the use of informal pressure is ineffective to secure adherence to current performance standards. In such circumstances the Director may apply to the Secretary of State to make regulations prescribing performance standards, which are then converted into a part of the undertaker's duty under s.94 and are enforceable under s.18 (s.94(3)). The Director must specify in his application the draft regulations, the sewerage undertaker or undertakers affected by the proposals, and a summary of the Director's reasons for making such application to the Secretary of State (subs. (2)).

Performance of sewerage undertaker's functions by local authorities etc.

Performance of sewerage undertaker's functions by local authorities etc.

97.—(1) A relevant authority may, in accordance with any arrangements which it has entered into for the purpose with any sewerage undertaker, carry out sewerage functions on that undertaker's behalf in relation to such area comprising the whole or any part of that authority's relevant area, together (where that authority are a local authority or an urban development corporation and the arrangements so provide) with parts of any adjacent relevant areas of other relevant authorities, as may be specified in the arrangements.

(2) Arrangements entered into for the purposes of this section may contain any such provision as may be agreed between the relevant authority and the sewerage undertaker but shall not affect the availability to any person, other than the relevant authority, of any remedy against the undertaker in respect of the carrying out of the undertaker's sewerage functions or of any failure to carry them out.

(3) It is hereby declared that, if arrangements entered into for the purposes of this section so provide, a relevant authority shall be entitled to

exercise on behalf of a sewerage undertaker any power which by or under any enactment is exercisable by the undertaker for the purposes of, or in connection with, the carrying out of the undertaker's sewerage functions.

(4) Where arrangements entered into for the purposes of this section provide for a local authority to carry out the sewerage functions of a sewerage undertaker on the undertaker's behalf, section 101 of the Local Government Act 1972 (delegation of functions), so far as it relates to the carrying out of functions by a committee, sub-committee or officer of a local authority, shall have effect in relation to those sewerage functions only in so far as the arrangements do not otherwise provide.

(5) In this section—
"new town" has the same meaning as in the New Towns Act 1981;
"relevant area"—
> (a) in relation to a local authority, means the area of the authority and the whole of any new town or urban development area any part of which is situated within the area of the authority;
> (b) in relation to the Commission for the New Towns, means any new town;
> (c) in relation to the development corporation for any new town, means that new town;
> (d) in relation to the Development Board for Rural Wales, means any new town situated within the area for which the Board is for the time being responsible; and
> (e) in relation to any urban development corporation for any urban development area, means that area;

"relevant authority" means any of the following, that is to say—
> (a) a local authority;
> (b) the Commission for the New Towns, a development corporation for a new town or the Development Board for Rural Wales;
> (c) the urban development corporation for any urban development area;

"sewerage functions," in relation to a sewerage undertaker, means any of the functions of the undertaker by virtue of its appointment under Chapter I of Part II of this Act as a sewerage undertaker, other than its functions relating to sewage disposal and its functions by virtue of Chapter III of this Part;
"urban development area" means any area so designated under Part XVI of the Local Government, Planning and Land Act 1980.

(6) Nothing in the Public Health Act 1875 (Support of Sewers) Amendment Act 1883 shall apply in relation to any sanitary work by virtue of this section; and in this section "sanitary work" has the same meaning as in that Act of 1883.

DEFINITIONS
"enactment": s.219(1).
"local authority": s.219(1).
"new town": subs. (5).
"relevant area": subs. (5).
"relevant authority": subs. (5).
"sewerage functions": subs. (5).
"urban development area": subs. (5).

GENERAL NOTE
This section provides sewerage undertakers with an unfettered discretion to enter into agency agreements with local authorities for the carrying out of sewerage functions (subs. (1)) but this does not affect any remedy against a sewerage undertaker for failure to comply with its sewerage functions (subs. (2)). Provided that such an arrangement has been entered into, a

"relevant authority", as defined in subs. (5), may exercise the sewerage undertaker's powers to enable it to carry out the undertaker's sewerage functions (subs. (3)).

Agency arrangements effected under s.97 authorise the authority to carry out sewerage functions in the relevant area except those relating to sewage disposal and the discharge of trade effluent into sewers (see definition of "sewerage functions" in subs. (5)).

Existing arrangements in force between a relevant authority and a water authority before September 1, 1989 will continue in force by virtue of Sched. 26, para. 15 to the Water Act 1989. These arrangements can be terminated or varied by agreement between the parties, but a sewerage undertaker may only end them unilaterally on the giving of reasonable notice to the relevant authority. If a termination notice was not given prior to September 1, 1989 it can only now take effect after April 1, 1992 (see Sched. 4A, para. (5)(1)(b) to the Water Act 1973).

Under subs. (2) the arrangements between a sewerage undertaker and a relevant authority will contain such provisions as "may be agreed" and will be likely to concern the authority's annual capital works programme and revenue expenditure programme.

The powers delegated to relevant authorities under subs. (3) may be delegated by the relevant authority to a committee, sub-committee or officer in accordance with s.101 of the Local Government Act 1972 (subs. (4)). Agency works do not have to be put out to tender under the provisions of Pt. I of the Local Government Act 1988 (s.3(3)).

CHAPTER II

PROVISION OF SEWERAGE SERVICES

Requisition of public sewer

Duty to comply with sewer requisition

98.—(1) It shall be the duty of a sewerage undertaker (in accordance with section 101 below) to provide a public sewer to be used for the drainage for domestic purposes of premises in a particular locality in its area if—

  (a) the undertaker is required to provide the sewer by a notice served on the undertaker by one or more of the persons who under subsection (2) below are entitled to require the provision of the sewer for that locality;

  (b) the premises in that locality the drainage of which would be by means of that sewer are—

      (i) premises on which there are buildings; or

      (ii) premises on which there will be buildings when proposals made by any person for the erection of any buildings are carried out;

    and

  (c) the conditions specified in section 99 below are satisfied in relation to that requirement.

(2) Each of the following persons shall be entitled to require the provision of a public sewer for any locality, that is to say—

  (a) the owner of any premises in that locality;

  (b) the occupier of any premises in that locality;

  (c) any local authority within whose area the whole or any part of that locality is situated;

  (d) where the whole or any part of that locality is situated in a new town, within the meaning of the New Towns Act 1981—

      (i) the Commission for the New Towns; and

      (ii) the Development Board for Rural Wales or the development corporation for the new town, according to whether or not the new town is situated within the area for which that Board is for the time being responsible;

    and

  (e) where the whole or any part of that locality is situated within an area designated as an urban development area under Part XVI of the Local Government, Planning and Land Act 1980, the urban development corporation.

(3) The duty of a sewerage undertaker under this section to provide a public sewer shall be owed to the person who requires the provision of the sewer or, as the case may be, to each of the persons who joins in doing so.

(4) Where a duty is owed by virtue of subsection (3) above to any person, any breach of that duty which causes that person to sustain loss or damage shall be actionable at the suit of that person; but, in any proceedings brought against a water undertaker in pursuance of this subsection, it shall be a defence for the undertaker to show that it took all reasonable steps and exercised all due diligence to avoid the breach.

(5) In this section the reference to domestic purposes, in relation to the drainage of premises in a particular locality to which a requirement under this section relates, is a reference—

(a) where there are buildings on premises in that locality, to such domestic sewerage purposes as are specified in relation to those buildings in the requirement; and

(b) where any person is proposing to erect buildings on premises in the locality, to such domestic sewerage purposes as are so specified in relation to the buildings and to times after the erection of the buildings.

DEFINITIONS
"domestic purposes": subs. (5).
"local authority": s.219(1).
"owner": s.219(1).
"public sewer": s.219(1).

GENERAL NOTE
This section imposes a duty on sewerage undertakers to provide a public sewer to drain premises for domestic purposes where a requisition is made by the persons specified in subs. (2), provided that the conditions in subs. (1) are met.

The section allows developers to be sure that a particular locality will be provided with a public sewer, even though this is in advance of the undertaker's forward planning and its general duty under s.94.

Breach of the duty owed by virtue of subs. (3) is actionable but is subject to the defence that the sewerage undertaker took all reasonable steps and exercised all due diligence to avoid the breach (subs. (4)). The definition of "domestic purposes" in subs. (5) is slightly different from that contained in ss.218 and 219(1).

Financial conditions of compliance

99.—(1) The conditions mentioned in section 98(1)(c) above are satisfied in relation to a requirement for the provision of a public sewer by a sewerage undertaker if—

(a) such undertakings as the undertaker may have reasonably required in accordance with subsection (2) below have been given by the person or persons who have required the provision of the sewer; and

(b) such security as the undertaker may have reasonably required has been provided for the discharge of any obligations imposed by those undertakings on any person who, under subsection (3) below, may be required to secure his undertakings.

(2) The undertakings which a sewerage undertaker may require for the purposes of subsection (1) above in respect of any public sewer are undertakings which—

(a) bind the person or persons mentioned in that subsection to pay to the undertaker, in respect of each of the twelve years following the provision of the sewer, an amount not exceeding the relevant deficit (if any) for that year on that sewer; and

(b) in the case of undertakings binding two or more persons, bind them either jointly and severally or with liability to pay apportioned in such manner as they may agree.

(3) For the purposes of subsection (1)(b) above a person may be required to secure his undertakings in relation to the provision of a public sewer if—
  (a) it was by virtue of section 98(2)(a) or (b) above that he required, or joined in requiring, the provision of the sewer; and
  (b) he is not a public authority.

(4) Where for the purposes of subsection (1)(b) above any sums have been deposited with a sewerage undertaker by way of security for the discharge of any obligation, the undertaker shall pay interest at such rate as may be determined either—
  (a) by the undertaker with the approval of the Director; or
  (b) in default of a determination under paragraph (a) above, by the Director,
on every sum of 50p so deposited for every three months during which it remains in the hands of the undertaker.

(5) An approval or determination given or made by the Director for the purposes of subsection (4) above—
  (a) may be given or made in relation to the provision of a particular public sewer, in relation to the provision of sewers of a particular description or in relation to the provision of public sewers generally; and
  (b) may be revoked at any time.

(6) Any dispute between a sewerage undertaker and any other person as to—
  (a) the undertakings or security required by the undertaker for the purposes of this section; or
  (b) the amount required to be paid in pursuance of any such undertaking,
shall be referred to the arbitration of a single arbitrator appointed by agreement between the undertaker and that person or, in default of agreement, by the President of the Institution of Civil Engineers.

(7) In this section "relevant deficit" has the meaning given by section 100 below.

Definitions
  "public authority": s.219(1).
  "public sewer": s.219(1).
  "relevant deficit": subs. (7).

General Note
  This section details the financial conditions which must be satisfied if a sewerage undertaker is to provide a public sewer in response to a requisition.
  The conditions referred to in s.98(1)(c) are satisfied if satisfactory undertakings are given by the person making the requisition and satisfactory security has been provided by that person to the undertaker (subs. (1)). Under subs. (2) the requisitioner must enter into an undertaking to pay to the undertaker during the 12 years following the provision of the public sewer an annual amount that does not exceed the relevant deficit on the sewer in that year (subs. (2)(a)) and where more than one person requisitions a public sewer then undertakings are taken which bind them jointly and severally.
  "The relevant deficit" is a new formula introduced by s.72 of the Water Act 1989 (and from which this section is derived) which is designed to iron out an anomaly under the formula adopted in earlier legislation.
  Section 17 of the Water Act 1973 was based on the assumption that a new sewer would be a satisfactory reasonable investment if sewerage charges for each of the first twelve years after connection would amount to one-eighth of the expense of providing the sewer. Converted to returns on investment, this formula did not allow for current levels of interest rates, and had the potential to result in uneconomic investment in new sewers by authorities which would then be subsidised by existing customers through higher charges. According to the consultation paper on water and sewerage law (Department of the Environment 1986), at interest rates of 12 per cent. a water authority would have received only £750 per £1000 invested. The new formula based on the concept of the "relevant deficit" is intended to remove such distortions and to require requisitioners to pay the full cost of investment. Where a requisitioner deposits funds as security in accordance with the provisions of s.99(1)(b), interest will be payable on such sum at a rate approved or determined by the Director (subs. (4)). The Director may give approval or

determination of the rate of interest which will apply to moneys held as security, either generally or in relation to a particular class of sewers or for an individual sewer. Such approvals or determinations may be revoked at any time save where the public sewer has been provided (subs. (5)). Any disputes between undertakers and requisitioners are referred to arbitration under the provisions of subs. (6).

Calculation of "relevant deficit" for the purposes of section 99

100.—(1) For the purposes of section 99 above the relevant deficit for any year on a public sewer is the amount (if any) by which the drainage charges payable for the use during that year of that sewer are exceeded by the annual borrowing costs of a loan of the amount required for the provision of that sewer.

(2) The annual borrowing costs of a loan of the amount required for the provision of a public sewer is the aggregate amount which would fall to be paid in any year by way of payments of interest and repayments of capital if an amount equal to so much of the costs reasonably incurred in providing that sewer as were not incurred in the provision of additional capacity had been borrowed, by the sewerage undertaker providing the sewer, on terms—

(a) requiring interest to be paid and capital to be repaid in twelve equal annual instalments; and

(b) providing for the amount of the interest to be calculated at such rate, and in accordance with such other provision, as may have been determined for the purposes of this subsection.

(3) A determination for the purposes of subsection (2) above shall be made either—

(a) by the undertaker with the approval of the Director; or

(b) in default of such a determination, by the Director.

(4) For the purposes of this section the costs reasonably incurred in providing a public sewer ("the new sewer") shall include—

(a) the costs reasonably incurred in providing such other public sewers and such pumping stations as it is necessary to provide in consequence of the provision of the new sewer; and

(b) such proportion (if any) as is reasonable of the costs reasonably incurred in providing any such additional capacity in an earlier public sewer as falls to be used in consequence of the provision of the new sewer.

(5) In subsection (4) above the reference to an earlier public sewer, in relation to the new sewer, is a reference to any public sewer which—

(a) has been provided in the period of twelve years immediately before the provision of the new sewer; and

(b) was so provided in pursuance of a public sewer requisition.

(6) Any reference in this section to the provision of additional capacity in a public sewer provided in pursuance of a requirement under any enactment is a reference to such works carried out or other things done in connection with the provision of that sewer as are carried out or done for the purpose of enabling that sewer to be used for purposes in addition to those for which it is necessary to provide the sewer in order to comply with the requirement.

(7) Any reference in this section to the drainage charges payable for the use during any year of any sewer provided by a sewerage undertaker is a reference to so much of the aggregate of any charges payable to the sewerage undertaker in respect of services provided in the course of that year as represents charges which—

(a) have been imposed by the undertaker in relation to such of the premises connected with that sewer as are premises where there are buildings; and

(b) are reasonably attributable to the use of that sewer for the drainage for domestic sewerage purposes of those premises or to the disposal of effluent drained for any such purpose from those premises.

(8) An approval or determination given or made by the Director for the purposes of subsection (2) above—

(a) may be given or made in relation to the provision of a particular public sewer, in relation to the provision of sewers of a particular description or in relation to the provision of public sewers generally; and

(b) may be revoked at any time except in relation to a public sewer that has already been provided.

(9) In this section "public sewer requisition" means—

(a) a requirement under section 98 above (including, by virtue of paragraph 1 of Schedule 2 to the Water Consolidation (Consequential Provisions) Act 1991, a requirement under section 71 of the Water Act 1989);

(b) a requirement under the provisions of section 16 of the Water Act 1973 (sewer requisitions); or

(c) a requirement under any local statutory provision corresponding to section 98 above or to any of the provisions of that section 16.

DEFINITIONS
"effluent": s.219(1).
"public sewer": s.219(1).
"public sewer requisition": subs. (9).
"relevant deficit": subs. (1).

GENERAL NOTE
This section is concerned with the calculation of the "relevant deficit" for the purposes of s.99. A person or persons who requisition a public sewer under s.99 are required to pay the full cost of investment over a 12-year period. This is achieved by basing the calculation on the "annual borrowing costs of a loan of the amount required for the provision of that sewer" as defined in subs. (2). The appropriate interest rate is determined by the undertaker with the approval of the Director or by the Director in default of determination under subs. (3). The costs which can be reasonably incurred in providing the new sewer are detailed in subs. (4) and include the provision of pumping stations or a proportion of the costs incurred in providing additional capacity in an existing public sewer which is now subject to increased use used in consequence of the provision of the new sewer.

Once the appropriate interest rate has been determined in accordance with the provisions of subs. (3), the rate cannot subsequently be altered for the new sewer will already have been provided (subs. (8)(b)). The formula used in s.100 thus excludes any costs associated with providing capacity in the sewer additional to the requirements of the requisition.

Determination of completion date and route for requisitioned sewer

101.—(1) A sewerage undertaker shall not be in breach of a duty imposed by section 98 above in relation to any locality unless—

(a) the period of six months beginning with the relevant day has expired; and

(b) the sewerage undertaker has not, before the end of that period, so laid the public sewer to be provided as to enable drains and private sewers to be used for the drainage of premises in that locality to communicate with the public sewer at the places determined under subsection (3) below.

(2) The period mentioned in subsection (1)(a) above may be extended—

(a) by agreement between the undertaker and the person or persons who required the provision of the public sewer; or

(b) where there is a dispute as to whether the period should be extended, by an arbitrator on a reference under subsection (4) below.

(3) The places mentioned in subsection (1)(b) above shall be—

(a) such places as are determined by agreement between the sewerage undertaker and the person or persons who required the provision of the public sewer; or

(b) in default of agreement, such places as are determined by an arbitrator on a reference under subsection (4) below to be the places at which it is reasonable, in all the circumstances, for drains or private sewers to be used for the drainage of premises in that locality to communicate with the public sewer.

(4) A reference for the purposes of subsection (3) or (4) above shall be to a single arbitrator appointed—

(a) by agreement between the undertaker and the person or persons who required the provision of the public sewer; or

(b) in default of agreement, by the President of the Institution of Civil Engineers.

(5) In this section "relevant day," in relation to a requirement to provide a public sewer for any locality, means the day after whichever is the later of the following, that is to say—

(a) the day on which the conditions specified in section 99 above are satisfied in relation to the requirement; and

(b) the day on which the places where drains or private sewers to be used for the drainage of premises in that locality will communicate with the public sewer are determined under subsection (3) above.

DEFINITIONS
"drains": s.219(1).
"public sewer": s.219(1).
"relevant day": subs. (5).

GENERAL NOTE
This section provides for the determination of the completion date for any sewer requisitioned under the provisions of s.98 and also contains provisions relating to the route of any requisitioned sewer.

Under subs. (1) a sewerage undertaker shall not be in breach of his s.98 duty to comply with a sewer requisition unless more than six months has elapsed from the "relevant day" (defined in subs. (5)) and the public sewer has not been laid so as to enable drains for private sewers to communicate with it.

The six-month time period in subs. (1)(a) may be extended by agreement or by reference to arbitration (subs. (2)). Contrast the six-month time limit in this section with the three-month time limit relating to a water supply requisition (s.44(1)(a)).

The provision of a public sewer (subs. (1)(b)) "to enable drains and private sewers to be used for the drainage of premises in that locality to communicate with the public sewers at the places determined at subs. (3))" is similar in content to s.16(3)(a) of the Water Act 1973. In *Leech (William) (Midlands)* v. *Severn-Trent Water Authority* [1980] J.P.L. 753 the court considered the interpretation of the similarly worded s.16(3)(a) of the Water Act 1973 and held that it implied effective communication, so that the water authority had to provide a pump if it was not possible to discharge into a public sewer by gravity. In the Court of Appeal (1982) 80 L.G.R. 102 it was confirmed that the authority was obliged to make the connection to the public sewer itself and the section did not entitle the authority merely to bring the sewer on to the land, leaving the owner to make subsequent connections.

Subsection (3) contains provisions relating to the determination of the routes of public sewers. Also note the general discussion relating to the phrase "at the places determined" in s.44.

Adoption etc. of sewers and disposal works

Adoption of sewers and disposal works

102.—(1) Subject to the following provisions of this section and to sections 103, 105 and 146(3) below, a sewerage undertaker may at any time declare that—

(a) any sewer which is situated within its area or which serves the whole or any part of that area; or

(b) any sewage disposal works which are so situated or which serve the whole or any part of that area, shall, as from such date as may be specified in the declaration, become vested in the undertaker.

(2) The owner, or any of the owners, of any sewer or sewage disposal works with respect to which a sewerage undertaker might make a declaration under this section may make an application to that undertaker requesting it to make a declaration under this section with respect to the sewer or works.

(3) A declaration or application under this section may be made with respect to a part only of a sewer.

(4) A sewerage undertaker which proposes to make a declaration under this section—

(a) shall give notice of its proposal to the owner or owners of the sewer or works in question; and

(b) shall take no further action in the matter until two months have elapsed without an appeal against the proposal being lodged under section 105 below or, as the case may be, until any appeal so lodged has been determined.

(5) A sewerage undertaker, in deciding whether a declaration should be made under this section, shall have regard to all the circumstances of the case and, in particular, to the following considerations, that is to say—

(a) whether the sewer or works in question is or are adapted to, or required for, any general system of sewerage or sewage disposal which the undertaker has provided, or proposes to provide, for the whole or any part of its area;

(b) whether the sewer is constructed under a highway or under land reserved by a planning scheme for a street;

(c) the number of buildings which the sewer is intended to serve, and whether, regard being had to the proximity of other buildings or the prospect of future development, it is likely to be required to serve additional buildings;

(d) the method of construction and state of repair of the sewer or works; and

(e) in a case where an owner objects, whether the making of the proposed declaration would be seriously detrimental to him.

(6) Any person who immediately before the making of a declaration under this section was entitled to use the sewer in question shall be entitled to use it, or any sewer substituted for it, to the same extent as if the declaration had not been made.

(7) No declaration may be made under this section in respect of any sewer or works the construction of which was completed before October 1, 1937.

DEFINITIONS
    "notice": s.219(1).
    "owner": s.219(1).
    "sewer": s.219(1).

GENERAL NOTE
    This section provides a power enabling sewerage undertakers to make a declaration vesting any sewer or sewage disposal works in the relevant undertaker either of its own volition (subs. (1)) or in response to an application made by the owner or any of the owners of any sewer or sewage disposal works (subs. (2)). The power does not extend to sewers and sewage disposal works constructed prior to October 1, 1937 (subs. (7)). An undertaker's declaration may relate to part of a sewer (subs. (3)).
    Prior to making the vesting declaration an undertaker must give two months' notice of its intention to all the owners of the sewer or works and if an appeal is lodged against the proposed adoption under s.105 the undertakers cannot proceed until the appeal has been determined (subs. (4)).
    In deciding whether a declaration ought to be made an undertaker must have regard to all the circumstances of the case, especially the five considerations contained in subs. (5). Subsection (5)(b) concerns access for repairs to sewers constructed under highways. Bearing in mind an

undertaker's powers of entry and power to prevent building over sewers, adoption should not be refused on this ground merely because sewers are in back gardens (see Department of the Environment appeal decision: Westfield Drive, Bolton-le-Sands, October 15, 1987, WS/5527/AB/17). Subsection (5)(c) does not provide a minimum figure in respect of the present or future number of buildings the sewer is serving or is likely to serve in the future. Each case is treated on its merits (see Department of the Environment appeal decisions: Portman Close, Dartford, February 5, 1987, WS/5274/AB/1). In subs. (5)(e) an owner may object to the proposed vesting if this would be seriously detrimental to him. The term "seriously detrimental" would include an increased likelihood that the sewer would overflow on to his land, a structural failure might result or some onerous liability might fall upon the owner in consequence of the declaration. Adoption is, however, likely to be considered as beneficial to the owner (see Department of the Environment appeal decision: Stennet Ave., Spalding, *Re* October 8, 1987, WS/5530/AB/22).

The Secretary of State in determining an appeal should not decide the matter on the least financial hardship that may be caused to a party to the proceedings (see *R.* v. *Secretary of State for Wales*, ex p. *Hutton* [1987] J.P.L. 711).

Adoption of cross-border sewers etc.

103.—(1) Where a sewerage undertaker is about to take into consideration the question of making a declaration under section 102 above with respect to—
(a) any sewer which is situated within the area of another sewerage undertaker or which, though situated within its own area, serves the whole or any part of the area of another sewerage undertaker; or
(b) any sewage disposal works which are situated within the area of another sewerage undertaker or which, though situated within its own area, serve the whole or any part of the area of another sewerage undertaker,
it shall give notice to the other undertaker.

(2) Where a sewerage undertaker is required to give notice under subsection (1) above to another undertaker, no declaration under section 102 above shall be made by the former undertaker until either—
(a) the other undertaker has consented to the declaration; or
(b) the Secretary of State, on an application made to him, has dispensed with the necessity for such consent, either unconditionally or subject to such conditions as he may think fit to impose.

(3) Where—
(a) a sewer or part of a sewer is vested, or any sewage disposal works are vested, in a relevant body; and
(b) in the case of a sewer, part of a sewer or works vested in railway undertakers or dock undertakers, the sewer or part in question is, or the works are, situated in or on land belonging to those undertakers and held or used by them for the purposes of their undertaking,
a sewerage undertaker shall not make a declaration under section 102 above with respect to the sewer or part or, as the case may be, with respect to the works, except on the application of the relevant body concerned.

(4) Where a sewerage undertaker makes a declaration under section 102 above with respect to—
(a) a sewer which is situated within the area of another sewerage undertaker; or
(b) any sewage disposal works which are so situated,
it shall forthwith give notice of the fact to that other undertaker.

(5) In this section "relevant body" means any sewerage undertaker, any local authority or county council or any railway undertakers or dock undertakers.

DEFINITIONS
"railway undertakers": s.219(1).
"relevant body": subs. (5).

GENERAL NOTE
   This section relates to the adoption of cross-border sewers and sewage disposal works. Where an undertaker is considering making a vesting declaration under s.102 it must give notice to an adjoining sewerage undertaker where the proposed declaration relates to any sewer or sewage disposal works which are either situated within the area of another sewerage undertaker or which serve the whole or any part of another sewerage undertaker's area (subs. (1)). No declaration can be made in such circumstances unless either the second sewerage undertaker consents to the declaration or the Secretary of State allows the adoption either unconditionally or subject to conditions (subs. (2)). A sewerage undertaker is prevented from making a declaration under s.102 in circumstances where part of the sewer or sewage disposal works are vested in any railway undertaker or dock undertaker and are situated in or on land belonging to those undertakers and used by them for their operational purposes (subs. (3)).
   Subsection (5) implements the first recommendation of the Law Commission's Report on the consolidation of the legislation relating to water (Cmnd. 1483, April 1981).
   Section 17(9) of the Public Health Act 1936, as amended, is now consolidated and applies to a declaration with respect to any sewer or sewage disposal works vested in another sewerage undertaker, a local authority or a county council.
   Where a sewerage undertaker makes a s.102 declaration with respect to a sewer or sewage disposal works situated in an area of another sewerage undertaker it must at once give notice of the declaration to the affected undertaker (subs. (4)).

Agreements to adopt sewer, drain or sewage disposal works, at future date

   104.—(1) Subject to subsection (7) and section 146(3) below, a sewerage undertaker may agree with any person constructing, or proposing to construct—
   (a) any sewer; or
   (b) any sewage disposal works,
that, if the sewer or works is or are constructed in accordance with the terms of the agreement, the undertaker will, upon the completion of the work, at some specified date or on the happening of some future event, declare the sewer or works to be vested in that undertaker.
   (2) A person constructing or proposing to construct a sewer may make an application to a sewerage undertaker requesting the undertaker to make an agreement under this section.
   (3) An application under subsection (2) above shall be accompanied and supplemented by all such information as the undertaker may reasonably require; but, subject to subsection (4) below and without prejudice to the effect (if any) of any other contravention of the requirements of this section in relation to such an application, a failure to provide information in pursuance of the obligation to supplement such an application shall not invalidate the application.
   (4) Where—
   (a) a person who has made an application to a sewerage undertaker under subsection (2) above has failed to comply with his obligation under this section to supplement that application with information required by the undertaker; and
   (b) that requirement was made by the undertaker at such a time before the end of the period within which the undertaker is required, by virtue of section 105 below, to respond to the application as gave that person a reasonable opportunity to provide the required information within that period,
the undertaker may delay its response to the application until a reasonable time after the required information is provided.
   (5) Any agreement made under this section by a sewerage undertaker shall be enforceable against the undertaker by the owner or occupier for the time being of any premises served by the sewer or works to which it relates.
   (6) The preceding provisions of this section shall apply also in relation to drains as if references to a sewer included references to a drain; but it shall be

a condition of any agreement under this section with respect to a drain that a declaration shall not be made before the drain has become a sewer.

(7) A sewerage undertaker shall not make an agreement under this section with respect to a sewer, drain or sewage disposal works situated within the area of another sewerage undertaker, until either—

(a) that other undertaker has consented to the making of the agreement; or

(b) the Secretary of State, on an application made to him, has dispensed with the necessity for such consent, either unconditionally or subject to such conditions as he may think fit to impose.

DEFINITIONS
"drains": s.219(1) and (2).
"sewer": s.219(1) and (2).

GENERAL NOTE
This section empowers sewerage undertakers to enter into agreements with developers to adopt sewers, drains or sewage disposal works if they are constructed in accordance with the terms of the relevant agreement. The sewerage undertaker will, either on completion of construction, or at some specified date or on the happening of some future event such as the construction of other works that link the new sewer to the general sewerage system, declare that the sewer, drain or sewage disposal works are vested in the undertaker (subs. (1)). An agreement under this section relating to drains is only effective where the relevant drains have become sewers (subs. (6)). A developer may request a sewerage undertaker to enter into such an agreement under subs. (2) in circumstances where either the developer is constructing or is proposing to construct a sewer. A developer's application under subs. (2) must be supported by all such information as the undertaker may reasonably require (subs. (3)) but an undertaker may delay responding to an application where information has not been provided by the developer (subs. (4)).

If the sewer, drain or sewage disposal works are situated within the area of another undertaker an agreement may not be made by the first undertaker until either the other undertaker has consented to the agreement or the Secretary of State has dispensed with the necessity for such consent either with or without conditions (subs. (7)). When effective the agreement is then enforceable against the undertaker by the owner or occupier for the time being of any premises served by the sewer under subs. (5) and recourse may also be had to s.33 of the Local Government (Miscellaneous Provisions) Act 1982.

Appeals with respect to adoption

105.—(1) An owner of any sewer or sewage disposal works may appeal to the Secretary of State if—

(a) he is aggrieved by the proposal of a sewerage undertaker to make a declaration under section 102 above; or

(b) he is aggrieved by the refusal of a sewerage undertaker to make such a declaration.

(2) Subject to section 104(4) above, a person constructing or proposing to construct a drain or sewer or any sewage disposal works may appeal to the Secretary of State where a sewerage undertaker—

(a) has refused an application under section 104 above;

(b) has offered to grant such an application on terms to which that person objects; or

(c) has failed, before the end of two months from the making of such an application, either to refuse the application or to give notice to the applicant of the terms on which it is prepared to grant the application.

(3) The time for the making of an appeal under subsection (1) above by the owner of any sewer or sewage disposal works shall be—

(a) in the case of an appeal by virtue of paragraph (a) of that subsection, any time within two months after notice of the proposal is served on that owner; and

(b) in the case of an appeal by virtue of paragraph (b) of that subsection, any time after receipt of notice of the undertaker's refusal or, if no such notice is given, at any time after the end of two months from the making of the application for the declaration.

(4) On the hearing of an appeal under this section, the Secretary of State may—

   (a) in the case of an appeal under subsection (1) above, allow or disallow the proposal of the sewerage undertaker or, as the case may be, make any declaration which the sewerage undertaker might have made; or

   (b) in the case of an appeal under subsection (2) above—

      (i) uphold the refusal of the undertaker to grant the application or to modify the terms offered; or

      (ii) on behalf of the undertaker, refuse the application or enter into any agreement into which the undertaker might have entered on the application;

and any declaration made under paragraph (a) above shall have the same effect as if it had been made by the undertaker in question.

(5) Where the Secretary of State makes a declaration under subsection (4)(a) above, he may, if he thinks fit—

   (a) specify conditions, including conditions as to the payment of compensation by the sewerage undertaker; and

   (b) direct that his declaration shall not take effect unless any conditions so specified are accepted.

(6) Where the Secretary of State makes an agreement under subsection (4)(b) above on behalf of a sewerage undertaker, he may do so on such terms as he considers reasonable or, as the case may be, on the terms offered by the undertaker subject to such modifications as he considers appropriate for ensuring that the terms of the agreement are reasonable.

(7) The Secretary of State, in deciding, on an appeal under this section, whether any declaration or agreement should be made, shall have regard to all the circumstances of the case and, in particular, to the considerations specified in section 102(5) above; and for the purposes of this subsection, in its application in relation to an appeal under subsection (2) above, paragraphs (a) to (e) of section 102(5) above shall have effect with the necessary modifications.

DEFINITIONS
  "drain": s.219(1).
  "owner": s.219(1).
  "sewer": s.219(1).

GENERAL NOTE

This section is concerned with rights of appeal regarding adoptions by sewerage undertakers of sewers or sewage disposal works.

An owner of any sewer or sewage disposal works may appeal to the Secretary of State against a sewerage undertaker's proposal to make a vesting declaration or if he himself makes an application to a sewerage undertaker for adoption and that application is refused (subs. (1)). In the case of developers who propose to construct drains, sewers or disposal works, an appeal may be made to the Secretary of State in three circumstances; where an undertaker has refused an application for an adoption agreement, or has offered to enter into such an agreement on unacceptable terms, or has failed to deal with the application for an adoption agreement within the two months specified in s.104(4) (subs. (2)).

The Secretary of State has wide powers under subs. (4) to allow or disallow an appeal or allow it subject to such conditions or modifications as he deems appropriate (see subss. (4), (5) and (6)). In deciding an appeal the Secretary of State must have regard to all the circumstances of the case and the considerations specified in s.102(5).

Communication of drains and private sewers with public sewers

Right to communicate with public sewers

  106.—(1) Subject to the provisions of this section—

(a) the owner or occupier of any premises in the area of a sewerage
    undertaker; or
(b) the owner of any private sewer draining premises in the area of any
    such undertaker,

shall be entitled to have his drains or sewer communicate with the public
sewers of that undertaker and thereby to discharge foul water and surface
water from those premises or that private sewer.

(2) Subject to the provisions of Chapter III of this Part, nothing in
subsection (1) above shall entitle any person—

(a) to discharge directly or indirectly into any public sewer—

    (i) any liquid from a factory, other than domestic sewage or
    surface or storm water, or any liquid from a manufacturing process;
    or

    (ii) any liquid or other matter the discharge of which into public
    sewers is prohibited by or under any enactment; or

(b) where separate public sewers are provided for foul water and for
    surface water, to discharge directly or indirectly—

    (i) foul water into a sewer provided for surface water; or

    (ii) except with the approval of the undertaker, surface water
    into a sewer provided for foul water; or

(c) to have his drains or sewer made to communicate directly with a
    storm-water overflow sewer.

(3) A person desirous of availing himself of his entitlement under this
section shall give notice of his proposals to the sewerage undertaker in
question.

(4) At any time within 21 days after a sewerage undertaker receives a
notice under subsection (3) above, the undertaker may by notice to the
person who gave the notice refuse to permit the communication to be made,
if it appears to the undertaker that the mode of construction or condition of
the drain or sewer is such that the making of the communication would be
prejudicial to the undertaker's sewerage system.

(5) For the purpose of examining the mode of construction and condition
of a drain or sewer to which a notice under subsection (3) above relates a
sewerage undertaker may, if necessary, require it to be laid open for
inspection.

(6) Any question arising under subsections (3) to (5) above between a
sewerage undertaker and a person proposing to make a communication as
to—

(a) the reasonableness of the undertaker's refusal to permit a communi-
    cation to be made; or

(b) as to the reasonableness of any requirement under subsection (5)
    above,

may, on the application of that person, be determined by a magistrates'
court.

(7) Sections 300 to 302 of the Public Health Act 1936 (which relate to the
determination of questions by courts of summary jurisdiction and to appeals
against such determinations) shall apply for the purposes of and in relation
to a determination on an application under subsection (6) above—

(a) as they apply for the purposes of and in relation to a determination by
    a magistrates' court under that Act; and

(b) in the case of section 302, as if the reference to a decision of a local
    authority included a reference to a decision of a sewerage undertaker.

(8) Where a person proposes under this section to make a communication
between a drain or sewer and such a public sewer in Greater London as is
used for the general reception of sewage from other public sewers and is not
substantially used for the reception of sewage from private sewers and
drains—

(a) the grounds on which a sewerage undertaker may refuse to permit the
    communication shall be such grounds as the undertaker thinks fit; and

(b) no application to a magistrates' court may be made under subsection (6) above in respect of any refusal under this subsection.

(9) In this section "factory" has the same meaning as in the Factories Act 1961.

DEFINITIONS
"drain": s.219(1) and (2).
"factory": subs. (9).
"sewer": s.219(1) and (2).
"surface water": s.219(1).

GENERAL NOTE
This section provides the owner or occupier of premises or the owner of a private sewer with a limited right to connect his drains or sewer to a public sewer for the discharge of foul water and surface water only (subs. (1)). Subsection (2) deals with the limitations on the right which does not extend to the discharge (other than domestic sewage or surface or storm water), from a factory or from a manufacturing process (subs. (2)(a)(i)). The sewerage undertaker also has power to insist that the connection to its sewers is made at a particular place (see *Beech Properties* v. *Wallis (G.E.) & Sons* [1976] 241 E.G. 685). Where a connection is to be made through land belonging to another person neither the owner of the pipe nor the sewerage undertaker may carry out any works until the landowner's consent has been obtained (see *Wood* v. *Ealing Tenants* [1907] 2 K.B. 390).

Before making the connection the owner or occupier must give the sewage undertaker notice of the proposed works (subs. (3)). On receipt of the notice an undertaker may, within 21 days, refuse to allow the applicant to make the connection if the undertaker considers that the way in which it is intended to be made, or the condition of the sewer or drain, is such as would be prejudicial to the undertaker's system (subs. (4)). An undertaker's right of refusal is restricted to the circumstances set out in subs. (4). An undertaker could not refuse to allow the connection on the basis that the system is inadequate to take the extra liquids resulting from the consideration (*Smeaton* v. *Ilford Corporation* [1954] Ch. 450), as that ought to have been dealt with when the existing sewerage system was planned. Nor can an undertaker impose a condition that the owner or occupier should pay the undertaker's costs in supervising any works to make the connection (*R.* v. *Greenwich Board of Works* [1884] 1 Cab. & E. 236).

Under subs. (5) an undertaker may require a drain or sewer to be opened up to enable the undertaker to confirm that it is suitably constructed. Disputes regarding whether the undertaker has acted reasonably in requiring the mode of construction of drains or sewers to be examined or is refusing to allow a connection will be determined by a magistrates' court under subs. (6). Subsection (8) is concerned with the restriction of an owner's or occupier's right to refer a dispute under subs. (6) where this relates to drains or sewers in Greater London.

Right of sewerage undertaker to undertake the making of communications with public sewers

107.—(1) Where a person gives to a sewerage undertaker notice under section 106 above of his proposal to have his drains or sewer made to communicate with a public sewer of that undertaker, the undertaker may—
  (a) within fourteen days after the receipt of the notice; or
  (b) if any question arising under the notice requires to be determined by a magistrates' court, within fourteen days after the determination of that question,
give notice to that person that the undertaker intends itself to make the communication.

(2) If, after a notice has been given to any person under subsection (1) above, that person proceeds himself to make the communication, he shall be guilty of an offence and liable, on summary conviction, to a fine not exceeding level 4 on the standard scale.

(3) Where a sewerage undertaker has given a notice under subsection (1) above—
  (a) the undertaker shall have all such rights in respect of the making of the communication as the person desiring it to be made would have; but
  (b) it shall not be obligatory on the undertaker to make the communication until either—

(i) there has been paid to the sewerage undertaker any such sum, not exceeding the undertaker's reasonable estimate of the cost of the work, as the undertaker may have required to be paid to it; or

(ii) there has been given to the undertaker such security for the payment of the cost of the work as it may reasonably have required.

(4) If any payment made to a sewerage undertaker under subsection (3) above exceeds the expenses reasonably incurred by it in the carrying out of the work in question, the excess shall be repaid by the undertaker; and, if and so far as those expenses are not covered by such a payment, the undertaker may recover the expenses, or the balance of them, from the person for whom the work was done.

(5) Sections 291, 293 and 294 of the Public Health Act 1936 (which provide for the means of, and for limitations on, the recovery of expenses incurred by a local authority) shall apply in relation to the recovery by a sewerage undertaker of any sums under this section as they apply in relation to the recovery of expenses under that Act by a local authority.

(6) For the purposes of this section, the making of the communication between a drain or private sewer and a public sewer includes all such work as involves the breaking open of a street.

DEFINITIONS
"drain": s.219(1), (2).
"notice": s.219(1).
"public sewer": s.219(1).
"sewer": s.219(1), (2).

GENERAL NOTE
This section provides a right for sewerage undertakers to make the connection between drains or sewers and the public sewerage system following service of a s.106 notice. In order to exercise the powers under this section a sewerage undertaker must serve notice on the person requiring the communication within 14 days of receiving the s.106 notice or within 14 days of the resolution by the magistrates' courts of any question arising under the provisions of s.106. It is the service of the s.101 notice that gives the sewerage undertaker all the rights which the owner or occupier of the relevant premises would have had (subs. (3)(a)). The undertaker may make the communication works conditional upon receipt of estimated reasonable costs or reasonable security. Should the person who served the s.106 notice complete the communication works himself, despite the service of a notice by a sewerage undertaker under this section, then he is guilty of an offence (subs. (2)). Note also a sewerage undertaker's powers under s.109(2).

Communication works by person entitled to communication

108.—(1) Where a sewerage undertaker does not under section 107 above elect itself to make a communication to which a person is entitled under section 106 above, the person making it shall—

(a) before commencing the work, give reasonable notice to any person directed by the undertaker to superintend the carrying out of the work; and

(b) afford any such person all reasonable facilities for superintending the carrying out of the work.

(2) For the purpose—

(a) of exercising his rights under section 106 above; or

(b) of examining, repairing or renewing any drain or private sewer draining his premises into a public sewer,

the owner or occupier of any premises shall be entitled to exercise the same powers as, for the purpose of carrying out its functions, are conferred on a sewerage undertaker by sections 158 and 161(1) below.

(3) The provisions of Part VI of this Act shall apply, with the necessary modifications, in relation to the power conferred by subsection (2) above as they apply in relation to the power conferred by sections 158 and 161(1) below.

GENERAL NOTE
This section is concerned with the powers which a person making a communication in pursuance of a s.106 notice has and also the provisions relating to supervision of the work which is carried out. The person entitled to make the communication will have the powers contained in s.15 (pipe laying in streets) and s.161(1) (carrying out works to deal with foul water and pollution). The person to whom notice will be given by virtue of subs. (1)(a) will be an officer of the sewerage undertaker appointed to supervise the communication works.

Unlawful communications

109.—(1) Any person who causes a drain or sewer to communicate with a public sewer—
  (a) in contravention of any of the provisions of section 106 or 108 above; or
  (b) before the end of the period mentioned in subsection (4) of that section 106,
shall be guilty of an offence and liable, on summary conviction, to a finc not exceeding level 4 on the standard scale.

(2) Whether proceedings have or have not been taken by a sewerage undertaker in respect of an offence under this section, such an undertaker may—
  (a) close any communication made in contravention of any of the provisions of section 106 or 108 above; and
  (b) recover from the offender any expenses reasonably incurred by the undertaker in so doing.

(3) Sections 291, 293 and 294 of the Public Health Act 1936 (which provide for the means of, and for limitations on, the recovery of expenses incurred by a local authority) shall apply in relation to the recovery by a sewerage undertaker of any sums under this section as they apply in relation to the recovery of expenses under that Act by a local authority.

DEFINITIONS
  "drain": s.219(1).
  "public sewer": s.219(1).
  "sewer": s.219(1) and (2).

GENERAL NOTE
This section sets out both the penalties for making an unlawful communication and the powers of a sewerage undertaker to close communications which are made in contravention of ss.106 and 108 and to recover expenses arising out of the closing of the communication. The person making the unlawful communication will not acquire any rights in the connection. If the sewerage undertaker acquiesced in the making of the communication it is possible that the sewerage undertaker will be estopped from closing the communication (*Clegg* v. *Castleford Local Board* (1874) W.N. 229).

Connections between public sewers

Determination of disputes with respect to cross boundary sewers

110.—(1) Where any part of a sewer is vested in a sewerage undertaker by virtue of section 70 of the Water Act 1989 (cross boundary sewers), the terms on which that part of that sewer—
  (a) communicates with such parts of that sewer or of any other sewer; or
  (b) discharges into any such sewage disposal works,
as immediately before September 1, 1989 were vested in the same water authority as that part of that sewer but, by virtue of that section, are vested in

another sewerage undertaker shall be determined, in default of agreement, by the Director.

(2) A determination by the Director under this section shall have effect as an agreement between the sewerage undertakers in question but may be varied or revoked by a subsequent determination made by the Director on the application of either of those undertakers, as well as by agreement between the undertakers.

(3) In making a determination under this section, the Director shall have regard to the desirability of a sewerage undertaker's recovering the costs resulting from its allowing the sewers of other sewerage undertakers to communicate with its sewers or to discharge into its sewage disposal works and of its securing a reasonable return on its capital.

DEFINITIONS
"sewer": s.219(1), (2).
"the Director": s.219(1).

GENERAL NOTE
This section provides the mechanism for resolving cross-boundary sewer disputes which may relate to the terms on which a cross-boundary communication was made or in relation to discharges into sewage disposal works. If the dispute cannot be resolved by agreement then the Director will make a determination. In reaching his decision, the Director will have regard to economic considerations contained in s.3, which mirror the Director's general duty contained in s.2(2). The Director's determination takes effect as an agreement between the relevant sewerage undertakers but the agreement may be varied or cancelled at a later date (subs. (2)).

Provisions protecting sewerage system

Restrictions on use of public sewers

111.—(1) Subject to the provisions of Chapter III of this Part, no person shall throw, empty or turn, or suffer or permit to be thrown or emptied or to pass, into any public sewer, or into any drain or sewer communicating with a public sewer—

(a) any matter likely to injure the sewer or drain, to interfere with the free flow of its contents or to affect prejudicially the treatment and disposal of its contents; or

(b) any such chemical refuse or waste steam, or any such liquid of a temperature higher than one hundred and ten degrees Fahrenheit, as by virtue of subsection (2) below is a prohibited substance; or

(c) any petroleum spirit or carbide of calcium.

(2) For the purposes of subsection (1) above, chemical refuse, waste steam or a liquid of a temperature higher than that mentioned in that subsection is a prohibited substance if (either alone or in combination with the contents of the sewer or drain in question) it is or, in the case of the liquid, is when so heated—

(a) dangerous;

(b) the cause of a nuisance; or

(c) injurious, or likely to cause injury, to health.

(3) A person who contravenes any of the provisions of this section shall be guilty of an offence and liable—

(a) on summary conviction, to a fine not exceeding the statutory maximum and to a further fine not exceeding £50 for each day on which the offence continues after conviction;

(b) on conviction on indictment, to imprisonment for a term not exceeding two years or to a fine or to both.

(4) For the purposes of so much of subsection (3) above as makes provision for the imposition of a daily penalty—

(a) the court by which a person is convicted of the original offence may fix

a reasonable date from the date of conviction for compliance by the
defendant with any directions given by the court; and
(b) where a court has fixed such a period, the daily penalty shall not be
imposed in respect of any day before the end of that period.
(5) In this section the expression "petroleum spirit" means any such—
(a) crude petroleum;
(b) oil made from petroleum or from coal, shale, peat or other bitumi-
nous substances; or
(c) product of petroleum or mixture containing petroleum,
as, when tested in the manner prescribed by or under the Petroleum (Consolidation) Act 1928, gives off an inflammable vapour at a temperature of less
than seventy-three degrees Fahrenheit.

DEFINITIONS
"drain": s.219(1) and (2).
"petroleum spirit": subs. (5).
"public sewer": s.219(1).
"sewer": s.219(1), (2).

GENERAL NOTE
This section is concerned with restrictions on the right in s.106 to discharge foul water and
surface water into a public sewer via any connecting drains or private sewers. Save for the
provisions in ss.118–141 relating to trade effluent the section prohibits the discharge into a
public sewer or any drain or sewer connecting thereto of any matter likely to injure the sewer or
drain or interfere with the flow of the sewerage system's contents. Such matter which would
damage either the sewer or sewerage treatment works will be prohibited under this section. The
prohibition in s.1 also extends to chemical refuse, waste steam, liquid at a temperature higher
than 110 degrees and any petroleum spirit or carbide of calcium.
The prohibited matter specified in subs. (1) is not an exhaustive list and reference should be
made to subs. (2), which deals with "cocktails" of substances which may either be dangerous, or
cause a nuisance or be injurious to health. Contravention of the section results in the committing of an offence and provision is made in subs. (3) for the imposition of a daily penalty where
there is a continuing offence committed. The courts can also give directions for compliance in
respect of a continuing offence (subs. (4)(a)). On conviction, on indictment the penalty may be
up to two years' imprisonment, or a fine, or both. Cynical offenders who continue to offend
because it is in their economic interests to do so may be restrained by way of an injunction.

Requirement that proposed drain or sewer be constructed so as to form part of general system

112.—(1) Where—
(a) a person proposes to construct a drain or sewer; and
(b) a sewerage undertaker considers that the proposed drain or sewer is,
or is likely to be, needed to form part of a general sewerage system
which that undertaker provides or proposes to provide,
the undertaker may require that person to construct the drain or sewer in a
manner differing, as regards material or size of pipes, depth, fall, direction
or outfall or otherwise, from the manner in which that person proposes, or
could otherwise be required by the undertaker, to construct it.
(2) If any person on whom requirements are imposed under this section by
a sewerage undertaker is aggrieved by the requirements, he may within 28
days appeal to the Secretary of State.
(3) On an appeal under subsection (2) above with respect to any requirements, the Secretary of State may either disallow the requirements or allow
them with or without modification.
(4) It shall be the duty of a person on whom requirements are imposed by a
sewerage undertaker under this section to comply with those requirements.
(5) The duty of any person by virtue of subsection (4) above to comply
with the requirements of a sewerage undertaker shall be owed to the
undertaker; and any breach of that duty which causes the undertaker to
sustain loss or damage shall be actionable at the suit of the undertaker.

(6) A sewerage undertaker which exercises the powers conferred on it by this section shall—

   (a) repay to the person constructing the drain or sewer the extra expenses reasonably incurred by that person in complying with the undertaker's requirements; and

   (b) until the drain or sewer becomes a public sewer, from time to time repay to that person so much of any expenses reasonably incurred by him in repairing or maintaining the drain or sewer as may be attributable to the undertaker's requirements having been imposed and complied with.

(7) Nothing in this section shall apply in relation to so much of any drain or sewer as is proposed to be constructed by any railway undertakers or dock undertakers in or on land which—

   (a) belongs to them; and

   (b) is held or used by them for the purposes of their undertaking.

DEFINITIONS
   "drain": s.219(1), (2).
   "sewer": s.219(1), (2).

GENERAL NOTE
   This section provides a sewerage undertaker with a power to require "a person", usually a developer, to construct a sewer or drain in accordance with the specifications of the sewerage undertaker. This situation will arise where the undertaker considers that the proposed sewer may be needed to form part of its general sewerage system. This section should be read in conjunction with the general duty to provide a sewerage system in s.94. Any person who considers that he has been adversely affected by the sewerage undertaker's requirements may appeal to the Secretary of State. Failure to comply with the undertaker's requirements will be a breach of duty owed to the sewerage undertaker, who may bring a civil action against the developer for any loss or damage caused by the breach (subss. (4) and (5)). Note also the provisions of s.104, which enable a sewerage undertaker and a developer to agree that a sewer constructed in accordance with the terms of an agreement under s.104 will, either on its completion, or on a specified date or on the occurrence of an event, for example, the construction of other works which link the newly constructed sewer to the general sewerage system, vest in that undertaker.

Power to alter drainage system of premises in area

113.—(1) Where any premises have a drain or sewer communicating with a public sewer or a cesspool, but that system of drainage, though sufficient for the effectual drainage of the premises—

   (a) is not adapted to the general sewerage system of the area; or

   (b) is, in the opinion of the sewerage undertaker for the area, otherwise objectionable,

the undertaker may, at its own expense, close the existing drain or sewer and fill up the cesspool, if any, and do any work necessary for that purpose.

(2) The power conferred on a sewerage undertaker by subsection (1) above shall be exercisable on condition only that the undertaker first provides, in a position equally convenient to the owner of the premises in question, a drain or sewer which—

   (a) is equally effectual for the drainage of the premises; and

   (b) communicates with a public sewer.

(3) A sewerage undertaker which proposes to carry out any work under this section shall give notice of its proposals to the owner of the premises in question.

(4) If the owner of the premises is aggrieved by the proposals, whether as regards the position or the sufficiency of the drain or sewer proposed to be provided for the drainage of the premises, he may appeal to a magistrates' court.

(5) Sections 300 to 302 of the Public Health Act 1936 (which relate to the determination of questions by courts of summary jurisdiction and to appeals

against such determinations) shall apply in relation to an appeal under subsection (4) above and to any determination on such an appeal—

  (a) as they apply in relation to appeals against any decision of a local authority under that Act and to determinations on any such appeal; and

  (b) in the case of section 302, as if the reference to a decision of a local authority included a reference to a decision of a sewerage undertaker.

(6) The Secretary of State may by regulations make provision with respect to consents and the conditions of consents for discharges of trade effluent into the sewer of a sewerage undertaker through a drain or sewer provided in pursuance of this section.

(7) In this section—

  "cesspool" includes a settlement tank or other tank for the reception or disposal of foul matter from buildings; and

  "trade effluent" has the same meaning as in Chapter III of this Part.

DEFINITIONS
  "cess pool": subs. (7).
  "drain": s.219(1) and (2).
  "public sewer": s.219(1).
  "sewer": s.219(1) and (2).
  "trade effluent": subs. (7) and s.141.

GENERAL NOTE
  This section empowers a sewerage undertaker to alter the drainage system of premises connected to a public sewer or cesspool in circumstances where the present arrangements do not conform to the undertaker's general sewerage system or where present arrangements are otherwise objectionable (subs. (1)). Prior to effecting the alterations to the drainage system the sewerage undertaker must provide an effectual alternative drainage system which connects with the public sewerage system (subs. (2)). The costs incurred in carrying out the alteration to the drainage system are borne entirely by the sewerage undertaker. In contrast to s.112(2), an owner of premises affected by the undertaker's proposals who is aggrieved has a right of appeal to a magistrates' court to determine any disputes relating to the substitute drainage system (subs. (4)). The utilisation of this power should be read in conjunction with a sewerage undertaker's general duty to provide and improve the sewerage system under s.94.

Power to investigate defective drain or sewer

114.—(1) Where it appears to a sewerage undertaker that there are reasonable grounds for believing—

  (a) that any drain connecting with a public sewer, or any private sewer so connecting, is in such a condition as to be injurious or likely to cause injury to health or as to be a nuisance; or

  (b) that any such drain or private sewer is so defective as to admit subsoil water,

the undertaker may examine the condition of the drain or sewer and, for that purpose, may apply any test, other than a test by water under pressure and, if the undertaker deems it necessary, open the ground.

(2) If on examination the drain or sewer is found to be in proper condition, the undertaker shall, as soon as possible, reinstate any ground which has been opened by it and make good any damage done by the undertaker.

DEFINITIONS
  "drain": s.219(1) and (2).
  "public sewer": s.219(1).

GENERAL NOTE
  This section provides a wide power for sewerage undertakers to carry out a wide range of tests, except a water pressure test, in order to confirm whether any drain or private sewer connecting with a public sewer is defective within the terms of subs. (1). The sewerage undertaker must have reasonable grounds for believing that the drains and sewers to be inspected are in a defective condition.

Use of pipes for sewerage purposes

Use of highway drains as sewers and vice versa

115.—(1) Subject to the provisions of this section, a relevant authority and a sewerage undertaker may agree that—

(a) any drain or sewer which is vested in the authority in their capacity as a highway authority may, upon such terms as may be agreed, be used by the undertaker for the purpose of conveying surface water from premises or streets;

(b) any public sewer vested in the undertaker may, upon such terms as may be agreed, be used by the authority for conveying surface water from roads repairable by the authority.

(2) Where a sewer or drain with respect to which a relevant authority and a sewerage undertaker propose to make an agreement under this section discharges, whether directly or indirectly, into the sewers or sewage disposal works of another sewerage undertaker, the agreement shall not be made without the consent of that other undertaker.

(3) Subject to subsection (4) below, a consent given by a sewerage undertaker for the purposes of subsection (2) above may be given on such terms as that undertaker thinks fit.

(4) Neither a relevant authority nor a sewerage undertaker shall—

(a) unreasonably refuse to enter into an agreement for the purposes of this section; or

(b) insist unreasonably upon terms unacceptable to the other party; and a sewerage undertaker shall not unreasonably refuse to consent to the making of such an agreement or insist unreasonably upon terms unacceptable to either party.

(5) Any question arising under this section as to whether or not any authority or undertaker is acting unreasonably shall be referred to the Secretary of State, whose decision shall be final.

(6) The powers by virtue of paragraph (a) of subsection (1) above of a relevant authority and a sewerage undertaker to enter into an agreement shall be exercisable by two relevant authorities as they would be exercisable if one of them were a sewerage undertaker.

(7) Nothing in this section shall be construed as limiting the rights of a relevant authority under section 264 of the Highways Act 1980.

(8) Part XII of the Public Health Act 1936 shall apply for the purposes of the provisions of this section which confer functions on relevant authorities as they apply for the purposes of the provisions of that Act.

(9) In this section "relevant authority" means a county council or any local authority except a non-metropolitan district council.

(10) The provisions of this section are subject to the provisions of section 146(4) below.

DEFINITIONS
   "a relevant authority": subs. (9).
   "drain": s.219(1) and (2).
   "highway authority": s.219(1).
   "public sewer": s.219(1).
   "sewer": s.219(1) and (2).
   "streets": s.219(1).
   "surface water": s.219(1).

GENERAL NOTE
   This section enables the class of highway authorities detailed in subs. (9) and sewerage undertakers to enter into reciprocal agreements whereby drains or sewers vested in the

authority may be used to convey surface water from premises or streets and conversely in relation to the use of public sewers by an authority for the conveyance of surface water from roads repairable by the local authority. In circumstances where the surface water will pass to the sewers or sewage disposal works of another sewerage undertaker, that sewerage undertaker must consent to the agreement (subs. (2)), and may impose such terms as he thinks fit upon its consent (subs. (3)). The Secretary of State will determine whether any party to the agreement or other sewerage undertaker from which a consent is sought is acting unreasonably in relation to the proposed agreement (subs. (5)).

Power to close or restrict use of public sewer

116.—(1) Subject to subsection (3) below, a sewerage undertaker may discontinue and prohibit the use of any public sewer which is vested in the undertaker.

(2) A discontinuance or prohibition under this section may be for all purposes, for the purpose of foul water drainage or for the purpose of surface water drainage.

(3) Before any person who is lawfully using a sewer for any purpose is deprived under this section by a sewerage undertaker of the use of the sewer for that purpose, the undertaker shall—

(a) provide a sewer which is equally effective for his use for that purpose; and

(b) at the undertaker's own expense, carry out any work necessary to make that person's drains or sewers communicate with the sewer provided in pursuance of this subsection.

DEFINITIONS
  "public sewer": s.219(1).
  "sewer": s.219(1), (2).

GENERAL NOTE
  This section provides a power for sewerage undertakers to discontinue and prohibit the use of any public sewer which is vested in the undertaker for all purposes, foul water drainage or surface water drainage. Before closing or restricting the use of the public sewer, the undertaker must provide persons lawfully using the sewer with an equally effective alternative and must bear the cost of connecting the lawful user's premises with the public sewer. A public sewer which has been closed continues to be a public sewer until it is removed or the rights in it are extinguished (*Blackdown Properties* v. *Ministry of Housing and Local Government* [1967] Ch. 115).

Interpretation of Chapter II

Interpretation of Chapter II

117.—(1) In this Chapter, except in so far as the context otherwise requires—

  "dock undertakers" means persons authorised by any enactment, or by any order, rule or regulation made under any enactment, to construct, work or carry on any dock, harbour, canal or inland navigation;

  "domestic sewerage purposes," in relation to any premises, means any one or more of the following purposes, that is to say—

      (a) the removal, from buildings on the premises and from land occupied with and appurtenant to the buildings, of the contents of lavatories;

      (b) the removal, from such buildings and from such land, of water which has been used for cooking or washing; and

      (c) the removal, from such buildings and such land, of surface water;

    but does not, by virtue of paragraph (b) of this definition, include the removal of any water used for the business of a laundry or for a business of preparing food or drink for consumption otherwise than on the premises.

(2) References in this Chapter to the construction of a sewer or of any sewage disposal works include references to the extension of any existing sewer or works.

(3) In this Chapter "local authority," in relation to the Inner Temple and the Middle Temple, includes, respectively, the Sub-Treasurer of the Inner Temple and the Under-Treasurer of the Middle Temple.

(4) Every application made or consent given under this Chapter shall be made or given in writing.

(5) Nothing in sections 102 to 109 above or in sections 111 to 116 above shall be construed as authorising a sewerage undertaker to construct or use any public or other sewer, or any drain or outfall—

(a) in contravention of any applicable provision of the Water Resources Act 1991; or

(b) for the purpose of conveying foul water into any natural or artificial stream, watercourse, canal, pond or lake, without the water having been so treated as not to affect prejudicially the purity and quality of the water in the stream, watercourse, canal, pond or lake.

(6) A sewerage undertaker shall so carry out its functions under sections 102 to 105, 112, 115 and 116 above as not to create a nuisance.

CHAPTER III

TRADE EFFLUENT

Consent for discharge of trade effluent into public sewer

Consent required for discharge of trade effluent into public sewer

118.—(1) Subject to the following provisions of this Chapter, the occupier of any trade premises in the area of a sewerage undertaker may discharge any trade effluent proceeding from those premises into the undertaker's public sewers if he does so with the undertaker's consent.

(2) Nothing in this Chapter shall authorise the discharge of any effluent into a public sewer otherwise than by means of a drain or sewer.

(3) The following, that is to say—

(a) the restrictions imposed by paragraphs (a) and (b) of section 106(2) above; and

(b) section 111 above so far as it relates to anything falling within paragraph (a) or (b) of subsection (1) of that section,

shall not apply to any discharge of trade effluent which is lawfully made by virtue of this Chapter.

(4) Accordingly, subsections (3) to (8) of section 106 above and sections 108 and 109 above shall have effect in relation to communication with a sewer for the purpose of making any discharge which is lawfully made by virtue of this Chapter as they have effect in relation to communication with a sewer for the purpose of making discharges which are authorised by subsection (1) of section 106 above.

(5) If, in the case of any trade premises, any trade effluent is discharged without such consent or other authorisation as is necessary for the purposes of this Chapter, the occupier of the premises shall be guilty of an offence and liable—

(a) on summary conviction, to a fine not exceeding the statutory maximum; and

(b) on conviction on indictment, to a fine.

DEFINITIONS
"drain": s.219(1), (2).

"effluent": s.219(1).
"public sewers": s.219(1).
"sewer": s.219(1), (2).
"trade effluent": s.141(1).
"trade premises": s.141(1), (2).

GENERAL NOTE

This section entitles occupiers of "trade premises" (defined in s.141) to discharge trade effluent into the public sewerage system provided that the sewerage undertaker's consent has been obtained (subs. (1)). Discharges may only be made via drains and sewers (subs. (2)) and a discharge made without the consent of a sewerage undertaker is an offence attracting the penalties specified in subs. (5).

The special provisions relating to trade effluent contained in Pt. VI, Chap. III of the Act exist to ensure that sewers and sewage treatment works can deal adequately and safely with the trade effluent discharged into the sewerage system. Where a discharge is lawfully made under this section the provisions contained in s.106(2)(a) and (b) (communication rights with public sewers) and s.111(1)(a) and (b) (restriction on the use of public sewers) do not apply.

The section gives effect to Recommendation No. 2 of the Law Commission's Report on the consolidation of the legislation relating to water (Cmnd. 1483, April, 1991) by clarifying that an agreement under s.7 of the Public Health (Drainage of Trade Premises) Act 1937, authorising the discharge of trade effluent into a public sewer, provides a defence to the offence under s.2(5)(a) of that Act, but that in doing so, it does not constitute a consent under that Act.

Consents on an application

Application for consent

119.—(1) An application to a sewerage undertaker for a consent to discharge trade effluent from any trade premises into a public sewer of that undertaker shall be by notice served on the undertaker by the owner or occupier of the premises.

(2) An application under this section with respect to a proposed discharge of any such effluent shall state—

(a) the nature or composition of the trade effluent;

(b) the maximum quantity of the trade effluent which it is proposed to discharge on any one day; and

(c) the highest rate at which it is proposed to discharge the trade effluent.

DEFINITIONS

"notice": s.219(1).
"owner": s.219(1).
"public sewer": s.219(1).
"trade effluent": s.141(1).
"trade premises": s.141(1), (2).

Applications for the discharge of special category effluent

120.—(1) Subject to subsection (3) below, where a notice containing an application under section 119 above is served on a sewerage undertaker with respect to discharges of any special category effluent, it shall be the duty of the undertaker to refer to the Secretary of State the questions—

(a) whether the discharges to which the notice relates should be prohibited; and

(b) whether, if they are not prohibited, any requirements should be imposed as to the conditions on which they are made.

(2) Subject to subsection (3) below, a reference which is required to be made by a sewerage undertaker by virtue of subsection (1) above shall be made before the end of the period of two months beginning with the day after the notice containing the application is served on the undertaker.

(3) There shall be no obligation on a sewerage undertaker to make a reference under this section in respect of any application if, before the end of the period mentioned in subsection (2) above, there is a refusal by the undertaker to give any consent on the application.

(4) It shall be the duty of a sewerage undertaker where it has made a reference under this section not to give any consent, or enter into any agreement, with respect to the discharges to which the reference relates at any time before the Secretary of State serves notice on the undertaker of his determination on the reference.

(5) Every reference under this section shall be made in writing and shall be accompanied by a copy of the notice containing the application in respect of which it is made.

(6) It shall be the duty of a sewerage undertaker, on making a reference under this section, to serve a copy of the reference on the owner or the occupier of the trade premises in question, according to whether the discharges to which the reference relates are to be by the owner or by the occupier.

(7) Subject to subsection (8) below, the duties of a sewerage undertaker under this section shall be enforceable under section 18 above by the Secretary of State.

(8) Where an application is made to the Secretary of State under section 18 above in respect of a failure by a sewerage undertaker to make a reference under this section, the Secretary of State may, instead of making an order under that section, proceed with the matter as if the application were the reference.

DEFINITIONS
"notice": s.219(1).
"owner": s.219(1).
"special category effluent": s.138.

GENERAL NOTE
This section is concerned with applications by owners of trade premises under s.119 where the discharge to which the consent application relates is a discharge of special category effluent (defined in s.138).

Where a special category effluent discharge application is made the undertaker is under a duty to refer to the Secretary of State the question whether the discharge should be prohibited or allowed subject to conditions. The application must be referred to the Secretary of State within two months of the date of the application unless during that period the undertaker has decided to refuse its consent to the application (subs. (3)). The appeals procedure in respect of a refusal of a special category effluent application is dealt with under s.123. The duties upon a sewerage undertaker under this section are enforceable by the Secretary of State under the s.18 enforcement procedures.

The special control relating to special category effluent under this section applies to discharges of effluent which either contain prescribed substances, or more than a prescribed quantity of such substances, or to effluent discharges that derive from a stipulated process or from a process that involves the use of a prescribed substance or more than the prescribed amount of such a substance. Substances or processes become prescribed where they are on the "red list" which comprises a list of harmful substances subject to the control of H.M. Inspectorate of Pollution. The prescribed substances are set out in Sched. 1 to the Trade Effluents (Prescribed Processes and Substances) Regulations 1989. In Sched. 2 to those Regulations are the prescribed processes. In addition substances or processes will be prescribed if they fall within the provisions of Art. 3.2 of the Aquatic Environment Directive (76/464/EEC). The section does not apply to "background concentrations" of prescribed substances.

Conditions of consent

121.—(1) The power of a sewerage undertaker, on an application under section 119 above, to give a consent with respect to the discharge of any trade effluent shall be a power to give a consent either unconditionally or subject to such conditions as the sewerage undertaker thinks fit to impose with respect to—
  (a) the sewer or sewers into which the trade effluent may be discharged;
  (b) the nature or composition of the trade effluent which may be discharged;

(c) the maximum quantity of trade effluent which may be discharged on any one day, either generally or into a particular sewer; and

(d) the highest rate at which trade effluent may be discharged, either generally or into a particular sewer.

(2) Conditions with respect to all or any of the following matters may also be attached under this section to a consent to the discharge of trade effluent from any trade premises—

(a) the period or periods of the day during which the trade effluent may be discharged from the trade premises into the sewer;

(b) the exclusion from the trade effluent of all condensing water;

(c) the elimination or diminution, in cases falling within subsection (3) below, of any specified constituent of the trade effluent, before it enters the sewer;

(d) the temperature of the trade effluent at the time when it is discharged into the sewer, and its acidity or alkalinity at that time;

(e) the payment by the occupier of the trade premises to the undertaker of charges for the reception of the trade effluent into the sewer and for the disposal of the effluent;

(f) the provision and maintenance of such an inspection chamber or manhole as will enable a person readily to take samples, at any time, of what is passing into the sewer from the trade premises;

(g) the provision, testing and maintenance of such meters as may be required to measure the volume and rate of discharge of any trade effluent being discharged from the trade premises into the sewer;

(h) the provision, testing and maintenance of apparatus for determining the nature and composition of any trade effluent being discharged from the premises into the sewer;

(i) the keeping of records of the volume, rate of discharge, nature and composition of any trade effluent being discharged and, in particular, the keeping of records of readings of meters and other recording apparatus provided in compliance with any other condition attached to the consent; and

(j) the making of returns and giving of other information to the sewerage undertaker concerning the volume, rate of discharge, nature and composition of any trade effluent discharged from the trade premises into the sewer.

(3) A case falls within this subsection where the sewerage undertaker is satisfied that the constituent in question, either alone or in combination with any matter with which it is likely to come into contact while passing through any sewers—

(a) would injure or obstruct those sewers, or make the treatment or disposal of the sewage from those sewers specially difficult or expensive; or

(b) in the case of trade effluent which is to be or is discharged—

    (i) into a sewer having an outfall in any harbour or tidal water; or

    (ii) into a sewer which connects directly or indirectly with a sewer or sewage disposal works having such an outfall,

would cause or tend to cause injury or obstruction to the navigation on, or the use of, the harbour or tidal water.

(4) In the exercise of the power conferred by virtue of subsection (2)(e) above, regard shall be had—

(a) to the nature and composition and to the volume and rate of discharge of the trade effluent discharged;

(b) to any additional expense incurred or likely to be incurred by a sewerage undertaker in connection with the reception or disposal of the trade effluent; and

(c) to any revenue likely to be derived by the undertaker from the trade effluent.

(5) If, in the case of any trade premises, a condition imposed under this section is contravened, the occupier of the premises shall be guilty of an offence and liable—

(a) on summary conviction, to a fine not exceeding the statutory maximum; and

(b) on conviction on indictment, to a fine.

(6) In this section "harbour" and "tidal water" have the same meanings as in the Merchant Shipping Act 1894.

(7) This section has effect subject to the provisions of sections 133 and 135(3) below.

DEFINITIONS

"harbour or tidal water": subs. (6).
"meter": s.219(1).
"records": s.219(1).
"sewer": s.219(1), (2).
"trade effluent": s.141(1).
"trade premises": s.141(1), (2).

GENERAL NOTE

This section provides sewerage undertakers with wide powers to grant applications for trade effluent discharges under s.119 either unconditionally or subject to a variety of conditions.

Under subs. (1) a sewerage undertaker may specify the sewer or sewers into which the discharge is made, the nature and composition of the discharge, its maximum daily quantity and highest rate of discharge. Under subs. (2) a sewerage undertaker may also impose conditions relating to the times during which trade effluent may be discharged into the sewerage system, the removal of condensing water from the discharge, the elimination or diminution of constituents of the trade effluent (before it enters the sewer), the temperature, acidity or alkalinity of the effluent, the payment of charges in respect of the trade effluent which the sewerage undertaker must dispose of, provision of inspection chambers and apparatus for testing the nature and composition of the effluent, provision of meters, keeping of records and provision of information relating to the volume, rate of discharge and nature and composition of the trade effluent.

Conditions may be imposed under the provisions of subs. (3) where an undertaker is satisfied that the nature of the effluent is likely to injure or obstruct the sewers or make the treatment or disposal especially difficult or expensive. Conditions may be imposed where trade effluent is to be discharged into a harbour or tidal waters and this might result in interference with navigation or the use of the harbour or tidal water.

In fixing charges under the provisions of subs. (2)(e), an undertaker must have regard to the nature and volume of effluent discharged, the likely additional expenses incurred in disposal of such effluent and the revenue likely to be derived from such disposal (subs. (4)). Subsection (5) deals with penalties that may be imposed regarding a failure to abide by the conditions upon an occupier of trade premises. The occupier of trade premises cannot make out a defence that he acted with due diligence.

A consent enures for the benefit of the trade premises and thus should a sewerage undertaker alter the sewerage system under s.113 the consent will apply to discharges from the substituted sewers. A discharge consent would be required in circumstances where the sewers serving new trade premises are connected to other premises having the benefit of a consent under this section (see *Yorkshire Dyeing and Proofing Co.* v. *Middleton Borough Council* [1953] 1 W.L.R. 393). The term "trade effluent" will include effluent which the trade itself produces even though such effluent would normally be classified as domestic sewage. This will apply to effluent directly produced in the course of running a business such as a laundry. See *Thames Water Authority* v. *Blue and White Launderettes* [1980] 1 W.L.R. 700.

Appeals to the Director with respect to decisions on applications etc.

122.—(1) Any person aggrieved by—

(a) the refusal of a sewerage undertaker to give a consent for which application has been duly made to the undertaker under section 119 above;

(b) the failure of a sewerage undertaker to give such a consent within the period of two months beginning with the day after service of the notice containing the application; or

(c) any condition attached by a sewerage undertaker to such a consent,
may appeal to the Director.

(2) On an appeal under this section in respect of a refusal or failure to give
a consent, the Director may give the necessary consent, either unconditionally or subject to such conditions as he thinks fit to impose for determining
any of the matters as respects which the undertaker has power to impose
conditions under section 121 above.

(3) On an appeal under this section in respect of a condition attached to a
consent, the Director may take into review all the conditions attached to the
consent, whether appealed against or not, and may—
- (a) substitute for them any other set of conditions, whether more or less
favourable to the appellant; or
- (b) annul any of the conditions.

(4) The Director may, under subsection (3) above, include provision as to
the charges to be made in pursuance of any condition attached to a consent
for any period before the determination of the appeal.

(5) On any appeal under this section, the Director may give a direction
that the trade effluent in question shall not be discharged until a specified
date.

(6) Any consent given or conditions imposed by the Director under this
section in respect of discharges of trade effluent shall have effect for the
purposes of this Chapter as if given or imposed by the sewerage undertaker
in question.

(7) The powers of the Director under this section shall be subject to the
provisions of sections 123, 128, 133, 135 and 137 below.

DEFINITIONS
    "the Director": s.219(1).
    "trade effluent": s.141(1).

GENERAL NOTE
    This section provides a right of appeal to the Director where a sewerage undertaker has
refused to give its consent to a discharge or has failed within two months to deal with the consent
application or in circumstances where the applicant is aggrieved about any condition attaching
to a consent. The Director has wide powers to allow, refuse or grant the consent subject to such
conditions as he thinks fit (subs. (2)). Where the appeal relates to a condition attached to a
consent the Director may review all the conditions and not merely the one which is appealed
against. In such circumstances the Director has wide powers both to substitute new conditions
and to cancel any condition (subs. (3)).

Appeals with respect to the discharge of special category effluent

123.—(1) Where a reference is made to the Secretary of State under
section 120 above, the period mentioned in paragraph (b) of subsection (1)
of section 122 above shall not begin to run for the purposes of that subsection, in relation to the application to which the reference relates, until the
beginning of the day after the Secretary of State serves notice on the
sewerage undertaker in question of his determination on the reference.

(2) If, on an appeal under section 122 above, it appears to the Director—
- (a) that the case is one in which the sewerage undertaker in question is
required to make a reference under section 120 above before giving a
consent; and
- (b) that the undertaker has not made such a reference, whether because
the case falls within subsection (3) of that section or otherwise,
the Director shall not be entitled to determine the appeal, otherwise than by
upholding a refusal, except where the conditions set out in subsection (3)
below are satisfied.

(3) The conditions mentioned in subsection (2) above are satisfied if the
Director—

    (a) has himself referred the questions mentioned in section 120(1) above to the Secretary of State; and

    (b) has been sent a copy of the notice of the Secretary of State's determination on the reference.

    (4) Every reference under this section shall be made in writing and shall be accompanied by a copy of the notice containing the application in respect of which the appeal and reference is made.

    (5) It shall be the duty of the Director, on making a reference under this section, to serve a copy of the reference—

    (a) on the owner or the occupier of the trade premises in question, according to whether the discharges to which the reference relates are to be by the owner or by the occupier; and

    (b) on the sewerage undertaker in question.

DEFINITIONS
    "notice": s.219(1).
    "owner": s.219(1).
    "trade premises": s.141(1), (2).

GENERAL NOTE
    This section makes provision to process appeals relating to special category effluent consent applications.

    An appeal under s.122(1)(b) cannot be made in circumstances where the consent application under s.119 relates to special category effluent and the sewerage undertaker has made a reference to the Secretary of State in accordance with the provisions of s.120. An appeal to the Director under s.122(1)(b) can be made two months after the day the Secretary of State serves notice on the sewerage undertaker as a result of the s.120 reference (subs. (1)).

    Subsection (2) provides a mechanism to ensure that references have been made to the Secretary of State in accordance with s.120 by either the sewerage undertaker or the Director. The Director can only determine the appeal in these circumstances where he has been sent a copy of the Secretary of State's determination on the s.120 reference (subs. (3)).

Variation of consents

    124.—(1) Subject to sections 128, 133 and 135(3) below, a sewerage undertaker may from time to time give a direction varying the conditions which have been attached to any of its consents under this Chapter to the discharge of trade effluent into a public sewer.

    (2) Subject to subsections (3) and (4) and section 125 below, no direction shall be given under this section with respect to a consent under this Chapter—

    (a) within two years from the date of the consent; or

    (b) where a previous direction has been given under this section with respect to that consent, within two years from the date on which notice was given of that direction.

    (3) Subsection (2) above shall not prevent a direction being given before the time specified in that subsection if it is given with the consent of the owner and occupier of the trade premises in question.

    (4) A direction given with the consent mentioned in subsection (3) above shall not affect the time at which any subsequent direction may be given.

    (5) The sewerage undertaker shall give to the owner and occupier of the trade premises to which a consent under this Chapter relates notice of any direction under this section with respect to that consent.

    (6) A notice under subsection (5) above shall—

    (a) include information as to the right of appeal conferred by subsection (1) of section 126 below; and

    (b) state the date, being a date not less than two months after the giving of the notice, on which (subject to subsection (2) of that section) the direction is to take effect.

(7) For the purposes of this section references to the variation of conditions include references to the addition or annulment of a condition and to the attachment of a condition to a consent to which no condition was previously attached.

DEFINITIONS
"owner": s.219(1).
"public sewer": s.219(1).
"trade effluent": s.141(1).
"trade premises": s.141(1), (2).

GENERAL NOTE
This section details the provisions in the Act relating to variations of trade effluent discharge consents. The provisions relating to variations of special category effluent consents are dealt with in s.127.

The section establishes the general rule that variation of the conditions relating to a trade effluent discharge may not be made within two years from the original date of the consent or alternatively two years from the previous variation given by a sewerage undertaker under this section. However, variations can be made at any time if made with the consent of the owner and occupier of the trade premises in question (subs. (3)). Variations in the consent conditions pursuant to subs. (3) do not affect the calculation of when variations can be made in accordance with the provisions of subs. (2). A sewerage undertaker must serve notice of any direction given under this section on the owner or occupier of the relevant trade premises (subs. (5)), and that notice will include details of the right of appeal under s.126(1).

Variations within time limit

125.—(1) A sewerage undertaker may give a direction under section 124 above before the time specified in subsection (2) of that section and without the consent required by subsection (3) of that section if it considers it necessary to do so in order to provide proper protection for persons likely to be affected by the discharges which could lawfully be made apart from the direction.

(2) Subject to section 134(3) below, where a sewerage undertaker gives a direction by virtue of subsection (1) above, the undertaker shall be liable to pay compensation to the owner and occupier of the trade premises to which the direction relates, unless the undertaker is of the opinion that the direction is required—

(a) in consequence of a change of circumstances which—

(i) has occurred since the beginning of the period of two years in question; and

(ii) could not reasonably have been foreseen at the beginning of that period;

and

(b) otherwise than in consequence of consents for discharges given after the beginning of that period.

(3) Where a sewerage undertaker gives a direction by virtue of subsection (1) above and is of the opinion mentioned in subsection (2) above, it shall be the duty of the undertaker to give notice of the reasons for its opinion to the owner and occupier of the premises in question.

(4) For the purposes of this section the circumstances referred to in subsection (2)(a) above may include the information available as to the discharges to which the consent in question relates or as to the interaction of those discharges with other discharges or matter.

(5) The Secretary of State may by regulations make provision as to the manner of determining the amount of any compensation payable under this section, including the factors to be taken into account in determining that amount.

DEFINITIONS
"owner": s.219(1).
"trade premises": s.141(1), (2).

GENERAL NOTE

This section provides a power for sewerage undertakers to give a direction varying the conditions of a trade effluent discharge consent where the undertaker considers that the variation is necessary to provide proper protection for persons likely to be affected by the discharges which would be lawful save for the implementation of this section. The power is available irrespective of the time specified in s.124(2) and agreement of the owner and occupier of trade premises in s.124(3).

Payment of compensation must be made by the undertaker to the owner and occupier of the trade premises unless there has been a change of circumstances which has occurred after the commencement of the two-year period in s.124(2) which could not reasonably have been foreseen at that time.

Subsection (3) imposes an obligation on a sewerage undertaker to give reasons for its direction where it holds the opinion set out in subs. (2). The Secretary of State is empowered to make regulations relating to the calculation of compensation payable under this section (subs. (5)).

Appeals with respect to variations of consent

126.—(1) The owner or occupier of any trade premises may—
(a) within two months of the giving to him under subsection (5) of section 124 above of a notice of a direction under that section; or
(b) with the written permission of the Director, at any later time,
appeal to the Director against the direction.

(2) Subject to subsection (3) below, if an appeal against a direction is brought under subsection (1) above before the date specified under section 124(6)(b) above in the notice of the direction, the direction shall not take effect until the appeal is withdrawn or finally disposed of.

(3) In so far as the direction which is the subject of an appeal relates to the making of charges payable by the occupier of any trade premises, it may take effect on any date after the giving of the notice.

(4) On an appeal under subsection (1) above with respect to a direction, the Director shall have power—
(a) to annul the direction given by the sewerage undertaker; and
(b) to substitute for it any other direction, whether more or less favourable to the appellant;
and any direction given by the Director may include provision as to the charges to be made for any period between the giving of the notice by the sewerage undertaker and the determination of the appeal.

(5) A person to whom notice is given in pursuance of section 125(3) above may, in accordance with regulations made by the Secretary of State, appeal to the Director against the notice on the ground that compensation should be paid in consequence of the direction to which the notice relates.

(6) On an appeal under subsection (5) above the Director may direct that section 125 above shall have effect as if the sewerage undertaker in question were not of the opinion to which the notice relates.

(7) Any consent given or conditions imposed by the Director under this section in respect of discharges of trade effluent shall have effect for the purposes of this Chapter as if given or imposed by the sewerage undertaker in question.

(8) The powers of the Director under this section shall be subject to the provisions of sections 133, 135 and 137 below.

DEFINITIONS
"owner": s.219(1).
"the Director": s.219(1).
"trade effluent": s.141(1).
"trade premises": s.141(1), (2).

Appeals regarding variation of consent discharges are dealt with by the Director and may be made within two months of the giving of the notice of the direction pursuant to s.124(5) or at any later time with the consent of the Director. Under subs. (4), on appeal, the Director has wide powers to revoke any direction given by a sewerage undertaker or substitute an alternative. The section also provides for an appeal to the Director relating to the provisions of s.125 which concern variations of consents within the time limits specified in s.124.

Review by the Secretary of State of consents relating to special category effluent

127.—(1) Where any person, as the owner or occupier of any trade premises, is (whether or not in accordance with a notice under section 132 below) for the time being authorised by virtue of a consent under this Chapter to make discharges of any special category effluent from those premises into a sewerage undertaker's public sewer, the Secretary of State may review the questions—

(a) whether the discharges authorised by the consent should be prohibited; and

(b) whether, if they are not prohibited, any requirements should be imposed as to the conditions on which they are made.

(2) Subject to subsection (3) below, the Secretary of State shall not review any question under this section unless—

(a) the consent or variation by virtue of which the discharges in question are made has not previously been the subject-matter of a review and was given or made—

(i) before September 1, 1989; or

(ii) in contravention of section 133 below;

(b) a period of more than two years has elapsed since the time, or last time, when notice of the Secretary of State's determination on any reference or review relating to that consent or the consent to which that variation relates was served under section 132 below on the owner or occupier of the trade premises in question; or

(c) there has, since the time, or last time, when such a notice was so served, been a contravention of any provision which was included in compliance with a requirement of a notice under section 132 below in the consent or variation by virtue of which the discharges in question are made.

(3) Subsection (2) above shall not apply if the review is carried out—

(a) for the purpose of enabling Her Majesty's Government in the United Kingdom to give effect to any Community obligation or to any international agreement to which the United Kingdom is for the time being a party; or

(b) for the protection of public health or of flora and fauna dependent on an aquatic environment.

DEFINITIONS
"notice": s.219(1).
"owner": s.219(1).
"public sewer": s.219(1).
"special category effluent": s.141(1).
"trade premises": s.141(1), (2).

GENERAL NOTE
This section provides the Secretary of State with a power to review consents in respect of special category effluent. In particular whether such discharges ought to be prohibited and in respect of conditions attaching to the relevant consent. Except to the extent that a review is necessary to enable effect to be given to any community obligation or international agreement or for the protection of public health or of flora and fauna dependent on the aquatic environment, then the Secretary of State may not review special category effluent consents unless the circumstances specified in subs. (2) appertain.

Application for variation of time for discharge

Application for variation of time for discharge

128.—(1) If, after a direction has been given under any of the preceding provisions of this Chapter requiring that trade effluent shall not be discharged until a specified date, it appears to the sewerage undertaker in question that in consequence—

(a) of a failure to complete any works required in connection with the reception and disposal of the trade effluent; or

(b) of any other exceptional circumstances,

a later date ought to be substituted for the date so specified in the direction, the undertaker may apply to the Director for such a substitution.

(2) The Director shall have power, on an application under subsection (1) above, to vary the direction so as to extend the period during which the trade effluent may not be discharged until the date specified in the application or, if he thinks fit, any earlier date.

(3) Not less than one month before making an application under subsection (1) above a sewerage undertaker shall give notice of its intention to the owner and occupier of the trade premises from which the trade effluent is to be discharged.

(4) The Director, before varying a direction on an application under subsection (1) above, shall take into account any representations made to him by the owner or occupier of the trade premises in question.

DEFINITIONS
"trade effluent": s.141(1).

GENERAL NOTE
  This section provides a power for sewerage undertakers to apply to the Director to vary the date when an owner or occupier of trade premises may commence discharging trade effluent arising from either a failure on the part of the undertaker to complete works for the reception and disposal of the effluent or due to any other exceptional circumstances. On such an application the Director has wide powers to extend the period prior to which trade effluent may be discharged into the sewers. If he thinks fit the Director may substitute an earlier date (subs. (2)). The Director is required to take into account any representations made to him by the owner or occupier of trade premises before reaching his decision (subs. (4)).

Agreements with respect the disposal etc. of trade effluent

Agreements with respect to the disposal etc. of trade effluent

129.—(1) Subject to sections 130 and 133 below, a sewerage undertaker may enter into and carry into effect—

(a) an agreement with the owner or occupier of any trade premises within its area for the reception and disposal by the undertaker of any trade effluent produced on those premises;

(b) an agreement with the owner or occupier of any such premises under which it undertakes, on such terms as may be specified in the agreement, to remove and dispose of substances produced in the course of treating any trade effluent on or in connection with those premises.

(2) Without prejudice to the generality of subsection (1) above, an agreement such as is mentioned in paragraph (a) of that subsection may, in particular, provide—

(a) for the construction or extension by the sewerage undertaker of such works as may be required for the reception or disposal of the trade effluent; and

(b) for the repayment by the owner or occupier, as the case may be, of the whole or part of the expenses incurred by the undertaker in carrying out its obligations under the agreement.

(3) It is hereby declared that the power of a sewerage undertaker to enter into an agreement under this section includes a power, by that agreement, to authorise such a discharge as apart from the agreement would require a consent under this Chapter.

GENERAL NOTE
  This section empowers sewerage undertakers to enter into agreements with owners or occupiers of any trade premises in its area relating to the disposal of trade effluent or substances produced in the course of treating trade effluent. Agreements relating to the reception and disposal of trade effluent may include provisions for the construction of additional works necessary for the treatment and disposal of the effluent and for payment of the whole or part of the undertaker's expenses incurred in fulfilling its obligations under such an agreement. By virtue of subs. (3) sewerage undertakers are enabled to authorise discharges of trade effluent without recourse to a consent application under s.119 where a s.129 agreement has been concluded. The section gives effect to Recommendation No. 2 of the Law Commission's Report on the consolidation of the legislation relating to water (Cmnd. 1483, April, 1991); see also the General Note to s.118.

Reference to the Secretary of State of agreements relating to special category effluent

130.—(1) Where a sewerage undertaker and the owner or occupier of any trade premises are proposing to enter into an agreement under section 129 above with respect to, or to any matter connected with, the reception or disposal of any special category effluent, it shall be the duty of the undertaker to refer to the Secretary of State the questions—
  (a) whether the operations which would, for the purposes of or in connection with the reception or disposal of that effluent, be carried out in pursuance of the proposed agreement should be prohibited; and
  (b) whether, if they are not prohibited, any requirements should be imposed as to the conditions on which they are carried out.

(2) It shall be the duty of a sewerage undertaker where it has made a reference under this section not to give any consent or enter into any agreement with respect to any such operations as are mentioned in subsection (1)(a) above at any time before the Secretary of State serves notice on the undertaker of his determination on the reference.

(3) Every reference under this section shall be made in writing and shall be accompanied by a copy of the proposed agreement.

(4) It shall be the duty of a sewerage undertaker, on making a reference under this section, to serve a copy of the reference on the owner or the occupier of the trade premises in question, according to whether it is the owner or occupier who is proposing to be a party to the agreement.

(5) Subject to subsection (6) below, the duties of a sewerage undertaker under this section shall be enforceable under section 18 above by the Secretary of State.

(6) Where an application is made to the Secretary of State under section 18 above in respect of a failure by a sewerage undertaker to make a reference under this section, the Secretary of State may, instead of making an order under that section, proceed with the matter as if the application were the reference.

This section imposes a duty on a sewerage undertaker to make a reference to the Secretary of State in circumstances where a proposed agreement under s.129 relates to special category effluent. Where such a reference is made the sewerage undertaker is under a duty not to give any consent or enter into any agreement prior to receiving the Secretary of State's determination (subs. (2)). An undertaker has a further duty (subs. (4)) to serve notice on the owner or occupier of the trade premises regarding the reference to the Secretary of State.

Review by the Secretary of State of agreements relating to special category effluent

131.—(1) Where any person, as the owner or occupier of any trade premises, is (whether or not in accordance with a notice under section 132 below) for the time being a party to any agreement under section 129 above with respect to, or to any matter connected with, the reception or disposal of special category effluent, the Secretary of State may review the questions—
  (a) whether the operations which, for the purposes of or in connection with the reception or disposal of that effluent, are carried out in pursuance of the agreement should be prohibited; and
  (b) whether, if they are not prohibited, any requirements should be imposed as to the conditions on which they are carried out.

(2) Subject to subsection (3) below, the Secretary of State shall not review any question under this section unless—
  (a) the agreement by virtue of which the operations in question are carried out has not previously been the subject-matter of a review and was entered into—
      (i) before September 1, 1989; or
      (ii) in contravention of section 133 below;
  (b) a period of more than two years has elapsed since the time, or last time, when notice of the Secretary of State's determination on any reference or review relating to that agreement was served under section 132 below on the owner or occupier of the trade premises in question; or
  (c) there has, since the time, or last time, when such a notice was so served, been a contravention of any provision which was included in compliance with a requirement of a notice under section 132 below in the agreement by virtue of which the operations in question are carried out.

(3) Subsection (2) above shall not apply if the review is carried out—
  (a) for the purpose of enabling Her Majesty's Government in the United Kingdom to give effect to any Community obligation or to any international agreement to which the United Kingdom is for the time being a party; or
  (b) for the protection of public health or of flora and fauna dependent on an aquatic environment.

(4) References in this section to an agreement include references to an agreement as varied from time to time by a notice under section 132 below.

DEFINITIONS
  "effluent": s.219(1).
  "notice": s.219(1).
  "special category effluent": s.138.
  "trade premises": s.141(1), (2).

GENERAL NOTE
This section provides a power for the Secretary of State to review agreements relating to the reception or disposal of special category effluent. The Secretary of State is empowered to consider whether there should be a prohibition relating to the reception or disposal of the special category effluent or alternatively, if there is no prohibition, whether those operations should be subject to conditions. The restrictions in s.127 regarding the circumstances in which

the Secretary of State may review consents relating to special category effluent similarly apply to agreements under this section and any agreement varied under the provisions of s.132.

References and reviews relating to special category effluent

Powers and procedure on references and reviews

132.—(1) This section applies to—
  (a) any reference to the Secretary of State under section 120, 123 or 130 above; and
  (b) any review by the Secretary of State under section 127 or 131 above.

(2) On a reference or review to which this section applies, it shall be the duty of the Secretary of State, before determining the questions which are the subject-matter of the reference or review—
  (a) to give an opportunity of making representations or objections to the Secretary of State—
      (i) to the sewerage undertaker in question; and
      (ii) to the following person, that is to say, the owner or the occupier of the trade premises in question, according to whether it is the owner or the occupier of those premises who is proposing to be, or is, the person making the discharges or, as the case may be, a party to the agreement;
  and
  (b) to consider any representations or objections which are duly made to him with respect to those questions by a person to whom he is required to give such an opportunity and which are not withdrawn.

(3) On determining any question on a reference or review to which this section applies, the Secretary of State shall serve notice on the sewerage undertaker in question and on the person specified in subsection (2)(a)(ii) above.

(4) A notice under this section shall state, according to what has been determined—
  (a) that the discharges or operations to which, or to the proposals for which, the reference or review relates, or such of them as are specified in the notice, are to be prohibited; or
  (b) that those discharges or operations, or such of them as are so specified, are to be prohibited except in so far as they are made or carried out in accordance with conditions which consist in or include conditions so specified; or
  (c) that the Secretary of State has no objection to those discharges or operations and does not intend to impose any requirements as to the conditions on which they are made or carried out.

(5) Without prejudice to section 133 below, a notice under this section, in addition to containing such provision as is specified in sub-paragraph (4) above, may do one or both of the following, that is to say—
  (a) vary or revoke the provisions of a previous notice with respect to the discharges or operations in question; and
  (b) for the purpose of giving effect to any prohibition or other requirement contained in the notice, vary or revoke any consent under this Chapter or any agreement under section 129 above.

(6) Nothing in subsection (1) or (2) of section 121 above shall be construed as restricting the power of the Secretary of State, by virtue of subsection (4)(b) above, to specify such conditions as he considers appropriate in a notice under this section.

(7) The Secretary of State shall have the same right of entry and other powers for the purposes of this section and any provision under which any reference or review to which this section applies is made as are conferred on a sewerage undertaker by section 171 below in relation to any other provision of this Chapter; and the provisions of that section accordingly have

effect with the necessary modifications in relation to the power conferred by this subsection.

(8) The Secretary of State shall send a copy of every notice served under this section to the Director.

DEFINITIONS
"notice": s.219(1).
"owner": s.219(1).
"trade premises": s.141(1), (2).

GENERAL NOTE
This section is concerned with the powers and procedures in respect of references made to the Secretary of State under s.120 (applications for the discharge of special category effluent), s.123 (appeals with respect to the discharge of special category effluent), s.130 (references to the Secretary of State in respect of special category effluent discharge agreements) reviews by the Secretary of State under s.127 (review of consents relating to special category effluent) and s.131 (agreements relating to special category effluent).

The section imposes a duty on the Secretary of State to allow representations or objections by sewerage undertakers, the person proposing to make the discharge or any person who proposes to be party to any agreement and unless those representations or objections are withdrawn the Secretary of State must consider them.

The Secretary of State has wide powers to allow or prohibit the operations which are the subject of the reference or make them subject to conditions. The Secretary of State may also vary or revoke a previous notice, consent or agreement.

Effect of determination on reference or review

133.—(1) Where a notice under section 132 above has been served on a sewerage undertaker, it shall be the duty—
  (a) of the undertaker; and
  (b) in relation to that undertaker, of the Director,
so to exercise the powers to which this section applies as to secure compliance with the provisions of the notice.

(2) This paragraph applies to the following powers, that is to say—
  (a) in relation to a sewerage undertaker, its power to give a consent under this Chapter, any of its powers under section 121 or 124 above and any power to enter into or vary an agreement under section 129 above; and
  (b) in relation to the Director, any of his powers under this Chapter.

(3) Nothing in subsection (1) or (2) of section 121 above shall be construed as restricting the power of a sewerage undertaker, for the purpose of complying with this section, to impose any condition specified in a notice under section 132 above.

(4) The duties of a sewerage undertaker under this section shall be enforceable under section 18 above by the Secretary of State.

DEFINITIONS
"notice": s.219(1).
"the Director": s.219(1).

GENERAL NOTE
This section imposes duties on the undertaker and Director to secure compliance with the provisions of any notice served by the Secretary of State under the provisions of s.132.

Compensation in respect of determinations made for the protection of public health etc.

134.—(1) Subject to subsection (2) below, the Secretary of State shall be liable to pay compensation to the relevant person in respect of any loss or damage sustained by that person as a result of any notice under section 132 above containing the Secretary of State's determination on a review which—
  (a) has been carried out for the protection of public health or of flora and fauna dependent on an aquatic environment; and

(b) but for being so carried out would have been prohibited by virtue of section 127(2) or 131(2) above.

(2) The Secretary of State shall not be required to pay any compensation under this section if the determination in question is shown to have been given in consequence of—

(a) a change of circumstances which could not reasonably have been foreseen at the time when the period of two years mentioned in section 127(2) or, as the case may be, section 131(2) above began to run; or

(b) consideration by the Secretary of State of material information which was not reasonably available to him at that time.

(3) No person shall be entitled to any compensation under section 125 above in respect of anything done in pursuance of section 133 above.

(4) In this section "the relevant person," in relation to a review, means the owner or the occupier of the trade premises in question, according to whether it is the owner or the occupier who makes the discharges to which the review relates or, as the case may be, is a party to the agreement to which it relates.

DEFINITIONS
"notice": s.219(1).
"relevant person": subs. (4).

GENERAL NOTE
This section is concerned with the liability of the Secretary of State to pay compensation arising out of determinations made by the Secretary of State under s.132 to protect public health or flora and fauna (and which the Secretary of State would otherwise have been prevented from reviewing by virtue of ss.127(2) and 131(2)). The Secretary of State is not required to pay compensation if the determination he made under s.132 was in consequence of a change of circumstances which could not reasonably have been foreseen or where material information has come to light which was not available to him at the relevant time. No other types of compensation are payable under the Act.

Supplemental provisions of Chapter III

Restrictions on power to fix charges under Chapter III

135.—(1) On any appeal under section 122 or 126(1) above conditions providing for the payment of charges to the sewerage undertaker in question shall not be determined by the Director except in so far as no provision is in force by virtue of a charges scheme under section 143 below in respect of any such receptions, discharges, removals or disposals of effluent or substances as are of the same description as the reception, discharge, removal or disposal which is the subject-matter of the appeal.

(2) In so far as any such conditions as are mentioned in subsection (1) above do fall to be determined by the Director, they shall be determined having regard to the desirability of that undertaker's—

(a) recovering the expenses of complying with its obligations in consequence of the consent or agreement to which the conditions relate; and

(b) securing a reasonable return on its capital.

(3) To the extent that subsection (1) above excludes any charges from a determination on an appeal those charges shall be fixed from time to time by a charges scheme under section 143 below but not otherwise.

DEFINITIONS
"effluent": s.219(1).
"the Director": s.219(1).

GENERAL NOTE
The Director's power to fix charges for the disposal of effluent on appeals under ss.122 and

126(1) only applies where there is no charges scheme in operation under s.143 setting charges in respect of the effluent which is the subject of the appeal (subs. (1)). On appeals under ss.122 and 126(1), where the Director is entitled to fix conditions relating to charges, he must fix them having regard to the desirability of the sewerage undertaker's need to recover its expenses and to secure a reasonable return on its capital. Note the Director's primary duty in s.2(2).

Evidence from meters etc.

136. Any meter or apparatus provided in pursuance of this Chapter in any trade premises for the purpose of measuring, recording or determining the volume, rate of discharge, nature or composition of any trade effluent discharged from those premises shall be presumed in any proceedings to register accurately, unless the contrary is shown.

DEFINITIONS
"meter": s.219(1).
"trade premises": s.141(1), (2).

Statement of case on appeal

137.—(1) At any stage of the proceedings on an appeal under section 122 or 126(1) above, the Director may, and if so directed by the High Court shall, state in the form of a special case for the decision of the High Court any question of law arising in those proceedings.

(2) The decision of the High Court on a special case under this section shall be deemed to be a judgment of the Court within the meaning of section 16 of the Supreme Court Act 1981 (which relates to the jurisdiction of the Court of Appeal); but no appeal to the Court of Appeal shall be brought by virtue of this subsection except with the leave of the High Court or of the Court of Appeal.

Meaning of "special category effluent"

138.—(1) Subject to subsection (2) below, trade effluent shall be special category effluent for the purposes of this Chapter if—
  (a) such substances as may be prescribed under this Act are present in the effluent or are present in the effluent in prescribed concentrations; or
  (b) the effluent derives from any such process as may be so prescribed or from a process involving the use of prescribed substances or the use of such substances in quantities which exceed the prescribed amounts.

(2) Trade effluent shall not be special category effluent for the purposes of this Chapter if it is produced, or to be produced, in any process which is a prescribed process designated for central control as from the date which is the determination date for that process.

(3) In subsection (2) above "determination date," in relation to a prescribed process, means—
  (a) in the case of a process for which authorisation is granted, the date on which the enforcing authority grants it, whether in pursuance of the application or, on an appeal, of a direction to grant it;
  (b) in the case of a process for which authorisation is refused, the date of refusal or, on appeal, of the affirmation of the refusal.

(4) In this section—
  (a) "authorisation," "enforcing authority" and "prescribed process" have the meanings given by section 1 of the Environmental Protection Act 1990; and
  (b) the references to designation for central control and to an appeal are references, respectively, to designation under section 4 of that Act and to an appeal under section 15 of that Act.

(5) Without prejudice to the power in subsection (3) of section 139 below, nothing in this Chapter shall enable regulations under this section to prescribe as special category effluent any liquid or matter which is not trade

effluent but falls to be treated as such for the purposes of this Chapter by virtue of an order under that section.

DEFINITIONS
"authorisation": s.1 of the Environmental Protection Act 1990.
"determination date": subs. (3).
"effluent": s.219(1).
"enforcing authority": s.1 of the Environmental Protection Act 1990.
"prescribed": s.219(1).
"prescribed process": s.1 of the Environmental Protection Act 1990.
"trade effluent": s.141(1).

GENERAL NOTE
The control of noxious substances contained in effluent has its legislative roots in the Public Health (Drainage of Trade Premises) Act 1937, the Public Health Act 1961, the Control of Pollution Act 1974 and more recently in the Water Act 1989 (see in particular s.74 of the Water Act 1989).
Sections 118 to 141 set out the legislative mechanisms to control discharges into the aquatic environment especially with regard to "special category effluent". The special controls relating to the discharge of "special category effluent" reflects the Government's new precautionary approach towards the control of dangerous substances discharged into the aquatic environment. In addition the Government is endeavouring to comply with the standards set by the EEC in its Directives, especially with regard to water quality (see Consultation Paper *Inputs of Dangerous Substances to Water* (DOE, 1988)). Reference should also be made to the Trade Effluents (Prescribed Processes and Substances) Regulations 1989 (S.I. 1989 No. 1156) which were made pursuant to s.74 of the Water Act 1989. Schedule 1 to the Regulations prescribes substances contained in List 1 of E.C. Directive 76/464/EEC on pollution caused by certain substances discharged into the aquatic environment and are intended to give effect to Art. 3, para. 2 of the Directive. Schedule 2 to the Regulations prescribes five types of process, including the manufacture of asbestos cement, paper or board, which are intended to give effect to Art. 3 of E.C. Directive 87/217/EEC regarding the prevention and reduction of environmental pollution by asbestos.
Reference should also be made to the Environmental Protection Act 1990, which details the system of integrated pollution control regarding emissions to air, water and land.

Power to apply Chapter III to other effluents

139.—(1) The Secretary of State may by order provide that, subject to section 138(5) above, this Chapter shall apply in relation to liquid or other matter of any description specified in the order which is discharged into public sewers as it applies in relation to trade effluent.

(2) An order applying the provisions of this Chapter in relation to liquid or other matter of any description may provide for it to so apply subject to such modifications (if any) as may be specified in the order and, in particular, subject to any such modification of the meaning for the purposes of this Chapter of the expression "trade premises" as may be so specified.

(3) The Secretary of State may include in an order under this section such provisions as appear to him expedient for modifying any enactment relating to sewage as that enactment applies in relation to the discharge into sewers of any liquid or other matter to which any provisions of this Chapter are applied by an order under this section.

(4) The Secretary of State may include in an order under this section such other supplemental, incidental and transitional provision as appears to him to be expedient.

(5) The power to make an order under this section shall be exercisable by statutory instrument; and no order shall be made under this section unless a draft of it has been laid before, and approved by a resolution of, each House of Parliament.

DEFINITIONS
"enactment": s.219(1).
"modifications": s.219(1).

"public sewers": s.219(1).
"sewers": s.219(1), (2).
"trade effluent": s.141(1), (2).

GENERAL NOTE
   This is an important section which provides the Secretary of State with a power to make an order by Statutory Instrument to extend the provisions of Pt. IV, Chap. III of this Act to "liquid or other matter" of a description specified in a subs. (2) order and effected via a Statutory Instrument (subs. (5)).

Pre-1989 Act authority for trade effluent discharges etc.

140. Schedule 8 to this Act shall have effect (without prejudice to the provisions of the Water Consolidation (Consequential Provisions) Act 1991 or to sections 16 and 17 of the Interpretation Act 1978) for the purpose of making provision in respect of certain cases where trade effluent was discharged in accordance with provision made before the coming into force of the Water Act 1989.

DEFINITIONS
   "trade effluent": s.141(1).

GENERAL NOTE
   This section introduces Sched. 8, which is concerned with transitional arrangements for trade effluent discharges operating prior to 1989.

Interpretation of Chapter III

Interpretation of Chapter III

141.—(1) In this Chapter, except in so far as the context otherwise requires—
      "special category effluent" has the meaning given by section 138 above;
      "trade effluent"—
            (a) means any liquid, either with or without particles of matter in suspension in the liquid, which is wholly or partly produced in the course of any trade or industry carried on at trade premises; and
            (b) in relation to any trade premises, means any such liquid which is so produced in the course of any trade or industry carried on at those premises,
         but does not include domestic sewage;
      "trade premises" means, subject to subsection (2) below, any premises used or intended to be used for carrying on any trade or industry.
   (2) For the purposes of this Chapter any land or premises used or intended for use (in whole or in part and whether or not for profit)—
      (a) for agricultural or horticultural purposes or for the purposes of fish farming; or
      (b) for scientific research or experiment,
shall be deemed to be premises used for carrying on a trade or industry; and the references to a trade or industry in the definition of "trade effluent" in subsection (1) above shall include references to agriculture, horticulture, fish farming and scientific research or experiment.
   (3) Every application or consent made or given under this Chapter shall be made or given in writing.
   (4) Nothing in this Chapter shall affect any right with respect to water in a river stream or watercourse, or authorise any infringement of such a right, except in so far as any such right would dispense with the requirements of this Chapter so far as they have effect by virtue of any regulations under section 138 above.

PART V

FINANCIAL PROVISIONS

CHAPTER I

CHARGES

Manner of fixing charges

Powers of undertakers to charge

142.—(1) Subject to the following provisions of this Chapter, the powers of every relevant undertaker shall include power—

(a) to fix charges for any services provided in the course of carrying out its functions and, in the case of a sewerage undertaker, charges to be paid in connection with the carrying out of its trade effluent functions; and

(b) to demand and recover charges fixed under this section from any persons to whom the undertaker provides services or in relation to whom it carries out trade effluent functions.

(2) Subject to subsection (3) below, the powers conferred by subsection (1) above shall be exercisable—

(a) by or in accordance with a charges scheme under section 143 below; or

(b) by or in accordance with agreements with the persons to be charged.

(3) Paragraph (b) of subsection (2) above shall have effect in relation to the exercise of powers with respect to charges in connection with the carrying out of a sewerage undertaker's trade effluent functions only in so far as provision for the fixing, demanding or recovery of such charges may be contained in an agreement entered into in accordance with section 129 above.

(4) Except in so far as this Chapter otherwise provides, a relevant undertaker may fix charges under this section by reference to such matters, and may adopt such methods and principles for the calculation and imposition of the charges, as appear to the undertaker to be appropriate.

(5) The powers in relation to which this section has effect shall not be exercised so as to contravene any local statutory provision which expressly provides that no charge shall be made for a particular service.

(6) Nothing in subsections (1) to (5) above or in any charges scheme under section 143 below shall affect any power of a relevant undertaker to fix charges under any power conferred otherwise than by virtue of this Chapter.

(7) References in this section to a sewerage undertaker's trade effluent functions are references to its functions under Chapter III of Part IV of this Act.

DEFINITIONS
 "functions": ss.217, 219(1).
 "services": s.219(1).
 "trade effluent functions": subs. (7).

GENERAL NOTE
 Sections 142 to 150 contain the statutory framework in respect of charges by both water and sewerage undertakers. The practical implications of these provisions are to be read in conjunction with the terms of the instrument of appointment made under s.6, and the policy of the Director General of Water Services when interpreting and enforcing the provisions of the instrument of appointment. In consequence, what may appear on the face of the Act to be discretionary powers available to undertakers are in effect quasi-contractual obligations under the conditions of the instrument of appointment, enforceable by s.18 orders and ultimately by a court injunction under s.22(4).

Charge conditions of the instrument of appointment

Conditions B and C of the model instrument of appointment provide the mechanism to regulate increases in charges by undertakers. Condition B concerns water supplies, sewerage services and trade effluent disposal. A formula is used to calculate the overall increase of charges which an undertaker may make. The formula RPI + K limits increases to the percentage change of the retail price index, together with an adjustment factor ("K"). The Director of Water Services is empowered to initiate reviews of the adjustment factor at five- and 10-yearly intervals and in establishing the relevant adjustment factor he will be guided by his general duty under s.2(2) of the Act to ensure that undertakers are able properly to finance the carrying out of their functions whilst paying heed to the need to secure "a reasonable return on capital". Undertakers may apply for a review of the adjustment factor at five-yearly intervals. The Director has a wide discretion to determine the adjustment factor ("K") subject to a right of appeal to the Monopolies and Mergers Commission. More frequent reviews of the "K" factor may arise as a result of "interim K determinations", which allow unexpected cost increases due to such items as new EEC requirements and other unanticipated obligations to be accommodated. The "interim K determination" was originally envisaged as an allowance for "cost pass through", but it is clear from the model instrument of appointment that this description no longer reflects the complex series of calculations that must be made before the "K" factor can be adjusted to take account of such additional costs. Undertakers cannot regard themselves as inevitably entitled to pass on unanticipated cost rises to their consumers if, for example, increases in costs could have been avoided by prudent management. Such considerations will form part of the equation when determining the "K" factor.

Condition C contains a simpler mechanism for controlling increases under s.146 in respect of connection charges and charges for highway drainage (so called infrastructure charges), by specifying a maximum limit that may be charged. This limit is tied to changes in the retail price index, but it may be reviewed by the Director as part of his five- or 10-year interval reviews of the adjustment factor.

Liability for charges

Section 142(1)(b) provides that charges are recoverable "from any persons to whom the undertaker provides services or in relation to whom it carries out trade effluent functions". In most cases this would be the current occupier of the premises provided with services by the undertaker. Where someone ceases to be an occupier, his liability may continue but different provisions apply in respect of both metered and non-metered supplies. For non-metered supplies, the occupier's liability ceases two working days following service by the consumer of a notice under s.62, even if he continues to occupy the premises (s.144(5)). In respect of metered supplies liability will continue even after ceasing occupation unless prior notice has been given (s.144(2) and (3)), but subject to overall limitations contained in s.144(4). Although it is the occupier who is normally liable, this can be subject to any contrary agreements made between the undertaker and another party (such as the non-occupying landlord) (s.144(1)). If that is the case, the undertaker would be obliged to seek recovery of any outstanding payments from the person who made the agreement rather than the actual occupier.

Charges scheme

Section 143 provides undertakers with a power to establish a charges scheme including trade effluent charges. Such a scheme does not override the power of undertakers to enter into individual agreements with trade effluent dischargers under s.143(5). Individual agreements could include provisions relating to capital contribution costs. Although s.143 is a discretionary power, condition D of the instrument of appointment requires undertakers to have in force at all times a charges scheme for domestic water supplies and sewerage services, which is freely available on request to consumers.

Charge basis and discrimination

Section 142(4) provides undertakers with a wide discretion as to the basis on which they may make charges. The section provides that a charges scheme may make different provisions in relation to different circumstances or localities. This would permit a different variation in charging rates between rural and urban areas but the wide discretion given to undertakers must be read in conjunction with the conditions of the instrument of appointment. Condition E requires an undertaker to ensure that charges show no undue preference or discrimination in respect of any class of customers. The statutory duties relating to the avoidance of discrimination and preference which appeared in previous legislation (s.31 of the Water Act 1973) are now part of the general duties of the Secretary of State and the Director under s.2(3)(a), which makes specific reference to the protection of the interests of customers and potential customers in rural areas.

After March 31, 2000, undertakers are prohibited from fixing charges by reference to rateable values (s.145). In consequence, standard flat rates or meter charges are likely in the future to form the basic methods of charging. The calculation of charges via the use of meters is permitted by the general power contained in s.142(4). Sections 140–149 contain specific provisions concerning the installation and maintenance of, and other matters connected with metering, and include a power for the Secretary of State to supplement those provisions by regulations (s.149).

Charges for new connections and infra-structure costs
Section 146 permits undertakers to charge for new connections even though no new mains or sewers may be required. Connections to existing water and sewerage systems may well lead to increased capital expenditure on improving or enlarging the infrastructure by the undertaker. Prior to the passing of the Water Act 1989 those costs would have been recoverable by ensuring that provision was made for them when undertakers calculated their overall standard and water sewerage charges. This meant that existing customers were subsidising new customers for the extra burden that was created on the existing systems. Where new development was involved an alternative was for the developer and local planning authority to enter into an agreement providing for capital sums to be paid to the undertaker. These agreements are now implemented under s.106 of the Town and Country Planning Act 1990 as amended by s.12 of the Planning and Compensation Act 1991. In practice, s.106 agreements are frequently used to secure infrastructure costs, but they depend upon local authority cooperation and cannot be imposed on an unwilling developer. In addition, there is perhaps less certainty now the water industry is privatised that planning authorities would feel obliged to accommodate the needs of water and sewerage undertakers which are no longer part of the public sector.
Section 146 is intended to introduce a new approach to this problem by means of a general prohibition on undertakers making initial connection charges whilst expressly permitting this in relation to new connections for domestic water supplies and domestic sewerage drainage. A maximum ceiling is placed on the level of infrastructure charges in accordance with condition D of the model instrument of appointment.

Resale of water
Section 150 contains a power to set maximum prices for the resale of water by persons other than undertakers.

Charges schemes

143.—(1) A relevant undertaker may make a scheme ("a charges scheme") which does any one or more of the following, that is to say—
  (a) fixes the charges to be paid for any services provided by the undertaker in the course of carrying out its functions;
  (b) in the case of a sewerage undertaker, requires such charges as may be fixed by the scheme to be paid to the undertaker where, in the circumstances set out in the scheme—
      (i) a notice containing an application for a consent is served on the undertaker under section 119 above;
      (ii) such a consent as is necessary for the purposes of Chapter III of Part IV of this Act is given by the undertaker; or
      (iii) a discharge is made in pursuance of such a consent; and
  (c) makes provision with respect to the times and methods of payment of the charges fixed by the scheme.
(2) The persons who may be required by a charges scheme to pay any charge fixed by virtue of subsection (1)(b) above shall be the person who serves the notice, the person to whom the consent is given or, as the case may be, any person who makes a discharge in pursuance of the consent at any time during the period to which, in accordance with the scheme, the charge relates.
(3) A charges scheme which requires the payment of charges where a discharge has been made in pursuance of such a consent as is mentioned in subsection (1)(b) above may impose—
  (a) a single charge in respect of the whole period for which the consent is in force;

(b) separate charges in respect of different parts of that period; or
(c) both such a single charge and such separate charges.
(4) A charges scheme may—
(a) make different provision for different cases, including different provision in relation to different circumstances or localities; and
(b) contain supplemental, consequential and transitional provision for the purposes of the scheme;
and such a scheme may revoke or amend a previous charges scheme.
(5) Nothing in any charges scheme shall affect—
(a) any power of a relevant undertaker to enter into such an agreement with any person in any particular case as determines the charges to be made for the services provided to that person by the undertaker; or
(b) the power of a sewerage undertaker to enter into any agreement under section 129 above on terms that provide for the making of payments to the undertaker.

DEFINITIONS
"functions": ss.217, 219(1).
"notice": s.219(1).
"services": s.219(1).

GENERAL NOTE
See also the General Note to s.142.
This section provides undertakers with a wide discretion to make charges schemes but this should be read in conjunction with condition D in the model instrument of appointment, which obliges undertakers to ensure that at all times they have a charges scheme in effect relating to firstly domestic water supplies and domestic drainage and secondly infrastructure charges under s.146(2). A charges scheme made under the provisions of s.143 may revoke or amend any previous scheme and contain provisions for transitional arrangements (subs. (4)).

Liability of occupiers etc. for charges

144.—(1) Subject to the following provisions of this section and except in so far as provision to the contrary is made by any agreement to which the undertaker is a party—
(a) supplies of water provided by a water undertaker shall be treated for the purposes of this Chapter as services provided to the occupiers for the time being of any premises supplied; and
(b) sewerage services provided by a sewerage undertaker shall be treated for the purposes of this Chapter as provided to the occupiers for the time being of any premises which—
(i) are drained by a sewer or drain connecting, either directly or through an intermediate sewer or drain, with such a public sewer of the undertaker as is provided for foul water or surface water or both; or
(ii) are premises the occupiers of which have, in respect of the premises, the benefit of facilities which drain to a sewer or drain so connecting.
(2) Subject to subsection (3) below, charges which, under the preceding provisions of this Chapter, are fixed in relation to any premises by reference to volume may be imposed so that a person is made liable in relation to those premises to pay charges for services provided by a relevant undertaker after that person has ceased to be the occupier of the premises.
(3) A person shall not be made liable by virtue of subsection (2) above for any charges fixed in relation to any premises by any relevant undertaker, except where—
(a) he fails to inform the undertaker of the ending of his occupation of the premises at least two working days before he ceases to occupy them; and

(b) the charges are in respect of a period ending no later than with the first relevant day.

(4) For the purposes of subsection (3) above, "the first relevant day," in relation to a case in which a person has ceased to be the occupier of any premises in relation to which charges are fixed by a relevant undertaker, means whichever of the following first occurs after he ceases to occupy the premises, that is to say—

(a) where that person informs the undertaker of the ending of his occupation of the premises less than two working days before, or at any time after, he ceases to occupy them, the twenty-eighth day after he so informs the undertaker;

(b) any day on which any meter would normally have been read in order for the amount of the charges to be determined;

(c) any day on which any other person informs the undertaker that he has become the new occupier of the premises.

(5) Where—

(a) any person who is the occupier of any premises to which a supply of water is provided by a water undertaker has served notice on the undertaker for the purposes of section 62 above; and

(b) that notice is given otherwise than in connection with that person's ceasing to be the occupier of the premises in a case in which provision is made by virtue of subsection (2) above for a person who has ceased to be the occupier of the premises to be made liable for any charges,

then, notwithstanding that that person continues to be the occupier of those premises, he shall not be liable to the undertaker (otherwise than in pursuance of a demand for a supply made since the service of the notice) for any charges in respect of any supply of water to those premises after the appropriate time.

(6) In subsection (5) above "the appropriate time," in relation to a case in which a notice has been served for the purposes of section 62 above, means whichever is the later of—

(a) the expiry of the notice; and

(b) the end of the period of two working days beginning with the service of the notice.

(7) In this section any reference to two working days is a reference to a period of 48 hours calculated after disregarding any time falling on—

(a) a Saturday or Sunday; or

(b) Christmas Day, Good Friday or any day which is a bank holiday in England and Wales under the Banking and Financial Dealings Act 1971.

(8) Where, in the case of any premises—

(a) the person who was liable, immediately before September 1, 1989, to pay charges in respect of a supply of water to those premises was the owner of those premises, rather than the occupier;

(b) that person was so liable (under section 54 of Schedule 3 to the Water Act 1945 or any other local statutory provision) otherwise than by virtue of an agreement; and

(c) the person who was in fact the occupier of the premises on that date has not ceased to be the occupier before the coming into force of this Act,

then the person who is the owner from time to time of those premises shall continue, until the person mentioned in paragraph (c) above does cease to be the occupier of the premises, to be the person liable and, accordingly, shall be treated for the purposes of this section as if he were the occupier of the premises.

DEFINITIONS
   "drain": s.219(1), (2).

"sewer": s.219(1), (2).
"surface water": s.219(1).
"the first relevant day": subs. (4).
"two working days": subs. (7).

GENERAL NOTE
See General Note to s.142.

This section reaffirms the general principle in previous legislation that liability for charges rests on the occupier of the premises, subject to any agreement to the contrary (for example where a landlord agrees to pay the charges). The Act provides no definition of an "occupier", but by analogy with rating cases, it implies someone with actual possession and control of premises. Under s.143(2) a different test for liability of charges applies in respect of discharge of trade effluent.

General restrictions on charging

Charging by reference to rateable value

145.—(1) Charges and other amounts to which this section applies shall not, by virtue of anything contained—
(a) in this Chapter;
(b) in any local statutory provision;
(c) in any charges scheme under section 143 above; or
(d) in any agreement entered into on or after September 1, 1989,
be recoverable by a relevant undertaker from any person if they have been fixed wholly or partly by reference to a rating valuation list or are otherwise determined, whether directly or indirectly, by reference to any value or other amount specified at any time in such a list.

(2) This section applies to—
(a) charges in respect of any services provided at any time after the end of March 31, 2000 by a relevant undertaker in the course of carrying out its functions; and
(b) amounts of any other description which such an undertaker, in exercise of any power conferred by or under any enactment, requires any person to pay in respect of any period ending after that date or in respect of anything done after that date,

(3) In this section "rating valuation list" means a list which is or has at any time been maintained, for the purposes of rating, under section 41 or 52 of the Local Government Finance Act 1988, section 67 of the General Rate Act 1967 or any other enactment.

DEFINITIONS
"functions": ss.217, 219(1).
"local statutory provision": s.219(1).
"rating valuation list": subs. (3).

GENERAL NOTE
See General Note to s.142.

The need to detach charges from being based upon rateable values arises from the introduction of the community charge, which replaced domestic rates, in 1990 under the Local Government Finance Act 1988. The section applies to charges for services provided after the end of March 31, 2000.

Connection charges etc. and charges for highway drainage

146.—(1) Subject to subsection (2) below, nothing in this Chapter or in any other enactment shall entitle any relevant undertaker to fix, demand or recover an initial charge for its becoming, or for its taking steps for the purpose of becoming—
(a) the person who provides a supply of water for domestic purposes to any premises; or

(b) the person who provides sewerage services for the purposes of the drainage for domestic sewerage purposes of any premises.

(2) Subject to subsection (3) below, nothing in subsection (1) above or in any other enactment shall be construed as prohibiting the fixing, demand or recovery by a relevant undertaker of—

(a) a charge for the connection to a water supply of premises which have never at any previous time (whether before or after the coming into force of the restriction contained in this section) been connected to a supply of water provided for domestic purposes by a water undertaker or by any other authority or body which at that time provided supplies of water in the course of carrying out functions under any enactment; or

(b) a charge for the connection to a public sewer of premises which have never at any previous time (whether before or after the coming into force of the restriction contained in this section) been connected to a sewer used for the drainage for domestic sewerage purposes of those premises by a sewerage undertaker or by any other authority or body which at that time provided sewerage services in the course of carrying out functions under any enactment.

(3) Nothing in this Chapter or in any other enactment or in the terms of any agreement under section 104 above shall authorise a sewerage undertaker to require any payment to be made to the undertaker in respect of the making by the undertaker of any declaration of vesting under Chapter II of Part IV of this Act or in respect of any agreement to make such a declaration.

(4) Nothing in this Chapter or in any other enactment shall authorise a sewerage undertaker to require any payment to be made to the undertaker by a highway authority in respect of the drainage of any highway or the disposal of the contents of any drain or sewer used for draining any highway.

(5) The preceding provisions of this section, so far as they restrict the making of certain charges, shall be without prejudice—

(a) to enactments by virtue of which a relevant undertaker may recover expenses incurred by it in carrying out works; and

(b) to the power of any such undertaker, by virtue of section 142(4) above, to fix the amount of any of its other charges by reference to such matters as it thinks appropriate.

(6) In this section "domestic sewerage purposes" has the same meaning as in Chapter II of Part IV of this Act.

DEFINITIONS
"domestic purposes": ss.218, 219(1).
"drainage for domestic purposes": subs. (6).
"highway": s.219(1).
"public sewer": s.219(1).
"sewerage services": s.219(1).

GENERAL NOTE
See General Note to s.142.

This section is derived from s.79 of the Water Act 1989, which provided a new power to undertakers to make infrastructure charges for new connections, and is distinct from requisitioning costs under ss.42 and 99.

Condition C of the model instrument of appointment provided a ceiling for both water and sewerage infrastructure charges in respect of the charging year commencing April 1, 1990 and for subsequent years charges are geared to increases or decreases in the retail price index, subject to periodic reviews at five- or 10-yearly intervals by the Director. A further ceiling is provided in respect of the aggregate charges that can be made in respect of a development site in any one charging year. Condition D of the model instrument of appointment provides that infrastructure charges must appear in the current charges scheme and that domestic consumers be given the option of paying by instalments over a 12-year period.

Charging for emergency use of water

147.—(1) Notwithstanding anything in section 142 above or in any charges scheme under section 143 above or in any agreement as to charges in respect of any supply of water, no charge may be made by any water undertaker in respect of—

(a) water taken for the purpose of extinguishing fires or taken by a fire authority for any other emergency purposes;

(b) water taken for the purpose of testing apparatus installed or equipment used for extinguishing fires or for the purpose of training persons for fire-fighting; or

(c) the availability of water for any purpose mentioned in paragraph (a) or (b) above.

(2) This section shall not prevent the making of charges in respect of work carried out at the request of or for the benefit of any person receiving a supply of water for the purposes mentioned in paragraph (a) or (b) of subsection (1) above.

(3) This section shall not have the effect, where any water is used or made available for any of the purposes mentioned in paragraph (a) or (b) of subsection (1) above, of requiring a reduction in the charges imposed in respect of the provision for other purposes of the supply from which that water is taken.

(4) In this section "fire authority" has the same meaning as in the Fire Services Act 1947.

DEFINITIONS
  "fire authority": subs. (4).

GENERAL NOTE
  This section provides that there will be no charge made by an undertaker where water is taken for the purposes of extinguishing a fire, for other emergency purposes, or for the purpose of testing fire-fighting equipment and training. Note also a water undertaker's duty under the provisions of s.57 to provide a water supply for fire-fighting purposes.

Metering

Restriction on charging for metering works

148.—(1) Subject to subsections (2) to (4) below and section 177 below, where any meter to be used in determining the amount of any charges is installed by or at the request of any relevant undertaker then, notwithstanding the provisions of any enactment or of any agreement to the contrary between the undertaker and any other person, the undertaker shall bear—

(a) the expenses of installing and connecting the meter;

(b) any expenses incurred in maintaining, repairing, disconnecting or removing the meter in accordance with any requirements of the undertaker; and

(c) any expenses incurred in carrying out any works for purposes connected with the installation and connection of the meter or with the maintenance, repair, disconnection or removal of the meter in accordance with any such requirements.

(2) Subject to subsection (3) below, subsection (1) above shall not require any relevant undertaker to bear, or prevent any such undertaker from recovering from any other person—

(a) any expenses incurred for the purpose of enabling a condition imposed by virtue of subsection (2)(c) or (d) of section 47 above to be satisfied;

(b) any sums which it is entitled to recover in pursuance of any terms or conditions determined under section 56 above;

(c) any sums which it is entitled to recover from that person by virtue of section 64(3)(b) above;

(d) any expenses incurred in relation to a meter which is or is to be used in determining the amount of—

(i) any charges which are to be paid in connection with the carrying out of a sewerage undertaker's functions under Chapter III of Part IV of this Act; or

(ii) any charges provision for which is contained in an agreement entered into in accordance with section 129 above;

(e) any expenses incurred in consequence of the exercise by the occupier of any premises of any option to be charged by the undertaker in relation to any premises by reference to volume rather than by reference to other matters.

(3) For the purposes of subsection (2) above the expenses which an undertaker may require someone else to bear, or may recover from another, by virtue of that subsection shall not include any expenses incurred for the purpose of enabling conditions such as are mentioned in paragraph (a) of that subsection to be satisfied in a case in which the conditions could not have been imposed but for the exercise by the undertaker of its power by virtue of paragraph (a), (b), (d) or (e) of section 64(2) above to require the provision of a separate service pipe to any premises.

(4) The occupier of any premises where any relevant undertaker installs or has installed a meter shall in all cases bear so much of the expenses referred to in subsection (1) above as is attributable to compliance with a request made by him in accordance with any regulations under section 149 below for the positioning, in a place other than that reasonably proposed by the undertaker, either of the meter or of any pipe or apparatus installed for the purpose of facilitating the use of the meter.

(5) Any dispute between a relevant undertaker and any other person (including another such undertaker)—

(a) as to whether the undertaker or that other person should bear any expenses under this section; or

(b) as to the amount of any expenses to be borne by any person under this section,

shall be referred to the arbitration of a single arbitrator appointed by agreement between the undertaker and that person or, in default of agreement, by the Director.

DEFINITIONS

"enactment": s.219(1).
"meter": s.219(1).
"surface pipe": s.219(1), (2).

GENERAL NOTE

This section is derived from Sched. 10 to the Water Act 1989 and makes provision that an undertaker must bear the costs of installation, maintenance, disconnection and removal of any meter installed by or at the request of an undertaker in order to determine an undertaker's charges. This applies even if the undertaker had entered into a contrary agreement with one of its customers.

An undertaker will however be able to recover its expenses relating to the installation of a meter which is required to be installed as a condition of connection to a water main. Similarly expenses can be recovered in respect of meters installed by virtue of a deemed condition under s.64(3)(b) where a requirement for separate service pipes has been served or as a condition imposed on the connection of a non-domestic supply. The consumer will also have to pay the expenses involved in positioning the meter if these differ from that which the undertaker may reasonably require. Any dispute regarding payment of costs incurred by an undertaker or a proportion thereof are referred to arbitration under subs. (5).

Further provision relating to charging by volume

149.—(1) The Secretary of State may by regulations make such provision, supplementing—
   (a) the provisions of this Chapter; and
   (b) so far as they relate to works for purposes connected with the fixing of charges in relation to any premises by reference to volume, the provisions of Part VI of this Act,
as he considers appropriate with respect to the installation of meters, with respect to the connection, disconnection, use, maintenance, authentication and testing of meters and with respect to any related matters.

(2) Without prejudice to the generality of subsection (1) above, regulations under that subsection may—
   (a) regulate the positioning, whether inside or outside the building or other premises in relation to which the meter is to be used, of any meter or of any pipes or apparatus appearing to any relevant undertaker to be required for the purpose of facilitating the use of any meter;
   (b) make any other provision which appears to the Secretary of State to be appropriate with respect to any such pipes or apparatus;
   (c) provide for a reading from a meter to be proved in such manner as may be prescribed and for a reading from a meter to be such evidence as may be prescribed of the volume of water supplied to, or of effluent discharged from, any premises;
   (d) fix the method of determining the amount of the charges to be paid where it appears that a meter has given, or may have given, an incorrect reading;
   (e) require a person who is not a relevant undertaker to pay the expenses incurred by such an undertaker in doing anything under the regulations or to pay contributions towards those expenses;
   (f) provide for the payment of compensation in respect of anything done by a relevant undertaker under the regulations;
   (g) require disputes arising under the regulations to be referred to arbitration;
   (h) repeal or amend any local statutory provision.

DEFINITIONS
   "effluent": s.219(1).
   "local statutory provision": s.219(1).
   "meter": s.219(1).
   "prescribed": s.219(1).

GENERAL NOTE
   See General Note to s.142.
   This section provides a power to the Secretary of State to make regulations supplementing the provisions of ss.142 to 150 regarding the installation, connection, disconnection, use, maintenance, authentication and testing of meters. Subsection (2) details the general remit of such regulations.

Charging for services provided with the help of an undertaker

Fixing maximum charges for services provided with the help of undertakers' services

150.—(1) The Director may from time to time by order fix maximum charges which a person who is not a relevant undertaker may recover from another such person in respect of water supplies or sewerage services provided to that other person with the help of services provided by a relevant undertaker.

(2) For the purposes of this section water supplies or sewerage services are provided to a person with the help of services provided by a relevant undertaker if—

(a) a facility for that person to have access to a supply of water provided by a water undertaker in pipes, or to make use of sewerage services provided by a sewerage undertaker, is made available to that person otherwise than by the undertaker;

(b) that person is provided with a supply of water in pipes by a person to whom the water is supplied, directly or indirectly, by a water undertaker; or

(c) that person is provided with sewerage services by a person who, for the purpose of providing those services, makes use of sewerage services provided, directly or indirectly, by a sewerage undertaker.

(3) It shall be the duty of the Director to publish any order under this section in such manner as he considers appropriate for the purpose of bringing it to the attention of persons likely to be affected by it.

(4) An order under this section may make different provision for different cases, including different provision in relation to different persons, circumstances or localities, and may fix a maximum charge either by specifying the maximum amount of the charge or by specifying a method of calculating that amount.

(5) Where a person pays a charge in respect of anything to which an order under this section relates and the amount paid exceeds the maximum charge fixed by the order, the amount of the excess shall be recoverable by that person from the person to whom he paid the charge.

DEFINITIONS
"services": s.219(1).
"sewerage services": s.219(1).

GENERAL NOTE
This section is derived from s.82 of the Water Act 1989 and arises out of concern regarding overcharging for the resale of water supplies or sewerage services by persons other than undertakers. The section provides the Director with a power to fix maximum prices for the resale of water supplies and sewerage services (subs. (1)). The Director is under a duty to publicise any such order he makes (subs. (3)). The provisions do not apply to all resales of water and by virtue of subs. (2) the sale of bottled water and provision of private water supplies are not intended to be included.
See also the "1990 Report of the Director General of Water Services", June 18, 1991, HMSO, p. 31. This addresses the problem of controlling the price at which landlords can recharge their tenants for water and sewerage services.

CHAPTER II

FINANCIAL ASSISTANCE FOR UNDERTAKERS

Financial contributions to rural services

151.—(1) Subject to subsection (2) below and to such conditions as the Treasury may determine, the Secretary of State, in any case in which it appears to him to be desirable to do so, may undertake to make a contribution out of money provided by Parliament towards the expenses incurred—

(a) by a water undertaker in providing a supply of water in a rural locality or in improving an existing supply of water in such a locality;

(b) by a sewerage undertaker in making adequate provision for the sewerage of a rural locality or for the disposal of such a locality's sewage.

(2) The Secretary of State shall not undertake to make a contribution under this section towards the expenses of making provision for the sewerage of a rural locality, or for the disposal of such a locality's sewage, unless

he is satisfied that the need for making the provision is due to anything done or proposed to be done—

(a) to supply water in pipes in that locality; or

(b) to increase the supply of water in pipes in that locality.

(3) An undertaking given by the Secretary of State under this section shall provide for the making of the contribution in the form of such lump sum payment or payments, or such periodical payments towards revenue expenditure, as may appear to the Secretary of State to be appropriate.

(4) The Secretary of State may withhold, or reduce the amount of, any contribution which he has undertaken to make towards the expenses incurred by a relevant undertaker in respect of any works or transaction, if it appears to him either—

(a) that any of the works have been carried out in an unsatisfactory manner;

(b) that—

(i) the effectiveness of any of the works is substantially less than as estimated in the proposals submitted to him by the relevant undertaker; and

(ii) the difference is due to any default, for which the undertaker is responsible, in the formulation of the proposals;

or

(c) that there has been any default in the carrying out of the transaction.

DEFINITIONS
"disposal": s.219(1).

GENERAL NOTE
This section provides the Secretary of State with a discretion to provide a financial contribution to water undertakers and sewerage undertakers to enable them to provide or improve water supplies or sewerage services in rural localities. Such a contribution will only be forthcoming if the Secretary of State is satisfied that the need for making the provision is due to anything done or proposed to be done in order to provide a water supply in that locality in pipes or to increase the provision of water supplies. The Treasury have the power by virtue of subs. (1) to make conditions relating to such financial contribution to rural communities.

Grants for national security purposes

152.—(1) The Secretary of State may, out of money provided by Parliament, make grants to relevant undertakers for the purpose of defraying or contributing towards any losses they may sustain by reason of compliance with directions given under section 208 below in the interests of national security.

(2) The approval of the Treasury shall be required for the making of grants under this section.

GENERAL NOTE
This section is derived from s.170(7) of the Water Act 1989. Grants may be made by the Secretary of State, subject to the approval of the Treasury, toward the cost of compliance with directions made under s.208, relating to interests of national security. Such grants can apply to costs incurred in respect of civil defence expenditure.

During the committee stage of the Water Act, the Under-Secretary of State indicated that the anticipated expenditure by the Government would be similar to the then current expenditure on civil defence by the water industry of £3,189,000. In order to defray costs, grant aid is available for up to 75 per cent. of expenditure but with full reimbursement for training, communications and full-time planning staff (Standing Committee D, col. 1532). The costs involved in other types of emergency expenditure are to be met by the undertakers themselves, who must make provision out of their general revenue.

Unforeseen substantial costs arising from civil emergency expenditure could be defrayed by customer price increases approved by the Director, using the procedure for reviewing the charges formula under the instrument of appointment discussed in the General Note to s.142.

Government financial assistance where special administration orders made

153.—(1) Where a special administration order is for the time being in force in relation to a company, the Secretary of State, may, with the consent of the Treasury—

(a) make to the company grants or loans of such sums as appear to him to be appropriate for the purpose of facilitating the achievement of the purposes of the order;

(b) agree to indemnify the person appointed to achieve the purposes of the order in respect of liabilities incurred and loss or damage sustained by that person in connection with the carrying out of his functions under the order.

(2) The Secretary of State may, with the consent of the Treasury, guarantee, in such manner and on such conditions as he may think fit, the repayment of the principal of, the payment of interest on and the discharge of any other financial obligation in connection with any sum which is borrowed from any person by a company in relation to which a special administration order is in force at the time when the guarantee is given.

(3) Without prejudice to any provision applied in relation to the company by Schedule 3 to this Act—

(a) the terms and conditions on which a grant is made to any company under this section may require the whole or a part of the grant to be repaid to the Secretary of State if there is a contravention of the other terms and conditions on which the grant is made; and

(b) any loans which the Secretary of State makes to a company under this section shall be repaid to him at such times and by such methods, and interest on the loans shall be paid to him at such rates and at such times, as he may, with the consent of the Treasury, from time to time direct.

(4) Any grant or loan made under this section and any sums required to be paid by the Secretary of State in respect of an indemnity given under this section shall be paid out of money provided by Parliament.

(5) Any sums received under subsection (3) above by the Secretary of State shall be paid into the Consolidated Fund.

DEFINITIONS
"damage": s.219(1).
"special administration order": ss.23, 219(1).

GENERAL NOTE
This section provides the Secretary of State, with the consent of the Treasury, with an important power to make grants or loans to ensure the continuity of an undertaker's functions until a replacement appointment is made. The following provisions of s.154 apply to any guarantee under subs. (2).

Guarantees under section 153

154.—(1) This section applies in relation to any guarantee given by the Secretary of State under section 153 above.

(2) Immediately after a guarantee to which this section applies is given, the Secretary of State shall lay a statement of the guarantee before each House of Parliament.

(3) Where any sum is paid out for fulfilling a guarantee to which this section applies, the Secretary of State shall, as soon as possible after the end of each financial year (beginning with that in which the sum is paid out and ending with that in which all liability in respect of the principal of the sum and in respect of the interest thereon is finally discharged), lay before each House of Parliament a statement relating to that sum.

(4) Any sums required by the Secretary of State for fulfilling a guarantee to which this section applies shall be paid out of money provided by Parliament.

(5) Without prejudice to any provision applied in relation to the relevant company by Schedule 3 to this Act, if any sums are paid out in fulfilment of a guarantee to which this section applies, the relevant company shall make to the Secretary of State, at such times and in such manner as the Secretary of State may from time to time direct—

(a) payments of such amounts as the Secretary of State may so direct in or towards repayment of the sums so paid out; and

(b) payments of interest, at such rate as the Secretary of State may so direct, on what is outstanding for the time being in respect of sums so paid out;

and the consent of the Treasury shall be required for the giving of a direction under this subsection.

(6) Any sums received by the Secretary of State under subsection (5) above shall be paid into the Consolidated Fund.

(7) In subsection (5) above "the relevant company" in relation to a guarantee, means the company which borrowed the sums in respect of which the guarantee was given.

DEFINITIONS
"the relevant company": subs. (7).

GENERAL NOTE
This provision details the procedures which are to be adopted where financial guarantees are given by the Secretary of State on behalf of the Government in circumstances where a special administration order has been made under either ss.24 or 25.

PART VI

UNDERTAKERS' POWERS AND WORKS

CHAPTER I

UNDERTAKERS' POWERS

Powers in relation to land

Compulsory purchase

155.—(1) A relevant undertaker may be authorised by the Secretary of State to purchase compulsorily any land anywhere in England and Wales which is required by the undertaker for the purposes of, or in connection with, the carrying out of its functions.

(2) The power of the Secretary of State under subsection (1) above shall include power—

(a) to authorise the acquisition of interests in and rights over land by the creation of new interests and rights; and

(b) by authorising the acquisition by a relevant undertaker of any rights over land which is to be or has been acquired by that undertaker, to provide for the extinguishment of those rights.

(3) Without prejudice to the generality of subsection (1) above, the land which a relevant undertaker may be authorised under that subsection to purchase compulsorily shall include land which is or will be required for the purpose of being given in exchange for, or for any right over, any other land which for the purposes of the Acquisition of Land Act 1981 is or forms part of a common, open space or a fuel or field garden allotment.

(4) Subject to section 188 below, the Acquisition of Land Act 1981 shall apply to any compulsory purchase under subsection (1) above of any land by

a relevant undertaker; and Schedule 3 to the said Act of 1981 shall apply to the compulsory acquisition under that subsection of rights by the creation of new rights.

(5) Schedule 9 to this Act shall have effect for the purpose of modifying enactments relating to compensation and the provisions of the Compulsory Purchase Act 1965 in their application in relation to the compulsory acquisition under subsection (1) above of a right over land by the creation of a new right.

(6) The provisions of Part I of the Compulsory Purchase Act 1965 (so far as applicable), other than sections 4 to 8, 10, 21, 27(1) and 31 and Schedule 4, shall apply in relation to any power to acquire land by agreement which is conferred (whether by virtue of the memorandum and articles of the company for the time being carrying out the functions of the undertaker or any enactment or otherwise) on a relevant undertaker, as if—

(a) any reference in those provisions to the acquiring authority were a reference to that undertaker; and

(b) any reference to land subject to compulsory purchase were a reference to land which may be purchased by agreement under that power.

DEFINITIONS
"enactments": s.219(1).
"functions": ss.217, 219(1).
"relevant undertaker": s.219(1).

GENERAL NOTE
This section provides undertakers, subject to the approval of the Secretary of State, with powers to purchase compulsorily land in England and Wales which is required by the undertaker for the performance of its functions. Note the additional compulsory purchase powers contained in s.167. The Acquisition of Land Act 1981 applies to any land compulsorily purchased under subs. (1) and thus compensation is calculated on the basis that the landowner is entitled to compensation based on the market value of his interest excluding any additional development value resulting from the undertaker's proposed scheme. Subsection (1) restricts the acquisition of land by this method to land which is required for the purpose of or in connection with the carrying out of the functions of the relevant undertaker. Such a limitation is designed to prevent an abuse of an undertaker's powers where land is acquired primarily for commercial reasons and not related to its primary functions of water supply and sewerage services.

Restriction on disposals of land

156.—(1) A company holding an appointment under Chapter I of Part II of this Act shall not dispose of any of its protected land, or of any interest or right in or over any of that land, except with the consent of, or in accordance with a general authorisation given by, the Secretary of State.

(2) A consent or authorisation for the purposes of this section—

(a) shall be set out in a notice served by the Secretary of State on the company which is or may be authorised, by virtue of the provision contained in the notice, to dispose of land or of interests or rights in or over land or, as the case may be, on every such company; and

(b) in the case of an authorisation, may be combined with an authorisation for the purposes of section 157 of the Water Resources Act 1991.

(3) A consent or authorisation for the purposes of this section may be given on such conditions as the Secretary of State considers appropriate.

(4) Without prejudice to the generality of subsection (3) above and subject to subsection (5) below, the conditions of a consent or authorisation for the purposes of this section may include—

(a) a requirement that, before there is any disposal, an opportunity of acquiring the land in question, or an interest or right in or over that land, is to be made available, in such manner and on such terms as may be specified in or determined under provision contained in the notice setting out the consent or authorisation, to such person as may be so specified or determined;

(b) a requirement that the company making the disposal has complied with such of the conditions of its appointment under Chapter I of Part II of this Act as relate to the disposal of its protected land or of any interest or right in or over that land;

(c) a requirement that the company, before making a disposal in a case in which the land in question is situated in a National Park, in the Broads or in an area of outstanding natural beauty or special scientific interest, should do one or both of the following, that is to say—

    (i) consult with the Countryside Commission (as respects land in England) or the Countryside Council for Wales (as respects land in Wales) and, in the case of an area of special scientific interest in England, with the Nature Conservancy Council for England; and

    (ii) enter into such agreements under section 39 of the Wildlife and Countryside Act 1981 (management agreements) or such covenants under subsection (6) below as the Secretary of State may determine;

(d) provision requiring determinations under or for the purposes of the consent or authorisation to be made, in such cases as are mentioned in paragraph (c) above, either by the Countryside Commission or the Countryside Council for Wales or only after consultation with that Commission or Council.

(5) A consent or authorisation shall not be given on any such condition as is mentioned in subsection (4)(a) above except where the Secretary of State is satisfied that the condition will have effect in relation only to—

(a) land which, or any interest in or right over which, was acquired by the relevant undertaker in question, or any predecessor of that undertaker, either compulsorily or at a time when the undertaker or that predecessor was authorised to acquire it compulsorily; or

(b) land situated in a National Park, in the Broads or in an area of outstanding natural beauty or special scientific interest.

(6) Where a company holding an appointment under Chapter I of Part II of this Act is proposing, in such a case as is mentioned in subsection (4)(c) above, to dispose of, or of any interest or right in or over, any of its protected land, it may enter into a covenant with the Secretary of State by virtue of which it accepts obligations with respect to—

(a) the freedom of access to the land that is to be afforded to members of the public or to persons of any description; or

(b) the use or management of the land;

and a covenant under this subsection shall bind all persons deriving title from or under that company and shall be enforceable by the Secretary of State accordingly.

(7) Section 3 above shall have effect for the purposes of this section as if every proposal which—

(a) is made by a company holding an appointment as a relevant undertaker with respect to land in a National Park, in the Broads or in an area of outstanding natural beauty or special scientific interest, or with respect to any interest or right in or over any such land; and

(b) is a proposal for which the Secretary of State's consent or authorisation is required under this section,

were a proposal relating to the functions of such an undertaker.

(8) In this section—

"area of outstanding natural beauty or special scientific interest" means an area which—

    (a) is for the time being designated as an area of outstanding natural beauty for the purposes of the National Parks and Access to the Countryside Act 1949; or

(b) is an area in relation to which a notification given, or having effect as if given, under section 28 of the Wildlife and Countryside Act 1981 (areas of special scientific interest) for the time being has effect;

and the reference in subsection (4)(c) above to an area of special scientific interest shall, accordingly, be construed as a reference to an area such as is mentioned in paragraph (b) of this definition; and "the Broads" has the same meaning as in the Norfolk and Suffolk Broads Act 1988.

DEFINITIONS

"area of outstanding natural beauty or special scientific interest": subs. (8).
"disposal": s.219(1).
"functions": ss.217, 219(1).
"notice": s.219(1).
"protected land": s.219(1).
"the Broads": subs. (8).

GENERAL NOTE

This section is concerned with important restrictions on disposals of land by undertakers.

It is estimated that water undertakers possess significant land holdings extending to some 430,000 acres, of which 180,000 acres are in national parks or areas of outstanding natural beauty. The section is designed to provide adequate protection against wide-scale land disposals by undertakers. The provisions of the section contain a number of mechanisms which are considered below.

Financial returns on sales of land

Conditions are included in each instrument of appointment relating to the disposal of land by undertakers, ensuring that customers benefit from disposals through reduced prices. In setting overall charges in respect of the provision of services (the RPI + K formula discussed in s.142) account is to be taken of the open market value of land already identified as surplus to requirements, and assuming a rate of flow of income arising from such sales. Where greater than forecast profits occur (for example because the undertaker has secured planning permission for a site or sold other lands not initially identified), the K factor would be reduced by the Director when carrying out his regular review of an undertaker's charging formula. The Director will review and reduce the K factor using a formula that 50 per cent. of the surplus receipts should directly benefit the consumer. A fall in an undertaker's receipts below that which has been forecast from disposals of land (for example due to the reduction in land prices) may result in an increase of the "K" factor. The instrument of appointment will also contain requirements that the prior authorisation or consent of the Director be obtained to ensure that realistic prices are being obtained for land which is to be disposed of and to prevent disposals to associated or subsidiary companies at less than the market value of such disposals. Note also the general duty on the Director in s.2(3) and the imposition of consent disposal conditions under s.156(4).

Protected land

The term "protected land" is defined in s.219(1) and includes all land held by undertakers on or after September 1, 1989 save for land acquired after that date and which relates to an undertaker's non-functional activities. Disposal of protected land may only occur with the consent of the Secretary of State or in accordance with the general authorisation procedure (subs. (3)).

Disposals and general environmental duties

The Secretary of State has a wide discretion under this section in determining whether to exercise his power to consent to a disposal of protected land but his discretion will still be subject to the general environmental duties set out in s.3. A disposal of land by undertakers is not a "function", and thus the general environmental duties will not generally apply, however s.156(7) extends the general environmental and recreational duties contained in s.3 to disposals of protected land within a national park, the Norfolk and Suffolk Broads, areas of outstanding natural beauty or sites of special scientific interest.

First offer requirements on disposal

The Secretary of State will use his consent conditions to ensure that an undertaker's land falling within a national park, the Broads, an area of outstanding natural beauty or a site of special scientific interest is offered for sale to the persons specified in subss. (4)(a) and (5)(b). The intention of those provisions is to require the first offer for the land or interest to be made by a conservation body approved by the Countryside Commission or Countryside Council for Wales, but at the market value of the land to be disposed of (*Hansard*, H.L. Vol. 508, cols. 950, 975).

Other protective measures

Consent conditions under s.156 may also be used in the event of a disposal of land within a national park, the Broads, an area of outstanding natural beauty, or a site of special scientific interest to ensure that the undertaker must firstly consult the Countryside Commission, Countryside Council for Wales or Nature Conservancy Council for England (subs. (4)(c)); secondly, enter into management agreements under s.39 of the Wildlife and Countryside Act 1981 (subs. (4)(c)); and thirdly, enter into covenants with the Secretary of State relating to freedom of access or the use and management of land (see subss. (4)(c) and (6)). Such covenants are declared to be binding on persons deriving title from the company (subs. (6)), and their effect may be to depress the market value of the land thereby making the purchase of it by conservation bodies more feasible if a "first offer" condition is attached.

Byelaws with respect to undertakers' waterways and land

157.—(1) Every relevant undertaker shall have power to make such byelaws as are mentioned in subsection (2) below with respect to any waterway owned or managed by that body and with respect to any land held or managed with the waterway.

(2) The byelaws referred to in subsection (1) above in relation to any waterway or to any land held or managed with any such waterway are byelaws for any of the following purposes, that is to say—

    (a) the preservation of order on or in any such waterway or land;

    (b) the prevention of damage to anything on or in any such waterway or land or to any such land;

    (c) securing that persons resorting to any such waterway or land so behave as to avoid undue interference with the enjoyment of the waterway or land by others.

(3) Without prejudice to the generality of any of the paragraphs of subsection (2) above, the byelaws mentioned in that subsection include byelaws—

    (a) regulating sailing, boating, bathing and fishing and other forms of recreation;

    (b) prohibiting the use of the waterway in question by boats which are not for the time being registered, in such manner as may be required by the byelaws, with the undertaker making the byelaws;

    (c) requiring the provision of such sanitary appliances as may be necessary for the purpose of preventing pollution;

    (d) providing for a contravention of the byelaws to constitute a summary offence punishable, on summary conviction, by a fine not exceeding level 5 on the standard scale or such smaller sum as may be specified in the byelaws; and

    (e) authorising the making of reasonable charges in respect of the registration of boats for the purposes of the byelaws.

(4) Schedule 10 to this Act shall have effect with respect to byelaws under this section.

(5) Byelaws made under this section shall cease to have effect at the end of the period of ten years beginning with the day on which they were made; but the Secretary of State may by order made by statutory instrument make provision in relation to any particular byelaws for those byelaws to continue to have effect for such period after the time when they would otherwise cease to have effect as may be specified in the order.

(6) In this section—

"boat" includes a vessel of any description, and "boating" shall be
     construed accordingly;
"waterway" has the same meaning as in the National Parks and Access
     to the Countryside Act 1949.

DEFINITIONS
  "boat": subs. (6)
  "damage": s.219(1).
  "relevant undertaker": s.219(1).
  "waterway": subs. (6).

GENERAL NOTE
  This section provides undertakers with an extensive power to make by-laws relating to any
waterway owned or managed by the undertaker and land associated with the waterway.
  The definition of "waterway" includes lakes, rivers, or other waters including reservoirs
which are suitable or which can be reasonably rendered suitable for sailing, boating, bathing or
fishing, together with any associated land.
  By-laws must relate either to the preservation of order on the waterway or associated land,
prevention of damage and to ensure that people using the waterway or associated land do so
without unduly interfering with others (subs. (2)). Schedule 10 of the Act sets out the procedure
which is to be followed in order to make the appropriate by-laws. Any by-law made by the
undertaker under s.157 will not have effect until confirmed by the Secretary of State under the
Sched. 10 procedure. By-laws made under s.157 cease to have effect once they are 10 years old
except to the extent that the Secretary of State makes an order by statutory instrument
continuing the by-law for such a period as the Secretary of State deems appropriate (subs. (5)).

Pipe-laying

Powers to lay pipes in streets

158.—(1) Subject to the following provisions of this section, to section
162(9) below and to the provisions of Chapter III of this Part, every relevant
undertaker shall, for the purpose of carrying out its functions, have power—
  (a) to lay a relevant pipe in, under or over any street and to keep that pipe
       there;
  (b) to inspect, maintain, adjust, repair or alter any relevant pipe which is
       in, under or over any street; and
  (c) to carry out any works requisite for, or incidental to, the purposes of
       any works falling within paragraph (a) or (b) above, including for
       those purposes the following kinds of works, that is to say—
         (i) breaking up or opening a street;
         (ii) tunnelling or boring under a street;
         (iii) breaking up or opening a sewer, drain or tunnel;
         (iv) moving or removing earth and other materials.
  (2) Without prejudice to the generality of subsection (1)(c) above, every
water undertaker shall have power to erect and keep in any street notices
indicating the position of such underground accessories for its relevant pipes
as may be used for controlling the flow of water in those pipes.
  (3) The power conferred by subsection (2) above shall include power to
attach any such notice as is mentioned in that subsection to any building,
fence or other structure which is comprised in premises abutting on the
street in question.
  (4) A stopcock fitted to any service pipe in a street shall be situated as near
as reasonably practicable to the boundary of the street; and a water undertaker shall consult with the highway authority concerned before determining
in accordance with this subsection where to fit a stopcock in a highway.
  (5) Where a water undertaker exercises its powers under this section for
the purpose of carrying out works of maintenance, repair or renewal in
relation to a service pipe belonging to a person other than the undertaker,
the undertaker shall be entitled to recover from the occupier of the premises

supplied by means of that pipe the expenses reasonably incurred by that undertaker in so exercising that power.

(6) Until the coming into force of its repeal by the New Roads and Street Works Act 1991 section 20 of the Highways Act 1980 (works in special roads) shall have effect as if the reference in that section to a power under any enactment to lay down or erect apparatus included a reference to any power to lay any relevant pipe which is conferred by this section.

(7) Subject to section 161(7) below, in this section references to a relevant pipe shall be construed—

(a) in relation to a water undertaker, as references to a water main (including a trunk main), resource main, discharge pipe or service pipe; and

(b) in relation to a sewerage undertaker, as references to any sewer or disposal main.

DEFINITIONS
"functions": ss.217, 219(1).
"highway authority": s.219(1).
"relevant pipe": subs. (7).
"relevant undertaker": s.219(1).
"street": s.219(1).

GENERAL NOTE
This section provides undertakers with power to lay, inspect, maintain and repair their pipes in, under or over any street. A "street" is defined in s.219(1) and will include any length of highway or square, court, or road, whether public or private, and will include a bridge or tunnel forming part of the highway. Subsection (1) empowers undertakers to carry out works which are incidental to the laying of pipes and these include breaking up a street, tunnelling or boring under it and moving or removing earth and materials from such works (subs. (1)(c)).

Provision is made for an undertaker to erect notices or attach them to structures abutting the street indicating the position of apparatus which controls the flow of water (subs. (2)). In addition stopcocks fitted to service pipes in any street will be placed as near as reasonably practicable to the street boundary following consultations with the relevant highway authority (subs. (4)).

No planning permission will be required for such works as long as they do not rise above ground level (GDO 1988, Sched. 2, Pts. 15 and 17E).

Power to lay pipes in other land

159.—(1) Subject to the following provisions of this section, to section 162(9) below and to the provisions of Chapter III of this Part, every relevant undertaker shall, for the purpose of carrying out its functions, have power—

(a) to lay a relevant pipe (whether above or below the surface) in any land which is not in, under or over a street and to keep that pipe there;

(b) to inspect, maintain, adjust, repair or alter any relevant pipe which is in any such land;

(c) to carry out any works requisite for, or incidental to, the purposes of any works falling within paragraph (a) or (b) above.

(2) Nothing in subsection (1) above shall authorise a water undertaker to lay a service pipe in, on or over any land except where—

(a) there is already a service pipe where that pipe is to be laid; or

(b) the undertaker is required to lay the pipe in, on or over that land by virtue of any of subsections (3) to (5) of section 46 above.

(3) The power conferred by virtue of paragraph (b) of subsection (1) above, and the power conferred in relation to that paragraph by virtue of paragraph (c) of that subsection shall be exercisable in relation to a service pipe irrespective of the person to whom the pipe belongs; but expenses incurred in exercising those powers in relation to any pipe shall be recoverable from the person to whom the pipe belongs only if and to the extent that that person has agreed to pay them.

(4) The powers conferred by this section shall be exercisable only after reasonable notice of the proposed exercise of the power has been given to the owner and to the occupier of the land where the power is to be exercised.

(5) Subject to subsection (6) below, in relation to any exercise of the powers conferred by this section for the purpose of laying or altering a relevant pipe, the minimum period that is capable of constituting reasonable notice for the purposes of subsection (4) above shall be deemed—

(a) where the power is exercised for the purpose of laying a relevant pipe otherwise than in substitution for an existing pipe of the same description, to be three months; and

(b) where the power is exercised for the purpose of altering an existing pipe, to be 42 days.

(6) Subsection (5) above shall not apply in the case of any notice given with respect to the exercise of any power in an emergency or for the purpose of—

(a) laying or altering a service pipe; or

(b) complying with a duty imposed under section 41 or 98 above.

(7) Subject to subsection (2) above, in this section "relevant pipe" has the same meaning as in section 158 above.

DEFINITIONS
 "functions": ss.217, 219(1).
 "owner": s.219(1).
 "reasonable notice": subs. (5).
 "relevant pipe": s.158(7),

GENERAL NOTE
 This section provides an undertaker with power to lay, inspect, maintain and repair pipes in other land not forming part of a street (including any associated works). The power may only be used for the purpose of carrying out an undertaker's functions (subs. (1)). Subsection (2) restricts an undertaker's power so that it may only be used where another service pipe already exists or as a result of a requisition made under s.46. Costs incurred by an undertaker in exercising the powers in subs. (1)(b) and (1)(c) may only be recovered from the person who is the owner of the relevant pipe if that person has agreed to pay those costs (subs. (3)).
 The powers conferred by this section to lay or alter a relevant pipe may only be exercised where reasonable notice is given under subs. (5). Where a new pipe is to be laid the requisite period of notice will be at least three months, but only 42 days' notice has to be given where an existing pipe has to be altered. The requirement to give reasonable notice under subs. (5) does not apply in an emergency or where the undertaker must give notice to lay a service pipe or comply with a duty imposed under ss.41 and 98.

Other works powers

Power to carry out works for sewerage purposes

160.—(1) A sewerage undertaker may, by agreement with the owner or occupier of any premises, carry out at that person's expense—

(a) any work in connection with the construction, laying, alteration or repair of a sewer or drain which that person is entitled to carry out; or

(b) any work which the undertaker has required that person to carry out under Part IV of this Act;

and for that purpose the undertaker shall have all such rights as that person would have.

(2) Sections 291, 293 and 294 of the Public Health Act 1936 (which provide for the means of, and for limitations on, the recovery of expenses incurred by a local authority) shall apply in relation to the recovery by a sewerage undertaker of any sums under this section as they apply in relation to the recovery of expenses under that Act by a local authority.

DEFINITIONS
 "drain": s.219(1), (2).

"local authority": s.219(1).
"owner": s.219(1).
"sewer": s.219(1), (2).

GENERAL NOTE
This section enables the sewerage undertaker to enter into an agreement with the owner or occupier of the premises (who is entitled to carry out sewerage works) that take advantage of an undertaker's desire to carry out those works.

Power to deal with foul water and pollution

161.—(1) Subject to the provisions of Chapter III of this Part, every relevant undertaker shall, for the purpose of carrying out its functions, have power—
   (a) to carry out in a street all such works as are requisite for securing that the water in any relevant waterworks is not polluted or otherwise contaminated; and
   (b) to carry out any works requisite for, or incidental to, the purposes of any works falling within paragraph (a) above, including for those purposes the following kinds of works, that is to say—
      (i) breaking up or opening a street;
      (ii) tunnelling or boring under a street;
      (iii) breaking up or opening a sewer, drain or tunnel;
      (iv) moving or removing earth and other materials;
and the provisions of section 158 above shall, so far as applicable, have effect in relation to the powers conferred by this subsection as they have effect in relation to the powers conferred by subsection (1) of that section.
   (2) Subject to the provisions of Chapter III of this Part, every relevant undertaker shall, for the purpose of carrying out its functions, have power—
   (a) to carry out on any land which is not in, under or over a street all such works as are requisite for securing that the water in any relevant waterworks is not polluted or otherwise contaminated; and
   (b) to carry out any works requisite for, or incidental to, the purposes of any works falling within paragraph (a) above;
and the provisions of section 159 above shall, so far as applicable, have effect in relation to the powers conferred by this subsection as they have effect in relation to the powers conferred by subsection (1) of that section.
   (3) Without prejudice to the powers conferred by subsections (1) and (2) above but subject to the provisions of Chapter III of this Part, every water undertaker shall have power, on any land which belongs to that undertaker or over or in which that undertaker has acquired the necessary easements or rights, to construct and maintain drains, sewers, watercourses, catchpits and other works for the purpose—
   (a) of intercepting, treating or disposing of any foul water arising or flowing upon that land; or
   (b) of otherwise preventing the pollution—
      (i) of any waters, whether on the surface or underground, which belong to the NRA or any water undertaker or from which the NRA or any water undertaker is authorised to take water;
      (ii) without prejudice to sub-paragraph (i) above, of any reservoir which belongs to or is operated by the NRA or any water undertaker or which the NRA or any water undertaker is proposing to acquire or construct for the purpose of being so operated; or
      (iii) of any underground strata from which the NRA or any water undertaker is for the time being authorised to abstract water in pursuance of a licence under Chapter II of Part II of the Water Resources Act 1991.
   (4) Where any water undertaker is proposing to carry out any such works as are mentioned in subsection (3) above and the proposed works will affect

any watercourse, the undertaker shall consult the NRA before carrying out the works.

(5) Without prejudice to the protective provisions of Chapter III of this Part, nothing in subsection (3) above shall authorise any water undertaker, without the consent of the navigation authority in question, to intercept or take any water which a navigation authority are authorised to take or use for the purposes of their undertaking.

(6) Any dispute as to whether any consent for the purposes of subsection (5) above is being unreasonably withheld shall be referred to the arbitration of a single arbitrator to be appointed by agreement between the parties to the dispute or, in default of agreement, by the President of the Institution of Civil Engineers.

(7) In section 158 above the references to the laying of a relevant pipe shall include references—

(a) to the laying of any drain or sewer for any of the purposes mentioned in subsection (3)(a) and (b) above; and

(b) to the construction of a watercourse for any of those purposes.

(8) In this section—

"the protective provisions of Chapter III of this Part" means the provisions of sections 183 to 191 below;

"relevant waterworks" means any waterworks which contain water which is or may be used by a water undertaker for providing a supply of water to any premises; and

"waterworks" includes any water main, resource main, service pipe or discharge pipe and any spring, well, adit, borehole, service reservoir or tank.

DEFINITIONS

"drain": s.219(1), (2).
"functions": ss.217, 219(1).
"protected provisions of Chapter III of this Part": subs. (8).
"relevant waterworks": subs. (8).
"sewer": s.219(1), (2).
"street": s.219(1), (5).
"underground strata": s.219(1).
"watercourse": s.219(1).
"waterworks": subs. (8).

GENERAL NOTE

Subsections (1) and (2) of this section provide undertakers with powers, for the purpose of carrying out their functions, to carry out works to ensure that water in any relevant waterworks is not polluted or contaminated. The power extends to relevant works both in a street and on other land.

Undertakers have additional anti-pollution powers (in respect of any land which belongs to them or in respect of which the undertaker has acquired easements and rights to construct and maintain drains, sewers, etc.) for the purpose of dealing with foul water or otherwise preventing the pollution of waters belonging to the National Rivers Authority or any other water undertaker. Undertakers are required to consult the National Rivers Authority where the proposed works detailed in subs. (3) will affect a watercourse (subs. (4)). Similarly the consent of any navigational authority is required where an undertaker's works under the provisions of subs. (3) are likely to interfere with the carrying out of the navigational authority's functions. In the event that an undertaker believes that a navigational authority is unreasonably refusing its consent then an application may be made for arbitration under subs. (6).

Works in connection with metering

162.—(1) Subject to the following provisions of this section, to section 148 above and to the provisions of Chapter III of this Part, where—

(a) any relevant undertaker has fixed any charges in relation to any premises by reference to volume or has given notice of its intention of so fixing any charges within the period specified in the notice; and

(b) there is either—
   (i) a service pipe which is connected with a water undertaker's water main and by which a supply of water is or could be provided to those premises or to any building in which those premises are contained; or
   (ii) a drain or private sewer which connects those premises with a public sewer,
the undertaker shall have power, in accordance with section 172 below or otherwise, to carry out any works specified in subsection (3) below.

(2) The power under subsection (1) above to carry out works specified in subsection (3) below shall include power to carry out any such works in a street; and the power conferred by virtue of subsection (1)(c) of section 158 above and subsection (6) of that section shall apply in relation to the power conferred by this subsection as they apply in relation to the powers conferred by that section.

(3) The works mentioned in subsections (1) and (2) above are, in relation to any premises—
   (a) works consisting in the installation and connection of any meter for use in determining the amount of any charges which have been or may be fixed in relation to the premises;
   (b) where the premises comprise a house which is one of two or more houses to which the supply of water is wholly or partly by the same service pipe, works consisting in the installation and connection, for any purpose connected with the installation or connection of such a meter, of a separate service pipe for that house;
   (c) works for the purpose of maintaining, repairing, disconnecting or removing—
      (i) any meter which has been installed for use in determining the amount of any charges which have been or may be fixed in relation to the premises; or
      (ii) any pipes or apparatus installed in the course of any works specified in this section;
      and
   (d) any other works appearing to the undertaker to be necessary or expedient for any purpose connected with the carrying out of any works specified in paragraph (a), (b) or (c) above, including the installation and connection of any pipes or other apparatus on the premises and the alteration or removal of any of the plumbing of the premises.

(4) A notice given for the purposes of subsection (1)(a) above may relate to particular premises or to any description of premises and shall be given—
   (a) by publishing the notice in the locality in which the premises to which it relates are situated in such a manner as the undertaker considers appropriate for bringing it to the attention of the persons likely to be affected by it; and
   (b) by serving a copy of the notice on the Secretary of State.

(5) Subject to subsection (6) below, any works carried out by a water undertaker by virtue of the provisions of this section shall be necessary works for the purposes of Chapter II of Part III of this Act.

(6) Nothing in this section shall prevent the exercise by a water undertaker of its power by virtue of subsection (3)(b) of section 64 above to impose a condition by virtue of subsection (2)(c) or (d) of section 47 above in a case where it has, under the said section 64, required the provision of a separate service pipe to any premises.

(7) Part II of Schedule 6 to this Act shall apply to the powers conferred by this section.

(8) Any dispute between a relevant undertaker and any other person (including another such undertaker) as to the exercise of any power under

this section to carry out any works on any premises shall be referred to the arbitration of a single arbitrator appointed—

(a) by agreement between the undertaker and that person; or

(b) in default of agreement, by the Director.

(9) Without prejudice to subsection (2) above, nothing in section 158, 159 or 161 above shall authorise the installation of any apparatus for measuring or showing the volume of water supplied to, or of effluent discharged from, any premises where that apparatus is to be used for the purpose only of determining the amount of any charges fixed, or to be fixed, in relation to those premises wholly or partly by reference to the volume of that water or effluent.

DEFINITIONS
"drain": s.219(1), (2).
"effluent": s.219(1).
"house": s.219(1).
"meter": s.219(1).
"notice": s.219(1).
"public sewer": s.219(1).
"service pipe": s.219(1), (2).
"street": s.219(1), (5).
"water main": s.219(1), (2).

GENERAL NOTE
This section provides undertakers with powers to carry out works relating to the installation and connection of meters and associated pipes or other apparatus (subs. (3)). In order to exercise the powers contained in subs. (3) an undertaker must already be charging the occupier by reference to a meter or has given notice that he intends to use that method. In addition there must also either be a service pipe in existence which is connected to the undertaker's water main or a drain or private sewer connecting the premises with a public sewer. Subsection (8) provides a mechanism for referring any dispute in relation to the exercise of these powers for power to arbitration.

Power to fit stopcocks

163.—(1) Subject to subsection (2) below and without prejudice to section 159 above, a water undertaker shall have power, at its own expense, to fit a stopcock to any service pipe by which a supply of water is or is to be provided to any premises by the undertaker, whether that pipe belongs to the undertaker or to any other person.

(2) A stopcock fitted in private premises by a water undertaker to any service pipe shall be situated as near as practicable to any street from which that pipe enters those premises.

DEFINITIONS
"service pipe": s.219(1), (2).
"stopcock": s.219(1).
"street": s.219(1), (5).

GENERAL NOTE
This section provides a water undertaker with a power, at its own expense, to fit a stopcock to any service pipe irrespective of whether that pipe belongs to the undertaker or to any other person. By subs. (2) a stopcock which is fitted in private premises by a water undertaker to a service pipe shall be as near as practicable to the street from which the service pipe enters the premises.

Agreements for works with respect to water source

164.—(1) A water undertaker may enter into agreements under this section with the owners and occupiers of any land, or with a local authority, with respect to the carrying out and maintenance by any party to the agreement of such works as the undertaker considers necessary—

(a) for the purpose of draining that land; or

(b) for more effectually collecting, conveying or preserving the purity of any water which the undertaker is for the time being authorised to take.

(2) Before entering into an agreement under this section with respect to the carrying out of works the carrying out of which would result in the discharge of any water into a watercourse otherwise than through public sewers, a water undertaker shall consult the NRA and, if the watercourse is subject to the jurisdiction of a navigation authority, that authority.

(3) An agreement under this section with the owner of any land which is expressed to be binding on and enforceable against the owner's successors in title to that land—

(a) may be registered under section 2 of the Land Charges Act 1972 as an obligation affecting land falling within Class D; and

(b) shall be so binding and enforceable unless it is void by reason of a failure so to register it.

(4) In this section the reference to a local authority includes a reference to a county council and to the Sub-Treasurer of the Inner Temple and the Under-Treasurer of the Middle Temple; and any expenses incurred by the Common Council of the City of London in the exercise of their functions under this section shall be defrayed as part of their general expenses.

DEFINITIONS
"local authority": s.219(1).
"navigation authority":s.219(1).
"owner": s.219(1).
"public sewer": s.219(1).
"water course": s.219(1).

GENERAL NOTE
This section gives a water undertaker a discretion to enter into agreements with owners and occupiers of land or with local authorities relating to works which the undertaker considers are necessary for the purpose of draining the land or alternatively for improving the collection, conveyance or preservation of the purity of any water which the undertaker is authorised to take (subs. (1)). Where such works would result in the discharge of water into a water course rather than a public sewer, a water undertaker must consult with either the National Rivers Authority or the relevant navigation authority (subs. (2)). Such agreements are registrable as local land charges if they are intended to bind successive owners in title and are registered as a local land charge (subs. (3)).

Powers to discharge water

Discharges for works purposes

165.—(1) Subject to the following provisions of this section and to section 166 below, where any water undertaker—

(a) is exercising or about to exercise any power conferred by section 158, 159, 161 or 163 above (other than the power conferred by section 161(3) above); or

(b) is carrying out, or is about to carry out, the construction, alteration, repair, cleaning, or examination of any reservoir, well, borehole, or other work belonging to or used by that undertaker for the purposes of, or in connection with, the carrying out of any of its functions,

the undertaker may cause the water in any relevant pipe or in any such reservoir, well, borehole or other work to be discharged into any available watercourse.

(2) Nothing in this section shall authorise any discharge which—

(a) damages or injuriously affects the works or property of any railway undertakers or navigation authority; or

(b) floods or damages any highway.

(3) If any water undertaker fails to take all necessary steps to secure that any water discharged by it under this section is as free as may be reasonably practicable from—
(a) mud and silt;
(b) solid, polluting, offensive or injurious substances; and
(c) any substances prejudicial to fish or spawn, or to spawning beds or food of fish,
the undertaker shall be guilty of an offence and liable, on summary conviction, to a fine not exceeding level 3 on the standard scale.

(4) In this section "relevant pipe" means any water main (including a trunk main), resource main, discharge pipe or service pipe.

DEFINITIONS
  "highway": s.219(1).
  "navigation authority": s.219(1).
  "railway undertaker": s.219(1).
  "relevant pipe": subs. (4).
  "watercourse": s.219(1).

GENERAL NOTE
  This section enables a water undertaker to discharge water into any available water course in the exercise of its powers to lay pipes, deal with foul water and pollution and fit stopcocks, or in circumstances where it is about to construct, alter, repair, clean or examine any reservoir, well, borehole or other work belonging to it or used by it for the exercise of its functions (subs. (1)). An undertaker's power to make such discharges is excluded where a discharge would damage or injuriously affect the works or property of any railway undertaker or navigation authority or where it would cause flooding or damage to any highway (subs. (2)).
  A water undertaker is under a duty to ensure that any water that it discharged is as free as may be reasonably practicable from the substances specified in subs. (3) and any undertaker failing to take such steps commits an offence.

Consents for certain discharges under section 165

166.—(1) Except in an emergency, no discharge through any pipe the diameter of which exceeds 229 millimetres shall be made under section 165 above except with the consent of the NRA and of any navigation authority which carries out functions in relation to—
(a) the part of the watercourse where the discharge is made; or
(b) any part of that watercourse which is less than three miles downstream from the place of the discharge.

(2) Where a water undertaker makes an application to any authority for a consent for the purposes of this section—
(a) that application shall be accompanied or supplemented by all such information as that authority may reasonably require; and
(b) the undertaker shall serve a copy of the application, and of any consent given on that application, on every person who—
    (i) is registered with the undertaker in respect of any premises which are within three miles of the place where the discharge to which the application relates is proposed to be made and are not upstream from that place; and
    (ii) has not agreed in writing that he need not be served with such a copy;
but, subject to subsection (4) below and without prejudice to the effect (if any) of any other contravention of the requirements of this section in relation to such an application, a failure to provide information in pursuance of the obligation to supplement such an application shall not invalidate the application.

(3) Subject to subsection (4) below, an application for a consent for the purposes of this section shall be determined—
(a) in the case of an application with respect to a particular discharge,

before the end of the period of seven days beginning with the day after
the application is made; and
(b) in any other case, before the end of the period of three months
beginning with that day;
and, subject to that subsection, where an application for any consent is
required to be determined within the period specified in paragraph (a)
above and is not so determined, the consent applied for shall be deemed to
have been given unconditionally.

(4) Where—
(a) an undertaker which has made an application to any authority for a
consent for the purposes of this section has failed to comply with its
obligation under subsection (2)(a) above to supplement that application with information required by that authority; and
(b) that requirement was made by that authority at such a time before the
end of the period within which that authority is required to determine
the application as gave the undertaker a reasonable opportunity to
provide the required information within that period,
that authority may delay his determination of the application until a reasonable time after the required information is provided.

(5) A consent for the purposes of this section may relate to a particular
discharge or to discharges of a particular description and may be made
subject to such reasonable conditions as may be specified by the person
giving it; but a consent for those purposes shall not be unreasonably
withheld.

(6) Any dispute as to whether a consent for the purposes of this section
should be given or withheld, or as to whether the conditions to which any
such consent is made subject are reasonable, shall be referred to the arbitration of a single arbitrator appointed by agreement between the parties to the
dispute or, in default of agreement, by the President of the Institution of
Civil Engineers.

(7) Where any discharge under section 165 above is made in an emergency
without the consent which, if there were no emergency, would be required
by virtue of this section, the undertaker which made the discharge shall, as
soon as practicable after making the discharge, serve a notice which—
(a) states that the discharge has been made; and
(b) gives such particulars of the discharge and of the emergency as the
persons served with the notice might reasonably require,
on every person on whom that undertaker would have been required to
serve the application for that consent or any copy of that application.

(8) If any water undertaker contravenes, without reasonable excuse, any
of the requirements of this section or any condition of a consent given for the
purposes of this section, it shall be guilty of an offence and liable, on
summary conviction, to a fine not exceeding level 3 on the standard scale.

(9) Nothing in this section shall require any consent to be obtained, or any
notice to be served, in respect of any discharge if the requirements of section
34 of the Water Act 1945 (temporary discharges into watercourses) in
relation to that discharge had been satisfied before September 1, 1989.

DEFINITIONS
"information": s.219(1).
"watercourse": s.219(1).

GENERAL NOTE
    This section is concerned with the requirement of consent for discharges under s.165 (except
in an emergency) in circumstances where the diameter of the pipe through which the discharge
is made exceeds 229 mm. The consent of the National Rivers Authority and any navigation
authority will be required where they exercise functions in relation to that part of the water
course where the discharge is made or alternatively any part of the water course which is less
than three miles downstream from the point of discharge (subs. (1)). Discharges authorised

before September 1, 1989 under the provisions of s.34 of the Water Act 1945 will not need consent (subs. (9)).

A water undertaker must keep a register of those owners or occupiers of premises which are situated within three miles of the place where the discharge is proposed to be made and the undertaker must serve those persons with a copy of his application unless they have agreed in writing that they need not be notified of the application (subs. (2)). A water undertaker must give the relevant authority (either the National Rivers Authority or the navigation authority) all such information as it may reasonably require (subs. (2)). Consent may be sought for a standard discharge and in such a case the application should be determined within seven days or it will be deemed to have been granted unconditionally. Non-standard discharge applications are required to be determined within three months (subs. (3)). A discharge consent may be granted subject to reasonable conditions but may not be unreasonably withheld (subs. (5)), and any dispute as to the grant or refusal of a consent or conditions attaching to it may be referred to arbitration under subs. (6).

Where a discharge is made in an emergency the water undertaker must notify those persons on whom it would have served a copy of any discharge consent application as soon as practicable (subs. (7)). Failure to comply without reasonable excuse with s.166 constitutes an offence under subs. (8).

Compulsory works orders

Compulsory works orders

167.—(1) Where a water undertaker is proposing, for the purposes of, or in connection with, the carrying out of any of its functions—

(a) to carry out any engineering or building operations; or

(b) to discharge water into any inland waters or underground strata, the undertaker may apply to the Secretary of State for an order under this section ("a compulsory works order").

(2) Subject to the following provisions of this section, the Secretary of State may, on an application under subsection (1) above, by order made by statutory instrument—

(a) confer such compulsory powers; and

(b) grant such authority,

as he considers necessary or expedient for the purpose of enabling any engineering or building operations or discharges of water to be carried out or made for the purposes of, or in connection with, the carrying out of the functions with respect to which the application was made.

(3) Schedule 11 to this Act shall have effect with respect to applications for compulsory works orders and with respect to such orders.

(4) Subject to the provisions of Schedule 11 to this Act, a compulsory works order may—

(a) without prejudice to section 155 above, confer power to acquire compulsorily any land, including—

(i) power to acquire interests in and rights over land by the creation of new rights and interests; and

(ii) power, by the compulsory acquisition by any water undertaker of any rights over land which is to be or has been acquired by that undertaker, to extinguish any such rights;

(b) apply for the purposes of the order, either with or without modifications, any of the relevant provisions of this Part of this Act which do not apply for those purposes apart from by virtue of this paragraph;

(c) make any authority granted by the order subject to such conditions as may be specified in the order;

(d) amend or repeal any local statutory provision;

(e) contain such supplemental, consequential and transitional provision as the Secretary of State considers appropriate.

(5) Without prejudice to any duty imposed by virtue of section 191 below, where—

   (a) the Secretary of State makes a compulsory works order authorising a water undertaker to carry out works for or in connection with the construction or operation of a reservoir or conferring compulsory powers for that purpose on such an undertaker; and

   (b) it appears to him that the works to be carried out may permanently affect the area in which they are situated and are not primarily intended to benefit the inhabitants of that area,

he may include in the order provision with respect to facilities for recreation or other leisure-time occupation for the benefit of those inhabitants.

(6) Nothing in any compulsory works order shall exempt any water undertaker from any restriction imposed by Chapter II of Part II of the Water Resources Act 1991 (abstraction and impounding of water).

(7) It is hereby declared that a compulsory works order may grant authority for discharges of water by a water undertaker where the undertaker has no power to take water, or to require discharges to be made, from the inland waters or other source from which the discharges authorised by the order are intended to be made; but nothing in so much of any such order as grants authority for any discharges of water shall have the effect of conferring any such power.

(8) In this section the reference to the relevant provisions of this Part is a reference to the provisions of this Part except sections 172 and 173, the provisions of Chapter II and any provision of this Part which is one of the relevant sewerage provisions.

DEFINITIONS
   "compulsory works order": subs. (1).
   "engineering or building operations": s.219(1).
   "functions": ss.217, 219(1).
   "inland waters": s.219(1).
   "modifications": s.219(1).
   "relevant sewerage provisions": s.219(1).
   "underground strata": s.219(1).

GENERAL NOTE
   This section enables a water undertaker to apply to the Secretary of State for an order granting it compulsory powers and authority to carry out engineering or building operations or to discharge water into any inland water or underground strata (subs. (1)). A compulsory works order may authorise an undertaker to acquire compulsorily land and interests in and rights over land by the creation of new rights and to buy other rights in order to extinguish them. Such an order may repeal or amend any local statutory enactments, impose conditions on the exercise of powers which it grants and contain such supplemental conditions as the Secretary of State considers appropriate. The order may also apply, with or without modifications, to any of the relevant provisions of Pt. VI of the Act which would not otherwise be available (subs. (4)). A compulsory works order cannot exempt the undertaker from a requirement to obtain an abstraction or impounding licence in respect of the authorised works (subs. (6)). While the order may authorise a specific discharge from an inland water or other source where necessary, the applicant will still need to obtain the power to make it under subs. (7).
   The section should also be read in conjunction with the provisions of Sched. 11 and s.155. Schedule 11 makes provision for compensation for loss and damage caused by the works detailed in subs. (1).

Entry to land etc. by water undertakers

Entry for works purposes

   168.—(1) Any person designated in writing for the purpose by a relevant undertaker may enter any premises for any of the purposes specified in subsection (2) below.

   (2) The purposes mentioned in subsection (1) above are—

(a) the carrying out of any survey or tests for the purpose of determining—
(i) whether it is appropriate and practicable for the undertaker to exercise any relevant works power; or
(ii) how any such power should be exercised;
or
(b) the exercise of any such power.

(3) The power, by virtue of subsection (1) above, of a person designated by a relevant undertaker to enter any premises for the purposes of carrying out any survey or tests shall include power—
(a) to carry out experimental borings or other works for the purpose of ascertaining the nature of the sub-soil; and
(b) to take away and analyse such samples of water or effluent or of any land or articles as the undertaker—
(i) considers necessary for the purpose of determining either of the matters mentioned in subsection (2)(a) above; and
(ii) has authorised that person to take away and analyse.

(4) Part II of Schedule 6 to this Act shall apply to the rights and powers conferred by this section.

(5) In this section "relevant works power" means any power conferred by any of the provisions of sections 158, 159, 161, 163 and 165 above, other than section 161(3).

Definitions
"effluent": s.219(1).
"relevant undertaker": s.219(1).
"relevant works power": subs. (5).

General Note
This section is concerned with the right of entry of persons duly designated by an undertaker in order to survey or test whether it would be appropriate to use the powers conferred by ss.153, 158, 159, 161 (except for subs. (3)), and 165 or to exercise any of those powers. Under subs. (3) the power to enter any premises in order to carry out any survey extends to making experimental borings to test the nature of the subsoil and to take away such samples of water or effluent or of any land or articles which the undertaker considers necessary.

Power to carry out surveys and to search for water

169.—(1) Without prejudice to the rights and powers conferred by section 168 above, any person designated in writing under this section by a water undertaker may enter any premises for any of the purposes specified in subsection (2) below.

(2) The purposes mentioned in subsection (1) above are the carrying out of any survey or tests for the purpose of determining—
(a) whether it would be appropriate for the undertaker to acquire any land, or any interest or right in or over land, for purposes connected with the carrying out of its functions; or
(b) whether it would be appropriate for the undertaker to apply for a compulsory works order under section 167 above and what compulsory powers it would be appropriate to apply for under that section.

(3) The power by virtue of subsection (1) above of a person designated under this section to enter any premises for the purpose of carrying out any survey or tests shall include power—
(a) to carry out experimental borings or other works for the purpose of ascertaining the nature of the sub-soil, the presence of underground water in the sub-soil or the quantity or quality of any such water;
(b) to install and keep monitoring or other apparatus on the premises for the purpose of obtaining the information on which any such determination as is mentioned in subsection (2) above may be made; and

(c) to take away and analyse such samples of water or of any land or
articles as the undertaker considers necessary for any of the purposes
so mentioned and has authorised that person to take away and
analyse.

(4) The powers conferred by this section shall not be exercised in any case
for purposes connected with the determination of—
(a) whether, where or how a reservoir should be constructed; or
(b) whether, where or how a borehole should be sunk for the purpose of
abstracting water from or discharging water into any underground
strata,
unless the Secretary of State has, in accordance with subsection (5) below,
given his written authorisation in relation to that case for the exercise of
those powers for those purposes.

(5) The Secretary of State shall not give his authorisation for the purposes
of subsection (4) above unless—
(a) he is satisfied that notice of the proposal to apply for the authorisation
has been given to the owner and to the occupier of the premises in
question; and
(b) he has considered any representations or objections with respect to
the proposed exercise of the powers under this section which—
(i) have been duly made to him by the owner or occupier of those
premises, within the period of fourteen days beginning with the day
after the giving of the notice; and
(ii) have not been withdrawn.

(6) Part II of Schedule 6 to this Act shall apply to the rights and powers
conferred by this section.

DEFINITIONS
"analyse": s.219(1).
"compulsory works order": s.167(1).
"functions": ss.217, 219(1).
"information": s.219(1).
"notice": s.219(1).
"owner": s.219(1).

GENERAL NOTE
This section provides representatives of water undertakers with powers to enter premises in
order to carry out surveys and tests to determine whether they should use their powers of
compulsory purchase under s.155 or apply for a compulsory works order. The consent of the
Secretary of State is only required under subs. (4) in respect of surveys or tests to determine the
siting and method of construction of a reservoir or borehole.

Entry etc. for other purposes

170.—(1) Any person designated in writing for the purpose by a water
undertaker may enter any premises for any of the following purposes, that is
to say—
(a) the carrying out of any survey or tests for the purpose of
determining—
(i) whether it is appropriate and practicable for the undertaker to
exercise any power under any provision of Part III of this Act to
disconnect any pipe or cut off any supply of water to any premises
or to carry out any works which it is authorised to carry out under
section 64(4), 66(3) or 75 above; or
(ii) how any such power should be exercised;
(b) the exercise of any such power;
(c) the monitoring and recording of—
(i) whether water supplied to any premises for domestic or food
production purposes is wholesome at the time of supply; or
(ii) the quality of the water from any source, or combination of

sources, which is or is to be used for supplying water to any
premises for those purposes,
    and the carrying out of any tests for that purpose.
(2) Any person designated for the purpose—
(a) by any water undertaker within whose area any waterworks are
situated; or
(b) by any water undertaker which takes water from any waterworks,
shall, on producing some duly authenticated document showing his
authority, have a right at all reasonable hours to enter any premises for the
purpose of ascertaining whether there is, or has been, any contravention of
section 72 above in relation to those waterworks.
(3) Any person designated in writing for the purpose by a water undertaker may—
(a) enter any premises for the purpose of—
    (i) ascertaining whether any provision contained in or made or
    having effect under this Act with respect to any water fittings or
    with respect to the waste or misuse of water is being, or has been,
    contravened;
    (ii) determining whether, and if so in what manner, any power or
    duty conferred or imposed on any person by regulations under
    section 74 above should be exercised or performed; or
    (iii) exercising any such power or performing any such duty;
    or
(b) carry out such inspections, measurements and tests on premises en-
    tered by that person or on water fittings or other articles found on any
    such premises, and take away such samples of water or of any land
    and such water fittings and other articles, as that person has been
    authorised to carry out or take away in accordance with regulations
    under that section.
(4) During any period when a prohibition or restriction under section 76
above is in force, any person designated for the purpose by the water
undertaker which imposed the prohibition or restriction shall, on producing
some duly authenticated document showing his authority, have a right at all
reasonable hours to enter any premises to which the prohibition or restriction applies for the purpose of ascertaining whether there is, or has been,
any contravention of the prohibition or restriction.
(5) The power by virtue of subsection (1) above of a person designated by
a water undertaker to enter any premises for the purpose of carrying out any
survey or tests shall include power to take away such samples of water or
effluent or of any land or articles as the undertaker—
(a) considers necessary for the purpose of determining any of the matters
    mentioned in paragraph (a) or (c) of that subsection; and
(b) has authorised that person to carry out or take away.
(6) Expressions used in this section and in any provision of Part III of this
Act in relation to which this section has effect shall have the same meaning in
this section as in that provision; and, without prejudice to the generality of
this provision, subsections (2) and (3) of section 68 above and the definitions
of "food production purposes" and "wholesome" in section 93(1) above
shall apply for the purposes of any power conferred by virtue of subsection
(1)(c)(i) above as they apply for the purposes of that section.
(7) Part I of Schedule 6 to this Act shall apply to the rights of entry
conferred by subsections (2) and (4) of this section; and Part II of that
Schedule shall apply to the rights and powers conferred by the other provisions of this section.
(8) The provisions of this section shall be without prejudice to the other
rights and powers conferred by this Part.

DEFINITIONS
    "domestic purposes": ss.218, 219(1).

"effluent": s.219(1).
"food production purposes": s.93(1).
"wholesome": s.93(1).

GENERAL NOTE

This section is concerned with the powers of entry of persons designated by water undertakers to carry out works in connection with their powers under s.64(4) (relating to the provision of separate service pipes), s.66(3) (regarding the power of undertakers to require the installation of cisterns), and s.75, which is concerned with the power to disconnect or carry out remedial works to prevent contamination or waste of water. The section also provides persons duly designated by water undertakers with powers to monitor and record water quality particularly relating to whether water supplies to any premises for domestic or food production purposes are wholesome at the time of supply. See the General Note to s.68 concerning the duty of water undertakers to supply water for domestic or food production purposes which is wholesome at the time of supply.

Under subs. (2) the officers of a water undertaker have a right at all reasonable hours to enter premises to ascertain whether there has been any contravention of the provisions of s.72 relating to the contamination of water sources. By virtue of subs. (3) the officers of a water undertaker may enter premises to ascertain whether any provisions in the Act relating to water fittings or in respect of waste or misuse of water have been contravened and with regard to the regulations made under the provisions of s.74 (for preventing contamination, waste, etc. and regarding water fittings) to determine in what way the powers and duties comprised in the regulations should be exercised and to perform the same. The powers of entry also include the right to carry out inspections and tests and the removal of samples.

Powers of entry under the section extend to the monitoring of temporary hosepipe bans under s.76. Reference should also be made to Sched. 6 to the Act.

Entry for sewerage purposes

171.—(1) Any person designated in writing for the purpose by a sewerage undertaker shall, on producing any duly authenticated document showing his authority, have a right to enter any premises at all reasonable hours—

(a) for the purpose of ascertaining whether there is or has been, on or in connection with the premises, any contravention of any of the relevant sewerage provisions which it is the function of the undertaker to enforce;

(b) for the purpose of ascertaining whether or not circumstances exist which would authorise or require the undertaker to take any action or carry out any works under any of the relevant sewerage provisions;

(c) for the purpose of taking action or carrying out any works authorised by or under any of the relevant sewerage provisions to be taken or carried out by the undertaker;

(d) generally for the purpose of carrying out the undertaker's functions under the relevant sewerage provisions.

(2) Part I of Schedule 6 to this Act shall apply to the right of entry conferred by subsection (1) above.

(3) Any person designated by a sewerage undertaker under subsection (1) above for the purpose of exercising any power under this section for the purposes of Chapter III of Part IV of this Act may, on any occasion on which he so exercises that power in relation to any premises, obtain and take away any sample of any trade effluent which is passing (either directly or through a private drain or sewer) from those premises into any of the undertaker's public sewers.

(4) The result of any analysis of a sample taken by any designated person under subsection (1) above shall not be admissible as evidence in any legal proceedings under Chapter III of Part IV of this Act unless the requirements of subsection (5) below are satisfied.

(5) The requirements mentioned in subsection (4) above are that the designated person shall—

(a) forthwith after taking the sample, notify his intention to have it analysed to the occupier of the trade premises in question;

(b) there and then divide the sample into three parts;
(c) cause each part to be placed in a suitable container which shall be sealed up and marked; and
(d) deliver one part to the occupier, retain one part for future comparison and, if he thinks fit to have an analysis made, submit one part to the analyst.

(6) In this section "trade effluent" and "trade premises" have the same meanings as in Chapter III of Part IV of this Act; and, accordingly, section 139 above shall have effect for the purposes of this section as it has effect for the purposes of that Chapter.

DEFINITIONS
"functions": ss.217, 219(1).
"relevant sewerage provisions": s.219(1).
"trade effluent": s.141.
"trade premises": s.141(1) and (2).

GENERAL NOTE
This section provides persons duly designated by water undertakers with powers of entry in order to ascertain whether any action is required in respect of a contravention of the "relevant sewerage provisions" as defined in s.219(1). Under subs. (3) sewerage undertakers in exercise of their powers under s.171 may take samples of trade effluent but those samples are only admissible in evidence in any subsequent proceedings if the conditions of subs. (5) are met.

Entry for metering purposes

172.—(1) Where the conditions set out in section 162(1) above are satisfied in relation to any premises, any person designated in writing for the purpose by the relevant undertaker in question may enter those premises, or any land occupied with those premises, for any of the purposes specified in subsection (2) below.

(2) The purposes mentioned in subsection (1) above are—
(a) the carrying out of any survey or tests for the purpose of determining—
    (i) whether the carrying out of any works by virtue of paragraph (a) or (b) of subsection (3) of section 162 above is practicable;
    (ii) whether it is necessary or expedient for any purpose connected with the carrying out of any works by virtue of either of those paragraphs for any other works to be carried out; or
    (iii) how any works specified in that subsection should be carried out;
(b) the carrying out of any works so specified;
(c) the inspection, examination or testing of any meter which is on those premises or of any pipes or apparatus installed in the course of any works which were carried out for any purpose that is connected with the installation, connection, testing, maintenance or repair of any such meter;
(d) the ascertainment from any meter of the volume of water supplied to, or of effluent discharged from, those premises.

(3) Part II of Schedule 6 to this Act shall apply in relation to the rights and powers conferred by the preceding provisions of this section.

(4) Where any meter or other recording apparatus is provided in any premises in pursuance of Chapter III of Part IV of this Act for the purpose of assessing any charge, a sewerage undertaker may (instead of exercising its powers under this section) for the purpose of reading that meter or apparatus exercise the power conferred by section 171 above as if that purpose were included in the purposes mentioned in subsection (1) of that section.

DEFINITIONS
"effluent": s.219(1).
"meter": s.219(1).

This section details the powers of entry of undertakers for metering purposes. The purposes for which entry may be made consist of surveying or testing premises to ascertain whether it is practicable to carry out the provisions of s.162(3)(a) and (b), the carrying out of any such work, the inspection and testing of any meter or associated pipes and apparatus and the need to read meters which register the volume of water supplied to or effluent discharged from premises.

Impersonation of persons entitled to entry

173.—(1) A person who, without having been designated or authorised for the purpose by a relevant undertaker, purports to be entitled to enter any premises or vessel in exercise of a power exercisable in pursuance of any such designation or authorisation shall be guilty of an offence and liable, on summary conviction, to a fine not exceeding level 4 on the standard scale.

(2) For the purposes of this section it shall be immaterial, where a person purports to be entitled to enter any premises or vessel, that the power which that person purports to be entitled to exercise does not exist or would not be exercisable even if that person had been designated or authorised by a relevant undertaker.

DEFINITIONS
"vessel": s.219(1).

GENERAL NOTE
An offence is committed under this section where a person attempts to enter any premises or vessel without proper designation or authorisation. The offence is made out in cases where there is impersonation as well as entry by officers of an undertaker who were not properly authorised or designated. The onus is on the undertaker to ensure that its officers possess the appropriate documentation.

CHAPTER II

PROTECTION OF UNDERTAKERS' WORKS, APPARATUS ETC.

Protection of apparatus in general

Offences of interference with works etc.

174.—(1) Subject to subsection (2) below, if any person without the consent of the water undertaker—
  (a) intentionally or recklessly interferes with any resource main, water main or other pipe vested in any water undertaker or with any structure, installation or apparatus belonging to any water undertaker; or
  (b) by any act or omission negligently interferes with any such main or other pipe or with any such structure, installation or apparatus so as to damage it or so as to have an effect on its use or operation,
that person shall be guilty of an offence and liable, on summary conviction, to a fine not exceeding level 3 on the standard scale.

(2) A person shall not be guilty of an offence under subsection (1) above—
  (a) by reason of anything done in an emergency to prevent loss or damage to persons or property; or
  (b) by reason of his opening or closing the stopcock fitted to a service pipe by means of which water is supplied to any premises by a water undertaker if—
      (i) he has obtained the consent of every consumer whose supply is affected by the opening or closing of that stopcock or, as the case may be, of every other consumer whose supply is so affected; and
      (ii) in the case of opening a stopcock, the stopcock was closed otherwise than by the undertaker.

(3) Any person who, without the consent of the water undertaker—

(a) attaches any pipe or apparatus—

    (i) to any resource main, water main or other pipe vested in a water undertaker; or

    (ii) to any service pipe which does not belong to such an undertaker but which is a pipe by means of which water is supplied by such an undertaker to any premises;

(b) makes any alteration in a service pipe by means of which water is so supplied, or in any apparatus attached to any such pipe; or

(c) subject to subsection (4) below, uses any pipe or apparatus which has been attached or altered in contravention of this section,

shall be guilty of an offence and liable, on summary conviction, to a fine not exceeding level 3 on the standard scale.

(4) In proceedings against any person for an offence by virtue of paragraph (c) of subsection (3) above it shall be a defence for that person to show that he did not know, and had no grounds for suspecting, that the pipe or apparatus in question had been attached or altered as mentioned in that subsection.

(5) If any person wilfully or negligently injures or suffers to be injured any water fitting belonging to a water undertaker, he shall be guilty of an offence and liable, on summary conviction, to a fine not exceeding level 1 on the standard scale.

(6) An offence under subsection (1) or (3) above shall constitute a breach of a duty owed to the water undertaker in question; and any such breach of duty which causes the undertaker to sustain loss or damage shall be actionable at the suit of the undertaker.

(7) The amount recoverable by virtue of subsection (6) above from a person who has committed an offence under subsection (3) above shall include such amount as may be reasonable in respect of any water wasted, misused or improperly consumed in consequence of the commission of the offence.

(8) A water undertaker may—

(a) do all such work as is necessary for repairing any injury done in contravention of subsection (5) above; and

(b) recover the expenses reasonably incurred by the undertaker in doing so from the offender summarily as a civil debt.

(9) In this section "consumer" and "water fitting" have the same meanings as in Part III of this Act; and in subsection (1) above the references to apparatus belonging to a water undertaker do not include references to any meter which belongs to such an undertaker and is used by it for the purpose of determining the amount of any charges which have been fixed by the undertaker by reference to volume.

DEFINITIONS

"consumer": subs. (9) and s.93(1).
"resource main": s.219(1), (2).
"service pipe": s.219(1), (2).
"stopcock": s.219(1).
"water fitting": subs. (9) and s.93(1).

GENERAL NOTE

This section makes provision for a number of offences arising out of interference with a water undertaker's works. The offence in subs. (1) is made out where a person interferes with the water transmission system either intentionally, recklessly or negligently. Subsection (2) provides that such a person shall not be guilty of an offence if the interference arose out of anything done in an emergency to prevent loss or damage or by reason of the operation of a stopcock with the consent of the persons affected. It is an offence by virtue of subs. (3) to attach any pipe or apparatus to the mains or service pipes supplying premises with water, together with the making of alterations to service pipes and using any pipe so altered. A person may also be guilty of an offence where he wilfully or negligently injures any water fitting belonging to a water undertaker.

Protection of meters

Offence of tampering with meter

175.—(1) If any person—
(a) so interferes with a meter used by any relevant undertaker in determining the amount of any charges fixed in relation to any premises as intentionally or recklessly to prevent the meter from showing, or from accurately showing, the volume of water supplied to, or of effluent discharged from, those premises; or
(b) carries out any works which he knows are likely to affect the operation of such a meter or which require the disconnection of such a meter,
he shall be guilty of an offence and liable, on summary conviction, to a fine not exceeding level 3 on the standard scale.

(2) A person shall not be guilty of an offence under this section in respect of anything done by him with the consent under section 176 below of the undertaker which uses the meter.

DEFINITIONS
  "effluent": s.219(1).
  "meter": s.219(1).
  "relevant undertaker": s.219(1).

GENERAL NOTE
  It is an offence under this section to interfere, either intentionally or recklessly, with a meter which is used by an undertaker to measure water supplied or effluent discharged from premises. In addition a person who knowingly carries out work likely to affect the operation of a meter commits an offence. Note the defence in subs. (2).

Consent for the purposes of section 175

176.—(1) Where an application is made to any relevant undertaker for a consent for the purposes of section 175 above, the undertaker—
(a) shall give notice of its decision with respect to the application as soon as reasonably practicable after receiving it; and
(b) subject to subsection (2) below, may make it a condition of giving any consent that the undertaker itself should carry out so much of any works to which the application relates as is specified in the notice of its decision.

(2) On such an application a relevant undertaker shall not refuse its consent, or impose any such condition as is mentioned in subsection (1)(b) above, unless it is reasonable to do so.

(3) Where any relevant undertaker has given a notice to any person imposing any such condition as is mentioned in subsection (1)(b) above, the undertaker—
(a) shall carry out those works as soon as reasonably practicable after giving the notice; and
(b) may recover from that person any expenses reasonably incurred by it in doing so.

(4) Any dispute between a relevant undertaker and any other person (including another such undertaker)—
(a) as to whether the undertaker or that other person should bear any expenses under subsection (3) above; or
(b) as to the amount of any expenses to be borne by any person under that subsection,

shall be referred to the arbitration of a single arbitrator appointed by agreement between the undertaker and that person or, in default of agreement, by the Director.

(5) Subsection (3) above shall not apply where the person who was given the notice notifies the undertaker that the carrying out of the works to which the condition relates is no longer required.

DEFINITIONS
"notice": s.219(1).
"relevant undertaker": s.219(1).
"the Director": s.219(1).

GENERAL NOTE
This section provides a mechanism whereby the consent of an undertaker may be obtained in respect of works which will affect the operation of any meter. An undertaker may grant or refuse its consent as soon as reasonably practicable after receiving the consent application. It may make a consent subject to a condition that the undertaker carries out the works referred to in the consent, however the undertaker must act reasonably (subs. (2)). Where an undertaker carries out any works in connection with the granting of a consent application it may recover its reasonable expenses (subs. (3)(b)) and disputes concerning who is to bear the cost of the relevant work may be referred to arbitration under the provisions of subs. (4).

Financial obligations with respect to any interference with a meter

177.—(1) A relevant undertaker which carries out any works made necessary by the commission of an offence under section 175 above shall be entitled to recover any expenses reasonably incurred in carrying out those works from the person who committed the offence.

(2) Any person who sustains any loss or damage in consequence of any failure by any relevant undertaker—
   (a) to comply with any obligation imposed on it by section 176 above; or
   (b) to exercise reasonable care in the performance of the duty imposed by subsection (3)(a) of that section,
shall be entitled to recover compensation from the undertaker.

(3) Any dispute between a relevant undertaker and any other person (including another such undertaker)—
   (a) as to whether the undertaker or that other person should bear any expenses under this section;
   (b) as to whether the undertaker should pay any compensation under this section; or
   (c) as to the amount of any expenses to be borne by any person under this section or as to the amount of any such compensation,
shall be referred to the arbitration of a single arbitrator appointed by agreement between the undertaker and that person or, in default of agreement, by the Director.

DEFINITIONS
"damage": s.219(1).

GENERAL NOTE
This section provides for the recovery of expenses by an undertaker who carries out work in consequence of the commission of an offence under s.175.
Under subs. (2) any person who sustains loss or damage arising out of an undertaker's failure to comply with s.176 including the carrying out of works specified in a consent application as soon as reasonably practicable may recover compensation from the undertaker under subs. (2) and any dispute arising out of subs. (2) may be referred to arbitration (subs. (3)).

Obstruction of sewerage works etc.

Obstruction of sewerage works etc.

178.—(1) A person who wilfully obstructs any person acting in the execution of any of the relevant sewerage provisions shall be guilty of an offence and liable, on summary conviction, to a fine not exceeding level 1 on the standard scale.

(2) If on a complaint made by the owner of any premises, it appears to a magistrates' court that the occupier of those premises is preventing the owner of those premises from carrying out any work which he is required to carry out by or under any of the relevant sewerage provisions, the court may order the occupier to permit the carrying out of the work.

(3) Sections 300 to 302 of the Public Health Act 1936 (which relate to the determination of questions by courts of summary jurisdiction and to appeals against such determinations) shall apply for the purposes of and in relation to the determination under subsection (2) above of any matter by a magistrates' court—

(a) as they apply for the purposes of or in relation to a determination by such a court under that Act; and

(b) in the case of section 302, as if the reference to a decision of a local authority included a reference to a decision of a sewerage undertaker.

DEFINITIONS
"local authority": s.219(1).
"owner": s.219(1).
"relevant sewerage provisions": s.219(1).

GENERAL NOTE
Subsection (1) of this section establishes an offence of wilful obstruction of the execution of an undertaker's relevant sewerage provisions. A person wilfully obstructs another if he intentionally and by his free will does an act which causes an obstruction (see *Arrowsmith* v. *Jenkins* [1963] 2 Q.B. 561). An obstruction is anything which makes it more difficult for the person exercising the right to carry out his duties (see *Lewis* v. *Cox* [1984] 3 W.L.R. 875).

Subsection (2) provides a mechanism whereby an owner of premises may lodge a complaint in a magistrates' court concerning an occupier's obstruction of an owner in the performance of his relevant sewerage provision obligations.

CHAPTER III

SUPPLEMENTAL PROVISIONS WITH RESPECT TO UNDERTAKERS' POWERS

Vesting of works in undertaker

Vesting of works in undertaker

179.—(1) Subject to subsection (3) below and to any provision to the contrary contained in an agreement between the relevant undertaker and the person in whom an interest in the pipe or works is or is to be vested—

(a) every relevant pipe which has been laid, in exercise of any power conferred by this Part or otherwise, by a relevant undertaker; and

(b) every sewage disposal works constructed by a sewerage undertaker, shall vest in the undertaker which laid it or, as the case may be, the undertaker which constructed them.

(2) In addition to the sewers and works which vest in a sewerage undertaker by virtue of subsection (1) above, the following shall also vest in such an undertaker, that is to say—

(a) every sewer or sewage disposal works with respect to which a declaration of vesting made by that undertaker under Chapter II of Part IV of this Act takes effect; and

(b) every sewer which is laid in the area of that undertaker under Part XI of the Highways Act 1980 (making up private streets) and is not a sewer belonging to a road maintained by a highway authority.

(3) Subsection (1) above shall not apply to a service pipe laid in a street other than the street in which the water main with which it connects is situated and shall not apply to a service pipe laid otherwise than in a street where that pipe is laid—

(a) in pursuance of the duty imposed by virtue of section 46(4) above; or
(b) in substitution for a service pipe belonging to a person other than the person who lays the replacement pipe.

(4) If any water fittings let for hire by a water undertaker are suitably marked, they—
(a) shall continue to be the property of and removable by the undertaker, even if they are fixed to some part of the premises in which they are situated or are laid in the soil under any premises; and
(b) shall not be subject to distress or to the landlord's remedy for rent or be liable to be taken in execution under any process of any court or in any proceedings in bankruptcy against a person in whose possession they are;

but nothing in this subsection shall affect the valuation for rating of any rateable hereditament.

(5) It is hereby declared that anything which, in pursuance of any arrangements under section 97 above, is done on behalf of a sewerage undertaker by a relevant authority within the meaning of that section is, subject to any provision to the contrary contained in any such arrangements, to be treated for the purposes of this section as done by the undertaker.

(6) The preceding provisions of this section are without prejudice, in relation to any company appointed to be a relevant undertaker, to the vesting of anything in that company by virtue of any scheme under Schedule 2 to this Act or of the exercise by any relevant undertaker of any power to acquire property by agreement or compulsorily.

(7) In this section—
  "relevant pipe"—
      (a) in relation to a water undertaker, means any water main (including a trunk main), resource main, discharge pipe or service pipe; and
      (b) in relation to a sewerage undertaker, means any sewer or disposal main;
    and
  "water fittings" has the same meaning as in Part III of this Act;
and water fittings let on hire by a water undertaker shall be treated as suitably marked for the purposes of this section if and only if they bear either such a distinguishing metal plate affixed to them or such a distinguishing brand or other mark conspicuously impressed or made on them as sufficiently indicates the undertaker as the actual owner of the fittings.

DEFINITIONS
  "highway authority": s.219(1).
  "relevant pipe": subs. (7).
  "service pipe": s.219(1), (2).
  "sewer": s.219(1), (2).
  "water fittings": subs. (7) and s.93(1).
  "water main" s.219(1).

GENERAL NOTE
  This section is concerned with the vesting of works in an undertaker. The general position is that the relevant pipe or works vests in the undertaker which laid or constructed the same but subs. (1) provides that this need not necessarily be the case if there is a contrary agreement entered into between an undertaker and a person with an interest in the pipe or works. Upon privatisation such agreements or schemes were made under Sched. 5 of the Water Act 1989. In addition, sewers or sewage disposal works vest in a sewerage undertaker where a vesting declaration has been made (see s.102) and sewers laid under Pt. XI of the Highways Act 1980 (sewers that do not belong to a road maintained by the Highways Authority).
  If an undertaker's appointment is terminated then its pipes and works would be transferred to a successor company under the provisions of Sched. 2 to the Act. This section does not affect property which is acquired compulsorily (see s.167) or by agreement. Note the provisions of

subs. (5) relating to the performance of a sewerage undertaker's functions by a local authority under s.97 and subs. (3) detailing exceptions to the general position.

Damage etc. caused by works

Compensation for damage caused by works etc.

180. Schedule 12 to this Act shall have effect for making provision for imposing obligations for the purpose of minimising the damage caused in the exercise of certain powers conferred on undertakers and for imposing obligations as to the payment of compensation.

GENERAL NOTE

This section introduces Sched. 12, which in turn sets out the compensation provisions relating to street works powers, pipe-laying works in private land, sewerage works, metering works and discharges for works purposes.

Complaints with respect to the exercise of works powers on private land

181.—(1) Subject to subsection (2) below, it shall be the duty of the Director to investigate any complaint made or referred to him with respect to the exercise by a relevant undertaker of any powers conferred on that undertaker by or by virtue of section 159 or 161(2) above.

(2) The Director shall not be required to investigate any such complaint as is mentioned in subsection (1) above if—

(a) the complaint appears to the Director to be vexatious or frivolous;

(b) the Director is not satisfied that the complaint has been brought by the complainant to the attention of the relevant undertaker in question and that that undertaker has been given a reasonable opportunity of investigating and dealing with it; or

(c) the complaint was first made to the Director or the appropriate customer service committee more than twelve months, or such longer period as the Director may for special reasons allow, after the matters to which the complaint relates first came to the notice of the complainant.

(3) Where the Director, in pursuance of his duty under this section, investigates a complaint with respect to the exercise of any powers by a relevant undertaker—

(a) it shall be the duty of that undertaker to provide the Director with all such information and assistance as he may reasonably require for the purposes of his investigation; and

(b) it shall be the duty of the Director, before giving any direction under subsection (4) below, to consider any representations made to him by the complainant or by that undertaker with respect to the subject-matter of the complaint.

(4) If on a complaint under subsection (1) above with respect to the exercise of any powers by a relevant undertaker, the Director is satisfied that that undertaker—

(a) has failed adequately to consult the complainant, before and in the course of exercising those powers, about the manner in which they are exercised; or

(b) by acting unreasonably in the manner of its exercise of those powers, has caused the complainant to sustain loss or damage or to be subjected to inconvenience,

the Director may direct the undertaker to pay to the complainant an amount, not exceeding £5,000, in respect of that failure, loss, damage or inconvenience.

(5) The Director shall not under subsection (4) above direct a relevant undertaker to pay any amount to a complainant in respect of any loss, damage or inconvenience for which compensation is recoverable under any

other enactment except in so far as it appears to him appropriate to do so by reason of any failure of the amount of any such compensation to reflect the fact that it was not reasonable for the undertaker to cause the complainant to sustain the loss or damage or to be subjected to the inconvenience.

(6) The duties of a relevant undertaker by virtue of subsection (3)(a) above shall be enforceable under section 18 above by the Director.

(7) A person to whom any amount is required, in pursuance of a direction under subsection (4) above, to be paid by a relevant undertaker shall be entitled to recover that amount from that undertaker by virtue of this section.

(8) The Secretary of State may by regulations substitute a different amount for the amount for the time being specified in subsection (4) above.

DEFINITIONS
  "relevant undertaker": s.219(1).
  "the Director": s.219(1).

GENERAL NOTE
  This section imposes on the Director a duty to investigate complaints regarding the exercise of works powers on private land by both water and sewerage undertakers under s.159 (powers to lay pipes in other land) and s.161(2) (power to deal with foul water and pollution).
  Subsection (2) details the circumstances in which the Director is not under any duty to investigate a complaint, for example, where the complaint appears to be vexatious or frivolous. Undertakers have a duty to provide the Director with information to facilitate the investigation of the complaint (subs. (3)(a)), and the Director is under a duty to consider representations made by both a complainant and an undertaker prior to making a determination (subs. (3)(b)).
  Where the Director is satisfied that the undertaker has failed to consult the owner or occupier about how best to exercise the works power, or has acted unreasonably so as to cause loss, damage or inconvenience, he may direct compensation payments up to a maximum of £5,000 (subs. (4)). The amount of money paid by an undertaker to a complainant is related to the nature of the unreasonable conduct rather than compensation for the exercise of the works power itself (subs. (5)).

Codes of practice with respect to work on private land

182.—(1) For the purposes of section 181 above it shall be the duty of every company holding an appointment under Chapter I of Part II of this Act as a relevant undertaker—

(a) as soon as reasonably practicable after its appointment takes effect, to submit to the Secretary of State for his approval a code of practice with respect to its exercise of any powers conferred by or by virtue of section 159 or 161(2) above; and

(b) if required to do so by the Secretary of State at any subsequent time, to submit proposed modifications of that code to the Secretary of State for his approval.

(2) The Secretary of State, if he considers it appropriate to do so for the purpose of promoting what appear to him to be desirable practices with respect to the exercise, by any company holding an appointment under Chapter I of Part II of this Act as a relevant undertaker, of any powers conferred by or by virtue of section 159 or 161(2) above, may at any time by order made by statutory instrument, in relation to that company—

(a) approve any code of practice with respect to the exercise of those powers which has been submitted to him (whether or not under subsection (1) above) by that company for his approval;

(b) approve any modifications of such a code which have been so submitted; or

(c) withdraw his approval for any such code or modification.

(3) A contravention of a code of practice as for the time being approved under this section in relation to a company shall not—

(a) affect the powers conferred on that company as a relevant undertaker by this Part;

(b) of itself entitle any person to be paid any amount under subsection (4) of section 181 above; or

(c) give rise to any criminal or civil liability;

but the Director shall take into account whether there has been any such contravention in determining whether to give a direction under that subsection to that company and in determining the amount to which any such direction relates.

(4) The Secretary of State shall not make an order under subsection (2) above unless he has first consulted all such persons as he considers it appropriate to consult.

(5) The duties of a relevant undertaker under subsection (1) above shall be enforceable under section 18 above by the Secretary of State.

DEFINITIONS
"modifications": s.219(1).

GENERAL NOTE
This section imposes a duty on undertakers to make and submit to the Secretary of State a code of practice relating to the use of the powers conferred by ss.159 and 161(2). The code of practice will be a statutory code (see subs. (2)) and the Secretary of State has wide powers to control its final format. Breach of any code does not in itself give rise to any civil or criminal liability (subs. (3)), nor are its obligations enforceable under the s.18 enforcement procedures (but a breach of the duty to submit a code will be). A breach of the statutory code will be taken into account by the Director in reaching his decision whether to direct an undertaker to pay compensation to a complainant (subs. (3)).

Protective provisions

Protection for particular undertakings

183. Schedule 13 to this Act shall have effect for the protection of particular undertakings in connection with the carrying out of works and other activities by relevant undertakers.

Power of certain undertakers to alter public sewers etc.

184.—(1) The NRA or the Civil Aviation Authority or any internal drainage board, dock undertakers, railway undertakers or airport operator may, after giving reasonable notice to the sewerage undertaker concerned, at their own expense and on substituting an equivalent, take up, divert or alter the level of any sewers, drains, culverts or other pipes which—

(a) are vested in the undertaker; and

(b) pass under or interfere with, or interfere with the alteration or improvement of, as the case may be—

(i) any watercourse or other works vested in or under the control of the NRA or that internal drainage board;

(ii) any property of the Civil Aviation Authority;

(iii) any river, canal towing path or works forming part of the undertaking of those dock undertakers;

(iv) the railway of the railway undertakers; or

(v) the airport in question.

(2) In subsection (1) above "an equivalent," in relation to any sewers, drains, culverts or pipes means other sewers, drains, culverts or pipes which will be equally effectual and will entail no additional expense for the sewerage undertaker in question.

(3) Any difference of opinion which arises under this section between a sewerage undertaker and any person as to whether any sewers, drains, culverts or pipes substituted or proposed to be substituted for sewers, drains, culverts or pipes of that undertaker—

(a) are or will be equally effectual; or

(b) entail or will entail additional expense for the sewerage undertaker, may, at the option of the party complaining, be referred to a single arbitrator appointed by agreement between the parties or, in default of agreement, by the President of the Institution of Civil Engineers.

(4) In this section—

"airport operator" means the person who is the airport operator for the purposes of Part V of the Airports Act 1986 in relation to an airport to which that Part of that Act applies; and

"dock undertakers" has the same meaning as in Chapter II of Part IV of this Act.

GENERAL NOTE

This section provides the National Rivers Authority, Civil Aviation Authority, internal drainage boards, dock undertakers, railway undertakers and airport operators with a power to alter public sewerage systems at their own expense and to substitute an effectual alternative. The section includes provision for arbitration in cases of dispute.

Duty to move pipes etc. in certain cases

185.—(1) Where any relevant pipe or other apparatus is for the time being kept installed by a relevant undertaker on, under or over any land, any person with an interest in that land or in adjacent land may by notice to the undertaker require the undertaker to alter or remove that pipe or apparatus on the ground that the alteration or removal of that pipe or apparatus is necessary to enable that person to carry out a proposed improvement of the land in which he has an interest.

(2) Subject to subsections (3) and (4) below, where a notice is served on a relevant undertaker under subsection (1) above, it shall be the duty of the undertaker to comply with the requirement contained in the notice except to the extent that that requirement is unreasonable.

(3) Nothing in this section shall require a relevant undertaker to alter or remove any pipe or apparatus which is kept installed in, under or over any street.

(4) A relevant undertaker may make it a condition of complying with the duty to which it is subject by virtue of a notice served by any person under subsection (1) above that such security as the undertaker may reasonably require has been provided for the discharge of any obligation of that person under subsection (5) below.

(5) Where a relevant undertaker carries out any works under this section by virtue of a notice having been served by any person under subsection (1) above, the undertaker shall be entitled to recover any expenses reasonably incurred in carrying out those works from that person.

(6) Where any sums have been deposited with a relevant undertaker by way of security for the discharge of any obligation under subsection (5) above, the undertaker shall pay interest at such rate as may be determined either—

(a) by the undertaker with the approval of the Director; or

(b) in default of a determination under paragraph (a) above, by the Director,

on every sum of 50p so deposited for every three months during which it remains in the hands of the undertaker.

(7) An approval or determination by the Director for the purposes of subsection (6) above may be given or made in relation to a particular case or description of cases or generally and may be revoked at any time.

(8) The duty of a relevant undertaker under this section shall be enforceable under section 18 above by the Director.

(9) In this section—

"improvement," in relation to any land, includes any development or change of use but does not include an improvement with respect to the supply of water, or the provision of sewerage services, to any premises; and

"relevant pipe" has the same meaning as in section 158 above.

<small>DEFINITIONS</small>
"improvement": subs. (9).
"notice": s.219(1).
"relevant pipe": subs. (9) and s.158.
"street": subs. (5).

<small>GENERAL NOTE</small>
This section obliges undertakers to remove or alter the location of mains and other pipes which would otherwise interfere with the development of land. An undertaker is entitled to recover its costs in carrying out such works from the person who requires the alteration or removal (subs. (5)). An undertaker is only under an obligation to comply with a notice served under this section if the removal or alteration of the pipe, etc. is not unreasonable (subs. (2)), and the decision as to whether the alteration or removal is reasonable will be that of the Director, who has power to enforce the duty by the s.18 enforcement procedure (subs. (8)). If there is no sensible alternative location for the relevant pipe then it is open to the Director to allow subs. (2) to operate. It is open to the undertaker to require security before discharging its obligation under the section (subs. (4)). The section does not apply to the alteration or removal of any pipe, etc. in a street (subs. (3)).

Protective provisions in respect of flood defence works and watercourses etc.

186.—(1) Nothing in this Act shall confer power on any person to do anything, except with the consent of the person who so uses them, which interferes—

(a) with any sluices, floodgates, groynes, sea defences or other works used by any person for draining, preserving or improving any land under any local statutory provision; or

(b) with any such works used by any person for irrigating any land.

(2) Without prejudice to the construction of subsection (1) above for the purposes of its application in relation to the other provisions of this Act, that subsection shall have effect in its application in relation to the relevant sewerage provisions as if any use of or injury to any such works as are mentioned in paragraph (a) or (b) of that subsection were such an interference as is mentioned in that subsection.

(3) Nothing in the relevant sewerage provisions shall authorise a sewerage undertaker injuriously to affect—

(a) any reservoir, canal, watercourse, river or stream, or any feeder thereof; or

(b) the supply, quality or fall of water contained in, or in any feeder of, any reservoir, canal, watercourse, river or stream,

without the consent of any person who would, apart from this Act, have been entitled by law to prevent, or be relieved against, the injurious affection of, or of the supply, quality or fall of water contained in, that reservoir, canal, watercourse, river, stream or feeder.

(4) Nothing in the relevant sewerage provisions, except sections 113 and 116 above, shall be taken to affect any right of drainage acquired by any person by prescription or otherwise before October 1, 1937.

(5) Where a relevant undertaker proposes, otherwise than in exercise of any compulsory powers, to construct or alter any relevant inland waters in any internal drainage district or to construct or alter any works on or in any such inland waters, the undertaker shall consult the drainage board for that district before doing so.

(6) A consent for the purposes of subsection (1) above may be given subject to reasonable conditions but shall not be unreasonably withheld.

(7) Any dispute—

(a) as to whether anything done or proposed to be done interferes or will interfere as mentioned in subsection (1) above;

(b) as to whether any consent for the purposes of this section is being unreasonably withheld;

(c) as to whether any condition subject to which any such consent has been given was reasonable; or

(d) as to whether the supply, quality or fall of water in any reservoir, canal, watercourse, river, stream or feeder is injuriously affected by the exercise of powers under the relevant sewerage provisions,

shall be referred (in the case of a dispute falling within paragraph (d) above, at the option of the party complaining) to the arbitration of a single arbitrator to be appointed by agreement between the parties or, in default of agreement, by the President of the Institution of Civil Engineers.

(8) In this section "relevant inland waters" means any inland waters other than any which form part of a main river for the purposes of Part IV of the Water Resources Act 1991.

(9) The provisions of this section shall be without prejudice to the provisions of Schedule 13 to this Act.

DEFINITIONS
  "local statutory provision": s.219(1).
  "relevant inland waters": subs. (8).
  "relevant sewerage provisions": s.219(1).

GENERAL NOTE
  This section imposes a prohibition on undertakers and others designed to prevent interference with flood defence works, drainage works and irrigation. The interests of undertakers are protected by virtue of subs. (6), which requires that the consent of the persons using the flood defence and irrigation works specified in subs. (1) be not unreasonably withheld. It will be for an arbitrator and not the Director to decide whether consent is being unreasonably withheld (subs. (7)). The section also extends to works by a sewerage undertaker which, it is claimed, injuriously affect any reservoir, canal, water course, river or stream (subs. (3)).

Works in tidal lands etc.

187.—(1) Nothing in any of the provisions of this Part relating to any relevant works power shall authorise any relevant undertaker to carry out any works at any place below the place to which the tide flows at mean high water springs, except in accordance with such plans and sections, and subject to such restrictions, as may, before the works are commenced, have been approved by the Secretary of State.

(2) An approval for the purposes of subsection (1) above shall be given to a relevant undertaker by the service on that undertaker of a notice containing the approval.

(3) In subsection (1) above the reference to a relevant works power is a reference to a power conferred by any of the relevant sewerage provisions or by any of sections 158, 159, 161, 163 and 165 above, except the power conferred by section 161(3).

DEFINITIONS
  "relevant sewerage provisions": s.219(1).
  "relevant works power": subs. (3).

GENERAL NOTE
  This section prohibits undertakers from carrying out works in tidal lands unless the approval of the Secretary of State is obtained prior to the commencement of the works.

Mineral rights

188. Schedule 14 to this Act (which makes provision with respect to the acquisition of mineral rights by relevant undertakers and with respect to the working of mines and minerals where pipes, sewers or other related works are affected) shall have effect and, in the case of the compulsory acquisition of land by virtue of this Act, shall have effect instead of Schedule 2 to the Acquisition of Land Act 1981 (mineral rights etc. in relation to compulsory purchase orders).

DEFINITIONS
"sewers": s.219(1), (2).

GENERAL NOTE
This section introduces Sched. 14, which deals with the acquisition of mineral rights and the working of mines and minerals by undertakers and, in cases of compulsory acquisition of land by virtue of the Act, replaces Sched. 2 to the Acquisition of Land Act 1981.

Power to sell minerals deriving from sewerage works

189.—(1) A sewerage undertaker may sell any materials which—
(a) have been removed by that undertaker from any premises, including any street, when carrying out works under, or otherwise carrying into effect the provisions of, the relevant sewerage provisions; and
(b) are not before the end of three days from the date of their removal claimed by the owner and taken away by him.

(2) Where a sewerage undertaker sells any materials under this section, they shall pay the proceeds to the person to whom the materials belonged after deducting the amount of any expenses recoverable by the undertaker from him.

(3) This section is subject to any rights conferred by virtue of paragraph 1 of Schedule 14 to this Act, does not apply to refuse removed by a sewerage undertaker and is not to be taken as prejudicing the determination of the rights and liabilities of a relevant undertaker when exercising a power in any case to which the preceding provisions of this section do not apply.

DEFINITIONS
"relevant undertaker": s.219(1).
"street": s.219(1), (5).

GENERAL NOTE
This section provides a power for sewerage undertakers to sell materials which derive from sewerage works. Although not defined, the term "materials" will include minerals. Materials obtained from any premises and any street may be sold unless claimed within three days of removal by the owner. The proceeds of sale of such materials must be paid by the undertaker to the owner, minus expenses. The section is subject to any rights conferred by para. 1 of Sched. 14 (see subs. (3)).

Saving for planning controls

190. Without prejudice to the operation of section 90 of the Town and Country Planning Act 1990 (planning permission deemed to be granted in certain cases) in relation to any provision made by or under this Act or any other enactment which by virtue of this Act or the Water Act 1989 relates to the functions of a relevant undertaker, nothing in this Act or in any such enactment shall be construed as authorising the carrying out of any development (within the meaning of that Act of 1990) without the grant of such planning permission as may be required by that Act of 1990.

DEFINITIONS
"enactment": s.219(1).
"functions": ss.217 and 219(1).
"relevant undertaker": s.219(1).

GENERAL NOTE
This section provides for a general saving of the requirements of the Town and Country Planning Act 1990 regarding development, within the meaning of that Act, carried out by an undertaker. Section 90 of the Town and Country Planning Act 1990 will apply to undertakers

and therefore, in appropriate cases, deemed planning permission will be granted for a range of developments connected with an undertaker's functions.

Duties to make recreational facilities available when building reservoirs in Wales

191.—(1) Where a water undertaker carries out any works for or in connection with the construction or operation of a reservoir in Wales which—

(a) permanently affect one or more communities; and

(b) are not primarily intended by that undertaker to benefit the inhabitants of that or those communities,

it shall be the duty of the undertaker to make available facilities for recreation or other leisure-time occupation for the benefit of those inhabitants or to assist others to make such facilities available.

(2) It shall be the duty of every water undertaker, in performing its duty under subsection (1) above, to consult—

(a) the community councils of the communities affected, in the case of communities having such councils; and

(b) in any case, the council of any district in which any community affected is situated.

(3) The duties of a water undertaker under this section shall be enforceable under section 18 above by the Secretary of State.

GENERAL NOTE

This section imposes a duty on water undertakers who are carrying out works in connection with the construction or operation of a reservoir to make available recreational facilities for those communities specified in subs. (1). Note that this duty is restricted to Wales. See also the general duty of undertakers to ensure the promotion of water and associated land for recreational purposes under s.3(5).

Interpretation of Part VI

Interpretation of Part VI

192.—(1) In this Part "discharge pipe" means a pipe from which discharges are or are to be made under section 165 above.

(2) In this Part references to maintaining a pipe include references to cleansing it and references to altering a pipe include references to altering its size or course, to moving or removing it and to replacing it with a pipe which is of the same description of relevant pipe (within the meaning of section 158 above) as the pipe replaced.

(3) The powers conferred by this Part on a relevant undertaker shall be exercisable both inside and outside the undertaker's area.

(4) In so far as any powers conferred by this Part on a relevant undertaker authorise the removal of any pipe or the alteration of its size or course, those powers shall be subject to such obligations by virtue of which the undertaker is required—

(a) to maintain a pipe or a connection with it; or

(b) to alter a pipe only where certain conditions are satisfied,

as are imposed on the undertaker by or under any enactment.

(5) The powers conferred by virtue of this Part are without prejudice to any power conferred by virtue of any agreement and are cumulative.

DEFINITIONS

"discharge pipe": subs. (1) and s.165.

GENERAL NOTE

This section relates to the interpretation of Pt. VI of the Act.

Part VII

Information Provisions

Reports

Reports by Director

193.—(1) The Director shall, as soon as practicable after December 31 each year, make to the Secretary of State a report on—
(a) his activities during that year; and
(b) the Monopolies Commission's activities during that year so far as relating to references made by him.
(2) Every such report shall—
(a) include a general survey of developments, during the year to which it relates, in respect of matters falling within the scope of the Director's functions; and
(b) set out any general directions given to the Director during that year under section 27(3) above.
(3) The Secretary of State shall lay a copy of every report made by the Director under subsection (1) above before each House of Parliament and shall arrange for copies of every such report to be published in such manner as he considers appropriate.
(4) The Director may also prepare such other reports as appear to him to be expedient with respect to any matters falling within the scope of his functions.
(5) The Director may arrange for copies of any report prepared under subsection (4) above to be published in such manner as he considers appropriate.
(6) In making or preparing any report under this section the Director shall have regard to the need for excluding, so far as that is practicable—
(a) any matter which relates to the affairs of an individual, where the publication of that matter would or might, in the opinion of the Director, seriously and prejudicially affect the interests of that individual; and
(b) any matter which relates specifically to the affairs of a particular body of persons, whether corporate or unincorporate, where publication of that matter would or might, in the opinion of the Director, seriously and prejudicially affect the interests of that body.

Definitions
"Monopolies Commission": s.219(1).
"the Director": s.219(1).

General Note
This section is concerned with the making and submission of annual reports to the Secretary of State relating to the activities of the Director and those of the Monopolies and Mergers Commission arising out of a reference made by the Director to the Monopolies Commission under s.14. The report will include both a general survey of the Director's activities during the year and any directions by the Secretary of State given to the Director under s.27(3) with which the Director must comply.

The Director has a discretion to prepare and publish other reports relating to his functions (subss. (4) and (5)). These provisions enable the Director to deal with particular issues by way of a report, or to respond to complaints by customer service committees by reporting his findings and conclusions. This power to publish incisive material is qualified by the requirement to have regard to the need to exclude items which would prejudicially affect the interest of individuals and companies (subs. (6)). The fact that the Director has no immunity from libel will also have a bearing on the content of such reports.

The Director has issued two annual reports to date. The second report for the year 1990/1991, "1990 Report of the Director General of Water Services", June 18, 1991, HMSO, gives a graphic account of the activities of the Director.

Reports by customer service committees

194.—(1) A customer service committee—
(a) shall prepare a report on any such matter as the Director may require; and
(b) may prepare a report concerning any matter which appears to the customer service committee to affect the interests of the customers or potential customers of a company allocated to the committee,

and, as soon as reasonably practicable after preparing a report under this subsection, a customer service committee shall send a copy of the report to the Director.

(2) As soon as reasonably practicable after the end of each financial year, a customer service committee shall prepare a report on its activities during that year and shall send a copy of that report to the Director.

(3) The Director may arrange for any report which has been sent to him by virtue of this section to be published in such manner as he considers appropriate.

(4) In publishing any report under this section the Director shall have regard to the need for excluding, so far as that is practicable, any such matters as are specified in section 193(6)(a) and (b) above.

DEFINITIONS
"customers or potential customers": s.219(1).
"financial year": s.219(1).

GENERAL NOTE
This section details the reports which customer service committees must send to the Director. These reports consist of reports on specific matters prepared in response to the Director's request, reports prepared by customer service committees at their own discretion on issues affecting customers or potential customers and annual reports on their activities. Customer service committees make reports under s.1(b) in respect of the company to which it is allocated. Customer service committees have no powers to publish independently of the Director. The Director has a discretion under the provisions of subs. (3) to publish any such report, but should he decide to publish, he must exclude matters which would injuriously affect the interest of either individuals or companies.

Registers, maps etc.

The Director's register

195.—(1) The Director shall, at such premises and in such form as he may determine, maintain a register for the purposes of Part II of this Act.

(2) Subject to any direction given under subsection (3) below, the Director shall cause to be entered in the register the provisions of—
(a) every appointment under Chapter I of Part II of this Act, every termination or transfer of any such appointment, every variation of the area for which any company holds any such appointment and every modification of the conditions of any such appointment;
(b) every direction, consent or determination given or made under any such appointment by the Secretary of State, the Monopolies Commission or the Director himself;
(c) every final enforcement order made under section 18 above, every provisional enforcement order made or confirmed under that section and every revocation of such a final or provisional enforcement order;
(d) every undertaking given to and accepted by the Secretary of State or the Director for the purposes of subsection (1)(b) of section 19 above and every notice under subsection (3) of that section; and
(e) every special administration order and every discharge of such an order.

(3) If it appears to the Secretary of State that the entry of any provision in the register would be against the public interest, he may direct the Director

not to enter that provision in the register; and the Director shall comply with any such direction.

(4) The contents of the register shall be available for inspection by the public at such times, and subject to the payment of such charges, as may be specified in an order made by the Secretary of State.

(5) Any person may, on the payment of such fee as may be specified in an order so made, require the Director to supply him with a copy of, or extract from, the contents of any part of the register, being a copy or extract which is certified by the Director to be a true copy or extract.

(6) The power to make an order under subsection (4) or (5) above shall be exercisable by statutory instrument subject to annulment in pursuance of a resolution of either House of Parliament.

(7) Any sums received by the Director under this section shall be paid into the Consolidated Fund.

DEFINITIONS
"final enforcement order": s.18(7).
"Monopolies Commission": s.219(1).
"provisional enforcement order": s.18(7).
"special administration order": ss.23 and 219(1).

GENERAL NOTE
This section obliges the Director to maintain a public register which will include important information relating to appointments, terminations and transfers relating to water and sewerage undertakers, final and provisional enforcement orders under s.18, undertakings pursuant to s.19(1)(b), special administration orders and other information. The information in the register should also be read in conjunction with the reports published by the Director under the provisions of ss.193 and 194. The Secretary of State may compel the Director to omit information from the register which he considers to be contrary to the public interest (subs. (3)). The grounds for exclusion are narrower than the equivalent registers held under s.36 of the Gas Act 1986 and s.19 of the Telecommunications Act 1984, which permit exclusion of information which would be "against the commercial interest of any person".

Trade effluent registers

196.—(1) It shall be the duty of every sewerage undertaker to secure that copies of—
   (a) every consent given or having effect as if given by the undertaker under Chapter III of Part IV of this Act;
   (b) every direction given or having effect as if given by the undertaker under that Chapter;
   (c) every agreement entered into or having effect as if entered into by the undertaker under section 129 above; and
   (e) every notice served on the undertaker under section 132 above,
are kept available, at all reasonable times, for inspection by the public free of charge at the offices of the undertaker.

(2) It shall be the duty of every sewerage undertaker, on the payment of such sum as may be reasonable, to furnish a person who requests it with a copy of, or of an extract from, anything kept available for inspection under this section.

(3) The duties of a sewerage undertaker under this section shall be enforceable under section 18 above by the Director.

DEFINITIONS
"notice": s.219(1).

GENERAL NOTE
This section imposes a duty on sewerage undertakers to maintain trade effluent registers available at all reasonable times for inspection by the public. There is no charge for inspection but a reasonable charge may be made for supplying any person with a copy of an extract from the register in compliance of its duty under subs. (2). The duties under this section are enforceable by the Director under the s.18 enforcement procedures.

Register for the purposes of works discharges

197.—(1) Every water undertaker shall keep a register of persons and premises for the purposes of section 166 above.

(2) A water undertaker shall enter the name and address of a person in that register in respect of any premises which abut on any watercourse if that person has requested to be so registered and is either—

(a) the owner or occupier of those premises; or

(b) an officer of an association of owners or occupiers of premises which abut on that watercourse and include those premises.

(3) If any water undertaker contravenes, without reasonable excuse, any of the requirements of this section, it shall be guilty of an offence and liable, on summary conviction, to a fine not exceeding level 3 on the standard scale.

DEFINITIONS
"owner": s.219(1).
"watercourse": s.219(1).

GENERAL NOTE
This section imposes a duty on water undertakers to maintain a register of persons and premises abutting water courses where the consent of those persons is required for discharges made under s.166. It is an offence to contravene, without reasonable excuse, the provisions of this section but the maintenance of such a register is not enforceable by the Director using s.18 enforcement procedures as it is on sewerage undertakers under s.196.

Maps of waterworks

198.—(1) Subject to subsections (4) and (5) below, it shall be the duty of every water undertaker to keep records of the location of—

(a) every resource main, water main or discharge pipe which is for the time being vested in that undertaker; and

(b) any other underground works, other than a service pipe, which are for the time being vested in that undertaker.

(2) It shall be the duty of every water undertaker to secure that the contents of any records for the time being kept by it under this section are available, at all reasonable times, for inspection by the public free of charge at an office of the undertaker.

(3) Any information which is required under this section to be made available by a water undertaker for inspection by the public shall be so made available in the form of a map.

(4) For the purpose of determining whether any failure to make a modification of any records kept under this section constitutes a breach of the duty imposed by subsection (1) above, that duty shall be taken to require any modification of the records to be made as soon as reasonably practicable after the completion of the works which make the modification necessary; and, where records kept under this section are modified, the date of the modification and of the completion of the works making the modification necessary shall be incorporated in the records.

(5) Nothing in this section shall require a water undertaker, at any time before September 1, 1999, to keep records of—

(a) any pipe which was laid before September 1, 1989; or

(b) any underground works which were completed before September 1, 1989,

unless those particulars were shown on August 31, 1989 on a map kept by a water authority or statutory water company under section 12 of Schedule 3 to the Water Act 1945 (maps of underground works).

(6) The reference in subsection (5) above to section 12 of Schedule 3 to the Water Act 1945 shall have effect, without prejudice to section 20(2) of the Interpretation Act 1978 (references to enactments to include references to enactments as amended, extended or applied), as including a reference to

that section as applied, with or without modifications, by any local statutory provision.

(7) The duties of a water undertaker under this section shall be enforceable under section 18 above by the Secretary of State.

(8) In this section "discharge pipe" has the same meaning as in Part VI of this Act.

DEFINITIONS
"discharge pipe": subs. (8).
"enactments": s.219(1).
"modification": s.219(1).
"records": s.219(1).
"resource main": s.219(1), (2).
"service pipe": s.219(1), (2).
"water main": s.219(1), (2).

GENERAL NOTE
This section imposes a duty on water undertakers to maintain records of the location of resource mains, water mains, discharge pipes (as defined by s.192(1)) and underground works other than a service pipe. Information under this section which is available to the public will be in map form. The term "map" is not defined, and is presumably intended to mean a visual record indicating geographical locations. The section does not provide any guidance as to the scale of such maps (subs. (3)).

Under subs. (2) it is the duty of every water undertaker to ensure that the contents of its records are available at all reasonable times for public inspection. The term "records" as defined in s.219(1) includes computer records and any other records kept otherwise than in a document. The duty to maintain maps of waterworks is enforceable by the Secretary of State under s.18.

Whilst it is the duty of water undertakers to keep records of the location of its waterworks under subs. (1), water undertakers are not required to keep records of pipes or works laid or completed before September 1, 1989 and may rely upon the particulars shown in the previous statutory maps kept pursuant to Sched. 3 to the Water Act 1945. A third party is entitled to rely upon the information contained in a water undertaker's map records to show the existence of works. If that information proves to be inaccurate then it is conceivable that a civil action could be taken against the water undertaker if damage or loss arises in consequence of the inaccurate map. In *Candler* v. *Crane, Christmas and Co.* [1951] 2 K.B. 164, Lord Denning dismissed the idea that map-makers could be liable for errors contained in their maps. However, given modern trends in liability for negligent misstatement, it is conceivable that Lord Denning's decision is open to challenge.

Sewerage undertakers are under a reciprocal duty by virtue of s.199 to keep and update sewer maps.

Sewer maps

199.—(1) Subject to subsections (6) to (8) below, it shall be the duty of every sewerage undertaker to keep records of the location and other relevant particulars—

(a) of every public sewer or disposal main which is vested in the undertaker;

(b) of every sewer in relation to which a declaration of vesting has been made by the undertaker under Chapter II of Part IV of this Act but has not taken effect; and

(c) of every drain or sewer which is the subject of any agreement to make such a declaration which has been entered into by the undertaker under section 104 above.

(2) For the purposes of this section the relevant particulars of a drain, sewer or disposal main are (in addition to its location) particulars—

(a) of whether it is a drain, sewer or disposal main and of the descriptions of effluent for the conveyance of which it is or is to be used; and

(b) of whether it is vested in the undertaker or, if it is not, of whether it is a sewer in relation to which a declaration has been made under Chapter

II of Part IV of this Act or a drain or sewer which is the subject of an agreement under section 104 above.

(3) The records kept by a sewerage undertaker under this section shall be kept separately in relation to the area of each local authority within whose area there is any drain, sewer or disposal main of which that undertaker is required to keep records and to whom the undertaker is required under section 200 below to provide copies of the contents of those records.

(4) It shall be the duty of every sewerage undertaker to secure that the contents of all the records for the time being kept by it under this section are available, at all reasonable times, for inspection by the public free of charge at an office of the undertaker.

(5) Any information which is required under this section to be made available by a sewerage undertaker for inspection by the public shall be so made available in the form of a map.

(6) For the purpose of determining whether any failure to make a modification of any records kept under this section constitutes a breach of the duty imposed by subsection (1) above, that duty shall be taken to require any modification of the records to be made as soon as reasonably practicable after the completion of the works which make the modification necessary; and, where records kept under this section are modified, the date of the modification and of the completion of the works making the modification necessary shall be incorporated in the records.

(7) Nothing in this section shall require a sewerage undertaker to keep records of any particulars of a drain, sewer or disposal main laid before September 1, 1989 if—

(a) the undertaker does not know of, or have reasonable grounds for suspecting, the existence of the drain, sewer or disposal main; or

(b) it is not reasonably practicable for the undertaker to discover the course of the drain, sewer or disposal main and it has not done so.

(8) Nothing in this section shall require a sewerage undertaker, at any time before September 1, 1999, to keep records of any particulars of any such drain, sewer or disposal main laid before September 1, 1989 as would not be excluded from its records by virtue of subsection (7) above unless—

(a) those particulars were shown on August 31, 1989 on a map kept by a local authority under section 32 of the Public Health Act 1936 (sewer maps); or

(b) it is a drain or sewer in relation to which a declaration of vesting, or an agreement to make such a declaration, has been made since August 31, 1989.

(9) The duties of a sewerage undertaker under this section shall be enforceable under section 18 above by the Secretary of State.

DEFINITIONS
    "disposal main": s.219(1), (2).
    "drain": s.219(1), (2).
    "effluent": s.219(1).
    "local authority": s.219(1).
    "modification": s.219(1).
    "public sewer": s.219(1).
    "records": s.219(1).
    "sewer": s.219(1), (2).

GENERAL NOTE
    This section imposes a duty on sewerage undertakers to keep records relating to drains, sewers and disposal mains. There is a reciprocal duty imposed on water undertakers in s.198 to keep records of waterworks.
    In addition to making provision for details of the location of drains, sewers or disposal mains in the form of a map, subs. (2) makes provision for additional information to be kept in respect of the description of effluent conveyed (subs. (2)(a)) and the status of the conducting media (subs. (2)(b)). The sewerage undertaker's "records", a term which includes computer records

and non-documentary records, are kept separately corresponding to the area of each local authority within whose area any drain or sewer or disposal main is situated and in respect of which the undertaker is obliged to keep records under s.200(3). Sewerage undertakers have a duty to ensure that their records are available at all reasonable times for public inspection and by virtue of subs. (5) any information which is required to be made available to the public will be in map form. The term "map" is not defined but presumably means a visual record indicating geographical locations. The scale of such maps is not specified in the section. See also the note to s.198 regarding potential liability for inaccurate maps.

The duty to keep sewer maps is enforceable by the Secretary of State using his s.18 enforcement powers. Under subs. (8) sewerage undertakers are not required to keep records of any drains, sewers or disposal mains laid before September 1, 1989 unless those particulars were shown on sewer maps kept by local authorities under s.32 of the Public Health Act 1936 or a vesting declaration or an agreement to make such a declaration has been made since August 31, 1989 in respect of a drain or sewer.

Provision of sewer maps to local authorities

200.—(1) It shall be the duty of every sewerage undertaker so to provide local authorities, free of charge, with—

(a) copies of the contents of records kept under section 199 above; and

(b) copies of any modifications of those records,

as to ensure that every local authority to whose area any of those records relate are at all times informed of the contents for the time being of the records relating to their area.

(2) A local authority shall secure that so much of any information provided to them by virtue of this section as consists in the contents for the time being of records kept by a sewerage undertaker under section 199 above is available, at all reasonable times, for inspection by the public free of charge at an office of the authority.

(3) Any information which is required under this section to be provided to a local authority or to be made available by a local authority for inspection by the public shall be so provided or made available in the form of a map.

(4) The duties of a sewerage undertaker under this section shall be enforceable under section 18 above by the Secretary of State.

(5) In this section and, accordingly, in section 199(3) above "local authority," in relation to the Inner Temple and the Middle Temple, includes, respectively, the Sub-Treasurer of the Inner Temple and the Under-Treasurer of the Middle Temple.

DEFINITIONS
"local authority": subs. (5) and s.219(1).
"modifications": s.219(1).
"records": s.219(1).

GENERAL NOTE
This section imposes a duty on sewerage undertakers to provide local authorities with free access to sewer maps. Under the provisions of subs. (2) local authorities must make available sewer map information supplied to them by sewerage undertakers, to the public at local authority offices, at all reasonable times, free of charge.

Local authorities require access to sewer maps in respect of their town and country planning and building control purposes.

Publication of certain information and advice

Publication of certain information and advice

201.—(1) The Secretary of State may arrange for the publication, in such form and in such manner as he considers appropriate, of such information relating to any matter which is connected with the carrying out by a company holding an appointment under Chapter I of Part II of this Act of the functions of a relevant undertaker as it may appear to him to be in the public interest to publish.

(2) The Director may arrange for the publication, in such form and in such manner as he considers appropriate, of such information and advice as it may appear to him to be expedient to give to any customer or potential customer of a company holding an appointment under Chapter I of Part II of this Act.

(3) In arranging for the publication of any such information or advice the Secretary of State or the Director shall have regard to the need for excluding, so far as that is practicable—

(a) any matter which relates to the affairs of an individual, where the publication of that matter would or might, in the opinion of the Secretary of State or (as the case may be) the Director, seriously and prejudicially affect the interests of that individual; and

(b) any matter which relates specifically to the affairs of a particular body of persons, whether corporate or unincorporate, where publication of that matter would or might, in the opinion of the Secretary of State or (as the case may be) the Director, seriously and prejudicially affect the interests of that body.

DEFINITIONS
"customer or potential customer": s.219(1).
"functions": ss.217 and 219(1).
"relevant undertaker": s.219(1).
"the Director": s.219(1).

GENERAL NOTE
This section provides the Secretary of State with a general power to publish information relating to the functions of both water and sewerage undertakers. In addition the Director is given a power to publish information and advice specifically for customers and potential customers of water and sewerage undertakers. Both the Secretary of State and the Director must have regard to the need to exclude prejudicial information adversely affecting the interests of individuals or companies (subs. (3)).

Powers to acquire and duties to provide information

Duties of undertakers to furnish the Secretary of State with information

202.—(1) It shall be the duty of a company holding an appointment as a relevant undertaker to furnish the Secretary of State with all such information relating to any matter which—

(a) is connected with, or with any proposals relating to, the carrying out by that company of the functions of a relevant undertaker; or

(b) is material to the carrying out by the Secretary of State of any of his functions under this Act, any of the other consolidation Acts or the Water Act 1989,

as the Secretary of State may reasonably require.

(2) Information required under this section shall be furnished in such form and manner, and be accompanied or supplemented by such explanations, as the Secretary of State may reasonably require.

(3) The information which a company may be required to furnish to the Secretary of State under this section shall include information which, although it is not in the possession of that company or would not otherwise come into the possession of that company, is information which it is reasonable to require that company to obtain.

(4) A requirement for the purposes of this section shall be contained in a direction which—

(a) may describe the information to be furnished in such manner as the Secretary of State considers appropriate;

(b) may require the information to be furnished on a particular occasion, in particular circumstances or from time to time; and

(c) may be given to a particular company, to companies of a particular description or to all the companies holding appointments under Chapter I of Part II of this Act.

(5) The obligations of a relevant undertaker under this section shall be enforceable under section 18 above by the Secretary of State.

(6) In this section "the other consolidation Acts" means the Water Resources Act 1991, the Statutory Water Companies Act 1991, so much of the Land Drainage Act 1991 as confers functions on the Secretary of State with respect to the NRA and the Water Consolidation (Consequential Provisions) Act 1991.

DEFINITIONS
"functions": ss.217 and 219(1).
"relevant undertaker": s.219(1).
"the other consolidation Acts": subs. (5).

GENERAL NOTE
This section imposes a duty on undertakers to furnish the Secretary of State with information relating either to the functions of the relevant undertaker or the functions of the Secretary of State under any of the consolidated water legislation. The section is enforced by the Secretary of State using the s.18 enforcement procedure (subs. (5)). Reference should also be made to the powers of the Secretary of State or Director to acquire information for enforcement purposes under the provisions of s.203, and conditions in the Instrument of Appointment, requiring the provision of information to the Director.

Power to acquire information for enforcement purposes

203.—(1) Where it appears to the Secretary of State or the Director that a company which holds an appointment as a relevant undertaker may be contravening, or may have contravened—

(a) any condition of its appointment; or

(b) any statutory or other requirement enforceable under section 18 above,

he may, for any purpose connected with such of his powers under Chapter II of Part II of this Act as are exercisable in relation to that matter, serve a notice under subsection (2) below on any person.

(2) A notice under this subsection is a notice signed by the Secretary of State or the Director and—

(a) requiring the person on whom it is served to produce, at a time and place specified in the notice, to—

(i) the Secretary of State or the Director; or

(ii) any person appointed by the Secretary of State or the Director for the purpose,

any documents which are specified or described in the notice and are in that person's custody or under his control; or

(b) requiring that person, if he is carrying on a business, to furnish, at the time and place and in the form and manner specified in the notice, the Secretary of State or the Director with such information as may be specified or described in the notice.

(3) No person shall be required under this section to produce any documents which he could not be compelled to produce in civil proceedings in the High Court or, in complying with any requirement for the furnishing of information, to give any information which he could not be compelled to give in evidence in any such proceedings.

(4) A person who, without reasonable excuse, fails to do anything required of him by a notice under subsection (2) above shall be guilty of an offence and liable, on summary conviction, to a fine not exceeding level 5 on the standard scale.

(5) A person who intentionally alters, suppresses or destroys any document which he has been required by any notice under subsection (2) above to produce shall be guilty of an offence and liable—

(a) on summary conviction, to a fine not exceeding the statutory maximum;

(b) on conviction on indictment, to a fine.

(6) If a person makes default in complying with a notice under subsection (2) above, the High Court may, on the application of the Secretary of State or the Director, make such order as the Court thinks fit for requiring the default to be made good; and any such order may provide that all the costs or expenses of and incidental to the application shall be borne by the person in default or by any officers of a company or other association who are responsible for its default.

(7) Nothing in this section shall be construed as restricting any power of the Secretary of State or the Director under section 202 above or the conditions of an appointment under Chapter I of Part II of this Act to require a company holding such an appointment to produce any document to him or to furnish him with any information.

DEFINITIONS
"notice": s.219(1).
"relevant undertaker": s.219(1).

GENERAL NOTE
The power given to the Secretary of State or the Director to acquire information for enforcement purposes under this section is not confined to water undertakers and sewerage undertakers. A notice requiring the provision of information or documentation may be served on any person under subs. (1). Unlike in s.202, failure to provide the information requested, without reasonable excuse (subs. (4)), and intentional destruction, suppression or alteration of documents (subs. (5)) are criminal offences. Redress may also be obtained in the High Court under subs. (6).

The intent of the section is to enable the Secretary of State or the Director to obtain documents and information which may be of relevance to s.18 enforcement procedures or applications for special administration orders under s.24. The restriction of disclosure of information in s.206 does not apply to such information as is required for the purposes of s.203. Reference should also be made to s.207, which deals with the offence of providing false information.

Provision of information to sewerage undertakers with respect to trade effluent discharge

204.—(1) The owner or occupier of any land on or under which is situated any sewer, drain, pipe, channel or outlet used or intended to be used for discharging any trade effluent into a sewer of a sewerage undertaker shall, when requested to do so by the undertaker—

(a) produce to the undertaker all such plans of the sewer, drain, pipe, channel or outlet as the owner or, as the case may be, occupier possesses or is able without expense to obtain;

(b) allow copies of the plans so produced by him to be made by, or under the directions of, the undertaker; and

(c) furnish to the undertaker all such information as the owner or, as the case may be, occupier can reasonably be expected to supply with respect to the sewer, drain, pipe, channel or outlet.

(2) A request by a sewerage undertaker for the purposes of this section shall be made in writing.

(3) Every person who fails to comply with this section shall be guilty of an offence and liable, on summary conviction to a fine not exceeding level 3 on the standard scale.

(4) Expressions used in this section and in Chapter III of Part IV of this Act have the same meanings in this section as in that Chapter; and, accordingly, section 139 above shall have effect for the purposes of this section as it has effect for the purposes of that Chapter.

DEFINITIONS
"drain": s.219(1), (2).
"owner": s.219(1).
"sewer": s.219(1), (2).
"trade effluent": subs. (4) and s.141.

GENERAL NOTE
This section imposes an obligation on the owners or occupiers of land through which trade effluent is discharged into a sewer, to supply undertakers with information and plans relating to the sewers, drains, etc. through which the effluent passes. Failure to provide the relevant information results in the commission of an offence (subs. (3)).

Exchange of metering information between undertakers

205.—(1) Where—
(a) different services are provided in relation to the same premises by different relevant undertakers;
(b) one of those undertakers has obtained a reading from a meter used in determining the amount of any charges fixed in relation to those premises;
(c) the charges in relation to those premises of another of those undertakers are fixed by reference to any matter to which the reading is relevant; and
(d) that other undertaker has agreed to bear a reasonable proportion of the expenses of obtaining the reading together with the reasonable expenses of the disclosure of the reading to it,
it shall be the duty of the undertaker who obtained the reading to disclose the reading to the other undertaker.
(2) Any dispute between a relevant undertaker and any other person (including another such undertaker)—
(a) as to the terms to be contained in any agreement for the purposes of subsection (1)(d) above; or
(b) as to the amount of any expenses to be borne by any person under any such agreement,
shall be referred to the arbitration of a single arbitrator appointed by agreement between the undertaker and that person or, in default of agreement, by the Director.
(3) The duties of a relevant undertaker under this section shall be enforceable under section 18 above by the Secretary of State.

DEFINITIONS
"meter": s.219(1).
"relevant undertakers": s.219(1).
"services": s.219(1).

GENERAL NOTE
This section imposes a duty on an undertaker to disclose a meter reading to another undertaker in circumstances where different services are provided to the same premises by those undertakers and there is an agreement relating to the exchange of information between them. Subsection (2) makes provision for arbitration.

Restriction on disclosure of information

Restriction on disclosure of information

206.—(1) Subject to the following provisions of this section, no information with respect to any particular business which—
(a) has been obtained by virtue of any of the provisions of this Act; and
(b) relates to the affairs of any individual or to any particular business,
shall, during the lifetime of that individual or so long as that business continues to be carried on, be disclosed without the consent of that individual or the person for the time being carrying on that business.

(2) No person shall disclose any information furnished to him under section 196 or 204 above or under Chapter III of Part IV of this Act except—
  (a) with the consent of the person by whom the information was furnished;
  (b) in connection with the execution of that Chapter;
  (c) for the purposes of any proceedings arising under that Chapter (including any appeal, application to the Secretary of State or the Director or an arbitration);
  (d) for the purposes of any criminal proceedings (whether or not so arising); or
  (e) for the purposes of any report of any proceedings falling within paragraph (c) or (d) above.

(3) Subsection (1) above does not apply to any disclosure of information which is made—
  (a) for the purpose of facilitating the carrying out by the Secretary of State, the Minister, the NRA, the Director, the Monopolies Commission or a county council or local authority of any of his, its or, as the case may be, their functions by virtue of this Act, any of the other consolidation Acts or the Water Act 1989;
  (b) for the purpose of facilitating the performance by a relevant undertaker of any of the duties imposed on it by or under this Act, any of the other consolidation Acts or the Water Act 1989;
  (c) in pursuance of any arrangements made by the Director under section 29(6) above or of any duty imposed by section 197(1)(a) or (2) or 203(1) or (2) of the Water Resources Act 1991 (information about water flow and pollution);
  (d) for the purpose of facilitating the carrying out by any person mentioned in Part I of Schedule 15 to this Act of any of his functions under any of the enactments or instruments specified in Part II of that Schedule;
  (e) for the purpose of enabling or assisting the Secretary of State to exercise any powers conferred on him by the Financial Services Act 1986 or by the enactments relating to companies, insurance companies or insolvency or for the purpose of enabling or assisting any inspector appointed by him under the enactments relating to companies to carry out his functions;
  (f) for the purpose of enabling an official receiver to carry out his functions under the enactments relating to insolvency or for the purpose of enabling or assisting a recognised professional body for the purposes of section 391 of the Insolvency Act 1986 to carry out its functions as such;
  (g) for the purpose of facilitating the carrying out by the Health and Safety Commission or the Health and Safety Executive of any of its functions under any enactment or of facilitating the carrying out by any enforcing authority, within the meaning of Part I of the Health and Safety at Work etc. Act 1974, of any functions under a relevant statutory provision, within the meaning of that Act;
  (h) for the purpose of facilitating the carrying out by the Comptroller and Auditor General of any of his functions under any enactment;
  (i) in connection with the investigation of any criminal offence or for the purposes of any criminal proceedings;
  (j) for the purposes of any civil proceedings brought under or by virtue of this Act, any of the other consolidation Acts, the Water Act 1989 or any of the enactments or instruments specified in Part II of Schedule 15 to this Act, or of any arbitration under this Act, any of the other consolidation Acts or that Act of 1989; or
  (k) in pursuance of a Community obligation.

(4) Nothing in subsection (1) above shall be construed—

(a) as limiting the matters which may be published under section 201 above or may be included in, or made public as part of, a report of the NRA, the Director, a customer service committee or the Monopolies Commission under any provision of this Act or of the Water Resources Act 1991; or

(b) as applying to any information which has been so published or has been made public as part of such a report or to any information exclusively of a statistical nature.

(5) Subject to subsection (6) below, nothing in subsection (1) above shall preclude the disclosure of information—

(a) if the disclosure is of information relating to a matter connected with the carrying out of the functions of a relevant undertaker and is made by one Minister of the Crown or government department to another; or

(b) if the disclosure is for the purpose of enabling or assisting any public or other authority for the time being designated for the purposes of this section by an order made by the Secretary of State to discharge any functions which are specified in the order.

(6) The power to make an order under subsection (5) above shall be exercisable by statutory instrument subject to annulment in pursuance of a resolution of either House of Parliament; and where such an order designates an authority for the purposes of paragraph (b) of that subsection, the order may—

(a) impose conditions subject to which the disclosure of information is permitted by virtue of that paragraph; and

(b) otherwise restrict the circumstances in which disclosure is so permitted.

(7) Any person who discloses any information in contravention of the preceding provisions of this section shall be guilty of an offence.

(8) A person who is guilty of an offence under this section by virtue of subsection (1) above shall be liable—

(a) on summary conviction, to a fine not exceeding the statutory maximum;

(b) on conviction on indictment, to imprisonment for a term not exceeding two years or to a fine or to both.

(9) A person who is guilty of an offence under this section by virtue of subsection (2) above shall be liable, on summary conviction, to imprisonment for a term not exceeding three months or to a fine not exceeding level 3 on the standard scale or to both.

(10) In this section "the other consolidation Acts" means the Water Resources Act 1991, the Statutory Water Companies Act 1991, the Land Drainage Act 1991 and the Water Consolidation (Consequential Provisions) Act 1991.

DEFINITIONS
"local authority": s.219(1).
"NRA": s.219(1).
"the Monopolies Commission": s.219(1).
"the other consolidation Acts": subs. (10).

GENERAL NOTE
This section creates a broad offence regarding the unauthorised disclosure of information obtained under the provisions of the Act and relating to a particular business or individual. The offence is subject to an extensive number of exceptions, mainly related to the functions of public bodies, including the duties, but not the powers, of undertakers. The section also gives effect to the recommendations of the Law Commission's Report on the consolidation of the legislation relating to water (Cmnd. 1483, April 1991), which addressed the problems of anomalies relating to s.174 of the Water Act 1989, from which this section is derived.

Provision of false information

207.—(1) If any person, in furnishing any information or making any application under or for the purposes of any provision of this Act, makes any statement which he knows to be false in a material particular, or recklessly makes any statement which is false in a material particular, he shall be guilty of an offence and liable—

(a) on summary conviction, to a fine not exceeding the statutory maximum;

(b) on conviction on indictment, to a fine.

(2) Proceedings for an offence under subsection (1) above shall not be instituted except by or with the consent of the Secretary of State, the Minister of Agriculture, Fisheries and Food or the Director of Public Prosecutions.

GENERAL NOTE

This section creates an offence of knowingly or recklessly supplying false information. Proceedings may be instituted only with the consent of the Secretary of State, the Minister of Agriculture, Fisheries and Food or the Director of Public Prosecutions.

The section gives effect to Recommendation No. 12 of the Law Commission's Report on the consolidation of the legislation relating to water (Cmnd. 1483, April 1991), which recommended that an offence corresponding to s.175 of the Water Act 1989 be applied to every provision consolidated in the Act.

PART VIII

MISCELLANEOUS AND SUPPLEMENTAL

Miscellaneous

Directions in the interests of national security

208.—(1) The Secretary of State may, after consultation with a relevant undertaker, give to that undertaker such directions of a general character as appear to the Secretary of State to be requisite or expedient in the interests of national security or for the purpose of mitigating the effects of any civil emergency which may occur.

(2) If it appears to the Secretary of State to be requisite or expedient to do so in the interests of national security or for the purpose of mitigating the effects of any civil emergency which has occurred or may occur, he may, after consultation with a relevant undertaker, give to that undertaker a direction requiring it to do, or not to do, a particular thing specified in the direction.

(3) It shall be the duty of a relevant undertaker, notwithstanding any other duty imposed on it (whether or not by or under this Act), to comply with any direction given to it by the Secretary of State under this section; and the duty of a relevant undertaker to comply with any such direction shall be enforceable under section 18 above by the Secretary of State.

(4) The Secretary of State shall lay before each House of Parliament a copy of every direction given under this section unless he is of the opinion that disclosure of the direction is against the interests of national security.

(5) A person shall not disclose, or be required by virtue of any enactment or otherwise to disclose, anything done by virtue of this section if the Secretary of State has notified him that the Secretary of State is of the opinion that disclosure of that thing is against the interests of national security.

(6) Any person who discloses any matter in contravention of subsection (5) above shall be guilty of an offence and liable, on conviction on indictment, to imprisonment for a term not exceeding two years or to a fine or to both.

(7) Any reference in this section to a civil emergency is a reference to any natural disaster or other emergency which, in the opinion of the Secretary of State, is or may be likely, in relation to any area—

(a) so to disrupt water supplies or sewerage services; or

(b) to involve such destruction of or damage to life or property in that area,

as seriously and adversely to affect all the inhabitants of that area, or a substantial number of them, whether by depriving them of any of the essentials of life or otherwise.

DEFINITIONS
"civil emergency": subs. (7).

GENERAL NOTE
This section empowers the Secretary of State to give directions to undertakers which are both general and specific for the purpose of mitigating the effects of a civil emergency or where such directions are necessary in the interests of national security.

The section is derived from s.170 of the Water Act 1989. During the passage of that Act an attempt was made to explain the phrase "requisite or expedient". It would appear that the word "requisite" applies to well-defined risks associated with serious consequences, such as the loss of a vital pumping station, whereas the word "expedient" could apply to circumstances where the risk is assessed to be lower, but where measures would still be prudent (see Colin Moynihan, Standing Committee D, col. 1524, March 2, 1989).

Breach of a direction given by the Secretary of State relating to non-disclosure carries a maximum penalty of imprisonment for two years and a fine.

Civil liability of undertakers for escapes of water etc.

209.—(1) Where an escape of water, however caused, from a pipe vested in a water undertaker causes loss or damage, the undertaker shall be liable, except as otherwise provided in this section, for the loss or damage.

(2) A water undertaker shall not incur any liability under subsection (1) above if the escape was due wholly to the fault of the person who sustained the loss or damage or of any servant, agent or contractor of his.

(3) A water undertaker shall not incur any liability under subsection (1) above in respect of any loss or damage for which the undertaker would not be liable apart from that subsection and which is sustained—

(a) by the NRA, a relevant undertaker or any statutory undertakers, within the meaning of section 336(1) of the Town and Country Planning Act 1990;

(b) by any public gas supplier within the meaning of Part I of the Gas Act 1986 or the holder of a licence under section 6(1) of the Electricity Act 1989;

(c) by any highway authority; or

(d) by any person on whom a right to compensation is conferred by section 82 of the New Roads and Street Works Act 1991.

(4) The Law Reform (Contributory Negligence) Act 1945, the Fatal Accidents Act 1976 and the Limitation Act 1980 shall apply in relation to any loss or damage for which a water undertaker is liable under this section, but which is not due to the undertaker's fault, as if it were due to its fault.

(5) Nothing in subsection (1) above affects any entitlement which a water undertaker may have to recover contribution under the Civil Liability (Contribution) Act 1978; and for the purposes of that Act, any loss for which a water undertaker is liable under that subsection shall be treated as if it were damage.

(6) Where a water undertaker is liable under any enactment or agreement passed or made before April 1, 1982, to make any payment in respect of any loss or damage the undertaker shall not incur liability under subsection (1) above in respect of the same loss or damage.

(7) In this section "fault" has the same meaning as in the Law Reform (Contributory Negligence) Act 1945.

(8) Until the coming into force of section 82 of the New Roads and Street Works Act 1991, subsection (3) above shall have effect as if for paragraph (d) there were substituted the following paragraphs—

> "(d) by any bridge authority, bridge managers, street authority or street managers within the meaning of the Public Utilities Street Works Act 1950; or
>
> (e) by any person on whom a right to compensation under section 26 of that Act of 1950 is conferred.";

but nothing in this section shall be taken to prejudice the power of the Secretary of State under that Act of 1991 to make an order bringing section 82 of that Act into force on different days for different purposes (including the purposes of this section).

DEFINITIONS
"damage": s.219(1).
"fault": subs. (7).

GENERAL NOTE
This section establishes an offence of strict liability in respect of any loss or damage that is caused by an escape of water from a water undertaker's pipes, irrespective of how that escape occurred. The definition of damage in s.219(1) includes death or personal injury. The offence as set out in subs. (1) is subject to a number of exceptions. A water undertaker will evade civil liability if the escape was due wholly to the fault of the person, or his servants, agents or contractors, who sustained the loss or damage and in respect of losses sustained by the bodies specified in subs. (3) (National Rivers Authority, gas suppliers, electricity suppliers, highway authorities and persons who have a right to compensation under s.82 of the New Roads and Street Works Act 1991).

An undertaker may reduce its liability where subs. (4) applies (contributory negligence). In addition, if the escape was due to the fault of a third party the water undertaker may recover a contribution from that person under the Civil Liability (Contributions) Act 1978 (subs. (5)). Liability might also be excluded under local Acts or agreements entered into with the plaintiff which took effect before April 1, 1982.

Offences

Offences by bodies corporate

210.—(1) Where a body corporate is guilty of an offence under this Act and that offence is proved to have been committed with the consent or connivance of, or to be attributable to any neglect on the part of, any director, manager, secretary or other similar officer of the body corporate or any person who was purporting to act in any such capacity, then he, as well as the body corporate, shall be guilty of that offence and shall be liable to be proceeded against and punished accordingly.

(2) Where the affairs of a body corporate are managed by its members, subsection (1) above shall apply in relation to the acts and defaults of a member in connection with his functions of management as if he were a director of the body corporate.

GENERAL NOTE
This section extends the liability for the commission of any offence under the Act by a body corporate to a director, manager or similar officer in circumstances where it is proved that the offence of the body corporate has been committed with the consent or connivance of, or is attributable to any neglect on the part of the senior company executives specified in subs. (1). An offence will also be made out where any person has purported to act in the capacity of the

senior officer of the company. Under subs. (2) where the affairs of the body corporate are managed by its members and it will be a member who has a management function who will be liable. Connivance will be viewed as culpable acquiescence in a course of conduct leading to the commission of an offence. The section also gives effect to recommendation No. 13 of the Law Commission's Report on the consolidation of the legislation relating to water (Cmnd. 1483, April 1991), which dealt with certain anomalies by applying the provisions of s.177 of the Water Act 1989 to this section and s.217 of the Water Resources Act 1991.

Limitation on right to prosecute in respect of sewerage offences

211. Proceedings in respect of an offence created by or under any of the relevant sewerage provisions shall not, without the written consent of the Attorney-General, be taken by any person other than—
    (a) a party aggrieved;
    (b) a sewerage undertaker; or
    (c) a body whose function it is to enforce the provisions in question.

DEFINITIONS
"relevant sewerage provisions": s.219(1).

GENERAL NOTE
This section provides for a limited class of persons who may, with the consent of the Attorney-General, institute proceedings in respect of an offence created by or under any of the relevant sewerage provisions.

Judicial disqualification

Judicial disqualification

212. No judge of any court or justice of the peace shall be disqualified from acting in relation to any proceedings to which a relevant undertaker is a party by reason only that he is or may become liable to pay a charge to that undertaker in respect of any service that is not the subject-matter of the proceedings.

GENERAL NOTE
Under this section a judge or Justice of the Peace will not be disqualified from dealing with an offence which is before him merely because he may be liable to pay a water undertaker or sewerage undertaker a charge for services that are not the subject matter of the proceedings before him.

Powers to make regulations

Powers to make regulations

213.—(1) The powers of the Secretary of State to make regulations under this Act shall be exercisable by statutory instrument subject (except in the case of regulations under section 8(1) or (2) above) to annulment in pursuance of a resolution of either House of Parliament.
    (2) Subject to subsection (3) below, the provisions of any regulations made by the Secretary of State under this Act may include—

(a) provision for any duty or other requirement imposed by the regulations on a water undertaker or sewerage undertaker to be enforceable under section 18 above by the Secretary of State, by the Director or by either of them;

(b) provision, where such a duty or requirement is so enforceable by either of them, for enforcement by the Director to be subject to such consent or authorisation as may be prescribed;

(c) provision which, in relation to the furnishing of any information or the making of any application under the regulations, makes provision corresponding to section 207 above;

(d) provision for anything that may be prescribed by the regulations to be determined under the regulations and for anything falling to be so determined to be determined by such persons, in accordance with such procedure and by reference to such matters, and to the opinion of such persons, as may be prescribed;

(e) different provision for different cases, including different provision in relation to different persons, circumstances or localities; and

(f) such supplemental, consequential and transitional provision as the Secretary of State considers appropriate.

(3) Except to the extent that they would do so apart from this section, the power to make regulations under section 113, 125 or 126 above or under section 214 below or Schedule 8 to this Act—

(a) shall not include the powers conferred by virtue of paragraphs (a) to (d) of subsection (2) above; and

(b) in the case of the power to make regulations under section 214 below, shall also not include the powers conferred by virtue of paragraphs (e) and (f) of that subsection.

DEFINITIONS
"prescribed": s.219(1).

GENERAL NOTE
The provisions of the Act establish the basic framework of control whereas the Secretary of State's power to make regulations under this section provide the detailed control. Regulations are effected by means of Statutory Instruments which are subject to annulment by either House of Parliament as provided in subs. (1). The Secretary of State has a wide discretion to make regulations, which may include those specified in subs. (2).

Section 14 of the Interpretation Act 1978 implies, unless a contrary intention is expressed, a power to revoke, amend or re-enact regulations made in pursuance of legislation (which includes powers to make regulations as in s.213).

Power to prescribe forms

214.—(1) The Secretary of State may by regulations prescribe the form of any notice or other document to be used for any of the purposes of the relevant sewerage provisions.

(2) If forms are prescribed under this section, those forms or forms to the like effect may be used in all cases to which those forms are applicable.

DEFINITIONS
"notice": s.219(1).
"prescribe": s.219(1).
"relevant sewerage provisions": s.219(1).

Local inquiries

Local inquiries

215.—(1) The Secretary of State may cause a local inquiry to be held in any case where he is authorised by any of the relevant sewerage provisions to determine any difference, to make any order, to give any consent or otherwise to act under any of those provisions.

(2) Subject to subsection (3) below, subsections (2) to (5) of section 250 of the Local Government Act 1972 (which contain supplementary provisions with respect to local inquiries held in pursuance of that section) shall apply to local inquiries under subsection (1) above or any of the other provisions of this Act as they apply to inquiries under that section.

(3) Subsection (4) of the said section 250 shall apply in accordance with subsection (2) above in relation to such local inquiries under this Act as are held with respect to any matter affecting the carrying out of any function of the NRA as if the reference to a local authority in that subsection included a reference to the NRA.

DEFINITIONS
"local authority": s.219(1).
"NRA": s.219(1).
"relevant sewerage provisions": s.219(1).

Construction of Act

Provisions relating to the service of documents

216.—(1) Any document required or authorised by virtue of this Act to be served on any person may be served—
(a) by delivering it to him or by leaving it at his proper address or by sending it by post to him at that address; or
(b) if the person is a body corporate, by serving it in accordance with paragraph (a) above on the secretary or clerk of that body; or
(c) if the person is a partnership, by serving it in accordance with paragraph (a) above on a partner or a person having the control of management of the partnership business.

(2) For the purposes of this section and section 7 of the Interpretation Act 1978 (which relates to the service of documents by post) in its application to this section, the proper address of any person on whom a document is to be served shall be his last known address, except that—
(a) in the case of service on a body corporate or its secretary or clerk, it shall be the address of the registered or principal office of the body;
(b) in the case of service on a partnership or a partner or a person having the control or management of a partnership business, it shall be the principal office of the partnership;
and for the purposes of this subsection the principal office of a company registered outside the United Kingdom or of a partnership carrying on business outside the United Kingdom is its principal office within the United Kingdom.

(3) If a person to be served by virtue of this Act with any document by another has specified to that other an address within the United Kingdom other than his proper address (as determined in pursuance of subsection (2) above) as the one at which he or someone on his behalf will accept documents of the same description as that document, that address shall also be treated as his proper address for the purposes of this section and for the purposes of the said section 7 in its application to this section.

(4) Where under any provision of this Act any document is required to be served on the owner, on a lessee or on the occupier of any premises then—
(a) if the name or address of the owner, of the lessee or, as the case may be, of the occupier of the premises cannot after reasonable inquiry be ascertained; or
(b) in the case of service on the occupier, if the premises appear to be or are unoccupied,

that document may be served either by leaving it in the hands of a person who is or appears to be resident or employed on the land or by leaving it conspicuously affixed to some building or object on the land.

(5) This section shall not apply to any document in relation to the service of which provision is made by rules of court.

DEFINITIONS
"owner": s.219(1).

GENERAL NOTE
This section sets out provisions relating to the service of documents under the Act and gives effect to Recommendation No. 14 of the Law Commission's Report on the consolidation of the legislation relating to water (Cmnd. 1483, April 1991) which recommended that a provision corresponding to s.187 of the Water Act 1989 be applied to all provisions in the water legislation consolidation but with the addition of a reference to lessees as set out in the report.

Construction of provision conferring powers by reference to undertakers' functions

217.—(1) The purposes to which this section applies shall be the construction of any enactment which, by reference to the functions of a relevant undertaker, confers any power on or in relation to that undertaker.

(2) For the purposes to which this section applies the functions of every relevant undertaker shall be taken to include joining with or acting on behalf of—

(a) the NRA;

(b) one or more other relevant undertakers; or

(c) the NRA and one or more other such undertakers,

for the purpose of carrying out any works or acquiring any land which at least one of the bodies with which it joins, or on whose behalf it acts, is authorised to carry out or acquire for the purposes of that body's functions under any enactment or of any function which is taken to be a function of that body for the purposes to which this section or section 3 of the Water Resources Act 1991 (functions of NRA for certain purposes) applies.

(3) For the purposes to which this section applies the functions of every relevant undertaker shall be taken to include the protection against pollution—

(a) of any waters, whether on the surface or underground, which belong to the NRA or any water undertaker or from which the NRA or any water undertaker is authorised to take water;

(b) without prejudice to paragraph (a) above, of any reservoir which belongs to or is operated by the NRA or any water undertaker or which the NRA or any water undertaker is proposing to acquire or construct for the purpose of being so operated; and

(c) of any underground strata from which the NRA or any water undertaker is for the time being authorised to abstract water in pursuance of a licence under Chapter II of Part II of the Water Resources Act 1991.

(4) For the purposes to which this section applies the functions of every relevant undertaker shall be taken to include the furtherance of research into matters in respect of which functions are conferred by or under this Act, the other consolidation Acts or the Water Act 1989 on the NRA, on water undertakers or on sewerage undertakers.

(5) For the purposes to which this section applies the functions of every relevant undertaker shall be taken to include the provision of houses and other buildings for the use of persons employed by that undertaker and the provision of recreation grounds for persons so employed.

(6) For the purposes to which this section applies the functions of every water undertaker shall be taken to include the provision of supplies of water in bulk, whether or not such supplies are provided for the purposes of, or in connection with, the carrying out of any other function of that undertaker.

(7) For the purposes to which this section applies the functions of every water undertaker shall be taken to include the doing of anything in pursuance of any arrangements under section 20 of the Water Resources Act 1991 between that undertaker and the NRA.

(8) In this section "the other consolidation Acts" has the same meaning as in section 206 above.

DEFINITIONS
"enactment": s.219(1).
"functions": ss.217 and 219(1).
"relevant undertaker": s.219(1).
"suppliers of water in bulk": s.219(1).
"the other consolidation Acts": subs. (8) and s.206.
"underground strata": s.219(1).

GENERAL NOTE
This is an important section which is concerned with the construction of provisions in any enactment contained in the Act or in any Act passed after the Act which confers powers by reference to an undertaker's functions. The extension of what is a "function" of an undertaker is important when one realises that the majority of an undertaker's duties and powers are confined to their functional activities, for example, their compulsory purchase powers under s.155, restriction on the disposal of an undertaker's protected land (s.156) and the mechanism to obtain a compulsory works order under s.167. Subsection (2) provides a power for undertakers and the National Rivers Authority to act jointly or enter into agency arrangements regarding carrying out works or acquiring land. By virtue of subs. (3) an undertaker's functions extend to protecting from pollution the types of water specified in the section. This seems to imply that undertakers and the National Rivers Authority (where it joins with an undertaker) have a residual duty to prevent pollution but do not have specific powers to take remedial action. The functions of a relevant undertaker also encompass research (subs. (4)), provision of houses and recreation grounds for employees (subs. (5)), bulk supplies of water (subs. (6)) and water management schemes (subs. (7)).

Meaning of "domestic purposes" in relation to water supply

218.—(1) Subject to the following provisions of this section, in this Act references to domestic purposes, in relation to a supply of water to any premises or in relation to any cognate expression, are references to the drinking, washing, cooking, central heating and sanitary purposes for which water supplied to those premises may be used.

(2) Where the whole or any part of the premises are or are to be occupied as a house, those purposes shall be taken to include—
   (a) the purposes of a profession carried on in that house or, where—
      (i) that house and another part of the premises are occupied together; and
      (ii) the house comprises the greater part of what is so occupied, in that other part; and
   (b) such purposes outside the house (including the washing of vehicles and the watering of gardens) as are connected with the occupation of the house and may be satisfied by a supply of water drawn from a tap inside the house and without the use of a hosepipe or similar apparatus.

(3) No such reference to domestic purposes shall be taken to include a reference—
   (a) to the use of a bath having a capacity, measured to the centre line of overflow or in such other manner as may be prescribed, of more than 230 litres;

(b) to the purposes of the business of a laundry; or
(c) to any purpose of a business of preparing food or drink for consumption otherwise than on the premises.

DEFINITIONS
"house": s.219(1).

GENERAL NOTE
This section details the precise meaning of "domestic purposes" where that phrase is used in relation to the supply of water to any premises. The section also gives effect to Recommendation No. 21 of the Law Commission's Report on the consolidation of the legislation relating to water (Cmnd. 1483, April 1991), clearing up an anomaly relating to the provision of water for central heating purposes.

General interpretation

219.—(1) In this Act, except in so far as the context otherwise requires—
"accessories," in relation to a water main, sewer or other pipe, includes any manholes, ventilating shafts, inspection chambers, settling tanks, wash-out pipes, pumps, ferrules or stopcocks for the main, sewer or other pipe, or any machinery or other apparatus which is designed or adapted for use in connection with the use or maintenance of the main, sewer or other pipe or of another accessory for it, but does not include any telecommunication apparatus (within the meaning of Schedule 2 to the Telecommunications Act 1984) unless it—
 (a) is or is to be situated inside or in the close vicinity of the main, sewer or other pipe or inside or in the close vicinity of another accessory for it; and
 (b) is intended to be used only in connection with the use or maintenance of the main, sewer or other pipe or of another accessory for it;
"analyse," in relation to any sample of land, water or effluent, includes subjecting the sample to a test of any description, and cognate expressions shall be construed accordingly;
"conservancy authority" means any person who has a duty or power under any enactment to conserve, maintain or improve the navigation of a tidal water, and is not a harbour authority or navigation authority;
"contravention" includes a failure to comply, and cognate expressions shall be construed accordingly;
"customer or potential customer," in relation to a company holding an appointment under Chapter I of Part II of this Act, means—
 (a) any person for or to whom that company provides any services in the course of carrying out the functions of a water undertaker or sewerage undertaker; or
 (b) any person who might become such a person on making an application for the purpose to the company;
"damage," in relation to individuals, includes death and any personal injury, including any disease or impairment of physical or mental condition;
"the Director" means the Director General of Water Services;
"disposal"—
 (a) in relation to land or any interest or right in or over land, includes the creation of such an interest or right and a disposal effected by means of the surrender or other termination of any such interest or right; and
 (b) in relation to sewage, includes treatment;
and cognate expressions shall be construed accordingly;

"disposal main" means (subject to subsection (2) below) any outfall pipe or other pipe which—

    (a) is a pipe for the conveyance of effluent to or from any sewage disposal works, whether of a sewerage undertaker or of any other person; and

    (b) is not a public sewer;

"domestic purposes," except in relation to sewers, shall be construed in accordance with section 218 above;

"drain" means (subject to subsection (2) below) a drain used for the drainage of one building or of any buildings or yards appurtenant to buildings within the same curtilage;

"effluent" means any liquid, including particles of matter and other substances in suspension in the liquid;

"enactment" includes an enactment contained in this Act or in any Act passed after this Act;

"engineering or building operations," without prejudice to the generality of that expression, includes—

    (a) the construction, alteration, improvement, maintenance or demolition of any building or structure or of any reservoir, watercourse, dam, weir, well, borehole or other works; and

    (b) the installation, modification or removal of any machinery or apparatus;

"financial year" means the 12 months ending with March 31;

"functions," in relation to a relevant undertaker, means the functions of the undertaker under or by virtue of any enactment and shall be construed subject to section 217 above;

"harbour authority" means a person who is a harbour authority within the meaning of the Prevention of Oil Pollution Act 1971 and is not a navigation authority;

"highway" and "highway authority" have the same meanings as in the Highways Act 1980;

"house" means any building or part of a building which is occupied as a dwelling-house, whether or not a private dwelling-house, or which, if unoccupied, is likely to be so occupied;

"information" includes anything contained in any records, accounts, estimates or returns;

"inland waters," has the same meaning as in the Water Resources Act 1991;

"limited company" means a company within the meaning of the Companies Act 1985 which is limited by shares;

"local authority" means the council of a district or of a London borough or the Common Council of the City of London;

"local statutory provision" means—

    (a) a provision of a local Act (including an Act confirming a provisional order);

    (b) a provision of so much of any public general Act as has effect with respect to a particular area, with respect to particular persons or works or with respect to particular provisions falling within any paragraph of this definition;

    (c) a provision of an instrument made under any provision falling within paragraph (a) or (b) above; or

    (d) a provision of any other instrument which is in the nature of a local enactment;

"meter" means any apparatus for measuring or showing the volume of water supplied to, or of effluent discharged from, any premises;

"micro-organism" includes any microscopic biological entity which is capable of replication;

"modifications" includes additions, alterations and omissions, and cognate expressions shall be construed accordingly;

"the Monopolies Commission" means the Monopolies and Mergers Commission;

"the NRA" means the National Rivers Authority;

"navigation authority" means any person who has a duty or power under any enactment to work, maintain, conserve, improve or control any canal or other inland navigation, navigable river, estuary, harbour or dock;

"notice" means notice in writing;

"owner," in relation to any premises, means the person who—

(a) is for the time being receiving the rack-rent of the premises, whether on his own account or as agent or trustee for another person; or

(b) would receive the rack rent if the premises were let at a rack rent,

and cognate expressions shall be construed accordingly;

"prescribed" means prescribed by regulations made by the Secretary of State;

"protected land," in relation to a company holding an appointment under Chapter I of Part II of this Act, means any land which, or any interest or right in or over which—

(a) was transferred to that company in accordance with a scheme under Schedule 2 to the Water Act 1989 or, where that company is a statutory water company, was held by that company at any time during the financial year ending with March 31, 1990;

(b) is or has at any time on or after September 1, 1989 been held by that company for purposes connected with the carrying out of its functions as a water undertaker or sewerage undertaker (including any functions which for the purposes for which section 218 above has effect are taken to be such functions by virtue of subsection (6) or (7) of that section); or

(c) has been transferred to that company in accordance with a scheme under Schedule 2 to this Act from another company in relation to which that land was protected land when the other company held an appointment under that Chapter;

"public authority" means any Minister of the Crown or government department, the NRA, any local authority or county council or any person certified by the Secretary of State to be a public authority for the purposes of this Act;

"public sewer" means a sewer for the time being vested in a sewerage undertaker in its capacity as such, whether vested in that undertaker by virtue of a scheme under Schedule 2 to the Water Act 1989 or Schedule 2 to this Act or under section 179 above or otherwise, and "private sewer" shall be construed accordingly;

"railway undertakers" means the British Railways Board, London Regional Transport or any other person authorised by any enactment, or by any order, rule or regulation made under any enactment, to construct, work or carry on any railway;

"records" includes computer records and any other records kept otherwise than in a document;

"the relevant sewerage provisions" means the following provisions of this Act, that is to say—

(a) Chapters II and III of Part IV (except sections 98 to 101 and 110 and so much of Chapter III of that Part as provides for regulations under section 138 or has effect by virtue of any such regulations);

(b) sections 160, 171, 172(4), 178, 184, 189, 196 and 204 and paragraph 4 of Schedule 12; and

(c) the other provisions of this Act so far as they have effect for the purposes of any provision falling within paragraph (a) or (b) of this definition;

"relevant undertaker" means a water undertaker or sewerage undertaker;

"resource main" means (subject to subsection (2) below) any pipe, not being a trunk main, which is or is to be used for the purpose of—

(a) conveying water from one source of supply to another, from a source of supply to a regulating reservoir or from a regulating reservoir to a source of supply; or

(b) giving or taking a supply of water in bulk;

"service pipe" means (subject to subsection (2) below) so much of a pipe which is, or is to be, connected with a water main for supplying water from that main to any premises as—

(a) is or is to be subject to water pressure from that main; or

(b) would be so subject but for the closing of some valve, and includes part of any service pipe;

"services" includes facilities;

"sewer" includes (without prejudice to subsection (2) below) all sewers and drains (not being drains within the meaning given by this subsection) which are used for the drainage of buildings and yards appurtenant to buildings;

"sewerage services" includes the disposal of sewage and any other services which are required to be provided by a sewerage undertaker for the purpose of carrying out its functions;

"special administration order" has the meaning given by section 23 above;

"statutory water company" means any company which was a statutory water company for the purposes of the Water Act 1973 immediately before September 1, 1989;

"stopcock" includes any box or pit in which a stopcock is enclosed and the cover to any such box or pit;

"street" has, subject to subsection (5) below, the same meaning as in Part III of the New Roads and Street Works 1991;

"subordinate legislation" has the same meaning as in the Interpretation Act 1978;

"substance" includes micro-organisms and any natural or artificial substance or other matter, whether it is in solid or liquid form or in the form of a gas or vapour;

"supply of water in bulk" means a supply of water for distribution by a water undertaker taking the supply;

"surface water" includes water from roofs;

"trunk main" means a water main which is or is to be used by a water undertaker for the purpose of—

(a) conveying water from a source of supply to a filter or reservoir or from one filter or reservoir to another filter or reservoir; or

(b) conveying water in bulk, whether in the course of taking a supply of water in bulk or otherwise, between different places outside the area of the undertaker, from such a place to any part of that area or from one part of that area to another part of that area;

"underground strata" means strata subjacent to the surface of any land;

"vessel" includes a hovercraft within the meaning of the Hovercraft Act 1968;

"water main" means (subject to subsection (2) below) any pipe, not being a pipe for the time being vested in a person other than the undertaker, which is used or to be used by a water undertaker for the purpose of making a general supply of water available to customers or potential customers of the undertaker, as distinct from for the purpose of providing a supply to particular customers;

"watercourse" includes all rivers, streams, ditches, drains, cuts, culverts, dykes, sluices, sewers and passages through which water flows except mains and other pipes which belong to the NRA or a water undertaker or are used by a water undertaker or any other person for the purpose only of providing a supply of water to any premises.

(2) In this Act—

(a) references to a pipe, including references to a main, a drain or a sewer, shall include references to a tunnel or conduit which serves or is to serve as the pipe in question and to any accessories for the pipe; and

(b) references to any sewage disposal works shall include references to the machinery and equipment of those works and any necessary pumping stations and outfall pipes;

and, accordingly, references to the laying of a pipe shall include references to the construction of such a tunnel or conduit, to the construction or installation of any such accessories and to the making of a connection between one pipe and another.

(3) Nothing in Part III or IV of this Act by virtue of which a relevant undertaker owes a duty to any particular person to lay any water main, resource main or service pipe or any sewer, disposal main or discharge pipe shall be construed—

(a) as conferring any power in addition to the powers conferred apart from those Parts; or

(b) as requiring the undertaker to carry out any works which it has no power to carry out.

(4) References in this Act to the fixing of charges in relation to any premises by reference to volume are references to the fixing of those charges by reference to the volume of water supplied to those premises, to the volume of effluent discharged from those premises, to both of those factors or to one or both of those factors taken together with other factors.

(5) Until the coming into force of Part III of the New Roads and Street Works Act 1991, the definition of "street" in subsection (1) above shall have effect as if the reference to that Part were a reference to the Public Utilities Street Works Act 1950; but nothing in this section shall be taken—

(a) to prejudice the power of the Secretary of State under that Act of 1991 to make an order bringing Part III of that Act into force on different days for different purposes (including the purposes of this section); or

(b) in the period before the coming into force of that Part, to prevent references in this Act to a street, where the street is a highway which passes over a bridge or through a tunnel, from including that bridge or tunnel.

(6) For the purposes of any provision of this Act by or under which power is or may be conferred on any person to recover the expenses incurred by that person in doing anything, those expenses shall be assumed to include such sum as may be reasonable in respect of establishment charges or overheads.

(7) References in this Act to the later or latest of two or more different times or days are, in a case where those times or days coincide, references to the time at which or, as the case may be, the day on which they coincide.

(8) Where by virtue of any provision of this Act any function of a Minister of the Crown is exercisable concurrently by different Ministers, that function shall also be exercisable jointly by any two or more of those Ministers.

(9) Sub-paragraph (1) of paragraph 1 of Schedule 2 to the Water Consolidation (Consequential Provisions) Act 1991 has effect (by virtue of sub-

paragraph (2)(b) of that paragraph) so that references in this Act to things done under or for the purposes of provisions of this Act or the Water Resources Act 1991 include references to things done, or treated as done, under or for the purposes of the corresponding provisions of the law in force before the commencement of this Act.

GENERAL NOTE

This section is a general interpretative section and gives effect to the following recommendations of the Law Commission in its Report on the consolidation of the legislation relating to water (Cmnd. 1483, April 1991): No. 15, relating to definition of "damage"; No. 17, relating to definition of "railway company"; No. 18, relating to definition of "owner"; No. 19, relating to definition of "street"; No. 20, relating to expenses that may be recovered.

Effect of local Acts

220. Subject to any provision to the contrary which is contained in Schedule 26 to the Water Act 1989 or in the Water Consolidation (Consequential Provisions) Act 1991, nothing in any local statutory provision passed or made before September 1, 1989 shall be construed as relieving any relevant undertaker from any liability arising by virtue of this Act in respect of any act or omission occurring on or after that date.

Other supplemental provisions

Crown application

221.—(1) Subject to the following provisions of this section, the provisions of this Act shall have effect in relation to land in which there is a Crown or Duchy interest as they have effect in relation to land in which there is no such interest.

(2) Subject to subsection (3) below, a power which is conferred by or under this Act in relation to land shall be exercisable in relation to any land in which there is a Crown or Duchy interest only with the consent of the appropriate authority.

(3) Subsection (2) above shall not require any consent to be given—

(a) for the exercise of any power in relation to any land in which there is a Crown or Duchy interest to the extent that that power would be so exercisable apart from subsection (1) above;

(b) for the imposition in relation to any premises in which there is a Crown or Duchy interest of any charges for a service provided by a relevant undertaker in the course of carrying out its functions; or

(c) for the purposes of any provision having effect by virtue of so much of section 167 above and Schedule 11 to this Act as relates to the granting of authority for discharges of water.

(4) A consent given for the purposes of subsection (2) above may be given on such financial and other conditions as the appropriate authority giving the consent may consider appropriate.

(5) In this section—

"the appropriate authority" has the same meaning as in section 293 of the Town and Country Planning Act 1990; and

"Crown or Duchy interest" means an interest belonging to Her Majesty in right of the Crown or of the Duchy of Lancaster, or to the Duchy of Cornwall, or belonging to a government department or held in trust for Her Majesty for the purposes of a government department;

and the provisions of subsection (3) of that section 293 as to the determination of questions shall apply for the purposes of this section.

GENERAL NOTE

Under the provisions of this section, undertakers are prevented from exercising their works powers in relation to Crown land unless they obtain the consent of the "appropriate authority", a term which is defined in subs. (5). Consent can be given subject to financial or other conditions. Subsection (3) details the circumstances in which consent is not required.

Application to Isles of Scilly

222.—(1) Subject to the provisions of any order under this section, nothing in this Act shall require or authorise any function, duty or power to be carried out, performed or exercised in relation to the Isles of Scilly by the NRA or any relevant undertaker; and references in the preceding provisions of this Act to England and Wales shall not include references to those Isles.

(2) The Secretary of State may, on the application of the Council of the Isles of Scilly, by order make provision with respect to the carrying out in those Isles of functions falling under this Act to be carried out in relation to other parts of England and Wales by the NRA or by a relevant undertaker.

(3) Without prejudice to the generality of the power conferred by subsection (2) above, an order under this section may apply any provision of this Act, of the Water Consolidation (Consequential Provisions) Act 1991 or of the Water Act 1989 in relation to the Isles of Scilly with or without modifications.

(4) The power of the Secretary of State to make an order under this section shall be exercisable by statutory instrument subject to annulment in pursuance of a resolution of either House of Parliament.

(5) An order under this section may—

(a) make different provision for different cases, including different provision in relation to different persons, circumstances or localities; and

(b) contain such supplemental, consequential and transitional provision as the Secretary of State considers appropriate, including provision saving provision repealed by or under any enactment.

(6) Chapter IV of Part III of this Act, except section 90, shall apply to the Isles of Scilly as if the Council of the Isles of Scilly were a water undertaker and the Isles were the area of the undertaker.

(7) The exception of section 90 above from the provisions of subsection (6) above shall be without prejudice to the power to make provision by an order under this section in relation to that section.

Short title, commencement and extent

223.—(1) This Act may be cited as the Water Industry Act 1991.

(2) This Act shall come into force on December 1, 1991.

(3) Except for the purpose of giving effect to any scheme under Schedule 2 to this Act, this Act extends to England and Wales only.

SCHEDULES

Section 1   SCHEDULE 1

THE DIRECTOR GENERAL OF WATER SERVICES

Remuneration, pensions etc.

1.—(1) There shall be paid to the Director such remuneration, and such travelling and other allowances, as the Secretary of State may determine.

(2) In the case of any such holder of the office of the Director as may be determined by the Secretary of State, there shall be paid such pension, allowances or gratuities to or in respect of him, or such payments towards provision for the payment of a pension, allowances or gratuities to or in respect of him, as may be so determined.

(3) If, when any person ceases to hold office as the Director, the Secretary of State determines that there are special circumstances which make it right that he should receive compensation, there may be paid to him a sum by way of compensation of such amount as may be determined by the Secretary of State.

(4) The approval of the Treasury shall be required for the making of a determination under this paragraph.

Staff

2.—(1) The Director may, with the approval of the Treasury as to numbers and terms and conditions of service, appoint such staff as he may determine.

(2) Anything authorised or required by or under any enactment to be done by the Director may be done by any member of the staff of the Director who has been authorised for the purpose, whether generally or specially, by the Director.

Expenses of the Director and his staff

3. There shall be paid out of money provided by Parliament—
(a) the remuneration of, and any travelling or other allowances payable under this Act to, the Director and any staff of the Director; and
(b) any expenses duly incurred by the Director or by any of his staff in consequence of the provisions of this Act.

Official seal

4. The Director shall have an official seal for the authentication of documents required for the purposes of his functions.

Documentary evidence

5. The Documentary Evidence Act 1868 shall have effect as if the Director were included in the first column of the Schedule to that Act, as if the Director and any person authorised to act on behalf of the Director were mentioned in the second column of that Schedule, and as if the regulations referred to in that Act included any document issued by the Director or by any such person.

Sections 10 and 23   SCHEDULE 2

TRANSITIONAL PROVISION ON TERMINATION OF APPOINTMENTS

Cases where Schedule applies

1.—(1) This Schedule shall apply in each of the cases specified in sub-paragraphs (2) and (3) below.

(2) The first case in which this Schedule applies is where—
(a) the Secretary of State or the Director is proposing to make an appointment or variation replacing a company as a relevant undertaker; and
(b) by virtue of that appointment a company ("the new appointee") will hold an appointment as the water undertaker or sewerage undertaker for an area which is or includes the whole or any part of the area for which, until the relevant date, another company ("the existing appointee") holds an appointment as the water undertaker or, as the case may be, sewerage undertaker.

(3) The second case in which this Schedule applies is where—
(a) the High Court has made a special administration order in relation to any company ("the existing appointee"); and
(b) it is proposed that on and after the relevant date another company ("the new appointee") should, without any such appointment or variation as is mentioned in sub-paragraph (2) above having been made, hold an appointment as water undertaker or sewerage undertaker for an area which is or includes the whole or any part of the area for which until that date the existing appointee holds an appointment as water undertaker or, as the case may be, sewerage undertaker.

(4) In this Schedule—
"existing appointee" and "new appointee" shall be construed in accordance with sub-paragraph (2) or (3) above according to whether this Schedule is applying in the case mentioned in the first or second of those sub-paragraphs;
"other appointees" means any companies, other than the existing appointee and the new appointee, which are likely on or at a time after the relevant date to be holding appointments as water undertakers or sewerage undertakers for any area which is or includes any part of the area for which the existing appointee has at any time held an appointment as water undertaker or sewerage undertaker;

"the relevant date" means—

>   (a) where this Schedule applies by virtue of sub-paragraph (2) above, the coming into force of the appointment or variation mentioned in paragraph (a) of that sub-paragraph; and
>
>   (b) where this Schedule applies by virtue of sub-paragraph (3) above, such day, being a day before the discharge of the special administration order takes effect, as the High Court may appoint for the purposes of this Schedule; and

"special administrator," in relation to a company in relation to which a special administration order has been made, means the person for the time being holding office for the purposes of section 23(1) of this Act.

Making and modification of transfer schemes

2.—(1) The existing appointee, acting with the consent of the new appointee and, in relation to the matters affecting them, of any other appointees, may make a scheme under this Schedule for the transfer of property, rights and liabilities from the existing appointee to the new appointee.

(2) A scheme under this Schedule shall not take effect unless it is approved by the Secretary of State or the Director.

(3) Where a scheme under this Schedule is submitted to the Secretary of State or the Director for his approval, he may, with the consent of the new appointee, of the existing appointee and, in relation to the matters affecting them, of any other appointees, modify the scheme before approving it.

(4) If at any time after a scheme under this Schedule has come into force in relation to the property, rights and liabilities of any company the Secretary of State considers it appropriate to do so and the existing appointee, the new appointee and, in relation to the provisions of the order which affect them, any other appointees consent to the making of the order, the Secretary of State may by order provide that that scheme shall for all purposes be deemed to have come into force with such modifications as may be specified in the order.

(5) An order under sub-paragraph (4) above may make, with effect from the coming into force of the scheme to which it relates, any such provision as could have been made by the scheme and, in connection with giving effect to that provision from that time, may contain such supplemental, consequential and transitional provision as the Secretary of State considers appropriate.

(6) In determining, in accordance with his duties under Part I of this Act, whether and in what manner to exercise any power conferred on him by this paragraph the Secretary of State or the Director shall have regard to the need to ensure that any provision for the transfer of property, rights and liabilities in accordance with a scheme under this Schedule allocates property, rights and liabilities to the different companies affected by the scheme in such proportions as appear to him to be appropriate in the context of the different functions which will, by virtue of this Act, be carried out at different times on and after the relevant date by the new appointee, by the existing appointee and by any other appointees.

(7) It shall be the duty of the new appointee, of the existing appointee and of any other appointees to provide the Secretary of State or the Director with all such information and other assistance as he may reasonably require for the purposes of, or in connection with, the exercise of any power conferred on him by this paragraph.

(8) A company which without reasonable excuse fails to do anything required of it by virtue of sub-paragraph (7) above shall be guilty of an offence and liable, on summary conviction, to a fine not exceeding level 5 on the standard scale.

(9) Without prejudice to the other provisions of this Act relating to the special administrator of a company, anything which is required by this paragraph to be done by a company shall, where that company is a company in relation to which a special administration order is in force, be effective only if it is done on the company's behalf by its special administrator.

Transfers by scheme

3.—(1) A scheme under this Schedule for the transfer of the existing appointee's property, rights and liabilities shall come into force on the relevant date and, on coming into force, shall have effect, in accordance with its provisions and without further assurance, so as to transfer the property, rights and liabilities to which the scheme relates to the new appointee.

(2) For the purpose of making any division of property, rights or liabilities which it is considered appropriate to make in connection with the transfer of property, rights and liabilities in accordance with a scheme under this Schedule, the provisions of that scheme may—

>   (a) create for the existing appointee, the new appointee or any other appointees an interest in or right over any property to which the scheme relates;
>
>   (b) create new rights and liabilities as between any two or more of those companies; and

(c) in connection with any provision made by virtue of paragraph (a) or (b) above, make incidental provision as to the interests, rights and liabilities of other persons with respect to the subject-matter of the scheme.

(3) A scheme under this Schedule may contain provision for the consideration to be provided by the new appointee and by any other appointees in respect of the transfer or creation of property, rights and liabilities by means of the scheme; and any such provision shall be enforceable in the same way as if the property, rights and liabilities had been created or transferred, and (if the case so requires) had been capable of being created or transferred, by agreement between the parties.

(4) The property, rights and liabilities of the existing appointee that shall be capable of being transferred in accordance with a scheme under this Schedule shall include—

(a) property, rights and liabilities that would not otherwise be capable of being transferred or assigned by the existing appointee;

(b) such property, rights and liabilities to which the existing appointee may become entitled or subject after the making of the scheme and before the relevant date as may be described in the scheme;

(c) property situated anywhere in the United Kingdom or elsewhere;

(d) rights and liabilities under enactments;

(e) rights and liabilities under the law of any part of the United Kingdom or of any country or territory outside the United Kingdom.

(5) The provision that may be made by virtue of sub-paragraph (2)(b) above includes—

(a) provision for treating any person who is entitled by virtue of a scheme under this Schedule to possession of a document as having given another person an acknowledgement in writing of the right of that other person to the production of the document and to delivery of copies thereof; and

(b) provision applying section 64 of the Law of Property Act 1925 (production and safe custody of documents) in relation to any case in relation to which provision falling within paragraph (a) above has effect.

(6) For the avoidance of doubt, it is hereby declared that the transfers authorised by paragraph (a) of sub-paragraph (4) above include transfers which, by virtue of that paragraph, are to take effect as if there were no such contravention, liability or interference with any interest or right as there would be, in the case of a transfer or assignment otherwise than in accordance with a scheme under this Schedule, by reason of any provision having effect (whether under any enactment or agreement or otherwise) in relation to the terms on which the existing appointee is entitled or subject to the property, right or liability in question.

Transfer of appointment

4.—(1) Where a scheme under this Schedule is made in the case specified in paragraph 1(3) above, the scheme may provide for the transfer to the new appointee, with such modifications as may be specified in the scheme, of the appointment under Chapter I of Part II of this Act which is held by the existing appointee.

(2) In such a case different schemes under this Schedule may provide for the transfer of such an appointment to different companies as respects different parts of the area to which the appointment relates.

Supplemental provisions of schemes

5.—(1) A scheme under this Schedule may contain supplemental, consequential and transitional provision for the purposes of, or in connection with, the provision for the transfers or any other provision made by the scheme.

(2) Without prejudice to the generality of sub-paragraph (1) above, a scheme under this Schedule may provide—

(a) that for purposes connected with any transfers made in accordance with the scheme (including the transfer of rights and liabilities under an enactment) the new appointee is to be treated as the same person in law as the existing appointee;

(b) that, so far as may be necessary for the purposes of or in connection with any such transfers, agreements made, transactions effected and other things done by or in relation to the existing appointee are to be treated as made, effected or done by or in relation to the new appointee;

(c) that, so far as may be necessary for the purposes of or in connection with any such transfers, references in any agreement (whether or not in writing) or in any deed, bond, instrument or other document to, or to any officer of, the existing appointee are to have effect with such modifications as are specified in the scheme;

(d) that proceedings commenced by or against the existing appointee are to be continued by or against the new appointee;

(e) that the effect of any transfer under the scheme in relation to contracts of employment with the existing appointee is not to be to terminate any of those contracts but is to be that periods of employment with the existing appointee are to count for all purposes as periods of employment with the new appointee;

(f) that disputes as to the effect of the scheme between the existing appointee and the new appointee, between either of them and any other appointee or between different companies which are other appointees are to be referred to such arbitration as may be specified in or determined under the scheme;

(g) that determinations on such arbitrations and certificates given jointly by two or more such appointees as are mentioned in paragraph (f) above as to the effect of the scheme as between the companies giving the certificates are to be conclusive for all purposes.

Duties of existing appointee after the scheme comes into force

6.—(1) A scheme under this Schedule may provide for the imposition of duties on the existing appointee and on the new appointee to take all such steps as may be requisite to secure that the vesting in the new appointee, by virtue of the scheme, of any foreign property, right or liability is effective under the relevant foreign law.

(2) The provisions of a scheme under this Schedule may require the existing appointee to comply with any directions of the new appointee in performing any duty imposed on the existing appointee by virtue of a provision included in the scheme under sub-paragraph (1) above.

(3) A scheme under this Schedule may provide that, until the vesting of any foreign property, right or liability of the existing appointee in the new appointee is effective under the relevant foreign law, it shall be the duty of the existing appointee to hold that property or right for the benefit of, or to discharge that liability on behalf of, the new appointee.

(4) Nothing in any provision included by virtue of this paragraph in a scheme under this Schedule shall be taken as prejudicing the effect under the law of any part of the United Kingdom of the vesting by virtue of the scheme in the new appointee of any foreign property, right or liability.

(5) A scheme under this Schedule may provide that, in specified cases, foreign property, rights or liabilities that are acquired or incurred by an existing appointee after the scheme comes into force are immediately to become property, rights or liabilities of the new appointee; and such a scheme may make the same provision in relation to any such property, rights or liabilities as can be made, by virtue of the preceding provisions of this paragraph, in relation to foreign property, rights and liabilities vested in the existing appointee when the scheme comes into force.

(6) References in this paragraph to any foreign property, right or liability are references to any property, right or liability as respects which any issue arising in any proceedings would have to be determined (in accordance with the rules of private international law) by reference to the law of a country or territory outside the United Kingdom.

(7) Any expenses incurred by an existing appointee in consequence of any provision included by virtue of this paragraph in a scheme under this Schedule shall be met by the new appointee.

(8) Duties imposed on a company by virtue of this paragraph shall be enforceable in the same way as if they were imposed by a contract between the existing appointee and the new appointee.

Further transitional provision and local statutory provisions

7.—(1) The Secretary of State may, if he thinks it appropriate to do so for the purposes of, or in connection with, any appointment or variation replacing a company as a relevant undertaker or any scheme under this Schedule, by order made by statutory instrument—

(a) make any provision which corresponds, in relation to any enactment referred to at the passing of the Water Act 1989 in Schedule 26 to that Act, to any provision originally made by that Schedule or makes similar provision in relation to any other enactment; or

(b) amend or repeal any local statutory provision.

(2) An order under this paragraph may—

(a) make provision applying generally in relation to local statutory provisions of a description specified in the order;

(b) make different provision for different cases, including different provision in relation to different persons, circumstances or localities; and

(c) contain such supplemental, consequential and transitional provision as the Secretary of State considers appropriate.

SCHEDULE 3

SPECIAL ADMINISTRATION ORDERS

PART I

MODIFICATIONS OF THE 1986 ACT

General application of provisions of 1986 Act

1. Where a special administration order has been made, sections 11 to 15, 17 to 23 and 27 of the 1986 Act (which relate to administration orders under Part II of that Act) shall apply, with the modifications specified in the following provisions of this Part of this Schedule—
   (a) as if references in those sections to an administration order were references to a special administration order and references to an administrator were references to a special administrator; and
   (b) where the company in relation to which the order has been made is a statutory water company that is not a limited company, as if references to a company included references to such a company.

Effect of order

2. In section 11 of the 1986 Act (effect of order), as applied by this Part of this Schedule—
   (a) the requirement in subsection (1)(a) that any petition for the winding up of the company shall be dismissed shall be without prejudice to the special administration order in a case where the order is made by virtue of section 25 of this Act;
   (b) the references in subsections (1)(b), (3)(b) and (4) to an administrative receiver, in relation to a statutory water company that is not a limited company, shall include references to any receiver whose functions in relation to that company correspond to those of an administrative receiver in relation to a limited company; and
   (c) the reference in subsection (3)(d) to proceedings shall include a reference to any proceedings under or for the purposes of section 18 of this Act.

Appointment of special administrator

3. In section 13 of the 1986 Act (appointment of administrator), as applied by this Part of this Schedule, for subsection (3) there shall be substituted the following subsection—
   "(3) an application for an order under subsection (2) may be made—
   (a) by the Secretary of State;
   (b) with the consent of the Secretary of State, by the Director General of Water Services;
   (c) by any continuing special administrator of the company or, where there is no such special administrator, by the company, the directors or any creditor or creditors of the company."

General powers of special administrator

4. In section 14 of the 1986 Act (general powers of administrator), as applied by this Part of this Schedule—
   (a) in subsection (1)(b), the reference to the powers specified in Schedule 1 to that Act shall be deemed to include a reference to a power to act on behalf of the company for the purposes of this Act, any local statutory provision or the exercise or performance of any power or duty which is conferred or imposed on the company by virtue of its holding an appointment under Chapter I of Part II of this Act; and
   (b) in subsection (4), the reference to a power conferred by the company's memorandum or articles of association shall be deemed to include a reference to a power conferred by a local statutory provision or by virtue of the company's holding such an appointment.

Power to deal with charged property

5.—(1) Section 15 of the 1986 Act (power to deal with charged property), as applied by this Part of this Schedule, shall have effect as follows.
   (2) In subsection (5)(b) (amount to be paid to chargeholder not to be less than open market value), for the words "in the open market by a willing vendor" there shall be substituted the words "for the best price which is reasonably available on a sale which is consistent with the purposes of the special administration order."
   (3) Subsections (7) and (8) (notice to registrar) shall not apply where the company in relation to which the special administration order is made is a statutory water company that is not a limited company.

Duties of special administrator

6.—(1) Section 17 of the 1986 Act (duties of administrator), as applied by this Part of this Schedule, shall have effect as follows.

(2) For subsection (2) there shall be substituted the following subsection—

"(2) Subject to any directions of the court, it shall be the duty of the special administrator to manage the affairs, business and property of the company in accordance with proposals, as for the time being revised under section 23, which have been prepared for the purposes of that section by him or any predecessor of his."

(3) In subsection (3), paragraph (a) (right of creditors to require the holding of a creditors' meeting) shall be omitted.

Discharge of order

7.—(1) Section 18 of the 1986 Act (discharge and variation of administration order), as applied by this Part of this Schedule, shall have effect as follows.

(2) For subsections (1) and (2) there shall be substituted the following subsection—

"(1) An application for a special administration order to be discharged may be made—
    (a) by the special administrator, on the ground that the purposes of the order have been achieved; or
    (b) by the Secretary of State or, with the consent of the Secretary of State, the Director General of Water Services, on the ground that it is no longer necessary that those purposes are achieved."

(3) In subsection (3), the words "or vary" shall be omitted.

(4) In subsection (4), the words "or varied" and "or variation" shall be omitted and for the words "to the registrar of companies" there shall be substituted—
    (a) where the company in relation to which the special administration order is made is a statutory water company that is not a limited company, the words "to the Director General of Water Services"; and
    (b) in any other case, the words "to the registrar of companies and to the Director General of Water Services."

Notice of making of order

8. In section 21(2) of the 1986 Act (notice of order to be given by administrator), as applied by this Part of this Schedule, for the words "to the registrar of companies" there shall be substituted—
    (a) where the company in relation to which the special administration order is made is a statutory water company that is not a limited company, the words "to the Director General of Water Services"; and
    (b) in any other case, the words "to the registrar of companies, to the Director General of Water Services."

Statement of proposals

9. In section 23 of the 1986 Act (statement of proposals), as applied by this Part of this Schedule, for subsections (1) and (2) there shall be substituted the following subsections—

"(1) Where a special administration order has been made, the special administrator shall, within three months (or such longer period as the court may allow) after the making of the order, send a statement of his proposals for achieving the purposes of the order—
    (a) to the Secretary of State and to the Director General of Water Services;
    (b) so far as he is aware of their addresses, to all creditors of the company; and
    (c) except where the company in relation to which the special administration order is made is a statutory water company that is not a limited company, to the registrar of companies;
and may from time to time revise those proposals.

(2) If at any time—
    (a) the special administrator proposes to make revisions of the proposals for achieving the purposes of the special administration order; and
    (b) those revisions appear to him to be substantial,
the special administrator shall, before making those revisions, send a statement of the proposed revisions to the Secretary of State, to the Director General of Water Services, (so far as he is aware of their addresses) to all creditors of the company and, except where the company in relation to which the special administration order is made is a statutory water company that is not a limited company, to the registrar of companies.

(2A) Where the special administrator is required by subsection (1) or (2) to send any person a statement before the end of any period or before making any revision of any proposals, he shall also, before the end of that period or, as the case may be, before making those revisions either—

(a) send a copy of the statement (so far as he is aware of their addresses) to all members of the company; or

(b) publish in the prescribed manner a notice stating an address to which members should write for copies of the statement to be sent to them free of charge."

Applications to court

10.—(1) Section 27 of the 1986 Act (protection of interests of creditors and members), as applied by this Part of this Schedule, shall have effect as follows.

(2) After subsection (1) there shall be inserted the following subsection—

"(1A) At any time when a special administration order is in force the Secretary of State or, with the consent of the Secretary of State, the Director General of Water Services may apply to the High Court by petition for an order under this section on the ground that the special administrator has exercised or is exercising, or proposing to exercise, his powers in relation to the company in a manner which—

(a) will not best ensure the achievement of the purposes of the order; or

(b) without prejudice to paragraph (a) above, involves either a contravention of the conditions of the company's appointment under Chapter I of Part II of the Water Industry Act 1991 or of any statutory or other requirement imposed on the company in consequence of that appointment."

(3) In subsection (3) (order not to prejudice or prevent voluntary arrangements or administrator's proposals), for paragraphs (a) and (b) there shall be substituted the words "the achievement of the purposes of the order."

(4) Subsections (4)(d) and (6) (power of court to order discharge) shall be omitted.

Part II

Supplemental

General adaptations and saving

11.—(1) Subject to the preceding provisions of this Schedule, references in the 1986 Act (except in sections 8 to 10 and 24 to 26), or in any other enactment passed before July 6, 1989, to an administration order under Part II of that Act, to an application for such an order and to an administrator shall include references, respectively, to a special administration order, to an application for a special administration order and to a special administrator.

(2) Subject as aforesaid and to sub-paragraph (3) below, references in the 1986 Act, or in any other enactment passed before July 6, 1989, to an enactment contained in Part II of that Act shall include references to that enactment as applied by section 24 of this Act or Part I of this Schedule.

(3) Sub-paragraphs (1) and (2) above shall apply in relation to a reference in an enactment contained in Part II of the 1986 Act only so far as necessary for the purposes of the operation of the provisions of that Part as so applied.

(4) The provisions of this Schedule shall be without prejudice to the power conferred by section 411 of the 1986 Act (company insolvency rules), as modified by sub-paragraphs (1) and (2) above.

Interpretation

12.—(1) In this Schedule "the 1986 Act" means the Insolvency Act 1986.

(2) In this Schedule, and in any modification of the 1986 Act made by this Schedule, "special administrator," in relation to a special administration order, means any person appointed in relation to that order for the purposes of section 23(1) of this Act; and in any such modification "special administration order" has the same meaning as in this Act.

Section 28   SCHEDULE 4

Customer Service Committees

Sub-committees

1. A customer service committee may, with the approval of the Director—

(a) establish local and other sub-committees through which the customer service committee may carry out such of its functions as it may determine;

(b) appoint such persons as it may determine (including persons who are not members of the committee) to be members of any such sub-committee; and
(c) regulate the procedure of any such sub-committee and, subject to paragraph 3 below, the terms and conditions of service of any person appointed to be a member of any such sub-committee.

Remuneration, pensions etc. of the chairman of a customer service committee

2.—(1) There shall be paid to the chairman of a customer service committee such remuneration, and such travelling and other allowances, as the Director may determine.
(2) There shall be paid—
(a) such pension, allowances or gratuities to or in respect of a person who has held or holds office as the chairman of a customer service committee; or
(b) such payments towards provision for the payment of a pension, allowances or gratuities to or in respect of such a person,
as may be determined by the Director.
(3) If, when any person ceases to hold office as such a chairman, the Director determines that there are special circumstances which make it right that that person should receive compensation, there may be paid to him a sum by way of compensation of such amount as may be determined by the Director.
(4) The approval of the Treasury shall be required for the making of a determination under this paragraph.

Expenses of other members of a customer service committee etc.

3. Subject to paragraph 2 above, neither the members of a customer service committee nor the members of any sub-committee of any such committee shall be paid any sums by the Director for or in respect of their services except—
(a) in the case of services as a member of a customer service committee, sums reimbursing the member for loss of remuneration, for travelling expenses or for any other out-of-pocket expenses; and
(b) in the case of services as a member of a sub-committee of a customer service committee, sums reimbursing the member for travelling expenses or for any other out-of-pocket expenses which do not relate to loss of remuneration.

Staff

4.—(1) The Director may, with the approval of the Treasury as to numbers and terms and conditions of service, appoint such officers and employees of a customer service committee or of any sub-committee of a customer service committee as he may determine.
(2) Anything authorised or required by or under this Act to be done by a customer service committee may be done by any of the officers or employees of the committee, or of any of its sub-committees, who has been authorised for the purpose, whether generally or specially, by the committee or, in accordance with the terms of its appointment, by a sub-committee of the committee.

Financial provisions

5.—(1) The following shall be paid by the Director out of money provided by Parliament, that is to say—
(a) any sums required to be paid to or in respect of any person under paragraph 2 or 3 above; and
(b) any expenses incurred by a customer service committee in accordance with any statement approved under sub-paragraph (3) below.
(2) A customer service committee shall prepare in respect of each financial year a statement of the expenses which it expects to incur in respect of that year—
(a) in relation to officers and employees of the committee and its sub-committees; or
(b) otherwise for the purposes of or in connection with, the carrying out of its functions;
and that statement shall be sent to the Director, in the case of the statement in respect of the financial year current at the establishment of the committee, as soon as practicable after the establishment of the committee and, in any other case, before the beginning of the financial year to which the statement relates.
(3) The Director shall consider any statement sent to him under sub-paragraph (2) above and shall either approve the statement or approve it with such modifications as he considers appropriate.

SCHEDULE 5

PROCEDURE FOR ORDERS RELATING TO PRESSURE AND CONSTANCY OF SUPPLY

Applications for orders

1.—(1) Where the Director or a water undertaker applies to the Secretary of State for an order under section 65(5) of this Act, the applicant shall—

(a) submit to the Secretary of State a draft of the order applied for;

(b) publish a notice with respect to the application, at least once in each of two successive weeks, in one or more newspapers circulating in the locality which would be affected by the provision proposed to be made by the order;

(c) not later than the date on which that notice is first published serve a copy of the notice on every affected local authority and every affected water undertaker; and

(d) publish a notice in the London Gazette which—

(i) states that the draft order has been submitted to the Secretary of State;

(ii) names every local authority on whom a notice is required to be served under this paragraph;

(iii) specifies a place where a copy of the draft order and of any relevant map or plan may be inspected; and

(iv) gives the name of every newspaper in which the notice required by virtue of paragraph (b) above was published and the date of an issue containing the notice.

(2) The notice required by virtue of sub-paragraph (1)(b) above to be published with respect to an application for an order shall—

(a) state the general effect of the order applied for;

(b) specify a place where a copy of the draft order and of any relevant map or plan may be inspected by any person free of charge at all reasonable times during the period of 28 days beginning with the date of the first publication of the notice; and

(c) state that any person may, within that period, by notice to the Secretary of State object to the making of the order.

(3) For the purposes of subsection (1)(c) above a local authority or a water undertaker which is not the applicant shall be affected by an application for an order if its area includes the whole or any part of the locality which would be affected by the provision proposed to be made by the order.

Supply of copies of draft orders

2. The applicant for an order under section 65(5) of this Act shall, at the request of any person and on payment by that person of such charge (if any) as the applicant may reasonably require, furnish that person with a copy of the draft order submitted to the Secretary of State under paragraph 1 above.

Modifications of proposals

3.—(1) On an application for an order under section 65(5) of this Act, the Secretary of State may make the order either in the terms of the draft order submitted to him or, subject to sub-paragraph (2) below, in those terms as modified in such manner as he thinks fit, or may refuse to make an order.

(2) The Secretary of State shall not make such a modification of a draft order submitted to him as he considers it likely adversely to affect any persons unless he is satisfied that the applicant for the order has given and published such additional notices, in such manner, as the Secretary of State may have required.

Consideration of objections etc.

4. Where an application for an order to which this Schedule applies has been made, the Secretary of State may, if he considers it appropriate to do so, hold a local inquiry before making any order on the application.

SUPPLEMENTAL PROVISIONS RELATING TO RIGHTS OF ENTRY

PART I

RIGHTS REQUIRING NOTICE FOR ENTRY TO NON-BUSINESS PREMISES

Notice of entry

1.—(1) Where this Part of this Schedule applies to any right of entry conferred by a provision of this Act, admission to any premises which are not business premises shall not be demanded as of right by virtue of that provision, unless 24 hours notice of the intended entry has been given to the occupier of the premises.

(2) In this paragraph "business premises" means—

(a) any factory; or

(b) any place in which persons are employed otherwise than in domestic service;

and in this sub-paragraph "factory" has the same meaning as in the Factories Act 1961.

Warrants to exercise right

2.—(1) Subject to sub-paragraph (3) below, if it is shown to the satisfaction of a justice of the peace, on sworn information in writing—

(a) that any one or more of the conditions specified in sub-paragraph (2) below is fulfilled in relation to any premises which a person is entitled to enter by virtue of a right of entry to which this Part of this Schedule applies; and

(b) that there is reasonable ground for entry to the premises for any purpose for which the right is exercisable,

the justice may by a warrant under his hand authorise that person to enter the premises, if need be by force.

(2) The conditions mentioned in sub-paragraph (1) above are—

(a) that admission to the premises has been refused to the person having the right to enter them;

(b) that such refusal is apprehended;

(c) that the premises are unoccupied or the occupier is temporarily absent;

(d) that the case is one of urgency;

(e) that an application for admission would defeat the object of the entry.

(3) A warrant under this Part of this Schedule shall not be issued by a justice of the peace in a case in which he is satisfied that the condition mentioned in paragraph (a) or (b) of sub-paragraph (2) above is fulfilled unless he is also satisfied—

(a) that notice of the intention to apply for a warrant has been given to the occupier;

(b) that a condition mentioned in either of paragraphs (c) and (d) of that sub-paragraph is also fulfilled in relation to the premises; or

(c) that the giving of such notice as is mentioned in paragraph (a) above would defeat the object of the entry.

(4) Every warrant under this Part of this Schedule shall continue in force until the purpose for which the entry is necessary has been fulfilled.

(5) A person leaving any unoccupied premises which he has entered by virtue of a warrant under this Part of this Schedule shall leave them as effectually secured against trespassers as he found them.

Supplementary power of person making entry

3. Any person entitled to enter any premises by virtue of a right to which this Part of this Schedule applies, or of a warrant under this Part of this Schedule, may take with him such other persons as may be necessary.

Obstruction of person exercising right

4. Any person who wilfully obstructs any person upon whom a right of entry has been conferred by virtue of—

(a) any provision of this Act relating to a right of entry to which this Part of this Schedule applies; or

(b) a warrant under this Part of this Schedule,

shall be guilty of an offence and liable, on summary conviction, to a fine not exceeding level 1 on the standard scale.

Duty of persons exercising rights to maintain confidentiality

5.—(1) Without prejudice to section 206 of this Act and subject to sub-paragraphs (2) and (3) below, any person who is admitted to any premises in compliance—

(a) with any provision of this Act relating to a right of entry to which this Part of this Schedule applies; or

(b) with a warrant under this Part of this Schedule,

shall be guilty of an offence under this paragraph if he discloses to any person any information obtained by him there with regard to any manufacturing process or trade secret.

(2) A person shall not be guilty of an offence under this paragraph in respect of any disclosure made in the performance of his duty.

(3) For the purposes of the application of this Part of this Schedule to the right conferred by section 171 of this Act, the reference to premises in subsection (1) above shall have effect as a reference only to business premises, within the meaning of paragraph 1 above.

(4) A person who is guilty of an offence under this paragraph, other than such a person as is mentioned in sub-paragraph (5) below, shall be liable—

    (a) on summary conviction, to imprisonment for a term not exceeding three months or to a fine not exceeding the statutory maximum or to both;

    (b) on conviction on indictment, to imprisonment for a term not exceeding three months or to a fine or to both.

(5) A person who is guilty of an offence under this paragraph by virtue of the application of this Part of this Schedule to the rights conferred by section 171 of this Act shall be liable, on summary conviction, to imprisonment for a term not exceeding three months or to a fine not exceeding level 3 on the standard scale or to both.

PART II

OTHER RIGHTS OF ENTRY AND RELATED POWERS

Notice of entry

6.—(1) Without prejudice to any power exercisable by virtue of a warrant under this Part of this Schedule, no person shall make an entry into any premises by virtue of any right or power to which this Part of this Schedule applies except—

    (a) in an emergency; or

    (b) at a reasonable time and after the required notice of the intended entry has been given to the occupier of the premises.

(2) For the purposes of this paragraph the required notice is—

    (a) in the case of the rights and powers conferred by virtue of any of sections 74(4), 84(2) and (3), 86(4) and 170(1)(c) and (3) of this Act, 24 hours' notice; and

    (b) in any other case, seven days' notice.

(3) For the purposes of the application of this Part of this Schedule to any right or power conferred by section 168 of this Act the reference in sub-paragraph (1) above to an emergency—

    (a) in relation to any entry to premises for the purposes of, or for purposes connected with, the exercise or proposed exercise of any power in relation to a street, includes a reference to any circumstances requiring the carrying out of emergency works within the meaning of Part III of the New Roads and Street Works Act 1991; and

    (b) in relation to any other entry to premises, includes a reference to any danger to property and to any interruption of a supply of water provided to any premises by any person and to any interruption of the provision of sewerage services to any premises.

(4) Until the coming into force of section 52 of the New Roads and Street Works Act 1991, sub-paragraph (3)(a) above shall have effect as if the reference to Part III of that Act were a reference to the Public Utilities Street Works Act 1950; but nothing in this sub-paragraph shall be taken to prejudice the power of the Secretary of State under that Act of 1991 to make an order bringing that section 52 into force on different days for different purposes (including the purposes of this paragraph).

(5) For the purposes of the application of this Part of this Schedule to the rights and other powers conferred by section 172 of this Act sub-paragraph (1) above shall have effect as if the power in an emergency to make an entry to any premises otherwise than at a reasonable time and after the required notice were omitted.

Warrant to exercise right or power

7.—(1) If it is shown to the satisfaction of a justice of the peace on sworn information in writing—

    (a) that there are reasonable grounds for the exercise in relation to any premises of a right or power to which this Part of this Schedule applies; and

    (b) that one or more of the conditions specified in sub-paragraph (2) below is fulfilled in relation to those premises,

the justice may by warrant authorise the relevant authority to designate a person who shall be authorised to exercise the right or power in relation to those premises in accordance with the warrant and, if need be, by force.

(2) The conditions mentioned in sub-paragraph (1)(b) above are—

    (a) that the exercise of the right or power in relation to the premises has been refused;

    (b) that such a refusal is reasonably apprehended;

    (c) that the premises are unoccupied;

(d) that the occupier is temporarily absent from the premises;
(e) that the case is one of urgency; or
(f) that an application for admission to the premises would defeat the object of the proposed entry.

(3) A justice of the peace shall not issue a warrant under this Part of this Schedule by virtue only of being satisfied that the exercise of a right or power in relation to any premises has been refused, or that a refusal is reasonably apprehended, unless he is also satisfied—
(a) that notice of the intention to apply for the warrant has been given to the occupier of the premises; or
(b) that the giving of such a notice would defeat the object of the proposed entry.

(4) For the purposes of the application of this Part of this Schedule to the rights and powers conferred by section 169 of this Act in a case to which subsection (4) of that section applies, a justice of the peace shall not issue a warrant under this Part of this Schedule unless he is satisfied that the Secretary of State has given his authorisation for the purposes of that subsection in relation to that case.

(5) Every warrant under this Part of this Schedule shall continue in force until the purposes for which the warrant was issued have been fulfilled.

Manner of exercise of right or power

8. A person designated as the person who may exercise any right or power to which this Part of this Schedule applies shall produce evidence of his designation and other authority before he exercises the right or power.

Supplementary powers of person making entry etc.

9. A person authorised to enter any premises by virtue of any right or power to which this Part of this Schedule applies shall be entitled, subject in the case of a right or power exercisable under a warrant to the terms of the warrant, to take with him on to the premises such other persons and such equipment as may be necessary.

Duty to secure premises

10. A person who enters any premises in the exercise of any right or power to which this Part of this Schedule applies shall leave the premises as effectually secured against trespassers as he found them.

Compensation

11.—(1) Where any person exercises any right or power to which this Part of this Schedule applies, it shall be the duty of the relevant authority to make full compensation to any person who has sustained loss or damage by reason of—
(a) the exercise by the designated person of that right or power or of any power to take any person or equipment with him when entering the premises in relation to which the right or power is exercised; or
(b) the performance of, or failure of the designated person to perform, the duty imposed by paragraph 10 above.

(2) Compensation shall not be payable by virtue of sub-paragraph (1) above in respect of any loss or damage if the loss or damage—
(a) is attributable to the default of the person who sustained it; or
(b) is loss or damage in respect of which compensation is payable by virtue of any other provision of this Act.

(3) Any dispute as to a person's entitlement to compensation under this paragraph or as to the amount of any such compensation, shall be referred to the arbitration of a single arbitrator appointed by agreement between the relevant authority and the person who claims to have sustained the loss or damage or, in default of agreement—
(a) by the President of the Lands Tribunal where the relevant authority is the Secretary of State; and
(b) by the Secretary of State, in any other case.

Obstruction of person exercising right or power

12. A person who intentionally obstructs another person acting in the exercise of any right or power to which this Part of this Schedule applies shall be guilty of an offence and liable, on summary conviction, to a fine not exceeding level 3 on the standard scale.

Interpretation of Part II

13.—(1) In this Part of this Schedule "relevant authority," in relation to a right or power to which this Part of this Schedule applies, means the person who, by virtue of—

(a) the provision by which the right or power is conferred; or

(b) (except in paragraph 7 above) the warrant,

is entitled to designate the person by whom the right or power may be exercised.

(2) References in this Part of this Schedule, except in paragraph 7 above, to a right or power to which this Part of this Schedule applies include references to a right or power exercisable by virtue of a warrant under this Part of this Schedule.

(3) For the purposes of paragraphs 10 and 11 above a person enters any premises by virtue of a right or power to which this Part of this Schedule applies notwithstanding that he has failed (whether by virtue of the waiver of the requirement by the occupier of the premises or otherwise) to comply with—

(a) any requirement to enter those premises at a reasonable time or after giving notice of his intended entry; or

(b) the requirement imposed by paragraph 8 above.

Section 91   SCHEDULE 7

Pre-1985 Fluoridation Schemes

Operation of pre-1985 schemes

1.—(1) Where in pursuance of any such arrangements entered into by a water authority or statutory water company before December 20, 1984 as have effect immediately before the coming into force of this Act as arrangements entered into by a water undertaker—

(a) a scheme for increasing the fluoride content of water supplied by the authority or company in any part of England and Wales was in operation immediately before that date; or

(b) work had been begun by the authority or company before that date for enabling such a scheme to be brought into operation,

that water undertaker may, while the conditions mentioned in sub-paragraph (2) below are satisfied, operate the scheme.

(2) The conditions referred to in sub-paragraph (1) above are that the arrangements require—

(a) fluoridation to be effected only by the addition of one or more of the compounds of fluorine mentioned in subsection (4) of section 87 of this Act; and

(b) the concentrations of fluoride in the water supplied to consumers to be maintained, so far as reasonably practicable, at one milligram per litre.

Supplies by other undertakers and revocation or variation of scheme

2.—(1) Where a water undertaker is operating a fluoridation scheme by virtue of this Schedule—

(a) subsections (6) and (7) of section 87 of this Act shall apply in relation to the scheme as they apply in relation to any scheme operated in exercise of the power conferred by that section or section 1 of the Water (Fluoridation) Act 1985;

(b) the scheme shall cease to have effect upon the appropriate authority giving to the undertaker reasonable notice of the authority's desire to terminate it; and

(c) the arrangements under which the scheme is operated may be varied to take account of any amendment of section 87(2) of this Act which is made under section 88 of this Act.

(2) In this paragraph "appropriate authority," in relation to a fluoridation scheme which is operated under this Schedule, means the Regional or District Health Authority to which the water undertaker concerned is answerable in accordance with the arrangements under which the scheme is operated.

Publicity and consultation

3.—(1) Section 89 of this Act (including the power of the Secretary of State under subsection (6) of that section to dispense with the other requirements of that section) shall apply where a District Health Authority propose to terminate a scheme which may be operated by virtue of this Schedule as it applies where such an authority propose to withdraw an application under section 87 of this Act.

(2) Accordingly, in subsection (7) of section 89 of this Act, the reference to the question whether an application under section 87 of this Act should be withdrawn shall be treated by

virtue of sub-paragraph (1) above as a reference to whether a scheme should be terminated under this Schedule.

SCHEDULE 8

PRE-1989 ACT TRANSITIONAL AUTHORITY FOR TRADE EFFLUENT DISCHARGES ETC.

Trade effluent agreements

1. Nothing in Chapter III of Part IV of this Act (except so far as it relates to special category effluent) or in the repeals made by the Water Consolidation (Consequential Provisions) Act 1991 shall affect—
   (a) any agreement with respect to any trade effluent to which a sewerage undertaker is a party by virtue of its having been duly made before July 1, 1937 between a predecessor of the undertaker and the owner or occupier of any trade premises; or
   (b) any agreement saved by section 63(8) of the Public Health Act 1961 (pre-1961 Act agreements with respect to discharges from premises used for farming or for scientific research or experiment).

Authorisations having effect as deemed consents under the Control of Pollution Act 1974

2.—(1) Where, by virtue of section 43(2) of the Control of Pollution Act 1974 there is, immediately before the commencement of this Act, a deemed consent for the purposes of the Public Health (Drainage of Trade Premises) Act 1937 which has effect under the Water Act 1989 in relation to any sewerage undertaker, that deemed consent shall have effect as a deemed consent for the purposes of Chapter III of Part IV of this Act subject to the following provisions of this paragraph.
   (2) The sewerage undertaker—
   (a) may at any time; and
   (b) shall if requested to do so by any person entitled to make a discharge in pursuance of the deemed consent,
by notice served on the owner and any occupier of the premises in question cancel the deemed consent and, subject to sub-paragraph (3) below, give its actual consent for such discharges as were authorised by the deemed consent.
   (3) An actual consent given under sub-paragraph (2) above shall be so given either conditionally or subject to any conditions which may be attached to consents by virtue of section 121 of this Act.
   (4) It is hereby declared that the provisions of Chapter III of Part IV of this Act with respect to the variation of conditions of a consent apply in relation to an actual consent under sub-paragraph (2) above as they apply in relation to any other actual consent under Chapter III of Part IV of this Act.
   (5) A notice signifying an actual consent under sub-paragraph (2) above shall indicate that a right of appeal is conferred under the following paragraph in respect of the notice.

Appeals in respect of consents under paragraph 2

3.—(1) A person on whom notice is served in pursuance of paragraph 2(2) above may, in accordance with regulations made by the Secretary of State, appeal to the Director.
   (2) Section 137 of this Act shall apply, with the necessary modifications, in relation to appeals under this paragraph as it applies in relation to appeals under section 122 of this Act.
   (3) On an appeal under this paragraph the Director may give the sewerage undertaker in question any such direction as he thinks fit with respect to the notice and it shall be the duty of the undertaker to comply with the direction.

Determinations of disputes as to transitional matters

4.—(1) Any dispute in so far as it—
   (a) arises after the commencement of this Act and relates to a deemed consent in respect of discharges previously authorised under section 4 of the Public Health (Drainage of Trade Premises) Act 1937; and
   (b) is a dispute as to the nature or composition of any trade effluent discharged from any trade premises into a sewer during any period, as to the quantity of trade effluent so discharged on any one day during any period or as to the rate of trade effluent so discharged during any period,
shall, unless the parties otherwise agree, be referred to the Director for determination.

(2) On a reference under this paragraph the Director may make such order in the matter as he thinks just.

(3) An order on a reference under this paragraph shall be final; but section 137 of this Act shall apply, with the necessary modifications, in relation to references under this paragraph as it applies in relation to appeals under section 122 of this Act.

Regulations as to residue of agreements

5. The Secretary of State may by regulations make provisions in relation to the provisions of any agreement to which subsection (1) of section 43 of the Control of Pollution Act 1974 applied and which apart from that section would be in force after the commencement of this Act—

(a) for determining, by arbitration or otherwise, whether any such agreement continues to have effect as relating to a matter other than the discharge of trade effluent into a sewerage undertaker's sewer;

(b) for determining, by arbitration or otherwise, what modifications (if any) are appropriate in consequence of any prescribed provision of section 43 of that Act or any provision of this Schedule re-enacting any such provision; and

(c) in a case in which the conditions on which any discharges authorised by such an agreement included, immediately before the coming into force of section 43 of that Act, a condition as to charges in respect of the discharges and other matters—

(i) for determining, by arbitration or otherwise, the proportion of the charges attributable to the discharges; and

(ii) for limiting accordingly the conditions which are to be treated by virtue of section 43 of that Act as included in the deemed consent which has effect by virtue of this Schedule.

Section 155   SCHEDULE 9

MODIFICATION OF COMPENSATION PROVISIONS ETC. IN RELATION TO THE CREATION OF NEW RIGHTS

Compensation enactments

1. Subject to the following provisions of this Schedule, the enactments for the time being in force with respect to compensation for the compulsory purchase of land shall apply with the necessary modifications as respects compensation in the case of a compulsory acquisition under section 155 of this Act of a right by the creation of a new right as they apply as respects compensation on the compulsory purchase of land and interests in land.

Adaptation of the Compulsory Purchase Act 1965

2.—(1) The Compulsory Purchase Act 1965 (in the following provisions of this Schedule referred to as "the 1965 Act") shall have effect with the modifications necessary to make it apply to the compulsory acquisition under section 155 of this Act of a right by the creation of a new right as it applies to the compulsory acquisition under that section of land, so that, in appropriate contexts, references in that Act to land are to be read (according to the requirements of the particular context) as referring to, or as including references to—

(a) the right acquired or to be acquired; or

(b) the land over which the right is or is to be exercisable.

(2) Without prejudice to the generality of sub-paragraph (1) above, Part I of the 1965 Act shall apply in relation to the compulsory acquisition under section 155 of this Act of a right by the creation of a new right with the modifications specified in the following provisions of this Schedule.

Section 7 of the 1965 Act

3. For section 7 of the 1965 Act (measure of compensation) there shall be substituted the following section—

"7. In assessing the compensation to be paid by the acquiring authority under this Act regard shall be had not only to the extent (if any) to which the value of the land over which the right is to be acquired is depreciated by the acquisition of the right but also to the damage (if any) to be sustained by the owner of the land by reason of its severance from other land of his, or injuriously affecting that other land by the exercise of the powers conferred by this or the special Act."

Section 8 of the 1965 Act

4. For subsection (1) of section 8 of the 1965 Act (protection for vendor against severance of house, garden, etc.) there shall be substituted the following subsections—

"(1) No person shall be required to grant any right over part only—
    (a) of any house, building or manufactory; or
    (b) of a park or garden belonging to a house,
if he is willing to sell the whole of the house, building, manufactory, park or garden, unless the Lands Tribunal determine that—
    (i) in the case of a house, building or manufactory, the part over which the right is proposed to be acquired can be made subject to that right without material detriment to the house, building or manufactory; or
    (ii) in the case of a park or garden, the part over which the right is proposed to be acquired can be made subject to that right without seriously affecting the amenity or convenience of the house;
and, if the Lands Tribunal so determine, the Tribunal shall award compensation in respect of any loss due to the acquisition of the right, in addition to its value; and thereupon the party interested shall be required to grant to the acquiring authority that right over the part of the house, building, manufactory, park or garden.

(1A) In considering the extent of any material detriment to a house, building or manufactory, or any extent to which the amenity or convenience of a house is affected, the Lands Tribunal shall have regard not only to the right which is to be acquired over the land, but also to any adjoining or adjacent land belonging to the same owner and subject to compulsory purchase."

Effect of deed poll

5. The following provisions of the 1965 Act (being provisions stating the effect of a deed poll executed in various circumstances where there is no conveyance by persons with interests in the land), that is to say—
    (a) section 9(4) (refusal by owners to convey);
    (b) paragraph 10(3) of Schedule 1 (owners under incapacity);
    (c) paragraph 2(3) of Schedule 2 (absent and untraced owners); and
    (d) paragraphs 2(3) and 7(2) of Schedule 4 (common land),
shall be so modified as to secure that, as against persons with interests in the land which are expressed to be overridden by the deed, the right which is to be compulsorily acquired is vested absolutely in the acquiring authority.

Section 11 of the 1965 Act

6. Section 11 of the 1965 Act (powers of entry) shall be so modified as to secure that, as from the date on which the acquiring authority have served notice to treat in respect of any right, they have power, exercisable in the like circumstances and subject to the like conditions, to enter for the purpose of exercising that right (which shall be deemed for this purpose to have been created on the date of service of the notice); and sections 12 (penalty for unauthorised entry) and 13 (entry on warrant in the event of obstruction) shall be modified correspondingly.

Section 20 of the 1965 Act

7. Section 20 of the 1965 Act (protection for interests of tenants at will etc.) shall apply with the modifications necessary to secure that persons with such interests as are mentioned in that section are compensated in a manner corresponding to that in which they would be compensated on a compulsory acquisition under section 155 of this Act of that land, but taking into account only to the extent (if any) of such interference with such an interest as is actually caused, or likely to be caused, by the exercise of the right in question.

Section 22 of the 1965 Act

8. Section 22 of the 1965 Act (protection of acquiring authority's possession where by inadvertence an estate, right or interest has not been got in) shall be so modified as to enable the acquiring authority, in circumstances corresponding to those referred to in that section, to continue entitled to exercise the right acquired, subject to compliance with that section as respects compensation.

Section 157   SCHEDULE 10

PROCEDURE RELATING TO BYELAWS UNDER SECTION 157

Confirmation of byelaws

1.—(1) No byelaw made by a relevant undertaker under section 157 of this Act shall have effect until confirmed by the Secretary of State under this Schedule.

(2) At least one month before it applies for the confirmation of any such byelaw, a relevant undertaker shall—

(a) cause a notice of its intention to make the application to be published in the London Gazette and in such other manner as it considers appropriate for the purpose of bringing the proposed byelaw to the attention of persons likely to be affected by it; and

(b) cause copies of the notice to be served on any persons carrying out functions under the enactment who appear to it to be concerned.

(3) For at least one month before an application is made by a relevant undertaker for the confirmation of any such byelaw, a copy of it shall be deposited at one or more of the offices of the relevant undertaker, including (if there is one) at an office in the area to which the area to which the byelaw would apply.

(4) A relevant undertaker shall provide reasonable facilities for the inspection free of charge of a byelaw deposited under sub-paragraph (3) above.

(5) Every person shall be entitled, on application to a relevant undertaker, to be furnished free of charge with a printed copy of a byelaw so deposited.

Confirmation with or without modifications

2.—(1) The Secretary of State, with or without a local inquiry, may refuse to confirm any byelaw submitted to him by a relevant undertaker for confirmation under this Schedule, or may confirm the byelaw either without or, if the relevant undertaker consents, with modifications.

(2) The relevant undertaker which has so submitted a byelaw shall, if so directed by the Secretary of State, cause notice of any proposed modifications to be given in accordance with his directions.

Commencement of byelaw

3.—(1) The Secretary of State may fix the date on which any byelaw confirmed under this Schedule is to come into force.

(2) If no date is so fixed, the byelaw shall come into force at the end of the period of one month beginning with the date of confirmation.

Availability of confirmed byelaws

4.—(1) Every byelaw made by a relevant undertaker and confirmed under this Schedule shall be printed and deposited at one or more of the offices of the relevant undertaker, including (if there is one) at an office in the area to which the byelaw applies; and copies of the byelaw shall be available at those offices, at all reasonable times, for inspection by the public free of charge.

(2) Every person shall be entitled, on application to a relevant undertaker and on payment of such reasonable sum as the relevant undertaker may determine, to be furnished with a copy of any byelaw so deposited by that undertaker.

Revocation of byelaws

5. Without prejudice to subsection (5) of section 157 of this Act and subject to paragraph 4(4) of Schedule 2 to the Water Consolidation (Consequential Provisions) Act 1991, if it appears to the Secretary of State that the revocation of a byelaw under that section is necessary or expedient, he may, after—

(a) giving notice to the relevant undertaker which made the byelaw;

(b) considering any representations made by that undertaker; and

(c) if required by that undertaker, holding a local inquiry,

revoke that byelaw.

Proof of byelaws etc.

6. The production of a printed copy of a byelaw purporting to be made by a relevant undertaker upon which is indorsed a certificate, purporting to be signed on its behalf, stating—

(a) that the byelaw was made by that undertaker;

(b) that the copy is a true copy of the byelaw;

(c) that on a specified date the byelaw was confirmed under this Schedule; and

(d) the date, if any, fixed under paragraph 3 above for the coming into operation of the byelaw,

shall be *prima facie* evidence of the facts stated in the certificate, and without proof of the handwriting or official position of any person purporting to sign the certificate.

SCHEDULE 11

Orders conferring Compulsory Works Powers

Applications for orders

1.—(1) Where a water undertaker applies to the Secretary of State for a compulsory works order, it shall—

(a) submit to the Secretary of State a draft of the order applied for;

(b) publish a notice with respect to the application, at least once in each of two successive weeks, in one or more newspapers circulating in each relevant locality;

(c) not later than the date on which that notice is first published—

    (i) serve a copy of the notice on each of the persons specified in relation to the application in sub-paragraph (3) below; and

    (ii) in the case of a draft order which would authorise the stopping-up or diversion of a footpath or bridleway, cause such a copy, together with a plan showing the general effect of the draft order so far as it relates to the footpath or bridleway, to be displayed in a prominent position at the ends of the part of the path or way to be stopped up or diverted;

and

(d) publish a notice in the London Gazette which—

    (i) states that the draft order has been submitted to the Secretary of State;

    (ii) names every local authority on whom a notice is required to be served under this paragraph;

    (iii) specifies a place where a copy of the draft order and of any relevant map or plan may be inspected; and

    (iv) gives the name of every newspaper in which the notice required by virtue of paragraph (b) above was published and the date of an issue containing the notice.

(2) The notice required by virtue of sub-paragraph (1)(b) above to be published with respect to an application for an order by a water undertaker shall—

(a) state the general effect of the order applied for;

(b) in the case of an application made wholly or partly for the purpose of enabling any discharges of water to be made—

    (i) contain particulars of the proposed discharges, stating the purposes of the discharges and specifying each place of discharge;

    (ii) specify the places at which the water to be comprised in the proposed discharges is to be taken and the treatment (if any) which the draft order proposes to require the water, or any of it, to receive before being discharged under the order; and

    (iii) state the effect which, in the opinion of the undertaker, the proposed discharges would have on the flow, level and quality of water in any inland waters or underground strata;

(c) specify a place where a copy of the draft order and of any relevant map or plan may be inspected by any person free of charge at all reasonable times during the period of 28 days beginning with the date of the first publication of the notice; and

(d) state that any person may, within that period, by notice to the Secretary of State object to the making of the order.

(3) The persons mentioned in sub-paragraph (1)(c) above in relation to an application for a compulsory works order a draft of which has been submitted to the Secretary of State are—

(a) the NRA;

(b) every local authority whose area is or includes the whole or any part of a relevant locality;

(c) every water undertaker, not being the applicant, whose area is or includes the whole or any part of such a locality;

(d) every navigation authority, harbour authority and conservancy authority which would be affected by, or has functions in relation to any inland waters which would be affected by, any provision proposed to be made by the order;

(e) every owner, lessee or occupier (except tenants for a month or for any period of less than a month) of any land in relation to which compulsory powers would become exercisable if the order were made in the terms of the draft order;

(f) every person who has given notice to the water undertaker requiring it to notify him of applications for compulsory works orders and has paid such reasonable charge as the undertaker may have required him to pay for being notified by virtue of this paragraph;

(g) such other persons as may be prescribed.

(4) In this paragraph "relevant locality," in relation to an application for an order a draft of which is submitted to the Secretary of State by a water undertaker, means—

(a) any locality which would be affected by any provision proposed to be made by the order for the purpose of enabling any engineering or building operations to be carried out; and

(b) where provision is proposed to be made by the order for the purpose of enabling discharges of water to be made, each locality in which the place of any of the proposed discharges is situated or in which there appears to that undertaker to be any inland waters or underground strata the flow, level or quality of water in which may be affected by any of the proposed discharges.

Supply of copies of draft orders

2. A water undertaker applying for a compulsory works order shall, at the request of any person and on payment by that person of such charge (if any) as the undertaker may reasonably require, furnish that person with a copy of the draft order submitted to the Secretary of State under paragraph 1 above and of any relevant map or plan.

Powers on an application

3.—(1) On an application for a compulsory works order, the Secretary of State may make the order either in the terms of the draft order submitted to him or, subject to sub-paragraphs (2) and (3) below, in those terms as modified in such manner as he thinks fit, or may refuse to make an order.

(2) The Secretary of State shall not make such a modification of a draft order submitted to him by any water undertaker as he considers is likely adversely to affect any persons unless he is satisfied that the undertaker has given and published such additional notices, in such manner, as the Secretary of State may have required.

(3) The Secretary of State shall not, unless all interested parties consent, make a compulsory works order so as to confer in relation to any land any powers of compulsory acquisition which would not have been conferred in relation to that land if the order were made in the terms of the draft order submitted to him under paragraph 1 above.

(4) Where, on an application by a water undertaker for a compulsory works order, the Secretary of State refuses to make an order, the undertaker shall, as soon as practicable after the refusal, notify the refusal to every person on whom it was, by virtue of paragraph 1(1)(c)(i) above, required to serve a copy of the notice with respect to the application.

(5) The duty of a water undertaker under sub-paragraph (4) above shall be enforceable under section 18 of this Act by the Secretary of State.

Consideration of objections etc.

4.—(1) If, where an application for a compulsory works order has been made by a water undertaker, any notice of an objection to it is received, before the end of the relevant period, by the Secretary of State from—

(a) any person on whom a notice under paragraph 1 or 3 above is required to be served; or

(b) from any other person appearing to the Secretary of State to be affected by the order as submitted to him or as proposed to be modified under paragraph 3 above,

then, unless the objection is withdrawn, the Secretary of State shall, before making the order, either cause a local inquiry to be held or afford to the objector and to the undertaker an opportunity of appearing before, and being heard by, a person appointed by the Secretary of State for the purpose.

(2) Where any objection received by the Secretary of State as mentioned in sub-paragraph (1) above relates to any powers of compulsory acquisition, the Secretary of State may require the objector to state in writing the grounds of his objection; and if the Secretary of State is satisfied that the objection relates exclusively to matters that can be dealt with in the assessment of compensation, he may disregard the objection for the purposes of that sub-paragraph.

(3) In this paragraph "the relevant period," in relation to an application for any order, means the period ending with whichever is the later of—

(a) the end of the period of 28 days beginning with the date of the first publication of the notice published with respect to the application for the purposes of paragraph 1(1)(b) above; and

(b) the end of the period of 28 days beginning with the date of the publication in the London Gazette of the notice published for the purposes of the application by virtue of paragraph 1(1)(d) above,

together, in the case of an application for an order modifications to which have been proposed by the Secretary of State, with any further periods specified with respect to the modifications in notices under paragraph 3(2) above.

Notice after making of order

5.—(1) As soon as practicable after a compulsory works order has been made, the undertaker on whose application it is made shall—

(a) publish a notice of the making of the order, at least once in each of two successive weeks, in one or more newspapers circulating in each relevant locality; and

(b) not later than the date on which that notice is first published—

(i) serve a copy of the notice on every person on whom that undertaker was, by virtue of paragraph 1(1)(c)(i) above, required to serve a copy of the notice with respect to the application for the order; and

(ii) in the case of an order authorising the stopping-up or diversion of a footpath or bridleway, cause such a copy, together with a plan showing the general effect of the order so far as it relates to the footpath or bridleway, to be displayed in a prominent position at the ends of the appropriate part of the path or way.

(2) The notice required by virtue of sub-paragraph (1)(a) above to be published with respect to a compulsory works order shall—

(a) state the general effect of the order;

(b) in the case of an order made wholly or partly for the purpose of enabling any discharges of water to be made—

(i) contain particulars of the discharges, stating the purposes of the discharges and specifying each place of discharge;

(ii) specify the places at which the water to be comprised in the discharges is to be taken and the treatment (if any) which the order requires the water, or any of it, to receive before being discharged under the order; and

(iii) state the effect which, in the opinion of the applicant undertaker, the discharges would have on the flow, level and quality of water in any inland waters or underground strata;

and

(c) specify a place where a copy of the order and of any relevant map or plan may be inspected by any person free of charge at all reasonable times.

(3) Where a compulsory works order has been made, the undertaker on whose application it was made shall, at the request of any person and on payment by that person of such charge (if any) as that undertaker may reasonably require, furnish that person with a copy of the order and of any relevant map or plan.

(4) The duties of a water undertaker under this paragraph shall be enforceable under section 18 of this Act by the Secretary of State.

(5) In this paragraph "relevant locality," in relation to any compulsory works order, means—

(a) any locality which is affected by any provision made by the order for the purpose of enabling any engineering or building operations to be carried out; and

(b) where provision is made by the order for the purpose of enabling discharges of water to be made, each locality in which the place of any of the discharges is situated or in which there appears to the undertaker which applied for the order to be any inland waters or underground strata the flow, level or quality of water in which may be affected by any of the discharges.

Compulsory acquisition provisions

6.—(1) Without prejudice to the provisions of Schedule 14 to this Act—

(a) Part I of the Compulsory Purchase Act 1965;

(b) section 4 and Part III of, and Schedule 3 to, the Acquisition of Land Act 1981; and

(c) the enactments for the time being in force with respect to compensation for the compulsory purchase of land,

shall apply in relation to so much of a compulsory works order as confers powers of compulsory acquisition as they apply in relation to a compulsory purchase order made by virtue of section 155 of this Act and, accordingly, shall so apply, where the case so requires, with the modifications made by Schedule 9 to this Act.

(2) Subject to the provisions of sub-paragraph (6) below, if any person aggrieved by a compulsory works order containing powers of compulsory acquisition, or by a certificate given under the special land provisions in connection with such an order, desires—

(a) to question the validity of the order, or of any provision of the order, on the grounds that any powers of compulsory acquisition conferred by the order are not authorised by this Act to be so conferred, or that any of the relevant requirements have not been complied with in relation to the order; or

(b) to question the validity of the certificate on the grounds that any of the relevant requirements have not been complied with in relation to the certificate, he may make an application for the purpose to the High Court at any time before the end of the period of six weeks beginning with the date on which notice of the making of the order is first published in accordance with paragraph 5 above or, as the case may be, notice of the giving of the certificate if first published in accordance with the special land provisions.

(3) On any application under sub-paragraph (2) above with respect to any order to certificate, the High Court—

(a) may by interim order suspend the operation of the order, or any provision of the order, or the certificate (either generally or in so far as it affects any property of the applicant to the High Court) until the final determination of the proceedings; and

(b) if satisfied—

(i) that any powers of compulsory acquisition conferred by the order are not authorised by this Act to be so conferred; or

(ii) that the interests of that applicant have been substantially prejudiced by a failure to comply with any of the relevant requirements in relation to the order or the certificate,

may quash the order, or any provision of the order, or the certificate (either generally or in so far as it affects any property of that applicant).

(4) Except as provided by sub-paragraph (2) above, the validity of any such order or certificate as is mentioned in that sub-paragraph shall not, either before or after the order or certificate has been made or given, be questioned in any legal proceedings whatsoever.

(5) Subject to any order of the High Court under sub-paragraph (3) above, any such order or certificate as is mentioned in sub-paragraph (2) above shall become operative (except, in the case of an order, where it is subject by virtue of the special land provisions to special parliamentary procedure) on the date on which notice of the making or giving of the order or certificate is published as mentioned in the said sub-paragraph (2).

(6) Where an order such as is mentioned in sub-paragraph (2) above is subject to special parliamentary procedure, sub-paragraphs (2) to (4) of this paragraph—

(a) shall not apply to the order if it is confirmed by Act of Parliament under section 6 of the Statutory Orders (Special Procedure) Act 1945; and

(b) in any other case, shall have effect as if the reference in sub-paragraph (2) of this paragraph to the date on which notice of the making of the order is first published in accordance with paragraph 5 above were a reference to the date on which the order becomes operative under the said Act of 1945.

(7) In this paragraph—

"the special land provisions" means the provisions, as applied by virtue of sub-paragraph (1) above, of Part III of the Acquisition of Land Act 1981 or, as the case may require, of Part II of Schedule 3 to that Act; and

"the relevant requirements," in relation to an order or certificate, means the requirements of this Schedule and such requirements of the special land provisions or of any other enactment as are applicable to that order or certificate by virtue of this paragraph.

Compensation in certain cases of compulsory acquisition

7. Where—

(a) in connection with any engineering or building operations to which a compulsory works order relates, a licence under Chapter II of Part II of the Water Resources Act 1991 is granted, or is deemed to be granted, to the water undertaker in question; and

(b) that licence is a licence to abstract water or to obstruct or impede the flow of any inland waters,

no compensation shall be payable by virtue of sub-paragraph (1) of paragraph 6 above in respect of any land or interest injuriously affected by the carrying out of these operations, in so far that land or interest is injuriously affected by the abstraction of water, or the obstruction or impeding of the flow, in accordance with the provisions of the licence.

Compensation in respect of powers other than acquisition powers

8.—(1) If the value of any interest in any relevant land is depreciated by the coming into force of so much of any compulsory works order as—

(a) confers compulsory powers, other than powers of compulsory acquisition, for the purpose of enabling any engineering or building operations to be carried out; and

(b) grants authority for the carrying out of the operations,

the person entitled to that interest shall be entitled to compensation from the applicant for the order of an amount equal to the amount of the depreciation.

(2) Where the person entitled to an interest in any relevant land sustains loss or damage which—

(a) is attributable to so much of any compulsory works order as—

      (i) confers compulsory powers, other than powers of compulsory acquisition, for the
      purpose of enabling any engineering or building operations to be carried out; and
      (ii) grants authority for the carrying out of the operations;
  (b) does not consist in depreciation of the value of that interest; and
  (c) is loss or damage for which he would have been entitled to compensation by way of
      compensation for disturbance, if his interest in that land had been compulsorily acquired
      under section 155 of this Act in pursuance of a notice to treat served on the date on which
      the order comes into force,
he shall be entitled to compensation from the applicant for the order in respect of that loss or
damage, in addition to compensation under sub-paragraph (1) above.

(3) Where any damage to, or injurious affection of, any land which is not relevant land is
attributable to so much of any compulsory works order as—
  (a) confers compulsory powers, other than powers of compulsory acquisition, for the pur-
      pose of enabling any engineering or building operations to be carried out; and
  (b) grants authority for the carrying out of the operations,
the applicant for the order shall pay compensation in respect of that damage or injurious
affection to every person entitled to an interest in that land.

(4) A person who sustains any loss or damage which is attributable to any discharge of water
made by a water undertaker in pursuance of a compulsory works order shall be entitled to
recover compensation from the undertaker in respect of the loss or damage.

(5) For the purposes of sub-paragraph (4) above any extra expenditure—
  (a) which it becomes reasonably necessary for any water undertaker or public authority
      (other than the undertaker making the discharge) to incur for the purpose of property
      carrying out any statutory functions; and
  (b) which is attributable to any such discharge of water as is mentioned in that
      sub-paragraph,
shall be deemed to be a loss sustained by the undertaker or public authority and to be so
attributable.

(6) Any question of disputed compensation under this paragraph, shall be referred to and
determined by the Lands Tribunal; and in relation to the determination of any such compensation the provisions of sections 2 and 4 of the Land Compensation Act 1961 shall apply, subject
to any necessary modifications.

(7) For the purpose of assessing any compensation under this paragraph, so far as that
compensation is in respect of loss or damage consisting in depreciation of the value of an
interest in land, the rules set out in section 5 of the Land Compensation Act 1961 shall, so far as
applicable and subject to any necessary modifications, have effect as they have effect for the
purpose of assessing compensation for the compulsory acquisition of an interest in land.

(8) Where the interest in land in respect of which any compensation falls to be assessed in
accordance with sub-paragraph (7) above is subject to a mortgage—
  (a) the compensation shall be assessed as if the interest were not subject to the mortgage;
  (b) a claim for compensation may be made by any mortgagee of the interest, but without
      prejudice to the making of a claim by the person entitled to the interest;
  (c) no such compensation shall be payable in respect of the interest of the mortgagee (as
      distinct from the interest which is subject to the mortgagee); and
  (d) any such compensation which is payable in respect of the interest which is subject to the
      mortgage shall be paid to the mortgagee, or, if there is more than one mortgagee, to the
      first mortgagee, and shall in either case be applied by him as if it were proceeds of sale.

(9) In this paragraph "relevant land," in relation to a compulsory works order, means any
land which is not land in relation to which powers of compulsory acquisition are conferred by
the order but is—
  (a) land where any operations for which authority is granted by the order are to be carried
      out;
  (b) land in relation to which compulsory powers are conferred by the order; or
  (c) land held with any land falling within paragraph (a) or (b) above.

Protection of public undertakings

9. The provisions of section 186 of this Act and of Part I of Schedule 13 to this Act shall apply,
as they apply in relation to the carrying out of works in exercise of powers under this Act, in
relation to the carrying out of works by virtue of an authority granted by so much of any
compulsory works order as makes provision other than provision conferring powers of compulsory acquisition.

Interpretation

10. In this Schedule—

"bridleway" and "footpath" have the same meanings as in the Highways Act 1980;

"compulsory works order" means an order under section 167 of this Act;

"powers of compulsory acquisition" means any such powers as are mentioned in subsection (4)(a) of section 167 of this Act;

and references to a tenant for a month or for any period of less than a month include references to a statutory tenant, within the meaning of the Landlord and Tenant Act 1985, and to a licensee under an assured agricultural occupancy, within the meaning of Part I of the Housing Act 1988.

Section 180   SCHEDULE 12

COMPENSATION ETC. IN RESPECT OF PIPE-LAYING AND OTHER WORKS POWERS

Compensation in respect of street works powers

1.—(1) This paragraph applies, in relation to a relevant undertaker, to the powers conferred on it in relation to streets by sections 158, 161 and 162 of this Act.

(2) It shall be the duty of every relevant undertaker—

(a) to do as little damage as possible in the exercise of the powers to which this paragraph applies; and

(b) to pay compensation for any loss caused or damage done in the exercise of those powers.

(3) Any dispute as to whether compensation should be paid under sub-paragraph (2) above, or as to the amount of any such compensation, shall be referred to the arbitration of a single arbitrator appointed by agreement between the parties to the dispute or, in default of agreement, by the Secretary of State.

(4) Until the coming into force of Part III of the New Roads and Street Works Act 1991, a payment of compensation under this paragraph shall be treated for the purposes of section 32 of the Public Utilities Street Works Act 1950 (provisions against duplication of compensation) as made under an enactment passed before that Act of 1950; but nothing in this sub-paragraph shall be taken to prejudice the power of the Secretary of State under that Act of 1991 to make an order bringing Part III of that Act into force on different days for different purposes (including the purposes of this paragraph).

Compensation in respect of pipe-laying works in private land

2.—(1) If the value of any interest in any relevant land is depreciated by virtue of the exercise, by any relevant undertaker, of any power to carry out pipe-laying works on private land, the person entitled to that interest shall be entitled to compensation from the undertaker of an amount equal to the amount of the depreciation.

(2) Where the person entitled to an interest in any relevant land sustains loss or damage which—

(a) is attributable to the exercise by any relevant undertaker of any power to carry out pipe-laying works on private land;

(b) does not consist in depreciation of the value of that interest; and

(c) is loss or damage for which he would have been entitled to compensation by way of compensation for disturbance, if his interest in that land had been compulsorily acquired under section 155 of this Act,

he shall be entitled to compensation from the undertaker in respect of that loss or damage, in addition to compensation under sub-paragraph (1) above.

(3) Where any damage to, or injurious affection of, any land which is not relevant land is attributable to the exercise by any relevant undertaker, of any power to carry out pipe-laying works on private land, the undertaker shall pay compensation in respect of that damage or injurious affection to every person entitled to an interest in that land.

(4) The Secretary of State may by regulations make provision requiring a relevant undertaker, where it is proposing or has begun, in a prescribed case, to exercise any power to carry out pipe-laying works on private land, to make advance payments on account of compensation that will become payable in respect of the exercise of that power.

(5) In this paragraph "relevant land," in relation to any exercise of a power to carry out pipe-laying works on private land, means the land where the power is exercised or land held with that land.

(6) In this paragraph the references to a power to carry out pipe-laying works on private land are references to any of the powers conferred by virtue of sections 159, 161(2) and 163 of this Act.

Assessment of compensation under paragraph 2

3.—(1) Any question of disputed compensation under paragraph 2 above shall be referred to and determined by the Lands Tribunal; and in relation to the determination of any such compensation the provisions of sections 2 and 4 of the Land Compensation Act 1961 shall apply, subject to any necessary modifications.

(2) For the purposes of assessing any compensation under paragraph 2 above, so far as that compensation is in respect of loss or damage consisting in depreciation of the value of an interest in land, the rules set out in section 5 of the Land Compensation Act 1961 shall, so far as applicable and subject to any necessary modifications, have effect as they have effect for the purpose of assessing compensation for the compulsory acquisition of an interest in land.

(3) Where the interest in land in respect of which any compensation falls to be assessed in accordance with sub-paragraph (2) above is subject to a mortgage—

(a) the compensation shall be assessed as if the interest were not subject to the mortgage;

(b) a claim for compensation may be made by any mortgagee of the interest, but without prejudice to the making of a claim by the person entitled to the interest;

(c) no such compensation shall be payable in respect of the interest of the mortgagee (as distinct from the interest which is subject to the mortgage); and

(d) any such compensation which is payable in respect of the interest which is subject to the mortgage shall be paid to the mortgagee or, if there is more than one mortgagee, to the first mortgagee, and shall in either case be applied by him as if it were proceeds of sale.

(4) Where, apart from this sub-paragraph, any person entitled to an interest in any land would be entitled under paragraph 2 above to an amount of compensation in respect of any works, there shall be deducted from that amount an amount equal to the amount by which the carrying out of the works has enhanced the value of any other land which—

(a) is contiguous or adjacent to that land; and

(b) is land to an interest in which that person is entitled in the same capacity.

Compensation in respect of sewerage works etc.

4.—(1) Subject to the following provisions of this paragraph, a sewerage undertaker shall make full compensation to any person who has sustained damage by reason of the exercise by the undertaker, in relation to a matter as to which that person has not himself been in default, of any of its powers under the relevant sewerage provisions.

(2) Subject to sub-paragraph (3) below, any dispute arising under this paragraph as to the fact of damage, or as to the amount of compensation, shall be referred to the arbitration of a single arbitrator appointed by agreement between the parties to the dispute or, in default of agreement, by the Secretary of State.

(3) If the compensation claimed under this paragraph in any case does not exceed £50, all questions as to the fact of damage, liability to pay compensation and the amount of compensation may, on the application of either party, be determined by, and any compensation awarded may be recovered before, a magistrates' court.

(4) Sections 300 and 301 of the Public Health Act 1936 (which relate to the determination of questions by courts of summary jurisdiction and to appeals against such determinations) shall apply for the purposes of and in relation to a determination on an application under sub-paragraph (3) above as they apply for the purposes of and in relation to a determination by a magistrates' court under that Act.

(5) No person shall be entitled by virtue of this paragraph to claim compensation on the ground that a sewerage undertaker has, in the exercise of its powers under the relevant sewerage provisions, declared any sewer or sewage disposal works, whether belonging to that person or not, to be vested in the undertaker.

Compensation in respect of metering works

5.—(1) Without prejudice to section 148 of this Act or to paragraph 11 of Schedule 6 to this Act or paragraph 1 above, where a person authorised by any relevant undertaker carries out any works by virtue of section 162 of this Act on any premises, the undertaker shall make good, or pay compensation for, any damage caused by that person or by any person accompanying him by or in connection with the carrying out of the works.

(2) Any dispute between a relevant undertaker and any other person (including another such undertaker)—

(a) as to whether the undertaker should pay any compensation under this paragraph; or

(b) as to the amount of any such compensation,

shall be referred to the arbitration of a single arbitrator appointed by agreement between the undertaker and that person or, in default of agreement, by the Director.

Compensation in respect of discharges for works purposes

6.—(1) It shall be the duty of every water undertaker—

(a) to cause as little loss and damage as possible in the exercise of the powers conferred on it by section 165 of this Act; and

(b) to pay compensation for any loss caused or damage done in the exercise of those powers.

(2) For the purposes of subsection (1) above any extra expenditure—

(a) which it becomes reasonably necessary for any other water undertaker or any sewerage undertaker or public authority to incur for the purpose of properly carrying out any statutory functions; and

(b) which is attributable to any discharge of water under section 165 of this Act,

shall be deemed to be a loss sustained by the undertaker or public authority and to have been caused in exercise of the powers conferred by that section.

(3) Any dispute as to whether compensation should be paid under sub-paragraph (1) above, or as to the amount of any such compensation, shall be referred to the arbitration of a single arbitrator appointed by agreement between the parties to the dispute or, in default of agreement, by the President of the Institution of Civil Engineers.

Section 183   SCHEDULE 13

PROTECTIVE PROVISIONS IN RESPECT OF CERTAIN UNDERTAKINGS

PART I

PROVISIONS APPLYING GENERALLY

General provisions protecting undertakings

1.—(1) Nothing in this Act conferring power on a relevant undertaker to carry out any works shall confer power to do anything, except with the consent of the persons carrying on an undertaking protected by this paragraph, which, whether directly or indirectly, so interferes or will so interfere—

(a) with works or property vested in or under the control of the persons carrying on that undertaking, in their capacity as such; or

(b) with the use of any such works or property,

as to affect injuriously those works or that property or the carrying on of that undertaking.

(2) Without prejudice to the construction of sub-paragraph (1) above for the purposes of its application in relation to the other provisions of this Act, that sub-paragraph shall have effect in its application in relation to the relevant sewerage provisions as if any use of, injury to or interference with any sluices, floodgates, sewers, groynes, sea defences or other works which are vested in or under the control of the NRA or an internal drainage board were such an interference with works or property vested in or under the control of the NRA or that board as to effect injuriously the works or property or the carrying on of the undertaking of the NRA or of that board.

(3) A consent for the purposes of sub-paragraph (1) above may be given subject to reasonable conditions but shall not be unreasonably withheld.

(4) Subject to the following provisions of his Schedule, any dispute—

(a) as to whether anything done or proposed to be done interferes or will interfere as mentioned in sub-paragraph (1) above;

(b) as to whether any consent for the purposes of this paragraph is being unreasonably withheld; or

(c) as to whether any condition subject to which any such consent has been given was reasonable,

shall be referred to the arbitration of a single arbitrator to be appointed by agreement between the parties to the dispute or, in default of agreement, by the President of the Institution of Civil Engineers.

(5) The following are the undertakings protected by this paragraph, that is to say—

(a) the undertakings of the NRA, the Civil Aviation Authority, the British Coal Corporation and the Post Office;

(b) the undertaking of any relevant undertaker;

(c) any undertaking consisting in the running of a telecommunications code system, within the meaning of Schedule 4 to the Telecommunications Act 1984;

(d) any airport to which Part V of the Airports Act 1986 applies;

(e) the undertaking of any public gas supplier within the meaning of Part I of the Gas Act 1986;

(f) the undertaking of any person authorised by a licence under Part I of the Electricity Act 1989 to generate, transmit or supply electricity;

(g) the undertaking of any navigation, harbour or conservancy authority or of any internal drainage board;

(h) the undertaking of any railway undertakers;

(i) any public utility undertaking carried on by a local authority under any Act or under any order having the force of an Act.

(6) For the purposes of this paragraph any reference in this paragraph, in relation to any such airport as is mentioned in sub-paragraph (5)(d) above, to the persons carrying on the undertaking is a reference to the airport operator.

Protection for statutory powers and jurisdiction

2. Nothing in any provision of this Act conferring power on a relevant undertaker to carry out any works shall confer power to do anything which prejudices the exercise of any statutory power, authority or jurisdiction from time to time vested in or exercisable by any persons carrying on an undertaking protected by paragraph 1 above.

Special protection for certain undertakings in respect of street works

3.—(1) Subject to the following provisions of this paragraph and without prejudice to the other provisions of this Schedule, the powers under the street works provisions to break up or open a street shall not be exercisable where the street, not being a highway maintainable at public expense (within the meaning of the Highways Act 1980)—

(a) is under the control or management of, or is maintainable by, railway undertakers or a navigation authority; or

(b) forms part of a level crossing belonging to any such undertakers or to such an authority or to any other person,

except with the consent of the undertakers or authority or, as the case may be, of the person to whom the level crossing belongs.

(2) Sub-paragraph (1) above shall not apply to any exercise of the powers conferred by the street works provisions for the carrying out of emergency works, within the meaning of Part III of the New Roads and Street Works Act 1991.

(3) A consent given for the purposes of sub-paragraph (1) above may be made subject to such reasonable conditions as may be specified by the person giving it but shall not be unreasonably withheld.

(4) Any dispute—

(a) as to whether a consent for the purposes of sub-paragraph (1) above should be given or withheld; or

(b) as to whether the conditions to which any such consent is made subject are reasonable,

shall be referred to the arbitration of a single arbitrator appointed by agreement between the parties to the dispute or, in default of agreement, by the President of the Institution of Civil Engineers.

(5) If any relevant undertaker contravenes, without reasonable excuse, the requirements of sub-paragraph (1) above, it shall be guilty of an offence and liable, on summary conviction, to a fine not exceeding level 3 on the standard scale.

(6) The restrictions contained in paragraphs (1) to (5) of section 32 of the Tramways Act 1870 (protection of tramways) shall apply in relation to any exercise of a power conferred by the street works provisions—

(a) as they apply in relation to the powers mentioned in that section; and

(b) as if references in that section to a tramway included references to a trolley vehicle system.

(7) In this paragraph "the street works provisions" means so much of sections 158, 161 and 162 of this Act as relates to powers exercisable in relation to streets.

(8) Until the coming into force of section 52 of the New Roads and Street Works Act 1991, sub-paragraph (2) above shall have effect as if the reference to Part III of that Act were a reference to the Public Utilities Street Works Act 1950; but nothing in this sub-paragraph shall be taken to prejudice the power of the Secretary of State under that Act of 1991 to make an order bringing that section 52 into force on different days for different purposes (including the purposes of this paragraph).

Protection for telecommunication systems

4. Paragraph 23 of Schedule 2 to the Telecommunications Act 1984 (which provides a procedure for certain cases where works involve the alteration of telecommunication apparatus) shall apply to every relevant undertaker for the purposes of any works carried out by that undertaker in exercise of any of the powers conferred by any enactment (including, in the case of a statutory water company, section 1 of the Statutory Water Companies Act 1991).

PART II

FURTHER PROTECTIVE PROVISIONS IN RESPECT OF SEWERAGE POWERS

Protection for dock undertakers

5.—(1) Subject to the provisions of this paragraph, nothing in the relevant sewerage provisions shall authorise a sewerage undertaker, without the consent of the dock undertakers concerned—

    (a) to interfere with any river, canal, dock, harbour, basin, lock or reservoir so as injuriously to affect navigation thereon or the use thereof or the access thereto, or to interfere with any towing path, so as to interrupt the traffic thereon;

    (b) to interfere with any bridges crossing any river, canal, dock, harbour or basin;

    (c) to carry out any works in, across or under any dock, harbour, basin, wharf, quay or lock, or any land which belongs to dock undertakers and is held or used by them for the purposes of their undertaking;

    (d) to carry out any works which will interfere with the improvement of, or the access to, any river, canal, dock, harbour, basin, lock, reservoir, or towing path, or with any works appurtenant thereto or any land necessary for the enjoyment or improvement thereof.

(2) For the purposes of this paragraph dock undertakers shall be deemed to be concerned with any river, canal, dock, harbour, basin, lock, reservoir, towing path, wharf, quay or land if—

    (a) it belongs to them and forms part of their undertaking; or

    (b) they have statutory rights of navigating on or using it or of demanding tolls or dues in respect of navigation thereon or the use thereof.

(3) A consent under this paragraph shall not be unreasonably withheld.

(4) Any dispute as to whether or not consent under this paragraph is unreasonably withheld shall be referred, if either party so require, to the arbitration of a single arbitrator appointed by agreement between the parties or, in default of agreement, by the President of the Institution of Civil Engineers.

(5) Upon an arbitration under this paragraph, the arbitrator shall determine—

    (a) whether any works which the sewerage undertaker proposes to carry out are such works as under this paragraph the undertaker is not entitled to carry out without the consent of any dock undertakers;

    (b) if they are such works, whether the injury, if any, to the undertakers will be of such a nature as to admit of being fully compensated by money; and

    (c) if the works are of such a nature, the conditions subject to which the sewerage undertaker may carry out the works, including the amount of the compensation (if any) to be paid by the sewerage undertaker to the dock undertakers.

(6) The sewerage undertaker in question shall not proceed to carry out any proposed works if, on an arbitration under this paragraph, the arbitrator determines—

    (a) that the proposed works are such works as the sewerage undertaker is not entitled to carry out without the consent of the dock undertakers; and

    (b) that the works would cause injury to the dock undertakers of such a nature as not to admit of being fully compensated by money,

but, in any other case, the sewerage undertaker may carry out the works subject to compliance with such conditions, including the payment of such compensation, as the arbitrator may have determined.

(7) Nothing in this paragraph shall be construed as limiting the powers of a sewerage undertaker under this Act in respect of the opening and the breaking up of streets and bridges for the purpose of constructing, laying and maintaining sewers, drains and pipes.

Protection for airports, railways etc.

6.—(1) Subject to the provisions of this paragraph, nothing in the relevant sewerage provisions shall authorise a sewerage undertaker, without the consent of the Civil Aviation Authority or, as the case may be, of the airport operator or railway undertakers concerned, to carry out any works along, across or under—

    (a) any property of the Civil Aviation Authority;

    (b) an airport to which Part V of the Airports Act 1986 applies; or

    (c) any railway of any railway undertakers.

(2) Sub-paragraphs (3) to (7) of paragraph 5 above shall apply for the purposes of this paragraph as they apply for the purposes of sub-paragraph (1) of that paragraph but as if references to the dock undertakers were references, as the case may require, to the Civil Aviation Authority, to the relevant airport operator or to the railway undertakers.

Saving for Part I and other powers

7. The provisions of this Part of this Schedule are without prejudice to the provisions of Part I of this Schedule or to any power conferred on a sewerage undertaker otherwise than by the relevant sewerage provisions.

Section 188   SCHEDULE 14

MINERAL RIGHTS

Acquisition of mineral rights

1.—(1) This paragraph applies in each of the following cases, that is to say—
  (a) where a relevant undertaker acquires any land (whether compulsorily in exercise of any power conferred by or under this Act or otherwise); and
  (b) where a relevant undertaker carries out any works in relation to any land for the purposes of, or in connection with, the carrying out of any of its functions.

(2) Subject to sub-paragraph (3) below, a relevant undertaker shall not, by virtue only of its acquisition of the land or the carrying out of the works, become entitled to any mines or minerals lying under the land; and, accordingly, any such mines or minerals shall be deemed to be excepted from any instrument by virtue of which the land vests in the relevant undertaker unless express provision to the contrary is contained—
  (a) where the land vests in the relevant undertaker by virtue of a conveyance, in the conveyance; or
  (b) where the land is acquired by the relevant undertaker in pursuance of any power of compulsory acquisition conferred by or under this Act, in the order authorising the acquisition.

(3) A relevant undertaker shall be entitled to such parts of any mines or minerals that lie under the land as it may be necessary for it to dig, carry away or use in carrying out any works for the purposes of constructing, making, erecting or laying any part of its undertaking.

Notice required for the working of underlying mines

2.—(1) If the owner of any mines or minerals underlying any part of a relevant undertaker's undertaking proposes to work them, he shall, not less than thirty days before the commencement of working, serve notice of his intention to do so on the relevant undertaker.

(2) On receipt of a notice under sub-paragraph (1) above the relevant undertaker may cause the mines or minerals to be inspected by a person designated by it for the purpose.

(3) Subject to sub-paragraph (5) and paragraph 3 below, if, where notice has been served under this paragraph, the relevant undertaker—
  (a) considers that the working of the underlying mines or minerals is likely to damage any part of its undertaking;
  (b) is willing to compensate the owner of the mines or minerals for the restriction imposed by virtue of this sub-paragraph; and
  (c) serves notice to that effect on the owner of the mines or minerals before the end of the period of thirty days mentioned in sub-paragraph (1) above,
the owner shall not work the mines or minerals except to such extent as may be determined by the relevant undertaker, and the relevant undertaker shall so compensate the owner.

(4) Any dispute as to the amount of any compensation payable by virtue of sub-paragraph (3) above shall be referred to and determined by the Lands Tribunal.

(5) If before the end of the period of thirty days mentioned in sub-paragraph (1) above, no notice has been served under sub-paragraph (3)(c) above by the relevant undertaker, the entitlement of the owner of the mines and minerals to work them shall be an entitlement to work them by proper methods and in the usual manner of working such mines or minerals in the district in question.

(6) If any damage to the undertaking of a relevant undertaker is caused by the working otherwise than as authorised by this paragraph of any mines or minerals underlying any part of its undertaking—
  (a) the owner of the mines or minerals shall, at his own expense, forthwith repair the damage; and
  (b) the relevant undertaker may, without waiting for the owner to perform his duty, repair the damage and may recover the expenses reasonably incurred by it in doing so from the owner.

Mining communications

3.—(1) If the working of any mines or minerals is prevented by reason of any of the preceding provisions of this Schedule, the owner of the mines or minerals may cut and make such communication works through the mines or minerals, or the strata in which they are situated, as are required for the ventilation, drainage and working of mines or minerals which are not underlying any part of the undertaking of the relevant undertaker in question.

(2) Communication works cut or made under this paragraph—

(a) shall not, in a case where—

> (i) the part of the undertaking in question was constructed, made, erected or laid in pursuance of an order made under any enactment or is situated on land acquired by the relevant undertaker in pursuance of any powers of compulsory acquisition; and

> (ii) the order authorising the works or acquisition designates dimensions or sections for the communication works,

exceed those dimensions or fail to conform to those sections; and

(b) in any other case, shall not be more than 2.44 metres high or more than 2.44 metres wide.

(3) Communication works cut or made under this paragraph shall not be cut or made on the land where the part of the undertaking is situated so as to cause damage to that part of the undertaking.

(4) Where works carried out under this paragraph by the owner of any mines or minerals cause loss or damage to the owner or occupier of land lying over the mines or minerals, the relevant undertaker shall pay full compensation to him for the loss or damage.

(5) Sub-paragraph (4) above shall not apply where the person sustaining the loss or damage is the owner of the mines.

(6) In this paragraph "communication works" means airways, headways, gateways or water levels.

Compensation relating to severance

4.—(1) Where mines or minerals underlying any part of a relevant undertaker's undertaking are situated so as, on two or more sides of that land, to extend beyond the land on which that part of the undertaking is situated, the relevant undertaker shall from time to time pay to the owner of the mines or minerals (in addition to any compensation under paragraph 2 above) any expenses and losses incurred by him in consequence of—

(a) the severance by the undertaking of the land lying over the mines;

(b) the interruption of continuous working of the mines in consequence of paragraph 2(3) above;

(c) the mines being so worked in accordance with restrictions imposed by virtue of this Act or any order made under this Act,

and shall pay for any minerals not purchased by the relevant undertaker which cannot be got or won by reason of the part of the undertaking in question being situated where it is or by reason of the requirement to avoid damage to any part of the relevant undertaker's undertaking.

(2) Any dispute as to whether any sum should be paid under this paragraph or as to the amount payable shall be referred to the arbitration of a single arbitrator appointed by agreement between the relevant undertaker and the owner of the mines or minerals or, in default of agreement, by the Secretary of State.

Powers of entry

5.—(1) Any person designated in writing for the purpose by a relevant undertaker may, for any purpose specified in sub-paragraph (2) below—

(a) enter on any land in which the mines or minerals are, or are thought to be, being worked, and which is in or near to the land where any part of that undertaker's undertaking is situated; and

(b) enter the mines and any works connected with the mines.

(2) The purposes mentioned in sub-paragraph (1) above are—

(a) carrying out any inspection under paragraph 2(2) above;

(b) ascertaining whether any mines or minerals have been worked so as to damage the undertaking of the relevant undertaker in question; and

(c) carrying out any works and taking any other steps which the relevant undertaker in question is authorised to carry out or take under paragraph 2(6) above.

(3) A person authorised to enter any premises under this paragraph may—

(a) make use of any equipment belonging to the owner of the mines or minerals in question; and

(b) use all necessary means for discovering the distance from any part of the undertaking of the relevant undertaker to the parts of the mines or the minerals which are, or are about to be, worked.

(4) Part II of Schedule 6 to this Act shall apply to the rights and other powers conferred by this paragraph.

No exemption for injury to mines and minerals

6. Nothing in any provision of this Act or of any order made under this Act shall be construed as exempting a relevant undertaker from any liability to which it would, apart from that provision, have been subject in respect of any damage to any mines or minerals underlying any part of its undertaking or in respect of any loss sustained in relation to any such mines or minerals by a person having an interest therein.

Interpretation

7.—(1) In this Schedule—

"conveyance" has the same meaning as in the Law of Property Act 1925;

"designated distance," in relation to any part of a relevant undertaker's undertaking, means, subject to sub-paragraph (6) below, thirty-seven metres;

"mines" means mines of coal, ironstone, slate or other minerals;

"owner," in relation to mines and minerals, includes a lessee or occupier; and

"underlying" in relation to any part of the undertaking of a relevant undertaker, means lying under, or within the designated distance from, that part of that undertaking.

(2) For the purposes of this Schedule the undertaking of a relevant undertaker shall be taken to consist of so much of any of the following as is for the time being vested in or held by that undertaker for the purposes of, or in connection with, the carrying out of any of its functions, that is to say—

(a) any buildings, reservoirs, wells, boreholes or other structures; and

(b) any pipes or other underground works particulars of which fall or would fall to be incorporated in any records kept under section 198 or 199 of this Act.

(3) References in this Schedule to the working of any mines or minerals include references to the draining of mines and to the winning or getting of minerals.

(4) For the purposes of this Schedule land shall be treated as acquired by a relevant undertaker in pursuance of powers of compulsory acquisition if it—

(a) was so acquired by a water authority established under section 2 of the Water Act 1973 or any predecessor of such a water authority or by a predecessor of a statutory water company; and

(b) is now vested in that undertaker in accordance with a scheme under Schedule 2 to the Water Act 1989 or Schedule 2 to this Act or otherwise.

(5) In relation—

(a) to any land treated by virtue of sub-paragraph (4) above as acquired in pursuance of powers of compulsory acquisition; or

(b) to any land acquired by a statutory water company before September 1, 1989 in pursuance of any such powers,

references in this Schedule to the order authorising the acquisition include references to any local statutory provision which immediately before September 1, 1989 had effect in relation to that land for the purposes of any provisions corresponding to the provisions of this Schedule.

(6) For the purposes of this Schedule where—

(a) any part of a relevant undertaker's undertaking was constructed, made, erected or laid in pursuance of an order made under any enactment or is situated on land acquired by the relevant undertaker in pursuance of any powers of compulsory acquisition; and

(b) the order authorising the works or acquisition designates any distance for the purposes of any enactment relating to mines or minerals underlying that part of the undertaking,

then for the purposes of this Schedule that distance shall be the designated distance in relation to that part of the undertaking, instead of the distance specified in sub-paragraph (1) above.

Section 206   SCHEDULE 15

DISCLOSURE OF INFORMATION

PART I

PERSONS IN RESPECT OF WHOSE FUNCTIONS DISCLOSURE MAY BE MADE

Any Minister of the Crown.
The Director General of Fair Trading.
The Monopolies Commission.
The Director General of Telecommunications.
The Civil Aviation Authority.
The Director General of Gas Supply.

The Director General of Electricity Supply.
A local weights and measures authority in England and Wales.

PART II

ENACTMENTS ETC. IN RESPECT OF WHICH DISCLOSURE MAY BE MADE

The Trade Descriptions Act 1968.
The Fair Trading Act 1973.
The Consumer Credit Act 1974.
The Restrictive Trade Practices Act 1976.
The Resale Prices Act 1976.
The Estate Agents Act 1979.
The Competition Act 1980.
The Telecommunications Act 1984.
The Airports Act 1986.
The Gas Act 1986.
The Consumer Protection Act 1987.
The Electricity Act 1989.
Any subordinate legislation made for the purpose of securing compliance with the Directive of the Council of the European Communities dated September 10, 1984 (No. 84/450/EEC) on the approximation of the laws, regulations and administrative provisions of the Member States concerning misleading advertising.

Table of Derivations

Notes:

1. The following abbreviations are used in this Table:—

1936	= The Public Health Act 1936 (c. 49)
1937	= The Public Health (Drainage of Trade Premises) Act 1937 (c. 40)
1945	= The Water Act 1945 (c. 42)
1948	= The Water Act 1948 (c. 22)
1961(F)	= The Factories Act 1961 (c. 34)
1961	= The Public Health Act 1961 (c. 64)
1963(L)	= The London Government Act 1963 (c. 33)
1973	= The Water Act 1973 (c. 37)
1974	= The Control of Pollution Act (c. 40)
1977	= The Criminal Law Act 1977 (c. 45)
1980	= The Highways Act 1980 (c. 66)
1981	= The Water Act 1981 (c. 12)
1981(SC)	= The Supreme Court Act 1981 (c. 54)
1982(CA)	= The Civil Aviation Act 1982 (c. 16)
1982(CJA)	= The Criminal Justice Act 1982 (c. 43)
1985	= The Local Government Act 1985 (c. 51)
1985	= The Water (Fluoridation) Act 1985 (c. 63)
1986(AA)	= The Airports Act 1986 (c. 31)
1986(GA)	= The Gas Act 1986 (c. 44)
1989	= The Water Act 1989 (c. 15)
1989(EA)	= The Electricity Act 1989 (c. 29)
1990(FS)	= The Food Safety Act 1990 (c. 16)
1990(EP)	= The Environmental Protection Act 1990 (c. 43)
1991(NR)	= The New Roads and Street Works Act 1991 (c. 22)
R: (followed by a number)	= The recommendation so numbered as set out in the Appendix to the Report of the Law Commission (Cm. 1483).

2. The functions originally vested in the Minister of Health under 1936 and 1937 have become vested in the Secretary of State as a result of the following transfer of functions orders ("TFOs"): S.I. 1951/142; S.I. 1951/1900; S.I. 1965/319; 1970/1681. Other TFOs, where applicable in relation to a provision re-enacted in this Bill, are specified at the appropriate place in column 2 of this Table.

3. General provisions contained in section 32 of the Magistrates' Courts Act 1980 (c. 43) and section 46 of the Criminal Justice Act 1982 (c. 48) provide, respectively, for the maximum fine on summary conviction of an either way offence to be the statutory maximum and for a reference to the amount of the maximum fine to which a person is liable in respect of a summary

offence to become a reference to a level on the standard scale. Where the effect of one of these enactments is consolidated it is not referred to separately in column 2 of this Table.

Provision of Act	Derivation
1	1989 s.5.
2	1989 s.7(1)–(4).
3	1989 ss.8(1)–(3), (5)–(7) & 20(8)(a)(i) & (c).
4	1989 ss.9 & 20(8)(a)(i) & (c); 1990(EP) Sched. 9, para. 17(2).
5	1989 s.10; 1990(EP) Sched. 9, para. 17(3).
6	1989 s.11(1)–(3), (5) & (8).
7	1989 ss.11(4)(part), (6) & (7) & 12(2).
8	1989 s.13(1), (2)(part), (3), (5) & (7).
9	
(1)	1989 s.13(2)(part).
(2)	1989 s.13(4).
(3) & (4)	1989 s.12(3) & (4).
(5)	1989 s.12(4) & (6).
10	1989 s.13(6).
11	1989 s.14(1), (3) & (8)–(10).
12	1989 s.14(2), (6) & (7).
13	1989 s.15.
14	1989 s.16.
15	1989 s.17.
16	1989 s.18.
17	1989 s.19.
18	1989 s.20(1)–(4) & (7)–(10).
19	1989 s.20(5), (6) & (8).
20	1989 s.21.
21	1989 s.22(1)–(3).
22	1989 s.22(4)–(8).
23	1989 s.23(2), (3), (8) & (9).
24	1989 s.23(1), (4)–(7) & (9).
25	1989 s.24(2).
26	1989 ss.24(1) & 23(9).
27	1989 s.26.
28	1989 s.6.
29	1989 s.27(1), (3) & (4).
30	1989 s.27(2).
31	1989 s.28.
32	1989 s.29(1), (3) & (4).
33	1989 s.29(3), (5), (6) & (10).
34	1989 s.30(1)–(5).
35	1989 ss.29(2), (8) & (9) & 30(6).
36	1989 s.12(1), (5) & (6).
37	1989 ss.37 & 38(6).
38	1989 s.38(1)–(3).
39	1989 s.38(4).
40	1989 s.39.
41	1989 s.40(1) & (2) & (6)–(8).
42	1989 s.41(1), (2) & (8)–(10).
43	1989 s.41(3)–(7) & (9).
44	1989 s.40(3)–(5) & (8).
45	1989 ss.42(1), (2) & (5), 44(1), (4) & (5) & 176.
46	1989 ss.42(3)–(5) & 44(1) & (4)–(6).
47	1989 s.43(1) & (2).
48	1989 s.43(3).
49	1989 s.43(4)–(6).
50	1989 s.43(7).
51	1989 ss.42(6), 44(2), (3) & (7) & 176.
52	1989 s.45(1)–(5).
53	1989 s.45(6).
54	1989 s.45(7) & (8).
55	1989 ss.46(1)–(3), (7)–(9) & 49(1)(part).
56	1989 s.46(4)–(6).

Provision of Act	Derivation
57	1989 s.47(1), (2), (4)–(9) & (11).
58	1989 s.47(3) & (6)–(11).
59	1989 s.48.
60	1989 s.49(1)–(3).
61	1989 s.49(1) & (4)–(6).
62	1989 s.49(1) & (7).
63	1989 s.49(8) & (9).
64	1989 s.50.
65	1989 s.51(1)–(4) & (7)–(9).
66	1989 s.51(5), (6) & (10).
67	1989 s.65.
68	1989 s.52; 1990(FS) s.55(2).
69	1989 s.53; 1990(FS) s.55(2).
70	1989 s.54.
71	1945 s.14(9), (10) & (12); 1948 s.5(4); 1977 Sched. 6; 1989 Sched. 25, para. 7(1).
72	1945 s.21(1), (3) & (4); 1989 Sched. 25, para. 7(4)(a) & (d); R: 21.
73	1989 s.61.
74	1989 s.62(1)–(4), (6) & (7) & Sched. 26, para. 19.
75	1989 s.63.
76	1945 s.16(1)–(4); 1977 Sched. 6; IA s.17; 1989 Sched. 25, para. 7(3)(a)–(c).
77	1989 s.56(1) & (4)–(6).
78	1989 s.56(2) & (3); 1990(FS) s.55(3).
79	1989 ss.55 & 56(2)(part).
80	1989 ss.57 & 164(3); 1990 (FS) s.55(4).
81	1989 s.58(1)–(4).
82	1989 s.58(5)–(10).
83	1989 s.164.
84	1945 ss.21(2) & (2A), 53 & 59; 1963(L) Sched. 11, Pt. I, para. 27; 1989 ss.59(2) & 62(4) & Sched. 25, para. 7(4)(b) & (c).
85	1989 s.59(1), (4) & (5).
86	1989 s.60(1)–(4) & (6).
87	1985 ss.1 & 5; 1989 Sched. 25, para. 73.
88	1985 ss.2 & 5; 1989 Sched. 25, para. 73.
89	1985 ss.4 & 5; 1989 Sched. 25, para. 73.
90	1989 s.172.
91	Introduces Sched. 7.
92	1989 s.171.
93	1989 ss.66 & 164(3) & Sched. 19, para. 11; 1990(FS) s.55(5) & (6).
94	1989 ss.67 & 68(6).
95	1989 s.68(1)–(3).
96	1989 s.68(4).
97	1989 s.73 & Sched. 25, para. 3.
98	1989 s.71(1)–(3), (7) & (8).
99	1989 s.72(1), (2) & (8)–(10).
100	1989 s.72(3)–(7) & (9).
101	1989 s.71(4)–(6) & (9).
102	1936 s.17(1), (2) & (4)–(6); 1973 s.14; 1989 Sched. 8, para. 1.
103	1936 s.17(7)–(9); 1973 s.14; 1989 Sched. 8, para. 1; R: 1.
104	1936 s.18(1)–(4); 1973 s.14; 1989 s.176 and Sched. 8, paras. 1 & 2(1).
105	1936 ss.17(3) & 18(4)–(6); 1973 s.14; 1989 s.176 and Sched. 8, paras. 1 & 2(1).
106	1936 ss.34(1) & (3), 303–302 & 343(1)(part); 1961(F) s.184 & Sched. 6, para. 1; 1973 s.14 & Sched. 8, para. 37; 1989 Sched. 8, paras. 1 & 2(6)(a).
107	1936 ss.36 & 291–294; 1973 s.14; 1974 Sched. 2, para. 9; 1982(CJA) s.38; 1989 Sched. 8, paras. 1 & 2(7).
108	1936 s.34(2) & (4); 1973 s.14; 1989 Sched. 8, paras. 1 & 2(6)(b).
109	1936 ss.34(5) & 291–294; 1973 s.14; 1974 Sched. 2, para. 8; 1982(CJA) s.38; 1989 Sched. 8, para. 1.

Provision of Act	Derivation
110	1989 s.70(3)–(5).
111	1936 ss.27, 297 & 343(1)(part); 1974 Sched. 2, para. 7.
112	1936 s.19; 1989 Sched. 8, para. 2(2).
113	1936 ss.42, 90(1)(part) & 300–302; 1973 s.14; 1974 s.43(6); 1989 Sched. 8, paras. 1 & 5(1)(a).
114	1936 ss.48 & 343(1)(part); 1973 Sched. 8, para. 39; 1989 Sched. 8, para. 1.
115	1936 s.21; 1973 s.14; 1980(H) Sched. 24, para. 4(b); 1985(LG) Sched. 4, para. 47; 1989 Sched. 8, paras. 1 & 2(3).
116	1936 s.22; 1973 s.14; 1989 Sched. 8, paras. 1 & 2(4).
117	1936 ss.30, 31, 90(5), 283 & 343(1); 1963(L) Sched. 11, Pt. I, paras. 1 & 24(b); 1973 s.14; 1989 ss.71(2) & (9), 72(7)(part) & Sched. 8, para. 1.
118	1937 ss.1 & 2(5) & (5A); 1961 s.69(1); 1973 s.14; 1989 Sched. 8, paras. 1 & 3(1)(c); R: 2.
119	1937 s.2(1); 1973 s.14; 1989 Sched. 8, paras. 1 & 3(1)(a).
120	1989 Sched. 9, paras. 1(1), (2), (4) & (5), 5 & 9.
121	1937 ss.2(3), (5) & (5A) & 14(1); 1961 ss.1(3) & 59; 1973 s.14; 1989 Sched. 8, paras. 1 & 3(1)(b) & (c).
122	1937 s.3; 1961 ss.61 & 66(2); 1973 s.14; 1989 Sched. 8, paras. 1 & 3(2) & (3).
123	1989 Sched. 9, para. 1(3)–(6).
124	1961 s.60(1)–(4), (6) & (8); 1973 s.14; 1989 Sched. 8, para. 1.
125	1974 s.45(1)–(3); 1989 Sched. 8, para. 5(3).
126	1961 s.60(5)–(7) & 66(2); 1973 s.14; 1974 s.45(4); 1989 Sched. 8, paras. 1 & 4(2) & (4) & 5(3) & (4).
127	1989 Sched. 9, para. 2.
128	1961 s.62; 1973 s.14; 1989 Sched. 8, paras. 1 & 4(2).
129	1936 s.90(5); 1937 ss.7(1) & (2) & 14(2); 1973 s.14; 1989 Sched. 8, para. 1; R: 2.
130	1989 Sched. 9, paras. 1(1), (4) & (5) & 5.
131	1989 Sched. 9, paras. 2.
132	1989 Sched. 9, paras. 3, 4(3) & 7.
133	1989 Sched. 9, paras. 4 & 5.
134	1989 Sched. 9, para. 6.
135	1989 Sched. 8, paras. 3(4) & 4(3).
136	1961 s.67(1).
137	1961 s.66(1); 1981(SC) Sched. 5.
138	1989 s.74; 1990(EP) Sched. 15, para. 28.
139	1961 s.64; TFOs: S.I. 1965/319; S.I. 1970/1681.
140	Introduces Sched. 8.
141	1936 s.283; 1937 ss.13 & 14(1); 1961 ss.1(3) & 63(1); 1973 s.14; 1989 Sched. 8, paras. 1 & 4(5).
142	1989 s.75.
143	1989 s.76.
144	1989 s.77 & Sched. 26, para. 16(10).
145	1989 s.80.
146	1989 s.79.
147	1989 s.81.
148	1989 Sched. 10, paras. 2(1)–(3) & (5) & 5.
149	1989 s.78(2) & (3).
150	1989 s.82.
151	1944 (c. 26) s.1(1), (4) & (5), 1955 (c.13) s.1; 1971 (c. 49) s. 1; 1989 Sched. 25, paras. 6 & 21; TFOs: S.I. 1951/142; S.I. 1951/1900; S.I. 1965/319; S.I. 1970/1681.
152	1989 s.170(7).
153	1989 s.25.
154	1989 s.184.
155	1989 s.151.
156	1989 s.152; 1990(EP) Sched. 8, para. 8 & Sched. 9, para. 17(4).
157	1989 ss.158 & 186.
158	1989 Sched. 19, paras. 1(1) & 2(1)–(3), (7) & (8).
159	1989 Sched. 19, paras. 1(1) & 4.

Provision of Act	Derivation
160	1936 ss.275 & 291–294; 1945 Sched. 4; 1973 s.14; 1989 Sched. 8, para. 1.
161	1989 s.154 & Sched. 19, paras. 1(2), 2(1)(c) & (d) & 4(1)(c) & (d).
162	1989 Sched. 10, paras. 1(1)–(3), (5) & (7) & 5 & Sched. 19, para. 1(5).
163	1989 Sched. 19, para. 5.
164	1945 ss.15, 53 & 59(1); 1963(L) Sched. 11, Pt. I, para. 27; 1972 (c. 61) s.18(6); 1973 Sched. 8, para. 49; 1989 Sched. 25, para. 7(2).
165	1989 Sched. 19, paras. 1(1) & 8(1), (5) & (6).
166	1989 s.176 & Sched. 19, para. 9(1) & (3)–(8) & Sched. 26, para. 43(1).
167	1989 ss.155 and 157(1).
168	1989 Sched. 19, para. 10(1)–(3).
169	1989 s.156(1)–(5).
170	1945 ss.16(5) & 21(2); 1948 s.6; 1989 ss.62(4) & 64(1)–(3) & (5) & Sched. 25, para. 7(3)(d) & (4); 1990(FS) s.55(2).
171	1936 s.287; 1937 s.10; 1973 s.14; 1974 Sched. 3, para. 10; 1989 Sched. 8, paras. 1, 2(9) & 3(7).
172	1961 s.67(2); 1989 Sched. 10, para. 1(1) & (4).
173	1989 s.180.
174	1945 s.35(4); 1977 s.31(6); 1989 s.167 & Sched. 25, para. 7(5)(b).
175	1989 Sched. 10, para. 3(1) & (2).
176	1989 Sched. 10, paras. 3(3) & (4) & 5.
177	1989 Sched. 10, paras. 3(5) & (6) & 5.
178	1936 ss.288 & 289; 1982(CJA) ss.35 & 38.
179	1945 s.35(2); 1989 s.153, Sched. 19, para. 1(1) & Sched. 25, para. 7(5)(a).
180	Introduces Sched. 12.
181	1989 s.162(1)–(5), (10) & (11).
182	1989 s.162(6)–(10).
183	Introduces Sched. 13.
184	1936 s.330 & 332; 1973 s.14; 1982(CA) Sched. 2, para. 1(2); 1986(AA) Sched. 2, para. 2; 1989 Sched. 8, para. 1.
185	1989 s.161.
186	1936 ss.331, 332, 334 & 339; 1973 s.14; 1989 s.160(4)–(7) & (9) & Sched. 8, para. 1.
187	1936 s.340; 1989 Sched. 19, para. 7; TFO: S.I. 1970/1537.
188	1989 s.159.
189	1936 s.276; 1973 s.14; 1989 Sched. 8, para. 1.
190	1989 s.163; 1990 (c. 11) Sched. 2, para. 81(2).
191	1989 s.157(2)–(4).
192	1936 s.328; 1989 Sched. 19, paras. 1(3), (4) & (6) & 11.
193	1989 s.35.
194	1989 s.36.
195	1989 s.31.
196	1937 s.7A; 1989 Sched. 8, para. 3(5).
197	1989 Sched. 19, para. 9(2) & (8).
198	1989 s.165.
199	1989 s.166(1), (2), (3)(b) & (5)–(9).
200	1989 s.166(3)(a), (4) & (8) & (9).
201	1989 s.34.
202	1989 s.32.
203	1989 s.33.
204	1937 s.9; 1973 s.14; 1974 Sched. 2, para. 14; 1982(CJA) s.38; 1989 Sched. 8, para. 1.
205	1989 Sched. 10, paras. 4 & 5.
206	1961 s.68; 1989 s.174 & Sched. 9, para. 8; R: 11.
207	1945 s.45; 1989 s.175 & Sched. 25, para. 7(8); R: 12.
208	1989 s.170(1)–(6) & (9).
209	1981 s.6; 1986(GA) Sched. 7, para. 2(6); 1989 Sched. 25, para. 63; 1989(EA) Sched. 16, para. 1(5); 1990 (c. 11) para. 46; 1991(NR) Sched. 8, para. 106.
210	1989 s.177; R: 13.
211	1936 s.298; 1973 s.14; 1989 Sched. 8, para. 1.
212	1989 s.182.

Provision of Act	Derivation
213	1936 s.319; 1946 (c. 36) ss.4(3) and 5(2); 1974 s.104; 1989 s.185.
214	1936 ss.283; 1937 s.14(2); 1961 s.1(3); 1973 s.14; 1989 s.189 (definition of "prescribed" & Sched. 8, paras. 1, 3(7) & 4(6).
215	1936 s.318; 1989 s.181 & Sched. 8, paras. 1 & 2(10).
216	1989 s.187; R: 14.
217	1989 s.188.
218	1989 s.189(2) & (3); R: 21.
219	1936 ss.90(4) & 343(1)(part); 1961 s.67(3); 1989 ss.43(8), 77(5), 78(4), 160(3), 166(9), 167(7) & 189 & Sched. 8, para. 2(12), Sched. 10, para. 6 & Sched. 19, paras. 1, 3(6), 8(8) & 11; 1991(NR) Sched. 8, para. 116(3); R: 15 & 17–20.
220	1989 s.191(6).
221	1936 s.341; 1989 s.192 & Sched. 8, para. 1; 1990 (c. 11) Sched. 2, para. 81(3).
222	1985 s.5(2); 1989 s.193 & Sched. 25, para. 73.
Sched. 1	1989 Sched. 3, paras. 1–5.
Sched. 2	1989 Sched. 5.
Sched. 3	1989 Sched. 6.
Sched. 4	1989 Sched. 4, paras. 1–5.
Sched. 5	1989 Sched. 7.
Sched. 6	
Pt. I	1936 ss.287 & 288; 1945 s.48; 1961(F) s.184 & Sched. 6, para. 1; 1973 s.14; 1989 Sched. 8, para. 1.
Pt. II	1989 ss.59(3), 60(5), 62(5), 64(4) & (5), 156(6), 178 & 179, Sched. 10, para. 1(6), Sched. 19, para. 10(4) & (5) & Sched. 21, para. 5(4); 1991(NR) Sched. 8, para. 116(4).
Sched. 7	1985 ss.3 & 4.
Sched. 8	1937 ss.4(4) & 7(4) & (5); 1961 s.63(8); 1973 s.14; 1974 Sched. 3, para. 9; 1989 Sched. 8, paras. 1, 3(2) & (4), 4(2) & 5(2).
Sched. 9	1989 Sched. 18.
Sched. 10	1989 Sched. 24.
Sched. 11	1989 Sched. 20.
Sched. 12	1936 ss.278 & 303; 1973 s.14; 1989 Sched. 8, para. 1, Sched. 10, paras. 1(2), 2(4) & 5 & Sched. 19, paras. 2(4)–(6), 6 & 8(2)–(4).
Sched. 13	1936 ss.333 & 334; 1973 s.14; 1982(CA) Sched. 2, para. 1(2); 1986(AA) Sched. 2, para. 2; 1989 s.160(1)–(3) & (6)–(8) & Sched. 8, para. 1, Sched. 10, para. 1(2) & Sched. 19, paras. 2(9) & 3; 1989(EA) Sched. 16, para. 37; 1991(NR) Sched. 8, para. 116(4).
Sched. 14	1989 Sched. 21.
Sched. 15	1989 s.174(2)(d) & (3).

TABLE OF DESTINATIONS

Public Health Act 1936
c.49

Public Health (Drainage of Trade Premises) Act 1937
c.40

Rural Water Supplies and Sewerage Act 1944
c.26

Water Act 1945
c.42

Statutory Instruments Act 1946
c.36

TABLE OF DESTINATIONS

WATER ACT 1948
c.22

RURAL WATER SUPPLIES AND SEWERAGE ACT 1955
c.13

PUBLIC HEALTH ACT 1961
c.64

FACTORIES ACT 1961
c.34

LONDON GOVERNMENT ACT 1963
c.33

RURAL WATER SUPPLIES AND SEWERAGE ACT 1971
c.49

LAND CHARGES ACT 1972
c.61

WATER ACT 1973
c.37

TABLE OF DESTINATIONS

CONTROL OF POLLUTION ACT 1974
c.40

CRIMINAL LAW ACT 1977
c.45

HIGHWAYS ACT 1980
c.66

WATER ACT 1981
c.12

SUPREME COURT ACT 1981
c.54

CIVIL AVIATION ACT 1982
c.16

CRIMINAL JUSTICE ACT 1982
c.43

WATER (FLUORIDATION) ACT 1985
c.63

LOCAL GOVERNMENT ACT 1985
c.51

AIRPORTS ACT 1986
c.31

TABLE OF DESTINATIONS

GAS ACT 1986
c.44

WATER ACT 1989
c.15

ELECTRICITY ACT 1989
c.29

TABLE OF DESTINATIONS

INDEX

References are to sections and Schedules

WATER RESOURCES ACT 1991*

(1991 c. 57)

[A table showing the derivation of the provisions of this Consolidation Act will be found at the end of the Act. The table has no official status.]

---

* Annotations by Jeremy Gibb, B.A., M.St., Dip.Law., Barrister, incorporating the annotations to the Water Act 1989 by Richard Macrory, M.A., Barrister, Lecturer in Law at Imperial College of Science and Technology, London.

CHAPTER II

ABSTRACTION AND IMPOUNDING

An Act to consolidate enactments relating to the National Rivers Authority and the matters in relation to which it exercises functions, with amendments to give effect to recommendations of the Law Commission.

[25th July 1991]

PARLIAMENTARY DEBATES
   Hansard, H.L. Vol. 528, cols. 484, 1738; Vol. 529, col. 746; H.C. Vol. 195, col. 1111.

INTRODUCTION
   This Act is part of the water consolidation and relates to the National Rivers Authority providing for the general duties of the Authority in relation to the water industry. Part II of the Act deals with water resources management covering general management functions, abstraction, impounding and drought. Part III deals with the control and prevention of pollution of water resources and flood defences. Various provisions are made relating to revenue giving a power to impose water resource charges. Powers are given to the Authority to enable it to carry out its functions in relation to this Act and duties are imposed on the Authority to guarantee publication of information and the keeping of registers to monitor its work.

ABBREVIATIONS
   C.O.P.A.   :   Control of Pollution Act 1974
   NCC   :   Nature Conservancy Council
   NRA   :   National Rivers Authority
   the Authority :   National Rivers Authority

PART I

PRELIMINARY

CHAPTER I

THE NATIONAL RIVERS AUTHORITY

The National Rivers Authority

1.—(1) There shall continue to be a body corporate, known as the National Rivers Authority, for the purpose of carrying out the functions specified in section 2 below.

(2) The Authority shall consist of not less than eight nor more than fifteen members of whom—

(a) two shall be appointed by the Minister; and

(b) the others shall be appointed by the Secretary of State.

(3) The Secretary of State shall designate one of the members appointed by him as the chairman of the Authority and may, if he thinks fit, designate another member of the Authority (whether or not appointed by him) as the deputy chairman of the Authority.

(4) In appointing a person to be a member of the Authority, the Secretary of State or, as the case may be, the Minister shall have regard to the desirability of appointing a person who has experience of, and has shown capacity in, some matter relevant to the functions of the Authority.

(5) The Authority shall not be regarded—

(a) as the servant or agent of the Crown, or as enjoying any status, immunity or privilege of the Crown; or

(b) by virtue of any connection with the Crown, as exempt from any tax, duty, rate, levy or other charge whatsoever, whether general or local;

and the Authority's property shall not be regarded as property of, or property held on behalf of, the Crown.

(6) The provisions of Schedule 1 to this Act shall have effect with respect to the Authority.

DEFINITIONS

"functions": s.3.

"the Minister": s.221(1).

GENERAL NOTE

This section sets out the structure, functions and duties of the National Rivers Authority, a non-departmental public body. It was established by the Water Act 1989, which provided for the privatisation and restructuring of the water industry in England and Wales. The Authority retains the regulatory and operational functions concerned with water management that it inherited from water authorities. The primary functions of the Authority encompass water pollution (Pt. III), water resource management including abstraction licensing (Pt. II), land drainage and flood protection (Pt. IV), together with the fishery and navigation functions formerly exercised by water authorities. In addition the Authority has general duties to promote conservation and recreational interests (s.16), and to pay particular regard to the duties imposed on water and sewerage undertakers which might be affected by the exercise of its powers (s.15(1)).

Although subs. (5) declares that the authority shall not be regarded as a servant or agent of the Crown, its close involvement in matters of Government policy is reflected in s.5, which gives the Secretary of State and the Minister of Agriculture, Fisheries, and Food the power to give the Authority directions of a general or specific nature in respect of its functions.

Part VI deals with the Authority's financial arrangements.

Subs. (2)

The Minister. References in the Act to the Minister mean the Minister for Agriculture, Fisheries and Food.

The Secretary of State. This can imply any one of Her Majesty's Principal Secretaries of State (Interpretation Act 1978, Sched. 1), but for administrative purposes under this Act the functions will be allocated to the Secretary of State for the Environment and the Secretary of State for Wales. The functions of the Secretary of State for Wales include shared responsibility for the NRA, joint appointment of the Director General of Water Services, initial appointment of water and sewerage undertakers in the previous area of the Welsh Water Authority, responsibility for enforcement functions related to those undertakers, and responsibility for pollution control, water quality, water resource management in Wales, and responsibility for land drainage and fisheries in the area of the Welsh water authority.

The Authority's functions

2.—(1) The functions of the Authority are—

(a) its functions with respect to water resources by virtue of Part II of this Act;

(b) its functions with respect to water pollution by virtue of Part III of this Act;

(c) its functions with respect to flood defence and land drainage by virtue of Part IV of this Act and the Land Drainage Act 1991 and the functions transferred to the Authority by virtue of section 136(8) of the Water Act 1989 and paragraph 1(3) of Schedule 15 to that Act (transfer of land drainage functions under local statutory provisions and subordinate legislation);

(d) its functions with respect to fisheries by virtue of Part V of this Act, the Diseases of Fish Act 1937, the Sea Fisheries Regulation Act 1966, the Salmon and Freshwater Fisheries Act 1975 and other enactments relating to fisheries;

(e) the functions as a navigation authority, harbour authority or conservancy authority which were transferred to the Authority by virtue of Chapter V of Part III of the Water Act 1989 or paragraph 23(3) of Schedule 13 to that Act or which are transferred to the Authority by any order or agreement under Schedule 2 to this Act; and

(f) the functions assigned to the Authority by any other enactment.

(2) Without prejudice to its duties under section 16 below, it shall be the duty of the Authority, to such extent as it considers desirable, generally to promote—

(a) the conservation and enhancement of the natural beauty and amenity of inland and coastal waters and of land associated with such waters;

(b) the conservation of flora and fauna which are dependent on an aquatic environment; and

(c) the use of such waters and land for recreational purposes;

and it shall be the duty of the Authority, in determining what steps to take in performance of the duty imposed by virtue of paragraph (c) above, to take into account the needs of persons who are chronically sick or disabled.

(3) It shall be the duty of the Authority to make arrangements for the carrying out of research and related activities (whether by the Authority or others) in respect of matters to which the functions of the Authority relate.

(4) The provisions of this Act relating to the functions of the Authority under Chapter II of Part II of this Act, and the related water resources provisions so far as they relate to other functions of the Authority, shall not apply to so much of any inland waters as—

(a) are part of the River Tweed;

(b) are part of the River Esk or River Sark at a point where either of the banks of the river is in Scotland; or

(c) are part of any tributary stream of the River Esk or the River Sark at a point where either of the banks of the tributary stream is in Scotland.

(5) The functions of the Authority specified in subsection (1)(c) above extend to the territorial sea adjacent to England and Wales in so far as—

(a) the area of any regional flood defence committee includes any area of that territorial sea; or

(b) section 165(2) or (3) below provides for the exercise of any power in the territorial sea.

(6) The area in respect of which the Authority shall carry out its functions relating to fisheries shall be the whole of England and Wales, together with—

(a) such part of the territorial sea adjacent to England and Wales as extends for six miles from the baselines from which the breadth of that sea is measured; and

(b) in the case of Part V of this Act, the Diseases of Fish Act 1937 and the Salmon and Freshwater Fisheries Act 1975, so much of the River Esk, with its banks and tributary streams up to their source, as is situated in Scotland,

but, in the case of Part V of this Act and those Acts, excluding the River Tweed.

(7) In this section—

"miles" means international nautical miles of 1,852 metres; and

"the River Tweed" means "the river" within the meaning of the Tweed Fisheries Amendment Act 1859, as amended by byelaws.

DEFINITIONS

"conservancy authority": s.221(1).
"enactment": s.221(1).
"functions": s.3.
"harbour authority": s.221(1).
"navigation authority": s.221(1).
"the Minister": s.221(1).

GENERAL NOTE

This section consolidates the functions of the Authority that were established under ss.8 and 143 of the 1989 Act, with the area limitations of ss.136(7) and 141(4) of that Act.

Subs. (2)

This provision must be read in the light of the general environmental and recreational duties under s.16.

Incidental functions of the Authority

3.—(1) This section has effect, without prejudice to section 2 above, for the purposes of section 4(1) below and the construction of any other enactment which, by reference to the functions of the Authority, confers any power on or in relation to the Authority.

(2) For the purposes to which this section applies the functions of the Authority shall be taken to include the protection against pollution—

(a) of any waters, whether on the surface or underground, which belong to the Authority or any water undertaker or from which the Authority or any water undertaker is authorised to take water;

(b) without prejudice to paragraph (a) above, of any reservoir which belongs to or is operated by the Authority or any water undertaker or which the Authority or any water undertaker is proposing to acquire or construct for the purpose of being so operated; and

(c) of any underground strata from which the Authority or any water undertaker is for the time being authorised to abstract water in pursuance of a licence under Chapter II of Part II of this Act.

(3) For the purposes to which this section applies the functions of the Authority shall be taken to include the furtherance of research into matters in respect of which functions are conferred by or under this Act, the other consolidation Acts or the Water Act 1989 on the Authority or on relevant undertakers.

(4) For the purposes to which this section applies the functions of the Authority shall be taken to include joining with or acting on behalf of one or more relevant undertakers for the purpose of carrying out any works or acquiring any land which at least one of the undertakers with which it joins, or on whose behalf it acts, is authorised to carry out or acquire for the purposes of—

(a) any function of that undertaker under any enactment; or

(b) any function which is taken to be a function of that undertaker for the purposes to which section 217 of the Water Industry Act 1991 applies.

(5) For the purposes to which this section applies the functions of the Authority shall be taken to include the provision of supplies of water in bulk, whether or not such supplies are provided for the purposes of, or in connection with, the carrying out of any other function of the Authority.

(6) For the purposes to which this section applies the functions of the Authority shall be taken to include the provision of houses and other buildings for the use of persons employed by the Authority and the provision of recreation grounds for persons so employed.

(7) In this section—

"the other consolidation Acts" means the Water Industry Act 1991, the Statutory Water Companies Act 1991, the Land Drainage Act 1991 and the Water Consolidation (Consequential Provisions) Act 1991;

"relevant undertaker" means a water undertaker or sewerage undertaker; and

"supply of water in bulk" means a supply of water for distribution by a water undertaker taking the supply.

DEFINITIONS

"enactment": s.221(1).
"the Authority": s.221(1).
"underground strata": s.221(1).
"water undertaker": s.221(1).

GENERAL NOTE

This is a significant section which expands the meaning of "functions" as it applies in this Act or any other enactment to the Authority or undertakers. For undertakers operating in the private sector, the distinction between functional and non-functional activity is crucial.

Subs. (2)

This declares that all functions of these bodies shall be taken to include protection against pollution against underground and surface waters, reservoirs, and underground strata used for abstraction. The rationale for this provision appears rather abstruse. The term "functions" can be taken to include duties and powers (although the Act makes no specific declaration to that effect), and subs. (2) could therefore imply that all such bodies have a duty to take action against pollution, but one for which no specific enforcement mechanism is provided. It may also be taken to imply that the bodies have residual powers to take such action, but, on general principles of statutory interpretation, these general powers cannot be taken to override specific provisions in the Act on this subject.

Subs. (4)

This empowers the authority and undertakers to act jointly or as agents for one another in acquiring land or carrying out works.

Incidental general powers of the Authority

4.—(1) The Authority—

(a) shall have power to do anything which, in the opinion of the Authority, is calculated to facilitate, or is conducive or incidental to, the carrying out of the Authority's functions; and

(b) without prejudice to the generality of that power, shall have power, for the purposes of, or in connection with, the carrying out of those functions, to institute criminal proceedings, to acquire and dispose of land and other property and to carry out such engineering or building operations at such places as the Authority considers appropriate.

(2) Subject to subsection (3) below, the Authority may provide for any person outside the United Kingdom advice or assistance, including training facilities, as respects any matter in which the Authority has skill or experience.

(3) Without prejudice to any power of the Authority apart from subsection (2) above to provide advice or assistance of the kind mentioned in that subsection, the power conferred by that subsection shall not be exercised except—

(a) with the consent in writing of the Secretary of State; and

(b) if the exercise of that power involves capital expenditure by the Authority, or the guaranteeing by the Authority of any liability, with that consent given with the approval of the Treasury;

and a consent under this subsection may be given subject to such conditions as the Secretary of State thinks fit.

(4) Without prejudice to subsection (1) above, the powers conferred by section 1 of the Local Authorities (Goods and Services) Act 1970 shall be exercisable by the Authority as if the Authority were a public body within the meaning of that section.

(5) Nothing in this section with respect to the carrying out of works shall be construed as conferring any power to do anything otherwise than for the purpose of giving the Authority capacity as a corporation to do that thing; and, accordingly, without prejudice to the provisions of Part VII of this Act, this section shall be disregarded for the purpose of determining whether the Authority is liable, on grounds other than an incapacity by virtue of its constitution, for any act or omission in exercise of a power to carry out works conferred by this section.

DEFINITIONS
"enactment": s.221(1).
"engineering or building operations": s.221(1).
"functions": s.3.

Subs. (1)
Under s.1(1), the National Rivers Authority is established as a body corporate, and therefore derives its legal capacity from statutory provisions. This section gives the Authority a number of residual powers.

Subss. (2)–(3)
These provisions permit the NRA to carry out overseas work such as consultancy or training advice, but subject to obtaining the consent of the Secretary of State. In addition, approval of the Treasury is required where the work involves capital expenditure or the guaranteeing of liabilities. The requirement for Government consent is justified on the grounds that the Authority is largely publicly funded, and the position can be contrasted with that of undertakers who, subject to the terms of their memorandum and articles, have no restrictions on overseas consultancy and similar work.

Subs. (4)
Section 1 of the Local Authorities (Goods and Services) Act 1970 allows the Authority to enter into agreements with local authorities for the supply of goods and certain services by the local authority.

Subs. (5)
Part VII of this Act concerns powers of compulsory purchase and acquisition. This subsection makes it clear that s.145 is concerned only with the legal capacity of the Authority, and does not in itself give the Authority statutory powers to interfere with property and other rights.

Ministerial directions to the Authority

5.—(1) Directions of a general or specific character may be given to the Authority—

(a) with respect to the carrying out of the Authority's functions mentioned in paragraphs (a), (b) and (e) of subsection (1) of section 2 above (other than its functions in connection with the making of applications for orders under section 94 below), by the Secretary of State;

(b) with respect to the making of applications for orders under section 94 below or with respect to the carrying out of its functions mentioned in paragraphs (c) and (d) of that subsection, by either of the Ministers; and

(c) with respect to anything not falling within paragraph (a) or (b) above which is connected with the carrying on of the Authority's activities generally, by the Ministers.

(2) Without prejudice to the generality of the power conferred by subsection (1) above, directions under that subsection may include such directions as the Secretary of State, the Minister or, as the case may be, both of them consider appropriate in order to enable Her Majesty's Government in the United Kingdom to give effect—

(a) to any Community obligations; or

(b) to any international agreement to which the United Kingdom is for the time being a party.

(3) The power to give a direction under this section shall be exercisable, except in an emergency, only after consultation with the Authority.

(4) Any power of the Secretary of State or the Minister otherwise than by virtue of this section to give directions to the Authority shall be without prejudice to the power conferred by this section.

(5) It shall be the duty of the Authority to comply with any direction which is given to the Authority, under this section or any of the other provisions of this Act, by either or both of the Ministers.

DEFINITIONS

"functions": s.3.

"the Authority": s.221(1).

"the Minister": s.221(1).

GENERAL NOTE

This important section delineates the relationship between the NRA and the Government. Similar statutory provisions concerning other public corporations are often qualified by permitting only "general" directions, or directions that are in the national interest. Here, the Authority's close involvement with policy issues is reflected in the very broad powers given to the Government to issue it with directions, though it must always be consulted first, otherwise than in an emergency (subs. (3)). A political check on over-zealous use of these powers is provided in s.187, which requires that the Annual Report of the Authority contain details of any directions issued under this section, though there is no requirement that directions be published at the time when they are made.

Three broad classes of directions are provided for under this section:

(1) Directions, general or specific, issued by the Secretary of State for the Environment concerning the Authority's functions in respect of pollution control, water resources, and navigation (subs. (1)(a)) (in Wales, the Secretary of State for Wales).

(2) Directions, general or specific, issued by the Minister of Agriculture, Fisheries and Food concerning the Authority's functions in respect of land drainage and flood defence, and fisheries, and its power to make an application to make an order creating a nitrate-sensitive area under s.94 (subs. (1)(b)).

(3) Directions, general or specific, issued individually or jointly by the Secretary of State for the Environment and the Minister for Agriculture, Fisheries and Food concerning other functions of the Authority not falling within the categories above (subs. (1)(c)).

Community and International Obligations

Subs. (2) expressly, though perhaps superfluously, provides that these powers may be used to implement Community obligations of any international agreement. There is no legal requirement that directions must be published or publicised. In recent years, the Department of the Environment has tended to make greater use of Circulars as a means of transmitting advice or instructions to regional water authorities rather than relying on the previous practice of less readily available letters to Chairmen of Water Authorities. Certainly, where Community obligations are concerned, the need for a transparent link between Government and implementation of Community obligations will be strong; indeed, case law in the European Court of Justice has held that "mere administrative practice" is not a sufficiently certain form in which to implement at least some types of Community obligations (see *E.C. Commission* v. *Belgium* (1982) C.M.L.R. 627).

Subs. (4)

Any power of the Secretary of State or the Minister otherwise than by virtue of this section to give Directions to the Authority. For other powers of direction under this Act, see: s.19 (general duties concerning water resource management); s.73 (emergency drought orders); s.196 (provision of information); s.207 (directions in interest on national security).

CHAPTER II

COMMITTEES WITH FUNCTIONS IN RELATION TO THE AUTHORITY

Advisory committees

The advisory committee for Wales

6.—(1) The Secretary of State shall continue to maintain the committee established under section 3 of the Water Act 1989 for advising him with respect to matters affecting or otherwise connected with the carrying out in Wales of the Authority's functions.

(2) The committee maintained under this section shall consist of such persons as may, from time to time, be appointed by the Secretary of State.

(3) The committee maintained under this section shall meet at least once a year.

(4) The Secretary of State shall pay to the members of the committee maintained under this section such sums reimbursing them for loss of remuneration, for travelling expenses and for other out-of-pocket expenses as he may, with the consent of the Treasury, determine.

GENERAL NOTE

Prior to the 1989 Act the Government intended to establish a non-statutory advisory committee to advise the Secretary of State for Wales on the Authority's functions as they affect Wales. As a result of sustained concern about Welsh interests being insufficiently reflected in that Act, this section was introduced during Report stage of the 1989 Act (old s.3) to give the committee a statutory form. The remit of the committee extends to Wales as a whole rather than solely the former area of the Welsh Water Authority, and in introducing the amendment to the 1989 Act, the Minister of State for Wales stated that its rôle was to ensure that the "Secretary of State for Wales is kept informed, and obtains a Welsh view, of NRA policies that affect Wales and of the needs of the NRA, if Welsh requirements are to be met" (*Hansard*, H.C. Vol. 149, col. 932; March 21, 1989).

Note also that one of the Regional Rivers Advisory Committees established under s.7 must cover all or most of Wales (s.7(2)). Further special provisions concerning Wales are included in s.184 (recreational facilities on reservoirs).

Regional rivers advisory committees

7.—(1) It shall be the duty of the Authority—

(a) to establish and maintain advisory committees, consisting of persons who are not members of the Authority, for the different regions of England and Wales;

(b) to consult the advisory committee for any region as to any proposals

of the Authority relating generally to the manner in which the
Authority carries out its functions in that region; and

(c) to consider any representations made to it by the advisory committee
for any region (whether in response to consultation under paragraph
(b) above or otherwise) as to the manner in which the Authority
carries out its functions in that region.

(2) The duty to establish and maintain advisory committees imposed by
subsection (1) above is a duty—

(a) to establish and maintain an advisory committee for each area which
the Authority considers it appropriate for the time being to regard as
a region of England and Wales for the purposes of this section; and

(b) to ensure that the persons appointed by the Authority to each such
committee are persons who appear to the Authority to have an
interest in matters likely to be affected by the manner in which the
Authority carries out any of its functions in the region in question;

and it shall be the duty of the Authority in determining the regions for which
advisory committees are established and maintained under this section to
ensure that one of those regions consists wholly or mainly of, or of most of,
Wales.

(3) There shall be paid by the Authority—

(a) to the chairman of an advisory committee established and maintained
under this section remuneration and such travelling and other allowances; and

(b) to any other members of that committee such sums reimbursing them
for loss of remuneration, for travelling expenses or for any other
out-of-pocket expenses,

as may, with the consent of the Treasury, be determined by the Secretary of
State.

(4) For the purposes of this section functions of the Authority which are
carried out in any area of Scotland or of the territorial sea which is adjacent
to any region for which an advisory committee is maintained shall be
regarded as carried out in that region.

DEFINITIONS
    "functions": s.3.

GENERAL NOTE
    The Authority is intended to operate on a strongly regional basis, initially matching the
catchment boundaries of former water authorities. This section introduces one of three types of
advisory committees required to be established in connection with the Authority's functions,
the others being Regional Flood Defence Committees (s.106) and Regional Fishery Advisory
Committees (s.8). The Regional Rivers Advisory Committees under this section replaced, at
the time of the Authority's creation, the former regional recreation and conservation committees set up under s.24A(2) of the Water Act 1973.
    Although these committees are expected to play an important advisory and consultative rôle,
and have general rights in this respect under subs. (1), the Act gives them no other specific
formal powers concerning production of documents and similar matters. The Public Bodies
(Admissions to Meetings) Act 1960 will continue to be applicable to them following their
insertion as sub-paragraphs (i), (j) and (k) of para. 1 of the Schedule to that Act by the Water
Act 1989.

Subs. (4)
    The reference to Scotland and the territorial sea relate to pollution control and fisheries
functions of the Authority (see Pts. III and V).

Regional and local fisheries advisory committees

8.—(1) It shall be the duty of the Authority—

(a) to establish and maintain advisory committees of persons who are not
members of the Authority but appear to it to be interested in salmon

fisheries, trout fisheries, freshwater fisheries or eel fisheries in the different parts of the controlled area; and

(b) to consult those committees as to the manner in which the Authority is to perform its duty under section 114 below.

(2) The duty to establish and maintain advisory committees imposed by subsection (1) above is a duty to establish and maintain—

(a) a regional advisory committee for each such region of the controlled area as the Authority considers it appropriate for the time being to regard as a region of that area for the purposes of this section; and

(b) such local advisory committees as the Authority considers necessary to represent the interests referred to in paragraph (a) of that subsection in the different parts of each such region;

and it shall be the duty of the Authority in determining the regions for which regional advisory committees are established and maintained under this section to ensure that one of those regions consists (apart from territorial waters) wholly or mainly of, or of most of, Wales.

(3) There shall be paid by the Authority—

(a) to the chairman of an advisory committee established and maintained under this section such remuneration and such travelling and other allowances; and

(b) to any other members of that committee such sums reimbursing them for loss of remuneration, for travelling expenses or for any other out-of-pocket expenses,

as may, with the consent of the Treasury, be determined by one of the Ministers.

(4) In this section "the controlled area" means the area specified in section 2(6) above in respect of which the Authority carries out functions under Part V of this Act.

Definitions
  "the Authority": s.221(1).
  "water authorities": s.221(1).

General Note
  This section and ss.114–116 give the NRA the fishery functions that were exercised by the water authorities prior to privatisation in 1989.

Subs. (1) requires the Authority to establish regional fisheries advisory committees, along the lines of those that had already been established by water authorities. Local advisory committees may also be set up. The exclusion of the Authority's board members from membership of these committees (subs. (1)(a)) was added as an amendment to the 1989 Act during Committee stage in the House of Lords out of concern that they should retain independence.

The Act provides no guidance on the precise functions of these committees, apart from being a consultee on how the Authority should exercise its general fishery duties (subs. (1)(b)), though, in practice, such committees have often exercised considerable delegated powers (such as setting fishing licence charges, and promoting byelaws). During Committee stage of the 1989 Act, the Government resisted amendments designed to give these committees a more executive rôle, but outlined the functions they should perform:

  "(The Regional Fisheries Advisory) Committees have played and will continue to play a very important and active rôle in the management of fisheries. The NRA will have a statutory duty to consult the RFAC on the way in which it carries out its responsibilities. The committees will be consulted about the setting of fishing licence duties and about fisheries contributions which should be levied on owners. It will thus have a major say in the collection and spending of revenue with the region, by its persuasive and expert advice on what the priorities should be. It will be fully involved in the development of all other NRA policy relevant to fisheries. However, we believe that the final decision, for both operational and management reasons, should rest with the NRA itself. After all, it is the authority which has the corporate statutory duty to maintain, improve and develop fisheries and which would be answerable to Ministers in default" (Baroness Trumpington, Hansard, H.L. Vol. 508, col. 313, May 23, 1989).

Sched. 17 of the 1989 Act replaced references to water authorities in fishery legislation with a reference to the Authority. Some other amendments were also included but the most significant concerned s.28 of the Salmon and Freshwater Fisheries Act 1975 relating to the making of orders authorising the levy of contributions from owners and occupiers of fisheries by the Authority. Such orders had been subject to special parliamentary procedure under Sched. 3 (paras. 9–11) of the 1975 Act, but the amendments under the Water Act 1989 replaced these provisions (considered by the Government to be anachronistic and a deterrent to the making of such orders) with a standard negative resolution procedure.

Flood defence committees

Continuance of regional flood defence committees

9.—(1) There shall continue to be committees, known as regional flood defence committees, for the purpose of carrying out the functions which fall to be carried out by such committees by virtue of this Act.

(2) Subject to Schedule 3 to this Act (which makes provision for the alteration of the boundaries of and the amalgamation of the areas of regional flood defence committees)—

(a) each regional flood defence committee shall have the same area as immediately before the coming into force of this section; but

(b) where under section 165(2) or (3) below any function of the Authority falls to be carried out at a place beyond the seaward boundaries of the area of any regional flood defence committee, that place shall be assumed for the purposes of this Act to be within the area of the regional flood defence committee to whose area the area of sea where that place is situated is adjacent.

(3) The Authority shall maintain a principal office for the area of each regional flood defence committee.

GENERAL NOTE

This section provides for the continuance of regional flood defence committees as established under s.137 of the 1989 Act. The Public Bodies (Admission to Meetings) Act 1960 applies to these committees (see note to s.7).

A committee appears to have a somewhat curious hybrid status, having semi-autonomous powers and a quasi-independent status from the Authority, but at the same time essentially acting as an agent in carrying out the Authority's land drainage functions. Regional flood defence committees are not expressly included as a relevant body to whom the environmental duties under s.16 apply, but on the delegated agent analysis, it would appear that they are equally bound by such duties. On a similar basis, the duties under s.17 (environmental duties with respect to sites of special interest) would be applicable on the grounds that they are activities of the Authority, a relevant body under that section.

Composition of regional flood defence committees

10.—(1) Subject to subsection (2) below, a regional flood defence committee shall consist of the following, none of whom shall be a member of the Authority, that is to say—

(a) a chairman and a number of other members appointed by the relevant Minister;

(b) two members appointed by the Authority;

(c) a number of members appointed by or on behalf of the constituent councils.

(2) Subject to section 11 below and to any order under Schedule 3 to this Act amalgamating the areas of any two or more regional flood defence committees—

(a) the total number of members of the regional flood defence committee for any area shall be the same as immediately before the coming into force of this section; and

(b) the number of members to be appointed to a regional flood defence committee for any area by or on behalf of each of the constituent councils or, as the case may be, jointly by or on behalf of more than one of them shall be the same number as fell to be so appointed immediately before the coming into force of this section.

(3) Where—

(a) the appointment of one or more members of a regional flood defence committee is (by virtue of subsection (2) above or an order under section 11(5) below), to be made jointly by more than one constituent council; and

(b) the councils by whom that appointment is to be made are unable to agree on an appointment,

the member or members in question shall be appointed by the relevant Minister on behalf of those councils.

(4) In appointing a person to be the chairman or a member of a regional flood defence committee under subsection (1)(a) or (c) or (3) above the relevant Minister or, as the case may be, a constituent council shall have regard to the desirability of appointing a person who has experience of, and has shown capacity in, some matter relevant to the functions of the committee.

(5) The councils of every county, metropolitan district or London borough any part of which is in the area of a regional flood defence committee shall be the constituent councils for the regional flood defence committee for that area, and the Common Council of the City of London shall be a constituent council for the regional flood defence committee for any area which comprises any part of the City.

(6) In this section "the relevant Minister"—

(a) in relation to the regional flood defence committee for an area the whole or the greater part of which is in Wales, means the Secretary of State; and

(b) in relation to any other regional flood defence committee, means the Minister.

DEFINITIONS
"constituent councils: subs. (5).
"relevant Minister": subs. (6).

GENERAL NOTE

Subs. (1)(c)
The maximum number of members is limited by s.11.

Subs. (4)
Under the Land Drainage Act 1976, the criteria for appointees was restricted to persons with "knowledge of or capacity in land drainage or agriculture". Here the qualifications have been greatly widened, and allow for the introduction of a wider range of expertise and experience.

Change of composition of regional flood defence committee

11.—(1) The Authority may, in accordance with the following provisions of this section, from time to time make a determination varying the total number of members of a regional flood defence committee.

(2) The Authority shall submit any determination under subsection (1) above to the relevant Minister.

(3) For the purposes of this section—

(a) the total number of members of a regional flood defence committee shall not be less than 11; and

(b) any determination by the Authority under subsection (1) above that a regional flood defence committee should consist of more than 17 members shall be provisional and shall take effect only if the relevant Minister makes an order under subsection (4) below.

(4) If the Authority submits a provisional determination to the relevant Minister with respect to any regional flood defence committee and he

considers that the committee should consist of more than 17 members, he may by order made by statutory instrument—

(a) confirm it; or

(b) substitute for the number of members determined by the Authority some other number not less than 17.

(5) Subject to the following provisions of this section, whenever—

(a) the total number of members of a regional flood defence committee is varied under this section; or

(b) the relevant Minister considers it necessary to make an order under this subsection in consequence of—

(i) the effect in relation to the whole or any part of the area of any regional flood defence committee of any rules or regulations made for the purposes of paragraphs 4 to 6 of Schedule 12A to the Local Government Finance Act 1988 (definition of relevant population); or

(ii) the alteration of the boundaries of the area of a regional flood defence committee,

the relevant Minister shall by order made by statutory instrument specify, in relation to times after the coming into force of the variation, rules or regulations or alteration, the number of members to be appointed to the committee by each of the constituent councils.

(6) An order under subsection (5) above shall be so framed that the total number of members appointed under section 10(1)(a) and (b) above is one less than the number of those appointed by or on behalf of constituent councils.

(7) For the purpose of determining for the purposes of subsection (5) above the number of persons to be appointed to a regional flood defence committee by or on behalf of each constituent council, the relevant Minister—

(a) shall have regard to the relevant population of any relevant area of that council; and

(b) where, having regard to the proportion which that population bears to the aggregate of the relevant populations of the relevant areas of all the constituent councils—

(i) he considers it to be inappropriate that that council should appoint a member of the committee; or

(ii) he considers that one or more members should be appointed jointly by that council and one or more other constituent councils,

may include provision to that effect in the order.

8. In this section—

"member," in relation to a regional flood defence committee, includes the chairman of the committee;

"relevant area," in relation to a council which is a constituent council in relation to any regional flood defence committee, means so much of the council's area as is included in the area of the committee;

"the relevant Minister" has the same meaning as in section 10 above;

"relevant population" has the same meaning as it has for the purposes of section 69 of the Local Government Finance Act 1988 (precepted authorities).

DEFINITIONS

"member": subs. (8).

"relevant area": subs. (8).

"relevant populations": subs. (8).

"the relevant Minister": subs. (8).

GENERAL NOTE

Subs. (5)

When regulations are made under Sched. 12A to the Local Government Finance Act 1988, membership of constituent councils will be allocated on a population basis as defined in the regulations rather than the pre-privatisation penny rate product basis.

Local flood defence schemes and local flood defence committees

12.—(1) A scheme, known as a local flood defence scheme, may be made by the Authority, in accordance with the following provisions of this section—

(a) for the creation in the area of a regional flood defence committee of one or more districts, to be known as local flood defence districts; and

(b) for the constitution, membership, functions and procedure of a committee for each such district, to be known as the local flood defence committee for that district.

(2) A regional flood defence committee may at any time submit to the Authority—

(a) a local flood defence scheme for any part of their area for which there is then no such scheme in force; or

(b) a scheme varying a local flood defence scheme or revoking such a scheme and, if the committee think fit, replacing it with another such scheme;

and references in the following provisions of this section and in section 13 below to local flood defence schemes are references to schemes under either of paragraphs (a) and (b) above.

(3) Before submitting a scheme to the Authority under subsection (2) above, a regional flood defence committee shall consult—

(a) every local authority any part of whose area will fall within the area to which the scheme is proposed to relate; and

(b) such organisations representative of persons interested in flood defence (within the meaning of Part IV of this Act) or agriculture as the regional flood defence committee consider to be appropriate.

(4) It shall be the duty of the Authority to send any scheme submitted to it under subsection (2) above to one of the Ministers.

(5) A local flood defence scheme may define a local flood defence district—

(a) by reference to the districts which were local land drainage districts immediately before September 1, 1989;

(b) by reference to the area of the regional flood defence committee in which that district is situated;

(c) by reference to a map;

or partly by one of those means and partly by another or the others.

(6) A local flood defence scheme may contain incidental, consequential and supplementary provisions.

(7) Either of the Ministers may approve a local flood defence scheme with or without modifications; and any scheme approved under this subsection shall come into force on a date fixed by the Minister approving it.

DEFINITIONS
  "local authority": s.221(1).
  "the Ministers": s.221(1).

GENERAL NOTE
  This provides for setting up of local flood defence committees along the lines of former local land drainage committees. See General Note to ss.9, 105 and 106.
  The Public Bodies (Admission to Meetings) Act 1960 also applies to such bodies (see note to s.7).

Subs. (3)(a)
  Every local authority. This provision, in conjunction with the definition of "local authority" in s.221(1), follows the recommendation of the Law Commission's report on the consolidation

of water legislation (Law Com. No. 198) to change the exclusion of London from local flood defence schemes (previously local land drainage schemes) by the Land Drainage Act 1976, as amended by the Water Act 1989.

Composition of local flood defence committees

13.—(1) Subject to subsections (2) and (3) below, a local flood defence scheme shall provide that any local flood defence committee to which it relates shall consist of not less than 11 and not more than 15 members.

(2) A regional flood defence committee may include in a local flood defence scheme which they submit to the Authority a recommendation that a committee to which the scheme relates should consist of a number of members greater than 15; and a scheme so submitted shall be taken to provide for the number of members of a committee if it contains a recommendation under this subsection relating to that committee.

(3) The power conferred on each of the Ministers by section 12(7) above shall include power to direct that a committee to which a recommendation under subsection (2) above relates shall consist either of the recommended number of members or of some other number of members greater than 15.

(4) A local flood defence committee shall consist of—

(a) a chairman appointed from among their own members by the regional flood defence committee;

(b) other members appointed by that committee; and

(c) members appointed, in accordance with and subject to the terms of the local flood defence scheme, by or on behalf of constituent councils.

(5) The number of members appointed to a local flood defence committee by or on behalf of constituent councils shall be one more than the total number of members appointed by the regional flood defence committee.

(6) In appointing a person to be a member of a local flood defence committee, the regional flood defence committee shall have regard to the desirability of appointing a person who has experience of, and has shown capacity in, some matter relevant to the functions of the committee to which he is appointed.

(7) The council of every county, metropolitan district or London borough any part of which is in a local flood defence district shall be the constituent councils for the local flood defence committee for that district, and the Common Council of the City of London shall be a constituent council for the local flood defence committee of any local flood defence district which comprises any part of the City.

DEFINITIONS
"constituent councils": s.221(1).
"the Ministers": s.221(1).

GENERAL NOTE

Subs. (6)
As with regional flood defence committees (s.10(4)), the qualifications have been widened from persons with "knowledge of or capacity in land drainage or agriculture" that were called for in local land drainage committees under the Land Drainage Act 1976.

Membership and proceedings of flood defence committees

14. Schedule 4 to this Act shall have effect in relation to regional flood defence committees and local flood defence committees.

GENERAL NOTE
Schedule 4 contains detailed provisions covering membership of regional and local flood defence committees (terms, qualification, disqualification, appointment of deputies and payment) and their proceedings. It is based on the Land Drainage Act 1976 (Sched. 1).

CHAPTER III

GENERAL DUTIES

General duties with respect to the water industry

15.—(1) It shall be the duty of the Authority, in exercising any of its powers under any enactment, to have particular regard to the duties imposed, by virtue of the provisions of Parts II to IV of the Water Industry Act 1991, on any water undertaker or sewerage undertaker which appears to the Authority to be or to be likely to be affected by the exercise of the power in question.

(2) It shall be the duty of each of the Ministers, in exercising—

(a) any power conferred by virtue of this Act, the Land Drainage Act 1991, the Water Industry Act 1991 or the Water Act 1989 in relation to, or to decisions of, the Authority; or

(b) any power which, but for any direction given by one of the Ministers, would fall to be exercised by the Authority,

to take into account the duty imposed on the Authority by subsection (1) above.

GENERAL NOTE

This section is fundamental to the regulatory framework of the Acts making up the consolidation of water legislation. It lays down primary and secondary considerations that will govern the relationship of the Secretary of State and the Director with undertakers in the exercise of their main regulatory functions and gives expression to underlying policy goals of the Act in a manner favoured by modern styles of legislative drafting.

The duties under this section apply to the powers and duties of the Secretary of State and the Director contained in the Water Industry Act 1991. Parts II – IV of the Water Industry Act 1991 are concerned with the appointment and regulation of undertakers, their duties with regard to water supply and the functions of sewerage undertakers. The two primary duties of the Secretary of State and the Director under that Act are to secure that the functions of undertakers are properly carried out throughout England and Wales and that undertakers are able to finance the proper carrying out of these functions, in particular by securing reasonable returns on their capital.

Legal significance of duties

Whatever their political and symbolic importance, there must be doubt whether these broadly drafted duties are themselves susceptible to judicial review. From an internal administrative perspective, they can probably best be viewed as gravitational rules, providing the administrator with policy priorities and justifications for decision-making. But this is not to say that they have no legal significance. Should particular decisions of the Director or Secretary of State be challenged in law, then these duties are likely to be considered by the courts in determining the policy and objectives of the legislation: see *Bromley London Borough Council* v. *Greater London Council* [1983] A.C. 768 and *Padfield* v. *Minister of Agriculture, Fisheries and Food* [1968] A.C. 997.

General environmental and recreational duties

16.—(1) It shall be the duty of each of the Ministers and of the Authority, in formulating or considering any proposals relating to any functions of the Authority—

(a) so far as may be consistent—

(i) with the purposes of any enactment relating to the functions of the Authority; and

(ii) in the case of the Secretary of State, with his duties under section 2 of the Water Industry Act 1991,

so to exercise any power conferred on him or it with respect to the proposals as to further the conservation and enhancement of natural beauty and the conservation of flora, fauna and geological or physiographical features of special interest;

(b) to have regard to the desirability of protecting and conserving buildings, sites and objects of archaelogical, architectural or historic interest; and

(c) to take into account any effect which the proposals would have on the
beauty or amenity of any rural or urban area on on any such flora,
fauna, features, buildings, sites or objects.

(2) Subject to subsection (1) above, it shall be the duty of each of the
Ministers and of the Authority, in formulating or considering any proposals
relating to the functions of the Authority—

(a) to have regard to the desirability of preserving for the public any
freedom of access to areas of woodland, mountains, moor, heath,
down, cliff or foreshore and other places of natural beauty;

(b) to have regard to the desirability of maintaining the availability to the
public of any facility for visiting or inspecting any building, site or
object of archaeological, architectural or historic interest; and

(c) to take into account any effect which the proposals would have on any
such freedom of access or on the availability of any such facility.

(3) Subsections (1) and (2) above shall apply so as to impose duties on the
Authority in relation to—

(a) any proposals relating to the functions of a water undertaker or
sewerage undertaker;

(b) any proposals relating to the management, by the company holding
an appointment as such an undertaker, of any land for the time being
held by that company for any purpose whatever (whether or not
connected with the carrying out of the functions of a water undertaker
or sewerage undertaker); and

(c) any proposal which by virtue of section 156(7) of the Water Industry
Act 1991 (disposals of protected land) falls to be treated for the
purposes of section 3 of that Act as a proposal relating to functions of
a water undertaker or sewerage undertaker,

as they apply in relation to proposals relating to the Authority's own functions but as if, for that purpose, the reference in subsection (1)(a) above to
enactments relating to the functions of the Authority were a reference to
enactments relating to that to which the proposal relates.

(4) Subject to obtaining the consent of any navigation authority, harbour
authority or conservancy authority before doing anything which causes
navigation which is subject to the control of that authority to be obstructed
or otherwise interfered with, it shall be the duty of the Authority to take such
steps as are—

(a) reasonably practicable; and

(b) consistent with the purposes of the enactments relating to the functions of the Authority,

for securing, so long as the Authority has rights to the use of water or land
associated with water, that those rights are exercised so as to ensure that the
water or land is made available for recreational purposes and is so made
available in the best manner.

(5) It shall be the duty of the Authority, in determining what steps to take
in performance of any duty imposed by virtue of subsection (4) above, to
take into account the needs of persons who are chronically sick or disabled.

(6) Nothing in this section or the following provisions of this Act shall
require recreational facilities made available by the Authority to be made
available free of charge.

(7) In this section "building" includes structure.

Definitions
"building": subs. (7).
"conservancy authority": s.221(1).
"enactments": s.221(1).

"functions": s.3.
"harbour authority": s.221(1).
"navigation authority": s.221(1).
"the Ministers": s.221(1).

GENERAL NOTE

This section imposes general environmental duties on the Secretary of State, the Minister of Agriculture, Fisheries and Food, and the NRA. It needs to be read alongside the more focused provisions of ss.17 and 18.

The language of these duties is modelled on that used for previous environmental duties imposed on water authorities under the Water Act 1973 and the Wildlife and Countryside Act 1981.

Subs. (1)

As to further the conservation and enhancement. See *Steinberg and Sykes* v. *Secretary of State for the Environment* (1989) J.P.L. 258, considering the phrase "preserving or enhancing the character or appearance of the conservation area" under s.277 of the Town and Country Planning Act 1971.

Subs. (3)

This is a significant provision which states that the environmental duties apply to land managed by undertakers whether for core business or non-core business, one of the few examples of statutory duties under this Act extending to non-functional activities. The environmental duties under this section extend to proposals for the disposal of protected land in National Parks, the Broads, areas of outstanding natural beauty, or sites of special scientific interest.

Subs. (6)

This provision must be read in light of the duty under subs. (2)(b). Though the latter provision does not provide a guarantee that existing freedom of access to land belonging to relevant bodies is preserved, it goes some way towards inhibiting the imposition of charges or other restrictions. During discussion of this provision as part of the Water Act 1989, the Government asserted that it would be impracticable or unreasonable for undertakers to charge for pursuits such as informal recreation and rambling, and that any costs associated with allowing free access in such cases would be borne by general service charges (*Hansard*, H.L. Vol. 507, col. 494, May 8, 1989).

Environmental duties with respect to sites of special interest

17.—(1) Where the Nature Conservancy Council for England or the Countryside Council for Wales are of the opinion that any area of land in England or, as the case may be, in Wales—

(a) is of special interest by reason of its flora, fauna or geological or physiographical features; and

(b) may at any time be affected by schemes, works, operations or activities of the Authority or by an authorisation given by the Authority,

that Council shall notify the fact that the land is of special interest for that reason to the Authority.

(2) Where a National Park authority or the Broads Authority is of the opinion that any area of land in a National Park or in the Broads—

(a) is land in relation to which the matters for the purposes of which sections 2(2) and 16 above have effect are of particular importance; and

(b) may at any time be affected by schemes, works, operations or activities of the Authority or by an authorisation given by the Authority,

the National Park authority or Broads Authority shall notify the fact that the land is such land, and the reasons why those matters are of particular importance in relation to the land, to the Authority.

(3) Where the Authority has received a notification under subsection (1) or (2) above with respect to any land, it shall consult the notifying body before carrying out or authorising any works, operations or activities which appear to the Authority to be likely—

(a) to destroy or damage any of the flora, fauna, or geological or phy siographical features by reason of which the land is of special interest; or

(b) significantly to prejudice anything the importance of which is one of the reasons why the matters mentioned in subsection (2) above are of particular importance in relation to that land.

(4) Subsection (3) above shall not apply in relation to anything done in an emergency where particulars of what is done and of the emergency are notified to the Nature Conservancy Council for England, the Countryside Council for Wales, the National Park authority in question or, as the case may be, the Broads Authority as soon as practicable after that thing is done.

(5) In this section—

"the Broads" has the same meaning as in the Norfolk and Suffolk Broads Act 1988; and

"National Park authority" means a National Park Committee or a joint or special planning board for a National Park.

DEFINITIONS

"National Park Authority": subs. (5).
"the Authority": s.221(1).
"the Broads": subs. (5).

GENERAL NOTE

This section elaborates the general duties under s.16 in respect of certain categories of land by requiring the NRA to consult certain bodies before undertaking potentially damaging operations and works. The NRA is also required to consult before granting an authorisation which may have similar effects. The requirements are not restricted to only the functional activities of water or sewerage undertakers.

These duties are enforceable by the Secretary of State by means of enforcement orders under the Water Industry Act 1991.

Subs. (1)

This relates to the Nature Conservancy Council and is modelled on s.22 of the Water Act 1973. Although the terminology is similar to that applied to sites of special scientific interest under s.28 of the Wildlife and Countryside Act 1981, it appears that the NCC is not constrained to include only those sites notified under that section. In many instances the provisions here will duplicate the SSSI procedures, but the main distinction is that here the NCC is not obliged to specify those operations which require prior notification. Under these provisions, the burden is on the body concerned to identify those works and operations which may destroy or damage features of the site and consult with the Council accordingly (subs. (3)(a)).

Subs. (2)

This concerns the National Parks Authorities and the Broads Authority. They are required to notify the Authority of land within their jurisdiction which is of "particular importance" in relation to the general environmental duties under s.16. The drafting is not elegant, but presumably is intended to allow the Authorities to refer back to any of the specific considerations in s.16. In contrast to the NCC, their notification to their Authority must be accompanied by reasons. The need to so do refers forward to subs. (3)(b), where the Authority is required to consult the Authorities before carrying out works and operations which may "prejudice" the considerations which gave the land its particular importance. Although again the responsibility is on the Authority to identify the works and operations that fall within this category, the implication is that it need only have regard to the reasons given by the Authorities on notification.

Codes of practice with respect to environmental and recreational duties

18.—(1) Each of the Ministers shall have power by order to approve any code of practice issued (whether by him or by another person) for the purpose of—

(a) giving practical guidance to the Authority with respect to any of the matters for the purposes of which sections 2(2), 16 and 17 above have effect; and

(b) promoting what appear to him to be desirable practices by the
      Authority with respect to those matters,
and may at any time by such an order approve a modification of such a code
or withdraw his approval of such a code or modification.

(2) A contravention of a code of practice as for the time being approved
under this section shall not of itself constitute a contravention of any requirement imposed by section 2(2), 16 or 17 above or give rise to any criminal or
civil liability; but each of the Ministers shall be under a duty to take into
account whether there has been or is likely to be any such contravention in
determining when and how he should exercise his powers in relation to the
Authority by virtue of this Act, the Land Drainage Act 1991, the Water
Industry Act 1991 or the Water Act 1989.

(3) The power of each of the Ministers to make an order under this section
shall be exercisable by statutory instrument subject to annulment in pursuance of a resolution of either House of Parliament.

(4) Neither of the Ministers shall make an order under this section unless
he has first consulted—
 (a) the Authority;
 (b) the Countryside Commission, the Nature Conservancy Council for
       England and the Countryside Council for Wales;
 (c) the Historic Buildings and Monuments Commission for England;
 (d) the Sports Council and the Sports Council for Wales; and
 (e) such water undertakers, sewerage undertakers and other persons as
       he considers it appropriate to consult.

DEFINITIONS
  "modification": s.221(1).
  "the Authority": s.221(1).
  "the Ministers": s.221(1).

GENERAL NOTE
  Codes of Practice under this section provide a mechanism for translating the general
environmental duties of undertakers into more specific requirements, and assist the use of
enforcement orders under the Water Industry Act 1991 in this context should they be required.
The Codes will apply to the National Rivers Authority, and as a means of enforcement, the
Secretary of State has power under s.5 to issue directions to the Authority. Although the
general duties under s.16 and the consultation requirements under s.17 apply to internal
drainage boards, the Codes of Practice under this section do not.

PART II

WATER RESOURCES MANAGEMENT

CHAPTER I

GENERAL MANAGEMENT FUNCTIONS

General management of resources by the Authority

19.—(1) It shall be the duty of the Authority to take all such action as it
may from time to time consider, in accordance (if any have been given for
the purposes of this section) with the directions of the Secretary of State, to
be necessary or expedient for the purpose—
 (a) of conserving, redistributing or otherwise augmenting water
       resources in England and Wales; and
 (b) of securing the proper use of water resources in England and Wales.

(2) Nothing in this section shall be construed as relieving any water
undertaker of the obligation to develop water resources for the purpose of
performing any duty imposed on it by virtue of section 37 of the Water
Industry Act 1991 (general duty to maintain water supply system).

DEFINITION
   "the Authority": s.221(1).

GENERAL NOTE

Subs. (1)
   This largely repeats the former general duty of water authorities under s.10 of the Water Act 1973 in respect of water resource management.
   The Directions of the Secretary of State. The power to give directions of both a general or specific character is contained in s.5 below.
   Redistributing. The Director General is empowered to settle disputes between water undertakers over bulk transfer agreements and in doing so must first consult the Authority if he considers that his decision would affect any of its functions. But the Authority has no veto over such agreements, nor can it initiate them.

Subs. (2)
   Duty imposed on it by virtue of section 37 of the Water Industry Act 1991. Under s.37 of that Act water undertakers are under a general duty to develop an efficient and economical system of water supply for premises in their area. This provision emphasises that, whatever the responsibilities of the Authority for water resource management, undertakers are still obliged to carry out strategic planning in this area. Note also that in exercising any of its powers the Authority must have particular regard for the undertaker's duties (s.15(1)).

Water resources management schemes

   20.—(1) It shall be the duty of the Authority so far as reasonably practicable to enter into and maintain such arrangements with water undertakers for securing the proper management or operation of—
   (a) the waters which are available to be used by water undertakers for the purposes of, or in connection with, the carrying out of their functions; and
   (b) any reservoirs, apparatus or other works which belong to, are operated by or are otherwise under the control of water undertakers for the purposes of, or in connection with, the carrying out of their functions.
as the Authority from time to time considers appropriate for the purpose of carrying out its functions under section 19(1) above.
   (2) Without prejudice to the power of the Authority and any water undertaker to include any such provision as may be agreed between them in arrangements under this section, such arrangements may—
   (a) make provision by virtue of subsection (1)(a) above with respect to the construction or installation of any reservoirs, apparatus or other works which will be used by the undertaker in the carrying out of its functions;
   (b) contain provision requiring payments to be made by the Authority to the undertaker; and
   (c) require the reference to and determination by the Secretary of State or the Director General of Water Services of questions arising under the arrangements.
   (3) The Authority shall send a copy of any arrangements entered into by it under this section to the Secretary of State; and the obligations of a water undertaker by virtue of any such arrangements shall be enforceable under section 18 of the Water Industry Act 1991 (enforcement orders) by the Secretary of State.

DEFINITION
   "functions": s.3.

GENERAL NOTE
   This section is intended to assist the Authority in performing its general water resource conservation duty under s.19. It enables the Authority to have some influence over the use of reservoirs, inter-river transfer schemes, and other assets which may be vested in water undertakers but which can have an important rôle to play in the conservation and redistribution of water.

Minimum acceptable flows

21.—(1) The Authority may, if it thinks it appropriate to do so, submit a draft statement to the Secretary of State containing, in relation to any inland waters that are not discrete waters—

(a) provision for determining the minimum acceptable flow for those waters; or

(b) where any provision for determining such a flow is for the time being in force in relation to those waters, provision for amending that provision or for replacing it with different provision for determining the minimum acceptable flow for those waters.

(2) The provision contained in any statement for determining the minimum acceptable flow for any inland waters shall, in relation to the inland waters to which it relates, set out—

(a) the control points at which the flow in the waters is to be measured;

(b) the method of measurement which is to be used at each control point; and

(c) the flow which is to be the minimum acceptable flow at each control point or, where appropriate, the flows which are to be the minimum acceptable flows at each such point for the different times or periods specified in the statement.

(3) Before preparing so much of any draft statement under this section as relates to any particular inland waters, the Authority shall consult—

(a) any water undertaker having the right to abstract water from those waters;

(b) any other water undertaker having the right to abstract water from any related underground strata;

(c) the drainage board for any internal drainage district from which water is discharged into those waters or in which any part of those waters is situated;

(d) any navigation authority, harbour authority or conservancy authority having functions in relation to those waters or any related inland waters;

(e) if those waters or any related inland waters are tidal waters in relation to which there is no such navigation authority, harbour authority or conservancy authority, the Secretary of State for Transport; and

(f) any person authorised by a licence under Part I of the Electricity Act 1989 to generate electricity.

(4) In determining the flow to be specified in relation to any inland waters under subsection (2)(c) above, the Authority shall have regard—

(a) to the flow of water in the inland waters from time to time;

(b) in the light of its duties under sections 2(2), 16 and 17 above, to the character of the inland waters and their surroundings; and

(c) to any water quality objectives established under Chapter I of Part III of this Act in relation to the inland waters or any other inland waters which may be affected by the flow in the inland waters in question.

(5) The flow specified in relation to any inland waters under subsection (2)(c) above shall be not less than the minimum which, in the opinion of the Authority, is needed for safeguarding the public health and for meeting (in respect of both quantity and quality of water)—

(a) the requirements of existing lawful uses of the inland waters, whether for agriculture, industry, water supply or other purposes; and

(b) the requirements, in relation to both those waters and other inland waters whose flow may be affected by changes in the flow of those waters, of navigation, fisheries or land drainage.

(6) The provisions of Schedule 5 to this Act shall have effect with respect to draft statements under this section and with respect to the approval of statements submitted as draft statements.

(7) The approval under Schedule 5 to this Act of a draft statement under this section shall bring into force, on the date specified in that approval, so much of that statement, as approved, as contains provision for determining, amending or replacing the minimum acceptable flow for any inland waters.

(8) For the purposes of subsection (3) above—

(a) underground strata are related underground strata in relation to any inland waters if—

    (i) a water undertaker has a right to abstract water from the strata; and

    (ii) it appears to the Authority, having regard to the extent to which the level of water in the strata depends on the flow of those waters, that the exercise of that right may be substantially affected by so much of the draft statement in question as relates to those waters;

(b) inland waters are related inland waters in relation to any other inland waters, where it appears to the Authority that changes in the flow of the other waters may affect the flow of the first-mentioned inland waters.

(9) For the purposes of subsection (5) above the Authority shall be entitled (but shall not be bound) to treat as lawful any existing use of any inland waters unless—

(a) by a decision given in any legal proceedings, it has been held to be unlawful; and

(b) that decision has not been quashed or reversed;

and in that subsection the reference to land drainage includes a reference to defence against water (including sea water), irrigation other than spray irrigation, warping and the provision of flood warning systems.

DEFINITIONS
"conservancy authority": s.221(1).
"discrete waters": s.221(1).
"functions": s.3.
"harbour authority": s.221(1).
"inland waters": s.221(1).
"navigation authority": s.221(1).
"the Authority": s.221(1).

GENERAL NOTE
This section follows the modification of s.19 of the Water Resources Act 1963 by s.127 of the Water Act 1989 by making the NRA now responsible, if it thinks it appropriate, for determining minimum acceptable flows for inland waters, and for submitting draft statements to the Secretary of State for approval.

The definition of "inland waters", following the Water Resources Act 1963, includes rivers, streams and other water sources, tidal and non-tidal, natural or artificial. Also following the 1963 Act, these provisions do not apply to land-locked lakes or ponds ("discrete waters") since these are not subject to abstraction licensing.

Copies of any minimum acceptable flows established under these procedures must be kept at the offices of the NRA and must be available for public inspection free of charge (Sched. 5).

Although the power to establish minimum acceptable flows has existed since 1963, none was formally determined by water authorities or their predecessors, mainly on the grounds of practical difficulties. In the *Consultation Paper on Water and Sewerage Law* (Department of the Environment, 1981), the Government proposed repealing the provisions completely. This has not been followed up, and they may now have more relevance, particularly in the light of the need to achieve water quality objectives and the general environment duties (ss.16–18). Whether they will be now subject to greater use largely rests with the discretion of the NRA, who need only prepare a statement "if it thinks it appropriate to do so," subject to the power of the Secretary of State to direct it to do so under s.22.

Directions to the Authority to consider minimum acceptable flow

22.—(1) If the Authority is directed by the Secretary of State to consider whether the minimum acceptable flow for any particular inland waters ought to be determined or reviewed, the Authority shall consider that matter as soon as reasonably practicable after being directed to do so.

(2) After considering any matter under subsection (1) above the Authority shall submit to the Secretary of State with respect to the inland waters in question either—

(a) such a draft statement as is mentioned in subsection (1) of section 21 above; or

(b) a draft statement that no minimum acceptable flow ought to be determined for those waters or, as the case may require, that the minimum acceptable flow for those waters does not need to be changed.

and subsections (6) and (7) of that section shall apply in relation to a draft statement under this subsection as they apply in relation to a draft statement under that section.

(3) Without prejudice to the generality of paragraph 4 of Schedule 5 to this Act, the power of the Secretary of State under that paragraph to alter a draft statement before approving it shall include power to substitute a statement containing or amending any such provision as is mentioned in subsection (2) of section 21 above for such a draft statement as is mentioned in subsection (2)(b) of this section.

Minimum acceptable level or volume of inland waters

23.—(1) Where it appears to the Authority, in the case of any particular inland waters, that it would be appropriate to measure the level or the volume (either instead of or in addition to the flow) the Authority may determine that sections 21 and 22 above shall apply in relation to those inland waters as if any reference to the flow were or, as the case may be, included a reference to the level or to the volume.

(2) Where the Authority makes a determination under subsection (1) above with respect to any inland waters, any draft statement prepared for the purposes of section 21 or 22 above, in so far as it relates to those waters, shall state—

(a) whether the level or the volume is to be measured; and

(b) whether it is to be measured instead of, or in addition to, the flow.

(3) Chapter II of this Part shall apply in relation to any inland waters with respect to which a determination has been made under subsection (1) above as if any reference in that Chapter to the flow were, or (as the case may be) included, a reference to the level or, as the case may be, the volume.

DEFINITIONS
  "the Authority": s.221(1).
  "inland waters": s.221(1).

GENERAL NOTE
  This section is taken from the Water Resources Act 1963 (s.22). See General Note to s.21.

CHAPTER II

ABSTRACTION AND IMPOUNDING

Restrictions on abstraction and impounding

Restrictions on abstraction

24.—(1) Subject to the following provisions of this Chapter and to any drought order under Chapter III of this Part, no person shall—

(a) abstract water from any source of supply; or

(b) cause or permit any other person so to abstract any water, except in pursuance of a licence under this Chapter granted by the Authority and in accordance with the provisions of that licence.

(2) Where by virtue of subsection (1) above the abstraction of water contained in any underground strata is prohibited except in pursuance of a licence under this Chapter, no person shall begin, or cause or permit any other person to begin—

(a) to construct any well, borehole or other work by which water may be abstracted from those strata;

(b) to extend any such well, borehole or other work; and

(c) to install or modify any machinery or apparatus by which additional quantities of water may be abstracted from those strata by means of a well, borehole or other work,

unless the conditions specified in subsection (3) below are satisfied.

(3) The conditions mentioned in subsection (2) above are—

(a) that the abstraction of the water or, as the case may be, of the additional quantities of water is authorised by a licence under this Chapter; and

(b) that—

(i) the well, borehole or work, as constructed or extended; or

(ii) the machinery or apparatus, as installed or modified,

fulfils the requirements of that licence as to the means by which water is authorised to be abstracted.

(4) A person shall be guilty of an offence if—

(a) he contravenes subsection (1) or (2) above; or

(b) he is for the purposes of this section the holder of a licence under this Chapter and, in circumstances not constituting such a contravention, does not comply with a condition or requirement imposed by the provisions, as for the time being in force, of that licence.

(5) A person who is guilty of an offence under this section shall be liable—

(a) on summary conviction, to a fine not exceeding the statutory maximum;

(b) on conviction on indictment, to a fine.

(6) The restrictions imposed by this section shall have effect notwithstanding anything in any enactment contained in any Act passed before the passing of the Water Resources Act 1963 on July 31, 1963 or in any statutory provision made or issued, whether before or after the passing of that Act, by virtue of such an enactment.

DEFINITIONS

"abstract": s.221(1).
"licence": s.72(1).
"source of supply": s.221(1).
"statutory provision": s.72(1).
"the Authority": s.221(1).
"underground strata": s.221(1).

GENERAL NOTE

The whole of Chapter II of Pt. II of the Act, dealing with abstraction and impounding, is taken from the Water Resources Act 1963. It reproduces the restrictions on abstraction and impounding that were then governed by individual water authorities, and the NRA has inherited their responsibilities and powers with regard to the granting of licences. The Water Act 1989 contained amendments to the Water Resources Act 1963 (Sched. 13 to the 1989 Act), which gave effect to this wholesale transfer of licensing powers to the NRA.

Abstraction. In addition to the definition to be found in s.221(1), the discharge of water from an overflow has not been said to constitute abstraction, as it flows undisturbed. However, the turning of a valve or tap so as to remove water from a reservoir does constitute abstraction (Decision Letter WS/3471/521/13, April 10, 1969).

Restrictions on impounding

25.—(1) Subject to the following provisions of this Chapter and to any

drought order under Chapter III of this Part, no person shall begin, or cause or permit any other person to begin, to construct or alter any impounding works at any point in any inland waters which are not discrete waters unless—
  (a) a licence under this Chapter granted by the Authority to obstruct or impede the flow of those inland waters at that point by means of impounding works is in force;
  (b) the impounding works will not obstruct or impede the flow of the inland waters except to the extent, and in the manner, authorised by the licence; and
  (c) any other requirements of the licence, whether as to the provision of compensation water or otherwise, are complied with.
  (2) A person shall be guilty of an offence if—
  (a) he contravenes subsection (1) above; or
  (b) he is for the purposes of this section the holder of a licence under this Chapter and, in circumstances not constituting such a contravention, does not comply with a condition or requirement imposed by the provisions, as for the time being in force, of that licence.
  (3) A person who is guilty of an offence under this section shall be liable—
  (a) on summary conviction, to a fine not exceeding the statutory maximum;
  (b) on conviction on indictment, to a fine.
  (4) Subject to subsection (5) below, the restrictions imposed by this section shall have effect notwithstanding anything in any enactment contained in any Act passed before the passing of the Water Resources Act 1963 on July 31, 1963 or in any statutory provision made or issued, whether before or after the passing of that Act, by virtue of such an enactment.
  (5) Subject to subsection (6) below, the restriction on impounding works shall not apply to the construction or alteration of any impounding works, if—
  (a) the construction or alteration of those works; or
  (b) the obstruction or impeding of the flow of the inland waters resulting from the construction or alterations of the works,
is authorised (in whatsoever terms, and whether expressly or by implication) by virtue of any such statutory provision as at the coming into force of this Act was an alternative statutory provision for the purposes of section 36(2) of the Water Resources Act 1963.
  (6) The provisions of this Chapter shall have effect in accordance with subsection (7) below where by virtue of any such provision as is mentioned in subsection (5) above and is for the time being in force—
  (a) any water undertaker or sewerage undertaker to which rights under that provision have been transferred in accordance with a scheme under Schedule 2 to the Water Act 1989 or Schedule 2 to the Water Industry Act 1991; or
  (b) any other person,
is authorised (in whatsoever terms, and whether expressly or by implication) to obstruct or impede the flow of any inland waters by means of impounding works (whether those works have already been constructed or not).
  (7) Where subsection (6) above applies, the provisions of this Chapter shall have effect (with the necessary modifications), where the reference is to the revocation or variation of a licence under this Chapter, as if—
  (a) any reference in those provisions to a licence under this Chapter included a reference to the authorisation mentioned in that subsection; and
  (b) any reference to the holder of such a licence included a reference to the undertaker or other person so mentioned.
  (8) In this Chapter "impounding works" means either of the following, that is to say—

(a) any dam, weir or other works in any inland waters by which water may be impounded;

(b) any works for diverting the flow of any inland waters in connection with the construction or alteration of any dam, weir or other works falling within paragraph (a) above.

DEFINITIONS
"discrete waters": s.221(1).
"impounding works": subs. (8).
"inland waters": s.221(1).
"licence": s.72(1).
"restriction on impounding works": subs. (1) and s.72(1).
"statutory provision": s.72(1).
"the Authority": s.221(1).

GENERAL NOTE
This section sets out the general restriction on the impounding of water from any inland water, apart from separate ponds, without a licence from the Authority (subs. (1)(a)). Impounding without a licence, or breaking the conditions of a licence, is an either way offence (subs. (2)). The circumstances in which impounding without a licence is not an offence are set out in subss. (5)–(7). These are restricted to statutory authorisation other than the Water Acts of 1958 and 1963 that were in force in 1963 (subs. (5)) and water undertakers or sewerage undertakers with such authorisations shall be treated as if they had licences (subs. (7)).
See s.36 for the power to grant a combined abstraction and impounding licence.

Rights to abstract or impound

Rights of navigation, harbour and conservancy authorities

26.—(1) The restriction on abstraction shall not apply to any transfer of water from one area of inland waters to another in the course of, or resulting from, any operations carried out by a navigation authority, harbour authority or conservancy authority in the carrying out of their functions as such an authority.

(2) The restriction on impounding works shall not apply to the construction or alteration of impounding works in the course of the performance by a navigation authority, harbour authority or conservancy authority of their functions as such an authority.

DEFINITIONS
"conservancy authority": s.221(1).
"harbour authority": s.221(1).
"inland waters": s.221(1).
"navigation authority": s.221(1).
"restriction on abstraction": s.72(1).
"restriction on impounding works": s.72(1).

GENERAL NOTE
This section excludes navigation, harbour and conservancy authorities from the requirement to obtain a licence for any transfer of water within inland waters. The only condition is that the authorities' actions should be performed in the course of their functions.

Rights to abstract small quantities

27.—(1) The restriction on abstraction shall not apply to any abstraction of a quantity of water not exceeding five cubic metres if it does not form part of a continuous operation, or of a series of operations, by which a quantity of water which, in aggregate, is more than five cubic metres is abstracted.

(2) The restriction on abstraction shall not apply to any abstraction of a quantity of water not exceeding 20 cubic metres if the abstraction—

(a) does not form part of a continuous operation, or of a series of operations, by which a quantity of water which, in aggregate, is more than 20 cubic metres is abstracted; and

(b) is with the consent of the Authority.

(3) The restriction on abstraction shall not apply to so much of any abstraction from any inland waters by or on behalf of an occupier of contiguous land as falls within subsection (4) below, unless the abstraction is such that the quantity of water abstracted from the inland waters by or on behalf of the occupier by virtue of this subsection exceeds 20 cubic metres, in aggregate, in any period of 24 hours.

(4) Subject to section 28 below, an abstraction of water falls within this subsection in so far as the water—

(a) is abstracted for use on a holding consisting of the contiguous land with or without other land held with that land; and

(b) is abstracted for use on that holding for either or both of the following purposes, that is to say—

(i) the domestic purposes of the occupier's household;

(ii) agricultural purposes other than spray irrigation.

(5) The restriction on abstraction shall not apply to the abstraction of water from underground strata, in so far as the water is abstracted by or on behalf of an individual as a supply of water for the domestic purposes of his household, unless the abstraction is such that the quantity of water abstracted from the strata by or on behalf of that individual by virtue of this subsection exceeds 20 cubic metres, in aggregate, in any period of 24 hours.

(6) For the purposes of this Chapter a person who is in a position to abstract water in such circumstances that, by virtue of subsection (3) or (5) above, the restriction on abstraction does not apply shall be taken to have a right to abstract water to the extent specified in that subsection.

(7) In the case of any abstraction of water from underground strata which falls within subsection (5) above, the restriction imposed by section 24(2) above shall not apply—

(a) to the construction or extension of any well, borehole or other work; or

(b) to the installation or modification of machinery or other apparatus, if the well, borehole or other work is constructed or extended, or the machinery or apparatus is installed or modified, for the purpose of abstracting the water.

(8) In this section "contiguous land," in relation to the abstraction of any water from inland waters, means land contiguous to those waters at the place where the abstraction is effected.

DEFINITIONS

"contiguous land": subs. (8).
"inland waters": s.221(1).
"restriction on abstraction": s.72(1).
"spray irrigation": s.72(1).
"the Authority": s.221(1).
"underground strata": s.221(1).

GENERAL NOTE

Abstractions of small quantities of water are exempted from the licensing system by this section in order to avoid a situation in which the Authority is overloaded with processing a large number of licences that would be of very little significance. For an amount under five cubic metres the restriction is lifted entirely (subs. (1)); for an amount under 20 cubic metres the restriction is lifted but the Authority's consent is required (subs. (2)). In both cases the quantity must not form a part of a larger abstraction operation.

Occupiers of land may abstract up to 20 cubic metres every 24 hours from an inland water that is next to their land (subs. (3)), but only if they use the water on a holding of which the land next to the water source is a part (subs. (4)(a)) and they use it for domestic or agricultural purposes but not for spray irrigation (subs. (4)(b)). (For the definition of "spray irrigation" see, in addition to s.221(1), the Spray Irrigation (Definition) Order 1965 (S.I. 1965 No. 1010)).

Abstraction from underground strata of up to 20 cubic metres every 24 hours is permitted but in this case for domestic purposes only (subs. (5)). By virtue of subs. (7) the building of wells or boreholes for domestic use within the 20 cubic metre a day limit does not require the licence that it would otherwise require under s.24(2).

Curtailment of rights under section 27

28.—(1) The provisions of this section shall have effect where a person ("the occupier") is entitled, by virtue of subsection (6) of section 27 above, to a protected right for the purpose of this Chapter by reason of his being the occupier of such a holding as is mentioned in subsection (4) of that section in relation to an abstraction falling within that subsection ("the holding").

(2) If it appears to the Authority that the occupier is entitled, as against other occupiers of land contiguous to the inland waters in question, to abstract water from those waters for use on part of the holding ("the relevant part"), but is not so entitled to abstract water for use on other parts of the holding—

(a) the Authority may serve on him a notice specifying the relevant part of the holding; and

(b) subject to the following provisions of this section, the notice shall have effect so as to require subsections (3) and (4) of section 27 above to be construed in relation to the holding as if the references in subsection (4) to use on the holding were references to use on the part of the holding specified in the notice.

(3) Where a notice is served under subsection (2) above and the occupier objects to the notice on the grounds—

(a) that he is entitled, as against other occupiers of land contiguous to the inland waters in question, to abstract water from those waters for use on every part of the holding; or

(b) that he is so entitled to abstract water for use on a larger part of the holding than that specified in the notice,

he may, within such period (not being less than 28 days from the date of service of the notice) and in such manner as may be prescribed, appeal to the court against the notice.

(4) On any appeal under subsection (3) above, the court shall determine the matter in dispute and, in accordance with its decision, confirm, quash or vary the Authority's notice and—

(a) where the court quashes a notice served under subsection (2) above, paragraph (b) of that subsection shall not have effect; and

(b) where the court varies such a notice, that paragraph shall have effect, but with the substitution, for the reference to the part of the holding specified in the notice, of a reference to the part specified in the notice as varied by the court.

(5) In this section—

"the court" means the county court for the district in which the holding, or the part of the holding which is contiguous to the inland waters in question, is situated; and

"entitled" (except in subsection (1) above) means entitled apart from this Chapter or any other statutory provision.

DEFINITIONS

"entitled": subs. (5).
"inland waters": s.221(1).
"notice": s.221(1).
"protected right": s.72(1).
"the Authority": s.221(1).
"the court": subs. (5).

GENERAL NOTE

Subs. (6) of s.27 gives a protected right to occupiers of land to abstract up to 20 cubic metres a day from an inland water next to their land, but only to be used on the holding of which the land next to the water source is a part. This section envisages a situation in which the layout of a holding is such that an occupier is able to extract water from a source but use it to irrigate land that is some distance away, or to cover a considerably greater area than other holdings that are also entitled to abstract water from the same source. It gives the Authority the power to restrict the occupier's use of the water to a part of the holding (subs. (2)(a)). Section 27 will then operate as if the part of the holding that the Authority has specified were the entire holding (subs. (2)(b)). The occupier can, within 28 days, appeal to the County Court (subs. (3)).

Rights to abstract for drainage purposes etc.

29.—(1) The restriction on abstraction shall not apply to any abstraction of water from a source of supply in the course of, or resulting from, any operations for purposes of land drainage.

(2) The restriction on abstraction shall not apply to any abstraction of water from a source of supply in so far as the abstraction (where it does not fall within subsection (1) above) is necessary—

(a) to prevent interference with any mining, quarrying, engineering, building or other operations (whether underground or on the surface); or

(b) to prevent damage to works resulting from any such operations.

(3) Where—

(a) water is abstracted, in the course of any such operations as are mentioned in subsection (2) above, from any excavation into underground strata in a case in which the level of water in the underground strata depends wholly or mainly on water entering it from those strata; and

(b) the abstraction is necessary as mentioned in that subsection,

the exemption conferred by that subsection shall apply notwithstanding that the water is used for the purposes of the operations.

(4) In the case of any abstraction of water from underground strata which falls within subsection (1) or (2) above, the restriction imposed by section 24(2) above shall not apply—

(a) to the construction or extension of any well, borehole or other work; or

(b) to the installation or modification of machinery or other apparatus,

if the well, borehole or other work is constructed or extended, or the machinery or apparatus is installed or modified, for the purpose of abstracting the water.

(5) In this section, "land drainage" includes the protection of land against erosion or encroachment by water, whether from inland waters or from the sea, and also includes warping and irrigation other than spray irrigation.

DEFINITIONS
"land drainage": subs. (5).
"restriction on abstraction": s.72(1).
"source of supply": s.221(1).
"spray irrigation": s.72(1).
"underground strata": s.221(1).

GENERAL NOTE
This section exempts abstractions in the course of land drainage and works that involve draining mines, quarries or building sites from the restriction on abstraction. The abstraction has to be necessary to prevent interference with (subs. (2)(a)) or damage to (subs. (2)(b)) such operations. Subsection (3) states that the use of abstracted water for the purposes of the operations, in the case of excavation into water-bearing underground strata, does not prevent the right to abstract in subs. (2) having effect. A typical situation that this subsection is designed to cover would be the use of water taken from a gravel pit to wash the gravel extracted from it. As with s.27(7), the requirement for a licence to build, extend or instal pumping equipment in a well or borehole (s.24(2)) does not apply in a situation that falls within subs. (3). See s.30 for notices that need to be served in respect of borings under this section.

Notices with respect to borings not requiring licences

30.—(1) Where any person—

(a) proposes to construct a well, borehole or other work which is to be used solely for the purpose of abstracting, to the extent necessary to prevent interference with the carrying out or operation of any underground works, water contained in underground strata; or

(b) proposes to extend any such well, borehole or other work,

he shall, before he begins to construct or extend the work, give to the Authority a notice of his intention in the prescribed form.

(2) Where a notice under subsection (1) above is given to the Authority by any person, the Authority may (subject to section 31 below) by notice to that person require him, in connection with the construction, extension or use of the work to which that person's notice relates, to take such reasonable measures for conserving water as are specified in the notice.

(3) The measures that may be specified in a notice under subsection (2) above shall be measures which, in the opinion of the Authority, will not interfere with the protection of the underground works in question.

(4) Any person who contravenes subsection (1) above or fails to comply with a notice under subsection (2) above shall be guilty of an offence and liable—

(a) on summary conviction, to a fine not exceeding the statutory maximum;

(b) on conviction on indictment, to a fine.

DEFINITIONS
"notice": s.221(1).
"prescribed": s.221(1).
"the Authority": s.221(1).

GENERAL NOTE
Construction of a well or borehole that falls under s.29 and therefore does not require a licence (s.29(4)) must nevertheless be brought to the attention of the Authority in advance under this section. The Authority then has the power to respond with a conservation notice specifying reasonable measures to be taken to conserve water (subs. (2)). The Authority must consider the safety of the operation when deciding on conservation measures (subs. (3)). Failing to give notice to the Authority of a proposed operation, or failing to observe a conservation notice, is an either way offence (subs. (4)).

The sinking of a borehole and the extraction of water will be an engineering or other operation or may be a change of use of land and thus requires planning permission under s.57 of the Town and Country Planning Act 1990. In some cases the planning authority will have to consider any relevant environmental impact under the Assessment of Environmental Effects Regulations 1988 (S.I. 1988 No. 1199, reg. 4(2), and Sched. 2, para. 2(b)(iii)).

See s.31 for appeals against conservation notices issued under this section.

Appeals against conservation notices under section 30

31.—(1) The person on whom a notice under section 30(2) above ("a conservation notice") is served may, by notice to the Secretary of State, appeal to him against the conservation notice on either or both of the following grounds, that is to say—

(a) that the measures required by the conservation notice are not reasonable;

(b) that those measures would interfere with the protection of the underground works in question.

(2) Any notice of appeal against a conservation notice shall be served within such period (not being less than 28 days from the date of service of the conservation notice) and in such manner as may be prescribed.

(3) Before determining an appeal against a conservation notice, the Secretary of State may, if he thinks fit—

(a) cause a local inquiry to be held; or

(b) afford to the appellant and the Authority an opportunity of appearing before, and being heard by, a person appointed by the Secretary of State for the purpose;

and the Secretary of State shall act as mentioned in paragraph (a) or (b) above is a request is made by the appellant or the Authority to be heard with respect to the appeal.

(4) On an appeal against a conservation notice the Secretary of State may confirm, quash or vary the notice as he may consider appropriate.

(5) The decision of the Secretary of State on any appeal against a conservation notice shall be final.

(6) The Secretary of State may be regulation make provision as to the manner in which appeals against conservation notices are to be dealt with, including provision requiring the giving of notices of, and information relating to, the making of such appeals or decisions on any such appeals.

DEFINITIONS
"notices": s.221(1).
"prescribed": s.221(1).
"the Authority": s.221(1).

GENERAL NOTE
Appeals against conservation notices issued by the Authority under s.30 may be framed either in terms of the reasonableness of the Authority's conditions or in terms of the protection of the operation (subs. (1)). The Secretary of State has a discretion to hold a local inquiry or a hearing of the parties (subs. (3)).
Section 250 of the Local Government Act 1972 applies to local inquiries held under this section. See also s.215 below.

Miscellaneous rights to abstract

32.—(1) The restriction on abstraction shall not apply to any abstraction by machinery or apparatus installed on a vessel, where the water is abstracted for use on that, or any other, vessel.

(2) The restriction on abstraction and the other restrictions imposed by section 24 above shall not apply to the doing of anything—
(a) for fire-fighting purposes (within the meaning of the Fire Services Act 1947); or
(b) for the purpose of testing apparatus used for those purposes or of training or practice in the use of such apparatus.

(3) The restriction on abstraction and the other restrictions imposed by section 24 above shall not apply—
(a) to any abstraction of water;
(b) to the construction or extension of any well, borehole or other work; or
(c) to the installation or modification of machinery or other apparatus,
if the abstraction, construction, extension, installation or modification is for any of the purposes specified in subsection (4) below and takes place with the consent of the Authority and in compliance with any conditions imposed by the Authority.

(4) The purposes mentioned in subsection (3) above are—
(a) the purpose of ascertaining the presence of water in any underground strata or the quality or quantity of any such water; and
(b) the purpose of ascertaining the effect of abstracting water from the well, borehole or other work in question on the abstraction of water from, or the level of water in, any other well, borehole or other work or any inland waters.

DEFINITIONS
"inland waters": s.221(1).
"restriction on abstraction": s.72(1).

"the Authority": s.221(1).
"vessel": s.221(1).

<small>GENERAL NOTE</small>

Also exempted from the general restriction on abstraction of water in s.24 are abstraction by a vessel for use on a vessel (subs. (1)), fire-fighting, including testing and training (subs. (2)), and tests of quality, quantity or the relationship between one well and another (subs. (4)).

Power to provide for further rights to abstract

33.—(1) Any of the relevant authorities, after consultation with the other relevant authorities (if any), may apply to the Secretary of State for an order excepting any one or more sources of supply from the restriction on abstraction, on the grounds that the restriction is not needed in relation to that source of supply or, as the case may be, those sources of supply.

(2) An application under this section may be made in respect of—

(a) any one or more areas of inland waters specified in the application or any class of inland waters so specified; or

(b) any underground strata described in the application, whether by reference to their formation on their location in relation to the surface of the land or in relation to other strata subjacent to that surface or partly in one way and partly in another;

and an order may be made under this section accordingly.

(3) For the purposes of this section—

(a) the Authority is a relevant authority in relation to every source of supply; and

(b) a navigation authority, harbour authority or conservancy authority having functions in relation to any inland waters is a relevant authority in relation to those inland waters.

(4) If, in the case of any source of supply—

(a) it appears to the Secretary of State, after consultation with the Authority, that the question whether the restriction on abstraction is needed in relation to that source of supply ought to be determined; but

(b) no application for an order under this section has been made,

the Secretary of State may direct the Authority to make an application under this section in respect to that source of supply.

(5) Schedule 6 to this Act shall have effect with respect to applications for orders under this section and with respect to the making of such orders; and the power to make any such order shall be exercisable by statutory instrument.

(6) On the coming into force of an order under this section—

(a) the restriction on abstraction and, in the case of any underground strata, the restriction imposed by subsection (2) of section 24 above shall cease to apply to any source of supply to which the order relates; and

(b) any licence granted under this Chapter which is for the time being in force shall cease to have effect in so far as it authorises abstraction from any such source of supply.

<small>DEFINITIONS</small>

"conservancy authority": s.221(1).
"inland waters": s.221(1).
"harbour authority": s.221(1).
"navigation authority": s.221(1).
"relevant authorities": subs. (3).
"source of supply": s.221(1).
"the Authority": s.221(1).
"underground strata": s.221(1).

GENERAL NOTE

This section provides the NRA with regard to all sources of supply, and the other authorities with regard to waters in their areas, with a mechanism whereby a source of supply can be taken out of the system restricting abstraction under s.24 on the grounds that restriction is not necessary. The Secretary of State may prompt the Authority to apply for a source of supply to be so excluded (subs. (4)), and this can include the Authority making such an application for an area that comes within the functional ambit of one of the other authorities (subs. (3)(a)).

Applications for a licence

Regulations with respect to applications

34.—(1) Any application for a licence under this Chapter shall be made in such manner as may be prescribed, and shall include such particulars, and be verified by such evidence, as may be prescribed.

(2) The Secretary of State may be regulations make provision as to the manner in which applications for the grant of licences under this Chapter are to be dealt with, including provision requiring the giving of notices of, and information relating to, the making of such applications or decisions on such applications.

(3) Without prejudice to the generality of subsection (2) above, provision shall be made by regulations under this section for securing that, in such circumstances as may be prescribed (being circumstances in which it appears to the Secretary of State that applications for licences under this Chapter would be of special concern to National Park planning authorities)—

(a) notice of any such application will be given to such one or more National Park planning authorities as may be determined in accordance with the regulations; and

(b) the matters to which the Authority or, as the case may be, the Secretary of State is to have regard in dealing with the application will include any representations made by any such National Park planning authority within such period and in such manner as may be prescribed.

(4) The preceding provisions of this section shall have effect subject to any express provision contained in, or having effect by virtue of, any other enactment contained in the Chapter; and any regulations made under this section shall have effect subject to any such express provision.

(5) In this section "National Park planning authority" means a local planning authority whose area consists of, or includes, the whole or any part of a National Park.

DEFINITIONS
  "enactment": s.221(1).
  "licence": s.72(1).
  "National Park planning authority": subs. (5).
  "notices": s.221(1).

GENERAL NOTE

The Water Resources (Licences) Regulations 1965 (S.I. 1965 No. 534) contain details of the forms, issued by the NRA, to be used in applications. The regulations prohibit the Authority from considering an application unless it is accompanied by a notice in the prescribed form, together with the required evidence (S.I. 1965 No. 534, reg. 6(4)).

Subs. (3)

This subsection imposes a duty on the Secretary of State and the Authority to consider representations from National Park planning authorities concerning any application for abstraction or impounding licences that would affect a National Park.

Restrictions on person who may make applications for abstraction licences

35.—(1) No application for a licence under this Chapter to abstract water shall be entertained unless it is made by a person entitled to make the application in accordance with the following provisions of this section.

(2) In relation to abstractions from any inland waters, a person shall be entitled to make the application if, at the place (or, if more than one, at each of the places) at which the proposed abstractions are to be effected, either—

(a) he is the occupier of land contiguous to the inland waters; or

(b) he satisfies the Authority that he has, or at the time when the proposed licence is to take effect will have, a right of access to such land.

(3) In relation to abstractions from underground strata, a person shall be entitled to make the application if either—

(a) he is the occupier of land consisting of or comprising those underground strata; or

(b) the following two conditions are satisfied, that is to say—

(i) the case is one in which water contained in an excavation into underground strata is to be treated as water contained in those strata by virtue of the level of water in the excavation depending wholly or mainly on water entering it from those strata; and

(ii) that person satisfies the Authority that he has, or at the time when the proposed licence is to take effect will have, a right of access to land consisting of, or comprising, those underground strata.

(4) Any reference in this section to a person who is the occupier of land of any description—

(a) includes a reference to a person who satisfies the Authority that he has entered into negotiations for the acquisition of an interest in land of that description such that, if the interest is acquired by him, he will be entitled to occupy that land; and

(b) without prejudice to the application of paragraph (a) above to a person who is or can be authorised to acquire land compulsorily, also includes any person who satisfies the Authority that by virtue of any enactment, the compulsory acquisition by that person of land of that description either has been authorised or can be authorised and has been intitiated.

(5) In subsection (4) above the reference to initiating the compulsory acquisition of land by a person is a reference to—

(a) the submission to the relevant Minister of a draft of an order which, if made by that Minister in the form of the draft, will authorise that person to acquire that land compulsorily, with or without other land; or

(b) the submission to the relevant Minister of an order which, if confirmed by that Minister as submitted will authorise that person to acquire that land compulsorily, with or without other land.

(6) In subsection (5) above "the relevant Minister," in relation to the compulsory acquisition of land by any person, means the Minister who, in accordance with the enactment mentioned in subsection (4)(b) above, is empowered to authorise that person to acquire land compulsorily.

DEFINITIONS

"enactment": s.221(1).
"initiating the compulsory acquisition of land": subs. (5).
"inland waters": s.221(1).
"licence": s.72(1).
"occupier of land": subs. (4).
"the Authority": s.221(1).
"the relevant Minister": subs. (6).
"underground strata": s.221(1).

GENERAL NOTE

This section restricts those who can apply for abstraction licences. For inland waters the applicant must be the occupier of, or have right of access to, land that is next to the source to which the application relates (subs. (2)). In the case of underground strata the applicant must be the occupier of the land comprising the underground strata or of land that contains an excavation that is filled with water that comes from the strata surrounding it (subs. (3)). Persons who are in the process of obtaining the right to occupy land or who are compulsorily purchasing it may apply for a licence if they can satisfy the Authority that the process that will lead to their acquisition of the appropriate rights has started (subs. (4)).

Application for combined abstraction and impounding licence

36. Where a licence under this Chapter is required by virtue of section 25 above for constructing or altering impounding works at a point in any inland waters, for the purpose of abstracting water from those waters at or near that point—

(a) an application may be made to the Authority for a combined licence under this Chapter to obstruct or impede the flow of those inland waters by means of impounding works at that point and to abstract the water; and

(b) the Authority shall have power (subject to the provisions of this Chapter as to procedure and as to the matters to be taken into account in dealing with applications for licences) to grant such a licence accordingly.

DEFINITIONS
    "flow": s.72(1).
    "impounding works": s.72(1).
    "inland waters": s.221(1).
    "licence": s.72(1).
    "the Authority": s.221(1).

Publication of application for licence

37.—(1) The Authority shall not entertain an application for a licence under this Chapter to abstract water or to obstruct or impede the flow of any inland waters by means of impounding works or for a combined licence, unless the application is accompanied—

(a) by a copy of a notice in the prescribed form; and

(b) by the prescribed evidence that the necessary notices of the application have been given.

(2) Subject to subsection (3) below, the necessary notices of any application have been given for the purposes of subsection (1) above if—

(a) the notice mentioned in paragraph (a) of that subsection has been published—
    (i) in the London Gazette; and
    (ii) at least once in each of two successive weeks, in one or more newspapers (other than the London Gazette) circulating in the relevant locality;
    and

(b) a copy of that notice has been served, not later than the date on which it was first published as mentioned in paragraph (a)(ii) above—
    (i) on any navigation authority, harbour authority or conservancy authority having functions in relation to any inland waters at a proposed point of abstraction or impounding;
    (ii) on the drainage board for any internal drainage district within which any such proposed point is situated; and
    (iii) on any water undertaker within whose area any such proposed point is situated.

(3) Where the licence applied for is exclusively for the abstraction of water from a source of supply that does not form part of any inland waters, the giving of the necessary notices shall not for the purposes of subsection (1) above require the service of any copy of the notice mentioned in paragraph

(a) of that subsection on any navigation authority, harbour authority, conservancy authority or drainage board.

(4) A notice for the purposes of the preceding provisions of this section, in addition to containing any other matters required to be contained in that notice, shall—

  (a) name a place within the relevant locality where a copy of the application, and of any map, plan or other document submitted with it, will be open to inspection by the public, free of charge, at all reasonable hours during a period specified in the notice in accordance with subsection (5) below; and

  (b) state that any person may make representations in writing to the Authority with respect to the application at any time before the end of that period.

(5) The period specified in a notice for the purposes of the preceding provisions of this section shall be a period which—

  (a) begins not earlier than the date on which the notice is first published in a newspaper other than the London Gazette; and

  (b) ends not less than 28 days from that date and not less than 25 days from the date on which the notice is published in the London Gazette.

(6) Where—

  (a) an application for a licence under this Chapter to abstract water is made to the Authority; and

  (b) the application proposes that the quantity of water abstracted in pursuance of the licence should not in any period of 24 hours exceed, in aggregate, 20 cubic metres or any lesser amount specified in the application,

the Authority may dispense with the requirements imposed by virtue of the preceding provisions of this section if and to the extent that it appears to the Authority appropriate to do so.

(7) In this section—

    "proposed point of abstraction or impounding," in relation to any application for a licence under this Chapter, means a place where a licence, if granted in accordance with the application, would authorise water to be abstracted or, as he case may be, would authorise inland waters to be obstructed or impeded by means of impounding works; and

    "relevant locality," in relation to an application for a licence under this Act, means the locality in which any proposed point of abstraction or impounding is situated.

DEFINITIONS

  "conservancy authority": s.221(1).
  "flow": s.72(1).
  "harbour authority": s.221(1).
  "inland waters": s.221(1).
  "licence": s.72(1).
  "navigation authority": s.221(1).
  "notice": s.221(1).
  "prescribed": s.221(1).
  "proposed point of abstraction or impounding": subs. (7).
  "relevant locality": subs. (7).
  "source of supply": s.221(1).
  "the Authority": s.221(1).

GENERAL NOTE

  This section sets out the publicity requirements for licence applications. Notice of applications for abstraction, impounding or combined licences must be published in the London Gazette and a local paper and served on the appropriate navigation, harbour or conservancy authority, drainage board or water undertaker (subs. (2)). Proof that these steps have been taken must accompany the application when it is submitted to the Authority (subs. (1)(b)). The applicant must also provide a copy of the application, with maps or plans, for inspection by the public and make clear that representations may be made to the Authority (subs. (4)).

Subs. (5)
This subsection sets out the minimum time that must be allowed for public access to the application and for representations to be made. The minimum period is 28 days from the publication of the notice of the application in a local paper, and 25 days from its publication in the London Gazette (if that date is later).

Subs. (6)
The Authority need not insist on the above procedures if the application is for an abstraction rate of less than 20 cubic metres per day that does not come within s.27 (rights to abstract small quantities).

Consideration of licence applications

General consideration of applications

38.—(1) The Authority shall not determine any application for a licence under this Chapter before the end of the period specified for the purposes of the application in accordance with section 37(5) above.

(2) Subject to the following provisions of this Chapter, on any application to the Authority for a licence under this Chapter, the Authority—
  (a) may grant a licence containing such provisions as the Authority considers appropriate; or
  (b) if, having regard to the provisions of this Chapter, the Authority considers it necessary or expedient to do so, may refuse to grant a licence.

(3) Without prejudice to section 39(1) below, the Authority, in dealing with any application for a licence under this Chapter, shall have regard to—
  (a) any representations in writing relating to the application which are received by the Authority before the end of the period mentioned in subsection (1) above; and
  (b) the requirements of the applicant, in so far as they appear to the Authority to be reasonable requirements.

DEFINITIONS
"licence": s.72(1).
"the Authority": s.221(1).

GENERAL NOTE
This section sets out the Authority's general power either to grant or to refuse a licence to abstract or impound water. The Authority is required to have regard to any representations that are produced, within the one-month time limit in s.37(5), by the public consultation process and to the reasonable requirements of the applicant.

Obligation to have regard to existing rights and privileges

39.—(1) The Authority shall not, except with the consent of the person entitled to the rights, grant a licence so authorising—
  (a) the abstraction of water; or
  (b) the flow of any inland waters to be obstructed or impeded by means of impounding works,
as to derogate from any rights which, at the time when the application is determined by the Authority, are protected rights for the purposes of this Chapter.

(2) In a case where an application for a licence under this Chapter relates to abstraction from underground strata, the Authority, in dealing with the application, shall have regard to the requirements of existing lawful uses of water abstracted from those strata, whether for agriculture, industry, water supply or other purposes.

(3) For the purposes of this Chapter a right is a protected right if it is such a right as a person is taken to have by virtue of section 27(6) above or section 48(1) below; and any reference in this Chapter to the person entitled to such a right shall be construed accordingly.

(4) Any reference in this Chapter, in relation to the abstraction of water or obstructing or impeding the flow of any inland waters by means of impounding works, to derogating from a right which is a protected right for the purposes of this Chapter is a reference to, as the case may be—
  (a) abstracting water; or
  (b) so obstructing or impeding the flow of any such waters,
in such a way, or to such an extent, as to prevent the person entitled to that right from abstracting water to the extent mentioned in section 27(6) above or, as the case may be, section 48(1) below.

(5) For the purposes of subsection (2) above the Authority shall be entitled (but shall not be bound) to treat as lawful any existing use of water from underground strata unless—
  (a) by a decision given in any legal proceedings, it has been held to be unlawful; and
  (b) that decision has not been quashed or reversed.

DEFINITIONS
  "abstraction": s.221(1).
  "flow": s.72(1).
  "impounding works": s.72(1).
  "inland waters": s.221(1).
  "licence": s.72(1).
  "protected right": subs. (3).
  "the Authority": s.221(1).
  "underground strata": s.221(1).

GENERAL NOTE
  This section prevents the Authority, unless with consent, from granting a licence that will interfere with a protected right under s.27(6) (rights to abstract small quantities for domestic or agricultural use) and s.48(1) (licence-holders in general). The latter of these two sections means that the Authority must have regard to existing licence-holders when it is considering an application for a new licence, and should not grant one if it would interfere with the abstraction or impounding operations of an existing licence-holder.

Obligation to take river flow etc. into account

40.—(1) Without prejudice to sections 38(3) and 39(1) above, subsection (2) or, as the case may be, subsection (3) below shall apply where any application for a licence under this Chapter relates to abstraction from any inland waters or to obstructing or impeding the flow of any inland waters by means of impounding works.

(2) If, in the case of such an application as is mentioned in subsection (1) above, the application is made at a time when no minimum acceptable flow for the inland waters in question has been detemined under Chapter I of this Part, the Authority, in dealing with the application, shall have regard to the considerations by reference to which, in accordance with section 21(4) and (5) above, a minimum acceptable flow for those waters would fall to be determined.

(3) If, in the case of such an application as is mentioned in subsection (1) above, the application is made at a time after a minimum acceptable flow for the waters in question has been determined under Chapter I of this Part, the Authority, in dealing with the application, shall have regard to the need to secure or, as the case may be, secure in relation to the different times or periods for which the flow is determined—
  (a) that the flow at any control point will not be reduced below the minimum acceptable flow at that point; or

(b) if it is already less than that minimum acceptable flow, that the flow at any control point will not be further reduced below the minimum acceptable flow at that point.

(4) Without prejudice to sections 38(3) and 39(1) above, where—

(a) an application for a licence under this Chapter relates to abstraction from underground strata; and

(b) it appears to the Authority that the proposed abstraction is likely to affect the flow, level or volume of any inland waters which are neither discrete waters nor waters comprised in an order under section 33 above,

subsection (2) or, as the case may be, subsection (3) above shall apply as if the application related to abstraction from those waters.

DEFINITIONS
"abstraction": s.221(1).
"discrete waters": s.221(1).
"flow": s.72(1).
"impounding works": s.72(1).
"inland waters": s.221(1).
"licence": s.72(1).
"minimum acceptable flow": s.221(1).
"the Authority": s.221(1).
"underground strata": s.221(1).

GENERAL NOTE
In addition to its obligation to consider public representations, the requirements of the applicant (s.38(3)) and existing rights (s.39(1)) when deciding on licence applications, this section obliges the Authority also to consider the effect of granting a licence on river flow. If a minimum acceptable flow has not been fixed, the issue should be considered as it would be in fixing one (subs. (2)), and if one has been fixed the Authority should have regard to the effect that the granting of the application would have on it (subs. (3)).

Call-in of applications

Secretary of State's power to call in applications

41.—(1) The Secretary of State may give directions to the Authority requiring applications for licences under this Chapter to be referred to him, instead of being dealt with by the Authority.

(2) A direction under this section—

(a) may relate either to a particular application or to applications of a class specified in the direction; and

(b) may except from the operation of the direction such classes of applications as may be specified in the direction in such circumstances as may be so specified.

DEFINITIONS
"licences": s.72(1).
"the Authority": s.221(1).

Consideration of called-in applications

42.—(1) Subject to the following provisions of this section and to section 46 below, the Secretary of State, on considering a called-in application—

(a) may determine that a licence shall be granted containing such provisions as he considers appropriate; or

(b) if, having regard to the provisions of this Act, he considers it necessary or expedient to do so, may determine that no licence shall be granted.

(2) Before determining a called-in application, the Secretary of State may, if he thinks fit—

(a) cause a local inquiry to be held; or
(b) afford to the applicant and the Authority an opportunity of appearing before, and being heard by, a person appointed by the Secretary of State for the purpose;

and the Secretary of State shall act as mentioned in paragraph (a) or (b) above if a request is made by the applicant or the Authority to be heard with respect to the application.

(3) The provisions of sections 37, 38(1) and (3), 39(2) and 40 above shall apply in relation to any called-in application as if—
(a) any reference in those provisions to the Authority, except the references in sections 37(4)(b) and (6)(a) and 38(3)(a), were a reference to the Secretary of State; and
(b) any reference to section 39(1) above were a reference to subsection (4) below.

(4) In determining any called-in application and, in particular, in determining what (if any) direction to give under subsection (5) below, the Secretary of State shall consider whether any such direction would require the grant of a licence which would so authorise—
(a) the abstraction of water; or
(b) the flow of any inland waters to be obstructed or impeded by means of impounding works,

as to derogate from rights which, at the time when the direction in question is given, are protected rights for the purposes of this Chapter.

(5) Where the decision of the Secretary of State on a called-in application is that a licence is to be granted, the decision shall include a direction to the Authority to grant a licence containing such provisions as may be specified in the direction.

(6) The decision of the Secretary of State on any called-in application shall be final.

(7) In this section "called-in application" means an application referred to the Secretary of State in accordance with directions under section 41 above.

DEFINITIONS
"called-in application": subs. (7).
"licence": s.72(1).
"the Authority": s.221(1).

GENERAL NOTE
This section mirrors for called-in applications the same obligations and powers set out in ss.38–40. The only distinction is the Secretary of State's discretion to hold a local inquiry or a hearing of the applicant and the Authority, and he must do one or the other if a request to be heard is made by either the applicant or the Authority (subs. (2)). A decision by the Secretary of State to grant a licence results not in the granting of one by him directly but in a direction to the Authority to do so (subs. (5)).

Section 250 of the Local Government Act 1972 applies to any local inquiry held under this section by virtue of s.215 below.

Appeals with respect to decisions on licence applications

Appeals to the Secretary of State

43.—(1) Where an application has been made to the Authority for a licence under this Chapter, the applicant may by notice appeal to the Secretary of State if—
(a) the applicant is dissatisfied with the decision of the Authority on the application; or
(b) the Authority fails within the period specified in subsection (2) below to give to the applicant either—
(i) notice of the Authority's decision on the application; or

(ii) notice that the application has been referred to the Secretary of State in accordance with any direction under section 41 above.

(2) The period mentioned in subsection (1)(b) above is—

(a) except in a case falling within paragraph (b) below, such period as may be prescribed; and

(b) where an extended period is at any time agreed in writing between the applicant and the Authority, the extended period.

(3) A notice of appeal under this section shall be served—

(a) in such manner as may be prescribed; and

(b) within such period as may be prescribed, being a period of not less than 28 days from, as the case may be—

(i) the date on which the decision to which it relates was notified to the applicant; or

(ii) the end of the period which, by virtue of subsection (2) above, is applicable for the purposes of subsection (1)(b) above.

(4) Where a notice is served under this section in respect of any application, the applicant shall, within the period prescribed for the purposes of subsection (3)(b) above, serve a copy of the notice on the Authority.

(5) Where any representations in writing with respect to an application were made within the period specified for the purposes of the application in accordance with section 37(5) above, the Secretary of State shall, before determining an appeal under this section in respect of the application, require the Authority to serve a copy of the notice of appeal on each of the persons who made those representations.

DEFINITIONS
"notice": s.72(1).
"prescribed": s.221(1).
"the Authority": s.221(1).

GENERAL NOTE
The right to appeal against a licence decision by the Authority is broad, since subs. (1) states that the applicant may appeal if dissatisfied or if the Authority has failed to respond to the application. The notice of appeal must be served on the Authority (subs. (4)), and the Authority must, in turn, serve it on any person who made representations to the Authority about the application (subs. (5)).

Determination of appeals

44.—(1) Subject to the following provisions of this Chapter, where an appeal is brought under section 43 above, the Secretary of State—

(a) may allow or dismiss the appeal or reverse or vary any part of the decision of the Authority, whether the appeal relates to that part of the decision or not; and

(b) may deal with the application as if it had been made to him in the first instance;

and for the purposes of this section an appeal by virtue of section 43(1)(b) above shall be taken to be an appeal against a refusal of the application.

(2) Before determining an appeal under section 43 above, the Secretary of State may, if he thinks fit—

(a) cause a local inquiry to be held; or

(b) afford to the applicant and the Authority an opportunity of appearing before, and being heard by, a person appointed by the Secretary of State for the purpose;

and the Secretary of State shall act as mentioned in paragraph (a) or (b) above if a request is made by the applicant or the Authority to be heard with respect to the appeal.

(3) The Secretary of State, in determining an appeal under section 43 above, shall take into account—

(a) any further representations in writing received by him, within the prescribed period, from the persons mentioned in section 43(5) above; and

(b) the requirements of the applicant, in so far as they appear to the Secretary of State to be reasonable requirements.

(4) In determining any appeal under section 43 above and, in particular, in determining what (if any) direction to give under subsection (6) below, the Secretary of State shall consider whether any such direction would require such a grant or variation of a licence as would so authorise—

(a) the abstraction of water; or

(b) the flow of any inland waters to be obstructed or impeded by means of impounding works,

as to derogate from rights which, at the time when the direction in question is given, are protected rights for the purposes of this Chapter.

(5) The provisions of sections 39(2) and 40 above shall apply in relation to any appeal under section 43 above as if—

(a) any reference in those provisions to the Authority, were a reference to the Secretary of State; and

(b) the references to sections 38(3) and 39(1) above were references to subsections (3) and (4) above.

(6) Where the decision on an appeal under section 43 above is that a licence is to be granted or to be varied or revoked, the decision shall include a direction to the Authority, as the case may be—

(a) to grant a licence containing such provisions as may be specified in the direction;

(b) to vary the licence so as to contain such provisions as may be so specified; or

(c) to revoke the licence.

(7) The decision of the Secretary of State on any appeal under section 43 above shall be final.

DEFINITIONS
   "abstraction": s.221(1).
   "flow": s.72(1).
   "impounding works": s.72(1).
   "inland waters": s.221(1).
   "the Authority": s.221(1).

GENERAL NOTE
   In considering an appeal the Secretary of State will weigh the interests of those enjoying protected rights and likely to be affected by the abstraction of water in accordance with the proposed licence against the agricultural or other advantages of it (Decision Letter WS/5530/733/66, March 3, 1987).
   The determination of appeals by the Secretary of State follows the same pattern as that of applications by the Authority (see ss.38–40).

Subs. (2)
   As with called-in applications (s.42), the Secretary of State may hold a local inquiry or hold a hearing with the Authority and the applicant present, and he must do one or the other if a request to be heard is made by either the applicant or the Authority.
   Section 250 of the Local Government Act 1972 applies to any local inquiry held under this section by virtue of s.215 below.

Subs. (3)
   The Secretary of State has a duty to take into account any further representations made by those persons that made representations to the Authority regarding the initial application.

Regulations with respect to appeals

   45.—(1) The Secretary of State may by regulations make provision as to the manner in which appeals against decisions on applications for the grant, revocation or variation of licences under this Chapter are to be dealt with, including provisions requiring the giving of notices of, and information relating to, the making of such appeals or decisions on any such appeals.

(2) Without prejudice to the generality of subsection (1) above, provision shall be made by regulations under this section for securing that, in prescribed circumstances (being circumstances in which it appears to the Secretary of State that applications for licences under this Chapter would be of special concern to National Park planning authorities)—

(a) notice of any appeal against the decision on such an application, will be served on any National Park planning authority who made representations falling within paragraph (b) of section 34(3) above; and

(b) the Secretary of State, in determining the appeal, will take account of any further representations made by such an authority within such period and in such manner as may be prescribed.

(3) Subsections (4) and (5) of section 34 above shall apply for the purposes of this section as they apply for the purposes of that section.

DEFINITIONS
"National Park planning authority": s.34(5).
"notices": s.221(1).
"prescribed": s.221(1).

Form, contents and effect of licences

Form and contents of licences

46.—(1) The Secretary of State may by regulations make provisions as to the form of licences under this Chapter or of any class of such licences; but any regulations under this subsection shall have effect subject to the following provisions of this section and to any other express provision contained in, or having effect by virtue of, any other enactment contained in this Chapter.

(2) Every licence under this Chapter to abstract water shall make—

(a) provision as to the quantity of water authorised to be abstracted in pursuance of the licence from the source of supply to which the licence relates during a period or periods specified in the licence, including provisions as to the way in which that quantity is to be measured or assessed for the purposes of this Chapter; and

(b) provision for determining, by measurement or assessment, what quantity of water is to be taken to have been abstracted during any such period by the holder of the licence from the source of supply to which the licence relates.

(3) Every licence under this Chapter to abstract water shall indicate the means by which water is authorised to be abstracted in pursuance of the licence, by reference either to specified works, machinery or apparatus or to works, machinery or apparatus fulfilling specified requirements.

(4) Every licence under this Chapter to abstract water, except a licence granted to the Authority, to a water undertaker or sewerage undertaker or to any person (not being a water undertaker) who proposes to abstract the water for the purpose of supplying it to others shall also specify the land on which, and the purposes for which, water abstracted in pursuance of the licence is to be used.

(5) Every licence under this Chapter to abstract water shall state whether the licence is to remain in force until revoked or is to expire at a time specified in the licence.

(6) Different provision may be made by the same licence with respect to any one or more of the following matters, that is to say—

(a) the abstraction of water during different periods;

(b) the abstraction of water from the same source of supply but at different points or by differenct means;

(c) the abstraction of water for use for different purposes;

and any such provision as is mentioned in subsection (2) above may be made separately in relation to each of the matters for which (in accordance with this subsection) different provision is made in the licence.

(7) Nothing in subsection (6) above shall be construed as preventing two or more licences from being granted to the same person to be held concurrently in respect of the same source of supply, if the licences authorise the abstraction of water at different points or by different means.

DEFINITIONS
"enactment": s.221(1).
"licences": s.72(1).
"source of supply": s.221(1).
"the Authority": s.221(1).

GENERAL NOTE
This section states that licences must include details of quantity over a period with method of measurement (subs. (2)), the authorised means of abstraction (subs. (3)) and the method of expiry (subs. (5)). In the case of an abstraction licence holder, other than the Authority, a water undertaker, or a person who is supplying water to others, the licence must also specify the area and purpose of water use (subs. (4)).

Holders of licence

47.—(1) Every licence under this Chapter to abstract water shall specify the person to whom the licence is granted.

(2) The person to whom a licence under this Chapter is granted to abstract water or to obstruct or impede any inland waters and, in the case of a licence to obstruct or impede any inland waters, no other person is the holder of the licence for the purposes of this Act.

(3) This section has effect subject to sections 49, 50 and 67 below and to any power under this Chapter to vary licences.

DEFINITIONS
"inland waters": s.221(1).
"licence": s.72(1).

General effect of licence

48.—(1) For the purposes of this Chapter a person who is for the time being the holder of a licence under this Chapter to abstract water shall be taken to have a right to abstract water to the extent authorised by the licence and in accordance with the provisions contained in it.

(2) In any action brought against a person in respect of the abstraction of water from a source of supply, it shall be a defence, subject to paragraph 2 of Schedule 7 to this Act, for him to prove—
   (a) that the water was abstracted in pursuance of a licence under this Chapter; and
   (b) that the provisions of the licence were complied with.

(3) In any action brought against a person in respect of any obstruction or impeding of the flow of any inland waters at any point by means of impounding works, it shall be a defence for him to prove—
   (a) that the flow was so obstructed or impeded in pursuance of a licence under this Chapter;
   (b) that the obstructing or impeding was in the manner specified in that licence and to an extent not exceeding the extent so specified; and
   (c) that the other requirements of the licence (if any) were complied with.

(4) Nothing in subsection (2) or (3) above shall exonerate a person from any action for negligence or breach of contract.

DEFINITIONS
"flow": s.72(1).

"impounding works": s.72(1).
"licence": s.72(1).

GENERAL NOTE
This section sets out the general effect of a licence (subs. (1)), and provides that the holding of a licence will be a defence to any action brought against a person in respect of either abstraction or impounding (subss. (2) and (3)). This defence does not extend to actions for negligence or breach of contract (subs. (4) and *Cargill* v. *Gotts* [1981] 1 W.L.R. 441).

Subs. (2)
Paragraph 2 of Sched. 7 to this Act. This provides that up until 1992 the holding of a licence of right under the 1989 Act will not be a defence to an action. Licences of Right under the 1989 Act (paras. 30 and 31 of Sched. 26 of that Act) gave licences to any person who had been abstracting water in the five years preceding the 1989 Act under the authorisation of the Water Resources Act 1963.

Succession to licences

Succession to licences to abstract where person ceases to occupy the relevant land

49.—(1) This section applies to a case where the holder of a licence under this Chapter to abstract water ("the prior holder") is the occupier of the whole of the land specified in the licence as the land on which water abstracted in pursuance of the licence is to be used ("the relevant land").

(2) If—

(a) the prior holder dies or, by reason of any other act or event, ceases to be the occupier of the whole of the relevant land and does not continue to be the occupier of any part of that land; and

(b) either immediately after the death of the prior holder or the occurrence of that other act or event or subsequently, another person ("the successor") becomes the occupier of the whole of the relevant land,

the prior holder shall cease (if he would not otherwise do so) to be the holder of the licence and the successor shall become the holder of the licence.

(3) Where the successor becomes the holder of a licence under subsection (2) above, he shall cease to be the holder of the licence at the end of the period of 15 months beginning with the date on which he became the occupier of the relevant land unless before the end of that period he has given to the Authority notice of the change in the occupation of the relevant land.

(4) Where any person who becomes the holder of a licence by virtue of the provisions of this section gives notice to the Authority in accordance with those provisions, the Authority shall vary the licence accordingly.

(5) Where, by virtue of the provisions of this section, any person ceases to be the holder of a licence in such circumstances that no other person thereupon becomes the holder of it, the licence shall cease to have effect.

(6) The preceding provisions of this section shall have effect without prejudice to any power to revoke or vary licences under this Chapter or to the powers conferred by section 50 below.

DEFINITIONS
"licence": s.72(1).
"the Authority": s.221(1).

GENERAL NOTE
This section allows for the transfer of licences to abstract to the new owner when land changes hands. There is a requirement on the successor to notify the Authority, in writing, of the change of occupation within 15 months of that change. If he fails to do so the licence lapses under subs. (3) and he would have to make a fresh application. If the successor does notify the Authority within the 15-month limit, the Authority is obliged to vary the licence by changing the holder to the new occupier (subs. (4)).

Succession where person becomes occupier of part of the relevant land

50.—(1) The Secretary of State may by regulations make provision, in relation to cases to which section 49 above applies, for conferring succession rights, in such circumstances as may be specified in the regulations, on a person who becomes the occupier of part of the relevant land after—

(a) the death of the prior holder; or

(b) the occurrence of any other act or event whereby the prior holder ceases to be the occupier of the relevant land or of part of that land.

(2) For the purposes of subsection (1) above succession rights are—

(a) a right to become the holder of the licence, subject to provisions corresponding to subsection (3) of section 49 above; or

(b) a right to apply for, and to the grant of, a new licence containing provisions (as to quantities of water and otherwise) determined, in accordance with the regulations made by the Secretary of State, by reference to the provisions of the original licence.

(3) The Secretary of State may by regulations make provision for conferring on the prior holder, where he—

(a) continues to be the occupier of part of the relevant land; but

(b) ceases to be the occupier of another part of that land,

a right, in such circumstances as may be specified in the regulations, to apply for, and to the grant of, a new licence containing such provisions as are mentioned in subsection (2)(b) above.

(4) Regulations under this section may provide that the provisions of this Chapter shall have effect in relation—

(a) to an application for a licence made by virtue of the regulations; or

(b) to a person entitled to make such an application,

subject to such modifications as may be specified in the regulations.

(5) Where any person who becomes the holder of a licence by virtue of the provisions of any regulations under this section gives notice to the Authority in accordance with those provisions, the Authority shall vary the licence accordingly.

(6) Where, by virtue of the provisions of any regulations under this section, any person ceases to be the holder of a licence in such circumstances that no other person thereupon becomes the holder of it, the licence shall cease to have effect.

(7) The preceding provisions of this section shall have effect without prejudice to the exercise of any power to revoke or vary licences under this Chapter.

DEFINITIONS

"licence": s.72(1).
"modifications": s.221(1).
"notice": s.221(1).
"relevant land": s.49(1).
"succession rights": subs. (2).
"the Authority": s.221(1).
"the prior holder": s.49(1).

GENERAL NOTE

Unlike s.49, which applies only when the whole of the land to which a licence applies changes hands, this section allows the Secretary of State to make provision for succession to a part of such land. Regulations may allow both the prior holder (subs. (3)) and the successor (subs. (1)) a right to a licence. Subs. (5) obliges the Authority to vary a licence in accordance with regulations made under this section.

See the Water Resources (Succession to Licences) Regulations 1969 (S.I. 1969 No. 976).

Modification of licences

Modification on application of licence holder

51.—(1) The holder of a licence under this Chapter may apply to the

Authority to revoke the licence and, on any such application, the Authority shall revoke the licence accordingly.

(2) The holder of a licence under this Chapter may apply to the Authority to vary the licence.

(3) Subject to subsection (4) below, the provisions of sections 37 to 44 above shall apply (with the necessary modifications) to applications under subsection (2) above, and to the variation of licences in pursuance of such applications, as they apply to applications for, and the grant of, licences under this Chapter.

(4) Where the variation proposed in an application under subsection (2) above is limited to reducing the quantity of water authorised to be abstracted in pursuance of the licence during one or more periods—

(a) sections 37 and 38(1) above shall not apply by virtue of subsection (3) above; and

(b) sections 43 and 44 above, as applied by that subsection, shall have effect as if subsection (5) of section 43 and paragraph (a) of section 44(3) were omitted.

DEFINITIONS
"licence": s.72(1).
"the Authority": s.221(1).

GENERAL NOTE

Subs. (4)
The effect of this subsection is to delete the requirements for publication of application details in s.37 if the variation applied for is merely to reduce the amount of water abstracted. In the event of an appeal the Secretary of State is not required to consider representations arising from the publication of application details (ss.43(5) and 44(3)(a)), although given the fact that the publication requirements do not apply it seems unlikely that there would be any in any event.

Proposals for modification at instance of the Authority or Secretary of State

52.—(1) Where it appears to the Authority that a licence under this Chapter should be revoked or varied, the Authority may formulate proposals for evoking or varying the licence.

(2) Where—

(a) it appears to the Secretary of State (either in consequence of representations made to the Secretary of State or otherwise) that a licence under this Chapter ought to be reviewed; but

(b) no proposals for revoking or varying the licence have been formulated by the Authority under subsection (1) above,

the Secretary of State may, as he may consider appropriate in the circumstances, give the Authority a direction under subsection (3) below.

(3) A direction under this subsection may—

(a) direct the Authority to formulate proposals for revoking the licence in question; or

(b) direct the Authority to formulate proposals for varying that licence in such manner as may be specified in the direction.

(4) Notice in the prescribed form of any proposals formulated under this section with respect to any licence shall—

(a) be served on the holder of the licence; and

(b) be published in the London Gazette and, at least once in each of two successive weeks, in one or more newspapers (other than the London Gazette) circulating in the relevant locality.

(5) If—

(a) a licence with respect to which any proposals are formulated under this section relates to any inland waters; and

(b) the proposals provide for variation of that licence,

a copy of the notice for the purposes of subsection (4) above shall, not later than the date on which it is first published otherwise than in the London

Gazette, be served on any navigation authority, harbour authority or conservancy authority having functions in relation to those waters at a place where the licence, if varied in accordance with the proposals, would authorise water to be abstracted or impounded.

(6) A notice for the purposes of subsection (4) above, in addition to any other matters required to be contained in that notice, shall—

(a) name a place within the relevant locality where a copy of the proposals, and of any map, plan or other document prepared in connection with them, will be open to inspection by the public, free of charge, at all reasonable hours during a period specified in the notice in accordance with subsection (7) below; and

(b) state that, at any time before the end of that period—

     (i) the holder of the licence may give notice in writing to the Authority objecting to the proposals; and

     (ii) any other person may make representations in writing to the Authority with respect to the proposals.

(7) The period specified in a notice for the purposes of subsection (6) above shall be a period which—

(a) begins not earlier than the date on which the notice is first published in a newspaper other than the London Gazette; and

(b) ends not less than 28 days from that date and not less than 25 days from the date on which the notice published in the London Gazette.

(8) In this section "the relevant locality" means the locality in which the place or places where the licence authorises water to be abstracted or impounded is or are situated.

DEFINITIONS
"conservancy authority": s.221(1).
"harbour authority": s.221(1).
"inland waters": s.221(1).
"licence": s.72(1).
"navigation authority": s.221(1).
"notice": s.221(1).
"prescribed": s.221(1).
"the Authority": s.221(1).
"the relevant locality": subs. (8).

GENERAL NOTE
This section allows either the Authority or the Secretary of State, through a direction to the Authority (subs. (3)), to make proposals to revoke or vary a licence. Where this process is set in motion the same requirements for publication as apply for licence applications (s.37) apply under this section (subss. (4)–(7)).

Modification in pursuance of proposals under section 52

53.—(1) Subject to the following provisions of this section, where the Authority has formulated any proposals under section 52 above with respect to any licence under this Chapter, it may—

(a) if the proposals are for the revocation of the licence, revoke the licence; and

(b) if the proposals are proposals for varying the licence, vary the licence in accordance with those proposals or, with the consent of the holder of the licence, in any other way.

(2) The Authority shall not proceed with any proposals formulated under section 52 above before the end of the period specified, in accordance with subsection (7) of that section, for the purposes in relation to those proposals of subsection (6) of that section.

(3) If no notice under subsection (4) below is given to the Authority before the end of the period mentioned in subsection (2) above, the Authority may proceed with the proposals.

(4) If the holder of the licence gives notice to the Authority objecting to the proposals before the end of the period mentioned in subsection (2) above, the Authority shall refer the proposals to the Secretary of State, with a copy of the notice of objection.

(5) Where the Authority proceeds with any proposals under subsection (3) above and the proposals are proposals for varying the licence, the provisions of sections 38(3), 39(1) and (2) and 40 above shall apply (with the necessary modifications) to any action of the Authority in proceeding with the proposals as they apply to the action of the Authority in dealing with an application for a licence.

DEFINITIONS
"licence": s.72(1).
"notice": s.221(1).
"the Authority": s.221(1).

GENERAL NOTE

Subs. (4)
An objection by the licence-holder to a proposal by the Authority for revocation or variation of the licence, if made within the one-month period from the date of publication of the proposal in a local paper, gives the licence-holder the right to have his objection considered by the Secretary of State. See s.54 for the procedure governing the Secretary of State's consideration.

Subs. (5)
The effect of this subsection is to reproduce a number of obligations applicable to the Authority's consideration of licence applications and apply them to its decision to proceed with a variation in the absence of a timely objection from the licence-holder. The obligations are:
(1) to have regard to any representations in writing, and the reasonable requirements of the applicant (s.38(3));
(2) to have regard to the rights of existing licence-holders (s.39(1)); and
(3) to take into account the effect on river flow (s.40).

Reference of modification proposals to the Secretary of State

54.—(1) Where any proposals of the Authority with respect to a licence are referred to the Secretary of State in accordance with subsection (4) of section 53 above, the Secretary of State shall consider—
(a) the proposals;
(b) the objection of the holder of the licence; and
(c) any representations in writing relating to the proposals with were received by the Authority before the end of the period mentioned in subsection (2) of that section,
and, subject to subsection (2) below, shall determine (according to whether the proposals are for the revocation or variation of the licence) the question whether the licence should be revoked or the question whether it should be varied as mentioned in subsection (1)(b) of that section.

(2) Before determining under this section whether a licence should be revoked or varied in a case in which proposals have been formulated under section 52 above, the Secretary of State may, if he thinks fit—
(a) cause a local inquiry to be held; or
(b) afford to the holder of the licence and the Authority an opportunity of appearing before, and being heard by, a person appointed by the Secretary of State for the purpose;
and the Secretary of State shall act as mentioned in paragraph (a) or (b) above if a request is made by the holder of the licence or the Authority to be heard with respect to the proposals.

(3) In determining under this section whether a licence should be varied and, if so, what directions should be given under subsection (5) below, the Secretary of State shall consider whether any such direction would require such a variation of the licence as would so authorise—

(a) the abstraction of water; or
(b) the flow of any inland waters to be obstructed or impeded by means of impounding works,
as to derogate from rights which, at the time when the direction is given, are protected rights for the purposes of this Chapter.

(4) The provisions of sections 39(2) and 40 above shall apply in relation to any proposals referred to the Secretary of State in accordance with section 53(4) above as if in those provisions.

(a) any reference to the Authority were a reference to the Secretary of State;
(b) any reference to the application were a reference to the proposals; and
(c) the references to sections 38(3) and 39(1) were references to subsections (1) and (3) above.

(5) Where the decision of the Secretary of State on a reference in accordance with section 53(4) above is that the licence in question should be revoked or varied, the decision shall include a direction to the Authority to revoke the licence or, as the case may be, to vary it so as to contain such provisions as may be specified in the direction.

(6) A decision of the Secretary of State under this section with respect to any proposals shall be final.

DEFINITIONS
"abstraction": s.221(1).
"flow": s.72(1).
"impounding works": s.72(1).
"inland waters": s.221(1).
"licence": s.72(1).
"the Authority": s.221(1).

GENERAL NOTE
This section governs the procedure to be followed in the consideration of a proposal for revocation or variation of a licence objected to by the licence-holder. As well as the proposals and the objection, the Secretary of State is obliged to consider representations produced by the public consultation process in s.52. As with ss.42 and 44 the Secretary of State may hold a local inquiry or a hearing of the parties, and must do one or the other if one of the parties requests to be heard (subs. (2)). The requirement to consider the rights of existing licence-holders in s.39 is reproduced in subs. (3), as are the requirements to consider the effect on other users of water from underground strata and on river flow (subs. (4)).

Section 250 of the Local Government Act 1972 applies to local inquiries held under this section by virtue of s.215 below.

Application for modification of licence by owner of fishing rights

55.—(1) Subject to the following provisions of this section and to Schedule 7 to this Act, where a licence under this Chapter authorises abstraction from any inland waters in respect of which no minimum acceptable flow has been determined under Chapter I of this Part, any person who is the owner of fishing rights in respect of those inland waters may apply to the Secretary of State for the revocation or variation of the licence.

(2) No application shall be made under this section in respect of any licence except at a time after the end of the period of one year beginning with the date on which the licence was granted but before a minimum acceptable flow has been determined in relation to the waters in question.

(3) Any application under this section made by a person as owner of fishing rights in respect of any inland waters shall be made on the grounds that, in his capacity as owner of those rights, he has sustained loss or damage which is directly attributable to the abstraction of water in pursuance of the licence in question and either—

(a) he is not entitled to a protected right for the purposes of this Chapter in respect of those inland waters; or

(b) the loss or damage which he has sustained in his capacity as owner of those rights is not attributable to any such breach of statutory duty as is mentioned in subsection (2) or (3) of section 60 below or is in addition to any loss or damage attributable to any such breach.

(4) Where an application is made under this section in respect of any licence, the applicant shall serve notice in the prescribed form on the Authority and on the holder of the licence, stating that each of them is entitled, at any time before the end of the period of 28 days beginning with the date of service of the notice, to make representations in writing to the Secretary of State with respect to the application.

(5) In this section and section 56 below "fishing rights," in relation to any inland waters, means any right (whether it is an exclusive right or a right in common with one or more other persons) to fish in those waters, where the right in question—

(a) constitutes or is included in an interest in land; or

(b) is exercisable by virtue of an exclusive licence granted for valuable consideration;

and any reference to an owner of fishing rights is a reference to the person for the time being entitled to those rights.

(6) In this section any reference to a right included in an interest in land is a reference to a right which is exercisable only by virtue of, and as a right incidental to, the ownership of that interest.

DEFINITIONS
"abstraction": s.221(1).
"fishing rights": subs. (5).
"inland waters": s.221(1).
"licence": s.72(1).
"minimum acceptable flow": s.221(1).
"notice": s.221(1).
"prescribed": s.221(1).
"protected right": s.72(1).

GENERAL NOTE
This section allows an owner of fishing rights who sustains loss or damage as a result of the abstraction operation of a licence-holder to ask the Authority to modify or revoke the licence. Such an application cannot be made until the licence has been in force for one year; neither can it be made if the level of the inland waters in question are governed by a minimum acceptable flow (subs. (2)). The situation envisaged by this section is one in which a licence-holder's abstraction is killing fish by reducing the water level. This situation should be ruled out by the setting of a minimum acceptable flow, hence s.55 provides transitional relief until the minimum acceptable flow procedure is applied more widely.

The application cannot be made if the owner of fishing rights is in any event the holder of a protected right (see s.39(3)) or has a claim against the Authority for breach of its statutory duty not to authorise derogation from such rights (see ss.39(1) and 60(2) and (3)).

Determination of application under section 55

56.—(1) The Secretary of State, in determining any application under section 55 above in respect of any licence, shall take into account any representations in writing received by him, within the period mentioned in subsection (4) of that section, from the Authority or from the holder of the licence.

(2) Before determining on an application under section 55 above whether a licence should be revoked or varied the Secretary of State may, if he thinks fit—

(a) cause a local inquiry to be held; or

(b) afford to the applicant, the holder of the licence and the Authority an opportunity of appearing before, and being heard by, a person appointed by the Secretary of State for the purpose;

and the Secretary of State shall act as mentioned in paragraph (a) or (b) above if a request is made by the applicant, the holder of the licence or the Authority to be heard with respect to the proposals.

(3) Subject to subsections (4) and (5) below, on an application under section 55 above in respect of any licence, the Secretary of State shall not determine that the licence shall be revoked or varied unless—

(a) the grounds of the application, as mentioned in subsection (3) of that section, are established to his satisfaction; and

(b) he is satisfied that the extent of the loss or damage which the applicant has sustained, as mentioned in that subsection, is such as to justify the revocation or variation of the licence.

(4) On an application under section 55 above in respect of any licence, the Secretary of State shall not determine that the licence shall be revoked or varied if he is satisfied that the fact that the abstraction of water in pursuance of the licence caused the loss or damage which the applicant has sustained, as mentioned in subsection (3) of that section, was wholly or mainly attributable to exceptional shortage of rain or to an accident or other unforeseen act or event not caused by, and outside the control of, the Authority.

(5) Where the Secretary of State determines, on an application under section 55 above, that a licence shall be varied, the variation shall be limited to that which, in the opinion of the Secretary of State, is requisite having regard to the loss or damage which the applicant as sustained as mentioned in subsection (3) of that section.

(6) Where the decision of the Secretary of State on an application under section 55 above in respect of any licence is that the licence should be revoked or varied, the decision shall include a direction to the Authority to revoke the licence or, as the case may be, to vary it so as to contain such provisions as may be specified in the direction.

(7) A decision of the Secretary of State on an application under section 55 above shall be final.

DEFINITIONS
"abstraction": s.221(1).
"licence": s.72(1).
"the Authority": s.221(1).

GENERAL NOTE
As with ss.42, 44 and 54, the Secretary of State may hold a local inquiry or a hearing under this section, and he must hold one or the other if any of the parties (applicant, licence-holder and Authority) requests a hearing (subs. (2)). The wording of subs. (3) puts the burden on the applicant to establish the grounds and the loss, which the Secretary of State must be satisfied is enough to justify modifying or revoking the licence. The licence-holder is also protected by subs. (4) if the low-water level is seen to be the result of an exceptional shortage of rain or an unforeseen accident. There is no guidance in the Act on how a shortage of rain is to be judged exceptional, and this therefore remains within the Secretary of State's discretion.

Emergency variation of licences for spray irrigation purposes

57.—(1) This section applies where at any time—

(a) one or more licences under this Chapter are in force in relation to a source of supply authorising water abstracted in pursuance of the licences to be used for the purpose of spray irrigation, or for that purpose together with other purposes; and

(b) by reason of exceptional shortage of rain or other emergency, it appears to the Authority that it is necessary to impose a temporary restriction on the abstraction of water for use for that purpose.

(2) Subject to subsections (3) and (4) below, where this section applies the Authority may serve a notice on the holder of any of the licences reducing, during such period as may be specified in the notice, the quantity of water authorised to be abstracted in pursuance of the licence from the source of

supply for use for the purpose of spray irrigation; and in relation to that period, the licence shall have effect accordingly subject to that reduction.

(3) The Authority shall not serve a notice under this section in respect of abstraction of water from underground strata unless it appears to the Authority that such abstraction is likely to affect the flow, level or volume of any inland waters which are neither discrete waters nor inland waters comprised in an order under section 33 above.

(4) In the exercise of the power conferred by this section in a case where there are two or more licences under this Chapter in force authorising abstraction from the same source of supply either at the same point or at points which, in the opinion of the Authority, are not far distant from each other—

(a) the Authority shall not serve a notice under this section on the holder of one of the licences unless a like notice is served on the holders of the other licences in respect of the same period; and

(b) the reductions imposed by the notices on the holders of the licences shall be so calculated as to represent, as nearly as appears to the Authority to be practicable, the same proportion of the quantity of water authorised by the licences (apart from the notices) to be abstracted for use for the purposes of spray irrigation.

(5) The provisions of this section shall have effect without prejudice to the exercise of any power conferred by sections 51 to 54 above.

DEFINITIONS
"abstraction": s.221(1).
"discrete waters": s.221(1).
"flow": s.72(1).
"inland waters": s.221(1).
"licences": s.72(1).
"notice": s.221(1).
"source of supply": s.221(1).
"spray irrigation": s.72(1).
"the Authority": s.221(1).
"underground strata": s.221(1).

GENERAL NOTE
This section allows the Authority to impose temporary restrictions on the abstraction of water by licence-holders who are using all or part of that water for spray irrigation during an exceptional shortage of rain or other emergency (subs. (1)). The restriction can also apply to underground strata, but only if it appears likely to affect the level of inland waters that are not exempted from the need for a licence by s.33 (subs. (3)). Under subs. (4) the Authority must ensure fairness between different licence-holders.

Revocation of licence for non-payment of charges

58.—(1) If the charges payable in respect of a licence under this Chapter are not paid within 28 days after notice demanding them has been served on the holder of the licence, the Authority may revoke the licence by the service of a notice of revocation on the holder of the licence.

(2) A notice demanding the payment of any charges which is served for the purposes of subsection (1) above shall—

(a) state that the licence in question may be revoked if the charges are not paid within 28 days after the service of the notice;

(b) set out the effect of revocation; and

(c) state that no compensation is payable in respect of a revocation under this section.

(3) Revocation of a licence under this section—

(a) shall take effect at such time, not being a time before the end of the period of 28 days after notice of revocation is served on the holder of the licence, as may be specified in that notice; and

(b) shall so take effect only if the charges in question are not paid before that time.

(4) A notice of revocation served under this section shall—

(a) set out the reason for the revocation; and

(b) state that the revocation will take effect only if the charges in question are not paid before the time specified in the notice.

DEFINITIONS
"licence": s.72(1).
"notice": s.221(1).

GENERAL NOTE
It is to be noted that a licence-holder who has his licence revoked due to non-payment of the Authority's charges in the 28-day limit loses any right to compensation that he might otherwise have had (subs. (2)(c)).

Regulations with respect to modification applications

59.—(1) The Secretary of State may by regulations make provision as to the manner in which applications for the revocation or variation of licences under this Chapter are to be dealt with, including provision requiring the giving of notices of, and information relating to, the making of such applications or decisions on any such applications.

(2) Subsection (1) above shall have effect subject to any express provision contained in, or having effect by virtue of, any other enactment contained in this Chapter; and any regulations made under this section shall have effect subject to any such express provision.

DEFINITIONS
"enactment": s.221(1).
"notices": s.221(1).

Remedies and compensation in respect of infringement of protected rights etc.

Liability of the Authority for derogation from protected right

60.—(1) A breach of the duty imposed by subsection (1) of section 39 above (including that duty as applied by section 51(3) or 53(5) above) shall neither invalidate the grant or variation of a licence nor be enforceable by any criminal proceedings, by prohibition or injunction or by action against any person other than the Authority.

(2) Instead, the duty referred to in subsection (1) above shall be enforceable, at the suit of any person entitled to a protected right for the purposes of this Chapter, by an action against the Authority for damages for breach of statutory duty.

(3) Where under any provision of this Chapter, the Authority is directed by the Secretary of State to grant or vary a licence, and the licence, as granted or varied in compliance with the direction, authorises derogation from protected rights, then—

(a) the grant or variation of the licence shall, as between the Authority and the person entitled to those rights, have effect as a breach on the part of the Authority of a statutory duty not to authorise derogation from those rights; and

(b) subsection (2) above shall apply in relation to that statutory duty as it applies in relation to the duty imposed by section 39(1) above.

(4) Subsection (3) above shall be without prejudice to the duty of the Authority, to comply with the direction in question, but that duty shall not afford any defence in an action brought by virtue of paragraph (b) of that subsection.

(5) In any action brought against the Authority in pursuance of this section it shall be a defence for the Authority to show that the fact, as the case may be—

(a) that the abstraction of water authorised by the licence, as granted or varied by the Authority, derogated from the plaintiff's protected right; or

(b) that the obstruction or impeding of the flow of the inland waters authorised by the licence, as so granted or varied, derogated from the plaintiff's protected right,

was wholly or mainly attributable to exceptional shortage of rain or to an accident or other unforeseen act or event not caused by, and outside the control of, the Authority.

(6) This section has effect subject to the provision made by Schedule 7 to this Act.

(7) In this section any reference to authorising a derogation from protected rights is a reference to so authorising—

(a) the abstraction of water; or

(b) the flow of any inland waters to be obstructed or impeded by means of impounding works,

as to derogate from rights which, at the time of the authorisation, are protected rights for the purposes of this Chapter.

DEFINITIONS
    "derogation from protected rights": subs. (7).
    "licence": s.72(1).
    "protected rights": s.72(1).
    "the Authority": s.221(1).

GENERAL NOTE
    This section confines the remedy available to the holder of a protected right, if that right has been interfered with by the Authority's action in granting a licence, to an action for breach of statutory duty. Such an action will still be available against the Authority even if the licence that has interfered with the protected right was granted at the direction of the Secretary of State (subs. (3)), and the Authority remains under a duty to carry out the direction but is unable to use it as a defence (subs. (4)). Should the Authority be liable in this way for the actions of the Secretary of State it can claim to be indemnified under s.63 below.

Subs. (6)
    Where the plaintiff in a breach of statutory duty action under this section holds a licence of right (deemed to have been given a licence at the coming into force of the Water Act 1989 as entitled to abstract under the Water Resources Act 1963) then the Authority does have available a defence to that action if it can show that such a licence-holder could have protected himself by making permissible alterations to his abstraction operation. (See para. 4 of Sched. 7).

Compensation where licence modified on direction of the Secretary of State

61.—(1) Where a licence is revoked or varied in pursuance of a direction under section 54 or 55 above and it is shown that the holder of the licence—

(a) has incurred expenditure in carrying out work which is rendered abortive by the revocation or variation; or

(b) has otherwise sustained loss or damage which is directly attributable to the revocation or variation,

the Authority shall pay him compensation in respect of that expenditure, loss or damage.

(2) For the purposes of this section, any expenditure incurred in the preparation of plans for the purposes of any work, or upon other similar matters preparatory to any work, shall be taken to be included in the expenditure incurred in carrying out that work.

(3) Subject to subsection (2) above and to Schedule 7 to this Act, no compensation shall be paid under this section—

    (a) in respect of any work carried out before the grant of the licence which is revoked or varied; or

    (b) in respect of any other loss or damage arising out of anything done or omitted to be done before the grant of that licence.

(4) No compensation shall be payable under this section in respect of a licence to abstract water, if it is shown that no water was abstracted in pursuance of the licence during the period of seven years ending with the date on which notice of the proposals for revoking or varying the licence was served on the holder of the licence.

(5) Any question of disputed compensation under this section shall be referred to and determined by the Lands Tribunal; and in relation to the determination of any such compensation the provisions of section 2 and 4 of the Land Compensation Act 1961 shall apply, subject to any necessary modifications.

(6) For the purpose of assessing any compensation under this section, in so far as that compensation is in respect of loss or damage consisting of depreciation of the value of an interest in land, the rules set out in section 5 of the Land Compensation Act 1961 shall, so far as applicable and subject to any necessary modifications, have effect as they have effect for the purpose of assessing compensation for the compulsory acquisition of an interest in land.

(7) Where the interest in land, in respect of which any compensation falls to be assessed in accordance with subsection (6) above, is subject to a mortgage—

    (a) the compensation shall be assessed as if the interest were not subject to the mortgage;

    (b) a claim for the compensation may be made by any mortgagee of the interest, but without prejudice to the making of a claim by the person entitled to the interest;

    (c) no such compensation shall be payable in respect of the interest of the mortgagee (as distinct from the interest which is subject to the mortgage);

    (d) any such compensation which is payable in respect of the interest which is subject to the mortgage shall be paid to the mortgagee or, if there is more than one mortgagee, to the first mortgagee, and shall in either case be applied by him as if it were proceeds of sale.

DEFINITIONS
    "licence": s.72(1).
    "the Authority": s.221(1).

GENERAL NOTE
    This section allows licence-holders to claim compensation for wasted expenditure or other loss suffered as a result of revocation or variation of their licences. Expenditure on planning is included (subs. (2)), but any amounts expended before the licence was originally granted is not (subs. (3)). A licence-holder who has not used his licence to abstract water for seven years by the time that the revocation or variation is proposed is also excluded from claiming compensation (subs. (4)).

Compensation for owner of fishing rights applying under section 55

62.—(1) Where a licence is revoked or varied on an application under section 55 above, the applicant shall be entitled to compensation from the Authority in respect of the loss or damage which he has sustained as mentioned in subsection (3) of that section.

(2) Where, on an application under section 55 above for the revocation or variation of a licence, the Secretary of State determines—

    (a) that the grounds of the application (as mentioned in subsection (3) of that section) have been established to his satisfaction; but

(b) that the licence shall not be revoked or varied in pursuance of that
     application,
he shall certify accordingly for the purposes of the following provisions of
this section.

(3) Unless within the period of six months from the date on which a
certificate under subsection (2) above is granted either—
  (a) notice to treat for the acquisition of the fishing rights of the applicant,
      or of an interest in land which includes those rights, has been served
      by the Authority; or
  (b) an offer has been made by the Authority to the owner of those rights
      to acquire them on compulsory purchase terms or, where the rights
      subsist only as rights included in an interest in land, to acquire that
      interest on such terms,
the owner of the fishing rights shall be entitled to compensation from the
Authority.

(4) The amount of the compensation payable under subsection (3) above
in respect of any fishing rights shall be the amount by which—
  (a) the value of those rights; or
  (b) where they subsist only as rights included in an interest in land, the
      value of that interest,
is depreciated by the operation of section 48(2) above in relation to the
licence to which the application related.

(5) Any question of disputed compensation under this section shall be
referred to and determined by the Lands Tribunal; and in relation to the
determination of any such compensation the provisions of sections 2 and 4 of
the Land Compensation Act 1961 shall apply, subject to any necessary
modifications.

(6) For the purposes of this section a right or interest is acquired on
compulsory purchase terms if it is acquired on terms that the price payable
shall be equal to and shall, in default of agreement, be determined in like
manner as the compensation which would be payable in respect thereof if
the right or interest were acquired compulsorily by the Authority.

(7) Where—
  (a) the Secretary of State, on an application under section 55 above,
      determines that the licence to which the application relates shall not
      be revoked or varied and grants a certificate under subsection (2)
      above; and
  (b) notice to treat for the acquisition of the fishing rights to which the
      application related, or of an interest in land in which those rights are
      included, has been served by the Authority within the period of six
      months from the date on which that certificate is granted,
then, for the purpose of assessing compensation in respect of any compulsory acquisition in pursuance of that notice to treat, no account shall be
taken of any depreciation of the value of the fishing rights, or of the interest
in question, which is applicable to the operation, in relation to that licence,
of section 48(2) above.

(8) Subsections (5) and (6) of section 55 above shall apply for construing
references in this section to fishing rights or to rights included in an interest
in land as they have effect for construing such references in that section.

DEFINITIONS
   "acquired on compulsory purchase terms": subs. (6).
   "licence": s.72(1).
   "notice": s.221(1).
   "the Authority": s.221(1).

GENERAL NOTE
   This section provides for compensation for loss by an owner of fishing rights who has suffered
as a result of the actions of a licence-holder. The compensation is available if the owner of

fishing rights has succeeded in his application under s.55 to have the offending licence revoked or varied (subs. (1)). It is also available if the s.55 application has failed (subs. (2)) and the Authority has not agreed to purchase, compulsorily or by agreement, the fishing rights in question (subs. (3)(a) and (b)).

Subs. (4)
In a situation where the offending licence has not been revoked and the Authority is not willing to buy the rights, the compensation will be the amount by which the value of the rights has been reduced by the actions of the licence-holder and his protection from a legal claim by the general defence in s.48(2).

Secretary of State to indemnify Authority in certain cases

63.—(1) Where—
   (a) the Authority is liable under section 60 above to pay damages to any person in consequence of the grant or variation of a licence in compliance with a direction given by the Secretary of State; and
   (b) the Authority pay to that person any sum in satisfaction of that liability,
then, whether an action for recovery of those damages has been brought or not, the Secretary of State may, if he thinks fit, pay to the Authority the whole or such part as he considers appropriate of the relevant amount.
   (2) If—
   (a) proposals for revoking or varying the licence, in a case falling within subsection (1) above, are formulated by the Authority, or an application with respect to any licence is made under section 55 above;
   (b) in consequence of those proposals or that application, the licence is revoked or varied; and
   (c) compensation in respect of the revocation or variation is payable by the Authority under section 61 above,
the Secretary of State may, if he thinks fit, pay to the Authority the whole or such part as he considers appropriate of the relevant amount.
   (3) Where—
   (a) the Secretary of State determines under section 55 above—
             (i) that a licence granted in compliance with a direction given by the Secretary of State shall be revoked or varied; or
             (ii) that a licence shall not be revoked or varied;
         and
   (b) in consequence of that determination, compensation is payable by the Authority under section 62 above,
the Secretary of State may, if he thinks fit, pay to the Authority the whole or such part as he considers appropriate of the relevant amount.
   (4) In this section "the relevant amount" means—
   (a) for the purposes of subsection (1) above, the amount of the sum paid by the Authority and, if an action has been brought against the Authority in respect of the liability mentioned in that subsection, the amount of any costs reasonably incurred by the Authority in connection with the action (including any costs of the plaintiff which the Authority was required to pay); and
   (b) for the purposes of subsections (2) and (3) above, the amount of the compensation and, if any question relating to that compensation is referred to the Lands Tribunal, the amount of any costs reasonably incurred by the Authority in connection with that reference (including any costs of the claimant which the Authority is required to pay).

DEFINITIONS
   "licence": s.72(1).
   "the Authority": s.221(1).
   "the relevant amount": subs. (4).

This section gives the Secretary of State a discretion to indemnify the Authority when it has paid damages or compensation under ss.60, 61 or 62 above. The discretion to indemnify includes settlements made by the Authority as a consequence of its liability under s.60 even if no action had been launched for breach of statutory duty (subs. (1)). The relevant amount to be considered by the Secretary of State when determining to what extent the Authority should be indemnified includes the Authority's costs, and so much of the plaintiff or applicant's costs as the Authority has been ordered to pay (subs. (4)).

Supplemental provisions of Chapter II

Abstracting and impounding by the Authority

64.—(1) The provisions of this Chapter shall have effect—
(a) in relation to the abstraction of water by the Authority from sources of supply; and
(b) in relation to the construction or alteration by the Authority of impounding works,
subject to such exceptions and modifications as may be prescribed.

(2) Regulations under this section may, in particular, provide for securing—
(a) that any licence required by the Authority in relation to the matters mentioned in subsection (1) above shall be granted (or be deemed to be granted) by the Secretary of State, and not be granted by the Authority;
(b) that, in such cases and subject to such conditions as may be prescribed, any licence so required by the Authority shall be deemed to be granted by the Secretary of State unless the Secretary of State requires an application for the licence to be made to him by the Authority; and
(c) that where a licence is deemed to be granted as mentioned in paragraph (b) above, the Authority shall give such notice of that fact as may be prescribed.

(3) Without prejudice to the preceding provisions of this section, section 52 above shall not apply in relation to any licence which by virtue of any regulations under this section is granted or deemed to have been granted by the Secretary of State, except in accordance with regulations under this section.

DEFINITIONS
"abstraction": s.221(1).
"impounding works": s.72(1).
"licence": s.72(1).
"prescribed": s.221(1).
"sources of supply": s.221(1).
"the Authority": s.221(1).

GENERAL NOTE
The Authority has deemed permission for works in the course of abstracting or impounding operations under Pt. 15 of Sched. 2 to the General Development Order 1988 (S.I. 1988 No. 1813), as amended by the Town and Country Planning General Development (Amendment) (No. 2) Order 1989 (S.I. 1989 No. 1590)).

The Authority, as a statutory body, will have deemed authority to interfere with the rights of riparian occupiers in the course of extracting water from a source of supply as long as any interference caused is a natural consequence of carrying out authorised operations (*Allen* v. *Gulf Oil Refining Co.* [1981] 2 W.L.R. 188, H.L.).

Subs. (3)
This subsection excludes licences granted to the Authority by the Secretary of State, or deemed to have been granted, from revocation or modification by the Authority. In practice, of course, it is difficult to see how the Authority can perform its regulatory functions in relation to itself.

Licences of right

65. Schedule 7 to this Act shall have effect for the purposes of giving effect to provisions conferring an entitlement to licences under this Chapter and with respect to licences granted in pursuance of that entitlement or the entitlement conferred by section 33 of the Water Resources Act 1963 or paragraph 30 or 31 of Schedule 26 to the Water Act 1989.

DEFINITION
"licences": s.72(1).

GENERAL NOTE
Schedule 7 deals with licences of right, acquired under the 1989 Act by persons holding rights to abstract under the Water Resources Act 1963 at the time of the coming into force of the 1989 Act. Special provisions apply to licences of right with respect to ss.48, 55, 60 and 61.

Inland waters owned or managed by British Waterways Board

66.—(1) This section applies to all inland water owned or managed by the British Waterways Board ("the Board"), except any such inland waters to which the Secretary of State may by order made by statutory instrument direct that this section shall not apply.

(2) In respect of abstraction from any inland waters to which this section applies—

(a) no person other than the Board or a person authorised for the purpose by the Board may be given a consent for the purposes of section 27(2) above;

(b) no person other than the Board shall be entitled to apply for a licence under this Chapter;

(c) in relation to any application by the Board for a licence under this Chapter—

(i) section 35 above shall not apply; and

(ii) section 37 above shall apply as if subsection (1) of that section did not require the service of any copy of the notice mentioned in paragraph (a) of that subsection on any navigation authority, harbour authority, conservancy authority or drainage board.

(3) Before making an order under subsection (1) above, the Secretary of State shall consult the Board and the Authority.

DEFINITIONS
"abstraction": s.221(1).
"conservancy authority": s.221(1).
"harbour authority": s.221(1).
"inland waters": s.221(1).
"licence": s.72(1).
"navigation authority": s.221(1).

GENERAL NOTE

Subs. (2)(a)
Section 27(2) concerns the abstraction of less than 20 cubic metres of water without a licence but with the consent of the Authority.

Subs. (2)(c)(i)
The effect of this subsection is to allow the British Waterways Board, unlike other applicants, to apply for an abstraction licence in relation to a source of supply where the Board is not the occupier of land next to that supply.

Ecclesiastical property

67.—(1) Where the relevant land belongs to a benefice—

(a) an application for a licence under this Chapter may be made by the Church Commissioners if the benefice is for the time being vacant; and

(b) any reference in this Chapter to the applicant for a licence shall be construed—

(i) in relation to any time when the benefice in question is vacant, as a reference to the Church Commissioners; and

(ii) in relation to any time when there is an incumbent of the benefice, as a reference to that incumbent.

(2) Where the relevant land belongs to a benefice, any licence under this Chapter shall provide that (notwithstanding anything in the preceding provisions of this Chapter) whoever is for the time being the incumbent of the benefice shall be the holder of the licence.

(3) Where a licence under this Chapter provides as mentioned in subsection (2) above—

(a) the licence shall not be required to specify the person to whom the licence is granted; and

(b) the licence shall be deemed to be held by the Church Commissioners at any time when the benefice in question is vacant.

(4) So much of any compensation falling to be paid under this Chapter as is payable—

(a) in respect of damage to land which is ecclesiastical property and to the owner of the fee simple in the land; or

(b) in respect of depreciation of the value of the fee simple in land which is ecclesiastical property,

shall be paid (where the fee is vested in any person other than the Church Commissioners) to them, instead of to the person in whom the fee simple is vested.

(5) Any sums paid under subsection (4) above to the Church Commissioners with reference to any land shall—

(a) if the land is not consecrated, be applied by them for the purposes for which the proceeds of a sale by agreement of the fee simple in the land would be applicable under any enactment or Measure authorising such a sale or disposing of the proceeds of such a sale; and

(b) if the land is consecrated, be applied by them in such manner as they may determine.

(6) Where—

(a) the Church Commissioners are required, by virtue of subsection (3)(b) above, to pay any fee or other charge in respect of a licence under this Chapter; and

(b) any moneys are then payable by the Commissioners to the incumbent of the benefice in question or subsequently become so payable.

the Commissioners shall be entitled to retain out of those moneys an amount not exceeding the amount of that fee or other charge.

(7) Where under any provision of this Chapter a document is required to be served on an owner of land and the land is ecclesiastical property, a copy of the document shall be served on the Church Commissioners.

(8) In this section—

"benefice" means an ecclesiastical benefice of the Church of England;

"ecclesiastical property" means land which—

(a) belongs to a benefice;

(b) is or forms part of a church subject to the jurisdiction of the bishop of any diocese of the Church of England or the site of a church so subject; or

(c) is or forms part of a burial ground so subject;

and

"the relevant land," in relation to a licence under this Chapter or an application for such a licence, means—

(a) the land on which water abstracted in pursuance of the licence is to be, or is proposed to be, used; or
(b) in the case of a licence for the purposes of section 25 above or an application for such a licence—
    (i) the land on which any part of the impounding works is to be, or is proposed to be, constructed; or
    (ii) in relation to an alteration of impounding works, the land on which any part of those works is situated or is to be, or is proposed to be, situated.

DEFINITIONS
  "benefice": subs. (8).
  "ecclesiastical property": subs. (8).
  "enactment": s.221(1).
  "licence": s.72(1).
  "the relevant land": subs. (8).

GENERAL NOTE
  The provisions of this section are restricted to the Church of England and have no application to any other religions. Neither do they apply to all land owned by the Church of England, but only to property held by an ecclesiastical officer, usually a rector or vicar.

Provision for appeals and references to tribunal

68.—(1) The Secretary of State may by order make provision for securing that, in such cases or classes or cases as may be specified in or determined under the order, appeals and references which in accordance with the provisions of this Chapter would, apart from the order, be appeals or references to the Secretary of State shall lie to a tribunal established in accordance with the provisions of the order, instead of being appeals or references to the Secretary of State.

(2) An order under this section shall not apply to references in pursuance of directions under section 41 above.

(3) The provisions of this Chapter relating to appeals or references to which an order under this section applies shall have effect, subject to such modifications as may be specified in the order, as they would have effect in relation to the like appeals or references if made to the Secretary of State.

(4) Provision may be made by an order under this section for appeals or references to the tribunal to be heard and determined by one or more members of the tribunal.

(5) If a tribunal is established in accordance with this section, the Secretary of State may pay to the members of the tribunal such remuneration, whether by way of salaries or by way of fees, and such reasonable allowances in respect of expenses properly incurred in the performance of their duties, as the Treasury may determine.

(6) The power of the Secretary of State to make an order under this section shall be exercisable by statutory instrument subject to annulment in pursuance of a resolution of either House of Parliament.

DEFINITION
  "modification": s.221(1).

GENERAL NOTE
  This section gives the Secretary of State the power, exercisable by statutory instrument, to set up a tribunal to exercise on his behalf his powers to determine appeals and references concerning abstraction or impounding licence decisions of the Authority. The powers in question are to be found in ss.31, 43–45 and 54. Applications that the Secretary of State has called in to consider himself under s.41, thus bypassing the Authority, are excluded from the remit of the tribunal (subs. (2)). This means that the tribunal can only function as an appellate body from decisions of the Authority, and not of the Secretary of State. Although not technically an exception to this rule, objections to modification proposals of the Authority

under s.52 could see the tribunal considering a decision that had in effect been taken by the Secretary of State under s.52(2).

Validity of decisions of Secretary of State and related proceedings

69.—(1) Except as provided by the following provisions of this section, the validity of a decision of the Secretary of State on—

(a) any appeal to the Secretary of State under this Chapter; or

(b) any reference to the Secretary of State in pursuance of a direction under section 41 above or in pursuance of section 53(4) above,

shall not be questioned in any legal proceedings whatsoever.

(2) If, in the case of any such appeal or reference, the Authority or the other party desires to question the validity of the decision of the Secretary of State on the grounds—

(a) that the decision is not within the powers of this Act; or

(b) that any of the requirements of, or of any regulations made under, this Chapter which are applicable to the appeal or reference have not been complied with,

the Authority or, as the case may be, the other party may, at any time within the period of six weeks beginning with the date on which the decision is made, make an application to the High Court under this section.

(3) On any application under this section, the High Court may by interim order suspend the operation of the decision to which the application relates until the final determination of the proceedings.

(4) If the High Court is satisfied, on an application under this section—

(a) that the decision to which the application relates is not within the powers of this Act; or

(b) that the interests of the person making the application under this section have been substantially prejudiced by a failure to comply with any of the requirements mentioned in subsection (2)(b) above,

the High Court may quash the decision.

(5) If an order is made establishing a tribunal under section 68 above, the preceding provisions of this section shall have effect in relation to any appeal or reference to that tribunal as they have effect in relation to an appeal or reference to the Secretary of State.

(6) In this section—

"decision" includes a direction; and

"other party"—

(a) in relation to an appeal, means the appellant;

(b) in relation to a reference in pursuance of a direction under section 41 above, means the applicant for the licence or, where that section applies by virtue of section 51(3) above, for the revocation or variation; and

(c) in relation to a reference in pursuance of section 53(4) above, means (subject, without prejudice to their application to the other provisions of this Chapter, to subsections (6) and (7) of section 25 above) the holder of the licence.

DEFINITIONS

"decision": subs. (6).

"licence": s.72(1).

"other party": subs. (6).

"the Authority": s.221(1).

GENERAL NOTE

The apparent contradiction between subs. (1) and the rest of the section can be explained by the experience of the legislature that even wording as clear as "shall not be questioned in any legal proceedings whatsoever" has not been held to be any bar to judicial review proceedings. As a result the rest of the section provides a statutory basis for the judicial review proceedings that would have been available to applicants with a case in any event.

Civil liability under Chapter II

70. Except in so far as this Act otherwise expressly provides and subject to the provisions of section 18 of the Interpretation Act 1978 (which relates to offences under two or more laws), the restrictions imposed by sections 24, 25 and 30 above shall not be construed as—

(a) conferring a right of action in any civil proceedings (other than proceedings for the recovery of a fine) in respect of any contravention of those restrictions;

(b) affecting any restriction imposed by or under any other enactment, whether contained in a public general Act or in a local or private Act; or

(c) derogating from any right of action or other remedy (whether civil or criminal) in proceedings instituted otherwise than under this Chapter.

DEFINITION
"enactment": s.221(1).

GENERAL NOTE
This section mirrors s.100 which repeats the approach in s.105(2) of the Control of Pollution Act 1974 by asserting the principle that the provisions of this Chapter of this Part of the Act shall not affect other areas of the law concerning abstraction or impounding of waters, whether criminal or civil. Section 18 of the Interpretation Act 1978 applies the basic rule against double jeopardy for criminal offences.

Modification of local enactments

71.—(1) If it appears to the Secretary of State by whom an order is made under a provision of this Chapter to which this section applies that any local enactment passed or made before the relevant date—

(a) is inconsistent with any of the provisions of that order; or

(b) requires to be amended or adapted, having regard to any of the provisions of that order,

the Secretary of State may by order appeal, amend or adapt that enactment to such extent, or in such manner, as he may consider appropriate.

(2) Any order under this section may include such transitional, incidental, supplementary and consequential provisions as the Secretary of State may consider necessary or expedient.

(3) The power to make an order under this section shall be exercisable by statutory instrument subject to annulment in pursuance of a resolution of either House of Parliament.

(4) This section applies to the following provisions of this Chapter, that is to say, section 33, 66, 68 and 72(5).

(5) In this section—

"local enactment" means—

(a) a local or private Act;

(b) a public general Act relating to London;

(c) an order or scheme made under an Act, confirmed by Parliament or brought into operation in accordance with special parliamentary procedure; or

(d) an enactment in a public general Act amending a local or private Act or any such order or scheme;

"relevant date" means the date which was the second appointed day for the purposes of section 133 of the Water Resources Act 1963.

(6) The provisions of this section shall have effect without prejudice to the exercise of any other power to repeal, amend or adapt local enactments which is conferred by any other enactment.

DEFINITIONS
"local enactment": subs. (5).
"relevant date": subs. (5).

General Note
This section gives the Secretary of State the power, exercisable by statutory instrument, to modify local enactments if they clash with any orders made concerning abstraction or impounding. The section only applies to orders made under ss.33, 66, 68 and 72(5) and not to regulations under ss.34, 45 and 59.

Interpretation of Chapter II

72.—(1) In this Chapter—
"derogate," in relation to a protected right, shall be construed in accordance with section 39(4) above;
"flow" shall be construed subject to section 23(3) above;
"impounding works" has the meaning given by section 25(8) above;
"licence," in relation to the variation or revocation of a licence, shall be construed subject to section 25(6) and (7) above;
"protected right" shall be construed in accordance with section 39(3) above;
"the restriction on abstraction" means the restriction imposed by section 24(1) above;
"the restriction on impounding works" means the restriction imposed by section 25(1) above;
"spray irrigation" means (subject to subsection (5) below) the irrigation of land or plants (including seeds) by means of water or other liquid emerging (in whatever form) from apparatus designed or adapted to eject liquid into the air in the form of jets or spray; and
"statutory provision" means a provision (whether of a general or special nature) which is contained in, or in any document made or issued under, any Act (whether of a general or special nature).
(2) References in this Chapter to a watercourse shall not include references—
(a) to any sewer or part of a sewer vested in—
(i) a sewerage undertaker;
(ii) a local authority or joint planning board;
(iii) the Commission for the New Towns or a development corporation for a new town;
(iv) a harbour board within the meaning of the Railway and Canal Traffic Act 1988;
or
(b) to any adit or passage constructed in connection with a well, borehole or other similar work for facilitating the collection of water in the well, borehole or work.
(3) Any reference in this Chapter to the doing of anything in pursuance of a licence under this Chapter is a reference to its being done—
(a) by the holder of such a licence; or
(b) by a person acting as a servant or agent of, or otherwise under the authority of, the holder of such a licence,
at a time when the licence is in force and in circumstances such that, if no such licence were in force, the doing of that thing would contravene a restriction imposed by this Chapter.
(4) For the purposes of this Chapter land shall be taken to be contiguous to any inland waters notwithstanding that it is separated from those water by a towpath or by any other land used, or acquired for use, in connection with the navigation of the inland waters, unless that other land comprises any building or works other than a lock, pier, wharf, landing-stage or similar works.
(5) The Ministers may by order direct that references to spray irrigation in this Chapter, and in any other enactments in which "spray irrigation" is given the same meaning as in this Chapter, or such of those references as may be specified in the order—
(a) shall be construed as not including spray irrigation if carried out by such

methods or in such circumstances or for such purposes as may be
specified in the order; and
(b) without prejudice to the exercise of the power conferred by virtue of
paragraph (a) above, shall be construed as including references to the
carrying out, by such methods or in such circumstances or for such
purposes as may be specified in the order, of irrigation of any such
description, other than spray irrigation, as may be so specified.
(6) The power of the Ministers to make an order under subsection (5) above
shall be exercisable by statutory instrument subject to annulment in pursuance of a resolution of either House of Parliament.

CHAPTER III

DROUGHT

Power to make ordinary and emergency drought orders

73.—(1) If the Secretary of State is satisfied that, by reason of an exceptional shortage of rain, a serious deficiency of supplies of water in any area
exists or is threatened then, subject to the following provisions of this
Chapter, he may by order (in this Chapter referred to as an "ordinary
drought order") make such provision authorised by this Chapter as appears
to him to be expedient with a view to meeting the deficiency.
(2) If the Secretary of State—
(a) is satisfied that, by reason of an exceptional shortage of rain, a serious
deficiency of supplies of water in any area exists or is threatened; and
(b) is further satisfied that the deficiency is such as to be likely to impair
the economic or social well-being of persons in the area,
then, subject to the following provisions of this Chapter, he may by order (in
this Chapter referred to as an "emergency drought order") make such
provision authorised by this Chapter as appears to him to be expedient with
a view to meeting the deficiency.
(3) Subject to section 76(3) below, the power to make a drought order in
relation to any area shall not be exercisable except where an application is
made to the Secretary of State—
(a) by the Authority; or
(b) by a water undertaker which supplies water to premises in that area.
(4) The power to make a drought order shall be exercisable by statutory
instrument; and Schedule 8 to this Act shall have effect with respect to the
procedure on an application for such an order.

DEFINITIONS
"drought order": s.221(1).
"the Authority": s.221(1).

GENERAL NOTE
Sections 73–81 concern the making of drought orders. They are taken from ss.131–135 of the
Water Act 1989, which were modelled on ss.1–4 of the Drought Act 1976 which they replaced,
with the necessary adjustments to take into account the different functions of the Authority and
water undertakers after privatisation.

General Drought Order
A general drought order (s.73) is made by the Secretary of State on the application of either
the NRA or a water undertaker. The criteria for making an order are that the Secretary of State
is satisfied that an "*exceptional shortage of rain*" has caused or threatens to cause a "*serious
deficiency of supplies of water*" in any area. Sched. 8 details the procedure for making the order,
and requires, *inter alia*, that the application be published in local newspapers, and that local
authorities, together with other specified public bodies and persons (depending on the nature of
the proposed provisions of the order) be given the opportunity to make representations to the
Secretary of State. Given that the effects of a drought order can be severe on water and
sewerage management, surprisingly there is no formal requirement for either the Authority or

the undertaker to consult each other before making an application. The Authority would be bound by its general duty under s.15 to have particular regard to the service duties of water and sewerage undertakers before taking such a step, and informal consultations might be a prudent method of discharging this obligation. Nevertheless, there may in practice be some very real tensions over who should initiate the procedures, especially as it is the applicant who can be liable to pay compensation to those affected by the order (see below). The drafting in subs. (3) does not appear to allow for joint applications, which might have been one sensible solution.

Effect of Drought Order

The provisions that may be included in a drought order are exceptionally broad, and may grant the Authority and/or water undertakers a wide range of powers. Section 74(1) relates to the Authority, which may be authorised, *inter alia*, to take water from any specified source, to discharge water to specified sources, and to prohibit or limit the taking of water from specified sources, even if the person concerned has a statutory or common law right to take such water (see s.77(2)). Subs. (2) specifies provisions that can relate to water undertakers, and includes giving undertakers the power to prohibit or limit the use of water for any purpose that has already been specified in a general direction given by the Secretary of State (subs. (2)(b)).

Although the order may also contain provisions that authorise the overriding of existing obligations and consents, including the modification of effluent discharge consents, the power to do so may be inhibited should this conflict with obligations under relevant EEC Directives, unless these contain their own derogation provisions. Section 80 makes it an offence to take, use, or discharge water in contravention of the provisions of a drought order.

Emergency Drought Order

The same procedure and basic criteria apply to an emergency drought order made under s.73, but in addition the Secretary of State must be satisfied that the shortage of water supplies poses a risk to the economic or social well-being of people living in the area. The order may contain the same provisions possible under a general drought order, but in addition water undertakers may be authorised to prohibit or limit the use of water for any purpose they think fit (rather than only for uses already specified by the Secretary of State) (s.75(2)(b)), and to supply water by means of stand-pipes or water tanks (s.75(2)(c)). The validity of an emergency drought order may last initially for only three months but may be extended by the Secretary of State up to another two months (s.75(4)). Another important distinction from general drought orders is that rights to compensation from those suffering loss or damage as a result of the order are strictly limited in the case of emergency drought orders.

Compensation

The provisions of drought orders may affect existing rights and cause loss or damage. Sched. 9 contains exclusive provisions relating to compensation, with amounts to be determined in the absence of agreement by the Lands Tribunal. Under both emergency and general drought orders, compensation may be payable for loss or damage caused by the entry and occupation of land as a result of the order (para. 1). In addition, but only for general drought orders, compensation may be payable where provisions have restricted the taking of water or its discharge, required the taking of water, and restricted or modified rights to discharge trade or sewerage effluent (including the modification of an effluent discharge consent) (para. 2). Claims under para. 2 must be made within six months after the relevant provision in an order has ceased to have effect (para. 4).

Subs. (4)

In addition to Sched. 8, which contains provision for the holding of a local inquiry (para. 2(1)), see the Drought Order (Inquiries Procedures) Rules 1984 (S.I. 1984 No. 999).

Provisions and duration of ordinary drought order

74.—(1) An ordinary drought order made on the application of the Authority may contain any of the following provisions, that is to say—
   (a) provision authorising the Authority (or persons authorised to do so by the Authority) to take water from any source specified in the order subject to any conditions or restrictions so specified;
   (b) provision authorising the Authority (or persons authorised to do so by the Authority) to discharge water to any place specified in the order subject to any conditions or restrictions so specified;
   (c) provision authorising the Authority to prohibit or limit the taking by any person (including a water undertaker) of water from a source

specified in the order if the Authority is satisfied that the taking of water from that source seriously affects the supplies available to the Authority, any water undertaker or any other person;

(d) provision suspending or modifying, subject to any conditions specified in the order, any restriction or obligation to which the Authority, any water undertaker or sewerage undertaker or any other person is subject as respects—

    (i) the taking of water from any source;

    (ii) the discharge of water;

    (iii) the supply of water (whether in point of quantity, pressure, quality, means of supply or otherwise); or

    (iv) the filtration or other treatment of water;

(e) provision authorising the Authority to suspend or vary, or attach conditions to, any consent specified in the order for the discharge of any effluent by any person, including any sewerage undertaker or water undertaker.

(2) An ordinary drought order made on the application of a water undertaker may contain any of the following provisions, that is to say—

(a) provision authorising the water undertaker to take water from any source specified in the order subject to any conditions or restrictions so specified;

(b) provision authorising the water undertaker to prohibit or limit the use of water for any purpose specified in the order, being a purpose for the time being set out in a direction given by the Secretary of State to water undertakers generally as a purpose which may be specified by virtue of this paragraph in any ordinary drought order;

(c) provision authorising the water undertakers to discharge water to any place specified in the order subject to any conditions or restrictions so specified;

(d) provision authorising the Authority to prohibit or limit the taking by any person of water from a source specified in the order if the Authority is satisfied that the taking of water from that source seriously affects the supplies available to the water undertaker;

(e) provision prohibiting or limiting the taking by the Authority of water for a source specified in the order if the taking of water from that source is determined, in accordance with provision made by the order, seriously to affect the supplies available to the water undertaker.

(f) provision suspending or modifying, subject to any conditions specified in the order, any restriction or obligation to which the water undertaker or any sewerage undertaker or other person is subject as respects—

    (i) the taking of water from any source;

    (ii) the discharge of water;

    (iii) the supply of water (whether in point of quantity, pressure, quality, means of supply or otherwise); or

    (iv) the filtration or other treatment of water;

(g) provision authorising the Authority to suspend or vary, or attach conditions to, any consent specified in the order for the discharge of any effluent by any person, including the company which applied for the order (whether in the capacity in which it made the application, in its capacity as a sewerage undertaker or in any other capacity).

(3) The period for which—

(a) an authorisation given by or under an ordinary drought order;

(b) a prohibition or limitation imposed by or under any such order; or

(c) a suspension or modification effected by or under any such order,

has effect shall expire before the end of the period of six months beginning with the day on which the order comes into force unless that period of six months is extended, in relation to that order, by virtue of the exercise by the Secretary of State of his power (subject to subsection (4) below) to amend the order.

(4) The power of the Secretary of State to amend an ordinary drought order shall not be exercised so as to extend the period of six months mentioned in subsection (3) above beyond the end of the period of one year beginning with the day on which that order came into force.

(5) Without prejudice to the following provisions of this Chapter, an ordinary drought order may—
  (a) make different provision for different cases, including different provision in relation to different persons, circumstances or localities; and
  (b) contain such supplemental, consequential and transitional provision as the Secretary of State considers appropriate.

DEFINITIONS
  "drought order": s.221(1).
  "effluent": s.221(1).
  "modification": s.221(1).
  "restriction or obligation": s.81.
  "take water": s.81.
  "the Authority": s.221(1).

GENERAL NOTE
  See General Note to s.73.

Provisions and duration of emergency drought order

75.—(1) An emergency drought order made on the application of the Authority may contain any of the provisions which could be included, by virtue of section 74(1) above, in an ordinary drought order made on the application of the Authority.

(2) An emergency drought order made on the application of a water undertaker may contain any of the following provisions, that is to say—
  (a) any provision which could be included, by virtue of subsection (2) of section 74 above, in an ordinary drought order made on the application of a water undertaker, except provision authorised by paragraph (b) of that subsection;
  (b) provision authorising the water undertaker to prohibit or limit the use of water for such purposes as the water undertaker thinks fit;
  (c) provision authorising the water undertaker—
      (i) to supply water in its area, or in any place within its area, by means of stand-pipes or water tanks; and
      (ii) to erect or set up and maintain stand-pipes or water tanks in any street in that area.

(3) The period for which—
  (a) an authorisation given by or under an emergency drought order;
  (b) a prohibition or limitation imposed by or under any such order; or
  (c) a suspension or modification effected by or under any such order,
has effect shall expire before the end of the period of three months beginning with the day on which the order comes into force unless that period of three months is extended, in relation to that order, by virtue of the exercise by the Secretary of State of his power (subject to subsection (4) below) to amend the order.

(4) The power of the Secretary of State to amend an emergency drought order shall not be exercised so as to extend the period of three months mentioned in subsection (3) above beyond the end of the period of five months beginning with the day on which that order came into force.

(5) Where powers have been conferred by an emergency drought order on any person—
  (a) the Secretary of State may give to that person such directions as he

considers necessary or expedient as to the manner in which, or the circumstances in which, any of those powers is or is not to be exercised;
(b) it shall be the duty of that person to comply with any such direction; and
(c) where that person is a water undertaker or sewerage undertaker, the duty to comply with any such direction shall be enforceable under section 18 of the Water Industry Act 1991 by the Secretary of State.
(6) The giving of a direction under subsection (5) above in relation to any power shall not affect—
(a) the validity of anything done in the exercise of that power before the giving of the direction; or
(b) any obligation or liability incurred before the giving of the direction.
(7) Without prejudice to the following provisions of this Chapter, an emergency drought order may—
(a) make different provision for different cases, including different provision in relation to different persons, circumstances or localities; and
(b) contain such supplemental, consequential and transitional provision as the Secretary of State considers appropriate.

DEFINITIONS
"drought order": s.221(1).
"obligation": s.81.
"the Authority": s.221(1).

GENERAL NOTE
See General Note to s.73.

Provisions of drought order restricting use of water

76.—(1) The following provisions apply where a drought order contains a provision authorising a water undertaker to prohibit or limit the use of water, that is to say—
(a) the power may be exercised in relation to consumers generally, a class of consumer or a particular consumer;
(b) the water undertaker shall take such steps as it thinks appropriate for bringing the prohibition or limitation to the attention of the persons to whom the prohibition or limitation will apply and, in particular, shall (as the undertaker thinks appropriate)—
(i) cause notice of the prohibition or limitation to be published in one or more local newspapers circulating within that part of the water undertaker's area which would be affected by the provision of the order; or
(ii) send notice of the prohibition or limitation to the persons to whom the prohibition or limitation will apply;
(c) the prohibition or limitation shall not come into operation until the end of the period of 72 hours beginning with the day on which the notice is published or, as the case may be, sent to the person in question.
(2) The Secretary of State may revoke or vary any direction given by him for the purposes of section 74(2)(b) above by a further direction for those purposes.
(3) Where any purpose set out in a direction given for the purposes of section 74(2)(b) above will cease, by virtue of the variation or revocation of the direction, to be one which may be specified in an ordinary drought order, the Secretary of State shall (without an application having been made to him) exercise his power to vary or revoke ordinary drought orders, in so far as any orders in force will be affected by the variation or revocation of the

direction, so as to make those orders conform to the variation or reflect the revocation.

(4) The revocation or variation of a direction under subsection (3) above shall not affect either—

(a) the validity of anything done in pursuance of an order before the giving of the further direction; or

(b) any obligation or liability accrued or incurred before the giving of the further direction.

DEFINITIONS
"drought order": s.221(1).
"obligation": s.81.

GENERAL NOTE
See General Note to s.73.

Provisions of drought order with respect to abstractions and discharges

77.—(1) Any drought order which—

(a) authorises the taking of water from a source from which water is supplied in an inland navigation; or

(b) suspends or modifies—

(i) a restriction as respects the taking of water from a source from which water is supplied to an inland navigation; or

(ii) an obligation to discharge compensation water into a canal or into any river or stream which forms part of, or from which water is supplied to, an inland navigation,

may include provision for prohibiting or imposing limitations on the taking of water from the inland navigation or for the suspension or modification of any obligation to which a navigation authority are subject as respects the discharge of water from the inland navigation.

(2) A prohibition or limitation by or under a drought order on the taking of water from any source may be imposed so as to have effect in relation to a source from which a person to whom the prohibition or limitation applies has a right to take water whether by virtue of an enactment or instrument, an agreement or the ownership of land.

(3) Where a drought order made in the application of a water undertaker confers power on the Authority—

(a) to prohibit or limit the taking of water from any source; or

(b) to suspend or vary, or attach conditions to, any consent for the discharge of any effluent,

the Authority shall exercise that power in such manner as will ensure, so far as reasonably practicable, that the supplies of water available to the water undertaker are not seriously affected.

(4) For the purposes of sections 125 to 129 below any water authorised by a drought order to be abstracted from a source of supply shall be treated as if it had been authorised to be so abstracted by a licence granted under Chapter II of this Part, whether the water undertaker to which the order relates is the holder of such a licence or not.

(5) Where—

(a) any drought order confers power on the Authority to suspend or vary, or attach conditions to, any consent for the discharge of any effluent; and

(b) the Authority exercises that power so as to restrict the discharge of effluent by a sewerage undertaker.

the sewerage undertaker may so modify any consents or agreements relating to the discharge by other persons of trade effluent as to enable it to comply with any requirements or conditions imposed on it by or under the order with respect to discharges from sewers or works of the undertaker.

(6) In this section—
    "compensation water" means water which a water undertaker or the
    Authority is under an obligation to discharge—
            (a) in accordance with the provisions of a licence under Chap-
        ter II of this Part into a source of supply; or
            (b) under any local statutory provision, into any river, stream,
        brook or other running water or into a canal;
        and
    "inland navigation" includes any canal or navigable river.

DEFINITIONS
    "compensation water": subs. (6).
    "drought order": s.221(1).
    "effluent": s.221(1).
    "enactment": s.221(1).
    "inland navigation": subs. (6).
    "navigation authority": s.221(1).
    "obligation": s.81.
    "sewers": s.221(1).
    "taking of water": s.81.
    "the Authority": s.221(1).

GENERAL NOTE
    See General Note to s.73.

Works under drought orders

78.—(1) A drought order may authorise the Authority or a water undertaker, subject to any conditions and restrictions specified in the order, to
carry out any works required for the performance of any duty or the exercise
of any power which is imposed or conferred by or under the order.
    (2) A drought order authorising the Authority or a water undertaker to
carry out any works—
    (a) may authorise the Authority or that undertaker for that purpose to
        enter upon any land specified in the order and to occupy and use the
        land to such extent and in such manner as may be requisite for the
        carrying out and maintenance of the works; and
    (b) may apply in relation to the carrying out of the works such of the
        provisions of Part VII of this Act or Part VI of the Water Industry Act
        1991 as appear to the Secretary of State to be appropriate, subject to
        such modifications as may be specified in the order.
    (3) The Secretary of State shall include in any drought order authorising
the Authority or a water undertaker to enter any land provisions requiring
the Authority or that undertaker to give to the occupier of the land and to
such other persons concerned with the land as may be specified in the order
not less than 24 hours' notice of any intended entry.
    (4) Subject to subsection (3) above, a drought order may make any such
provision in relation to provisions of the order authorising any person to
enter any land as corresponds to provision having effect by virtue of section
173 below or to provision contained in Part II of Schedule 6 to the Water
Industry Act 1991.
    (5) Any works to be carried out under the authority of an emergency
drought order shall be included in the definition of emergency works in
section 52 of the New Roads and Street Works Act 1991.
    (6) Until the coming into force of section 52 of the New Roads and Street
Works Act 1991, subsection (5) above shall have effect as if the reference to
that section were a reference to section 39(1) of the Public Utilities Street
Works Act 1950; but nothing in this section shall be taken to prejudice the
power of the Secretary of State under that Act of 1991 to make an order

bringing that section 52 into force on different days for different purposes (including the purposes of this section).

DEFINITIONS
    "drought order": s.221(1).
    "restrictions": s.81.
    "the Authority": s.221(1).

GENERAL NOTE
    No planning permission will be required for authorised works or those necessary in connection with a drought order as they have deemed permissions under Pt. 15, Class A and Pt. 17, Class E of Sched. 2 to the General Development Order 1988 (S.I. 1988 No. 1813).

Compensation and charges where drought order made

79.—(1) Schedule 9 to this Act shall have effect with respect to the payment of compensation where a drought order has been made.

(2) Except as provided by Schedule 9 to this Act, neither the Authority nor any water undertaker or sewerage undertaker shall incur any liability to any person for loss or damage sustained by reason of anything done in pursuance of any drought order or of any omission in pursuance of such an order.

(3) Nothing in any drought order shall affect the right of the Authority, a water undertaker or a sewerage undertaker, in the event of an interruption or diminution of the supply of water, to recover any fixed or minimum charge which might have been recovered from any person by the Authority or that undertaker if there had been no such interruption or diminution.

DEFINITIONS
    "damage": s.221(1).
    "drought order": s.221(1).
    "the Authority": s.221(1).

GENERAL NOTE
    Compensation will be payable if the damage sustained by the claimant was the natural and reasonable consequence of the order and if it was not too remote. This may allow the recovery of expenditure incurred before the order came into operation (*Bateman* v. *Welsh Water Authority* (Ref./84/1985) (1986) 27 R.V.R. 10).

Offences against drought order

80.—(1) If any person—
    (a) takes or uses water in contravention of a prohibition or limitation imposed by or under any drought order or takes or uses water otherwise than in accordance with any condition or restriction so imposed; or
    (b) discharges water otherwise than in accordance with any condition or restriction imposed by or under such an order,
he shall be guilty of an offence under this section.

(2) If any person—
    (a) fails to construct or maintain in good order a gauge, weir or other apparatus for measuring the flow of water which he was required to construct or maintain by any drought order; or
    (b) fails to allow some person authorised for the purpose by or under any such order to inspect and examine any such apparatus or any records made thereby or kept by that person in connection therewith or to take copies of any such records,
he shall be guilty of an offence under this section.

(3) In any proceedings against any person for an offence under this section it shall be a defence for that person to show that he took all reasonable precautions and exercised all due diligence to avoid the commission of the offence.

(4) A person who is guilty of an offence under this section shall be liable—
(a) on summary conviction, to a fine not exceeding the statutory maximum;
(b) on conviction on indictment, to a fine.

DEFINITION
"drought order": s.221(1).

GENERAL NOTE
See General Note to s.73.

Interpretation of Chapter III

81. In this Chapter—
(a) references to the taking of water include references to the collection, impounding, diversion or appropriation of water; and
(b) references to an obligation or to a restriction include references to an obligation or, as the case may be, to a restriction which is imposed by or under any enactment or agreement.

DEFINITION
"enactment": s.221(1).

PART III

CONTROL OF POLLUTION OF WATER RESOURCES

CHAPTER I

QUALITY OBJECTIVES

Classification of quality of waters

82.—(1) The Secretary of State may, in relation to any description of controlled waters (being a description applying to some or all of the waters of a particular class or of two or more different classes), by regulations prescribe a system of classifying the quality of those waters according to criteria specified in the regulations.

(2) The criteria specified in regulations under this section in relation to any classification shall consist of one or more of the following, that is to say—
(a) general requirements as to the purposes for which the waters to which the classification is applied are to be suitable;
(b) specific requirements as to the substances that are to be present in or absent from the water and as to the concentrations of substances which are or are required to be present in the water;
(c) specific requirements as to other characteristics of those waters;
and for the purposes of any such classification regulations under this section may provide that the question whether prescribed requirements are satisfied may be determined by reference to such samples as may be prescribed.

DEFINITIONS
"controlled waters": s.104.
"substance": s.221(1).

GENERAL NOTE

The New Controls
Part III of the Act (ss.82–104) contains a statutory system of controls over pollution of inland, coastal, and other waters as defined in this section, which reproduce the structure of the 1989 Act which replaced the provisions under Pt. II of the Control of Pollution Act 1974 (C.O.P.A.) as they applied to England and Wales.

In many respects, the provisions build upon the C.O.P.A. model of regulating discharges by consents but subject to the important change that the NRA, rather than water authorities or their successors, has the lead responsibility for implementation and enforcement of the controls (although the Secretary of State has the power to give it general or specific directions in respect of its functions under this part (s.5)).

The 1989 Act also introduced a number of other significant legal changes. For the first time, water quality objectives and targets for achieving them were given statutory form. The NRA was given the power to make charges for consents and set consent conditions requiring pre-treatment or other process requirements. The emphasis on precautionary measures, together with the need to control diffuse as well as point sources of pollution, was reflected in other new provisions, in line with policy objectives outlined in the Government consultation paper *The Water Environment: the Next Steps* (Department of the Environment, 1986). Previous provisions in C.O.P.A. 1974 concerning general precautionary standards and the establishment of water protection zones are re-enacted in a strengthened and more explicit form (s.93). A new power to prevent and regulate the entry of nitrate from agricultural activities by the establishment of nitrate-sensitive areas was introduced by the 1989 Act (s.94 of this Act). For further discussion of the policy background and current levels of pollution, see the Third Report of the House of Commons Environment Committee Session 1986–87, Pollution of Rivers and Estuaries (1987), and the Third Special Report of the Environment Committee Session 1987–88, Pollution of Rivers and Estuaries—Observations by the Government on the Third Report of the Committee in Session 1986–87 (1988).

Objectives of the New System

The following three sections, taken from the Water Act 1989 (ss.104–106), allow for a system of statutory water quality objectives to act as the key criteria against which policy and control decisions of the NRA, such as the attachment of conditions on discharge consents, are to be set. These provisions allow the creation of what is in effect a statutory national policy concerning water pollution, and both the Secretary of State and the NRA are under a general duty to achieve the objectives (s.84). The justification for the new system was explained in the Government's observations of the Third Report of the House of Commons Select Committee on the Environment Pollution of Rivers and Estuaries (1987):

"The system is thus intended to assist coherent development of policy and effective implementation. In particular it will:

—clarify priorities between areas and different types of improvement;

—require pollution control authorities and all those water users they regulate, to follow standards and practices compatible with the achievement of the objectives;

—allow necessary investment levels to be identified and planned for by the utility companies and industrial discharges" (para. 1.21, Select Committee on the Environment, Third Special Report, Observations by the Government on the Third Report of the Committee in Session 1986–87 (1988)).

Water Quality Classifications

Section 82 empowers the Secretary of State to establish, by regulations, classification systems for controlled waters which logically precede and form the basis of the heart of the new procedures—the setting of objectives under s.83. In 1978, a system for classifying inland waters into five categories of water quality ranging from "good" to "bad" was developed by the then National Water Council and adopted by water authorities for administrative purposes: see National Water Council, River Water Quality, The Next State (1978). But the system has no statutory base, and rested uneasily with the process of implementing EEC water pollution Directives, where both the Commission and the European Court favour implementation within national jurisdictions to be achieved by more formal mechanisms.

The section is drafted to give the maximum possible discretion to the Secretary of State. There is no obligation on him to develop classifications for all types of controlled waters, though a statutory water quality objective cannot be established in the absence of a classification under this section (s.83(1)(a)). Similarly, the type of criteria that may be incorporated within any particular classification has been left open-ended, and may be related to specified purposes for particular waters, concentrations of substances, any other characteristics, or a combination of any or all three. A number of amendments were proposed during Committee stage of the 1989 Act in the House of Lords which would have required specific reference to nature conservation interests within the classifications. In resisting these on the grounds that they would inhibit flexibility, Lord Hesketh for the Government nevertheless gave a commitment that they would be incorporated at some stage in the future:

"Will nature conservation be included as a goal in the statutory quality objectives which will be framed in terms of the classifications? The answer is yes. We have already had discussions with the Nature Conservancy Council on how best to do this. There is no simple method, as what may be good for one type of conservation site may be damaging for another. However, we have no doubt that our discussions with the Council will produce a generally acceptable means of setting objectives designed to promote conservation" (*Hansard*, H.L. Vol. 508, col. 183, May 23, 1989).

The first set of classifications made under the then s.104 of the 1989 Act related to inland waters, based on their suitability for abstraction for drinking water, and reflect the mandatory values in Annex II of E.C. Directive 75/440 concerning the quality required of surface water intended for the abstraction of drinking water: Surface Water (Classification) Regulations 1989 (S.I. 1989 No. 1148).

Revision of Classifications
The classifications under this section are made by regulations, and can be revised by subsequent regulations. This section contains no other formal consultative or other procedural requirements to be followed before any such change takes place, but in themselves the classifications have no legal effect. To do so, they must be incorporated in "Water Quality Objectives" established under s.83, and the Secretary of State may only vary such objectives after following the review contained in s.83(3) and (4).

Water quality objectives

83.—(1) For the purpose of maintaining and improving the quality of controlled waters the Secretary of State may, by serving a notice on the Authority specifying—
  (a) one or more of the classifications for the time being prescribed under section 82 above; and
  (b) in relation to each specified classification, a date,
establish the water quality objectives for any waters which are, or are included in, waters of a description prescribed for the purposes of that section.
  (2) The water quality objectives for any waters to which a notice under this section relates shall be the satisfaction by those waters, on and at all times after each date specified in the notice, of the requirements which at the time of the notice were the requirements for the classification in relation to which that date is so specified.
  (3) Where the Secretary of State has established water quality objectives under this section for any waters he may review objectives for those waters if—
  (a) five years or more have elapsed since the service of the last notice under subsection (1) or (6) of this section to be served in respect of those waters; or
  (b) the Authority, after consultation with such water undertakers and other persons as it considers appropriate, requests a review;
and the Secretary of State shall not exercise his power to establish objectives for any waters by varying the existing objectives for those waters except in consequence of such a review.
  (4) Where the Secretary of State proposes to exercise his power under this section to establish or vary the objectives for any waters he shall—
  (a) give notice setting out his proposal and specifying the period (not being less than three months from the date of publication of the notice) within which representations or objections with respect to the proposal may be made; and
  (b) consider any representations or objections which are duly made and not withdrawn;
and, if he decides, after considering any such representations or objections, to exercise his power to establish or vary those objectives, he may do so either in accordance with the proposal contained in the notice or in accordance with that proposal as modified in such manner as he considers appropriate.
  (5) A notice under subsection (4) above shall be given—

(a) by publishing the notice in such manner as the Secretary of State considers appropriate for bringing it to the attention of persons likely to be affected by it; and

(b) by serving a copy of the notice on the Authority.

(6) If, on a review under this section or in consequence of any representations or objections made following such a review for the purposes of subsection (4) above, the Secretary of State decides that the water quality objectives for any waters should remain unchanged, he shall serve notice of that decision on the Authority.

DEFINITIONS
"controlled water": s.104.
"notice": s.221(1).
"the Authority": s.221(1).

GENERAL NOTE

Subs. (1)
For the purpose of maintaining or improving the quality of controlled waters. The Secretary of State may only specify objectives in order to maintain or improve water quality, and this qualification will apply to any further establishment of objectives following subsequent reviews. It does not necessarily preclude a subsequent downgrading of a particular water quality objective, although the wording is ambiguous. Certainly, in such cases, the Secretary of State would have to show why such downgrading would maintain or improve water quality, *e.g.* by allowing resources to be spent more effectively on improvements elsewhere. The procedure for establishing both initial and subsequent water quality objectives is contained in subss. (4) and (5).

By serving a notice. The notice specifying the objective served by the Secretary of State must be placed on the public register maintained by the NRA under s.190. Potential dischargers and members of the public will therefore be able to determine the statutory water quality objective covering any particular area of water.

Subs. (3)
He may review objectives. No variation of existing objectives may take place unless a review under this subsection has been carried out. Reviews may take place only (i) at intervals of at least five years or (ii) on request of the NRA, after consultation with water undertakers and others it thinks appropriate.

Subss. (4) and (5)
These subsections cover the procedure to be followed by the Secretary of State before initial establishment of objectives or their subsequent variation. He is required to give at least three months' notice, publish notice of his proposal and consider representations. Equivalent statutory provisions often specify publication in the London Gazette and/or in local newspapers. Under these subsections the Secretary of State is given wide discretion as to how best to publicise the notice, but his powers are not totally unfettered since they must be exercised "for bringing it to the attention of persons likely to be affected by it". In addition to any publicity given under these provisions, the notice must also be placed in the public register set up under s.190.

General duties to achieve and maintain objectives etc.

84.—(1) It shall be the duty of the Secretary of State and of the Authority to exercise the powers conferred on him or it by or under the water pollution provisions of this Act (other than the preceding provisions of this Chapter and sections 104 and 192 below) in such manner as ensures, so far as it is practicable by the exercise of those powers to do so, that the water quality objectives specified for any waters in—

(a) a notice under section 83 above; or

(b) a notice under section 30C of the Control of Pollution Act 1974 (which makes corresponding provision for Scotland),

are achieved at all times.

(2) It shall be the duty of the Authority, for the purposes of the carrying out of its functions under the water pollution provisions of this Act—

(a) to monitor the extent of pollution in controlled waters; and

(b) to consult, in such cases as it may consider appropriate, with river purification authorities in Scotland.

DEFINITIONS
"controlled waters": s.104.
"functions": s.3.
"the Authority": s.221(1).

GENERAL NOTE

Subs. (1)
This is an important general duty requiring both the Authority and the Secretary of State to exercise their powers to secure the achievement of the statutory water objectives at all times. The duty is, however, qualified by the phrase "so far as it is practicable", and it only applies to the pollution control powers under this Chapter of the Act. In theory, the duty itself might be enforceable by way of judicial review, though in respect of the Authority, the Secretary of State has the power to issue general or specific Directions (s.5) which might be considered a more appropriate alternative remedy. In any event, in practice its existence will prove more relevant in providing underlining criteria against which operational decisions, including the granting of discharge consents, are taken.
A notice under section 30C of the Control of Pollution Act 1974. The inclusion of this reference is to ensure that both the Secretary of State and the NRA have regard to Scottish Water Quality Objectives when taking decisions which may affect Scottish waters. There is a reciprocal provision in the new s.30D of C.O.P.A. 1974 as amended by Sched. 23.

Subs. (2)
To monitor the extent of pollution in controlled waters. This is a new duty not explicitly contained in previous water pollution legislation. Prescribed particulars of samples of water or effluent taken in carrying out this duty must be placed on the public register maintained under s.190.

CHAPTER II

POLLUTION OFFENCES

Principal offences

Offences of polluting controlled waters

85.—(1) A person contravenes this section if he causes or knowingly permits any poisonous, noxious or polluting matter or any solid waste matter the enter any controlled waters.

(2) A person contravenes this section if he causes or knowingly permits any matter, other than trade effluent or sewage effluent, to enter controlled waters by being discharged from a drain or sewer in contravention of a prohibition imposed under section 86 below.

(3) A person contravenes this section if he causes or knowingly permits any trade effluent or sewage effluent to be discharged—
  (a) into any controlled waters; or
  (b) from land in England and Wales, through a pipe, into the sea outside the seaward limits of controlled waters.

(4) A person contravenes this section if he causes or knowingly permits any trade effluent or sewage effluent to be discharged, in contravention of any prohibition imposed under section 86 below, from a building or from any fixed plant—
  (a) on to or into any land; or
  (b) into any waters of a lake or pond which are not inland freshwaters.

(5) A person contravenes this section if he causes or knowingly permits any matter whatever to enter any inland freshwaters so as to tend (either directly or in combination with other matter which he or another person causes or permits to enter those waters) to impede the proper flow of the

waters in a manner leading, or likely to lead, to a substantial aggravation
of—
(a) pollution due to other causes; or
(b) the consequences of such pollution.
(6) Subject to the following provisions of this Chapter, a person who
contravenes this section or the conditions of any consent given under this
Chapter for the purposes of this section shall be guilty of an offence and
liable—
(a) on summary conviction, to imprisonment for a term not exceeding
three months or to a fine not exceeding £20,000 or to both;
(b) on conviction on indictment, to imprisonment for a term not exceeding two years or to a fine or to both.

DEFINITIONS
"contravention": s.221(1).
"controlled waters": s.104.
"drains": s.221(1).

GENERAL NOTE
This section contains key water pollution offences which, coupled with the defence provided
in s.88, provide the legal basis for a system of regulation based on consents. These offences
largely repeat what was previously contained in ss.31 and 32 of C.O.P.A. 1974, but with some
important structural differences. While C.O.P.A. 1974 contained two distinct types of offences
in different sections (essentially relating to one-off pollution incidents whether accidental or
not, and to regular discharge through outlet pipes), the Water Act 1989 conflated these into one
section with one set of defences. In contrast to previous legislation, discharges of trade or
sewage effluent from buildings or fixed plant on to land (which may indirectly reach waters or
groundwater) are no longer an offence in themselves. Such land discharges must also be in
breach of a "prohibition under this section" as defined in s.86(1), a device which should allow
the controls to be applied to these sorts of discharges in a rather more purposeful and focused
manner than under previous law. Finally, the politically controversial defence of "good
agricultural practice" which applied to s.31 of C.O.P.A. 1974 was not re-enacted by the 1989
Act.

Subs. (1)
Causes or knowingly permits. The alternative wording implies two distinct offences: see
Mcleod v. *Buchanan* [1940] 2 All E.R. 179. Where a defendant has been charged with the
"causes" offence, it is not necessary to show that the defendant acted intentionally or negligently, and a common sense approach to the word in its everyday usage should be adopted:
Alphacell v. *Woodward* [1972] A.C. 824, *Wrothwell (F.J.H.)* v. *Yorkshire Water Authority*
[1984] Crim.L.R. 43; and for a useful restatement of principles, see *Southern Water Authority* v.
Pegrum [1989] Crim.L.R. 442. The chain of causation may be broken by, *e.g.* intervention of a
third party such as a trespasser: *Impress (Worcester)* v. *Rees* [1971] 2 All E.R. 357. The courts
have held that the notion of causing in the offence implies some positive participation by the
defendant—merely standing by is not sufficient: *Price* v. *Cromack* [1975] 1 W.L.R. 988,
Lockhart v. *National Coal Board* [1981] S.C.C.R. 9. In such cases, a charge based on "knowingly permitting" may be appropriate.
Poisonous, noxious, or polluting matter. The provision in s.11 of the Rivers (Prevention of
Pollution) Act 1951, namely that an innocuous discolouration of water was not in itself
poisonous, noxious or polluting, has not been repeated in subsequent legislation. In practice,
though there is no case-law on the point, some water authorities have taken the view that the
phrase implies harm or potential harm to some organism or similar feature; where only
discolouration takes place, it must therefore be shown that it could interfere with growth of
water plants and organisms by restricting their access to sunlight.
Solid waste matter. Although the phrase receives no statutory definition, it would include
items of litter, discharged canisters, etc., and it is not necessary to show that they are poisonous,
noxious or polluting.
Matter, other than trade effluent or sewage effluent. This category, which applies to, say,
discharges of rainwater or domestic run-offs, is now no longer an offence unless covered by a
relevant prohibition issued under s.86.

Subs. (6)
Or the conditions of any consent. In *Severn Trent River Authority* v. *Express Food Group*

(1989) 153 J.P. 126 a decision concerning the similarly worded offence under s.32 of C.O.P.A. 1974, it was held that only one offence was committed for each discharge, however many consent conditions were broken. Although the formulation is a little different here, it would appear that the same reasoning would apply to this offence.

On summary conviction. The penalties were increased by the 1989 Act (s.107); under C.O.P.A. 1974 the possibility of imprisonment on summary conviction applied only to the offence relating to noxious, poisonous, or polluting entries.

Prohibition of certain discharges by notice or regulations

86.—(1) For the purposes of section 85 above a discharge of any effluent or other matter is, in relation to any person, in contravention of a prohibition imposed under this section if, subject to the following provisions of this section—

(a) the Authority has given that person notice prohibiting him from making or, as the case may be, continuing the discharge; or

(b) the Authority has given that person notice prohibiting him from making or, as the case may be, continuing the discharge unless specified conditions are observed, and those conditions are not observed.

(2) For the purposes of section 85 above a discharge of any effluent or other matter is also in contravention of a prohibition imposed under this section if the effluent or matter discharged—

(a) contains a prescribed substance or a prescribed concentration of such a substance; or

(b) derives from a prescribed process or from a process involving the use of prescribed substances or the use of such substances in quantities which exceed the prescribed amounts.

(3) Nothing in subsection (1) above shall authorise the giving of a notice for the purposes of that subsection in respect of discharges from a vessel; and nothing in any regulations made by virtue of subsection (2) above shall require any discharge from a vessel to be treated as a discharge in contravention of a prohibition imposed under this section.

(4) A notice given for the purposes of subsection (1) above shall expire at such time as may be specified in the notice.

(5) The time specified for the purposes of subsection (4) above shall not be before the end of the period of three months beginning with the day on which the notice is given, except in a case where the Authority is satisfied that there is an emergency which requires the prohibition in question to come into force at such time before the end of that period as may be so specified.

(6) Where, in the case of such a notice for the purposes of subsection (1) above as (but for this subsection) would expire at a time at or after the end of the said period of three months, an application is made before that time for a consent under this Chapter in respect of the discharge to which the notice relates, that notice shall be deemed not to expire until the result of the application becomes final—

(a) on the grant or withdrawal of the application;

(b) on the expiration, without the bringing of an appeal with respect to the decision on the application, of any period prescribed as the period within which any such appeal must be brought; or

(c) on the withdrawal or determination of any such appeal.

DEFINITIONS
    "contravention": s.221(1).
    "notice": s.221(1).
    "prescribed": s.221(1).
    "vessel": s.221(1).

GENERAL NOTE

Subs. (1)

A prohibition imposed under this section. This is a new procedure designed to ensure that the broadly worded offences under s.85(2) and (4) are more effectively focused and applied only to those types of discharge which most require control. Unless the discharge contains one or more substances prescribed in regulations, the Authority must give notice before the prohibition takes effect. Normally, there must be at least three months' notice, but the prohibition could take immediate effect where the Authority is satisfied that there is an emergency (subs. (5)). This latter provision was the result of an amendment accepted by the Government during Report stage of the 1989 Act in the House of Lords. Although drafted in the present tense, the phrase *there is an emergency* appears to be broad enough to encompass the immediate likelihood of a discharge taking place with serious consequences. Note that only the person served with a notice can be subsequently charged with the offence.

Those conditions not observed. Although the overall offence is one of strict liability, it is suggested that the non-observance of conditions in a prohibition notice must be accompanied by knowledge or recklessness.

Subs. (3)

Discharges from a vessel. The effect of this provision is that discharges from vessels will be covered only by the offences under s.85(1) ("noxious, poisonous, or polluting") or s.85(5) (impeding flow leading to aggravated pollution).

Discharges into and from public sewers etc.

87.—(1) For the purposes of section 85 above where—

(a) any sewage effluent is discharged as mentioned in subsection (3) or (4) of that section from any sewer or works vested in a sewerage undertaker; and

(b) the undertaker did not cause or knowingly permit the discharge but was bound (either unconditionally or subject to conditions which were observed) to receive into the sewer or works matter included in the discharge,

the undertaker shall be deemed to have caused the discharge.

(2) A sewerage undertaker shall not be guilty of an offence under section 85 above by reason only of the fact that a discharge from a sewer or works vested in the undertaker contravenes conditions of a consent relating to the discharge if—

(a) the contravention is attributable to a discharge which another person caused or permitted to be made into the sewer or works;

(b) the undertaker either was not bound to receive the discharge into the sewer or works or was bound to receive it there subject to conditions which were not observed; and

(c) the undertaker could not reasonably have been expected to prevent the discharge into the sewer or works.

(3) A person shall not be guilty of an offence under section 85 above in respect of a discharge which he caused or permitted to be made into a sewer or works vested in a sewerage undertaker if the undertaker was bound to receive the discharge there either unconditionally or subject to conditions which were observed.

DEFINITIONS

"sewage effluent": s.221(1).

"sewer": s.221(1).

GENERAL NOTE

Subs. (1)(b)

Was bound . . . to receive into the sewer. The effect of this provision is to impose a heavy duty on water undertakers to ensure proper treatment of those discharges into their sewers which they are bound to receive. The obligation is mirrored by the defence in subs. (2), which in effect provides that an undertaker will not be strictly liable for those discharges which are not lawfully made into its sewers. For discharges to sewers which an undertaker is bound to receive, see, in particular, s.34 of the Public Health Acts 1936 and the Public Health (Drainage of Premises) Act 1937.

Defence to principal offences in respect of authorised discharges

88.—(1) Subject to the following provisions of this section, a person shall not be guilty of an offence under section 85 above in respect of the entry of any matter into any waters or any discharge if the entry occurs or the discharge is made under and in accordance with, or as a result of any act or omission under and in accordance with—

(a) a consent given under this Chapter or under Part II of the Control of Pollution Act 1974 (which makes corresponding provision for Scotland);

(b) an authorisation for a prescribed process designated for central control granted under Part I of the Environmental Protection Act 1990;

(c) a waste management or disposal licence;

(d) a licence granted under Part II of the Food and Environment Protection Act 1985;

(e) section 163 below or section 165 of the Water Industry Act 1991 (discharges for works purposes);

(f) any local statutory provision or statutory order which expressly confers power to discharge effluent into water; or

(g) any prescribed enactment.

(2) Schedule 10 to this Act shall have effect, subject to section 91 below, with respect to the making of applications for consents under this Chapter for the purposes of subsection (1)(a) above and with respect to the giving, revocation and modification of such consents.

(3) Nothing in any disposal licence shall be treated for the purposes of subsection (1) above as authorising—

(a) any such entry or discharge as is mentioned in subsections (2) to (4) of section 85 above; or

(b) any act or omission so far as it results in any such entry or discharge.

(4) In this section—

"disposal licence" means a licence issued in pursuance of section 5 of the Control of Pollution Act 1974;

"statutory order" means—

(a) any order under section 168 below or section 167 of the Water Industry Act 1991 (compulsory works orders); or

(b) any order, byelaw, scheme or award made under any other enactment, including an order or scheme confirmed by Parliament or brought into operation in accordance with special parliamentary procedure;

and

"waste management licence" means such a licence granted under Part II of the Environmental Protection Act 1990.

DEFINITIONS

"disposal licence": subs. (4).

"prescribed": s.221(1).

"statutory order": subs. (4).

"waste management licence": subs. (4).

GENERAL NOTE

This section provides various defences to the offence under s.85. These largely repeat those previously available under Pt. II of C.O.P.A. 1974, with the exception that the defence of "good agricultural practice" under s.31(2)(c) of C.O.P.A. 1974 is no longer available.

Subs. (1)

A disposal licence. This refers to the system of licensing waste disposal facilities and disposal sites under Pt. I of C.O.P.A. 1974. Licences are granted by waste disposal authorities, normally local authorities, who must consult the NRA before granting a licence (s.5(4) of C.O.P.A. 1974 as amended under Sched. 22 to the 1989 Act). Run-offs or leachate from land-fill disposal sites can give rise to water pollution, and the drafting here is designed to ensure no duplication of controls. The qualification in subs. (3) is to make it clear that a disposal licence cannot authorise direct discharges into waters.

Subs. (2)

Compliance with a consent is a defence to the pollution offences. Depending on the terms of the order establishing a water protection zone under s.93, consents may also be required for carrying out activities within it, but consent procedures are to be provided in regulations made under s.96(1). Similarly, for nitrate-sensitive areas under s.94, specific consent procedures will be established by regulations made under s.96(2).

The procedures contained in Sched. 10 build upon the provisions concerning consent applications contained in Pt. II of C.O.P.A. 1974 which were, in terms of providing opportunities for public participation, something of an innovation in British pollution control legislation. For the power to charge for consents see s.131.

For provisions concerning appeals and "called-in" applications, see Control of Pollution (Consent for Discharges etc.) (Secretary of State Functions) Regulations 1989 (S.I. 1989 No. 1151).

Other defences to principal offences

89.—(1) A person shall not be guilty of an offence under section 85 above in respect of the entry of any matter into any waters or any discharge if—

(a) the entry is caused or permitted, or the discharge is made, in an emergency in order to avoid danger to life or health;

(b) that person takes all such steps as are reasonably practicable in the circumstances for minimising the extent of the entry or discharge and of its polluting effects; and

(c) particulars of the entry or discharge are furnished to the Authority as soon as reasonably practicable after the entry occurs.

(2) A person shall not be guilty of an offence under section 85 above by reason of his causing or permitting any discharge of trade or sewage effluent from a vessel.

(3) A person shall not be guilty of an offence under section 85 above by reason only of his permitting water from an abandoned mine to enter controlled waters.

(4) A person shall not, otherwise than in respect of the entry of any poisonous, noxious or polluting matter into any controlled waters, be guilty of an offence under section 85 above by reason of his depositing the solid refuse of a mine or quarry on any land so that it falls or is carried into inland freshwaters if—

(a) he deposits the refuse on the land with the consent of the Authority;

(b) no other site for the deposit is reasonably practicable; and

(c) he takes all reasonably practicable steps to prevent the refuse from entering those inland freshwaters.

(5) A highway authority or other person entitled to keep open a drain by virtue of section 100 of the Highways Act 1980 shall not be guilty of an offence under section 85 above by reason of his causing or permitting any discharge to be made from a drain kept open by virtue of that section unless the discharge is made in contravention of a prohibition imposed under section 86 above.

(6) In this section "mine" and "quarry" have the same meanings as in the Mines and Quarries Act 1954.

DEFINITIONS

"drain": s.221(1).
"highway": s.221(1).
"mine": subs. (6).
"vessel": s.221(1).

GENERAL NOTE

Subs. (1)(a)
An emergency in order to avoid danger to life or health. The 1989 Water Bill originally contained the phrase "to the public". This phrase was substituted by a Government amendment during Committee stage of the 1989 Act in the House of Lords, on the grounds that the defence should apply where risks to employees occurred as well as to members of the public. It also has the apparently unintended effect of encompassing other living animals such as threatened livestock. Where a defendant reasonably believed that an emergency existed but was in fact mistaken in doing so, it is suggested that the defence would still be applicable, though there is no case law on this point.

Offences in connection with deposits and vegetation in rivers

Offences in connection with deposits and vegetation in rivers

90.—(1) A person shall be guilty of an offence under this section if, without the consent of the Authority, he—
(a) removes from any part of the bottom, channel or bed of any inland freshwaters a deposit accumulated by reason of any dam, weir or sluice holding back the waters; and
(b) does so by causing the deposit to be carried away in suspension in the waters.

(2) A person shall be guilty of an offence under this section if, without the consent of the Authority, he—
(a) causes or permits a substantial amount of vegetation to be cut or uprooted in any inland freshwaters, or to be cut or uprooted so near to any such waters that it falls into them; and
(b) fails to take all reasonable steps to remove the vegetation from those waters.

(3) A person guilty of an offence under this section shall be liable, on summary conviction, to a fine not exceeding level 4 on the standard scale.

(4) Nothing in subsection (1) above applies to anything done in the exercise of any power conferred by or under any enactment relating to land drainage, flood prevention or navigation.

(5) In giving a consent for the purposes of this section the Authority may make the consent subject to such conditions as it considers appropriate.

(6) The Secretary of State may by regulations provide that any reference to inland freshwaters in subsection (1) or (2) above shall be construed as including a reference to such coastal waters as may be prescribed.

DEFINITIONS
"coastal waters": s.104.
"enactment": s.221(1).
"inland waters": s.104.
"prescribed": s.221(1).

GENERAL NOTE
This section creates a specific offence relating to activity which gives rise to disturbances and obstruction in water courses, without necessarily causing pollution. It is modelled on the previous offence under s.49 of C.O.P.A. 1974. The offence can be extended by regulations to cover coastal waters (subs. (6)).

Subs. (1) and (2)
Without the consent of the Authority. Conditions may be attached to the consent (subs. (5)), and for further provisions concerning the procedure, see s.99 and Sched. 10.

Appeals in respect of consents under Chapter II

91.—(1) This section applies where the Authority, otherwise than in pursuance of a direction of the Secretary of State—

(a) on an application for a consent under this Chapter for the purposes of section 88(1)(a) above, has refused a consent for any discharges;

(b) in giving a discharge consent, has made that consent subject to conditions;

(c) has revoked a discharge consent, modified the conditions of any such consent or provided that any such consent which was unconditional shall be subject to conditions;

(d) has, for the purpose of paragraph 7(1) or (2) of Schedule 10 to this Act, specified a period in relation to a discharge consent without the agreement of the person who proposes to make, or makes, discharges in pursuance of that consent;

(e) has refused a consent for the purposes of section 89(4)(a) above for any deposit; or

(f) has refused a consent for the purposes of section 90 above for the doing of anything by any person or, in giving any such consent, made that consent subject to conditions.

(2) The person, if any, who applied for the consent in question, or any person whose deposits, discharges or other conduct is or would be authorised by the consent may appeal against the decision to the Secretary of State.

(3) The Secretary of State may by regulations provide for the conduct and disposal of appeals under this section.

(4) Without prejudice to the generality of the power conferred by subsection (3) above, regulations under that subsection may, with prescribed modifications, apply any provision of paragraphs 1(3) to (6), 2(1) and 4(4) to (6) of Schedule 10 to this Act in relation to appeals under this section.

(5) If, on an appeal under this section the Secretary of State is of the opinion that the decision of the Authority should be modified or reversed, he may give the Authority such directions as he thinks appropriate for requiring it—

(a) to give a consent, either unconditionally or, in the case of a discharge consent or a consent for the purposes of section 90 above, subject to such conditions as may be specified in the direction;

(b) to modify the conditions of any discharge consent or any consent for the purposes of section 90 above or to provide that any discharge consent which is unconditional shall be subject to such conditions as made be specified in the direction;

(c) to modify in accordance with the direction any provision specifying a period for the purposes of paragraph 7 of Schedule 10 to this Act.

(6) In complying with a direction under subsection (5) above to give a consent the Authority shall not be required to comply with any requirement imposed by paragraph 3 of Schedule 10 to this Act.

(7) Nothing in any direction under subsection (5) above or in anything done in pursuance of any such direction shall be taken to affect the lawfulness or validity of anything which was done—

(a) in pursuance of any decision o the Authority which is to be modified or reversed under the direction; and

(b) before the direction is complied with.

(8) In this section "discharge consent" means such a consent under this Chapter for any discharges or description of discharges as is given for the purposes of section 88(1)(a) above either on an application for a consent or, by virtue of paragraph 5 of Schedule 10 to his Act, without such an application having been made.

"discharge consent": subs. (8).
"the Authority": s.221(1).
"the Secretary of State": s.221(1).

GENERAL NOTE
No formal requirements are specified for the making of applications, but this section provides a mechanism for appeals to the Secretary of State against refusal or imposition of conditions.

CHAPTER III

POWERS TO PREVENT AND CONTROL POLLUTION

Requirements to take precautions against pollution

92.—(1) The Secretary of State may by regulations make provision—
(a) for prohibiting a person from having custody or control of any poisonous, noxious or polluting matter unless prescribed works and prescribed precautions and other steps have been carried out or taken for
the purpose of preventing or controlling the entry of the matter into
any controlled waters;
(b) for requiring a person who already has custody or control of, or makes
use of, any such matter to carry out such works for that purpose and to
take such precautions and other steps for that purpose as may be
prescribed.
(2) Without prejudice to the generality of the power conferred by subsection (1) above, regulations under that subsection may—
(a) confer power on the Authority—
(i) to determine for the purposes of the regulations the circumstances in which a person is required to carry out works or to take
any precautions or other steps; and
(ii) by notice to that person, to impose the requirement and to
specify or describe the works, precautions or other steps which
that person is required to carry out or take;
(b) provide for appeals to the Secretary of State against notices served by
the Authority in pursuance of provision made by virtue of paragraph
(a) above; and
(c) provide that a contravention of the regulations shall be an offence the
maximum penalties for which shall not exceed the penalties specified
in subsection (6) of section 85 above.

DEFINITIONS
"controlled waters": s.104.
"notice": s.221(1).
"prescribed": s.221(1).

GENERAL NOTE
This section re-enacts the power to make regulations given under s.31(4) of C.O.P.A. 1974, but which had never been exercised. The type of precautionary measure envisaged, primarily aimed at risks of spillages entering waters, was described in the Government Consultation document *The Water Environment: the Next Steps* (Department of the Environment, 1981) as one that would provide a major instrument of water environment policy after privatisation. During Committee stage of the 1989 Act in the House of Lords, the Government confirmed that initial regulations under [this] section would cover construction standards for silage and slurry stores, and oil facilities.

Subs. (2)(a) and (b)
The regulations give the Authority the power to serve what are, in effect, improvement notices, a significant provision introduced by the 1989 Act designed to ensure more effective enforcement of the requirements specified.

In determining when and how to exercise its powers under any regulations made under this section, the Authority is obliged to take into account whether there has been or is likely to be a breach of a Code of Good Agricultural Practice approved under s.97.

Water protection zones

93.—(1) Where the Secretary of State considers, after consultation (in the case of an area wholly or partly in England) with the Minister, that subsection (2) below is satisfied in relation to any area, he may by order make provision—

(a) designating that area as a water protection zone; and

(b) prohibiting or restricting the carrying on in the designated area of such activities as may be specified or described in the order.

(2) For the purposes of subsection (1) above this subsection is satisfied in relation to any area if (subject to subsection (3) below) it is appropriate, with a view to preventing or controlling the entry of any poisonous, noxious or polluting matter into controlled waters, to prohibit or restrict the carrying on in that area of activities which the Secretary of State considers are likely to result in the pollution of any such waters.

(3) The reference in subsection (2) above to the entry of poisonous, noxious or polluting matter into controlled waters shall not include a reference to the entry of nitrate into controlled waters as a result of, or of anything done in connection with, the use of any land for agricultural purposes

(4) Without prejudice to the generality of the power conferred by virtue of subsection (1) above, an order under this section may—

(a) confer power on the Authority to determine for the purposes of the order the circumstances in which the carrying on of any activities is prohibited or restricted and to determine the activities to which any such prohibition or restriction applies;

(b) apply a prohibition or restriction in respect of any activities to cases where the activities are carried on without the consent of the Authority or in contravention of any conditions subject to which any such consent is given;

(c) provide that a contravention of a prohibition or restriction contained in the order or of a condition of a consent given for the purposes of any such prohibition or restriction shall be an offence the maximum penalties for which shall not exceed the penalties specified in subsection (6) of section 85 above;

(d) provide (subject to any regulations under section 96 below) for anything falling to be determined under the order by the Authority to be determined in accordance with such procedure and by reference to such matters and to the opinion of such persons as may be specified in the order;

(e) make different provision for different cases, including different provision in relation to different persons, circumstances or localities; and

(f) contain such supplemental, consequential and transitional provision as the Secretary of State considers appropriate.

(5) The power of the Secretary of State to make an order under this section shall be exercisable by statutory instrument subject to annulment in pursuance of a resolution of either House of Parliament; but the Secretary of State shall not make such an order except on an application made by the Authority in accordance with Schedule 11 to this Act and otherwise in accordance with that Schedule.

DEFINITIONS
  "controlled waters": s.124(1).
  "the Minister": s.189(1).

This is another example of a legal mechanism aimed at anticipating and preventing water pollution arising from activities which are unsuited to control by licensing of direct discharges. The section is modelled on previous powers which existed under s.31(5) of the Control of Pollution Act 1974 but which were never used, though the provisions are now rather more specific and powerful, and the creation of zones is made simpler. In the Consultation Document *The Water Environment: the Next Steps* (Department of the Environment, 1986) it was noted that "an effective protection zone policy would be a major advance in water pollution control policy".

Nitrate sensitive areas

94.—(1) Where the relevant Minister considers that it is appropriate to do so with a view to achieving the purpose specified in subsection (2) below in relation to any land, he may by order make provision designating that land, together with any other land to which he considers it appropriate to apply the designation, as a nitrate sensitive area.

(2) The purpose mentioned in subsection (1) above is preventing or controlling the entry of nitrate into controlled waters as a result of, or of anything done in connection with, the use for agricultural purposes of any land.

(3) Where it appears to the relevant Minister, in relation to any area which is or is to be designated by an order under this section as a nitrate sensitive area, that it is appropriate for provision for the imposition of requirements, prohibitions or restrictions to be contained in an order under this section (as well as for him to be able to enter into such agreements as are mentioned in section 95 below), he may, by a subsequent order under this section or, as the case may be, by the order designating that area—

(a) with a view to achieving the purpose specified in subsection (2) above, require, prohibit or restrict the carrying on, either on or in relation to any agricultural land in that area, of such activities as may be specified or described in the order; and

(b) provide for such amounts (if any) as may be specified in or determined under the order to be paid by one of the Ministers, to such persons as may be so specified or determined, in respect of the obligations imposed in relation to that area on those persons by virtue of paragraph (a) above.

(4) Without prejudice to the generality of subsection (3) above, provision contained in an order under this section by virtue of that subsection may—

(a) confer power on either of the Ministers to determine for the purposes of the order the circumstances in which the carrying on of any activities is required, prohibited or restricted and to determine the activities to which any such requirement, prohibition or restriction applies;

(b) provide for any requirement to carry on any activity not to apply in cases where one of the Ministers has consented to a failure to carry on that activity and any conditions on which the consent has been given are complied with;

(c) apply a prohibition or restriction in respect of any activities to cases where the activities are carried on without the consent of one of the Ministers or in contravention of any conditions subject to which any such consent is given;

(d) provide that a contravention of a requirement, prohibition or restriction contained in the order or in a condition of a consent given in relation to or for the purposes of any such requirement, prohibition or restriction shall be an offence the maximum penalties for which shall not exceed the penalties specified in subsection (6) of section 85 above;

(e) provide for amounts paid in pursuance of any provision contained in the order to be repaid at such times and in such circumstances, and with such interest, as may be specified in or determined under the order; and

(f) provide (subject to any regulations under section 96 below) for anything falling to be determined under the order by any person to be determined in accordance with such procedure and by reference to such matters and to the opinion of such persons as may be specified in the order.

(5) An order under this section may—

(a) make different provision for different cases, including different provision in relation to different persons, circumstances or localities; and

(b) contain such supplemental, consequential and transitional provision as the relevant Minister considers appropriate.

(6) The power of the relevant Minister to make an order under this section shall be exercisable by statutory instrument subject to annulment in pursuance of a resolution of either House of Parliament; but the relevant Minister shall not make such an order except in accordance with any applicable provisions of Schedule 12 to this Act.

(7) In this section and in Schedule 12 to this Act "the relevant Minister"—

(a) in relation to the making of an order in relation to an area which is wholly in England or which is partly in England and partly in Wales, means the Ministers; and

(b) in relation to the making of an order in relation to an area which is wholly in Wales, means the Secretary of State.

DEFINITIONS
"agricultural": s.221(1).
"controlled waters": s.104.
"relevant Minister": subs. (7).

GENERAL NOTE
The enabling powers in this and the following section provide for the creation of nitrate-sensitive areas, a new form of designation aimed at reducing the amount of nitrate leaching from agricultural land into controlled waters. They can be viewed as complementary to s.93 (water protection zones) but differ from them in three fundamental respects. The water protection zones are restricted to prohibiting and restricting activities, while nitrate-sensitive areas may provide for positive action to be required of farmers (such as the construction of silage facilities) in addition to prohibitions and restrictions (subs. (3)(a)). The second major difference is that with nitrate-sensitive areas, financial compensation may be payable in respect of obligations resulting from the designation (subs. (3)(b)). Finally, it is the Minister of Agriculture, Fisheries and Food (in England) who makes the designation with the consent of the Treasury rather than the Secretary of State for the Environment. Depending on the terms of the designation order, operation of the scheme may involve both the Department of the Environment and the Ministry of Agriculture, Fisheries and Food.

Effects of Designation
Sections 94 and 95 are drafted to give maximum flexibility, but in broad terms they envisage three types of nitrate-sensitive areas, though in practice designations could involve a combination of all three.
(i) Voluntary Areas (s.95(2) and (3)). Within these areas, management agreements may be entered into voluntarily by farmers in return for compensation, an approach building upon existing arrangements under the Wildlife and Countryside Act 1981, and the method that is planned to be adopted initially.
(ii) Mandatory Areas without Compensation (subss. (3)(a) and (4)(a)). Here, specified activities may be required, prohibited or restricted. Consent systems may be included (subs. (4)(b) and (c)) and contraventions sanctioned by criminal offences (subs. (4)(d)).
(iii) Mandatory Areas with Compensation. The difference here is that provision may be included for paying compensation to those affected by the resulting obligations (subs. (3)(b)).

Designation Procedures
Sched. 12 specifies the procedures that must be followed before an order is made. The initiative for establishing any type of nitrate-sensitive area rests with the National Rivers

Authority to make an application to the relevant Minister to make an order, though either the Secretary of State or the Minister of Agriculture, Fisheries and Food has the power to direct it to do so (s.5(1)(b)). Before making an application, the Authority must first be satisfied that nitrate pollution is occurring or is likely to occur as a result of agricultural activities, and that other provisions are not sufficient to deal with the problem. No more procedural requirements are laid down for voluntary areas, though in Committee stage of the 1989 Act, the Government made a commitment that it would announce the fact that a particular area had been proposed by the Authority and that the Government were seriously considering this, including undertaking a detailed agricultural survey (*Hansard*, H.L. Vol. 508, col. 252, May 23, 1989).

Agreements in nitrate sensitive areas

95.—(1) Where—
(a) any area has been designated as a nitrate sensitive area by an order under section 94 above; and
(b) the relevant Minister considers that it is appropriate to do so with a view to achieving the purpose mentioned in subsection (2) of that section,
he may, subject to such restrictions (if any) as may be set out in the order, enter into an agreement falling within subsection (2) below.

(2) An agreement falls within this subsection if it is one under which, in consideration of payments to be made by the relevant Minister—
(a) the owner of the freehold interest in any agricultural land in a nitrate sensitive area; or
(b) where the owner of the freehold interest in any such land has given his written consent to the agreement being entered into by any person having another interest in that land, that other person,
accepts such obligations with respect to the management of that land or otherwise as may be imposed by the agreement.

(3) An agreement such as is mentioned in subsection (2) above between the relevant Minister and a person having an interest in any land shall bind all persons deriving title from or under that person to the extent that the agreement is expressed to bind that land in relation to those persons.

(4) In this section "the relevant Minister"—
(a) in relation to an agreement with respect to land which is wholly in England, means the Minister;
(b) in relation to an agreement with respect to land which is wholly in Wales, means the Secretary of State; and
(c) in relation to an agreement with respect to land which is partly in England and partly in Wales, means either of the Ministers.

DEFINITIONS
"agricultural": s.221(1).
"the relevant Minister": subs. (4).

GENERAL NOTE
See General Note to s.94.

Agricultural Tenants
Voluntary management agreements may only be entered into by tenants with the written agreement of the freeholder (subs. (2)(b)), but are not binding on subsequent tenants under subs. (3) since they derive their title from the landlord rather than the previous tenant. The Agricultural Holdings Act 1986 was amended by the 1989 Act (Sched. 25, para. 75) to ensure that obligations arising under a nitrate-sensitive area, whether as a result of a voluntary agreement or mandatory provisions, are to be excluded by an Agricultural Lands Tribunal in determining whether there has been a failure to farm in accordance with the rules of good husbandry. It seems likely that for the purposes of a rent arbitration under the Agricultural Holdings Act 1986, voluntary participation within a nitrate-sensitive area leading to compensation would be a "relevant factor" (see *Hansard*, H.L. Vol. 508, col. 225, May 23, 1989).

Regulations with respect to consents required by virtue of section 93 or 94

96.—(1) The Secretary of State may, for the purposes of any orders under

section 93 above which require the consent of the Authority to the carrying on of any activities, by regulations make provision with respect to—
  (a) applications for any such consent;
  (b) the conditions of any such consent;
  (c) the revocation or variation of any such consent;
  (d) appeals against determinations on any such application;
  (e) the exercise by the Secretary of State of any power conferred on the Authority by the orders;
  (f) the imposition of charges where such an application has been made, such a consent has been given or anything has been done in pursuance of any such consent; and
  (g) the registration of any such application or consent.
(2) The Ministers may, for the purposes of any orders under section 94 above which require the consent of either of those Ministers to the carrying on of any activities or to any failure to carry on any activity, by regulations make provision with respect to—
  (a) applications for any such consent;
  (b) the conditions of any such consent;
  (c) the revocation or variation of any such consent;
  (d) the reference to arbitration of disputes about determinations on any such application;
  (e) the imposition of charges where such an application has been made, such a consent has been given or there has been any act or omission in pursuance of any such consent; and
  (f) the registration of any such application or consent.
(3) Without prejudice to the generality of the powers conferred by the preceding provisions of this section, regulations under subsection (1) above may apply (with or without modifications) any enactment having effect in relation to consents under Chapter II of this Part.

DEFINITIONS
  "the Authority": s.221(1).
  "the Minister": s.221(1).

GENERAL NOTE
  See General Notes to ss.93 and 94.

Codes of good agricultural practice

97.—(1) The Ministers may by order made by statutory instrument approve any code of practice issued (whether by either or both of the Ministers or by another person) for the purpose of—
  (a) giving practical guidance to persons engaged in agriculture with respect to activities that may affect controlled waters; and
  (b) promoting what appear to them to be desirable practices by such persons for avoiding or minimising the pollution of any such waters,
and may at any time by such an order approve a modification of such a code or withdraw their approval of such a code or modification.
(2) A contravention of a code of practice as for the time being approved under this section shall not of itself give rise to any criminal or civil liability, but the Authority shall take into account whether there has been or is likely to be any such contravention in determining when and how it should exercise—
  (a) its power, by giving a notice under subsection (1) of section 86 above, to impose a prohibition under that section; and
  (b) any powers conferred on the Authority by regulations under section 92 above.
(3) The Ministers shall not make an order under this section unless they have first consulted the Authority.

DEFINITIONS
"agriculture": s.221(1).
"controlled waters": s.104.
"the Ministers": s.221(1).

GENERAL NOTE
Compliance with a Ministerial Code of Good Agriculture Practice was a statutory defence to the main water pollution offence under the Control of Pollution Act 1974. Though rarely successfully invoked, its presence on the statute book was heavily criticised, and this provision was not repeated in the 1989 Act, from which this section is taken: See House of Commons Environment Committee, Third Report *Pollution of Rivers and Estuaries* (1988). A Code of Practice approved under this section provides no defence to an offence under this Part of the Act, nor will non-compliance in itself give rise to criminal or civil liability (subs. (2)). There will still, however, be some legal incentive to comply with a Code. The Authority must take into account compliance or non-compliance with a Code in two situations:

(1) Before issuing a relevant prohibition notice under s.86(1), which has the effect of applying the pollution controls to discharges of effluent from buildings or plant on to land or land-locked ponds; and

(2) When exercising powers conferred to the Authority under regulations made under s.90, requiring preventive precautions to be taken in respect of storage of potentially harmful materials such as silage.

CHAPTER IV

SUPPLEMENTAL PROVISIONS WITH RESPECT TO WATER POLLUTION

Radioactive substances

98.—(1) Except as provided by regulations made by the Secretary of State under this section, nothing in this Part shall apply in relation to radioactive waste within the meaning of the Radioactive Substances Act 1960.

(2) The Secretary of State may by regulations—
(a) provide for prescribed provisions of this Part to have effect with such modifications as he considers appropriate for dealing with such waste;
(b) make such modifications of the said Act of 1960 or, in relation to such waste, of any other enactment as he considers appropriate in consequence of the provisions of this Part and of any regulations made by virtue of paragraph (a) above.

GENERAL NOTE
By regulations. See Control of Pollution (Radioactive Waste) Regulations 1989 (S.I. 1989 No. 1158).

Consents required by the Authority

99.—(1) The Secretary of State may by regulations—
(a) make provision modifying the water pollution provisions of this Act in relation to cases in which consents under Chapter II of this Part are required by the Authority; and
(b) for the purposes of the application of the provisions of this Part in relation to discharges by the Authority, make such other modifications of those provisions as may be prescribed.

(2) Without prejudice to the generality of subsection (1) above, regulations under this section may provide for such consents as are mentioned in paragraph (a) of that subsection to be required to be given by the Secretary of State (instead of by the Authority) and, in prescribed cases, to be deemed to have been so given.

DEFINITIONS
"prescribed": s.221(1).
"regulations": s.221(1).

GENERAL NOTE
See General Note to s.88.

Subs. (1)(a)
See Control of Pollution (Discharges by the National Rivers Authority) Regulations 1989
(S.I. 1989 No. 1157).

Civil liability in respect of pollution and savings

100. Except in so far as this Part expressly otherwise provides and subject
to the provisions of section 18 of the Interpretation Act 1978 (which relates
to offences under two or more laws), nothing in this Part—
  (a) confers a right of action in any civil proceedings (other than proceed-
      ings for the recovery of a fine) in respect of any contravention of this
      Part or any subordinate legislation, consent or other instrument
      made, given or issued under this Part;
  (b) derogates from any right of action or other remedy (whether civil or
      criminal) in proceedings instituted otherwise than under this Part; or
  (c) affects any restriction imposed by or under any other enactment,
      whether public, local or private.

DEFINITION
"enactment": s.221(1).

GENERAL NOTE
This section repeats the approach in s.105(2) of the Control of Pollution Act 1974 by asserting
the principle that the provisions of this Part of the Act shall not affect other areas of the law
concerning pollution of waters, whether criminal or civil. Section 18 of the Interpretation Act
1978 applies the basic rule against double jeopardy for criminal offences.

Limitation for summary offences under Part III

101. Notwithstanding anything in section 127 of the Magistrates' Courts
Act 1980 (time limit for summary proceedings), a magistrates' court may try
any summary offence under this Part, or under any subordinate legislation
made under this Part, if the information is laid not more than 12 months after
the commission of the offence.

GENERAL NOTE
Not more than twelve months. The standard six-month time limit for the commencement of
proceedings for summary offences is extended for all summary offences under this Chapter.
The predecessor to s.121 of the Water Act 1989 (from which this section is taken) contained in
s.87(3) of the Control of Pollution Act 1974 applied only to offences concerning entry of
polluting matter under s.31 of that Act.

Power to give effect to international obligations

102. The Secretary of State shall have power by regulations to provide that
the water pollution provisions of this Act shall have effect with such modifications as may be prescribed for the purpose of enabling Her Majesty's
Government in the United Kingdom to give effect—
  (a) to any Community obligations; or
  (b) to any international agreement to which the United Kingdom is for
      the time being a party.

GENERAL NOTE
This section gives the Secretary of State the power to modify certain provisions of the Act by
regulations in order to give effect to a Community obligation or an international agreement.
With respect to Community obligations, these provisions appear on strict legal grounds
superfluous, since s.2(2) of the European Communities Act 1972 already provides a broad
general power to make regulations needed to implement any Community obligations, and since
by s.2(4) such regulations may include "any such provision (of any such extent) as might be

made by Act of Parliament," they may amend or in other ways modify existing primary legislation. The powers, however, are not precisely co-extensive, since Sched. 2, para. 1(1), of the European Communities Act 1972 provides some limitation on the scope of regulations made under the Act which are not paralleled here.

Transitional pollution provisions

103. The provisions of this Part shall have effect subject to the provisions of Schedule 13 to this Act (which reproduce transitional provision originally made in connection with the coming into force of provisions of the Water Act 1989).

Meaning of "controlled waters" etc. in Part III

104.—(1) References in this Part to controlled waters are references to waters of any of the following classes—
  (a) relevant territorial waters, that is to say, subject to subsection (4) below, the waters which extend seaward for three miles from the baselines from which the breadth of the territorial sea adjacent to England and Wales is measured;
  (b) coastal waters, that is to say, any waters which are within the area which extends landward from those baselines as far as—
        (a) the limit of the highest tide; or
        (b) in the case of the waters of any relevant river or watercourse, the fresh-water limit of the river or watercourse,
     together with the waters of any enclosed dock which adjoins waters within that area;
  (c) inland freshwaters, that is to say, the waters of any relevant lake or pond or of so much of any relevant river or watercourse as is above the fresh-water limit;
  (d) ground waters, that is to say, any waters contained in underground strata;
and, accordingly, in this Part "coastal waters," "controlled waters," "ground waters," "inland freshwaters" and "relevant territorial waters" have the meanings given by this subsection.
  (2) In this Part any reference to the waters of any lake or pond or of any river or watercourse includes a reference to the bottom, channel or bed of any lake, pond, river or, as the case may be, watercourse which is for the time being dry.
  (3) In this section—
     "fresh-water limit," in relation to any river or watercourse, means the place for the time being shown as the fresh-water limit of that river or watercourse in the latest map deposited for that river or watercourse under section 192 below;
     "miles" means international nautical miles of 1,852 metres;
     "lake or pond" includes a reservoir of any description;
     "relevant lake or pond" means (subject to subsection (4) below) any lake or pond which (whether it is natural or artificial or above or below ground) discharges into a relevant river or watercourse or into another lake or pond which is itself a relevant lake or pond;
     "relevant river or watercourse" means (subject to subsection (4) below) any river or watercourse (including an underground river or watercourse and an artificial river or watercourse) which is neither a public sewer nor a sewer or drain which drains into a public sewer.
  (4) The Secretary of State may by order provide—
  (a) that any area of the territorial sea adjacent to England and Wales is to be treated as if it were an area of relevant territorial waters for the

purposes of this Part and of any other enactment in which any expression is defined by reference to the meanings given by this section;

(b) that any lake or pond which does not discharge into a relevant river or watercourse or into a relevant lake or pond is to be treated for those purposes as a relevant lake or pond;

(c) that a lake or pond which does so discharge and is of a description specified in the order is to be treated for those purposes as if it were not a relevant lake or pond;

(d) that a watercourse of a description so specified is to be treated for those purposes as if it were not a relevant river or watercourse.

(5) An order under this section may—

(a) contain such supplemental, consequential and transitional provision as the Secretary of State considers appropriate; and

(b) make different provision for different cases, including different provision in relation to different persons, circumstances or localities.

(6) The power of the Secretary of State to make an order under this section shall be exercisable by statutory instrument subject to annulment in pursuance of a resolution of either House of Parliament.

DEFINITIONS
"underground strata": s.221(1).
"watercourse": s.221(1).

GENERAL NOTE
Section 104 specifies the various types of waters to which these pollution controls will apply, known generically as "controlled waters". It makes little change to previous coverage under C.O.P.A. 1974 but the terminology used is rather less obscure.

Subs. (1)(a)
Relevant territorial waters. Although the Territorial Sea Act 1987 extended U.K. territorial waters to 12 miles, the three-mile limit under C.O.P.A. 1974 has been preserved, but jurisdiction may be extended to other areas of the territorial sea by order of the Secretary of State (subs. (4)). These powers are likely to be used in respect of certain estuaries which would otherwise fall outside the controls. The N.R.A.'s jurisdiction is also extended beyond the three-mile limit in the case of pipes discharging effluent beyond these limits (s.85(3)).

Coastal waters. This category will include all estuarine waters up to the fresh-water limits of rivers and watercourses. Since most of the offences under this Part of the Act apply to all controlled waters, the distinction between coastal and inland waters will therefore have little legal significance, though note that the offence under s.90 (deposits and vegetation) is applicable only to inland waters.

Inland waters. For all other Parts of the Act, the definition of "inland waters" is based upon the definition of the term in s.135 of the Water Resources Act 1963 (as amended by Sched. 13 to the Water Act 1989). This rather confusingly includes tidal rivers, estuaries or arms of the sea.

Lakes and ponds. These include reservoirs, but the controls do not apply to land-locked lakes, ponds, or reservoirs (*i.e.* those not discharging into rivers or other waters) unless they have been specified in order by the Secretary of State under subs. (4)(b). The Controlled Waters (Lakes and Ponds) Order 1989 (S.I. 1989 No. 1149) has been made under this section.

Although excluded from the general definition of controlled waters, such lakes or ponds are covered by the offence relating to the discharge of trade or sewage effluence under s.87. Other forms of pollution of lakes and ponds not falling within these controls may be dealt with by local authorities under the statutory nuisance provisions in the Public Health Act 1936–see ss.92(1) and 259(1) of that Act.

Ground waters. Groundwater contamination is increasingly recognised as a potential problem area, and the controls now apply to waters contained in all underground strata. Under C.O.P.A. 1974, underground waters had to be specified by water authorities if they were to be covered by controls, a restriction largely made redundant by the adoption of E.C. Directives on the subject, making no such distinction—see in particular E.C. Directive on The Protection of Groundwater Against Pollution Caused by Certain Dangerous Substances 80/68/EEC, where the definition of groundwater is "all water which is below the surface of the ground in the saturation zone and in direct contact with the ground or subsoil" (Art. 1(2)(a)).

PART IV

FLOOD DEFENCE

General

General functions with respect to flood defence

105.—(1) Subject to section 106 below, the Authority shall in relation to England and Wales exercise a general supervision over all matters relating to flood defence.

(2) For the purpose of carrying out its flood defence functions the Authority shall from time to time carry out surveys of the areas in relation to which it carries out those functions.

(3) In the exercise of the powers conferred by the following provisions of this Part and the other flood defence provisions of this Act due regard shall be had to the interests of fisheries, including sea fisheries.

(4) Nothing in the following provisions of this Part or the other flood defence provisions of this Act shall prejudice or affect the provisions of Part V of this Act or the Salmon and Freshwater Fisheries Act 1975 or any right, power or duty conferred or imposed by that Part or that Act.

DEFINITIONS
"flood defence": s.113(1).
"flood defence functions": s.221(1).
"the Authority": s.221(1).

GENERAL NOTE
Part IV (ss.105–113) is concerned with flood protection and land drainage. Although the term "flood defence" is now used in preference to land drainage in order to reflect modern priorities, the Water Act 1989, from which Pt. IV is taken, essentially preserved the arrangements under the Land Drainage Act 1976, by transferring the responsibilities under that Act from water authorities to the Authority. This Part establishes an institutional structure for the discharge of those functions through committees that match those that existed before the 1989 Act. Internal drainage boards continue to exercise their functions within internal drainage districts.

Section 105 establishes the general supervisory duty of the Authority with respect to flood defence and land drainage, based on the former duty of water authorities under s.1 of the Land Drainage Act 1976. The Act largely maintains the previous system of financing land drainage and flood defence, with revenue from local authority levies (changed from precepts under the Local Government Finance Act 1988), contributions from internal drainage boards under s.84 of the Land Drainage Act 1976, special drainage charges under s.50 of the 1976 Act and general drainage charges under s.134; the Authority is required to confine these revenues to its flood defence functions.

Schedule 4 is concerned with the establishment and composition of the regional flood defence committees. Any reference to a regional land drainage committee in the Land Drainage Act was replaced by a reference to a regional flood defence committee by the Water Act 1989 (Sched. 15, para. 1 to that Act).

Obligation to carry out flood defence functions through committees

106.—(1) Without prejudice to any scheme for the appointment of local flood defence committees and subject to subsection (2) below, the Authority shall arrange for all its functions relating to flood defence under the following provisions of this Act and the Land Drainage Act 1991 to be carried out by regional flood defence committees, so that those functions of the Authority are carried out—

(a) in relation to the area of each regional flood defence committee, by the committee for that area; and

(b) in cases involving the areas of more than one regional flood defence committee, by such committee, or jointly by such committees, as may be determined in accordance with arrangements made by the Authority.

(2) The Authority shall not make arrangements for the carrying out by any other body, or by any committee, of any of its functions with respect to—

(a) the issuing of levies (within the meaning of the Local Government Finance Act 1988); or

(b) the making of drainage charges under Chapter II of Part VI of this Act;

and nothing in this section shall enable the Authority to authorise any such other body or any committee to borrow money for purposes connected with the Authority's functions relating to flood defence.

(3) The Authority may give a regional flood defence committee a direction of a general or specific character as to the carrying out of any function relating to flood defence, other than one of its internal drainage functions, so far as the carrying out of that function appears to the Authority likely to affect materially the Authority's management of water for purposes other than flood defence.

(4) It shall be the duty of a regional flood defence committee to comply with any direction under subsection (3) above.

(5) In subsection (3) above "internal drainage functions" means the functions of the Authority under sections 108, 139 and 140 below and the following provisions of the Land Drainage Act 1991, that is to say—

(a) sections 2 to 9 (transfer to the Authority and supervision by the Authority of the functions of internal drainage boards);

(b) sections 38, 39 and 47 (differential drainage rates and exemptions from such rates);

(c) sections 57 and 58(1) (provisions with respect to contributions by the Authority to the expenses of internal drainage boards and the expenses of the Authority as such a board).

DEFINITIONS

"functions relating to flood defence": s.221(1).
"internal drainage function": subs. (5).
"the Authority": s.221(1).

GENERAL NOTE

Subs. (4)

Issuing of levies within the meaning of the Local Government Finance Act 1988. On March 31, 1990, the power to raise precepts under the Land Drainage Act was abolished (s.117 of the Local Government Finance Act 1988), and regulations under s.74 of that Act are now required to authorise the making of levies on local authorities.

Subs. (5)

A direction of a general or specific character. Regional flood defence committees have considerable autonomy in their day-to-day operations, but this important provision establishes in what circumstances the Authority can go beyond a general supervisory rôle in its relationship with them. Concern has sometimes been expressed at the damaging environmental consequences of actions by former regional land drainage committees, and in exercising its powers here the Authority would be bound to bear in mind its environmental duties under s.16.

Main river functions

Main river functions under the Land Drainage Act 1991

107.—(1) This section has effect for conferring functions in relation to main rivers on the Authority which are functions of drainage boards in relation to other watercourses.

(2) Notwithstanding subsection (3) of section 21 of the Land Drainage Act 1991 (power to secure compliance with drainage obligations), the powers of the Authority in relation to a main river shall, by virtue of this section, include the powers which under that section are exercisable otherwise than

in relation to a main river by the drainage board concerned; and the provisions of that section shall have effect accordingly.

(3) The powers of the Authority in relation to a main river shall, by virtue of this section, include the powers which under section 25 of the Land Drainage Act 1991 (powers for securing the maintenance of flow of watercourses) are exercisable in relation to an ordinary watercourse by the drainage board concerned; and the provisions of that section and section 27 of that Act shall have effect accordingly.

(4) Sections 33 and 34 of the Land Drainage Act 1991 (commutation of obligations) shall have effect where—

(a) any person is under an obligation imposed on him by reason of tenure, custom, prescription or otherwise to do any work in connection with the drainage of land (whether by way of repairing banks or walls, maintaining watercourses or otherwise); and

(b) that work is in connection with a main river,

as they have effect in relation to an obligation to do work otherwise than in connection with a main river but as if the Authority were under a duty to take steps to commute the obligation and the references in those sections to the drainage board for the internal drainage district where the works fall to be done were omitted.

(5) In this section—

(a) references to the exercise of a power in relation to a main river shall include a reference to its exercise in connection with a main river or in relation to the banks of such a river or any drainage works in connection with such a river; and

(b) expressions used both in this section and in a provision applied by this section have the same meanings in this section as in that provision.

(6) The functions of the Authority by virtue of this section are in addition to the functions of the Authority which by virtue of the provisions of the Land Drainage Act 1991 are exercisable by the Authority concurrently with an internal drainage board.

DEFINITIONS
  "functions": s.3.
  "main river": s.113(1).
  "the Authority": s.221(1).
  "watercourse": s.113(1).

GENERAL NOTE
  Sections 107–111 are based on the Land Drainage Act 1976 and the arrangements that existed under that Act are preserved, with the Authority taking over responsibility for flood defence for main rivers. Reference to the Land Drainage Act 1991 is required for an examination of the Authority's powers.

Schemes for transfer to the Authority of functions in relation to main river

108.—(1) The Authority may at any time prepare and submit to either of the Ministers for confirmation a scheme making provision for the transfer to the Authority from any drainage body of—

(a) all rights, powers, duties, obligations and liabilities (including liabilities incurred in connection with works) over or in connection with a main river; and

(b) any property held by the drainage body for the purpose of, or in connection with, any functions so transferred;

and the Authority shall prepare such a scheme and submit it to one of the Ministers if it is directed to do so by that Minister.

(2) A scheme prepared and submitted under subsection (1) above may make provisions for any matter supplemental to or consequential on the transfers for which the scheme provides.

(3) The Minister to whom a scheme is submitted under this section may by order made by statutory instrument confirm that scheme; and Schedule 14 to this Act shall have effect with respect to the procedure to be followed in connection with the making of such an order and with respect to challenges to such orders.

(4) An order under this section may contain provisions with respect to the persons by whom all or any of the expenses incurred by the Ministers or other persons in connection with the making or confirmation of the order, or with the making of the scheme confirmed by the order, are to be borne.

(5) Where, under a scheme made by the Authority under this section, liabilities incurred in connection with drainage works are transferred to the Authority from a local authority, the Authority may require the local authority to make contributions to the Authority towards the discharge of the liabilities.

(6) If the amount to be paid by a local authority by way of contributions required under subsection (5) above is not agreed between the Authority and the local authority, it shall be referred to the arbitration of a single arbitrator appointed—

(a) by agreement between them; or

(b) in default of agreement, by the Ministers.

(7) The relevant Minister shall by regulations provide for the payment, subject to such exceptions or conditions as may be specified in the regulations, of compensation by the Authority to any officer or other employee of a drainage body who suffers loss of employment or loss or diminution of emoluments which is attributable to a scheme under this section or anything done in pursuance of such a scheme.

(8) Regulations under subsection (7) above may include provision—

(a) as to the manner in which and the persons to whom any claim for compensation by virtue of the regulations is to be made; and

(b) for the determination of all questions arising under the regulations.

(9) In this section—

"drainage body" means an internal drainage board or any other body having power to make or maintain works for the drainage of land;

"the relevant Minister"—

(a) in relation to employees of a drainage body wholly in Wales, means the Secretary of State;

(b) in relation to employees of a drainage body partly in Wales, means the Ministers; and

(c) in any other case, means the Minister.

DEFINITIONS
"drainage body": subs. (9).
"main river": s.113(1).
"the Authority": s.221(1).
"the relevant Minister": subs. (9).

GENERAL NOTE
Under this section the Authority has wide discretion and power, subject to the approval of the relevant Minister, to take over the activities of local authorities in relation to main rivers. This includes the transfer of property (subs. (1)(b)) and the power to require the local authority to pay off any liabilities that the Authority inherits from it (subs. (5)).

Structures in, over or under a main river

109.—(1) No person shall erect any structure in, over or under a watercourse which is part of a main river except with the consent of and in accordance with plans and sections approved by the Authority.

(2) No person shall, without the consent of the Authority, carry out any work of alteration or repair on any structure in, over or under a watercourse

which is part of a main river if the work is likely to affect the flow of water in the watercourse or to impede any drainage work.

(3) No person shall erect or alter any structure designed to contain or divert the floodwaters of any part of a main river except with the consent of and in accordance with plans and sections approved by the Authority.

(4) If any person carries out any work in contravention of this section the Authority may—

(a) remove, alter, or pull down the work; and

(b) recover from that person the expenses incurred in doing so.

(5) Subsections (1) and (2) above shall not apply to any work carried out in an emergency; but a person carrying out any work excepted from those subsections by this subsection shall inform the Authority in writing as soon as practicable—

(a) of the carrying out of the work; and

(b) of the circumstances in which it was carried out.

(6) Nothing in this section shall be taken to affect any enactment requiring the consent of any government department for the erection of a bridge or any powers exercisable by any government department in relation to a bridge.

DEFINITIONS
"main river": s.113(1).
"the Authority": s.221(1).
"watercourse": s.113(1).

Applications for consents and approvals under section 109

110.—(1) The Authority may require the payment of an application fee by a person who applies to it for its consent under section 109 above; and the amount of that fee shall be £50 or such other sum as may be specified by order made by the Ministers.

(2) A consent or approval required under section 109 above—

(a) shall not be unreasonably withheld;

(b) shall be deemed to have been given if it is neither given nor refused within the relevant period; and

(c) in the case of a consent, may be given subject to any reasonable condition as to the time at which and the manner in which any work is to be carried out.

(3) For the purposes of subsection (2)(b) above the relevant period is—

(a) in the case of a consent, the period of two months after whichever is the later of—

(i) the day on which application for the consent is made; and

(ii) if at the time when that application is made an application fee is required to be paid, the day on which the liability to pay that fee is discharged;

and

(b) in the case of an approval, the period of two months after application for the approval is made.

(4) If any question arises under this section whether any consent or approval is unreasonably withheld or whether any condition imposed is reasonable, the question shall—

(a) if the parties agree to arbitration, be referred to a single arbitrator appointed by agreement between the parties or, in default of agreement, by the President of the Institution of Civil Engineers; and

(b) if the parties do not agree to arbitration, be referred to and determined by the Ministers or the Secretary of State, according to whether the determination falls to be made in relation to England or Wales.

(5) The power of the Ministers to make an order under subsection (1) above shall be exercisable by statutory instrument subject to annulment in pursuance of a resolution of either House of Parliament.

DEFINITIONS
  "relevant period": subs. (3).
  "the Authority": s.221(1).
  "the Ministers": s.221(1).

Arrangements with certain authorities

Arrangements with navigation and conservancy authorities

111.—(1) Subject to subsection (2) below, the Authority with a view to improving the drainage of any land, may enter into an arrangement with a navigation authority or conservancy authority for any of the following purposes, that is to say—
  (a) the transfer to the Authority of—
      (i) the whole or any part of the undertaking of the navigation authority or conservancy authority or of any of the rights, powers, duties, liabilities and obligations of that authority; or
      (ii) any property vested in that authority as such;
  (b) the alteration or improvement by the Authority of any of the works of the navigation authority or conservancy authority;
  (c) the making of payments by the Authority to the navigation authority or conservancy authority or by that authority to the Authority in respect of any matter for which provision is made by the arrangement.
(2) The exercise by the Authority of its power to enter into an arrangement under this section shall require the approval of the Ministers.
(3) Where the Authority is intending to enter into an arrangement under this section it shall publish a notice of its intention in such manner as may be directed by either of the Ministers.
(4) Where an arrangement has been made under this section, the Authority shall cause a notice under subsection (5) below to be published in the London Gazette in such form as may be prescribed by regulations made by one of the Ministers.
(5) A notice under this subsection is a notice—
  (a) stating that the arrangement has been made; and
  (b) specifying the place at which a copy of the arrangement may be inspected by persons interested.

DEFINITIONS
  "conservancy authority": s.221(1).
  "navigation authority": s.221(1).
  "notice": s.221(1) and subs. (5).
  "the Authority": s.221(1).
  "the Ministers": s.221(1).

GENERAL NOTE
  This section gives the Authority similar powers to those granted with respect to local authorities (s.108) but in contrast to that section the Authority may seek the approval of the relevant Minister for an arrangement with a navigation or conservancy authority without the submission of a scheme.

Supplemental

Flood defence regulations

112. The Ministers shall each have power by regulations to make provision generally for the purpose of carrying into effect the provisions of this Part and the other flood defence provisions of this Act.

DEFINITIONS
"flood defence provisions": s.221(1).
"the Ministers": s.221(1).

Interpretation of Part IV

113.—(1) In this Part—
"banks" means banks, walls or embankments adjoining or confining, or constructed for the purposes of or in connection with, any channel or sea front, and includes all land and water between the bank and low-watermark;
"drainage" includes—
    (a) defence against water, including sea water;
    (b) irrigation other than spray irrigation; and
    (c) warping;
"flood defence" means the drainage of land and the provision of flood warning systems;
"main river" (subject to section 137(4) below) means a watercourse shown as such on a main river map and includes any structure or appliance for controlling or regulating the flow of water into, in or out of the channel which—
    (a) is a structure or appliance situated in the channel or in any part of the banks of the channel; and
    (b) is not a structure or appliance vested in or controlled by an internal drainage board;
"watercourse" shall be construed as if for the words from "except" onwards in the definition in section 221(1) below there were substituted the words "except a public sewer."
(2) If any question arises under this Part—
(a) whether any work is a drainage work in connection with a main river; or
(b) whether any proposed work will, if constructed, be such a drainage work,
the question shall be referred to one of the Ministers for decision or, if either of the parties so requires, to arbitration.
(3) Where any question is required under subsection (2) above to be referred to arbitration it shall be referred to the arbitration of a single arbitrator appointed—
(a) by agreement between the parties; or
(b) in default of agreement, by the President of the Institution of Civil Engineers, on the application of either party.
(4) Nothing in this Part shall affect the powers exercisable by the Authority under any local Act, as they existed immediately before the coming into force of this Act.

PART V

GENERAL CONTROL OF FISHERIES

General fisheries duty of the Authority

114. It shall be the duty of the Authority to maintain, improve and develop salmon fisheries, trout fisheries, freshwater fisheries and eel fisheries.

DEFINITION
"the Authority": s.221(1).

GENERAL NOTE
This section repeats the general duty applicable to water authorities under s.18(1) of the

Water Act 1973. The Authority is also required to establish regional fisheries advisory committees under s.8 (see the General Note to that section).

Fisheries orders

115.—(1) Subject to the following provisions of this section, each of the
Ministers shall have power, on an application made to him by the Authority,
by order made by statutory instrument to make provision in relation to an
area defined by the order for the modification, in relation to the fisheries in
that area—
  (a) of any provisions of the Salmon and Freshwater Fisheries Act 1975
      relating to the regulation of fisheries;
  (b) of section 156 below; or
  (c) of any provisions of a local Act relating to any fishery in that area.
(2) An order under this section—
  (a) may contain such supplemental, consequential and transitional provi-
      sion, including provision for the payment of compensation to persons
      injuriously affected by the order, as may appear to be necessary or
      expedient in connection with the other provisions of the order; but
  (b) shall not apply to any waters in respect of which either of the Ministers
      has granted a licence under section 29 of the Salmon and Freshwater
      Fisheries Act 1975 (fish rearing licences).
(3) Before either of the Ministers makes an order under this section he
shall—
  (a) send to the Authority a copy of the draft order; and
  (b) notify the Authority of the time within which, and the manner in
      which, objections to the draft order may be made to him.
(4) Neither of the Ministers shall make an order under this section unless
the Authority has caused notice of—
  (a) that Minister's intention to make the order;
  (b) the place where copies of the draft order may be inspected and
      obtained; and
  (c) the matters notified under subsection (3)(b) above,
to be published in the London Gazette and, if it is directed to do so by one of
the Ministers, in such other manner as that Minister thinks best adapted for
informing persons affected.
(5) Before either of the Ministers makes an order under this section he—
  (a) shall consider any objection which may be duly made to the draft
      order; and
  (b) may cause a public local inquiry to be held with respect to any such
      objections.
(6) A statutory instrument containing an order under this section shall be
subject to annulment in pursuance of a resolution of either House of Parliament; and, where a statutory instrument is laid before Parliament for the
purposes of this paragraph, a copy of the report of any local inquiry held with
respect to objections considered in connection with the making of the order
contained in that instrument shall be so laid at the same time.
(7) Where—
  (a) any fishery, land or foreshore proposed to be comprised in an order
      under this section; or
  (b) any fishery proposed to be affected by any such order; or
  (c) any land over which it is proposed to acquire an easement under any
      such order,
belongs to Her Majesty in right of the Crown or forms part of the possessions
of the Duchy of Lancaster or the Duchy of Cornwall or belongs to, or is
under the management of, any government department, the order may be
made by one of the Ministers only if he has previously obtained the consent
of the appropriate authority.
(8) In subsection (7) above "the appropriate authority"—

(a) in the case of any foreshore under the management of the Crown Estate Commissioners or of any fishery or land belonging to Her Majesty in right of the Crown, means those Commissioners;
(b) in the case of any foreshore, fishery or land forming part of the possessions of the Duchy of Lancaster, means the Chancellor of the Duchy;
(c) in the case of any foreshore, fishery or land forming part of the possessions of the Duchy of Cornwall, means the Duke of Cornwall or the persons for the time being empowered to dispose for any purpose of the land of the Duchy;
(d) in the case of any foreshore, fishery or land which belongs to or is under the management of a government department, means that government department.

(9) In this section "foreshore" includes the shore and bed of the sea and of every channel, creek, bay, estuary and navigable river as far as the tide flows.

DEFINITIONS
"foreshore": subs. (9).
"the appropriate authority": subs. (8).
"the Authority": s.221(1).
"the Ministers": s.221(1).

GENERAL NOTE
This section is based on the Salmon and Freshwater Fisheries Act 1975 (s.28). It gives the Authority, through the relevant Minister, a wide power to alter any legislation relating to fisheries in a particular area. An order under this section may include provision for compensation (subs. (2)(a)).

Power to give effect to international obligations

116. Each of the Ministers shall have power by regulations to provide that the provisions of this Part or of any other enactment relating to the carrying out by the Authority of such of its functions as relate to fisheries shall have effect with such modifications as may be prescribed by the regulations for the purpose of enabling Her Majesty's Government in the United Kingdom to give effect—
(a) to any Community obligations; or
(b) to any international agreement to which the United Kingdom is for the time being a party.

DEFINITIONS
"enactment": s.221(1).
"functions": s.3.
"modifications": s.221(1).
"the Authority": s.221(1).
"the Ministers": s.221(1).

GENERAL NOTE
This section gives either the Secretary of State or the Minister of Agriculture, Fisheries and Food the power to modify certain provisions of the Act by regulations in order to give effect to a Community obligation or an international agreement. The power under this section does not extend beyond Pt. V (General Control of Fisheries). Section 102 performs the same function for Pt. III (Control of Pollution). See the General Note to that section for the relationship between these provisions and the European Communities Act 1972.

PART VI

FINANCIAL PROVISIONS IN RELATION TO THE AUTHORITY

CHAPTER I

GENERAL FINANCIAL PROVISIONS

General financial duties

117.—(1) Subject to section 118 below, the Ministers may, after consultation with the Authority and with the Treasury's approval determine the financial duties of the Authority, and different determinations may be made for different functions and activities of the Authority.

(2) The Ministers shall give the Authority notice of every determination under this section, and such a determination may—

(a) relate to a period beginning before the date on which it is made;

(b) contain supplemental provisions; and

(c) be varied by a subsequent determination.

(3) Subject to sections 118(1) and 119(2) below, where it appears to the Secretary of State that the Authority has a surplus, whether on capital or revenue account, the Secretary of State may, after consultation with the Treasury and the Authority, direct the Authority to pay to him such amount not exceeding the amount of that surplus as may be specified in the direction.

(4) Any sum received by the Secretary of State under subsection (3) above shall be paid into the Consolidated Fund.

DEFINITIONS
  "the Authority": s.221(1).
  "the Ministers": s.221(1).

GENERAL NOTE
  Part VI, based on Sched. 1 to the Water Act 1989, deals with the Authority's financial arrangements. These include the provision of Government grant-aid, borrowings and loans, but an underlying policy aim is that the Authority should recover the maximum possible revenue from activities. Finance for land drainage and flood defence continues on much the same basis as it did before privatisation, with an added provision for long-term capital borrowing from the Government (s.152), as do the recovery of costs for water resource management through abstraction licence charges, and charges in connection with fishery navigation functions. A provision, introduced at privatisation, for charging for the cost of discharge consents and associated monitoring to the person making the discharge is retained.
  Shortfall in recovery of costs of these latter activities will be made by an annual grant-in-aid which replaced the environmental service charge formerly made by water authorities prior to privatisation (s.146).
  Under the transfer schemes of the Water Act 1989 (Sched. 2 to that Act) the Authority inherited from water authorities property, rights and liabilities appropriate to its functions. Its estimated staff of 6,500 are similarly mostly former authority employees.

Special duties with respect to flood defence revenue

118.—(1) Revenue raised by the Authority as mentioned in subsection (2) below—

(a) shall, except for any amount falling within subsection (3) below, be spent only in the carrying out of the Authority's flood defence functions in or for the benefit of the local flood defence district in which it is raised; and

(b) shall be disregarded in determining the amount of any surplus for the purposes of section 117(3) above.

(2) The revenue referred to in subsection (1) above is revenue raised by the Authority in a local flood defence district—

(a) by virtue of any regulation under section 74 of the Local Government Finance Act 1988 (power to issue levies);

(b) by general drainage charges under sections 134 to 136 below;

(c) by special drainage charges under sections 137 and 138 below; or

(d) by contributions required under section 139(1) below.

(3) An amount falls within this subsection if it is an amount which the Authority considers it appropriate—

(a) to set aside towards research or related activities or towards meeting the Authority's adminstrative expenses; or

(b) to be paid by way of contribution towards expenses incurred by the Authority or any regional flood defence committee under arrangements made for the purposes of section 106(1)(b) above.

(4) Any amount specified in a resolution under section 58(1)(b) of the Land Drainage Act 1991 in relation to any local flood defence district (allocation of revenue in lieu of contributions) shall be treated for the purposes of this section as if it were revenue actually raised by contributions required under section 139(1) below.

(5) For the purposes of this section, the following sums, that is to say—

(a) any sums held by the Authority by virtue of any transfer of property, rights or liabilities from a water authority in accordance with a scheme under Schedule 2 to the Water Act 1989, in so far as those sums represent amounts which the water authority was required by virtue of paragraph 31 of Schedule 3 to the Water Act 1973 to spend only in the discharge of their land drainage functions in or for the benefit of a particular local land drainage district; and

(b) any sums raised by the Authority in a flood defence district by virtue of a precept issued under section 46 of the Land Drainage Act 1976,

shall be treated as revenue raised by the Authority as mentioned in subsection (2) above in the corresponding local flood defence district or, as the case may be, in that local flood defence district.

(6) For the purposes of this section so much of the area of a regional flood defence committee as is an area in relation to which no local flood defence scheme is in force shall be treated as a single local flood defence district.

DEFINITION
"the Authority": s.221(1).

GENERAL NOTE
This section prevents the Authority from spending revenue raised by levies on local authorities, general drainage charges, special drainage charges and contributions from internal drainage boards (subs. (2)) on anything other than flood defence functions. It also excludes such revenue from the surplus that can be claimed back from the Authority by the Secretary of State under s.117(3). Revenue expended on research or related activities, as well as the Authority's administrative costs, is excluded from the general requirement to restrict revenue to flood defence (subs. (3)).

Duties with respect to certain funds raised under local enactments

119.—(1) The funds which the Authority are required at the coming into force of this section under subsection (1) of section 88 of the Water Resources Act 1963 (funds held for particular purposes under local statutory provisions) to use only for particular purposes and any interest in any such funds shall not be used except for the purposes for which they could be used by virtue of that subsection.

(2) Any funds to which subsection (1) above applies shall be disregarded in determining the amount of any surplus under section 117(3) above.

DEFINITION
"the Authority": s.221(1).

Section 88(1) of the Water Resources Act 1963 refers to funds "created under any local Act for fishery purposes" and the effect of this section is to prevent the Authority from using such funds for general expenses. As with s.118, such funds are excluded from the calculation of any surplus that may be claimed back from the Authority by the Secretary of State (subs. (2)).

Contributions between the Authority and certain other authorities

120.—(1) Where, on the application of a navigation authority, harbour authority or conservancy authority, it appears to the Authority that any works constructed or maintained by the applicants have made, or will make, a beneficial contribution towards the fulfilment of the purposes of the Authority's water resources functions, the Authority shall contribute towards the expenditure incurred or to be incurred by the applicants in constructing or maintaining those works.

(2) Where, on the application of the Authority, it appears to a navigation authority, harbour authority or conservancy authority that any works constructed or maintained by the Authority in the carrying out of its water resources functions have made, or will make, a beneficial contribution towards the carrying out of the functions of the authority to whom the application is made, that authority shall contribute to the Authority towards the expenditure incurred or to be incurred by the Authority in constructing or maintaining those works.

(3) Subject to the following provisions of this section, the sums to be paid by way of contribution and the terms and conditions on which they are to be paid shall be such as the Authority and the other authority concerned may agree to be appropriate.

(4) If on any application under this section—

(a) the Authority or, as the case may be, the other authority to whom the application is made refuses to make a contribution; or

(b) the Authority and the other authority concerned are unable to agree as to the sums to be contributed or the terms and conditions on which they are to be contributed,

the Authority or the other authority concerned may refer the matter in dispute to the Secretary of State.

(5) On a reference under subsection (4) above the Secretary of State may either—

(a) determine that matter himself; or

(b) refer it for determination to an arbitrator appointed by him for the purpose;

and where any decision has been made by the Secretary of State or an arbitrator under this subsection, the decision shall be final and a contribution shall be made in accordance with the decision as if the sums, terms or conditions determined under this subsection had been agreed to be appropriate as mentioned in subsection (3) above.

(6) Any expenditure incurred by a navigation authority, harbour authority or conservancy authority in paying any contribution under this section shall be defrayed in the like manner as any corresponding expenditure of that authority; and that authority shall have the same powers for the purpose of raising money required for paying any such contribution as they would have for the purpose of raising money required for defraying any corresponding expenditure of that authority.

(7) In subsection (6) above the references to corresponding expenditure of a navigation authority, harbour authority or conservancy authority, in relation to the payment of a contribution in respect of any works, are references to expenditure incurred by the authority in performing the functions in respect of which it is claimed by the Authority that the works have made, or will make, such a beneficial contribution as is mentioned in subsection (2) above.

(8) References in this section to the water resources functions of the Authority are references to the functions of the Authority under Part II of this Act or under any provisions not contained in that Part which are related water resources provisions in relation to Chapter II of that Part.

DEFINITIONS
"conservancy authority": s.221(1).
"harbour authority": s.221(1).
"navigation authority": s.221(1).
"the Authority": s.221(1).
"water resources functions": subs. (8).

GENERAL NOTE
  This section allows for cooperation between the National Rivers Authority and navigation, harbour and conservancy authorities in that either the Authority or one of the authorities engaged in construction or maintenance of any works can claim a contribution from each other if benefit will result. Resolution of disputes is in the hands of the Secretary of State (subs. (4)), who may determine it himself or appoint an arbitrator (subs. (5)).

Accounts of the Authority

121.—(1) It shall be the duty of the Authority—
  (a) to keep proper accounts and proper records in relation to the accounts; and
  (b) to prepare in respect of each accounting year a statement of accounts giving a true and fair view of the state of affairs and the income and expenditure of the Authority.
  (2) Every statement of accounts prepared by the Authority in accordance with this section shall comply with any requirement which the Ministers have, with the consent of the Treasury, notified in writing to the Authority and which relates to any of the following matters, namely—
  (a) the information to be contained in the statement;
  (b) the manner in which that information is to be presented;
  (c) the methods and principles according to which the statement is to be prepared.
  (3) Subject to subsection (4) below, in this section and section 122 below "accounting year," in relation to the Authority, means a financial year.
  (4) If the Secretary of State so directs in relation to any accounting year of the Authority, that accounting year shall end with such date other than the next 31st March as may be specified in the direction; and, where the Secretary of State has given such a direction, the following accounting year shall begin with the day after the date so specified and, subject to any further direction under this subsection, shall end with the next 31st March.

DEFINITIONS
  "accounting year": s.221(1) and subs. (3).
  "the Authority": s.221(1).
  "the Ministers": s.221(1).

Audit

122.—(1) The accounts of the Authority shall be audited by auditors appointed for each accounting year by the Secretary of State.
  (2) A person shall not be qualified for appointment for the purposes of subsection (1) above unless he is—
  (a) a member of a body of accountants established in the United Kingdom and recognised for the purposes of section 389(1)(a) of the Companies Act 1985; or
  (b) a member of the Chartered Institute of Public Finance and Accountancy;
but a firm may be so appointed if each of its members is qualified to be so appointed.

(3) A copy of any accounts of the Authority which are audited under subsection (1) above and of the report made on those accounts by the auditors shall be sent to each of the Ministers as soon as reasonably practicable after the report is received by the Authority; and the Secretary of State shall lay a copy of any accounts or report sent to him under this subsection before Parliament.

(4) The Comptroller and Auditor General shall be entitled to inspect the contents of all books, papers and other records of the Authority relating to, or to matters dealt with in, the accounts required to be kept by virtue of section 121 above; and, accordingly, section 6 of the National Audit Act 1983 (examinations of economy, efficiency and effectiveness) shall apply to the Authority.

(5) In this section "accounts," in relation to the Authority, includes any statement under section 121 above.

DEFINITIONS
"accounts": subs. (5).
"the Authority": s.221(1).
"the Ministers": s.221(1).

CHAPTER II

REVENUE PROVISIONS

Water resources charges

Power to make scheme imposing water resources charges

123.—(1) Where—
(a) an application is made for any licence under Chapter II of Part II of this Act or for the variation of, or of the conditions of, any such licence;
(b) a licence under that Chapter to abstract water is granted to any person or there is a variation of any such licence or of the conditions of any such licence; or
(c) a licence under that Chapter to abstract water is for the time being in force,
the Authority may require the payment to it of such charges as may be specified in or determined under a scheme made by it under this section.

(2) The persons who shall be liable to pay charges which are required to be paid by virtue of a scheme under this section shall be—
(a) in the case of a charge by virtue of subsection (1)(a) above, the person who makes the application; and
(b) in the case of a charge by virtue of subsection (1)(b) or (c) above, the person to whom the licence is granted or, as the case may be, the person holding the licence which is varied or is in force.

(3) Provision made by a scheme for the purposes of subsection (1)(c) above may impose a single charge in respect of the whole period for which a licence is in force or separate charges in respect of different parts of that period or both such a single charge and such separate charges.

(4) The Authority shall not make a scheme under this section unless its provisions have been approved by the Secretary of State under section 124 below.

(5) A scheme under this section may—
(a) make provision with respect to the times and methods of payment of the charges which are required to be paid by virtue of the scheme;
(b) make different provision for different cases, including different provision in relation to different circumstances or localities; and
(c) contain supplemental, consequential and transitional provision for the purposes of the scheme;

and such a scheme may revoke or amend a previous scheme under this section.

(6) It shall be the duty of the Authority to take such steps as it considers appropriate for bringing the provisions of any scheme under this section which is for the time being in force to the attention of persons likely to be affected by them.

(7) A scheme under this section shall have effect subject to any provision made by or under section 58 above or sections 125 to 130 below.

DEFINITION
"the Authority": s.221(1).

GENERAL NOTE
Abstraction charges form a significant part of the Authority's revenue, and this section empowers the Authority to impose charges in accordance with a scheme submitted to the Secretary of State for approval. Section 124(1) and (2) prescribes the procedure to be followed for the approval of such a scheme.

Under s.30 of the Water Act 1973, water authorities charged for abstraction licences in accordance with a charges scheme which had to indicate both the method and principles which underlay it. The common method was to provide for a base standard charge in pence per cubic metre abstracted, which was multiplied up or down according to various factors such as the location and quality of return of water, and the time of year. The provisions under ss.123 and 124 are not so specific on the need to indicate principles, but the Authority is likely to follow a similar pattern, and the procedures for making such a scheme are now considerably more formalised, requiring the approval of the Secretary of State and providing opportunities for public representation (s.124(1)–(3)).

Subs. (5)(b)
Including different provisions in relation to different circumstances or localities. This allows considerable flexibility in fixing charges, although qualified by the obligation under s.124(3) (b), to avoid undue preference or discrimination. Apart from permitting seasonal variations to be taken into account, it should allow higher charges to be made in areas where minimum acceptable river flows have been established under s.21.

Approval of scheme under section 123

124.—(1) Before submitting a scheme under section 123 above to the Secretary of State for his approval the Authority shall, in such manner as it considers appropriate for bringing it to the attention of persons likely to be affected by the scheme, publish a notice—

(a) setting out its proposals; and

(b) specifying the period within which representations or objections with respect to the proposals may be made to the Secretary of State.

(2) Where any proposed scheme under section 123 above has been submitted to the Secretary of State for his approval, it shall be the duty of the Secretary of State, in determining whether or not to approve the scheme or to approve it subject to modifications—

(a) to consider any representations or objections duly made to him and not withdrawn; and

(b) to have regard to the matters specified in subsection (3) below.

(3) The matters mentioned in subsection (2) above are—

(a) the desirability of ensuring that the amounts recovered by the Authority by way of charges fixed by or under schemes under section 123 above are the amounts which, taking one year with another, are required by the Authority for recovering such amounts as the Secretary of State may consider it appropriate to attribute to the expenses incurred by the Authority in carrying out its functions under Part II of this Act; and

(b) the need to ensure that no undue preference is shown, and that there is no undue discrimination, in the fixing of charges by or under any scheme under that section.

(4) For the purposes of subsection (3)(a) above—

(a) the Secretary of State shall take into account any determinations under section 117 above in determining the amounts which he considers it appropriate to attribute to the expenses incurred by the Authority in carrying out its functions under Part II of this Act; and

(b) those amounts may include amounts in respect of the depreciation of, and the provision of a return on, such of the Authority's assets as are held by it for purposes connected with the carrying out of those functions.

(5) The consent of the Treasury shall be required for the giving of an approval to a scheme under section 123 above.

DEFINITIONS
"modifications": s.221(1).
"notice": s.221(1).
"the Authority": s.221(1).

GENERAL NOTE
See General Note to s.123.

Subs. (3)(a)
This provision has significant economic implications, and establishes two important guiding principles in determining the charges scheme. First, the revenue from abstraction charges cannot be used to cross-subsidise the Authority's other functions, such as those connected with pollution control, land drainage or fishery protection. Conversely, the revenue is not confined solely to the costs of the abstraction licence system, but can be related to other water resource functions of the Authority, such as the costs associated with arrangements made with water undertakers concerning their river-regulating reservoirs under s.20 (see debate on the 1989 Act: *Hansard*, H.L. Vol. 508, col. 299, May 23, 1989).

Specific exemptions from water resources charges

125.—(1) No charges, other than those for the purpose of recovering administrative expenses attributable to the exercise by the Authority of its functions in relation to the application for the licence, shall be levied in respect of water authorised by a licence to be abstracted for use in the production of electricity or any other form of power by any generating station or apparatus of a capacity of not more than five megawatts.

(2) No charges shall be levied in respect of water authorised by a licence to be abstracted from underground strata, in so far as—

(a) the water is authorised to be abstracted for use for agricultural purposes other than spray irrigation; and

(b) the quantity of water authorised to be abstracted from the strata in any period of 24 hours does not exceed 20 cubic metres in aggregate.

DEFINITIONS
"agricultural": s.221(1).
"functions": s.3.
"underground strata": s.221(1).

Agreements containing exemptions from charges

126.—(1) The Authority may, on the application of any person who is liable to pay charges to the Authority for the abstraction of water under a licence under Chapter II of Part II of this Act, make an agreement with him either exempting him from the payment of charges or providing for charges to be levied on him at reduced rates specified in the agreement.

(2) In the exercise of its powers under subsection (1) above in relation to any person, the Authority shall have regard to—

(a) the extent to which any works constructed at any time by that person or any works to be constructed by him have made, or will make, a beneficial contribution towards the fulfilment of the purposes of the functions of the Authority under any enactment;

(b) any financial assistance which that person has rendered, or has agreed to render, towards the carrying out of works by the Authority in the performance of those functions; and

(c) any other material considerations.

(3) The Secretary of State may give directions as to the exercise by the Authority of its powers under subsection (1) above.

(4) Without prejudice to the exercise of the power conferred by subsection (3) above, if on any application under this section—

(a) the Authority refuses to make an agreement with the applicant as mentioned in subsection (1) above; or

(b) the applicant objects to the terms of such an agreement as proposed by the Authority and that objection is not withdrawn,

the applicant or the Authority may refer the question in dispute to the Secretary of State.

(5) On a reference under subsection (4) above—

(a) the Secretary of State shall determine the question in dispute, having regard to the matters to which, in accordance with subsection (2) above, the Authority was required to have regard in relation to the applicant; and

(b) may give directions to the Authority requiring it to make an agreement with the applicant in accordance with his decision.

(6) Section 68 above shall have effect for the purposes of so much of this section as relates to a reference to the Secretary of State as if references in that section to Chapter II of Part II of this Act included references to this section.

(7) Any decision of the Secretary of State on a reference under subsection (4) above shall be final; and section 69 above shall apply in relation to the decision on a reference under this section as it applies in relation to a decision on a reference such as is mentioned in subsection (1)(b) of that section, but as if references to the other party were references to the applicant.

DEFINITION
  "the Authority": s.221(1).

GENERAL NOTE
  This section follows a similar pattern to that allowing the Authority to enter into financial arrangements with navigation, harbour and conservancy authorities to share the costs of mutually beneficial works. In the case of a reference to the Secretary of State under subs. (4), the Secretary of State will consider all the matters to which the Authority must have regard but his view is that any works done by the applicant only justify a reduction or exemption if they are beneficial to water resources generally, as distinct from being of benefit to the abstractor alone (Decision Letter WS/3468/565/2, June 25, 1970).

Subs. (6)
  This enables the Secretary of State to pass on his powers to resolve disputes to a tribunal. Section 68 allows the Secretary of State to establish the tribunal to determine appeals with respect to decisions on licence applications (abstraction and impounding). Section 43 governs those appeals.

Subs. (7)
  Determinations of either the Secretary of State or the tribunal can be challenged in the High Court on the grounds that the decision is *ultra vires* or that there has been prejudice caused by breach of procedural requirements. Section 69 sets out in shortened form the challenge that would in any event be available under the general principles of judicial review.

Special charges in respect of spray irrigation

    127.—(1) Where a person ("the applicant") is for the time being the holder of a licence under Chapter II of Part II of this Act to abstract water ("the applicant's licence"), and in accordance with the provisions of that licence—

    (a) the water is to be used on land of which the applicant is the occupier; and

    (b) the purposes for which water abstracted in pursuance of the licence is to be used consist of or include spray irrigation,

the applicant may apply to the Authority to make an agreement with him under this section and, subject to the following provisions of this section and sections 128 and 129 below, the Authority may make such an agreement accordingly.

(2) During any period for which an agreement under this section is in force, the following charges shall be payable by the applicant to the Authority in respect of the applicant's licence, in so far as it relates to water authorised to be abstracted and used on the relevant land, that is to say—

    (a) basic charges calculated, in accordance with the agreement, by reference to the quantity of water authorised to be so abstracted and used from time to time in pursuance of the licence; and

    (b) supplementary charges calculated, in accordance with the agreement, by reference to the quantity of water which is measured or assessed as being abstracted from time to time by or on behalf of the applicant from the source of supply to which the applicant's licence relates for use on the relevant land.

(3) In determining—

    (a) whether to make an agreement with the applicant under this section; and

    (b) the charges to be leviable under such an agreement,

the Authority shall have regard to the extent to which, in any year within the period proposed to be specified in the agreement as the period for which it is made, the quantity of water referred to in paragraph (a) of subsection (2) above is likely to exceed the quantity referred to in paragraph (b) of that subsection.

(4) Where the applicant's licence authorises water abstracted in pursuance of the licence to be used on the relevant land for purposes which include spray irrigation and other purposes—

    (a) any agreement made under this section shall provide for apportioning, as between those purposes respectively, the quantity referred to in paragraph (a) of subsection (2) above and the quantity referred to in paragraph (b) of that subsection;

    (b) subsection (2) above shall have effect as if in each of those paragraphs the reference to the quantity of water mentioned in that paragraph were a reference to so much of that quantity as in accordance with the agreement is apportioned to the purpose of spray irrigation; and

    (c) in subsection (3) above any reference to either of those paragraphs shall be construed as a reference to that paragraph as modified by paragraph (b) of this subsection.

(5) An application under subsection (1) above may be made by a person who has applied for, but is not yet the holder of, a licence under Chapter II of Part II of this Act to abstract water; and, in relation to an application so made or to an agreement made on such an application—

    (a) the reference in that subsection to the provisions of the applicant's licence shall be construed as a reference to the proposals contained in the application for a licence; and

    (b) any other reference in this section or in section 128 or 129 below to the applicant's licence shall be construed as a reference to any licence granted to the applicant in pursuance of the application mentioned in paragraph (a) above or in pursuance of an appeal consequential upon the application so mentioned.

(6) In this section and sections 128 and 129 below—
"the applicant" and "the applicant's licence" shall be construed, subject to subsection (5) above, in accordance with subsection (1) above;
"the relevant land" means the land on which the applicant's licence, as for the time being in force, authorises water abstracted in pursuance of the licence to be used for purposes which consist of or include spray irrigation; and
"year" means a period of 12 months beginning—
(a) with the date on which an agreement under this section comes into force or is proposed to come into force; or
(b) with an anniversary of that date.

DEFINITIONS
"spray irrigation": s.145.
"the applicant": subs. (6).
"the applicant's licence": subs. (6).
"the Authority": s.221(1).
"the relevant land": subs. (6).
"year": subs. (6).

GENERAL NOTE
Sections 127–129 deal with the Authority's power to levy special charges on holders of abstraction licences who are using them for spray irrigation. The purpose of the special charges is to reconcile the Authority's need to ensure that water is available to meet the total maximum quantity authorised by licence, with the fact that the actual requirements for spray irrigation are particularly variable from season to season according to rainfall. Section 127 enables the charge payable to be fixed partly on the basis of the quantity of water authorised (subs. (2)(a)) and partly on the basis of the quantity actually abstracted (subs. (2)(b)).

Duration of agreement under section 127

128.—(1) The period specified in an agreement under section 127 above as the period for which it is made shall not be less than five years.
(2) An agreement under section 127 above shall remain in force until the occurrence of whichever of the following events first occurs, that is to say—
(a) the period specified in the agreement, as mentioned in subsection (1) above, comes to an end;
(b) the applicant's licence expires or is revoked;
(c) the applicant ceases to be the occupier of the relevant land or, if he has previously ceased to be the occupier of a part or parts of that land, ceases to be the occupier of the remainder of it;
(d) the agreement is terminated under subsection (4) below.
(3) At any time while an agreement under section 127 above is in force, the applicant may apply to the Authority to terminate the agreement.
(4) If, on an application for the termination of an agreement under section 127 above, the Authority is satisfied that, by reason of any change of circumstances since the agreement was made, it ought to be terminated, it may terminate the agreement, either unconditionally or subject to such conditions (whether as to any payment to be made by the applicant or otherwise) as the Authority and the applicant may agree.

DEFINITIONS
"the applicant": s.127(6).
"the Authority": s.221(1).

Directions and appeals with respect to exercise of powers under sections 127 and 128

129.—(1) The Secretary of State may give directions as to the exercise by the Authority of its powers under sections 127 and 128 above.
(2) Without prejudice to the exercise of the power conferred by subsection (1) above, if on any application under section 127 or 128 above—

(a) the Authority refuses to make or terminate an agreement under section 127 above; or

(b) the applicant objects to the proposals of the Authority—
> (i) as to the terms of such an agreement; or
> (ii) as to the conditions subject to which such an agreement is to be terminated,

and that objection is not withdrawn,

the applicant or the Authority may refer the question in dispute to the Secretary of State.

(3) On a reference under subsection (2) above—

(a) the Secretary of State shall determine the question in dispute, having regard to the matters to which, in accordance with subsection (3) of section 127 above, the Authority would be required to have regard in relation to the applicant on an application under that section; and

(b) may give directions to the Authority requiring it to make an agreement with the applicant in accordance with his decision.

(4) Section 68 above shall have effect for the purposes of so much of this section as relates to a reference to the Secretary of State as if references in that section to Chapter II of Part II of this Act included references to this section.

(5) Any decision of the Secretary of State on a reference under subsection (2) above shall be final; and section 69 above shall apply in relation to the decision on a reference under this section as it applies in relation to a decision on a reference such as is mentioned in subsection (1)(b) of that section, but as if references to the other party were references to the applicant.

DEFINITIONS
"the applicant": s.127(6).
"the Authority": s.221(1).

GENERAL NOTE
Appeals and dispute resolution for spray irrigation charges follow the same pattern as for agreements for financial contributions to mutually beneficial works (s.120) and agreements for exemptions from charges (s.126).

Subss. (4) and (5)
These repeat s.126(6) and (7) above. See the Note to that section.

Charges in respect of abstraction from waters of British Waterways Board

130.—(1) Where the British Waterways Board are the holders of a licence under Chapter II of Part II of this Act authorising abstraction from any inland waters to which section 66 above applies, then, the charges which, apart from this subsection, would be payable in respect of that licence either—

(a) shall be reduced to such extent, and as so reduced shall be payable subject to such conditions; or

(b) shall not be payable,

as the Board and the Authority may agree or, in default of such agreement, the Secretary of State may determine.

(2) Where—

(a) a person other than the British Waterways Board is the holder of a licence under Chapter II of Part II of this Act authorising abstraction from any inland waters to which section 66 above applies; and

(b) any charges in respect of that licence are payable,

the Authority shall pay to the Board such proportion of those charges, subject to such conditions, as the Board and the Authority may agree, or, in default of such agreement, the Secretary of State may determine.

DEFINITIONS
"inland waters": s.221(1).
"the Authority": s.221(1).

GENERAL NOTE
The effect of this section is that where water is abstracted from an inland water owned or managed by the British Waterways Board (s.66) the Authority is obliged to reduce (subs. (1)(a)) or waive charges for abstraction if the Board holds the licence. If the Authority receives charges for a licence held by a person other than the Board for abstraction from inland waters owned or managed by the Board then the Authority shall pay all or some of those charges to the Board (subs. (2)).

Charges in connection with control of pollution

Power to make scheme of charges

131.—(1) Where—
(a) an application is made to the Authority for a Part III consent;
(b) the Authority gives a Part III consent otherwise than in a case where an application for a consent was made under paragraph 1 of Schedule 10 to this Act; or
(c) a Part III consent is for the time being in force,
the Authority may require the payment to it of such charges as may be specified in or determined under a scheme made by it under this section.

(2) The persons who shall be liable to pay charges which are required to be paid by virtue of a scheme under this section shall be—
(a) in the case of a charge by virtue of subsection (1)(a) above, the person who makes the application;
(b) in the case of a charge by virtue of subsection (1)(b) above, any person who is authorised to do anything by virtue of the consent and on whom the instrument giving the consent is served; and
(c) in the case of a charge by virtue of subsection (1)(c) above, any person who makes a discharge in pursuance of the consent at any time during the period to which, in accordance with the scheme, the charge relates.

(3) Provision made by a scheme for the purposes of subsection (2)(c) above may impose a single charge in respect of the whole period for which the consent is in force or separate charges in respect of different parts of that period or both such a single charge and such separate charges.

(4) The Authority shall not make a scheme under this section unless its provisions have been approved by the Secretary of State under section 132 below.

(5) A scheme under this section may—
(a) make provision with respect to the times and methods of payment of the charges which are required to be paid by virtue of the scheme;
(b) make different provision for different cases, including different provision in relation to different persons, circumstances or localities; and
(c) contain supplemental, consequential and transitional provision for the purposes of the scheme;
and such a scheme may revoke or amend a previous scheme under this section.

(6) It shall be the duty of the Authority to take such steps as it considers appropriate for bringing the provisions of any scheme under this section which is for the time being in force to the attention of persons likely to be affected by them.

(7) In this section "a Part III consent" means a consent for the purposes of section 88(1)(a), 89(4)(a) or 90 above.

DEFINITIONS
"a Part III consent": subs. (7).
"the Authority": s.221(1).

GENERAL NOTE
See s.88(2) and Sched. 10 for the provisions governing applications for consents, and s.99 for the power of the Secretary of State to make regulations modifying the water pollution provisions of the Act in cases where consents are required. This section is based on Sched. 12 of the Water Act 1989.

Approval of scheme under section 131

132.—(1) Before submitting a scheme under section 131 above to the Secretary of State for his approval the Authority shall, in such manner as it considers appropriate for bringing it to the attention of persons likely to be affected by it, publish a notice—

(a) setting out its proposals; and

(b) specifying the period within which representations or objections with respect to the proposals may be made to the Secretary of State.

(2) Where any proposed scheme under section 131 above has been submitted to the Secretary of State for his approval, it shall be the duty of the Secretary of State, in determining whether or not to approve the scheme or to approve it subject to modifications—

(a) to consider any representations or objections duly made to him and not withdrawn; and

(b) to have regard to the matters specified in subsection (3) below.

(3) The matters mentioned in subsection (2) above are—

(a) the desirability of ensuring that the amount recovered by the Authority by way of charges fixed by or under schemes under section 131 above does not exceed, taking one year with another, such amount as appears to the Secretary of State to be reasonably attributable to the expenses incurred by the Authority in carrying out its functions under the consent provisions and otherwise in relation to discharges into controlled waters; and

(b) the need to ensure that no undue preference is shown, and that there is no undue discrimination, in the fixing of charges by or under the scheme.

(4) The consent of the Treasury shall be required for the giving of the Secretary of State's approval to a scheme under section 131 above.

(5) In this section—

"the consent provisions" means the provisions of Schedule 10 to this Act, together with the provisions of section 91 above and of this section and section 131 above;

"controlled waters" has the same meaning as in Part III of this Act.

DEFINITIONS
"controlled waters": subs. (5).
"notice": s.221(1).
"the Authority": s.221(1).
"the consent provisions": subs. (5).
"year": s.221(1).

Levies by the Authority on local authorities

Power to authorise the Authority to issue levies

133. For the purposes of its flood defence functions the Authority shall be a levying body within the meaning of section 74 of the Local Government Finance Act 1988 (power to make regulations authorising a levying body to issue a levy); and that section shall have effect accordingly.

DEFINITION
"the Authority": s.221(1).

General drainage charges

Raising of general drainage charges

134.—(1) Subject to subsection (2) below, the Authority may raise at an amount per hectare of chargeable land in a local flood defence district a charge to be known as a general drainage charge and to be levied in accordance with sections 135 and 136 below.

(2) The Authority shall not levy a general drainage charge in respect of any local flood defence district unless the regional flood defence committee for the area in which that district is situated have recommended that such a charge should be raised.

(3) For the purposes of this section and sections 135 and 136 below the area of a regional flood defence committee in relation to which no local flood defence scheme is in force shall be treated as a single local flood defence district; and any parts of such an area in relation to which no such scheme is in force shall be treated as included in a single such district.

DEFINITIONS
"chargeable land": s.145.
"the Authority": s.221(1).

GENERAL NOTE
For the general structure of the financial arrangements for flood defence see the General Note to s.105.

Amount, assessment etc. of general drainage charge

135.—(1) A general drainage charge raised by the Authority for a local flood defence district for any year shall be at a uniform amount per hectare of chargeable land in that district.

(2) The uniform amount referred to in subsection (1) above shall be ascertained, subject to subsection (3) below, by multiplying the relevant quotient determined in accordance with section 136 below by one penny and by such number as may be specified by either of the Ministers by order made for the purposes of this subsection.

(3) The number specified in an order under this section for the purposes of subsection (2) above shall (apart from any adjustment made to it to take account of rough grazing land) be such as the Minister making the order considers will secure, so far as reasonably practicable, that the amount specified in paragraph (a) below will be equal to the amount specified in paragraph (b) below, that is to say—
  (a) the aggregate amount produced by any charge levied by reference to a relevant quotient determined under section 136 below; and
  (b) the aggregate amount which, if the chargeable land in the local flood defence district had been liable to be rated for the financial year beginning in 1989, would have been produced by a rate levied on the land at an amount in the pound (of rateable value) equal to that quotient multiplied by one penny.

(4) An order under this section may be made so as to apply either—
  (a) to all general drainage charges; or
  (b) to the general drainage charges proposed to be raised in any one or more local flood defence districts specified in the order;
and any such order applying to more than one local flood defence district may make different provision as respects the different districts to which it applies.

(5) Schedule 15 to this Act shall have effect with respect to the assessment, incidence, payment and enforcement of general drainage charges.

(6) The power of each of the Ministers to make an order under this section shall be exercisable by statutory instrument subject to annulment in pursuance of a resolution of either House of Parliament.

GENERAL NOTE
See General Note to s.105.

Subs. (2)
Relevant quotient. For the method of calculation of the relevant quotient, see s.136.

Determination of the relevant quotient

136.—(1) The relevant quotient for the purposes of section 135(2) above shall, in relation to any local flood defence district, be determined by the application of the following formula—

$$\left(\frac{A}{B} \times \frac{D}{E} \right) \div C = \text{relevant quotient}$$

where—
  "A" means the aggregate amount demanded by the precepts issued in respect of that district under subsection (3) of section 46 of the Land Drainage Act 1976 in respect of the financial year beginning in 1989.
  "B" means the aggregate amount of the estimated penny rate products on the basis of which the aggregate amount so demanded was apportioned in pursuance of subsection (1) of that section in respect of that financial year;
  "C" means the amount ascertained by dividing the aggregate amount so demanded by the number of the relevant population of that disrrict for the financial year beginning in 1990;
  "D" means the aggregate amount of the levies issued by the Authority in respect of that disrrict under the National Rivers Authority (Levies) Regulations 1990 for the financial year in respect of which the drainage charge in question is raised; and
  "E" means the relevant population of that disrrict for the financial year in respect of which that charge is raised.
(2) For the purposes of this section the relevant population of a local flood defence district for any financial year is the aggregate of—
  (a) the relevant population for that year of the area of each charging authority the whole of whose area falls within that district; and
  (b) the relevant population of such parts of the areas of any other charging authorities as fall within that district.
(3) For the purposes of subsection (2) above—
  (a) the relevant population for any financial year of the area of an English charging authority shall be taken to be the relevant population of that area for that year as calculated under paragraph 4 of Schedule 12A to the Local Government Finance Act 1988;
  (b) the relevant population for any financial year of the area of a Welsh charging authority shall be taken to be the relevant population of that area for that year as calculated in accordance with rules for the time being effective (as regards that year) under regulations made under paragraph 5(1) of that Schedule;

  (c) the relevant population for any financial year of any part of the area of a charging authority shall be taken to be the relevant population of that part of that area for that year as calculated in accordance with rules for the time being effective (as regards that year) under regulations made under paragraph 6(2) of that Schedule;
and, accordingly, any such regulations as are mentioned in paragraph (b) or (c) above shall have effect for the purposes of this section as they have effect for the purposes of section 69 of that Act.

  (4) In this section "charging authority" has the same meaning as in the Local Government Finance Act 1988.

DEFINITIONS
  "charging authority": subs. (4).
  "financial year": s.221(1).
  "the Authority": s.221(1).

GENERAL NOTE
  Local authority precepts were changed to levies by the Local Government Finance Act 1988.

Special drainage charges

Special drainage charges in interests of agriculture

  137.—(1) Where it appears to the Authority that the interests of agriculture require the carrying out, improvement or maintenance of drainage works in connection with any watercourses in the area of any regional flood defence committee, the Authority may submit to either of the Ministers for confirmation a scheme under this section with respect to those watercourses.

  (2) A scheme under this section with respect to any watercourses is a scheme—

    (a) designating those watercourses, and any watercourses connected with them, for the purposes of this section; and

    (b) making provision for the raising, in accordance with section 138 below, of a charge (known as a "special drainage charge") for the purpose of meeting the expenses of drainage works in connection with the designated watercourses and any expenses arising from such works.

  (3) A scheme under this section shall designate for the purposes of the special drainage charge so much of the area of the regional flood defence committee as consists of land which, in the opinion of the Authority, is agricultural land that would benefit from drainage works in connection with the designated watercourses.

  (4) The watercourses designated in any scheme under this section shall, if the scheme is confirmed, be treated for the purposes of this Act and the Land Drainage Act 1991 as part of a main river.

  (5) A scheme under this section—

    (a) may make provision for any of the matters referred to in subsections (1) and (2) of section 108 above; and

    (b) may provide for the revocation or amendment of, and for the retransfer of property, rights, powers, duties, obligations and liabilities transferred by, any previous scheme under this section.

  (6) Schedule 16 to this Act shall have effect with respect to the making and confirmation of schemes under this section.

  (7) For the purposes of this section—

    (a) the reference to expenses of drainage works is a reference to expenses incurred in the construction, improvement or maintenance of drainage works;

    (b) the expenses of any drainage works which may be necessary in consequence of other drainage works, and so much of any contribution made under section 57 of the Land Drainage Act 1991 as is fairly attributable to such expenses, shall be deemed to be expenses arising from those other drainage works; and

(c) the expenses of any drainage works shall be taken (without prejudice to section 221(5) below) to include a proper proportion of the cost of the officers and buildings and establishment of the authority carrying them out.

(8) In this section and Schedule 16 to this Act "watercourse" has the same meaning as in Part IV of this Act.

Levying and amount of special drainage charge

138.—(1) A special drainage charge shall be levied by the Authority in respect of chargeable land included in the area designated for the purposes of the charge by the scheme authorising it ("the relevant chargeable land").

(2) The special drainage charge raised for any year shall be at a uniform amount per hectare of the relevant chargeable land.

(3) The uniform amount referred to in subsection (2) above shall be determined by the regional flood defence committee for the area which includes the relevant chargeable land but shall exceed neither—

(a) an amount to be specified in the scheme as the maximum amount of the charge or such greater amount as may be authorised for the purposes of the scheme by an order made by one of the Ministers on the application of the Authority; nor

(b) 25 pence or such other amount as may be substituted for 25 pence by an order made by one of the Ministers and approved by a resolution of the House of Commons.

(4) Before either of the Ministers makes an order under subsection (3)(a) above he shall—

(a) consult with such of the associations and persons concerned as he considers appropriate;

(b) cause a notice of his intention to make the order, and of the time (which shall not be less than 30 days) within which objections to the proposed order may be made to him, to be published in such manner as he thinks best adapted for informing persons affected;

(c) if he considers it necessary, afford such persons an opportunity of appearing before and being heard by a person appointed by him for the purpose; and

(d) consider the report of the person so appointed and any objections duly made.

(5) An order under subsection (3)(b) above may be made so as to apply—

(a) to special drainage charges in general; or

(b) to the special drainage charges proposed to be raised in respect of such areas of regional flood defence committees as may be specified in the order; or

(c) to special drainage charges proposed to be raised in pursuance of one or more schemes made under section 137 above and so specified;

and any such order applying to the charges proposed to be raised in respect of more than one area of a regional flood defence committee, or authorised by more than one such scheme, may make different provision for the charges in respect of different areas or, as the case may be, the charges authorised by the different schemes.

(6) The power of each of the Ministers to make an order under subsection (3)(b) above shall be exercisable by statutory instrument; and section 14 of the Interpretation Act 1978 (power to revoke or amend orders made by statutory instrument) shall apply to the power to make orders under subsection (3)(a) above as it applies, by virtue of this subsection, to the power to make orders under subsection (3)(b) above.

(7) Schedule 15 to this Act shall have effect with respect to the assessment, incidence, payment and enforcement of special drainage charges.

Revenue from internal drainage boards

Contributions from internal drainage boards

139.—(1) Subject to subsections (2) and (3) below, the Authority shall by resolution require every internal drainage board to make towards the expenses of the Authority such contribution as the Authority may consider to be fair.

(2) Subject to subsection (3) below, where an internal drainage district ("the main internal drainage district") comprises two or more other internal districts ("minor internal drainage districts"), the Authority shall not require the drainage board for that district to make any contribution towards the expenses of the Authority except in respect of such part, if any, of that district as is not situated within any minor internal drainage district.

(3) Notwithstanding subsection (2) above, the Authority, after determining what contribution should be made by the drainage board for each of the minor internal drainage districts, may, if it thinks fit, require the drainage board for the main internal drainage district to pay direct to the Authority an amount equal to the aggregate of those contributions.

(4) If the Authority make a requisition under subsection (3) above, the drainage board of the main internal drainage district shall raise the amount paid by them under that subsection to the Authority by means of drainage rates levied by them within, or special levies issued in respect of, the main internal drainage district or, as the case may be, such part of that district as is situated within a minor internal drainage district.

(5) Without prejudice to subsection (3) of section 140 below, a resolution under this section may be acted upon by the Authority forthwith, notwithstanding that the time for bringing an appeal under that section has not expired or that an appeal so brought is pending.

DEFINITIONS
   "agricultural land": s.145.
   "drainage works": s.221(1).
   "main river": s.221(1).
   "minor internal drainage districts": subs. (2).
   "the Authority": s.221(1).
   "the main internal drainage district": subs. (2).
   "the Ministers": s.221(1).
   "watercourse": subs. (8) and s.221(1).

Appeals in respect of resolutions under section 139

140.—(1) If—
   (a) an internal drainage board is aggrieved by a resolution of the Authority under section 139 above determining the amount of any contribution; or
   (b) the council of any county or London borough is aggrieved by any such resolution on the ground that the amount of the contribution required to be made by an internal drainage board is inadequate,
the board or council may, within six weeks after the date on which notice of the resolution is given by the Authority to the internal drainage board in question, appeal to the relevant Minister against the resolution.

(2) On an appeal under this section the relevant Minister may, after—
   (a) considering any objections made to him; and
   (b) if he thinks fit, holding a local public inquiry,
make such an order in the matter as he thinks just.

(3) Where the Authority has acted on a resolution by virtue of section 139(5) above and an appeal is brought in respect of the resolution, the

relevant Minister shall by his order direct such adjustment to be made in respect of any sums recovered or paid in pursuance of the resolution as may be necessary for giving effect to his decision.

(4) Where the relevant Minister makes an order under this section, he shall lay before Parliament particulars of the matter in respect of which the appeal was made and of the reasons for his order.

(5) Compliance with any order made by the relevant Minister under this section may be enforced by mandamus.

(6) In this section "the relevant Minister"—

(a) in relation to an internal drainage district wholly in Wales or the drainage board for such a district, means the Secretary of State;

(b) in relation to an internal drainage district partly in Wales or the drainage board for such a district, means the Ministers; and

(c) in any other case, means the Minister.

DEFINITIONS
"relevant Minister": subs. (6).
"the Authority": s.221(1).

GENERAL NOTE

Subs. (2)(b)
See s.215 below for the application of s.250 of the Local Government Act 1972 to local inquiries held under this section.

Precepts for recovery of contributions from internal drainage boards

141.—(1) The Authority may issue precepts to internal drainage boards requiring payment of any amount required to be contributed by those boards under section 139 above.

(2) An internal drainage board shall pay, in accordance with any precept issued to them under this section, the amount thereby demanded.

(3) It shall be the duty of the Authority to prepare, in such form as the relevant Minister may direct, a statement of—

(a) the purposes to which the amount demanded by any precept issued by the Authority under this section is intended to be applied; and

(b) the basis on which it is calculated;

and an internal drainage board shall not be liable to pay the amount demanded by any such precept until they have received such a statement.

(4) Compliance with any precept issued by the Authority in accordance with this section may be enforced by mandamus.

(5) In this section "the relevant Minister" has the same meaning as in section 140 above.

DEFINITIONS
"the Authority": s.221(1).
"the relevant Minister": subs. (5) and s.140(6).

Fisheries contributions

Fisheries contributions

142.—(1) Each of the Ministers shall have power, on an application made to him by the Authority, by order made by statutory instrument to make provision in relation to an area defined by the order—

(a) for the imposition on the owners and occupiers of fisheries in that area of requirements to pay contributions to the Authority, of such amounts as may be determined under the order, in respect of the expenses of the carrying out in relation to that area of the Authority's functions with respect to fisheries;

(b) for such contributions to be paid or recovered in such manner, and to be refundable, in such circumstances as may be specified in or determined under the order.

(2) Subsections (2) to (9) of section 115 above shall have effect in relation to the power conferred by subsection (1) above as they have effect in relation to the power conferred by subsection (1) of that section.

(3) The reference in this section to the owners and occupiers of fisheries shall have the same meaning as any such reference in the Salmon and Freshwater Fisheries Act 1975.

DEFINITIONS
  "functions": s.3.
  "owners and occupiers of fisheries": subs. (3).
  "the Authority": s.221(1).
  "the Ministers": s.221(1).

Navigation tolls

Power of Authority to levy navigation tolls

143.—(1) Where any navigable waters—
  (a) in England and Wales; or
  (b) in so much of the territorial sea adjacent to England and Wales as is included in the area of a regional flood defence committee,
are not subject to the control of any navigation authority, harbour authority or conservancy authority, the Authority may apply to the Secretary of State for an order imposing tolls in respect of the navigation of vessels in those waters.

(2) An order under this section shall not be made unless the Secretary of State is satisfied that the cost of the maintenance or works in connection with the waters to which the order relates has been or will be increased as a result of the use of those waters for purposes of navigation.

(3) Schedule 17 to this Act shall have effect with respect to the making of orders under this section.

(4) Any tolls payable under this section in respect of the navigation of a vessel in any water referred to in subsection (1) above—
  (a) may be demanded from the person in charge of the vessel by any person authorised for that purpose by the Authority; and
  (b) if not paid on demand, may be recovered from either the person in charge of the vessel or the owner of the vessel.

DEFINITIONS
  "conservancy authority": s.221(1).
  "harbour authority": s.221(1).
  "navigation authority": s.221(1).
  "vessels": s.221(1).

GENERAL NOTE
  The Authority's power to levy navigation tolls under this section is confined to areas not controlled by a navigation, harbour or conservancy authority (subs. (1)), and also to situations in which the Authority can satisfy the Secretary of State that it will suffer, or is suffering, additional expense as a result of the passage of vessels through the waters in question (subs. (2)).

Incidental power of the Authority to impose charges

Incidental power of the Authority to impose charges

144. Without prejudice to the generality of its powers by virtue of section 4(1)(a) above and subject to any such express provision with respect to

charging by the Authority as is contained in the preceding provisions of this Chapter or any other enactment, the Authority shall have power to fix and recover charges for services and facilities provided in the course of carrying out its functions.

DEFINITIONS
  "enactment": s.221(1).
  "functions": s.221(1).
  "the Authority": s.221(1).

Interpretation of Chapter II

Interpretation of Chapter II

145. In this Chapter—
  "agricultural buildings" has the meaning provided by section 26(4) of
      the General Rate Act 1967 as amended by the Rating Act 1971;
  "agricultural land" means—
        (a) land used as arable, meadow or pasture ground only;
        (b) land used for a plantation or a wood or for the growth of
    saleable underwood; and
        (c) land exceeding one tenth of a hectare used for the purpose
    of poultry farming, market gardens, nursery grounds, orchards
    or allotments, including allotment gardens within the meaning
    of the Allotments Act 1922,
    but does not include land occupied together with a house as a park,
    gardens (other than as aforesaid) or pleasure grounds, land kept or
    preserved mainly or exclusively for purposes of sport or recreation
    or land used as a racecourse;
  "chargeable land" means the agricultural land and agricultural build-
      ings in so much of the area of a regional flood defence committee as
      does not fall within an internal drainage district, excluding rough
      grazing land and woodlands other than commercial woodlands;
  "commercial woodlands" means woodlands managed on a commercial
      basis with a view to the realisation of profits;
  "drainage" has the same meaning as in Part IV above;
  "drainage charge" means general drainage charge or special drainage
      charge;
  "rough grazing land" means land of either of the following descriptions,
      that is to say—
        (a) land used as pasture ground on which the vegetation
    consists solely or mainly of one or more of the following, that is
    to say, bracken, gorse, heather, rushes and sedge; and
        (b) land so used which is unsuitable for mowing by machine
    and on which the vegetation consists solely or mainly of grass of
    poor feeding value; and
  "spray irrigation" has the same meaning as in Chapter II of Part II of
      this Act.

CHAPTER III

GRANTS AND LOANS

Grants to the Authority

Revenue grants

146.—(1) The Secretary of State may, with the approval of the Treasury, make grants to the Authority of such amounts as he thinks fit.

(2) The payment by the Secretary of State of a grant under this section shall be on such terms as he may, with the approval of the Treasury, provide.

(3) The Secretary of State shall—

(a) prepare in respect of each financial year an account of the sums paid by him to the Authority under this section; and

(b) before the end of September in the following financial year send that account to the Comptroller and Auditor General;

and the form of the account and the manner of preparing it shall be such as the Treasury may direct.

(4) The Comptroller and Auditor General shall examine, certify and report on each account sent to him under this section and shall lay copies of it and of his report before each House of Parliament.

DEFINITIONS
"financial year": s.221(1).
"the Authority": s.221(1).

Grants for drainage works

147.—(1) Subject to subsection (2) below, the relevant Minister may make grants towards expenditure incurred by the Authority in—

(a) the improvement of existing drainage works; or

(b) the construction of new drainage works.

(2) Grants under subsection (1) above shall be—

(a) of such amounts as the Treasury may from time to time sanction; and

(b) subject to such conditions as may, with the approval of the Treasury, be prescribed by regulations made by the relevant Minister.

(3) No grant shall be made under subsection (1) above towards expenditure incurred in connection with any improvement or construction unless—

(a) the plans and sections for it have been approved by the relevant Minister; and

(b) the relevant Minister is satisfied that the work is being or has been properly carried out.

(4) The relevant Minister may, with the approval of the Treasury, make grants to the Authority in respect of expenditure properly incurred by it with a view to carrying out drainage works, being expenditure towards which, if the works had been properly carried out, a grant would have been payable under subsection (1) above.

(5) Where the Authority is about to incur—

(a) such expenditure in respect of any work as is expenditure towards which, if the work is properly carried out, a grant will be payable under subsection (1) above; or

(b) expenditure in respect of which it appears to the relevant Minister that a grant will be payable under subsection (4) above,

the relevant Minister may, with the approval of the Treasury, make advances to the Authority on account of the expenditure.

(6) In this section "the relevant Minister"—

(a) in relation to Wales, means the Secretary of State; and

(b) in relation to England, means the Minister.

DEFINITIONS
"drainage works": s.221(1).
"the Authority": s.221(1).
"the relevant Minister": subs. (6).

Grants towards cost of flood warning systems

148.—(1) The relevant Minister may make grants, of such amounts as the Treasury may from time to time sanction, towards expenditure incurred by the Authority in providing or installing apparatus, or carrying out other engineering or building operations, for the purposes of a flood warning system.

(2) No grant shall be payable under this section towards expenditure incurred in connection with any work unless—

(a) the work has been approved by the relevant Minister; and

(b) the relevant Minister is satisfied that the work is being or has been properly carried out.

(3) Grants under this section shall be made subject to such conditions as may be imposed by the relevant Minister with the approval of the Treasury.

(4) Where any such expenditure as is mentioned in subsection (1) above is about to be incurred by the Authority, the relevant Minister may, with the approval of the Treasury, make advances to the Authority on account of the expenditure.

(5) In this section—

"flood warning system" means any system whereby, for the purpose of providing warning of any danger of flooding, information with respect to—

(a) rainfall, as measured at a particular place within a particular period; or

(b) the level or flow of any inland water, or part of an inland water, at a particular time; or

(c) other matters appearing to the Authority to be relevant for that purpose,

is obtained and transmitted, whether automatically or otherwise, with or without provision for carrying out calculations based on such information and for transmitting the results of those calculations;

"inland water" means any of the following in any part of Great Britain, that is to say—

(a) any river, stream or other watercourse, whether natural or artificial and whether tidal or not;

(b) any lake or pond, whether natural or artificial, and any reservoir or dock; and

(c) any channel, creek, bay, estuary or arm of the sea;

"rainfall" includes any fall of snow, hail or sleet; and

"the relevant Minister" has the same meaning as in section 147 above.

DEFINITIONS

"flood warning system": subs. (5).

"inland water": subs. (5).

"rainfall": subs. (5).

"the Authority": s.221(1).

"the relevant Minister": subs. (5).

Other grants in respect of exercise of powers under Part VII for drainage purposes

149.—(1) The relevant Minister may, with the approval of the Treasury, make to the Authority grants in respect of expenditure incurred by the Authority, and advances on account of expenditure to be incurred by the Authority, in connection with the Authority's functions by virtue of section 165(1)(b) or (c) below—

(a) in making payments arising from the exercise of any power of the Authority by virtue of this Act to acquire land by agreement or compulsorily;

(b) in providing housing accommodation for persons employed or to be employed by the Authority in controlling works of such a kind or so located that those persons are or will be required to reside in the vicinity of the works;

(c) for making payments by virtue of any provision having effect under section 177 below in respect of injury sustained by any person by reason of the exercise by the Authority of any powers under section 165 below;

(d) in paying compensation by virtue of any provision having effect under section 177 below in respect of injury sustained by reason of the exercise by the Authority of its powers under section 167 below.

(2) The relevant Minister may, with the approval of the Treasury, make to the Authority grants in respect of, or advances on account of, expenditure incurred or to be incurred in carrying out works for the rebuilding or repair of any bridge maintained by the Authority, other than works appearing to the relevant Minister to be maintenance works of a routine kind.

(3) The relevant Minister may, with the approval of the Treasury, make to the Authority grants in respect of the cost of any works executed by the Authority in pursuance of section 165(4) below.

(4) In this section "the relevant Minister" has the same meaning as in section 147 above.

DEFINITIONS
  "the Authority": s.221(1).
  "the relevant Minister": subs. (4).

GENERAL NOTE
  The grants under this section are confined to the Authority's functions with respect to flood defence and drainage.

Grants for national security purposes

150.—(1) The Secretary of State may make grants to the Authority for the purpose of defraying or contributing towards any losses it may sustain by reason of compliance with directions given under section 207 below in the interests of national security.

(2) The approval of the Treasury shall be required for the making of grants under this section.

DEFINITION
  "the Authority": s.221(1).

GENERAL NOTE
  Under this section grants may be made to the Authority towards the costs of compliance with directions made under s.207, but only when made in the interests of national security. This can include the costs of required civil defence measures. During Committee stage of the 1989 Act, the Under-Secretary of State stated that the Government expected that the total costs of such measures would be little different from the then current expenditure on civil defence by the water industry of £3,189,000. Grant aid for that sum was mostly set at 75 per cent. but with 100 per cent. for training, communications and full-time planning staff (Standing Committee D, col. 1532, March 2, 1989). The costs involved in other types of emergency expenditure are to be met by the bodies concerned, with undertakers expected to make provision out of general revenue.

Borrowing by the Authority

Borrowing powers of the Authority

151.—(1) The Authority shall be entitled to borrow in accordance with the following provisions of this section, but not otherwise.

(2) Subject to subsection (4) below, the Authority may, with the consent of either of the Ministers and with the approval of the Treasury, borrow temporarily in sterling, by way of overdraft or otherwise, from persons other than the Ministers, such sums as it may require for meeting its obligations and carrying out its functions.

(3) Subject to subsection (4) below, the Authority may borrow, otherwise than by way of temporary loan, such sums in sterling from either of the Ministers as it may require for capital purposes in connection with the carrying out of its flood defence functions.

(4) The aggregate amount outstanding in respect of the principal of sums borrowed under this section by the Authority shall not at any time exceed £100 million or such greater sum, not exceeding £160 million, as the Ministers may specify by order made by statutory instrument.

(5) No order shall be made under subsection (4) above unless a draft of the order has been laid before the House of Commons and has been approved by a resolution of that House.

DEFINITIONS
  "flood defence functions": s.221(1).
  "functions": s.3.
  "the Authority": s.221(1).
  "the Ministers": s.221(1).

Loans to the Authority

152.—(1) Each of the Ministers shall have power, with the approval of the Treasury, to lend any sums to the Authority which the Authority has power to borrow under section 151(3) above.

(2) Any loan made by one of the Ministers under this section shall be repaid to him at such times and by such methods, and interest on the loan shall be paid to him at such rates and at such times, as that Minister may with the approval of the Treasury from time to time determine.

(3) Any sums required by either of the Ministers for making a loan under this section shall be paid out of money provided by Parliament; and any sums received by either of them in pursuance of subsection (2) above shall be paid into the Consolidated Fund.

(4) Each of the Ministers shall—
  (a) prepare in respect of each financial year an account of the sums lent by him to the Authority under this section; and
  (b) before the end of September in the following financial year send that account to the Comptroller and Auditor General;
and the form of the account and the manner of preparing it shall be such as the Treasury may direct.

(5) The Comptroller and Auditor General shall examine, certify and report on each account sent to him under this section and shall lay copies of it and of his report before each House of Parliament.

DEFINITIONS
  "financial year": s.221(1).
  "the Authority": s.221(1).
  "the Ministers": s.221(1).

Treasury guarantees of the Authority's borrowing

153.—(1) Each of the Ministers shall have power, with the consent of the

Treasury, to guarantee, in such manner and on such conditions as he may think fit, the repayment of the principal of, the payment of interest on and the discharge of any other financial obligation in connection with any sum which the Authority borrows from any person.

(2) Immediately after a guarantee is given under this section the Minister who gave it shall lay a statement of the guarantee before each House of Parliament.

(3) Where any sum is paid out for fulfilling a guarantee under this section the Minister who gave the guarantee shall, as soon as possible after the end of each financial year (beginning with that in which the sum is paid out and ending with that in which all liability in respect of the principal of the sum and in respect of the interest thereon is finally discharged), lay before each House of Parliament a statement relating to that sum.

(4) Any sums required by either of the Ministers for fulfilling a guarantee under this section shall be paid out of money provided by Parliament.

(5) If any sums are paid out in fulfilment of a guarantee under this section, the Authority shall make to the Minister who gave the guarantee, at such times and in such manner as that Minister may from time to time direct—

(a) payments of such amounts as that Minister may so direct in or towards repayment of the sums so paid out; and

(b) payments of interest, at such rate as that Minister may so direct, on what is outstanding for the time being in respect of sums so paid out;

and the consent of the Treasury shall be required for the giving of a direction under this subsection.

(6) Any sums received by either of the Ministers under subsection (5) above shall be paid into the Consolidated Fund.

DEFINITIONS
"financial year": s.221(1).
"the Authority": s.221(1).
"the Ministers": s.221(1).

PART VII

LAND AND WORKS POWERS

CHAPTER I

POWERS OF THE AUTHORITY

Provisions in relation to land

Compulsory purchase etc.

154.—(1) The Authority may be authorised by either of the Ministers to purchase compulsorily any land anywhere in England and Wales which is required by the Authority for the purposes of, or in connection with, the carrying out of its functions.

(2) The power of each of the Ministers under subsection (1) above shall include power—

(a) to authorise the acquisition of interests in, and rights over, land by the creation of new interests and rights; and

(b) by authorising the acquisition by the Authority of any rights over land which is to be or has been acquired by the Authority, to provide for the extinguishment of those rights.

(3) Without prejudice to the generality of subsection (1) above, the land which the Authority may be authorised under that subsection to purchase compulsorily shall include land which is or will be required for the purpose of being given in exchange for, or for any right over, any other land which for

the purposes of the Acquisition of Land Act 1981 is or forms part of a common, open space or a fuel or field garden allotment.

(4) Subject to section 182 below, the Acquisition of Land Act 1981 shall apply to any compulsory purchase under subsection (1) above of any land by the Authority; and Schedule 3 to the said Act of 1981 shall apply to the compulsory acquisition under that subsection of rights by the creation of new rights.

(5) Schedule 18 to this Act shall have effect for the purpose of modifying enactments relating to compensation and the provisions of the Compulsory Purchase Act 1965 in their application in relation to the compulsory acquisition under subsection (1) above of a right over land by the creation of a new right.

(6) The provisions of Part I of the Compulsory Purchase Act 1965 (so far as applicable), other than sections 4 to 8, 10, 21, 27(1) and 31 and Schedule 4, shall apply in relation to any power to acquire land by agreement which is conferred, by virtue of any provision of this Act (including section 4 above) or otherwise, on the Authority as if—

(a) any reference in those provisions to the acquiring authority were a reference to the Authority; and

(b) any reference to land subject to compulsory purchase were a reference to land which may be purchased by agreement under that power.

DEFINITIONS
"functions": s.3.
"the Authority": s.221(1).
"the Minister": s.189(1).

GENERAL NOTE
This section gives powers of compulsory purchase of land in England and Wales to the Authority.

Under subs. (4), the procedures of the Acquisition of Land Act 1981 apply to compulsory purchase under subs. (1). As was made clear during Parliamentary debate on the 1989 Act, the "Point Gourde" principle applies to the computation of compensation; *i.e.* the land-owner is entitled to compensation based on the market value of his interest but excluding any additional development value resulting from the proposed scheme for the purpose of which the land has been acquired.

Accretions of land resulting from drainage works

155.—(1) If the relevant Minister certifies that, as the result of—

(a) any drainage works carried out or improved, or proposed to be carried out or improved, by the Authority in connection with the tidal waters of a main river; or

(b) any drainage works transferred from a drainage body to the Authority in pursuance of this Act or the Land Drainage Act 1991,

there has been or is likely to be any accretion of land, the powers of the Authority by virtue of this Act, for the purpose of carrying out its functions, to acquire land or any interest in or right over land by agreement or compulsorily shall include power so to acquire the land mentioned in subsection (2) below.

(2) The land mentioned in subsection (1) above is—

(a) the accretion of land or the land to which the accretion will, if it takes place, be added, together with any right to reclaim or embank the accretion; and

(b) such other land as is reasonably required for the purpose of reclamation of the accretion or for the enjoyment of it when reclaimed.

(3) An agreement or order with respect to the acquisition of any land or rights by virtue of this section may provide for the transfer to the Authority of any liability for the upkeep, maintenance and repair of any bank or drainage work or of any other like liability.

(4) Where the value of any land or right is increased by the carrying out or proposed carrying out of drainage works by the Authority the amount of the increase shall not be taken into account in assessing the compensation in respect of the compulsory acquisition of it.

(5) Where, by reason of a certificate having been given by the relevant Minister under this section in relation to any drainage works, the Authority has acquired any land or right and a grant has been made out of public moneys for defraying the cost or part of the cost of the carrying out of the works, the Authority shall—

(a) on being so required by the Crown Estate Commissioners; and

(b) on payment by the Commissioners to the Authority of the sum paid by the Authority in respect of the acquisition of the land or right, together with the amount of any costs incurred by the Authority in connection with the acquisition,

transfer the land or right to the Commissioners or to any person nominated by them.

(6) If the Authority, on being so required by the Crown Estate Commissioners in pursuance of subsection (5) above, fail to transfer to the Commissioners any land or right, the relevant Minister may by a vesting order transfer the land or right to the Commissioners or to a person nominated by them; and, for the purposes of this subsection, the relevant Minister shall be deemed to be a competent authority within the meaning of section 9 of the Law of Property Act 1925.

(7) In this section—

"banks" has the same meaning as in Part IV of this Act;

"drainage body" has the same meaning as in section 108 above;

"the relevant Minster"—

(a) in relation to England, means the Minister; and

(b) in relation to Wales, means the Secretary of State.

DEFINITIONS

"banks": subs. (7).

"drainage body": subs. (7).

"functions": s.3.

"the Authority": s.221(1).

"the relevant Minister": subs. (7).

GENERAL NOTE

Subs. (4)

This enshrines the "Point Gourde" principle for the computation of compensation. See General Note to s.154.

Acquisition of land etc. for fisheries purposes

156.—(1) Without prejudice to section 4 above, the powers conferred on the Authority by that section and section 154 above include power to purchase or take on lease (either by agreement or, if so authorised, compulsorily)—

(a) any dam, fishing weir, fishing mill dam, fixed engine or other artificial obstruction and any fishery attached to or worked in connection with any such obstruction;

(b) so much of the bank adjoining a dam as may be necessary for making or maintaining a fish pass for the purposes of section 10 of the Salmon and Freshwater Fisheries Act 1975; and

(c) for the purpose of erecting and working a fixed engine, any fishery land or foreshore together with any easement over any adjoining land necessary for securing access to the fishery land or foreshore so acquired.

(2) Without prejudice to section 4 above, the Authority may—

(a) either alter or remove an obstruction acquired in the exercise of the powers mentioned in subsection (1) above; or

(b) by itself or its lessees use or work in any lawful manner the obstruction for fishing purposes and exercise the right by any fishery so acquired, subject, in the case of an obstruction or fishery acquired by way of lease, to the terms of the lease.

(3) Expressions used in this section and in the Salmon and Freshwater Fisheries Act 1975 have the same meanings in this section as in that Act.

DEFINITIONS
"dam": subs. (3).
"fishing weir": subs. (3).
"fishing mill dam": subs. (3).

GENERAL NOTE
Any land acquired under this section that is below the mean spring high-water mark is controlled by s.38 of the Salmon and Freshwater Fisheries Act 1975 as a result of s.181 below.

Restriction on disposals of compulsorily acquired land

157.—(1) The Authority shall not dispose of any of its compulsorily acquired land, or of any interest or right in or over any of that land, except with the consent of, or in accordance with a general authorisation given by one of the Ministers.

(2) A consent or authorisation for the purposes of this section—
(a) shall be set out in a notice served on the Authority by the Minister who is giving the consent or authorisation; and
(b) in the case of an authorisation, may be combined with an authorisation for the purposes of section 156 of the Water Industry Act 1991 (restrictions on disposals of land by a water or sewerage undertaker).

(3) A consent or authorisation for the purposes of this section may be given on such conditions as the Minister who is giving it considers appropriate.

(4) Without prejudice to the generality of subsection (3) above, the conditions of a consent or authorisation for the purposes of this section may include a requirement that, before there is any disposal, an opportunity of acquiring the land in question, or an interest or right in or over that land, is to be made available to such person as may be specified in or determined under provision contained in the notice setting out the consent or authorisation in question.

(5) A requirement under subsection (4) above may require the opportunity to be made available in such manner and on such terms as may be specified in or determined under provision contained in the notice setting out the consent or authorisation in question.

(6) In this section "compulsorily acquired land," in relation to the Authority, means any land of the Authority which—
(a) was acquired by the Authority compulsorily under the provisions of section 154 above or of an order under section 168 below;
(b) was acquired by the Authority at a time when it was authorised under those provisions to acquire the land compulsorily;
(c) being land which has been transferred to the Authority in accordance with a scheme under Schedule 2 to the Water Act 1989, was acquired by a predecessor of the Authority compulsorily under so much of any enactment in force at any time before September 1, 1989, as conferred powers of compulsory acquisition; or
(d) being land which has been so transferred, was acquired by such a predecessor at a time when it was authorised to acquire the land by virtue of any such powers as are mentioned in paragraph (c) above.

DEFINITIONS
"compulsorily acquired land": subs. (6).
"disposal": s.221(1).

"notice": s.221(1).
"the Authority": s.221(1).
"the Ministers": s.221(1).

GENERAL NOTE
This section mirrors the restrictions on disposal of compulsorily acquired land by water companies in s.156 of the Water Industry Act 1991. The restrictions are of more significance for water companies than for the Authority, since they possess extensive land-holdings—around 430,000 acres, of which some 180,000 acres are in national parks or areas of outstanding natural beauty. This section and s.156 of the Water Industry Act 1991 resulted from one of a number of amendments introduced by the Government during the final stages of the 1989 Water Bill's progress through Parliament in response to concern that there would be inadequate protection against wide-scale land disposal by undertakers following privatisation.

Application of Crichel Down rules
Subsequent disposal of compulsorily acquired land by the Authority requires the consent or general authorisation of the Secretary of State or Minister. The consent may be specific or under the terms of a general authorisation. During Parliamentary proceedings covering the 1989 Act, the then Environment Minister, Michael Howard, indicated that the Government was considering a formula for general authorisations that would in appropriate cases apply the so-called Crichel Down rules, *i.e.* former owners would be given the first opportunity to repurchase at current market prices land compulsorily purchased within the last 25 years, or, in the case of agricultural land, 35 years (Standing Committee D, col. 1511, March 2, 1989).

Works agreements for water resources purposes

Works agreements for water resources purposes

158.—(1) Without prejudice to the generality of the powers of the Authority by virtue of section 4 above but subject to subsection (2) below, those powers shall include power to enter into an agreement with any water undertaker, with any sewerage undertaker, with any local authority or joint planning board, or with the owner or occupier of any land, with respect to any one or more of the following matters, that is to say—
  (a) the carrying out by any party to the agreement of works which the Authority considers necessary or expedient in connection with the carrying out of any of the Authority's functions by virtue of Part II of this Act;
  (b) the maintenance by any party to the agreement of works carried out in pursuance of the agreement;
  (c) provision for the Authority to use, or have access to, any land for any purpose connected with the carrying out of any of those functions;
  (d) the manner in which any reservoir is to be operated.
(2) The Secretary of State may by a direction to the Authority direct that, in such cases or classes of cases as are specified in the direction, the Authority shall not enter into any such agreement as is mentioned in subsection (1) above except with his consent.
(3) An agreement such as is mentioned in subsection (1) above may contain such incidental and consequential provisions (including provisions of a financial character) as appear to the Authority necessary or expedient for the purposes of the agreement.
(4) Where an agreement such as is mentioned in subsection (1) above is made with an owner of land, other than registered land, and the agreement provides that the provisions of this subsection shall have effect in relation to the agreement—
  (a) the agreement may be registered as a land charge under the Land Charges Act 1972 as if it were a charge affecting land falling within paragraph (iii) of Class D;
  (b) the provisions of section 4 of that Act (which relates to the effect of non-registration) shall apply as if the agreement were such a land charge; and

(c) subject to the provisions of section 4 of that Act, the agreement shall be binding upon any successor of that owner to the same extent as it is binding upon that owner, notwithstanding that it would not have been binding upon that successor apart from the provisions of this paragraph.

(5) Where an agreement such as is mentioned in subsection (1) above is made with an owner of land which is registered land, and the agreement provides that the provisions of this subsection shall have effect in relation to the agreement—

(a) notice of the agreement may be registered under section 59(2) of the Land Registration Act 1925 as if it were a land charge (other than a local land charge) within the meaning of that Act;

(b) the provisions of that Act shall apply accordingly as if the agreement were such a land charge; and

(c) where notice of the agreement has been so registered, the agreement shall be binding upon any successor of that owner to the same extent as it is binding upon that owner, notwithstanding that it would not have been binding upon that successor apart from the provisions of this paragraph.

(6) In this section—

"registered land" has the same meaning as in the Land Registration Act 1925; and

"successor," in relation to an agreement with the owner of any land, means a person deriving title or otherwise claiming under that owner, otherwise than in right of an interest or charge to which the interest of the owner was subject immediately before the following time, that is to say—

(a) where the land is not registered land, the time when the agreement was made; and

(b) where the land is registered land, the time when the notice of the agreement was registered.

DEFINITIONS
"functions": s.3.
"owner": s.221(1).
"registered land": subs. (6).
"successor": subs. (6).
"the Authority": s.221(1).

GENERAL NOTE
This section gives the Authority the power, in addition to its general powers under s.4 but subject to a possible requirement of Ministerial consent (subs. (2)), to enter into an agreement for works with water or sewerage undertakers, local authorities, planning boards or land-owners. For unregistered land the agreement may be registered as a Class D land charge (subs. (4)); for registered land as a land charge under the Land Registration Act 1925 (subs. (5)). This gives such agreements the power to bind successive owners.

General pipe-laying powers

Powers to lay pipes in streets

159.—(1) Subject to the following provisions of this Part, the Authority shall, for the purpose of carrying out its functions, have power—

(a) to lay a relevant pipe in, under or over any street and to keep that pipe there;

(b) to inspect, maintain, adjust, repair or alter any relevant pipe which is in, under or over any street; and

(c) to carry out any works requisite for, or incidental to, the purposes of any works falling within paragraph (a) or (b) above, including for those purposes the following kinds of works, that is to say—

      (i) breaking up or opening a street;
      (ii) tunnelling or boring under a street;
      (iii) breaking up or opening a sewer, drain or tunnel;
      (iv) moving or removing earth and other materials.

(2) Without prejudice to the generality of subsection (1)(c) above, the Authority shall have power to erect and keep in any street notices indicating the position of such underground accessories for its relevant pipes as may be used for controlling the flow of water in those pipes.

(3) The power conferred by subsection (2) above shall include power to attach any such notice as is mentioned in that subsection to any building, fence or other structure which is comprised in premises abutting on the street in question.

(4) Until the coming into force of its repeal by the New Roads and Street Works Act 1991 section 20 of the Highways Act 1980 (works in special roads) shall have effect as if the reference in that section to a power under any enactment to lay down or erect apparatus included a reference to any power to lay any pipe which is conferred by this section.

(5) In this section references to a relevant pipe are references to a resource main or discharge pipe and references to laying such a pipe shall include references—

    (a) to the laying of any drain or sewer for any of the purposes specified in subsection (6) below; and

    (b) to the construction of a watercourse for any of those purposes.

(6) The purposes mentioned in subsection (5) above are—

    (a) intercepting, treating or disposing of any foul water arising or flowing upon any land; or

    (b) otherwise preventing the pollution—

        (i) of any waters, whether on the surface or underground, which belong to the Authority or any water undertaker or from which the Authority or any water undertaker is authorised to take water;

        (ii) without prejudice to sub-paragraph (i) above, of any reservoir which belongs to or is operated by the Authority or any water undertaker or which the Authority or any water undertaker is proposing to acquire or construct for the purpose of being so operated; or

        (iii) of any underground strata from which the Authority or any water undertaker is for the time being authorised to abstract water in pursuance of a licence under Chapter II of Part II of this Act.

(7) References in this section to maintaining a pipe include references to cleansing it and references to altering a pipe include references to altering its size or course, to moving or removing it and to replacing it with a pipe which is of the same description of relevant pipe as the pipe replaced.

DEFINITIONS
    "functions": s.3.
    "relevant pipe": subs. (5).
    "street": s.221(1).
    "the Authority": s.221(1).
    "underground strata": s.221(1).

GENERAL NOTE
    Sections 159 and 160 are taken from Sched. 19 to the Water Act 1989. This re-enacted many of the provisions in previous legislation, covering street works as well as works on private land, and including compensation provisions. Sched. 19 of the 1989 Act consolidated the previous separate and complex legislation relating to water and sewerage into a single set of powers. Section 160(1) repeats the power to lay pipes on private land simply by giving "reasonable notice" to the owner and occupier of the land concerned (as defined in s.160(3): see *Hutton* v.

Esher Urban District Council [1974] Ch. 167, where the Court of Appeal held that the power was broad enough to warrant demolition of a private dwelling-house if that was necessarily involved in the works.

Power to law pipes in other land

160.—(1) Subject to the following provisions of this Part, the Authority shall, for the purpose of carrying out its functions, have power—

(a) to lay a relevant pipe (whether above or below the surface) in any land which is not in, under or over a street and to keep that pipe there;

(b) to inspect, maintain, adjust, repair or alter any relevant pipe which is in any such land;

(c) to carry out any works requisite for, or incidental to, the purposes of any works falling within paragraph (a) or (b) above.

(2) The powers conferred by this section shall be exercisable only after reasonable notice of the proposed exercise of the power has been given to the owner and to the occupier of the land where the power is to be exercised.

(3) Subject to subsection (4) below, in relation to any exercise of the powers conferred by this section for the purpose of laying or altering a relevant pipe, the minimum period that is capable of constituting reasonable notice for the purposes of subsection (2) above shall be deemed—

(a) where the power is exercised for the purpose of laying a relevant pipe otherwise than in substitution for an existing pipe of the same description, to be three months; and

(b) where the power is exercised for the purpose of altering an existing pipe, to be 42 days.

(4) In this section references to a relevant pipe are references to a resource main or discharge pipe; and subsection (7) of section 159 above shall apply for the purposes of this section as it applies for the purposes of that section.

DEFINITIONS
  "functions": s.3.
  "relevant pipe": subs. (4).
  "street": s.221(1).
  "the Authority": s.221(1).

GENERAL NOTE
  See General Note to s.159.

Anti-pollution works

Anti-pollution works and operations

161.—(1) Subject to subsection (2) below, where it appears to the Authority that any poisonous, noxious or polluting matter or any solid waste matter is likely to enter, or to be or to have been present in, any controlled waters, the Authority shall be entitled to carry out the following works and operations, that is to say—

(a) in a case where the matter appears likely to enter any controlled waters, works and operations for the purpose of preventing it from doing so; or

(b) in a case where the matter appears to be or to have been present in any controlled waters, works and operations for the purpose—

(i) of removing or disposing of the matter;

(ii) of remedying or mitigating any pollution caused by its presence in the waters; or

(iii) so far as it is reasonably practicable to do so, of restoring the waters, including any flora and fauna dependent on the aquatic environment of the waters, to their state immediately before the matter became present in the waters.

(2) Nothing in subsection (1) above shall entitle the Authority to impede or prevent the making of any discharge in pursuance of a consent given under Chapter II of Part III of this Act.

(3) Where the Authority carries out any such works or operations as are mentioned in subsection (1) above, it shall, subject to subsection (4) below, be entitled to recover the expenses reasonably incurred in doing so from any person who, as the case may be—

(a) caused or knowingly permitted the matter in question to be present at the place from which it was likely, in the opinion of the Authority, to enter any controlled waters; or

(b) caused or knowingly permitted the matter in question to be present in any controlled waters.

(4) No such expenses shall be recoverable from a person for any works or operations in respect of water from an abandoned mine which that person permitted to reach such a place as is mentioned in subsection (3) above or to enter any controlled waters.

(5) Nothing in this section—

(a) derogates from any right of action or other remedy (whether civil or criminal) in proceedings instituted otherwise than under this section; or

(b) affects any restriction imposed by or under any other enactment, whether public, local or private.

(6) In this section—

"controlled waters" has the same meaning as in Part III of this Act; and "mine" has the same meaning as in the Mines and Quarries Act 1954.

DEFINITIONS

"controlled waters": s.104(1) and subs. (6).
"expenses": s.221(5).
"mine": subs. (6).
"the Authority": s.221(1).

GENERAL NOTE

This section gives the Authority important powers to take preventive action to forestall pollution of controlled waters, to take remedial steps where pollution has already occurred, and to recover the reasonable costs of doing so from the person responsible. They are modelled on the provisions in s.46(4)–(7) of the C.O.P.A. 1974, which were confined to inland waters.

The initial provisions of s.46 of C.O.P.A. 1974 have not been repeated here. They gave a general power to remedy and restore waters where pollution has been caused by consented discharges. These provisions were never brought into force, and reliance has now been placed on making more effective the preventive mechanisms such as those under ss.92 and 93.

Subs. (1)

Likely to enter any controlled waters. The phrase implies that there should be some degree of proximity, in both time and space. The NRA could, for example, use these powers to remove leaky oil drums deposited near a river bank, but they would be inappropriate where the risk of entry of polluting matters into the waters is slight. Powers of entry on to premises to exercise these powers are available under s.169.

Subs. (2)

Any discharge in pursuance of a consent. The NRA is not entitled under this section to do anything to impede the continuation of a consented discharge even if it has caused or is likely to continue to cause pollution. If that is the case, it should seek a revocation or variation of the consent (Sched. 10, paras. 6 and 7).

Other powers to deal with foul water and pollution

162.—(1) Without prejudice to the powers conferred by section 161 above and subsections (2) and (3) below, the Authority shall have power, on any land—

(a) which belongs to the Authority; or

(b) over or in which the Authority has acquired the necessary easements or rights,

to construct and maintain drains, sewers, watercourses, catchpits and other works for the purpose of intercepting, treating or disposing of any foul water arising or flowing on that land or of otherwise preventing any such pollution as is mentioned in section 159(6)(b) above.

(2) Subject to the following provisions of this Part, the Authority shall, for the purpose of carrying out its functions, have power—

(a) to carry out in a street all such works as are requisite for securing that the water in any relevant waterworks is not polluted or otherwise contaminated; and

(b) to carry out any works requisite for, or incidental to, the purposes of any works falling within paragraph (a) above, including for those purposes the following kinds of works, that is to say—

    (i) breaking up or opening a street;

    (ii) tunnelling or boring under a street;

    (iii) breaking up or opening a sewer, drain or tunnel;

    (iv) moving or removing earth and other materials;

and the provisions of section 159 above shall, so far as applicable, have effect in relation to the powers conferred by this subsection as they have effect in relation to the powers conferred by subsection (1) of that section.

(3) Subject to the following provisions of this Part, the Authority shall, for the purpose of carrying out its functions, have power—

(a) to carry out on any land which is not in, under or over a street all such works as are requisite for securing that the water in any relevant waterworks is not polluted or otherwise contaminated; and

(b) to carry out any works requisite for, or incidental to, the purposes of any works falling within paragraph (a) above;

and the provisions of section 160 above shall, so far as applicable, have effect in relation to the powers conferred by this subsection as they have effect in relation to the powers conferred by subsection (1) of that section.

(4) Without prejudice to the provisions of sections 178 to 184 below, nothing in subsection (1) above shall authorise the Authority, without the consent of the navigation authority in question, to intercept or take any water which a navigation authority are authorised to take or use for the purposes of their undertaking.

(5) Any dispute as to whether any consent for the purposes of subsection (4) above is being unreasonably withheld shall be referred to the arbitration of a single arbitrator to be appointed by agreement between the parties to the dispute or, in default of agreement, by the President of the Institution of Civil Engineers.

(6) In this section—

"relevant waterworks" means any waterworks which contain water which is or may be used by a water undertaker for providing a supply of water to any premises;

"service pipe" and "water main" have the same meanings as in the Water Industry Act 1991;

"waterworks" includes any water main, resource main, service pipe or discharge pipe and any spring, well, adit, borehole, service reservoir or tank.

<small>DEFINITIONS</small>

  "drains": s.221(1).

  "navigation authority": s.221(1).

  "relevant waterworks": subs. (6).

  "service pipe": subs. (6).

  "sewers": s.221(1).

  "street": s.221(1).

  "the Authority": s.221(1).

"underground strata": s.221(1).
"water main": subs. (6).
"watercourse": s.221(1).

GENERAL NOTE
Section 162 is an enabling power allowing the Authority to carry out anti-pollution work on its own land or on land over which it possesses easements or other rights.

Subs. (1)
Without prejudice to the powers conferred by s.161 above. The reference is to the powers to carry out remedial works in response to pollution incidents.

Powers to discharge water

Discharges for works purposes

163.—(1) Subject to the following provisions of this section and to section 164 below, where the Authority—

(a) is carrying out, or is about to carry out, the construction, alteration, repair, cleaning, or examination of any reservoir, well, borehole or other work belonging to or used by the Authority for the purposes of, or in connection with, the carrying out of any of its functions; or

(b) is exercising or about to exercise any power conferred by section 159, 160 or 162(2) or (3) above,

the Authority may cause the water in any relevant pipe or in any such reservoir, well, borehole or other work to be discharged into any available watercourse.

(2) Nothing in this section shall authorise any discharge which—

(a) damages or injuriously affects the works or property of any railway company or navigation authority; or

(b) floods or damages any highway.

(3) If the Authority fails to take all necessary steps to secure that any water discharged by it under this section is as free as may be reasonably practicable from—

(a) mud and silt;

(b) solid, polluting, offensive or injurious substances; and

(c) any substances prejudicial to fish or spawn, or to spawning beds or food of fish,

it shall be guilty of an offence and liable, on summary conviction, to a fine not exceeding level 3 on the standard scale.

(4) In this section—

"railway company" means the British Railways Board, London Regional Transport or any other person authorised by any enactment, or by any order, rule or regulation made under any enactment, to construct, work or carry on a railway; and

"relevant pipe" has the same meaning as in section 159 above.

DEFINITIONS
"functions": s.3.
"highway": s.221(1).
"navigation authority": s.221(1).
"railway company": subs. (4).
"relevant pipe": subs. (4).
"the Authority": s.221(1).

GENERAL NOTE

Subs. (4)
This subsection gives effect to one of the recommendations of the Law Commission (Law Com. No. 198) to alter the wording of the Water Act 1989 (s.160(3)(h)) from persons whose authorisation is conferred "by" an enactment to include the wider wording of "or by any order, rule or regulation made under any enactment". This change brings the definition of a railway company into agreement with that in the Public Health Act 1936. The Law Commission gave

this as their reason for making the recommendation: "it seems unlikely that Parliament was intending in the 1989 Act to exclude any railway undertakers who are afforded protection under the provisions left in the 1936 Act from protection under the 1989 Act".

Consents for certain discharges under section 163

164.—(1) Except in an emergency, no discharge through any pipe the diameter of which exceeds 229 millimetres shall be made under section 163 above except with such consent as may be prescribed.

(2) Where the Authority makes an application to any person for a consent for the purposes of this section—

(a) that application shall be accompanied or supplemented by all such information as that person may reasonably require; and

(b) the Authority shall serve a copy of the application, and of any consent given on that application, on every person who—

    (i) is registered with the Authority in respect of any premises which are within three miles of the place where the discharge to which the application relates is proposed to be made and are not upstream from that place; and

    (ii) has not agreed in writing that he need not be served with such a copy;

but, subject to subsection (4) below and without prejudice to the effect (if any) of any other contravention of the requirements of this section in relation to such an application, a failure to provide information in pursuance of the obligation to supplement such an application shall not invalidate the application.

(3) Subject to subsection (4) below, an application for a consent for the purposes of this section shall be determined—

(a) in the case of an application with respect to a particular discharge, before the end of the period of seven days beginning with the day after the application is made; and

(b) in any other case, before the end of the period of three months beginning with that day;

and, subject to that subsection, where an application for any consent is required to be determined within the period specified in paragraph (a) above and is not so determined, the consent applied for shall be deemed to have been given unconditionally.

(4) Where—

(a) the Authority, having made an application to any person for a consent for the purposes of this section, has failed to comply with its obligation under subsection (2)(a) above to supplement that application with information required by that person; and

(b) that requirement was made by that person at such a time before the end of the period within which he is required to determine the application as gave the Authority a reasonable opportunity to provide the required information within that period,

that person may delay his determination of the application until a reasonable time after the required information is provided.

(5) A consent for the purposes of this section may relate to a particular discharge or to discharges of a particular description and may be made subject to such reasonable conditions as may be specified by the person giving it; but a consent for those purposes shall not be unreasonably withheld.

(6) Any dispute as to whether a consent for the purposes of this section should be given or withheld, or as to whether the conditions to which any such consent is made subject are reasonable, shall be referred to the arbitration of a single arbitrator appointed by agreement between the parties to the dispute or, in default of agreement, by the President of the Institution of Civil Engineers.

(7) Where any discharge under section 163 above is made in an emergency without the consent which, if there were no emergency, would be required by virtue of this section, the Authority shall, as soon as practicable after making the discharge, serve a notice which—
 (a) states that the discharge has been made; and
 (b) gives such particulars of the discharge and of the emergency as the persons served with the notice might reasonably require,
on every person on whom the Authority would have been required to serve the application for that consent or any copy of that application.

(8) If the Authority contravenes, without reasonable excuse, any of the requirements of this section or any condition of a consent given for the purposes of this section, it shall be guilty of an offence and liable, on summary conviction, to a fine not exceeding level 3 on the standard scale.

(9) Nothing in this section shall require any consent to be obtained, or any notice to be served, in respect of any discharge if the requirements of section 34 of the Water Act 1945 (temporary discharges into watercourses) in relation to that discharge had been satisfied before September 1, 1989.

DEFINITIONS
 "pipe": s.221(2).
 "the Authority": s.221(1).

GENERAL NOTE
 The effect of this section is to require the NRA to serve a copy of its application to make a discharge for works purposes, with explanatory information (subs. (2)(a)), on any person registered with the Authority within three miles of the site of the proposed discharge (unless they are upstream of the site) (subs. (2)(b)). If the Authority makes a discharge in an emergency it has to notify those people to whom it would have had to apply for consent (subs. (7)). Disputes are to be referred to arbitration (subs. (6)) and any contravention of the section by the Authority is made a summary criminal offence (subs. (8)).

Flood defence and drainage works

General powers to carry out flood defence and drainage works

165.—(1) The Authority shall have power, in connection with a main river—
 (a) to maintain existing works, that is to say, to cleanse, repair or otherwise maintain in a due state of efficiency any existing watercourse or any drainage work;
 (b) to improve any existing works, that is to say, to deepen, widen, straighten or otherwise improve any existing watercourse or remove or alter mill dams, weirs or other obstructions to watercourses, or raise, widen or otherwise improve any existing drainage work;
 (c) to construct new works, that is to say, to make any new watercourse or drainage work or erect any machinery or do any other act (other than an act referred to in paragraph (a) or (b) above) required for the drainage of any land.

(2) The Authority shall also have power, irrespective of whether the works are in connection with a main river, to maintain, improve or construct drainage works for the purpose of defence against sea water or tidal water; and that power shall be exercisable both above and below the low-water mark.

(3) The Authority may construct all such works and do all such things in the sea or in any estuary as may, in its opinion, be necessary to secure an adequate outfall for a main river.

(4) The Authority may by agreement with any person carry out, improve or maintain, at that person's expense, any drainage works which that person is entitled to carry out, improve or maintain; but for the purposes of this subsection the expense to be borne by that person shall not include the

amount of any grant paid under section 149(3) above in respect of the works in question.

(5) The Authority may enter into an agreement with any local authority or with any navigation authority for the carrying out by that authority, on such terms as to payment or otherwise as may be specified in the agreement, of any work in connection with a main river which the Authority is authorised to carry out.

(6) Nothing in subsections (1) to (3) above authorises any person to enter on the land of any person except for the purpose of maintaining existing works.

(7) In this section "watercourse" has the same meaning as in Part IV of this Act; and subsections (2) and (3) of section 113 above shall apply for the purposes of determining any question arising under this section as to—

(a) whether any work is a drainage work in connection with a main river; or

(b) whether any proposed work will, if constructed, be such a drainage work,

as they apply for the purposes of that Part.

DEFINITIONS
"main river": s.221(1).
"navigation authority": s.221(1).
"the Authority": s.221(1).
"watercourse": subs. (7).

Power to carry out works for purpose of providing flood warning system

166.—(1) Without prejudice to its other powers by virtue of section 4 above, Part IV of this Act and this Part, the Authority shall have power—

(a) to provide and operate flood warning systems;

(b) to provide, install and maintain apparatus required for the purposes of such systems;

(c) to carry out any other engineering or building operations so required.

(2) Subsection (1) above shall not be construed as authorising, on the part of the Authority, any act or omission which, apart from that subsection, would be actionable at the suit of any person on any grounds other than a limitation imposed by law on the capacity of the Authority by virtue of its constitution.

(3) The Authority may exercise the powers conferred by subsection (1)(b) or (c) above in an area in Scotland as if—

(a) its functions in relation to the areas of the regional flood defence committees whose areas are adjacent to Scotland were functions in relation to that area in Scotland; and

(b) that area in Scotland were included in the areas of each of those committees;

but the powers conferred by this subsection are subject (except in the case of a power to maintain apparatus) to prior consultation with the local authority (within the meaning of section 1 of the Flood Prevention (Scotland) Act 1961) for the area in Scotland in question.

(4) In this section "flood warning system" has the same meaning as in section 148 above.

DEFINITIONS
"flood warning system": subs. (4).
"the Authority": s.221(1).

Power to dispose of spoil in connection with flood defence works

167.—(1) Subject to subsection (2) below, the Authority may—

(a) without making payment for it appropriate and dispose of any matter

removed in the course of the carrying out of any work for widening, deepening or dredging any watercourse; and
(b) deposit any matter so removed on the banks of the watercourse, or on such width of land adjoining the watercourse as is sufficient to enable the matter in question to be removed and deposited by mechanical means in one operation.

(2) Subsection (1) above shall not authorise the deposit of any matter if the matter deposited would constitute a statutory nuisance within the meaning of Part III of the Environmental Protection Act 1990.

(3) The Authority and the council of any district or London borough may enter into an agreement providing—
(a) for the disposal by the council of any matter removed as mentioned in subsection (1) above; and
(b) for the payment by the Authority to the council, in respect of the disposal of the matter by the council, of such sum as may be provided by the agreement.

(4) In this section "banks" and "watercourse" have the same meanings as in Part IV of this Act.

DEFINITIONS
"banks": subs. (4) and s.113(1).
"the Authority": s.221(1).
"watercourse": subs. (4) and s.113(1).

Compulsory works orders

Compulsory works orders

168.—(1) Where the Authority is proposing, for the purposes of, or in connection with, the carrying out of any of its functions—
(a) to carry out any engineering or building operations; or
(b) to discharge water into any inland waters or underground strata,
the Authority may apply to either of the Ministers for an order under this section ("a compulsory works order").

(2) Subject to the following provisions of this section, the Ministers shall each have power, on an application under subsection (1) above, by order made by statutory instrument—
(a) to confer such compulsory powers; and
(b) to grant such authority,
as he considers necessary or expedient for the purpose of enabling any engineering or building operations or discharges of water to be carried out or made for the purposes of, or in connection with, the carrying out of the functions with respect to which the application was made.

(3) Schedule 19 to this Act shall have effect with respect to applications for compulsory works orders and with respect to such orders.

(4) Subject to the provisions of Schedule 19 to this Act, a compulsory works order may—
(a) without prejudice to section 154 above, confer power to acquire compulsorily any land, including—
(i) power to acquire interests in and rights over land by the creation of new rights and interests; and
(ii) power, by the compulsory acquisition by the Authority of any rights over land which is to be or has been acquired by the Authority, to extinguish any such rights;
(b) apply for the purposes of the order, either with or without modifications, any of the relevant provisions of this Part which do not apply for those purposes apart from by virtue of this paragraph;
(c) make any authority granted by the order subject to such conditions as may be specified in the order;

(d) amend or repeal any local statutory provision;
(e) contain such supplemental, consequential and transitional provision as the Minister making the order considers appropriate;
and section 156(1) above shall apply in relation to the powers conferred by virtue of this section as it applies in relation to the power conferred by section 154 above.

(5) Without prejudice to any duty imposed by virtue of section 184 below, where—
(a) either of the Ministers makes a compulsory works order authorising the Authority to carry out works for or in connection with the construction or operation of a reservoir or conferring compulsory powers for that purpose on the Authority; and
(b) it appears to him that the works to be carried out may permanently affect the area in which they are situated and are not primarily intended to benefit the inhabitants of that area,
he may include in the order provision with respect to facilities for recreation or other leisure-time occupation for the benefit of those inhabitants.

(6) Nothing in any compulsory works order shall exempt the Authority from any restriction imposed by Chapter II of Part II of this Act.

(7) It is hereby declared that a compulsory works order may grant authority for discharges of water by the Authority where the Authority has no power to take water, or to require discharges to be made, from the inland waters or other source from which the discharges authorised by the order are intended to be made; but nothing in so much of any such order as grants authority for any discharges of water shall have the effect of conferring any such power.

(8) In this section the reference to the relevant provisions of this Part is a reference to the provisions of this Part except sections 155 to 158 and 165 to 167 above.

DEFINITIONS
"functions": s.3.
"inland waters": s.221(1).
"the Authority": s.221(1).
"the Ministers": s.221(1).
"underground strata": s.221(1).

GENERAL NOTE

Subs. (4)
Section 154 gives the Authority its power of compulsory purchase of land required for the carrying out of its functions; s.156(1) extends that power to include dams, weirs or sections of bank required for fisheries purposes. The effect of incorporating s.156 in subs. (4) is therefore to include fisheries works in the area of works that can be enforced using a compulsory works order.

Subs. (5)
Without prejudice to any duty imposed by virtue of s.184 below. Section 184 imposes a duty on the Authority to make recreational facilities available when building reservoirs in Wales.

CHAPTER II

POWERS OF ENTRY

Powers of entry for enforcement purposes

169.—(1) Any person designated in writing for the purpose by either of the Ministers or by the Authority may—
(a) enter any premises or vessel for the purpose of ascertaining whether any provision of an enactment to which this section applies, of any subordinate legislation or other instrument made by virtue of any such enactment or of any byelaws made by the Authority is being or has been contravened; and

(b) carry out such inspections, measurements and tests on any premises
or vessel entered by that person or of any articles found on any such
premises or vessel, and take away such samples of water or effluent or
of any land or articles, as that Minister or the Authority—
     (i) considers appropriate for the purpose mentioned in para-
graph (a) above; and
     (ii) has authorised that person to carry out or take away.

(2) The powers which by virtue of subsection (1) above are conferred in
relation to any premises for the purpose of enabling either of the Ministers
or the Authority to determine whether any provision made by or under any
of the water pollution provisions of this Act is being or has been contravened
shall include power, in order to obtain the information on which that
determination may be made—
(a) to carry out experimental borings or other works on those premises;
and
(b) to install and keep monitoring and other apparatus there.

(3) This section applies to any enactment contained in this Act and to any
other enactment under or for the purposes of which the Authority carries
out functions.

DEFINITIONS
"enactment": s.221(1).
"the Authority": s.221(1).
"the Ministers": s.221(1).
"vessel": s.221(1).

GENERAL NOTE
This section gives powers of entry and inspection to persons authorised by the Ministers and
the NRA in connection with their functions under Pts. II–V of the Act (pollution control, water
resource management, flood defence and land drainage, and fishery protection), the Water
Resources Act 1963, the Land Drainage Act 1976, and any other piece of legislation under
which the Authority carries out a function (subs. (3)). The powers are wide, but are based on
ss.111–113 of the Water Resources Act 1963 (which were repealed under Sched. 24 of the 1989
Act) and ss.91 and 92 of the C.O.P.A. 1974 (which remain in force).

Power of entry for certain works purposes

170.—(1) Any person designated in writing for the purpose by the
Authority may enter any premises for any of the purposes specified in
subsection (2) below.

(2) The purposes mentioned in subsection (1) above are—
(a) the carrying out of any survey or tests for the purpose of
determining—
     (i) whether it is appropriate and practicable for the Authority
to exercise any relevant works power; or
     (ii) how any such power should be exercised;
(b) the exercise of any such power.

(3) The power by virtue of subsection (1) above of a person designated by
the Authority to enter any premises for the purposes of carrying out any
survey or tests shall include power—
(a) to carry out experimental borings or other works for the purpose of
ascertaining the nature of the sub-soil; and
(b) to take away and analyse such samples of water or effluent or of any
land or articles as the Authority considers necessary for the purpose
of determining either of the matters mentioned in subsection (2)(a)
above and has authorised that person to take away and analyse.

(4) In this section "relevant works power" means any power conferred by
any of the provisions of sections 159, 160, 162(2) and (3) and 163 above.

DEFINITIONS
"effluent": s.221(1).

"relevant works power": subs. (4).
"the Authority": s.221(1).

Power to carry out surveys and to search for water

171.—(1) Without prejudice to the rights and powers conferred by the other provisions of this Chapter, any person designated in writing under this section by the Authority may enter any premises for any of the purposes specified in subsection (2) below.

(2) The purposes mentioned in subsection (1) above are the carrying out of any survey or tests for the purpose of determining—

(a) whether it would be appropriate for the Authority to acquire any land, or any interest or right in or over land, for purposes connected with the carrying out of its functions; or

(b) whether it would be appropriate for the Authority to apply for an order under section 168 above and what compulsory powers it would be appropriate to apply for under that section.

(3) The power by virtue of subsection (1) above of a person designated under this section to enter any premises for the purpose of carrying out any survey or tests shall include power—

(a) to carry out experimental borings or other works for the purpose of ascertaining the nature of the sub-soil, the presence of underground water in the sub-soil or the quantity or quality of any such water;

(b) to install and keep monitoring or other apparatus on the premises for the purpose of obtaining the information on which any such determination as is mentioned in subsection (2) above may be made; and

(c) to take away and analyse such samples of water or of any land or articles as the Authority considers necessary for any of the purposes so mentioned and has authorised that person to take away and analyse.

(4) The powers conferred by this section shall not be exercised in any case for purposes connected with the determination of—

(a) whether, where or how a reservoir should be constructed; or

(b) whether, where or how a borehole should be sunk for the purpose of abstracting water from or discharging water into any underground strata,

unless the Secretary of State has, in accordance with subsection (5) below, given his written authorisation in relation to that case for the exercise of those powers for those purposes.

(5) The Secretary of State shall not give his authorisation for the purposes of subsection (4) above unless—

(a) he is satisfied that notice of the proposal to apply for the authorisation has been given to the owner and to the occupier of the premises in question; and

(b) he has considered any representation or objections with respect to the proposed exercise of the powers under this section which—

(i) have been duly made to him by the owner or occupier of those premises, within the period of 14 days beginning with the day after the giving of the notice; and

(ii) have not been withdrawn.

DEFINITIONS
"notice": s.221(1).
"owner": s.221(1).
"the Authority": s.221(1).
"underground strata": s.221(1).

GENERAL NOTE
This section gives certain powers to representatives of the Authority to enter premises in order to carry out surveys and associated works to determine whether they should use powers of

compulsory purchase under s.154 or apply for a compulsory works order under s.168. The powers are based on those in s.8 of the Water Act 1948 (which was repealed by the 1989 Act), but consent of the Secretary of State is no longer required in all cases, being needed only where the circumstances in subs. (4) apply.

Powers of entry for other purposes

172.—(1) Any person designated in writing for the purpose by either of the Ministers or the Authority may enter any premises or vessel for the purpose of—

(a) determining whether, and if so in what manner, any power or duty conferred or imposed on either of the Ministers or on the Authority by virtue of any enactment to which this section applies (including a power of either or both of the Ministers to make subordinate legislation) should be exercised or, as the case may be, performed; or

(b) exercising or performing any power or duty which is so conferred or imposed.

(2) Any person designated in writing for the purpose by either of the Ministers or the Authority may—

(a) carry out such inspections, measurements and tests on any premises or vessel entered by that person under this section or of any articles found on any such premises or vessel; and

(b) take away such samples of water or effluent or of any land or articles, as that Minister or the Authority considers appropriate for any purpose mentioned in subsection (1) above and has authorised that person to carry out or take away.

(3) The powers which by virtue of subsections (1) and (2) above are conferred in relation to any premises for the purpose of enabling either of the Ministers or the Authority to determine whether or in what manner to exercise or perform any power or duty conferred or imposed on him or it by or under the water pollution provisions of this Act shall include power, in order to obtain the information on which that determination may be made—

(a) to carry out experimental borings or other works on those premises; and

(b) to install and keep monitoring and other apparatus there.

(4) This section applies to any enactment contained in this Act and to any other enactment under or for the purposes of which the Authority carries out functions.

DEFINITIONS
  "enactment": s.221(1).
  "the Authority": s.221(1).
  "the Ministers": s.221(1).
  "vessel": s.221(1).

GENERAL NOTE
  This section adds general powers of entry to those contained in the preceding three sections. The wording of subs. (1)(a) is extremely broad and gives the Authority and the Ministers a wide discretion to authorise entry.

Powers of entry: supplemental provisions

173. Schedule 20 to this Act shall have effect with respect to the powers of entry and related powers which are conferred by the preceding provisions of this Chapter.

GENERAL NOTE
  Sched. 20 covers the requirement to serve a notice before exercising any of the powers of entry available, otherwise than in an emergency, the power to apply for a warrant, the duty to secure premises after entry, compensation for loss and damage and the summary offence of obstructing a person exercising a power of entry.

Impersonation of persons exercising powers of entry

174.—(1) A person who, without having been designated or authorised for the purpose by the Authority, purports to be entitled to enter any premises or vessel in exercise of a power exercisable in pursuance of any such designation or authorisation shall be guilty of an offence and liable, on summary conviction, to a fine not exceeding level 4 on the standard scale.

(2) For the purposes of this section it shall be immaterial, where a person purports to be entitled to enter any premises or vessel, that the power which that person purports to be entitled to exercise does not exist, or would not be exercisable, even if that person had been designated or authorised by the Authority.

DEFINITIONS
  "the Authority": s.221(1).
  "vessel": s.221(1).

GENERAL NOTE
  This is a new offence. Although it is primarily aimed at impersonation, it could also be applicable to officers of the Authority who attempt to enter without proper designation or authorisation.

CHAPTER III

PROVISIONS SUPPLEMENTAL TO LAND AND WORKS POWERS

Vesting of pipes in the Authority

Vesting of pipes in the Authority

175.—(1) Subject to any provision to the contrary contained in an agreement between the Authority and the person in whom an interest in the pipe is or is to be vested, every pipe which—
  (a) is a relevant pipe for the purposes of section 159 or 160 above; and
  (b) has been laid, in exercise of any power conferred by Chapter I of this Part or otherwise, by the Authority,
shall vest in the Authority.

(2) Subsection (1) above is without prejudice to the vesting of anything in the Authority by virtue of the exercise by the Authority of any power to acquire property by agreement or compulsorily.

DEFINITIONS
  "pipes": s.221(2).
  "relevant pipe": s.160(4).
  "the Authority": s.221(1).

GENERAL NOTE
  This section should be read in conjunction with ss.159 and 160, which give wide powers to the Authority to lay pipes and sewers. It provides for the vesting of pipes and other works in the Authority.

Offence of interference with works etc.

Offence of interference with works etc.

176.—(1) Subject to subsection (2) below, if any person without the consent of the Authority—
  (a) intentionally or recklessly interferes with any resource main or other pipe vested in the Authority or with any structure, installation or apparatus belonging to the Authority; or
  (b) by any act or omission negligently interferes with any such main or

other pipe or with any such structure, installation or apparatus so as to damage it or so as to have an effect on its use or operation,
that person shall be guilty of an offence and liable, on summary conviction, to a fine not exceeding level 3 on the standard scale.

(2) A person shall not be guilty of an offence under subsection (1) above—

(a) by reason of anything done in an emergency to prevent loss or damage to persons or property; or

(b) by reason of his opening or closing the stopcock fitted to a service pipe by means of which water is supplied to any premises by a water undertaker if—

(i) he has obtained the consent of every consumer whose supply is affected by the opening or closing of that stopcock or, as the case may be, of every other consumer whose supply is so affected; and

(ii) in the case of opening a stopcock, the stopcock was closed otherwise than by the undertaker.

(3) Any person who without the consent of the Authority—

(a) attaches any pipe or apparatus to any resource main or other pipe vested in the Authority; or

(b) subject to subsection (4) below, uses any pipe or apparatus which has been attached or altered in contravention of this section,
shall be guilty of an offence and liable, on summary conviction, to a fine not exceeding level 3 on the standard scale.

(4) In proceedings against any person for an offence by virtue of paragraph (b) of subsection (3) above it shall be a defence for that person to show that he did not know, and had no grounds for suspecting, that the pipe or apparatus in question had been attached or altered as mentioned in that subsection.

(5) An offence under subsection (1) or (3) above shall constitute a breach of a duty owed to the Authority; and any such breach of duty which causes the Authority to sustain loss or damage shall be actionable at the suit of the Authority.

(6) The amount recoverable by virtue of subsection (5) above from a person who has committed an offence under subsection (3) above shall include such amount as may be reasonable in respect of any water wasted, misused or improperly consumed in consequence of the commission of the offence.

(7) In this section "service pipe" and "stopcock" have the same meanings as in the Water Industry Act 1991, and "consumer" has the same meaning as in Part III of that Act.

DEFINITIONS
"consumer": subs. (7).
"pipe": s.221(2).
"resource main": s.186(1).
"service pipe": subs. (7).
"stop-cock": subs. (7).
"the Authority": s.221(1).

GENERAL NOTE
The offences created in this section are derived from ss.67 and 68 of Sched. 3 to the Water Act 1945, which was repealed by the Water Act 1989.

Subs. (3)
Attaches any pipe or apparatus. A prior version of this offence was held to apply to a hose-pipe temporarily attached to a pipe without consent (*Cambridge University and Town Waterworks Co.* v. *Hancock* (1910) 103 L.T. 562).

Compensation etc. in respect of exercise of works powers

Compensation etc. in respect of exercise of works powers

177. Schedule 21 to this Act shall have effect for making provision for imposing obligations as to the payment of compensation in respect of the exercise of the powers conferred on the Authority by sections 159 to 167 above and otherwise for minimising the damage caused by the exercise of those powers.

DEFINITION
"the Authority": s.221(1).

Protective provisions

Protection for particular undertakings

178. Schedule 22 to this Act shall have effect for the protection of particular undertakings in connection with the carrying out of works and other activities by the Authority.

DEFINITION
"the Authority": s.221(1).

GENERAL NOTE
Sched. 22 is an important provision prohibiting the Authority from carrying out works which would interfere with the carrying out of the functions of a wide range of undertakings specified in para. 1(4) without the consent of the body concerned. The interests of the Authority are protected by requiring that consent shall not be unreasonably withheld. The provisions of the Public Utilities Street Works Act 1950 continue to apply to works involving the breaking up of streets.

Protective provisions in respect of flood defence works and watercourses etc.

179.—(1) Nothing in this Act shall confer power on any person to do anything, except with the consent of the person who so uses them, which interferes—

(a) with any sluices, floodgates, groynes, sea defences or other works used by any person for draining, preserving or improving any land under any local statutory provision; or

(b) with any such works used by any person for irrigating any land.

(2) Where the Authority proposes, otherwise than in exercise of any compulsory powers—

(a) to construct or alter any such inland waters in any internal drainage district as do not form part of a main river; or

(b) to construct or alter any works on or in any such inland waters,

the Authority shall consult the internal drainage board for that district before doing so.

(3) A consent for the purposes of subsection (1) above may be given subject to reasonable conditions but shall not be unreasonably withheld.

(4) Any dispute—

(a) as to whether anything done or proposed to be done interferes or will interfere as mentioned in subsection (1) above;

(b) as to whether any consent for the purposes of this section is being unreasonably withheld; or

(c) as to whether any condition subject to which any such consent has been given was reasonable,

shall be referred to the arbitration of a single arbitrator to be appointed by agreement between the parties or, in default of agreement, by the President of the Institution of Civil Engineers.

(5) The provisions of this section shall be without prejudice to the provisions of Schedule 22 to this Act.

DEFINITIONS
"inland waters": s.221(1).
"local statutory provision": s.221(1).
"main river": s.221(1).
"the Authority": s.221(1).

GENERAL NOTE
This section protects flood and sea defences from any of the Act's provisions that might otherwise give the Authority power to carry out works that would interfere with them. However, the Authority is protected by subs. (3), which states that if a consent to works that do so interfere is requested, it shall not be unreasonably withheld. Disputes are to be referred to arbitration (subs. (4)).

Power of navigation authorities etc. to divert the Authority's watercourses

180.—(1) Where any watercourses under the control of the Authority pass under or interfere with, or with the improvement or alteration of, any river, canal, dock, harbour, basin or other work (including any towing-path adjacent thereto) which belongs to or is under the jurisdiction of any relevant authority, the relevant authority may, at their own expense and on substituting for those watercourses other equally effective watercourses—
   (a) take up, divert or alter the level of those watercourses; and
   (b) do all such matters and things as may be necessary in connection with the works authorised to be done by them under this section.

(2) If any question arises under this section between the Authority and any relevant authority as to whether any watercourses substituted or proposed to be substituted by the relevant authority for any existing watercourses are as effective as the existing watercourses, that question shall be referred to the arbitration of a single arbitrator appointed by agreement between the parties or, in default of agreement, by the President of the Institution of Civil Engineers on the application of either party.

(3) In this section—
   "relevant authority" means any navigation authority, harbour authority or conservancy authority; and
   "watercourse" has the same meaning as in Part IV of this Act.

DEFINITIONS
"conservancy authority": s.221(1).
"harbour authority": s.221(1).
"navigation authority": s.221(1).
"relevant authority": subs. (3).
"the Authority": s.221(1).
"watercourses": subs. (3) and s.113(1).

GENERAL NOTE
This section gives navigation, harbour and conservancy authorities the power to divert watercourses controlled by the NRA, on condition that they provide an adequate alternative. Disputes are to be referred to arbitration (subs. (2)).

Works in tidal lands etc.

181.—(1) Nothing in any of the provisions of this Part relating to any relevant works power shall authorise the Authority to carry out any works at any place below the place to which the tide flows at mean high water springs, except in accordance with such plans and sections, and subject to such restrictions, as may, before the works are commenced, have been approved by the Secretary of State.

(2) An approval for the purposes of subsection (1) above shall be given to the Authority by the service on the Authority of a notice containing the approval.

(3) Section 38 of the Salmon and Freshwater Fisheries Act 1975 (tidal lands etc.) shall apply to any proposed construction, alteration or extension

under section 156 above as it applies to any proposed construction, alteration or extension under that Act.

(4) Section 74 of the Land Drainage Act 1991 (application to Crown and tidal lands), so far as it relates to lands below the high-water mark of ordinary spring tides shall apply, as it applies in relation to that Act, to the flood defence provisions of this Act.

(5) In subsection (1) above the reference to a relevant works power is a reference to a power conferred by any of sections 159, 160, 162(2) and (3) and 163 above.

DEFINITIONS
  "notice": s.221(1).
  "relevant works power": subs. (5).
  "the Authority": s.221(1).

GENERAL NOTE
  Any works that are contemplated by the Authority anywhere below the high water mark are excluded by this section from any of the preceding general works powers; as a result they will always require the approval of the Secretary of State.

Subs. (3)
  Section 156 extends the Authority's powers of compulsory purchase to include dams, weirs and river banks required by the Authority for fisheries purposes. This subsection extends the provisions concerning tidal land in the Salmon and Freshwater Fisheries Act 1975 to any land acquired by the Authority under s.156.

Mineral rights

182. Schedule 23 to this Act (which makes provision with respect to the acquisition of mineral rights by the Authority and with respect to the working of mines and minerals where pipes, sewers or other related works are affected) shall have effect and, in the case of the compulsory acquisition of land by virtue of this Act, shall have effect instead of Schedule 2 to the Acquisition of Land Act 1981 (mineral rights etc. in relation to compulsory purchase orders).

DEFINITIONS
  "pipes": s.221(2).
  "sewer": s.221(1).
  "the Authority": s.221(1).

GENERAL NOTE
  Sched. 23 is taken from Sched. 20 of the 1989 Act, which replaced the provisions in Pt. IV of Sched. 3 of the Water Act 1945 concerning minerals and works conducted by water undertakers, and those in the Acquisition of Land Act 1981 concerning mineral rights in compulsorily purchased land.

Saving for planning controls etc.

183.—(1) Without prejudice to the operation of section 90 of the Town and Country Planning Act 1990 (planning permission deemed to be granted in certain cases) in relation to any provision made by or under this Act or any other enactment which by virtue of this Act or the Water Act 1989 relates to the functions of the Authority, nothing in this Act or in any such enactment shall be construed as authorising the carrying out of any development (within the meaning of that Act of 1990) without the grant of such planning permission as may be required by that Act of 1990.

(2) Nothing in the flood defence provisions of this Act shall authorise any person to carry out any works or do anything in contravention of any of the provisions of the Ancient Monuments and Archaelogical Areas Act 1979.

DEFINITIONS
  "enactment": s.221(1).

"the Authority": s.221(1).
"water undertaker": ss.11 and 189(1).

GENERAL NOTE
This section provides for a general saving of the requirements of the Town and Country Planning Act 1990 in relation to developments by the Authority. The Authority and water and sewerage undertakers were deemed to be statutory undertakers for specified provisions of the Town and Country Planning Act 1971 by the 1989 Act (Sched. 25, para. 1(2)(xvi) of that Act). The general development order will continue to grant deemed planning permission for a range of developments connected with the Authority's functions.

Duties to make recreational facilities available when building reservoirs in Wales

184.—(1) Where the Authority carries out any works for or in connection with the construction or operation of a reservoir in Wales which—
  (a) permanently affect one or more communities; and
  (b) are not primarily intended by the Authority to benefit the inhabitants of that or those communities,
it shall be the duty of the Authority to make available facilities for recreation or other leisure-time occupation for the benefit of those inhabitants or to assist others to make such facilities available.
  (2) It shall be the duty of the Authority, in performing its duty under subsection (1) above, to consult—
  (a) the community councils of the communities affected, in the case of communities having such councils; and
  (b) in any case, the council of any district in which any community affected is situated.

DEFINITION
"the Authority": s.221(1).

GENERAL NOTE
This section is based on ss.20 and 21 of the Water Act 1973, which were repealed by the Water Act 1989, but, unlike those provisions, is restricted to reservoirs.

Savings in respect of existing drainage obligations

Savings in respect of existing drainage obligations

185.—(1) Nothing in the flood defence provisions of this Act shall operate to release any person from an obligation to which section 21 of the Land Drainage Act 1991 applies.
  (2) The functions of the Authority as respects the doing of any work under the flood defence provisons of this Act are not to be treated as in any way limited by the fact that some other person is under an obligation, by reason of tenure, custom, prescription or otherwise, to do that work.

DEFINITIONS
"functions": s.3.
"the Authority": s.221(1).

GENERAL NOTE
This section operates to preserve existing drainage obligations, reproduced in the Land Drainage Act 1991 from the Land Drainage Act 1976, and to ensure that the Authority's flood defence functions are not restricted by any existing obligations of any sort on any person.

Interpretation of Part VII

Interpretation of Part VII

186.—(1) In this Part—

"discharge pipe" means a pipe from which discharges are or are to be made under section 163 above;

"resource main" means any pipe, not being a trunk main within the meaning of the Water Industry Act 1991, which is or is to be used for the purpose of—

    (a) conveying water from one source of supply to another, from a source of supply to a regulating reservoir or from a regulating reservoir to a source of supply; or

    (b) giving or taking a supply of water in bulk.

(2) In subsection (1) above—

"source of supply" shall be construed without reference to the definition of that expression in section 221 below; and

"supply of water in bulk" has the same meaning as in section 3 above.

(3) The powers conferred by Chapter I of this Part shall be without prejudice to the powers conferred on the Authority by any other enactment or by any agreement.

DEFINITIONS
  "enactment": s.221(1).
  "pipe": s.221(2).
  "the Authority": s.221(1).

PART VIII

INFORMATION PROVISIONS

Annual report and publication of information

Annual report of the Authority

187.—(1) As soon as reasonably practicable after the end of each financial year the Authority shall prepare a report on its activities during that year and shall send a copy of that report to each of the Ministers.

(2) Every such report shall set out any directions under section 5 above which have been given to the Authority during the year to which the report relates.

(3) The Secretary of State shall lay a copy of every such report before each House of Parliament and shall arrange for copies of every such report to be published in such manner as he considers appropriate.

(4) The Authority's annual report shall be in such form and contain such information as may be specified in any direction given to the Authority by the Ministers.

DEFINITION
  "the Ministers": s.221(1).

GENERAL NOTE
  The restrictions on disclosure (s.204) do not apply to material contained in this or any other report of the Authority (s.204(4)).

Duty of Authority to publish certain information

188. It shall be the duty of the Authority—

(a) to collate and publish information from which assessments can be made of the actual and prospective demand for water, and of actual and prospective water resources, in England and Wales; and

(b) so far as it considers it appropriate to do so, to collaborate with others in collating and publishing any such information or any similar information in relation to places outside England and Wales.

DEFINITION
  "the Authority": s.221(1).

This section imposes a duty on the Authority to carry out research relating to its functions, whether by itself and or contracted out. The duty to publish the material under this section should assist water undertakers in performing their basic supply duty under s.37 of the Water Industry Act 1991.

Registers etc. to be kept by the Authority

Register of abstraction and impounding licences

189.—(1) The Authority shall keep, in such manner as may be prescribed, registers containing such information as may be prescribed with respect—
   (a) to applications made for the grant, revocation or variation of licences under Chapter II of Part II of this Act, including information as to the way in which such applications have been dealt with; and
   (b) to persons becoming the holders of such licences by virtue of section 49 above of this Act or regulations made under section 50 above.
   (2) Every register kept by the Authority under this section shall also contain such information as may be prescribed with respect—
   (a) to applications made in accordance with regulations under section 64 above; and
   (b) to licences granted or deemed to be granted, and licences revoked or varied, in accordance with regulations made under that section.
   (3) Subject to any regulations under this section, the information which the Authority is required to keep in registers under this section shall continue to include the information which immediately before September 1, 1989, was contained in a register kept by a water authority under section 53 of the Water Resources Act 1963.
   (4) The contents of every register kept under this section shall be available, at such place as may be prescribed, for inspection by the public at all reasonable hours.

DEFINITION
   "the Authority": s.221(1).

GENERAL NOTE
   The registers that the Authority is obliged to keep must include information on applications to abstract and impound water (subs. (1)(a)), licences that have been gained by succession where land changes hands (subs. (1)(b)) and licences granted or deemed to be granted to the Authority itself by the Secretary of State (subs. (2)).
   Details of the information that is to be held in the registers are set out in the Water Resources (Licences) Regulations 1965 (S.I. 1965 No. 574, reg. 17).

Pollution control register

190.—(1) It shall be the duty of the Authority to maintain, in accordance with regulations made by the Secretary of State, registers containing prescribed particulars of—
   (a) any notices of water quality objectives or other notices served under section 83 above;
   (b) applications made for consents under Chapter II of Part III of this Act;
   (c) consents given under that Chapter and the conditions to which the consents are subject;
   (d) certificates issued under paragraph 1(7) of Schedule 10 to this Act;
   (e) the following, that is to say—
           (i) samples of water or effluent taken by the Authority for the purposes of any of the water pollution provisions of this Act;
           (ii) information produced by analyses of those samples;

(iii) such information with respect to samples of water or effluent taken by any other person, and the analyses of those samples, as is acquired by the Authority from any person under arrangements made by the Authority for the purposes of any of those provisions; and

(iv) the steps taken in consequence of any such information as is mentioned in any of sub-paragraphs (i) to (iii) above;

and

(f) any matter about which particulars are required to be kept in any register under section 20 of the Environmental Protection Act 1990 (particulars about authorisations for prescribed processes etc.) by the chief inspector under Part I of that Act.

(2) It shall be the duty of the Authority—

(a) to secure that the contents of registers maintained by the Authority under this section are available, at all reasonable times, for inspection by the public free of charge; and

(b) to afford members of the public reasonable facilities for obtaining from the Authority, on payment of reasonable charges, copies of entries in any of the registers.

(3) Section 101 above shall have effect in relation to any regulations under this section as it has effect in relation to any subordinate legislation under Part III of this Act.

DEFINITIONS
"effluent": s.221(1).
"prescribed": s.221(1).
"the Authority": s.221(1).

GENERAL NOTE
The material to be contained in public registers maintained under this section is largely a re-enactment of the provisions in the C.O.P.A. 1974. But there are two significant additions. First, details of water quality objectives laid down by the Secretary of State under s.83 are now included, together with notices proposing subsequent variations of objectives (subs. (1)(a)). Secondly, information concerning water or effluent samples taken by persons other than the Authority may now be included (such as a discharger or independent consultant). This removes an unnecessary restriction in the pre-1989 legislation.

Subs. (1)
In accordance with regulations. See Control of Pollution (Registers) Regulations 1989 (S.I. 1989 No. 1160).
See s.209 for procedures required when samples are to be used in legal proceedings.

Subs. (2)
Not more than twelve months. The standard six-month time limit for the commencement of proceedings for summary offences is extended for all summary offences under this Chapter. The predecessor to this section contained in s.87(3) of the Control of Pollution Act 1974 applied only to offences concerning entry of polluting matter under s.31 of that Act.

Register for the purposes of works discharges

191.—(1) The Authority shall keep a register of persons and premises for the purposes of section 164 above.

(2) The Authority shall enter the name and address of a person in that register in respect of any premises which abut on any watercourse if that person has requested to be so registered and is either—

(a) the owner or occupier of those premises; or

(b) an officer of an association of owners or occupiers of premises which abut on that watercourse and include those premises.

(3) If the Authority contravenes, without reasonable excuse, any of the requirements of this section, it shall be guilty of an offence and liable, on summary conviction, to a fine not exceeding level 3 on the standard scale.

DEFINITION
"the Authority": s.221(1).

GENERAL NOTE
Sections 163–164 require the Authority to apply to persons within three miles of a point where it wanted to discharge water during the course of any works for consent, and to let them know if it had made any discharge in an emergency. The offence in subs. (3) is additional to the offence in s.163(3), but it is still subject to the condition that the owner or occupier must request to be registered.

Maps of fresh-water limits

192.—(1) The Secretary of State—
  (a) shall deposit maps with the Authority showing what appear to him to be the fresh-water limits of every relevant river or watercourse; and
  (b) may from time to time, if he considers it appropriate to do so by reason of any change of what appears to him to be the fresh-water limit of any river or watercourse, deposit a map showing a revised limit for that river or watercourse.
    (2) It shall be the duty of the Authority to keep any maps deposited with it under subsection (1) above available, at all reasonable times, for inspection by the public free of charge.
    (3) In this section "relevant river or watercourse" has the same meaning as in section 104 above.

DEFINITIONS
"relevant river or watercourse": subs. (3) and s.104.
"the Authority": s.221(1).

GENERAL NOTE

Subs. (1)(a)
Above the fresh-water limit. Maps deposited under subs. (2) provide conclusive evidence of these limits.

Main river maps

193.—(1) Subject to section 194 below, the Authority shall—
  (a) keep the main river map for the area of a regional flood defence committee at the principal office of the Authority for that area; and
  (b) provide reasonable facilities for inspecting that map and taking copies of and extracts from it;
and any local authority whose area is wholly or partly within the area of a regional flood defence committee shall, on application to the Authority, be entitled to be furnished with copies of the main river map for the area of that committee on payment of such sum as may be agreed between the Authority and that local authority.
    (2) For the purposes of this Act a main river map is a map relating to the area of a regional flood defence committee which—
  (a) shows by a distinctive colour the extent to which any watercourse in that area is to be treated as a main river, or part of a main river, for the purposes of this Act; and
  (b) indicates (by a distinctive colour or otherwise) which (if any) of those watercourses are watercourses designated in a scheme made under section 137 above;
and, subject to section 194 below, references in this Act to a main river map, in relation to the area of a regional flood defence committee, include so much of any map as, by virtue of paragraph 38 of Schedule 26 to the Water Act 1989, has effect as such a map at the coming into force of this Act.

(3) A main river map—

(a) shall be conclusive evidence for all purposes as to what is a main river; and

(b) shall be taken for the purposes of the Documentary Evidence Act 1868, as it applies to either of the Ministers, to be a document within the meaning of that Act and to have been issued by that Minister.

(4) In this section and section 194 below "watercourse" has the same meaning as in Part IV of this Act.

DEFINITIONS

"main river": s.221(1).
"main river map": subs. (2).
"the Authority": s.221(1).
"watercourse": subs. (4) and s.113(1).

GENERAL NOTE

This section requires the Authority to keep a map indicating main rivers for the area of every regional flood defence committee. It must be available for public inspection (subs. (1)(a)) and copies must be made available to local authorities (subs. (1)). Main river maps provide conclusive evidence of their limits (subs. (3)).

Subs. (2)

Section 137 deals with special drainage charges, and the main river map is therefore required to show areas that are liable to such charges.

Amendment of main river maps

194.—(1) Either of the Ministers may at any time send the Authority one or more new maps to be substituted for the whole or part of a main river map and containing a statement to that effect.

(2) A statement contained in a map in pursuance of subsection (1) above shall specify the date on which the substitution is to take effect and the substitution shall take effect in accordance with the statement.

(3) Where—

(a) the area of a regional flood defence committee is altered so as to affect any of the particulars shown on the main river map for that area; or

(b) one of the Ministers confirms a scheme under section 137 above; or

(c) the Authority applies to one of the Ministers for the variation of a main river map, so far as it shows the extent to which any watercourse is to be treated as a main river or part of a main river,

the Ministers shall each be under a duty to ensure that such action as he considers appropriate is taken under subsection (4) below.

(4) The action referred to in subsection (3) above is action by one of the Ministers—

(a) requiring the Authority to send him any part of the main river map in question, altering it and sending it back to the Authority; or

(b) preparing a new main river map and sending it to the Authority; or

(c) notifying the Authority that he does not intend to vary the main river map in question.

(5) Before one of the Ministers alters a map or prepares a new map by virtue of subsection (3)(c) above, he shall—

(a) give notice of his intention to do so in such manner as he thinks best adapted for informing persons affected; and

(b) consider any objections made to him within the time and in the manner specified in that notice;

and he may then alter or prepare the map either in accordance with the proposals contained in the notice or otherwise.

DEFINITIONS

"main river": s.221(1).

"main river map": s.193(2).
"notice": s.221(1).
"the Authority": s.221(1).
"the Ministers": s.221(1).

GENERAL NOTE
This section allows the Ministers to amend main river maps. The requirement that there should be a statement to accompany any amendment, and that it should specify the date of the amendment, is designed to avoid confusion. Similarly, the requirement on the Ministers in subs. (4) to keep the Authority informed of any alteration of the area of a regional flood defence committee, any new special drainage scheme or variation of the extent to which a watercourse is a main river (subs. (3)(a–c)) is designed to ensure that main river maps remain reliable and up to date. The Ministers are also required to give notice of an intention to alter a map and consider objections, but having considered objections they may proceed with an alteration different from that originally proposed without starting the consultation process again (subs. (5)).

Maps of waterworks

195.—(1) Subject to subsections (4) and (5) below, it shall be the duty of the Authority to keep records of the location of—
  (a) every resource main or discharge pipe which is for the time being vested in the Authority; and
  (b) any other underground works which are for the time being vested in the Authority.
(2) It shall be the duty of the Authority to secure that the contents of any records for the time being kept by it under this section are available, at all reasonable times, for inspection by the public free of charge at an office of the Authority.
(3) Any information which is required under this section to be made available by the Authority for inspection by the public shall be so made available in the form of a map.
(4) For the purpose of determining whether any failure to make a modification of any records kept under this section constitutes a breach of the duty imposed by subsection (1) above, that duty shall be taken to require any modification of the records to be made as soon as reasonably practicable after the completion of the works which make the modification necessary; and, where records kept under this section are modified, the date of the modification and of the completion of the works making the modification necessary shall be incorporated in the records.
(5) Nothing in this section shall require the Authority, at any time before September 1, 1999, to keep records of—
  (a) any pipe which was laid before September 1, 1989; or
  (b) any underground works which were completed before September 1, 1989,
unless those particulars were shown on August 31, 1989, on a map kept by a water authority or statutory water company under section 12 of Schedule 3 to the Water Act 1945 (maps of underground works).
(6) The reference in subsection (5) above to section 12 of Schedule 3 to the Water Act 1945 shall have effect, without prejudice to section 20(2) of the Interpretation Act 1978 (references to enactments to include references to enactments as amended, extended or applied), as including a reference to that section as applied, with or without modifications, by any local statutory provision.
(7) In this section—
  "discharge pipe" and "resource main" have the same meanings as in Part VII of this Act;
  "underground works" does not include a service pipe within the meaning of the Water Industry Act 1991.

DEFINITIONS
  "discharge pipe": subs. (7).
  "enactment": s.221(1).
  "modifications": s.221(1).
  "pipe": s.221(2).
  "records": s.221(1).
  "resource main": subs. (7).
  "the Authority": s.221(1).
  "underground works": subs. (7).

GENERAL NOTE

The duty of the Authority and water undertakers to maintain maps of water and resource mains and other underground works derives from the former duty of water authorities to prepare and keep maps of underground works under s.12 of Sched. 3 to the Water Act 1945 (the Waterworks Code), which was repealed by the 1989 Act. The term "records," as used in the section, is defined in s.221 to include computer records and other non-documentary forms, but subs. (3) requires that information be made available to the public in the form of a "map". The term "map" is not statutorily defined, but must be presumed to imply a visual record indicating geographical locations. Rather surprisingly, the provisions (in contrast to the former Water-works Code) provide no minimum requirement as to the scale of such maps.

Clearly, it is in the interest of the Authority to ensure that the records are accurate, though under subs. (5) they are effectively given 10 years' grace in respect of existing works, and may rely upon the particulars shown in the previous statutory maps. A third party may rely upon the information contained in a map to show the existence or non-existence of particular works. Should the information be inaccurate due to the negligence of the Authority or undertaker, it may be that a civil action could be taken should damage result. Although Lord Denning in *Candler* v. *Crane, Christmas & Co.* [1951] 2 K.B. 164 dismissed the idea that map-makers could be liable for errors contained in their maps, it is possible that modern trends in liability for negligent misstatements mean that the issue is less clear-cut.

Subs. (4)

Failure to make modification. The duty under subs. (1) to "keep records" implies the need to update existing records, and the wording of subs. (4), which elaborates on the implication of the duty to modify, confirms this interpretation.

Provision and acquisition of information etc.

Provision of information by the Authority to the Ministers

196.—(1) It shall be the duty of the Authority to furnish the Secretary of State or the Minister with all such information relating to—
  (a) the Authority's property;
  (b) the carrying out and proposed carrying out of its functions; and
  (c) its responsibilities generally,
as he may reasonably require.

(2) Information required under this section shall be furnished in such form and manner, and be accompanied or supplemented by such explanations, as the Secretary of State or the Minister may reasonably require.

(3) The information which the Authority may be required to furnish to either of the Ministers under this section shall include information which, although it is not in the possession of the Authority or would not otherwise come into the possession of the Authority, is information which it is reasonable to require the Authority to obtain.

(4) A requirement for the purposes of this section shall be contained in a direction which—
  (a) may describe the information to be furnished in such manner as the Secretary of State or the Minister considers appropriate; and
  (b) may require the information to be furnished on a particular occasion, in particular circumstances or from time to time.

(5) For the purposes of this section the Authority shall—
  (a) permit any person authorised by one of the Ministers for the purpose

to inspect and make copies of the contents of any accounts or other records of the Authority; and
(b) give such explanation of them as that person or the Secretary of State or the Minister may reasonably require.

DEFINITIONS
"functions": s.3.
"the Authority": s.221(1).
"the Minister": s.221(1).

GENERAL NOTE
This section, as with s.5, emphasises the close working relationship that the Authority and Government are expected to have. Section 204 (restrictions against disclosure) would not apply to the provisions here, because of the exceptions in s.204(2).

Provision of information about water flow etc.

197.—(1) It shall be the duty of the Authority—
(a) to provide a water undertaker with all such information to which this section applies as is in the possession of the Authority and is reasonably requested by the undertaker for purposes connected with the carrying out of its functions; and
(b) to provide reasonable facilities to all persons—
　　(i) for the inspection of the contents of any records kept by the Authority and containing information to which this section applies; and
　　(ii) for the taking of copies of, or of extracts from, any such records.
(2) It shall be the duty of every water undertaker to provide the Authority with all such information to which this section applies as is in the possession of the undertaker and is reasonably requested by the Authority for purposes connected with the carrying out of any of its functions.
(3) Where records of the flow, level or volume of any inland waters, other than discrete waters, are kept by a person other than a water undertaker, the Authority shall have the right at all reasonable times—
(a) to inspect the contents of any of those records; and
(b) to take copies of, or of extracts from, the contents of any of those records;
and any person who, without reasonable excuse, refuses or fails to permit the Authority to exercise its right under this subsection shall be guilty of an offence and liable, on summary conviction, to a fine not exceeding level 1 on the standard scale.
(4) Information provided to a water undertaker or to the Authority under subsection (1) or (2) above shall be provided in such form and in such manner and at such times as the undertaker or, as the case may be, the Authority may reasonably require; and the duties of the Authority under subsection (1) above shall extend to information provided to or obtained by the Authority under subsection (2) or (3) above.
(5) Information or facilities provided under subsection (1) or (2) above to the Authority, to a water undertaker, to a local authority or joint planning board, or to an internal drainage board, shall be provided free of charge; and facilities provided under subsection (1) above to other persons may be provided on terms requiring the payment by persons making use of the facilities of such reasonable charges as the Authority may determine.
(6) The duties of a water undertaker under subsection (2) above shall be enforceable under section 18 of the Water Industry Act 1991 by the Secretary of State.
(7) This section applies to information about the flow, level or volume of any inland waters or any water contained in underground strata, about

rainfall or any fall of snow, hail or sleet or about the evaporation of any water.

DEFINITIONS
DEFINITIONS
    "discrete waters": s.221(1).
    "functions": s.3.
    "inland waters": s.221(1).
    "local authority": s.221(1).
    "the Authority": s.221(1).
    "underground strata": s.221(1).

GENERAL NOTE
    This section concerns the exchange of information held by the Authority and other parties about flows and levels of inland or underground waters, and other matters specified in subs. (7).

The Authority and Water Undertakers
    This section places the Authority and water undertakers under reciprocal duties to exchange without costs (subs. (5)) information that each may collect concerning the flow, level, or volume of inland waters and underground strata, and related information, as defined in subs. (7). It mirrors the duties to exchange information concerning pollution incidents in s.203, and is designed to ensure that, despite the demise of integrated water management with privatisation, information flows between the bodies involved are maintained. The Secretary of State, rather than the courts, will have the crucial rôle in making sure that both the NRA and water undertakers respect the spirit of the provisions. The duties imposed on the Authority by this section can be enforced by a direction issued by the Secretary of State under s.5.

The Authority and Other Parties
    The section also has legal implications for parties other than the NRA and water undertakers. Under subs. (3), third parties who hold records concerning the flow, level or volume of inland waters (other than land-locked lakes or ponds) are required to grant the NRA access to them, and can be prosecuted for failing to do so "without reasonable excuse"—a phrase as yet undefined. Under subs. (1), the NRA must provide third parties with reasonable facilities for access to the information which it holds on the matters specified in subs. (7), including information it has collected from water undertakers or third parties, though, in contrast to water undertakers, other parties cannot specify the form in which it should be provided. It may charge for doing so, with the exception of water undertakers, local authorities, county councils, joint planning boards, and internal drainage boards who must be provided the information free of charge (subs. (5)). It appears that the general restrictions on disclosure under s.204 would not apply here to the Authority since they would be protected by s.204(2).

Information about underground water

198.—(1) Any person who, for the purpose of searching for or abstracting water, proposes to sink a well or borehole intended to reach a depth of more than 50 feet below the surface shall, before he begins to do so, give notice to the Natural Environment Research Council of his intention to do so.

(2) Any person sinking any such well or borehole as is mentioned in subsection (1) above shall—
    (a) keep a journal of the progress of the work and, on completion or abandonment of the work, send a complete copy of the journal to the Natural Environment Research Council;
    (b) send to that Council particulars of any test made before completion or abandonment of the work of the flow of water;
    (c) allow any person authorised by that Council for the purpose, on production of some duly authenticated document showing his authority, at all reasonable times to exercise any of the rights specified in subsection (5) below.

(3) The journal required to be kept under this section shall include measurements of—
    (a) the strata passed through; and
    (b) the levels at which water is struck and subsequently rests.

(4) The particulars required to be sent to the Natural Environment Research Council under subsection (2)(b) above shall specify—

(a) the rate of flow throughout the test;
(b) the duration of the test;
(c) where practicable, the water levels during the test and afterwards until the water returns to its natural level; and
(d) where the well or borehole is sunk in connection with an existing pumping station, the rate of pumping at the existing works during the test.

(5) The rights mentioned in subsection (2)(c) above are the rights, subject to section 205 below—
(a) to have free access to the well or borehole;
(b) to inspect the well or borehole and the material extracted from it;
(c) to take specimens of any such material and of water abstracted from the well or borehole; and
(d) to inspect and take copies of or extracts from the journal required to be kept under this section.

(6) Where the person sinking a well or borehole on any land is not the occupier of the land, the obligation imposed on that person by virtue of subsection (2)(c) above shall be the obligation of the occupier as well.
(7) Where—
(a) any person contracts to sink any well or borehole on land belonging to or occupied by another; and
(b) the carrying out of the work is under the control of the contractor, the contractor and no other person shall be deemed for the purposes of this section to be the person sinking the well or borehole.

(8) Any person who fails to comply with any obligation imposed on him by this section shall be guilty of an offence and liable, on summary conviction—
(a) to a fine not exceeding level 3 on the standard scale; and
(b) where the the offence continues after conviction, to a further fine of £20 for every day during which it so continues.

GENERAL NOTE

This section requires any person sinking a well or borehole deeper than 50 feet to notify the Natural Environment Research Council in advance (subs. (1)). The Council is entitled to information on the strata passed through and the level at which water is struck (subs. (3)) as well as rate of flow from the well (subs. (4)). The Council is entitled to inspect the well or borehole, take specimens, and inspect the journal that any person sinking a well is obliged to keep (subs. (5)). Occupiers of land who are not themselves engaged in sinking a well are nevertheless obliged to co-operate (subs. (6)), and a contractor in control of the work is deemed to be the person sinking the well (subs. (7)). Failure to comply is a summary offence, with an additional provision for a daily fine if the offence continues after conviction (subs. (8)).

See s.205 for the confidentiality of information obtained by the Council under this section.

Notice etc. of mining operations which may affect water conservation

199.—(1) Where a person proposes to construct or extend a boring for the purpose of searching for or extracting minerals, he shall, before he begins to construct or extend the boring, give to the Authority a notice of his intention in the prescribed form.

(2) The provisions of subsections (2) and (3) of section 30 above and of section 31 above shall apply where a notice is served under subsection (1) above as they apply where a notice is served under subsection (1) of that section 30 but as if the references in subsection (3) of that section 30 and in subsection (1) of that section 31 to interference with the protection of the underground works in question were a reference to interference with the winning of minerals.

(3) Sections 68 to 70 above shall apply for the purposes of subsection (2) above as they apply for the purposes of the provisions applied by that subsection.

(4) Any person who contravenes subsection (1) above or fails to comply with a conservation notice given by virtue of subsection (2) above shall be guilty of an offence and liable—
  (a) on summary conviction, to a fine not exceeding the statutory maximum;
  (b) on conviction on indictment, to a fine.

DEFINITIONS
  "notice": s.221(1).
  "prescribed": s.221(1).
  "the Authority": s.221(1).

GENERAL NOTE
  This section requires notice to be given to the NRA of any new or extended boring extracting minerals (or searching for them) (subs. (1)). Subs. (2) allows the Authority to require that reasonable measures to conserve water are taken during the work (s.30(2)); an appeal against the reasonableness of the requirements may be lodged with the Secretary of State, who may determine it with or without a hearing or a local inquiry (s.31(3)).

Gauges and records kept by other persons

200.—(1) Subject to subsection (3) below, any person other than the Authority, who proposes to install a gauge for measuring and recording the flow, level or volume of any inland waters other than discrete waters—
  (a) shall give notice to the Authority of his proposal to install the gauge; and
  (b) shall not begin the work of installing it before the end of the period of three months beginning with the date of service of the notice or such shorter period as the Authority may in any particular case allow.
(2) Not more than one month after any such work as is mentioned in paragraph (b) of subsection (1) above is completed, the person required to give notice under that subsection shall give notice to the Authority stating where the records obtained by means of the gauge are to be kept.
(3) Subsections (1) and (2) above shall not apply—
  (a) to any gauge installed for the sole purpose of indicating the level of any inland waters for the benefit of persons who fish in them; or
  (b) to any gauge which is removed at or before the end of the period of 28 days beginning with the date on which it is installed.
(4) Any person who contravenes subsection (1) or (2) above shall be guilty of an offence and liable, on summary conviction, to a fine not exceeding level 1 on the standard scale.

DEFINITIONS
  "discrete waters": s.221(1).
  "inland waters": s.221(1).
  "notice": s.221(1).
  "records": s.221(1).
  "the Authority": s.221(1).

GENERAL NOTE
  This section gives the Authority access to the records of any measurements of water flow in any inland waters other than land-locked ponds. Any person wanting to instal a gauge for measuring flow, other than a level indicator for fishing (subs. (3)(a)), for longer than a month (subs. (3)(b)), must notify the Authority three months before installation (subs. (1)(b)). The location of the records, including computer records, must be notified to the Authority within one month of installation (subs. (2)) and a failure to notify the Authority, wait the appropriate time before installation, or identify the records in the appropriate time, is a summary offence (subs. (4)).

Power to require information with respect to abstraction

201.—(1) The Authority may give directions requiring any person who is abstracting water from a source of supply, at such times and in such form as may be specified in the directions, to give such information to the Authority as to the abstraction as may be so specified.

(2) Where—

(a) directions are given to any person under this section; and

(b) that person considers that they are unreasonable or unduly onerous,

he may make representations to the Secretary of State with respect to the directions.

(3) Subject to subsection (4) below, where representations are made to the Secretary of State under subsection (2) above, he may, if he thinks fit, give a direction under this section requiring the Authority to revoke or modify the direction.

(4) Subsection (3) above shall not apply to any directions in so far as they require the occupier of any land to give any prescribed particulars as to the quantity or quality of water abstracted by him or on his behalf from any source of supply.

(5) Any person who fails to comply with any directions given by the Authority under this section shall be guilty of an offence and liable, on summary conviction, to a fine not exceeding level 1 on the standard scale.

DEFINITIONS
"abstraction": s.221(1).
"source of supply": s.221(1).
"the Authority": s.221(1).

GENERAL NOTE

This section gives the Authority a general power to require information from any person abstracting water from any inland waters or underground strata. Representations to the Secretary of State that the Authority's request is unreasonable or unduly onerous (subs. (2)) may result in a direction to the Authority to revoke or modify its request (subs. (3)). Despite this procedure, the Authority is guaranteed access to data on the quantity or quality of water abstracted by any occupier of land (subs. (4)).

Information and assistance required in connection with the control of pollution

202.—(1) It shall be the duty of the Authority, if and so far as it is requested to do so by either of the Ministers, to give him all such advice and assistance as appears to it to be appropriate for facilitating the carrying out by him of his functions under the water pollution provisions of this Act.

(2) Subject to subsection (3) below, either of the Ministers or the Authority may serve on any person a notice requiring that person to furnish him or, as the case may be, it, within a period or at times specified in the notice and in a form and manner so specified, with such information as is reasonably required by the Minister in question or by the Authority for the purpose of carrying out any of his or, as the case may be, its functions under the water pollution provisions of this Act.

(3) Each of the Ministers shall have power by regulations to make provision for restricting the information which may be required under subsection (2) above and for determining the form in which the information is to be so required.

(4) A person who fails without reasonable excuse to comply with the requirements of a notice served on him under this section shall be guilty of an offence and liable, on summary conviction, to a fine not exceeding level 5 on the standard scale.

(5) Notwithstanding anything in section 127 of the Magistrates' Courts Act 1980 (time limit for summary proceedings), a magistrates' court may try any summary offence under this section if the information is laid not more than 12 months after the commission of the offence.

DEFINITIONS
    "functions": s.3.
    "notice": s.221(1).
    "the Authority": s.221(1).
    "the Ministers": s.221(1).

GENERAL NOTE
    The powers given in subs. (2) to the Secretary of State and the NRA are closely modelled on those contained in s.93 of the C.O.P.A. 1974.

Subs. (5)
    Not more than 12 months. The standard six-month time limit for the commencement of proceedings for summary offences is extended, as it is for all summary offences under Pt. III.

Exchange of information with respect to pollution incidents etc.

203.—(1) It shall be the duty of the Authority to provide a water undertaker with all such information to which this section applies as is in the possession of the Authority and is reasonably requested by the undertaker for purposes connected with the carrying out of its functions.

(2) It shall be the duty of every water undertaker to provide the Authority with all such information to which this section applies as is in the possession of the undertaker and is reasonably requested by the Authority for purposes connected with the carrying out of any of its functions.

(3) Information provided to a water undertaker or to the Authority under subsection (1) or (2) above shall be provided in such form and in such manner and at such times as the undertaker or, as the case may be, the Authority may reasonably require.

(4) Information provided under subsection (1) or (2) above to a water undertaker or to the Authority shall be provided free of charge.

(5) The duties of a water undertaker under subsection (2) above shall be enforceable under section 18 of the Water Industry Act 1991 by the Secretary of State.

(6) This section applies to information—
(a) about the quality of any controlled waters or of any other waters; or
(b) about any incident in which any poisonous, noxious or polluting matter or any solid waste matter has entered any controlled waters or other waters.

(7) In this section "controlled waters" has the same meaning as in Part III of this Act.

DEFINITIONS
    "controlled waters": subs. (7) and 104.
    "functions": s.3.
    "the Authority": s.221(1).

GENERAL NOTE
    This section is aimed at ensuring reciprocal exchanges of information between the Authority and water undertakers concerning the quality of waters and pollution incidents, and it supplements the powers available to the Authority under s.202. Although drafted with a view to positive co-operation, in practice its implementation could raise difficult questions. Does the water undertaker have to disclose self-incriminating information about its activities, which could lead to prosecution by the Authority? And, if the water and sewerage undertaker are one and the same body, it is unclear whether the obligation is restricted to information held in its capacity as a water undertaker only. Similarly, the Authority itself might be reluctant to provide information if it concerned an incident under investigation with a view to possible prosecution. Ultimately, resolving a dispute on these issues would be a matter of judgment by the Secretary of State, since enforcement of the duty rests with him—by means of s.18 (of the Water Industry Act 1991) orders against water undertakers (subs. (5)) and specific directions to the Authority (s.5)).
    The restrictions on subsequent disclosure of information under s.204 do not apply to information provided under this section (s.204(2)(c)).

Restriction on disclosure of information

Restriction on disclosure of information

204.—(1) Subject to the following provisions of this section, no information with respect to any particular business which—
  (a) has been obtained by virtue of any of the provisions of this Act; and
  (b) relates to the affairs of any individual or to any particular business,
shall, during the lifetime of that individual or so long as that business continues to be carried on, be disclosed without the consent of that individual or the person for the time being carrying on that business.

(2) Subsection (1) above does not apply to any disclosure of information which is made—
  (a) for the purpose of facilitating the carrying out by either of the Ministers, the Authority, the Director General of Water Services, the Monopolies Commission or a local authority of any of his, its or, as the case may be, their functions by virtue of this Act, any of the other consolidation Acts or the Water Act 1989;
  (b) for the purpose of facilitating the performance by a water undertaker or sewerage undertaker of any of the duties imposed on it by or under this Act, any of the other consolidation Acts or the Water Act 1989;
  (c) in pursuance of any duty imposed by section 197(1)(a) or (2) or 203(1) or (2) above or of any arrangements made by the Director General of Water Services under section 29(6) of the Water Industry Act 1991;
  (d) for the purpose of facilitating the carrying out by any person mentioned in Part I of Schedule 24 to this Act of any of his functions under any of the enactments or instruments specified in Part II of that Schedule;
  (e) for the purpose of enabling or assisting the Secretary of State to exercise any powers conferred on him by the Financial Services Act 1986 or by the enactments relating to companies, insurance companies or insolvency or for the purpose of enabling or assisting any inspector appointed by him under the enactments relating to companies to carry out his functions;
  (f) for the purpose of enabling an official receiver to carry out his functions under the enactments relating to insolvency or for the purpose of enabling or assisting a recognised professional body for the purposes of section 391 of the Insolvency Act 1986 to carry out its functions as such;
  (g) for the purpose of facilitating the carrying out by the Health and Safety Commission or the Health and Safety Executive of any of its functions under any enactment or of facilitating the carrying out by any enforcing authority, within the meaning of Part I of the Health and Safety at Work etc. Act 1974, of any functions under a relevant statutory provision, within the meaning of that Act;
  (h) for the purpose of facilitating the carrying out by the Comptroller and Auditor General of any of his functions under any enactment;
  (i) in connection with the investigation of any criminal offence or for the purposes of any criminal proceedings;
  (j) for the purposes of any civil proceedings brought under or by virtue of this Act, any of the other consolidation Acts, the Water Act 1989 or any of the enactments or instruments specified in Part II of Schedule 24 to this Act, or of any arbitration under this Act, any of the other consolidation Acts or that Act of 1989; or
  (k) in pursuance of a Community obligation.

(3) Nothing in subsection (1) above shall be construed—
  (a) as limiting the matters which may be included in, or made public as part of, a report of—

(i) the Authority;

(ii) the Director General of Water Services;

(iii) a customer service committee maintained under the Water Industry Act 1991; or

(iv) the Monopolies Commission,

under any provision of this Act or that Act of 1991;

(b) as limiting the matters which may be published under section 201 of that Act; or

(c) as applying to any information which has been made public as part of such a report or has been so published or to any information exclusively of a statistical nature.

(4) Subject to subsection (5) below, nothing in subsection (1) above shall preclude the disclosure of information—

(a) if the disclosure is of information relating to a matter connected with the carrying out of the functions of a water undertaker or sewerage undertaker and is made by one Minister of the Crown or government department to another; or

(b) if the disclosure is for the purpose of enabling or assisting any public or other authority for the time being designated for the purposes of this section by an order made by the Secretary of State to discharge any functions which are specified in the order.

(5) The power to make an order under subsection (4) above shall be exercisable by statutory instrument subject to annulment in pursuance of a resolution of either House of Parliament; and where such an order designates an authority for the purposes of paragraph (b) of that subsection, the order may—

(a) impose conditions subject to which the disclosure of information is permitted by virtue of that paragraph; and

(b) otherwise restrict the circumstances in which disclosure is so permitted.

(6) Any person who discloses any information in contravention of the preceding provisions of this section shall be guilty of an offence and liable—

(a) on summary conviction, to a fine not exceeding the statutory maximum;

(b) on conviction on indictment, to imprisonment for a term not exceeding two years or to a fine or to both.

(7) In this section "the other consolidation Acts" means the Water Industry Act 1991, the Statutory Water Companies Act 1991, the Land Drainage Act 1991 and the Water Consolidation (Consequential Provisions) Act 1991.

DEFINITIONS
"enactments": s.221(1).
"functions": s.3.
"local authority": s.221(1).
"the Authority": s.221(1).
"the Ministers": s.221(1).
"the other Consolidation Acts": subs. (7).

GENERAL NOTE
This section creates a very broad offence concerning disclosure of information obtained under the Act which relates to the particular business of any individual, and is disclosed without their consent. The offence is subject to an extensive number of exceptions, mainly related to the functions of public bodies, and including the duties (but not powers) of water and sewerage undertakers.

Subs. (2)(a), (b) and (j) have been amended from the corresponding subsections of s.174 of the Water Act 1989 in line with the recommendation of the Law Commission (Law Com. No. 198, para. 11) to include functions or duties under "this Act, any of the other consolidation Acts or the Water Act 1989". In the 1989 Act, the functions or duties were restricted to those imposed by that Act.

Confidentiality of information relating to underground water etc.

205.—(1) The person sinking any such well or borehole as is mentioned in section 198 above or, if it is a different person, the owner or occupier of the land on which any such well or borehole is sunk may by notice to the Natural Environment Research Council require that Council to treat as confidential—

(a) any copy of or extract from the journal required to be kept under that section; or

(b) any specimen taken in exercise of the rights specified in subsection (5) of that section.

(2) Subject to subsections (3) and (4) below, the Natural Environment Research Council shall not, without the consent of the person giving the notice, allow any matter to which any notice under subsection (1) above relates to be published or shown to any person who is not an officer of that Council or of a department of the Secretary of State.

(3) Subsection (2) above shall not prohibit any matter from being published or shown to any person in so far as it contains or affords information as to water resources and supplies.

(4) If at any time the Natural Environment Research Council give notice to any person that in their opinion his consent for the purposes of subsection (2) above is being unreasonably withheld—

(a) that person may, within three months after the giving of the notice, appeal to the High Court for an order restraining that Council from acting as if consent had been given; and

(b) that Council may proceed as if consent had been given if either no such appeal is brought within that period or the High Court, after hearing the appeal, do not make such an order.

(5) Any person who fails to comply with any obligation imposed on him by the preceding provisions of this section shall be guilty of an offence and liable, on summary conviction—

(a) to a fine not exceeding level 3 on the standard scale; and

(b) where the offence continues after conviction, to a further fine of £20 for every day during which it so continues.

(6) If any person who is admitted to any premises in compliance with section 198(2)(c) above discloses to any person any information obtained by him there with regard to any manufacturing process or trade secret, he shall unless the disclosure is in performance of his duty, be guilty of an offence and liable—

(a) on summary conviction, to imprisonment for a term not exceeding three months or to a fine not exceeding the statutory maximum or to both;

(b) on conviction on indictment, to imprisonment for a term not exceeding three months or to a fine or to both.

DEFINITION
"notice": s.221(1).

GENERAL NOTE
It is to be noted that the requirement of confidentiality only arises if the Council is served with a written notice. If the Council is refused consent to publish any information it may serve a notice saying that it regards the withholding of consent as unreasonable. Having done so, it may publish the information if the person concerned has not appealed to the High Court within three months, or if the appeal has been turned down (subs. (4)). The balance is therefore tilted in favour of disclosure.

Subs. (6)
This subsection creates an offence that is separate from the rest of the section in that it deals not with information relating to water flow but with trade secrets and manufacturing processes.

It is designed to guard against the abuse of the Council's powers of entry for unfair commercial competition.

Making of false statements etc.

Making of false statements etc.

206.—(1) If, in furnishing any information or making any application under or for the purposes of any of the following provisions of this Act, that is to say, the provisions of—
  (a) Part I, other than Schedule 2;
  (b) sections 19 and 20 and Chapter III of Part II;
  (c) Part III;
  (d) Part VI, other than sections 133 to 143 and 147 to 149;
  (e) Part VII, other than sections 155, 156, 158, 165 to 167 and the other provisions of that Part so far as they relate to those sections;
  (f) this Part, other than sections 189, 193, 194, 198 to 201 and 205; and
  (g) Part IX, except so far as it relates to a provision of this Act in relation to which this subsection does not apply,
any person makes any statement which he knows to be false in a material particular, or recklessly makes any statement which is false in a material particular, he shall be guilty of an offence under this section.

(2) If—
  (a) in giving any information which he is required to give under Chapter II of Part II of this Act or any of the related water resources provisions or under Schedule 2 to this Act, any person knowingly or recklessly makes a statement which is false in a material particular; or
  (b) for the purpose of obtaining a licence under that Chapter, any person knowingly makes a statement which is false in a material particular,
that person shall be guilty of an offence under this section.

(3) Where—
  (a) the provisions contained in a licence under Chapter II of Part II of this Act in pursuance of paragraph (b) of subsection (2) of section 46 above, or of that paragraph as modified by subsection (6) of that section, require the use of a meter, gauge or other device; and
  (b) such a device is used for the purposes of those provisions,
any person who wilfully alters or interferes with that device so as to prevent it from measuring correctly shall be guilty of an offence under this section.

(4) If, in keeping any record or journal or in furnishing any information which he is required to keep or furnish under section 198 or 205 above, any person knowingly or recklessly makes any statement which is false in a material particular, he shall be guilty of an offence under this section.

(5) A person who is guilty of an offence under this section by virtue of subsection (1) above shall be liable—
  (a) on summary conviction, to a fine not exceeding the statutory maximum;
  (b) on conviction on indictment, to a fine;
and proceedings for an offence by virtue of subsection (1) above shall not be instituted except by or with the consent of one of the Ministers or the Director of Public Prosecutions.

(6) A person who is guilty of an offence under this section by virtue of subsection (2) or (3) above shall be liable—
  (a) on summary conviction, to imprisonment for a term not exceeding three months or to a fine not exceeding the statutory maximum or to both;
  (b) on conviction on indictment, to imprisonment for a term not exceeding two years or to a fine or to both.

(7) A person who is guilty of an offence under this section by virtue of subsection (4) above shall be liable—

(a) on summary conviction, to imprisonment for a term not exceeding three months or to a fine not exceeding the statutory maximum or to both;

(b) on conviction on indictment, to imprisonment for a term not exceeding three months or to a fine or to both.

DEFINITION
"record": s.221(1).

GENERAL NOTE
This section sets out broad offences for making false statements in any of the situations in which the Act calls for information to be furnished, and in any of the applications for any of the various licences that the Authority has the power to grant. The *mens rea* of the offences includes recklessness for subss. (1), (2)(a) and (4). For subs. (2)(b) (abstraction licence application) and subs. (3) (altering a meter), recklessness is not sufficient. All of the offences under this section are indictable.

PART IX

MISCELLANEOUS AND SUPPLEMENTAL

Miscellaneous

Directions in the interests of national security etc.

207.—(1) The Secretary of State may, after consultation with the Authority, give to the Authority such directions of a general character as appear to the Secretary of State to be requisite or expedient in the interests of national security or for the purpose of mitigating the effects of any civil emergency which may occur.

(2) If it appears to the Secretary of State to be requisite or expedient to do so in the interests of national security or for the purpose of mitigating the effects of any civil emergency which has occurred or may occur, he may, after consultation with the Authority, give to the Authority a direction requiring it to do, or not to do, a particular thing specified in the direction.

(3) The duty of the Authority to comply with a direction under this section is a duty which has effect notwithstanding any other duty imposed on it (whether or not by or under this Act).

(4) The Secretary of State shall lay before each House of Parliament a copy of every direction given under this section unless he is of the opinion that disclosure of the direction is against the interests of national security.

(5) A person shall not disclose, or be required by virtue of any enactment or otherwise to disclose, anything done by virtue of this section if the Secretary of State has notified him that the Secretary of State is of the opinion that disclosure of that thing is against the interests of national security.

(6) Any person who discloses any matter in contravention of subsection (5) above shall be guilty of an offence and liable, on conviction on indictment, to imprisonment for a term not exceeding two years or to a fine or to both.

(7) Any reference in this section to a civil emergency is a reference to any natural disaster or other emergency which, in the opinion of the Secretary of State, is or may be likely, in relation to any area—

(a) so to disrupt water supplies or sewerage services; or

(b) to involve such destruction of or damage to life or property in that area,

as seriously and adversely to affect all the inhabitants of that area, or a substantial number of them, whether by depriving them of any of the essentials of life or otherwise.

(8) In this section "sewerage services" has the same meaning as in the Water Industry Act 1991.

"civil emergency": subs. (7).
"sewerage services": subs. (8).
"the Authority": s.221(1).

GENERAL NOTE

This section gives wide powers to the Secretary of State to give both general directions (subs. (1)) and specific directions (subs. (2)) to the Authority in the interest of national security or for mitigating the effects of a civil emergency. The phrase "civil emergency" is explained in subs. (9). The section is modelled on similar provisions in the Telecommunications Act 1984.

Subs. (1)

To be requisite or expedient. An attempt to explain the difference between these two words was made by the Under-Secretary of State during Committee stage of the 1989 Act: "The word 'requisite' applies to well-defined risks associated with serious consequences, such as the loss of a vital pumping station. The word 'expedient' could apply to circumstances where the risk is assessed to be lower but where measures would still be prudent" (Standing Committee D, col. 1524, March 2, 1989).

Civil liability of the Authority for escapes of water etc.

208.—(1) Where an escape of water, however caused, from a pipe vested in the Authority causes loss or damage, the Authority shall be liable, except as otherwise provided in this section, for the loss or damage.

(2) The Authority shall not incur any liability under subsection (1) above if the escape was due wholly to the fault of the person who sustained the loss or damage or of any servant, agent or contractor of his.

(3) The Authority shall not incur any liability under subsection (1) above in respect of any loss or damage for which the Authority would not be liable apart from that subsection and which is sustained—

(a) by any water undertaker or sewerage undertaker or by any statutory undertakers, within the meaning of section 336(1) of the Town and Country Planning Act 1990;

(b) by any public gas supplier within the meaning of Part I of the Gas Act 1986 or the holder of a licence under section 6(1) of the Electricity Act 1989;

(c) by any highway authority; or

(d) by any person on whom a right to compensation is conferred by section 82 of the New Roads and Street Works Act 1991.

(4) The Law Reform (Contributory Negligence) Act 1945, the Fatal Accidents Act 1976 and the Limitation Act 1980 shall apply in relation to any loss or damage for which the Authority is liable under this section, but which is not due to the Authority's fault, as if it were due to its fault.

(5) Nothing in subsection (1) above affects any entitlement which the Authority may have to recover contribution under the Civil Liability (Contribution) Act 1978; and for the purposes of that Act, any loss for which the Authority is liable under that subsection shall be treated as if it were damage.

(6) Where the Authority is liable under any enactment or agreement passed or made before April 1, 1982, to make any payment in respect of any loss or damage the Authority shall not incur liability under subsection (1) above in respect of the same loss or damage.

(7) In this section "fault" has the same meaning as in the Law Reform (Contributory Negligence) Act 1945.

(8) Until the coming into force of section 82 of the New Roads and Street Works Act 1991, subsection (3) above shall have effect as if for paragraph (d) there were substituted the following paragraphs—

"(d) by any bridge authority, bridge managers, street authority or street managers within the meaning of the Public Utilities Street Works Act 1950; or

(e) by any person on whom a right to compensation under section 26 of that Act of 1950 is conferred.";

but nothing in this section shall be taken to prejudice the power of the Secretary of State under that Act of 1991 to make an order bringing section 82 of that Act into force on different days for different purposes (including the purposes of this section).

DEFINITIONS
"enactment": s.221(1).
"fault": subs. (7).
"pipe": s.221(2).
"the Authority": s.221(1).

GENERAL NOTE
This section states that the Authority shall be liable for loss and damage caused by an escape of water, unless that escape was wholly the fault of the person who has suffered (subss. (1) and (2)). The Authority's liability is limited both by the restriction of a number of organisations (subs. (3)) and by the exclusion of any liability arising under any pre 1982 legislation (subs. (6)).

Evidence of samples and abstractions

209.—(1) Subject to subsection (2) below, the result of the analysis of any sample taken on behalf of the Authority in exercise of any power conferred by this Act shall not be admissible in any legal proceedings in respect of any effluent passing from any land or vessel unless the person who took the sample—

(a) on taking the sample notified the occupier of the land or the owner or master of the vessel of his intention to have it analysed;

(b) there and then divided the sample into three parts and caused each part to be placed in a container which was sealed and marked; and

(c) delivered one part to the occupier of the land or the owner or master of the vessel and retained one part, apart from the one he submitted to be analysed, for future comparison.

(2) If it is not reasonably practicable for a person taking a sample to comply with the requirements of subsection (1) above on taking the sample, those requirements shall be treated as having been complied with if they were complied with as soon as reasonably practicable after the sample was taken.

(3) Where, in accordance with the provisions contained in a licence in pursuance of paragraph (b) of subsection (2) of section 46 above, or in pursuance of that paragraph as read with subsection (6) of that section, it has been determined what quantity of water is to be taken—

(a) to have been abstracted during any period from a source of supply by the holder of the licence; or

(b) to have been so abstracted at a particular point or by particular means, or for use for particular purposes,

that determination shall, for the purposes of any proceedings under Chapter II of Part II of this Act or any of the related water resources provisions, be conclusive evidence of the matters to which it relates.

(4) In relation to any proceedings in respect of effluent passing from a public sewer or other outfall belonging to a sewerage undertaker into any water, this section shall have effect as if the references to the occupier of the land were references to the sewerage undertaker in which the sewer or outfall is vested.

DEFINITIONS
"analyse": s.221(1).

"effluent": s.221(1).
"public sewer": s.221(1).
"sewer": s.221(1).
"the Authority": s.221(1).

GENERAL NOTE

This important section prescribes circumstances in which the results of sample analyses may only be used in court proceedings if the "three-way" sample procedure was used at the time of taking it. The requirement is based on s.113(2) of the Water Resources Act 1963 which, via the 1989 Act, it replaces.

In determining whether the section is applicable, three key questions must be asked:

(1) Is the evidence based on "the analysis" of a sample? If no analysis is involved, the section does not apply, and the Authority or other prosecutor may rely upon visual or other forms of evidence without the need of "three-way" sampling. The leading case is *Trent River Board* v. *Wardle* [1957] Crim.L.R. 196, where it was held that exposing a fish to a sample of effluent did not amount to an "analysis". Note, however, that s.221 of this Act now defines the term to include subjecting a sample to a test of any kind.

(2) If the evidence is based on a sample analysis, was the sample taken on behalf of the Authority? If it was, then it will be admissible only if the three-way procedure was followed at the time or, where subs. (2) is applicable, "as soon as reasonably practicable" afterwards. The effect of the requirement is that where the Authority undertakes prosecutions, whether against water undertakers or other industrial dischargers, evidence relating to its sample analyses must have involved the three-way procedure. The public registers concerning water pollution maintained by the Authority under s.190 of this Act will contain particulars of samples and of their analyses taken both by the NRA and others under arrangement with the NRA to the extent prescribed by regulations. Under Control of Pollution (Registers) Regulations 1989 (S.I. 1989 No. 1160), the entries relating to samples will now distinguish those taken for routine monitoring purposes and those where the statutory sampling procedure under this section has been followed. Where the information in the register is based on a sample taken by or on behalf of the Authority, it would seem that the three-way procedure must have been followed if it is to be admissible in court proceedings, whether the prosecution is undertaken by the Authority or a private person (simply determining the content of a sample involves an "analysis")—though see Jackson S., Private Prosecutions under the Control of Pollution Act 1974 (1988) 2 Environment Law 3.

(3) If the evidence is based on a sample analysis, was the sample taken by some other person or body not acting on behalf of the Authority? If this is the case, then the results may be admissible despite the absence of the three-way procedure. The Act does not prohibit private prosecutions, and although a court is likely to give greater credibility to evidence based on more controlled three-way procedures, evidence from single samples or other types of evidence is admissible. Some sample evidence on the public register maintained by the Authority may be derived from samples taken by dischargers or others "under arrangements" made by the Authority. It is arguable that evidence of such samples may be admissible without the requirement of the "three-way" procedure, provided that the terms of the arrangement do not imply that the sample is being taken "on behalf of the Authority", the critical phrase in subs. (1).

Subs. (1)

Notified the occupier. It is not necessary for the sampler to be accompanied by the occupier at the time of taking the sample. Powers of entry are contained in ss.169 and 173 (entry by justice's warrant). Where residential premises are involved, seven days' notice is required in the absence of an emergency or a justice's warrant.

Delivered one part to the occupier. The implication is that the sample must actually be delivered to the occupier or owner, and cannot simply be left at unoccupied premises.

Byelaws

Byelaw-making powers of the Authority

210.—(1) Schedule 25 to this Act shall have effect for conferring powers on the Authority to make byelaws for purposes connected with the carrying out of its functions.

(2) Schedule 26 to this Act shall have effect in relation to byelaws made by the Authority, whether by virtue of subsection (1) above or by virtue of any other enactment.

DEFINITIONS
　"enactment": s.221(1).
　"the Authority": s.221(1).

Enforcement of byelaws

211.—(1) If any person contravenes any byelaws made by virtue of paragraph 1 of Schedule 25 to this Act, he shall be guilty of an offence and liable, on summary conviction—

(a) to a fine not exceeding level 1 on the standard scale; and

(b) if the contravention is continued after conviction, to a fine not exceeding £5 for each day on which it is so continued.

(2) Byelaws made by virtue of paragraph 2 or 3 of that Schedule may contain provision providing for a contravention of the byelaws to constitute a summary offence punishable, on summary conviction, by a fine not exceeding level 5 on the standard scale or such smaller sum as may be specified in the byelaws.

(3) A person who contravenes any byelaws made by virtue of paragraph 4 or 6 of that Schedule shall be guilty of an offence and liable, on summary conviction, to a fine not exceeding level 4 on the standard scale or, in the case of byelaws made by virtue of paragraph 4, such smaller sum as may be specified in the byelaws.

(4) If any person acts in contravention of any byelaw made by virtue of paragraph 5 of that Schedule he shall be guilty of an offence and liable, on summary conviction—

(a) to a fine not exceeding level 5 on the standard scale; and

(b) if the contravention is continued after conviction, to a further fine not exceeding £40 for each day on which it is so continued.

(5) Without prejudice to any proceedings by virtue of subsection (1) or (4) above, the Authority may—

(a) take such action as it considers necessary to remedy the effect of any contravention of byelaws made by virtue of paragraph 1 of Schedule 25 to this Act;

(b) take such action as may be necessary to remedy the effect of any person's contravention of byelaws made by virtue of paragraph 5 of that Schedule; and

(c) recover the expenses reasonably incurred by the Authority in taking any action under paragraph (a) or (b) above from the person in default.

(6) So much of the Salmon and Freshwater Fisheries Act 1975 as makes provision with respect to or by reference to offences under that Act shall have effect as if an offence consisting in a contravention of byelaws made by virtue of paragraph 6 of Schedule 25 to this Act were an offence under that Act.

(7) Section 70 above shall apply in relation to any restrictions imposed by byelaws made by virtue of paragraph 1 of Schedule 25 to this Act as it applies in relation to restrictions imposed by the provisions of Chapter II of Part II of this Act which are mentioned in that section; and sections 100 and 101 above shall have effect in relation to contraventions of byelaws made by virtue of paragraph 4 of that Schedule as they have effect in relation to contraventions of provisions of Part III of this Act.

DEFINITION
　"the Authority": s.221(1).

GENERAL NOTE

Subs. (7)
　The effect of this subsection is to extend the normal limitation period of six months for summary offences to 12 for offences created under Sched. 25 (s.101) and to prevent the byelaws giving rise to civil liabilities or restricting any other liabilities or offences (s.70).

Compensation in respect of certain fisheries byelaws

212.—(1) Where—

(a) the owner or occupier of any fishery by notice to the Authority claims that the fishery is injuriously affected by a byelaw made for any of the purposes specified in subsection (2) below; and

(b) that claim is made at any time before the end of 12 months after the confirmation of the byelaw,

the claim and the amount of compensation to be paid, by way of annual payment or otherwise, for the damage (if any) to the fishery shall be determined, in default of agreement, by a single arbitrator appointed by one of the Ministers.

(2) The purposes mentioned in subsection (1)(a) above are the following purposes specified in paragraph 6(2) of Schedule 25 to this Act, that is to say—

(a) prohibiting the use for taking salmon, trout, or freshwater fish of any instrument (not being a fixed engine) in such waters and at such times as are prescribed by the byelaw;

(b) specifying the nets and other instruments (not being fixed engines) which may be used for taking salmon, trout, freshwater fish and eels and imposing requirements as to the use of such nets and other instruments;

(c) imposing requirements as to the construction, design, material and dimensions of any such nets or instruments, including in the case of nets the size of mesh.

(3) Where by virtue of this section any compensation is payable under any award by way of an annual payment—

(a) the Authority or the person entitled to the annual payment may at any time after the end of five years from the date of the award require it to be reviewed by a single arbitrator appointed by one of the Ministers; and

(b) the compensation to be paid after the review shall be such, if any, as may be determined by that arbitrator.

(4) Expressions used in this section and in the Salmon and Freshwater Fisheries Act 1975 have the same meanings in this section as in that Act.

Definitions
   "notice": s.221(1).
   "owner": s.221(1).
   "the Authority": s.221(1).
   "the Ministers": s.221(1).

General Note
   This section allows fishery owners to claim compensation for the effect of byelaws made by the Authority prohibiting or limiting their use of nets and other instruments (subs. (2)(a) and (b)). If not agreed the compensation will be determined by an arbitrator (subs. (1)) and the amount may be reviewed at the request of either party after five years (subs. (3)).

Local inquiries

General powers to hold local inquiries

213.—(1) Without prejudice to any other provision of this Act by virtue of which a local inquiry is authorised or required to be held, each of the Ministers shall have power to cause a local inquiry to be held in any case where it appears to him expedient to do so—

(a) in connection with any matter arising under Chapter II of Part II of this Act or the related water resources provisions; or

(b) otherwise in connection with any of the Authority's functions.

(2) Without prejudice as aforesaid, the Secretary of State may cause a local inquiry to be held in any case in which he considers it appropriate for such an inquiry to be held—
  (a) for the purposes of the establishment or review under section 83 above of any water quality objectives or otherwise in connection with any of the water pollution provisions of this Act;
  (b) with a view to preventing or dealing with pollution of any controlled waters; or
  (c) in relation to any other matter relevant to the quality of any such waters.

(3) In this section "controlled waters" has the same meaning as in Part III of this Act.

DEFINITIONS
  "controlled waters": subs. (3) and s.104.
  "the Authority's functions": s.3.
  "the Ministers": s.221(1).

GENERAL NOTE
  This section gives the Ministers a general power to hold a local inquiry in addition to any of the specific powers to do so found elsewhere in the Act. See s.215 applying the provisions of s.250 of the Local Government Act 1972 to any such inquiry.

Power to hold inquiries for flood defence purposes etc.

214.—(1) Each of the Ministers shall have power to cause such inquiries to be held as he considers necessary or desirable for the purposes of the flood defence provisions of this Act.

(2) Subject to subsection (3) below, the person appointed to hold any inquiry under subsection (1) above or otherwise under the flood defence provisions of this Act may for the purposes of the inquiry—
  (a) by summons require any person to attend, at a time and place stated in the summons, to give evidence or to produce any documents in his custody or under his control relating to any matter in question at the inquiry; and
  (b) take evidence on oath and for that purpose administer oaths.

(3) No person shall be required, in obedience to a summons under this section, to attend to give evidence or to produce any documents, unless the necessary expenses of his attendance are paid or tendered to him; and nothing in this section shall empower a person holding an inquiry to require the production of the title, or of any instrument relating to the title, of any land which is not the property of a local authority.

(4) Any person who—
  (a) refuses or deliberately fails to attend in obedience to a summons under this section, or to give evidence; or
  (b) deliberately alters, suppresses, conceals, destroys, or refuses to produce any book or other document which he is required or is liable to be required to produce for the purposes of this section,
shall be guilty of an offence and liable, on summary conviction, to imprisonment for a term not exceeding six months or to a fine not exceeding level 3 on the standard scale or to both.

(5) Where either of the Ministers causes an inquiry to be held under this section—
  (a) the costs incurred by him in relation to the inquiry shall be paid by such authority or party to the inquiry as he may direct; and
  (b) the Minister in question may cause the amount of the costs so incurred to be certified;
and any amount so certified and directed to be paid by any authority or person shall be recoverable from that authority or person by that Minister summarily as a civil debt.

(6) Where either of the Ministers causes an inquiry to be held under this section—

　(a) he may make orders as to the costs of the parties at the inquiry and as to the parties by whom the costs are to be paid; and

　(b) every such order may be made a rule of the High Court on the application of any party named in the order.

(7) Section 42 of the Housing and Planning Act 1986 (recovery of Minister's costs in connection with inquiries) shall apply where either of the Ministers is authorised by virtue of subsection (5) above to recover costs incurred by him in relation to an inquiry as it applies where a Minister is so authorised by virtue of an enactment specified in subsection (1) of that section.

Definitions
　"enactment": s.221(1).
　"the Ministers": s.221(1).

General Note

Subss. (5)–(7)
　These subsections perform a similar function to s.250 of the Local Government Act 1972, which, by virtue of s.215, applies to all other local inquiries under the Act. The effect of subss. (5)–(7) is to allow the Minister to decide the issue of costs at a local inquiry and to recover costs from the NRA or any other parties to the inquiry.

Procedure at local inquiries

215.—(1) Subject to subsection (2) below, subsections (2) to (5) of section 250 of the Local Government Act 1972 (which contain supplementary provisions with respect to local inquiries held in pursuance of that section) shall apply to local inquiries under any provision of this Act, other than a provision in relation to which section 214 above has effect, as they apply to inquiries under that section of that Act of 1972.

(2) Subsection (4) of section 250 of that Act of 1972 shall apply in accordance with subsection (1) above in relation to such local inquiries under this Act as are held with respect to any matter affecting the carrying out of any function of the Authority as if the reference to a local authority in that subsection included a reference to the Authority.

Definitions
　"function": s.3.
　"local authority": s.221(1).
　"the Authority": s.221(1).

General Note

Subs. (2)
　Subsection (4) of section 250. Under this subsection, the Secretary of State may recover his costs in relation to the inquiry from a local authority or other party to the inquiry. The effect of subs. (2) is to allow the Secretary of State to recover costs from the NRA as well, if it is a party to the inquiry.

Offences etc.

Enforcement: powers and duties

216.—(1) Without prejudice to its powers of enforcement in relation to the other provisions of this Act, it shall be the duty of the Authority to enforce the provisions to which this section applies.

(2) No proceedings for any offence under any provision to which this section applies shall be instituted except—

　(a) by the Authority; or

　(b) by, or with the consent of, the Director of Public Prosecutions.

(3) This section applies to Chapter II of Part II of this Act and the related water resources provisions.

DEFINITION
"the Authority": s.221(1).

GENERAL NOTE
This section imposes a duty on the Authority to enforce the provisions relating to abstraction and impounding. In this area, unlike the pollution offences, private prosecutions are excluded by subs. (2).

Criminal liabilities of directors and other third parties

217.—(1) Where a body corporate is guilty of an offence under this Act and that offence is proved to have been committed with the consent or connivance of, or to be attributable to any neglect on the part of, any director, manager, secretary or other similar officer of the body corporate or any person who was purporting to act in any such capacity, then he, as well as the body corporate, shall be guilty of that offence and shall be liable to be proceeded against and punished accordingly.

(2) Where the affairs of a body corporate are managed by its members, subsection (1) above shall apply in relation to the acts and defaults of a member in connection with his functions of management as if he were a director of the body corporate.

(3) Without prejudice to subsections (1) and (2) above, where the commission by any person of an offence under the water pollution provisions of this Act is due to the act or default of some other person, that other person may be charged with and convicted of the offence whether or not proceedings for the offence are taken against the first-mentioned person.

GENERAL NOTE
Under this section, officers or members (if performing a management function) of bodies corporate may be criminally liable in addition to the body corporate itself (subs. (1) and (2)). Third parties who have caused another to commit a pollution offence may also be proceeded against, regardless of whether the person caused to commit the offence is proceeded against (subs. (3)).

This section gives effect to the recommendation of the Law Commission (Law Com. No. 198, para. 13) that the consolidation of previous legislation in this Act and the Water Industry Act 1991 should not maintain the distinction between the approach of s.177 of the 1989 Act and earlier provisions in the Water Resources Act 1963 and others. Under the 1963 Act provisions about bodies governed by their members were confined to nationalised industries. This approach, and other similar offences under other Acts now consolidated, has been discarded in favour of the universal application of the form found in this section.

Judicial disqualification

Judicial disqualification

218. No judge of any court or justice of the peace shall be disqualified from acting in relation to any proceedings to which the Authority is a party by reason only that he is or may become liable to pay a charge to the Authority in respect of any services or facilities that are not the subject-matter of the proceedings.

DEFINITION
"the Authority": s.221(1).

Powers to make regulations

Powers to make regulations

219.—(1) Any power of one or both of the Ministers to make regulations under any provision of this Act shall be exercisable by statutory instrument subject (except in the case of regulations made by virtue of paragraph 1(3) of Schedule 15 to this Act) to annulment in pursuance of a resolution of either House of Parliament.

(2) Subject to subsection (3) below, the provisions of any regulations made by one or both the Ministers under this Act may include—

(a) provision for any duty or other requirement imposed by the regulations on a water undertaker or sewerage undertaker to be enforceable under section 18 of the Water Industry Act 1991 by the Secretary of State, by the Director or by either of them;

(b) provision, where such a duty or requirement is so enforceable by either of them, for enforcement by the Director to be subject to such consent or authorisation as may be prescribed;

(c) provision which, in relation to the furnishing of any information or the making of any application under the regulations, makes provision corresponding to section 206(1) and (5) above;

(d) provision for anything that may be prescribed by the regulations to be determined under the regulations and for anything falling to be so determined to be determined by such persons, in accordance with such procedure and by reference to such matters, and to the opinion of such persons, as may be prescribed;

(e) different provision for different cases, including different provision in relation to different persons, circumstances or localities; and

(f) such supplemental, consequential and transitional provision as the Minister or Ministers exercising the power considers or consider appropriate.

(3) The powers to make regulations under any of the provisions of Chapter II of Part II, under any of the flood defence provisions of this Act or under section 189 or 199 above or paragraph 10 of Schedule 2 to this Act—

(a) shall not, except to the extent that they would do so apart from this section, include any of the powers conferred by subsection (2) above; but

(b) in the case of the powers conferred by section 108(7) above and paragraph 10 of Schedule 2 to this Act, shall include power to make different provision in relation to different classes of person.

DEFINITIONS
"flood defence provisions": s.221(1).
"prescribed": s.221(1).
"the Ministers": s.221(1).

GENERAL NOTE

Subs. (3)
   The effect of this subsection is to exclude all powers to make regulations that arise in relation to abstraction and impounding or flood defence from the powers contained in subs. (2).

Construction of Act

Provisions relating to service of documents

220.—(1) Any document required or authorised by virtue of this Act to be served on any person may be served—

(a) by delivering it to him or by leaving it at his proper address or by sending it by post to him at that address; or

(b) if the person is a body corporate, by serving it in accordance with paragraph (a) above on the secretary or clerk of that body; or

(c) if the person is a partnership, by serving it in accordance with paragraph (a) above on a partner or a person having the control or management of the partnership business.

(2) For the purposes of this section and section 7 of the Interpretation Act 1978 (which relates to the service of documents by post) in its application to this section, the proper address of any person on whom a document is to be served shall be his last known address, except that—

(a) in the case of service on a body corporate or its secretary or clerk, it shall be the address of the registered or principal office of the body;

(b) in the case of service on a partnership or a partner or a person having the control or management of a partnership business, it shall be the address of the principal office of the partnership;

and for the purposes of this subsection the principal office of a company registered outside the United Kingdom, or of a partnership carrying on business outside the United Kingdom, is its principal office within the United Kingdom.

(3) If a person to be served by virtue of this Act with any document by another has specified to that other an address within the United Kingdom other than his proper address (as determined in pursuance of subsection (2) above) as the one at which he or someone on his behalf will accept documents of the same description as that document, that address shall also be treated as his proper address for the purposes of this section and for the purposes of the said section 7 in its application to this section.

(4) Where under any provision of this Act any document is required to be served on the owner, on a lessee or on the occupier of any premises then—

(a) if the name or address of the owner, of the lessee or, as the case may be, of the occupier of the premises cannot after reasonable inquiry be ascertained; or

(b) in the case of service on the occupier, if the premises appear to be or are unoccupied,

that document may be served either by leaving it in the hands of a person who is or appears to be resident or employed on the land or by leaving it conspicuously affixed to some building or object on the land.

(5) This section shall not apply to any document in relation to the service of which provision is made by rules of court.

General interpretation

221.—(1) In this Act, except in so far as the context otherwise requires—

"abstraction," in relation to water contained in any source of supply, means the doing of anything whereby any of that water is removed from that source of supply, whether temporarily or permanently, including anything whereby the water is so removed for the purpose of being transferred to another source of supply; and "abstract" shall be construed accordingly;

"accessories," in relation to a main, sewer or other pipe, includes any manholes, ventilating shafts, inspection chambers, settling tanks, wash-out pipes, pumps, ferrules or stopcocks for the main, sewer or other pipe, or any machinery or other apparatus which is designed or adapted for use in connection with the use or maintenance of the main, sewer or other pipe or of another accessory for it, but does not include any telecommunication apparatus (within the meaning of Schedule 2 to the Telecommunications Act 1984) unless it—

(a) is or is to be situated inside or in the close vicinity of the main, sewer or other pipe or inside or in the close vicinity of another accessory for it; and

(b) is intended to be used only in connection with the use or maintenance of the main, sewer or other pipe or of another accessory for it;

and in this definition "stopcock" has the same meaning as in the Water Industry Act 1991;

"agriculture" has the same meaning as in the Agriculture Act 1947 and "agricultural" shall be construed accordingly;

"analyse," in relation to any sample of land, water or effluent, includes subjecting the sample to a test of any description, and cognate expressions shall be construed accordingly;

"the Authority" means the National Rivers Authority;

"conservancy authority" means any person who has a duty or power under any enactment to conserve, maintain or improve the navigation of a tidal water and is not a navigation authority or harbour authority;

"constituent council," in relation to regional flood defence committees and local flood defence committees, shall be construed in accordance with sections 10(5) and 13(7) above, respectively;

"contravention" includes a failure to comply, and cognate expressions shall be construed accordingly;

"damage," in relation to individuals, includes death and any personal injury (including any disease or impairment of physical or mental condition);

"discrete waters" means inland waters so far as they comprise—

(a) a lake, pond or reservoir which does not discharge to any other inland waters; or

(b) one of a group of two or more lakes, ponds or reservoirs (whether near to or distant from each other) and of watercourses or mains connecting them, where none of the inland waters in the group discharges to any inland waters outside the group;

"disposal"—

(a) in relation to land or any interest or right in or over land, includes the creation of such an interest or right and a disposal effected by means of the surrender or other termination of any such interest or right; and

(b) in relation to sewage, includes treatment;

and cognate expressions shall be construed accordingly;

"drain" has, subject to subsection (2) below, the same meaning as in the Water Industry Act 1991;

"drainage" in the expression "drainage works" has the meaning given by section 113 above for the purposes of Part IV of this Act;

"drought order" means an ordinary drought order under subsection (1) of section 73 above or an emergency drought order under subsection (2) of that section;

"effluent" means any liquid, including particles of matter and other substances in suspension in the liquid;

"enactment" includes an enactment contained in this Act or in any Act passed after this Act;

"engineering or building operations," without prejudice to the generality of that expression, includes—

(a) the construction, alteration, improvement, maintenance or demolition of any building or structure or of any reservoir, watercourse, dam, weir, well, borehole or other works; and

(b) the installation, modification or removal of any machinery or apparatus;

"financial year" means the 12 months ending with March 31;

"flood defence functions," in relation to the Authority, means the functions of the Authority mentioned in section 2(1)(c) above and any other functions of the Authority under any of the flood defence provisions of this Act;

"flood defence provisions," in relation to this Act, means any of the following provisions of this Act, that is to say—

(a) Part IV;

(b) sections 133 to 141 (including Schedule 15), 143, 147 to 149, 155, 165 to 167, 180, 193, 194, 214, Schedule 4 and paragraph 5 of Schedule 25; and

(c) any other provision so far as it relates to a provision falling within paragraph (a) or (b) above;

"harbour" has the same meaning for the purposes of the flood defence provisions of this Act as in the Merchant Shipping Act 1894;

"harbour authority" (except in the flood defence provisions of this Act, in which it has the same meaning as in the Merchant Shipping Act 1894) means a person who is a harbour authority within the meaning of the Prevention of Oil Pollution Act 1971 and is not a navigation authority;

"highway" has the same meaning as in the Highways Act 1980;

"information" includes anything contained in any records, accounts, estimates or returns;

"inland waters" means the whole or any part of—

    (a) any river, stream or other watercourse (within the meaning of Chapter II of Part II of this Act), whether natural or artificial and whether tidal or not;

    (b) any lake or pond, whether natural or artificial, or any reservoir or dock, in so far as the lake, pond, reservoir or dock does not fall within paragraph (a) of this definition; and

    (c) so much of any channel, creek, bay, estuary or arm of the sea as does not fall within paragraph (a) or (b) of this definition;

"joint planning board" has the same meaning as in the Town and Country Planning Act 1990;

"local authority" means the council of any county, district or London borough or the Common Council of the City of London;

"local statutory provision" means—

    (a) a provision of a local Act (including an Act confirming a provisional order);

    (b) a provision of so much of any public general Act as has effect with respect to a particular area, with respect to particular persons or works or with respect to particular provisions falling within any paragraph of this definition;

    (c) a provision of an instrument made under any provision falling within paragraph (a) or (b) above; or

    (d) a provision of any other instrument which is in the nature of a local enactment;

"main river" means a main river within the meaning of Part IV of this Act;

"main river map" has, subject to section 194 above, the meaning given by section 193(2) above;

"micro-organism" includes any microscopic, biological entity which is capable of replication;

"minimum acceptable flow," in relation to any inland waters, means (except in sections 21 and 22 above and subject to section 23(3) above) the minimum acceptable flow as for the time being contained in provisions which are in force under section 21(7) above in relation to those waters;

"the Minister" means the Minister of Agriculture, Fisheries and Food;

"the Ministers" means the Secretary of State and the Minister;

"modifications" includes additions, alterations and omissions, and cognate expressions shall be construed accordingly;

"mortgage" includes any charge or lien on any property for securing money or money's worth, and "mortgagee" shall be construed accordingly;

"navigation authority" means any person who has a duty or power under any enactment to work, maintain, conserve, improve or control any canal or other inland navigation, navigable river, estuary, harbour or dock;

"notice" means notice in writing;

"owner," in relation to any premises, means the person who—

(a) is for the time being receiving the rack-rent of the premises, whether on his own account or as agent or trustee for another person; or

(b) would receive the rack-rent if the premises were let at a rack-rent,

but for the purposes of Schedule 2 to this Act, Chapter II of Part II of this Act and the related water resources provisions does not include a mortgagee not in possession, and cognate expressions shall be construed accordingly;

"prescribed" means prescribed by regulations made by the Secretary of State or, in relation to regulations made by the Minister, by those regulations;

"public authority" means any Minister of the Crown or government department, the Authority, any local authority or any person certified by the Secretary of State to be a public authority for the purposes of this Act;

"public sewer" means a sewer for the time being vested in a sewerage undertaker in its capacity as such, whether vested in that undertaker by virtue of a scheme under Schedule 2 to the Water Act 1989, section 179 of or Schedule 2 to the Water Industry Act 1991 or otherwise;

"records" includes computer records and any other records kept otherwise than in a document;

"the related water resources provisions," in relation to Chapter II of Part II of this Act, means the provisions of sections 21 to 23 above (including Schedule 5), of sections 120, 123 to 130, 158, 189, 199 to 201, 206(2) and (3), 209(3), 211(1), 213(1), and 216 above and of paragraph 1 of Schedule 25 to this Act;

"sewage effluent" includes any effluent from the sewage disposal or sewerage works of a sewerage undertaker but does not include surface water;

"sewer" has, subject to subsection (2) below, the same meaning as in the Water Industry Act 1991;

"source of supply" means—

(a) any inland waters except, without prejudice to subsection (3) below in its application to paragraph (b) of this definition, any which are discrete waters; or

(b) any underground strata in which water is or at any time may be contained;

"street" has, subject to subsection (4) below, the same meaning as in Part III of the New Roads and Street Works 1991;

"subordinate legislation" has the same meaning as in the Interpretation Act 1978;

"substance" includes micro-organisms and any natural or artificial substance or other matter, whether it is in solid or liquid form or in the form of a gas or vapour;

"surface water" includes water from roofs;

"trade effluent" includes any effluent which is discharged from premises used for carrying on any trade or industry, other than surface water and domestic sewage, and for the purposes of this definition any premises wholly or mainly used (whether for profit or not) for agricultural purposes or for the purposes of fish farming or for scientific research or experiment shall be deemed to be premises used for carrying on a trade;

"underground strata" means strata subjacent to the surface of any land;

"vessel" includes a hovercraft within the meaning of the Hovercraft Act 1968;

"watercourse" includes (subject to sections 72(2) and 113(1) above) all rivers, streams, ditches, drains, cuts, culverts, dykes, sluices,

sewers and passages through which water flows, except mains and
other pipes which—
     (a) belong to the Authority or a water undertaker; or
     (b) are used by a water undertaker or any other person for the
purpose only of providing a supply of water to any premises,
"water pollution provisions," in relation to this Act, means the following provisions of this Act—
     (a) the provisions of Part III of this Act;
     (b) sections 161, 190, 202, 203 and 213(2) above; and
     (c) paragraph 4 of Schedule 25 to this Act and section 211
above so far as it relates to byelaws made under that paragraph.
  (2) References in this Act to a pipe, including references to a main, a drain
or a sewer, shall include references to a tunnel or conduit which serves or is
to serve as the pipe in question and to any accessories for the pipe; and,
accordingly, references to the laying of a pipe shall include references to the
construction of such a tunnel or conduit, to the construction or installation of
any such accessories and to the making of a connection between one pipe
and another.
  (3) Any reference in this Act to water contained in underground strata is a
reference to water so contained otherwise than in a sewer, pipe, reservoir,
tank or other underground works constructed in any such strata; but for the
purposes of this Act water for the time being contained in—
    (a) a well, borehole or similar work, including any adit or passage con-
       structed in connection with the well, borehole or work for facilitating
       the collection of water in the well, borehole or work; or
    (b) any excavation into underground strata, where the level of water in
       the excavation depends wholly or mainly on water entering it from
       those strata,
shall be treated as water contained in the underground strata into which the
well, borehole or work was sunk or, as the case may be, the excavation was
made.
  (4) Until the coming into force of Part III of the New Roads and Street
Works Act 1991, the definition of "street" in subsection (1) above shall have
effect as if the reference to that Part were a reference to the Public Utilities
Street Works Act 1950; but nothing in this section shall be taken—
    (a) to prejudice the power of the Secretary of State under that Act of 1991
       to make an order bringing Part III of that Act into force on different
       days for different purposes (including the purposes of this section); or
    (b) in the period before the coming into force of that Part, to prevent
       references in this Act to a street, where the street is a highway which
       passes over a bridge or through a tunnel, from including that bridge or
       tunnel.
  (5) For the purposes of any provision of this Act by or under which power
is or may be conferred on any person to recover the expenses incurred by
that person in doing anything, those expenses shall be assumed to include
such sum as may be reasonable in respect of establishment charges or
overheads.
  (6) References in this Act to the later or latest of two or more different
times or days are, in a case where those times or days coincide, references to
the time at which or, as the case may be, the day on which they coincide.
  (7) For the purposes of this Act—
    (a) references in this Act to more than one Minister of the Crown, in
       relation to anything falling to be done by those Ministers, are refer-
       ences to those Ministers acting jointly; and
    (b) any provision of this Act by virtue of which any function of a Minister
       of the Crown is exercisable concurrently by different Ministers, shall
       have effect as providing for that function also to be exercisable jointly
       by any two or more of those Ministers.

(8) Sub-paragraph (1) of paragraph 1 of Schedule 2 to the Water Consolidation (Consequential Provisions) Act 1991 has effect (by virtue of sub-paragraph (2)(b) of that paragraph) so that references in this Act to things done under or for the purposes of provisions of this Act, the Water Industry Act 1991 or the Land Drainage Act 1991 include references to things done, or treated as done, under or for the purposes of the corresponding provisions of the law in force before the commencement of this Act.

(9) Subject to any provision to the contrary which is contained in Schedule 26 to the Water Act 1989 or in the Water Consolidation (Consequential Provisions) Act 1991, nothing in any local statutory provision passed or made before September 1, 1989, shall be construed as relieving any water undertaker or sewerage undertaker from any liability arising by virtue of this Act in respect of any act or omission occurring on or after that date.

Other supplemental provisions

Crown application

222.—(1) Subject to the following provisions of this section, the provisions of this Act shall have effect in relation to land in which there is a Crown or Duchy interest as they have effect in relation to land in which there is no such interest.

(2) Chapter II of Part II of this Act and the related water resources provisions shall not apply—

(a) to anything done by or on behalf of the Crown; or

(b) to any land which is in the occupation of a government department or any other land in which there is a Crown or Duchy interest and which is occupied in right of that interest.

(3) Nothing in this Act, as read with the other provisions of this section, shall be construed—

(a) as conferring any power of levying drainage charges in respect of lands below the high-water mark of ordinary spring tides; or

(b) as authorising the Authority to require the Crown to make any payment to the Authority in respect of any premises.

(4) Subject to subsection (2) and (3) above and to subsection (5) below, where a power is conferred in relation to land by or under any provision of this Act other than one of the flood defence provisions—

(a) that power shall be exercisable in relation to any land in which there is a Crown or Duchy interest only with the consent of the appropriate authority; and

(b) a consent for the purposes of this subsection may be given on such financial and other conditions as the appropriate authority giving the consent may consider appropriate.

(5) Subsection (4) above shall not require any consent to be given—

(a) for the exercise of any power in relation to any land in which there is a Crown or Duchy interest to the extent that that power would be so exercisable apart from subsection (1) above; or

(b) for the purposes of any provision having effect by virtue of so much of section 168 above and Schedule 19 to this Act as relates to the granting of authority for discharges of water.

(6) Section 74 of the Land Drainage Act 1991 (Crown application), so far as it relates to land in which there is a Crown or Duchy interest, shall apply in relation to the flood defence provisions of this Act as it applies in relation to that Act; but nothing in this subsection shall affect any power conferred by this Act for the purposes both of the Authority's functions under those provisions and of other functions of the Authority.

(7) In this section—

"the appropriate authority" has the same meaning as in section 293 of the Town and Country Planning Act 1990; and

"Crown or Duchy interest" means an interest belonging to Her Majesty in right of the Crown or of the Duchy of Lancaster, or to the Duchy of Cornwall, or belonging to a government department or held in trust for Her Majesty for the purposes of a government department.

(8) The provisions of subsection (3) of section 293 of the Town and Country Planning Act 1990 (questions relating to Crown application) as to the determination of questions shall apply for the purposes of this section.

(9) Nothing in this section shall be construed as requiring any provision of this Act having effect otherwise than in relation to land to be construed as imposing any liability on the Crown to which the Crown would not be subject apart from this section.

DEFINITIONS
"Crown or Duchy interest": subs. (7).
"the appropriate authority": subs. (7).

Exemption for visiting forces

223.—(1) Chapter II of Part II of this Act and the related water resources provisions shall not apply—
  (a) to anything done by a member of a visiting force in his capacity as a member of that force; or
  (b) to any land occupied by or for the purposes of a visiting force.

(2) In this section "visiting force" means any such body, contingent or detachment of the forces of any country as is a visiting force for the purposes of any of the provisions of the Visiting Forces Act 1952.

DEFINITION
"visiting force": subs. (2).

Application to Isles of Scilly

224.—(1) Subject to the provisions of any order under this section, nothing in this Act shall require or authorise any function, duty or power to be carried out, performed or exercised in relation to the Isles of Scilly by the Authority; and references in the preceding provisions of this Act to England and Wales shall not include references to those Isles.

(2) The Secretary of State may, on the application of the Council of the Isles of Scilly, by order make provision with respect to the carrying out in those Isles of functions falling under this Act to be carried out in relation to other parts of England and Wales by the Authority.

(3) Without prejudice to the generality of the power conferred by subsection (2) above, an order under this section may apply any provision of this Act, of the Water Consolidation (Consequential Provisions) Act 1991 or of the Water Act 1989 in relation to the Isles of Scilly with or without modifications.

(4) The power of the Secretary of State to make an order under this section shall be exercisable by statutory instrument subject to annulment in pursuance of a resolution of either House of Parliament.

(5) An order under this section may—
  (a) make different provision for different cases, including different provision in relation to different persons, circumstances or localities; and
  (b) contain such supplemental, consequential and transitional provision as the Secretary of State considers appropriate, including provision saving provision repealed by or under any enactment.

DEFINITIONS
"enactment": s.221(1).
"functions": s.3.
"modifications": s.221(1).

Short title, commencement and extent

225.—(1) This Act may be cited as the Water Resources Act 1991.

(2) This Act shall come into force on December 1, 1991.

(3) Subject to subsections (4) to (6) of section 2 and to section 224 above, to the extension of section 166(3) above to Scotland and to the extension, by virtue of any other enactment, of any provision of this Act to the territorial sea, this Act extends to England and Wales only.

(4) Nothing in this Act, so far as it extends to Scotland, shall authorise the Authority to acquire any land in Scotland compulsorily.

SCHEDULES

Section 1   SCHEDULE 1

THE NATIONAL RIVERS AUTHORITY

Membership

1.—(1) Subject to the following provisions of this paragraph, a member shall hold and vacate office in accordance with the terms of his appointment and shall, on ceasing to be a member, be eligible for re-appointment.

(2) A member may at any time by notice to the appropriate Minister resign his office.

(3) The appropriate Minister may remove a member if he is satisfied—

(a) that that member has been absent from meetings of the Authority for a period of more than three consecutive months without the permission of the Authority;

(b) that that member has been adjudged bankrupt, that his estate has been sequestrated or that he has made a composition or arrangement with, or granted a trust deed for, his creditors; or

(c) that that member is unable or unfit to carry out the functions of a member.

Remuneration, pensions etc.

2.—(1) The Authority shall pay to its members such remuneration, and such travelling and other allowances, as may be determined by the appropriate Minister.

(2) The Authority shall, if so required by the appropriate Minister—

(a) pay such pension, allowances or gratuities to or in respect of a person who has been or is a member; or

(b) make such payments towards provision for the payment of a pension, allowances or gratuities to or in respect of such a person,

as may be determined by the appropriate Minister.

(3) If, when any member ceases to hold office, the appropriate Minister determines that there are special circumstances which make it right that that member should receive compensation, the Authority shall pay to him a sum by way of compensation of such amount as may be so determined.

(4) Without prejudice to the other provisions of this Schedule—

(a) the Authority may enter into a contract with any person under which, in consideration of payments made by the Authority by way of premium or otherwise, that person undertakes to pay to the Authority such sums as may be provided in the contract in the event of any member of the Authority or of any of its committees meeting with a personal accident, whether fatal or not, while he is engaged on the business of the Authority;

(b) any sum received by the Authority under any such contract shall, after deduction of any expenses incurred in the recovery of that sum, be paid by the Authority to, or to the personal representatives of, the person in respect of whose accident the sum is received;

and the provisions of the Life Assurance Act 1774 shall not apply to any such contract.

(5) The approval of the Treasury shall be required for the making of a determination under this paragraph.

Staff

3.—(1) The Authority may, with the approval of the Secretary of State as to terms and conditions of service, appoint such officers and employees as it may determine.

(2) No member or other person shall be appointed by the Authority to act as chief executive of the Authority unless the Secretary of State has consented to the appointment of that person.

(3) The Authority may—

(a) pay such pensions, allowances or gratuities to or in respect of any persons who have been or are its officers or employees as it may, with the approval of the Secretary of State, determine;

(b) make such payments as it may so determine towards provision for the payment of pensions, allowances or gratuities to or in respect of any such persons;

(c) provide and maintain such schemes as it may so determine (whether contributory or not) for the payment of pensions, allowances or gratuities to or in respect of any such persons.

(4) Any reference in sub-paragraph (3) above to pensions, allowances or gratuities to or in respect of any such persons as are mentioned in that subparagraph includes a reference to pensions, allowances or gratuities by way of compensation to or in respect of any of the Authority's officers or employees who suffer loss of office or employment or loss or diminution of emoluments.

(5) If any person—

(a) on ceasing to be an officer or employee of the Authority, becomes a member; and

(b) was by reference to his office or employment with the Authority a participant in a pension scheme maintained by the Authority for the benefit of any of its officers or employees,

the Authority may, with the approval of the Secretary of State, make provision for him to continue to participate in that scheme, on such terms and conditions as it may with the consent of the Secretary of State determine, as if his service as a member were service as an officer or employee of the Authority.

(6) Provision made by virtue of sub-paragraph (5) above shall be without prejudice to paragraph 2 above.

(7) The consent of the Treasury shall be required for the giving of an approval under this paragraph.

Proceedings of Authority

4. Subject to the following provisions of this Schedule and to section 106 of this Act, the Authority may regulate its own procedure (including quorum).

Delegation of powers

5. Subject to section 106 of this Act, anything authorised or required by or under any enactment to be done by the Authority may be done—

(a) by any member, officer or employee of the Authority who has been authorised for the purpose, whether generally or specially, by the Authority; or

(b) by any committee or sub-committee of the Authority which has been so authorised.

Interests of members

6.—(1) A member who is in any way directly or indirectly interested in any matter that is brought up for consideration at a meeting of the Authority shall disclose the nature of his interest to the meeting; and, where such a disclosure is made—

(a) the disclosure shall be recorded in the minutes of the meeting; and

(b) the member shall not take any part in any deliberation or decision of the Authority, or of any of its committees or sub-committees, with respect to that matter.

(2) For the purposes of sub-paragraph (1) above, a general notification given at a meeting of the Authority by a member to the effect that—

(a) he is a member of a specified company or firm; and

(b) is to be regarded as interested in any matter involving that company or firm,

shall be regarded as a sufficient disclosure of his interest in relation to any such matter.

(3) A member need not attend in person at a meeting of the Authority in order to make a disclosure which he is required to make under this paragraph if he takes reasonable steps to secure that the disclosure is made by a notice which is taken into consideration and read at the meeting.

(4) The Secretary of State may, subject to such conditions as he considers appropriate, remove any disability imposed by virtue of this paragraph in any case where the number of members of the Authority disabled by virtue of this paragraph at any one time would be so great a proportion of the whole as to impede the transaction of business.

(5) The power of the Secretary of State under sub-paragraph (4) above includes power to remove, either indefinitely or for any period, a disability which would otherwise attach to any member, or members of any description, by reason of such interests, and in respect of such matters, as may be specified or described by the Secretary of State.

(6) Nothing in this paragraph precludes any member from taking part in the consideration or discussion of, or voting on, any question whether an application should be made to the Secretary of State for the exercise of the power conferred by sub-paragraph (4) above.

(7) In this paragraph references to a meeting of the Authority include references to a meeting of any of its committees or sub-committees.

Vacancies and defective appointments

7. The validity of any proceedings of the Authority shall not be affected by a vacancy amongst the members or by a defect in the appointment of a member.

Minutes

8.—(1) Minutes shall be kept of proceedings of the Authority, of its committees and of its sub-committees.

(2) Minutes of any such proceedings shall be evidence of those proceedings if they are signed by a person purporting to have acted as chairman of the proceedings to which the minutes relate or of any subsequent proceedings in the course of which the minutes were approved as a correct record.

(3) Where minutes of any such proceedings have been signed as mentioned in sub-paragraph (2) above, those proceedings shall, unless the contrary is shown, be deemed to have been regularly convened and constituted.

Application of seal and proof of instruments

9.—(1) The application of the seal of the Authority shall be authenticated by the signature of any member, officer or employee of the Authority who has been authorised for the purpose, whether generally or specially, by the Authority.

(2) In this paragraph the reference to the signature of a person includes a reference to a facsimile of a signature by whatever process reproduced; and, in paragraph 10 below, the word "signed" shall be construed accordingly.

Documents served etc. by or on the Authority

10.—(1) Any document which the Authority is authorised or required by or under any enactment to serve, make or issue may be signed on behalf of the Authority by any member, officer or employee of the Authority who has been authorised for the purpose, whether generally or specially, by the Authority.

(2) Every document purporting to be an instrument made or issued by or on behalf of the Authority and to be duly executed under the seal of the Authority, or to be signed or executed by a person authorised by the Authority for the purpose, shall be received in evidence and be treated, without further proof, as being so made or issued unless the contrary is shown.

(3) Any notice which is required or authorised, by or under any enactment not contained in this Act, to be given, served or issued by or to the Authority shall be in writing.

Interpretation

11. In this Schedule—
    "the appropriate Minister," in relation to any person who is or has been a member, means the Minister or the Secretary of State, according to whether that person was appointed as a member by the Minister or the Secretary of State; and
    "member" means any member of the Authority, including the chairman and the deputy chairman.

Section 2   SCHEDULE 2

Orders and Agreements for Transfer of Navigation, Harbour and Conservancy Functions

Powers to transfer functions or property

1.—(1) The Authority may at any time apply to the Ministers for an order under this Schedule transferring to the Authority any of the functions or property of a navigation authority, harbour authority or conservancy authority.

(2) The power to make an order under this Schedule shall be exercisable by statutory instrument.

(3) Any transfer of functions or property which could be effected by an order under this Schedule may, with the consent of the Ministers, be effected by agreement between the Authority and the other body concerned.

(4) Where, in accordance with this paragraph, the authority may apply for an order transferring any functions or property of another body, that body may itself apply for such an order.

(5) For the purposes of this Schedule the references in sub-paragraph (1) above to a navigation authority, to a harbour authority and to a conservancy authority shall each include a reference to a body which no longer has any members but which, if it had members, would be such an authority.

Consultation with affected body

2.—(1) Before determining whether to make an order on an application under paragraph 1 above, the Ministers shall—
   (a) consult whichever of the following is not the applicant, that is to say, the Authority and the body from which any functions or property are proposed in the application to be transferred; and
   (b) consider any representations made with respect to the application by the Authority or, as the case may be, by any such body.
(2) Sub-paragraph (1) above shall not require the Ministers to consult, or consider representations from, any body which no longer has any members.

Public consultation

3.—(1) If the Ministers propose to make an order on an application under paragraph 1 above, they shall prepare a draft order, and shall cause notice of their intention to make an order—
   (a) to be published in the London Gazette and in such other manner as they think best adapted for informing persons affected; and
   (b) to be served on—
      (i) the Authority;
      (ii) any body (other than one no longer having any members) from which any functions or property are proposed to be transferred; and
      (iii) any such navigation authority, harbour authority or conservancy authority not falling within paragraph (ii) above as appears to the Ministers to be affected by the proposals.
(2) A notice under sub-paragraph (1) above shall specify—
   (a) the place where copies of the draft order, and of any map to which it refers, may be inspected and obtained; and
   (b) the time (not being less than 28 days) within which, and the manner in which, objections to the draft order may be made.
(3) Before making any order on an application under paragraph 1 above, the Ministers—
   (a) shall consider any objections which may be duly made to the draft order; and
   (b) may, if they think fit, cause a local inquiry to be held with respect to any such objections; and, in making the order, the Ministers may make such modifications in the terms of the draft as appear to them desirable.

Supplemental provisions of order

4.—(1) An order under this Schedule may contain such incidental, supplementary, consequential and transitional provisions as the Ministers consider necessary or expedient.
(2) Without prejudice to the generality of sub-paragraph (1) above, the provision that may be included in an order by virtue of that sub-paragraph shall include such provisions as the Ministers consider necessary or expedient with respect to—
   (a) the transfer of assets and liabilities, the payment of compensation and other financial adjustments;
   (b) the amendment, adaptation or repeal of local enactments; and
   (c) the application, subject to such modifications as may be specified in the order, of provisions corresponding to those originally made by or under Part IX of the Water Resources Act 1963.

Objection to final order by affected bodies

5.—(1) After making an order under this Schedule, the Ministers, if an objection—
   (a) has been duly made by the Authority or any other body on which notice is required to be served under paragraph 3 above; and
   (b) has not been withdrawn,
shall serve notice of the making of the order and of the effect of the order on the Authority or, as the case may be, that body.
(2) Where a notice is required to be served under sub-paragraph (1) above, the order shall not have effect before the end of a period of 28 days from the date of service of that notice.
(3) If, within the period of 28 days mentioned in sub-paragraph (2) above, any body (including the Authority) on which notice has been served under sub-paragraph (1) above gives

notice to one of the Ministers objecting to the order, and the objection is not withdrawn, the order shall be subject to special parliamentary procedure.

Public notice of order

6.—(1) After making an order under this Schedule, the Ministers shall publish in the London Gazette, and in such other manner as they think best adapted for informing persons affected, a notice—

(a) stating that the order has been made; and

(b) naming a place where a copy of the order may be seen at all reasonable hours.

(2) In the case of an order to which sub-paragraph (1) of paragraph 5 above applies, a notice under sub-paragraph (1) above—

(a) shall not be published until the end of the period of 28 days mentioned in sub-paragraph (2) of that paragraph; and

(b) shall state whether or not the order is to be subject to special parliamentary procedure.

Challenge of order

7.—(1) Subject to sub-paragraph (3) below, if any person aggrieved by an order under this Schedule desires to question its validity on the ground—

(a) that it is not within the powers of this Schedule; or

(b) that any requirement of this Schedule has not been complied with in relation to the order,

he may, within six weeks after the first publication of the notice required by paragraph 6 above, make an application for the purpose to the High Court.

(2) Where an application under sub-paragraph (1) above is duly made to the High Court, that Court, if satisfied—

(a) that the order is not within the powers of this Schedule; or

(b) that the interests of the applicant have been substantially prejudiced by any requirements of this Schedule not having been complied with,

may quash the order either generally or in so far as it affects the applicant.

(3) The preceding provisions of this paragraph—

(a) shall not apply to any order which is confirmed by Act of Parliament under section 6 of the Statutory Orders (Special Procedure) Act 1945; and

(b) shall have effect in relation to any other order which is subject to special parliamentary procedure by virtue of the provisions of this Schedule as if, for the reference to the first publication of the notice required by paragraph 6 above, there were substituted a reference to the date on which the order becomes operative under that Act of 1945.

(4) Except as provided by this paragraph, the validity of an order under this Schedule shall not, either before or after the order has been made, be questioned in any legal proceedings whatsoever.

Effect of order or agreement

8.—(1) Where, by virtue of an order or agreement under this Schedule, property is transferred to the Authority on the terms that—

(a) the body from which it is transferred shall continue liable for the repayment of, and payment of interest on, any sum borrowed in connection with the property; and

(b) the Authority shall make payments to that body in respect of amounts paid by that body by reason of its continuing so liable,

any payment so made by the Authority shall be deemed to be a capital payment or an annual payment, according as the amount in respect of which it is made was paid in or towards repayment of the loan or by way of interest thereon.

(2) Property vested in the Authority by virtue of an order or agreement under this Schedule shall not be treated as so vested by way of sale for the purpose of section 12 of the Finance Act 1895 (which provides for charging stamp duty in the case of certain statutory transfers by way of sale).

Ministers' expenses

9.—(1) The costs incurred by the Ministers in connection with the making and notification of an order under this Schedule shall be paid by the applicant for the order; and, if there is more than one, the Ministers may apportion the costs between the applicants.

(2) The Ministers may require any applicant for an order under this Schedule to give security for the payment of any costs payable by the applicant under this paragraph.

(3) The reference in sub-paragraph (1) above to any costs incurred in connection with the making and notification of an order under this Schedule includes a reference to any costs incurred in relation to any such order under the Statutory Orders (Special Procedure) Act 1945.

Compensation for officers and staff

10.—(1) The Ministers shall by regulations make provision requiring the payment by the Authority, subject to such exceptions or conditions as may be prescribed, of compensation to or in respect of persons who—

(a) are, or but for any military or other designated service of theirs would be, the holders of any such situation, place or employment as may be prescribed; and

(b) suffer loss of employment, or loss or diminution of emoluments, in consequence of any order or agreement under this Schedule.

(2) Regulations under this paragraph may be so framed as to have effect as from a date earlier than that on which they are made; but so much of any regulations as provides that any provision is to have effect as from a date earlier than that on which they are made shall not place any person other than the Authority in a worse position than he would have been in if the regulations had been so framed as to have effect only as from the date on which they are made.

(3) Regulations made under this paragraph may include provision as to the manner in which, and the person to whom, any claim for compensation under this paragraph is to be made, and for the determination of all questions arising under the regulations.

(4) In this paragraph "military or other designated service" means any such service in any of Her Majesty's forces or other employment (whether or not in the service of Her Majesty) as may be prescribed by regulations under this paragraph.

Power to amend local enactments

11.—(1) If it appears to the Ministers by whom an order is made under this Schedule that any local enactment passed or made before the relevant date—

(a) is inconsistent with any of the provisions of that order; or

(b) requires to be amended or adapted, having regard to any of the provisions of that order, those Ministers may by order repeal, amend or adapt that enactment to such extent, or in such manner, as they may consider appropriate.

(2) Any order under this paragraph may include such transitional, incidental, supplementary and consequential provisions as the Ministers may consider necessary or expedient.

(3) The power to make an order under this paragraph shall be exercisable by statutory instrument subject to annulment in pursuance of a resolution of either House of Parliament.

(4) In this paragraph "relevant date" means the date which was the second appointed day for the purposes of section 133 of the Water Resources Act 1963.

(5) The provisions of this paragraph shall have effect without prejudice to the exercise of any other power to repeal, amend or adapt local enactments which is conferred by any other enactment.

Interpretation

12.—(1) In this Schedule "local enactment" means—

(a) a local or private Act;

(b) a public general Act relating to London;

(c) an order or scheme made under an Act, confirmed by Parliament or brought into operation in accordance with special parliamentary procedure; or

(d) an enactment in a public general Act amending a local or private Act or any such order or scheme.

(2) References in this Schedule to the Ministers, in a case in which all the functions in question are exercisable in Wales and all the property in question is situated there, shall have effect as references to the Secretary of State.

Section 9   SCHEDULE 3

BOUNDARIES OF REGIONAL FLOOD DEFENCE AREAS

Power to make order

1.—(1) The relevant Minister may by order made by statutory instrument—

(a) alter the boundaries of the area of any regional flood defence committee; or

(b) provide for the amalgamation of any two or more such areas.

(2) Where an order under this Schedule makes provision by reference to anything shown on a main river map, that map shall be conclusive evidence for the purposes of the order of what is shown on the map.

(3) The power to make an order under this Schedule shall include power to make such supplemental, consequential and transitional provision as the relevant Minister considers appropriate.

(4) In the case of an order under this Schedule amalgamating the areas of any two or more regional flood defence committees, the provision made by virtue of sub-paragraph (3) above may include provision determining—

(a) the total number of members of the amalgamated committee; and

(b) the total number of such members to be appointed by the constituent councils of that committee;

and subsections (6) and (7) of section 11 of this Act shall apply in relation to so much of an order under this Schedule as is made by virtue of this sub-paragraph as they apply in relation to an order under subsection (5) of that section.

(5) In this paragraph and the following paragraphs of this Schedule "the relevant Minister"—

(a) in relation to any alteration of the boundaries of an area where the whole or any part of that area is in Wales, means the Ministers;

(b) in relation to the amalgamation of any two or more areas where the whole or any part of any one of those areas is in Wales, means the Ministers; and

(c) in any other case, means the Minister.

Consultation and notice of intention to make order

2.—(1) Before making an order under this Schedule, the relevant Minister shall—

(a) consult such persons or representative bodies as he considers it appropriate to consult at that stage;

(b) prepare a draft order;

(c) publish a notice complying with sub-paragraph (2) below in the London Gazette and in such other manner as he considers appropriate for bringing the draft order to the attention of persons likely to be affected by it if it is made.

(2) A notice for the purposes of sub-paragraph (1)(c) above with respect to a draft order shall—

(a) state the relevant Minister's intention to make the order and its general effect;

(b) specify the places where copies of the draft order and of any map to which it refers may be inspected by any person free of charge at all reasonable times during the period of 28 days beginning with the date on which the notice is first published otherwise than in the London Gazette; and

(c) state that any person may within that period by notice in writing to the relevant Minister object to the making of the order.

(3) The relevant Minister shall also cause copies of the notice and of the draft order to be served on every person carrying out functions under any enactment who appears to him to be concerned.

Objections to draft order and making of order

3.—(1) Before making an order under this Schedule, the relevant Minister—

(a) shall consider any representations or objections which are duly made with respect to the draft order and are not withdrawn; and

(b) may, if he thinks fit, cause a local inquiry to be held with respect to any such representations or objections.

(2) Where notice of a draft order has been published and given in accordance with paragraph 2 above and any representations or objections considered under sub-paragraph (1) above, the relevant Minister may make the order either in the terms of the draft or in those terms as modified in such manner as he thinks fit, or may decide not to make the order.

(3) The relevant Minister shall not make a modification of a draft order in so far as the modification is such as to include in the area of any regional flood defence committee any tidal waters which, if the order had been made in the form of the draft, would have been outside the area of every regional flood defence committee.

Procedure for making of order

4.—(1) Where the relevant Minister makes an order under this Schedule, he shall serve notice of the making of the order on every person (if any) who—

(a) is a person on whom notice is required to have been served under paragraph 2(3) above; and

(b) has duly made an objection to the making of the order that has not been withdrawn.

(2) Where a notice is required to be served under sub-paragraph (1) above with respect to any order, the order shall not have effect before the end of a period of 28 days from the date of service of the last notice served under that sub-paragraph.

(3) If before an order takes effect under sub-paragraph (2) above—

(a) any person who has been served with a notice under sub-paragraph (1) above with respect to that order serves notice objecting to the order on the Minister (or, in the case of an order made jointly by the Ministers, on either of them); and

(b) the objection is not withdrawn,

the order shall be subject to special parliamentary procedure.

(4) A statutory instrument containing an order under this Schedule which is not subject to special parliamentary procedure under sub-paragraph (3) above shall be subject to annulment in pursuance of a resolution of either House of Parliament.

Notice after making of order

5.—(1) Subject to sub-paragraph (2) below, after making an order under this Schedule, the relevant Minister shall publish in the London Gazette, and in such other manner as he considers appropriate for bringing the order to the attention of persons likely to be affected by it, a notice—

(a) stating that the order has been made; and

(b) naming the places where a copy of the order may be inspected at all reasonable times.

(2) In the case of an order to which sub-paragraph (2) of paragraph 4 above applies, the notice—

(a) shall not be published until the end of the period of 28 days referred to in that sub-paragraph; and

(b) shall state whether or not the order is to be subject to special parliamentary procedure.

Questioning of order in courts

6.—(1) Subject to sub-paragraph (3) below, if any person desires to question the validity of an order under this Schedule on the ground—

(a) that it is not within the powers of this Schedule; or

(b) that any requirement of this Schedule has not been complied with,

he may, within six weeks after the date of the first publication of the notice required by paragraph 5 above, make an application for the purpose to the High Court.

(2) On an application under this paragraph the High Court, if satisfied—

(a) that the order is not within the powers of this Schedule; or

(b) that the interests of the applicant have been substantially prejudiced by a failure to comply with any of the requirements of this Schedule,

may quash the order either generally or in so far as it affects the applicant.

(3) Sub-paragraph (1) above—

(a) shall not apply to any order which is confirmed by Act of Parliament under section 6 of the Statutory Orders (Special Procedure) Act 1945; and

(b) shall have effect in relation to any other order which is subject to special parliamentary procedure by virtue of the provisions of this Schedule as if the reference to the date of the first publication of the notice required by paragraph 5 above were a reference to the date on which the order becomes operative under that Act of 1945.

(4) Except as provided by this paragraph the validity of an order under this Schedule shall not, either before or after the order has been made, be questioned in any legal proceedings whatsoever.

Section 14 SCHEDULE 4

MEMBERSHIP AND PROCEEDINGS OF REGIONAL AND LOCAL FLOOD DEFENCE COMMITTEES

PART I

MEMBERSHIP OF FLOOD DEFENCE COMMITTEES

Terms of membership

1.—(1) Members of a flood defence committee (that is to say a regional flood defence committee or a local flood defence committee), other than those appointed by or on behalf of one or more constituent councils, shall hold and vacate office in accordance with the terms of their appointment.

(2) The first members of a local flood defence committee appointed by or on behalf of any one or more constituent councils—

(a) shall come into office on the day on which the committee comes into existence or, in the case of a member who is for any reason appointed after that day, on the day on which the appointment is made; and

(b) subject to the following provisions of this Schedule, shall hold office until the end of May in such year as may be specified for the purposes of this paragraph in the scheme establishing the committee.

(3) Any members of a flood defence committee appointed by or on behalf of any one or more constituent councils who are not members to whom sub-paragraph (2) above applies—

(a) shall come into office at the beginning of the June next following the day on which they are appointed; and

(b) subject to the following provisions of this Schedule, shall hold office for a term of four years.

(4) If for any reason any such member as is mentioned in sub-paragraph (3) above is appointed on or after the day on which he ought to have come into office, he shall—

(a) come into office on the day on which he is appointed; and

(b) subject to the following provisions of this Schedule, hold office for the remainder of the term.

(5) References in this paragraph and the following provisions of this Schedule to a member of a flood defence committee include references to the chairman of such a committee.

Membership of constituent council as qualification for membership of committee

2.—(1) Members of a flood defence committee appointed by or on behalf of any one or more constituent councils may be members of that council, or one of those councils, or other persons.

(2) Any member of a flood defence committee appointed by or on behalf of a constituent council who at the time of his appointment was a member of that council shall, if he ceases to be a member of that council, also cease to be a member of the committee with whichever is the earlier of the following—

(a) the end of the period of three months beginning with the date when he ceases to be a member of the council; and

(b) the appointment of another person in his place.

(3) For the purposes of sub-paragraph (2) above a member of a council shall not be deemed to have ceased to be a member of the council by reason of retirement if he has been re-elected a member of the council not later than the date of his retirement.

Disqualification for membership of committee

3.—(1) Subject to the following provisions of this paragraph, a person shall be disqualified for appointment as a member of a flood defence committee if he—

(a) is a paid officer of the Authority; or

(b) is a person who has been adjudged bankrupt, or whose estate has been sequestrated or who has made a composition or arrangement with, or granted a trust deed for, his creditors; or

(c) within the period of five years before the day of his appointment, has been convicted, in the United Kingdom, the Channel Islands or the Isle of Man, of any offence and has had passed on him a sentence of imprisonment (whether suspended or not) for a period of not less than three months without the option of a fine; or

(d) is disqualified for being elected or for being a member of a local authority under Part III of the Local Government Finance Act 1982 (accounts and audit) or Part III of the Representation of the People Act 1983 (legal proceedings).

(2) Where a person is disqualified under sub-paragraph (1) above by reason of having been adjudged bankrupt, the disqualification shall cease—

(a) unless the bankruptcy order made against that person is previously annulled, on his discharge from bankruptcy; and

(b) if the bankruptcy order is so annulled, on the date of the annulment.

(3) Where a person is disqualified under sub-paragraph (1) above by reason of having had his estate sequestrated, the disqualification shall cease—

(a) unless the sequestration is recalled or reduced, on the person's discharge under section 54 of the Bankruptcy (Scotland) Act 1985; and

(b) if the sequestration is recalled or reduced, on the date of the recall or reduction.

(4) Where a person is disqualified under sub-paragraph (1) above by reason of his having made a composition or arrangement with, or having granted a trust deed for, his creditors, the disqualification shall cease—

(a) if he pays his debts in full, on the date on which the payment is completed; and

(b) in any other case, at the end of five years from the date on which the terms of the deed of composition or arrangement, or of the trust deed, are fulfilled.

(5) For the purposes of sub-paragraph (1)(c) above the date of the conviction shall be taken to be—

(a) the ordinary date on which the period allowed for making an appeal or application with respect to the conviction expires; or

(b) if such an appeal or application is made, the date on which it is finally disposed of or abandoned or fails by reason of non-prosecution.

(6) Section 92 of the Local Government Act 1972 (proceedings for disqualification) shall apply in relation to disqualification under this paragraph for appointment as a member of a flood defence committee as it applies in relation to disqualification for acting as a member of a local authority.

Vacation of office by disqualifying event

4.—(1) The office of a member of a flood defence committee shall become vacant upon the fulfilment of any of the following conditions, that is to say—
(a) the person holding that office is adjudged bankrupt, is a person whose estate is sequestrated or makes a composition or arrangement with, or grants a trust deed for, his creditors;
(b) that person is convicted, in the United Kingdom, the Channel Islands or the Isle of Man, of any offence and has passed on him a sentence of imprisonment (whether suspended or not) for a period of not less than three months without the option of a fine;
(c) that person is disqualified for being elected or for being a member of a local authority under Part III of the Local Government Finance Act 1982 (accounts and audit) or Part III of the Representation of the People Act 1983 (legal proceedings); or
(d) that person has, for a period of six consecutive months been absent from meetings of the committee, otherwise than by reason of illness or some other cause approved during the period by the committee.

(2) For the purposes of sub-paragraph (1)(d) above, the attendance of a member of a flood defence committee—
(a) at a meeting of any sub-committee of the committee of which he is a member; or
(b) at any joint committee to which he has been appointed by that committee,
shall be treated as attendance at a meeting of the committee.

Resignation of office by members of regional committee

5.—(1) The chairman of a regional flood defence committee may resign his office at any time by giving notice to the chairman of the Authority and to one of the Ministers.

(2) Any other member of such a committee may resign his office at any time by giving notice to the chairman of the committee and also, if he was appointed by one of the Ministers, to that Minister.

Resignation of office by members of local committee

6.—(1) The chairman of a local flood defence committee may resign his office at any time by giving notice to the chairman of the regional flood defence committee.

(2) Any other member of a local flood defence committee may resign his office at any time by giving notice to the chairman of that local flood defence committee.

Appointments to fill casual vacancies

7.—(1) Where, for any reason whatsoever, the office of a member of a flood defence committee becomes vacant before the end of his term of office, the vacancy—
(a) shall, if the unexpired portion of the term of office of the vacating member is six months or more, be filled by the appointment of a new member; and
(b) may be so filled in any other case.

(2) A person appointed by virtue of sub-paragraph (1) above to fill a casual vacancy shall hold office for so long only as the former member would have held office.

Eligibility of previous members for re-appointment

8. Subject to the provisions of this Schedule, a member of a flood defence committee shall be eligible for reappointment.

Appointment of deputies

9.—(1) Subject to the following provisions of this paragraph, a person nominated by one or more constituent councils may act as deputy for a member of a flood defence committee appointed by or on behalf of that council or those councils and may, accordingly, attend and vote at a meeting of the committee, instead of that member.

(2) A person nominated under sub-paragraph (1) above as deputy for a member of a flood defence committee may, by virtue of that nomination, attend and vote at a meeting of a sub-committee of that committee which—

(a) has been appointed by that committee under Part II of this Schedule; and

(b) is a committee to which the member for whom he is a deputy belongs.

(3) A person acting as deputy for a member of a flood defence committee shall be treated for the purposes for which he is nominated as a member of that committee.

(4) A person shall not act as deputy for a member of a flood defence committee unless his nomination has been notified to such officer of the Authority as is appointed to receive such nominations.

(5) A nomination under this paragraph shall be in writing and may apply either to a particular meeting or to all meetings during a stated period or until the nomination is revoked.

(6) A person shall not act as deputy for more than one member of a flood defence committee.

(7) Nothing in this paragraph shall entitle a person to attend and vote at a meeting of a local flood defence committee by reason of his nomination as deputy of a member of a regional flood defence committee.

Payments to past and present chairmen and to members

10.—(1) The Authority shall pay to any person who is a chairman of a flood defence committee such remuneration and allowances as may be determined by the relevant Minister with the consent of the Treasury.

(2) If the relevant Minister so determines in the case of any person who is or has been chairman of a flood defence committee, the Authority shall pay or make arrangements for the payment of a pension in relation to that person in accordance with the determination.

(3) If a person ceases to be chairman of a flood defence committee and it appears to the relevant Minister that there are special circumstances which make it right that that person should receive compensation in respect of his ceasing to be chairman, the relevant Minister may require the Authority to pay to that person a sum of such amount as that Minister may determine with the consent of the Treasury.

(4) The Authority may pay to any person who is a member of a flood defence committee such allowances as may be determined by the relevant Minister with the consent of the Treasury.

(5) In this paragraph—

"pension," in relation to any person, means a pension (whether contributory or not) of any kind payable to or in respect of him, and includes an allowance, gratuity or lump sum so payable and a return of contributions with or without interest or any other addition; and

"the relevant Minister"—

(a) in relation to the regional flood defence committee for an area the whole or the greater part of which is in Wales and in relation to any local flood defence committee for any district comprised in the area of such a regional flood defence committee, means the Secretary of State; and

(b) in relation to any other flood defence committee, means the Minister.

Part II

Proceedings of Flood Defence Committees

Appointment of sub-committees, joint sub-committees etc.

11.—(1) For the purpose of carrying out any functions in pursuance of arrangements under paragraph 12 below—

(a) a flood defence committee may appoint a sub-committee of the committee;

(b) two or more regional or two or more local flood defence committees may appoint a joint sub-committee of those committees;

(c) any sub-committee may appoint one or more committees of that sub-committee ("under sub-committees").

(2) The number of members of any sub-committee and their terms of office shall be fixed by the appointing committee or committees or, in the case of an under sub-committee, by the appointing sub-committee.

(3) A sub-committee appointed under this paragraph may include persons who are not members of the appointing committee or committees or, in the case of an under sub-committee, the committee or committees of whom they are an under sub-committee; but at least two thirds of the members appointed to any such sub-committee shall be members of that committee or those committees, as the case may be.

(4) A person who is disqualified for being a member of a flood defence committee shall be disqualified also for being a member of a sub-committee or under sub-committee appointed under this paragraph.

Delegation of functions to sub-committees etc.

12.—(1) Subject to section 106 of this Act and to any other express provision contained in any enactment, a flood defence committee may arrange for the carrying out of any of their functions—

(a) by a sub-committee, or an under sub-committee of the committee or an officer of the Authority; or

(b) by any other regional or, as the case may be, local flood defence committee;

and two or more regional or two or more local flood defence committees may arrange to carry out any of their functions jointly or may arrange for the carrying out of any of their functions by a joint sub-committee of theirs.

(2) Where by virtue of this paragraph any functions of a flood defence committee or of two or more such committees may be carried out by a sub-committee, then, unless the committee or committees otherwise direct, the sub-committee may arrange for the carrying out of any of those functions by an under sub-committee or by an officer of the Authority.

(3) Where by virtue of this paragraph any functions of a flood defence committee or of two or more such committees may be carried out by an under sub-committee, then, unless the committee or committees or the sub-committee otherwise direct, the under sub-committee may arrange for the carrying out of any of those functions by an officer of the Authority.

(4) Any arrangements made by a flood defence committee under this paragraph for the carrying out of any function shall not prevent the committee from discharging their functions themselves.

(5) References in the preceding provisions of this paragraph to the carrying out of any functions of a flood defence committee include references to the doing of anything which is calculated to facilitate, or is conducive or incidental to, the carrying out of any of those functions.

(6) A regional flood defence committee shall not, under this paragraph, make arrangements for the carrying out in a local flood defence district of any functions which fall to be carried out there by the local flood defence committee.

Rules of procedure

13.—(1) A flood defence committee may, with the approval of the relevant Minister, make rules for regulating the proceedings of the committee.

(2) Nothing in section 105 or 106 of this Act shall entitle the Authority to make any arrangements or give any directions for regulating the proceedings of any flood defence committee.

(3) In this paragraph "relevant Minister" has the same meaning as in paragraph 10 above.

Declarations of interest etc.

14.—(1) Subject to the following provisions of this paragraph, the provisions of sections 94 to 98 of the Local Government Act 1972 (pecuniary interests of members of local authorities) shall apply in relation to members of a flood defence committee as those provisions apply in relation to members of local authorities.

(2) In their application by virtue of this paragraph those provisions shall have effect in accordance with the following provisions—

(a) for references to meetings of the local authority there shall be substituted references to meetings of the committee;

(b) in section 94(4), for the reference to provision being made by standing orders of a local authority there shall be substituted a reference to provisions being made by directions of the committee;

(c) in section 96, for references to the proper officer of the local authority there shall be substituted a reference to an officer of the Authority appointed for the purposes of this paragraph; and

(d) section 97 shall apply as it applies to a local authority other than a parish or community council.

(3) Subject to sub-paragraph (4) below, a member of a flood defence committee shall be disqualified, for so long as he remains such a member and for 12 months after he ceases to be such a member, for appointment to any paid office by the Authority or any regional flood defence committee.

(4) Sub-paragraph (3) above shall not disqualify any person for appointment to the office of chairman of a local flood defence committee.

Authentication of documents

15.—(1) Any notice or other document which a flood defence committee are required or authorised to give, make or issue by or under any enactment may be signed on behalf of the committee by any member of the committee or any officer of the Authority who is generally or specifically authorised for that purpose by a resolution of the committee.

(2) Any document purporting to bear the signature of a person expressed to be authorised as mentioned in sub-paragraph (1) above shall be deemed, unless the contrary is shown, to be duly given, made or issued by authority of the committee.

(3) In this paragraph "signature" includes a facsimile of a signature by whatever process reproduced.

Proof and validity of proceedings

16.—(1) A minute of the proceedings of a meeting of a flood defence committee, purporting to be signed at that or the next ensuing meeting by—
(a) the chairman of the meeting to the proceedings of which the minute relates; or
(b) by the chairman of the next ensuing meeting,
shall be evidence of the proceedings and shall be received in evidence without further proof.

(2) Where a minute has been signed as mentioned in sub-paragraph (1) above in respect of a meeting of a committee or sub-committee, then, unless the contrary is shown—
(a) the meeting shall be deemed to have been duly convened and held;
(b) all the proceedings had at any such meeting shall be deemed to have been duly had; and
(c) that committee or sub-committee shall be deemed to have been duly constituted and have had power to deal with the matters referred to in the minute.

(3) The validity of any proceedings of a flood defence committee shall not be affected by any vacancy among the members of the committee or by any defect in the appointment of such a member.

Section 21   SCHEDULE 5

PROCEDURE RELATING TO STATEMENTS ON MINIMUM ACCEPTABLE FLOW

Application of Schedule

1.—(1) This Schedule applies in the case of any draft statement prepared under section 21 or 22 of this Act.

(2) References in this Schedule, in relation to a statement for amending the provision for determining the minimum acceptable flow of any inland waters, to the inland waters to which the statement relates are references to the inland waters to which the proposed amendment relates.

Notice of proposed statement

2.—(1) Before submitting the draft statement to the Secretary of State, the Authority shall publish a notice—
(a) stating the general effect of the draft statement;
(b) specifying the place where a copy of the draft statement, and of any relevant map or plan, may be inspected by any person free of charge at all reasonable times during the period of 28 days beginning with the date of first publication of the notice; and
(c) stating that any person may within that period, by notice in writing to the Secretary of State, object to the approval of the statement.

(2) A notice under this paragraph shall be published either—
(a) at least once in each of two successive weeks, in one or more newspapers circulating in the locality in which the inland waters to which the draft statement relates are situated; or
(b) in any other manner which, in any particular case, may be certified by the Secretary of State to be expedient in that case.

(3) Not later than the date on which the notice is first published in pursuance of sub-paragraph (2) above, the Authority shall serve a copy of the notice on—
(a) every local authority or joint planning board whose area comprises any inland waters to which the draft statement relates;
(b) any water undertaker having the right to abstract water from any such inland waters;
(c) any other water undertaker which was consulted in relation to the draft statement in pursuance of section 21(3)(b) of this Act;
(d) the drainage board for any internal drainage district which comprises any such inland waters or from which water is discharged into any such inland waters;
(e) any navigation authority, harbour authority or conservancy authority having functions in relation to any such waters or any related inland waters;
(f) if any such waters or any related inland waters are tidal waters in relation to which there is

no such navigation authority, harbour authority or conservancy authority, the Secretary of State for Transport;

(g) any person authorised by a licence under Part I of the Electricity Act 1989 to generate electricity; and

(h) every person who—

    (i) has given notice to the Authority requesting it to notify him of action taken in connection with the determination of a minimum acceptable flow for any inland waters to which the draft statement relates; and

    (ii) if the Authority have required him to pay a reasonable charge for being so notified, has paid that charge.

(4) The Authority shall also publish a notice in the London Gazette—

(a) stating that the draft statement has been submitted to the Secretary of State;

(b) naming the areas in respect of which a copy of a notice is required to be served under sub-paragraph (3)(a) above;

(c) specifying a place where a copy of the draft statement and of any relevant map or plan may be inspected; and

(d) where the notice required by sub-paragraph (1) above is published in a newspaper, giving the name of the newspaper and the date of an issue containing the notice.

(5) In this paragraph "related inland waters" has the same meaning as for the purposes of subsection (3) of section 21 of this Act is given by subsection (8) of that section.

Duty to provide copy of draft statement

3. The Authority shall, at the request of any person, furnish him with a copy of the draft statement on payment of such charge as the Authority thinks reasonable.

Approval of draft statement

4.—(1) The Secretary of State may approve the statement either in the form of the draft or in that form as altered in such manner as he thinks fit.

(2) Where the Secretary of State—

(a) proposes to make any alteration of a statement before approving it; and

(b) considers that any persons are likely to be adversely affected by it,

the Authority shall give and publish such additional notices, in such manner, as the Secretary of State may require.

(3) Sub-paragraph (4) below shall apply if, before the end of—

(a) the period of 28 days referred to in sub-paragraph (1) of paragraph 2 above;

(b) the period of 25 days from the publication in the London Gazette of the notice under sub-paragraph (4) of that paragraph; or

(c) any period specified in notices under sub-paragraph (2) above,

notice of an objection is received by the Secretary of State from any person on whom a notice is required by this Schedule to be served, or from any other person appearing to the Secretary of State to be affected by the draft statement, either as prepared in draft or as proposed to be altered.

(4) Where this sub-paragraph applies and the objection in question is not withdrawn, the Secretary of State, before approving the statement, shall either—

(a) cause a local inquiry to be held; or

(b) afford to the objector and to the Authority an opportunity of appearing before, and being heard by, a person appointed by the Secretary of State for the purpose.

(5) Where under this paragraph an objection is received by the Secretary of State from—

(a) the drainage board for any internal drainage district which comprises any inland waters to which the draft statement relates or, as the case may be, from which water is discharged into any such inland waters; or

(b) such an association or person claiming to represent a substantial fishery interest affected by the statement as is certified by the Minister to appear to him to represent such an interest,

sub-paragraphs (1) to (4) above and paragraph 5 below shall have effect as if references to the Secretary of State (except the first reference in sub-paragraph (3) above) were references to the Ministers.

Notice and inspection of approved statement

5.—(1) Where a statement is approved under this Schedule, whether in the form of the draft proposed by the Authority or with alterations, the Secretary of State shall give notice to the Authority—

(a) stating that the statement has been approved, either without alteration or with alterations specified in the notice; and

(b) specifying the date (not being earlier than 28 days after the date of the notice under this paragraph) on which the statement shall have effect;

and the Authority shall forthwith publish the notice.

(2) The Authority shall keep a copy of every statement, as approved under this Schedule, available at its offices for inspection by the public, free of charge, at all reasonable times.

Section 33   SCHEDULE 6

ORDERS PROVIDING FOR EXEMPTION FROM RESTRICTIONS ON ABSTRACTION

Notice of draft order

1.—(1) An application to the Secretary of State for an order under section 33 of this Act ("an exemption order") shall be accompanied by a draft of the proposed order.

(2) Before submitting a draft exemption order to the Secretary of State, the applicant authority shall publish a notice—

(a) stating the general effect of the draft order;

(b) specifying the place where a copy of the draft order, and of any relevant map or plan, may be inspected by any person free of charge at all reasonable times during the period of 28 days beginning with the date of first publication of the notice; and

(c) stating that any person may within that period, by notice to the Secretary of State, object to the making of the order.

(3) A notice under this paragraph shall be published either—

(a) at least once in each of two successive weeks, in one or more newspapers circulating in the locality in which the sources of supply to which the draft order relates are situated; or

(b) in any other manner which, in any particular case, may be certified by the Secretary of State to be expedient in that case.

(4) Not later than the date on which the notice is first published in pursuance of sub-paragraph (2) above, the applicant authority shall serve a copy of the notice on—

(a) the Authority, if it is not the applicant;

(b) every local authority or joint planning board whose area comprises any source of supply to which the draft order relates;

(c) any water undertaker having the right to abstract water from any such source of supply;

(d) any other water undertaker having the right to abstract water from any related underground strata;

(e) the drainage board for any internal drainage district which comprises any such source of supply or from which water is discharged into any such source of supply;

(f) any navigation authority, harbour authority or conservancy authority having functions in relation to any such source of supply or any related inland waters;

(g) if any such source of supply or any related inland waters are tidal waters in relation to which there is no such navigation authority, harbour authority or conservancy authority, the Secretary of State for Transport; and

(h) any person authorised by a licence under Part I of the Electricity Act 1989 to generate electricity.

(5) Where an application for an exemption order is made, the applicant authority shall also publish a notice in the London Gazette—

(a) stating that the draft exemption order has been submitted to the Secretary of State;

(b) naming the areas in respect of which a copy of a notice is required to be served under sub-paragraph (4)(b) above;

(c) specifying a place where a copy of the draft order and of any relevant map or plan may be inspected; and

(d) where the notice required by sub-paragraph (1) above is published in a newspaper, giving the name of the newspaper and the date of an issue containing the notice.

(6) For the purposes of this paragraph—

(a) underground strata are related underground strata in relation to any source of supply if—

(i) a water undertaker has a right to abstract water from the strata; and

(ii) it appears to the applicant authority, having regard to the extent to which the level of water in those strata depends on the flow of the waters in that source of supply, that the exercise of that right may be substantially affected by so much of the draft order in question as relates to that source of supply;

(b) inland waters are related inland waters in relation to any source of supply, where it appears to the applicant authority that changes in the flow of the waters of the source of supply may affect the flow of the waters in the inland waters in question.

Duty to provide copy of draft order

2. Where an application for an exemption order is made, the applicant authority shall, at the request of any person, furnish him with a copy of the draft exemption order on payment of such charge as the Authority thinks reasonable.

Making of order

3.—(1) Where an application for an exemption order is made, the Secretary of State may make the exemption order either in the form of the draft or in that form as altered in such manner as he thinks fit.

(2) Where the Secretary of State—

(a) proposes to make any alteration of an exemption order before making it; and

(b) considers that any persons are likely to be adversely affected by it,

the applicant authority shall give and publish such additional notices, in such manner, as the Secretary of State may require.

(3) Sub-paragraph (4) below shall apply if before the end of—

(a) the period of 28 days referred to in sub-paragraph (2) of paragraph 1 above;

(b) the period of 25 days from the publication in the London Gazette of the notice under sub-paragraph (5) of that paragraph; or

(c) any period specified in notices under sub-paragraph (2) above,

notice of an objection is received by the Secretary of State from any person on whom a notice is required by this Schedule to be served, from any other person appearing to the Secretary of State to be affected by the exemption order (either as prepared in draft or as proposed to be altered) or, in the case of a draft order submitted under section 33(4) of this Act, from the Authority.

(4) Where this sub-paragraph applies and the objection in question is not withdrawn, the Secretary of State, before making the order, shall either—

(a) cause a local inquiry to be held; or

(b) afford to the objector and to the applicant authority an opportunity of appearing before, and being heard by, a person appointed by the Secretary of State for the purpose.

(5) Where the exemption order (whether as prepared in draft or as proposed to be altered) relates to any tidal water in respect of which there is no relevant authority for the purposes of section 33 of this Act except the Authority, sub-paragraphs (1) to (4) above and paragraph 4 below shall have effect as if references to the Secretary of State (except the first reference in sub-paragraph (3) above) were references to the Secretary of State and the Secretary of State for Transport.

Notice and inspection of final order

4.—(1) Where an exemption order is made under section 33 of this Act, whether in the form of the draft proposed by the applicant authority or with alterations, the Secretary of State shall give notice to the applicant authority and (if it is not the applicant authority) to the Authority—

(a) stating that the exemption order has been made, either without alteration or with alterations specified in the notice; and

(b) specifying the date (not being earlier than 28 days after the date of the notice under this paragraph) on which the order shall have effect;

and the Authority shall forthwith publish the notice.

(2) The Authority shall keep a copy of every order made under section 33 of this Act available at its offices for inspection by the public, free of charge, at all reasonable times.

Sections 48, 55, 60, 61 and 65   SCHEDULE 7

LICENCES OF RIGHT

Applications for licences of right under paragraph 30 or 31 of Schedule 26 to the Water Act 1989

1.—(1) Paragraphs 30 and 31 of Schedule 26 to the Water Act 1989 shall continue to apply (notwithstanding the repeals made by the Water Consolidation (Consequential Provisions) Act 1991 but subject to the following provisions of this Schedule) in relation—

(a) to any application made under either of those paragraphs which is outstanding immediately before the coming into force of this Act; and

(b) to any appeal against a determination made, on an application under either of those paragraphs, either before the coming into force of this Act or, thereafter, by virtue of paragraph (a) above;

but for the purposes of any such application or appeal any reference in those paragraphs to a provision of the Water Resources Act 1963 which is re-enacted in this Act shall have effect, in relation to a time after the coming into force of this Act, as a reference to the corresponding provision of this Act.

(2) Where an application for the grant of a licence by virtue of paragraph 30 or 31 of Schedule 26 to the Water Act 1989 has been made before the end of the period within which such an application was required to be made under that paragraph, then—

(a) sections 24 and 48 of this Act and Part II of the Gas Act 1965 shall have effect, until the application is disposed of, as if the licence had been granted on the date of the application and the provisions of the licence had been in accordance with the proposals contained in the application; and

(b) for the purposes of those sections and Part II of the said Act of 1965 any licence granted on the application shall be treated as not having effect until the application has been disposed of.

(3) For the purposes of this paragraph an application for the grant of a licence by virtue of paragraph 30 or 31 of Schedule 26 to the Water Act 1989 above shall be taken to be disposed of on (but not before) the occurrence of whichever of the following events last occurs, that is to say—

(a) the grant, on the determination of the application by the Authority, of a licence the provisions of which are in accordance with the proposals contained in the application;

(b) the expiration, without a notice of appeal having been given, of the period (if any) within which the applicant is entitled to give notice of appeal against the decision on the application;

(c) the determination or withdrawal of an appeal against that decision;

(d) the grant, variation or revocation, in compliance with a direction given by the Secretary of State in consequence of such an appeal, of any licence;

and in this sub-paragraph any reference to a decision includes a reference to a decision which is to be treated as having been made by virtue of any failure of the Authority to make a decision within a specified time.

(4) Subject to the other provisions of this Schedule, any licence granted by virtue of this paragraph shall have effect as a licence under Chapter II of Part II of this Act; and, so far as necessary for the purposes of this paragraph, anything done under or for the purposes of a provision of the Water Resources Act 1963 applied by paragraph 30 or 31 of Schedule 26 to the 1989 Act, shall have effect as if that paragraph applied the corresponding provision of this Act and that thing had been done under or for the purposes of that corresponding provision.

Section 48 of this Act

2. Subsection (2) of section 48 of this Act shall not afford any defence to an action brought before September 1, 1992 if the licence referred to in that subsection is a 1989 Act licence of right; and there shall be no defence afforded to such an action by that subsection as applied by paragraph 1(2) above.

Section 55 of this Act

3. No application shall be made under section 55 of this Act (variation of licence on application of owner of fishing rights) in respect of any 1989 Act licence of right.

Section 60 of this Act

4.—(1) Where the plaintiff in any action brought against the Authority in pursuance of section 60 of this Act (liability of the Authority for derogation from protected right) is entitled to a protected right for the purposes of Chapter II of Part II of this Act by reason only that he is the holder of, or has applied for, a licence of right, it shall be a defence for the Authority to prove—

(a) that the plaintiff could have carried out permissible alterations in the means whereby he abstracted water from the source of supply in question; and

(b) that, if he had carried out such alterations, the abstraction or, as the case may be, the obstruction or impeding of the flow of the inland waters authorised by the licence to which the action relates would not have derogated from his protected right for the purposes of that Chapter;

and subsection (3) of that section (liability of Authority for compliance with direction requiring derogation from protected rights) shall not apply to a direction given in consequence of an appeal against the decision of the Authority on an application for the grant of a 1989 Act licence of right.

(2) In this paragraph "permissible alterations"—

(a) in relation to a person who is the holder of a licence of right, means any alteration of works, or modification of machinery or apparatus, which would fulfil the requirements of the licence as to the means whereby water is authorised to be abstracted;

(b) in relation to a person who is not the holder of a licence of right, but to whose application for such a licence paragraph 1 above applies, means any alteration of works, or modification of machinery or apparatus, by means of which he abstracted water from the source of supply in question during the period of five years ending with September 1, 1989, being an alteration or modification which would be within the scope of the licence if granted in accordance with the application.

Section 61 of this Act

5.—(1) No compensation shall be payable under section 61 of this Act (compensation for revocation or variation of a licence) in respect of the revocation or variation of a 1989 Act licence of right if the revocation or variation is for giving effect to the decision of the court in an action in respect of which paragraph 2 above has effect or in any proceedings in consequence of such an action.

(2) Nothing in section 61(3) of this Act (compensation not payable in respect of works etc. carried out before the grant of a licence) shall apply in relation to any licence of right.

Licences of right

6.—(1) In this Schedule references to a licence of right are references to—
(a) any 1989 Act licence of right, that is to say, a licence granted (whether or not by virtue of paragraph 1 above) under paragraph 30 or 31 of Schedule 26 to the Water Act 1989; or
(b) any licence which, having been granted in pursuance of an application under section 33 of the Water Resources Act 1963 (or in pursuance of an appeal consequential on such an application), has effect after the coming into force of this Act by virtue of sub-paragraph (2) below.

(2) The repeal by the Water Consolidation (Consequential Provisions) Act 1991 of paragraph 29(4) of Schedule 26 to the Water Act 1989 shall not prevent any licence granted as mentioned in paragraph (b) of sub-paragraph (1) above from continuing (in accordance with paragraph 1 of Schedule 2 to that Act of 1991 and subject to the preceding provisions of this Schedule) to have effect after the coming into force of this Act as a licence under Chapter II of Part II of this Act.

Section 73   SCHEDULE 8

Proceedings on Applications for Drought Orders

1.—(1) The applicant for a drought order shall—
(a) cause notice of the application to be served on the persons specified in the Table set out in sub-paragraph (2) below;
(b) cause a notice of the application to be published in one or more local newspapers circulating within the area affected by the order; and
(c) cause a notice of the application to be published in the London Gazette.
(2) The said Table is as follows—

Table

All orders	(a) The Authority (where it is not the applicant).
	(b) Every local authority (not being a county council) and water undertaker (not being the applicant) whose area would be affected by the order.
Orders which suspend or modify any enactment or any order or scheme made or confirmed under any enactment.	Such persons (if any) as are specified by name in the enactment, order or scheme as being persons for whose protection it was enacted or made.
Orders concerning the taking of water from a source or the discharge of water or effluent to a place.	(a) Every local authority (not being a county council) in whose area the source, or the place at which water or effluent is to be discharged, is situated.
	(b) Every drainage board for an internal district in which the source, or the place at which water or effluent is to be discharged, is situated.

	(c) Every navigation authority exercising functions over any watercourse affected by the order.
	(d) If the order concerns any consent relating to the discharge of sewage effluent or trade effluent, the person to whom the consent was given.
Orders which authorise the carrying out of any works.	(a) Every local authority (not being a county council) within whose area the works are situated.
	(b) If the order authorises the carrying out of works in, under or over a watercourse, every drainage board for an internal drainage district within which the works, or any part of the works, are situated.
Orders which authorise the occupation and use of land.	Every owner, lessee and occupier of the land.
Orders which prohibit or limit the taking of water.	Every named person to whom the prohibition or limitation applies.

(3) A notice for the purposes of this paragraph of an application for drought order—

(a) shall state the general effect of the application;

(b) shall specify a place within the area affected by the order where a copy of any relevant map or plan may be inspected by any person free of charge at all reasonable times within a period of seven days from the date on which it is served or, as the case may be, published;

(c) shall state that objections to the application may be made to the Secretary of State within seven days from the date on which it is served or, as the case may be, published; and

(d) in the case of an application for an order authorising the occupation and use of land, shall specify the land to which the application relates.

(4) A notice sent in a letter in pursuance of section 220 of this Act to an address to which it may be sent in pursuance of that section shall not be treated as having been properly served for the purposes of this paragraph unless the sender takes such steps as are for the time being required to secure that the letter is transmitted in priority to letters of other descriptions.

Objections to and making of orders

2.—(1) If any objection is duly made with respect to an application for a drought order and is not withdrawn then, subject to the provisions of this paragraph, the Secretary of State shall, before making the order, either—

(a) cause a local inquiry to be held; or

(b) afford an opportunity—

  (i) to the objector; and

  (ii) if the objector avails himself of the opportunity, to the applicant and to any other persons to whom it appears to the Secretary of State expedient to afford the opportunity,

of appearing before and being heard by a person appointed by the Secretary of State for the purpose.

(2) Subject to sub-paragraph (3) below, where, on an application for a drought order, it appears to the Secretary of State that a drought order is required to be made urgently if it is to enable the deficiency of supplies of water to be effectively met, he may direct that the requirements of sub-paragraph (1) above shall be dispensed with in relation to the application.

(3) Nothing in sub-paragraph (2) above shall authorise the Secretary of State to fail to consider any objection to a proposed drought order which has been duly made and not withdrawn.

(4) Notwithstanding anything in sub-paragraph (1) above, the Secretary of State may—

(a) require any person who has made an objection to a proposed drought order to state in writing the grounds of his objection; and

(b) disregard the objection for the purposes of this paragraph if the Secretary of State is satisfied—

  (i) that the objection relates exclusively to matters which can be dealt with on a reference under Schedule 9 to this Act or by any person by whom compensation is to be assessed; or

(ii) in a case where the order is one confined to the extension of a period specified in a previous order, that the objection is one that has in substance been made with respect to the application for that previous order.

(5) Subject to the requirements of this paragraph, the Secretary of State, upon being satisfied that the proper notices have been published and served, may, if he thinks fit, make the order in respect of which the application is made with or without modifications.

(6) The Secretary of State may hold a local inquiry on any application for a drought order notwithstanding that he is not required to do so by this paragraph.

Notice after making of order

3. After a drought order has been made, the person on whose application it was made shall cause to be published (in the manner in which notice of the application was required under paragraph 1 above to be published) a notice—

(a) stating that the order has been made; and

(b) naming a place where a copy of it may be inspected.

Section 79   SCHEDULE 9

Compensation in respect of Drought Orders

Compensation to be made in the case of all drought orders

1. Where a drought order has been made, compensation in respect of the entry upon or occupation or use of land shall be made by the applicant for the order to—

(a) the owners and occupiers of the land; and

(b) all other persons interested in the land or injuriously affected by the entry upon, occupation or use of the land,

for loss or damage sustained by reason of the entry upon, occupation or use of the land.

Compensation to be made in the case of ordinary orders only

2.—(1) This paragraph shall apply for determining the compensation to be made, in addition to any made under paragraph 1 above, where an ordinary drought order has been made.

(2) Compensation in respect of the taking of water from a source or its taking from a source otherwise than in accordance with a restriction or obligation which has been suspended or modified shall be made by the applicant for the order to—

(a) the owners of the source of water; and

(b) all other persons interested in the source of water or injuriously affected by the taking of the water,

for loss or damage sustained by reason of the taking of the water.

(3) Compensation in respect of water's being discharged or not discharged to any place or its being discharged otherwise than in accordance with a restriction or obligation (whether relating to the treatment or discharge of the water) which has been suspended or modified shall be made by the applicant for the order to—

(a) the owners of the place of discharge; and

(b) all other persons interested in the place of discharge or injuriously affected by the discharge or lack of discharge,

for loss or damage sustained by reason of the water being discharged or not discharged or being discharged otherwise than in accordance with the restriction or obligation.

(4) Compensation in respect of the imposition of a prohibition or limitation on the taking of water from a source shall be made by the applicant for the order, to any persons to whom the prohibition or limitation applies, for loss or damage sustained by reason of the prohibition or limitation.

(5) Compensation in respect of a power to make discharges of sewage effluent or trade effluent in pursuance of any consent shall be made by the applicant for the order, to any person who has been exercising that power, for loss or damage sustained by reason of the suspension or variation of the consent or the attachment of conditions to the consent.

Claims for compensation: general

3.—(1) A claim for compensation under this Schedule shall be made by serving upon the applicant a notice stating the grounds of the claim and the amount claimed.

(2) Any question as to the right of a claimant to recover compensation, or as to the amount of compensation recoverable, shall, in default of agreement, be referred to, and determined by, the Lands Tribunal.

Claims for compensation under paragraph 2

4.—(1) A claim for compensation under paragraph 2 above may be made at any time not later than six months after the end of the period for which the order authorises, as the case may be—

(a) the taking or discharge of water;

(b) the imposition of a prohibition or limitation on the taking of water;

(c) the suspension or modification of any restriction or obligation; or

(d) the suspension or variation of, or attachment of conditions to, any consent relating to the discharge of sewage effluent or trade effluent.

(2) Where a claim for compensation under paragraph 2 above is made during the continuance of the ordinary drought order, the Lands Tribunal may, if it thinks fit, award a sum representing the loss or damage which is likely to be sustained by the claimant in respect of each day on which, as the case may be—

(a) water is taken or discharged;

(b) water is not discharged or is discharged otherwise than in accordance with an obligation or restriction; or

(c) sewage effluent or trade effluent is discharged otherwise than in accordance with a consent originally given.

(3) In assessing the compensation to be made under paragraph 2(2) above the Lands Tribunal may, if it thinks fit, have regard to the amount of water which, on an equitable apportionment of the water available from the source between the claimant, the applicant and other persons taking water from the source, may fairly be apportioned to the claimant.

(4) In assessing the compensation to be made under paragraph 2(3) above in respect of the lack of discharge of compensation water, the Lands Tribunal may, if it thinks fit, have regard to the amount of water which, under the conditions existing by reason of the shortage of rain, would have been available to the claimant during the period during which the deficiency of supplies of water is continued, if the applicant in relation to whom the obligation was imposed had never carried on its undertaking.

(5) In sub-paragraph (4) above "compensation water" has the same meaning as in section 77 of this Act.

Section 88   SCHEDULE 10

D<small>ISCHARGE</small> C<small>ONSENTS</small>

Applications for consents

1.—(1) An application for a consent, for the purposes of section 88(1)(a) of this Act, for any discharges shall be made to the Authority.

(2) An application under this paragraph shall be accompanied or supplemented by all such information as the Authority may reasonably require; but, subject to paragraph 2(4) below and without prejudice to the effect (if any) of any other contravention of the requirements of this Schedule in relation to such an application, a failure to provide information in pursuance of this sub-paragraph, shall not invalidate an application.

(3) An application made in accordance with this paragraph which relates to proposed discharges at two or more places may be treated by the Authority as separate applications for consents for discharges at each of those places.

(4) Where an application is made in accordance with this paragraph the Authority shall—

(a) publish notice of the application, at least once in each of two successive weeks, in a newspaper or newspapers circulating in—

(i) the locality or localities in which the places are situated at which it is proposed in the application that the discharges should be made; and

(ii) the locality or localities appearing to the Authority to be in the vicinity of any controlled waters which the Authority considers likely to be affected by the proposed discharges;

(b) publish a copy of that notice in an edition of the London Gazette published no earlier than the day after the publication of the last of the notices to be published by virtue of paragraph (a) above;

(c) send a copy of the application to every local authority or water undertaker within whose area any of the proposed discharges is to occur;

(d) in the case of an application which relates to proposed discharges into coastal waters, relevant territorial waters or waters outside the seaward limits of relevant territorial waters, serve a copy of the application on each of the Ministers.

(5) The Authority shall be entitled, on an application made in accordance with this paragraph, to disregard the provisions of paragraphs (a) to (c) of sub-paragraph (4) above if it

proposes to give the consent applied for and considers that the discharges in question will have no appreciable effect on the waters into which it is proposed that they should be made.

(6) Where notice of an application under this paragraph is published by the Authority under sub-paragraph (4) above, the Authority shall be entitled to recover the expenses of publication from the applicant.

(7) If a person who proposes to make or has made an application under this paragraph ("the relevant application")—

    (a) applies to the Secretary of State within the prescribed period for a certificate providing that the provisions of sub-paragraph (4) above and subsection (1) of section 190 of this Act shall not apply to—

        (i) the relevant application;

        (ii) any consent given or conditions imposed on the relevant application;

        (iii) any sample of effluent taken from a discharge for which consent is given on the relevant application; or

        (iv) information produced by analysis of such a sample;

    and

    (b) satisfies the Secretary of State that it would be contrary to the public interest or would prejudice, to an unreasonable degree, some private interest, by disclosing information about a trade secret, if a certificate were not issued under this sub-paragraph,

the Secretary of State may issue a certificate to that person providing that those provisions shall not apply to such of the things mentioned in paragraph (a) above as are specified in the certificate.

Consideration and determination of applications

2.—(1) It shall be the duty of the Authority to consider any written representations or objections with respect to an application under paragraph 1 above which are made to it in the period of six weeks beginning with the day of the publication of notice of the application in the London Gazette and are not withdrawn.

(2) On an application under paragraph 1 above the Authority shall be under a duty, if the requirements of that paragraph are complied with, to consider whether to give the consent applied for, either unconditionally or subject to conditions, or to refuse it.

(3) Subject to sub-paragraph (4) and paragraph 3(5) below, on an application made in accordance with paragraph 1 above, the consent applied for shall be deemed to have been refused if it is not given within the period of four months beginning with the day on which the application is received or within such longer period as may be agreed in writing between the Authority and the applicant.

(4) Where—

    (a) any person, having made an application to the Authority for a consent, has failed to comply with his obligation under paragraph 1(2) above to supplement that application with information required by the Authority; and

    (b) that requirement was made by the Authority at such a time before the end of the period within which the Authority is required to determine the application as gave that person a reasonable opportunity to provide the required information within that period,

the Authority may delay its determination of the application until a reasonable time after the required information is provided.

(5) The conditions subject to which a consent may be given under this paragraph shall be such conditions as the Authority may think fit and, in particular, may include conditions—

    (a) as to the places at which the discharges to which the consent relates may be made and as to the design and construction of any outlets for the discharges;

    (b) as to the nature, origin, composition, temperature, volume and rate of the discharges and as to the periods during which the discharges may be made;

    (c) as to the steps to be taken, in relation to the discharges or by way of subjecting any substance likely to affect the description of matter discharged to treatment or any other process, for minimising the polluting effects of the discharges on any controlled waters;

    (d) as to the provision of facilities for taking samples of the matter discharged and, in particular, as to the provision, maintenance and use of manholes, inspection chambers, observation wells and boreholes in connection with the discharges;

    (e) as to the provision, maintenance and testing of meters for measuring or recording the volume and rate of the discharges and apparatus for determining the nature, composition and temperature of the discharges;

    (f) as to the keeping of records of the nature, origin, composition, temperature, volume and rate of the discharges and, in particular, of records of readings of meters and other recording apparatus provided in accordance with any other condition attached to the consent; and

(g) as to the making of returns and the giving of other information to the Authority about the nature, origin, composition, temperature, volume and rate of the discharges;

and it is hereby declared that a consent may be given under this paragraph subject to different conditions in respect of different periods.

(6) A consent for any discharges which is given under this paragraph is not limited to discharges by a particular person and, accordingly, extends to discharges which are made by any person.

Notification of proposal to give consent

3.—(1) This paragraph applies where the Authority proposes to give its consent under paragraph 2 above on an application in respect of which such representations or objections as the Authority is required to consider under sub-paragraph (1) of that paragraph have been made.

(2) It shall be the duty of the Authority to serve notice of the proposal on every person who made any such representations or objection; and any such notice shall include a statement of the effect of sub-paragraph (3) below.

(3) Any person who made any such representations or objection may, within the period of 21 days beginning with the day on which the notice of the proposal is served on him, in the prescribed manner request the Secretary of State to give a direction under paragraph 4(1) below in respect of the application.

(4) It shall be the duty of the Authority not to give its consent on the application before the end of the period of 21 days mentioned in sub-paragraph (3) above and, if within that period—

(a) a request is made under sub-paragraph (3) above in respect of the application; and

(b) the person who makes that request serves notice of it on the Authority,

the Authority shall not give its consent on the application unless the Secretary of State has served notice on the Authority stating that he declines to comply with the request.

(5) Any period during which the Authority is prohibited by virtue of sub-paragraph (4) above from giving its consent on the application shall be disregarded in determining whether the application is deemed to have been refused under paragraph 2(3) above.

Reference to Secretary of State of certain applications for consent

4.—(1) The Secretary of State may, either in consequence of representations or objections made to him or otherwise, direct the Authority to transmit to him for determination such applications for consent under paragraph 1 above as are specified in the direction or are of a description so specified.

(2) Where a direction is given to the Authority under this paragraph, the Authority shall comply with the direction and inform every applicant to whose application the direction relates of the transmission of his application to the Secretary of State.

(3) Paragraphs 1(4) to (6) and 2(1) above shall have effect in relation to an application transmitted to the Secretary of State under this paragraph with such modifications as may be prescribed.

(4) Where an application is transmitted to the Secretary of State under this paragraph, the Secretary of State may at any time after the application is transmitted and before it is granted or refused—

(a) cause a local inquiry to be held with respect to the application; or

(b) afford the applicant and the Authority an opportunity of appearing before, and being heard by, a person appointed by the Secretary of State for the purpose.

(5) The Secretary of State shall exercise his power under sub-paragraph (4) above in any case where a request to be heard with respect to the application is made to him in the prescribed manner by the applicant or by the Authority.

(6) Where under this paragraph the Secretary of State affords to an applicant and the Authority an opportunity of appearing before, and being heard by, a person appointed for the purpose, it shall be the duty of the Secretary of State to afford an opportunity of appearing before, and being heard by, that person to every person who has made any representations or objection to the Secretary of State with respect to the application in question.

(7) It shall be the duty of the Secretary of State, if the requirements of this paragraph and of any regulations made under it are complied with, to determine an application for consent transmitted to him by the Authority under this paragraph by directing the Authority to refuse its consent or to give its consent under paragraph 2 above (either unconditionally or subject to such conditions as are specified in the direction).

(8) In complying with a direction under sub-paragraph (7) above to give a consent the Authority shall not be required to comply with any requirement imposed by paragraph 3 above.

(9) Without prejudice to any of the preceding provisions of this paragraph, the Secretary of State may by regulations make provision for the purposes of, and in connection with, the consideration and disposal by him of applications transmitted to him under this paragraph.

Consents without applications

5.—(1) If it appears to the Authority—
  (a) that a person has caused or permitted effluent or other matter to be discharged in contravention—
      (i) of the obligation imposed by virtue of section 85(3) of this Act; or
      (ii) of any prohibition imposed under section 86 of this Act;
  and
  (b) that a similar contravention by that person is likely,
the Authority may, if it thinks fit, serve on him an instrument in writing giving its consent, subject to any conditions specified in the instrument, for discharges of a description so specified.
  (2) A consent given under this paragraph shall not relate to any discharge which occurred before the instrument containing the consent was served on the recipient of the instrument.
  (3) Sub-paragraphs (5) and (6) of paragraph 2 above shall have effect in relation to a consent given under this paragraph as they have effect in relation to a consent given under that paragraph.
  (4) Where a consent has been given under this paragraph, the Authority shall, as soon as practicable after giving it—
  (a) publish notice of the consent, at least once in each of two successive weeks, in a newspaper or newspapers circulating in—
      (i) the locality or localities in which the places are situated at which discharges may be made in pursuance of the consent; and
      (ii) the locality or localities appearing to the Authority to be in the vicinity of any controlled waters which it considers likely to be affected by the discharges;
  (b) publish a copy of that notice in an edition of the London Gazette published no earlier than the day after the publication of the last of the notices to be published by virtue of paragraph (a) above;
  (c) send a copy of the instrument containing the consent to every local authority within whose area any of the discharges authorised by the consent may occur;
  (d) in the case of a consent which relates to discharges into coastal waters, relevant territorial waters or waters outside the seaward limits of relevant territorial waters, serve a copy of the instrument containing the consent on each of the Ministers.
  (5) It shall be the duty of the Authority to consider any written representations or objections with respect to a consent under this paragraph which are made to it in the period of six weeks beginning with the day of the publication of notice of the consent in the London Gazette and are not withdrawn.
  (6) Where notice of a consent is published by the Authority under sub-paragraph (4) above, the Authority shall be entitled to recover the expenses of publication from the person on whom the instrument containing the consent was served.

Revocation of consents and alteration and imposition of conditions

6.—(1) It shall be the duty of the Authority to review from time to time the consents given under paragraphs 2 and 5 above and the conditions (if any) to which the consents are subject.
  (2) Subject to such restrictions on the exercise of the power conferred by this sub-paragraph as are imposed under paragraph 7 below, where the Authority has reviewed a consent under this paragraph, it may by a notice served on the person making a discharge in pursuance of the consent—
  (a) revoke the consent;
  (b) make modifications of the conditions of the consent; or
  (c) in the case of an unconditional consent, provide that it shall be subject to such conditions as may be specified in the notice.
  (3) If on a review under sub-paragraph (1) above it appears to the Authority that no discharge has been made in pursuance of the consent to which the review relates at any time during the preceding 12 months, the Authority may revoke the consent by a notice served on the owner or occupier of the land from which discharges would be made in pursuance of the consent.
  (4) If it appears to the Secretary of State appropriate to do so—
  (a) for the purpose of enabling Her Majesty's Government in the United Kingdom to give effect to any Community obligation or to any international agreement to which the United Kingdom is for the time being a party;

(b) for the protection of public health or of flora and fauna dependent on an aquatic environment; or

(c) in consequence of any representations or objections made to him or otherwise,

he may, subject to such restrictions on the exercise of the power conferred by virtue of paragraph (c) above as are imposed under paragraph 7 below, at any time direct the Authority, in relation to a consent given under paragraph 2 or 5 above, to do anything mentioned in sub-paragraph (2)(a) to (c) above.

(5) The Authority shall be liable to pay compensation to any person in respect of any loss or damage sustained by that person as a result of the Authority's compliance with a direction given in relation to any consent by virtue of sub-paragraph (4)(b) above if—

(a) in complying with that direction the Authority does anything which, apart from that direction, it would be precluded from doing by a restriction imposed under paragraph 7 below; and

(b) the direction is not shown to have been given in consequence of—

(i) a change of circumstances which could not reasonably have been foreseen at the beginning of the period to which the restriction relates; or

(ii) consideration by the Secretary of State of material information which was not reasonably available to the Authority at the beginning of that period.

(6) For the purposes of sub-paragraph (5) above information is material, in relation to a consent, if it relates to any discharge made or to be made by virtue of the consent, to the interaction of any such discharge with any other discharge or to the combined effect of the matter discharged and any other matter.

Restriction on variation and revocation of consent and previous variation

7.—(1) Each instrument signifying the consent of the Authority under paragraph 2 or 5 above shall specify a period during which no notice by virtue of paragraph 6(2) or (4)(c) above shall be served in respect of the consent.

(2) Each notice served by the Authority by virtue of paragraph 6(2) or (4)(c) above (except a notice which only revokes a consent) shall specify a period during which a subsequent such notice which alters the effect of the first-mentioned notice shall not be served.

(3) The period specified under sub-paragraph (1) or (2) above in relation to any consent shall not, unless the person who proposes to make or makes discharges in pursuance of the consent otherwise agrees, be less than the period of two years beginning—

(a) in the case of a period specified under sub-paragraph (1) above, with the day on which the consent takes effect; and

(b) in the case of a period specified under sub-paragraph (2) above, with the day on which the notice specifying that period is served.

(4) A restriction imposed under sub-paragraph (1) or (2) above shall not prevent the service by the Authority of a notice by virtue of paragraph 6(2) or (4)(c) above in respect of a consent given under paragraph 5 above if—

(a) the notice is served not more than three months after the beginning of the period specified in paragraph 5(5) above for the making of representations and objections with respect to the consent; and

(b) the Authority or, as the case may be, the Secretary of State considers, in consequence of any representations or objections received by it or him within that period, that it is appropriate for the notice to be served.

Section 93　　　　　　　SCHEDULE 11

Water Protection Zone Orders

Applications for orders

1.—(1) Where the Authority applies to the Secretary of State for an order under section 93 of this Act, it shall—

(a) submit to the Secretary of State a draft of the order applied for;

(b) publish a notice with respect to the application, at least once in each of two successive weeks, in one or more newspapers circulating in the locality proposed to be designated as a water protection zone by the order;

(c) not later than the date on which that notice is first published serve a copy of the notice on every local authority and water undertaker whose area includes the whole or any part of that locality; and

(d) publish a notice in the London Gazette which—

(i) states that the draft order has been submitted to the Secretary of State;

(ii) names every local authority on whom a notice is required to be served under this paragraph;

(iii) specifies a place where a copy of the draft order and of any relevant map or plan may be inspected; and

(iv) gives the name of every newspaper in which the notice required by virtue of paragraph (b) above was published and the date of an issue containing the notice.

(2) The notice required by virtue of sub-paragraph (1)(b) above to be published with respect to an application for an order shall—

(a) state the general effect of the order applied for;

(b) specify a place where a copy of the draft order and of any relevant map or plan may be inspected by any person free of charge at all reasonable times during the period of 28 days beginning with the date of the first publication of the notice; and

(c) state that any person may, within that period, by notice to the Secretary of State object to the making of the order.

Supply of copies of draft orders

2. Where the Authority has applied for an order under section 93 of this Act, it shall, at the request of any person and on payment by that person of such charge (if any) as the Authority may reasonably require, furnish that person with a copy of the draft order submitted to the Secretary of State under paragraph 1 above.

Modifications of proposals

3.—(1) On an application for an order under section 93 of this Act, the Secretary of State may make the order either in the terms of the draft order submitted to him or, subject to sub-paragraph (2) below, in those terms as modified in such manner as he thinks fit, or may refuse to make an order.

(2) The Secretary of State shall not make such a modification of a draft order submitted to him as he considers is likely adversely to affect any persons unless he is satisfied that the Authority has given and published such additional notices, in such manner, as the Secretary of State may have required.

(3) Subject to sub-paragraph (2) above and to the service of notices of the proposed modification on such local authorities as appear to him to be likely to be interested in it, the modifications that may be made by the Secretary of State of any draft order include any modification of the area designated by the draft order as a water protection zone.

Consideration of objections etc.

4. Without prejudice to section 213 of this Act, where an application for an order under section 93 of this Act has been made, the Secretary of State may, if he considers it appropriate to do so, hold a local inquiry before making any order on the application.

Section 94   SCHEDULE 12

Nitrate Sensitive Area Orders

Part I

Applications by the Authority for Designation Orders

Orders made only on application

1.—(1) Subject to sub-paragraphs (2) and (3) below, the relevant Minister shall not make an order under section 94 of this Act by virtue of which any land is designated as land comprised in a nitrate sensitive area, except with the consent of the Treasury and on an application which—

(a) has been made by the Authority in accordance with paragraph 2 below; and

(b) in identifying controlled waters by virtue of sub-paragraph (2)(a) of that paragraph, identified the controlled waters with respect to which that land is so comprised by the order.

(2) This paragraph shall not apply to an order which reproduces or amends an existing order without adding any land appearing to the relevant Minister to constitute a significant area to the land already comprised in the areas for the time being designated as nitrate sensitive areas.

Procedure for applications

2.—(1) The Authority shall not for the purposes of paragraph 1 above apply for the making of any order under section 94 of this Act by which any land would be comprised in the areas for the time being designated as nitrate sensitive areas unless it appears to the Authority—

(a) that pollution is or is likely to be caused by the entry of nitrate into controlled waters as a result of, or of anything done in connection with, the use of particular land in England and Wales for agricultural purposes; and

(b) that the provisions for the time being in force in relation to those waters and that land are not sufficient, in the opinion of the Authority, for preventing or controlling such an entry of nitrate into those waters.

(2) An application under this paragraph shall identify—

(a) the controlled waters appearing to the Authority to be the waters which the nitrate is or is likely to enter; and

(b) the land appearing to the Authority to be the land the use of which for agricultural purposes, or the doing of anything in connection with whose use for agricultural purposes, is resulting or is likely to result in the entry of nitrate into those waters.

(3) An application under this paragraph shall be made—

(a) where the land identified in the application is wholly in Wales, by serving a notice containing the application on the Secretary of State; and

(b) in any other case, by serving such a notice on each of the Ministers.

PART II

ORDERS CONTAINING MANDATORY PROVISIONS

Publication of proposal for order containing mandatory provisions

3.—(1) This paragraph applies where the relevant Minister proposes to make an order under section 94 of this Act which—

(a) makes or modifies any such provision as is authorised by subsection (3)(a) of that section; and

(b) in doing so, contains provision which is not of one of the following descriptions, that is to say—

(i) provision reproducing existing provisions without modification and in relation to substantially the same area; and

(ii) provision modifying any existing provisions so as to make them less onerous.

(2) The relevant Minister shall, before making any such order as is mentioned in sub-paragraph (1) above—

(a) publish a notice with respect to the proposed order, at least once in each of two successive weeks, in one or more newspapers circulating in the locality in relation to which the proposed order will have effect;

(b) not later than the date on which that notice is first published, serve a copy of the notice on—

(i) the Authority;

(ii) every local authority and water undertaker whose area includes the whole or any part of that locality; and

(iii) in the case of an order containing any such provision as is authorised by section 94(3)(b) of this Act, such owners and occupiers of agricultural land in that locality as appear to the relevant Minister to be likely to be affected by the obligations in respect of which payments are to be made under that provision; and

(c) publish a notice in the London Gazette which—

(i) names every local authority on whom a notice is required to be served under this paragraph;

(ii) specifies a place where a copy of the proposed order and of any relevant map or plan may be inspected; and

(iii) gives the name of every newspaper in which the notice required by virtue of paragraph (a) above was published and the date of an issue containing the notice.

(3) The notice required by virtue of sub-paragraph (2)(a) above to be published with respect to any proposed order shall—

(a) state the general effect of the proposed order;

(b) specify a place where a copy of the proposed order, and of any relevant map or plan, may be inspected by any person free of charge at all reasonable times during the period of 42 days beginning with the date of the first publication of the notice; and

(c) state that any person may, within that period, by notice to the Secretary of State or, as the case may be, to one of the Ministers object to the making of the order.

Supply of copies of proposed orders

4. The Secretary of State and, in a case where he is proposing to join in making the order, the Minister shall, at the request of any person and on payment by that person of such charge (if any) as the Secretary of State or the Minister may reasonably require, furnish that person with a copy of any proposed order of which notice has been published under paragraph 3 above.

Modifications of proposals

5.—(1) Where notices with respect to any proposed order have been published and served in accordance with paragraph 3 above and the period of 42 days mentioned in sub-paragraph (3)(b) of that paragraph has expired, the relevant Minister may—

(a) make the order either in the proposed terms or, subject to sub-paragraph (2) below (but without any further compliance with paragraph 3 above), in those terms as modified in such manner as he thinks fit; or

(b) decide not to make any order.

(2) The relevant Minister shall not make such a modification of a proposed order of which notice has been so published and served as he considers is likely adversely to affect any persons unless he has given such notices as he considers appropriate for enabling those persons to object to the modification.

(3) Subject to sub-paragraph (2) above and to the service of notices of the proposed modification on such local authorities as appear to him to be likely to be interested in it, the modifications that may be made by the relevant Minister include any modification of any area designated by the proposed order as a nitrate sensitive area.

(4) For the purposes of this Schedule it shall be immaterial, in a case in which a modification such as is mentioned in sub-paragraph (3) above incorporates land in England in an area which (but for the modification) would have been wholly in Wales, that any requirements of paragraph 3 above in relation to the proposed order have been complied with by the Secretary of State, rather than by the Ministers.

Consideration of objections etc.

6. Without prejudice to section 213 of this Act, where notices with respect to any proposed order have been published and served in accordance with paragraph 3 above, the Secretary of State or, as the case may be, the Ministers may, if he or they consider it appropriate to do so, hold a local inquiry before deciding whether or not to make the proposed order or to make it with modifications.

Consent of Treasury for payment provisions

7. The consent of the Treasury shall be required for the making of any order under section 94 of this Act the making of which does not require the consent of the Treasury by virtue of paragraph 1 above but which contains any such provision as is authorised by subsection (3)(b) of that section.

Section 103   SCHEDULE 13

Transitional Water Pollution Provisions

Transitional power to transfer power of determination with respect to water pollution matters to the Authority

1. Where by virtue of the provisions of Schedule 2 to the Water Consolidation (Consequential Provisions) Act 1991 in relation to anything having effect under paragraph 21 of Schedule 26 to the Water Act 1989 any matter falls to be determined by the Secretary of State in accordance with any of the provisions of Part III of this Act (other than section 91), that matter shall, if the Secretary of State refers the matter to the Authority for determination, be determined by the Authority instead.

Order under section 32(3) of the 1974 Act

2.—(1) Except in so far as the Secretary of State by order otherwise provides, section 85 of this Act shall not apply to any discharges which are of a kind or in any area specified in an order which was made under subsection (3) of section 32 of the Control of Pollution Act 1974 (preservation of existing exemptions) and is in force for the purposes of paragraph 22(1) of Schedule 26 to the Water Act 1989 immediately before the coming into force of this Act.

(2) The Secretary of State may by order require the Authority to publish in a manner specified in the order such information about the operation of any provision made by or under this paragraph as may be so specified.

(3) The power to make an order under this paragraph shall be exercisable by statutory instrument subject to annulment in pursuance of a resolution of either House of Parliament.

Pre-1989 transitional provisions

3.—(1) A consent which has effect, in accordance with paragraph 24(2) of Schedule 26 to the Water Act 1989 and paragraph 1 of Schedule 2 to the Water Consolidation (Consequential Provisions) Act 1991, as a consent given for the purposes of Chapter II of Part III of this Act in respect of an application which itself has effect, by virtue of paragraph 21 of that Schedule 26 and that paragraph 1, as an application made under Schedule 10 to this Act shall cease to have effect on the disposal of that application by—
  (a) the giving of an unconditional consent on that application;
  (b) the expiration, without an appeal under section 91 of this Act being brought, of the period of three months beginning with the date on which notice is served on the applicant that the consent applied for is refused or is given subject to conditions; or
  (c) the withdrawal or determination of any such appeal.
(2) Particulars of consents to which sub-paragraph (1) above applies shall not be required to be contained in any register maintained under section 190 of this Act.

Discharge consents on application of undertakers etc.

4.—(1) The repeal by the Water Consolidation (Consequential Provisions) Act 1991 of sub-paragraphs (2) and (6) of paragraph 25 of Schedule 26 to the Water Act 1989 shall not affect any provision made under section 113(2) of that Act for the purposes of either of those sub-paragraphs; and, accordingly any such provision shall have effect in accordance with Schedule 2 to that Act of 1991 as if made in exercise of a power conferred by section 99 of this Act.
(2) If the Secretary of State determines that this sub-paragraph is to apply in relation to any application which is deemed by virtue of paragraph 25(2)(a) of Schedule 26 to the Water Act 1989 and Schedule 2 to the Water Consolidation (Consequential Provisions) Act 1991 to have been made to the Authority by the successor company of a water authority—
  (a) that application shall be treated as having been transmitted to the Secretary of State in accordance with a direction under paragraph 4 of Schedule 10 to this Act; but
  (b) the Authority shall not be required, by virtue of sub-paragraph (2) of that paragraph 4, to inform that company that the application is to be so treated.
(3) Where an application is deemed to have been so made by the successor company of a water authority, then, whether or not it is treated under sub-paragraph (2) above as having been transmitted to the Secretary of State, the following provisions shall apply in relation to the application and, except in so far as the Secretary of State otherwise directs, shall so apply instead of paragraphs 1(4) to (6) and 2(1) or, as the case may be, paragraph 4(3) of Schedule 10 to this Act, that is to say—
  (a) the application shall not be considered by the Secretary of State or the Authority unless the company has complied with such directions (if any) as may be given by the Secretary of State with respect to the publicity to be given to the application;
  (b) the Secretary of State or, as the case may be, the Authority shall be under a duty to consider only such representations and objections with respect to the application as have been made in writing to the Secretary of State or the Authority before the end of such period as he may determine and as are not withdrawn; and
  (c) the Secretary of State shall have power to direct the Authority (pending compliance with any direction under paragraph (a) above or pending his or, as the case may be, its consideration of the application, representations and objections) to give such a temporary consent under Chapter II of Part III of this Act, or to make such temporary modifications of the conditions of any existing consent, as may be specified in the direction.
(4) The power of the Secretary of State to make a determination or give a direction under sub-paragraph (2) or (3) above shall be exercisable generally in relation to applications of any such description as he may consider appropriate (as well as in relation to a particular application) and, in the case of a direction to give a temporary consent or to make a temporary modification, shall include—
  (a) power to require a temporary consent to be given either unconditionally or subject to such conditions falling within paragraph 2(5) of Schedule 10 to this Act as may be specified in the direction;
  (b) power, where the direction relates to a description of applications, to require the temporary consent given in pursuance of the direction to be a general consent relating to cases of such a description as may be so specified; and
  (c) power, where the direction is in respect of an application falling to be considered by the

Authority, to require the consent or modification to be given or made so as to continue to have effect until the Authority's determination on the application becomes final—

(i) on the expiration, without the bringing of an appeal against the determination, of the prescribed period for the bringing of such an appeal; or

(ii) on the withdrawal or determination of any such appeal.

(5) Without prejudice to the provisions of Schedule 2 to the Water Consolidation (Consequential Provisions) Act 1991, a consent to which sub-paragraph (7) of paragraph 25 of the Water Act 1989 applies immediately before the coming into force of this Act by virtue of its conditions including a condition that is contravened where there is a failure by more than a specified number of samples to satisfy specified requirements, shall continue to have effect as if the only samples falling to be taken into account for the purposes of that condition were samples taken on behalf of the Authority in exercise, at a time after August 31, 1989, of a power conferred by the Water Act 1989 or a corresponding provision of this Act.

(6) References in this paragraph to the successor company of a water authority shall be construed in accordance with the Water Act 1989.

Section 108   SCHEDULE 14

ORDERS TRANSFERRING MAIN RIVER FUNCTIONS TO THE AUTHORITY

Procedure on application for order

1. As soon as any scheme under section 108 of this Act has been submitted to one of the Ministers, the Authority shall—

(a) send copies of the scheme to every internal drainage board, local authority, navigation authority, harbour authority and conservancy authority affected by it; and

(b) publish, in one or more newspapers circulating in the area affected by the scheme, a notice stating—

(i) that the scheme has been submitted to that Minister;

(ii) that a copy of it is open to inspection at a specified place; and

(iii) that representations with respect to the scheme may be made to that Minister at any time within one month after the publication of the notice.

Order making procedure etc.

2.—(1) Before either of the Ministers makes an order under section 108 of this Act, he shall cause notice of—

(a) the intention to make it;

(b) the place where copies of the draft order may be inspected and obtained; and

(c) the period within which, and the manner in which, objections to the draft order may be made,

to be published in the London Gazette and in such other manner as he thinks best adapted for informing persons affected and to be sent to the persons specified in sub-paragraph (2) below.

(2) The persons referred to in sub-paragraph (1) above are—

(a) every county council or London borough council in whose area any part of the area proposed to be affected by the order is situated and, if any part of that area is situated in the City of London, the Common Council of the City of London;

(b) the Authority and every drainage body, navigation authority, harbour authority or conservancy authority that is known to the Minister in question to be exercising jurisdiction within the area proposed to be affected by the order.

(3) In sub-paragraph (2) above "drainage body" has the same meaning as in section 108 of this Act.

Determination of whether to make order

3.—(1) Before either of the Ministers makes an order under section 108 of this Act he—

(a) shall consider any objections duly made to the draft order; and

(b) may, in any case, cause a public local inquiry to be held with respect to any objections to the draft order.

(2) Each of the Ministers may, in making an order under section 108 of this Act, make such modifications in the terms of the draft as appear to him to be desirable and may confirm the scheme to which the order relates either with or without modifications.

Notice of orders

4. As soon as may be after an order under section 108 of this Act has effect one of the

Ministers shall publish in the London Gazette, and in such other manner as he thinks best adapted for informing persons affected, a notice—
(a) stating that the order has come into force; and
(b) naming a place where a copy of it may be seen at all reasonable hours.

Challenge to orders

5.—(1) If any person aggrieved by an order under section 108 of this Act desires to question its validity on the ground—
(a) that it is not within the powers of this Act; or
(b) that any requirement of this Act has not been complied with,
he may, within six weeks of the date of the publication of the notice mentioned in paragraph 4 above, make an application for the purpose to the High Court.

(2) Where an application is duly made to the High Court under this paragraph, the High Court, if satisfied—
(a) that the order is not within the powers of this Act; or
(b) that the interests of the applicant have been substantially prejudiced by any requirements of this Act not having been complied with,
may quash the order either generally or in so far as it affects the applicant.

(3) Except by leave of the Court of Appeal, no appeal shall lie to the House of Lords from a decision of the Court of Appeal in proceedings under this paragraph.

(4) Subject to the preceding provisions of this paragraph an order under section 108 of this Act shall not at any time be questioned in any legal proceedings whatsoever.

Power to make regulations for purposes of Schedule etc.

6. The Ministers may make regulations in relation to—
(a) the publication of notices under paragraph 2 or 4 above;
(b) the holding of public local inquiries under this Schedule and procedure at those inquiries; and
(c) any other matters of procedure respecting the making of orders under section 108 of this Act.

Sections 135 and 138   SCHEDULE 15

SUPPLEMENTAL PROVISIONS WITH RESPECT TO DRAINAGE CHARGES

Raising of drainage charge

1.—(1) A drainage charge—
(a) shall be raised by the Authority in writing under the common seal of the Authority; and
(b) shall be deemed to be raised on the date on which a resolution is passed by the Authority authorising their seal to be affixed to the charge.

(2) Every drainage charge shall be raised for a year ending on March 31 and shall be raised before or during the year for which it is raised.

(3) Without prejudice to their powers by virtue of section 112 of this Act, the Ministers shall each have power by regulations to prescribe the forms of drainage charges and of demands for drainage charges.

Publication of drainage charge

2.—(1) A drainage charge shall not be valid unless notice of the charge is given by the Authority in accordance with sub-paragraph (2) below within ten days of the date on which it is raised.
(2) The notice must—
(a) state the amount of the charge and the date on which it was raised; and
(b) be published in one or more newspapers circulating in the area in respect of which the charge was raised.

Occupiers liable for drainage charge

3.—(1) Subject to paragraphs 4 and 5 below—
(a) drainage charges shall be levied on the occupiers of chargeable land in the local flood defence district or, as the case may be, the designated area; and
(b) sub-paragraphs (2) to (4) below shall have effect with respect to the assessment of persons to a drainage charge with respect to any land ("the relevant land") and their liability in regard to the charge.

(2) A drainage charge shall be assessed on the person who at the date of the raising of the charge is the occupier of the relevant land.

(3) The full amount of a drainage charge may be recovered by the Authority from any person who is the occupier of the relevant land at any time during the period for which the charge is raised; but a person who is in occupation of the relevant land for part only of the period for which the charge is raised shall be liable, by virtue of sub-paragraph (4) below, to bear a proportionate part only of the charge.

(4) If a person who is in occupation of the relevant land for part only of a period for which a drainage charge is raised is required under sub-paragraph (3) above to pay the full amount of the charge, he may (subject to any agreement to the contrary) recover, from any other person who has been in occupation of the land for part of that period, the amount which that other person is liable to bear.

Cases where identity of occupiers in doubt

4.—(1) The Authority may serve on the owner of any land a notice requiring him to state in writing the name and address of any person known to him as being an occupier of that land.

(2) The owner of any land shall be guilty of an offence if—

(a) he fails without reasonable excuse to comply with a notice under sub-paragraph (1) above;

(b) he makes any statement in respect of the information required by such a notice which he knows to be false in a material particular; or

(c) he recklessly makes any statement in respect of the information required by such a notice which is false in a material particular.

(3) A person guilty of an offence under sub-paragraph (2) above shall be liable, on summary conviction, to a fine not exceeding level 4 on the standard scale; and a person convicted by virtue of paragraph (a) of that sub-paragraph shall be liable to a further conviction by virtue of that paragraph if, after conviction, he continues without reasonable excuse to comply with the notice in question.

(4) Where the name of any person liable to be assessed to any drainage charge is not known to the Authority, it shall be sufficient to assess him to the charge by the description of the "occupier" of the premises (naming them) in respect of which the assessment is made, without further name or description.

(5) For the purposes of this Schedule the owner of any land shall be deemed to be its occupier during any period during which it is unoccupied.

(6) Sub-paragraphs (1) to (3) above shall be without prejudice to the provisions of Part VIII of this Act.

Arrangements for owner of land to pay drainage charge

5.—(1) Subject to paragraph 6 below, the Authority may make arrangements with the owner of any chargeable land for any drainage charges which may be raised by the Authority for any period in respect of the land to be levied on the owner, instead of on the occupier of the land.

(2) Where arrangements under this paragraph are made—

(a) the charges in question shall be levied on the owner, instead of on the occupier; and

(b) any reference to an occupier in the provisions of this Schedule (except in this paragraph and paragraph 6 below) shall be construed accordingly.

(3) Subject to sub-paragraph (4) below, where in pursuance of any arrangements under this paragraph the owner of any land pays drainage charges in respect of the land to the Authority either—

(a) before the end of the period of two months beginning with the date of the service on him of the demand for the charges; or

(b) before the end of one-half of the period for which the charges are raised,

the Authority shall make to him an allowance equal to ten per cent. of the full amount of the charges.

(4) No allowance shall be made under sub-paragraph (3) above in respect of charges which, apart from this paragraph, are payable for any period by the owner in pursuance of paragraph 4(5) above.

(5) Where arrangements are made under this paragraph, it shall be the duty of the Authority to give notice of the arrangements, forthwith after they are made, to the occupier of the land affected by them.

(6) The owner of any land who is a party to any arrangements under this paragraph in respect of the land may recover from the occupier of the land a sum equal to the amount of any drainage charges in respect of the land which, apart from the arrangements, would be payable by the occupier.

Power of occupier to prevent arrangements under paragraph 5

6.—(1) The occupier of any chargeable land may, by notice given to the Authority, determine—

(a) that no arrangements under paragraph 5 above shall be made in respect of the land; and

(b) that any such arrangements previously made shall cease to have effect so far as they relate to the land and any drainage charge to be raised for a period beginning after the date on which the notice takes effect;

and may, by a notice so given, revoke any determination under this sub-paragraph so far as it prohibits the making of any such arrangements in respect of the land.

(2) A notice under sub-paragraph (1) above shall take effect on the day following that on which it is given to the Authority.

(3) Where notice is given to the Authority under sub-paragraph (1) above, it shall be the duty of the Authority to send a copy of the notice to the owner of the land to which it relates.

Assessment of chargeable land to drainage charge

7.—(1) Where land is chargeable land during part only of the year for which a drainage charge is raised, a proportionate part only of the charge shall be payable in respect of that land; and any amount overpaid shall be repaid.

(2) Where the area of chargeable land in respect of which, apart from this sub-paragraph, a sum is payable by any person by way of a drainage charge consists of or includes a fraction of a hectare, then for the purpose of calculating that sum the fraction shall be disregarded if it is less than one-half and treated as one hectare in any other case.

Partial exemption of commercial woodlands

8.—(1) The sum payable by way of a drainage charge in respect of chargeable land consisting of commercial woodlands shall be calculated as if the area of the land were one-fifth of its actual area.

(2) In the application of paragraph 7(2) above to chargeable land to which sub-paragraph (1) above applies the area ascertained in pursuance of sub-paragraph (1) above (and not the area of which it is one-fifth) shall be treated as the area in relation to which paragraph 7(2) above has effect.

Returns with respect to land

9.—(1) The Authority may serve on any person appearing to it to be the occupier of any land a notice requiring him to furnish a return under sub-paragraph (2) below to the Authority within 28 days beginning with the date of service of the notice on him.

(2) The return required of a person by a notice under sub-paragraph (1) above is a return, in writing and in such form as may be specified in the notice, containing such particulars as may reasonably be required for the purpose of enabling the Authority to determine—

(a) how much (if any) of the land occupied by that person is chargeable land; and

(b) how much (if any) consists of commercial woodlands.

(3) If any person on whom notice has been served under sub-paragraph (1) above—

(a) fails without reasonable excuse to comply with the notice;

(b) in a return made in pursuance of such a notice, makes any statement which he knows to be false in a material particular; or

(c) in any such return recklessly makes any statement which is false in a material particular, he shall be guilty of an offence.

(4) A person guilty of an offence under sub-paragraph (3) above shall be liable, on summary conviction, to a fine not exceeding level 4 on the standard scale; and a person convicted by virtue of paragraph (a) of that sub-paragraph shall be liable to a further conviction by virtue of that paragraph if, after conviction, he continues without reasonable excuse to comply with the notice in question.

(5) This paragraph shall be without prejudice to the provisions of Part VIII of this Act.

Power to correct erroneous assessments etc.

10.—(1) The Authority may, as respects any drainage charge raised by it for the current or the preceding year, make such amendments in any demands or other documents relating to the charge as appear to the Authority necessary in order to make the raising, levying and collection of the charge conform with this Act.

(2) In particular, the Authority may—

(a) correct any clerical or arithmetical error;

(b) correct any erroneous insertions or omissions or any misdescriptions;

(c) make such additions or corrections as appear to the Authority to be necessary by reason of any change in the occupation of any chargeable land or any property ceasing to be chargeable land.

(3) The Authority shall serve a notice of any amendment made by the Authority in pursuance of this paragraph on the occupier of all land affected thereby.

(4) Where an amendment is made in pursuance of this paragraph—

(a) any amount overpaid shall be repaid or allowed; and

(b) any amount underpaid may be recovered as if it were arrears of the charge.

Appeals against demands for drainage charges

11.—(1) If any person is aggrieved by—

(a) a demand for a drainage charge made on him as the occupier of chargeable land; or

(b) an amendment of such a demand,

he may appeal to the county court for the area in which the land or any part of it is situated.

(2) Notice of appeal under this paragraph, specifying the grounds of appeal, must be given within the required period—

(a) to the court to which the appeal is made;

(b) to the Authority; and

(c) if the appeal relates to land not in the occupation of the appellant, to the occupier of the land.

(3) For the purposes of sub-paragraph (2) above the required period is 28 days after the date on which the demand is made or, as the case may be, notice of the amendment is served on the appellant.

(4) On an appeal under this paragraph the court shall, as it thinks just, either confirm the demand or annul or modify it.

Recovery of drainage charges

12.—(1) Arrears of any drainage charge may be recovered by the Authority in the same manner in which arrears of a non-domestic rate may be recovered under the Local Government Finance Act 1988 by a charging authority within the meaning of that Act.

(2) Without prejudice to its powers by virtue of section 4 of this Act and paragraph 5 of Schedule 1 to this Act, the Authority may by resolution authorise any member or officer of the Authority, either generally or in respect of particular proceedings—

(a) to institute or defend on its behalf any proceedings in relation to a drainage charge; or

(b) notwithstanding that he is not qualified to act as a solicitor, to appear on the Authority's behalf in any proceedings before a magistrates' court for the issue of a warrant of distress for failure to pay a drainage charge.

(3) In proceedings for the recovery of arrears of a drainage charge the defendant shall not be entitled to raise by way of defence any matter which might have been raised on an appeal under paragraph 11 above.

(4) The Authority shall not be required to demand or enforce payment of a drainage charge in any case where the amount of the charge is insufficient to justify the expense of collection.

Use of certain authorities as agents for assessment, collection etc. of drainage charges

13.—(1) The Authority and any relevant authority may enter into agreements for—

(a) the doing by the relevant authority, as agents of the Authority, of anything required for the purpose of the assessment to and recovery of a drainage charge in respect of any relevant land; and

(b) the making by the Authority to the relevant authority of payments in respect of anything so done.

(2) The Authority may make arrangements with either of the Ministers for the exercise by him on behalf of the Authority, in such cases as may be determined in pursuance of the arrangements, of the powers conferred on the Authority by paragraph 9 above.

(3) Any arrangements under sub-paragraph (2) above shall contain provision for the reimbursement by the Authority of any expenses incurred by the Minister in question in pursuance of the arrangements.

(4) In this paragraph—

"relevant authority" means the council of any district or London borough or any internal drainage board; and

"relevant land", in relation to an agreement with any relevant authority, means—

(a) where the relevant authority is a district or London borough council, the chargeable land within the council's area; and

(b) where the relevant authority is an internal drainage board, such land as may be specified in the agreement.

SCHEDULE 16

SCHEMES IMPOSING SPECIAL DRAINAGE CHARGES

Submission of scheme

1.—(1) Before submitting a special charges scheme to either of the Ministers, the Authority shall consult organisations appearing to it to represent the interests of persons engaged in agriculture in the area designated in the scheme.

(2) As soon as any special charges scheme has been submitted to either of the Ministers, the Authority shall—

(a) send copies of the scheme to—

(i) the council of any county, district or London borough wholly or partly within the relevant area;

(ii) the drainage board for any internal drainage district within the relevant area; and

(iii) every organisation appearing to the Authority to represent the interests of persons engaged in agriculture in the relevant area; and

(b) publish, in one or more newspapers circulating in the area affected by the scheme, a notice stating—

(i) that the scheme has been submitted to that Minister;

(ii) that a copy of it is open to inspection at a specified place; and

(iii) that representations with respect to the scheme may be made to that Minister at any time within one month after the publication of the notice.

(3) Where the Authority submit a special charges scheme which designates any watercourse wholly or partly within an internal drainage district, then (unless the Authority is the drainage board for that district) the scheme must be accompanied either—

(a) by a statement of the drainage board for that district that they have consented to the designation; or

(b) by a statement that they have not consented thereto and a further statement setting out the reasons why the watercourse should nevertheless be designated for the purposes of section 137 of this Act.

(4) For the purposes of sub-paragraph (2) above "the relevant area" is the area designated in the scheme.

Confirmation of scheme

2.—(1) Subject to the following provisions of this Schedule the Minister to whom a special charges scheme has been submitted may by order made by statutory instrument confirm the scheme either with or without modifications.

(2) Neither of the Ministers shall confirm a special charges scheme unless he is satisfied that the scheme is reasonable and financially sound, having regard to all the circumstances, and in particular to any contributions from local authorities and internal drainage boards which, if the scheme is confirmed, are likely to be available to the Authority in addition to the special drainage charge authorised by the scheme.

(3) An order confirming a special charges scheme may contain provisions with respect to the persons by whom all or any of the expenses incurred by either of the Ministers or by other persons in connection with the making or confirmation of the order, or the making of the scheme, are to be borne.

Notice of proposed order

3.—(1) Before either of the Ministers makes an order confirming a special charges scheme he shall cause notice of—

(a) the intention to make it;

(b) the place where copies of the draft order may be inspected and obtained; and

(c) the period within which, and the manner in which, objections to the draft order may be made,

to be published in the London Gazette and in such other manner as he thinks best adapted for informing persons affected and to be sent to the persons specified in sub-paragraph (2) below.

(2) The persons referred to in sub-paragraph (1) above are—

(a) every county council or London borough council in whose area any part of the area proposed to be affected by the order is situated and, if any part of that area is situated in the City of London, the Common Council of the City of London; and

(b) the Authority and every drainage body, navigation authority, harbour authority or conservancy authority that is known to the Minister in question to be exercising jurisdiction within the area proposed to be affected by the order.

(3) In sub-paragraph (2) above "drainage body" has the same meaning as in section 108 of this Act.

Determination of whether to make order

4.—(1) Before either of the Ministers makes an order confirming a special charges scheme, he—
   (a) shall consider any objections duly made to the draft order; and
   (b) may, in any case, cause a public local inquiry to be held with respect to any objections to the draft order.
(2) Each of the Ministers shall have power, in making an order confirming a special charges scheme, to make such modifications in the terms of the draft as appear to him to be desirable.

Procedure and other matters after the making of an order

5.—(1) After either of the Ministers has made an order confirming a special charges scheme, the order (together with a notice under sub-paragraph (2) below) shall be published in such manner as he thinks best adapted for informing the persons affected.
(2) A notice under this sub-paragraph is a notice—
   (a) that the Minister in question has made the order; and
   (b) that the order will become final and have effect unless, within such period of not less than 30 days as may be specified in the notice, a memorial praying that the order shall be subject to special parliamentary procedure is presented to that Minister, by a person who is affected by the order and has such interest as may be prescribed by regulations made by one of the Ministers as being sufficient for the purpose.

Orders subject to special parliamentary procedure

6.—(1) If—
   (a) no such memorial as is mentioned in paragraph 5(2) above has been presented within the period so mentioned in respect of any order confirming a special charges scheme; or
   (b) every such memorial has been withdrawn,
the Minister who made the order shall confirm the order and it shall thereupon have effect.
   (2) If such a memorial has been presented in respect of such an order and has not been withdrawn, the order shall be subject to special parliamentary procedure.
   (3) An order confirming a special charges scheme shall in any event be subject to special parliamentary procedure if the Minister who makes the order so directs.
   (4) The Minister who makes an order confirming a special charges scheme may, at any time before it has been laid before Parliament, revoke, either wholly or partially, any order that is subject to special parliamentary procedure.

Notice of unconfirmed orders

7. As soon as may be after an unconfirmed order has effect, the Minister who made the order shall publish in the London Gazette, and in such other manner as he thinks best adapted for informing persons affected, a notice—
   (a) stating that the order has come into force; and
   (b) naming a place where a copy of it may be seen at all reasonable hours.

Challenge to unconfirmed orders

8.—(1) If any person aggrieved by an unconfirmed order desires to question its validity on the ground—
   (a) that it is not within the powers of this Act; or
   (b) that any requirement of this Act has not been complied with,
he may, within six weeks of the relevant date, make an application for the purpose to the High Court.
   (2) Where an application is duly made to the High Court under this paragraph, the High Court, if satisfied—
   (a) that the order is not within the powers of this Act; or
   (b) that the interests of the applicant have been substantially prejudiced by any requirements of this Act not having been complied with,
may quash the order either generally or in so far as it affects the applicant.
   (3) Except by leave of the Court of Appeal, no appeal shall lie to the House of Lords from a decision of the Court of Appeal in proceedings under this paragraph.
   (4) Subject to the preceding provisions of this paragraph an unconfirmed order shall not at any time be questioned in any legal proceedings whatsoever.

(5) In this paragraph "the relevant date," in relation to an order, means—
(a) where the order is subject to special parliamentary procedure, the date on which the order becomes operative under the Statutory Orders (Special Procedure) Act 1945;
(b) where the order is not subject to special parliamentary procedure, the date of the publication of the notice mentioned in paragraph 7 above.

Power to make regulations for purposes of Schedule

9. The Ministers may make regulations in relation to—
(a) the publication of notices under this Schedule;
(b) the holding of public local inquiries under this Schedule and procedure at those inquiries; and
(c) any other matters of procedure respecting the making of orders confirming a special charges scheme.

Interpretation

10.—(1) In this Schedule—
"special charges scheme" means a scheme under section 137 of this Act; and
"unconfirmed order" means an order confirming a special charges scheme, other than one which is itself confirmed under section 6 of the Statutory Orders (Special Procedure) Act 1945.
(2) Section 113 of this Act shall apply for the interpretation of this Schedule as it applies for the interpretation of Part IV of this Act.

Section 143   SCHEDULE 17

Orders with respect to Navigation Tolls

Orders to be made by statutory instrument

1. The power to make an order under section 143 of this Act shall be exercisable by statutory instrument.

Inquiries

2.—(1) The Secretary of State may hold inquiries for the purposes of section 143 of this Act as if those purposes were purposes of the Ministry of Transport Act 1919; and section 20 of that Act (power to hold inquiries) shall have effect accordingly.
(2) The Secretary of State may make such order as to the payment of costs incurred by him in connection with any such inquiry as he may think just.

Notice of order

3.—(1) After the Secretary of State has made an order under section 143 of this Act, the order, together with a notice under sub-paragraph (2) below, shall be published in such manner as he thinks best adapted for informing the persons affected.
(2) A notice under this sub-paragraph is a notice—
(a) that the Secretary of State has made the order; and
(b) that the order will become final and have effect unless, within such period of not less than 30 days as may be specified in the notice, a memorial praying that the order shall be subject to special parliamentary procedure is presented to the Secretary of State, by a person who is affected by the order and has such an interest as may be prescribed as being sufficient for the purpose.

Orders subject to special parliamentary procedure

4.—(1) If—
(a) no such memorial as is mentioned in paragraph 3(2) above has been presented within the period so mentioned in respect of any order under section 143 of this Act; or
(b) every such memorial has been withdrawn,
the Secretary of State shall confirm the order and it shall thereupon have effect.
(2) If such a memorial has been presented in respect of such an order and has not been withdrawn, the order shall be subject to special parliamentary procedure.
(3) An order under section 143 of this Act shall, in any event, be subject to special parliamentary procedure if the Secretary of State so directs.
(4) The Secretary of State may, at any time before it has been laid before Parliament, revoke, either wholly or partially, any order under section 143 of this Act that is subject to special parliamentary procedure.

SCHEDULE 18

Modification of Compensation Provisions etc. in relation to the Creation of New Rights

Compensation enactments

1. Subject to the following provisions of this Schedule, the enactments for the time being in force with respect to compensation for the compulsory purchase of land shall apply with the necessary modifications as respects compensation in the case of a compulsory acquisition under section 154 of this Act of a right by the creation of a new right as they apply as respects compensation on the compulsory purchase of land and interests in land.

Adaptation of the Compulsory Purchase Act 1965

2.—(1) The Compulsory Purchase Act 1965 (in the following provisions of this Schedule referred to as "the 1965 Act") shall have effect with the modifications necessary to make it apply to the compulsory acquisition under section 154 of this Act of a right by the creation of a new right as it applies to the compulsory acquisition under that section of land, so that, in appropriate contexts, references in that Act to land are to be read (according to the requirements of the particular context) as referring to, or as including references to—
    (a) the right acquired or to be acquired; or
    (b) the land over which the right is or is to be exercisable.
(2) Without prejudice to the generality of sub-paragraph (1) above, Part I of the 1965 Act shall apply in relation to the compulsory acquisition under section 154 of this Act of a right by the creation of a new right with the modifications specified in the following provisions of this Schedule.

Section 7 of the 1965 Act

3. For section 7 of the 1965 Act (measure of compensation) there shall be substituted the following section—
    "7. In assessing the compensation to be paid by the acquiring authority under this Act regard shall be had not only to the extent (if any) to which the value of the land over which the right is to be acquired is depreciated by the acquisition of the right but also to the damage (if any) to be sustained by the owner of the land by reason of its severance from other land of his, or injuriously affecting that other land by the exercise of the powers conferred by this or the special Act."

Section 8 of the 1965 Act

4. For subsection (1) of section 8 of the 1965 Act (protection for vendor against severance of house, garden, etc.) there shall be substituted the following subsections—
    "(1) No person shall be required to grant any right over part only—
        (a) of any house, building or manufactory; or
        (b) of a park or garden belonging to a house,
    if he is willing to sell the whole of the house, building, manufactory, park or garden, unless the Lands Tribunal determine that—
        (i) in the case of a house, building or manufactory, the part over which the right is proposed to be acquired can be made subject to that right without material detriment to the house, building or manufactory; or
        (ii) in the case of a park or garden, the part over which the right is proposed to be acquired can be made subject to that right without seriously affecting the amenity or convenience of the house;
    and, if the Lands Tribunal so determine, the Tribunal shall award compensation in respect of any loss due to the acquisition of the right, in addition to its value; and thereupon the party interested shall be required to grant to the acquiring authority that right over the part of the house, building, manufactory, park or garden.
    (1A) In considering the extent of any material detriment to a house, building or manufactory, or any extent to which the amenity or convenience of a house is affected, the Lands Tribunal shall have regard not only to the right which is to be acquired over the land, but also to any adjoining or adjacent land belonging to the same owner and subject to compulsory purchase."

Effect of deed poll

5. The following provisions of the 1965 Act (being provisions stating the effect of a deed poll executed in various circumstances where there is no conveyance by persons with interests in the land), that is to say—
    (a) section 9(4) (refusal by owners to convey);

(b) paragraph 10(3) of Schedule 1 (owners under incapacity);

(c) paragraph 2(3) of Schedule 2 (absent and untraced owners); and

(d) paragraphs 2(3) and 7(2) of Schedule 4 (common land),

shall be so modified as to secure that, as against persons with interests in the land which are expressed to be overridden by the deed, the right which is to be compulsorily acquired is vested absolutely in the acquiring authority.

Section 11 of the 1965 Act

6. Section 11 of the 1965 Act (powers of entry) shall be so modified as to secure that, as from the date on which the acquiring authority have served notice to treat in respect of any right, they have power, exercisable in the like circumstances and subject to the like conditions, to enter for the purpose of exercising that right (which shall be deemed for this purpose to have been created on the date of service of the notice); and sections 12 (penalty for unauthorised entry) and 13 (entry on warrant in the event of obstruction) shall be modified correspondingly.

Section 20 of the 1965 Act

7. Section 20 of the 1965 Act (protection for interests of tenants at will etc.) shall apply with the modifications necessary to secure that persons with such interests as are mentioned in that section are compensated in a manner corresponding to that in which they would be compensated on a compulsory acquisition under section 154 of this Act of that land, but taking into account only the extent (if any) of such interference with such an interest as is actually caused, or likely to be caused, by the exercise of the right in question.

Section 22 of the 1965 Act

8. Section 22 of the 1965 Act (protection of acquiring authority's possession where by inadvertence an estate, right or interest has not been got in) shall be so modified as to enable the acquiring authority, in circumstances corresponding to those referred to in that section, to continue entitled to exercise the right acquired, subject to compliance with that section as respects compensation.

Section 168   SCHEDULE 19

ORDERS CONFERRING COMPULSORY WORKS POWERS

Applications for orders

1.—(1) Where the Authority applies to either of the Ministers for a compulsory works order, it shall—

(a) submit to that Minister a draft of the order applied for;

(b) publish a notice with respect to the application, at least once in each of two successive weeks, in one or more newspapers circulating in each relevant locality;

(c) not later than the date on which that notice is first published—

(i) serve a copy of the notice on each of the persons specified in relation to the application in sub-paragraph (3) below; and

(ii) in the case of a draft order which would authorise the stopping-up or diversion of a footpath or bridleway, cause such a copy, together with a plan showing the general effect of the draft order so far as it relates to the footpath or bridleway, to be displayed in a prominent position at the ends of the part of the path or way to be stopped up or diverted;

and

(d) publish a notice in the London Gazette which—

(i) states that the draft order has been submitted to that Minister;

(ii) names every local authority on whom a notice is required to be served under this paragraph;

(iii) specifies a place where a copy of the draft order and of any relevant map or plan may be inspected; and

(iv) gives the name of every newspaper in which the notice required by virtue of paragraph (b) above was published and the date of an issue containing the notice.

(2) The notice required by virtue of sub-paragraph (1)(b) above to be published with respect to an application for an order by the Authority shall—

(a) state the general effect of the order applied for;

(b) in the case of an application made wholly or partly for the purpose of enabling any discharges of water to be made—

(i) contain particulars of the proposed discharges, stating the purposes of the discharges and specifying each place of discharge;

(ii) specify the places at which the water to be comprised in the proposed discharges is to be taken and the treatment (if any) which the draft order proposes to require the water, or any of it, to receive before being discharged under the order; and

(iii) state the effect which, in the opinion of the Authority, the proposed discharges would have on the flow, level and quality of water in any inland waters or underground strata;

(c) specify a place where a copy of the draft order and of any relevant map or plan may be inspected by any person free of charge at all reasonable times during the period of 28 days beginning with the date of the first publication of the notice; and

(d) state that any person may within that period, by notice to the Minister applied to, object to the making of the order.

(3) The persons mentioned in sub-paragraph (1)(c) above in relation to an application for a compulsory works order a draft of which has been submitted to either of the Ministers are—

(a) every local authority whose area is or includes the whole or any part of a relevant locality and which is not a county council;

(b) every water undertaker whose area is or includes the whole or any part of such a locality;

(c) every navigation authority, harbour authority and conservancy authority which would be affected by, or has functions in relation to any inland waters which would be affected by, any provision proposed to be made by the order;

(d) every owner, lessee or occupier (except tenants for a month or for any period of less than a month) of any land in relation to which compulsory powers would become exercisable if the order were made in the terms of the draft order;

(e) every person who has given notice to the Authority requiring it to notify him of applications for compulsory works orders and has paid such reasonable charge as the Authority may have required him to pay for being notified by virtue of this paragraph;

(f) such other persons as may be prescribed.

(4) In this paragraph "relevant locality," in relation to an application for an order, means—

(a) any locality which would be affected by any provision proposed to be made by the order for the purpose of enabling any engineering or building operations to be carried out; and

(b) where provision is proposed to be made by the order for the purpose of enabling discharges of water to be made, each locality in which the place of any of the proposed discharges is situated or in which there appears to the Authority to be any inland waters or underground strata the flow, level or quality of water in which may be affected by any of the proposed discharges.

Supply of copies of draft orders

2. Where the Authority is applying for a compulsory works order, it shall, at the request of any person and on payment by that person of such charge (if any) as the Authority may reasonably require, furnish that person with a copy of any draft order submitted to either of the Ministers under paragraph 1 above and of any relevant map or plan.

Powers on an application

3.—(1) On an application for a compulsory works order, the Minister or the Secretary of State may make the order either in the terms of the draft order submitted or, subject to sub-paragraphs (2) and (3) below, in those terms as modified in such manner as he thinks fit, or may refuse to make an order.

(2) Neither of the Ministers shall make such a modification of a draft order as he considers is likely adversely to affect any persons unless he is satisfied that the Authority has given and published such additional notices, in such manner, as he may have required.

(3) Neither of the Ministers shall, unless all interested parties consent, make a compulsory works order so as to confer in relation to any land any powers of compulsory acquisition which would not have been conferred in relation to that land if the order were made in the terms of the draft order submitted under paragraph 1 above.

(4) Where one of the Ministers refuses, on an application for a compulsory works order, to make an order, the Authority shall, as soon as practicable after the refusal, notify the refusal to every person on whom it was, by virtue of paragraph 1(1)(c)(i) above, required to serve a copy of the notice with respect to the application.

Consideration of objections etc.

4.—(1) If, where an application for a compulsory works order has been made, either of the Ministers receives any notice of an objection to it, before the end of the relevant period, from—

(a) any person on whom a notice under paragraph 1 or 3 above is required to be served; or

(b) from any other person appearing to that Minister to be affected by the order as submitted or as proposed to be modified under paragraph 3 above,

then, unless the objection is withdrawn, the Minister or the Secretary of State shall, before making the order, either cause a local inquiry to be held or afford to the objector and to the Authority an opportunity of appearing before, and being heard by, a person appointed by him for the purpose.

(2) Where any objection received by one of the Ministers as mentioned in subparagraph (1) above relates to any powers of compulsory acquisition, the Minister or the Secretary of State—

(a) may require the objector to state in writing the grounds of his objection; and

(b) if he is satisfied that the objection relates exclusively to matters that can be dealt with in the assessment of compensation, may disregard the objection for the purposes of that sub-paragraph.

(3) In this paragraph "the relevant period," in relation to an application for any order, means the period ending with whichever is the later of—

(a) the end of the period of 28 days beginning with the date of the first publication of the notice published with respect to the application for the purposes of paragraph 1(1)(b) above; and

(b) the end of the period of 25 days beginning with the date of the publication in the London Gazette of the notice published for the purposes of the application by virtue of paragraph 1(1)(d) above,

together, in the case of an application for an order modifications to which have been proposed by the Minister considering the application, with any further periods specified with respect to the modifications in notices under paragraph 3(2) above.

Notice after making of order

5.—(1) As soon as practicable after a compulsory works order has been made, the Authority shall—

(a) publish a notice of the making of the order, at least once in each of two successive weeks, in one or more newspapers circulating in each relevant locality; and

(b) not later than the date on which that notice is first published—

(i) serve a copy of the notice on every person on whom the Authority was, by virtue of paragraph 1(1)(c)(i) above, required to serve a copy of the notice with respect to the application for the order; and

(ii) in the case of an order authorising the stopping-up or diversion of a footpath or bridleway, cause such a copy, together with a plan showing the general effect of the order so far as it relates to the footpath or bridleway, to be displayed in a prominent position at the ends of the appropriate part of the path or way.

(2) The notice required by virtue of sub-paragraph (1)(a) above to be published with respect to a compulsory works order shall—

(a) state the general effect of the order;

(b) in the case of an order made wholly or partly for the purpose of enabling any discharges of water to be made—

(i) contain particulars of the discharges, stating the purposes of the discharges and specifying each place of discharge;

(ii) specify the places at which the water to be comprised in the discharges is to be taken and the treatment (if any) which the order requires the water, or any of it, to receive before being discharged under the order; and

(iii) state the effect which, in the opinion of the applicant, the discharges would have on the flow, level and quality of water in any inland waters or underground strata; and

(c) specify a place where a copy of the order and of any relevant map or plan may be inspected by any person free of charge at all reasonable times.

(3) Where a compulsory works order has been made, the Authority shall, at the request of any person and on payment by that person of such charge (if any) as the Authority may reasonably require, furnish that person with a copy of the order and of any relevant map or plan.

(4) In this paragraph "relevant locality," in relation to any compulsory works order, means—

(a) any locality which is affected by any provision made by the order for the purpose of enabling any engineering or building operations to be carried out; and

(b) where provision is made by the order for the purpose of enabling discharges of water to be made, each locality in which the place of any of the discharges is situated or in which there appears to the Authority to be any inland waters or underground strata the flow, level or quality of water in which may be affected by any of the discharges.

Compulsory acquisition provisions

6.—(1) Without prejudice to the provisions of Schedule 23 to this Act—

(a) Part I of the Compulsory Purchase Act 1965;

(b) section 4 and Part III of, and Schedule 3 to, the Acquisition of Land Act 1981; and

(c) the enactments for the time being in force with respect to compensation for the compulsory purchase of land,

shall apply in relation to so much of a compulsory works order as confers powers of compulsory acquisition as they apply in relation to a compulsory purchase order made by virtue of section 154 of this Act and, accordingly, shall so apply, where the case so requires, with the modifications made by Schedule 18 to this Act.

(2) Subject to the provisions of sub-paragraph (6) below, if any person aggrieved by a compulsory works order containing powers of compulsory acquisition, or by a certificate given under the special land provisions in connection with such an order, desires—

(a) to question the validity of the order, or of any provision of the order, on the grounds that any powers of compulsory acquisition conferred by the order are not authorised by this Act to be so conferred, or that any of the relevant requirements have not been complied with in relation to the order; or

(b) to question the validity of the certificate on the grounds that any of the relevant requirements have not been complied with in relation to the certificate,

he may make an application for the purpose to the High Court at any time before the end of the period of six weeks beginning with the date on which notice of the making of the order is first published in accordance with paragraph 5 above or, as the case may be, notice of the giving of the certificate is first published in accordance with the special land provisions.

(3) On any application under sub-paragraph (2) above with respect to any order or certificate, the High Court—

(a) may by interim order suspend the operation of the order, or any provision of the order, or of the certificate (either generally or in so far as it affects any property of the applicant to the High Court) until the final determination of the proceedings; and

(b) if satisfied—

(i) that any powers of compulsory acquisition conferred by the order are not authorised by this Act to be so conferred; or

(ii) that the interests of that applicant have been substantially prejudiced by a failure to comply with any of the relevant requirements in relation to the order or the certificate,

may quash the order, or any provision of the order, or the certificate (either generally or in so far as it affects any property of that applicant).

(4) Except as provided by sub-paragraph (2) above, the validity of any such order or certificate as is mentioned in that sub-paragraph shall not, either before or after the order or certificate has been made or given, be questioned in any legal proceedings whatsoever.

(5) Subject to any order of the High Court under sub-paragraph (3) above, any such order or certificate as is mentioned in sub-paragraph (2) above shall become operative (except, in the case of an order, where it is subject by virtue of the special land provisions to special parliamentary procedure) on the date on which notice of the making or giving of the order or certificate is published as mentioned in the said sub-paragraph (2).

(6) Where an order such as is mentioned in sub-paragraph (2) above is subject to special parliamentary procedure, sub-paragraphs (2) to (4) of this paragraph—

(a) shall not apply to the order if it is confirmed by Act of Parliament under section 6 of the Statutory Orders (Special Procedure) Act 1945; and

(b) in any other case, shall have effect as if the reference in sub-paragraph (2) of this paragraph to the date on which notice of the making of the order is first published in accordance with paragraph 5 above were a reference to the date on which the order becomes operative under the said Act of 1945.

(7) In this paragraph—

"the special land provisions" means the provisions, as applied by virtue of sub-paragraph (1) above, of Part III of the Acquisition of Land Act 1981 or, as the case may require, of Part II of Schedule 3 to that Act; and

"the relevant requirements," in relation to an order or certificate, means the requirements of this Schedule and such requirements of the special land provisions or of any other enactment as are applicable to that order or certificate by virtue of this paragraph.

Compensation in certain cases of compulsory acquisition

7. Where—

(a) in connection with any engineering or building operations to which a compulsory works order relates, a licence under Chapter II of Part II of this Act is granted, or is deemed to be granted, to the Authority; and

(b) that licence is a licence to abstract water or to obstruct or impede the flow of any inland waters,

no compensation shall be payable by virtue of sub-paragraph (1) of paragraph 6 above in respect of any land or interest injuriously affected by the carrying out of those operations, in so far as that land or interest is injuriously affected by the abstraction of water, or the obstruction or impeding of the flow, in accordance with the provisions of the licence.

Compensation in respect of powers other than acquisition powers

8.—(1) If the value of any interest in any relevant land is depreciated by the coming into force of so much of any compulsory works order as—

(a) confers compulsory powers, other than powers of compulsory acquisition, for the purpose of enabling any engineering or building operations to be carried out; and

(b) grants authority for the carrying out of the operations,

the person entitled to that interest shall be entitled to compensation from the Authority of an amount equal to the amount of the depreciation.

(2) Where the person entitled to an interest in any relevant land sustains loss or damage which—

(a) is attributable to so much of any compulsory works order as—

(i) confers compulsory powers, other than powers of compulsory acquisition, for the purpose of enabling any engineering or building operations to be carried out; and

(ii) grants authority for the carrying out of the operations;

(b) does not consist in depreciation of the value of that interest; and

(c) is loss or damage for which he would have been entitled to compensation by way of compensation for disturbance, if his interest in that land had been compulsorily acquired under section 154 of this Act in pursuance of a notice to treat served on the date on which the order comes into force,

he shall be entitled to compensation from the Authority in respect of that loss or damage, in addition to compensation under sub-paragraph (1) above.

(3) Where any damage to, or injurious affection of, any land which is not relevant land is attributable to so much of any compulsory works order as—

(a) confers compulsory powers, other than powers of compulsory acquisition, for the purpose of enabling any engineering or building operations to be carried out; and

(b) grants authority for the carrying out of the operations,

the Authority shall pay compensation in respect of that damage or injurious affection to every person entitled to an interest in that land.

(4) A person who sustains any loss or damage which is attributable to any discharge of water made by the Authority in pursuance of a compulsory works order shall be entitled to recover compensation from the Authority in respect of the loss or damage.

(5) For the purposes of sub-paragraph (4) above any extra expenditure—

(a) which it becomes reasonably necessary for any water undertaker or public authority (other than the Authority) to incur for the purpose of properly carrying out any statutory functions; and

(b) which is attributable to any such discharge of water as is mentioned in that sub-paragraph,

shall be deemed to be a loss sustained by the undertaker or public authority and to be so attributable.

(6) Any question of disputed compensation under this paragraph, shall be referred to and determined by the Lands Tribunal; and in relation to the determination of any such compensation the provisions of sections 2 and 4 of the Land Compensation Act 1961 shall apply, subject to any necessary modifications.

(7) For the purpose of assessing any compensation under this paragraph, so far as that compensation is in respect of loss or damage consisting in depreciation of the value of an interest in land, the rules set out in section 5 of the Land Compensation Act 1961 shall, so far as applicable and subject to any necessary modifications, have effect as they have effect for the purpose of assessing compensation for the compulsory acquisition of an interest in land.

(8) Where the interest in land in respect of which any compensation falls to be assessed in accordance with sub-paragraph (7) above is subject to a mortgage—

(a) the compensation shall be assessed as if the interest were not subject to the mortgage;

(b) a claim for compensation may be made by any mortgagee of the interest, but without prejudice to the making of a claim by the person entitled to the interest;

(c) no such compensation shall be payable in respect of the interest of the mortgagee (as distinct from the interest which is subject to the mortgage); and

(d) any such compensation which is payable in respect of the interest which is subject to the mortgage shall be paid to the mortgagee, or, if there is more than one mortgagee, to the first mortgagee, and shall in either case be applied by him as if it were proceeds of sale.

(9) In this paragraph "relevant land," in relation to a compulsory works order, means any land which is not land in relation to which powers of compulsory acquisition are conferred by the order but is—

(a) land where any operations for which authority is granted by the order are to be carried out;

(b) land in relation to which compulsory powers are conferred by the order; or

(c) land held with any land falling within paragraph (a) or (b) above.

Protection of public undertakings

9. The provisions of section 179 and paragraphs 1, 2 and 5 of Schedule 22 to this Act shall apply, as they apply in relation to the carrying out of works in exercise of the powers specified in those provisions, in relation to the carrying out of works by virtue of an authority granted by so much of any compulsory works order as makes provision other than provision conferring powers of compulsory acquisition.

Interpretation

10. In this Schedule—
"bridleway" and "footpath" have the same meanings as in the Highways Act 1980;
"compulsory works order" means an order under section 168 of this Act;
"powers of compulsory acquisition" means any such powers as are mentioned in subsection (4)(a) of section 168 of this Act;
and references to a tenant for a month or for any period of less than a month include references to a statutory tenant, within the meaning of the Landlord and Tenant Act 1985, and to a licensee under an assured agricultural occupancy, within the meaning of Part I of the Housing Act 1988.

Section 173   SCHEDULE 20

SUPPLEMENTAL PROVISIONS WITH RESPECT TO POWERS OF ENTRY

Notice of entry

1.—(1) Without prejudice to any power exercisable by virtue of a warrant under this Schedule, no person shall make an entry into any premises or vessel by virtue of any power conferred by sections 169 to 172 of this Act except—

(a) in an emergency; or

(b) at a reasonable time and after the required notice of the intended entry has been given to the occupier of the premises or vessel.

(2) For the purposes of this paragraph the required notice is seven days' notice; but such notice shall not be required in the case of an exercise of a power conferred by section 169 or 172 above, except where the premises in question are residential premises, the vessel in question is used for residential purposes or the entry in question is to be with heavy equipment.

(3) For the purposes of the application of this paragraph to the power conferred by section 170 of this Act the reference in sub-paragraph (1) above to an emergency—

(a) in relation to an entry to premises for the purposes of, or for purposes connected with, the exercise or proposed exercise of any power in relation to a street, includes a reference to any circumstances requiring the carrying out of emergency works within the meaning of Part III of the New Roads and Street Works Act 1991; and

(b) in relation to any other entry to premises, includes a reference to any danger to property and to any interruption of a supply of water provided to any premises by any person and to any interruption of the provision of sewerage services to any premises.

(4) Until the coming into force of section 52 of the New Roads and Street Works Act 1991, sub-paragraph (3) above shall have effect as if the reference to Part III of that Act were a reference to the Public Utilities Street Works Act 1950; but nothing in this sub-paragraph shall be taken to prejudice the power of the Secretary of State under that Act of 1991 to make an order bringing that section 52 into force on different days for different purposes (including the purposes of this paragraph).

Warrant to exercise power

2.—(1) If it is shown to the satisfaction of a justice of the peace on sworn information in writing—

(a) that there are reasonable grounds for the exercise in relation to any premises or vessel of a power conferred by sections 169 to 172 of this Act; and

(b) that one or more of the conditions specified in sub-paragraph (2) below is fulfilled in relation to those premises or that vessel,

the justice may by warrant authorise the relevant authority to designate a person who shall be authorised to exercise the power in relation to those premises, or that vessel, in accordance with the warrant and, if need be, by force.

(2) The conditions mentioned in sub-paragraph (1)(b) above are—

(a) that the exercise of the power in relation to the premises or vessel has been refused;

(b) that such a refusal is reasonably apprehended;

(c) that the premises are unoccupied or the vessel is unoccupied;

(d) that the occupier is temporarily absent from the premises or vessel;

(e) that the case is one of urgency; or

(f) that an application for admission to the premises or vessel would defeat the object of the proposed entry.

(3) A justice of the peace shall not issue a warrant under this Schedule by virtue only of being satisfied that the exercise of a power in relation to any premises or vessel has been refused, or that a refusal is reasonably apprehended, unless he is also satisfied—

(a) that notice of the intention to apply for the warrant has been given to the occupier of the premises or vessel; or

(b) that the giving of such a notice would defeat the object of the proposed entry.

(4) For the purposes of the application of this Schedule to the powers conferred by section 171 of this Act in a case to which subsection (4) of that section applies, a justice of the peace shall not issue a warrant under this Schedule unless he is satisfied that the Secretary of State has given his authorisation for the purposes of that subsection in relation to that case.

(5) Every warrant under this Schedule shall continue in force until the purposes for which the warrant was issued have been fulfilled.

Manner of exercise of powers

3. A person designated as the person who may exercise any power to which this Schedule applies shall produce evidence of his designation and other authority before he exercises the power.

Supplementary powers of person making entry etc.

4. A person authorised to enter any premises or vessel by virtue of any power to which this Schedule applies shall be entitled, subject in the case of a power exercisable under a warrant to the terms of the warrant, to take with him on to the premises or vessel such other persons and such equipment as may be necessary.

Duty to secure premises

5. A person who enters any premises or vessel in the exercise of any power to which this Schedule applies shall leave the premises or vessel as effectually secured against trespassers as he found them.

Compensation

6.—(1) Where any person exercises any power to which this Schedule applies, it shall be the duty of the relevant authority to make full compensation to any person who has sustained loss or damage by reason of—

(a) the exercise by the designated person of that power or of any power to take any person or equipment with him when entering the premises or vessel in relation to which the power is exercised; or

(b) the performance of, or failure of the designated person to perform, the duty imposed by paragraph 5 above.

(2) Compensation shall not be payable by virtue of sub-paragraph (1) above in respect of any loss or damage if the loss or damage—

(a) is attributable to the default of the person who sustained it; or

(b) is loss or damage in respect of which compensation is payable by virtue of any other provision of this Act.

(3) Any dispute as to a person's entitlement to compensation under this paragraph, or as to the amount of any such compensation, shall be referred to the arbitration of a single arbitrator appointed by agreement between the relevant authority and the person who claims to have sustained the loss or damage or, in default of agreement—

(a) by the President of the Lands Tribunal where the relevant authority is one of the Ministers; and

(b) by one of the Ministers, where the Authority is the relevant authority.

Obstruction of person exercising power

7. A person who intentionally obstructs another person acting in the exercise of any power to which this Schedule applies shall be guilty of an offence and liable, on summary conviction, to a fine not exceeding level 3 on the standard scale.

Interpretation

8.—(1) In this Schedule—

"relevant authority," in relation to a power to which this Schedule applies, means one of the Ministers or the Authority, according to who is entitled, by virtue of the provision by which the power is conferred or, as the case may be, the warrant, to designate the person by whom the power may be exercised; and

"sewerage services" has the same meaning as in the Water Industry Act 1991.

(2) References in this Schedule to a power to which this Schedule applies are references to any power conferred by Chapter II of Part VI of this Act, including a power exercisable by virtue of a warrant under this Schedule.

(3) For the purposes of paragraphs 5 and 6 above a person enters any premises or vessel by virtue of a power to which this Schedule applies notwithstanding that he has failed (whether by virtue of the waiver of the requirement by the occupier of the premises or otherwise) to comply with—

(a) any requirement to enter those premises at a reasonable time or after giving notice of his intended entry; or

(b) the requirement imposed by paragraph 3 above.

Section 177 SCHEDULE 21

COMPENSATION ETC. IN RESPECT OF CERTAIN WORKS POWERS

Compensation in respect of street works powers

1.—(1) This paragraph applies, in relation to the Authority, to the powers conferred on it in relation to streets by sections 159 and 162 of this Act.

(2) It shall be the duty of the Authority—

(a) to do as little damage as possible in the exercise of the powers to which this paragraph applies; and

(b) to pay compensation for any loss caused or damage done in the exercise of those powers.

(3) Any dispute as to whether compensation should be paid under sub-paragraph (2) above, or as to the amount of any such compensation, shall be referred to the arbitration of a single arbitrator appointed by agreement between the parties to the dispute or, in default of agreement, by the Secretary of State.

(4) Until the coming into force of Part III of the New Roads and Street Works Act 1991, a payment of compensation under this paragraph shall be treated for the purposes of section 32 of the Public Utilities Street Works Act 1950 (provisions against duplication of compensation) as made under an enactment passed before that Act of 1950; but nothing in this sub-paragraph shall be taken to prejudice the power of the Secretary of State under that Act of 1991 to make an order bringing Part III of that Act into force on different days for different purposes (including the purposes of this paragraph).

Compensation in respect of pipe-laying work on private land

2.—(1) If the value of any interest in any relevant land is depreciated by virtue of the exercise by the Authority of any power to carry out pipe-laying works on private land, the person entitled to that interest shall be entitled to compensation from the Authority of an amount equal to the amount of the depreciation.

(2) Where the person entitled to an interest in any relevant land sustains loss or damage which—

(a) is attributable to the exercise by the Authority of any power to carry out pipe-laying works on private land;

(b) does not consist in depreciation of the value of that interest; and

(c) is loss or damage for which he would have been entitled to compensation by way of compensation for disturbance, if his interest in that land had been compulsorily acquired under section 154 of this Act, he shall be entitled to compensation from the Authority in respect of that loss or damage, in addition to compensation under sub-paragraph (1) above.

(3) Where any damage to, or injurious affection of, any land which is not relevant land is attributable to the exercise by the Authority, of any power to carry out pipe-laying works on private land, the Authority shall pay compensation in respect of that damage or injurious affection to every person entitled to an interest in that land.

(4) The Secretary of State may by regulations make provision requiring the Authority, where it is proposing or has begun, in a prescribed case, to exercise any power to carry out pipe-laying works on private land, to make advance payments on account of compensation that will become payable in respect of the exercise of that power.

(5) In this paragraph "relevant land," in relation to any exercise of a power to carry out pipe-laying works on private land, means the land where the power is exercised or land held with that land.

(6) In this paragraph the references to a power to carry out pipe-laying works on private land are references to any of the powers conferred by virtue of section 160 or 162(3) of this Act.

Assessment of compensation under paragraph 2

3.—(1) Any question of disputed compensation under paragraph 2 above shall be referred to and determined by the Lands Tribunal; and in relation to the determination of any such compensation the provisions of sections 2 and 4 of the Land Compensation Act 1961 shall apply, subject to any necessary modifications.

(2) For the purpose of assessing any compensation under paragraph 2 above, so far as that compensation is in respect of loss or damage consisting in depreciation of the value of an interest in land, the rules set out in section 5 of the Land Compensation Act 1961 shall, so far as applicable and subject to any necessary modifications, have effect as they have effect for the purpose of assessing compensation for the compulsory acquisition of an interest in land.

(3) Where the interest in land in respect of which any compensation falls to be assessed in accordance with sub-paragraph (2) above is subject to a mortgage—

   (a) the compensation shall be assessed as if the interest were not subject to the mortgage;
   (b) a claim for compensation may be made by any mortgagee of the interest, but without prejudice to the making of a claim by the person entitled to the interest;
   (c) no such compensation shall be payable in respect of the interest of the mortgagee (as distinct from the interest which is subject to the mortgage); and
   (d) any such compensation which is payable in respect of the interest which is subject to the mortgage shall be paid to the mortgagee, or, if there is more than one mortgagee, to the first mortgagee, and shall in either case be applied by him as if it were proceeds of sale.

(4) Where, apart from this sub-paragraph, any person entitled to an interest in any land would be entitled under paragraph 2 above to an amount of compensation in respect of any works, there shall be deducted from that amount an amount equal to the amount by which the carrying out of the works has enhanced the value of any other land which—

   (a) is contiguous or adjacent to that land; and
   (b) is land to an interest in which that person is entitled in the same capacity.

Compensation in respect of discharges for works purposes

4.—(1) It shall be the duty of the Authority—
   (a) to cause as little loss and damage as possible in the exercise of the powers conferred on it by section 163 of this Act; and
   (b) to pay compensation for any loss caused or damage done in the exercise of those powers.

(2) For the purposes of sub-paragraph (1) above any extra expenditure—
   (a) which it becomes reasonably necessary for any water undertaker, sewerage undertaker or public authority (other than the Authority itself) to incur for the purpose of properly carrying out any statutory functions; and
   (b) which is attributable to any discharge of water under section 163 of this Act,
shall be deemed to be a loss sustained by the undertaker or public authority and to have been caused in exercise of the powers conferred by that section.

(3) Any dispute as to whether compensation should be paid under sub-paragraph (1) above, or as to the amount of any such compensation, shall be referred to the arbitration of a single arbitrator appointed by agreement between the parties to the dispute or, in default of agreement, by the President of the Institution of Civil Engineers.

Compensation in respect of flood defence and drainage works

5.—(1) Where injury is sustained by any person by reason of the exercise by the Authority of any powers under section 165(1) to (3) of this Act, the Authority shall be liable to make full compensation to the injured party.

(2) In case of dispute, the amount of any compensation under sub-paragraph (1) above shall be determined by the Lands Tribunal.

(3) Where injury is sustained by any person by reason of the exercise by the Authority of its powers under subsection (1)(b) of section 167 of this Act—

(a) the Authority may, if it thinks fit, pay to him such compensation as it may determine; and

(b) if the injury could have been avoided if those powers had been exercised with reasonable care, the provisions of sub-paragraphs (1) and (2) above shall apply as if the injury had been sustained by reason of the exercise by the Authority of its powers under section 165(1) to (3) of this Act.

Section 178   SCHEDULE 22

PROTECTION FOR PARTICULAR UNDERTAKINGS

General provisions protecting undertakings

1.—(1) Nothing in any of the provisions of this Act conferring power on the Authority to carry out any works shall confer power to do anything, except with the consent of the persons carrying on an undertaking protected by this paragraph, which, whether directly or indirectly, so interferes or will so interfere—

(a) with works or property vested in or under the control of the persons carrying on that undertaking, in their capacity as such; or

(b) with the use of any such works or property,

as to affect injuriously those works or that property or the carrying on of that undertaking.

(2) A consent for the purposes of sub-paragraph (1) above may be given subject to reasonable conditions but shall not be unreasonably withheld.

(3) Subject to the following provisions of this Schedule, any dispute—

(a) as to whether anything done or proposed to be done interferes or will interfere as mentioned in sub-paragraph (1) above;

(b) as to whether any consent for the purposes of this paragraph is being unreasonably withheld; or

(c) as to whether any condition subject to which any such consent has been given was reasonable,

shall be referred to the arbitration of a single arbitrator to be appointed by agreement between the parties to the dispute or, in default of agreement, by the President of the Institution of Civil Engineers.

(4) The following arc the undertakings protected by this paragraph, that is to say—

(a) the undertakings of the Civil Aviation Authority, the British Coal Corporation and the Post Office;

(b) the undertaking of any water undertaker or sewerage undertaker;

(c) any undertaking consisting in the running of a telecommunications code system, within the meaning of Schedule 4 to the Telecommunications Act 1984;

(d) any airport to which Part V of the Airports Act 1986 applies;

(e) the undertaking of any public gas supplier within the meaning of Part I of the Gas Act 1986;

(f) the undertaking of any person authorised by a licence under Part I of the Electricity Act 1989 to generate, transmit or supply electricity;

(g) the undertaking of any navigation authority, harbour authority or conservancy authority or of any internal drainage board;

(h) the undertaking of any railway company;

(i) any public utility undertaking carried on by a local authority under any Act or under any order having the force of an Act.

(5) For the purposes of this paragraph any reference in this paragraph, in relation to any such airport as is mentioned in sub-paragraph (4)(d) above, to the persons carrying on the undertaking is a reference to the airport operator.

(6) The reference in sub-paragraph (1) above to the provisions of this Act conferring power to carry out works includes (without prejudice to the extent of that reference apart from this sub-paragraph) a reference to any provisions of any order under section 108 of this Act by virtue of which any such power is conferred.

Protection for statutory powers and jurisdiction

2.—(1) Subject to sub-paragraph (2) below, nothing in—

(a) any provision of this Act conferring power on the Authority to carry out any works; or

(b) any of the flood defence provisions of this Act,

shall confer power to do anything which prejudices the exercise of any statutory power, authority or jurisdiction from time to time vested into exercisable by any persons carrying on an undertaking protected by paragraph 1 above.

(2) Nothing in this paragraph shall be taken to exclude the application of section 109 of this Act to any work executed by persons carrying on an undertaking protected by paragraph 1 above.

(3) Sub-paragraph (6) of paragraph 1 above shall apply for the purposes of sub-paragraph (1) above as it applies for the purposes of sub-paragraph (1) of that paragraph.

(4) This paragraph shall be without prejudice to any power under this Act to transfer the functions of any authority.

Special protection for certain undertakings in respect of street works

3.—(1) Subject to the following provisions of this paragraph and without prejudice to the other provisions of this Schedule, the powers under the street works provisions to break up or open a street shall not be exercisable where the street, not being a highway maintainable at public expense (within the meaning of the Highways Act 1980)—

  (a) is under the control or management of, or is maintainable by, a railway company or a navigation authority; or

  (b) forms part of a level crossing belonging to such a company or authority or to any other person,

except with the consent of the company or authority or, as the case may be, of the person to whom the level crossing belongs.

(2) Sub-paragraph (1) above shall not apply to any exercise of the powers conferred by the street works provisions for the carrying out of emergency works, within the meaning of Part III of the New Roads and Street Works Act 1991.

(3) A consent given for the purposes of sub-paragraph (1) above may be made subject to such reasonable conditions as may be specified by the person giving it but shall not be unreasonably withheld.

(4) Any dispute—

  (a) as to whether a consent for the purposes of sub-paragraph (1) above should be given or withheld; or

  (b) as to whether the conditions to which any such consent is made subject are reasonable,

shall be referred to the arbitration of a single arbitrator appointed by agreement between the parties to the dispute or, in default of agreement, by the President of the Institution of Civil Engineers.

(5) If the Authority contravenes, without reasonable excuse, the requirements of sub-paragraph (1) above, it shall be guilty of an offence and liable, on summary conviction, to a fine not exceeding level 3 on the standard scale.

(6) The restrictions contained in paragraphs (1) to (5) of section 32 of the Tramways Act 1870 (protection of tramways) shall apply in relation to any exercise of a power conferred by the street works provisions—

  (a) as they apply in relation to the powers mentioned in that section; and

  (b) as if references in that section to a tramway included references to a trolley vehicle system.

(7) In this paragraph "the street works provisions" means sections 159 and 162(2) of this Act.

(8) Until the coming into force of section 52 of the New Roads and Street Works Act 1991, sub-paragraph (2) above shall have effect as if the reference to Part III of that Act were a reference to the Public Utilities Street Works Act 1950; but nothing in this sub-paragraph shall be taken to prejudice the power of the Secretary of State under that Act of 1991 to make an order bringing that section 52 into force on different days for different purposes (including the purposes of this paragraph).

Protection for railways in connection with carrying out of flood defence functions

4.—(1) Without prejudice to the preceding provisions of this Schedule, nothing in the flood defence provisions of this Act shall authorise any person, except with the consent of the railway company in question, to interfere with—

  (a) any railway bridge or any other work connected with a railway; or

  (b) the structure, use or maintenance of a railway or the traffic on it.

(2) A consent for the purposes of sub-paragraph (1) above may be given subject to reasonable conditions but shall not be unreasonably withheld.

(3) Subject to the following provisions of this Schedule, any dispute—

  (a) as to whether anything interferes, or will interfere, as mentioned in sub-paragraph (1) above;

(b) as to whether any consent for the purposes of this paragraph is being unreasonably withheld; or

(c) as to whether any condition subject to which any such consent has been given was reasonable,

shall be referred to the arbitration of a single arbitrator to be appointed by agreement between the parties to the dispute or, in default of agreement, by the President of the Institution of Civil Engineers.

Protection for telecommunication systems

5. Paragraph 23 of Schedule 2 to the Telecommunications Act 1984 (which provides a procedure for certain cases where works involve the alteration of telecommunication apparatus) shall apply to the Authority for the purposes of any works carried out by the Authority in exercise of any of the powers conferred by any enactment (including section 4(1) of this Act).

Interpretation

6. In this Schedule "railway company" means the British Railways Board, London Regional Transport or any other person authorised by any enactment, or by any order, rule or regulation made under any enactment, to construct, work or carry on a railway.

Section 182   SCHEDULE 23

MINERAL RIGHTS

Acquisition of mineral rights

1.—(1) This paragraph applies in each of the following cases, that is to say—

(a) where the Authority acquires any land (whether compulsorily in exercise of any power conferred by or under this Act or otherwise); and

(b) where the Authority carries out any works in relation to any land for the purposes of, or in connection with, the carrying out of any of its functions.

(2) Subject to sub-paragraph (3) below, the Authority shall not, by virtue only of its acquisition of the land or the carrying out of the works, become entitled to any mines or minerals lying under the land; and, accordingly, any such mines or minerals shall be deemed to be expected from any instrument by virtue of which the land vests in the Authority unless express provision to the contrary is contained—

(a) where the land vests in the Authority by virtue of a conveyance, in the conveyance; or

(b) where the land is acquired by the Authority in pursuance of any power of compulsory acquisition conferred by or under this Act, in the order authorising the acquisition.

(3) The Authority shall be entitled to such parts of any mines or minerals that lie under the land as it may be necessary for it to dig, carry away or use in carrying out any works for the purpose of constructing, making, erecting or laying any part of its undertaking.

Notice required for the working of underlying mines

2.—(1) If the owner of any mines or minerals underlying any part of the Authority's undertaking proposes to work them, he shall, not less than thirty days before the commencement of working, serve notice of his intention to do so on the Authority.

(2) On receipt of a notice under sub-paragraph (1) above the Authority may cause the mines or minerals to be inspected by a person designated by it for the purpose.

(3) Subject to sub-paragraph (5) and paragraph 3 below, if, where notice has been served under this paragraph, the Authority—

(a) considers that the working of the underlying mines or minerals is likely to damage any part of its undertaking;

(b) is willing to compensate the owner of the mines or minerals for the restriction imposed by virtue of this sub-paragraph; and

(c) serves notice to that effect on the owner of the mines or minerals before the end of the period of thirty days mentioned in sub-paragraph (1) above,

the owner shall not work the mines or minerals except to such extent as may be determined by the Authority, and the Authority shall so compensate the owner.

(4) Any dispute as to the amount of any compensation payable by virtue of sub-paragraph (3) above shall be referred to and determined by the Lands Tribunal.

(5) If before the end of the period of thirty days mentioned in sub-paragraph (1) above, no notice has been served under sub-paragraph (3)(c) above by the Authority, the entitlement of the owner of the mines and minerals to work them shall be an entitlement to work them by

proper methods and in the usual manner of working such mines or minerals in the district in question.

(6) If any damage to the undertaking of the Authority is caused by the working otherwise than as authorised by this paragraph of any mines or minerals underlying any part of its undertaking—

(a) the owner of the mines or minerals shall, at his own expense, forthwith repair the damage; and

(b) the Authority may, without waiting for the owner to perform his duty, repair the damage and may recover the expenses reasonably incurred by it in doing so from the owner.

Mining communications

3.—(1) If the working of any mines or minerals is prevented by reason of any of the preceding provisions of this Schedule, the owner of the mines or minerals may cut and make such communication works through the mines or minerals, or the strata in which they are situated, as are required for the ventilation, drainage and working of mines or minerals which are not underlying any part of the undertaking of the Authority.

(2) Communication works cut or made under this paragraph—

(a) shall not, in a case where—

(i) the part of the undertaking in question was constructed, made, erected or laid in pursuance of an order made under any enactment or is situated on land acquired by the Authority in pursuance of any powers of compulsory acquisition; and

(ii) the order authorising the works or acquisition designates dimensions or sections for the communication works,

exceed those dimensions or fail to conform to those sections; and

(b) in any other case, shall not be more than 2.44 metres high or more than 2.44 metres wide.

(3) Communication works cut or made under this paragraph shall not be cut or made on the land where the part of the undertaking is situated so as to cause damage to that part of the undertaking.

(4) Where works carried out under this paragraph by the owner of any mines or minerals cause loss or damage to the owner or occupier of land lying over the mines or minerals, the Authority shall pay full compensation to him for the loss or damage.

(5) Sub-paragraph (4) above shall not apply where the person sustaining the loss or damage is the owner of the mines.

(6) In this paragraph "communication works" means airways, headways, gateways or water levels.

Compensation relating to severance

4.—(1) Where mines or minerals underlying any part of the Authority's undertaking are situated so as, on two or more sides of that land, to extend beyond the land on which that part of the undertaking is situated, the Authority shall from time to time pay to the owner of the mines or minerals (in addition to any compensation under paragraph 2 above) any expenses and losses incurred by him in consequence of—

(a) the severance by the undertaking of the land lying over the mines;

(b) the interruption of continuous working of the mines in consequence of paragraph 2(3) above;

(c) the mines being so worked in accordance with restrictions imposed by virtue of this Act or any order made under this Act,

and shall pay for any minerals not purchased by the Authority which cannot be got or won by reason of the part of the undertaking in question being situated where it is or by reason of the requirement to avoid damage to any part of the Authority's undertaking.

(2) Any dispute as to whether any sum should be paid under this paragraph, or as to the amount payable, shall be referred to the arbitration of a single arbitrator appointed by agreement between the Authority and the owner of the mines or minerals or, in default of agreement, by the Secretary of State.

Powers of entry

5.—(1) Any person designated in writing for the purpose by the Authority may, for any purpose specified in sub-paragraph (2) below—

(a) enter on any land in which the mines or minerals are, or are thought to be, being worked, and which is in or near to the land where any part of the Authority's undertaking is situated; and

(b) enter the mines and any works connected with the mines.

(2) The purposes mentioned in sub-paragraph (1) above are—

(a) carrying out any inspection under paragraph 2(2) above;

(b) ascertaining whether any mines or minerals have been worked so as to damage the undertaking of the Authority; and

(c) carrying out any works and taking any other steps which the Authority in question is authorised to carry out or take under paragraph 2(6) above.

(3) A person authorised to enter any premises under this paragraph may—

(a) make use of any equipment belonging to the owner of the mines or minerals in question; and

(b) use all necessary means for discovering the distance from any part of the undertaking of the Authority to the parts of the mines or the minerals which are, or are about to be, worked.

(4) Schedule 20 to this Act shall apply in relation to the powers conferred by this paragraph as it applies to the powers conferred by sections 169 to 172 of this Act.

No exemption for injury to mines and minerals

6. Nothing in any provision of this Act or of any order made under this Act shall be construed as exempting the Authority from any liability to which it would, apart from that provision, have been subject in respect of any damage to any mines or minerals underlying any part of its undertaking or in respect of any loss sustained in relation to any such mines or minerals by a person having an interest therein.

Interpretation

7.—(1) In this Schedule—

"conveyance" has the same meaning as in the Law of Property Act 1925;

"designated distance," in relation to any part of the Authority's undertaking, means, subject to sub-paragraph (6) below, thirty-seven metres;

"mines" means mines of coal, ironstone, slate or other minerals;

"owner," in relation to mines and minerals, includes a lessee or occupier; and

"underlying," in relation to any part of the Authority's undertaking, means lying under, or within the designated distance from, that part of that undertaking.

(2) For the purposes of this Schedule the Authority's undertaking shall be taken to consist of so much of any of the following as is for the time being vested in or held by the Authority for the purpose of, or in connection with, the carrying out of any of its functions, that is to say—

(a) any buildings, reservoirs, wells, boreholes or other structures; and

(b) any pipes or other underground works particulars of which fall or would fall to be incorporated in any records kept under section 195 of this Act.

(3) References in this Schedule to the working of any mines or minerals include references to the draining of mines and to the winning or getting of minerals.

(4) For the purposes of this Schedule land shall be treated as acquired by the Authority in pursuance of powers of compulsory acquisition if it—

(a) was so acquired by a water authority or any predecessor of a water authority; and

(b) is now vested in the Authority in accordance with a scheme under Schedule 2 to the Water Act 1989 or otherwise.

(5) In relation to any land treated by virtue of sub-paragraph (4) above as acquired in pursuance of powers of compulsory acquisition, references in this Schedule to the order authorising the acquisition include references to any local statutory provision which immediately before 1st September 1989 had effect in relation to that land for the purposes of any provisions corresponding to the provisions of this Schedule.

(6) For the purposes of this Schedule where—

(a) any part of the Authority's undertaking was constructed, made, erected or laid in pursuance of an order made under any enactment or is situated on land acquired by the Authority in pursuance of any powers of compulsory acquisition; and

(b) the order authorising the works or acquisition designates any distance for the purposes of any enactment relating to mines or minerals underlying that part of the undertaking,

then for the purposes of this Schedule that distance (instead of the distance specified in subsection (1) above) shall be the designated distance in relation to that part of the undertaking.

Section 204   SCHEDULE 24

DISCLOSURE OF INFORMATION

PART I

PERSONS IN RESPECT OF WHOSE FUNCTIONS DISCLOSURE MAY BE MADE

Any Minister of the Crown.

The Director General of Fair Trading.
The Monopolies and Mergers Commission.
The Director General of Telecommunications.
The Civil Aviation Authority.
The Director General of Gas Supply.
The Director General of Electricity Supply.
A local weights and measures authority in England and Wales.

PART II

ENACTMENTS ETC. IN RESPECT OF WHICH DISCLOSURE MAY BE MADE

The Trade Descriptions Act 1968.
The Fair Trading Act 1973.
The Consumer Credit Act 1974.
The Restrictive Trade Practices Act 1976.
The Resale Prices Act 1976.
The Estate Agents Act 1979.
The Competition Act 1980.
The Telecommunication Act 1984.
The Airports Act 1986.
The Gas Act 1986.
The Consumer Protection Act 1987.
The Electricity Act 1989.
Any subordinate legislation made for the purpose of securing compliance with the Directive of the Council of the European Communities dated 10th September 1984 (No. 84/450/EEC) on the approximation of the laws, regulations and administrative provisions of the member States concerning misleading advertising.

Section 210   SCHEDULE 25

BYELAW-MAKING POWERS OF THE AUTHORITY

Byelaws for regulating use of inland waters

1.—(1) Subject to the following provisions of this paragraph but without prejudice to the powers conferred by the following provisions of this Schedule, where it appears to the Authority to be necessary or expedient to do so for the purposes of any of the functions specified in paragraphs (a), (c) and (d) of section 2(1) of this Act, the Authority may make byelaws—

(a) prohibiting such inland waters as may be specified in the byelaws from being used for boating (whether with mechanically propelled boats or otherwise), swimming or other recreational purposes; or

(b) regulating the way in which any inland waters so specified may be used for any of those purposes.

(2) Byelaws made by the Authority under this paragraph shall not apply to—

(a) any tidal waters or any discrete waters;

(b) any inland waters in relation to which functions are exercisable by a navigation authority, harbour authority or conservancy authority other than the Authority; or

(c) any reservoir belonging to, and operated by, a water undertaker.

(3) Byelaws made in respect of any inland waters by virtue of this paragraph may—

(a) include provision prohibiting the use of the inland waters by boats which are not for the time being registered with the Authority in such manner as the byelaws may provide; and

(b) authorise the Authority to make reasonable charges in respect of the registration of boats in pursuance of the byelaws.

Byelaws for regulating the use of navigable waters etc.

2.—(1) The Authority shall have power to make such byelaws as are mentioned in sub-paragraph (3) below with respect to any inland waters in relation to which—

(a) there is a public right of navigation; and

(b) the condition specified in sub-paragraph (2) below is satisfied,

and with respect to any land associated with such waters.

(2) For the purposes of this paragraph the condition mentioned in sub-paragraph (1) above is satisfied in relation to any waters if navigation in those waters—

(a) is not for the time being subject to the control of any navigation authority, harbour authority or conservancy authority; or

(b) is subject to the control of such a navigation authority, harbour authority or conservancy authority as is prescribed for the purposes of this paragraph by reason of its appearing to the Secretary of State to be unable for the time being to carry out its functions.

(3) The byelaws referred to in sub-paragraph (1) above in relation to any inland waters or to any land associated with any such waters are byelaws for any of the following purposes, that is to say—

(a) the preservation of order in or on any such waters or land;

(b) the prevention of damage to anything in or on any such waters or land or to any such land;

(c) securing that persons resorting to any such waters or land so behave as to avoid undue interference with the enjoyment of the waters or land by others.

(4) Without prejudice to the generality of any of the paragraphs of sub-paragraph (3) above or to the power conferred on the Authority by virtue of paragraph 4 below, the byelaws mentioned in that sub-paragraph include byelaws—

(a) regulating sailing, boating, bathing and fishing and other forms of recreation;

(b) prohibiting the use of the inland waters in question by boats which are not for the time being registered, in such manner as may be required by the byelaws, with the Authority;

(c) requiring the provision of such sanitary appliances as may be necessary for the purpose of preventing pollution; and

(d) authorising the making of reasonable charges in respect of the registration of boats for the purposes of the byelaws.

(5) In this paragraph "boat" includes a vessel of any description, and "boating" shall be construed accordingly.

Byelaws for regulating the use of the Authority's waterways etc.

3.—(1) The Authority shall have power to make such byelaws as are mentioned in sub-paragraph (2) below with respect to any waterway owned or managed by the Authority and with respect to any land held or managed with the waterway.

(2) The byelaws referred to in sub-paragraph (1) above in relation to any waterway or to any land held or managed with any such waterway are byelaws for any of the following purposes, that is to say—

(a) the preservation of order on or in any such waterway or land;

(b) the prevention of damage to anything on or in any such waterway or land or to any such land;

(c) securing that persons resorting to any such waterway or land so behave as to avoid undue interference with the enjoyment of the waterway or land by others.

(3) Without prejudice to the generality of any of the paragraphs of sub-paragraph (2) above or to the power conferred on that Authority by virtue of paragraph 4 below, the byelaws mentioned in that sub-paragraph include byelaws—

(a) regulating sailing, boating, bathing and fishing and other forms of recreation;

(b) prohibiting the use of the waterway in question by boats which are not for the time being registered, in such manner as may be required by the byelaws, with the Authority;

(c) requiring the provision of such sanitary appliances as may be necessary for the purpose of preventing pollution; and

(d) authorising the making of reasonable charges in respect of the registration of boats for the purposes of the byelaws.

(4) In this paragraph—

"boat" and "boating" have the same meanings as in paragraph 2 above; and

"waterway" has the same meaning as in the National Parks and Access to the Countryside Act 1949.

Byelaws for controlling certain forms of pollution

4.—(1) The Authority may by byelaws make such provision as the Authority considers appropriate—

(a) for prohibiting or regulating the washing or cleaning in any controlled waters of things of a description specified in the byelaws;

(b) for prohibiting or regulating the keeping or use or any controlled waters of vessels of a description specified in the byelaws which are provided with water closets or other sanitary appliances.

(2) In this paragraph—

"controlled waters" has the same meaning as in Part III of this Act; and

"sanitary appliance," in relation to a vessel, means any appliance which—

(a) not being a sink, bath or shower bath, is designed to permit polluting matter to pass into the water where the vessel is situated; and

(b) is prescribed for the purposes of this paragraph.

Byelaws for flood defence and drainage purposes

5.—(1) The Authority may make such byelaws in relation to any particular locality or localities as it considers necessary for securing the efficient working of any drainage system including the proper defence of any land against sea or tidal water.

(2) Without prejudice to the generality of sub-paragraph (1) above and subject to sub-paragraph (3) below, the Authority may, in particular, make byelaws for any of the following purposes, that is to say—

(a) regulating the use and preventing the improper use of any watercourses, banks or works vested in the Authority or under its control or for preserving any such watercourses, banks or works from damage or destruction;

(b) regulating the opening of sluices and flood gates in connection with any such works as are mentioned in paragraph (a) above;

(c) preventing the obstruction of any watercourse vested in the Authority or under its control by the discharge into it of any liquid or solid matter or by reason of any such matter being allowed to flow or fall into it;

(d) compelling the persons having control of any watercourse vested in the Authority or under its control, or of any watercourse flowing into any such watercourse, to cut the vegetable growths in or on the bank of the watercourse and, when cut, to remove them.

(3) No byelaw for any purpose specified in sub-paragraph (2)(a) above shall be valid if it would prevent reasonable facilities being afforded for enabling a watercourse to be used by stock for drinking purposes.

(4) Notwithstanding anything in this Act, no byelaw made by the Authority under this paragraph shall conflict with or interfere with the operation of any byelaw made by a navigation authority, harbour authority or conservancy authority.

(5) In this paragraph "banks" and "watercourse" have the same meanings as in Part IV of this Act.

Byelaws for purposes of fisheries functions

6.—(1) The Authority shall have power, in relation to any part or parts of the area in relation to which it carries out its functions relating to fisheries under Part V of this Act, to make byelaws generally for the purposes of—

(a) the better execution of the Salmon and Freshwater Fisheries Act 1975; and

(b) the better protection, preservation and improvement of any salmon fisheries, trout fisheries, freshwater fisheries and eel fisheries.

(2) Subject to paragraph 7(1) below, the Authority shall have power, in relation to any part or parts of the area mentioned in sub-paragraph (1) above, to make byelaws for any of the following purposes, that is to say—

(a) prohibiting the taking or removal from any water, without lawful authority, of any fish, whether alive or dead;

(b) prohibiting or regulating—

(i) the taking of trout or any freshwater fish of a size less than such as may be prescribed by the byelaw; or

(ii) the taking of fish by any means within such distance as is specified in the byelaw above or below any dam or any other obstruction, whether artificial or natural;

(c) prohibiting the use for taking salmon, trout, or freshwater fish of any instrument (not being a fixed engine) in such waters and at such times as may be prescribed by the byelaws;

(d) specifying the nets and other instruments (not being fixed engines) which may be used for taking salmon, trout, freshwater fish and eels, imposing requirements as to the use of such nets and other instruments and regulating the use, in connection with fishing with rod and line, of any lure or bait specified in the byelaw;

(e) authorising the placing and use of fixed engines at such places, at such times and in such manner as may be prescribed by the byelaws;

(f) imposing requirements as to the construction, design, material and dimensions of any such nets, instruments or engines as are mentioned in paragraphs (d) and (e) above, including in the case of nets the size of mesh;

(g) requiring and regulating the attachment to licensed nets and instruments of marks, labels or numbers, or the painting of marks or numbers or the affixing of labels or numbers to boats, coracles or other vessels used in fishing;

(h) prohibiting the carrying in any boat or vessel whilst being used in fishing for salmon or trout of any net which is not licensed, or which is without the mark, label or number prescribed by the byelaws; and

(i) prohibiting or regulating the carrying in a boat or vessel during the annual close season for salmon of a net capable of taking salmon, other than a net commonly used in the area to which the byelaw applies for sea fishing and carried in a boat or vessel commonly used for that purpose.

(3) Subject to the provisions of Schedule 1 to the Salmon and Freshwater Fisheries Act 1975 (duty to make byelaws about close season), the Authority shall have power, in relation to any part or parts of the area mentioned in sub-paragraph (1) above, to make byelaws for any of the following purposes, that is to say—

(a) fixing or altering any such close season or close time as is mentioned in paragraph 3 of that Schedule;

(b) dispensing with a close season for freshwater fish or rainbow trout;

(c) determining for the purposes of the Salmon and Freshwater Fisheries Act 1975 the period of the year during which gratings need not be maintained;

(d) prohibiting or regulating fisheries with rod and line between the end of the first hour after sunset on any day and the beginning of the last hour before sunrise on the following morning;

(e) determining the time during which it shall be lawful to use a gaff in connection with fishing with rod and line for salmon or migratory trout;

(f) authorising fishing with rod and line for eels during the annual close season for freshwater fish.

(4) Subject to paragraph 7(2) below, the Authority shall have power, in relation to any part or parts of the area mentioned in sub-paragraph (1) above, to make byelaws for the purpose of regulating the deposit or discharge in any waters containing fish of any liquid or solid matter specified in the byelaw which is detrimental to salmon, trout or freshwater fish, or the spawn or food of fish.

(5) The Authority shall have power, in relation to any part or parts of the area mentioned in sub-paragraph (1) above, to make byelaws for the purpose of requiring persons to send to the Authority returns, in such form, giving such particulars and at such times as may be specified in the byelaws—

(a) of the period or periods during which they have fished for salmon, trout, freshwater fish or eels,

(b) of whether they have taken any; and

(c) if they have, of what they have taken.

(6) Byelaws made under this paragraph may be made to apply to the whole or any part or parts of the year.

(7) Expressions used in this paragraph and in the Salmon and Freshwater Fisheries Act 1975 have the same meanings in this paragraph as in that Act.

Restrictions on powers to make byelaws for fisheries purposes

7.—(1) The Authority shall not make any byelaws by virtue of paragraph 6(2)(e) above in relation to any place within the sea fisheries district of a local fisheries committee except with the consent of that committee.

(2) The Authority shall not make byelaws by virtue of paragraph 6(4) above so as to prejudice any powers of a sewerage undertaker to discharge sewage in pursuance of any power given by a public general Act, a local Act or a provisional order confirmed by Parliament.

Section 210   SCHEDULE 26

PROCEDURE RELATING TO BYELAWS MADE BY THE AUTHORITY

Confirmation of byelaws

1.—(1) No byelaw made by the Authority shall have effect until confirmed by the relevant Minister under this Schedule.

(2) At least one month before it applies for the confirmation of any byelaw, the Authority shall—

(a) cause a notice of its intention to make the application to be published in the London Gazette and in such other manner as it considers appropriate for the purpose of bringing the proposed byelaw to the attention of persons likely to be affected by it; and

(b) cause copies of the notice to be served on any persons carrying out functions under any enactment who appear to it to be concerned.

(3) For at least one month before an application is made by the Authority for the confirmation of any byelaw, a copy of it shall be deposited at one or more of the offices of the Authority, including (if there is one) at an office in the area to which the byelaw would apply.

(4) The Authority shall provide reasonable facilities for the inspection free of charge of a byelaw deposited under sub-paragraph (3) above.

(5) Every person shall be entitled, on application to the Authority, to be furnished free of charge with a printed copy of a byelaw so deposited.

Confirmation with or without modifications

2.—(1) Subject to sub-paragraph (3) below, the relevant Minister, with or without a local inquiry, may refuse to confirm any byelaw submitted to him by the Authority for confirmation under this Schedule, or may confirm the byelaw either without or, if the Authority consents, with modifications.

(2) The Authority shall, if so directed by the relevant Minister, cause notice of any proposed modifications to be given in accordance with his directions.

(3) A byelaw made by the Authority under paragraph 4 of Schedule 25 to this Act shall be confirmed without a local inquiry only if—

(a) no written objection to its confirmation has been received by the relevant Minister;

(b) every objection to its confirmation which has been so received has been withdrawn; or

(c) in the opinion of that Minister the person making the objection has no material interest in the controlled waters to which the byelaw relates;

and in relation to any such byelaw sub-paragraph (1) above shall have effect with the substitution for the words "if the Authority consents" of the words "after consultation with the Authority."

Commencement of byelaw

3.—(1) The relevant Minister may fix the date on which any byelaw confirmed under this Schedule is to come into force.

(2) If no date is so fixed in relation to a byelaw, it shall come into force at the end of the period of one month beginning with the date of confirmation.

Availability of confirmed byelaws

4.—(1) Every byelaw made by the Authority and confirmed under this Schedule shall be printed and deposited at one or more of the offices of the Authority, including (if there is one) at an office in the area to which the byelaw applies; and copies of the byelaw shall be available at those offices, at all reasonable times, for inspection by the public free of charge.

(2) Every person shall be entitled, on application to the Authority and on payment of such reasonable sum as the Authority may determine, to be furnished with a copy of any byelaw so deposited by the Authority.

Revocation of byelaws

5. If it appears to the relevant Minister that the revocation of a byelaw is necessary or expedient, he may—

(a) after giving notice to the Authority and considering any representations or objections made by the Authority; and

(b) if required by the Authority, after holding a local inquiry,

revoke that byelaw.

Proof of byelaws

6. The production of a printed copy of a byelaw purporting to be made by the Authority upon which is indorsed a certificate, purporting to be signed on its behalf, stating—

(a) that the byelaw was made by the Authority;

(b) that the copy is a true copy of the byelaw;

(c) that on a specified date the byelaw was confirmed under this Schedule; and

(d) the date, if any, fixed under paragraph 3 above for the coming into force of the byelaw,

shall be prima facie evidence of the facts stated in the certificate, and without proof of the handwriting or official position of any person purporting to sign the certificate.

Meaning of "the relevant Minister"

7. In this Schedule "the relevant Minister"—

(a) in relation to byelaws which—

(i) are made by virtue of paragraph 5 of Schedule 25 to this Act or by virtue of section 136(8) of the Water Act 1989 as read with the savings in paragraphs 1 and 5 of Schedule 2 to the Water Consolidation (Consequential Provisions) Act 1991 (transfer of land drainage functions under local statutory provisions); and

(ii) have effect in the area of a regional flood defence committee the whole or the
    greater part of whose area is in England,
  means the Minister;
(b) in relation to byelaws made by virtue of paragraph 6 of that Schedule 25 or by virtue of
    any provision amended by Schedule 17 to the Water Act 1989 (fisheries functions of the
    Authority), means the Secretary of State or the Minister; and
(c) in relation to any other byelaws, means the Secretary of State.

Table of Derivations

Notes:

1. The following abbreviations are used in this Table:—

1945	= The Water Act 1945 (c. 42)
1963	= The Water Resources Act 1963 (c. 38)
1965	= The Science and Technology Act 1965 (c. 4)
1973	= The Water Act 1973 (c. 37)
1975	= The Salmon and Freshwater Fisheries Act 1975 (c. 51)
1976	= The Land Drainage Act 1976 (c. 70)
1977	= The Criminal Law Act 1977 (c. 45)
1980(LG)	= The Local Government, Planning and Land Act 1980 (c. 65)
1981	= The Water Act 1981 (c. 12)
1982(CJA)	= The Criminal Justice Act 1982 (c.43)
1983	= The Water Act 1983 (c. 23)
1984	= The Telecommunications Act 1984 (c. 12)
1985(LG)	= The Local Government Act 1985 (c. 51)
1986(GA)	= The Gas Act 1986 (c. 44)
1989	= The Water Act 1989 (c. 15)
1989(EA)	= The Electricity Act 1989 (c. 29)
1990	= The Environmental Protection Act 1990 (c. 43)
1991(NR)	= The New Roads and Street Works Act 1991 (c. 22)
R: (followed by a number)	= The recommendation so numbered as set out in the Appendix to the Report of the Law Commission (Cm. 1483).

2. Transfer of functions orders ("TFOs"), where applicable in relation to a provision
re-enacted in the Bill, are specified at the appropriate place in column 2 of the Table.

3. General provisions contained in section 32 of the Magistrates' Courts Act 198 (c. 43) and
section 46 of the Criminal Justice Act 1982 (c. 48) provide, respectively, for the maximum fine
on summary conviction of an either way offence to be the statutory maximum and for a
reference to the amount of the maximum fine to which a person is liable in respect of a summary
offence to become a reference to a level on the standard scale. Where the effect of one of these
enactments is consolidated it is not referred to separately in column 2 of this Table.

Provision of Act	Derivation
1	1989 s.1.
2	1963 s.126(3) & (4); 1989 s.1(1), 8(4) & (5), 136(7) & (8), 141(4) & (7), 142(1) & 143(1), 189(1) (definition of "function") & Sched. 13, paras. 23(3) & 27.
3	1989 s.188.
4	1989 s.144 & 145(1)(a) & (b), (2) & (3).
5	1989 s.146; Sched. 12, paras. 4(7) & 6(4).
6	1989 s.3.
7	1989 s.2.
8	1989 s.141(1)(b) & (c), (2) & (3).
9	1989 ss.136(6) & (7) & 137(1)–(2).
10	1989 s.137(3), (7), (10) & (11) & 138(1) & (8).
11	1989 ss.137(11) & 138(2)–(7) & (9).
12	1976 s.4; 1989 s.139(1) and Sched. 15, paras. 1 & 2. TFO: S.I. 1978/272 Sched. 3, para 7(2); R: 6.
13	1976 s.5(1)–(6) & (8); 1985(LG) Sched. 7, para. 2 & S.I. 1986/208 Sched. 1, Pt. II, para. 2; 1989 Sched. 15, paras. 1 & 3.
14	1976 s.5(7); 1989 ss.137(8) & 139(3) & Sched. 15, para. 1.
15	1989 s.7(6) & (7).
16	1989 ss.8(1)–(3), (5)–(7) & 152(8).

Provision of Act	Derivation
17	1989 s.9; 1990 Sched. 9, para. 17(2).
18	1989 s.10; 1990 Sched. 9, para. 17(3).
19	1989 s.125.
20	1989 s.126.
21	1963 ss.19(1), (3)–(7) & 135(1)(part) & (5); 1973 Sched. 8, para. 85; 1989 s.127; 1989(EA) Sched. 16, para. 10; TFOs: S.I. 1965/145 Sched. 1; S.I. 1970/1537 Art. 2(1); S.I. 1970/1681 Sched. 3, para. 9(1); S.I. 1974/692 Sched. 1, Pt. III; S.I. 1983/1127 Art. 2(3).
22	1963 s.19(2) & (6); 1989 s.127(2) & (5).
23	1963 s.22; 1973 s.9; 1989 Sched. 13, paras. 1 and 4.
24	1963 ss.23, 49 & 128(1); 1976 (c. 44) s.5(8); 1989 Sched. 13, paras. 1 & 5 & Sched. 25, para. 2.
25	1963 ss.36(1)–(3), (5) & (6), 48, 49 & 128(1); 1976 (c. 44) s.5(8); 1989 Sched. 13, paras. 1, 12 & 16 & Sched. 25, para. 2.
26	1963 s.24(6) & 36(4).
27	1963 s.24(1)–(3) & (5) & 26(1)(b); 1989 Sched. 13, para. 6.
28	1963 ss.24(2)(proviso) & 55; 1973 s.9; 1989 Sched. 13, para 1.
29	1963 s.24(4), (5) & (10); 1973 Sched. 8, para. 78.
30	1963 s.78(1)–(3) & (7); 1973 s.9; 1989 Sched. 13, paras. 1 & 20.
31	1963 s.78(4)–(6).
32	1963 s.24(7)–(9); 1973 s.9; 1989 Sched. 13, para. 1.
33	1963 ss.25 & 134(4); 1973 s.9; 1989 Sched. 13, paras. 1 & 7.
34	1963 s.54(1)–(3) & (5).
35	1963 s.27; 1968 (c. 35) s.1; 1973 s.9; 1989 Sched. 13, para. 1.
36	1963 s.37(3); 1973 s.9; 1989 Sched. 13, para. 1.
37	1963 ss.28 & 37(5); 1973 s.9; 1989 Sched. 13, paras. 1 & 8.
38	1963 ss.28(3) (part), 29(3) & (8) & 37(5); 1973 s.9; 1989 Sched. 13, para. 1.
39	1963 ss.26(1) & (2), 29(2) & (7)(a), 36(6), 37(5) & 135(5); 1973 s.9; 1989 Sched. 13, paras. 1 & 9(1).
40	1963 ss.29(4)–(6) & (7)(b) & 37(5); 1973 s.9; 1989 Sched. 13, paras. 1 & 9(2).
41	1963 s.38(1) & (2); 1973 s.9 & Sched. 8, para. 79; 1989 Sched. 13, paras. 1 & 13.
42	1963 ss.38(3) & (4) 41(1)–(4) & (7)–(9); 1973 s.9; 1989 Sched. 13, paras. 1 & 14(2).
43	1963 ss.39(1), (2) & (4) & 40; 1973 s.9; 1989 Sched. 13, para. 1.
44	1963 ss.39(3)–(6), 40 & 41(1), (5) & (7)–(9); 1989 Sched. 13, paras. 1 & 14(1).
45	1963 s.54(2), (3) & (5).
46	1963 s.30(1)–(3) & (5)–(7) & 54(4); 1973 s.9; 1989 Sched. 13, paras. 1 & 10.
47	1963 ss.30(4), 31(4) & 37(1).
48	1963 ss.26(1)(a), 31(1) & (3) 37(2).
49	1963 s.32(1), (2), (6) & (7); 1973 s.9; 1989 Sched. 13, paras. 1 & 11.
50	1963 s.32(3), (4), (6) & (7); 1973 s.9; 1989 Sched. 13, para. 1.
51	1963 s.42; 1973 s.9; 1989 Sched. 13, para. 1.
52	1963 s.43(1)–(5) & (9); 1973 s.9; 1989 Sched. 13, para. 1.
53	1963 s.43(5)–(8); 1973 s.9; 1989 Sched. 13, para 1.
54	1963 s.44; 1973 s.9; 1989 Sched. 13, para. 1.
55	1963 s.47(1)–(3) & (11); 1973 s.9; Sched. 13, para. 1.
56	1963 s.47(3)–(5); 1973 s.9; 1989 Sched. 13, para. 1.
57	1963 s.45; 1973 s.9; 1989 Sched. 13, paras. 1 & 15.
58	1963 s.64; 1989 Sched. 13, para. 19.
59	1963 s.54(2) & (5).
60	1963 s.50; 1973 s.9; 1989 Sched. 13, para. 1.
61	1963 ss.46 & 47(6); 1973 s.9; 1989 Sched. 13, para 1.
62	1963 ss.47(7)–(10) & 71(3); 1973 s.9; 1989 Sched. 13, para 1.
63	1963 s.51; 1973 s.9; 1989 Sched. 13, para. 1.
64	1963 ss.43(1) & 52; 1973 s.9; 1989 Sched. 13, para 1.
65	Introduces Sched. 7.
66	1963 s.131(1), (2) & (8) & 134(4); 1989 Sched. 13, para. 29; TFOs: S.I. 1965/319; S.I. 1970/1681.

Provision of Act	Derivation
67	1963 s.132; 1989 Sched. 13, para. 30.
68	1963 ss.116 & 134(4) & (6); TFOs: S.I. 1965/319 Sched. 3, para. 2.
69	1963 s.117; 1973 s.9; 1989 Sched. 13, para. 1.
70	1963 s.135(8); IA s.17.
71	1963 ss.133(2)–(4), 134(4) & (6) & 135(1).
72	1963 ss.105, 134(4) & (6) & 135(1), (3), (6) & (7); 1973 Sched. 8, para. 86; 1989 Sched. 13, para. 31(1)(e) & (3).
73	1989 ss.131(1), (2) & (8) & 132(1), (2) & (9).
74	1989 ss.131(3)–(4) & (9) & 133(7)(b) & (c).
75	1989 s.132(3), (4), (6), (7) & (10) & 133(7)(b) & (c).
76	1989 ss.131(5)–(7) & 132(5).
77	1963 s.128(2); 1989 ss.133(1)–(4) & 135(1) & Sched. 13, para. 28.
78	1989 ss.132(8) & 133(5), (6) & (7)(a); 1991(NR) Sched. 8, para. 116(2).
79	1989 ss.131(8), 132(9) & 133(8) & Sched. 14, para. 4.
80	1989 s.134.
81	1989 s.135(2).
82	1989 s.104.
83	1989 s.105.
84	1989 s.106.
85	1989 s.107(1) & (6); 1990 s.145(1).
86	1989 s.107(2)–(4).
87	1989 s.107(5) & 108(7) & (8).
88	1989 s.108(1) & (9) & 113(1) & Sched 19, para. 8(7); 1990 Sched. 15, para. 29.
89	1989 ss.108(2)–(6) & 124(1).
90	1989 s.109.
91	1989 Sched. 12, para. 8.
92	1989 s.110.
93	1989 s.111(1)–(3) & (5).
94	1989 s.112(1), (4)–(7) & (9).
95	1989 s.112(2), (3) & (9).
96	1989 s.111(4) & 112(8).
97	1989 s.116.
98	1989 s.123.
99	1989 s.113(2) & (3).
100	1989 s.122.
101	1989 s.121(2).
102	1989 s.171.
103	Introduces Sched. 13.
104	1989 ss.103(1), (2) (part) & (4) to (6) & 124.
105	1976 s.113; 1989 s.136(1).
106	1989 s.136(3)–(5) & (9).
107	1976 ss.8(1), 18, 24(2) & (3), 26; 1989 Sched. 15, paras. 1 & 9(1).
108	1976 ss.10(1), (3) & (4), 94, 109(1), (5)(b) & (6) & 116(1); 1989 Sched. 15, para. 1; S.I. 1991/983; TFO: S.I. 1978/272 Sched. 3, para. 7(5) & (8).
109	1976 s.29(1), (2), (4), (6) & (7); 1989 Sched. 15, para. 1.
110	1976 ss.29(2A), (3), (5) & (9) & 109(1) & (2); 1989 Sched. 15, paras. 1, 13 & 35; TFO: S.I. 1978/272 Sched. 3, para. 7(3).
111	1976 s.23(2)–(5); 1984 Sched. 4, para. 66(1); 1989 Sched. 15, paras. 1 & 8; TFO: S.I. 1978/272 Sched. 3, para. 7(4) & (6).
112	1976 s.95; TFO: S.I. 1978/272 Sched. 3, para. 7.
113	1976 s.8(2) & (3), 114(1) & 116; 1989 Sched. 15, para. 1; TFO: S.I. 1978/272 Sched. 3, para. 7(5).
114	1989 s.141(1)(a).
115	1975 s.28(3)–(6) & Sched. 3, paras. 7–9 & 13; 1989 Sched. 17, paras. 1 & 7(7)(a) & (14)(a) & (b); TFO: S.I. 1978/272 Sched. 3, para. 6.
116	1989 s.171.
117	1989 Sched. 1, para. 15(1)–(3) & (5).
118	1989 Sched. 1, paras. 15(4) & 16.
119	1963 s.88 & 1989 Sched. 1, para. 15(4) & Sched. 13, para. 1.
120	1963 s.91 & 135(1) & (2); 1989 Sched. 13, paras, 1, 24 & 31; TFOs: S.I. 1976/1775; S.I. 1979/571 Art. 3(5); S.I. 1981/238 Arts. 2 & 3(4); R: 16.
121	1989 Sched. 1, para. 21.

Provision of Act	Derivation
122	1989 Sched. 1, para. 22.
123	1989 s.129(1)–(3) & (7)–(9).
124	1989 s.129(3)–(6).
125	1963 s.60(5A) & (6); 1973 s.9 & Sched. 8, para. 80(3); 1989 Sched. 13, paras. 1 & 18(2) & (3).
126	1963 ss.60(1)–(5), 116 & 117; 1973 s. 9 & Sched. 8, para. 80(1); 1989 Sched. 13, paras. 1 & 18(1); TFOs: S.I. 1965/319 Sched. 3, para. 2 & S.I. 1970/1681.
127	1963 s.63(1)–(3), (8), (10) & (11); 1973 s.9; 1989 Sched. 13, para. 1.
128	1963 s.63(4)–(6); 1973 s.9; 1989 Sched. 13, para. 1.
129	1963 ss.63(7), 116 & 117.
130	1963 s.131(6) & (7); 1973 s.9; 1989 Sched. 13, para 1; TFOs: S.I. 1965/319; S.I. 1970/1681.
131	1989 Sched. 12, para. 9(1)–(3), (7) & (8).
132	1989 Sched. 12, para. 9(3)–(6).
133	1989 Sched. 25, para. 80(1).
134	1976 ss.48 & 89(2); S.I. 1978/319 Sched. para. 2; 1989 Sched. 15, paras. 1 & 20; S.I. 1990/214 reg. 2.
135	1976 s.49 & 109(1) & (2); S.I. 1978/319 Sched. para. 3; 1989 Sched. 15, paras. 1 & 21. S.I. 1990/214 regs. 3 & 4; TFO: S.I. 1978/272 Sched. 3, para. 7(5).
136	S.I. 1990/214 reg. 3.
137	1976 ss.50(1)–(4) & (9) & 116(4); 1989 Sched. 15, paras. 1 & 22; TFO: S.I. 1978/272 Sched. 3, para 7(5).
138	1976 ss.51 & 109(1) & (3); S.I. 1978/319 Sched. para. 4; 1989 Sched. 15, paras. 1 & 23.
139	1976 s.84(1)–(3) & (5); 1989 Sched. 15, para. 1; S.I. 1990/72 reg. 3A(1); S.I. 1991/523 reg. 3.
140	1976 s.84(5)–(8); 1989 Sched. 15, para. 1; TFO: S.I. 1978/272 Sched. 3, para. 7(4).
141	1976 s.85; 1989 Sched. 15, para. 1; TFO: S.I. 1978/272 Sched. 3, para. 7(4).
142	1975 s.28(3)(a) & (b), 1989 Sched. 17, para. 7(7)(a).
143	1976 s.88(1), (2) & (5); 1989 Sched. 15, paras. 1 & 29.
144	1989 ss.145(1)(c) & 189(1).
145	1976 ss.89(1) & 116(1); S.I. 1978/319 Sched. para. 6; 1989 Sched. 15, paras. 1 & 30.
146	1989 Sched. 1, para. 17.
147	1976 s.90(1)–(5); 1989 Sched. 15, para. 1; TFO: S.I. 1978/272 Sched. 3, para. 7(3).
148	1976 ss.32(5) & 92; 1989 Sched. 15, para. 1; TFO: S.I. 1978/272 Sched. 3, para. 7(3).
149	1976 s.90(6) & (7); 1989 Sched. 15, paras. 1 & 31; TFO: S.I. 1978/272 Sched. 3, para. 7(3).
150	1989 s.170(7) & (8).
151	1989 Sched. 1, para. 18.
152	1989 Sched. 1, para. 19.
153	1989 s.184 & Sched. 1, para. 20.
154	1989 s.151.
155	1976 ss.36 & 116; 1989 Sched. 15, paras. 1 & 16; TFO: S.I. 1978/272 Sched. 3, para. 7(3).
156	1975 Sched. 3, paras. 37 and 38; 1989 Sched. 17, paras. 1 and 7(14)((e) & (f).
157	1989 s.152.
158	1963 ss.81 & 135(1); 1972 (c. 61) s. 18(6); 1973 s.9; 1989 Sched. 13, paras. 1 & 22.
159	1989 s.154(1) & (5) & Sched. 19, paras. 1 & 2(1), (2) & (8).
160	1989 Sched. 19, paras. 1 & 4(1), (4) & (5).
161	1989 ss.115, 122 & 124.
162	1989 s.154(1), (3) & (4) & Sched. 19, paras. 1(2), 2(1)(c) & (d) & 4(1)(c) & (d).
163	1989 Sched. 19, para. 8(1), (5), (6) & (8); R: 17.

Provision of Act	Derivation
164	1989 s.176 & Sched. 19, para. 9(1) & (3)–(8) & Sched. 26, para. 43.
165	1976 ss.8(2), 17, 22, 23(1), 90(7) & 116(4); 1989 Sched. 15, paras. 1 & 5.
166	1976 s.32; 1989 Sched. 15, para. 1 & 14.
167	1976 s.33(1)–(3) & (5); 1989 Sched. 15, para. 1; 1990 Sched. 15, para. 18.
168	1975 Sched. 3, para. 37; 1989 ss.155 & 157(1) & Sched. 17, para. 7(4)(e).
169	1989 s.147(1), (2) & (4).
170	1989 Sched. 19, para. 10(1)–(3).
171	1989 s.156(1)–(5).
172	1989 s.147(1), (2) & (4).
173	Introduces Sched. 20.
174	1989 s.180.
175	1989 s.153(2) & (6).
176	1989 s.167.
177	Introduces Sched. 21.
178	Introduces Sched. 22.
179	1989 s.160(4)–(7) & (9).
180	1976 s.106; 1989 Sched. 15, para. 1.
181	1975 s.38; 1976 s.115; 1989 Sched. 17, para. 1 & Sched. 19, para. 7.
182	1989 s.159.
183	1976 s.111; 1979 (c. 46) Sched. 4, para. 16; 1989 s.163; 1990 (c. 11) Sched. 2, para. 81(2).
184	1989 s.157(2) & (3).
185	1976 s.24(1) & 26(12); 1989 Sched. 15, para. 1.
186	1989 Sched. 19, paras. 1 & 11.
187	1989 s.150.
188	1989 s.143(2).
189	1963 s.53; 1973 s.9; 1989 Sched. 13, paras. 1 & 17.
190	1989 s.117 & 121; 1990 Sched. 15, para. 30.
191	1989 Sched. 19, para. 9(2) & (8).
192	1989 s.103(2) & (3).
193	1976 s.9(1), (7), (8), (10) & (11); 1989 Sched. 15, paras. 1 & 4 & Sched. 26, para. 38; TFO: S.I. 1978/272 Sched. 3, para. 7(5).
194	1976 s.9(3), (5) & (6); 1989 Sched. 15, paras. 1 & 4; TFO: S.I. 1978/272 Sched. 3, para. 7(5).
195	1989 s.165.
196	1989 s.149.
197	1989 s.130.
198	1945 s.7(1)–(5) & (7); 1965 Sched. 2; 1977 Sched. 1.
199	1963 s.78(2)–(3) & (7); 1973 s.9; 1989 Sched. 13, paras. 1 & 20.
200	1963 s.17; 1973 s.9; 1982(CJA) s.38; 1989 Sched. 13, paras. 1 & 3.
201	1963 s.114; 1973 s.9; 1982(CJA) s.38; 1989 Sched. 13, para. 1.
202	1989 ss.118 & 121.
203	1989 s.119.
204	1989 s.174; R: 11.
205	1945 ss.7(6) & (7) & 48(6); 1949 (c. 11) s.1(1); 1977 Sched. 1; TFOs: S.I. 1951/142 Sched.; S.I. 1951/1900 art. 1; S.I. 1965/319 Sched. 3; S.I. 1970/1681 Sched. 1.
206	1945 s.45; 1963 s.115; 1989 s.175.
207	1989 s.170(1)–(6) & (9).
208	1981 s.6; 1986(GA) Sched. 7, para. 2(6); 1989 Sched. 25, para. 63; 1989(EA) Sched. 16, para. 1(5); 1990 (c. 11) Sched., para. 46; 1991(NR) Sched. 8, para. 106.
209	1963 s.31(5); 1989 s.148.
210	1975 s.28(6) & (8); 1989 s.186 & Sched. 17, para. 7(7)(b).
211	1963 ss.79(8) & (9) & 135(8); 1975 s.28(7) & Sched. 4, Pt. I, para. 1(2); 1976 s.34(4) & (5); 1977 Sched. 6; 1982(CJA) s.38; 1989 ss.114(2), 121, 122 & 158(d).
212	1975 Sched. 3, paras. 17 & 18; 1989 Sched,. 17, para. 1; TFO: S.I. 1978/272 Sched. 3, para. 6.
213	1963 s.109(1); 1973 s.9; 1989 s.120 & Sched. 13, para. 1; TFOs: S.I. 1965/319 Sched. 3, para. 2; S.I. 1978/272 Sched. 3, para. 2(7).

Provision of Act	Derivation
214	1976 s.96; 1982(CJA) s.38; 1986 (c.63) s.42; TFO: S.I. 1978/272 Sched. para. 7.
215	1963 s.109(2); 1989 s.181 & Sched. 13, para. 26 & Sched. 17, para. 7(16).
216	1963 s.118(1) & (2); 1973 s.9; 1989 Sched. 13, para. 1.
217	1963 s.118(3) & (4); 1989 ss.121(1) & 177; R; 13.
218	1989 ss.182 & 189(1) (definition of "services").
219	1963 s.134; 1989 ss.185 & 189(1) (definition of "prescribed").
220	1945 s.56; 1963 s.120; 1989 s.187 & Sched. 25, para. 7(10); R: 14.
221	1945 s.59(1) (definition of "owner"); 1963(L) Sched. 14, para. 10; 1963 ss.2, 19(7), 120(5) & 135; 1976 ss.32(5) & 116; 1981 s.6(7)(b); 1985(LG) Sched. 7, para. 9; 1989 ss.124, 127(6), 130(8), 135(1), 189 & 191(6) & Sched. 13, paras. 2 & 31 & Sched. 15, para. 38; 1990 (c. 11) Sched. 2, para. 81(1); 1991(NR) Sched. 8, para. 116(3). R: 6, 15, 16 & 20.
222	1963 s.123(1) & (5); 1976 s.115; 1989 s.192; 1990 (c.11) Sched. 2, para. 81(3).
223	1963 s.123(1) & (5).
224	1989 s.193.
225	1989 ss.141(6) & 194.
Sched. 1	1963 s.120(5); 1976 s.35; 1989 Sched. 1, Pt. I, paras. 1–10 & 14 & Sched. 15, para. 1.
Sched. 2	1963 ss.83, 106, 133(2)–(4), 134(4) & 135(1) & (2) & Sched. 10; 1973 s.9 & Sched. 8, para. 83; 1989 Sched. 13, paras. 1, 23, 25 & 33; TFOs: S.I. 1976/1775 Sched. 3, para. 7; S.I. 1979/571 Art. 3(5); S.I. 1981/238 Arts. 2 & 3(4); R: 16.
Sched. 3	1989 Sched. 16.
Sched. 4	1976 Sched. 1; 1982 (c. 32) Sched. 5, para. 7; 1983 Sched. 4, paras. 5 & 6; 1985 (c. 65) Sched. 8, para 29; 1989 Sched. 15, paras. 1 & 39; TFO: S.I. 1978/272 Sched. 3, para. 7(5).
Sched. 5	1963 s.135(1) & Sched. 7; 1973 s.9; 1989 Sched. 13, paras. 1 and 32; 1989(EA) Sched. 16, para. 10; TFOs: S.I. 1970/1681 Sched. 3, para. 9(1); 1983/1127 Art. 2(3).
Sched. 6	1963 ss.25(5)–(8) & 135(1) & Sched. 7; 1973 s.9; 1989 Sched. 13, paras. 1 and 32; 1989(EA) Sched. 16, para. 10; TFOs: S.I. 1965/145 Sched. 1; S.I. 1970/1537 art. 2(1); S.I. 1970/1681 Sched. 3, para. 9; S.I. 1974/692 Sched. 1, Pt. III; S.I. 1983/1127 Art. 2(3); R: 4.
Sched. 7	1963 ss.46(3) & 50(4) & (5); 1989 Sched. 26, paras. 30–33.
Sched. 8	1989 Sched. 14, paras. 1–3.
Sched. 9	1989 s.135(1) & Sched. 14, paras. 5–8.
Sched. 10	1989 s.176 & Sched. 12, paras. 1–7.
Sched. 11	1989 Sched. 7.
Sched. 12	1989 Sched. 11.
Sched. 13	1989 Sched. 26, Pt. III.
Sched. 14	1976 s.10(2) & (3) & 109(5)(b) & Sched. 3, paras. 1–4 & 9–14; TFO: S.I. 1978/272 Sched. 3, para. 7(12).
Sched. 15	1976 ss.52–61; 1989 Sched. 15, paras. 1, 24 & 25; S.I. 1978/319 Sched. 5, para. 5; S.I. 1990/214 reg. 5; TFO: S.I. 1978/272 Sched. 3, para. 7(5).
Sched. 16	1976 ss.50(4)–(8) & 109(6); 1989 Sched. 15, para. 1; S.I. 1991/83; TFO: S.I. 1978/272 Sched. 3, para. 7(5).
Sched. 17	1976 ss.88(3) & (4) & 109(1), (4) & (5) & Sched. 3, paras. 5 to 8.
Sched. 18	1989 Sched. 18.
Sched. 19	1989 Sched. 20.
Sched. 20	1989 ss.147(3), 156(6), 178 & 179 & Sched. 19, para. 10(4) & (5); 1991(NR) Sched. 8, para. 116(4).
Sched. 21	1976 ss.17(5) & 33(4); 1989 Sched. 15, para. 1 & Sched. 19, paras. 2(4)–(6), 6 & 8(2)–(4).
Sched. 22	1976 ss.29(8) & 112; 1984 Sched. 4, para. 66(2); 1984 (c. 32) Sched. 6, para. 12; 1986 (c. 31) Sched. 2, para. 5; 1986 (c. 44) Sched. 7, para. 25; 1987 (c. 3) Sched. 1, para. 32; 1989 s.160(1)–(3), (6) & (8) Sched. 15, para. 37 & Sched. 19, paras. 2(9) & (3); 1989 (c. 29) Sched. 16, paras. 21 & 37; 1991(NR) Sched. 8, para. 116(4); R: 17.
Sched. 23	1989 Sched. 21.
Sched. 24	1989 s.174(2)(d) & (3).

Provision of Act	Derivation
Sched. 25	1963 s.79(3)–(6); 1973 s.9; 1975 Sched. 3, paras. 14–16 & 19–36; 1976 s.34; 1986 (c. 62) s.33(3); 1989 ss.114, 158, Sched. 13, para. 21, Sched. 15, para. 15(1) & Sched. 17, para. 7(14)(c) & (d); R: 5.
Sched. 26	1989 Sched. 24.

TABLE OF DESTINATIONS

WATER ACT 1945
c.42

RAILWAY AND CANAL COMMISSION (ABOLITION) ACT 1949
c.11

WATER RESOURCES ACT 1963
c.38

SCIENCE AND TECHNOLOGY ACT 1965
c.4

WATER RESOURCES ACT 1968
c.35

LAND CHARGES ACT 1972
c.61

WATER ACT 1973
c.37

THE SALMON AND FRESHWATER FISHERIES ACT 1975
c.51

TABLE OF DESTINATIONS

THE LAND DRAINAGE ACT 1976
c.70

CRIMINAL LAW ACT 1977
c.45

ANCIENT MONUMENTS AND ARCHAEOLOGICAL AREAS ACT 1979
c.46

WATER ACT 1981
c.12

57–263

TABLE OF DESTINATIONS

CRIMINAL JUSTICE ACT 1982
c.43

LOCAL GOVERNMENT FINANCE ACT 1982
c.32

WATER ACT 1983
c.23

TELECOMMUNICATIONS ACT 1984
c.12

LONDON REGIONAL TRANSPORT ACT 1984
c.32

LOCAL GOVERNMENT ACT 1985
c.51

INSOLVENCY ACT 1985
c.65

GAS ACT 1986
c.44

AIRPORTS ACT 1986
c.31

SALMON ACT 1986
c.62

TABLE OF DESTINATIONS

Housing and Planning Act 1986
c.63

Coal Industry Act 1987
c.3

Electricity Act 1989
c.29

Water Act 1989
c.15

ENVIRONMENTAL PROTECTION ACT 1990
c.43

PLANNING (CONSEQUENTIAL PROVISIONS) ACT 1990
c.11

NEW ROADS AND STREET WORKS ACT 1991
c.22

TABLE OF DESTINATIONS

INDEX

STATUTORY WATER COMPANIES ACT 1991

(1991 c. 58)

[A table showing the derivation of the provisions of this Consolidation Act will be found at the end of the Act. The table has no official status.]

ARRANGEMENT OF SECTIONS

PART I

POWERS OF STATUTORY WATER COMPANIES

General powers

An Act to consolidate certain enactments relating to statutory water companies. [25th July 1991]

PARLIAMENTARY DEBATES
Hansard, H.L. Vol. 528, cols. 484, 1738; Vol. 529, cols. 746, 1006; H.C. Vol. 195, col. 1110.

INTRODUCTION AND GENERAL NOTE
As at September 1989, there were some 29 statutory water companies in England and Wales. They were established under Private Acts of Parliament in the 19th century; Acts with evocative names such as the Frimley and Farnborough District Water Act 1893, the South Essex Waterworks Act 1861 or the Sunningdale District Water Act 1877.

---

* Annotations by William Wilson, LL.M., Barrister, Middle Temple.

The Victorian local Acts contained special provisions concerning the constitution and financial arrangements of such water companies. There were restrictions on dividends, borrowing, capital and the use of profits.

The main structural provisions regulating these companies survived, as did the companies themselves, the passing of the Water Acts of 1945 and 1973. By the time of the reorganisation of the water industry ushered in by the Water Act 1989, however, the constitution of, and restrictions upon, such companies had come to be seen as unduly restrictive and preventing diversification. There was also some concern at the fact that the companies were not registered, where the second European Directive on Company Law (O.J.E.E.C. 1977 No. L 26/1) required companies to be registered.

The Water Act 1989 accordingly introduced a new régime for statutory water companies. They were to be allowed to convert to public limited company or private limited company status. Significant financial controls, on dividends, borrowing, capital and the use of profits were lifted. A procedure was introduced whereby they could pass by a majority a special resolution proposing the substitution of a memorandum and articles for a local statutory constitution, and registration under the Companies Act 1985 for local statutes, which would be repealed. The special resolution had to be approved by order of the Secretary of State, in a statutory instrument to be laid before both Houses of Parliament. Minority holders of shares, stock and debentures were given the right to challenge the process in the High Court.

The Water Act 1989 provided (s.11(4)(a)) that as it took effect, statutory water companies would be appointed as the "water undertakers" for their respective areas. They thus became subject to the main provisions of that Act relating to the powers, duties and functions of water undertakers. Under the Water Industry Act 1991 (s.6(5)), as they become limited companies they will also be able to become sewerage undertakers. Important provisions in s.14 of the Water Act 1989 (subss. (4) and (5)) allowed the initial instrument of appointment to postpone setting conditions on the way the companies fixed charges. The companies were given a right to make representations to the Secretary of State on this area.

Under the Water Act 1989, the statutory water companies began to convert to limited companies. For examples of the statutory instruments approving the special resolutions, substituting a memorandum and articles for local statutory constitutions and making consequential repeals of local Acts, see:—

The East Surrey Water (Constitution and Regulation) Order 1989 (S.I. 1989 No. 2101)
The Essex Water Company (Constitution and Regulation) Order 1991 (S.I. 1991 No. 1596)
The Mid Southern Water Company (Constitution and Regulation) Order 1991 (S.I. 1991 No. 1733).

Consolidation of the water legislation foreshadowed by the Law Commission's *"Report on the Consolidation of the Legislation Relating to Water"* (Cm. 1483, April 1991), was approved by both Houses of Parliament without significant debate. The provisions relating to statutory water companies in the Water Act 1989 (ss.98–102) were re-enacted in the present Statutory Water Companies Act 1991.

Arrangement of the Act
Part I deals with the powers of statutory water companies.
Section 1 deals with their general powers.
Sections 2–3 cover their powers to issue redeemable stock.
Sections 4–8 relax restrictions on capital, borrowing, dividends, payment of interest, applications of profits and the mode of sale of shares or stock, with minority holders being given a right of appeal to the High Court challenging the modifications of financial controls.
Section 9 applies part of Pt. XIII of the Companies Act 1985 (arrangements and reconstructions) to statutory water companies.
Section 10 allows the appointment of one officer of the company as a director by a modified procedure.

Part II concerns the conversion of statutory water companies to limited companies.
Section 11 allows for their registration under the Companies Act 1985.
Section 12 concerns their adoption of a memorandum and articles, with the Secretary of State's order bringing the new constitution into being as the local statutory provisions cease to have effect.
Section 13 allows the High Court wide powers to cancel or confirm a resolution for conversion on its being challenged by minority holders.
Section 14 formally permits the Secretary of State's constituting order to make consequential amendments of local statutory provisions.

Part III contains supplemental provisions.
Section 15 covers general interpretation.

Section 16 introduces important disclosure of information provisions from the Water Industry Act 1991.

Section 17 is the short title, commencement and extent section.

PART I

POWERS OF STATUTORY WATER COMPANIES

General powers

General powers of companies holding appointments

1.—(1) Subject to the following provisions of this section, a statutory water company holding an appointment under Chapter I of Part II of the Water Industry Act 1991 as a water undertaker for any area—

(a) shall have power to do anything (whether in that area or elsewhere) which, in the opinion of the company, is calculated to facilitate, or is conducive or incidental to, the carrying out of the functions which are functions of the company by virtue of the appointment; and

(b) without prejudice to the generality of that power, shall have power, for the purposes of, or in connection with, the carrying out of those functions—

(i) to acquire and dispose of land and other property;

(ii) to carry out such engineering or building operations at such places (whether in that area or elsewhere) as the company considers appropriate; and

(iii) to supply water fittings to any person to whom they supply water and to install, repair and alter such a person's water fittings, whether or not supplied by the company.

(2) Without prejudice to the generality of the power conferred by virtue of paragraph (a) of subsection (1) above, a company such as is mentioned in that subsection shall have power—

(a) to provide for any person outside the United Kingdom advice or assistance, including training facilities, as respects any matter in which the company has skill or experience;

(b) to become a member of any body formed for the purpose of promoting the interests of water undertakers or any description of water undertakers; and

(c) to make donations and incur expenditure for the benefit of its officers and employees and in particular to pay, or make provision (whether by contributory or non-contributory schemes or otherwise) for the payment of, pensions, allowances or gratuities to or in respect of any persons who have been or are officers or employees of the company.

(3) Nothing in this section with respect to the carrying out of works shall be construed as conferring any power otherwise than for the purpose of removing such a limitation on the capacity of a statutory water company as would, apart from this section, exist by virtue of the company's constitution.

(4) Accordingly, without prejudice to the provisions of Part VI of the Water Industry Act 1991, this section shall be disregarded for the purpose of determining whether a statutory water company is liable, on grounds other than such a limitation as is mentioned in subsection (3) above, for any act or omission in exercise of a power to carry out works conferred by this section.

(5) Nothing in this section shall be construed as authorising a statutory water company to carry on the business of a manufacturer of water fittings.

(6) In this section "supply," in relation to water fittings, has the same meaning as it has in Part II of the Consumer Protection Act 1987 by virtue of section 46 of that Act.

DEFINITIONS
"disposal": s.15(1).

"engineering or building operations": s.15(1).
"functions": s.15(1); s.217 of the Water Industry Act 1991.
"statutory water company": s.15(1); s.38(1) of the Water Act 1973.
"supply": subs. (6); s.46 of the Consumer Protection Act 1987.
"water fittings": s.15(1); s.93(1) of the Water Industry Act 1991.
"water undertaker": s.6 of the Water Industry Act 1991.

GENERAL NOTE
This section substantially re-states s.97 of the Water Act 1989.

Subs. (1)
A statutory water company appointed under the Water Industry Act 1991 as a water undertaker is generally empowered as such in terms of its own constitution. Section 6(5) of the Water Industry Act 1991 allows a limited company or a statutory water company to be appointed as a water undertaker, but only a limited company may be appointed as a sewerage undertaker. The functions of water and sewerage undertakers are widely enough defined by s.217 of the Water Industry Act 1991 to include, for example, the provision of houses and recreation grounds for a company's employees, and participation in relevant research. It seems that the legislation aims to avoid some of the questions on companies' powers, for example to grant pensions, which have occupied company lawyers for so long.

Subs. (3)
Without this restriction of the scope of the section, a statutory water company might be able, for example, to carry out building works without regard to planning legislation.

Subs. (5)
It seems curious that a statutory water company may supply, instal, repair and alter water fittings but not manufacture them. Provision is made in s.74 of the Water Industry Act 1991 for regulations to govern, *inter alia*, the safety and accuracy of water fittings and the way in which they are installed. Breach of these regulations will be a summary offence, and s.84 of that Act confers rights of entry upon local authorities to check compliance with them.

Powers to issue redeemable stock

Powers to issue redeemable stock

2. —(1) This section applies, subject to the following provisions of this Act, to every statutory water company which—
    (a) has created or issued any redeemable stock; or
    (b) has authority to create and issue any stock.
    (2) Subject to the following provisions of this section and to section 3 below, a company to which this section applies may from time to time issue, so as to be redeemable, any stock created by them or any redeemed stock.
    (3) No redeemed stock shall be issued under this section except for the purpose of effecting the redemption of redeemable stock under the provisions of section 3 below unless the issue is authorised by a resolution of a general meeting of the company.
    (4) No new stock shall be created, nor shall any redeemed stock be issued by a statutory water company, so as to make the total amount of any particular class of stock exceed the amount of stock of that class which the company is for the time being authorised to create except during an interval of three months between—
    (a) the creation or, in the case of redeemed stock, the issue of the stock; and
    (b) the completion of the redemption of redeemable stock for the purpose of redeeming which the stock of that particular class is proposed to be created or issued.
    (5) Where any preference stock is created or issued by a statutory water company as mentioned in subsection (4) above, the amount raised by means of that stock shall, for the purposes of any enactment, statutory order or resolution regulating the borrowing powers of the company, be deemed during any such interval as is so mentioned not to have been raised.

(6) In this section and section 3 below—
"issue" includes reissue;
"preference stock" includes preference shares;
"redeemable stock" means stock issued so as to be redeemable;
"redeemed stock" means redeemable stock which has been redeemed and is available for issue under the provisions of this section or section 3 below; and
"stock" means preference stock or debenture stock.

DEFINITIONS
"issue": subs. (6).
"preference stock": subs. (6).
"redeemable stock": subs. (6).
"redeemed stock": subs. (6).
"stock": subs. (6).

GENERAL NOTE
Statutory water companies were given the power to issue redeemable preference or debenture stock by the Statutory Companies (Redeemable Stock) Act 1915. Sections 2 and 3 of the Statutory Water Companies Act 1991, and the definitions in s.2 of that Act, are taken from s.41 of the Water Act 1945, as applied specifically to statutory water companies by Sched. 25, para. 6 to the Water Act 1989.

Subs. (3)
The requirement for a general meeting of the company to authorise certain issues of redeemed stock should be noted.

Subs. (5)
The statutory predecessor of this subsection, s.41(3)(b) of the Water Act 1945, was considered in *Sutton District Water Co.* v. *I.R.C.* [1982] S.T.C. 459 which concerned the scope of the exemption.

Terms and conditions of issue and redemption of redeemable stock

3.—(1) Subject to the following provisions of this section and to section 4 below, redeemable stock issued by a company to which section 2 above applies—
(a) shall bear such rate of dividend or interest; and
(b) shall be redeemable at such time, in such manner and subject otherwise to such terms and conditions,
as the company may have determined before issuing the stock.
(2) The terms and conditions of redemption upon which any redeemable stock is issued by a company to which section 2 above applies shall be stated—
(a) in any offer by the company of any of the stock for sale; and
(b) in every certificate of the stock;
and a term or condition which is not so stated shall not be binding upon the holder of the stock.
(3) Redeemable stock may be redeemed either—
(a) by paying off the stocks; or
(b) by issuing, to an assenting holder of the stock, other stock in substitution for the redeemable stock;
and for the purpose of raising money to pay off, or of providing stock in substitution for, any redeemable stock, a company to which section 2 above applies may (subject to subsections (4) and (5) of that section) create new stock or issue redeemed stock, in either case, so as to be redeemable or irredeemable, as the company thinks fit.
(4) A company to which section 2 above applies shall not redeem any redeemable stock out of revenue; but any discount allowed on the issue of redeemable stock, or any premium payable on redemption, may be written off out of revenue.

(5) The redemption, by a company to which section 2 above applies, of any preference stock issued so as to be redeemable shall not affect the validity of any mortgage or of any debenture stock if the grant or issue of the mortgage or debenture stock by the company was lawful in the circumstances existing at the date of the grant or issue.

DEFINITIONS
  "issue": s.2(6).
  "preference stock": s.2(6).
  "redeemable stock": s.2(6).
  "redeemed stock": s.2(6).
  "stock": s.2(6).

GENERAL NOTE
  See General Note to s.2.

Subs. (2)
  It should be noted that terms or conditions of redemption not stated on any certificate or offer for sale of redeemable stock will not be binding on the holder.

Relaxation of restrictions affecting raising of capital

Relaxation of limits on capital, borrowing and dividends

4.—(1) Subject to the following provisions of this section and to section 5 below, so much of any provision contained in any local statutory provision, or having effect by virtue of anything done under any relevant provision, as—
  (a) imposes any limit to which this section applies in relation to any statutory water company; or
  (b) otherwise relates to any such limit,
shall have effect subject to such modifications as may be approved by special resolution of the company.

(2) This section applies, in relation to a statutory water company, to the following limits (whether they are expressed by reference to a specified sum or percentage or by reference to the respective proportions of, or of different descriptions of, capital raised and sums borrowed or to any other matter), that is to say—
  (a) a limit on the amount of capital, or of capital of a particular description, that may be raised by the company;
  (b) a limit on the amount that may be borrowed, or borrowed in a particular way or in particular circumstances, by the company; and
  (c) a limit on the dividends payable on shares or stock in the company, or on shares or stock of a particular description.

(3) Where there is a division of the shares or stock of a statutory water company into different classes, no modification of a limit falling within subsection (2)(c) above shall have effect by virtue of this section unless a consent to or approval of the modification has been given under subsection (4) below in respect of each class the rights attached to which are varied in consequence of the modification.

(4) A consent or approval is given for the purposes of subsection (3) above in respect of a class of shares or stock if—
  (a) consent in writing to the modification has been given by not less than three-quarters, in nominal value, of the members of the company holding shares or stock of that class; or
  (b) a resolution approving the modification is passed by not less than three-quarters, in nominal value, of the members of the company holding shares or stock of that class who are present (whether in person or by proxy) at a meeting of which not less than 21 days'

notice, specifying the intention to propose the resolution, has been duly given.

(5) For the purpose of determining whether the requirements of sub-section (3) above are satisfied in relation to any two or more classes of shares or stock in a statutory water company, it shall be immaterial that consents and approvals have been given in respect of different classes in accordance with different paragraphs of subsection (4) above.

(6) Provision having effect by virtue of a resolution passed in accordance with this section may be modified by a subsequent such resolution.

(7) The modifications that may be made by virtue of this section do not include, in the case of a limit falling within subsection (2)(a) above, any modification having the effect of reducing the authorised share capital, or the authorised capital stock, of the statutory water company in question.

(8) In this section—

"relevant provision" means section 3(1) above, section 41(5) of the Water Act 1945, the provisions of the Statutory Companies (Redeemable Stock) Act 1915 or any local statutory provision;

"special resolution", in relation to a statutory water company, means a resolution passed by a majority of not less than three-quarters of such of the members of the company as (being entitled to do so) vote (whether in person or by proxy) at a meeting of the company of which not less than 21 days' notice, specifying the intention to propose the resolution, has been duly given;

and in computing any majority for the purposes of the definition of "special resolution" the regulations contained in any local statutory provision as to the number of votes to which each member is entitled shall apply.

DEFINITIONS
"consent or approval": subs. (4).
"local statutory provision": s.15(1).
"modification": subs. (7); s.15(1).
"notice": s.15(1).
"relevant provision": subs. (8).
"special resolution": subs. (8).

GENERAL NOTE
This section re-enacts s.98(1)–(4) and (8)–(10) of the Water Act 1989, while s.98(5)–(7) of that Act are re-enacted in s.5 following. The section allows statutory water companies to pass special resolutions modifying statutory limits on their ability to raise capital, borrow money and pay dividends on shares and stock (subss. (1) and (2)). Special resolutions for these purposes are defined in subs. (8) as requiring a majority of at least three-quarters of members present and entitled to vote at a meeting called for the purpose. Modifications of dividend limits on shares or stock require further consent of a three-quarters majority of members of the company holding the classes of shares or stock affected (subss. (3) and (4)).

Subs. (7)
Permitted modifications of limits on capital under this section do not include reduction of authorised share capital.

Subs. (8)
Local statutory provisions, defined in s.15(1), apply in relation to the number of votes to which each member of a company is entitled for the purposes of passing a special resolution.

Appeals to the court in respect of applications under section 4

5.—(1) Where subsection (3) of section 4 above applies in relation to a modification specified in a resolution passed for the purposes of that section, the holders of not less, in the aggregate, than 15 per cent., in nominal value, of the issued shares or stock of any class of shares or stock of the company (being persons who have not for the purposes of that section consented to the modification or voted in favour of any resolution for the modification) may apply to the High Court to have the modification cancelled.

(2) An application to the High Court under this section—
(a) may be made on behalf of the shareholders or stockholders entitled to make the application by such one or more of their number as they may appoint in writing for the purpose; but
(b) shall not be made in relation to any modification more than 21 days after the date of the giving of the last consent or approval to the modification to be given for the purposes of section 4(1) or (3) above.
(3) Where an application is made under this section—
(a) the modification to which it relates shall have no effect unless and until it is confirmed by the High Court; and
(b) the High Court, after hearing the applicant and any other persons who apply to that Court to be heard and appear to that Court to be interested in the application—
(i) if satisfied, having regard to all the circumstances of the case, that the variation would unfairly prejudice the shareholders or stockholders of the class represented by the applicant, may disallow the modifications; and
(ii) if not so satisfied, shall confirm it.
(4) The decision of the High Court on an application under this section shall be final.

DEFINITIONS
"consent or approval": s.4(4).
"modification": s.4(7); s.15(1).
"notice": s.15(1).
"resolution for the modification": s.4(4)(b).

GENERAL NOTE
See General Note to s.4. Minority holders of 15 per cent. in nominal value of any class of shares or stock affected, provided that they have not consented or voted in favour, may challenge the modification of dividend limits in the High Court on the grounds of unfair prejudice. The High Court may disallow or confirm the modification.

Subs. (1)
At first sight, the phrase "modification specified in a resolution" appears to limit this right of challenge to situations where a resolution had been passed under s.4(4)(b) rather than the written consent procedure under s.4(4)(a) being used. However, the right of challenge appears to apply to both circumstances, because of the general requirement under s.4 for a special resolution to authorise modifications, as well as the consent or approval for dividend modifications required by s.4(4).

Subs. (2)
An application under this section must be made within 21 days of the consent or approval challenged.

Relaxation of restrictions on payment of interest

6. Nothing in so much of any local statutory provision as imposes a requirement—
(a) as to the rate of interest at which sums may be borrowed by a statutory water company; or
(b) as to the rate at which interest on sums so borrowed is to be paid, shall apply in relation to any borrowing by a statutory water company after August 31, 1989.

DEFINITIONS
"local statutory provision": s.15(1) and (3).

GENERAL NOTE
This section and s.7 following re-enact s.99(1) and s.99(2)–(4) of the Water Act 1989 respectively. The two sections relax restrictions in local statutory provisions, on the interest

rates which can be paid on borrowings, on the maintenance of reserve and contingency funds, and on carrying forward amounts to the credit of the profit and loss account of statutory water companies.

Relaxation of restrictions on applications of profits

7.—(1) Notwithstanding the provisions of any local statutory provision, every statutory water company shall have power to form and maintain reserve and contingency funds by setting apart such sums in such circumstances, and to invest those funds in such manner, as it thinks fit.

(2) Nothing in subsection (1) above shall authorise any failure by a statutory water company to meet any obligation imposed on it by virtue of any local statutory provision to pay any sum to any other person.

(3) Nothing in any local statutory provision shall have effect so as to impose a limit on the amount that may be carried forward at the end of any period to the credit of the profit and loss (net revenue) account of a statutory water company.

DEFINITIONS
"local statutory provision": s.15(1) and (3).

GENERAL NOTE
See General Note to s.6. This section relaxes restrictions on the application of profits.

Subs. (2)
This subsection continues one theme of this Act, as being an enabling Act aimed at the constitution of statutory water companies rather than seeking to alter their status *vis-à-vis* third parties.

Relaxation of restrictions on mode of sale of shares or stock

8. Nothing in any local statutory provision shall have effect—
  (a) so as to require any shares or stock in a statutory water company to be offered for sale to the public; or
  (b) so as to require any offer for the sale of any such shares or stock to be an offer for sale by auction or tender.

DEFINITIONS
"local statutory provision": s.15(1) and (3).

GENERAL NOTE
This section sets aside the requirements of any local statutory provision that shares or stock in a statutory water company be offered for sale to the public or offered for sale by auction or tender. It re-enacts s.100 of the Water Act 1989.

Arrangements and reconstructions

Arrangements and reconstructions by certain companies

9.—(1) Part XIII of the 1985 Act (arrangements and reconstructions) shall have effect in relation to statutory water companies that are not limited companies with such modifications as may be prescribed by regulations made by the Secretary of State.

(2) Section 213 of the Water Industry Act 1991 (procedure for making regulations and supplemental powers) shall apply in relation to the making of regulations under this section as it applies in relation to the making of regulations under that Act.

(3) In this section "limited company" means a company, within the meaning of the 1985 Act, which is limited by shares.

DEFINITIONS
"limited company": subs. (3); s.1(2)(a) of the Companies Act 1985.
"the 1985 Act": s.15(1).

GENERAL NOTE

Part XIII of the Companies Act 1985, entitled "Arrangements and Reconstructions", covers the following areas:

"s.425 Power of company to compromise with creditors and members.

s.426 Information as to compromise to be circulated.

s.427 Provisions for facilitating company reconstruction or amalgamation.

s.428 Power to acquire shares of dissenting majority.

s.429 Dissentient's right to compel acquisition of his shares.

s.430 Provisions supplementing ss.428, 429".

These provisions were in turn based upon ss.206–209 of the Companies Act 1948.

Part XIII of the Companies Act 1985 was applied to statutory water companies that were not limited companies by Sched. 25, para. 71(2) to the Water Act 1989, "with such modifications as may be prescribed". Such modifications were prescribed in the Companies Act 1985 (Modifications for Statutory Water Companies) Regulations 1989 (S.I. 1989 No. 1461), which came into force on September 1, 1989. These Regulations have the effects of applying only ss.425 and 426 of Pt. XIII of the Companies Act 1985 to statutory water companies. The effect of a court order allowing a compromise or arrangement under s.425(2) of the Companies Act 1985 is stayed until the memorandum and articles are in place by virtue of the Secretary of State's order.

Subs. (1)

This substantially re-enacts Sched. 25, para. 71(2) to the Water Act 1989, allowing the Secretary of State to prescribe modifications to the application of the provisions by regulations.

Subs. (2)

This subsection adopts the procedures for making regulations set out in s.213 of the Water Industry Act 1991. That section in turn is based on the provisions of s.185 of the Water Act 1989 and its statutory predecessors, including what are now the usual very wide powers to make regulations covering "such supplemental, consequential and transitional provisions as the Secretary of State considers appropriate".

Power to appoint officers as directors

Power to appoint officers as directors

10.—(1) Notwithstanding anything in the Companies Clauses Consolidation Act 1845 ("the 1845 Act"), as applied to any company, but subject to any provision of a memorandum and articles having effect by virtue of an order under section 12 below and to any modification of any such memorandum and articles, the following provisions of this section shall have effect in relation to any statutory water company.

(2) Any person employed as chief engineer, general manager or secretary of the company may (whether or not he is a shareholder of the company) be appointed a director of the company either by the directors or in the manner provided by the 1845 Act.

(3) No appointment shall be made by virtue of this section if the appointment would increase the number of the directors of the company in question beyond the maximum number prescribed by any provision of any enactment or statutory order relating to the company; and not more than one director of the company shall hold office by virtue of this section at the same time.

(4) A person appointed by virtue of this section—

(a) shall not cease to be a director by reason that he is employed as mentioned in subsection (2) above; but

(b) if he was appointed by the directors, shall cease to be a director as from the date of the next ordinary general meeting of the company unless his appointment is approved at that meeting by a majority of the votes of the proprietors of the company entitled to vote or voting (whether personally or by proxy) at the meeting.

(5) The provisions of the 1845 Act requiring directors to retire by rotation shall have effect as if a person appointed by virtue of this section were not a director.

DEFINITIONS
"enactment": s.15(1).
"memorandum and articles": s.15(1).
"modification": s.15(1).
"order under section 12": s.12(1)(c).
"statutory order": s.15(1).
"the 1845 Act": subs. (1).

GENERAL NOTE
For provisions as to directors in the Companies Clauses Consolidation Act 1945, see Volume 8 of that Act, entitled Companies, and in particular:
    s.81 Number of directors.
    s.82 Power to vary number of directors.
    s.83 Election of directors.
    s.88 Rotation of directors.
This section is based upon s.43 of the Water Act 1945, as adapted for statutory water companies by Sched. 25, para. 7(7) to the Water Act 1989.

Subs. (3)
Only one director of the company at a time shall hold office "by virtue of this section"; other directors will therefore be subject to general company law provisions governing, for example, rotation.

Subs. (4)(b)
The reference in this subsection to the "proprietors of the company", not defined in s.15(1), is taken from s.43(d)(ii) of the Water Act 1945. The term "proprietors" is used in the context used for "members of the company" elsewhere in the Act; see, for example, s.4(8), definition of "special resolution".

PART II

CONVERSION OF STATUTORY WATER COMPANIES

Registration of statutory water companies under the Companies Act 1985

11.—(1) Chapter II of Part XXII of the 1985 Act (registration of companies not formed under that Act) shall have effect in relation to statutory water companies as if—
  (a) any reference in that Chapter to a joint stock company included a reference to such a statutory water company as would not fall to be treated as a joint stock company for the purposes of that Chapter apart from this paragraph; and
  (b) any reference in that Chapter to an Act of Parliament included a reference to a local statutory provision which is not contained in an Act of Parliament.

(2) It is hereby declared that nothing in the 1985 Act, the Water Act 1989, the Water Industry Act 1991 or this Act shall be construed as requiring a statutory water company to which a certificate has been issued under section 688 of the 1985 Act (certificates of registration under Chapter II of Part XXII) to be treated for the purposes of those Acts or any other purposes as if it had been a different person in law before the issue of that certificate.

DEFINITIONS
"certificate issued under section 688 of the 1985 Act": s.688 of the Companies Act 1985.
"certificate of registration under Chapter II of Pt. XXII": s.688 of the Companies Act 1985.
"company's becoming a registered water company": s.15(2).
"joint stock company": s.683 of the Companies Act 1985.
"local statutory provision": s.15(1).

"statutory water companies": s.15(1).
"the 1985 Act": s.15(1).

GENERAL NOTE

This section re-enacts s.101(1) of the Water Act 1989. Together with s.12 following, which re-enacts s.101(2)–(5) and (7) and (8) of the Water Act 1989, this section allows statutory water companies to register under the Companies Acts and to adopt a new memorandum and articles without any need for a new Private Act. Sections 11 and 12 of the Statutory Water Companies Act 1991 are the heart of the Act. This s.11 follows the route of joining the statutory water company to the Companies Act 1985 registration procedure as if it were a joint stock company, while re-stating that the fact of registration is not to affect its continuing legal personality. For the effects of registration under s.680 of the Companies Act 1985 on such areas as vesting of property, existing liabilities and pending actions in law, see Sched. 21 to the Companies Act 1985.

Subs. (2)

Sched. 21 to the Companies Act 1985 (see General Note above) now needs to be read subject to this re-statement in respect of companies' legal personality.

Adoption of memorandum and articles

12.—(1) Where—
(a) provision for the constitution and regulation of a statutory water company holding an appointment under Chapter I of Part II of the Water Industry Act 1991—
    (i) is contained in local statutory provisions having effect in accordance with paragraph 5 of Schedule 21 to the 1985 Act (enactments to have effect as if contained in memorandum and articles); or
    (ii) would, apart from this subsection, be so contained if the company became a registered water company;
(b) the company has by special resolution proposed (whether before or after becoming a registered water company) that provision contained in a memorandum and articles shall have effect in substitution for those local statutory provisions;
(c) the proposal that a memorandum and articles shall so have effect in relation to the company has been approved by order made by the Secretary of State; and
(d) in the case of a company that has not already done so, the company becomes a registered water company,
those local statutory provisions shall cease to have effect on such date as may, for the purposes of this subsection, be specified or described in that order and the proposed memorandum and articles shall come into force on that date subject to any modifications, terms or conditions contained in any order made by the High Court under section 13 below.

(2) The Secretary of State shall not make an order for the purposes of subsection (1)(c) above in relation to a proposal by any company unless it appears to him—
(a) that neither an application under section 13 below with respect to the company's proposal nor an appeal with respect to the subject-matter of such an application is pending and that the period within which any such application or appeal may be made or brought has expired; and
(b) where there is—
    (i) a division of the shares or stock of the company into different classes; and
    (ii) such a proposed difference between the memorandum and articles and the local statutory provisions which they will replace as will vary the rights attached to any such class,

that a consent to or approval of the difference has been given under subsection (3) below in respect of each class the rights attached to which would be varied if the order were made.

(3) A consent to or approval of a proposal is given for the purposes of subsection (2)(b) above in respect of a class of shares or stock if—

(a) consent in writing to the proposal has been given by the holders of not less than three-quarters, in nominal value, of the issued shares or stock of that class; or

(b) an extraordinary resolution approving the proposal is passed at a separate general meeting of holders of shares or stock of that class.

(4) For the purpose of determining whether the requirements specified in subsection (2)(b) above are satisfied in relation to any two or more classes of shares or stock in a company, it shall be immaterial that consents and approvals have been given in respect of different classes in accordance with different paragraphs of subsection (3) above.

(5) Where an order has been made for the purposes of subsection (1)(c) above in relation to any company—

(a) nothing in sections 1 to 8 above shall have effect on and after the date specified or described in the order so as to confer powers in relation to the company in addition to those conferred by virtue of the company's memorandum and articles;

(b) on and after that date, the memorandum and articles which come into force by virtue of the order shall have effect, in accordance with section 14 and the other provisions of the 1985 Act, as if they were the company's registered memorandum and articles; and

(c) the company shall, before the end of the period of 15 days beginning with the day after that date, deliver to the registrar of companies a printed copy of the memorandum and articles which have so come into force.

(6) Subsection (3) of section 6 of the 1985 Act (penalty for default in delivering documents to the registrar of companies) shall apply in relation to the obligation imposed by subsection (5)(c) above as it applies in relation to the obligations imposed by subsection (1) of that section.

(7) The power to make an order for the purposes of subsection (1)(c) above shall be exercisable by statutory instrument subject to annulment in pursuance of a resolution of either House of Parliament.

(8) In this section—

"extraordinary resolution"—

(a) in relation to a meeting held after the company in question has become a registered water company, means an extraordinary resolution within the meaning of the 1985 Act; and

(b) in relation to a meeting held before that company becomes a registered water company, means such a resolution as would be a special resolution within the meaning of section 4 above if the meeting were a meeting of the company;

"registrar of companies" has the same meaning as in the 1985 Act; and

"special resolution"—

(a) in relation to a time after the company in question has become a registered water company, means (subject to subsection (2) of section 13 below) a special resolution within the meaning of the 1985 Act; and

(b) in relation to a time before that company becomes a registered water company, means (subject to that subsection) a special resolution within the meaning of section 4 above.

DEFINITIONS

"company's becoming a registered water company": s.15(2).
"consent to or approval of": subs. (3).

"extraordinary resolution": subs. (8); s.378(1) of the Companies Act 1985 (after company becomes a registered water company): subs. (8); s.4(8) (before company becomes a registered water company).

"holding an appointment under Chapter I of Pt. II of the Water Industry Act 1991": subs. (1)(a); s.6(1) of the Water Industry Act 1991.

"joint stock company": s.683 of the Companies Act 1985.

"local statutory provision": s.15(1).

"memorandum and articles": s.15(1).

"modifications": s.15(1).

"registrar of companies": subs. (8); s.744 of the Companies Act 1985.

"special resolution": subs. (8); s.378(2) of the Companies Act 1985 (after company becomes a registered water company): subs. (8); s.4(8) (before company becomes a registered water company).

"statutory water company": s.15(1).

"the 1985 Act": s.15(1).

GENERAL NOTE

See General Note to s.11.

A statutory water company becomes a registered water company upon the issue to it of a certificate of registration under s.688 of the Companies Act 1985 (s.15(2)). The consequences of such registration would include statutory provisions constituting or regulating such companies being deemed to be part of the companies' memorandum and articles of association (Sched. 21, para. 5 to the Companies Act 1985). This section lays down the route by which statutory water companies can achieve the substitution of a memorandum and articles for a statutory constitution. Two main requirements are (i) consent of at least a three-quarters majority of the shareholders by special resolution (s.12(1)(b) and (8)), and (ii) approval of the proposal by order of the Secretary of State (s.12(1)(c) and (2)).

Subs. (2) and (3)

The Secretary of State shall not make an order allowing the proposed substitution of memorandum and articles for statutory constitution unless (1) there is no challenge to the proposal pending under s.13, and the time limit for such a challenge has passed (subs. (2)(a)), or (2) where the proposed substitution will vary any class rights (subs. (2)(b)), the holders of at least three-quarters in nominal value of the issued shares or stock of that class either consent in writing (subs. (3)(a)) or approve by passing an extraordinary resolution (subs. (3)(b)).

Subs. (5)

Once the requirements of the section have been met, the local statutory provisions defining the company's constitution cease to have effect on the date specified in the order. The memorandum and articles become the limits of the company's constitution, bind the company and its members (subs. 5(b)), and the company has 15 days to deliver the memorandum and articles to the registrar of companies, with a fine for default (subs. 6).

Subs. (7)

The parliamentary procedure for an order by the Secretary of State under this section is by way of statutory instrument subject to annulment by a resolution of either House of Parliament.

Review by High Court of resolution substituting memorandum and articles

13.—(1) Where a special resolution has been passed containing a proposal, in relation to a company, for a memorandum and articles to have effect as mentioned in subsection (1) of section 12 above, an application for the resolution to be cancelled may be made to the High Court—

  (a) by the holders of not less, in the aggregate, than 15 per cent., in nominal value, of the company's issued share capital or issued stock;

  (b) by the holders of not less, in the aggregate, than 15 per cent., in nominal value, of the issued shares or stock of any class in respect of which a consent to or approval of the proposal to which the resolution relates is required for the purposes of subsection (2)(b) of that section; or

  (c) if the resolution incorporates a modification of the company's objects, by the holders of not less than 15 per cent. of such of the company's debentures as entitle the holders to object under this section to such a modification;

but an application under this section shall not be made by any person who has consented to or voted in favour of the proposal (whether for the purposes of subsection (1) or for the purposes of subsection (2)(b) of that section).

(2) Accordingly, in the case of such a special resolution for the purposes of section 12(1) above as incorporates a modification of the company's objects—

(a) the same notice as is given for the purposes of that resolution to members of the company is required to be given to the holders of debentures entitling the holders to object under this section to a modification of the company's objects; and

(b) in the absence of any local statutory provision regulating the giving of that notice, that notice shall be given in accordance with the provisions regulating the giving of the notice to the members.

(3) An application under this section—

(a) may be made on behalf of the persons entitled to make it by such one or more of their number as they may appoint in writing for the purpose; but

(b) shall not be made in relation to any special resolution more than 21 days after the date of the last resolution, consent or approval to be passed or given—

(i) for the purposes of subsection (1)(b) or (2)(b) of section 12 above; or

(ii) for the purposes, in connection with the company's becoming a registered water company, of section 681 of the 1985 Act (procedural requirements for registration).

(4) The powers of the High Court on an application under this section shall be to do one or more of the following, that is to say—

(a) to make an order, on such terms and conditions as it thinks fit, cancelling the resolution to which the application relates or confirming the proposal contained in that resolution either subject to such modifications of the proposed memorandum and articles as may be specified in the order or without modifications;

(b) if it thinks fit, to adjourn the proceedings in order that arrangements may be made to the Court's satisfaction for the purchase of the interests of dissentient members or for the payment of compensation to such members,

(c) to give such directions and make such orders as it thinks expedient for facilitating or carrying into effect any such arrangement; and

(d) to require that provision contained in any memorandum and articles, as confirmed by the Court, shall not at any time be modified in the respects specified in the Court's order except with the leave of the Court.

(5) Without prejudice to the powers conferred by subsection (4)(c) above, an order of the High Court under this section may (if the Court thinks fit) provide for—

(a) the purchase by a company of the shares or stock of any members of the company; and

(b) the reduction accordingly of the company's capital;

and an order which so provides shall not confirm a proposal for a memorandum and articles to have effect in substitution for any local statutory provisions except subject to such modifications (if any) as may be required in consequence of that purchase and reduction.

(6) The High Court shall not on an application under this section confirm any proposal in so far as it incorporates such an alteration of a company's

objects as could not be made under section 4 of the 1985 Act (alteration of objects) if the company were entitled to alter its objects under that section.

(7) The debentures entitling the holders to object under this section to a modification of a company's objects are any debentures secured on the company's undertaking which—

(a) were issued or first issued before July 6, 1989; or
(b) form part of the same series as any debentures so issued but have been issued on or after that date;

and in this section "debentures" has the same meaning as in the 1985 Act.

DEFINITIONS

"company's becoming a registered water company": s.15(2).
"consent to or approval of" for the purposes of s.12(2)(b): s.12(3).
"debentures": subs. (7); s.744 of the Companies Act 1985.
"debentures entitling the holders to object under this section": subs. (7).
"local statutory provision": s.15(1).
"memorandum and articles": s.15(1).
"modifications": s.15(1).

GENERAL NOTE

See General Note to s.12. This section re-enacts s.102 of the Water Act 1989.

A special resolution proposing to substitute a memorandum and articles for a statutory constitution may be challenged by an application to the High Court by the holders of 15 per cent.: (1) in nominal value of the company's issued share capital or issued stock (subs. (1)(a)); (2) in nominal value of the issued shares or stock of any class where the proposal will vary class rights (subs. (1)(b) and s.12(2)(b)(ii)); or (3) of such of the company's debentures (see subs. (7)) as entitle the holders to object under this section to such a modification (subs. (1)(c)) *provided* that such applicants did not consent or vote for the proposal.

Subs. (2)

Debenture holders must also be given the same notice of a special resolution in order that they have an opportunity to challenge the decision in the High Court.

Subs. (3)(b)

Applications to the High Court must be made within 21 days of the relevant resolution, consent, approval or assent.

Subss. (4) and (5)

The High Court may (1) cancel the resolution, on terms or conditions or not; (2) confirm the proposal in the resolution, with modifications or not; (3) adjourn proceedings to allow arrangements to be made to purchase dissentients' interests, or to pay them compensation (a late addition to the Water Act 1989 at Report stage of the House of Lords, to allow more effective action by the Court); (4) give directions and make orders to facilitate or carry into effect such arrangements; (5) require parts of the memorandum and articles not to be modified except with leave of the Court; (6) allow for purchase by the company of any member's shares or stock, and the consequent reduction of its capital, in which case the conversion to a "memorandum and articles" constitution is subject to those arrangements.

The criterion of "unfair prejudice" for a High Court challenge under s.5 is absent from this section, which specifies no criteria on which the court must be satisfied before reaching a decision. This anomaly was noted as between s.98 and s.102 of the Water Act 1989, and appears to have been carried over into the consolidated legislation.

Power to amend local statutory provisions

14.—(1) Where the Secretary of State makes an order for the purposes of section 12(1)(c) above in relation to any company and it appears to him to be appropriate to do so for the purposes of, or in consequence of, the approval contained in the order, he may by order repeal or amend any local statutory provision.

(2) The power to make an order under this section shall be exercisable by statutory instrument subject to annulment in pursuance of a resolution of either House of Parliament.

(3) An order under this section may—

(a) make different provision for different cases, including different provision in relation to different persons, circumstances or localities; and

(b) contain such supplemental, consequential and transitional provision as the Secretary of State considers appropriate.

DEFINITIONS
"local statutory provision": s.15(1).

GENERAL NOTE
This section re-enacts s.101(6) and (7) of the Water Act 1989. Where the Secretary of State makes an order under s.12(1)(c) (for a memorandum and articles to replace a statutory constitution), this section allows him or her to repeal or amend the relevant local statutory provision, and make "tidying up" orders. The further orders are made by statutory instrument subject to annulment by Parliamentary resolution.

PART III

SUPPLEMENTAL

General interpretation

15.—(1) In this Act, except in so far as the context otherwise requires—

"the 1985 Act" means the Companies Act 1985;

"disposal," in relation to land or any interest or right in or over land, includes the creation of such an interest or right and a disposal effected by means of the surrender or other termination of any such interest or right;

"enactment" includes an enactment contained in this Act or in any Act passed after this Act;

"engineering or building operations," without prejudice to the generality of that expression, includes—

(a) the construction, alteration, improvement, maintenance or demolition of any building or structure or of any reservoir, watercourse, dam, weir, well, borehole or other works; and

(b) the installation, modification or removal of any machinery or apparatus;

"functions," in relation to a water undertaker, means the functions of the undertaker under or by virtue of any enactment and shall be construed subject to section 217 of the Water Industry Act 1991 (extension of meaning of "functions" in relation to undertakers);

"local statutory provision" means, subject to subsection (3) below—

(a) a provision of a local Act (including an Act confirming a provisional order);

(b) a provision of so much of any public general Act as has effect with respect to a particular area, with respect to particular persons or works or with respect to particular provisions falling within any paragraph of this definition;

(c) a provision of an instrument made under any provision falling within paragraph (a) or (b) above; and

(d) a provision of any other instrument which is in the nature of a local enactment;

"memorandum and articles" means a document containing only such provision as may be contained in a memorandum and articles of association registered under the 1985 Act;

"modifications" includes—

(a) additions, alterations and omissions; and

(b) in relation to any provision imposing a limit to which section 4 above applies in relation to any statutory water company, the removal of that limit and the replacement of that

provision with a provision imposing a different such limit in relation to that company;
and cognate expressions shall be construed accordingly;
"notice" means notice in writing;
"statutory order" means an order or scheme made under any Act of Parliament, including an order or scheme confirmed by Parliament;
"statutory water company" means any company which was a statutory water company for the purposes of the Water Act 1973 immediately before September 1, 1989; and
"water fittings" has the same meaning as in Part III of the Water Industry Act 1991.

(2) In this Act a reference to a company's becoming a registered water company is a reference to the issue to that company (whether before or on or after September 1, 1989) of a certificate under section 688 of the 1985 Act.

(3) The references in sections 6 to 8 of this Act to a local statutory provision shall not include a reference to any provision contained in any enactment or instrument passed or made on or after September 1, 1989.

(4) Section 216 of the Water Industry Act 1991 (manner of serving notices etc.) shall apply in relation to the service of any document by virtue of this Act as it applies in relation to the service of any document by virtue of that Act.

GENERAL NOTE

Subs. (4)
Section 216 of the Water Industry Act 1991 (provisions relating to the service of documents) is based upon s.187 of the Water Act 1989, and Recommendation 14 of the Law Commission's "Report on the Consolidation of the Legislation Relating to Water" (Cm. 1483, April 1991).

Information provisions

16. Sections 206 and 207 of the Water Industry Act 1991 (confidentiality of information and offence of providing false information) shall have effect in relation to the provisions of this Act as they have effect in relation to the provisions of that Act.

DEFINITIONS
"the Director": s.219(1) of the Water Industry Act 1991.
"functions": s.219(1) of the Water Industry Act 1991.
"local authority": s.219 of the Water Industry Act 1991.
"the Monopolies Commission": s.219(1) of the Water Industry Act 1991.
"the NRA": s.219 of the Water Industry Act 1991.
"relevant undertaker": s.219 of the Water Industry Act 1991.
"the other consolidation Acts": s.206(10) of the Water Industry Act 1991.

GENERAL NOTE
For the origins of the relevant provisions, see:
(1) s.206 of the Water Industry Act 1991; s.174 of the Water Act 1989 and Recommendation 11 of the Law Commission's Report (Cm. 1483), cited in the General Note to s.15 above;
(2) s.207 of the Water Industry Act 1991; s.175 and Sched. 25, para. 8 to the Water Act 1989 and Recommendation 12 of the Law Commission's Report (Cm. 1483).

Section 206 of the Water Industry Act 1991
This section consists of a general prohibition on disclosure of information obtained by virtue of the Act's provisions and relating to an individual or business. It then sets out a very long list of exceptions relating to the functions of public bodies and the duties of water and sewerage contractors. It adds an offence of disclosure of information outside them (subs. (7)). As such, the section resembles the "disclosure of information" sections of other recent legislation, such as the Financial Services Act 1986.

Section 207 of the Water Industry Act 1991

Deliberate or reckless provision of false information under the Act is a criminal offence carrying a fine.

Short title, commencement and extent

17.—(1) This Act may be cited as the Statutory Water Companies Act 1991.

(2) This Act shall come into force on December 1, 1991.

(3) This Act extends to England and Wales only.

Table of Derivations

Note: The following abbreviations are used in this Table:—

1945   = The Water Act 1945 (c. 42)
1989   = The Water Act 1989 (c. 15)

Provision of Act	Derivation
1	1989 s.97.
2	1945 ss.41(1), (2) & (3) (proviso) & 59(1); 1989 Sched. 25, para. 7(6).
3	1945 s.41(3) (except proviso) & (4)–(6); 1989 Sched. 25, para. 7(6).
4	1989 s.98(1)–(4) & (8)–(10).
5	1989 s.98(5)–(7).
6	1989 s.99(1).
7	1989 s.99(2)–(4).
8	1989 s.100.
9	1989 ss.185 & 189(1) & Sched. 25, para. 71(2).
10	1945 ss.43 & 59(1); 1989 Sched. 25, para. 7(7).
11	1989 s.101(1).
12	1989 s.101(2)–(5), (7) & (8).
13	1989 s.102.
14	1989 s.101(6) & (7).
15	1945 s.59(1); 1989 ss.97(4), 98(9), 101(8), 187 & 189(1) (part).
16	1989 ss.174 & 175.
17	Short title, commencement and extent.

TABLE OF DESTINATIONS

WATER ACT 1945
c. 42

WATER ACT 1989
c. 15

INDEX

References are to sections

LAND DRAINAGE ACT 1991*

(1991 c. 59)

[A table showing the derivation of the provisions of this Consolidation Act will be found at the end of the Act. The table has no official status.]

ARRANGEMENT OF SECTIONS

PART I

INTERNAL DRAINAGE BOARDS

Constitution etc. of boards

---

* Annotations by Simon Jackson, Solicitor.

An Act to consolidate the enactments relating to internal drainage boards, and to the functions of such boards and of local authorities in relation to land drainage, with amendments to give effect to recommendations of the Law Commission.   **[25th July 1991]**

PARLIAMENTARY DEBATES
Hansard, H.L. Vol. 528, cols. 484, 1738; Vol. 529, col. 746; H.C. Vol. 195, col. 1111.

INTRODUCTION AND GENERAL NOTE
This Act forms part of a comprehensive consolidation of water legislation following on from the Water Act 1989, which abolished water authorities and created the National Rivers

Authority (NRA) and the private water undertakers. The Water Act 1989 resulted in large-scale amendments to earlier Acts, in particular the Water Resources Act 1963 and the Land Drainage Act 1976, reflecting the radically altered structure of the water industry. The consolidation is a logical step to bring land drainage legislation into a single Act and incorporate the substantial transitional provisions brought in by the Water Act 1989.

Land drainage law comprised in the Act is at root derived from the Land Drainage Act 1930 and, before that, piecemeal legislation stretching back to the sixteenth century. The legislation was updated in the 1976 Act, which concerned itself with land drainage in the fields of both flood prevention and improvement of land use. This Act concerns itself solely with the latter. The duties of the NRA in relation to flood prevention, and also its duties in relation to main rivers, are now contained in the Water Resources Act 1991.

The Act therefore concentrates on the permissive powers granted to the relevant bodies to maintain and improve existing drainage works and create new drainage works. These powers are primarily vested in internal drainage boards. The boards cover geographical areas of the country where drainage of land is required to benefit and protect land use in their area. Land drainage powers and duties are also vested in the NRA and local authorities, and the Act deals in detail with the relationship between the three bodies. As indicated above, the NRA is solely responsible for the efficient drainage of main rivers. The NRA keeps available for public inspection a map showing main rivers under its control. In some geographical areas land drainage functions are in fact operated by the NRA.

Whilst the Act re-enacts substantial parts of the 1976 Act, it also incorporates material from subsequent Acts which impinge on the provisions of the 1976 Act. These can be summarised as follows:

(1) the subsequent creation of the NRA and its interrelationship with Internal Drainage Boards;

(2) the greater environmental duties and obligations to consult other bodies as to the environmental impact of drainage works and the exercise of powers;

(3) the revaluation of land drainage rates consequent on the abolition of the general rating system.

As to the latter, the Act contains the framework for the first revaluation for land drainage purposes. That revaluation is to be completed by the end of 1992 and the new valuations will be effective from April 1, 1993. Until then, the current valuation system is governed by the provisions saved by virtue of para. 15 of Sched. 2 to the Water Consolidation (Consequential Provisions) Act 1991.

The Act also puts into effect the recommendations of the Law Commission *Report on the Consolidation of Legislation Relating to Water 1990*. These were as follows:

(1) an amendment to clarify the exercise by the Minister of powers to make regulations governing procedure for election to an Internal Drainage Board;

(2) consolidation to ensure that common provisions apply to all determinations of disputes as to whether a river is a main river or not;

(3) consolidation of penalties that can be imposed for breach of provisions in the Act preventing the placing of obstructions in water courses;

(4) ironing out an inconsistency regarding authority to make payments to Internal Drainage Board chairmen.

At the end of the Act there is a table of derivations which gives the source of each section, for the most part being the 1976 Act.

ARRANGEMENT OF THE ACT

Part I   *Internal drainage boards*
Ss.1–6   Definition of internal drainage districts and boards; the procedure for reviewing boundaries of districts; procedure for initiating schemes to reorganise drainage districts; powers to make the NRA a drainage board; transfer of powers back from the NRA; compensation provision consequent on schemes and order under ss.3–5.

Ss.7–11   Environmental and recreational duties of drainage authorities generally and specifically with respect to sites of special interest.

Part II   *The drainage provisions*
Ss.14–22   General powers of boards and local authorities; disposal of spoil; local authority exercise of powers and control of those powers; drainage of small areas; arrangement with other bodies; enforcement powers; ministerial powers.

SCHEDULES

ABBREVIATIONS

the 1976 Act	:	Land Drainage Act 1976
Drainage Authority	:	an internal drainage board, or the NRA or a local authority, as the case may be
Drainage Board	:	an internal drainage board or the NRA, as the case may be
IDB	:	Internal Drainage Board
NRA	:	National Rivers Authority
SSSI	:	Site of Special Scientific Interest

PART I

INTERNAL DRAINAGE BOARDS

Constitution etc. of boards

Internal drainage districts and boards

1.—(1) For the purposes of the drainage of land, there shall continue to be—

(a) districts, known as internal drainage districts, which shall be such areas within the areas of the regional flood defence committees as will derive benefit, or avoid danger, as a result of drainage operations; and

(b) boards, known as internal drainage boards, each of which shall be the drainage board for an internal drainage district;

and, subject to the following provisions of this Part, the internal drainage districts which were such districts immediately before the coming into force of this section, and the boards for those districts, shall continue as such districts and boards.

(2) An internal drainage board shall—

(a) exercise a general supervision over all matters relating to the drainage of land within their district; and

(b) have such other powers and perform such other duties as are conferred or imposed on internal drainage boards by this Act.

(3) Subject to subsections (4) and (6) below, an internal drainage board shall be a body corporate and shall consist of—

(a) members who shall be elected and hold office in accordance with provisions made by or under Schedule 1 to this Act; and

(b) members appointed in accordance with those provisions by charging authorities.

(4) The first members of an internal drainage board shall be persons appointed by the relevant Minister, together with any persons appointed as mentioned in subsection (3)(b) above.

(5) Subject to subsection (6) below, Schedule 2 to this Act shall have effect with respect to the proceedings of internal drainage boards.

(6) The following provisions, that is to say, the provisions of Schedule 1 to this Act, except so far as it relates to the appointment of members by a charging authority, the provisions of Schedule 2 to this Act and the provisions of subsection (3) above, so far as it requires members of an internal drainage board to be elected, shall have effect in relation to an internal drainage board in existence on August 1, 1930 only to such an extent as—

(a) those provisions are applied to the board by a scheme made or having effect as if made under section 3 below; or

(b) immediately before the coming into force of this Act, corresponding provision otherwise applied in relation to that board by virtue of section 7(4) of the Land Drainage Act 1976.

DEFINITIONS
"charging authority": s.72.
"drainage": s.72.
"minister": s.72.

GENERAL NOTE
This section provides for the continuation of internal drainage districts and boards which already exist by virtue of the 1976 Act and earlier legislation. Internal drainage districts coincide with Regional Flood Defence Committee areas: see s.9 of the Water Resources Act 1991.
Membership of an IDB is made up in part of appointees put forward by charging authorities who contribute to the funds of IDBs and in part members elected by those eligible to vote.

Essentially those who pay drainage rates are able to vote and also stand to be elected as members. The ratio of elected to appointed members is governed by the proportions in which the ratepayers on the one hand and the charging authorities on the other contribute to the expenses of the IDB.

Schedule 1 to the Act sets out in detail the provisions relating to the constitution of IDBs. It also provides that the Minister shall make regulations to govern the conduct of elections. These are contained in the Land Drainage (Election of Drainage Board) Regulations 1938 (S.I. 1938 No. 558) as amended by the Land Drainage (Election of Internal Drainage Boards) (Amendment) Regulations 1977 (S.I. 1977 No. 366).

Where a new IDB is created it shall for the initial period comprise members appointed by the Minister and the charging authorities.

Schedule 2 to the Act sets out the procedure which IDBs shall adopt.

Schedules 1 and 2 do not have effect with respect to the constitution or conduct of IDBs already in existence on August 1, 1930, unless those IDBs have been subjected to a reorganisation scheme in the interim, or in future are so subjected as provided by s.3 of the Act.

Review of boundaries of internal drainage districts

2.—(1) Subject to subsection (7) below, where—
  (a) a petition for the alteration of the boundaries of an internal drainage district is made to the NRA by a sufficient number of qualified persons or by a qualified authority; and
  (b) the boundaries of that district have for a period exceeding ten years been neither reviewed on such a petition nor altered,
the NRA shall review those boundaries.

(2) Subject to subsection (7) below, where a petition under subsection (1) above is received by the NRA in the circumstances mentioned in subsection (1)(b) above, the NRA shall—
  (a) inform the relevant Minister; and
  (b) publish, in one or more newspapers circulating in the internal drainage district, a notice stating—
      (i) that the petition has been received;
      (ii) that a review of the boundaries is being undertaken; and
      (iii) that the representations may be made to the NRA within a period (which shall not be less than thirty days) stated in the notice.

(3) In carrying out any review required by this section the NRA shall—
  (a) consult the drainage board for the internal drainage district in question, unless it is itself the drainage board; and
  (b) consider any representations duly made to it.

(4) Within six months after a petition under this section is made or such longer period as the relevant Minister may allow, the NRA shall inform the relevant Minister—
  (a) whether, as a result of the review, it proposes to submit to him a scheme under section 3 below; and
  (b) if so, what provision it proposes to make by the scheme.

(5) Subject to subsection (6) below, where—
  (a) the NRA does not propose, as a result of the review, to submit to the relevant Minister a scheme under section 3 below; but
  (b) it appears to the NRA that an order under section 38 below, or an order varying or revoking such an order, should be made by the drainage board for the internal drainage district in question,
the NRA may direct the drainage board to make such an order in such terms as may be specified in the direction.

(6) If an internal drainage board to which a direction has been given under subsection (5) above object to the direction, the direction shall have no effect unless it is confirmed (with or without modifications) by the relevant Minister.

(7) This section does not require the NRA to carry out a review or publish any notice on a petition which, in the opinion of the relevant Minister, is frivolous.

DEFINITIONS
"internal drainage district": s.1(1)(a).
"Minister": s.72(1).
"qualified authority": s.72(1).
"qualified persons": s.72(2).

GENERAL NOTE
Section 2 provides a machinery for reviewing the boundaries of internal drainage districts. A petition to apply for a change can only be made by qualifying persons or by a qualifying authority. If no review has been carried out for more than 10 years then the NRA, as reviewing body, must give full publicity to the intended review petitioned for and consult. Three options are open to the NRA. It can make no change; it can reorganise the district (see notes to s.3 below); or it can sub-divide the district into different regions (see notes to s.38 below). The Act does not specify the form of the petition.

Schemes for reorganisation of internal drainage districts etc.

3.—(1) The NRA—
(a) may at any time (in consequence of a review under section 2 above or otherwise) prepare and submit to the relevant Minister for confirmation a scheme making provision for any of the matters specified in subsection (2) below; and
(b) shall prepare and so submit such a scheme if it is directed to do so by the relevant Minister.
(2) The matters mentioned in subsection (1) above are—
(a) the alteration of the boundaries of any internal drainage district;
(b) the amalgamation of the whole or any part of any internal drainage district with any other such district;
(c) the abolition as from such date as may be specified in the scheme of Commissioners of Sewers exercising jurisdiction within the area for which the NRA carries out functions that are flood defence functions within the meaning of the Water Resources Act 1991;
(d) the abolition or reconstitution of any internal drainage district and of the drainage board for that district;
(e) the constitution of new internal drainage districts;
(f) the constitution of internal drainage boards for all or any of the separate internal drainage districts constituted by the scheme;
(g) where it appears desirable so to provide in the case of any internal drainage board, the amendment of the method of constituting that board so far as is necessary to secure that members of the board shall include persons elected as such in accordance with the provisions for that purpose contained in section 1 above and Schedule 1 to this Act;
(h) the making of alterations in, and the addition of supplemental provisions to, the provisions of any local Act or of any award made under any such Act, where such alterations or supplemental provisions are necessary or expedient for enabling the area for the benefit of which drainage works are authorised by the local Act or award to be drained effectually;
(i) any matters supplemental to or consequential on the matters mentioned in paragraphs (a) to (h) above for which it appears necessary or desirable to make provision, including the transfer to the NRA or an internal drainage board of any property, rights, powers, duties, obligations and liabilities vested in or to be discharged by the NRA or by the internal drainage board affected by the scheme.
(3) A scheme under this section may provide for the revocation or amendment of, and for the retransfer of property, rights, powers, duties, obligations and liabilities transferred by, any previous scheme under this section.
(4) A soon as any scheme under this section has been submitted to the relevant Minister, the NRA shall—
(a) send copies of the scheme to every internal drainage board, local

authority, navigation authority, harbour authority and conservancy authority affected by it; and
(b) publish in one or more newspapers circulating in the area affected by the scheme a notice stating—
(i) that the scheme has been submitted to that Minister; and
(ii) that a copy of it is open to inspection at a specified place; and
(iii) that representations with respect to the scheme may be made to that Minister at any time within one month after the publication of the notice.

(5) The relevant Minister may by order made by statutory instrument confirm any scheme submitted to him under this section, either with or without modifications.

(6) Schedule 3 to this Act shall apply with respect to an order confirming a scheme under this section.

(7) An order confirming a scheme under this section may contain provisions with respect to the persons by whom all or any of the expenses incurred by the relevant Minister or other persons in connection with the making or confirmation of the order, or the making of the scheme, are to be borne.

(8) Where the boundaries of an internal drainage district are altered under this section, all powers exercisable under any local Act by the drainage board for the district with respect to land included in it shall be exercisable with respect to land added to the district, except so far as provision is otherwise made by the scheme effecting the alteration or by the order confirming that scheme.

DEFINITIONS
"internal drainage board": s.1(1)(b).
"internal drainage district": s.1(1)(a).
"Minister": s.72(1).

GENERAL NOTE
Section 3 vests wide powers in the NRA to reorganise internal drainage districts, either as a result of a petition under s.2 (see above), at its own instance, or if directed to do so by the relevant Minister.
Subsection (2) sets out the scope of what the NRA may include in a scheme of reorganisation.
The section gives power to the NRA to vary matters originally provided for by a Local Act.
There is a duty on the NRA to serve details on the relevant IDB and to consult it. Reorganisation schemes are subject to ministerial approval.
Commissioners of Sewers exist where created under relevant Local Acts.
Schedule 3 sets out detailed procedures which must be adopted by the relevant Minister before any s.2 scheme is confirmed. It gives power to order a local inquiry; the power for persons affected to have the Order made subject to special parliamentary procedure; the right for an aggrieved person to apply to the High Court on the basis either that the Minister has acted *ultra vires*, or that a requirement of the Act has not been complied with.

Powers to make the NRA a drainage board

4.—(1) The relevant Minister may, on a petition for the purpose presented to him by the NRA, by order made by statutory instrument transfer to the NRA the powers, duties, liabilities, obligations and property (including deeds, maps, books, papers and other documents) of the drainage board for any internal drainage district.

(2) On a transfer under this section, the NRA shall for the purposes of this Act become the drainage board for the district in question; and any expenses incurred by the NRA as the drainage board for that district shall be defrayed under and in accordance with the powers transferred by the order under this section and not in any other manner.

(3) Without prejudice to the preceding provisions of this section, a scheme under section 3 above which makes provision for the constitution of a new internal drainage district may provide—
(a) for the NRA to be constituted the drainage board for that district; and

(b) for conferring on the NRA in relation to that district the powers and duties of an internal drainage board;

and any expenses incurred by the NRA as the internal drainage board for such a district shall be defrayed under and in accordance with the powers so conferred and not in any other manner.

(4) Schedule 3 to this Act shall apply with respect to an order under this section.

(5) An order under this section may contain provisions with respect to the persons by whom all or any of the expenses incurred by the relevant Minister or other persons in connection with the making or confirmation of the order are to be borne.

DEFINITIONS
"internal drainage board": s.1(1)(b).
"internal drainage district": s.1(1)(a).
"Minister": s.72(1).

GENERAL NOTE
Section 4 gives power to the NRA, either by presenting a petition to the relevant minister or by virtue of s.3 reorganisation schemes (see above), to ask the Minister to constitute the NRA as the drainage board in place of the existing board.
The provisions of Sched. 3 (see notes to s.3 above) apply.

Transfer of functions etc. back from the NRA

5.—(1) Where—
(a) the NRA is (whether by virtue of a scheme under section 3 above or an order under section 4 above) the drainage board for an internal drainage district; and
(b) a petition for constituting an internal drainage board for that district is made to the NRA by a sufficient number of qualified persons or by a qualified authority,

the relevant Minister may by order made by statutory instrument constitute an internal drainage board for that district and transfer to it the property and liabilities of the NRA, so far as vested in or incurred by the NRA in its capacity as the drainage board for that district.

(2) On receiving such a petition as is mentioned in subsection (1) above the NRA shall send a copy of it to the relevant Minister.

(3) The NRA shall inform the relevant Minister, within six months of the date on which such a petition is received, whether in its opinion an order under subsection (1) above ought to be made.

(4) Before making an order under subsection (1) above the relevant Minister shall consider the views expressed by the NRA in accordance with subsection (3) above.

(5) Schedule 3 to this Act shall apply with respect to an order under this section.

(6) An order under this section may contain provisions with respect to the persons by whom all or any of the expenses incurred by the relevant Minister or other persons in connection with the making or confirmation of the order are to be borne.

DEFINITIONS
"internal drainage board": s.1(1)(b).
"qualified authority": s. 72(1).
"qualified persons": s. 72(1).

GENERAL NOTE
This is a reverse provision to that contained in s.4, so that qualified persons can apply to the Minister for an IDB to be created to take over land drainage functions from the NRA. The Ministers must consider views expressed by the NRA. Schedule 3 (see notes on s.3 above) applies.

Schemes and orders under sections 3 to 5: compensation for loss of office

6.—(1) The appropriate Minister shall by regulations provide for the payment, subject to such exceptions or conditions as may be specified in the regulations, of compensation—

(a) if it is specified for the purpose in the regulations, by the NRA; or

(b) by such internal drainage board or boards as may be so specified,

to any officer or other employee of a drainage body who suffers loss of employment or loss or diminution of emoluments which is attributable to a scheme under section 3 above or anything done in pursuance of such a scheme.

(2) The appropriate Minister shall by regulations provide for the payment, subject to such exceptions or conditions as may be specified in the regulations, of compensation by the NRA—

(a) to any officer or other employee of an internal drainage board who suffers loss of employment or loss or diminution of emoluments which is attributable to an order under section 4 above or anything done in pursuance of such an order;

(b) to any officer or other employee of the NRA who suffers loss of employment or loss or diminution of emoluments which is attributable to an order under section 5 above or anything done in pursuance of such an order.

(3) Regulations under this section may include provision—

(a) as to the manner in which and the persons to whom any claim for compensation by virtue of the regulations is to be made; and

(b) for the determination of all questions arising under the regulations;

and may make different provision for different classes of person.

(4) In this section "the appropriate Minister"—

(a) in relation to employees of a drainage body wholly in Wales, means the Secretary of State;

(b) in relation to employees of a drainage body partly in Wales, means the Ministers; and

(c) in any other case, means the Minister;

but in relation to employees of the NRA, the powers and duties conferred or imposed on the appropriate Minister by this section shall be exercisable or, as the case may be, shall fall to be performed by either of the Ministers.

DEFINITIONS

"appropriate Minister": subs. (4).
"internal drainage board": s.1(1)(b).
"Minister": s.72(1).

GENERAL NOTE

Section 6 imposes a duty on the relevant Minister to make regulations providing for compensation for loss of office as a result of schemes and orders under ss.3–5 (see above). Compensation is payable by the NRA except where appropriate in a s.3 scheme, when an IDB may be liable to pay.

The material regulations are contained in the Land Drainage (Compensation) Regulations 1977 (S.I. 1977 No. 339).

General provision with respect to functions of drainage boards

Supervision of drainage boards by the NRA

7.—(1) The NRA may, for the purpose of securing—

(a) the efficient working and maintenance of existing drainage works; and

(b) the construction of such new drainage works as may be necessary,

give such general or special directions as it considers reasonable for the guidance of the internal drainage boards with respect to the exercise and performance by those boards of their powers and duties as such.

(2) Without prejudice to subsection (1) above, an internal drainage board shall not—

(a) except with the consent of the NRA, construct any drainage works or alter any existing drainage works, if the construction or alteration will in any way affect the interests of, or the working of any drainage works belonging to, any other drainage board; or

(b) otherwise than by way of maintaining an existing work, construct or alter any structure, appliance or channel for the discharge of water from their district into a main river except on such terms as may be agreed between the NRA and the internal drainage board or, in default of agreement, be determined by the relevant Minister.

(3) The consent of the NRA for the purposes of subsection (2)(a) above shall not be unreasonably withheld and may be given subject to reasonable conditions.

(4) If an internal drainage board acts in contravention of subsection (2) above, the NRA shall—

(a) have power itself to carry out and maintain any works and do any things which are, in its opinion, necessary in order to prevent or remedy any damage which may result, or has resulted, from the action of the internal drainage board; and

(b) be entitled to recover from that board the amount of any expenses reasonably incurred by the NRA in the exercise of that power.

(5) If any question arises under this section—

(a) whether the consent of the NRA is unreasonably withheld;

(b) whether any condition subject to which any consent of the NRA is given is reasonable; or

(c) whether any expenses have been reasonably incurred by the NRA in pursuance of this section;

that question shall be referred to the relevant Minister for decision.

(6) Where the relevant Minister gives any decision under this section, he shall make and cause to be laid before Parliament a report giving particulars of the question referred to him and of the reasons for his decision.

DEFINITIONS
"internal drainage board": s.1(1)(b).
"main river": s.72(1); see also Introduction and General Note.
"Minister": s.72(1).

GENERAL NOTE
Section 7 acknowledges the major rôle vested in the NRA in connection with main rivers and many other drainage and flood prevention duties and powers now contained in the Water Resources Act 1991. It also re-enacts similar provisions from the 1976 Act. It gives power to make directions; requires NRA consent before an IDB may construct or alter any drainage works, structure, appliance or channel; and gives default powers where an IDB acts without consent.

As to the meaning of the word "structure" see *Hobday* v. *Nicol* [1944] 1 All E.R. 302.

Concurrent powers of NRA

8. The powers of an internal drainage board in relation to their district under sections 21 and 23 below shall be exercisable concurrently with that board by the NRA and references in those sections and in section 24 below to the drainage board concerned shall be construed accordingly.

DEFINITIONS
"internal drainage board": s.1(1)(b).

GENERAL NOTE
See notes to ss.21, 23, and 24 below.

Default powers of the NRA

9.—(1) Subject to subsections (2) and (3) below but without prejudice to section 8 above, where in the opinion of the NRA any land is injured or likely to be injured by flooding or inadequate drainage that might be remedied wholly or partially by the exercise of drainage powers vested in any internal drainage board which either—

(a) are not being exercised at all; or

(b) in the opinion of the NRA, are not being exercised to the necessary extent,

the NRA may exercise all or any of those powers and also any power vested in that board for the purpose of defraying expenses incurred in the exercise by that board of those powers or for any purposes incidental to the exercise of those powers.

(2) Before exercising any powers under subsection (1) above the NRA shall give to the internal drainage board in whose default it proposes to exercise the powers not less than thirty days' notice of its intention to do so.

(3) If, before the end of the period of notice specified under subsection (2) above, the internal drainage board in question intimate in writing to the NRA their objection to the exercise by the NRA of the powers, the NRA shall not exercise the powers except with the consent of the relevant Minister.

(4) The relevant Minister may, if he thinks fit, cause a public local inquiry to be held with respect to an objection for the purposes of subsection (3) above.

(5) Where in pursuance of this section the NRA is exercising the powers of the drainage board for an internal drainage district, any person authorised in that behalf by the NRA may, so far as is reasonably necessary for the purpose of, and in connection with, the exercise by the NRA of those powers, at all reasonable times inspect and take copies of any deeds, maps, books, papers or other documents which—

(a) are in the possession of the board; and

(b) relate to land drainage or the provision of flood warning systems in that district.

(6) Any person who intentionally obstructs or impedes any person authorised as mentioned in subsection (5) above in the exercise of his powers under this section shall be liable, on summary conviction, to a fine not exceeding level 4 on the standard scale.

DEFINITIONS
  "internal drainage board": s.1(1)(b).
  "internal drainage district": s.1(1)(a).

GENERAL NOTE
  Section 9 gives default powers to the NRA to exercise the powers of an IDB if the former considers that the latter is not exercising them properly or at all. An IDB has a chance to object to the exercise of default powers and in that case ministerial approval is required, if deemed necessary after a public inquiry. When exercising powers the NRA may inspect and take copies of relevant documents in the possession of an IDB.
  Obstruction of the NRA in exercising default powers is an offence with a penalty not exceeding level 4.
  The current limits of the standard scale fine levels are : Level 1—£50; Level 2—£100; Level 3—£400; Level 4—£1,000; Level 5—£2,000.
  There is no statutory definition of injury in subs. (1).

Exercise of default powers by local authorities

10.—(1) The NRA may, on the application of the council of any county, metropolitan district or London borough, direct that the powers conferred by section 9 above on the NRA shall, as respects land in the area of the council, be exercisable by that council instead of by the NRA.

(2) If the NRA refuses to comply with any application under subsection (1) above, the council by which the application was made may appeal against the refusal to the relevant Minister and he may, if he thinks fit, require the NRA to comply with the application.

(3) Without prejudice to the power of the NRA to give a new direction, the NRA may—

(a) subject to the consent of the relevant Minister; and

(b) on giving the council concerned not less than six months' notice of its intention to do so,

revoke any direction given under subsection (1) above.

General Note

This section gives powers to a local authority to apply to the NRA to exercise the default powers under s.9 above.

Arrangements between drainage authorities

11.—(1) The NRA may enter into an agreement with any internal drainage board for the carrying out by the board, on such terms as to payment or otherwise as may be specified in the agreement, of any work in connection with a main river which the NRA is authorised to carry out.

(2) Notwithstanding any restriction by reference to a main river of the powers conferred on the NRA by section 165 of the Water Resources Act 1991, the NRA may—

(a) with the consent of an internal drainage board, carry out and maintain in that board's district any works which the board might carry out or maintain, on such terms as to payment or otherwise as may be agreed between the board and the NRA; or

(b) agree to contribute to the expense of the carrying out or maintenance of any works by any internal drainage board.

(3) An internal drainage board may—

(a) with the consent of an internal drainage board for any other district, carry out and maintain in that other district any works which the first-mentioned board might carry out or maintain within their own district, on such terms as to payment or otherwise as may be agreed between the boards; or

(b) agree to contribute to the expense of the carrying out or maintenance of any works by the internal drainage board for any other district.

(4) Any expense incurred by an internal drainage board under subsection (3) above shall be defrayed as if the expense had been incurred in their own district.

Definitions

"internal drainage board": s.1(1)(b).

General Note

Section 165 of the Water Resources Act 1991 vests in the NRA its powers in relation to main rivers, which are analogous to those contained in s.14 (see below).

Section 11 gives flexible powers for the NRA and an IDB to carry out work on each other's behalf and for similar arrangements between IDBs. See also s.17(4) of the Act, which authorises an IDB to carry out work outside its own district for the benefit of its own district.

The NRA or an IDB may carry out such work on behalf of a person authorised to have work carried out even if the land is in a nature reserve (see s.22 of the National Parks and Access to Countryside Act 1949).

Duties with respect to the environment and recreation

General environmental and recreational duties

12.—(1) It shall be the duty of each of the Ministers, of the NRA and of every internal drainage board, in formulating or considering any proposals relating to any functions of such a board (including, in the case of such a board, their own functions)—

   (a) so far as may be consistent—

         (i) with the purposes of any enactment relating to the functions of such a board; and

         (ii) in the case of the Secretary of State, with his duties under section 2 of the Water Industry Act 1991,

     so to exercise any power conferred with respect to the proposals on that Minister, the NRA or, as the case may be, the board as to further the conservation and enhancement of natural beauty and the conservation of flora, fauna and geological or physiographical features of special interest;

   (b) to have regard to the desirability of protecting and conserving buildings, sites and objects of archaeological, architectural or historic interest; and

   (c) to take into account any effect which the proposals would have on the beauty or amenity of any rural or urban area or on any such flora, fauna, features, buildings, sites or objects.

(2) Subject to subsection (1) above, it shall be the duty of each of the Ministers, of the NRA and of every internal drainage board, in formulating or considering any proposals relating to any functions of such a board (including, in the case of such a board, their own functions)—

   (a) to have regard to the desirability of preserving for the public any freedom of access to areas of woodland, mountains, moor, heath, down, cliff or foreshore and other places of natural beauty;

   (b) to have regard to the desirability of maintaining the availability to the public of any facility for visiting or inspecting any building, site or object of archaeological, architectural or historic interest; and

   (c) to take into account any effect which the proposals would have on any such freedom of access or on the availability of any such facility.

(3) Subsections (1) and (2) above shall apply so as to impose duties on an internal drainage board in relation to—

   (a) any proposals relating to the functions of the NRA or of a water undertaker or sewerage undertaker;

   (b) any proposals relating to the management, by the company holding an appointment as such an undertaker, of any land for the time being held by that company for any purpose whatever (whether or not connected with the carrying out of the functions of a water undertaker or sewerage undertaker); and

   (c) any proposal which by virtue of section 156(7) of the Water Industry Act 1991 (disposals of protected land) falls to be treated for the purposes of section 3 of that Act as a proposal relating to the functions of a water undertaker or sewerage undertaker,

as they apply in relation to proposals relating to the functions of an internal drainage board but as if, for that purpose, the reference in subsection (1)(a) above to enactments relating to the functions of such a board were a reference to enactments relating to that to which the proposal relates.

(4) Subject to obtaining the consent of any navigation authority, harbour authority or conservancy authority before doing anything which causes navigation which is subject to the control of that authority to be obstructed or otherwise interfered with, it shall be the duty of every internal drainage board to take such steps as are—

   (a) reasonably practicable; and

   (b) consistent with the purposes of the enactments relating to the functions of that board,

for securing, so long as that board have rights to the use of water or land associated with water, that those rights are exercised so as to ensure that the water or land is made available for recreational purposes and is so made available in the best manner.

(5) It shall be the duty of every internal drainage board, in determining what steps to take in performance of any duty imposed by virtue of subsection (4) above, to take into account the needs of persons who are chronically sick or disabled.

(6) Nothing in this section or the following provisions of this Act shall require recreational facilities made available by an internal drainage board to be made available free of charge.

(7) In this section—
    "building" includes structure; and
    "harbour authority" means a harbour authority within the meaning of the Prevention of Oil Pollution Act 1971.

DEFINITIONS
    "building": subs. (7).
    "conservancy authority": s.72(1).
    "internal drainage board": s.1(1)(b).
    "Minister": s.72(1).
    "navigation authority": s.72(1).

GENERAL NOTE
    Section 12 consolidates the introduction in the Water Act 1989 of new environmental and recreational duties re-enacted in the Water Resources Act 1991. It acknowledges heightened public interest in the environment and requirements for recreational availability. Drainage authorities are primarily concerned with wetland areas and this section recognises the special environmental importance of those areas, and the impact which the exercise of drainage authority powers may have on those wetlands. European Community Environmental Directives may also affect the exercise by drainage authorities of their powers. See, for example, the *Leybucht Dikes* case discussed at p. 152 *et seq.* of Water Law 1991, Vol. 2, Issue 5. This was a case brought against the German government for breach of Directive 79/409, which deals with conservation of birds and in particular bird habitats.

Subs. (1)
    This sets out the environmental duties imposed on the Ministers, NRA and IDBs in the exercise of their functions. In the case of subs. (1)(a) (furthering and enhancing natural beauty and conservation) it is effective where consistent with the exercise of their statutory functions. Subss. (1)(b) and (1)(c) are not so qualified.

Subs. (2)
    This sets out the (non-qualified) recreational duties and imposes duties on IDBs to make land or water subject to their control available (but not free of charge) for recreational purposes where availability is reasonably practicable and consistent with its statutory functions.
    Breach of the duties contained in this section may render a drainage authority liable to have its decision judicially reviewed if a person is aggrieved by a decision made by that authority which is in breach of its duties under this section. The ability to bring judicial review proceedings is determined by the *locus standi* of the party bringing the application (see *R.* v. *Poole Borough Council*, ex p. *Beebee* (1991) 2 P.L.R. 27). For consideration of this case see [1991] J.P.L., p. 293 *et seq.* This case involved representatives of the Worldwide Fund for Nature and the British Herpetological Society applying for a review of the decision by Poole Borough Council granting itself planning permission for a development of land at Canford Heath, part of which was an SSSI. The Nature Conservancy Council were statutory consultees but failed to persuade the council not to proceed. The applicants also failed to persuade the NCC to apply for judicial review, and therefore did so themselves.
    The judge accepted that both applicants did have *locus standi* (albeit that the WWF were brought into the action by consent), although not parties to the original consultation and decision.

Environmental duties with respect to sites of special interest

13.—(1) Where the Nature Conservancy Council for England or the Countryside Council for Wales are of the opinion that any area of land in England or, as the case may be, in Wales—

(a) is of special interest by reason of its flora, fauna or geological or physiographical features; and

(b) may at any time be affected by schemes, works, operations or activities of an internal drainage board,

that Council shall notify the fact that the land is of special interest for that reason to every internal drainage board whose works, operations or activities may affect the land.

(2) Where a National Park authority or the Broads Authority is of the opinion that any area of land in a National Park or in the Broads—

(a) is land in relation to which the matters for the purposes of which section 12 above has effect are of particular importance; and

(b) may at any time be affected by schemes, works, operations or activities of an internal drainage board,

the National Park authority or Broads Authority shall notify the fact that the land is such land, and the reasons why those matters are of particular importance in relation to the land, to every internal drainage board whose works, operations or activities may affect the land.

(3) Where an internal drainage board have received a notification under subsection (1) or (2) above with respect to any land, the board shall consult the notifying body before carrying out any works, operations or activities which appear to the board to be likely—

(a) to destroy or damage any of the flora, fauna, or geological or physiographical features by reason of which the land is of special interest; or

(b) significantly to prejudice anything the importance of which is one of the reasons why the matters mentioned in subsection (2) above are of particular importance in relation to that land.

(4) Subsection (3) above shall not apply in relation to anything done in an emergency where particulars of what is done and of the emergency are notified to the Nature Conservancy Council for England, the Countryside Council for Wales, the National Park authority in question or, as the case may be, the Broads Authority as soon as practicable after that thing is done.

(5) In this section—

"the Broads" has the same meaning as in the Norfolk and Suffolk Broads Act 1988; and

"National Park authority" means a National Park Committee or a joint or special planning board for a National Park.

DEFINITIONS
"broads": subs. (5).
"internal drainage board": s.1(1)(b).
"national park authority": subs. (5).

GENERAL NOTE

Section 13 consolidates the provision for notification and consultation brought in by s.9 of the Water Act 1989, and alterations to the constitution and functions of the Nature Conservancy Council (as was) in the Environmental Protection Act 1990.

The section allows the Nature Conservancy organisation, National Park Authority or Broads Authority to notify an IDB if land is of special interest. Following such notification an IDB must consult the relevant body before carrying out works, operations or activities which may fall within subs. 3(a) or (b).

Emergency operations are exempted subject to *ex post facto* notification: see *Southern Water Authority* v. *Nature Conservancy Council* (1991) 135 S.J.L.B. 53 for consideration of the extent of the duty of consultation.

In addition to the duty under subs. (2), any drainage body in the Norfolk and Suffolk Broads area must comply with the Code of Practice issued by the Broads Authority under para. 33 of Sched. 3 to the Norfolk and Suffolk Broads Authority Act 1988. (See also note to s.12 regarding *locus standi* in cases of applications for judicial review).

PART II

PROVISIONS FOR FACILITATING OR SECURING THE DRAINAGE OF LAND

General powers

General drainage powers of boards and local authorities

14.—(1) Subject to section 11 above and subsection (4) and section 17 below—

  (a) every drainage board acting within the internal drainage district for which they are the drainage board; and

  (b) every local authority acting either—

      (i) for the purpose of carrying out works in pursuance of a scheme under section 18 below; or

      (ii) so far as may be necessary for the purpose of preventing flooding or mitigating any damage caused by flooding in their area,

shall have the powers specified in subsection (2) below.

(2) The powers mentioned in subsection (1) above are the powers, otherwise than in connection with a main river or the banks of such a river—

  (a) to maintain existing works, that is to say, to cleanse, repair or otherwise maintain in a due state of efficiency any existing watercourse or drainage work;

  (b) to improve any existing works, that is to say, to deepen, widen, straighten or otherwise improve any existing watercourse or remove or alter mill dams, weirs or other obstructions to watercourses, or raise, widen or otherwise improve any existing drainage work;

  (c) to construct new works, that is to say, to make any new watercourse or drainage work or erect any machinery or do any other act (other than an act referred to in paragraph (a) or (b) above) required for the drainage of any land.

(3) Subject to section 11 above and subsection (4) and section 17 below, an internal drainage board or local authority that desire, otherwise than in connection with a main river or the banks of such a river, to carry out any drainage works for the benefit of their district or area in lands outside that district or area shall have the same powers for that purpose as are conferred by this Act on persons interested in land which is capable of being drained or improved and desiring to carry out drainage works for that purpose.

(4) Nothing in this section—

  (a) authorises any person to enter on the land of any person except for the purpose of maintaining existing works; or

  (b) authorises a county council to exercise any power except in accordance with section 16 below.

(5) Where injury is sustained by any person by reason of the exercise by a drainage board or local authority of any of their powers under this section, the board or authority shall be liable to make full compensation to the injured person.

(6) In case of dispute, the amount of the compensation payable under subsection (5) above shall be determined by the Lands Tribunal.

(7) Any expenses incurred by an internal drainage board under subsection (3) above shall be defrayed as if the expenses had been incurred in their district.

DEFINITIONS

  "construct": subs. (2)(c).

  "improve": subs. (2)(b).

  "internal drainage district": s.1(1)(a).

  "main river": s.72(1).

  "maintain": subs. (2)(a).

GENERAL NOTE

Section 14, which substantially re-enacts s.17 of the 1976 Act, is the section that sets out the powers vested in the drainage authority (as defined in subs. (1)). The powers are defined in subs. (2). Subs. (3) gives the drainage authority the power to exercise its powers as if it were in effect a private landowner, subject to the qualifications set out in subs. (4) and also to the requirements for consents from third party authorities provided for in ss.11 and 17, and the qualifications in subs. (4).

Subsections (5) and (6) set out compensation provisions, whereby parties suffering injury as a result of the exercise of powers under this section can obtain compensation, if necessary, through the Lands Tribunal.

Subs. (2)

The powers granted under this section are permissive and not mandatory. Hence a drainage authority will not generally be liable for damage caused as a result of failure to exercise these powers (see *East Sussex Catchment Board* v. *Kent* [1940] 4 All E.R. 527). This may be different if the power derives originally from a Local Act which imposed a duty. It is also possible that authorities may be liable in nuisance for the consequences of the exercise or failure to exercise their powers if they knew or ought to have known the consequences of their acts or omissions. See *Russell* v. *Barnet London Borough* (1984) E.G. 975 and *Leakey* v. *National Trust for Places of Historic Interest and Natural Beauty* [1980] Q.B. 485.

Any person suffering damage will therefore have a choice between pursuing a claim at common law or claiming statutory compensation.

Subss. (5) and (6)

Statutory compensation, if not agreed, is determined by the Lands Tribunal [address 48/49 Chancery Lane, London WC2A 1JR]. Proceedings are commenced by a Notice of Reference, and follow Lands Tribunal rules, copies of which are available from the Tribunal. The claimant will need to show that the works in question caused the damage in question. He will also need to show that but for the Act, the authority would have been liable at common law.

Compensation can be for interference with rights, *e.g.* fishing rights (see *Burgess* v. *Gwynedd River Authority* (1972) 24 P. & C.R. 150). It can also be for damage to property itself when the compensation is determined by the difference in value of the property before and after the works have been done (see *Farmer Giles* v. *Wessex Water Authority* [1990] 18 E.G. 102).

As to the environmental and recreational duties and obligations in relation to the exercise of s.14 powers, see ss.12 and 13 and the general notes to those sections.

Disposal of spoil by boards and local authorities

15.—(1) Subject to subsections (2) and (3) and sections 16 and 17 below, an internal drainage board or local authority may—
  (a) without making payment for it, appropriate and dispose of any matter removed in the course of the carrying out of any work for widening, deepening or dredging any ordinary watercourse; and
  (b) deposit any matter so removed on the banks of such a watercourse, or on such width of land adjoining such a watercourse as is sufficient to enable the matter to be removed and deposited by mechanical means in one operation.

(2) The powers conferred on a local authority by this section shall not be exercisable except—
  (a) for the purpose of carrying out works in pursuance of a scheme under section 18 below; or
  (b) so far as may be necessary for the purpose of preventing flooding or mitigating any damage caused by flooding in their area.

(3) Subsection (1) above shall not authorise the deposit of any matter if the matter deposited would constitute a statutory nuisance within the meaning of Part III of the Environmental Protection Act 1990.

(4) Where injury is sustained by any person by reason of the exercise by an internal drainage board or local authority of their powers under subsection (1)(b) above—
  (a) the board or authority may, if they think fit, pay to him such compensation as they may determine; and
  (b) where the injury could have been avoided if those powers had been

exercised with reasonable care, subsections (5) and (6) of section 14 above shall apply as if the injury had been sustained by reason of the exercise by the board or authority of their powers under that section.

(5) An internal drainage board or local authority, on the one hand, and the council of any district or London borough, on the other, may enter into an agreement providing—

(a) for the disposal by the council or any matter removed as mentioned in subsection (1) above; and

(b) for the payment by the board or authority to the council, in respect of the disposal of the matter by the council, of such sum as may be provided by the agreement.

DEFINITIONS
"internal drainage board": s.1(1)(b).
"ordinary watercourse": s.72(1).

GENERAL NOTE
This section deals with the disposal of spoil (as defined in subs. (1)(a)) as a consequence of the exercise of drainage powers. The meaning of the expression of "one operation" defined in subs. (1)(b) was considered in the case of *Stapleford* v. *Severn Trent Water Authority* (1989) 291 R.V.R. 85 as meaning a single operation of one machine and does not embrace operations by other machines.

Drainage authorities are given discretionary powers to pay compensation for damage suffered as a result of disposal of spoil (subs. (4)(a)) but must pay compensation if the damage could have been avoided. They may also (subs. (5)) pay a district council or London Borough to remove such spoil.

See ss.14 and 15 as to environmental duties and duties to notify which may be of relevance. See also *Southern Water Authority* v. *Nature Conservancy Council* (1991) 135 S.J.L.B. 53.

As to subs. (3), statutory nuisance, see s.79 of the Environmental Protection Act 1990 *et seq.* Section 79(1)(e) would appear to be relevant.

Exercise of local authority powers under sections 14 and 15

16.—(1) Subject to subsection (3) below, where the powers conferred by section 14 or 15 above on a non-metropolitan district council are not exercised by that council, they may be exercised by the county council—

(a) at the request of the council of the district; or

(b) after not less than six weeks' notice given in writing by the county council to the district council.

(2) Subject to subsection (3) below, where the powers conferred by section 14(1) above on a metropolitan district council or London borough council or the Common Council of the City of London are not exercised by that council, they may be exercised by the NRA—

(a) at the request of the council; or

(b) after not less than six weeks' notice given in writing by the NRA to the council;

and any expenses incurred by the NRA under subsection (3) above shall be recoverable from the council concerned by the NRA summarily as a civil debt.

(3) Where the council to whom a notice has been given for the purposes of subsection (1)(b) or (2)(b) above—

(a) appeal against the notice to the Secretary of State before it expires; and

(b) inform the county council or, as the case may be, the NRA of the appeal,

the powers to which the notice relates shall not be exercised in pursuance of the notice by the county council or, as the case may be, the NRA unless it is confirmed by the Secretary of State.

DEFINITIONS
"Secretary of State": s.72(1).

GENERAL NOTE
This section gives power for a county council to accept on request or require the transfer of drainage functions exercisable by a district council. Analogous arrangements exist between Metropolitan and London Boroughs and the NRA.

Where a district council or metropolitan authority objects to the exercise by the county council or NRA respectively of its drainage powers, it may appeal to the Secretary of State, who shall either confirm the proposed exercise of powers or not.

Supervision of local authority powers under sections 14 to 16

17.—(1) A local authority shall not carry out or maintain any drainage works authorised by sections 14 to 16 above in connection with any water-course except with the consent of, and in accordance with any reasonable conditions imposed by, the NRA.

(2) Before giving any consent or imposing any condition under subsection (1) above with respect to any drainage works in connection with a water-course under the control of an internal drainage board the NRA shall consult with the internal drainage board.

(3) A consent required under subsection (1) above—

(a) shall not be reasonably withheld; and

(b) shall be deemed to have been given if it is neither given nor refused within two months after application for it is made.

(4) Any question arising under this section whether the consent of the NRA is unreasonably withheld, or whether any condition imposed by the NRA is reasonable, shall be referred to and determined by the Ministers.

(5) Subsection (1) above shall not apply to any work carried out in an emergency, but a local authority carrying out any work excepted by this subsection shall, as soon as practicable, inform the NRA in writing of the carrying out of the work and of the circumstances in which it was carried out.

DEFINITIONS
"internal drainage board": s.1(1)(b).
"Ministers": s.72(1).

GENERAL NOTE
This section vests in the NRA a supervisory rôle where any local authority exercises drainage powers under the Act. Any works by a local authority require NRA consent on the terms set out in subss. (3) and (4), unless carried out in an emergency. The Act does not define the word "emergency".

Drainage of small areas

18.—(1) Where—

(a) the NRA is of the opinion that any land is capable of improvement by drainage works but that the constitution for that purpose of an internal drainage district would not be practicable; or

(b) a local authority other than a district council is of that opinion in relation to any land in their area,

the NRA or, as the case may be, that local authority may, in accordance with the provisions of a scheme made by it or them under this section, enter on the land and carry out such drainage works as appear to it or them desirable.

(2) Schedule 4 to this Act shall have effect with respect to the making of a scheme under this section.

(3) A scheme under this section must state—

(a) the works proposed to be carried out;

(b) the area to be improved by the works;

(c) the estimated expenses (including administrative expenses) of the carrying out of the works;

(d) the maximum amount to be recoverable by the NRA or local authority in respect of those expenses; and

(e) the manner in which the expenses of carrying out and maintaining the works are to be apportioned amongst the lands comprised in the area to be improved.

(4) Subject to subsection (6) and (7) below, the amount stated in a scheme in pursuance of subsection (3)(c) above shall not exceed an amount equal to £50 for each hectare in the area to be improved.

(5) The following expenses, that is to say—

(a) those incurred by the NRA or a local authority under this section in the carrying out of drainage works, to an amount not exceeding the amount stated in the scheme in pursuance of subsection (3)(d) above; and

(b) those incurred by the NRA or a local authority in maintaining works carried out by the NRA or, as the case may be, that authority under this section,

shall, according to the apportionment provided for by the scheme, be recoverable by the NRA or that authority from the several owners of the lands to which the scheme relates.

(6) Each of the Ministers shall have power to exempt a scheme from the limit imposed by subsection (4) above if it appears to him that the works proposed to be carried out are urgently required in the public interest.

(7) Each of the Ministers shall have power by order made by statutory instrument from time to time to vary the limit imposed by subsection (4) above; but no such order shall have effect unless it is approved by a resolution of each House of Parliament.

(8) A scheme made under this section shall be a local land charge.

DEFINITIONS
"internal drainage district": s.1(1)(a).
"Ministers": s.72(1).

GENERAL NOTE
Section 18 sets out arrangements for the execution and maintenance of drainage works in small areas by the NRA or local authorities, as the case may be. Small areas are land areas which would not in themselves justify the creation of an IDB.

Where a local authority exercises its powers under this section it must consult the NRA (Sched. 4, para. 1).

The NRA or local authority must give proper publicity to the scheme (see Sched. 4) and the Minister must determine whether or not the scheme is to proceed if there are objections. A public inquiry may be held. Subsection (3) sets out the various matters which a scheme must state.

Subsection (4) provides that the maximum amount recoverable from land owners whose land is affected by the scheme shall not exceed £50 per hectare.

The Ministers do, however, have discretion to increase this limit if the works are urgent.

Arrangements as to works etc. with navigation and conservancy authorities

19.—(1) Subject to subsections (2) and (3) below, an internal drainage board, with a view to improving the drainage of any land situated in their district, may enter into an arrangement with a navigation authority or conservancy authority for any of the following purposes, that is to say—

(a) the transfer to the board of—

(i) the whole or any part of the undertaking of the navigation authority or conservancy authority or of any of the rights, powers, duties, liabilities and obligations of that authority; or

(ii) any property vested in that authority as such;

(b) the alteration or improvement by the board of any of the works of the navigation authority or conservancy authority;

(c) the making of payments by the board to the navigation authority or conservancy authority or by that authority to the board in respect of any matter for which provision is made by the arrangement.

(2) An internal drainage board shall not enter into any arrangement under this section in relation to a main river or the banks of a main river or in relation to any drainage works in connection with a main river.

(3) The exercise by an internal drainage board of their power to enter into an arrangement under this section shall require the approval of the relevant Minister and the Secretary of State.

(4) Where an internal drainage board are intending to enter into an arrangement under this section, they shall publish a notice of their intention in such manner as may be directed by the relevant Minister.

(5) Where an arrangement has been made under this section, an internal drainage board shall cause a notice under subsection (6) below to be published in the London Gazette in such form as may be prescribed by regulations made by the relevant Minister.

(6) A notice under this subsection is a notice—

(a) stating that the arrangement has been made; and

(b) specifying the place at which a copy of the arrangement may be inspected by persons interested.

DEFINITIONS
"conservation authority": s.72(1).
"internal drainage board": s.1(1)(b).
"main river": s.72(1).
"Minister": s.72(2).
"navigation authority": s.72(1).
"Secretary of State": s.72(2).

GENERAL NOTE
Section 19 gives an IDB the power to enter into arrangements with navigation and/or conservation authorities, so as to take over the functions of that authority with a view to improving the drainage of any land in its district.

The section sets out the procedure to be adopted when such arrangements are entered into and afterwards.

Arrangements with other persons for carrying out drainage works

20.—(1) Subject to subsection (3) below, an internal drainage board may, by agreement with any person and at that person's expense, carry out and maintain, whether within or outside their district, any drainage works which that person is entitled to carry out and maintain.

(2) Any local authority other than the council of a non metropolitan district may, by agreement with any person and at that person's expense, carry out within the local authority's area any drainage works which that person is entitled to carry out.

(3) The powers conferred on an internal drainage board by subsection (1) above shall not be exercisable in connection with a main river, the banks of such a river or any drainage works in connection with a main river.

(4) The obligation of any person under this section to meet the expenses of any works shall be subject to section 59(6) below.

DEFINITIONS
"internal drainage board": s.1(1)(b).

GENERAL NOTE
Section 20 gives power to drainage authorities, except county councils, to undertake drainage work on due payment on behalf of any person authorised to have works carried out.

Such work may be grant-aided (see s.59). If so, that charge for the works will be net of the grant element.

Enforcement of obligations to repair watercourses, bridges, etc.

21.—(1) This section applies to any obligation to which any person was subject, before the commencement of this Act, by reason of tenure, custom, prescription or otherwise, except an obligation under an enactment re-enacted in this Act or the Water Resources Act 1991.

(2) If any person—

(a) is liable, by reason of any obligation to which this section applies, to do any work in relation to any watercourse, bridge or drainage work (whether by way of repair, maintenance or otherwise); and

(b) fails to do the work,

the drainage board concerned may serve a notice on that person requiring him to do the necessary work with all reasonable and proper despatch.

(3) Subject to section 107(2) of the Water Resources Act 1991, the powers conferred by this section shall not be exercisable in connection with a main river, the banks of such a river or any drainage works in connection with such a river.

(4) If any person fails, within seven days, to comply with a notice served on him under subsection (2) above by the drainage board concerned, the board may do all such things as are necessary for that purpose.

(5) Any expenses reasonably incurred, in the exercise of their powers under this section, by the drainage board concerned may be recovered from the person liable to repair.

(6) Subject to section 8 above, references in this section to the drainage board concerned—

(a) in relation to any watercourse, bridge or drainage works in an internal drainage district, are references to the drainage board for that district; and

(b) in relation to any other watercourse, bridge or drainage works, are references to the NRA.

DEFINITIONS

"drainage board": subs. (6).

"main river": s.72(1).

GENERAL NOTE

This section concerns drainage or other works which third parties are bound to carry out. It gives drainage boards power to compel third parties to carry out these works, and default powers if they do not.

Section 107(2) of the Water Resources Act 1991 relates to the NRA's powers over main rivers.

Powers of Ministers to authorise landowners to carry out drainage works

22.—(1) Where—

(a) any persons interested in any land are of the opinion that it is capable of improvement by drainage works; but

(b) the works cannot be carried out by reason of the objection or disability of any person whose land would be entered upon, cut through or interfered with by or for the purposes of the works,

those persons may present an application to the appropriate Minister for an order under this section authorising them to carry out such drainage works as are expedient with a view to the improvement of the land.

(2) An application for an order under this section—

(a) shall be in the prescribed form; and

(b) shall contain particulars of the proposed works and the persons by whom they are to be carried out and such further particulars as the appropriate Minister may prescribe or require;

and the applicants shall give such security for expenses as may be required by the appropriate Minister.

(3) Notice of any application for an order under this section, of the place where it can be inspected and of the period within which objections to the

proposed works may be made to the appropriate Minister shall be given in the prescribed manner—
  (a) to all persons not parties to the application whose lands are proposed to be entered upon, cut through or interfered with;
  (b) to the NRA; and
  (c) to any internal drainage board for any district within which all or any of the proposed works are to be carried out.

(4) If, where an application for an order under this section has been made—
  (a) an objection to the proposed works has been made to the appropriate Minister, within the prescribed period, by any person interested or in any way affected by the proposed works; and
  (b) that objection is not withdrawn,
the appropriate Minister shall forthwith cause a public inquiry to be held in the locality in which the proposed works are to be carried out.

(5) On an application for an order under this section, the appropriate Minister—
  (a) where either no objection has been made as mentioned in subsection (4) above or every such objection has been withdrawn; or
  (b) in any other case, after receiving the report of the inquiry under subsection (4) above,
shall, in his discretion, either refuse to authorise the carrying out of the proposed works or by order authorise the carrying out of the works with or without alteration.

(6) Subject to subsection (7) below, the persons authorised by an order under this section to carry out works shall have full power to carry out the works and to maintain them for ever thereafter.

(7) Where an order under this section is made, every person interested in the land affected by the order (other than any person who is one of those authorised to carry out the works) shall be entitled to compensation for any injury suffered by him in respect of that interest by reason of the works; and, in case of a dispute as to the amount of the compensation payable, the amount shall be determined by the Lands Tribunal.

(8) No order of the appropriate Minister under this section shall authorise any work whereby the streams, reservoirs or feeders supplying any ornamental waters will be cut through, diverted or interfered with otherwise than by agreement and with the consent of the persons to whom such ornamental waters belong.

(9) In this section "the appropriate Minister"—
  (a) in relation to England, means the Minister; and
  (b) in relation to Wales, means the Secretary of State.

DEFINITIONS
  "appropriate minister": subs. (9).
  "internal drainage board": s.1(1)(b).
  "minister": s.72(2).

GENERAL NOTE
  Section 22 gives power to the Minister, on application by interested landowners, to authorise the carrying out by them of drainage works to improve land where those works entail cutting through or interfering with the land of another person, who objects to the proposed works. Regulations as to the "prescribed form" and "manner" (see subss. (2) and (3)) are contained in S.O. 1932, 64, reg. 6(1).
  The section sets out the parties to be consulted (subs. (3)); provisions for an inquiry (subs. (4)); and compensation (subs. (7)). Subsection (8) contains a protection in favour of the owners of ornamental waters (this expression is not defined).
  The exercise of ministerial discretion under this section will be subject to the environmental duties imposed by s.12 and elsewhere.

Control of flow of watercourses etc.

Prohibition on obstructions etc. in watercourses

23.—(1) No person shall—
(a) erect any mill dam, weir or other like obstruction to the flow of any ordinary watercourse or raise or otherwise alter any such obstruction; or
(b) erect any culvert that would be likely to affect the flow of any ordinary watercourse or alter any culvert in a manner that would be likely to affect any such flow,

without the consent in writing of the drainage board concerned.

(2) The drainage board concerned may require the payment of an application fee by a person who applies to them for their consent under this section; and the amount of that fee shall be £50 or such other sum as may be specified by order made by the Ministers.

(3) Where an application is made to the drainage board concerned for their consent under this section—
(a) the consent is not to be unreasonably withheld; and
(b) if the board fail within two months after the relevant day to notify the applicant in writing of their determination with respect to the application, they shall be deemed to have consented.

(4) In subsection (3) above "the relevant day," in relation to an application for a consent under this section, means whichever is the later of—
(a) the day on which the application is made; and
(b) if at the time when the application is made an application fee is required to be paid, the day on which the liability to pay that fee is discharged.

(5) If any question arises under this section whether the consent of the drainage board concerned is unreasonably withheld, that question shall be referred to a single arbitrator to be agreed between the parties or, failing such agreement, to be appointed by the President of the Institution of Civil Engineers on the application of either party.

(6) Nothing in this section shall apply—
(a) to any works under the control of a navigation authority, harbour authority or conservancy authority; or
(b) to any works carried out or maintained under or in pursuance of any Act or any order having the force of an Act.

(7) The power of the Ministers to make an order under subsection (2) above shall be exercisable by statutory instrument subject to annulment in pursuance of a resolution of either House of Parliament.

(8) Subject to section 8 above, references in this section and section 24 below to the drainage board concerned—
(a) in relation to a watercourse in an internal drainage district, are references to the drainage board for that district; and
(b) in relation to any other watercourse, are references to the NRA.

DEFINITIONS
"conservancy authority": s.72(1).
"drainage board concerned": subs. (8).
"harbour": s.72(1).
"Ministers": s.72(1).
"navigation": s.72(1).
"ordinary watercourse": s.72(1).
"relevant day": subs. (4).

GENERAL NOTE
Section 23 substantially re-enacts s.28 of the 1976 Act and gives a drainage board controls over obstruction in non-main rivers analogous to those given to the NRA by s.109 of the Water Resources Act 1991.

The matters set out at subs. (1)(a) and (b) are subject to consent being given by the drainage board, such consent not to be unreasonably withheld.

Subsection (5) provides for an arbitration procedure if an applicant considers that consent has been unreasonably withheld.

The Act does not define the words "mill", "dam", "weir" or "culvert".

Contraventions of prohibition on obstructions etc.

24.—(1) If any obstruction is erected or raised or otherwise altered, or any culvert is erected or altered, in contravention of section 23 above, it shall constitute a nuisance in respect of which the drainage board concerned may serve upon such person as is specified in subsection (2) below a notice requiring him to abate the nuisance within a period to be specified in the notice.

(2) The person upon whom a notice may be served under subsection (1) above is—

(a) in a case where the person by whom the obstruction has been erected or raised or otherwise altered has, at the time when the notice is served, power to remove the obstruction, that person; and

(b) in any other case, any person having power to remove the obstruction.

(3) If any person acts in contravention of, or fails to comply with, any notice served under subsection (1) above he shall be guilty of an offence and liable, on summary conviction—

(a) to a fine not exceeding level 5 on the standard scale; and

(b) if the contravention or failure is continued after conviction, to a further fine not exceeding £40 for every day on which the contravention or failure is so continued.

(4) If any person acts in contravention of, or fails to comply with, any notice served under subsection (1) above, the drainage board concerned may, without prejudice to any proceedings under subsection (3) above—

(a) take such action as may be necessary to remedy the effect of the contravention or failure; and

(b) recover the expenses reasonably incurred by them in doing so from the person in default.

DEFINITIONS
    "drainage board": s.23(8).

GENERAL NOTE
    Section 24 contains the enforcement provisions which tie in with s.23. Where a person contravenes s.23 it is a nuisance and the drainage board may serve a notice to abate that nuisance. Failure to comply with such a notice is an offence and gives the drainage board default powers to remove the obstruction and recover the expense of so doing. Maximum fines at level 5 are currently £2,000.

Powers to require works for maintaining flow of watercourse

25.—(1) Subject to section 26 below, where any ordinary watercourse is in such a condition that the proper flow of water is impeded, then, unless the condition is attributable to subsidence due to mining operations (including brine pumping), the drainage board or local authority concerned may, by notice served on a person falling within subsection (3) below, require that person to remedy that condition.

(2) For the purposes of this section in its application in relation to any watercourse—

(a) the drainage board concerned is the drainage board for the internal drainage district in which the watercourse is situated; and

(b) the local authority concerned is the local authority for the area where the land as respects which the powers under this section are exercisable is situated;

but references in this section to the drainage board concerned shall, in relation to a watercourse which is not in an internal drainage district, be construed as references to the NRA.

(3) Subject to subsection (4) below, a notice under this section in relation to a watercourse may be served on—

(a) any person having control of the part of the watercourse where any impediment occurs; or

(b) any person owning or occupying land adjoining that part; or

(c) any person to whose act or default the condition of the watercourse mentioned in subsection (1) above is due.

(4) No notice under this section requiring any person to carry out any work on land not owned or occupied by him shall be served without the consent of the owner and the occupier of the land, except in a case where it is not practicable, after reasonable inquiry, to ascertain the name and address of the owner or occupier.

(5) A notice under this section shall indicate—

(a) the nature of the works to be carried out and the period within which they are to be carried out; and

(b) the right of appeal to a magistrates' court and the period within which such an appeal may be brought under section 27 below.

(6) Subject to the right of appeal provided by section 27 below, if the person upon whom a notice is served under this section fails to carry out the works indicated by the notice within the period so indicated—

(a) the drainage board or local authority concerned may themselves carry out the works and recover from that person the expenses reasonably incurred by them in doing so; and

(b) without prejudice to their right to exercise that power, that person shall be guilty of an offence and liable, on summary conviction, to a fine not exceeding level 4 on the standard scale.

(7) In proceedings by the drainage board or local authority concerned for the recovery of any expenses under subsection (6) above it shall not be open to the defendant to raise any question which he could not have raised on an appeal under section 27 below.

(8) Nothing in this section shall affect the right of an owner or occupier to recover from the other, under the terms of any lease or other contract, the amount of any expenses incurred by him under this section or recovered from him by the drainage board or local authority concerned.

DEFINITIONS

"internal drainage district": s.1(1)(a).
"ordinary watercourse": s.72(1).

GENERAL NOTE

This section vests power in drainage boards (as defined in subs. (2)) and local authorities to ensure that a proper flow of water in ordinary watercourses (*i.e.* non-main rivers) is not impeded. The section gives default powers to carry out necessary works and recover expenses, where a notice has been served on a person (as defined by subs. (3)) and not complied with. This notice must comply with subs. (5).

Subsection (6)(b) additionally creates an offence of impeding ordinary watercourses. Maximum fine is at level 4, currently £1,000.

See notes to s.27 as to the appeals procedure.

Competing jurisdictions under section 25

26.—(1) Before exercising their powers under section 25 above in relation to any watercourse or part of a watercourse a local authority shall, according to whether or not the watercourse or part is in an internal drainage district, notify either the drainage board for that district or the NRA.

(2) Where a local authority have powers (otherwise than under section 25 above) for securing the appropriate flow of water in any watercourse under

their jurisdiction, the powers conferred by section 25 above shall not be exercised by any body in relation to that watercourse except—
  (a) by agreement with the local authority; or
  (b) where, after reasonable notice from the body, the local authority either fail to exercise their powers or exercise them improperly.
(3) Where any watercourse is under the jurisdiction of a navigation authority, harbour authority, conservancy authority or board of conservators which are exercising their powers, section 25 above shall not apply to the watercourse except with the consent of that authority or board.
(4) Nothing in this section shall apply in relation to section 25 above in its application to main rivers by virtue section 107(3) of the Water Resources Act 1991 (main river functions of NRA).

DEFINITIONS
  "conservancy authority": s.72(1).
  "harbour": s.72(1).
  "navigation": s.72(1).
  "watercourse": s.72(1).

Appeals against notices under section 25

27.—(1) A person served with a notice under section 25 above may, within twenty-one days from the date on which the notice is served on him, appeal to a magistrates' court on any of the following grounds, that is to say—
  (a) that the notice or requirement is not justified by that section;
  (b) that there has been some informality, defect or error in, or in connection with, the notice;
  (c) that the body which served the notice has refused unreasonably to approve the carrying out of alternative works, or that the works required by the notice to be carried out are otherwise unreasonable in character or extent, or are unnecessary;
  (d) that the period within which the works are to be carried out is not reasonably sufficient for the purpose;
  (e) that the notice might lawfully have been served on another person and that it would have been equitable for it to have been so served;
  (f) that some other person ought to contribute towards the expenses of carrying out any works required by the notice.
(2) The procedure on an appeal under this section shall be by way of complaint for an order and in accordance with the Magistrates' Courts Act 1980.
(3) For the purposes of the time limit for bringing an appeal under this section the making of the complaint shall be treated as the bringing of the appeal.
(4) In so far as an appeal under this section is based on the ground of some informality, defect or error in, or in connection with, the notice, the court shall dismiss the appeal if it is satisfied that the informality, defect or error was not a material one.
(5) In the case of an appeal under this section, the appellant—
  (a) may serve a copy of his notice of appeal on any person having an estate or interest in the part of the watercourse where the impediment occurs or land adjoining that part; and
  (b) shall, where the grounds upon which the appeal under this section is brought include a ground specified in subsection (1)(e) or (f) above, serve a copy of his notice of appeal on each other person referred to.
(6) On the hearing of an appeal under this section the court may make such order as it thinks fit—
  (a) with respect to the person by whom any work is to be carried out and the contribution to be made by any other person towards the cost of the work; or

(b) as to the proportions in which any expenses which may become recoverable by the body which served the notice are to be borne by the appellant and such other person.

(7) In exercising its powers under subsection (6) above the court shall have regard—

(a) as between an owner and an occupier, to the terms and conditions (whether contractual or statutory) of the tenancy and to the nature of the works required; and

(b) in any case, to the degree of benefit to be derived by the different persons concerned.

(8) A person aggrieved by an order, determination or other decision of a magistrates' court under this section may appeal to the Crown Court.

(9) Where upon an appeal under this section a court varies or reverses any decision of a body which has served a notice under section 25 above, it shall be the duty of that body to give effect to the order of the court.

GENERAL NOTE
Section 27 re-enacts s.19 of the 1976 Act. It gives power to appeal to the magistrates' court against a notice served under s.25, on one or more of the grounds listed at subs. (1)(a).

The section provides a procedure for serving notice of appeal on third parties, and gives power to the magistrates to apportion the costs of complying with a notice under s.25 between different parties where it thinks fit (subs. (6)).

A right of further appeal exists to the Crown Court (subs. (8)).

Where the court varies or reverses a decision of the drainage board the local authority must give effect to the order.

See s.51 *et seq* of the Magistrates' Court Act 1980 for details of the procedure referred to in subs. (2).

Restoration and improvement of ditches

Orders requiring the cleansing of ditches etc.

28.—(1) Where a ditch is in such a condition as—

(a) to cause injury to any land; or

(b) to prevent the improvement of the drainage of any land,
the Agricultural Land Tribunal, on the application of the owner or occupier of the land, may if they think fit make an order requiring the person or persons named in the order to carry out such remedial work as may be specified in the order.

(2) An order under this section with respect to a ditch may name—

(a) any person who is an owner or occupier of land through which the ditch passes or which abuts on the ditch; and

(b) any person who, though not such an owner or occupier, has a right to carry out the work specified in the order or any part of it.

(3) Where an order under this section names more than one person it may either—

(a) require each of those persons to carry out a specified part of the work specified in the order; or

(b) subject to subsection (4) below, require all those persons jointly to carry out the whole of that work.

(4) Where the Agricultural Land Tribunal make an order requiring persons jointly to carry out any work, the Tribunal, without prejudice to those persons' joint liability, may, if they think fit, specify in the order the proportions in which those persons are to contribute to the cost of doing so.

(5) In this section—

"ditch" includes a culverted and a piped ditch but does not include a watercourse vested in, or under the control of, a drainage body; and

"remedial work", in relation to a ditch, means work—

(a) for cleansing the ditch, removing from it any matter which impedes the flow of water or otherwise putting it in proper order; and

(b) for protecting it.

DEFINITIONS
"ditch": subs. (5).
"drainage body": s.72.
"remedial work": subs. (5).

GENERAL NOTE
The word "ditch" is not defined other than the specific amplification in subs. (5).

The constitution and procedure of the Agricultural Lands Tribunal are set out in the Agriculture Act 1948. For procedure before the Tribunal, see the Agricultural Lands Tribunals (Rules) Order 1978 (S.I. 1978 No. 259).

Effect of order under section 28

29.—(1) An order under section 28 above shall be sufficient authority for any person named in the order—

(a) to do the work specified in relation to him in the order; and

(b) so far as may be necessary for that purpose, to enter any land so specified.

(2) Where at the end of three months, or such longer period as may be specified in the order, any work specified in an order under section 28 above has not been carried out, the appropriate Minister or any drainage body authorised by him, either generally or in a particular case, may—

(a) carry out the work;

(b) enter any land which it is necessary to enter for that purpose; and

(c) recover from any person named in the order the expenses reasonably incurred in carrying out under this subsection any work which ought to have been carried out by that person;

and those expenses may include any compensation payable in connection with the work under subsection (5) below.

(3) A person entitled by virtue of this section to enter any land—

(a) may take with him such other persons and such equipment as may be necessary; and

(b) if the land is unoccupied, shall, on leaving it, leave it as effectually secured against trespassers as he found it.

(4) Before entering any land under the powers conferred by virtue of this section the person entering it shall give not less than seven days' notice to the occupier of the land.

(5) Where any person sustains any injury by reason of the exercise of any power conferred by virtue of this section then, unless the power was exercised in or for the purpose of the carrying out of any work which that person was required to carry out by an order under section 28 above, the person exercising the power shall be liable to make full compensation to the person sustaining the injury.

(6) In the case of dispute the amount of the compensation payable under subsection (5) above shall be determined by the Lands Tribunal.

(7) The services for which provision may be made under section 1 of the Agriculture Act 1986 (provision of agricultural goods and services) shall include such services to the owner or occupier of any land as may enable him to carry out any work which he is authorised to carry out in exercise of any power conferred by virtue of this section.

(8) In this section "the appropriate Minister"—

(a) in relation to England, means the Minister; and

(b) in relation to Wales, means the Secretary of State.

DEFINITIONS
   "appropriate minister": subs. (8).
   "drainage body": s.72(1).

GENERAL NOTE
   Section 29 gives power to the Minister or, by delegation, a drainage body to carry out work and recover the expense of so doing in default of the person(s) carrying out the works who is liable to do so under a s.28 Order.
   It also gives necessary powers of entry where required to comply with a s.28 Order, subject to due notice being given (subs. (4)) and payment of compensation (subs. (5)).
   For the procedure before the Lands Tribunal (subs. (6)), see the note to s.14.

Authorisation of drainage works in connection with a ditch

   30.—(1) Where the drainage of any land requires—
   (a) the carrying out of any work in connection with a ditch passing through other land;
   (b) the replacement or construction of such a ditch; or
   (c) the alteration or removal of any drainage work in connection with such a ditch,
the Agricultural Land Tribunal, on the application of the owner or occupier of the first-mentioned land, may if they think fit make an order under this section.
   (2) An order under this section is an order authorising the applicant for the order—
   (a) for the purpose mentioned in subsection (1) above, to carry out such work as may be specified in the order; and
   (b) so far as may be necessary for that purpose, to enter any land so specified.
   (3) Subsections (3) to (7) of section 29 above shall apply in relation to the powers conferred by virtue of an order under this section as they apply in relation to the powers conferred by virtue of that section.
   (4) In this section "ditch" has the same meaning as in section 28 above.

DEFINITIONS
   "ditch": s.28(5) and General Note to that section.

GENERAL NOTE
   See the note to s.28 for procedure in relation to Agricultural Lands Tribunal.

Composition and incidental powers of Agricultural Land Tribunal

   31.—(1) The Lord Chancellor shall draw up for each Agricultural Land Tribunal, and from time to time revise, a panel of persons appearing to him to be experienced in matters relating to the drainage of land.
   (2) For each hearing by an Agricultural Land Tribunal of an application under section 28 or 30 above one of the members of the Tribunal shall, instead of being a person nominated in accordance with paragraph 16(1)(b) of Schedule 9 to the Agriculture Act 1947, be a person nominated by the chairman from the panel drawn up under this section.
   (3) Paragraph 16A of Schedule 9 to the Agriculture Act 1947 (which provides for the exercise of the power of making nominations if the chairman is prevented from doing so) shall apply to nominations under this section.
   (4) For the purposes of deciding any application under section 28 or 30 of this Act the Agricultural Land Tribunal may authorise any of its members or any other person to enter and inspect any land.
   (5) Subsections (3) to (6) of section 29 above shall apply in relation to the power conferred by virtue of subsection (4) above as they apply in relation to the powers conferred by virtue of that section.

See the note to s.28 for notes on the procedure before the Agricultural Lands Tribunal.

PART III

POWERS TO MODIFY EXISTING OBLIGATIONS

Variation of awards

32.—(1) Where any award made under any public or local Act contains any provision which in any manner affects or relates to the drainage of land, including any provision affecting the powers or duties of any drainage body or other person with respect to the drainage of land, the NRA—
   (a) may submit to the appropriate Minister for confirmation a scheme for revoking, varying or amending that provision; and
   (b) shall submit such a scheme if it is directed to do so by the appropriate Minister on an application under subsection (2) below.
   (2) An application may be made to the appropriate Minister for such a direction as is mentioned in subsection (1)(b) above by any person who is under any obligation imposed by the award or by any internal drainage board.
   (3) An application under sub-section (2) above shall not be entertained unless—
   (a) the applicant has requested the NRA to submit a scheme under this section; and
   (b) the NRA has either refused to do so or failed to do so within six months or has submitted a scheme different from that which was requested.
   (4) A scheme under this section with respect to any award may—
   (a) provide for commuting, on the basis on which the obligations to which section 33 below relates are to be commuted, the obligation of any person under the award to repair or maintain any drainage works;
   (b) contain such incidental, consequential or supplemental provisions as are necessary or proper for the purposes of the scheme;
   (c) be revoked or varied by a subsequent scheme under this section.
   (5) The appropriate Minister may by order made by statutory instrument confirm any scheme submitted to him under this section, either with or without modifications.
   (6) Schedule 3 to this Act shall apply with respect to an order confirming a scheme under this section.
   (7) An order confirming a scheme under this section may contain provisions with respect to the persons by whom all or any of the expenses incurred by the appropriate Minister or other persons in connection with the making or confirmation of the order, or the making of the scheme, are to be borne.
   (8) In this section "the appropriate Minister"—
   (a) in relation to England, means the Minister; and
   (b) in relation to Wales, means the Secretary of State.

DEFINITIONS
   "appropriate Minister": subs. (8).
   "internal drainage board": s.1(1)(b).
   "minister": s.72(2).

GENERAL NOTE
   Schedule 3 sets out the procedure to be adopted by the Minister and the manner in which his decision can be challenged. See also notes to s.3 above.

Commutation of obligations

33.—(1) Where—

(a) any person is under an obligation imposed on him by reason of tenure, custom, prescription or otherwise to do any work in connection with the drainage of land (whether by way of repairing banks or walls, maintaining watercourses or otherwise); and

(b) without prejudice to section 107(4) of the Water Resources Act 1991 (application of this section to main rivers), that work is otherwise than in connection with a main river,

the NRA or the drainage board for the internal drainage district where the work falls to be done may commute the obligation with the consent of the appropriate Minister.

(2) Where the NRA or an internal drainage board propose to commute any obligation to which this section applies, the NRA or board shall give, in such manner as the appropriate Minister may direct, notice of—

(a) the proposal;

(b) the terms on which it is to be commuted; and

(c) the period within which objection to the proposal may be made.

(3) If within one month of any notice being given under subsection (2) above the person on whom the obligation is imposed gives notice to the NRA or board of his objection to the proposal, the question whether the NRA or board shall proceed to commute the obligation shall be referred to the appropriate Minister.

(4) The decision of the appropriate Minister on a reference under subsection (3) above shall be final.

(5) Nothing in this section shall apply to any obligation imposed by section 25 above.

(6) In this section and section 34 below "the appropriate Minister"—

(a) in relation to the NRA, means either of the Ministers; and

(b) in relation to an internal drainage board, means the relevant Minister.

DEFINITIONS

"appropriate Minister": subs. (6).
"internal drainage board": s.1(1)(b).
"internal drainage district": s.1(1)(a).
"main river": s.72(1).

GENERAL NOTE

Section 33 applies where a drainage authority wishes to commute, *i.e.* practically, take over, land drainage work carried on by a person by reason of "tenure, custom, prescription or otherwise". This phrase is limited to obligations imposed on land, not on purely contractual obligations (see *Eton Rural District Council* v. *Thames Conservators* [1950] Ch. 540).

The drainage authority must give notice in accordance with subs. (2) of its proposal to commute, so that the person has an opportunity to object to the Minister.

The section does not (see subs. (5)) apply to obligations to do works pursuant to s.25 (see above). This section cross-refers to s.107(4) of the Water Resources Act 1991, which provides that the NRA must commute obligations relating to main rivers rather than discretionary powers which exist under this section.

The regulations as to the manner in which notice must be given under s.2 are contained in S.O. 1932, No. 64, reg. 1, and reg. 4 of the Land Drainage (River Authorities) General Regulations 1965 (S.I. 1965 No. 443).

Financial consequences of commutation

34.—(1) Where any obligation is commuted under section 33 above, any person who would, but for the commutation, be entitled to any exemption in respect of drainage rates (either absolutely as being the person subject to the obligation or conditionally on performance of the obligation) shall be entitled absolutely to a like exemption.

(2) The sum to be paid in respect of the commutation of any obligation under section 33 above shall be such sum as the NRA or internal drainage

board in question may, in accordance with the provisions of subsection (4) below, by order determine; and the sum so determined shall—

(a) be payable by way either of a capital sum or of a terminal annuity for a period not exceeding 30 years, at the option of the owner;

(b) be charged on the land in respect of which the obligation existed; and

(c) have priority over any other incumbrances (whenever created) charged on that land by the owner thereof, other than charges (whenever created) under the Improvement of Land Act 1864.

(3) Any capital sum or terminable annuity fixed under this section shall, notwithstanding any agreement to the contrary between the owner and any lessee of the land, be payable by the owner.

(4) For the purpose of determining the sum to be paid in respect of the commutation of any obligation, the NRA or internal drainage board in question shall—

(a) ascertain the amount which, in the opinion of the NRA or, as the case may be, that board, fairly represents the probable average annual cost, taking one year with another, of carrying out and maintaining in a due state of efficiency the works which are required to be carried out and maintained by virtue of the obligation to be commuted; and

(b) fix the capital sum or terminable annuity to be paid in respect of the commutation accordingly.

(5) In fixing any such capital sum or terminable annuity no account shall be taken of so much of the probable annual average cost as, in the opinion of the NRA or, as the case may be, the internal drainage board in question, is attributable to the fact that, by reason of—

(a) improvements effected since January 1, 1900 in the drainage of the land drained by a main river; or

(b) alterations effected since that date in the method of cultivation thereof,

the volume of water which is discharged into a main river at any time is greater than it would have been if those improvements or alterations had not been effected.

(6) If any person is aggrieved by any determination of the NRA or an internal drainage board under this section as regards the sum to be paid in respect of the commutation of any obligation, he may, at any time within three months after the date on which the NRA or board notify him of the determination, require the matter to be referred to the arbitration of a single arbitrator to be appointed, in default of agreement, by the President of the Institution of Civil Engineers.

(7) On any reference under subsection (6) above the arbitrator may either confirm, vary or set aside the determination of the NRA or internal drainage board in question, as he thinks proper.

(8) An order under this section may contain provisions with respect to the persons by whom all or any of the expenses incurred by the appropriate Minister or other persons in connection with the making or confirmation of the order are to be borne.

(9) A record of any such charge as is mentioned in subsection (2) above shall be entered in a register to be kept for the purpose by an authorised officer of the NRA or internal drainage board; and a copy of any such record purporting to be certified by such an officer as a true copy shall be receivable in evidence in all legal proceedings.

DEFINITIONS
  "internal drainage board": s.1(1)(b).
  "main river": s.72(1).

GENERAL NOTE
  Section 34 entitles the drainage authority to recover from the person whose drainage

obligation has been commuted to a payment either a single amount or a terminable annuity (not defined) not exceeding 30 years.

The drainage authority assesses the amount of the sum to be paid, based on the cost saved by the person whose obligation has been commuted, but ignoring the matters referred to in subs. (5).

Any aggrieved person may refer the assessment to an independent arbitrator (subss. (6) and (7)).

Pursuant to subs. (2), the sum paid shall be a charge on the land. If it is an annual payment then it is a rent charge and must be registered at the Land Charges Registry as a Class A charge. The drainage authority must keep a register of all charges open for inspection.

Powers to vary navigation rights

35.—(1) Subject to the following provisions of this section, where, on an application made to him for that purpose by the NRA and (except where the application is made in connection with a main river) the drainage boards for every internal drainage district within which any of the waters to which that application relates are situated—

    (a) it appears to either of the Ministers that a navigation authority is not exercising at all, or is not exercising to the necessary extent, the powers vested in it; and

    (b) it appears to him desirable to do so with a view to securing the better drainage of any land,

he may by order made by statutory instrument revoke, vary or amend the provisions of any local Act relating to navigation rights over any canal, river or navigable waters or to the powers and duties of the navigation authority with respect to any canal, river or navigable waters.

(2) Without prejudice to the generality of the power conferred by subsection (1) above, an order under this section may extinguish, vary or suspend, during such period as the Minister making the order may think proper, any such rights, powers or duties as are mentioned in that subsection.

(3) The power of each of the Ministers to make an order under this section—

    (a) shall be exercisable only after consultation with the Secretary of State for the Environment; and

    (b) shall not be exercisable in relation to any waters within the ebb and flow of the tide at ordinary spring tides except with the consent of the Secretary of State for Transport.

(4) An order made under this section may contain such incidental, consequential or supplemental provisions as appear to the Minister making the order to be necessary or proper for the purposes of the order.

(5) Schedule 3 to this Act shall apply with respect to an order under this section.

DEFINITIONS
    "internal drainage district": s.1(1)(a).
    "main river": s.72(1).
    "Minister(s)": s.72(2).
    "navigation authority": s.72(1).

GENERAL NOTE
    Section 35 gives power to a drainage authority to apply to the Minister for an order to "revoke, vary or amend" any Local Act to enable the drainage authority to take over the functions of a navigation authority in order to secure better drainage of land.

    Both Secretaries of State for the Environment and Transport must be consulted (subs. (3)).

    The section applies both to main rivers and non-main rivers (subs. (1)).

    Schedule 3 applies in relation to an order made under this section (see notes to s.3 above).

PART IV

FINANCIAL PROVISIONS

CHAPTER I

PROVISION FOR THE EXPENSES OF INTERNAL DRAINAGE BOARDS

Raising and apportionment of expenses

Raising of the expenses of internal drainage boards

36.—(1) The expenses under this or any other Act of the drainage board for an internal drainage district (including any contribution made by the board towards expenses of the NRA) shall, in so far as they are not met by contributions from the NRA, be raised by means of—

(a) drainage rates made by the board under and in accordance with Chapter II of this Part or, in relation to any time before April 1, 1993, the provisions saved by virtue of paragraph 15 of Schedule 2 to the Water Consolidation (Consequential Provisions) Act 1991; and

(b) special levies issued by the board under and in accordance with regulations made under section 75 of the Local Government Finance Act 1988.

(2) The expenses of a drainage board which are raised by means of drainage rates in respect of the financial year beginning in 1993 and subsequent financial years shall be defrayed out of such rates without regard to the purpose for which any such expenses were incurred.

DEFINITIONS
"internal drainage district": s.1(1)(a).

GENERAL NOTE
Section 36 contains the principal power for an internal drainage board or the NRA if it is exercising the powers of an IDB to raise income by levying rates. The powers are analogous to those contained in earlier land drainage Acts.

The position is complicated by the fact that a new basis for assessing rates will come into effect on April 1, 1993. Later sections in the Act set out in detail how rates will be assessed from that date on.

In the interim period rates are assessed by existing legislation, which is saved by para. 15 of Sched. 2 to the Water Consolidation (Consequential) Provisions Act 1991. This paragraph provides that until April 1993 when the new rate is levied, the drainage board will be empowered to levy rates under provisions in the 1976 Act and the Internal Drainage Boards (Finance) Regulations 1990 notwithstanding the provisions of this Act.

Schedule 2 of the Water Consolidation (Consequential) Provisions Act 1991, also contains other savings regarding qualifications of electors and elections to IDBs until the new rating system comes into effect.

Apportionment of drainage expenses

37.—(1) Subject to any provision made by or under section 38 below, the following provision shall have effect with respect to the raising by a drainage board for any internal drainage district of their expenses for the financial year beginning in 1993 and each subsequent financial year, that is to say—

(a) the proportion of the expenses of the board which shall be raised from the proceeds of drainage rates shall be equal to the agricultural proportion, determined for that year in accordance with the following provisions of this section, of land values in that district; and

(b) the proportion of the expenses of the board which shall be raised from the proceeds of special levies shall be such as to raise the balance of the expenses of the board remaining after deduction of the amount to be raised for that year from the proceeds of drainage rates.

(2) The drainage board for every internal drainage district, before February 15, 1993 and before February 15 in every subsequent year, shall determine for the financial year beginning on the following April 1—

(a) the aggregate annual value of the chargeable properties in that district; and

(b) the aggregate value of all other land in that district;

and the agricultural proportion for any financial year of land values in that district shall be the amount determined for that year under paragraph (a) above divided by the sum of that amount and the amount determined for that year under paragraph (b) above.

(3) A determination made under subsection (2) above for any financial year shall be made as at December 31 preceding that financial year.

(4) For the purposes of this section the annual value of a chargeable property shall be its annual value for the purposes of Chapter II of this Part.

(5) For the purposes of this section the value of other land in an internal drainage district shall be taken to be—

(a) in the case of a hereditament shown in the local non-domestic rating list of a charging authority on April 1, 1990, one-third of the relevant proportion of the rateable value shown for that hereditament in respect of that date in that list on December 31, 1992;

(b) in the case of domestic property shown in a valuation list on March 31, 1990, one-third of the relevant proportion of the rateable value shown for it in the list on that date multiplied by a factor of 6.73;

(c) in the case of a hereditament which—

    (i) is neither one to which paragraph (a) above applies nor domestic property to which paragraph (b) above applies; but

    (ii) was shown on March 31, 1990 in the register maintained for the drainage board for that district in accordance with the Registers of Drainage Boards Regulations 1968,

one third of the annual value shown for that hereditament in that register on that date multiplied by a factor of 8.02;

(d) in the case of any land to which none of paragraphs (a) to (c) applies, the amount calculated by multiplying—

    (i) the area of the land, expressed in hectares and parts of a hectare; by

    (ii) such a unit value per hectare as represents the average value per hectare of all land to which those paragraphs do apply if the average is calculated by reference to the values determined in accordance with those paragraphs.

(6) In paragraphs (a) and (b) of subsection (5) above—

"relevant proportion," in relation to the rateable value of any hereditament, means the proportion of that value which the area of the part of the hereditament lying within the internal drainage district in question bears to the total area of that hereditament; and

"valuation list" means a valuation list maintained under Part V of the General Rate Act 1967.

DEFINITIONS
"internal drainage district": s.1(1)(a).
"relevant proportion": subs. (6).
"valuation list": subs. (6).

GENERAL NOTE
This section sets out the manner in which rates shall be raised after April 1, 1993. A drainage board may arise its finance first from annual drainage rates and, as to any balance, from special levies (subs. (1)).

A drainage board has to assess the agricultural proportion of land values in its area. To do this it first has to determine the aggregate annual value of (a) chargeable properties in its area and (b) the aggregate value of non-chargeable properties in its area.

Chargeable properties' annual values are assessed in accordance with ss.40–54 of the Act.

The aggregate values of non-chargeable properties are to be ascertained in accordance with subs. (5). The agricultural proportion is equal to the aggregate value of chargeable properties and the value of non-chargeable properties divided by the aggregate value of chargeable properties.

The regulations referred to at subs. (5)(c)(ii) are Registers of Drainage Boards Regulations 1968 (S.I. 1968 No. 672).

Division of district for purposes of drainage rates and special levies

Orders sub-dividing a district for the purposes of raising expenses

38.—(1) A drainage board for an internal drainage district, after consultation with the NRA, may—

(a) for the purpose of levying differential drainage rates or issuing differential special levies, from time to time by order divide that district into sub-districts; and

(b) if, having regard to all the circumstances, they think that it is just to do so, exercise their powers, under Chapter II of this Part or any regulations made under section 75 of the Local Government Finance Act 1988, to make and levy differential drainage rates or issue differential special levies.

(2) Any order made under this section in respect of an internal drainage district may determine the proportions of the expenses of the drainage board for that district which are to be raised in the respective sub-districts within that district.

(3) Where an order made under this section is in force in respect of an internal drainage district and the order does not determine the proportions of the expenses of the drainage board for that district which are to be raised in the respective sub-districts, the amount to be raised in the respective sub-districts shall be determined as follows, that is to say—

(a) expenses incurred in connection with new works or the maintenance or improvement of existing works in each sub-district shall be raised in that sub-district; and

(b) there shall be raised in each sub-district a proportionate part—

(i) of the charges incurred by the board in respect of contributions to the NRA under section 139 of the Water Resources Act 1991 (contributions from internal drainage boards to NRA), or amounts specified under section 58 below as corresponding to such contributions; and

(ii) of other expenses and charges not directly attributable to the maintenance of particular works.

(4) Where an order under this section is in force in respect of an internal drainage district, the proportions of the expenses of the drainage board for that district raised in a sub-district which shall be raised by means of drainage rates and special levies respectively shall, in respect of the financial year beginning in 1993 and each subsequent financial year, bear the same proportion to each other as are borne to each other by the following amounts, that is to say—

(a) the aggregate of the annual values of the chargeable properties in that sub-district; and

(b) the aggregate of the values of other land in that sub-district;

and subsections (2) to (6) of section 37 above shall have effect in respect of each sub-district for the purpose of determining those aggregate amounts as they have effect in respect of an internal drainage district for the purpose of determining the amounts specified in subsection (2)(a) and (b) of that section.

(5) When an order is made under this section by the drainage board for an internal drainage district, the board shall—

(a) submit the order to the relevant Minister; and

(b) forthwith thereafter publish, in one or more newspapers circulating in that district, a notice under subsection (6) below.

(6) A notice under this subsection is a notice stating—

(a) that the order has been submitted to the relevant Minister;

(b) that a copy of the order is open to inspection at a specified place; and
(c) that representations with respect to the order may be made to the relevant Minister within one month after the publication of the notice.

(7) Where an order is submitted to the relevant Minister under this section—
(a) he shall forthwith take into consideration the order; and
(b) the order shall have no effect unless and until it is confirmed by him.

DEFINITIONS
"internal drainage district": s.1(1)(a).

GENERAL NOTE
Section 38 allows a drainage board to sub-divide its district for the purpose of levying different rates and levies in different districts.

The drainage board must consult the NRA and the sub-division shall be by way of an order which complies with the requirements of subss. (5), (6) and (7).

The order may state the proportions in which each sub-district shall bear the drainage board's overall expenses. If the order is silent, the proportions shall be as provided in subs. (3).

Petition for sub-division of internal drainage district

39.—(1) Subject to subsection (6) below, where a petition for the making, variation or revocation of an order under section 38 above is made to the drainage board for an internal drainage district by a sufficient number of qualified persons or by a qualified authority, the board—
(a) shall consider the petition; and
(b) if so directed by a direction under subsection (2) below, shall make, vary or revoke the order, either in accordance with the petition or in accordance with the petition as modified by the direction.

(2) A direction under this subsection is a direction given—
(a) if the NRA is the board, by either of the Ministers; and
(b) in any other case, by the NRA.

(3) Where an internal drainage board object to a direction under subsection (2) above given by the NRA, the direction shall have no effect unless confirmed (with or without modifications) by the relevant Minister.

(4) Subject to subsection (6) below, where a petition under this section is received by the drainage board for an internal drainage district, the board shall—
(a) inform the NRA or, if the NRA is the board, one of the Ministers; and
(b) publish a notice under subsection (5) below in one or more newspapers circulating in that district.

(5) A notice under this subsection is a notice—
(a) that the petition has been received;
(b) that the making, variation or revocation of an order under section 38 above will be considered; and
(c) that representations may be made to the drainage board within a period (which shall not be less than thirty days) stated in the notice.

(6) This section does not require the drainage board for an internal drainage district to consider any petition or publish any notice of a petition if—
(a) they have received a petition under this section within the period of ten years immediately preceding the making of the first-mentioned petition;
(b) they have, within that period, by an order made in exercise of the powers conferred by section 38 above, divided their district into sub-districts or varied or abolished any sub-district; or
(c) the petition is frivolous in the opinion of the NRA or, if the NRA is the board, of either of the Ministers.

(7) After considering a petition under this section and not later than six months after it is received, a drainage board shall inform the NRA or, as the case may be, one of the Ministers—

(a) whether they propose to make, vary or revoke any order under section 38 above; and

(b) if they propose to make or vary such an order, of the terms of the order or variation they propose to make.

DEFINITIONS
"internal drainage board": s.1(1)(b).
"Ministers": s.72(1).
"qualified authority": s.72(1).
"qualified persons": s.72(2).

GENERAL NOTE
Section 39 gives qualified persons or a qualified authority the power to petition for the making, revocation or varying of sub-districts. The procedures to be adopted by the drainage board are set out in subss. (2)–(5) and (7).
Subsection (6) qualifies the power given in subs. (1).

CHAPTER II

DRAINAGE RATES

Levying of drainage rates

Levying of drainage rates

40.—(1) In respect of financial years beginning in or after 1993, the drainage board for an internal drainage district may make a drainage rate in respect of agricultural land and buildings.

(2) Every drainage rate made under this Chapter by the drainage board for an internal drainage district shall be assessed and levied, subject to and in accordance with this Chapter and any order under section 38 above, on the occupiers of hereditaments in the district; but for the purposes of this subsection and the following provisions of this Chapter the owner of a hereditament shall be deemed to be its occupier during any period during which it is unoccupied.

(3) Every drainage rate shall be made in respect of a financial year and, without prejudice to section 50 below or any corresponding provision of any local Act, the drainage board for an internal drainage district shall not make more than one rate in respect of the same financial year.

(4) Every drainage rate shall be made before February 15 in the financial year preceding that in respect of which it is made, but is not invalid merely because it is made on or after that date.

DEFINITIONS
"agricultural building": s.72(1).
"agricultural land": s.72(1).
"internal drainage district": s.1(1)(a).

GENERAL NOTE
Section 40 gives the drainage board the power to levy rates on agricultural land and buildings. The rate is levied on the occupier of a hereditament, and shall be made before February 15 each year.
This section only applies after April 1, 1993. For the situation until that date, see the Water Consolidation (Consequential Provisions) Act 1991.

Rates charged by reference to annual value of agricultural land and buildings

41.—(1) Subject to section 38 above and section 47 below, a rate made by the drainage board for an internal drainage district shall be assessed at a uniform amount per pound throughout the district on the annual value of the agricultural land or agricultural buildings in respect of which it is made.

(2) For the purposes of this Chapter the annual value of any chargeable property shall (subject to sections 43 and 44 below) be the amount, determined in accordance with section 42 below, which is equal to the yearly rent, in respect of a holding comprising the chargeable property, at which the holding might reasonably be expected to have been let, by a prudent and willing landlord to a prudent and willing tenant, on a tenancy from year to year commencing on April 1, 1988 and on the relevant terms.

(3) For the purposes of subsection (2) above chargeable property is let on the relevant terms if—

(a) the tenancy incorporates the terms set out in subsection (4) below; and

(b) the property is let on the terms relating to maintenance, repair and insurance of fixed equipment which are set out in the Schedule to the Agriculture (Maintenance, Repair and Insurance of Fixed Equipment) Regulations 1973.

(4) The terms mentioned in subsection (3)(a) above are—

(a) a covenant by the tenant, in the event of the destruction by fire of harvested crops grown on the holding for consumption on it, to return to the holding the full equivalent manurial value of the crops destroyed, in so far as the return of that value is required for the fulfilment of his responsibilities to farm in accordance with the rules of good husbandry;

(b) a covenant by the tenant to insure against damage by fire all dead stock on the holding and all harvested crops grown on the holding for consumption on it;

(c) a power for the landlord to re-enter on the holding in the event of the tenant not performing his obligations under the tenancy agreement;

(d) a covenant by the tenant not to assign sub-let or part with possession of the holding or any part of it without the landlord's consent in writing.

(5) In determining for the purposes of subsection (2) above the yearly rents at which a property might reasonably be expected to have been let, any liability for the payment of drainage rates shall be disregarded, but account shall be taken of all other relevant factors, including, in every case—

(a) the character and situation of the holding (including the locality in which it is situated);

(b) the productive capacity of the holding and its related earning capacity; and

(c) the level of rents for comparable lettings current on April 1, 1988.

(6) In determining for the purposes of subsection (5) above the level of rents current on April 1, 1988 for comparable lettings—

(a) accounts may be taken of any available evidence with respect to the rents which are or were payable in respect of tenancies of comparable agricultural holdings on terms (other than terms fixing the rent payable) similar to those assumed for the holding in question; but

(b) the following shall be disregarded—

(i) any element of the rents in question which is due to appreciable scarcity of comparable holdings available for letting on such terms compared with the number of persons seeking to become tenants of such holdings on such terms;

(ii) any element of those rents which is due to the fact that the tenant of, or a person tendering for, a comparable holding is in occupation of other land in the vicinity of that holding that may conveniently be occupied with that holding; and

(iii) any effect on those rents which is due to any allowances or reductions made in consideration of the charging of premiums.

(7) In this section—
"productive capacity," in relation to a holding, means the productive
    capacity of the holding determined (taking into account fixed
    equipment and any other available facilities on the holding) on the
    assumption that the holding is in the occupation of a competent
    tenant practising a system of farming suitable to the holding; and
"related earning capacity," in relation to the productive capacity of a
    holding, means the extent to which, in the light of that productive
    capacity, a competent tenant practising such a system of farming
    could reasonably be expected to profit from farming that holding.

DEFINITIONS
   "agricultural buildings": s.72(1).
   "agricultural land": s.72(1).
   "internal drainage district": s.1(1)(a).
   "productive capacity": subs. (7).
   "related earnings capacity": subs. (7).

GENERAL NOTE
   Section 41 imposes a duty on drainage boards to set a uniform rate across its district, based on
the annual value of agricultural land and buildings in its district. This duty is qualified by the
provisions for sub-division from payment of rates (see notes to s.47).
   The annual value of agricultural land and buildings is assessed by determining a yearly
notional rent that would be payable for the agricultural land and/or buildings in question on the
bases set out at subs. (2)(b). The regulations referred to at subs. (3)(b) are contained in S.I.
1987 No. 1473.
   This section adopts the principle of revaluation for rating purposes initiated by the Water Act
1989. For appeal provisions, see s.43.

Determination and modification of annual value

Determination of annual value

   42.—(1) Without prejudice to sections 43 and 44 below, the drainage
board for every internal drainage district shall, not later than December 31,
1992, determine the annual value for the purposes of section 41 above of
each chargeable property in their district on that date.
   (2) Where after December 31, 1992—
   (a) any property in an internal drainage district becomes chargeable
       property;
   (b) any property consisting of agricultural land or buildings becomes part
       of an internal drainage district,
then, as soon as practicable after the date ("the valuation date") on which
the property has become chargeable property or, as the case may be, part of
that district, the drainage board for that district shall determine the annual
value for the purposes of section 41 above of that property.
   (3) A determination made under subsection (2) above shall have effect
from the valuation date.
   (4) Where any drainage board make a determination under this section,
they shall serve notice of the determination, together with a statement in
writing of the right of appeal under section 45 below, on the occupier of the
property to which the determination relates.
   (5) For the purpose of enabling the drainage board for an internal drainage district to comply with their obligations under subsections (1) and (2)
above, the occupier of a chargeable property shall afford reasonable facilities for inspecting the property to the drainage board for the internal
drainage district in which the property lies and to the officers and agents of
that board.

DEFINITIONS
   "internal drainage district": s.1(1)(a).

Section 42 imposes a duty on drainage boards to complete the revaluation by December 31, 1992 and to serve notice of the valuation on the occupier of the property in question, and notice of the rights of appeal.

It also imposes a continuing duty to determine the annual value of any agricultural land and/or buildings which come into existence in its district after 1992. Subs. (5) imposes obligations on occupiers of chargeable properties to give access for inspection.

As to powers of entry by drainage board officials, see s.64 below.

Adjustment of annual values to secure fair distribution of rating burden

43.—(1) If the drainage board for any internal drainage district are of the opinion that the amount of the annual value of any chargeable property in that district should be increased or reduced, having regard to changes in the relevant circumstances, for the purpose of securing that the burden of the drainage rates payable in respect of all chargeable properties in the district is fairly distributed so far as reasonably practicable among the persons liable to pay those rates, the board may make a determination of annual value under this section.

(2) If the occupier of any chargeable property in a drainage district is of the opinion that, having regard to changes in the relevant circumstances, the amount of the annual value of the property should be altered for the purpose mentioned in subsection (1) above—

(a) he may request the drainage board in writing to make a determination under this section in respect of the property; and

(b) the board shall either comply with the request or, if they consider that no alteration of the value is required for that purpose, determine that the request be refused.

(3) A determination of annual value under this section shall be a determination in accordance with section 44 below specifying as the annual value of the chargeable property in question such greater or smaller amount than the amount of the annual value as the board, having regard—

(a) to the changes in the relevant circumstances; and

(b) to any other alterations of annual values under this section made or proposed by the board,

consider just for the purpose mentioned in subsection (1) above.

(4) For the purposes of this section a change in the relevant circumstances, in relation to any chargeable property, is a change in the circumstances by reference to which the annual value of the property in question, or of any other chargeable property in the district in question, was fixed.

DEFINITIONS
"chargeable property": s.72(1).
"internal drainage district": s.1(1)(a).

GENERAL NOTE
Section 43 gives power to both drainage boards and occupiers of chargeable properties to value or apply for a variation of the annual value assessed for the chargeable property. "Relevant circumstances" are not defined but will presumably include the matters set out in s.41(2)–(7).

Effect of determinations under section 43

44.—(1) Where a drainage board make a determination under section 43 above, they shall serve notice of the determination, together with a statement in writing of the rights of appeal conferred by section 45 below, on the occupier of the chargeable property to which the determination relates.

(2) Subject to section 46 below (and notwithstanding anything in section 41 above), where a determination of annual value under section 43 above is made in pursuance of section 43(1) above, the annual value of the property in question shall, for the purposes of any drainage rate made after the effective date, be that specified in the determination.

(3) Subject to section 46 below (and notwithstanding anything in section 41 above), where a determination of annual value under section 43 above is made in pursuance of section 43(2) above, the annual value of the property in question shall for the purposes of—

(a) any drainage rate made in respect of any period included in the financial year in which the request for the determination was made; and

(b) any drainage rate made in respect of any subsequent period,

be that specified in the determination.

(4) Where—

(a) the annual value of any chargeable property is altered by a determination under section 43 above which is made in pursuance of subsection (2) of that section;

(b) drainage rates for any period in respect of the chargeable property have been or are subsequently paid by reference to its annual value before the alteration; and

(c) the period is one for which, in accordance with subsection (3) above, the amount of those rates falls to be assessed on the value specified in the determination,

that amount shall be recalculated accordingly and any sum overpaid shall be repaid or allowed, and any sum underpaid may be recovered as if it were arrears of drainage rates.

(5) In this section "the effective date," in relation to a determination under section 43 above, means the date on which notice of the determination is served in pursuance of subsection (1) above on the occupier of the chargeable property to which the determination relates.

DEFINITIONS
"chargeable property": s.72(1).

GENERAL NOTE
Section 44 provides that a drainage board shall give notice of a determination under s.43, and the date of service shall be the effective date for recalculating rates payable if the annual value has been altered. This is deferred if an appeal is made under s.46 (see below).

Appeals against determinations of annual value

45.—(1) Subject to the following provisions of this section, where a determination under section 42 of 43 above is made by the drainage board for an internal drainage district, the occupier of the land in respect of which the determination is made may appeal, in accordance with this section, against the determination.

(2) An occupier who wishes to appeal under this section against any determination must, before the end of—

(a) the period of twenty-eight days beginning with the date of service on him of notice of the determination; or

(b) such longer period as the drainage board which made the determination may allow, either generally or in any particular case,

serve on the board a notice objecting to the determination and stating the grounds of the objection.

(3) Where notice of objection to a determination is served in pursuance of subsection (2) above, the drainage board which made the determination, if they think fit, may, before the end of the period of twenty-eight days beginning with the date of service of the notice on them—

(a) cancel the determination; and

(b) subject to subsection (4) below, make in its place a fresh determination under section 42 or, as the case may be, section 43 above;

and section 46(7) below shall have effect in relation to the cancellation and the other provisions of this Chapter shall have effect in relation to the fresh determination accordingly.

(4) Where notice of objection is served in pursuance of subsection (2) above in respect of a determination made by a drainage board under section 43 above, the board—

(a) may cancel the determination in accordance with subsection (3) above without making a fresh determination in its place; and

(b) where they do so, shall serve notice of cancellation on the person by whom the notice of objection was served on them.

(5) Where—

(a) notice of objection to a determination is served in pursuance of subsection (2) above and is not withdrawn before the end of the period mentioned in subsection (3) above; and

(b) the drainage board which made the determination do not cancel it in accordance with subsection (3) above,

that board shall, forthwith after the end of that period, transmit the notice and a note of the determination to the clerk of the appropriate tribunal.

(6) The transmission in pursuance of subsection (5) above of the notice of objection to a determination by a drainage board shall constitute the lodging of an appeal against the determination, by the person who served the notice on the board, to a valuation and community charge tribunal constituted in accordance with section 46 below.

(7) In subsection (5) above "the appropriate tribunal," in relation to a determination under section 42 or 43 above, means—

(a) the valuation and community charge tribunal established, in accordance with regulations under Schedule 11 to the Local Government Finance Act 1988, for the area in which the land to which the determination relates is situated; or

(b) where different parts of that land are situated in different areas for which such tribunals are established, such one of those tribunals as may be determined by or under the Drainage Rates (Appeals) Regulations 1970.

DEFINITIONS

"appropriate tribunal": subs. (7).

"internal drainage district": s.1(1)(a).

GENERAL NOTE

Section 45 sets out the procedure for appealing against a determination of annual value under ss.42 or 43. The notice of appeal must be served within 28 days of service of the notice of determination. Subss. (3)–(5) set out the options open to the drainage board on receipt of a notice of appeal. If the drainage board declines to alter its valuation the notice of appeal is transmitted to the valuation and community charge tribunal, and the transmission shall constitute notice of appeal to that Tribunal. For the procedure before the Tribunal, see s.46 below.

The regulations referred to at subs. (7) are contained in the Drainage Rates (Appeals) Regulations 1970 (S.I. 1970 No. 1152).

Hearing and determination of appeals under section 45

46.—(1) It shall be the duty of the president of the valuation and community charge tribunal to whose clerk a notice of objection is transmitted in pursuance of section 45 above to arrange for the appeal to which the notice relates to be heard and determined.

(2) Subsections (5) and (6) of section 88 of the 1967 Act shall apply—

(a) to the constitution of the tribunal to hear and determine an appeal against a determination under section 42 or 43 above; and

(b) to the rehearing of such an appeal in case of such a failure to agree as is mentioned in subsection (6) of section 88 of that Act.

(3) On the hearing of an appeal to a valuation and community charge tribunal against a determination under section 42 or 43 above the following persons, that is to say—

(a) the person whose notice of objection to the determination in question has resulted in the hearing;

(b) any other person who is the occupier of any land to which the determination relates; and

(c) the drainage board by which the determination was made,

shall be entitled to appear and be heard as parties to the appeal and to call witnesses and to examine any witness before the tribunal.

(4) On an appeal to a valuation and community charge tribunal against a determination under section 42 or 43 above, the tribunal—

(a) shall sit in public, unless the tribunal otherwise orders, on being satisfied, on the application of a party to the appeal, that the interests of that party would be prejudicially affected; and

(b) shall have power to administer oaths and to take evidence on oath;

but, subject to that and to the Drainage Rates (Appeals) Regulations 1970, the procedure of such a tribunal in relation to such an appeal shall be such as the tribunal may determine.

(5) The tribunal which is convened under this section to determine an appeal against a determination under section 42 or 43 above shall, after hearing the persons mentioned in subsection (3) above or such of them as desire to be heard, do one of the following—

(a) quash the determination to which the appeal relates; or

(b) alter the determination in such manner as the tribunal thinks just; or

(c) dismiss the appeal.

(6) Section 77 of the 1967 Act (which provides for appeals from valuation and community charge tribunals to the Lands Tribunal) shall have effect in relation to a decision of a valuation and community charge tribunal on an appeal against a determination under section 42 or 43 above as if—

(a) for the reference to section 76 of that Act there were substituted a reference to the preceding provisions of this section; and

(b) the words from "and the valuation officer" onwards were omitted.

(7) Where a determination under section 42 or 43 above of the amount of the annual value of any property is quashed or altered on appeal or is cancelled in accordance with section 45 above, then (except in so far as the parties agree otherwise)—

(a) that amount of the annual value shall be recalculated accordingly; and

(b) any sum overpaid shall be repaid or allowed and any sum underpaid may be recovered as if it were arrears of drainage rates.

(8) Where a determination under section 42 or 43 above which has been quashed is subsequently restored on appeal—

(a) the amount of any drainage rate falling to be recalculated in consequence of the appeal shall (except in so far as the parties agree otherwise) be recalculated accordingly; and

(b) any sum overpaid shall be repaid or allowed and any sum underpaid may be recovered as if it were arrears of drainage rates.

(9) In this section "the 1967 Act" means the General Rate Act 1967.

DEFINITIONS
"the 1967 Act": General Rate Act 1967.

GENERAL NOTE
Section 46 imposes a duty on the valuation and community charge tribunal to hear appeals under ss.42 and 43 above. Its procedure is governed by the relevant sections in the 1967 Act, subject as appropriate to the Drainage Rates (Appeals) Regulations 1970 (S.I. 1970 No. 1152).

Appeals from the valuation and community charge tribunal are made to the Lands Tribunal (see subs. (6)). Subss. (7) and (8) contain provisions as to adjustment of rates where an appeal alters a determination.

Power to grant exemptions from rating

Power to grant exemptions from rating

47.—(1) The drainage board for an internal drainage district, after consultation with the NRA, may by order determine that no rates shall be levied by them on the occupiers of hereditaments in any portion of the district which, in their opinion, ought (either by reason of its height above sea level or for any other reason) to be exempted wholly from rating.

(2) Subsections (5) to (7) of section 38 above shall apply in relation to orders made under this section as they apply in relation to orders made under that section.

(3) Where the occupier of any hereditament in an internal drainage district requests the drainage board for the district to make or amend an order under this section so as to exempt from drainage rates the portion of the district in which the hereditament is situated, the board—

(a) shall consider the request; and

(b) if so directed under this section, shall comply with it.

(4) Where a request under subsection (3) above is refused by the drainage board for an internal drainage district, the person making it may appeal—

(a) to the NRA; or

(b) if the board is the NRA, to the relevant Minister;

and the NRA or, as the case may be, the relevant Minister may direct the board to make or amend the order as requested.

(5) Where a request under subsection (3) above is neither refused nor complied with within three months after it is made, it shall be treated for the purposes of subsection (4) above as having been refused.

DEFINITIONS
   "internal drainage district": s.1(1)(a).
   "Minister": s.72(1).

GENERAL NOTE
   Section 47 gives power to a drainage board either at its own instance, after consultation with the NRA, or on an application by a ratepayer in occupation of hereditaments exempt from the payment of rates.
   If a drainage board refuses to exempt the ratepayer, the ratepayer may appeal to the NRA, or, if the drainage board is the NRA, the Minister.

Making and assessment of rates

Procedure for making of rate

48.—(1) A drainage rate shall—

(a) be made by the drainage board for an internal drainage district in writing under the common seal of the board; and

(b) be treated as made on the date on which a resolution is passed by the board authorising their seal to be affixed to the rate.

(2) A drainage rate made by a drainage board shall not be valid unless notice of it stating—

(a) the amount of the rate;

(b) the amounts of the board's expenses to be raised by means of drainage rates and special levies, respectively; and

(c) the date on which the rate was made,

is given by the board in accordance with subsection (3) below within ten days of its being made.

(3) A notice under subsection (2) above of a rate made by the drainage board for any internal drainage district may, as the board think fit, either—

(a) be affixed in one or more public or conspicuous places in that district; or

(b) be published in one or more newspapers circulating in that district.

(4) Every drainage rate shall be in the prescribed form.

"internal drainage district": s.1(1)(a).

GENERAL NOTE

As to the meaning of drainage rate, see s.40 *et seq.* The prescribed form in subs. (4) is provided for in Form 2 of the General Drainage Charges (Forms) Regulations 1990 (S.I. 1990 No. 564).

Assessment for rating

49.—(1) This section shall have effect with respect to the assessment of persons to a drainage rate in respect of any hereditament ("the relevant hereditament") and the liability of the occupier of that hereditament in respect of the rate.

(2) Every rate shall be assessed on the person who at the date of the making of the rate is the occupier of the relevant hereditament.

(3) The full amount of a drainage rate may be recovered by the drainage board in question from any person who is the occupier of the relevant hereditament at any time during the period in respect of which the rate is made; but a person who is in occupation of any hereditament for part only of the period in respect of which a drainage rate is made shall be liable, by virtue of subsection (4) below, to bear a proportionate part only of the rate.

(4) If a person who is in occupation of the relevant hereditament for part only of a period for which a drainage rate is raised is required under subsection (3) above to pay the full amount of the rate, he may (subject to any agreement to the contrary) recover, from any other person who has been in occupation of the relevant hereditament for part of that period, the amount which that other person is liable to bear.

(5) Where the name of any person liable to be assessed to any drainage rate is not known to the board, it shall be sufficient to assess him by the description of "the occupier" of the premises (naming them) in respect of which the assessment is made, without further name or description.

(6) Every demand for a drainage rate shall be in the prescribed form.

(7) Where the value on which a drainage rate is assessed would, apart from this subsection, include a fraction of a pound, the fraction shall—

(a) if greater than fifty pence, be treated as one pound; and

(b) in any other case, disregarded.

DEFINITIONS

"relevant hereditament": subs. (1).

GENERAL NOTE

Section 49 provides that the person who shall pay the drainage rate is the person in occupation of the relevant hereditament. Where the drainage board does not know the name of the occupier the assessment can be addressed to "the occupier" (subs. (5)).

Subsection (4) gives power to an occupier to recover a proportion of the drainage rate from any other person who has occupied the relevant hereditament for part of the period for which the occupier has paid the rate.

Amendments as respects drainage rates

50.—(1) The drainage board for an internal drainage district may at any time make such amendments in the current or last preceding drainage rate as appear to them necessary in order to make the rate conform with this Part and, in particular, may—

(a) correct any clerical or arithmetical error;

(b) correct any erroneous insertions or omissions or any misdescriptions;

(c) make such additions or corrections as appear to the board to be necessary by reason of—

  (i) any change in the occupation of any hereditament; or
  (ii) any property previously rated as a single hereditament becoming liable to be rated in parts.
(2) The drainage board for an internal drainage district shall serve notice of any amendment made by them in pursuance of this section on the occupier of every hereditament affected by it.
(3) Where an amendment is made in pursuance of this section—
(a) any amount overpaid shall be repaid or allowed; and
(b) any amount underpaid may be recovered as if it were arrears of the rate.

DEFINITIONS
  "internal drainage district": s.1(1)(a).

Other appeals against drainage rates

51.—(1) Subject to the following provisions of this section, if any person, as occupier of any hereditament in a drainage district, is aggrieved, upon any ground other than a ground upon which he might have appealed in pursuance of section 45 above—
(a) by a drainage rate; or
(b) by an amendment of a drainage rate,
he may appeal against the rate, or the rate as amended, to the Crown Court.
  (2) Notice of appeal under this section, specifying the grounds of the appeal, must be given within twenty-eight days after, as the case may be—
(a) the date on which the rate is made; or
(b) the date on which notice of the amendment is served on the appellant,
to the Crown Court, to the internal drainage board in question and also, if the appeal relates to a hereditament not in the occupation of the appellant, to the occupier of that hereditament.
  (3) On an appeal under this section, the Crown Court shall, as it thinks just, either confirm the rate or annul or modify it.
  (4) The appellant and the respondent to an appeal under this section may agree in writing to refer the matter in dispute to the arbitration of such person as may be agreed between them or, in default of agreement, as may be appointed by the relevant Minister.
  (5) In the event of a reference under subsection (4) above, the costs of and incidental to the hearing before the arbitrator and his award shall be in the discretion of the arbitrator and, if not agreed by the parties, shall be taxed as part of the costs of the appeal to the Crown Court.

DEFINITIONS
  "internal drainage board": s.1(1)(b).
  "Minister": s.72(1).

GENERAL NOTE
  Section 51 deals with appeals against a drainage rate other than appeals against determination of annual value. Such appeals may, *inter alia*, be applicable where a person disputes that he was an occupier for the purposes of s.49.

Supplemental and enforcement provisions

Registers of drainage hereditaments

52.—(1) It shall be the duty of the drainage board for each internal drainage district to prepare in the prescribed form and within the prescribed period, or such longer period as the relevant Minister may allow in any particular case—
(a) a register containing the prescribed information in respect of the drainage hereditaments in that district; and

(b) a map showing the prescribed particulars of such of those hereditaments as are of the prescribed description.

(2) It shall be the duty of the drainage board for each internal drainage district—

(a) to maintain the register and map prepared by them in pursuance of subsection (1) above; and

(b) to alter the register or map in such circumstances and in such manner, and within such periods, as may be prescribed.

(3) It shall be the duty of the drainage board for each internal drainage district to keep the register and map maintained by them in pursuance of subsection (2) above open to inspection at prescribed places by members of the public at all reasonable times.

DEFINITIONS
"internal drainage district": s.1(1)(a).
"Minister": s.72(1).

GENERAL NOTE
Section 52 imposes duties on drainage boards to prepare and maintain prescribed information and maps and make them available for inspection. The relevant regulations are contained in the Register of Drainage Board Regulations 1968 (S.I. 1968 No. 1672).

Power to require information

53.—(1) The drainage board for an internal drainage district may serve on the owner of any hereditament in the district in respect of which a drainage rate is levied a notice requiring him to state in writing the name and address of any person known to him as being an occupier of that hereditament.

(2) A person shall be guilty of an offence under this section if, where a notice is served on him under subsection (1) above, he—

(a) fails without reasonable excuse to comply with the notice; or

(b) in pursuance of the notice—

(i) makes any statement in respect of the information required which he knows to be false in a material particular; or

(ii) recklessly makes any statement in respect of that information which is false in a material particular.

(3) A person guilty of an offence under this section shall be liable, on summary conviction, to a fine not exceeding level 4 on the standard scale.

(4) Where—

(a) a person is convicted of an offence under this section in respect of a failure to comply with a notice; and

(b) the failure continues after conviction,

then, unless he has a reasonable excuse for the continuance of the failure, he shall be guilty of a further offence under this section and shall be liable, on summary conviction, to be punished accordingly.

DEFINITIONS
"internal drainage district": s.1(1)(a).

GENERAL NOTE
The current maximum fine under level 4 is £1,000.

Powers for enforcing payment

54.—(1) Arrears of any drainage rates made under this Chapter may be recovered by the drainage board for an internal drainage district in the same manner in which arrears of a non-domestic rate may be recovered under the Local Government Finance Act 1988 by a charging authority.

(2) The drainage board for an internal drainage district may by resolution authorise any member or officer of the board, either generally or in respect of particular proceedings—

(a) to institute or defend on their behalf proceedings in relation to a drainage rate; or

(b) notwithstanding that he is not qualified to act as a solicitor, to appear on their behalf in any proceedings before a magistrates' court for the issue of a warrant of distress for failure to pay a drainage rate.

(3) In proceedings for the recovery of arrears of a drainage rate the defendant shall not be entitled to raise by way of defence any matter which might have been raised on an appeal under section 45 or 51 above.

(4) The powers conferred by this section are in addition to, and not in substitution for, the powers conferred by any provision of any local Act on any drainage board in relation to arrears of drainage rates; and for the purposes of any such provisions a rate made under this Chapter shall be treated, subject to subsection (5) below, as a rate to which those provisions apply.

(5) Notwithstanding anything in any local Act—

(a) no distress for arrears of any rate made under this Chapter shall be levied on the goods or chattels of any person other than a person from whom the arrears may be recovered by virtue of subsection (1) above; and

(b) no proceedings shall be taken, whether by action or otherwise, for the enforcement of any charge on land created by a local Act for securing payment of arrears of any rate made under this Chapter.

(6) The drainage board for an internal drainage district shall not be required to enforce payment of any drainage rate in any case where the amount payable is, in their opinion, insufficient to justify the expense of collection.

DEFINITIONS
"internal drainage district": s.1(1)(a).

GENERAL NOTE
Subsection (3) provides that a ground that would entitle a ratepayer to appeal under ss.45 or 51 (see above) is no defence. If such a ground exists, the ratepayer should appeal in accordance with those sections and an adjustment to the rates will be made if the appeal is successful pursuant to s.46(8) or (9), or by inference following an order under s.51(3).

CHAPTER III

FURTHER FINANCIAL PROVISIONS

Powers of internal drainage boards and local authorities to borrow etc.

55.—(1) Subject to the following provisions of this section, an internal drainage board may borrow, on the security of their property or income—

(a) for the purpose of defraying any costs, charges or expenses incurred by them in the execution of this Act; or

(b) for the purpose of discharging any loan contracted by them under this Act or any provision re-enacted, whether directly or indirectly, by this Act.

(2) The council of a county or London borough and the Common Council of the City of London may borrow for the purposes of this Act.

(3) The consent of the relevant Minister shall be required for any borrowing by an internal drainage board under this section other than a borrowing for the purpose of discharging any loan previously contracted.

(4) Money borrowed by an internal drainage board under this section may be borrowed for such period not exceeding fifty years as the board, with the consent of the relevant Minister, may in each case determine.

(5) Where the drainage board for an internal drainage district borrow any sums in respect of which they have determined that some part only of that district shall be liable, the money borrowed shall be repayable only out of

rates levied on, or special levies issued or contributions received in respect of, that part of the drainage district.

(6) The provisions of the Commissioners Clauses Act 1847 as to mortgages shall be incorporated with the provisions of this section so far as it relates to borrowing by an internal drainage board.

(7) Where the owner of any land comprised within any internal drainage district is authorised to invest money on real security, he shall, unless the instrument authorising the investment provides to the contrary, have power to invest money on a first mortgage of the drainage rates leviable by the drainage board for that district.

(8) The reference in subsection (1) above to an internal drainage board borrowing on the security of their property or income is a reference to their borrowing on the security of any property vested in the board or on the security of—

(a) any rates to be levied by the board under this Act;

(b) any special levies to be issued by the board in accordance with regulations under section 75 of the Local Government Finance Act 1988; or

(c) any contributions to be paid to the board under this Act.

DEFINITIONS
  "internal drainage board": s.1(1)(b).
  "internal drainage district": s.1(1)(a).
  "Minister": s.72(1).

GENERAL NOTE
  As to the relevant regulations under s.75 of the Local Government Finance Act 1988, see notes to s.36.

Concurrent power of boards to impose navigation tolls

56.—(1) The power of the NRA under section 143 of the Water Resources Act 1991 to make an application for the imposition of tolls in respect of navigation shall, in the case of waters within an internal drainage district which do not form part of a main river, be exercisable by the drainage board for that district, concurrently with the NRA.

(2) Subsection (4) of section 143 of the Water Resources Act 1991 shall have effect in relation to tolls imposed, by virtue of this section, on the application of an internal drainage board as if the reference in that subsection to the NRA were a reference to that board.

DEFINITIONS
  "internal drainage district": s.1(1)(a).
  "main river": s.72(1).

GENERAL NOTE
  Section 143 of the Water Resources Act 1991 sets out the procedure whereby the NRA can apply to the Minister for an order allowing it to charge tolls, where the exercise of navigation creates expense, and where no navigation authority exists. Section 143(4) sets out how tolls may be levied.

Contributions by the NRA to expenses of internal drainage boards

57.—(1) Where it appears to the drainage board for any internal drainage district that, by reason—

(a) of the quantity of water which that district receives from lands at a higher level; or

(b) of the period that will elapse before that district obtains any relief from operations of the NRA on a main river,

it is fair that a contribution towards their expenses should be made by the NRA, they may make an application to the NRA for a contribution.

(2) On an application under subsection (1) above the NRA may resolve to make to the internal drainage board such contribution, if any, as may be specified in the resolution.

(3) A resolution under this section may be acted upon by the NRA forthwith, notwithstanding that the period for bringing an appeal under subsection (4) below has not expired or that an appeal so brought is pending.

(4) If—

(a) an internal drainage board is aggrieved by a resolution of the NRA under this section determining the amount of any contribution or refusing to make a contribution; or

(b) the council of any county or London borough is aggrieved by any such resolution on the ground that the contribution to be made by the NRA is excessive.

the board or council may, within six weeks after the date on which notice of the resolution is given by the NRA to the internal drainage board in question, appeal to the relevant Minister against the resolution.

(5) On an appeal under this section the relevant Minister may, after considering any objections made to him and, if he thinks fit, holding a public local inquiry, make such an order in the matter as he thinks just.

(6) Where—

(a) the NRA has acted on a resolution by virtue of subsection (3) above; and

(b) an appeal is brought in respect of the resolution,

the relevant Minister shall by his order direct such adjustment to be made in respect of any sums paid in pursuance of the resolution as may be necessary for giving effect to his decision.

(7) Where the relevant Minister makes an order under this section, he shall lay before Parliament particulars of the matter in respect of which the appeal was made and of the reasons for his order.

(8) Compliance with any order made by the relevant Minister under this section may be enforced by mandamus.

DEFINITIONS
"internal drainage board": s.1(1)(b).
"internal drainage district": s.1(1)(a).
"Minister": s.72(1).

GENERAL NOTE
Section 57 sets out the procedure for IDBs to obtain contributions from the NRA where the IDB is put to additional expense by reason of the NRA failing to provide relief by necessary operations on main rivers.

Subsection (3) gives a right of appeal to the Minister if the IDB is unhappy with the amount of the contribution, or to a county council or London Borough if it feels that the contribution is excessive, given that the council has to contribute to the NRA's expenses by precept.

Allocation of NRA revenue for its functions as an internal drainage board

58.—(1) Where the NRA is the drainage board for an internal drainage district (whether by virtue of section 3 or 4 above), it may by resolution specify an amount as corresponding to the amount of any contribution which, if it were not the drainage board for that district, it would—

(a) make to that drainage board under section 57 above; or

(b) require from that board under section 139 of the Water Resources Act 1991 (contributions from internal drainage boards to NRA expenses).

(2) Where any amount is specified under subsection (1) above, then, according as that amount is specified by virtue of paragraph (a) or (b) of that subsection—

(a) expenses incurred by the NRA as the drainage board for the internal drainage district in question shall, to the extent of that amount, be defrayed out of revenue received by it otherwise than as that board; or

(b) expenses incurred by the NRA as such shall be defrayed out of sums received by it as that board.

(3) The NRA shall publish any resolution under this section in one or more newspapers circulating in the internal drainage district in question.

(4) Where a sufficient number of qualified persons or the council of any county or London borough are aggrieved—

(a) by a resolution of the NRA under this section;

(b) whether on the ground that it is too small or on the ground that it is too large, by the amount specified in such a resolution; or

(c) by the failure of the NRA to pass such a resolution,

they may appeal to the relevant Minister.

(5) An appeal under subsection (4) above, other than an appeal on the ground that the NRA has failed to pass a resolution under this section, must be made within six weeks after the date on which the NRA published the resolution in respect of which it is made.

(6) On an appeal under subsection (4) above the relevant Minister may, after considering any objections made to him, make such an order in the matter as he thinks just.

(7) An order under subsection (6) above shall be treated as an order on an appeal under section 57(5) above or, as the case may require, under section 140 of the Water Resources Act 1991 (appeals with respect to resolutions requiring contributions from internal drainage boards).

DEFINITIONS
"internal drainage district": s.1(1)(a).
"Minister": s.72(1).

GENERAL NOTE
Section 58 contains reciprocal provisions to s.57 above where an IDB is increasing the NRA's expense in exercising its functions in relation to main rivers. It also provides for funding arrangements where the drainage board is the NRA itself (see s.4 above).

Grants to drainage bodies

59.—(1) The appropriate Minister may make grants towards expenditure incurred by internal drainage boards or by other drainage bodies (except the NRA) in the exercise of their functions in carrying out drainage schemes.

(2) Grants under subsection (1) above shall be of such amounts and subject to such conditions as may be approved by the Treasury.

(3) Where a drainage body are about to incur in respect of any work expenditure which, if the work is properly carried out, a grant will be payable under subsection (1) above, the appropriate Minister may, with the approval of the Treasury, make advances to that body on account of the expenditure.

(4) The appropriate Minister may, with the approval of the Treasury, make grants to drainage bodies in respect of expenditure properly incurred by them with a view to carrying out drainage works, being expenditure towards which, if the works had been properly carried out, a grant would have been payable under subsection (1) above.

(5) Where a drainage body are about to incur expenditure in respect of which it appears to the appropriate Minister that a grant will be payable under subsection (4) above, he may, with the approval of the Treasury, make advances to the body on account of the expenditure.

(6) The appropriate Minister may, with the approval of the Treasury, make grants to an internal drainage board or a local authority in respect of the cost of any works carried out by the board or authority in pursuance of section 20 above; and the reference to expense in that section shall be

construed as excluding the amount of any grant paid under this subsection in respect of the works in question.

(7) The appropriate Minister may, with the approval of the Treasury, make to an internal drainage board grants in respect of expenditure incurred by the board, and advances on account of expenditure to be incurred by the board, in carrying out works for the rebuilding or repair of any bridge maintained by the board, other than works appearing to the appropriate Minister to be maintenance works of a routine kind.

(8) In this section "the appropriate Minister"—

(a) in relation to England, means the Minister; and

(b) in relation to Wales, means the Secretary of State.

DEFINITIONS
"appropriate Minister": subs. (8) and s.72(1).
"internal drainage board": s.1(1)(b).

GENERAL NOTE

Subs. (6)
See notes to s.20 above.

Power of local authority to contribute to expenses of drainage works

60.—(1) A local authority may contribute, or undertake to contribute, to the expenses of the carrying out or maintenance of any drainage works by a drainage body such an amount as, having regard to the public benefit to be derived therefrom, appears to the local authority to be proper.

(2) Without prejudice to section 55(2) above, the making of contributions under this section shall be a purpose for which a local authority may borrow.

(2) References in this section to a local authority include references to the Sub-Treasurer of the Inner Temple and to the Under Treasurer of the Middle Temple.

Land drainage expenses of local authorities

61.—(1) Subject to any express provision to the contrary contained in this Act or in Chapter II of Part VI of the Water Resources Act 1991, the expenses of the council of a metropolitan district or London borough under this Act or the flood defence provisions of that Act shall be defrayed as general expenses or, if and so far as the council think fit, as special expenses charged on such parts of the metropolitan district or, as the case may be, borough as the council think fit.

(2) The reference in subsection (1) above to the flood defence provisions of the Water Resources Act 1991 shall have the same meaning as is given, by virtue of section 221(1) of that Act, to any such reference in that Act.

PART V

MISCELLANEOUS AND SUPPLEMENTAL

Powers to acquire and dispose of land

Powers of internal drainage boards and local authorities to acquire land

62.—(1) An internal drainage board may, for any purpose in connection with the performance of any of their functions—

(a) acquire land inside or outside their district by agreement; or

(b) if authorised by the relevant Minister, acquire any such land compulsorily.

(2) The exercise of the powers conferred on local authorities by sections 14 to 17 above and section 66 below shall be included in the purposes for which the council of any district or London borough or the Common Council

of the City of London may be authorised by the Secretary of State to purchase land compulsorily; and subsections (1) and (3) of section 16 above shall apply in relation to the powers conferred by this subsection as they apply in relation to the powers conferred by section 14 above.

(3) The Acquisition of Land Act 1981 shall apply in relation to the compulsory acquisition of land in pursuance of subsection (1) or (2) above.

(4) An internal drainage board may exercise the powers conferred by subsection (1) above so as to acquire interests in or rights over land by way of securing the creation of new interests or rights in their favour (as well as by acquiring interests or rights already in existence).

(5) Where an internal drainage board exercise their powers under this section so as to acquire compulsorily an interest in or right over land by way of securing compulsorily the creation in their favour of a new interest or right—

(a) the enactments relating to compensation for the compulsory purchase of land shall, in their application to such acquisition, have effect with the necessary modifications; and

(b) the Acquisition of Land Act 1981 and the Compulsory Purchase Act 1965 shall, in their application to such compulsory acquisition, have effect with such modifications as may be prescribed.

(6) Where an internal drainage board propose to acquire by agreement any land belonging to Her Majesty in right of the Duchy of Lancaster—

(a) the Chancellor and Council of that Duchy may sell the land to the board; and

(b) the land may be granted to them, and the proceeds of sale shall be paid and dealt with, as if the land had been sold under the authority of the Duchy of Lancaster Lands Act 1855.

DEFINITIONS
"internal drainage board": s.1(1)(a).
"Minister": s.72(1).

Power of internal drainage boards to dispose of land

63.—(1) Subject to the following provisions of this section, an internal drainage board may dispose of land held by them in any manner they wish.

(2) Except with the consent of the relevant Minister, an internal drainage board shall not dispose of land under this section, otherwise than by way of a short tenancy, for a consideration less than the best that can reasonably be obtained.

(3) Except with the consent of the relevant Minister, an internal drainage board shall not dispose under this section, otherwise than by way of a short tenancy, of land which has been acquired by them (whether before or after the commencement of this Act) either—

(a) compulsorily; or

(b) at a time when they were authorised to acquire it compulsorily, by agreement.

(4) For the purposes of this section a disposal of land is a disposal by way of a short tenancy if it consists of—

(a) the grant of a term not exceeding seven years; or

(b) the assignment of a term which at the date of the assignment has not more then seven years to run.

DEFINITIONS
"internal drainage board": s.1(1)(a).
"Minister": s.72(1).

Powers of entry for internal drainage boards and local authorities

64.—(1) Any person authorised by an internal drainage board or local authority, after producing (if so required) a duly authenticated document showing his authority, may at all reasonable times—

(a) enter any land for the purpose of exercising any functions of the board or, as the case may be, any functions under this Act of that authority;

(b) without prejudice to paragraph (a) above, enter and survey any land (including the interior of any mill through which water passes or in connection with which water is impounded) and take levels of the land and inspect the condition of any drainage work on it; and

(c) inspect and take copies of any Acts of Parliament, awards or other documents which—

(i) are in the possession of any internal drainage board, local authority or navigation authority;

(ii) relate to the drainage of land; and

(iii) confer any powers or impose any duties on that board or authority.

(2) A person entitled under this section to enter any land—

(a) may take with him such other persons and such equipment as may be necessary; and

(b) if the land is unoccupied, shall, on leaving it, leave it as effectually secured against trespassers as he found it.

(3) Except in an emergency, admission to any land shall not be demanded as of right under this section, unless notice of the intended entry—

(a) has been given to the occupier; and

(b) if the land is used for residential purposes or the demand if for admission with heavy equipment, has been given not less than seven days before the demand is made.

(4) Where injury is sustained by any person by reason of the exercise by an internal drainage board or local authority of any of their powers under this section, the board or authority shall be liable to make full compensation to the injured person.

(5) In case of dispute, the amount of the compensation payable under subsection (4) above shall be determined by the Lands Tribunal.

(6) If any person intentionally obstructs or impedes any person exercising a power conferred by this section, he shall be guilty of an offence and liable, on summary conviction, to a fine not exceeding level 4 on the standard scale.

(7) This section shall not apply in relation to land belonging to Her Majesty in right of the Crown or the Duchy of Lancaster, in relation to land belonging to the Duchy of Cornwall or in relation to land belonging to a government department.

(8) This section shall be without prejudice to any other enactment conferring powers of entry.

DEFINITIONS
"internal drainage board": s.1(1)(b).

GENERAL NOTE
Section 64 gives powers of entry to IDBs and local authorities to enter land for the purposes of exercising their functions under the Act.

The expression "duly authenticated document" in subs. (1) is not defined.

As to the procedure before the Lands Tribunal (subs. (5)), see notes to s.14. The current upper limit for level 4 (subs. (5)) is £1,000.

Subordinate legislation

Land drainage regulations

65.—(1) Each of the Ministers shall have power to make regulations—

(a) for the purpose of prescribing anything which may be prescribed under this Act (other than under section 74 below); and

(b) generally for the purposes of carrying this Act into effect.

(2) The power to make regulations under this section or any other provision of this Act shall be exercisable by statutory instrument subject to annulment in pursuance of a resolution of either House of Parliament.

DEFINITIONS
   "Ministers": s.72(1).

Powers to make byelaws

66.—(1) Subject to the following provisions of this section and to any other enactment contained in this Act or the Water Resources Act 1991, an internal drainage board or a local authority, except (subject to subsection (8) below) a county council, may make such byelaws as they consider necessary for securing the efficient working of the drainage system in their district or area.

(2) Without prejudice to the generality of subsection (1) above but subject as aforesaid, an internal drainage board or local authority, other than a county council, may, in particular, make byelaws for any of the following purposes, that is to say—
   (a) regulating the use and preventing the improper use of any watercourses, banks or works vested in them or under their control or for preserving any such watercourse, banks or works from damage or destruction;
   (b) regulating the opening of sluices and flood gates in connection with any such works as are mentioned in paragraph (a) above;
   (c) preventing the obstruction of any watercourse vested in them or under their control by the discharge into it of any liquid or solid matter or by reason of any such matter being allowed to flow or fall into it;
   (d) compelling the persons having control of any watercourse vested in the board or local authority or under their control, or of any watercourse flowing into any such watercourse, to cut the vegetable growths in or on the bank of the watercourse and, when cut, to remove them.

(3) The powers conferred by subsections (1) and (2) above—
   (a) shall not be exercisable by an internal drainage board in connection with a main river, the banks of such a river or any drainage works in connection with such a river; and
   (b) shall be exercisable by a local authority only so far as may be necessary for the purpose of preventing flooding or remedying or mitigating any damage caused by flooding.

(4) No byelaw for any purpose specified in subsection (2)(a) above shall be valid if it would prevent reasonable facilities being afforded for enabling a watercourse to be used by stock for drinking purposes.

(5) Byelaws made under this section shall not be valid until they are confirmed—
   (a) in the case of byelaws made by an internal drainage board, by the relevant Minister;
   (b) in the case of byelaws made by a local authority, in relation to any area of England, by the Minister; and
   (c) in the case of byelaws made by a local authority in relation to any area of Wales, by the Secretary of State.
and Schedule 5 to this Act and section 236 of the Local Government Act 1972 (procedure for byelaws) shall have effect, respectively, in relation to byelaws made under this section by an internal drainage board and in relation to byelaws made under this section by a local authority.

(6) If any person acts in contravention of, or fails to comply with, any byelaw made under this section he shall be guilty of an offence and liable, on summary conviction—

(a) to a fine not exceeding level 5 on the standard scale; and
(b) if the contravention or failure is continued after conviction, to a further fine not exceeding £40 for every day on which the contravention or failure is so continued.

(7) If any person acts in contravention of, or fails to comply with, any byelaw made under this section by an internal drainage board or local authority, the board or authority may, without prejudice to any proceedings under subsection (6) above—

(a) take such action as may be necessary to remedy the effect of the contravention or failure; and
(b) recover the expenses reasonably incurred by them in doing so from the person in default.

(8) For the purposes of this section—

(a) subsections (1) and (3) of section 16 above shall apply in relation to the powers conferred by this section as they apply in relation to the powers conferred by section 14 above; and
(b) section 17 above shall apply in relation to the carrying out by a local authority of any drainage works authorised by subsection (7) above as it applies in relation to the carrying out of any drainage works authorised by section 14(1) above;

but nothing in this section shall authorise the carrying out of any works in connection with a main river.

(9) Notwithstanding anything in this Act, no byelaw made by an internal drainage board or local authority under this section shall conflict with or interfere with the operation of any byelaw made by a navigation authority, harbour authority or conservancy authority.

DEFINITIONS
    "conservancy authority": s.72(1).
    "harbour authority": s.72(1).
    "internal drainage board": s.1(1)(b).
    "main river": s.72(1).
    "Minister": s.72(1).
    "navigation authority": s.72(1).
    "watercourses": s.72(1).

GENERAL NOTE

Subs. (6)
    The current maximum under level 5 is £2,000.
    See Sched. 5 for the procedure to be adopted by an IDB when making a byelaw, and provisions for inspection once made.

Protective provisions

Protection for particular undertakings and savings in respect of works

67.—(1) Subject to subsection (2) below, Schedule 6 to this Act shall have effect for the protection of particular undertakings in connection with the carrying out of works and other activities under this Act.

(2) Schedule 6 to this Act shall not apply in relation to the carrying out of works under this Act by the NRA; but sections 179 and 183 of, and Schedule 22 to, the Water Resources Act 1991 (protective provisions for flood defence works and for certain undertakings) shall apply in relation to the carrying out of works under this Act by the NRA as they apply in relation to carrying out of works by the NRA under the flood defence provisions of that Act.

(3) Nothing in this Act shall authorise any person to carry out any works or do anything in contravention of any of the provisions of the Ancient Monuments and Archaeological Areas Act 1979.

(4) In the exercise of the powers conferred by this Act due regard shall be had to the interests of fisheries, including sea fisheries.

(5) Nothing in this Act shall prejudice or affect the provisions of Part V of the Water Resources Act 1991 (fisheries functions of the NRA) or of the Salmon and Freshwater Fisheries Act 1975 or any right, power or duty conferred or imposed by those provisions.

(6) The reference in subsection (2) above to the flood defence provisions of the Water Resources Act 1991 shall have the same meaning as is given, by virtue of section 221(1) of that Act, to any such reference in that Act.

(7) Without prejudice to paragraph 1 of Schedule 2 to the Water Consolidation (Consequential Provisions) Act 1991, any provisions for the protection of any authorities or persons contained in any local Act, so far as by virtue of section 114(2) of the Land Drainage Act 1976 (protection under local Acts) they applied immediately before the commencement of this Act in relation to the exercise by any internal drainage board or local authority of powers under any enactment re-enacted by this Act, shall apply to the like extent in relation to the exercise by that board or authority of powers under the corresponding provisions of this Act.

(8) Nothing in this Act shall affect any powers of an internal drainage board under any local Act so far as they existed immediately before the commencement of this Act.

Definitions
"internal drainage board": s.1(1)(b).

General Note
Section 67 contains provisions dealing with potential conflicts with the operations of other statutory undertakers (see subs. (1) and Sched. 6), and conflicts with other duties in other Acts.

The Ancient Monuments and Archaeological Areas Act 1979 requires consent for any act that may damage or destroy a monument or archaeological site. "Fisheries" and "sea fisheries" are not defined in the Act. See Bates, "Water and Drainage Law", section 16.02 *et seq.* for a definition of fisheries. Sea fisheries are in fact salt-water fisheries. See the Fisheries Act 1981 for definition of "sea fish".

Subsection (5) provides that NRA fisheries at Pt. V of the Water Resources Act 1991 and in the Salmon and Freshwater Fisheries Act 1975, *e.g.* s.28, are not prejudiced by any part of this Act.

Subsections (7) and (8) deal with the relationship between obligations in this Act and Local Acts already in existence.

Actions by a drainage authority which offend subss. (3), (4) or (5) may render the authority liable to proceedings for breach of statutory duty or liable to have decisions judicially reviewed.

Power of navigation authorities etc. to divert sewers

68.—(1) Where any watercourses under the control of an internal drainage board pass under or interfere with, or with the improvement or alteration of, any river, canal, dock, harbour, basin or other work (including any towing-path adjacent thereto) which belongs to or is under the jurisdiction of any relevant authority, the relevant authority may, at their own expense and on substituting for those watercourses other equally effective watercourses—

(a) take up, divert or alter the level of those watercourses; and

(b) do all such matters and things as may be necessary in connection with the works authorised to be done by them under this section.

(2) If any question arises under this section between any internal drainage board and any relevant authority as to whether any watercourses substituted or proposed to be substituted by the relevant authority for any existing watercourses are as effective as the existing watercourses, that question shall be referred to a single arbitrator to be agreed between the parties or, failing

such agreement, to be appointed by the President of the Institution of Civil Engineers on the application of either party.

(3) In this section "relevant authority" means any navigation authority, harbour authority or conservancy authority.

DEFINITIONS
"internal drainage board": s.1(1)(b).
"relevant authority": subs. (3) and s.72(1).
"watercourses": s.72(1).

GENERAL NOTE
The maximum fine under level 3 (subs. (4)) is currently £1,000.
It is felt that s.69(6)(b) would make more sense if the words "a rule" in the first line read "an order".

Information provisions

Power to hold inquiries for land drainage purposes etc.

69.—(1) Each of the Ministers shall have power to cause such inquiries to be held as he considers necessary or desirable for the purposes of this Act.

(2) Subject to subsection (3) below, the person appointed to hold any inquiry under subsection (1) above or otherwise under this Act may for the purposes of the inquiry—

(a) by summons require any person to attend, at a time and place stated in the summons, to give evidence or to produce any documents in his custody or under his control relating to any matter in question at the inquiry; and

(b) take evidence on oath and for that purpose administer oaths.

(3) No person shall be required, in obedience to a summons under this section, to attend to give evidence or to produce any documents, unless the necessary expenses of his attendance are paid or tendered to him; and nothing in this section shall empower a person holding an inquiry to require the production of the title, or of any instrument relating to the title, of any land which is not the property of a local authority.

(4) Any person who—

(a) refuses or deliberately fails to attend in obedience to a summons under this section, or to give evidence; or

(b) deliberately alters, suppresses, conceals, destroys, or refuses to produce any book or other document which he is required or is liable to be required to produce for the purposes of this section,

shall be guilty of an offence and liable, on summary conviction, to imprisonment for a term not exceeding six months or to a fine not exceeding level 3 on the standard scale or to both.

(5) Where either of the Ministers causes an inquiry to be held under this Act—

(a) the costs incurred by him in relation to the inquiry shall be paid by such authority or party to the inquiry as he may direct; and

(b) the Minister in question may cause the amount of the costs so incurred to be certified;

and any amount so certified and directed to be paid by any authority or person shall be recoverable from that authority or person by that Minister summarily as a civil debt.

(6) Where either of the Ministers causes an inquiry to be held under this section—

(a) he may make orders as to the costs of the parties at the inquiry and as to the parties by whom the costs are to be paid; and

(b) every such order may be made a rule of the High Court on the application of any party named in the order.

(7) Section 42 of the Housing and Planning Act 1986 (recovery of Minister's costs in connection with inquiries) shall apply where either of the Ministers is authorised by virtue of subsection (5) above to recover costs incurred by him in relation to an inquiry as it applies where a Minister is so authorised by virtue of an enactment specified in subsection (1) of that section.

Confidentiality of information obtained by NRA etc.

70. Section 204 of the Water Resources Act 1991 (confidentiality of information) shall have effect in relation to information obtained by virtue of the provisions of this Act so far as they relate to functions exercisable by or in relation to the NRA as it has effect in relation to the information obtained as mentioned in that section.

GENERAL NOTE

Section 206 of the Water Resources Act 1991 in fact contains confidentiality provisions and provides that information which has been obtained by virtue of the Act and relates to the affairs of an individual or a particular business shall not be disclosed except with the consent of that individual or business. The remaining part of the section sets out numerous qualifications to the duty of confidentiality. Section 70 only relates to informations in the hands of the NRA. This section has created practical difficulties in relation to the provision of information by the NRA to third parties to assist in civil claims. The NRA's legal department has issued guidelines as to what information it is willing to disclose.

Construction of Act

Service of documents

71.—(1) A notice required or authorised to be served under or by virtue of this Act by any person shall be in writing.

(2) Any document required or authorised by virtue of this Act to be served on any person may be served—

(a) by delivering it to him or by leaving it at his proper address or by sending it by post to him at that address; or

(b) if the person is a body corporate, by serving it in accordance with paragraph (a) above on the secretary or clerk of that body; or

(c) if the person is a partnership, by serving it in accordance with paragraph (a) above on a partner or a person having the control of management of the partnership business.

(3) For the purposes of this section and section 7 of the Interpretation Act 1978 (which relates to the service of documents by post) in its application to this section, the proper address of any person on whom a document is to be served shall be his last known address, except that—

(a) in the case of service on a body corporate or its secretary or clerk, it shall be the address of the registered or principal office of the body;

(b) in the case of service on a partnership or a partner or a person having the control or management of a partnership business, it shall be the principal office of the partnership;

and for the purposes of this subsection the principal office of a company registered outside the United Kingdom or of a partnership carrying on business outside the United Kingdom is its principal office within the United Kingdom.

(4) If a person to be served by virtue of this Act with any document by another has specified to that other an address within the United Kingdom other than his proper address (as determined in pursuance of subsection (3) above) as the one at which he or someone on his behalf will accept

documents of the same description as that document, that address shall also be treated as his proper address for the purposes of this section and for the purposes of the said section 7 in its application to this section.

(5) Where under any provision of this Act any document is required to be served on the owner, on a lessee or on the occupier of any premises then—

(a) if the name or address of the owner, of the lessee or, as the case may be, of the occupier of the premises cannot after reasonable inquiry be ascertained; or

(b) in the case of service on the occupier, if the premises appear to be or are unoccupied,

that document may be served either by leaving it in the hands of a person who is or appears to be resident or employed on the land or by leaving it conspicuously affixed to some building or object on the land.

(6) This section shall not apply to any document in relation to the service of which provision is made by rules of court.

Interpretation

72.—(1) In this Act, unless the context otherwise requires—
"agricultural buildings" has the meaning provided by paragraphs 2 to 8 of Schedule 5 to the Local Government Finance Act 1988;
"agricultural land" has the meaning provided by paragraphs 2 and 4 to 8 of that Schedule;
"banks" means banks, walls or embankments adjoining or confining, or constructed for the purposes of or in connection with, any channel or sea front, and includes all land between the bank and low-watermark;
"chargeable property" means a hereditament comprising agricultural land or agricultural buildings in respect of which drainage rates may be assessed under Chapter II of Part IV of this Act;
"charging authority" has the same meaning as in the Local Government Finance Act 1988;
"conservancy authority" means any person who has a duty or power under any enactment to conserve, maintain or improve the navigation of a tidal water and is not a navigation authority or a harbour authority within the meaning of the Prevention of Oil Pollution Act 1971;
"drainage" includes defence against water (including sea water), irrigation, other than spray irrigation, and warping;
"drainage body" means the NRA, an internal drainage board or any other body having power to make or maintain works for the drainage of land;
"financial year" means the twelve months ending with March 31;
"harbour" and "harbour authority" have the same meanings as in the Merchant Shipping Act 1894;
"land" includes water and any interests in land or water and any easement or right in, to or over land or water;
"local authority" means the council of a county, district or London borough or the Common Council of the City of London;
"main river" has the same meaning as in the Water Resources Act 1991;
"the Minister" means the Minister of Agriculture, Fisheries and Food;
"the Ministers" means the Minister and the Secretary of State, and in relation to anything which falls to be done by the Ministers, means those Ministers acting jointly;
"the NRA" means the National Rivers Authority;
"navigation authority" means any person who has a duty or power under any enactment to work, maintain, conserve, improve or

control any canal or other inland navigation, navigable river, estuary, harbour or dock;

"ordinary watercourse" means a watercourse that does not form part of a main river;

"prescribed" means prescribed by regulations under section 65 above;

"qualified authority," in relation to an internal drainage district, means a charging authority for an area wholly or partly included in that district;

"qualified persons" shall be construed in accordance with subsection (2) below;

"the relevant Minister"—

 (a) in relation to internal drainage districts which are neither wholly nor partly in Wales or to the boards for such districts, means the Minister;

 (b) in relation to internal drainage districts which are partly in Wales or to the boards for such districts, means the Ministers; and

 (c) in relation to internal drainage districts which are wholly in Wales or to the boards for such districts, means the Secretary of State;

"watercourse" includes all rivers and streams and all ditches, drains, cuts, culverts, dikes, sluices, sewers (other than public sewers within the meaning of the Water Industry Act 1991) and passages, through which water flows.

(2) Subject to the provisions of paragraph 19 of Schedule 2 to the Water Consolidation (Consequential Provisions) Act 1991 (which makes provision with respect to qualification under this subsection by reference to drainage rates levied on land in respect of years beginning before 1993), where any provision of this Act refers, in relation to an internal drainage district, to the making of any appeal or petition by a sufficient number of qualified persons—

(a) the persons who are qualified are the occupiers of any land in the district in respect of which a drainage rate is levied; and

(b) subject to subsection (3) below, their number shall be sufficient if (but only if)—

 (i) they are not less than forty; or

 (ii) they are not less than one-fifth of the number of persons who are qualified to make the petition or appeal; or

 (iii) the assessable value for the purposes of the last drainage rate levied in the district of all the land in respect of which they are qualified persons is not less than one-fifth of the assessable value of all the land in respect of which that rate was levied.

(3) In relation to a district divided into sub-districts the persons qualified to make a petition under section 39 above as being the occupiers of land in one of the sub-districts shall also be sufficient in any case where the condition in subsection (2)(b)(ii) or (iii) above would be satisfied if the sub-district were an internal drainage district.

(4) The references to the assessable value of any land in paragraph (b) of subsection (2) above are references to the amount which for the purposes of the drainage rate mentioned in that paragraph would be the annual value of the land.

(5) References in this Act to the carrying out of drainage works include references to the improvement of drainage works.

(6) Nothing in this Act shall operate to release any person from an obligation to which section 21 above applies; and the functions of the NRA or any internal drainage board as respects the doing of any work under this Act are not to be treated as in any way limited by the fact that some other

person is under an obligation, by reason of tenure, custom, prescription or otherwise, to do that work.

(7) Where by virtue of any provision of this Act any function of a Minister of the Crown is exercisable concurrently by different Ministers, that function shall also be exercisable jointly by any two or more of those Ministers.

(8) This Act so far as it confers any powers on the NRA shall have effect subject to the provisions of the Water Resources Act 1991.

(9) The powers conferred by this Act on the Common Council of the City of London shall be exercisable as respects that City.

(10) Sub-paragraph (1) of paragraph 1 of Schedule 2 to the Water Consolidation (Consequential Provisions) Act 1991 has effect (by virtue of sub-paragraph (2)(b) of that paragraph) so that references in this Act to things done under or for the purposes of provisions of this Act or the Water Resources Act 1991 include references to things done, or treated as done, under or for the purposes of the corresponding provisions of the law in force before the commencement of this Act.

Disputes as to whether works connected with main river

73.—(1) If any question arises under this Act—
(a) whether any work is a drainage work in connection with a main river; or
(b) whether any proposed work will, if constructed, be such a drainage work,
the question shall be referred to one of the Ministers for decision or, if either of the parties so requires, to arbitration.

(2) Where any question is required under subsection (1) above to be referred to arbitration it shall be referred to the arbitration of a single arbitrator appointed—
(a) by agreement between the parties; or
(b) in default of agreement, by the President of the Institution of Civil Engineers on the application of either party.

DEFINITIONS
"main river": s.72(1).
"Ministers": s.72(1).

Other supplemental provisions

Application to Crown

74.—(1) Subject as otherwise expressly provided in this Act, this Act shall apply to land belonging to Her Majesty in right of the Crown or the Duchy of Lancaster, to land belonging to the Duchy of Cornwall and to land belonging to a government department.

(2) For the purposes of this Act the following shall be deemed to be the owner of land to which this section applies by virtue of this section, that is to say—
(a) in the case of land belonging to Her Majesty in right of the Crown, the Crown Estate Commissioners or the Secretary of State, according as the land is under the management of those Commissioners or the Secretary of State;
(b) in the case of land belonging to Her Majesty in right of the Duchy of Lancaster, the Chancellor of the Duchy; and
(c) in the case of land belonging to the Duchy of Cornwall, such person as the Duke of Cornwall or the possessor for the time being of the Duchy of Cornwall appoints.

(3) Notwithstanding subsection (1) above but subject to subsection (4) below, nothing in this Act shall—

(a) authorise the compulsory acquisition of any land belonging to Her Majesty in right of the Crown or the Duchy of Lancaster, or of any land belonging to the Duchy of Cornwall or a government department;

(b) operate as a grant—

(i) by or on behalf of Her Majesty as owner (whether in right of the Crown or of the Duchy of Lancaster) of any tidal lands; or

(ii) by or on behalf of the Duchy of Cornwall as owner of any such lands,

of any estate or interest in or right over any of those lands or any part of them; or

(c) authorise any person to do any work on, over or under, or to use for any purpose, any tidal lands or any lands belonging to Her Majesty in right of the Crown or of the Duchy of Lancaster, to the Duchy of Cornwall, or to any government department, except—

(i) with the consent of the owner of the land or, in the case of tidal lands, of the owner of the land and of the Secretary of State; and

(ii) in accordance with the approved plans and sections and subject to the prescribed restrictions and conditions;

or

(d) confer any power of levying drainage rates in respect of tidal lands.

(4) Nothing in subsection (3)(c) above shall apply to work done in maintaining existing works on tidal lands, or on land not in occupation of Her Majesty, the Duke of Cornwall or a government department.

(5) Section 222 of the Water Resources Act 1991 (Crown application) shall have effect in relation to the provisions of this Act so far as they confer powers on the NRA as it applies in relation to the provisions of that Act.

(6) In this section—

"tidal lands" means lands below the high-water mark of ordinary spring tides but, for the purposes of subsection (3)(c) above, does not include any lands which are protected, by means of walls, embankments or otherwise, from the incursion of the tides; and

"approved" and "prescribed" mean, respectively, approved and prescribed by the Secretary of State or, as the case may be, the owner of the lands, before the commencement of the work in question.

Application to Isles of Scilly

75.—(1) Subject to the provisions of any order under this section, nothing in this Act shall require or authorise any function, duty or power to be carried out, performed or exercised in relation to the Isles of Scilly by the NRA.

(2) The Secretary of State may, on the application of the Council of the Isles of Scilly, by order make provision with respect to the carrying out in those Isles of functions falling under this Act to be carried out in relation to other parts of England and Wales by the NRA.

(3) Without prejudice to the generality of the power conferred by subsection (2) above, an order under this section may apply any provision of this Act, of the Water Consolidation (Consequential Provisions) Act 1991 or of the Water Act 1989 in relation to the Isles of Scilly with or without modifications.

(4) The power of the Secretary of State to make an order under this section shall be exercisable by statutory instrument subject to annulment in pursuance of a resolution of either House of Parliament.

(5) An order under this section may—

(a) make different provision for different cases, including different provision in relation to different persons, circumstances or localities; and

(b) contain such supplemental, consequential and transitional provision as the Secretary of State considers appropriate, including provision saving provision repealed by or under any enactment.

Short title, commencement and extent

76.—(1) This Act may be cited as the Land Drainage Act 1991.

(2) This Act shall come into force on December 1, 1991.

(3) This Act extends to England and Wales only.

SCHEDULES

SCHEDULE 1

MEMBERS OF INTERNAL DRAINAGE BOARDS

PART 1

ELECTION OF MEMBERS

Election rules

1.—(1) An election of members of an internal drainage board shall be conducted in accordance with rules contained in regulations made by the relevant Minister—

(a) for the preparation of registers of electors and for securing that the registers are open to inspection;

(b) with respect to the holding and conduct of elections, including provisions as to returning officers, nominations, polls and the counting of votes; and

(c) for allowing any person or body of persons entitled to vote at an election to vote by a deputy.

(2) Provision made by virtue of sub-paragraph (1)(a) above may include provision with respect to the making of objections to entries in registers and with respect to the hearing and determination of such objections.

Eligibility of electors

2.—(1) Subject to sub-paragraphs (2) and (3) below, the electors for members of an internal drainage board shall be the persons who at the date of the election occupy land in the board's district on which a drainage rate has been levied in the year immediately preceding.

(2) A person shall not be entitled to be an elector by reason of his occupation of land if at the date of the election any amount demanded in respect of any drainage rate levied on that land has remained unpaid for more than a month.

(3) For the purposes of this paragraph the owner of any hereditament shall be deemed to be its occupier during any period during which it is unoccupied.

(4) The preceding provisions of this paragraph and paragraph 3 below shall have effect subject to the provisions of paragraph 17 of Schedule 2 to the Water Consolidation (Consequential Provisions) Act 1991 (which makes provision with respect to electors who qualify by reference to drainage rates made in respect of years beginning before 1993).

Number of votes for each elector

3.—(1) Each elector at an election of members of an internal drainage board shall be entitled, in accordance with the following table, to one or more votes, according to the assessable value of the property in respect of which the elector is entitled to vote—

Table

Assessable value	Number of votes
Less than £50	1 vote
Not less than £50 but less than £100	2 votes
Not less than £100 but less than £150	3 votes
Not less than £150 but less than £200	4 votes
Not less than £200 but less than £250	5 votes
Not less than £250 but less than £500	6 votes
Not less than £500 but less than £1,000	8 votes
£1,000 or more	10 votes

(2) In sub-paragraph (1) above, the reference to the assessable value of any land is a reference to the amount which for the purposes of any drainage rate levied at the relevant date would be the annual value of the land.

(3) In this paragraph "the relevant date" means the date as at which the qualifications of electors is determined for the purposes of the election in accordance with rules made under paragraph 1 above.

Qualification for election

4.—(1) A person shall not be qualified for election as a member of an internal drainage board unless he is—

  (a) both the owner and the occupier of not less than four hectares of land in respect of which a drainage rate may be levied by the board and which is situated in the electoral district for which he is a candidate for election; or

  (b) the occupier, whether under tenancies of year to year or otherwise, of not less than eight hectares of such land as aforesaid; or

  (c) the occupier of land which is of an assessable value of £30 or upwards and is situated in the electoral district for which he is a candidate for election; or

  (d) a person nominated as a candidate for election by the person (whether an individual or a body of persons) who is both the owner and the occupier of land which—

    (i) is situated in the electoral district in question; and

    (ii) is either of not less than four hectares in extent or of an assessable value of £30 or upwards.

(2) A person shall not be qualified for the purposes of sub-paragraph (1) above as being an occupier of any land or, as being the owner and occupier of any land or a person nominated by the owner and occupier of any land, if at the date of the election any amount demanded in respect of any drainage rate levied on that land has remained unpaid for more than one month.

(3) In sub-paragraph (1) above, the reference to the assessable value of any land is a reference to the amount which for the purposes of any drainage rate levied at the relevant date would be the annual value of the land.

(4) The preceding provisions of this paragraph shall have effect subject to the provisions of paragraph 18 of Schedule 2 to the Water Consolidation (Consequential Provisions) Act 1991 (which makes provision with respect to relevant dates falling before April 1, 1993).

(5) In this paragraph "the relevant date" means the date as at which the qualifications of candidates for the election in question are determined in accordance with rules made under paragraph 1 above.

Part II

Members Appointed by Charging Authorities

Appointment of members by charging authorities

5.—(1) The charging authority for any area wholly or partly included in an internal drainage district may appoint a member or members of the internal drainage board having power, by virtue of regulations under the Local Government Finance Act 1988, to issue special levies to that authority.

(2) In appointing a person to be a member of an internal drainage board a charging authority shall have regard to the desirability of appointing a person who—

  (a) has knowledge of experience (including knowledge of the internal drainage district in question or commercial experience) of some matter relevant to the functions of the board; and

  (b) has shown capacity in such a matter.

(3) This paragraph has effect subject to the restrictions on appointments which are imposed by paragraph 6 below or, as the case may require, paragraph 16 of Schedule 2 to the Water Consolidation (Consequential Provisions) Act 1991 (number of appointed members of internal drainage board allowed in period ending with March 31, 1993).

Numbers of members appointed by charging authorities

6.—(1) The number of appointed members of an internal drainage board—
(a) shall be determined, in accordance with the following provisions of this paragraph, for the period April 1, 1993 to March 31, 1996 and each succeeding three-year period beginning with April 1; and
(b) shall be so determined in relation to each drainage board by reference to the amounts ascertained, on December 31 preceding the relevant three-year period, as the amounts in respect of which that board makes drainage rates and issue special levies in the financial year preceding that period.

(2) The number of appointed members of an internal drainage board—
(a) shall not exceed by more than one the number of other members of the board; and
(b) subject to paragraph (a) above, shall be such that the number of appointed members bears, as nearly as possible, the same proportion to the maximum number of all the members of the board as the aggregate amount of special levies issued by the board bears to the amount of the expenses of the board in respect of which drainage rates have been made and special levies have been issued.

(3) If more than one charging authority is entitled to appoint members of an internal drainage board under paragraph 5 above—
(a) each such authority may appoint the number of members of the board calculated by multiplying the maximum number of appointed members by the relevant fraction for that authority and disregarding any fraction in the resulting product; and
(b) where in respect of the board—
(i) any such authority has appointed a member; or
(ii) the calculation referred in paragraph (a) above results in respect of each such authority in a product of less than one,
the charging authorities shall, unless they otherwise agree, jointly appoint the number of members of the board representing the difference between the maximum number of appointed members and the aggregate number of members that may be appointed by individual charging authorities or, as the case may be, constituting the maximum number of appointed members.

(4) For the purposes of sub-paragraph (3) above the relevant fraction, in relation to a charging authority, is the fraction which identifies how much of the aggregate amount of the special levies issued by the internal drainage board in question consists in a special levy issued to that authority.

(5) In this paragraph "appointed members," in relation to an internal drainage board, means members of the board appointed by one or more charging authorities under this Part of this Schedule or, at a time before the commencement of this Act, under the corresponding provisions of the Internal Drainage Boards (Finance) Regulations 1990.

PART III

SUPPLEMENTAL PROVISIONS WITH RESPECT TO MEMBERS

Terms of office etc. of members

7.—(1) Subject to the following provisions of this Part of this Schedule, elected members of an internal drainage board shall come into office on November 1, next after the day on which they are elected and shall hold office for a term of three years.

(2) Subject as aforesaid, the terms of appointment of a member of an internal drainage board who is appointed by one or more charging authorities shall be determined by the authority or authorities by which he is appointed.

(3) Subject as aforesaid, the members of an internal drainage board who are appointed by the relevant Minister as first members of that board shall hold office until the end of one year from November 1 next following the day on which they are appointed.

Resignation etc. of elected members

8.—(1) An elected member of an internal drainage board may resign his office by notice given to the chairman of the board.

(2) If an elected member of an internal drainage board is absent from meetings of the board for more than six months consecutively, he shall, unless his absence is due to illness or some other reason approved by the board, vacate his office at the end of that six months.

Insolvency of members or candidates

9.—(1) A person who is an undischarged bankrupt or who has at any time within the preceding five years made a composition or arrangement with, or granted a trust deed for, his creditors shall be ineligible for election as a member of an internal drainage board and also for being a member of such a board.

(2) If—

(a) an elected member of an internal drainage board is adjudged bankrupt;

(b) the estate of such a member is sequestrated; or

(c) such a member makes a composition or arrangement with, or grants a trust deed for, his creditors,

he shall vacate his office.

Filling casual vacancies

10.—(1) Subject to sub-paragraph (2) below, if for any reason whatsoever the place of an elected member of an internal drainage board becomes vacant before the end of his term of office, the vacancy shall be filled by the election by the board of a new member.

(2) Where the unexpired portion of the term of office of the vacating member is less than six months, the vacancy need not be filled.

(3) A person elected to fill a casual vacancy shall hold office so long as the vacating member would have held office.

Eligibility of vacating member of board

11. Subject to the preceding provisions of this Schedule, a vacating member of an internal drainage board shall be eligible for re-election or re-appointment.

Meaning of "elected member"

12. References in this Part of this Schedule to an elected member, in relation to an internal drainage board, are references to any member of that board other than a member appointed by one or more charging authorities.

Section 1   SCHEDULE 2

Expenses and Proceedings etc. of Internal Drainage Boards

Payment of expenses etc. of members and officers

1.—(1) The relevant Minister may, if he thinks fit, by order authorise an internal drainage board to pay to the chairman of the board, for the purpose of enabling him to meet the expenses of his office, such allowance as may be specified in the order.

(2) An internal drainage board may pay any reasonable expenses incurred by their members and officers in—

(a) attending meetings of the board or a committee or sub-committee thereof;

(b) carrying out inspections necessary for the discharge of the functions of the board; or

(c) attending conferences or meetings convened by one or more internal drainage boards, or by any association of internal drainage boards, for the purpose of discussing matters connected with the discharge of the functions of internal drainage boards;

and may pay any reasonable expenses incurred by their members or officers in purchasing reports of the proceedings of any such conference or meeting.

(3) Without prejudice to the other provisions of this Schedule—

(a) an internal drainage board may enter into a contract with any person under which, in consideration of payments made by the board by way of premium or otherwise, that person undertakes to pay to the board such sums as may be provided in the contract in the event of any member of the board or of any of its committees meeting with a personal accident, whether fatal or not, while he is engaged on the business of the board;

(b) any sum received by an internal drainage board under any such contract shall, after deduction of any expenses incurred in the recovery of that sum, be paid by the board to, or to the personal representatives of, the person in respect of whose accident the sum is received;

and the provisions of the Life Assurance Act 1774 shall not apply to any such contract.

Payments etc. to staff

2.—(1) An internal drainage board may pay to persons employed by them such reasonable remuneration as they think fit.

(2) An internal drainage board may provide housing accommodation for persons employed by them (and may, accordingly, acquire land for that purpose under section 62 of this Act).

Proceedings of internal drainage board

3.—(1) An internal drainage board may, with the approval of the relevant Minister, make rules—

(a) for regulating the proceedings of the board, including quorum, place of meetings and notices to be given of meetings;

(b) with respect to the appointment of a chairman and a vice-chairman;

(c) for enabling the board to constitute committees; and

(d) for authorising the delegation to committees of any of the powers of the board and for regulating the proceedings of committees, including quorum, place of meetings and notices to be given of meetings.

(2) The first meeting of an internal drainage board shall be held on such day and at such time and place as may be fixed by the relevant Minister; and the relevant Minister shall cause notice of the meeting to be sent by post to each member of the board not less than fourteen days before the appointed day.

(3) Any member of an internal drainage board who is interested in any company with which the board has, or proposes to make, any contract shall—

(a) disclose to the board the fact and nature of his interest; and

(b) take no part in any deliberation or decision of the board relating to such contract; and such disclosure shall be forthwith recorded in the minutes of the board.

(4) A minute of the proceedings of a meeting of an internal drainage board, or of a committee of such a board, purporting to be signed at that or the next ensuing meeting by a person describing himself as, or appearing to be, the chairman of the meeting to the proceedings of which the minute relates—

(a) shall be evidence of the proceedings; and

(b) shall be received in evidence without further proof.

(5) Until the contrary is proved—

(a) every meeting in respect of the proceedings of which a minute has been so signed shall be deemed to have been duly convened and held;

(b) all the proceedings had at any such meeting shall be deemed to have been duly had; and

(c) where the proceedings at any such meeting are the proceedings of a committee, the committee shall be deemed to have been duly constituted and to have had power to deal with the matters referred to in the minute.

(6) The proceedings of an internal drainage board shall not be invalidated by any vacancy in the membership of the board or by any defect in the appointment or qualification of any member of the board.

Annual report

4.—(1) An internal drainage board shall—

(a) before such date in every year as the relevant Minister may fix, send to that Minister a report of their proceedings during the preceding year and

(b) at the same time send a copy of the report to the NRA and to the council of every county and London borough in which any part of the board's district is situated.

(2) Every such report shall be in such form and shall contain particulars with respect to such matters as the relevant Minister may direct.

Accounts

5.—(1) An internal drainage board shall—

(a) as soon as the accounts of the board have been audited, send a copy of them to the relevant Minister; and

(b) at the same time, send a copy of the accounts to the NRA and to the council of every county of London borough in which any part of the board's district is situated.

(2) A copy of the audited accounts of an internal drainage board shall be kept at the office of the board and any person who is liable to pay drainage rates in the board's district shall be entitled, without payment, to inspect and take copies of, or extracts from, that copy.

SCHEDULE 3

PROCEDURE WITH RESPECT TO CERTAIN ORDERS

Application and interpretation of Schedule

1.—(1) This Schedule applies to the following orders under this Act, that is to say—

(a) any order confirming a scheme under section 3 or 32 of this Act; and

(b) any order under section 4, 5 or 35 of this Act.

(2) References in this Schedule to an unconfirmed order are references to any order to which this Schedule applies other than one confirmed under section 6 of the Statutory Orders (Special Procedure) Act 1945.

(3) In this Schedule "the appropriate Minister," in relation to any order or proposed order, means the Minister or Ministers by whom the order is being or has been made or, as the case may be, by whom the proposal to make the order has been made.

Notice of proposed order

2.—(1) Before making an order to which this Schedule applies the appropriate Minister shall cause notice of—

(a) his intention to make it;

(b) the place where copies of the draft order may be inspected and obtained; and

(c) the period within which, and the manner in which, objections to the draft order may be made,

to be published in the London Gazette and in such other manner as he thinks best adapted for informing persons affected and to be sent to the persons specified in sub-paragraph (2) below.

(2) The persons referred to in sub-paragraph (1) above are—

(a) every county council or London borough council in whose area any part of the area proposed to be affected by the order is situated and, if any part of that area is situated in the City of London, the Common Council of the City of London;

(b) every drainage body, navigation authority, harbour authority or conservancy authority that is known to the appropriate Minister to be exercising jurisdiction within the area proposed to be affected by the order.

Determination of whether to make order

3.—(1) Before making an order to which this Schedule applies the appropriate Minister—

(a) shall consider any objections duly made to the draft order; and

(b) may, in any case, cause a public local inquiry to be held with respect to any objections to the draft order.

(2) The appropriate Minister, in making an order to which this Schedule applies, may make such modifications in the terms of the draft as appear to him to be desirable.

Procedure and other matters after the making of an order

4.—(1) After the appropriate Minister has made an order to which this Schedule applies, the order, together with a notice under sub-paragraph (2) below, shall be published in such manner as he thinks best adapted for informing the persons affected.

(2) A notice under this sub-paragraph is a notice—

(a) that the appropriate Minister has made the order; and

(b) that the order will become final and have effect unless, within such period of not less than thirty days as may be specified in the notice, a memorial praying that the order shall be subject to special parliamentary procedure is presented to that Minister by a person who—

(i) is affected by the order; and

(ii) has such interest as may be prescribed as being sufficient for the purpose.

Orders subject to special parliamentary procedure

5.—(1) If, in the case of any order to which this Schedule applies, either—

(a) no such memorial as is mentioned in paragraph 4(2) above has been presented within the period so mentioned; or

(b) every memorial so presented has been withdrawn,

the appropriate Minister shall confirm the order and it shall thereupon have effect.

(2) If such a memorial has been presented in respect of such an order and has not been withdrawn, the order shall be subject to special parliamentary procedure.

(3) An order to which this Schedule applies shall, in any event, be subject to special parliamentary procedure if the appropriate Minister so directs.

(4) The appropriate Minister may, at any time before it has been laid before Parliament, revoke, either wholly or partially, any order to which this Schedule applies which is subject to special parliamentary procedure.

Notice of unconfirmed orders

6. As soon as may be after an unconfirmed order has effect, the appropriate Minister shall publish in the London Gazette, and in such other manner as he thinks best adapted for informing persons affected, a notice—

(a) stating that the order has come into force; and

(b) naming a place where a copy of it may be seen at all reasonable hours.

Challenge to unconfirmed orders

7.—(1) If any person aggrieved by an unconfirmed order desires to question its validity on the ground—

(a) that it is not within the powers of this Act; or

(b) that any requirement of this Act has not been complied with,

he may, within six weeks of the relevant date, make an application for the purpose of the High Court.

(2) Where an application is duly made to the High Court under this paragraph, the High Court, if satisfied—

(a) that the order is not within the powers of this Act; or

(b) that the interests of the applicant have been substantially prejudiced by any requirements of this Act not having been complied with,

may quash the order either generally or in so far as it affects the applicant.

(3) Except by leave of the Court of Appeal, no appeal shall lie to the House of Lords from a decision of the Court of Appeal in proceedings under this paragraph.

(4) Subject to the preceding provisions of this paragraph, an unconfirmed order shall not at any time be questioned in any legal proceedings whatsoever.

(5) In this paragraph "the relevant date," in relation to any order to which this Schedule applies, means—

(a) where the order is subject to special parliamentary procedure, the date on which the order becomes operative under the Statutory Orders (Special Procedure) Act 1945;

(b) where the order is not subject to special parliamentary procedure, the date of the publication of the notice mentioned in paragraph 6 above.

Power to make regulations for purposes of Schedule etc.

8. The Ministers may make regulations in relation to—

(a) the publication of notices under this Schedule;

(b) the holding of public local inquiries under this Schedule and procedure at those inquiries; and

(c) any other matters of procedure respecting the making of orders to which this Schedule applies.

Section 18   SCHEDULE 4

Schemes for Small Drainage Works

Consultation and notice with respect to proposed scheme

1.—(1) Before making a scheme under section 18 of this Act, a local authority shall consult the NRA.

(2) Before making a scheme under section 18 of this Act, the NRA or a local authority shall give a notice under this paragraph—

(a) to the owners and occupiers of land within the area to which the scheme relates; and

(b) to any other persons appearing to the NRA or, as the case may be, that local authority to be affected by the scheme.

(3) A notice under this paragraph is a notice in the prescribed manner of—

(a) the intention of making the scheme; ·

(b) the place where a draft of it can be inspected; and

(c) the period (which shall not be less than thirty days) within which objections to it may be made to the NRA or local authority.

Objections to scheme

2.—(1) Where any objections to a scheme are duly made and are not withdrawn—

(a) the NRA or local authority shall send a copy of the draft scheme, together with copies of the objections, to one of the Ministers; and

(b) the scheme shall not be made unless the draft is confirmed, with or without modifications, by one of the Ministers.

(2) Before either of the Ministers confirms a scheme under this paragraph, he shall either—

(a) cause a public local inquiry to be held; or

(b) give to—

    (i) the NRA or, as the case may be, the local authority; and

    (ii) the persons by whom the objections are made,

an opportunity of appearing before and being heard by a person appointed by him for the purpose.

Notice of scheme after it is made

3.—(1) Where a scheme is made by the NRA or a local authority under section 18 of this Act, the NRA or, as the case may be, that authority shall send copies of the scheme to the owners and occupiers of land in the area to which it relates.

(2) Where the NRA makes such a scheme it shall also notify the council of any county, district or London borough in which any of that land is situated.

Section 66   SCHEDULE 5

BYELAWS

Publicity for application for confirmation

1.—(1) An internal drainage board shall, at least one month before they apply for the confirmation of any byelaw—

(a) cause a notice of their intention to make the application to be published in the London Gazette and in such other manner as they think best adapted for informing persons affected; and

(b) cause copies of the notice to be served on any public authorities who appear to them to be concerned.

(2) For at least one month before an application is made for the confirmation of any byelaw, a copy of it shall be deposited at the offices of the relevant drainage board.

(3) The relevant drainage board shall provide reasonable facilities for the inspection, without charge, of a byelaw deposited under sub-paragraph (2) above.

(4) Any person on application to the relevant drainage board shall be entitled to be furnished free of charge with a printed copy of such a byelaw.

Confirmation

2.—(1) The relevant Minister, with or without a local inquiry, may—

(a) refuse to confirm any byelaw submitted for confirmation under this Schedule; or

(b) confirm any such byelaw either without or, if the relevant drainage board consent, with modifications.

(2) The relevant drainage board shall, if so directed by the relevant Minister, cause notice of any proposed modifications to be given in accordance with his directions.

Commencement of byelaw

3.—(1) The relevant Minister may fix the date on which any confirmed byelaw is to come into force.

(2) If no date is fixed in relation to a byelaw under sub-paragraph (1) above, the byelaw shall come into force at the end of the period of one month beginning with the date of confirmation.

Publicity for confirmed byelaw

4.—(1) Any byelaw confirmed under this Schedule shall be printed and deposited at the office of the relevant drainage board and copies of it shall, at all reasonable hours, be open to public inspection without charge.

(2) Any person, on application to the relevant drainage board, shall be entitled to be furnished with a copy of any confirmed byelaw, on payment of such reasonable sum as the relevant drainage board may determine.

Revocation of byelaw

5. If it appears to the relevant Minister that the revocation of a byelaw is necessary or expedient, he may, after—

(a) giving notice to the relevant drainage board and considering any objections raised by them; and

(b) if required by them, holding a local inquiry,

revoke that byelaw.

Proof of byelaws

6. The production of a printed copy of a byelaw purporting to be made by an internal drainage board upon which is indorsed a certificate, purporting to be signed on their behalf, stating—

(a) that the byelaw was made by that board;

(b) that the copy is a true copy of the byelaw;

(c) that on a specified date the byelaw was confirmed; and

(d) the date (if any) fixed under any enactment for the coming into force of the byelaw,

shall be *prima facie* evidence of the facts stated in the certificate and without proof of the handwriting or official position of any person purporting to sign the certificate.

Interpretation

7. In this Schedule "the relevant drainage board," in relation to a byelaw, means the internal drainage board which made the byelaw.

Section 67   SCHEDULE 6

PROTECTION FOR PARTICULAR UNDERTAKINGS

Undertakings protected by Schedule

1.—(1) The following are the undertakings protected by this Schedule, that is to say—

(a) the undertakings of the NRA, the Civil Aviation Authority, the British Coal Corporation and the Post Office;

(b) the undertaking of any water undertaker or sewerage undertaker;

(c) any undertaking consisting in the running of a telecommunications code system, within the meaning of Schedule 4 to the Telecommunications Act 1984;

(d) any airport to which Part V of the Airports Act 1986 applies;

(e) the undertaking of any public gas supplier within the meaning of Part I of the Gas Act 1986;

(f) the undertaking of any person authorised by a licence under Part I of the Electricity Act 1989 to generate, transmit or supply electricity;

(g) the undertaking of any navigation authority, harbour authority or conservancy authority;

(i) any public utility undertaking carried on by a local authority under any Act or under any order having the force of an Act.

(2) For the purposes of this Schedule any reference in this Schedule, in relation to any such airport as is mentioned in sub-paragraph (1)(d) above, to the persons carrying on the undertaking is a reference to the airport operator.

Protection for statutory powers and jurisdiction

2. Without prejudice to any power under this Act to transfer the functions of any authority or to vary navigation rights, nothing in this Act shall confer power to do anything which prejudices the exercise of any statutory power, authority or jurisdiction from time to time vested in or exercisable by any persons carrying on an undertaking protected by this Schedule.

General provisions protecting undertakings

3. Nothing in this Act or in any order under this Act shall authorise any person, except with the consent of the persons carrying on an undertaking protected by this Schedule, to do any work which, whether directly or indirectly, interferes or will interfere—

(a) with the works or any property which is vested in, or under the control of, the persons carrying on that undertaking, in their capacity as such; or

(b) with the use of any such works or property,

in such a manner as to affect injuriously those works or that property or the carrying on of that undertaking.

Special protection for railways etc.

4. Without prejudice to the preceding provisions of this Schedule, nothing in the provisions of

this Act shall authorise any person, except with the consent of the British Railways Board, London Regional Transport or, as the case may be, the railway company in question, to interfere with—

(a) any railway bridge or any other work connected with a railway; or

(b) the structure, use or maintenance of a railway or the traffic on it.

Conditions of consent and grounds for refusal

5. A consent for the purposes of paragraph 3 or 4 above may be given subject to reasonable conditions but shall not be unreasonably withheld.

Determination of disputes

6. If any question arises under this Schedule—

(a) as to whether anything done or proposed to be done interferes or will interfere as mentioned in paragraph 3 or 4 above;

(b) as to whether any consent for the purposes of this Schedule is being unreasonably withheld; or

(c) as to whether any condition subject to which any such consent has been given was reasonable,

that question shall be referred to a single arbitrator to be agreed between the parties or, failing such an agreement, to be appointed by the President of the Institution of Civil Engineers.

Table of Derivations

Notes:

1. The following abbreviations are used in this Table:—

1976	= The Land Drainage Act 1976 (c. 70)
1980(MCA)	= The Magistrates' Courts Act 1980 (c. 43)
1982(CJA)	= The Criminal Justice Act 1982 (c. 48)
1984	= The Telecommunications Act 1984 (c. 12)
1985(LG)	= The Local Government Act 1985 (c. 51)
1989	= The Water Act 1989 (c. 15)
1989(EA)	= The Electricity Act 1989 (c. 29)
1990	= The Environmental Protection Act 1990 (c. 43)
R: (followed by a number	= The recommendation so numbered as set out in the Appendix to the Report of the Law Commission (Cm. 1483).

2. Transfer of functions orders ("TFOs"), where applicable in relation to a provision re-enacted in the consolidation Bills, are specified at the appropriate place in column 2 of the Table.

3. General provisions contained in section 32 of the Magistrates' Courts Act 1980 (c. 43) and section 46 of the Criminal Justice Act 1982 (c. 48) provide, respectively, for the maximum fine on summary conviction of an either way offence to be the statutory maximum and for a reference to the amount of the maximum fine to which a person is liable in respect of a summary offence to become a reference to a level on the standard scale. Where the effect of one of these enactments is consolidated it is not referred to separately in column 2 of this Table.

Provision of Act	Derivation
1	1976 ss.6 & 7 & Sched. 2, para. 2; 1989 s.140; S.I. 1990/72 reg. 19(1) & (2); TFO: S.I. b1978/272 Sched. 3, para. 7(4) & (13).
2	1976 s.14; 1989 Sched. 15, para. 1; TFO: S.I. 1978/272 Sched. 3, para. 7(4).
3	1976 ss.11(1) & (3)–(5), 109(1), (5) & (6) & 114(3); 1989 Sched. 15, para. 1; S.I. 1991/983; TFO: S.I. 1978/272 Sched. 3, para. 7(4).
4	1976 ss.11(2) & 12 & 109(1) & (6); 1989 Sched. 15, para. 1; S.I. 1991/983; TFO: S.I. 1978/272 Sched. 3, para. 7(4).
5	1976 ss.13 & 109(1) & (6); 1989 Sched. 15, para. 1; S.I. 1991/983; TFO: S.I. 1978/272 Sched. 3, para. 7(4).
6	1976 s.94; 1989 Sched. 15, paras. 1 & 33; TFO: S.I. 1978/272 Sched. 3, para. 7(8).
7	1976 ss.15 & 116(4); 1989 Sched. 15, para. 1; TFO: S.I. 1978/272 Sched. 3, para. 7(4).
8	1976 ss.24(2) & 28(1); 1989 Sched. 15, paras. 9(1) & 12(1).

Provision of Act	Derivation
9	1976 ss.16(1)–(4) & 116(1); 1982(CJA) s.38; 1989 Sched. 15, para. 1; TFO: S.I. 1978/272 Sched. 3, para. 7(4).
10	1976 s.16(5)–(7); 1985(LG) Sched. 7, para. 2; 1989 Sched. 15, para. 1; TFO: S.I. 1978/272 Sched. 3, para. 7(4).
11	1976, s.21; 1989 Sched. 15, paras. 1 & 6.
12	1989 ss.8(1)–(3), (5)–(7) & 152(8).
13	1989 s.9; 1990 Sched. 9, para. 17(2).
14	1976 ss.17, 98(1) & (7) & 100(3); 1989 Sched. 15, paras. 1 & 5.
15	1976 ss.8(1), 33, 98(1) & (7) & 100(3); 1989 Sched. 15, para. 1; 1990 Sched. 15, para. 18.
16	1976 s.98(5), (5A) & (6); 1985(LG) Sched. 7, para. 6; 1989 Sched. 15, para. 1.
17	1976 ss.98(8)–(13) & 116(4); 1989 Sched. 15, para. 1.
18	1976 ss.30, 31(4)–(6), 100(1) & 109(1); 1989 Sched. 15, paras. 1 & 34; S.I. 1978/319 Sched. para. 1; TFO: S.I. 1978/272 Sched. 3, para. 7(5).
19	1976 ss.8(1) & 23(2)–(5); 1984 Sched. 4, para. 66(1); 1989 Sched. 15, paras. 1 & 8; TFOs: S.I. 1978/272 Sched. 3, para. 7(4) & (6); R: 16.
20	1976 ss.8(1), 22, 99 & 116(4); 1985(LG) Sched. 7, para. 7; 1989 Sched. 15, para. 7.
21	1976 ss.8(1); 24(2) & (3); 1989 Sched. 15, paras. 1 & 9(1).
22	1976 s.93; 1989 Sched. 15, para. 32; TFO: S.I. 1978/272 Sched. 3, para. 7(3).
23	1976 ss.28(1)–(3) & (10)–(11A), 109(1) & (2) & 116(4); 1989 Sched. 15, paras. 1, 12 & 35.
24	1976 s.28(4)–(9); 1989 Sched. 15, para. 1; R: 9.
25	1976 ss.8(1), 18(1)–(7) & 97(1); 1982(CJA) s.38; 1989 Sched. 15, para. 1.
26	1976 ss.18(8)–(11) & 97(3); 1989 Sched. 15, para. 1.
27	1976 s.19; 1980(MCA) Sched. 7, para. 147; 1989 Sched. 15, para. 1.
28	1976 s.40.
29	1976 ss.40(2), 43 & 44; 1986 (c. 49) Sched. 3, para. 3; TFO: S.I. 1978/272 Sched. 3, para. 7(3).
30	1976 ss.40(4), 41, 43(3) & 44.
31	1976 ss.42 & 44.
32	1976 ss.25 & 109(1), (5) & (6); 1989 Sched. 15, para. 1; S.I. 1991/983; TFO: S.I. 1978/272 Sched. 3, para. 7(3).
33	1976 ss.18(10) & 26(1)–(3); 1989 Sched. 15, para. 1; TFO: S.I. 1978/272 Sched. 3, para. 7(4) & (5).
34	1976 ss.26(4)–(11) & 109(6); 1989 Sched. 15, para. 1 & 10; S.I. 1991/983; TFO: S.I. 1978/272 Sched. 3, para. 7(4) & (5).
35	1976 ss.8(1), 27 & 109(1) & (5); 1989 Sched. 15, paras. 1 & 11; TFOs: S.I. 1978/272 Sched. 3, para. 7(4) & (5); S.I. 1983/1127 art. 1(2)(a).
36	S.I. 1990/72 regs. 3 & 6(1).
37	S.I. 1990/72 regs. 15, 16 & 18.
38	1976 ss.68(1), (5) & (6); 1989 Sched. 15, paras. 1 & 28; S.I. 1990/72 reg. 17; TFO: S.I. 1978/272 Sched. 3, para. 7(4).
39	1976 s.69(2)–(6); 1989 Sched. 15, para. 1; TFO: S.I. 1978/272 Sched. 3, para. 7(4) & (5).
40	1976 ss.63(3) & 83; 1989 Sched. 15, para. 1; S.I. 1990/72 regs. 5, 6(1) & (1)–(3).
41	1976 s.64(1); 1989 Sched. 15, para. 27; S.I. 1990/72 regs. 2 & 7(1) & Sched.
42	S.I. 1990/72 reg. 7(2), (3) & (5); S.I. 1991/523 reg. 5.
43	1976 s.67(1)–(3) & (8); S.I. 1990/72 reg. 6(2).
44	1976 s.67(4)–(7); S.I. 1990/72 regs. 6(2) & 8(6).
45	1976 s.78; S.I. 1989/440 Sched. 2, para. 4; S.I. 1990/72 regs. 3, 5, 6(2) & 7(4); TFO: S.I. 1978/272 Sched. 3, para. 7(3).
46	1976 s.79; S.I. 1989/440 Sched. 2, para. 4; S.I. 1990/72 reg. 6(2).
47	1976 s.68(4)–(9); 1989 Sched. 15, paras. 1 & 28; S.I. 1990/72 reg. 6(2); TFO: S.I. 1978/272 Sched. 3, para. 7(4).
48	1976 ss.72(1) & (4) & 74; S.I. 1990/72 reg. 8(4).
49	1976 ss.71 & 72(4)–(6); S.I. 1990/72 reg. 6(2)(c).
50	1976 s.76; S.I. 1990/72 reg. 6(2).
51	1976 s.77; S.I. 1990/72 reg. 6(2); TFO: S.I. 1978/272 Sched. 3, para. 7(4).
52	1976 s.75; TFO: S.I. 1978/272 Sched. 3, para. 7(4).

Provision of Act	Derivation
53	1976 s.82; 1982(CJA) s.38.
54	1976 ss.72(7) & 80; S.I. 1990/72 reg. 8(7) & (8).
55	1976 ss.87, 104 & 107.
56	1976 ss.8(1) & 88; 1989 Sched. 15, paras. 1 & 29.
57	1976 s.84(4)–(8); 1989 Sched. 15, para. 1; TFO: S.I. 1978/272 Sched. 3, para. 7(4).
58	1976 s.86; 1989 Sched. 15, para. 1; TFO: S.I. 1978/272 Sched. 3, para. 7(4).
59	1976 s.91; 1989 Sched. 15, para. 1; TFO: S.I. 1978/272 Sched. 3, para. 7(3).
60	1976 s.102.
61	1976 s.110(3); 1985(LG) Sched. 7, para. 8.
62	1976 ss.37 & 98(3), (5) & (6); IA s.17; 1981 (c. 67) Sched. 4, para. 1; 1989 Sched. 15, para. 17; TFO: S.I. 1978/272 Sched. 3, para. 7(4).
63	1976 s.38; TFO: S.I. 1978/272 Sched. 3, para. 7(4).
64	1976 ss.39 & 103; 1982(CJA) s.38.
65	1976 ss.95 & 109(1) & (2); TFO: S.I. 1978/272 Sched. 3, para. 7(9).
66	1976 ss.8(1), 34 & 98 & Sched. 4, para. 1; 1982(CJA) s.38; 1989 Sched. 15, para. 15; TFO: S.I. 1978/272 Sched. 3, para. 7(3).
67	1976 ss.111, 113 & 114; 1979 (c. 46) Sched. 4, para. 16; 1989 S. 160.
68	1976 s.106.
69	1976 s.96; 1982(CJA) s.38; 1986 (c. 63) s.42; TFO: S.I. 1978/272 Sched. para. 7(9).
70	1989 s.174; R: 11.
71	1976 s.108; 1989 s.187; R: 14.
72	1976 ss.24(1), 26(12) 104A & 116; 1985 Sched. 7, para. 9; S.I. 1986/208 Sched. 1, Pt. II, para. 4; S.I. 1990/72 regs. 2, 6(2), 7(6), 8(5) & 9(3); S.I. 1991/523 reg. 5(c); R: 16.
73	1976 s.8(2); TFO: S.I. 1978/272 Sched. 3, para. 7(5); R: 8.
74	1976 s.115; 1989 s.192.
75	1989 s.193.
Sched. 1	1976 ss.7(3) & 83 & Sched. 2, paras. 1–6 & Pt. II, S.I. 1978/319 Sched. para. 7(4); 1989 Sched. 15, para. 40; S.I. 1990/72 regs. 6, 7(6), 19 & 20; S.I. 1991/523 regs. 5(c) & 7; TFO: S.I. 1978/272 Sched. 3, para. 7(4); R: 7.
Sched. 2	1976 s.35 & Sched. 2, paras. 8 to 21; 1989 Sched. 15, para. 1; TFO: S.I. 1978/272 Sched. 3, para. 7(4); R: 10.
Sched. 3	1976 109(4) & Sched. 3; TFO: S.I. 1978/272 Sched. 3, para. 7(4), (5) & (12).
Sched. 4	1976 ss.31(1)–(3) & 100(1) & (2); 1989 Sched. 15, para. 1; TFO: S.I. 1978/272 Sched. 3, para. 7(5).
Sched. 5	1976 Sched. 4, paras. 2–11; 1989 Sched. 15, para. 41; TFO: S.I. 1978/272 Sched. 3, para. 7(4).
Sched. 6	1976 s.112; 1984 (c. 12) Sched. 4, para 66(1); 1984 (c. 32) Sched. 6, para. 12; 1986 (c. 31) Sched. 2, para. 5; 1986 (c. 44) Sched. 7, para. 25; 1987 (c. 3) Sched. 1, para. 32; 1989 Sched. 15, para. 37; 1989(EA) Sched. 16, para. 21.

TABLE OF DESTINATIONS

LAND DRAINAGE ACT 1976
c.70

TABLE OF DESTINATIONS

TABLE OF DESTINATIONS

ELECTRICITY ACT 1989
c.29

1989	c.29
Sched. 16,	
para. 21 ....Sched. 6	

WATER ACT 1989
c.15

1989	c.15	1989	c.15	1989	c.15
s.9 .... s.13		Sched. 15,		Sched. 15—*cont.*	
8(1)......... 12		para. 1 ..... 2, 3, 4, 5, 6,		para. 10 34	
(2)......... 12			7, 9, 10, 11, 14,	11 35	
(3)......... 12			15, 16, 17, 18,	12 23	
(5)......... 12			19, 21, 23, 24,	(1).. 8	
(6)......... 12			25, 26, 27, 32,	15 66	
(7)......... 12			33, 34, 35, 38,	17 62	
140 1			39, 40, 46, 56,	27 41	
152(8)...... 12			57, 58, 59,	28 .... 38, 47	
160 67			Sched. 1,	29 56	
174 70			Sched. 3	32 22	
187 71		5 14		33 6	
192 74		6 11		34 18	
193 75		7 20		35 23	
		8 19		37 ....Sched. 6	
		9(1)... 8, 21		41 ....Sched. 5	

ENVIRONMENTAL PROTECTION ACT 1990
c.43

1990	c.43
Sched. 9,	
para. 17(2) .. s.13	
18 15	

THE LAW COMMISSION'S REPORT ON THE CONSOLIDATION OF WATER LEGISLATION 1990
(CMND. 1483)

Rec. 7 ....Sched. 1
8 .... s.73
9 24
10 ......Sched. 2
11 70
14 71
16 .... 19, 72

TRANSFER OF FUNCTIONS ORDERS (STATUTORY INSTRUMENTS)

S.I. 1978/272...... s.22, 29, 32,		S.I. 1978/319...... 18		S.I. 1990/72—*cont.*	
Sched. 3,	45, 59, 66	Sched.,		reg. 6(2)(c) . 49	
para. 7(3)		para. 1		7(1).... 41	
(4)... 1, 2, 3, 4,		7(4)...Sched. 1		(2).... 42	
5, 7, 9, 10,		1986/208...... 72		(3).... 42	
19, 33, 34,		Sched. 1,		(4).... 45	
35, 38, 39,		Pt. II,		(5).... 42	
51, 52, 57,		para. 4		(6).... 72, Sched.	
58, 62, 63,		1983/1127..... 35		1	
Sched. 1,		Art. 1(2)(a)		8(1)–(3) 40	
Sched. 2,		1989/440...... 45, 46		(4).... 48	
Sched. 3,		Sched. 2,		(5).... 72	
Sched. 5		para. 4		(6).... 44	
(5)... 18, 33, 34,		1990/72....... 41, 72		(7).... 54	
35, 39, 73,		reg. 2		(8).... 54	
Sched. 3,		3 ..... 36, 45		9(3).... 72	
Sched. 4		5 ..... 40, 45		15 37	
(6)... 19		6 .....Sched. 1		16 37	
(8)... 6		(1).... 36, 40		17 38	
(9)... 65, 69		(2).... 43, 44, 45,		18 37	
(12)..Sched. 3		46, 47, 50,		19 .....Sched. 1	
(13).. 1		51, 72		(1)... 1	
				(2)... 1	

INDEX

References are to sections

AGRICULTURAL LAND TRIBUNAL,
  composition of, 31(1)
  incidental power of, 31(5)
APPLICATION,
  Crown to, 74
  Isles of Scilly, to, 75

BY-LAWS,
  commencement of, Sched. 5(3)
  confirmation of, Sched. 5(2)
  proof of, Sched. 5(6)
  publicity for, Sched. 5(4)
  revocation of, Sched. 5(5)

DEFAULT POWER,
  NRA, of, 9
DEFINITIONS,
  ditch, 28(5)
  generally, 72
  harbour, 12(7)
  national park authority, 13(5)
  remedial work, 28(5)
DISPUTES,
  arbitration provisions, 73
  determination of, Sched. 6(6)
DITCHES,
  authorisation of drainage works, 30
  definitions of, 28(5)
  orders to restore, 28
  persons liable for restoration of, 28(2)
DRAINAGE DISTRICTS,
  division of, 38
  petitions for division of, 39
  power of the NRA, 2(2)
  reorganisation of, 3
  review of boundaries, 2
DRAINAGE OF SMALL AREAS,
  area to be improved, 18(3)(b)
  estimated expenses, 18(3)(c)
  limits on expenditure, 18(4)
  local authorities, exercise by, 10
  power of minister to exempt from expendi-
    ture limits, 18(6)
DRAINAGE RATES,
  appeals against, 51
  assessment for, 49
  calculation of, 42
  determination of annual value, 42
  levying of, 40
  power to grant exemption from, 47
  procedure for making, 48
DRAINAGE REGISTER,
  duty to keep, 52(1)

DRAINAGE REGISTER—*cont.*
  duty to provide information, 53

ENVIRONMENT,
  conservation of buildings, historic sites,
    etc, 12(1)(b)
  duty to consider freedom of access, 12(2)
  duty to consider the disabled, 12(5)
  duty to consider, 12(1)
  generally, 12–13
  national parks, 13(2)
  recreational use of water, 12(4)
  special interest sites, 113
EXPENSES OF INTERNAL DRAINAGE BOARDS,
  apportionment of, 37
  calculation of, 37
  division of districts for the purposes of
    determining, 38
  payment of officers, Sched. 2(1)
  payments to staff, Sched. 2(2)
  raising of, 36(2)

FINANCE,
  allocation of revenue, 58
  contributions of local authorities, 60
  contributions of NRA, 57
  enforcing payment, 54
  grants to drainage boards, 59
  power to borrow, 55
  power to impose tolls, 5

INTERNAL DRAINAGE BOARDS,
  agreements with conservancy authorities,
    19
  agreements with navigation authorities, 19
  annual report, Sched. 2(4)
  applications to obstruct water course, 23
  commutation of obligations, 33
  constitution, 1
  disposal of spoil, 15
  election of members, Sched. 1, 1–4
  expenses incurred by, 119(4)
  financial consequences of commutation, 34
  members of, 1(4)
  obligation to repair, 21
  power of entry, 64
  power to acquire land, 62
  power to dispose of land, 63
  power to impose charges for use of recrea-
    tional land and water, 12(6)
  power to make by-laws, 66
  power generally, 14

WATER CONSOLIDATION (CONSEQUENTIAL PROVISIONS) ACT 1991

(1991 c. 60)

ARRANGEMENT OF SECTIONS

An Act to make provision for consequential amendments and repeals, and for transitional and transitory matters and savings, in connection with the consolidation of certain enactments in the Water Resources Act 1991, the Water Industry Act 1991, the Land Drainage Act 1991 and the Statutory Water Companies Act 1991; and to repeal certain related enactments which are spent or unnecessary.   [25th July 1991]

PARLIAMENTARY DEBATES
   Hansard, H.L. Vol. 528, cols. 484, 744, 1738; Vol. 529, col. 746; H.C. Vol. 195, col. 1111.

INTRODUCTION
   This Act makes all consequential amendments and repeals in connection with the four main Acts.

Interpretation

1.—(1) In this Act "the consolidation Acts" means—
(a) the Water Resources Act 1991, the Water Industry Act 1991, the Land Drainage Act 1991 and the Statutory Water Companies Act 1991; and
(b) so much of this Act as re-enacts provisions repealed by this Act.
(2) In this Act—
   "the 1989 Act" means the Water Act 1989;
   "the 1976 Act" means the Land Drainage Act 1976;
   "commencement" means the commencement of the consolidation Acts and of so much of this Act as gives effect to any repeal;
   "local statutory provision" means—
        (a) a provision of a local Act (including an Act confirming a provisional order);
        (b) a provision of so much of any public general Act as has effect with respect to a particular area, with respect to particular persons or works or with respect to particular provisions falling within any paragraph of this definition;
        (c) a provision of an instrument made under any provision falling within paragraph (a) or (b) above; or
        (d) a provision of any other instrument which is in the nature of a local enactment;
   "modifications" includes additions, alterations and omissions, and cognate expressions shall be construed accordingly;

"the NRA" means the National Rivers Auhority;
"subordinate legislation" has the same meaning as in the Interpretation
Act 1978.

Consequential amendments, transitional and transitory provisions and savings

2.—(1) The enactments mentioned in Schedule 1 to this Act shall have effect subject to the amendments there specified (being amendments consequential on the re-enactment of provisions in the consolidation Acts).

(2) The transitional provisions, transitory provisions and savings contained in Schedule 2 to this Act shall have effect.

(3) The powers under sections 190(1) and 194(5) of the 1989 Act and the powers under paragraph 2 of Schedule 17 to that Act (by virtue of which consequential amendments, transitional provisions and savings may be made in connection with the coming into force of provisions of that Act)—

(a) shall not be restricted in consequence of any repeal made by this Act or of any provision of the consolidation Acts; but

(b) shall be exercisable in relation to any provision of those Acts to the same extent as, before the coming into force of this Act, they were exercisable in relation to any corresponding provision of that Act.

(4) The repeals made by this Act shall not affect the following powers to amend local statutory provisions, that is to say—

(a) the power conferred by section 317 of the Public Health Act 1936;

(b) the power conferred by section 12 of the Public Health (Drainage of Trade Premises) Act 1937 and section 69(2) of the Public Health Act 1961;

(c) the power conferred by section 133(1) of the Water Resources Act 1963;

(d) the powers conferred by section 191 of the 1989 Act;

but those powers, to the extent that they are exercisable by reference to the effect or operation of, or to things done under, any provision repealed by this Act, shall also be exercisable by reference to the effect or operation of, or to things done under, any corresponding provision of the consolidation Acts.

(5) The provisions having effect by virtue of this section shall be without prejudice to sections 16 and 17 of the Interpretation Act 1978 (effect of repeals) and subsections (3) and (4) above shall also be without prejudice to the generality of the provisions of paragraphs 1 and 2 of Schedule 2 to this Act.

Repeals etc.

3.—(1) Subject to the provisions having effect by virtue of section 2 above, the enactments mentioned in Part I of Schedule 3 to this Act (which include spent and unnecessary enactments) are hereby repealed to the extent specified in the third column of that Part of that Schedule.

(2) Subject as aforesaid, the subordinate legislation mentioned in Part II of Schedule 3 to this Act is hereby revoked to the extent specified in the third column of that Part of that Schedule.

Short title, commencement and extent

4.—(1) This Act may be cited as the Water Consolidation (Consequential Provisions) Act 1991.

(2) This Act shall come into force on December 1, 1991.

(3) Subject to subsections (4) to (7) below, this Act extends to England and Wales only.

(4) Subject to the provisions—

(a) of any order under section 224 of the Water Resources Act 1991,

section 222 of the Water Industry Act 1991 or section 75 of the Land
Drainage Act 1991 (Isles of Scilly); and
  (b) of any order under section 193 of the Water Act 1989 (Isles of Scilly)
       which, by virtue of paragraph 1 of Schedule 2 to this Act, has effect in
       relation to any provisions of the consolidation Acts as an order falling
       within paragraph (a) above,
nothing in this Act shall require or authorise any function, duty or power to
be carried out, performed or exercised in relation to the Isles of Scilly by the
NRA or any water undertaker or sewerage undertaker.

(5) This Act, so far as it gives effect to amendments of the following
enactments, that is to say—
  (a) the Parliamentary Commissioner Act 1967;
  (b) the House of Commons Disqualification Act 1975; and
  (c) the Northern Ireland Assembly Disqualification Act 1975,
extends to the whole United Kingdom.

(6) This Act so far as it gives effect to amendments of the Environmental
Protection Act 1990 extends to Great Britain.

(7) This Act, so far as it gives effect to the amendments in Schedule 1 to
this Act of the following enactments, that is to say—
  (a) sections 30D(1) and 31(2)(b)(iv) of the Control of Pollution Act 1974;
       and
  (b) the Water (Fluoridation) Act 1985,
extends to Scotland only.

SCHEDULES

Section 2   SCHEDULE 1

CONSEQUENTIAL AMENDMENTS

The Public Health Act 1875 (c. 55)

1. A person shall not be guilty of an offence under section 68 of the Public Health Act 1875
(offences of causing pollution of certain waters) in respect of any entry of matter into any
controlled waters (within the meaning of Part III of the Water Resources Act 1991) which
occurs—
  (a) under and in accordance with a consent under Chapter II of Part III of the Water
       Resources Act 1991 or under Part II of the Control of Pollution Act 1974 (which makes
       corresponding provision for Scotland); or
  (b) as a result of any act or omission under and in accordance with such a consent.

The Public Health Act 1936 (c. 39)

2.—(1) Section 48 of the Public Health Act 1936 shall cease to have effect in relation to a
drain or private sewer connecting with a public sewer; and, accordingly, for the word "relevant"
in subsection (1) of that section there shall be substituted the word "local."

(2) In section 227 of that Act of 1936—
  (a) in paragraph (a), for the words "paragraph 2 of Schedule 19 to the Water Act 1989" there
       shall be substituted the words "section 158 of the Water Industry Act 1991";
  (b) in paragraph (b), for the words "paragraph 2" there shall be substituted the words
       "section 158"; and
  (c) in the words after paragraph (b), for the word "Schedule" there shall be substituted the
       word "Act."

(3) Section 330 of that Act of 1936 shall cease to have effect in relation to any sewers, drains,
culverts or pipes vested in a sewerage undertaker.

(4) In section 343(1) of that Act of 1936, for the definitions of "land drainage authority" and
"public sewer" there shall be substituted, respectively, the following definitions—
  " 'land drainage authority' means the National Rivers Authority or an internal drainage
     board; and
  'public sewer' means a sewer for the time being vested in a sewerage undertaker in its
     capacity as such, whether vested in that undertaker by virtue of a scheme under
     Schedule 2 to the Water Act 1989 or Schedule 2 to the Water Industry Act 1991 or
     under section 179 of that Act of 1991 or otherwise;".

The Agriculture (Miscellaneous Provisions) Act 1941 (c. 50)

3. In section 15 of the Agriculture (Miscellaneous Provisions) Act 1941, for the definitions of "drainage," "drainage authority," "internal drainage board" and "internal drainage district" there shall be substituted the following definitions—
" 'drainage' has the same meaning as in the Land Drainage Act 1991;
'drainage authority' means the National Rivers Authority or an internal drainage board;".

The Fire Services Act 1947 (c. 41)

4.—(1) In section 14(4) of the Fire Services Act 1947, for the words "section 20 of the Water Act 1989" there shall be substituted the words "section 18 of the Water Industry Act 1991."
(2) In section 15(2) of that Act of 1947, for the words "sections 47(1) and 81(1) of the Water Act 1989" there shall be substituted the words "sections 57(1) and 147(1) of the Water Industry Act 1991."

The Requisitioned Land and War Works Act 1948 (c. 17)

5. In section 15(4)(c) of the Requisitioned Land and War Works Act 1948, for the words from "paragraphs 2 and 3" to "1989" there shall be substituted the words "section 158 of the Water Industry Act 1991."

The Coast Protection Act 1949 (c. 74)

6. In section 49(1) of the Coast Protection Act 1949, for the definitions of "catchment board" and "drainage authority" there shall be substituted the following definition—
" 'drainage authority' means the National Rivers Authority or an internal drainage board;".

The National Parks and Access to the Countryside Act 1949 (c. 97)

7. In section 114(1) of the National Parks and Access to the Countryside Act 1949, for the definition of "drainage authority" there shall be substituted the following definition—
" 'drainage authority' means the National Rivers Authority or an internal drainage board;".

The Coal-Mining (Subsidence) Act 1957 (c. 59)

8.—(1) In section 5 of the Coal-Mining (Subsidence) Act 1957—
(a) in subsection (2), for the words from "main river" to "shall make" there shall be substituted the words "main river within the meaning of Part IV of the Water Resources Act 1991, shall make"; and
(b) in subsection (7), for the words from "main river" to "that Act" there shall be substituted the words "main river within the meaning of Part IV of the Water Resources Act 1991, or outside any internal drainage district as defined by the Land Drainage Act 1991."
(2) This paragraph shall have no effect after the coming into force of the repeal of section 5 of that Act of 1957 by the Coal Mining Subsidence Act 1991.

The Radioactive Substances Act 1960 (c. 34)

9.—(1) In Part I of Schedule 1 to the Radioactive Substances Act 1960, at the end the following paragraphs shall be inserted appropriately numbered—
". Sections 72, 111 and 113(6) and Chapter III of Part IV of the Water Industry Act 1991 and paragraphs 2 to 4 of Schedule 8 to that Act so far as they re-enact provisions of sections 43 and 44 of the Control of Pollution Act 1974.
. Sections 82, 84, 85, 86, 87(1), 88(2), 92, 93, 99, 161, 190, 202, 203 and 213 of the Water Resources Act 1991.
. Section 18 of the Water Act 1945 so far as it continues to have effect by virtue of Schedule 2 to the Water Consolidation (Consequential Provisions) Act 1991 or by virtue of provisions of the Control of Pollution Act 1974 not having been brought into force."
(2) Without prejudice to paragraph 2 of Schedule 2 to this Act, the references to provisions of the Water Resources Act 1991 which are inserted by virtue of sub-paragraph (1) above in Part I of Schedule 1 to that Act of 1960 shall have effect subject to the power conferred by section 98 of that Act of 1991.

The Public Bodies (Admission to Meetings) Act 1960 (c. 67)

10. In paragraph 1 of the Schedule to the Public Bodies (Admission to Meetings) Act 1960—

(a) in sub-paragraph (j), for the words "section 2 or 141 of the Water Act 1989" there shall be substituted the words "section 7 or 8 of the Water Resources Act 1991"; and

(b) in sub-paragraph (k), for the words "established and maintained under section 6 of that Act" there shall be substituted the words "maintained under section 28 of the Water Industry Act 1991."

The Public Health Act 1961 (c. 64)

11. In section 54 of the Public Health Act 1961—

(a) in subsection (4), for the words from "controlled by" to "internal drainage board" and "the board" there shall be substituted, respectively, the words "controlled by the National Rivers Authority or any internal drainage board" and the words "that Authority or, as the case may be, that board"; and

(b) in subsection (10), for the words from "byelaws," in the first place where it occurs, onwards there shall be substituted the words "byelaws made by virtue of paragraph 5 of Schedule 25 to the Water Resources Act 1991 or section 66 of the Land Drainage Act 1991."

The Pipe-lines Act 1962 (c. 58)

12. In section 66(1) of the Pipe-lines Act 1962, for the definition of "river works consent" there shall be substituted the following definition—

" 'river works consent' means a consent given under section 109 of the Water Resources Act 1991;".

The Harbours Act 1964 (c. 40)

13.—(1) References in the Harbours Act 1964 to river works powers shall include references to any powers which are conferred by section 4 or 165 of the Water Resources Act 1991, or by or under Part VII of that Act or Part VI of the Water Industry Act 1991 and to any powers conferred by section 14 of the Land Drainage Act 1991.

(2) In section 27(2) of that Act of 1964—

(a) in paragraph (c), for the words from "under" to "that Act" there shall be substituted the words "under section 142 of the Water Resources Act 1991"; and

(b) in paragraph (e), for the words "the Water Resources Act 1963" there shall be substituted the words "Chapter II of Part II of the Water Resources Act 1991."

The Gas Act 1965 (c. 36)

14.—(1) In section 15 of the Gas Act 1965—

(a) in subsection (1), for the words "section 26 of the Water Resources Act 1963" there shall be substituted the words "Chapter II of Part II of the Water Resources Act 1991 or within the meaning of that Chapter so far as it applies in relation to any application for a licence which is a licence of right for the purposes of Schedule 7 to the Water Resources Act 1991)"; and

(b) in subsection (5)(b), for the words "section 129 of the Water Act 1989" there shall be substituted the words "section 123 of the Water Resources Act 1991."

(2) In section 23(5) of that Act of 1965, for the words "the Water Resources Act 1963" there shall be substituted the words "Chapter II of Part II of the Water Resources Act 1991."

(3) In Part II of Schedule 4 to that Act of 1965—

(a) in paragraph 4, for the words "section 26 of the Water Resources Act 1963" there shall be substituted the words "Chapter II of Part II of the Water Resources Act 1991 or within the meaning of that Chapter so far as it applies in relation to any application for a licence which is a licence of right for the purposes of Schedule 7 to the Water Resources Act 1991)"; and

(b) in paragraph 5(4)(b), for the words "section 129 of the Water Act 1989" there shall be substituted the words "section 123 of the Water Resources Act 1991."

The Public Works Loans Act 1965 (c. 63)

15. In Schedule 1 to the Public Works Loans Act 1965—

(a) in paragraph 1, for the words "section 87 of the Land Drainage Act 1976 or with any other enactment" there shall be substituted the words "any enactment"; and

(b) in paragraph 2, after the words "as so incorporated" there shall be inserted the words "or as incorporated with section 55 of the Land Drainage Act 1991."

The Sea Fisheries Regulation Act 1966 (c. 38)

16. In section 18(3) of the Sea Fisheries Regulation Act 1966, for the words "section 186 of

the Water Act 1989" there shall be substituted the words "section 210(2) of the Water Resources Act 1991."

The Parliamentary Commissioner Act 1967 (c. 13)

17. In Schedule 2 to the Parliamentary Commissioner Act 1967, in the note 9 inserted by the 1989 Act, for the words from "(that is to say" to "1976)" there shall be substituted the words "(within the meaning of the Water Resources Act 1991)."

The Sea Fish (Conservation) Act 1967 (c. 84)

18. In section 18(1) of the Sea Fish (Conservation) Act 1967 (enforcement of orders relating to salmon and migratory trout)—
(a) for the words "subsection (4) of section 141 of the Water Act 1989" there shall be substituted the words "subsection (6) of section 2 of the Water Resources Act 1991"; and
(b) for paragraph (b) there shall be substituted the following paragraph—
  "(b) the provisions of sections 169 and 172 of the Water Resources Act 1991 and, in relation to those sections, of Schedule 20 to that Act (which confer powers of entry) shall apply as if section 4 of this Act, and any order under section 5 or 6 of this Act, were an enactment to which the said sections 169 and 172 applied."

The Transport Act 1968 (c. 73)

19. In section 109(3)(b) of the Transport Act 1968, for the words "the Ministers (as defined in section 82(9) of the Water Resources Act 1963" there shall be substituted the words "the Ministers (for the purposes of Schedule 2 to the Water Resources Act 1991)."

The Local Authorities (Goods and Services) Act 1970 (c. 39)

20. The powers conferred by section 1 of the Local Authorities (Goods and Services) Act 1970 (supply of goods and services by local authorities to public bodies) shall be exercisable by a local authority, within the meaning of that section, as if the NRA was a public body within the meaning of that section; and the powers of a local authority under that Act shall be deemed to include power to enter into an agreement for the collection and recovery by the authority, on behalf of any water undertaker or sewerage undertaker, of any charges fixed by the undertaker under Chapter I of Part V of the Water Industry Act 1991.

The Land Charges Act 1972 (c. 61)

21. In paragraph 1(d) of Schedule 2 to the Land Charges Act 1972—
(a) for the words "the Land Drainage Act 1976" there shall be substituted the words "the Land Drainage Act 1991" (with a corresponding amendment of the Chapter number); and
(b) for the words "Section 26(6)" there shall be substituted the words "Section 34(2)."

The Local Government Act 1972 (c. 70)

22.—(1) In section 73(1) of the Local Government Act 1972, for the words from "conferred" to "or," in the first place where it occurs, there shall be substituted the words "conferred by the Water Resources Act 1991, the Land Drainage Act 1991 or."
(2) In section 138(3) of that Act of 1972—
(a) in paragraph (a), for the words "within the meaning of the Land Drainage Act 1930" there shall be substituted the words "within the meaning of Part IV of the Water Resources Act 1991"; and
(b) in paragraph (b), for the words from "section" to the end of paragraph (b) there shall be substituted the words "sections 14 to 17, 62(2) and (3) and 66 of the Land Drainage Act 1991."

The Land Compensation Act 1973 (c. 41)

23. In sections 44(2) and 58(2) of the Land Compensation Act 1973, for the words "Schedule 18 to the Water Act 1989" there shall be substituted the words "Schedule 9 to the Water Industry Act 1991 or of Schedule 18 to the Water Resources Act 1991."

The Fair Trading Act 1973 (c. 41)

24.—(1) The Director General of Fair Trading shall consult with the Director General of Water Services before publishing under section 124 of the Fair Trading Act 1973 (publication of information or advice) any information or advice which the latter Director has power to publish under section 201(2) of the Water Industry Act 1991.

(2) Section 125(1) of that Act of 1973 (annual and other reports) shall not apply to activities of the Monopolies and Mergers Commission on which the Director General of Water Services is required to report by section 193(1) of the Water Industry Act 1991.

(3) In section 133(2)(a) of that Act of 1973, after the words "or the Water Act 1989," there shall be inserted the words "the Water Industry Act 1991 or any of the other consolidation Acts (within the meaning of section 206 of that Act of 1991)."

The Local Government Act 1974 (c. 7)

25. In section 25(1) of the Local Government Act 1974, in paragraph (d), for the words from "(that is to say" to "1976)" there shall (without prejudice to anything saved by paragraph 3 of Schedule 26 to the 1989 Act) be substituted the words "(within the meaning of the Water Resources Act 1991)."

The Consumer Credit Act 1974 (c. 39)

26. In section 174(3)(a) of the Consumer Credit Act 1974, after the words "or the Water Act 1989," there shall be inserted the words "the Water Industry Act 1991 or any of the other consolidation Acts (within the meaning of section 206 of that Act of 1991)."

The Control of Pollution Act 1974 (c. 40)

27.—(1) In section 30D(1) of the Control of Pollution Act 1974, for the words "section 105 of the Water Act 1989" there shall be substituted the words "section 83 of the Water Resources Act 1991."

(2) In section 31(2)(b)(iv) of that Act of 1974, for the words "Chapter I of Part III of the Water Act 1989" there shall be substituted the words "Chapter II of Part III of the Water Resources Act 1991."

The House of Commons Disqualification Act 1975 (c. 24)

28. In Part III of Schedule 1 to the House of Commons Disqualification Act 1975 (other disqualifying offices)—
(a) in the entry relating to a chairman of a customer service committee established under section 6 of the Water Act 1989, for the words "established under section 6 of the Water Act 1989" there shall be substituted the words "maintained under section 28 of the Water Industry Act 1991"; and
(b) in the entry relating to directors of companies holding appointments under Chapter I of Part II of the Water Act 1989, for the words "Water Act 1989" there shall be substituted the words "Water Industry Act 1991."

The Northern Ireland Assembly Disqualification Act 1975 (c. 25)

29. In Part III of Schedule 1 to the Northern Ireland Assembly Disqualification Act 1975 (other disqualifying offices)—
(a) in the entry relating to a chairman of a customer service committee established under section 6 of the Water Act 1989, for the words "established under section 6 of the Water Act 1989" there shall be substituted the words "maintained under section 28 of the Water Industry Act 1991"; and
(b) in the entry relating to directors of companies holding appointments under Chapter I of Part II of the Water Act 1989, for the words "Water Act 1989" there shall be substituted the words "Water Industry Act 1991."

The Salmon and Freshwater Fisheries Act 1975 (c. 51)

30.—(1) A person shall not be guilty of an offence under section 4 of the Salmon and Freshwater Fisheries Act 1975 (offences of causing pollution of certain waters) in respect of any entry of matter into any controlled waters (within the meaning of Part III of the Water Resources Act 1991) which occurs—
(a) under and in accordance with a consent under Chapter II of Part III of the Water Resources Act 1991 or under Part II of the Control of Pollution Act 1974 (which makes corresponding provision for Scotland); or
(b) as a result of any act or omission under and in accordance with such a consent.

(2) In section 5(5) of that Act of 1975, for paragraph (c) there shall be substituted the following paragraph—
"(c) section 85(1) of the Water Resources Act 1991;".

(3) In section 39(5) of that Act of 1975, after the words "this section" there shall be substituted the words "the Water Resources Act 1991."

(4) In section 41(1) of that Act of 1975, for the definition of "inland water" there shall be substituted the following definition—

" 'inland water' means any area of inland waters within the meaning of the Water Resources Act 1991;".

(5) Section 215 of the Water Resources Act 1991 shall apply in relation to a local inquiry under that Act of 1975 as it applies in relation to a local inquiry under a provision of that Act of 1991 to which that section applies.

(6) In paragraph 39 of Schedule 3 to that Act of 1975, for the words "the said section 145" there shall be substituted the words "section 4 of the Water Resources Act 1991."

The Restrictive Trade Practices Act 1976 (c. 34)

31. In section 4(1)(a) of the Restrictive Trade Practices Act 1976, after the words "or the Water Act 1989," there shall be inserted the words "the Water Industry Act 1991 or any of the other consolidation Acts (within the meaning of section 206 of that Act of 1991)."

The Interpretation Act 1978 (c. 30)

32. In Schedule 1 to the Interpretation Act 1978, in the definitions of "sewerage undertaker" and "water undertaker," for the words "section 11 of the Water Act 1989" there shall be substituted the words "section 6 of the Water Industry Act 1991."

The Estate Agents Act 1979 (c. 38)

33. In section 10(3)(a) of the Estate Agents Act 1979, after the words "or the Water Act 1989," there shall be inserted the words "the Water Industry Act 1991 or any of the other consolidation Acts (within the meaning of section 206 of that Act of 1991)."

The Competition Act 1980 (c. 21)

34. In section 19(3)(l) of the Competition Act 1980, at the end there shall be inserted the words "the Water Industry Act 1991 or any of the other consolidation Acts (within the meaning of section 206 of that Act of 1991)."

The Local Government, Planning and Land Act 1980 (c. 65)

35. In section 185(2) of the Local Government, Planning and Land Act 1980—
(a) for paragraph (b), there shall be substituted the following paragraph—
   "(b) on any inland waters (within the meaning of the Water Resources Act 1991) in respect of which the National Rivers Authority may make byelaws by virtue of paragraph 1 of Schedule 25 to that Act";
(b) the reference in paragraph (c) to the definition of a "navigation authority" in subsection (1) of section 135 of the Water Resources Act 1963 shall continue to have effect notwithstanding the repeal and re-enactment of provisions of that section.

The Highways Act 1980 (c. 66)

36.—(1) In section 100(5) and (6) of the Highways Act 1980, for the words "Schedule 19 to the Water Act 1989" there shall be substituted the words "sections 158, 159, 163, 165 and 168 of the Water Industry Act 1991."

(2) In section 339 of that Act of 1980, for the words "Land Drainage Act 1976," in each place where they occur, there shall be substituted the words "Land Drainage Act 1991."

The Fisheries Act 1981 (c. 29)

37. In Schedule 4 to the Fisheries Act 1981, for paragraph 6 there shall be substituted the following paragraph—

"Offences against byelaws relating to salmon and other freshwater fishing

"6. Any offence under section 211 of the Water Resources Act 1991 consisting in a contravention of a byelaw made for any of the following purposes mentioned in paragraph 6(2) of Schedule 25 to that Act—
   (a) prohibiting the taking or removal from any water without lawful authority of any fish, whether alive or dead;
   (b) prohibiting or regulating the taking of trout or any freshwater fish of a size less than that prescribed by the byelaw;

(c) prohibiting the use for taking salmon, trout, or freshwater fish of any instrument (not being a fixed engine) in such waters and at such times as are prescribed by the byelaw;

(d) specifying the nets and other instruments (not being fixed engines) which may be used for taking salmon, trout, freshwater fish and eels and imposing requirements as to the use of such nets and other instruments;

(e) imposing requirements as to the construction, design, material and dimensions of any such nets or instruments, including in the case of nets the size of mesh;

(f) prohibiting the carrying in any boat or vessel whilst being used in fishing for salmon or trout of any net which is not licensed, or which is without the mark, label or number prescribed by the byelaw;

(g) prohibiting or regulating the carrying in a boat or vessel during the annual close season for salmon of a net capable of taking salmon, other than a net commonly used in the area to which the byelaw applies for sea fishing and carried in a boat or vessel commonly used for that purpose."

The Telecommunications Act 1984 (c. 12)

38.—(1) In section 98(9) of the Telecommunications Act 1984, in paragraph (a) of the definition of "water main," for the words from "within," in the first place where it occurs, to "that Act" there shall be substituted the words "or resource main within the meaning of the Water Industry Act 1991."

(2) In section 101(3)(j) of that Act of 1984, at the end there shall be inserted the words "the Water Industry Act 1991 or any of the other consolidation Acts (within the meaning of section 206 of that Act of 1991)."

The Building Act 1984 (c. 55)

39.—(1) The Building Act 1984 shall be amended as follows.

(2) In section 18(5)—

(a) in the definition of "disposal main," for the words "paragraph 1 of Schedule 19 to the Water Act 1989" there shall be substituted the words "the Water Industry Act 1991"; and

(b) in the definition of "map of sewers," for the words "section 166 of the Water Act 1989" there shall be substituted the words "section 199 of the Water Industry Act 1991."

(3) In section 25(7)—

(a) for the words "section 65 of the Water Act 1989" there shall be substituted the words "section 67 of the Water Industry Act 1991"; and

(b) for the words "Chapter II of Part II" there shall be substituted the words "Chapter III of Part III."

(4) In section 82, for the words "section 167 of the Water Act 1989" there shall be substituted the words "section 174 of the Water Industry Act 1991 or section 176 of the Water Resources Act 1991."

(5) In section 101—

(a) in subsection (1), for the words "paragraphs 2 and 3 of Schedule 19 to the Water Act 1989," the words "they apply" and the words "that Schedule" there shall be substituted, respectively, the words "section 158 of the Water Industry Act 1991," the words "it applies" and the words "that section"; and

(b) in subsection (2), for the words "Those paragraphs" there shall be substituted the words "That section."

(6) In section 126, in the definition of "public sewer," for the words "Public Health Act 1936" there shall be substituted the words "Water Industry Act 1991."

The Companies Act 1985 (c. 6)

40.—(1) In sections 425(6)(a) and 460(2) of the Companies Act 1985 (compromises with creditors and protection of minorities by the Secretary of State), any reference to a company or body corporate which is liable to be wound up includes a reference to a company or body corporate which would be so liable but for section 25 of the Water Industry Act 1991.

(2) In section 459(3) of that Act of 1985, for the words "the Water Act 1989" there shall be substituted the words "the Statutory Water Companies Act 1991."

The Business Names Act 1985 (c. 7)

41. In section 1(1)(c) of the Business Names Act 1985 (persons subject to Act), the reference to a company capable of being wound up includes a reference to a company which would be so capable but for section 25 of the Water Industry Act 1991.

The Water (Fluoridation) Act 1985 (c. 63)

42. In section 1 of the Water (Fluoridation) Act 1985, after subsection (6) there shall be inserted the following subsection—

"(7) In subsection (6) above, the reference to water to which fluoride has been added by a statutory water undertaker in exercise of the power conferred by this section includes a reference to water to which fluoride has been added by a water undertaker in exercise of the power conferred by section 87 of the Water Industry Act 1991."

The Agricultural Holdings Act 1986 (c. 5)

43. In paragraphs 9 to 11 of Part II of Schedule 3 to the Agricultural Holdings Act 1986, for the words "section 112 of the Water Act 1989," wherever they occur, there shall be substituted the words "section 94 or 95 of the Water Resources Act 1991."

The Airports Act 1986 (c. 31)

44. In section 74(3)(k) of the Airports Act 1986, at the end there shall be inserted the words "the Water Industry Act 1991 or any of the other consolidation Acts (within the meaning of section 206 of that Act of 1991)."

The Gas Act 1986 (c. 44)

45. In section 42(3)(l) of the Gas Act 1986, at the end there shall be inserted the words "the Water Industry Act 1991 or any of the other consolidation Acts (within the meaning of section 206 of that Act of 1991)."

The Insolvency Act 1986 (c. 45)

46. In section 413(2) of the Insolvency Act 1986, for the words "section 23 or 24 of or Schedule 6 to the Water Act 1989" there shall be substituted the words "any of sections 23 to 26 of the Water Industry Act 1991 or Schedule 3 to that Act."

The Norfolk and Suffolk Broads Act 1988 (c. 4)

47. In section 25(1) of the Norfolk and Suffolk Broads Act 1988, in paragraph (b) of the definition of "statutory undertaker," for the words "the Land Drainage Act 1976" there shall be substituted the words "the Land Drainage Act 1991."

The Local Government Act 1988 (c. 9)

48. In section 25(2)(b) of the Local Government Act 1988, for the words "section 40 or 71 of the Water Act 1989" there shall be substituted the words "section 41 or 98 of the Water Industry Act 1991."

The Local Government Finance Act 1988 (c. 41)

49. In Schedule 5 to the Local Government Finance Act 1988—
(a) in paragraph 10(1)(b), for the words "section 28(3)(a) of that Act" there shall be substituted the words "section 142(1)(a) of the Water Resources Act 1991"; and
(b) for sub-paragraph (2) of paragraph 14 there shall be substituted the following sub-paragraph—
   "(2) 'Drainage authority' means the National Rivers Authority or any internal drainage board and 'main river' and 'watercourse' have the same meanings, respectively, as they have in the Water Resources Act 1991 and the Land Drainage Act 1991."

The Water Act 1989 (c. 15)

50.—(1) The Water Act 1989 shall be amended as follows.
(2) In section 174—
(a) in each of paragraphs (a) and (b) of subsection (2), after the word "Act" there shall be inserted the words "or any of the water consolidation Acts";
(b) for paragraph (c) of that subsection there shall be substituted the following paragraph—
   "(c) in pursuance of any duty imposed by section 197(1)(a) or (2) or 203(1) or (2) of the Water Resources Act 1991 or of any arrangements made by the Director under section 29(6) of the Water Industry Act 1991;"
(c) in paragraph (j) of that subsection, after the word "Act," in the first place where it occurs, there shall be inserted the words ", any of the water consolidation Acts" and,

after that word, in the second place where it occurs, there shall be inserted the words "or any of those Acts";

(d) in subsection (4)(a), for the words "section 34 above" and the words "this Act" there shall be substituted, respectively, the words "section 201 of the Water Industry Act 1991" and the words "the water consolidation Acts"; and

(e) after subsection (7) there shall be inserted the following subsection—

"(8) In this section 'the water consolidation Acts' means the Water Resources Act 1991, the Water Industry Act 1991, the Statutory Water Companies Act 1991, the Land Drainage Act 1991 and the Water Consolidation (Consequential Provisions) Act 1991."

(3) In Schedule 26—

(a) in paragraph 6(2), after the words "this Act" there shall be inserted the words "or Chapter I of Part V of the Water Industry Act 1991";

(b) in paragraph 15(1), for the words "and are" there shall be substituted the words "continue to have effect (notwithstanding the repeal of sub-paragraph (2) of this paragraph) in accordance with paragraph 1 of Schedule 2 to the Water Consolidation (Consequential Provisions) Act 1991 and were";

(c) in paragraph 40(3), in the words after paragraph (b), for the words "that subsection" there shall be substituted the words "section 28(3) of the Salmon and Freshwater Fisheries Act 1975";

(d) in paragraph 41(5), for the words "section 20 of this Act" there shall be substituted the words "section 18 of the Water Industry Act 1991";

(e) in paragraph 49, for the words "section 8 or 157 of this Act or otherwise by virtue of this Act" there shall be substituted the words "by virtue of any enactment"; and

(f) in paragraph 54(2), for the words "Chapter VI of Part II of this Act" there shall be substituted the words "the Statutory Water Companies Act 1991."

The Electricity Act 1989 (c. 29)

51.—(1) In section 57(3)(n) of the Electricity Act 1989, at the end there shall be inserted the words "the Water Industry Act 1991 or any of the other consolidation Acts (within the meaning of section 206 of that Act of 1991)."

(2) In paragraph 3(1)(c) of Schedule 4 to that Act of 1989, for the words "Schedule 19 to the Water Act 1989" there shall be substituted the words "section 159 of the Water Resources Act 1991 or section 158 of the Water Industry Act 1991 which (whether or not it is in a street) is."

The Companies Act 1989 (c. 40)

52. In section 152(11) of the Companies Act 1989, for the words from "include" onwards there shall be substituted the words "include sections 32 to 34 of the Water Industry Act 1991 and any reference under section 32 of that Act."

The Capital Allowances Act 1990 (c. 1)

53. In section 18(9) of the Capital Allowances Act 1990, in the definition of "sewerage undertaking," for the words "the Water Act 1989" there shall be substituted the words "the Water Industry Act 1991."

The Town and Country Planning Act 1990 (c. 8)

54. In section 264(4)(a) of the Town and Country Planning Act 1990, for the words "or the Water Act 1989" there shall be substituted the words "the Water Act 1989 or the Water Industry Act 1991."

The Food Safety Act 1990 (c. 16)

55. In section 55(1) of the Food Safety Act 1990, for the words "Chapter II of Part II of the Water Act 1989" there shall be substituted the words "Part III of the Water Industry Act 1991."

The Environmental Protection Act 1990 (c. 43)

56.—(1) In section 1 of the Environmental Protection Act 1990—

(a) in subsection (6), for the words "Chapter I of Part III of the Water Act 1989" there shall be substituted the words "Part III of the Water Resources Act 1991"; and

(b) in subsection (11)(c), for the words "the Public Health Act 1936" there shall be substituted the words "the Water Industry Act 1991."

(2) In section 7(12) of that Act of 1990, for paragraph (e) there shall be substituted the following paragraph—

"(e) the Water Resources Act 1991; and."

(3) In section 20(9) of that Act of 1990, for the words "section 117(1)(f) of the Water Act 1989" there shall be substituted the words "section 190(1)(f) of the Water Resources Act 1991."

(4) In section 28(3) of that Act of 1990, for the words "Chapter I of Part III of the Water Act 1989" there shall be substituted the words "Chapter I of Part III of the Water Resources Act 1991."

The New Roads and Street Works Act 1991 (c. 22)

57.—(1) In section 89 of the New Roads and Street Works Act 1991, for the words "the Water Act 1989" there shall be substituted the words "the Water Industry Act 1991."

(2) In paragraph 7(3) of Schedule 4 to that Act of 1991, for the words "Water Act 1989" there shall be substituted the words "Water Industry Act 1991."

The Planning and Compensation Act 1991 (c. 34)

58. In Part I of Schedule 18 to the Planning and Compensation Act 1991, after the entries relating to the Planning (Hazardous Substances) Act 1990 there shall be inserted the following entries—

"Paragraph 1 of Schedule 9 to the Water Resources Act 1991	Date of entry upon or occupation or use of land
Paragraph 2(2) of (3) of that Schedule	Date of the ordinary drought order
Paragraph 2(4) of that Schedule	Date of decision to prohibit or limit the taking of water
Paragraph 2(5) of that Schedule	Date of suspension or variation of consent to make discharges or of the attachment of conditions to such consent
Paragraph 2(1) of Schedule 21 to that Act	Date of claim
Paragraph 2(2) or (3) of that Schedule	In the case of damage sustained by reason of expenditure, the date on which the damage is sustained; otherwise the date of claim
Paragraph 4(1)(b) of that Schedule	Date loss is caused or damage done
Paragraph 5(1) of that Schedule (including that provision as applied by paragraph 5(3)(b) of that Schedule)	Date of claim
Paragraph 2(1) of Schedule 12 to the Water Industry Act 1991	Date of claim
Paragraph 2(2) or (3) of that Schedule	In the case of damage sustained by reason of expenditure, the date on which the damage is sustained, otherwise the date of claim
Paragraph 6(1)(b) of that Schedule	Date loss is caused or damage done
Section 14 of the Land Drainage Act 1991 (including that provision as applied by section 25(4)(b))	Date of claim
Section 22 of that Act	Date of claim
Section 29(5) of that Act (including that provision as applied by sections 30(3) and 31(5))	Date of claim"

The Coal Mining Subsidence Act 1991 (c. 45)

59. In section 36(8) of the Coal Mining Subsidence Act 1991, in the definition of "main river," for the words "the Land Drainage Act 1976" there shall be substituted the words "Part IV of the Water Resources Act 1991."

Section 2   SCHEDULE 2

Transitional and Transitory Provisions and Savings

Part I

General Transitional Provisions and Savings

Principal transitional provision

1.—(1) Subject to Part II of this Schedule, any subordinate legislation, application or appointment made, consent or approval given, licence or certificate issued or other thing done under or for the purposes of any enactment repealed by this Act, and anything which has effect as something so made, given, issued or done, shall have effect, so far as necessary for the purposes specified in sub-paragraph (2) below, as made, given, issued or done under the corresponding provision of the consolidation Acts.

(2) The purposes mentioned in sub-paragraph (1) above are—

(a) the purpose of preserving and continuing the validity and effect after commencement of anything which has been made, given, issued or otherwise done under or for the purposes of any enactment repealed by this Act, and of anything so far as it is treated as a thing so made, given, issued or done; and

(b) the purpose of including references to things which have been so made, given, issued or done before commencement, or which are treated as if they were, in references in the consolidation Acts, in any other enactment and in any subordinate legislation or document to things made, given, issued or otherwise done under or for the purposes of any provision of the consolidation Acts.

(3) Subject to sub-paragraphs (1) and (2) above, a reference in any Act or in any subordinate legislation or document to any enactment repealed by this Act shall have effect after commencement as a reference to the corresponding enactment contained in the consolidation Acts.

(4) Without prejudice to the preceding provisions of this paragraph, where—

(a) by virtue of any enactment repealed by this Act, any subordinate legislation, consent, licence, document or other thing has effect immediately before commencement subject to modifications specified or described in that enactment; and

(b) with those modifications that subordinate legislation, consent, licence, document or other thing would continue, in accordance wih sub-paragraphs (1) and (2) above, to have effect after commencement as something made, given, issued or done under or for the purposes of any provision of the consolidation Acts,

then, notwithstanding the repeal, the modifications shall continue to have effect, and those sub-paragraphs shall have effect in relation to that subordinate legislation, consent, licence, document or other thing accordingly.

(5) Without prejudice to the preceding provisions of this paragraph, anything which immediately before commencement is treated for the purposes of an enactment repealed by this Act as done by or in relation to a particular person shall continue to be treated as done by or in relation to that person for the purposes of the corresponding provisions of the consolidation Acts, and sub-paragraphs (1) and (2) above shall have effect accordingly.

(6) The repeal by this Act of any provision which authorised any instrument under an enactment repealed by this Act to be made without—

(a) such consultation; or

(b) such compliance with any other requirements,

as would be required in respect of an instrument under the corresponding provision of the consolidation Acts shall not prevent any instrument which in pursuance of that provision has been so made from having effect, in accordance with sub-paragraphs (1) and (2) above, as if made under that corresponding provision.

(7) Where—

(a) any period of time is specified in any enactment repealed by this Act to which a provision of the consolidation Acts corresponds; and

(b) that period is current for the purposes of that enactment at commencement,

so much of the period as has expired before commencement shall be taken into account, in relation to anything which is treated by virtue of this Schedule as done under that provision, as if that provision had been in force when the period began to run.

(8) References in this paragraph to an enactment repealed by this Act include references to any provision of subordinate legislation which is revoked by this Act.

Savings for powers to make, amend or challenge subordinate legislation and for certain specific instruments

2.—(1) Without prejudice to the provisions of paragraph 1 above—

(a) the powers to make subordinate legislation under the Local Government Finance Act 1988 and section 149 of the Local Government and Housing Act 1989 (power to make provision in connection with the arrangements for financing local government); and

(b) any other powers to make subordinate legislation modifying any provision reproduced in the consolidation Acts, including the power to amend or revoke any subordinate legislation reproduced in those Acts,

shall be exercisable in relation to the provisions of those Acts to the like extent as they were exercisable in relation to the enactment or subordinate legislation to which those provisions correspond.

(2) Where provision contained in any subordinate legislation is reproduced in any enactment contained in sections 134 to 136 of the Water Resources Act 1991, Chapter I or II of Part IV of, or Part II of Schedule 1 to, the Land Drainage Act 1991 or Part II of this Schedule, that enactment shall not have any greater effect by virtue of being contained in an enactment than it would have had if it had continued to be contained in the subordinate legislation in question.

(3) The repeal by this Act of paragraph 23 of Schedule 13 to the 1989 Act shall not affect the operation in relation to the NRA, in accordance with sub-paragraph (3) of that paragraph, of any provision of an order under section 82 of the Water Resources Act 1963 which was made before September 1, 1989.

(4) The repeal by this Act of section 106 of the Water Resources Act 1963 shall not affect the powers conferred by that section in relation to the provisions of section 5 or Part IX of that Act or in relation to any order under section 10 of that Act.

(5) The repeal by this Act of sections 45 to 47, 89 and 110 of the 1976 Act shall not affect the operation of those sections so far as—

(a) they have effect by virtue of any subordinate legislation made, under the Local Government Finance Act 1988 and section 149 of the Local Government and Housing Act 1989, for the purpose of or in connection with the issue of levies by the NRA; or

(b) they have effect in relation to any precept issued before April 1, 1990.

(6) The repeal by this Act of sub-paragraph (2) of paragraph 71 of Schedule 25 to the 1989 Act (power to modify Part XII of the Companies Act 1985) shall not affect the continuing validity of anything done by virtue of the power conferred by that sub-paragraph to make regulations in relation to times before September 1, 1989.

Byelaws: prevention of waste of water etc.

3.—(1) Subject to section 74(6) of the Water Industry Act 1991—

(a) any byelaws made or having effect as if made under section 17 of the 1945 Act and in force immediately before commencement by virtue of paragraph 19 of Schedule 26 to the 1989 Act; and

(b) section 19 of the 1945 Act so far as it relates to any such byelaws,

shall continue to have effect (notwithstanding the repeals made by this Act) with the modifications for which that paragraph provides and as if every duty imposed on a water undertaker by virtue of those modifications were enforceable under section 18 of the Water Industry Act 1991 by the Secretary of State.

(2) Notwithstanding any repeal by the 1989 Act or this Act, Part V of the 1945 Act shall accordingly have effect in relation to any provisions having effect under the said paragraph 19 and this paragraph as it had effect in relation to those provisions immediately before September 1, 1989.

(3) In this paragraph and paragraph 4 below "the 1945 Act" means the Water Act 1945.

Byelaws preventing pollution

4.—(1) Where immediately before commencement any byelaws have effect by virtue of paragraph 57 of Schedule 26 to the 1989 Act as if the power conferred by any enactment repealed by this Act included a power to make those byelaws, those byelaws shall continue to have effect as if the corresponding enactment contained in the consolidation Acts contained such a power.

(2) Notwithstanding any repeal made by the 1989 Act or this Act, the provisions of subsections (2) to (5) of section 18 of the 1945 Act and of subsections (2), (4) and (5) of section 19 of the 1945 Act and, in relation to those provisions, the provisions of Part V of the 1945 Act shall have effect in relation to any byelaws under section 18 of the 1945 Act which have effect by virtue of paragraph 57(1) and (2) of Schedule 26 to the 1989 Act and the preceding provisions of this Schedule—

(a) as they had effect in relation to those byelaws immediately before September 1, 1989; but

(b) as if any references in those provisions of sections 18 and 19 of the 1945 Act to the statutory water undertakers who made the byelaws were references to the relevant body;

and every duty imposed on a water undertaker by virtue of paragraph (b) above shall be enforceable under section 18 of the Water Industry Act 1991 by the Secretary of State.

(3) Without prejudice to the power of the Secretary of State under the Control of Pollution Act 1974 to bring the repeal of section 18 of the 1945 Act into force, the power of the Secretary of State under section 93 of the Water Resources Act 1991 to make an order for the purposes specified in that section shall include power, by an order under that section—

(a) to modify the operation of the provisions of this Schedule in relation to any byelaws under the said section 18 that have effect by virtue of those provisions; and

(b) to revoke or amend any such byelaws.

(4) Without prejudice to the power conferred by virtue of sub-paragraph (3) above, the Secretary of State shall not be required to hold a local inquiry before exercising his power, under paragraph 5 of Schedule 10 to the Water Industry Act 1991 or under paragraph 5 of Schedule 26 to the Water Resources Act 1991, to revoke any byelaw having effect by virtue paragraph 57(2) of Schedule 26 to the 1989 Act and this Schedule.

(5) The repeal by this Act of subsections (8) and (9) of section 79 of the Water Resources Act 1963 shall not affect the application of those subsections (pending the repeal of subsection (1) of that section) in relation to any byelaws made by virtue of that subsection (1).

(6) The repeal by this Act of paragraph 26 of Schedule 26 to the 1989 Act (byelaws under the Rivers (Prevention of Pollution) Act 1951) shall not prevent any order made under that paragraph from continuing, subject to any modification required by paragraph 1(2)(b) above, to have effect; nor shall it affect any power to revoke, amend or re-enact any such order.

(7) In this paragraph "the relevant body," in relation to any byelaws—

(a) in the case of byelaws made by a statutory water company, means that company;

(b) in the case of byelaws made by a water authority under section 22(6) of the Countryside Act 1968 (byelaws with respect to certain waterways) with respect to any waterway or land which—

(i) is owned by the water authority's successor company (within the meaning of the 1989 Act); or

(ii) without being owned by the NRA, is managed by that company,

means that company; and

(c) in any other case, means the NRA.

Savings for local statutory provisions

5.—(1) Notwithstanding the repeal by this Act of subsection (8) of section 136 of the 1989 Act, any local statutory provision having effect with modifications by virtue of that subsection shall continue to have effect with those modifications after commencement.

(2) Notwithstanding the repeal by this Act of sub-paragraph (3) of paragraph 1 of Schedule 15 to the 1989 Act and the provisions of the 1976 Act by virtue of which the scheme or order in question was made or treated as made, the functions transferred to the NRA by that sub-paragraph shall continue to be functions of the NRA after commencement as if the scheme or order had been made under the corresponding provisions of the consolidation Acts.

(3) The revocation by this Act of any provisions of the Internal Drainage Boards (Finance) Regulations 1990 shall not affect the operation of those provisions (by virtue of regulation 4 of those regulations) in relation to any local Act.

(4) Section 11 of the Sevenoaks Water Order 1934 (protective provisions for the benefit of the British Railways Board) shall continue to have effect notwithstanding the repeal by this Act of the Water Supplies (Exceptional Shortage Orders) Act 1934.

(5) This paragraph shall be without prejudice to any power to amend local statutory provisions which is saved by virtue of section 2 of this Act.

Saving for transfer schemes

6.—(1) The repeal by this Act of provisions contained in Schedule 26 to the 1989 Act (transitional provisions) shall be without prejudice to the effect of any scheme made under Schedule 2 to that Act and, in particular, of any provision contained in such a scheme by virtue of paragraph 2(3)(c) of that Schedule 2.

(2) The repeal by this Act of sub-paragraph (3) of paragraph 29 of Schedule 26 to the 1989 Act shall not prevent any direction under that sub-paragraph from continuing (subject to any such modifications as are required by virtue of sub-paragraph (2)(b) of paragraph 1 above) to have effect in relation to any application which has effect—

(a) by virtue of a scheme under Schedule 2 to the 1989 Act, as an application by the successor company of a water authority; and

(b) by virtue of paragraph 1 above, as an application for a licence under Part II of the Water Resources Act 1991.

Water enterprise mergers before the transfer date

7. The repeal by this Act of sections 29 and 30 of the 1989 Act (merger of water enterprises) shall not apply to those sections in so far as they have effect in relation to mergers taking place before September 1, 1989.

Non-domestic supplies

8. The repeal by this Act of paragraph 8 of Schedule 26 to the 1989 Act shall not affect the power to make a determination under sub-paragraph (2) of that paragraph on any reference

which remains outstanding at commencement; and any such determination shall have effect, after it is made, as a determination of the Director General of Water Services for the purposes of section 55 of the Water Industry Act 1991.

Sewer requisitions

9.—(1) Without prejudice to paragraph 1 above, any duty which has effect under sub-paragraph (1) of paragraph 14 of Schedule 26 to the 1989 Act as a duty owed by a sewerage undertaker under section 71 of that Act shall have effect after commencement as owed by that undertaker under section 98 of the Water Industry Act 1991; and, accordingly, sub-paragraph (5) of that paragraph 14 shall have effect for the purposes of anything saved by this sub-paragraph as it has effect for the purposes of anything saved by sub-paragraph (3) of that paragraph.

(2) The repeal by this Act of section 72 of the 1989 Act shall be without prejudice to the application of subsection (8) of that section by paragraph 14(4) of Schedule 26 to that Act.

Appeals with respect to sewerage matters etc. begun before September 1, 1989

10. The repeals made by this Act shall not affect anything saved by virtue of sub-paragraph (2) of paragraph 13 of Schedule 26 to the 1989 Act (saving for certain appeals and reference); but any determination made after commencement by virtue of that sub-paragraph under an enactment repealed by this Act shall have effect as if made by the Director General of Water Services under the corresponding provision of the Water Industry Act 1991.

Savings in respect of charging provisions

11.—(1) Notwithstanding its repeal by the 1989 Act, section 4 of the Public Utility Transfers and Water Charges Act 1988 (approval of metering trials schemes) shall apply, with the necessary modifications, to so much of any scheme made by a water undertaker under section 143 of the Water Industry Act 1991 as amends or revokes any scheme which—
  (a) was made in accordance with the said section 4 before September 1, 1989 and was either in force immediately before that date or due to come into force after that date; and
  (b) continues in force by virtue of paragraph 1 above as a scheme under that section 143.

(2) The repeal by this Act of sub-paragraph (6) of paragraph 16 of Schedule 26 to the 1989 Act shall not prevent any regulations which have effect in accordance with that sub-paragraph from continuing to have effect after commencement in accordance with paragraph 1 above as if the power in section 149 of the Water Industry Act 1991 included power to make or revoke any such provision as might have been made by virtue of section 5(3)(e) of the Public Utility Transfers and Water Charges Act 1988.

Commissioners of Sewers

12. Commissioners of Sewers in existence immediately before commencement—
  (a) shall continue (subject to any scheme under section 3 of the Land Drainage Act 1991 or to any other scheme under that Act affecting their powers) to have the powers then exercisable by them or, in so far as those powers were exercisable under an enactment repealed by this Act, the corresponding powers under the Land Drainage Act 1991; and
  (b) shall have those powers subject to the same conditions, restrictions and qualifications or, in so far as the enactments imposing those conditions, restrictions or qualifications are repealed by this Act, the corresponding conditions, restrictions and qualifications in the Land Drainage Act 1991.

PART II

TRANSITORY PROVISIONS IN RESPECT OF FLOOD DEFENCE AND LAND DRAINAGE

Disqualification for membership of regional flood defence committee

13. Where a person is disqualified for membership of a regional flood defence committee by virtue of having been adjudged bankrupt before the coming into force of the Insolvency Act 1986, the rules applicable apart from the repeals made by this Act, rather than paragraph 3(2) of Schedule 4 to the Water Resources Act 1991, shall apply for determining when that disqualification shall cease.

Savings in relation to local flood defence schemes

14.—(1) Where immediately before commencement—

(a) any scheme or committee falls to be treated as a local flood defence scheme or a local flood defence committee by virtue of subsection (2) of section 139 of the 1989 Act; or

(b) any person holds office in accordance with subsection (4) of that section,

that scheme or committee shall continue to be so treated or, as the case may be, that person shall continue so to hold office, notwithstanding the provisions of section 13 of, or Schedule 4 to, the Water Resources Act 1991 or the repeal of any enactment by this Act.

(2) Where a person is disqualified for membership of a local flood defence committee by virtue of having been adjudged bankrupt before the coming into force of the Insolvency Act 1986, the rules applicable apart from the repeals made by this Act, rather than paragraph 3(2) of Schedule 4 to the Water Resources Act 1991, shall apply for determining when that disqualification shall cease.

Drainage rates etc. for the financial years beginning before 1993

15.—(1) The repeals and revocations made by this Act shall not affect—

(a) any provisions regulating, in relation to a drainage district or sub-district, the apportionment for any financial year beginning before 1993 between drainage rates and special levies of any expenses of an internal drainage board; or

(b) the powers of the drainage board for any internal drainage district to make a drainage rate, or to levy differential drainage rates, in respect of a financial year beginning before 1993;

and the applicable provisions of the 1976 Act and of the Internal Drainage Boards (Finance) Regulations 1990 shall continue, notwithstanding those repeals and revocations, to have effect (instead of any provisions of the Land Drainage Act 1991) for the purposes of, and in connection with, the making or levying of any such apportionment or rate and otherwise in relation to drainage rates made in respect of any such financial year.

(2) Where—

(a) any order has been made under section 68 of the 1976 Act or is made under that section by virtue of sub-paragraph (1) above or any other thing has been or is done under or for the purposes of any provision having effect by virtue of that sub-paragraph in relation to drainage rates made in respect of a financial year beginning before 1993; and

(b) apart from the repeals and revocations made by this Act, that order or thing would have effect both in relation to a rate so made and in relation to drainage rates made in respect of one or more financial years beginning in or after 1993,

that order or other thing shall have effect in relation to the drainage rates made in respect of the latter years as if it had been made or done under or for the purposes of the corresponding provision of Part IV of the Land Drainage Act 1991; and references in that Act, in any other enactment or in any subordinate legislation or document to orders made under that Act or to any other thing done under or for the purposes of that Act shall be construed accordingly.

(3) References in paragraphs 17 to 19 below, in relation to any drainage rate made for a financial year beginning before 1993, to section 64 of the 1976 Act include references to that section as it has effect, subject to the provisions of the Internal Drainage Boards (Finance) Regulations 1990, by virtue of sub-paragraph (1) above.

Restrictions on appointed members of internal drainage boards until 1993

16.—(1) In the period ending with March 31, 1993 the number of appointed members of an internal drainage board—

(a) shall not exceed two-fifths of the number of all the members of the board; and

(b) subject to paragraph (a) above, shall be such that the number of appointed members bears, as nearly as possible, the same proportion to the maximum number of all the members of the board as the first of the following amounts bears to the second, that is to say—

(i) the aggregate amount raised by the board by means of drainage rates assessed on land other than agricultural land and agricultural buildings in respect of the financial year beginning in 1989 (including any amount payable to the board under an agreement made under section 81 of the 1976 Act); and

(ii) the total amount raised by that board by means of drainage rates in respect of that financial year.

(2) If, in that period, more than one charging authority is entitled to appoint members of an internal drainage board under paragraph 5 of Schedule 1 to the Land Drainage Act 1991—

(a) each such authority may appoint the number of members of the board calculated by multiplying the maximum number of appointed members by the relevant fraction for that authority and disregarding any fraction in the resulting product; and

(b) where in respect of the board—

(i) any such authority has appointed a member; or

(ii) the calculation referred in paragraph (a) above results in respect of each such authority in a product of less than one,

the charging authorities shall, unless they otherwise agree, jointly appoint the number of members of the board representing the difference between the maximum number of appointed members and the aggregate number of members that may be appointed by individual charging authorities or, as the case may be, constituting the maximum number of appointed members.

(3) For the purposes of sub-paragraph (2) above the relevant fraction, in relation to a charging authority, is the fraction which bears the same proportion to one as the aggregate for that authority of the values specified in sub-paragraph (4) below bears to the sum of such aggregate values for all the local charging authorities whose areas lie within the board's district.

(4) The values mentioned in sub-paragraph (3) above are, in relation to any internal drainage board, the following values for the area of every charging authority whose area lies wholly within the internal drainage district of that board and for such parts of the areas of other charging authorities as lie within that district, that is to say—

(a) the rateable values shown, on January 1, 1990, for hereditaments in the valuation lists maintained under Part V of the General Rate Act 1967;

(b) the annual values of hereditaments, other than agricultural land and agricultural buildings shown on January 1, 1990 in the register maintained by the board by virtue of the Registers of Drainage Boards Regulations 1968.

(5) In this paragraph—

"agricultural buildings" has the meaning provided by paragraphs 2 to 8 of Schedule 5 to the Local Government Finance Act 1988;

"agricultural land" has the meaning provided by paragraphs 2 and 4 to 8 of that Schedule;

"appointed members," in relation to an internal drainage board, means members of the board appointed by one or more charging authorities under Part II of Schedule 1 to the Land Drainage Act 1991 or, at a time before commencement, under the corresponding provisions of the Internal Drainage Boards (Finance) Regulations 1990;

"charging authority" has the same meaning as in the Land Drainage Act 1991.

Qualification of electors of members of internal drainage boards—pre 1993 rates

17.—(1) Paragraph 2 of Schedule 1 to the Land Drainage Act 1991 (persons entitled to vote in elections of internal drainage board members) shall have effect until the beginning of the financial year beginning in 1993 as if—

(a) in sub-paragraph (1), for the reference to occupying land on which a drainage rate has been levied there were substituted a reference to owning or occupying such land; and

(b) sub-paragraph (2) prevented a person from being entitled to be an elector in respect of his ownership of any land if any amount in respect of an owner's drainage rate levied on that land remained unpaid for more than a month at the date of the election.

(2) In paragraph 3(1) of that Schedule, a reference to the assessable value of any land, in relation to a relevant date before April 1, 1993, is a reference to the annual value on which any such drainage rate would be assessable in accordance with section 64 of the 1976 Act.

(3) In this paragraph "the relevant date" has the same meaning as in paragraph 3 of Schedule 1 to that Act of 1991.

Qualification for election to internal drainage board—pre 1993 rates

18.—(1) Paragraph 4 of Schedule 1 to the Land Drainage Act 1991, shall have effect until the beginning of the financial year beginning in 1993, as if—

(a) in paragraphs (a) and (d) of sub-paragraph (1), the requirement for the purposes of those paragraphs that a person who is the owner of land such as is mentioned in those paragraphs should also be its occupier were omitted; and

(b) in paragraph (c) of that sub-paragraph, the reference to the occupier of any such land as is mentioned in that paragraph were a reference to person who is the owner or the occupier of any such land.

(2) Subject to sub-paragraph (3) below, a person shall not, by virtue of paragraph 4(1)(a), (c) or (d) of Schedule 1 to the Land Drainage Act 1991 and sub-paragraph (1) above, be qualified for election as being the owner of any land or a person nominated by the owner of any land if at the date of the election any amount demanded in respect of any owner's drainage rate levied in respect of that land remains unpaid.

(3) Sub-paragraph (2) above shall not apply if—

(a) the date of the election falls less than 6 months after the beginning of the period for which the unpaid rate was made; or

(b) the land was occupied, when the amount was demanded, by a person who, as between the owner and the occupier, was liable to pay the owner's drainage rate.

(4) In paragraph 4(1) of Schedule 1 to the Land Drainage Act 1991, a reference to the assessable value of land is, in relation to a relevant date before April 1, 1993, a reference to the annual value on which any such a drainage rate would be assessable in accordance with section 64 of the 1976 Act.

(5) In this paragraph "the relevant date" has the same meaning as in paragraph 4 of Schedule 1 to the Land Drainage Act 1991.

Qualification for making certain applications—pre-1993 rates

19.—(1) Subsections (2) and (3) of section 72 of the Land Drainage Act 1991 (qualification for making certain applications) shall have effect in relation to qualification by reference to a drainage rate made in respect of a financial year beginning before 1993, as if a reference in those subsections to the occupiers of any land included a reference to the owners of the land.

(2) In paragraph (b)(iii) of subsection (2) of that section, a reference to the assessable value of land is, where the rate referred to in that paragraph was made for a year beginning before 1993, a reference to the annual value on which any such drainage rate would be assessable in accordance with section 64 of the 1976 Act.

Section 3   SCHEDULE 3

                     REPEALS AND REVOCATIONS

                              PART I

                             REPEALS

Chapter	Short title	Extent of repeal
24 & 25 Geo 5. c. 20.	The Water Supplies (Exceptional Shortage Orders) Act 1934.	The whole Act.
26 Geo. 5 & 1 Edw. 8. c. 49.	The Public Health Act 1936.	Sections 17 to 19. Sections 21 and 22. Section 27. Sections 30 and 31. Section 34. Section 36. Section 42. In section 48, in subsection (1), the words "directly or" and subsection (1A). In section 90, in subsection (4), the words from "and any reference" onwards and subsection (5). In section 278(3), the words from "on", in the first place where it occurs, to "them, or". In section 339, the proviso.
1 Edw. 8 & 1 Geo. 6. c. 40.	The Public Health (Drainage of Trade Premises) Act 1937.	Sections 1 to 3. Section 4(5). Sections 7 and 7A. Sections 9 and 10. Sections 13 and 14.
7 & 8 Geo. 6. c. 26.	The Rural Water Supplies and Sewerage Act 1944.	The whole Act.
8 & 9 Geo. 6. c. 42.	The Water Act 1945.	Section 7. Section 14(9), (10) and (12). Sections 15 and 16. Section 21. Section 35(2) and (4). Section 41. Section 43. Section 45. Section 48. Section 53.

Chapter	Short title	Extent of repeal
11 & 12 Geo. 6. c. 22.	The Water Act 1948.	Section 56. Section 59. Section 5(4). Section 6.
3 & 4 Eliz. 2. c. 13.	The Rural Water Supplies and Sewerage Act 1955.	The whole Act.
6 & 7 Eliz. 2. c. 69.	The Opencast Coal Act 1958.	In section 51(1), the definition of "drainage authority".
8 & 9 Eliz. 2. c. 34.	The Radioactive Substances Act 1960.	In Part I of Schedule 1, in paragraph 3 the words "twenty-seven", paragraphs 5, 6 and 8B, the paragraph 8F inserted by Schedule 25 to the Water Act 1989 and the paragraph 8G inserted by the Control of Pollution (Radioactive Waste) Regulations 1989.
9 & 10 Eliz 2. c. 64.	The Public Health Act 1961.	Section 1(3). Sections 59 to 64. Sections 66 to 68. Section 69(1).
1963 c. 33.	The London Government Act 1963.	In Part I of Schedule 11, paragraph 27. In Schedule 9, paragraphs 11 and 17 of Part II and Part III. In Schedule 14, paragraph 10.

1963 c. 38.	The Water Resources Act 1963.	Section 2.
		Section 17.
		Section 19.
		Sections 22 to 32.
		Sections 36 to 55.
		Section 60.
		Sections 63 and 64.
		Section 71(3).
		Section 78.
		Section 79(3) to (6), (8) and (9).
		Sections 81 and 82.
		Section 88.
		Section 91.
		Sections 105 and 106.
		Section 109.
		Sections 114 to 118.
		Section 120.
		Section 123.
		Section 126(3) and (4).
		Section 128(1) and (2).
		Sections 131 and 132.
		Section 133(2).
		Section 134(1), (2) and (6)(c).
		In section 135—
		  (a) subsection (1), except in so far as it defines "local enactment", "performance" and "repeal"; and
		  (b) subsections (2), (3) and (5) to (8).
		Schedule 7.
		Schedule 10.

1964 c. 40.	The Harbours Act 1964.	In section 58, the words "(within the meaning of the Land Drainage Act 1930)".
1965 c. 4.	The Science and Technology Act 1965.	In Schedule 2, the entry relating to section 7 of the Water Act 1945.
1965 c. 36.	The Gas Act 1965.	Section 28(5).
1967 c. 22.	The Agriculture Act 1967.	In section 50(3)(h), the words "(within the meaning of the Land Drainage Act 1930)".

Chapter	Short title	Extent of repeal
1968 c. 13.	The National Loans Act 1968.	In section 6(1), the words "section 1(3)(b) of the Rural Water Supplies and Sewerage Act 1955".
1968 c. 35.	The Water Resources Act 1968.	The whole Act.
1971 c. 49.	The Rural Water Supplies and Sewerage Act 1971.	The whole Act.
1972 c. 70.	The Local Government Act 1972.	In Schedule 13, paragraph 24.
1973 c. 37.	The Water Act 1973.	Section 14(4). In Schedule 8, paragraphs 37, 39, 49, 78, 79, 80(1) and (3), 83, 85 and 86.
1974 c. 40.	The Control of Pollution Act 1974.	Section 43. Section 44(1), (3), (5) and (6). Section 45. In Schedule 2, paragraphs 6 to 9, 14 and 16. In Schedule 3, paragraphs 8 to 10.
1975 c. 51.	The Salmon and Freshwater Fisheries Act 1975.	In section 6(3)(c), the words "under this Act". In section 28, subsections (3) to (8). In Schedule 3, paragraphs 7 to 9 and 13 to 38.
1976 c. 55.	The Agriculture (Miscellaneous Provisions) Act 1976.	In Schedule 3, the entries relating to the Land Drainage Act 1961 and sections 21(1), 23(1) and 24(1) of the Agriculture (Miscellaneous Provisions) Act 1968.
1976 c. 70.	The Land Drainage Act 1976.	Sections 4 to 19. Sections 21 to 61. Sections 63 and 64. Sections 67 to 69. Sections 71 and 72. Sections 74 to 79. Section 80(2) to (4). Sections 82 to 100. Section 102 to 104A. Sections 106 to 115. Section 116, except so much of subsection (1) as defines "drainage", "land", "land drainage", "land drainage functions" and "the London excluded area". Section 117(1) and (3). In section 118(3), the words "Save as provided by section 32(4) above." Schedules 1 to 4. Schedule 6. In Schedule 7, paragraphs 6 and 8. Schedule 8.
1977 c. 45.	The Criminal Law Act 1977.	In Schedule 1, the entry relating to section 7 of the Water Act 1945. In Schedule 6, the entries relating to sections 14 and 16 of the Water Act 1945.
1979 c. 46.	The Ancient Monuments and Archaeological Areas Act 1979.	In Schedule 4, paragraph 16.
1980 c. 43.	The Magistrates' Courts Act 1980.	In Schedule 7, paragraph 147.
1980 c. 65.	The Local Government, Planning and Land Act 1980.	Section 181.
1980 c. 66.	The Highways Act 1980.	In Schedule 24, paragraph 4.
1981 c. 12.	The Water Act 1981.	Section 6.
1981 c. 54.	The Supreme Court Act 1981.	In Schedule 5, the entry relating to the Public Health Act 1961.

Chapter	Short title	Extent of repeal
1981 c. 67.	The Acquisition of Land Act 1981.	In Schedule 4, in paragraph 1, the entry relating to the Land Drainage Act 1976.
1982 c. 32.	The Local Government Finance Act 1982.	In Schedule 5, paragraph 7.
1983 c. 23.	The Water Act 1983.	In Schedule 4, paragraphs 5 and 6.
1983 c. 55.	The Value Added Tax Act 1983.	In section 20(3)(c), the words "within the meaning of the Land Drainage Act 1976".
1984 c. 12.	The Telecommunications Act 1984.	In Schedule 4, paragraph 66(1) and (2).
1984 c. 32.	The London Regional Transport Act 1984.	In Schedule 6, paragraph 12.
1985 c. 51.	The Local Government Act 1985.	In Schedule 4, paragraph 47. In Schedule 7, paragraphs 2 and 5 to 9.
1985 c. 63.	The Water (Fluoridation) Act 1985.	The whole Act.
1985 c. 65.	The Insolvency Act 1985.	In Schedule 8, paragraph 29.
1986 c. 31.	The Airports Act 1986.	In Schedule 2, paragraph 5.
1986 c. 44.	The Gas Act 1986.	In Schedule 7, paragraphs 2(6) and 25.
1986 c. 49.	The Agriculture Act 1986.	In Schedule 3, paragraph 3.
1986 c. 62.	The Salmon Act 1986.	Section 33(3).
1986 c. 63.	The Housing and Planning Act 1986.	Section 42(1)(b).
1987 c. 3.	The Coal Industry Act 1987.	In Schedule 1, paragraph 32.
1989 c. 15.	The Water Act 1989.	In section 1, subsections (1) to (5). Sections 2 and 3. In section 5, subsections (1) to (4). In section 6, subsections (1) to (7). Sections 7 to 10. Section 11(1) to (8). Sections 12 to 68. Section 70(3) to (5). Sections 71 to 82. Sections 97 to 136. In section 137, subsections (1) to (8), (10) and (11). Section 138. Section 139(1) to (5). Section 140. Section 141(1) to (4) and (7). Section 142(1). Sections 143 to 167. Sections 170 to 172. Section 176. Sections 178 to 182. In section 184— (a) in subsection (1), the words "25(2) or" and the words from "or by" onwards; (b) in subsections (3) and (5), the words "or the Minister"; and (c) in subsection (4), the words from the beginning to "Schedule 6 to this Act". In section 185(1), the words "(except in the case of regulations under section 13(1) above)". Section 186. Section 188. In section 189— (a) subsection (1) except in so far as it defines "the 1945 Act", "the 1973 Act", "the Authority", "contravention", "the Director", "disposal" and

Chapter	Short title	Extent of repeal
		cognate expressions, "enactment", "holding company", "information", "local statutory provision", "the Minister", "modifications" and cognate expressions, "sewer", "subordinate legislation", "statutory water company", "successor company", "transfer date" and "water authority"; and (b) subsections (2) to (5) and (8). In section 192(3), paragraph (c) and the word "or" immediately preceding it. In Schedule 1, paragraphs 1 to 10 and 14 to 23. In Schedule 3, paragraphs 1 to 5. In Schedule 4, paragraphs 1 to 5. Schedules 5 to 7. In Schedule 8, paragraphs 1 and 2(1) to (10) and (12) and paragraphs 3 to 5. Schedules 9 to 16. In Schedule 17, paragraphs 6(b) and 7(2), 7(a), 14(a) to (f) and (g)(i) and (16). Schedules 18 to 21. Schedule 24. In Schedule 25— (a) paragraph 2; (b) in paragraph 3(1), the words from "or in" onwards; (c) paragraphs 6, 7, 10, 21, 27(4) and 31(1); (d) in paragraph 32(5), the words after paragraph (b); (e) paragraph 40; (f) in paragraph 45, sub-paragraphs (1) and (2); and (g) paragraphs 61(5), 63, 71(1) and (2), 72, 73 and 80(1). In Schedule 26— (a) in paragraph 5, sub-paragraphs (2) to (4); (b) paragraphs 7 to 12; (c) paragraph 13(1); (d) in paragraph 14, sub-paragraphs (1) and (2) and in sub-paragraph (5) the words "(1) or"; (e) in paragraph 15, sub-paragraph (2); (f) in paragraph 16, sub-paragraphs (1), (2), (5) to (7) and (10); (g) paragraphs 18 and 19; (h) paragraphs 21 to 39; (i) in paragraph 40, sub-paragraph (2) and in sub-paragraph (3), the words from the beginning to the end of paragraph (b) and the word "and" immediately after that paragraph; (j) in paragraph 41, sub-paragraphs (2) and (3) and in sub-paragraph (4), the words "or (2)"; (k) paragraphs 42 to 45; (l) paragraph 48; (m) paragraph 50; (n) paragraph 56; and (o) in paragraph 57, sub-paragraphs (1) to (5) and (7).

Chapter	Short title	Extent of repeal
1989 c. 29.	The Electricity Act 1989.	In Schedule 16, paragraphs 1(1)(vi) and (5), 3(1)(a), 10, 21 and 37.
1990 c.11.	The Planning (Consequential Provisions) Act 1990.	In Schedule 2, paragraphs 46 and 81(1) and (2).
1990 c. 16.	The Food Safety Act 1990.	Section 55(2) to (6).
1990 c. 43.	The Environmental Protection Act 1990.	Section 145(1). In Schedule 8, paragraph 8. In Schedule 9, paragraph 17. In Schedule 15, paragraphs 18, 28, 29 and 30.
1991 c. 22.	The New Roads and Street Works Act 1991.	In Schedule 8, paragraphs 110 and 122.
1991 c. 34.	The Planning and Compensation Act 1991.	In Part I of Schedule 18, the entries relating to the Land Drainage Act 1976 and the Water Act 1989.

PART II

REVOCATIONS OF SUBORDINATE LEGISLATION

Number	Citation	Extent of revocation
S.I. 1978/319.	The Land Drainage Act 1976 (Amendment) Regulations 1978.	The whole instrument.
S.I. 1986/208.	The Local Government Act 1985 (Land Drainage Functions) Order 1986.	In Part II of Schedule 1, paragraphs 2 to 4.
S.I. 1989/440.	The Valuation and Community Charge Tribunal (Transfer of Jurisdiction) Regulations 1989.	In regulation 6(3), the words "section 79(8) of the Land Drainage Act 1976". In Part II of Schedule 2, paragraph 4.
S.I. 1989/1158.	The Control of Pollution (Radioactive Waste) Regulations 1989.	In regulation 4, the words from "and accordingly" onwards.
S.I. 1990/72.	The Internal Drainage Boards (Finance) Regulations 1990.	Regulations 3 and 3A. Regulations 6 to 8. Regulation 9(3). Regulation 15(1) and (3). Regulations 16 to 20. Schedule.
S.I. 1990/214.	The Drainage Charges Regulations 1990.	The whole instrument.
S.I. 1991/523.	The Internal Drainage Boards (Finance) (Amendment) Regulations 1991.	Regulations 3 to 5. In regulation 6, the words "and 17(4)(b)(ii)". Regulations 7 and 8.
S.I. 1991/983.	The Local Government Finance (Consequential Amendment) Order 1991.	The whole instrument.

INDEX

References are to sections

STATUTE LAW REVISION (ISLE OF MAN) ACT 1991

(1991 c. 61)

ARRANGEMENT OF SECTIONS

SECT.
1. Repeals.
2. Short title and extent.

       SCHEDULES:
           Schedule 1—Repealing Acts.
           Schedule 2—Miscellaneous Repeals.

An Act to revise the statute law by repealing obsolete, spent, unnecessary or superseded enactments so far as they continue to form part of the law of the Isle of Man.   [25th July 1991]

PARLIAMENTARY DEBATES
   Hansard, H.L. Vol. 528, col. 1864; Vol. 530, cols. 268, 988.

INTRODUCTION
   The Act is intended to repeal approximately 700 obsolete enactments of the Westminster Parliament which although have ceased to have force in the U.K. still form part of the law in the Isle of Man. The anomaly arose due to the omissions of those enactments listed in Sched. 1 to extend to the Isle of Man, though since 1973 Statute Law (Repeals) Acts have expressly provided for such effect.

Repeals

   1.—(1) The enactments which were repealed (whether for the whole or any part of the United Kingdom) by the Acts specified in Schedule 1 to this Act are hereby repealed so far as they extend to the Isle of Man.

   (2) The Acts specified in Schedule 2 to this Act are hereby repealed so far as they extend to the Isle of Man.

Short title and extent

   2.—(1) This Act may be cited as the Statute Law Revision (Isle of Man) Act 1991.

   (2) This Act extends only to the Isle of Man.

SCHEDULES

Section 1(1)   SCHEDULE 1

REPEALING ACTS

Statute Law Revision Act 1861 (c.101).
Statute Law Revision Act 1863 (c.125).
Statute Law Revision Act 1867 (c.59).
Statute Law Revision Act 1871 (c.116).
Statute Law Revision Act 1872 (c.63).
Statute Law Revision (No. 2) Act 1872 (c.97).
Statute Law Revision Act 1873 (c.91).
Statute Law Revision Act 1874 (c.35).
Statute Law Revision (No.2) Act 1874 (c.96).
Statute Law Revision Act 1875 (c.66).
Statute Law Revision Act 1883 (c.39).
Statute Law Revision Act 1887 (c.59).
Statute Law Revision Act 1892 (c.19).

Statute Law Revision Act 1893 (c.14).
Statute Law Revision (No. 2) Act 1893 (c.54).
Statute Law Revision Act 1894 (c.56).
Statute Law Revision Act 1898 (c.22).
Statute Law Revision Act 1908 (c.49).
Statute Law Revision Act 1927 (c.42).
Statute Law Revision Act 1948 (c.62).
Statute Law Revision Act 1950 (c.6).
Statute Law Revision Act 1953 (c.5).
Statute Law Revision Act 1958 (c.46).
Statute Law Revision Act 1959 (c.68).
Statute Law Revision Act 1963 (c.30).
Statute Law Revision Act 1964 (c.79).
Statute Law Revision Act 1966 (c.5).
Statute Law (Repeals) Act 1969 (c.52).
Statute Law (Repeals) Act 1971 (c.52).

Section 1(2)   SCHEDULE 2

MISCELLANEOUS REPEALS

Chapter	Short Title or Subject
26 Hen. 8. c.3.	First fruits and tenths.
26 Hen. 8. c.17.	First fruits and tenths.
27 Hen. 8. c.8.	First fruits and tenths.
32 Hen. 8. c.38.	Marriage Act 1540.
33 Hen. 8. c.6.	Crossbows and handguns.
5 Eliz. 1. c.1.	Supremacy of the Crown.
23 Eliz. 1. c.1.	Religion.
27 Eliz. 1. c.2.	Jesuits, seminary priests.
29 Eliz. 1. c.6.	Religion.
1 Jac. 1. c.4.	Jesuits, seminary priests, recusants, &c.
3 Jac. 1. c.1.	Observance of 5th November.
7 Jac. 1. c.4. (Pr.).	Assurance of the Isle of Man.
12 Car. 2. c.14.	Observance of 29th May.
1 Geo. 1. St. 2. c.13.	Security of the Crown.
3 Geo. 4. c.60.	Importation of corn.
4 & 5 Will. 4. c.34.	Greenwich Hospital.
5 & 6 Vict. c.14.	Corn duties.
8 & 9 Vict. c.117.	Poor Removal Act 1845.
18 & 19 Vict. c.27.	Newspaper postage.
22 & 23 Vict. c.30.	Coinage.
29 & 30 Vict. c.65.	Colonial Branch Mint Act 1866.
32 & 33 Vict. c.71.	Bankruptcy Act 1869.
39 & 40 Vict. c.59.	Appellate Jurisdiction Act 1876.
54 & 55 Vict. c.21.	Savings Banks Act 1891.
54 & 55 Vict. c.69.	Penal Servitude Act 1891.
63 & 64 Vict. c.56	Military Lands Act 1900.
4 & 5 Geo. 5. c.14.	Currency and Bank Notes Act 1914.
4 & 5 Geo. 5. c.50.	Merchant Shipping (Convention) Act 1914.
4 & 5 Geo. 5. c.59.	Bankruptcy Act 1914.
8 & 9 Geo. 5. c.55.	School Teachers (Superannuation) Act 1918.
7 & 8 Geo. 6. c.43.	Matrimonial Causes (War Marriages) Act 1944.
11 & 12 Geo. 6. c.10.	Emergency Laws (Miscellaneous Provisions) Act 1947.

INDEX

References are to sections

ARMED FORCES ACT 1991*

(1991 c. 62)

Arrangement of Sections

Part I

Continuance of Services Acts

Part II

Amendments Relating to the Armed Forces and Other Persons Subject to Provisions of the Services Acts

Young offenders

Stoppages and compensation orders

Courts-martial

Deduction of maintenance payments etc. from pay

Naval and marine pay and pensions

Part III

Protection of Children of Service Families

Part IV

Supplementary

---

* Annotations by Professor Peter Rowe, Head of the Department of Law, University of Liverpool.

An Act to continue the Army Act 1955, the Air Force Act 1955 and the Naval Discipline Act 1957; to amend those Acts and other enactments relating to the armed forces; to make provision for compensation for miscarriages of justice before courts-martial; to make provision for orders for the assessment and emergency protection of children forming part of or staying with service families abroad; and for connected purposes.

[July 25, 1991]

INTRODUCTION AND GENERAL NOTE

The Army has no permanent legal basis. Article 9 of the Bill of Rights 1688 declared that "the raising or keeping of a standing Army within the Kingdom in time of peace, unless it be with the consent of Parliament, is against law". From that date until 1955 Parliament showed its consent to a standing army by annual Mutiny Acts (which gradually laid down a code of military discipline) and then by an Army Act of 1881. Thereafter, an annual continuation Act was passed until 1955 when the Army Act, the basis of the modern law, was enacted. It is, in its turn, subject to annual continuation Orders in Council, passed by affirmative resolutions of both Houses of Parliament.

The Royal Air Force was established in 1917 by the Air Force (Constitution) Act of that year and it became the Royal Air Force in 1920. Its legal basis became virtually identical with that of the Army, by the Air Force Act 1955, and it became subject to the same continuation procedures.

The history of the Royal Navy was entirely different. It was never subject to the Bill of Rights and since it normally conducted its activities outside the jurisdiction its members were bound by Articles of War made under the Royal prerogative. It is now governed by the Naval Discipline Act 1957, an Act in many ways quite different from the 1955 Acts dealing with the other services. It is for this reason that separate sections in the Armed Forces Act 1991 are required to amend it.

The 1955 Acts came into force in 1957, along with the Naval Discipline Act, and were to last for one year unless continued by an annual Order in Council for a maximum period of five years. An Act of Parliament would then be required to keep the 1955 and the 1957 Acts in being. The Army and Air Force Act 1961 and subsequently the Armed Forces Act 1961 was enacted to achieve this and the pattern of using an Act of Parliament to make amendments to the earlier Acts has been repeated ever since, with an Armed Forces Act being passed every five years. During the passage of the Armed Forces Act 1981 the Minister responsible compared the process of quinquennial review to a naval refit in the following statement. "Once every five years we take the Army Act 1955, the Air Force Act 1955 and the Naval Discipline Act 1957 out of the legislative waters and let the experts swarm all over them, tapping here and prodding there, to consider whether any provisions need amendment, strengthening or scrapping." This process occurs in a Select Committee on each Armed Forces Bill and was carried out in 1990–91, the Special Report being published on April 24, 1991 (H.C. Paper 179). The Select Committee itself described the process of establishing a Select Committee on a Bill as "nowadays a procedural rarity."

As a result of these procedures there have been many amendments to the Army Act 1955, the Air Force Act 1955 and the Naval Discipline Act 1957 (hereafter styled the Service Discipline Acts). The Select Committee concluded that this process of constant amendment to Acts that had been in force for 34 years was "frankly a mess" and recommended that the Government should "provide parliamentary time within the next five years for legislation to consolidate service law". The relevant Acts are most conveniently to be found in the Manual of Military Law (Part I and separate Civilian Supplement), the Manual of Air Force law and the Manual of Naval Law, all published by HMSO.

By s.209 of (and Sched. 5 to) the 1955 Acts and s.118 of the 1957 Act civilians may be subject to Service law (a term which encompasses air force and naval law). When the armed forces are not on active service this can only occur if civilians accompany the armed forces abroad. The largest category of civilians subject to Service law is the families of serving members stationed overseas. Pt. III of this Act deals with the protection of children of service families who are outside the U.K.

There is a clear pattern in the various Armed Forces Acts, repeated in this Act, of bringing Service law into line, so far as is possible, with civilian law. Indeed, the Lewis Committee (Report of the Army and Air Force Court-Martial Committee, Cmnd. 7608, 1946) had stated that "In the matter of legal safeguards, citizens should be no worse off when they are in the Forces than in civil life unless considerations of discipline or other circumstances make such a disadvantage inevitable". The Select Committee on the Armed Forces Bill 1990–91 sought to do this by adding a new clause to the Bill to abolish the death penalty presently available for five military offences (see, for example, ss.24, 25, 26, 31 and 32 of the Army Act 1955). This clause was defeated in the House of Commons (*Hansard*, H.C. Vol. 193, col. 83). The Select Committee also recommended that "homosexual conduct of a kind that is legal in civilian law should not constitute an offence under Service law" (para. 41, p. xiv). Homosexual conduct can presently be charged as an offence, for example, under s.66 of the Army Act 1955 as disgraceful conduct of an indecent kind. In 1990 the Army dismissed six soldiers following conviction by court-martial for a homosexual offence and administratively discharged 24 (males and females). The Act contains no amendment to the pre-existing law.

APPLICATION

The Act applies to Scotland, Northern Ireland, the Channel Islands and the Isle of Man.

The Army Act 1955, the Air Force Act 1955 and the Naval Discipline Act 1957 apply to Scotland and to Northern Ireland (see s.216 of the Army Act 1955, s.214 of the Air Force Act 1955 and s.125 of the Naval Discipline Act 1957). For amendment of the application of these Acts to the Channel Islands and to the Isle of Man, see s.24 of this Act.

ABBREVIATIONS

AA 1955	:	Army Act 1955.
AFA 1955	:	Air Force Act 1955.
NDA 1957	:	Naval Discipline Act 1957.
Service Discipline Acts and Service Law	:	the three above Acts.
SSAFA	:	Soldiers', Sailors' and Airmen's Families Association.

PART I

CONTINUANCE OF SERVICES ACTS

Continuance of Services Acts

1.—(1) The 1955 Acts and the 1957 Act shall, instead of expiring on December 31, 1991, continue in force until August 31, 1992, and shall then expire unless continued in force in accordance with the following provisions of this section.

(2) Subject to subsection (3) below, Her Majesty may from time to time by Order in Council provide for the 1955 Acts and the 1957 Act to continue in force for a period not exceeding twelve months beyond the day on which they would otherwise expire.

(3) No Order in Council shall be made under subsection (2) above so as to continue the 1955 Acts and the 1957 Act beyond the end of the year 1996.

(4) No recommendation shall be made to Her Majesty in Council to make an Order under subsection (2) above unless a draft thereof has been laid before Parliament and approved by a resolution of each House of Parliament.

GENERAL NOTE

This section continues the Service Discipline Acts for a further year and thereafter until 1996, subject to annual continuation Orders in Council passed by affirmative resolutions of both Houses of Parliament. Clause 1 of the Armed Forces Bill in 1971 had proposed that the need to pass annual continuation orders should no longer be required, but this was rejected by the 1975–76 Select Committee on the Bill and, subsequently, by Parliament.

Subsection (1) of the 1991 Bill, as originally drafted, and in keeping with earlier Armed Forces Acts, had provided that the Service Discipline Acts would continue after August 31, 1991. This depended on the Armed Forces Act receiving the Royal Assent before this date. It became clear in June 1991 that it might not, in fact, do so. In order to prevent the lapsing of the Service Discipline Acts, an additional Order in Council was passed to continue these Acts in force until December 31, 1991 (see *Hansard*, H.C. Vol. 193, col. 90). By virtue of s.1(3) of the Armed Forces Act 1986 no continuation order is permitted to extend the Service Discipline Acts beyond the end of the year 1991. The Royal Assent was, in fact, given on July 25 and the original date by which the Service Discipline Acts would expire, August 31, 1992, was restored in subs. (1).

PART II

AMENDMENTS RELATING TO THE ARMED FORCES AND OTHER PERSONS SUBJECT TO PROVISIONS OF THE SERVICES ACTS

Young offenders

Young offenders: custodial sentences

2.—(1) Section 71A of each of the 1955 Acts (juveniles) and, subject to the modifications in subsection (6) below, section 43A of the 1957 Act (juveniles) shall each be amended in accordance with subsections (2) to (5) below.

(2) In subsection (1B)—

(a) after the words "imprisonment for life" there shall be inserted "then, subject to subsection (1E) below"; and

(b) paragraph (a) shall be omitted.

(3) After subsection (1C) there shall be inserted the following subsections—

"(1D) Subject to subsections (3) and (4) below, the only custodial sentences that a court may award where a peron under 21 years of age is convicted or found guilty of an offence are—

(a) a custodial order under section 71AA of this Act or under paragraph 10 of Schedule 5A to this Act; and

(b) a sentence of custody for life under subsection (1A) or (1B) above.

(1E) A court may not—

(a) make a custodial order under section 71AA of this Act; or

(b) pass a sentence of custody for life under subsection (1B) above;

unless it is satisfied—

(i) that the circumstances, including the nature and the gravity of the offence, are such that if the offender were aged 21 or over the court would pass a sentence of imprisonment; and

(ii) that he qualifies for a custodial sentence.

(1F) An offender qualifies for a custodial sentence if—

(a) he has a history of failure to respond to non-custodial sentences and is unable or unwilling to respond to them; or

(b) only a custodial sentence would be adequate to protect the public from serious harm from him; or

(c) the offence of which he has been convicted or found guilty was so serious that a non-custodial sentence for it cannot be justified."

(4) In subsection (4)—

(a) for the words "A person under 17 years of age" there shall be substituted "In any case where—

(a) a person aged 14 or over but under 17 years of age is";

(b) for the words "may be sentenced by the court, if it" there shall be substituted "or

(b) a person under 14 years of age is found guilty of manslaughter, and, in either case, the court"; and

(c) after the word "suitable" there shall be inserted "the court may sentence that person."

(5) After subsection (6) there shall be inserted the following subsection—

"(7) A sentence of detention under section 71(1)(e) of this Act shall be treated for the purposes of this section as a non-custodial sentence and references in this section to a custodial sentence shall be construed accordingly."

(6) The modifications of the amendments in subsections (2) to (5) above in their application to section 43A of the 1957 Act are—

(a) for "section 71AA," in each place where it occurs in the amendment in subsection (3) above, there shall be substituted "section 43AA";

(b) for "Schedule 5A" in the amendment in subsection (3) above there shall be substituted "Schedule 4A"; and

(c) for "section 71(1)(e)" in the amendment in subsection (5) above there shall be substituted "section 43(1)(e)."

GENERAL NOTE

The minimum age for entry to each of the three Services is (or in the case of the Royal Air Force will shortly be) 16 for males and 17 for females. Sections 71A of the 1955 Acts and 43A of the 1957 Act will therefore apply to young Service offenders, but also to others who are subject to Service law. Thus, by s.209 of and Sched. 5 to the Army Act 1955 (and corresponding sections in the other Service Discipline Acts) the families of members of the armed forces serving abroad will also be subject to this section. The major difference between these two groups of young offenders is that this section applies to both groups only in respect of custody for life and serious offences under s.71A (as amended by subs. (4) below). When dealing with other custodial sentences it is concerned only with Service offenders (under s.71AA of the 1955 Acts). In relation to civilian offenders comparable provisions are to be found in s.5 below.

The changes introduced by this section are intended to bring Service law into line with civilian law. Thus, by s.1(1) of the Criminal Justice Act 1982 an offender under the age of 21 cannot be sentenced to imprisonment. A court-martial can impose only two types of custodial sentence on young offenders: custody for life (under s.71A(1)(A) or (B) of the 1955 Acts and s.43A(1)(A) or (B) of the 1957 Act) or a custody order (for Service offenders only under s.71AA of the 1955 Acts or s.43AA of the 1957 Act). In order to pass a custodial sentence upon a young offender a court-martial must be satisfied that the conditions in subs. (3) (adding subss. (1E) and (1F) to s.71A of the 1955 Acts and s.43A of the 1957 Act) are met. These are derived from s.1(4A) of the Criminal Justice Act 1982 (as amended by s.123 of the Criminal Justice Act 1988).

Subs. (4)

This subsection amends the Service Discipline Acts in a case where the offender is either aged 14 or over but is under 21 and has been convicted by a court-martial of an offence which, if committed by an adult, is punishable by a term of 14 years' imprisonment, or where a person under the age of 14 is convicted by court-martial of manslaughter. He may be sentenced to a period of detention as the Secretary of State may direct. It should be remembered that a court-martial has no jurisdiction over civilians for offences committed in the U.K. unless the armed forces are on active service. Civilian offenders under this subsection will therefore have been convicted by court-martial in respect of offences committed outside the U.K.

Subs. (5)

A serviceman under the age of 21 may be sentenced to a period of military detention (see s.71(e) of the 1955 Acts), either within his own unit (if the sentence is of short duration) or at the Military Correction and Training Centre at Colchester (or the Royal Naval detention quarters at Plymouth). If this were to be considered as a custodial sentence the limitations imposed under subs. (3) above would apply to it. The object of this subsection, therefore, is to exclude from these limitations the right of a court-martial to pass a sentence of detention upon an offender aged under 21 years.

Subs. (6)

This subsection refers to the sections in the Naval Discipline Act equivalent to those in the 1955 Acts.

Young service offenders: minimum period of custodial orders etc.

3.—(1) In section 71AA of each of the 1955 Acts and in section 43AA of the 1957 Act (young service offenders: custodial orders), in subsection (1) the words "subject to subsection (1A) below" shall be omitted and after the words "period to be specified in the order" there shall be inserted "being not less than 21 days and."

(2) Subsection (1A) of each of those sections shall be omitted.

(3) Subject to subsection (4) below, in subsection (1B) of each of those sections for the words from "there is" to "in respect of him" there shall be substituted "it is satisfied as mentioned in sub-paragraphs (i) and (ii) of subsection (1E) of section 71A of this Act with respect to any person."

(4) In the application of subsection (3) above to section 43AA of the 1957 Act, for "section 71A" there shall be substituted "section 43A."

GENERAL NOTE

This section provides that the minimum period of a custodial sentence passed on a young Service offender is 21 days if the offender is aged 18 or over and a minimum period of two months if the offender is younger than 18.

Reasons to be given where custodial sentence awarded to young offender

4.—(1) After section 71AA of each of the 1955 Acts there shall be inserted the following section—

> **"Reasons to be given where custodial sentence awarded to young offender**
>
> 71AB.—(1) This section applies where a court—
> (a) makes a custodial order under section 71AA of this Act, or
> (b) passes a sentence of custody for life under section 71A(1B) of this Act.
> (2) It shall be the duty of the court—
> (a) to state in open court and to record in the proceedings that it is satisfied that the offender qualifies for a custodial sentence under one or more of the paragraphs of subsection (1F) of section 71A of this Act, the paragraph or paragraphs in question, and why it is so satisfied; and
> (b) to explain to the offender in open court and in ordinary language why it is passing a custodial sentence on him.
> (3) Where a court makes a custodial order and, in accordance with its duty under subsection (2) above, makes the statement required by paragraph (a) of that subsection, the matters stated shall be specified in the order (made under Imprisonment and Detention Rules) pursuant to which the offender is committed into custody."

(2) After section 43AA of the 1957 Act there shall be inserted the following section—

> **"Reasons to be given where custodial sentence awarded to young offender**
>
> 43AB.—(1) This section applies where a court—
> (a) makes a custodial order under section 43AA of this Act, or
> (b) passes a sentence of custody for life under section 43A(1B) of this Act.
> (2) It shall be the duty of the court—
> (a) to state in open and to record in the proceedings that it is satisfied that the offender qualifies for a custodial sentence under one or more of the paragraphs of subsection (1F) of section 43A of this Act, the paragraph or paragraphs in question, and why it is so satisfied; and
> (b) to explain to the offender in open court and in ordinary language why it is passing a custodial sentence on him.
> (3) Where a court makes a custodial order and, in accordance with its duty under subsection (2) above, makes the statement required by

paragraph (a) of that subsection, the matters stated shall be specified in the committal order."

GENERAL NOTE

This section follows the lead given in the civilian field by s.2(4) of the Criminal Justice Act 1982 (as amended by s.123(5) of the Criminal Justice Act 1988). Where a custodial sentence is passed on an offender under the age of 21 years it must be stated in open court that the court is satisfied that the offender qualifies for a custodial sentence and it must be explained to him why such a sentence is being passed.

There is no requirement, apart from this section, in the Service Discipline Acts for a court-martial to give reasons for its decisions on finding or sentence. This section therefore makes a considerable change. There is an additional duty on the court to record in the proceedings that it has, in effect, complied with the section. The reason for this is that the President of a court-martial is required to keep a record of the proceedings.

Subs. (2)

This makes a corresponding alteration to the Naval Discipline Act 1957.

Young civilian offenders: custodial orders

5.—(1) In Schedule 5A to each of the 1955 Acts and Schedule 4A to the 1957 Act (powers of court on trial of civilian), paragraph 10 (custodial orders) shall be amended in accordance with the following provisions of this section.

(2) Subject to subsection (9) below, in sub-paragraph (1)—
(a) for the words "subsection (1A) below" there shall be substituted "sub-paragraphs (1A) and (1AA) below"; and
(b) for the words from "in accordance" to the end of paragraph (b) there shall be substituted—
"for a period, to be specified in the order, which—
(a) shall not be less than 21 days;
(b) shall not exceed the maximum period for which he could have been sentenced to imprisonment if he had attained the age of 21; and
(c) if the order is made by a Standing Civilian Court, shall not exceed six months."

(3) In sub-paragraph (1A) the words from the beginning to "appropriate and" shall be omitted.

(4) After sub-paragraph (1A) there shall be inserted the following sub-paragraphs—
"(1AA) The court may not make a custodial order unless it is satisfied—
(a) that the circumstances, including the nature and the gravity of the offence, are such that if the offender were aged 21 or over the court would pass a sentence of imprisonment; and
(b) that he qualifies for a custodial sentence.
(1AB) An offender qualifies for a custodial sentence if—
(a) he has a history of failure to respond to non-custodial sentences and is unable or unwilling to respond to them; or
(b) only a custodial sentence would be adequate to protect the public from serious harm from him; or
(c) the offence of which he has been convicted or found guilty was so serious that a non-custodial sentence for it cannot be justified."

(5) In sub-paragraph (1B) for the words from "there is" to "in respect of him" there shall be substituted "it is satisfied as mentioned in paragraphs (a) and (b) of sub-paragraph (1AA) above with respect to an offender."

(6) Subject to subsection (10) below, for sub-paragraphs (3A) and (3B) there shall be substituted the following sub-paragraphs—

"(3A) Where the court makes a custodial order it shall be its duty—
(a) to state in open court and to record in the proceedings that it is satisfied that the offender qualifies for a custodial sentence under one or more of the paragraphs of sub-paragraph (1AB) above, the paragraph or paragraphs in question, and why it is so satisfied; and
(b) to explain to the offender in open court and in ordinary language why it is passing a custodial sentence on him.

(3B) Where the court makes a custodial order and, in accordance with its duty under sub-paragraph (3A) above, makes the statement required by paragraph (a) of that sub-paragraph, the matters stated shall be specified in the order (made under Imprisonment and Detention Rules) pursuant to which the offender is committed into custody."

(7) For sub-paragraph (4) there shall be substituted the following sub-paragraphs—
"(4) If a person is outside the United Kingdom at the time a custodial order is made in respect of him, he shall as soon as practicable be removed to the United Kingdom.

(4A) A person in respect of whom a custodial order has been made shall be detained in such appropriate institution as the Secretary of State may direct, and any enactment applying to persons detained in any such institution shall apply to a person so detained under this paragraph."

(8) In sub-paragraph (6), in each of paragraphs (a), (b) and (c) after the words "where the offender is" there shall be inserted "in or."

(9) In the application of subsection (2) above to paragraph 10 of Schedule 4A to the 1957 Act, for paragraph (b) there shall be substituted—
"(b) for the words from "in accordance" to the end of paragraph (b) there shall be substituted "for a period to be specified in the order, being not less than 21 days and not exceeding the maximum period for which he could have been sentenced to imprisonment if he had attained the age of 21"."

(10) In the application of subsection (6) above to paragraph 10 of Schedule 4A to the 1957 Act, for the words from "order (made under" onwards there shall be substituted "committal order."

GENERAL NOTE
Sections 2–4 deal principally with the Service offender, although the young civilian offender sentenced to a custodial sentence for life and one sentenced to be detained as the Secretary of State may direct under s.71A(4) of the 1955 Acts will also be covered by these sections. Section 5 is concerned with the young civilian offender sentenced by a court-martial or a Standing Civilian Court to a custodial sentence. There are approximately 50,000 young civilians who are subject to Service law, through living with their parents, where the father is a member of the armed forces stationed outside the U.K. The vast majority of these young civilians will be in Germany. The NATO Status of Forces Agreement 1951 and the Supplementary Agreement of 1964 determine the issue of a conflict of jurisdiction between the British military authorities and the German prosecution offices with the result that the crimes committed by British young civilians will be dealt with by the British military authorities, either by court-martial or by Standing Civilian Court. The latter court was established by the Armed Forces Act 1976 (ss.6–8) and its jurisdiction, procedures and powers of sentence are modelled on a magistrates' court in England and Wales.

Subs. (1)
Schedule 5A to the 1955 Acts and Sched. 4A to the 1957 Act deal with the range of sentences available to a court-martial or a Standing Civilian Court, para. 10 dealing with custodial sentences.

Subs. (2)
This amends para. 10(1) by providing that the minimum period for a custody order is 21 days and the maximum is the time that a person over the age of 21 might be sentenced. If the order is

made by a Standing Civilian Court it cannot exceed six months, since this is the maximum period of custody that this court may impose in all circumstances (AFA 1976, s.8(1)).

Subs. (3)
  This deletes sub-para. (1A) to enable the following subsection to be added.

Subs. (4)
  This subsection adds the grounds for making a custodial order against a young civilian offender and is similar to s.2 above.

Subs. (5)
  This subsection requires a small textual amendment in the light of the preceding subsection.

Subs. (6)
  This subsection imposes the duty upon a court-martial or a Standing Civilian Court to give reasons to the young offender sentenced to a custody order in terms similar to s.4 above.

Subs. (7).
  Paragraph 10(4) of Sched. 5A to the 1955 Acts had assumed that all young civilian offenders would be sentenced by a court outside the U.K. In most cases this will occur, but since a court-martial may sit at any place (s.91 of the 1955 Acts) it is possible for it to hear a case in the U.K., provided that the offence was committed abroad. The convicted offender would serve his sentence at a civilian young offenders' institution.

Subs. (9)
  This makes an amendment to the NDA 1957 similar to subs. (2) above. There is no reference to a Standing Civilian Court since that court has no jurisdiction over those subject to Naval law.

Abolition of reception orders

6. In Schedule 5A to each of the 1955 Acts and in Schedule 4A to the 1957 Act the following provisions (which refer to reception orders made in respect of civilians under 17 found guilty of certain offences) shall cease to have effect—
  (a) in paragraph 2 the definition of "reception order";
  (b) paragraphs 6 to 9; and
  (c) in paragraph 15(3), in the third column of the Table, paragraph 2.

GENERAL NOTE
  This section abolishes the power of courts-martial and Standing Civilian Courts to sentence a civilian under the age of 17 years to a reception order, whereby he would be committed to the care of a local authority in the U.K. The civilian equivalent was the care order imposed by a court following conviction of an offence. This power was abolished by s.90(2) of the Children Act 1989. This section therefore brings Service law into line with civilian law.

Stoppages and compensation orders

Stoppages under the 1955 Acts: personal injuries and limits

7.—(1) In section 71 of each of the 1955 Acts (scale of punishments and supplementary provisions)—
  (a) in subsection (1), in paragraph (k) after the word "expense" there shall be inserted "personal injury"; and
  (b) after subsection (5) there shall be inserted the following subsections—
    "(6) Unless the Secretary of State by order provides that this sub-section shall no longer apply, the stoppages awarded by a court-martial in respect of any offence occasioning personal injury of which a person is convicted or any other such offence which is taken into consideration in determining sentence shall not exceed such sum as is for the time being specified by an order made by the Secretary of State.
    (7) The power to make an order under subsection (6) above shall be exercisable by statutory instrument subject to annulment in pursuance of a resolution of either House of Parliament."

(2) In section 225 of the Army Act 1955 and section 223 of the Air Force Act 1955 (general provisions as to interpretation) in subsection (1) in the definition of "stoppages" the words from "for any expense" onwards shall be omitted.

GENERAL NOTE

Under s.71 of the 1955 Acts a court-martial may impose stoppages (or deductions from pay) of a serviceman upon conviction for any loss or damage caused as a result of the offence. This can be particularly effective since the court-martial "represents" the convicted serviceman's employer and can easily arrange for the necessary deductions to be made.

This section adds to the powers of the court-martial by permitting it also to order such stoppages where the accused is convicted of an offence occasioning personal injury. There is a similar power in s.35 of the Powers of Criminal Courts Act 1973 and a limit of £2,000 in the magistrates' court (Magistrates' Courts Act 1980, s.40(1)). There is no limit in the Crown Court. There is guidance issued to magistrates' courts concerning the level of compensation for particular injuries and it is anticipated that this will also guide courts-martial. These guidelines are set out in Blackstone's Criminal Practice at E12.8. It is anticipated that regulations will be made to deal with the case where a court-martial is minded to fine a Service offender and also to impose stoppages for personal injury. Preference will be given to the imposition of stoppages (see Select Committee on the Armed Forces Bill, 1990–91, p. 178. Compare s.9(5) in relation to civilians).

Subs. (1)

This amends s.71 of each of the 1955 Acts. It adds a new subs. (6) to s.71. The Act enables a limit to be imposed to the amount of compensation to be awarded, despite the fact that no limit is imposed for the Crown court, of similar status to the court-martial. The limit will be set by an order made by the Secretary of State. This is likely to be the same amount set for magistrates' courts (currently £2,000). Problems may arise where an offender is convicted of more than one offence or where more than one offender is jointly convicted. It is likely in these circumstances that the court-martial would only award a sum up to the maximum permissible per offender (even if there are multiple offences). See Select Committee on the Armed Forces Bill, 1990–91, p. 177.

An award of compensation to a victim under this Act would not be a bar to a civil action by him for the same injuries. In the civil action he would give credit for the amount awarded by the court-martial (see Select Committee on the Armed Forces Bill, 1990–91, para. 111 and see Sched. 2, para. 9). By the Crown Proceedings (Armed Forces) Act 1987 the former bar, established by s.10 of the Crown Proceedings Act 1947, whereby one serviceman could not sue another in tort where the injuries were caused while on duty or on Service property, has been repealed (although it may be reinstated by the 1987 Act).

Stoppages under the 1957 Act: personal injuries and limits

8.—(1) In section 43 of the 1957 Act (scale of punishments and supplementary provisions)—

(a) in subsection (1), in paragraph (1) after the word "expense," in both places where it occurs, there shall be inserted "personal injury"; and

(b) after subsection (6) there shall be inserted the following subsections—

"(7) Unless the Secretary of State by order provides that this subsection shall no longer apply, the stoppages awarded in respect of any offence occasioning personal injury of which a person is convicted or any other such offence which is taken into consideration in determining sentence shall not exceed such sum as is for the time being specified by an order made by the Secretary of State.

(8) The power to make an order under subsection (7) above shall be exercisable by statutory instrument subject to annulment in pursuance of a resolution of either House of Parliament."

(2) In section 49 of the 1957 Act (summary trial), after subsection (5) there shall be inserted the following subsection—

"(6) The reference in the proviso to subsection (5) above to stoppages does not include a reference to stoppages for personal injury."

GENERAL NOTE

This makes similar provision in the NDA 1957, although the power is also available to commanding officers in the Royal Navy. The reason for this is that these officers have more extensive powers of punishment than their Army or Royal Air Force counterparts. At every quinquennial review by a Select Committee on the Armed Forces Bill the Royal Navy is required to justify these wider powers and does so largely on the basis that while serving at sea it is more difficult to arrange a court-martial than is the case for the other two services.

Subs. (2)
This limits the power to impose stoppages for personal injuries to commanding officers.

Compensation orders for personal injuries on trial of civilians

9.—(1) In the following enactments relating to the powers of a court on the trial of a civilian—
    (a) Schedule 5A to each of the 1955 Acts, and
    (b) Schedule 4A to the 1957 Act,
paragraph 11 (compensation orders) shall be amended in accordance with the following provisions of this section.

(2) In sub-paragraph (1) for the words "loss or damage, other than personal injury" there shall be substituted "personal injury, loss or damage."

(3) Subject to subsection (6) below, after sub-paragraph (1) there shall be inserted the following sub-paragraph—

"(1A) Unless the Secretary of State by order provides that this sub-paragraph shall no longer apply, the sum specified in a compensation order made by a court-martial for any personal injury shall not exceed such sum as is for the time being specified in sub-paragraph (2) below or such larger sum as may for the time being be specified by an order made by the Secretary of State; and the power to make an order under this sub-paragraph shall be exercisable by statutory instrument subject to annulment in pursuance of a resolution of either House of Parliament."

(4) In sub-paragraph (4) the words from "and no such order" onwards shall be omitted and after that sub-paragraph there shall be inserted the following sub-paragraphs—

"(4A) A compensation order may only be made in respect of injury, loss or damage which was due to an accident arising out of the presence of a motor vehicle on a road if—
    (a) it is in respect of damage which is treated by sub-paragraph (3) above as resulting from an offence of unlawfully obtaining any property; or
    (b) it is in respect of injury, loss or damage as respects which—
        (i) the offender is uninsured in relation to the use of the vehicle; and
        (ii) compensation is not payable under any arrangements specified by the Secretary of State for the purposes of this paragraph;
and, where a compensation order is made in respect of injury, loss or damage due to such an accident, the amount to be paid may include an amount representing the whole or part of any loss of or reduction in preferential rates of insurance attributable to the accident.

(4B) For the purposes of sub-paragraph (4A) above, a person is not uninsured in relation to the use of a vehicle if—
    (a) the vehicle is in the public service of the Crown; or
    (b) the use of the vehicle is exempted from insurance by section 144 of the Road Traffic Act 1988 or paragraph (2) or paragraph (3) of Article 90 of the Road Traffic (Northern Ireland) Order 1981."

(5) After sub-paragraph (5) there shall be inserted the following sub-paragraph—

"(6) Where the court considers—
   (a) that it would be appropriate both to impose a fine and to make a compensation order, but
   (b) that the person concerned has insufficient means to pay both an appropriate fine and appropriate compensation,
the court shall give preference to compensation (though it may impose a fine as well)."

(6) Subsection (3) above shall not apply in relation to paragraph 11 of Schedule 4A to the 1957 Act; but after sub-paragraph (1) of that paragraph there shall be inserted the following sub-paragraph—

"(1A) Unless the Secretary of State by order provides that this sub-paragraph shall no longer apply, the sum specified in a compensation order made for any personal injury shall not exceed such sum as is for the time being specified in paragraph 11(2) of Schedule 5A to the Army Act 1955 or such larger sum as may for the time being be specified by an order made by the Secretary of State; and the power to make an order under this sub-paragraph shall be exercisable by statutory instrument subject to annulment in pursuance of a resolution of either House of Parliament."

GENERAL NOTE

This enacts a power similar to ss.7 and 8 but applies it to the trial of civilians whether by court-martial or by Standing Civilian Court (see para. 2(1) of Sched. 5A to the 1955 Acts).

Subs. (3)

The new paragraph (1A) refers only to a compensation order made by a court-martial. The reason for this is that the powers of a Standing Civilian Court are limited to those possessed by a magistrates' court. The limit of personal injury compensation applicable at any one time to magistrates' courts will also apply to Standing Civilian Courts and hence no order of the Secretary of State will be required.

Subs. (4)

Paragraph 11(4) of Sched. 5A to the 1955 Acts states (as amended by this subsection) that "No compensation shall be made in respect of loss suffered by the dependants of a person in consequence of his death." The new subsection limits compensation to a victim of a road accident in the manner described. Sub-para. (a) to this subsection refers to a case (detailed in para. 11(3) of Sched. 5A to the 1955 Acts and Sched. 4A to the 1957 Act) where property that has been unlawfully obtained and is subsequently recovered has been damaged while outside the control of the owner.

Subs. (5)

Unlike ss.7 and 8, this subsection directs a court-martial or a Standing Civilian Court as to a preference where the court is minded to fine the offender and also to award compensation to his victim.

Subs. (6)

This makes a minor amendment to the NDA 1957, required because of a slight textual difference between Sched. 4A (to the NDA 1957) and Sched. 5A to the 1955 Acts.

Courts-martial

Compensation for miscarriages of justice

10.—(1) Subject to subsection (2) below, when—
   (a) a person has been convicted by a court-martial, and
   (b) subsequently his conviction has been reversed or he has been pardoned on the ground that a new or newly discovered fact shows beyond reasonable doubt that there has been a miscarriage of justice,
the Secretary of State shall pay compensation for the miscarriage of justice to the person who has suffered punishment as a result of such conviction or, if he is dead, to his personal representatives, unless the non-disclosure of the unknown fact was wholly or partly attributable to the person convicted.

(2) No payment of compensation under this section shall be made unless an application for such compensation has been made to the Secretary of State.

(3) The question whether there is a right to compensation under this section shall be determined by the Secretary of State.

(4) If the Secretary of State determines that there is a right to such compensation, the amount of the compensation shall be assessed by an assessor appointed by the Secretary of State.

(5) In this section "reversed" shall be construed as referring to a conviction having been quashed—

(a) on an appeal out of time; or

(b) on a reference under section 34 of the Courts-Martial (Appeals) Act 1968.

(6) For the purposes of this section a person suffers punishment as a result of a conviction when sentence is passed on him for the offence of which he was convicted.

(7) Schedule 1 to this Act shall have effect.

GENERAL NOTE

This section is a further example of Service law being brought into line with civilian law. The comparable power in relation to a conviction by a civilian court is s.133 of the Criminal Justice Act 1988. *Ex gratia* payments have been made previously by the Ministry of Defence. Indeed, the Select Committee in 1990–91 was informed that a payment of £30,000 was made in 1987 (para. 153). This form of compensation will be retained in addition to the compensation provisions contained in this section.

Subs. (1)

Compensation is available for the person who has suffered *punishment*. This section applies to a person convicted by a court-martial. The person convicted by a court-martial may be either a serviceman or a civilian (who was, at the time of the offence subject to Service law) or a civilian who appealed from a Standing Civilian Court to a court-martial (see Armed Forces Act 1976, Sched. 3, para. 18(5), which states that the appeal shall take the form of a rehearing of that charge). Section 71 of the 1955 Acts lists the punishments that can be imposed by a court-martial. These are in descending order with death as the most severe punishment. The reason for placing punishments in this order is that, for historical reasons, many offence-creating sections of the Service Discipline Acts impose a punishment of "death or any lesser punishment".

Subs. (5)

It is clearly intended that the normal procedure of appeal to the Court-Martial Appeal Court is to apply. The time limits for appeal are set out in s.8 of the Courts-Martial (Appeals) Act 1968 and Courts-Martial Appeal Rules 1968, r. 6(1)(b). Time starts to run from the date of promulgation of the court-martial decision and not from the date the sentence was passed by the court. The reason for this is that the findings and sentence of a court-martial (although not a Standing Civilian Court nor a Naval court-martial) are subject to confirmation.

Withdrawal of election to be tried by court-martial under the 1955 Acts: officers, warrant officers and civilians

11.—(1) In section 79 of each of the 1955 Acts (further proceedings on charges against officers and warrant officers), in subsection (6) after the words "so elects" there shall be inserted "and does no subsequently in accordance with Queen's Regulations withdraw his election."

(2) In section 209 of each of those Acts (application of Acts to civilians), in subsection (3) (modifications), in paragraph (d) after the words "so elects" there shall be inserted "and does not subsequently in accordance with Rules of Procedure withdraw his election."

GENERAL NOTE

In the 1955 Acts an officer, or a warrant officer, can be dealt with summarily (by "the appropriate superior authority"). That superior authority is directed by s.79 of the 1955 Acts to investigate the charge and determine whether the accused is guilty or not. If the decision is one of guilt and it is proposed to impose a forfeiture of pay, or any punishment more severe than a severe reprimand (for the list of punishments see s.79(5) of the 1955 Acts) the accused must be offered the opportunity to elect trial by court-martial instead. If he so elects he is, by this section, given the opportunity to withdraw it and to be dealt with summarily. A similar power to withdraw an election had been given to non-commissioned officers and soldiers (and their Royal Air Force equivalents) by s.78(5) of the 1955 Acts (see also Queen's Regulations (1975) 6.088). This avoids the need to convene a court-martial if the accused changes his mind.

No such change is necessary to the NDA 1957 since officers in the Royal Navy are subject only to court-martial and not to summary proceedings. A similar provision is made for civilians subject to Service law by s.209 of the 1955 Acts.

Powers of naval courts-martial

12.—(1) In section 90 of the 1957 Act (suspension of sentences), in subsection (1) for the words "any such case" there shall be substituted "any case where a sentence is suspended under this subsection" and after that subsection there shall be inserted the following subsection—

"(1A) Where any person has been sentenced under this Act by a court-martial to imprisonment or detention, the court-martial may itself exercise the power under subsection (1) above to order the suspension of the sentence."

(2) In Schedule 4A to the 1957 Act (powers of courts-martial on trial of civilian), in paragraph 4(7) (offences relating to community supervision orders to be treated as offences against provisions of Part II of that Act) for the words "Part II" there shall be substituted "Part I."

GENERAL NOTE

This section gives power to Naval courts-martial to suspend sentences of imprisonment or detention. Such a power is not available to Army and Royal Air Force courts-martial since their findings, unlike a Naval court-martial, are subject to confirmation and the confirming officer has this power (see s.120 of the 1955 Acts).

Damage to public or service property etc.

13.—(1) In the Army Act 1955, in Schedule 3 (alternative offences of which accused may be convicted by court-material), after the paragraphs in the first and second columns numbered 7B there shall be inserted—

"7C. Wilfully damaging public or service property or property belonging to another person subject to military law.	7C. By wilful neglect causing damage to public or service property or property belonging to another person subject to military law."

(2) The paragraphs set out in subsection (1) above shall also be inserted in the first and second columns of Schedule 3 to the Air Force Act 1955 after the paragraphs numbered 7B, but with the substitution for the words "military law," in each place where they occur, of the words "air-force law."

GENERAL NOTE

Schedule 3 to the 1955 Acts lists alternative offences of which an accused may be convicted at a court-martial. The principal section is s.98(6) which provides that where an accused is charged before a court-martial with an offence specified in the first column of Sched. 3 he may be convicted of the offence specified in the second column. Thus, the added sub-para. 7C to Sched. 3 enables a court-martial to convict an accused of the alternative offence in the right-hand paragraph (or second column). These are offences respectively by s.44(1)(a) and (1)(b) of the 1955 Acts, although the level of punishment is the same for both offences. The nature of this procedure is to enable a court-martial to convict where the alternative offence is not included in the charge sheet. It applies only to purely Service offences (listed in Sched. 3) and not to civilian offences, charged under s.70 of the 1955 Acts (for which see s.98(5)). For the alternative conviction of an attempt, see s.98(2), (3), (4) of the 1955 Acts.

Deduction of maintenance payments etc. from pay

Deductions from pay in respect of liabilities for maintenance: the 1955 Acts.

14.—(1) Section 150 of each of the 1955 Acts (enforcement of maintenance and affiliation orders by deduction from pay) shall be amended in accordance with subsections (2) to (4) below.

(2) In subsection (1), in paragraph (a) the words "or child" shall be omitted and after that paragraph there shall be inserted the following paragraph—

"(aa) the maintenance of any child of his or his wife or of any other child who has been treated by them both as a child of their family; or."

(3) After subsection (1) there shall be inserted the following subsection—

"(1A) Without prejudice to any enactment or rule of law relating to adoption or legitimation, in subsection (1)(aa) above any reference to a child of the defendant or his wife shall be construed without regard to whether or not the father and mother of the child have or had been married to each other at any time."

(4) In subsection (5)—

(a) in the paragraph beginning "references to a wife" the words "or child," in both places where they occur, shall be omitted; and

(b) the paragraph beginning "references to a child" shall be omitted.

(5) At the end of section 151 of each of the 1955 Acts (deductions from pay for maintenance of wife or child) there shall be added, and be deemed always to have been added, the following subsection—

"(6) Without prejudice to any enactment or rule of law relating to adoption or legitimation, references in this section to a child of any person shall be construed without regard to whether the father and mother of the child have or had been married to each other at any time."

(6) The amendments made by the preceding provisions of this section do not affect the operation,—

(a) in England and Wales, of section 1 of the Family Law Reform Act 1987; or

(b) in Scotland, of section 1 of the Law Reform (Parent and Child) (Scotland) Act 1986.

GENERAL NOTE

This section makes a number of amendments to ss.150 and 151 of the 1955 Acts. Section 150 enables an order made by a civilian court in the U.K. to be enforced against a person subject to the 1955 Acts. Thus, a soldier whose wife secures a maintenance order against him in a court in (say) Liverpool can have this enforced through deduction of pay of her soldier husband. Section 151 enables an officer appointed by the Defence Council to order a deduction from pay where he is satisfied that the soldier is neglecting, without reasonable cause, to maintain his wife. There are approximately 2,300 such orders currently in operation (Select Committee Report, 1990–91, para. 206). Generally, no deductions from the pay of a soldier or airman may be made unless authorised by the 1955 Acts or by Royal Warrant (s.144 of the 1955 Acts) and for assignments of, or charges on, pay, pensions bounty or grants, see s.203 of the 1955 Acts and s.16 of this Act.

In both ss.150 and 151 orders can be made in respect of children and the following subsections make amendments to the principal sections as to the meaning of "child".

Subs. (2)

This amendment is designed to ensure that the word "child" is wide enough to encompass a child within the new para. (aa). It follows the pattern set by s.105(1) of the Children Act 1989 (with suitable amendments to delete references to foster children).

Subs. (3)

This amendment provides that the marital status of the father and mother of the child, and thus the concept of illegitimacy, is irrelevant. See also subs. (6) of this section.

Subs. (4)

Since subss. (2) and (3) of this section provide new interpretations of the word "child", the references in s.150(5) are no longer necessary and are deleted.

Subs. (5)

This makes an amendment to s.151 of the 1955 Acts similar to subs. (3) above. The difference is that, unlike subs. (3), this provision has retrospective effect. See also subs. (6) of this section.

Subs. (6)

Section 1 of the Family Law Reform Act 1969 and (for Scotland) s.1 of the Law Reform (Parent and Child) (Scotland) Act 1986 abolish the concept of illegitimacy but they only have effect within their own individual territorial boundaries. Service law applies to those subject to it (see the Introduction and General Note at the beginning of the annotation) wherever the armed forces happen to be serving. Subsections (3) and (5) ensure that the abolition of the concept of illegitimacy applies in the Service context, wherever the Serviceman happens to be. This subsection is designed to ensure that the Armed Forces Act 1991 has no effect on the status of the earlier Acts of 1969 and 1986 referred to in it.

Deductions from naval and marine pay in respect of liabilities for maintenance

15.—(1) In the Naval Forces (Enforcement of Maintenance Liabilities) Act 1947, section 1 (deductions from pay in respect of liabilities for maintenance etc.) shall be amended in accordance with subsections (2) to (4) below.

(2) In subsection (1)—

(a) for paragraph (a) there shall be substituted the following paragraphs—

"(a) for the maintenance of the wife of that person;

(aa) for the maintenance of any child of that person or his wife or of any other child who has been treated by them both as a child of their family;";

(b) in paragraph (b) for the words from "and any such children" onwards there shall be substituted "or any such child as is mentioned in paragraph (aa) above"; and

(c) after paragraph (b) there shall be added the following paragraph—

"(c) for the payment of any sum adjudged as costs, or awarded as expenses, incurred in proceedings on appeal against, or for the variation, revocation or revival of, any such order or decree."

(3) After subsection (2) there shall be inserted the following subsections—

(2A) For the purposes of this section—

(a) if, in proceedings in connection with the dissolution or annulment of a marriage, an order has been made for the payment of any periodical or other sum in respect of the maintenance of the person who, if the marriage had subsisted, would have been the wife of any such person as is mentioned in subsection (1) above, references in this section to that person's wife include references to the person in whose favour the order was made;

(b) any reference to an order or decree of any court in Her Majesty's dominions includes a reference to an order registered in a court in the United Kingdom under Part I of the Maintenance Orders (Reciprocal Enforcement) Act 1972 or registered under Part I of the Civil Jurisdiction and Judgments Act 1982 in a court in any territory to which that Act for the time being extends; and

(c) without prejudice to any enactment or rule of law relating to adoption or legitimation, references to a child of a person or his wife shall be construed without regard to whether or not the father and mother of the child have or had been married to each other at any time.

(2B) In relation to women members of Her Majesty's naval forces, within the meaning of the Naval Discipline Act 1957, references in this section to a wife shall be construed as references to a husband."

(4) Subsections (3) and (5) shall be omitted.

(5) In section 101 of the 1957 Act (service of proceedings for maintenance etc.), in subsection (5) (definition of "maintenance order") for paragraphs (a) and (b) there shall be substituted the following paragraphs—

"(a) the maintenance of the wife of the person against whom the order is made; or

(b) the maintenance of any child of that person or his wife or of any other child who has been treated by them both as a child of their family; or."

(6) After subsection (5) of section 101 of the 1957 Act there shall be inserted the following subsections—

"(5A) In subsection (5) above—

(a) references to the wife of a person include, in relation to an order made in proceedings in connection with the dissolution or annulment of a marriage, references to a person who would have been his wife if the marriage had subsisted; and

(b) without prejudice to any enactment or rule of law relating to adoption or legitimation, references to a child of a person or his wife shall be construed without regard to whether or not the father and mother of the child have or had been married to each other at any time.

(5B) In relation to women members of Her Majesty's naval forces, references in this section to a wife shall be construed as references to a husband."

(7) The amendments made by the preceding provisions of this section do not affect the operation,—

(a) in England and Wales, of section 1 of the Family Law Reform Act 1987; or

(b) in Scotland, of section 1 of the Law Reform (Parent and Child) (Scotland) Act 1986.

GENERAL NOTE
This section makes changes to the NDA 1957 comparable to those contained in s.14 relating to the 1955 Acts.

Naval and marine pay and pensions

New provisions as to assignments, charges and court orders in respect of naval and marine pay, pensions etc.

16.—(1) In the 1957 Act, after section 128F there shall be inserted the following section—

"**Avoidance of assignment of or charge on naval pay and pensions etc.**

128G.—(1) Every assignment of or charge on, and every agreement to assign or charge, any pay, pensions, bounty, grants or other allowances in the nature thereof payable to any person in respect of his or any other person's service in Her Majesty's naval forces shall be void.

(2) Save as expressly provided by this Act, no order shall be made by any court the effect of which would be to restrain any person from receiving anything which by virtue of this section he is precluded from assigning and to direct payment thereof to another person.

(3) Nothing in this section—

(a) shall apply to the making or variation of attachment of earnings orders; or

(b) shall prejudice any enactment providing for the payment of any sum to a bankrupt's trustee in bankruptcy for distribution among creditors.

(4) In the application of this section to Northern Ireland at any time before the coming into operation of the Insolvency (Northern Ireland) Order 1989, for the reference in subsection (3) above to a bankrupt's trustee in bankruptcy there shall be substituted a reference to an assignee in bankruptcy."

(2) Subsection (1) above has effect in place of sections 4 and 5 of the Naval and Marine Pay and Pensions Act 1865.

(3) In section 2 of the Naval Pensions Act 1884 (application of 1865 Act etc. to Greenwich Hospital pensions) after the words "Act 1865," in the second place where they occur, there shall be inserted "or section 128G of the Naval Discipline Act 1957."

(4) In section 59(3) of the Reserve Forces Act 1980 (which applies sections 3 and 5 of the Naval and Marine Pay and Pensions Act 1865 in relation to pay, bounty and allowances payable as mentioned in that provision)—
   (a) for the words "Sections 3 and 5" there shall be substituted "Section 3"; and
   (b) after "1865" there shall be inserted "and section 128G of the Naval Discipline Act 1957."

GENERAL NOTE

Subs. (1)
   The clear intention of this subsection is to bring the NDA 1957 into line with s.203 of the 1955 Acts, to which it is almost identical. It replaces (see subs. (2)) ss.4 and 5 of the Naval and Marine Pay and Pensions Act 1865, which contained earlier provisions relating to the subject-matter of this subsection. The reason for this amendment to the NDA 1957 was explained to the Select Committee on the Armed Forces Bill 1990–91 as follows: "It was questions raised on the ambit of sections 4 and 5 of the 1865 Act which caused us to look at it. There were no questions raised on the ambit of the provisions of the [1955 Acts] but we are now bringing them all into line. So it is not a question of the Navy being behind, only that the provisions were worded differently thus causing confusion" (para. 217). Section 203 of the Army Act 1955 was discussed in *Roberts* v. *Roberts* [1986] 1 W.L.R. 437, where it was held that an order by a registrar that the husband, a serving soldier, pay as a lump sum a quarter of his terminal grant if, and when it became due, to the wife, was void under s.203 of the Army Act 1955. The court also relied on *Walker* v. *Walker* [1983] Fam. 68. See also *Ranson* v. *Ranson* [1988] 1 W.L.R. 183. Compare the position had a pension or gratuity been received in *Roberts* v. *Roberts*.
   The SDAs clearly permit a serviceman to be sentenced to stoppages of pay (see also ss.7 and 8 of this Act) and allow the military or naval authorities to deduct pay (see ss.14 and 15 of this Act). These actions clearly do not fall foul of s.203 of the 1955 Acts or this new section inserted into the NDA 1957 by virtue of s.128G(2). For the same reason, the Attachment of Earnings Act 1971 does not apply in respect of pay and allowances (but it does in respect of a pension) of a debtor who is a member of the armed forces: express reference is to be found in ss.22(5) and 24(2)(b) of that Act.

Subss. (2), (3), (4)
   These give effect to the amendment to the NDA 1957 contained in subs. (1) above.

PART III

PROTECTION OF CHILDREN OF SERVICE FAMILIES

Power to make service family child assessment orders

   17.—(1) Subject to subsection (2) below, the power to make an order under this section (in this Part of this Act referred to as an "assessment order") is exercisable only with respect to a child who—
   (a) forms part of the family of a person subject to service law serving in a country or territory outside the United Kingdom or of a civilian in a corresponding position; and
   (b) resides outside the United Kingdom with that family or another such family.

(2) The power to make an assessment order is also exercisable with respect to a child who, though not falling within paragraph (a) of subsection (1) above, is staying (for however short a time) with such a family as is referred to in that paragraph and is so exercisable as if he resided with that family; and any reference in the following provisions of this Part of this Act to a person with whom a child was at any time residing shall be construed accordingly.

(3) On an application made with respect to a child by a person authorised in that behalf by regulations, the officer having jurisdiction may make an assessment order with respect to the child if, but only if, he is satisfied that—

(a) the applicant has reasonable cause to suspect that the child is suffering, or is likely to suffer, significant harm;

(b) an assessment of the state of the child's health or development or of the way in which he has been treated is required to enable the applicant to determine whether or not the child is suffering, or is likely to suffer, significant harm; and

(c) it is unlikely that such an assessment will be made, or be satisfactory, in the absence of an assessment order.

(4) A person making an application for an assessment order with respect to a child shall take such steps as are reasonably practicable to ensure that, before the application is considered, notice of the application is given to—

(a) the child;

(b) his parents;

(c) any other person who has parental responsibility for him;

(d) any other person caring for the child or with whom the child is residing immediately before the making of the application;

(e) any person in whose favour a contact order is in force with respect to the child; and

(f) any person who is allowed to have contact with the child by virtue of an order under section 34 of the Children Act 1989.

(5) An assessment order shall not be made with respect to any child if the officer to whom the application is made is satisfied—

(a) that there are grounds for making a protection order with respect to the child; and

(b) that he ought to make such an order rather than an assessment order;

and an officer to whom an application for an assessment order is made may treat the application as an application for a protection order.

(6) Regulations may make provision with respect to the procedure to be followed on and in connection with the making of an assessment order.

DEFINITIONS
See s.23.

GENERAL NOTE
Part III of the Act, in dealing with the protection of the children of Service families, attempts to bring Service law into line, so far as is possible, with civilian law, particularly with the Children Act 1989. This part of the Act will apply only to children of Service families outside the U.K. A Service child within the U.K. will be subject to the "ordinary" civilian law. Section 209 of the 1955 Acts and Schedule 5 to those Acts subject civilians who are within the limits of the command of any officer commanding a body of the regular forces outside the U.K. to Service law. Thus, the wife and children of a serviceman, along with relatives staying with them, will be so subject. This will include a great many children. Social work outside the U.K. is provided by SSAFA Social Work Service, recruited from those having obtained relevant qualifications and experience in the U.K. Case conferences, similar to those operating in the U.K., will therefore take place. Prior to this Act a child could be subject to a place of safety order under s.14 of the Armed Forces Act 1981. In 1990, six children were subjected to such an order (see Select Committee on the Armed Forces Bill 1990–91, p. 155). The protection order made under s.19 replaces the place of safety order. The assessment order is similar to s.43 and the protection order to ss.44 and 45, both of the Children Act 1989. See generally White, Carr and Lowe, *A Guide to the Children Act 1989.*

Subs. (1)
This is in line with the normal rule for the subjection of civilians to Service law. Schedule 5 to the 1955 Acts also subjects certain civilians, such as SSAFA social workers, to Service law. The children of such a worker would come within this subsection.

Subs. (2)
This is an exceptional provision to cover a visitor to a family whose members are subject to Service law. It would include, for instance, a boarding-school friend staying with such a family during the school holidays. Normally such a child would not be subject to military jurisdiction.

Subs. (3)
The assessment order may only be made by a person authorised by (subsequent) regulations. It is likely to be a SSAFA social worker or a Service medical officer (Select Committee on the Armed Forces Bill 1990–91, para. 262). The grounds upon which an order can be made are identical to those contained in s.43(1)(a), (b) and (c) of the Children Act 1989.

Subs. (4)
This requirement to give notice prior to the consideration of the application is similar to s.43(11) of the Children Act 1989.

Subs. (5)
Protection orders are made by virtue of s.19 of this Act. Where one is indicated it should be made. See the similar provision in s.43(4) of the Children Act 1989.

Content, effect, variation and discharge of assessment orders

18.—(1) An assessment order shall—
(a) specify the date by which the assessment is to begin; and
(b) have effect for such period, not exceeding seven days beginning with that date, as may be specified in the order.

(2) Where an assessment order is in force with respect to a child, it shall be the duty of any person who is in a position to produce the child—
(a) to produce him to such person as may be named in the order; and
(b) to comply with such directions relating to the assessment of the child as the officer making the order considers appropriate to include in the order.

(3) Subject to subsection (4) below, an assessment order authorises any person carrying out the assessment, or any part of the assessment, to do so in accordance with the terms of the order.

(4) If the child to whom an assessment order relates is of sufficient understanding to make an informed decision, he may refuse to submit to a medical or psychiatric examination or other assessment.

(5) The child to whom an assessment order relates may only be kept away from home—
(a) in accordance with directions included in the order; and
(b) if it is necessary for the purposes of the assessment; and
(c) for such period or periods as may be specified in the order.

(6) Where the child to whom an assessment order relates is to be kept away from home, the order shall contain such directions as the officer making it considers appropriate with regard to the contact that the child must be allowed to have with other persons while away from home.

(7) In such circumstances and subject to such conditions as may be prescribed by regulations, an assessment order may be varied or discharged on an application made, in such manner as may be so prescribed, by—
(a) the child to whom the order relates;
(b) a parent of his;
(c) any other person who has parental responsibility for him;
(d) any other person caring for the child or with whom the child was residing immediately before the making of the application;

(e) any person in whose favour a contact order is in force with respect to the child; or

(f) any person who is allowed to have contact with the child by virtue of an order under section 34 of the Children Act 1989.

(8) A person subject to service law or a civilian in a corresponding position who intentionally obstructs any person exercising a power conferred on him by virtue of the making of an assessment order shall be liable on conviction to a fine or to any less punishment provided by the Army Act 1955, the Air Force Act 1955 or the 1957 Act, as the case may require.

(9) Any offence under subsection (8) above shall be treated,—

(a) if the offender is subject to military law or a civilian to whom Part II of the Army Act 1955 is applied by section 209 of that Act, as if it were an offence against a provision of Part II of that Act which is triable by court-martial under that Act;

(b) if the offender is subject to air-force law or a civilian to whom Part II of the Air Force Act 1955 is applied by section 209 of that Act, as if it were an offence against a provision of Part II of that Act which is triable by court-martial under that Act;

(c) if the offender is subject to the 1957 Act or a civilian to whom Parts I and II of that Act are applied by section 118 of that Act, as if it were an offence against a provision of Part I of that Act which is triable by court-martial under that Act.

(10) Any power conferred by this section to give directions shall be exercisable subject to, and in accordance with, any provision made by regulations.

DEFINITIONS
See s.23.

GENERAL NOTE

Subs. (1)
This is identical to s.43(5) of the Children Act 1989. In White, Carr and Lowe, *A Guide to the Children Act 1989*, the authors explain that "since the order shall not have effect for a period exceeding seven days . . ., it seems likely that it will be primarily a medical assessment, as a social work assessment normally takes rather longer" (p. 97).

Subs. (2)
This is similar to s.43(6) of the Children Act 1989.

Subs. (3)
This is identical to s.43(7) of the Children Act 1989.

Subs. (4)
This is similar to s.43(8) of the Children Act 1989. It is anticipated that the decision as to whether the child is of sufficient understanding to refuse to submit to a medical or psychiatric examination or other assessment would be made by the commanding officer of the person subject to Service law (usually the father of the child), who might wish to seek advice (see Select Committee on the Armed Forces Bill 1990–91, para. 264). Even if he decided that the child was not of sufficient understanding to refuse and therefore the examination could proceed *quaere* whether a medical officer would proceed to examine an obviously unwilling child. If he was ordered to do so by the commanding officer it is unlikely that this order would be one which the medical officer would be required to obey (see, for example, s.34 of the 1955 Acts, where a person subject to military law commits an offence if he disobeys any lawful command. The issue would clearly turn on whether the order was a lawful one).

Subs. (5)
This is identical to s.43(9) of the Children Act 1989.

Subs. (6)
This is identical to s.43(10) of the Children Act 1989.

Subs. (7)
For definitions, see s.23 of this Act.

Subs. (8)
This offence can be committed by anyone subject to Service law. Thus the serviceman or his wife who intentionally obstructs the relevant person would commit an offence under Service law. The Select Committee on the Armed Forces Bill 1990–91 was told that the fine, in the case of a serviceman, would be a maximum of 28 days' pay (para. 268). This is in line with s.71(5) of the 1955 Acts. The phrase "or any less punishment" is one common to the structure of the Service Discipline Acts. See, for example, s.71 of the 1955 Acts, where the sentences that may be imposed by a court-martial are listed in order of severity, with death at the top and minor punishments at the bottom. Thus, lesser punishments than a fine include severe reprimand, reprimand, stoppages of pay (by way of compensation) and minor punishments. For a civilian, see Sched. 5A to the 1955 Acts.

Subs. (9)
This subsection gives jurisdiction to a court-martial to try the offence created in subs. (8). This is necessary since there is no general offence of contempt of Service jurisdiction. However, contempt of a court-martial is an offence by s.57 (and for civilians, additionally, s.209) (proviso) of the 1955 Acts.

Power to make orders for the emergency protection of children of service families

19.—(1) Subject to subsection (2) below, the power to make an order under this section (in this Part of this Act referred to as a "protection order") is exercisable only with respect to a child who—
  (a) forms part of the family of a person subject to service law serving in a country or territory outside the United Kingdom or of a civilian in a corresponding position; and
  (b) resides outside the United Kingdom with that family or another such family.

(2) The power to make a protection order is also exercisable with respect to a child who, though not falling within paragraph (a) of subsection (1) above, is staying (for however short a time) with such a family as is referred to in that paragraph and is so exercisable as if he resided with that family; and any reference in the following provisions of this Part of this Act to a person with whom a child was at any time residing shall be construed accordingly.

(3) On an application made by any person with respect to a child, the officer having jurisdiction may make a protection order with respect to the child if, but only if, he is satisfied that—
  (a) there is reasonable cause to believe that the child is likely to suffer significant harm if he is not removed to accommodation provided by or on behalf of the applicant; or
  (b) there is reasonable cause to believe that the child is likely to suffer significant harm if he does not remain in the place in which he is then being accommodated (whether or not that is the place where he is resident); or
  (c) in the case of an application made by a designated person—
        (i) the applicant has reasonable cause to suspect that a child is suffering, or is likely to suffer, significant harm;
        (ii) the applicant is making enquiries with respect to the child's welfare; and
        (iii) those enquiries are being frustrated by access to the child being unreasonably refused to the applicant or a person authorised by the applicant to seek access and the applicant has reasonable cause to believe that access to the child is required as a matter of urgency.

(4) No protection order shall be made without affording—
  (a) the child to whom it is proposed that the order should relate,

(b) his parents,
(c) any other person who has parental responsibility for him, and
(d) any other person with whom he was residing immediately before the
making of the application for the order

an opportunity to make representations to the officer to whom the application for the order is made, except where it appears to that officer that it would be undesirable to do so in the interests of the child or that it would be impracticable, or would cause unnecessary delay, to communicate with any parent of the child or with any such other person as is mentioned in paragraph (c) or paragraph (d) above.

(5) Any person—
(a) seeking access to a child in connection with enquiries of a kind
mentioned in subsection (3)(c) above, and
(b) purporting to be a designated person or a person authorised by a
designated person to seek such access,

shall, on being asked to do so, produce some duly authenticated document as evidence that he is such a person.

(6) Regulations may—
(a) prescribe the descriptions of persons who for the purposes of this
section are designated persons; and
(b) make provision with respect to the procedure to be followed on and in
connection with the making of protection orders.

(7) This section and sections 20 to 22 below have effect in place of section 14 of the Armed Forces Act 1981 (temporary removal to and detention in a place of safety abroad of children of service families in need of care or control).

DEFINITIONS
See s.23.

GENERAL NOTE

Subss. (1) and (2)
These are similar to those contained in s.17 (*q.v.*).

Subs. (3)
The grounds upon which a protection order can be made are similar to those contained in s.44 of the Children Act 1989 (where it is styled an emergency protection order), with all references to local authorities being deleted, since this order can only be made while the child is overseas (see subs. (1) above). The order is to be made by an officer having jurisdiction (for which see s.23(2)), unlike s.44 of the Children Act 1989, where it is made by the court. The application can be made by any person. This is wide enough to cover a neighbour or grandparent (see Select Committee on the Armed Forces Bill 1990–91, para. 273). For the power to appoint a designated person, see subs. (6)(a). This is likely to be a SSAFA officer, a medical officer or a member of the Naval Personnel and Family Service (see Select Committee on the Armed Forces Bill 1990–91, para. 272).

Subs. (4)
There is no comparable provision in the Children Act 1989, although see s.95, where the court may order the attendance of the child, and s.47(4) for the obligation on the part of the police to inform the child's parents where in an emergency the child has been taken into police protection.

Subs. (5)
This is identical to s.44(3) of the Children Act 1989.

Content and effect of protection orders

20.—(1) A protection order shall name the person on whose application it was made (in this Part of this Act referred to as "the responsible person") and, wherever it is reasonably practicable to do so, the order shall also name the child to whom it relates; and where it does not name that child it shall describe him as clearly as possible.

(2) Where a protection order is in force with respect to a child—

(a) it shall be the duty of any person who is in a position to do so to comply with any request to produce the child to the responsible person; and

(b) the order authorises—

(i) the removal of the child at any time to accommodation provided by or on behalf of the responsible person and his being kept there; or

(ii) the prevention of the child's removal from any service hospital, or other place, in which he was being accommodated immediately before the making of the order.

(3) Where a protection order is in force with respect to a child, the responsible person—

(a) shall only exercise a power given by virtue of subsection (2)(b) above in order to safeguard the welfare of the child;

(b) shall comply with the requirements of any regulations made for the purposes of this subsection; and

(c) subject to paragraphs (a) and (b) above, shall do what is reasonable in all the circumstances of the case for the purpose of safeguarding or promoting the child's welfare (having regard in particular to the duration of the order).

(4) The officer making a protection order may give such directions (if any) as he considers appropriate with respect to all or any of the following matters—

(a) whether the responsible person, in exercising any power under the order, should be accompanied by a person having a medical, nursing or other appropriate qualification;

(b) any contact which is, or is not, to be allowed between the child and any named person; and

(c) any medical or psychiatric examination or other assessment of the child which is, or is not, to be carried out;

but, where a direction is given under paragraph (c) above for the carrying out of an examination or other assessment, the child may, if he is of sufficient understanding to make an informed decision, refuse to submit to the examination or assessment.

(5) Where a protection order is in force with respect to a child and—

(a) the responsible person has exercised the power given by subsection (2)(b)(i) above but it appears to him that it is safe for the child to be returned; or

(b) the responsible person has exercised the power given by subsection (2)(b)(ii) above but it appears to him that it is safe for the child to be allowed to be removed from the place in question,

he shall return the child or (as the case may be) allow him to be removed.

(6) Where he is required by subsection (5) above to return the child, the responsible person shall—

(a) return him to the care of the person from whose care he was removed; or

(b) if that is not reasonably practicable, return him to the care of—

(i) a parent of his;

(ii) any person who is not a parent of his but who has parental responsibility for him; or

(iii) such other person as the responsible person (with the agreement of the officer having jurisdiction) considers appropriate.

(7) Where the responsible person has been required by subsection (5) above to return the child, or to allow him to be removed, he may again exercise his powers with respect to the child (at any time while the protection order remains in force) if it appears to him that a change in the circumstances of the case makes it necessary for him to do so.

(8) Where a protection order has been made with respect to a child, the responsible person shall, subject to any direction given under subsection (4) above, allow the child reasonable contact with—

(a) his parents;

(b) any other person who has parental responsibility for him;

(c) any other person with whom he was residing immediately before the making of the application for the order;

(d) any person in whose favour a contact order is in force with respect to him;

(e) any person who is allowed to have contact with the child by virtue of an order under section 34 of the Children Act 1989; and

(f) any person acting on behalf of any of those persons.

(9) A person subject to service law or a civilian in a corresponding position who intentionally obstructs any person exercising the power under subsection (2)(b) above to remove, or prevent the removal of, a child shall be liable on conviction to a fine or to any less punishment provided by the Army Act 1955, the Air Force Act 1955 or the 1957 Act, as the case may require.

(10) Any offence under subsection (9) above shall be treated,—

(a) if the offender is subject to military law or a civilian to whom Part II of the Army Act 1955 is applied by section 209 of that Act, as if it were an offence against a provision of Part II of that Act which is triable by court-martial under that Act;

(b) if the offender is subject to air-force law or a civilian to whom Part II of the Air Force Act 1955 is applied by section 209 of that Act, as if it were an offence against a provision of Part II of that Act which is triable by court-martial under that Act;

(c) if the offender is subject to the 1957 Act or a civilian to whom Parts I and II of that Act are applied by section 118 of that Act, as if it were an offence against a provision of Part I of that Act which is triable by court-martial under that Act.

(11) Any directions given under subsection (4) above shall be set out in the protection order, and—

(a) the power to give such directions shall be exercisable subject to, and in accordance with, any provision made by regulations; and

(b) any direction given in the exercise of that power may be varied or revoked at any time subject to, and in accordance with, any provision so made.

DEFINITIONS
See s.23.

GENERAL NOTE

Subs. (1)
This is similar to s.44(14) of the Children Act 1989. Once the order is made the applicant becomes the "responsible person".

Subs. (2)
This is similar to s.44(4) of the Children Act 1989. The accommodation concerned might be a Service hospital or Service foster parents (see Select Committee on the Armed Forces Bill 1990–91, para. 271).

Subs. (3)
This is similar to s.44(5) of the Children Act 1989.

Subs. (4)
This is similar to s.44(6) and (7) of the Children Act 1989. There is no equivalent provision in the Children Act to subs. 4(a). The right of the child to submit to a medical examination is similar to the right contained in s.18(4) (see also the discussion above).

Subs. (5)
This is similar to s.44(10) of the Children Act 1989.

Subs. (6)
This is similar to s.44(11) of the Children Act 1989.

Subs. (7)
This is similar to s.44(12) of the Children Act 1989.

Subs. (8)
This is similar to s.44(13) of the Children Act 1989.

Subs. (9)
This is similar to s.18(8) (see also the discussion of it above).

Subs. (10)
This is similar to s.18(9) (see also the discussion of it above).

Duration of protection orders

21.—(1) A protection order shall specify the period for which it is to have effect, being—
  (a) in a case where the order is made by an officer other than a superior officer, a period not exceeding the period of eight days beginning with the date of the order; and
  (b) in a case where the order is made by a superior officer, a period not exceeding the period of twenty-eight days beginning with the date of the order.
(2) Where a protection order has been made with respect to a child and it appears at any time to the officer having jurisdiction—
  (a) that the period for which the order is to have effect is less than the maximum period applicable under subsection (1) above in relation to a protection order made by that officer; and
  (b) that there is reasonable cause to believe that the child concerned is likely to suffer significant harm if the effect of the order is not extended or further extended,
that officer may by an order (in this Part of this Act referred to as an "extension order") continue the effect of the protection order until a time no later after the making of the protection order than the end of that maximum period.
(3) No extension order shall be made without affording—
  (a) the child to whom the protection order relates,
  (b) his parents,
  (c) any other person who has parental responsibility for him, and
  (d) any other person with whom he was residing immediately before the making of the application for the protection order,
an opportunity to make representations to the officer by whom the case is being considered, except where it appears to that officer that it would be undesirable to do so in the interests of the child or that it would be impracticable, or would cause unnecessary delay, to communicate with any parent of the child or with any such other person as is mentioned in paragraph (c) or paragraph (d) above.
(4) Where a child is removed under a protection order to accommodation in the United Kingdom—
  (a) the order shall not authorise his being kept in that accommodation after the end of the period of twenty-four hours beginning with his arrival in that accommodation; but
  (b) the powers conferred by the Children Act 1989, the Social Work (Scotland) Act 1968 and the Children and Young Persons Act (Northern Ireland) 1968 shall be exercisable with respect to the child as if everything which was relevant to the question of whether a protection order should be made were relevant, notwithstanding that the child

has been removed under the order, to the question whether the conditions for the exercise of any of those powers are satisfied.

(5) Without prejudice to the power to vary or revoke any direction previously given under subsection (4) of section 20 above, an officer making an extension order may exercise the power to give such directions and subsection (11) of that section shall have effect accordingly.

DEFINITIONS
See s.23.

GENERAL NOTE

Subs. (1)
This subsection follows the pattern of the Children Act 1989 of imposing a limit of eight days to the protection order. (See s.45(1) of the 1989 Act). The order may be made by a superior officer for up to 28 days, a period therefore wider than that under the Children Act. The reason given to the Select Committee on the Armed Forces Bill 1990–91 for this increased power was that such an order could only be made overseas and "we think we need to make provision for that greater period of time in order both to let us assess the case, and make any necessary arrangements with the local authorities in the U.K. and, as necessary, get the child back to the U.K. (para. 345). Note the power to review such orders in s.22 (not available under the Children Act 1989). For power to determine who is a superior officer, see s.23(2). It is likely to be someone higher in military rank than the commanding officer.

Subs. (2)
An extension to the protection order may be made, but not beyond the maximum period stated in subs. (1). By s.44(5) and (6) of the Children Act 1989 an emergency protection order can only be extended once for a further period of seven days, making the maximum time by which the order can remain in force 15 days.

Subs. (3)
This is similar to s.19(4) (see also the discussion above).

Subs. (4)
The effect of this subsection is that if a child is removed from overseas to the U.K., by virtue of a protection order imposed under this Act the protection order will expire 24 hours after his arrival in the U.K. He will then be subject to the powers contained in the Children Act 1989. It is for this reason that the maximum period of a protection order under this section of the Act is 28 days. Such a period will enable all the necessary arrangements to be made prior to the arrival of the child in the U.K.

Subs. (5)
Where an extension to the protection order is made, the officer making it may make such directions as are permitted by s.20(4) or revoke any previously made.

Review and discharge or protection orders

22.—(1) Subsections (2) to (4) below apply in relation to a protection order in any case where—
   (a) the order as originally made has effect for a period exceeding eight days; or
   (b) by an extension order the effect of the protection order is continued for a period exceeding seven days beginning with the date of the extension order.

(2) If, during the period of six days beginning with the date of the protection order or during any other period of six days while the protection order continues to have effect,—
   (a) no extension order is made continuing the effect of the protection order, and
   (b) no review of the protection order is carried out in accordance with subsection (4) below,

then, subject to subsection (3) below, on the day immediately following the end of that six-day period a superior officer shall carry out a review of the protection order in accordance with subsection (4) below.

(3) Subsection (2) above does not require a review of a protection order to be carried out on the day following any six-day period if—

(a) the order ceases to have effect at the end of that period or on that following day; or

(b) on that following day an extension order is made continuing the effect of the protection order.

(4) A superior officer carrying out a review of a protection order shall consider whether—

(a) if the child were returned by the responsible person, or

(b) where section 20(2)(b)(ii) above applies, if the child were allowed to be removed from the place in which he was being accommodated immediately before the making of the order,

any of the conditions in paragraphs (a) to (c) of subsection (3) of section 19 above would be satisfied; and if in his opinion none of those conditions would be satisfied he shall discharge the order.

(5) Without prejudice to the possibility of the discharge of a protection order on a review under the preceding provisions of this section, if an application is made by—

(a) the responsible person,

(b) the child to whom the order relates,

(c) a parent of his,

(d) any other person who has parental responsibility for him, or

(e) any other person with whom he was residing immediately before the making of the application for the order,

then, in such circumstances and subject to such conditions as may be prescribed by regulations, the officer having jurisdiction may discharge the order.

(6) Regulations may make provision as to the procedure to be followed on a review of a protection order (including provision as to the making of representations by any persons).

(7) Without prejudice to the power to vary or revoke any direction previously given under subsection (4) of section 20 above, if, on carrying out a review of a protection order or on an application under subsection (5) above, the officer dealing with the matter does not discharge the order, he may exercise the power to give directions under subsection (4) of section 20 above and subsection (11) of that section shall have effect accordingly.

DEFINITIONS
See s.23.

GENERAL NOTE

Subs. (1)
This subsection enables a review of protection orders made for the periods specified in it. Thus an order made by a superior officer for a period exceeding eight days (but not exceeding 28 days) or an extension order is made for a period longer than seven days. There is therefore no review where the original protection order is made by a. commanding officer for (say) seven days.

Subs. (2)
The review begins on the seventh day after the beginning of a protection order while it continues in force and has not been extended.
The review process is continuous at the same periods and subject to the same conditions.

Subs. (5)
This is similar to s.45(8) of the Children Act 1989.

Subs. (7)
This is similar to s.21(5) (see also the discussion above).

Interpretation of Part III

23.—(1) In this Part of this Act—

"accommodation" means any service hospital or other suitable place the occupier of which is willing temporarily to receive the child to whom a protection order relates, whether situated in the United Kingdom, the country or territory where the child resides or elsewhere;

"assessment order" has the meaning given by section 17 above;

"child" means a person under the age of eighteen;

"civilian in a corresponding position" has the same meaning as in section 13 of the Armed Forces Act 1981;

"contact order" has the meaning given by section 8(1) of the Children Act 1989;

"extension order" has the meaning given by section 21(2) above;

"officer having jurisdiction" and "superior officer" shall be construed in accordance with subsection (2) below;

"parental responsibility" has the meaning given by section 3 of the Children Act 1989;

"parents" shall be construed in accordance with subsection (3) below;

"protection order" has the meaning given by section 19 above.

"regulations" means regulations made by the Secretary of State by statutory instrument subject to annulment in pursuance of a resolution of either House of Parliament;

"the responsible person," in relation to a protection order, has the meaning given by section 20(1) above;

"service hospital" means a military, air-force or naval unit or establishment or a ship at or in which medical or surgical treatment is provided for persons subject to service law; and

"service law" means military law, air-force law or the 1957 Act.

(2) Regulations may make provision for determining—

(a) who, in relation to an assessment order or a protection order, is at any time the officer having jurisdiction for the purposes of any of the provisions of this Part of this Act; and

(b) who, in relation to a protection order, is at any time a superior officer for the purposes of sections 21 and 22 above.

(3) Any reference in this Part of this Act to the parents of a child shall be construed without regard to whether they are or have been married to each other at any time; and this subsection is without prejudice to—

(a) the operation of section 1 of the Family Law Reform Act 1987 as part of the law of England and Wales or section 1 of the Law Reform (Parent and Child) (Scotland) Act 1986 as part of the law of Scotland; and

(b) any enactment or rule of law relating to adoption or legitimation.

(4) Any power under this Part of this Act to make regulations may make different provision for different cases and for different purposes.

GENERAL NOTE

Subs. (3)

The need for this subsection was discussed in relation to s.14(3), (5) and 6).

PART IV

SUPPLEMENTARY

Application of Services Acts, including provisions of this Act, to Channel Islands and Isle of Man

24.—(1) In section 216 of the Army Act 1955 and section 214 of the Air Force Act 1955 (application of those Acts to the Channel Islands and the Isle of Man) for subsection (1) there shall be substituted the following subsection—

"(1) This Act extends to the Channel Islands and the Isle of Man subject to the following provisions of this section and to such modifications as Her Majesty may by Order in Council specify; and, where any such modification refers to any law for the time being in force in any of the Channel Islands or the Isle of Man, the modification may be expressed to have effect for all purposes of this Act (and not only in the application of this Act to the Channel Islands or the Isle of Man, as the case may be)."

(2) In section 125 of the 1957 Act (application of that Act to the Channel Islands and the Isle of Man) for subsection (1) there shall be substituted the following subsection—

"(1) This Act extends to the Channel Islands and the Isle of Man subject to subsection (2) below and to such modifications as Her Majesty may by Order in Council specify; and, where any such modification refers to any law for the time being in force in any of the Channel Islands or the Isle of Man, the modification may be expressed to have effect for all purposes of this Act (and not only in the application of this Act to the Channel Islands or the Isle of Man, as the case may be)."

(3) Section 216(4) of the Army Act 1955, section 214(4) of the Air Force Act 1955 and section 125(3) of the 1957 Act (which contain specific modifications in relation to the Channel Islands and the Isle of Man) shall cease to have effect.

(4) Section 216 of the Army Act 1955 and section 214 of the Air Force Act 1955 shall each apply in relation to the provisions of section 10 and Part III of this Act as if those provisions were comprised in the Army Act 1955 of the Air Force 1955, as the case may require.

(5) Section 125 of the 1957 Act shall apply in relation to the provisions of—

(a) the Naval Forces (Enforcement of Maintenance Liabilities) Act 1947, and

(b) section 10 and Part III of this Act,

as if those provisions were comprised in the 1957 Act.

GENERAL NOTE

The Service Discipline Acts have always applied to the Isle of Man and to the Channel Islands, and s.216(4) of the Army Act 1955 (and similar provisions in the other Service Discipline Acts) referred to specific statutes of the Tynwald on the Isle of Man. Should the Tynwald amend any of its Acts there was no provision in the Army Act to make a suitable amendment. Section 216(4) (see subs. (3)) is abolished and a power to make modifications by Order in Council to references within the Service Discipline Acts to local laws of the Tynwald and the Channel Islands is given (see subss. (1) and 2)).

Subs. (4)

The effect of this subsection is that the relevant sections of the 1955 Acts apply to s.10 and Pt. III of this Act. Thus, a child against whom a protection order is in force may be brought back to the Channel Islands. After a period of 24 hours following his arrival there the local law relating to children in need of protection will apply.

Subs. (5)

This subsection gives a similar effect to Naval law.

The 1955 Acts and the 1957 Act

25.—In this Act—
"the 1955 Acts" means the Army Act 1955 and the Air Force Act 1955; and
"the 1957 Act" means the Naval Discipline Act 1957.

Minor and consequential amendments and repeals

26.—(1) Schedule 2 to this Act, which contains minor amendments and amendments consequential on the provisions of this Act, shall have effect.

(2) The enactments specified in Schedule 3 to this Act, which include some that are spent, are hereby repealed to the extent specified in the third column of that Schedule.

Short title and commencement

27.—(1) This Act may be cited as the Armed Forces Act 1991.

(2) Subject to subsection (4) below, Parts II and III of this Act, sections 24 and 26 above and Schedules 2 and 3 to this Act shall come into force on such day as the Secretary of State may by order made by statutory instrument appoint; and different days may be so appointed for different provisions and for different purposes.

(3) An order under subsection (2) above may contain such transitional provisions and savings as appear to the Secretary of State to be necessary or expedient in connection with the provisions brought into force by the order.

(4) The repeal by this Act of section 1 of the Armed Forces Act 1986 shall come into force on January 1, 1992.

SCHEDULES

Section 10   SCHEDULE 1

ASSESSORS OF COMPENSATION FOR MISCARRIAGES OF JUSTICE

1. A person may only be appointed to be an assessor for the purposes of section 10 of this Act if he is—
   (a) a person who has a 7 year general qualification, within the meaning of section 71 of the Courts and Legal Services Act 1990;
   (b) an advocate or solicitor in Scotland;
   (c) a member of the Bar of Northern Ireland or solicitor of the Supreme Court of Northern Ireland of at least 7 years' standing;
   (d) a person who holds or has held judicial office in any part of the United Kingdom; or
   (e) a member (whether the chairman or not) of the Criminal Injuries Compensation Board.

2. A person shall hold and vacate office as an assessor in accordance with the terms of his appointment.

3. A person shall vacate office as an assessor—
   (a) if he ceases to be qualified for appointment as an assessor, or
   (b) on attaining the age of 72,
unless the Secretary of State considers that it is in the interests of the efficient operation of section 10 of this Act that he should continue to hold office.

4. A person may at any time resign his office as an assessor by giving the Secretary of State notice in writing to that effect.

5. Subject to paragraph 6 below, the Secretary of State may at any time remove a person from office as an assessor if satisfied that—
   (a) he has been convicted of a criminal offence;
   (b) he has become bankrupt, has made an arrangement with his creditors, has had his estate sequestrated or has granted a trust deed for his creditors or a compensation contract;
   (c) he is incapacitated by physical or mental illness; or
   (d) he is otherwise unable or unfit to perform his duties.

6. The power conferred by paragraph 5 above shall only be exercisable,—
   (a) in the case of a person who qualifies for appointment under paragraph 1(a) or paragraph 1(c) above, with the consent of the Lord Chancellor;
   (b) in the case of a person who qualifies for appointment under paragraph 1(b) above, with the consent of the Lord President of the Court of Session;
   (c) in the case of a person who qualifies for appointment under paragraph 1(d) above by virtue of holding or having held judicial office in England and Wales or Northern Ireland, with the consent of the Lord Chancellor; and
   (d) in the case of a person who qualifies for appointment under paragraph 1(d) above by virtue of holding or having held judicial office in Scotland, with the consent of the Lord President of the Court of Session.

7. An assessor shall be paid such remuneration and allowances as the Secretary of State may, with the approval of the Treasury, determine.

GENERAL NOTE

This is similar to Sched. 12 to the Criminal Justice Act 1988.

Section 26   SCHEDULE 2

MINOR AND CONSEQUENTIAL AMENDMENTS

Removal of offender to United Kingdom before confirmation of sentence

1. In section 71AA(2) of each of the 1955 Acts (young service offenders: custodial orders) and in section 127(2) of each of those Acts (country in which sentence of imprisonment or detention to be served) the words "after the confirmation of the sentences is completed" shall be omitted.

Power to impose imprisonment for default in payment of fines

2. In section 71B of each of the 1955 Acts and in section 43B of the 1957 Act (power to impose imprisonment for default in payment of fines), in subsection (2) (which refers to the Table in section 31(3A) of the Powers of Criminal Courts Act 1973) for the words from "from time to time" to "the Magistrates' Courts Act 1980" there shall be substituted "for the time being in force."

Evidence of child of tender years

3.—(1) In section 93 of each of the 1955 Acts (administration of oaths)—
(a) in the proviso to subsection (2) (which relates to the evidence of a child of tender years and the corroboration thereof) the words from "so however" to the end of the proviso shall be omitted; and
(b) after subsection (2) there shall be inserted the following subsection—
   "(2A) Unsworn evidence admitted by virtue of the proviso to subsection (2) above may corroborate evidence (sworn or unsworn) given by any other person."
(2) In section 60 of the 1957 Act (administration of oaths)—
(a) the proviso to subsection (3) (which relates to the corroboration of evidence given by a child of tender years) shall be omitted; and
(b) after that subsection there shall be inserted the following subsection—
   "(3A) Unsworn evidence admitted by virtue of subsection (3) above may corroborate evidence (sworn or unsworn) given by any other person."

Rules of evidence

4.—(1) In section 99 of each of the 1955 Acts (rules of evidence), in subsection (1) after the words "subject to section 99A below" there shall be inserted "to Schedule 13 to the Criminal Justice Act 1988 (evidence before courts-martial etc.)."
(2) In the Armed Forces Act 1976, in Schedule 3 (Standing Civilian Courts), in paragraph 11 (rules of evidence) after the words "paragraph 12 below" there shall be inserted "and to Schedule 13 to the Criminal Justice Act 1988 (evidence before courts-martial etc.)."

Finality of trials

5.—(1) Each of the 1955 Acts shall be amended in accordance with the following provisions of this paragraph.
(2) In section 133 (jurisdiction of civil courts), in subsection (1) for the words "an offence substantially the same as that offence" there shall be substituted "the same, or substantially the same offence."
(3) In section 134 (persons not to be tried under those Acts for offences already disposed of), in subsection (1) for the words "that offence" there shall be substituted "the same, or substantially the same offence."

Enactments requiring fiat of Attorney General etc. in connection with proceedings

6.—(1) In section 204A of each of the 1955 Acts (fiat of Attorney General etc. not required in connection with proceedings under the Act, other than subsections (1) and (3) of section 132) for the words "subsections (1) and (3)" there shall be substituted "subsection (3A)."
(2) In section 129A of the 1957 Act (fiat of Attorney General etc. not required in connection with proceedings under the Act, other than section 52(3)(b)) for the words "section 52(3)(b)" there shall be substituted "section 52(3)."

Recognizance by parent or guardian on conviction of civilian under 17

7. In Schedule 4A to the 1957 Act (powers of court on trial of civilian) in paragraph 14(1)

(order requiring parent or guardian to enter into a recognizance in respect of person under 17 found guilty of an offence) for the amount specified as the maximum amount of the recognizance there shall be substituted "£1,000."

Power of Courts-Martial Appeal Court to order retrial

8. In section 19 of the Courts-Marital (Appeals) Act 1968 (power to authorise retrial in certain cases), in subsection (1) the words from "the appeal against conviction" to "and" shall be omitted.

Compensation orders

9.—(1) In section 38 of the Powers of Criminal Courts Act 1973 (effect of compensation order on subsequent award of damages in civil proceedings)—
- (a) in subsection (1) after the words "compensation order" there shall be inserted "or a service compensation order or award";
- (b) in subsection (2) after the word "order" there shall be inserted "or award"; and
- (c) at the end of the section there shall be added the following subsection—
    "(3) In this section a "service compensation order or award" means—
    - (a) an order requiring the payment of compensation under paragraph 11 of Schedule 5A to the Army Act 1955, of Schedule 5A to the Air Force Act 1955 or of Schedule 4A to the Naval Discipline Act 1957; or
    - (b) an award of stoppages payable by way of compensation under any of those Acts."

(2) In section 67 of the Criminal Justice (Scotland) Act 1980 (effect of compensation order on subsequent award of damages in civil proceedings)—
- (a) in subsection (1) after the words "compensation order" there shall be inserted "or a service compensation order or award";
- (b) in subsections (2) and (3) after the word "order," in every place where it occurs, there shall be inserted "or award"; and
- (c) at the end of the section there shall be added the following subsection—
    "(4) In this section a "service compensation order or award" means—
    - (a) an order requiring the payment of compensation under paragraph 11 of Schedule 5A to the Army Act 1955, of Schedule 5A to the Air Force Act 1955 or of Schedule 4A to the Naval Discipline Act 1957; or
    - (b) an award of stoppages payable by way of compensation under any of those Acts."

(3) In Article 5 of the Criminal Justice (Northern Ireland) Order 1980 (effect of compensation order on subsequent award of damages in civil proceedings)—
- (a) in paragraph (1) after the words "compensation order" there shall be inserted "or a service compensation order or award";
- (b) in paragraphs (2) and (3) after the word "order," in every place where it occurs, there shall be inserted "or award"; and
- (c) at the end of the Article there shall be added the following paragraph—
    "(4) In this Article a "service compensation order or award" means—
    - (a) an order requiring the payment of compensation under paragraph 11 of Schedule 5A to the Army Act 1955, of Schedule 5A to the Air Force Act 1955 or of Schedule 4A to the Naval Discipline Act 1957; or
    - (b) an award of stoppages payable by way of compensation under any of those Acts."

(4) In Schedule 7 to the Criminal Justice Act 1988 (compensation payable by Criminal Injuries Compensation Board), in paragraph 13 (reduction of compensation by reference to damages etc.) at the end of sub-paragraph (b) there shall be inserted—
    "or
- (c) any order under paragraph 11 (compensation orders) of Schedule 5A to the Army Act 1955, of Schedule 5A to the Air Force Act 1955 or of Schedule 4A to the Naval Discipline Act 1957; or
- (d) any award of stoppages under any of the Acts referred to in sub-paragraph (c) above."

Powers of Standing Civilian Courts

10. In section 8 of the Armed Forces Act 1976 (powers of Standing Civilian Courts in relation to civilians), in subsection (1) for the words "and to section 71A" "there shall be substituted "and to the restrictions imposed by section 71A."

Removal or amendment of spent or obsolete expressions

11.—(1) In section 131 of each of the 1955 Acts (trial and punishment of service offences notwithstanding offender ceasing to be subject to military or air-force law), in subsection (1) the word "reconsideration" shall be omitted.

(2) In section 145 of each of the 1955 Acts (forfeiture of pay for absence from duty), in subsection (1), in paragraph (b)—
(a) the words "corrective training, preventive detention" shall be omitted; and
(b) for the words from "an order or sentence" to the end of the paragraph there shall be substituted—
      "(i) an order or sentence of a civil court;
      (ii) a revocation of a licence under section 62 of the Criminal Justice Act 1967; or
      (iii) an order of recall under section 23 of the Prison Act (Northern Ireland) 1953."

(3) In the 1957 Act, in section 129 (jurisdiction of civil courts), in subsection (2) the words "corrective training, preventive detention" shall be omitted.

(4) In the Reserve Forces Act 1980, in Schedule 6 (general provisions as to evidence in proceedings under Parts IV and V of that Act) paragraph 1(7A) shall be omitted.

GENERAL NOTE

Para. 1
This enables an offender sentenced to a custodial order made against him to be returned to the U.K. prior to confirmation of the finding or sentence. There may be some time-lapse between the court-martial and confirmation, and suitable accommodation might be available only in the U.K.

Para. 3
This enables unsworn evidence of a child to corroborate other evidence, whether sworn or not. It takes account of the amendment of civilian law made by s.34 of the Criminal Justice Act 1988.

Para. 4
This formally makes s.99 of the 1955 Acts subject to Sched. 13 to the Criminal Justice Act 1988 (Evidence before courts-martial, etc.). A similar amendment is made in respect of the Standing Civilian Court.

Section 26   SCHEDULE 3

ENACTMENTS REPEALED

Chapter	Short title	Extent of repeal
28 & 29 Vict. c. 73.	The Naval and Marine Pay and Pensions Act 1865.	Sections 4 and 5.
10 & 11 Geo. 6 c. 24.	The Naval Forces (Enforcement of Maintenance Liabilities) Act 1947.	In section 1 subsections (3) and (5). Section 2.
3 & 4 Eliz. 2 c. 18.	The Army Act 1955.	Section 71A(1B)(a). In section 71AA, in subsection (1) the words "subject to subsection (1A) below", subsection (1A) and in subsection (2) the words from "after" to "completed". In section 93, in the proviso to subsection (2) the words from "so however" onwards. In section 122(1) the words "this Part of". In section 127(2) the words from "after" to "completed". In section 131(1) the words "reconsideration". In section 145(1)(b) the words "corrective training, preventive detention". In section 150, in subsection (1)(a) the words "or child" and in subsection (5) the words "or child", in both places where they occur, and the paragraph beginning "references to a child".

Chapter	Short title	Extent of repeal
		Section 216(4).
		In section 225(1), in the definition of "stoppages" the words from "for any expense" onwards.
		In Schedule 5A, in paragraph 2 the definition of "reception order", paragraphs 6 to 9, in paragraph 10(1A) the words from the beginning to "appropriate and", in pararaph 11(4) the words from "and no such order" onwards and, in paragraph 15(3), in the third column of the Table paragraph 2.
3 & 4 Eliz. 2 c. 19.	The Air Force Act 1955.	Section 71A(1B)(a).
		In section 71AA, in subsection (1) the words "subject to subsection (1A) below", subsection (1A) and in subsection (2) the words from "after" to "completed".
		In section 93, in the proviso to subsection (2) the words from "so however" onwards.
		In section 122(1) the words "this Part of".
		In section 127(2) the words from "after" to "completed".
		In section 131(1) the word "reconsideration".
		In section 145(1)(b) the words "corrective training, preventive detention".
		In section 150, in subsection (1)(a) the words "or child" and in subsection (5) the words "or child", in both places where they occur, and the paragraph beginning "references to a child".
		Section 214(4).
		In section 223(1), in the definition of "stoppages" the words from "for any expense" onwards.
		In Schedule 5A, in paragraph 2 the definition of "reception order", paragraphs 6 to 9, in paragraph 10(1A) the words from the beginning to "appropriate and", in paragraph 11(4) the words from "and no such order" onwards and, in paragraph 15(3), in the third column of the Table paragraph 2.
5 & 6 Eliz. 2 c.53.	The Naval Discipline Act 1957.	Section 43A(1B)(a).
		In section 43AA, in subsection (1) the words "subject to subsection (1A) below" and subsection (1A).
		In section 60 the proviso to subsection (3).
		Section 125(3).
		In section 129(2) the words "corrective training, preventive detention".
		In Schedule 4A, in paragraph 2 the definition of "reception order", paragraphs 6 to 9, in paragraph 10(1A) the words from the beginning to "appropriate and", in paragraph 11(4) the words from "and no such order" onwards and, in paragraph 15(3), in the third column of the Table paragraph 2.

Chapter	Short title	Extent of repeal
1968 c. 20.	The Courts-Martial (Appeals) Act 1968.	In section 8(1A)(a), "6" and the words "reception orders". In section 19(1) the words from "the appeal against conviction" to "and".
1974 c. 53.	The Rehabilitation of Offenders Act 1974.	Section 5(5)(h).
S.I. 1978/1908 (N.I. 27).	The Rehabilitation of Offenders (Northern Ireland) Order 1978.	Article 6(5)(d).
1980 c. 9.	The Reserve Forces Act 1980.	In Schedule 6 paragraph 1(7A).
1981 c. 55.	The Armed Forces Act 1980.	Section 14.
1982 c. 14.	The Reserve Forces Act 1982.	In section 2 subsections (4) and 5).
1986 c. 21.	The Armed Forces Act 1986.	Section 1. Section 13. In Schedule 1, in paragraph 12 sub-paragraphs (3) and (5).
1989 c. 41.	The Children Act 1989.	In Schedule 12 paragraphs 8, 10 and 18. In Schedule 14 paragraph 15(1)(b) and, in paragraph 16, in sub-paragraph (1) the words "or (b)", sub-paragraph (2)(b) and the word "or" immediately preceding it and sub-paragraph (3).

INDEX

References are to sections and Schedules

BRITISH RAILWAYS BOARD (FINANCE) ACT 1991

(1991 c. 63)

An Act to alter the limits under section 42(6) of the Transport Act 1968 relating to the indebtedness of the British Railways Board and the limits on the amount of compensation payable in respect of certain public service obligations of the Board.   [25th July 1991]

PARLIAMENTARY DEBATES
Hansard, H.C Vol. 194, col. 1100; H.L. Vol. 531, col. 820.

INTRODUCTION
    S.1 of this Act increases the limit, under s.42(6) of the Transport Act 1968, on the aggregate amount outstanding in respect of the principal of any money borrowed by the British Railways Board under s.19 of the Transport Act 1962, together with the Board's commencing capital debt, to £3,000m. The maximum sum to which the limit may be raised further by the Secretary of State is increased to £5,000m.
    The Act makes further provisions relating to the grant paid to the British Railways Board as compensation for public service obligations imposed on the Board.

Increased borrowing limit for British Railways Board

    1.—(1) In section 42(6) of the Transport Act 1968 (which, as amended by section 1 of the Transport (Finance) Act 1982, limits the aggregate amount outstanding in respect of the principal of money borrowed by the British Railways Board and its commencing capital debt to £1,100 million or such greater sum not exceeding £1,300 million as the Secretary of State may by order specify) for the words from "shall not exceed" to "as the Minister" there shall be substituted "shall not exceed £3,000 million or such greater sum not exceeding £5,000 million as the Secretary of State".
    (2) Section 1 of the Transport (Finance) Act 1982, which is superseded by subsection (1) above, is hereby repealed.

Increased limit relating to compensation

    2.—(1) In subsection (4) of section 3 of the Railways Act 1974 (which, as set out in section 2 of the Transport (Finance) Act 1982, provides that the power to give directions relating to compensation under certain Community regulations is to be so exercised that the aggregate of compensation payable for periods after the end of 1978 is limited to £6,000 million or such greater sum not exceeding £10,000 million as may be specified by Order in Council) after the words "end of 1978" there shall be inserted "and ending before 1st April 1992".
    (2) After subsection (5) of section 3 of the Railways Act 1974 there shall be inserted the following subsections—
    "(5A) The power of giving directions under subsection (1) above shall be so exercised that the aggregate amount of any compensation payable under the relevant transport regulations, for periods ending after 1st April 1992, in respect of all obligations imposed by directions under that subsection shall not exceed £3,000 million or such greater sum not exceeding £5,000 million as the Secretary of State may by order made by statutory instrument specify.
    (5B) No order shall be made under subsection (5A) above unless a draft of the order has been approved by a resolution of the Commons House of Parliament."

Short title

    3. This Act may be cited as the British Railways Board (Finance) Act 1991.

INDEX

References are to sections

BREEDING OF DOGS ACT 1991

(1991 c. 64)

An Act to extend powers of inspection for the purposes of the Breeding of Dogs Act 1973 to premises not covered by a licence under that Act.

[25th July 1991]

PARLIAMENTARY DEBATES
Hansard, H.C. Vol. 193, col. 656; H.L. Vol. 531, cols. 427, 734.

INTRODUCTION

This Act empowers justices of the peace to issue warrants authorising the search of premises by authorised persons if there are reasonable grounds for suspecting that an offence against s.1(1) of the Breeding of Dogs Act 1973 has been or is being committed. The section of the 1973 Act requires that establishments used for the breeding of dogs are licensed. No warrant is to be issued in relation to any premises which is for the time being used as a private dwelling.

Conviction of an offence under the Act may lead to disqualification from keeping a breeding establishment for dogs for an appropriate period; any persons who intentionally obstruct the exercise of powers under the Act will be liable to a fine not exceeding level three on the standard scale.

Power to inspect premises not covered by licence under Breeding of Dogs Act 1973

1.—(1) If a justice of the peace is satisfied by information on oath laid by any officer of a local authority authorised in writing for the purposes of this section by the authority, or any veterinary surgeon or veterinary practitioner so authorised, that there are reasonable grounds for suspecting that an offence against section 1(1) of the Breeding of Dogs Act 1973 (breeding establishments for dogs to be covered by a licence) has been or is being committed at any premises in the area of the authority, the justice may issue a warrant authorising any such officer, surgeon or practitioner to enter those premises, by reasonable force if need be, and inspect them and any animals or any thing found there.

(2) No warrant shall be issued under subsection (1) above authorising entry to any premises for the time being used as a private dwelling.

(3) The reference in subsection (2) above to premises for the time being used as a private dwelling does not include a reference to any garage, outhouse or other structure (whether or not forming part of the same building as the premises) which belongs to or is usually enjoyed with the premises.

(4) A warrant issued under subsection (1) above—

(a) may authorise persons to accompany the person who is executing the warrant; and

(b) shall continue in force for the period of one month commencing with the date of issue.

(5) The power of entry conferred by the warrant may be exercised at all reasonable times and any person entering the premises in exercise of that power shall—

(a) produce the warrant if so required; and

(b) comply with such precautions (if any) as the justice of the peace may specify to prevent the spread among animals of infectious or contagious diseases.

(6) In the application of this section to Scotland, any reference to a justice of the peace shall include a reference to a sheriff and the reference in subsection (1) to written information on oath shall be construed as a reference to evidence on oath.

(7) In this section "local authority", "veterinary practitioner" and "veterinary surgeon" have the same meanings as in the Breeding of Dogs Act 1973.

Offence and disqualification

2.—(1) Any person who intentionally obstructs or delays any person in the exercise of his powers of entry or inspection under section 1 above is guilty of an offence and liable on summary conviction to a fine not exceeding level 3 on the standard scale.

(2) Where a person is convicted of an offence under subsection (1) above, the court by which he is convicted may disqualify him from keeping a breeding establishment for dogs for such period as the court thinks fit; and whilst that disqualification is in force, no licence shall be granted to him under section 1 of the Breeding of Dogs Act 1973.

(3) In the application of this section to Scotland, "breeding establishment" includes any premises where a business of rearing puppies for sale is carried on.

Short title, commencement and extent

3.—(1) This Act may be cited as the Breeding of Dogs Act 1991.

(2) This Act shall come into force at the end of the period of two months beginning with the date on which it is passed.

(3) This Act does not extend to Northern Ireland.

INDEX

References are to section numbers

DANGEROUS DOGS ACT 1991

(1991 c. 65)

ARRANGEMENT OF SECTIONS

An Act to prohibit persons from having in their possession or custody dogs belonging to types bred for fighting; to impose restrictions in respect of such dogs pending the coming into force of the prohibition; to enable restrictions to be imposed in relation to other types of dog which present a serious danger to the public; to make further provision for securing that dogs are kept under proper control; and for connected purposes.

[25th July 1991]

PARLIAMENTARY DEBATES
Hansard, H.C. Vol. 192, cols. 605, 644; Vol. 195, cols. 1264, 1266; H.L. Vol. 530, cols. 510, 1405; Vol. 531, col. 281; Vol. 531, col. 700.

INTRODUCTION
This Act was introduced to Parliament as a response to increased public outrage at the number of attacks suffered by persons from certain breeds of dogs. The Act imposes restrictions on the owning and breeding of dogs bred for fighting, specifically the pit bull terrier and the Japanese tosa. The Secretary of State is empowered to designate any other breed he perceives as being bred for fighting. The restrictions include the prohibition of breeding from such named species, of selling such animals and the condition that all such dogs must be muzzled and leashed in public; the Secretary of State may specify the type of muzzle or lead suitable for the purpose. A further offence is created of allowing a dog to be dangerously out of control in a public place, the resulting sentence being either imprisonment or a fine. Further provisions are also made establishing the means to destroy animals and disqualify certain persons from owning a dog and to regulate the seizure of animals and the entering of premises by the police when executing their powers under this Act.

Dogs bred for fighting

1.—(1) This section applies to—
(a) any dog of the type known as the pit bull terrier;
(b) any dog of the type known as the Japanese tosa; and
(c) any dog of any type designated for the purposes of this section by an order of the Secretary of State, being a type appearing to him to be bred for fighting or to have the characteristics of a type bred for that purpose.

(2) No person shall—
(a) breed, or breed from, a dog to which this section applies;
(b) sell or exchange such a dog or offer, advertise or expose such a dog for sale or exchange;
(c) make or offer to make a gift of such a dog or advertise or expose such a dog as a gift;
(d) allow such a dog of which he is the owner or of which he is for the time being in charge to be in a public place without being muzzled and kept on a lead; or

(e) abandon such a dog of which he is the owner or, being the owner or for the time being in charge of such a dog, allow it to stray.

(3) After such day as the Secretary of State may by order appoint for the purposes of this subsection no person shall have any dog to which this section applies in his possession or custody except—

(a) in pursuance of the power of seizure conferred by the subsequent provisions of this Act; or

(b) in accordance with an order for its destruction made under those provisions;

but the Secretary of State shall by order make a scheme for the payment to the owners of such dogs who arrange for them to be destroyed before that day of sums specified in or determined under the scheme in respect of those dogs and the cost of their destruction.

(4) Subsection (2)(b) and (c) above shall not make unlawful anything done with a view to the dog in question being removed from the United Kingdom before the day appointed under subsection (3) above.

(5) The Secretary of State may by order provide that the prohibition in subsection (3) above shall not apply in such cases and subject to compliance with such conditions as are specified in the order and any such provision may take the form of a scheme of exemption containing such arrangements (including provision for the payment of charges or fees) as he thinks appropriate.

(6) A scheme under subsection (3) or (5) above may provide for specified functions under the scheme to be discharged by such persons or bodies as the Secretary of State thinks appropriate.

(7) Any person who contravenes this section is guilty of an offence and liable on summary conviction to imprisonment for a term not exceeding six months or a fine not exceeding level 5 on the standard scale or both except that a person who publishes an advertisement in contravention of subsection 2(b) or (c)—

(a) shall not on being convicted be liable to imprisonment if he shows that he published the advertisement to the order of someone else and did not himself devise it; and

(b) shall not be convicted if, in addition, he shows that he did not know and had no reasonable cause to suspect that it related to a dog to which this section applies.

(8) An order under subsection (1)(c) above adding dogs of any type to those to which this section applies may provide that subsections (3) and (4) above shall apply in relation to those dogs with the substitution for the day appointed under subsection (3) of a later day specified in the order.

(9) The power to make orders under this section shall be exercisable by statutory instrument which, in the case of an order under subsection (1) or (5) or an order containing a scheme under subsection (3), shall be subject to annulment in pursuance of a resolution of either House of Parliament.

Other specially dangerous dogs

2.—(1) If it appears to the Secretary of State that dogs of any type to which section 1 above does not apply present a serious danger to the public he may by order impose in relation to dogs of that type restrictions corresponding, with such modifications, if any, as he thinks appropriate, to all or any of those in subsection (2)(d) and (e) of that section.

(2) An order under this section may provide for exceptions from any restriction imposed by the order in such cases and subject to compliance with such conditions as are specified in the order.

(3) An order under this section may contain such supplementary or transitional provisions as the Secretary of State thinks necessary or expedient and may create offences punishable on summary conviction with

imprisonment for a term not exceeding six months or a fine not exceeding level 5 on the standard scale or both.

(4) In determining whether to make an order under this section in relation to dogs of any type and, if so, what the provisions of the order should be, the Secretary of State shall consult with such persons or bodies as appear to him to have relevant knowledge or experience, including a body concerned with animal welfare, a body concerned with veterinary science and practice and a body concerned with breeds of dogs.

(5) The power to make an order under this section shall be exercisable by statutory instrument and no such order shall be made unless a draft of it has been laid before and approved by a resolution of each House of Parliament.

Keeping dogs under proper control

3.—(1) If a dog is dangerously out of control in a public place—

(a) the owner; and

(b) if different, the person for the time being in charge of the dog,

is guilty of an offence, or, if the dog while so out of control injures any person, an aggravated offence, under this subsection.

(2) In proceedings for an offence under subsection (1) above against a person who is the owner of a dog but was not at the material time in charge of it, it shall be a defence for the accused to prove that the dog was at the material time in the charge of a person whom he reasonably believed to be a fit and proper person to be in charge of it.

(3) If the owner or, if different, the person for the time being in charge of a dog allows it to enter a place which is not a public place but where it is not permitted to be and while it is there—

(a) it injures any person; or

(b) there are grounds for reasonable apprehension that it will do so,

he is guilty of an offence, or, if the dog injures any person, an aggravated offence, under this subsection.

(4) A person guilty of an offence under subsection (1) or (3) above other than an aggravated offence is liable on summary conviction to imprisonment for a term not exceeding six months or a fine not exceeding level 5 on the standard scale or both; and a person guilty of an aggravated offence under either of those subsections is liable—

(a) on summary conviction, to imprisonment for a term not exceeding six months or a fine not exceeding the statutory maximum or both;

(b) on conviction on indictment, to imprisonment for a term not exceeding two years or a fine or both.

(5) It is hereby declared for the avoidance of doubt that an order under section 2 of the Dogs Act 1871 (order on complaint that dog is dangerous and not kept under proper control)—

(a) may be made whether or not the dog is shown to have injured any person; and

(b) may specify the measures to be taken for keeping the dog under proper control, whether by muzzling, keeping on a lead, excluding it from specified places or otherwise.

(6) If it appears to a court on a complaint under section 2 of the said Act of 1871 that the dog to which the complaint relates is a male and would be less dangerous if neutered the court may under that section make an order requiring it to be neutered.

(7) The reference in section 1(3) of the Dangerous Dogs Act 1989 (penalties) to failing to comply with an order under section 2 of the said Act of 1871 to keep a dog under proper control shall include a reference to failing to comply with any other order made under that section; but no order shall be made under that section by virtue of subsection (6) above where the matters complained of arose before the coming into force of that subsection.

Destruction and disqualification orders

4.—(1) Where a person is convicted of an offence under section 1 or 3(1) or (3) above or of an offence under an order made under section 2 above the court—

(a) may order the destruction of any dog in respect of which the offence was committed and shall do so in the case of an offence under section 1 or an aggravated offence under section 3(1) or (3) above; and

(b) may order the offender to be disqualified, for such period as the court thinks fit, for having custody of a dog.

(2) Where a court makes an order under subsection (1)(a) above for the destruction of a dog owned by a person other than the offender, then, unless the order is one that the court is required to make, the owner may appeal to the Crown Court against the order.

(3) A dog shall not be destroyed pursuant to an order under subsection (1)(a) above—

(a) until the end of the period for giving notice of appeal against the conviction or, where the order was not one which the court was required to make, against the order; and

(b) if notice of appeal is given within that period, until the appeal is determined or withdrawn,

unless the offender and, in a case to which subsection (2) above applies, the owner of the dog give notice to the court that made the order that there is to be no appeal.

(4) Where a court makes an order under subsection (1)(a) above it may—

(a) appoint a person to undertake the destruction of the dog and require any person having custody of it to deliver it up for that purpose; and

(b) order the offender to pay such sum as the court may determine to be the reasonable expenses of destroying the dog and of keeping it pending its destruction.

(5) Any sum ordered to be paid under subsection (4)(b) above shall be treated for the purposes of enforcement as if it were a fine imposed on conviction.

(6) Any person who is disqualified for having custody of a dog by virtue of an order under subsection (1)(b) above may, at any time after the end of the period of one year beginning with the date of the order, apply to the court that made it (or a magistrates' court acting for the same petty sessions area as that court) for a direction terminating the disqualification.

(7) On an application under subsection (6) above the court may—

(a) having regard to the applicant's character, his conduct since the disqualification was imposed and any other circumstances of the case, grant or refuse the application; and

(b) order the applicant to pay all or any part of the costs of the application;

and where an application in respect of an order is refused no further application in respect of that order shall be entertained if made before the end of the period of one year beginning with the date of the refusal.

(8) Any person who—

(a) has custody of a dog in contravention of an order under subsection (1)(b) above; or

(b) fails to comply with a requirement imposed on him under subsection (4)(a) above,

is guilty of an offence and liable on summary conviction to a fine not exceeding level 5 on the standard scale.

(9) In the application of this section to Scotland—

(a) in subsection (2) for the words "Crown Court against the order" there shall be substituted the words " High Court of Justiciary against the order within the period of seven days beginning with the date of the order";

(b) for subsection (3)(a) there shall be substituted—
  "(a) until the end of the period of seven days beginning with the date of the order";
(c) for subsection (5) there shall be substituted—
  "(5) Section 411 of the Criminal Procedure (Scotland) Act 1975 shall apply in relation to the recovery of sums ordered to be paid under subsection (4)(b) above as it applies to fines ordered to be recovered by civil diligence in pursuance of Part II of that Act."; and
(d) in subsection (6) the words "(or a magistrates' court acting for the same petty sessions area as that court)" shall be omitted.

Seizure, entry of premises and evidence

5.—(1) A constable or an officer of a local authority authorised by it to exercise the powers conferred by this subsection may seize—
(a) any dog which appears to him to be a dog to which section 1 above applies and which is in a public place—
    (i) after the time when possession or custody of it has become unlawful by virtue of that section; or
    (ii) before that time, without being muzzled and kept on a lead;
(b) any dog in a public place which appears to him to be a dog to which an order under section 2 above applies and in respect of which an offence against the order has been or is being committed; and
(c) any dog in a public place (whether or not one to which that section or such an order applies) which appears to him to be dangerously out of control.

(2) If a justice of the peace is satisfied by information on oath, or in Scotland a justice of the peace or sheriff is satisfied by evidence on oath, that there are reasonable grounds for believing—
(a) that an offence under any provision of this Act or of an order under section 2 above is being or has been committed; or
(b) that evidence of the commission of any such offence is to be found,
on any premises he may issue a warrant authorising a constable to enter those premises (using such force as is reasonably necessary) and to search them and seize any dog or other thing found there which is evidence of the commission of such an offence.

(3) A warrant issued under this section in Scotland shall be authority for opening lockfast places and may authorise persons named in the warrant to accompany a constable who is executing it.

(4) Where a dog is seized under subsection (1) or (2) above and it appears to a justice of the peace, or in Scotland a justice of the peace or sheriff, that no person has been or is to be prosecuted for an offence under this Act or an order under section 2 above in respect of that dog (whether because the owner cannot be found or for any other reason) he may order the destruction of the dog and shall do so if it is one to which section 1 above applies.

(5) If in any proceedings it is alleged by the prosecution that a dog is one to which section 1 or an order under section 2 above applies it shall be presumed that it is such a dog unless the contrary is shown by the accused by such evidence as the court considers sufficient; and the accused shall not be permitted to adduce such evidence unless he has given the prosecution notice of his intention to do so not later than the fourteenth day before that on which the evidence is to be adduced.

Dogs owned by young persons

6. Where a dog is owned by a person who is less than sixteen years old any reference to its owner in section 1(2)(d) or (e) or 3 above shall include a reference to the head of the household, if any, of which that person is a member or, in Scotland, to the person who has his actual care and control.

Muzzling and leads

7.—(1) In this Act—
(a) references to a dog being muzzled are to its being securely fitted with a muzzle sufficient to prevent it biting any person; and
(b) references to its being kept on a lead are to its being securely held on a lead by a person who is not less than sixteen years old.

(2) If the Secretary of State thinks it desirable to do so he may by order prescribe the kind of muzzle or lead to be used for the purpose of complying, in the case of a dog of any type, with section 1 or an order under section 2 above; and if a muzzle or lead of a particular kind is for the time being prescribed in relation to any type of dog the references in subsection (1) above to a muzzle or lead shall, in relation to any dog of that type, be construed as references to a muzzle or lead of that kind.

(3) The power to make an order under subsection (2) above shall be exercisable by statutory instrument subject to annulment in pursuance of a resolution of either House of Parliament.

Power to make corresponding provision for Northern Ireland

8. An Order in Council under paragraph 1(1)(b) of Schedule 1 to the Northern Ireland Act 1974 (legislation for Northern Ireland in the interim period) which states that it is made only for purposes corresponding to the purposes of this Act—
(a) shall not be subject to paragraph 1(4) and (5) of that Schedule (affirmative resolution of both Houses of Parliament); but
(b) shall be subject to annulment in pursuance of a resolution of either House.

Expenses

9. Any expenses incurred by the Secretary of State in consequence of this Act shall be paid out of money provided by Parliament.

Short title, interpretation, commencement and extent

10.—(1) This Act may be cited as the Dangerous Dogs Act 1991.
(2) In this Act—
"advertisement" includes any means of bringing a matter to the attention of the public and "advertise" shall be construed accordingly;
"public place" means any street, road or other place (whether or not enclosed) to which the public have or are permitted to have access whether for payment or otherwise and includes the common parts of a building containing two or more separate dwellings.

(3) For the purposes of this Act a dog shall be regarded as dangerously out of control on any occasion on which there are grounds for reasonable apprehension that it will injure any person, whether or not it actually does so, but references to a dog injuring a person or there being grounds for reasonable apprehension that it will do so do not include references to any case in which the dog is being used for a lawful purpose by a constable or a person in the service of the Crown.

(4) Except for section 8, this Act shall not come into force until such day as the Secretary of State may appoint by an order made by statutory instrument and different days may be appointed for different provisions or different purposes.

(5) Except for section 8, this Act does not extend to Northern Ireland.

INDEX

References are to section numbers

BRITISH TECHNOLOGY GROUP ACT 1991

(1991 c. 66)

ARRANGEMENT OF SECTIONS

Vesting of property etc. of NRDC and NEB in a successor company

An Act to provide for the vesting of the property, rights and liabilities of the National Research Development Corporation and the National Enterprise Board in a company nominated by the Secretary of State and for the subsequent dissolution of the Corporation and Board; and for connected purposes.   [22nd October 1991]

PARLIAMENTARY DEBATES
Hansard, H.C. Vol. 185, cols. 735, 803; Vol. 189, col. 167; Vol. 196, vol. 739; H.L. Vol. 529, col. 430; Vol. 530, col. 711; Vol. 531, cols. 597, 1007, 1422.
The Bill was considered in Standing Committee G from February 19 to March 12, 1991.

INTRODUCTION

This Act facilitates the transfer of the assets and liabilities of the National Research Development Corporation and the National Enterprise Board to a company nominated by the Secretary of State. It also provides for the shares in this successor company to be issued to the Government and for the dissolution of the Corporation and the Board. The Development of Inventions

Act 1967 (which regulates the Corporation) is repealed, as is the Industry Act 1975, Pt.I and Scheds. 1 and 2 (which regulates the Board).

Vesting of property etc. of NRDC and NEB in a successor company

Vesting of property etc. of NRDC and NEB in a successor company

1.—(1) On such day as the Secretary of State may by order appoint all the property, rights and liabilities to which—
  (a) the National Research Development Corporation; or
  (b) the National Enterprise Board,
was entitled or subject immediately before that day shall, subject to section 2 below, become by virtue of this section property, rights and liabilities of a company nominated for the purposes of this section by the Secretary of State; and references in this Act to the appointed day or to the successor company are references to the day so appointed or to the company so nominated respectively.

(2) The Secretary of State may, after consulting the Corporation and Board mentioned in subsection (1) above (in this Act referred to as "the Corporation" and "the Board"), by order nominate for the purposes of this section any company formed and registered under the Companies Act 1985; but on the appointed day the company in question must be a company limited by shares which is wholly owned by the Crown.

(3) References in this Act to property, rights and liabilities of the Corporation or Board are references to all such property, rights and liabilities, whether or not capable of being transferred or assigned by the Corporation or Board.

(4) It is hereby declared for the avoidance of doubt that—
  (a) any reference in this Act to property of the Corporation or Board is a reference to property of the Corporation or Board whether situated in the United Kingdom or elsewhere; and
  (b) any reference in this Act to rights or liabilities of the Corporation or Board is a reference to rights to which the Corporation or Board is entitled, or (as the case may be) liabilities to which it is subject, whether under the law of the United Kingdom or of any part of the United Kingdom or under the law of any country or territory outside the United Kingdom.

(5) An order under this section appointing a day under subsection (1) above or nominating any company for the purposes of this section may be varied or revoked by a subsequent order at any time before any property, rights or liabilities of the Corporation or Board vest in any company by virtue of this section.

(6) Schedule 1 to this Act shall have effect for the purpose of supplementing the provisions of this section.

Extinguishment of NRDC reserve and NEB public dividend capital

2.—(1) There shall be extinguished immediately before the appointed day—
  (a) the reserve established by the Corporation under section 10 of the Development of Inventions Act 1967; and
  (b) any liability of the Board to the Secretary of State in respect of the Board's public dividend capital.

(2) Subsection (1)(b) above shall not operate to extinguish any liability of the Board under paragraph 5(3) or (3A) of Schedule 2 to the Industry Act 1975 which accrued before the appointed day.

Provisions relating to Government holdings in successor company

Initial Government holding in the successor company

3.—(1) As a consequence of the vesting in the successor company by virtue of section 1 above of property, rights and liabilities of the Corporation and the Board, the successor company shall issue such securities of the company as the Secretary of State may from time to time direct; and any such securities shall, as the Secretary of State may so direct—

(a) be issued to the Treasury or the Secretary of State, or

(b) be allotted to the Treasury or the Secretary of State and subsequently issued to the persons for the time being entitled to be issued with them (who may include the Treasury or the Secretary of State).

(2) The Secretary of State shall not give a direction under subsection (1) above at a time when the successor company has ceased to be wholly owned by the Crown.

(3) Securities to be issued or allotted in pursuance of this section shall be issued or allotted at such time or times, and (subject to subsection (4) below) on such terms, as the Secretary of State may direct.

(4) Any shares issued in pursuance of this section—

(a) shall be of such nominal value as the Secretary of State may direct; and

(b) shall be issued as fully paid and treated for the purposes of the Companies Act 1985 as if they had been paid up by virtue of the payment to the successor company of their nominal value in cash.

(5) The Secretary of State may not exercise any power conferred on him by this section, or dispose of any securities issued or of any rights to securities initially allotted to him in pursuance of this section, without the consent of the Treasury.

(6) Any dividends or other sums received by the Treasury or the Secretary of State in right of, or on the disposal of, any securities or rights acquired by virtue of this section shall be paid into the Consolidated Fund.

Government investment in securities of the successor company

4.—(1) Subject to section 6(5) below, the Treasury or, with the consent of the Treasury, the Secretary of State may at any time acquire—

(a) securities of the successor company; or

(b) rights to subscribe for any such securities.

(2) The Secretary of State may not dispose of any securities or rights acquired by him by virtue of this section without the consent of the Treasury.

(3) Any expenses incurred by the Treasury or the Secretary of State in consequence of the provisions of this section shall be paid out of money provided by Parliament.

(4) Any dividends or other sums received by the Treasury or the Secretary of State in right of, or on the disposal of, any securities or rights acquired by virtue of this section shall be paid into the Consolidated Fund.

Exercise of functions through nominees

5.—(1) The Treasury or, with the consent of the Treasury, the Secretary of State may, for the purposes of section 3 or 4 above, appoint any person to act as the nominee, or one of the nominees, of the Treasury or the Secretary of State; and—

(a) securities of the successor company may be issued or allotted in pursuance of section 3 above to any nominee of the Treasury or the Secretary of State appointed for the purposes of that section and may be issued to any person entitled to be issued with the securities following their initial allotment to any such nominee, and

(b) any such nominee appointed for the purposes of section 4 above may acquire securities or rights under that section,

in accordance with directions given from time to time by the Treasury or, with the consent of the Treasury, by the Secretary of State.

(2) Any person holding any securities or rights as a nominee of the Treasury or the Secretary of State by virtue of subsection (1) above shall hold and deal with them (or any of them) on such terms and in such manner as the Treasury or, with the consent of the Treasury, the Secretary of State may direct.

Target investment limit for Government shareholding

6.—(1) As soon after the date when the successor company ceases to be wholly owned by the Crown as he considers expedient, and in any case not later than six months after that date, the Secretary of State shall by order fix a target investment limit in relation to the shares for the time being held in the successor company by virtue of any provision of this Act by the Treasury and their nominees and by the Secretary of State and his nominees ("the Government shareholding").

(2) The target investment limit shall be expressed as a proportion of the voting rights which are exercisable in all circumstances at general meetings of the successor company ("the ordinary voting rights").

(3) The first target investment limit fixed under this section shall be equal to the proportion of the ordinary voting rights which is carried by the Government shareholding at the time when the order fixing the limit is made.

(4) The Secretary of State may from time to time by order fix a new target investment limit in place of the one previously in force under this section; but—

(a) any new limit must be lower than the one it replaces; and

(b) an order under this section may only be revoked by an order fixing a new limit.

(5) It shall be the duty of the Treasury and of the Secretary of State so to exercise—

(a) their powers under section 4 above and any power to dispose of any shares held by virtue of any provision of this Act, and

(b) their power to give directions to their respective nominees,

as to secure that the Government shareholding does not carry a proportion of the ordinary voting rights exceeding any target investment limit for the time being in force under this section.

(6) Notwithstanding subsection (5) above, the Treasury or the Secretary of State may take up, or direct any of their respective nominees to take up, any rights for the time being available to them or him, or to that nominee, as an existing holder of shares or other securities of the successor company; but if, as a result, the proportion of the ordinary voting rights carried by the Government shareholding at any time exceeds the target investment limit, it shall be the duty of the Treasury or (as the case may be) the Secretary of State to comply with subsection (5) above as soon after that time as is reasonably practicable.

(7) For the purposes of this section the temporary suspension of any of the ordinary voting rights shall be disregarded.

Offers for sale of securities etc.

7. Where an offer for sale of any securities of the successor company is to be made by or on behalf of the Crown or any invitation or advertisement is to be issued by or on behalf of the Crown in connection with the offer, the Secretary of State shall consult such persons appearing to him to be representative of the universities of the United Kingdom as he considers appropriate.

Financial provisions relating to successor company

Financial structure of successor company

8.—(1) If the aggregate nominal value of the securities of the successor company issued in pursuance of section 3 above is for the time being less than the amount of the reserve and public dividend capital extinguished by virtue of section 2 above a sum equal to the amount of the difference shall be carried by the successor company to a reserve ("the statutory reserve").

(2) The statutory reserve may only be applied by the successor company in paying up unissued shares of the company to be allotted to its members as fully paid bonus shares except to the extent that the Secretary of State directs, with the consent of the Treasury, that it may be applied as if it were profits available for distribution within the meaning of section 263(1) of the Companies Act 1985 (distributions to be made out of profits).

(3) No direction shall be given by the Secretary of State under subsection (2) above at a time when the successor company has ceased to be wholly owned by the Crown.

(4) Notwithstanding subsection (2) above, no part of the statutory reserve shall count as an undistributable reserve of the successor company for the purposes of section 264(3)(d) of the Companies Act 1985 (restriction on distribution of assets); but for the purpose of determining under section 264 whether the successor company may make a distribution at any time, any amount for the time being standing to the credit of the statutory reserve (excluding any amount which under subsection (2) above is authorised to be, but has not yet been, applied as if it were profits available for distribution) shall be treated for the purposes of section 264(3)(c) as if it were unrealised profits of the company.

(5) For the purposes of any statutory accounts of the successor company—

(a) all the property, rights and liabilities to which the Corporation or Board was entitled or subject immediately before the end of the last financial year of the Corporation or Board ending before the appointed day shall be taken to have been vested in the successor company by virtue of section 1 above, and to have been so vested immediately after the end of that year; and

(b) the value or amount (as at the time of vesting) of any asset or liability of the Corporation or Board taken to have been vested in the successor company by virtue of paragraph (a) above shall be taken to be the value or (as the case may be) the amount assigned to that asset or liability for the purposes of the corresponding statement of accounts prepared by the Corporation or Board in respect of the financial year referred to in that paragraph.

(6) For the purposes of any statutory accounts of the successor company the amount to be included in respect of any item shall be determined as if anything done by the Corporation or Board (whether by way of acquiring, revaluing or disposing of any asset, or incurring, revaluing or discharging any liability, or by carrying any amount to any provision or reserve, or otherwise) had been done by the successor company.

Accordingly (but without prejudice to the generality of the preceding provision) the amount to be included from time to time in any reserves of the successor company as representing its accumulated realised profits shall be determined as if any profits realised and retained by the Corporation or Board had been realised and retained by the company.

(7) References in this section to the statutory accounts of the successor company are to any accounts prepared by that company for the purposes of any provision of the Companies Act 1985 (including group accounts).

Loans by Secretary of State to successor company

9.—(1) As from the appointed day the Secretary of State may, with the consent of the Treasury, make loans to the successor company; but no loan shall be made by him under this section at a time when that company has ceased to be wholly owned by the Crown.

(2) The Treasury may issue to the Secretary of State out of the National Loans Fund any sums necessary to enable him to make loans under this section.

(3) Any loan made by the Secretary of State under this section shall be repaid to him at such times and by such methods, and interest on it shall be paid to him at such rates and at such times, as he may, with the consent of the Treasury, from time to time direct.

(4) Any sums received by the Secretary of State under subsection (3) above shall be paid into the National Loans Fund.

(5) The Secretary of State shall in respect of each financial year prepare, in such form and manner as the Treasury may direct, an account of—

(a) sums issued to him under subsection (2) above;

(b) sums received by him under subsection (3) above; and

(c) the disposal by him of sums so issued or received;

and shall send the account to the Comptroller and Auditor General not later than the end of November in the following financial year; and the Comptroller and Auditor General shall examine, certify and report on the account and lay copies of it, together with his report, before each House of Parliament.

Temporary restrictions on successor company's borrowings etc.

10.—(1) If the articles of association of the successor company confer on the Secretary of State powers exercisable with the consent of the Treasury for, or in connection with, restricting the sums of money which may during any period be borrowed or raised by the successor company and its subsidiaries, taken as a whole, those powers shall be exercisable in the national interest notwithstanding any rule of law and the provisions of any enactment.

(2) For the purposes of this section any alteration of the articles of association of the successor company which—

(a) has the effect of conferring or extending any such power as is mentioned in subsection (1) above, and

(b) is made at a time when that company has ceased to be wholly owned by the Crown,

shall be disregarded.

Dissolution of the Corporation and Board

Dissolution of the Corporation and Board

11.—(1) The Corporation and Board shall continue in existence after the appointed day until dissolved in accordance with subsection (2) below; and in relation to each of those bodies the period of its continued existence after the appointed day is referred to in this Act as "the transitional period".

(2) If in the case of either of those bodies the Secretary of State is satisfied that nothing further remains to be done by it under Schedule 3 to this Act, he may, after consulting that body and the successor company, by order dissolve that body on a day specified in the order.

Supplementary provisions

Corporation tax

12.—(1) Subject to subsection (2) below, the successor company shall be treated for the purposes of the Corporation Tax Acts as if it were the same person as the Corporation and the Board.

(2) Notwithstanding subsection (1) above, section 345 of the Income and Corporation Taxes Act 1988 (computation of chargeable gains) shall apply to the successor company without regard to any allowable losses of the Corporation or the Board.

(3) Any share issued by the successor company in pursuance of section 3 above shall be treated for the purposes of the Corporation Tax Acts as if it had been issued wholly in consideration of a subscription paid to that company of an amount equal to the nominal value of the share.

(4) Any debenture issued by the successor company in pursuance of that section shall be treated for the purposes of those Acts as if it had been issued—

(a) wholly in consideration of a loan made to that company of an amount equal to the principal sum payable under the debenture; and

(b) wholly and exclusively for the purposes of the trade carried on by that company

Application of Trustee Investments Act 1961 in relation to investment in the successor company

13.—(1) For the purpose of applying paragraph 3(b) of Part IV of Schedule 1 to the Trustee Investments Act 1961 (which provides that shares and debentures of a company shall not count as wider-range and narrower-range investments respectively within the meaning of that Act unless the company has paid dividends in each of the five years immediately preceding that in which the investment is made) in relation to investment in shares or debentures of the successor company during the calendar year in which the appointed day falls ("the first investment year") or during any year following that year, the successor company shall be deemed to have paid a dividend as there mentioned—

(a) in any year preceding the first investment year which is included in the relevant five years; and

(b) in the first investment year, if that year is included in the relevant five years and the successor company does not in fact pay such a dividend in that year.

(2) In subsection (1) above "the relevant five years" means the five years immediately preceding the year in which the investment in question is made or proposed to be made.

Orders

14.—(1) Any power of the Secretary of State to make an order under this Act shall be exercisable by statutory instrument.

(2) Any statutory instrument containing an order made by the Secretary of State under section 6 above or 17(1) below shall be subject to annulment in pursuance of a resolution of either House of Parliament.

Administrative expenses

15. Any administrative expenses incurred by the Secretary of State or the Treasury in consequence of the provisions of this Act shall be paid out of money provided by Parliament.

Interpretation

16.—(1) In this Act—
"the appointed day" means the day appointed under section 1(1) above;
"the Board" means the National Enterprise Board;
"the Corporation" means the National Research Development Corporation;
"debenture" includes debenture stock;
"financial year", in relation to the Corporation, means a year ending on 31st March and, in relation to the Board, means the accounting year as defined in section 37(1) of the Industry Act 1975;
"securities", in relation to a company, includes shares, debentures, bonds and other securities of the company, whether or not constituting a charge on the assets of the company;
"shares" includes stock;
"the successor company" means the company nominated for the purposes of section 1 above;
"the transitional period" has the meaning given by section 11(1) above.
(2) A company shall be regarded for the purposes of this Act as wholly owned by the Crown at any time when each of the issued shares of the company is held by, or by a nominee of, the Treasury or the Secretary of State.

Consequential amendments, repeals and transitional provisions

17.—(1) The Secretary of State may by order make—
(a) such consequential modifications of any provision contained in any Act (whether public general or local) passed, or subordinate legislation made, before the appointed day as appear to him to be necessary or expedient in connection with any reference in that Act or subordinate legislation to the Corporation or the Board;
(b) such transitional or saving provision as appears to him to be necessary or expedient in connection with the coming into force of any provision of this Act;
and any provision of an order made under this subsection after the appointed day may be made so as to have effect as from that or any later day.
(2) The enactments mentioned in Schedule 2 to this Act (which include certain spent enactments) are hereby repealed to the extent specified in the third column of that Schedule.
(3) The transitional provisions and savings contained in Schedule 3 to this Act shall have effect.

Short title, commencement and extent

18.—(1) This Act may be cited as the British Technology Group Act 1991.
(2) Subject to subsections (3) and (4) below, this Act shall come into force on the appointed day.
(3) Sections 1, 2, 7, 14, 16(1), this section and paragraph 1 of Schedule 1 shall come into force at the passing of this Act.
(4) Parts II and III of Schedule 2 shall come into force on the dissolution of the Corporation or, as the case may be, the Board.
(5) Except for sections 3 to 6, 8 to 10 and 13, this Act extends to Northern Ireland.

SCHEDULES

Section 1(6)   SCHEDULE 1

PROVISIONS SUPPLEMENTARY TO S.1

Preparation for transfer to successor company

1. Without prejudice to any powers of the Corporation or Board apart from this paragraph, the Corporation and Board may each do before the appointed day anything which in their opinion is appropriate for the purpose of facilitating the vesting in the successor company by virtue of section 1 of this Act of the property, rights and liabilities of the Corporation or Board.

Provisions as to vesting of property etc.

2. Any agreement made, transaction effected or other thing done by, to or in relation to the Corporation or Board which is in force or effective immediately before the appointed day shall have effect as from that day as if made, effected or done by, to or in relation to the successor company, in all respects as if the successor company were the same person, in law, as the Corporation and the Board; and accordingly references to the Corporation or Board—
   (a) in any agreement (whether or not in writing) and in any deed, bond or instrument,
   (b) in any process or other document issued, prepared or employed for the purpose of any proceeding before any court or other tribunal or authority, and
   (c) in any other document whatever (other than an enactment) relating to or affecting any property, right or liability of the Corporation or Board which vests by virtue of section 1 of this Act in the successor company,
shall be taken as from the appointed day as referring to the successor company.
3. Where immediately before the appointed day there is in force an agreement which—
   (a) confers or imposes on the Corporation or Board any rights or liabilities which vest in the successor company by virtue of section 1 of this Act, and
   (b) refers (in whatever terms and whether expressly or by implication) to a member or officer of the Corporation or Board,
the agreement shall have effect, in relation to anything falling to be done on or after that day, as if for that reference there were substituted a reference to such person as that company may appoint or, in default of appointment, to the officer of that company who corresponds as nearly as may be to the member or officer of the Corporation or Board in question.
4.—(1) It is hereby declared for the avoidance of doubt that—
   (a) the effect of section 1 of this Act in relation to any contract of employment with the Corporation or Board in force immediately before the appointed day is merely to modify the contract (as from that day) by substituting the successor company as the employer (and not to terminate the contract or vary it in any other way); and
   (b) that section is effective to vest the rights and liabilities of the Corporation or Board under any agreement or arrangement for the payment of pensions, allowances or gratuities in the successor company along with all other rights and liabilities of the Corporation or Board.
(2) Accordingly, for the purposes of any such agreement or arrangement as it has effect as from the appointed day—
   (a) any period of employment with, or with a subsidiary of, the Corporation or Board, and
   (b) any period of employment which would, immediately before that day, have been treated as such employment for the purposes of any such agreement or arrangement,
shall count as employment with, or with that subsidiary of, the successor company.

Disqualification of certain directors of successor company

5. In the House of Commons Disqualification Act 1975, in Part III of Schedule 1 (other disqualifying offices) there shall be inserted at the appropriate place—
   "Director of the successor company (within the meaning of the British Technology Group Act 1991) being a director nominated or appointed by a Minister of the Crown or by a person acting on behalf of the Crown";
and a corresponding amendment shall be made in Part III of Schedule 1 to the Northern Ireland Assembly Disqualification Act 1975.

SCHEDULE 2

REPEALS

PART I

REPEALS ON APPOINTED DAY

Chapter	Short title	Extent of repeal
1967 c. 32.	The Development of Inventions Act 1967.	Sections 2 to 13. Section 15(3) to (8). In the Schedule, paragraphs 4 to 8.
1972 c. 11.	The Superannuation Act 1972.	In Schedule 4 the entry relating to the National Research Development Corporation.
1975 c. 68.	The Industry Act 1975.	Part I except section 1. In section 13(2) the words "the Board or" in both places. In section 14(1) and (4) the words "or the Board". In section 16(1)(b) and (4) the words "or the Board". In section 19(3)(i) the words "the Board or". In section 20(3) the words ", the Board". Section 26. In section 37, in subsection (1) the definitions of "accounting year" and "wholly owned subsidiary" and subsections (2) and (4). In Schedule 1, paragraphs 7 to 10, 18, 19 and 20. Schedule 2.
1979 c. 32.	The Industry Act 1979.	In section 1, in subsection (1) the words "section 8 of the Industry Act 1975", "the National Enterprise Board" and "that Board and", in subsections (5) and (7) the figure "8" and in subsection (6) the figure "8(4)(b)" and the words "the Board or". In the Schedule the entry relating to the Industry Act 1975.
1980 c. 33.	The Industry Act 1980.	Section 1(1). In section 2, in subsection (1) the words "the National Enterprise Board" and paragraph (a) and in subsections (2) and (3) the words "the National Enterprise Board". Section 4(1). Section 5(3) and (5). Section 6(1). Section 8(1). In section 21(2) the words "section 2(2) of the Industry Act 1975" and "the National Enterprise Board".
1980 c. 65.	The Local Government, Planning and Land Act 1980.	In section 170(2) the words "and the National Enterprise Board".
1981 c. 6.	The Industry Act 1981.	Section 1.
1981 c. 68.	The Broadcasting Act 1981.	In section 65(2) the words "each of section 9 of the Industry Act 1975 and". In Part II of Schedule 3 the entry relating to section 9 of the Industry Act 1975.

Chapter	Short title	Extent of repeal
1983 c. 29.	The Miscellaneous Financial Provisions Act 1983.	In Schedule 2 the entry relating to the Industry Act 1975.
1985 c. 9.	The Companies Consolidation (Consequential Provisions) Act 1985.	In Schedule 2 the entry relating to section 12(3) of the Development of Inventions Act 1967, in the entry relating to section 37(1) of the Industry Act 1975 the words from "and in the definition of 'wholly-owned subsidiary' " onwards and the entries relating to Schedules 1 and 2 to that Act.
1986 c. 60.	The Financial Services Act 1986.	In Schedule 16, paragraph 10.
1988 c. 50.	The Housing Act 1988.	In Schedule 9, in paragraph 4(b) the words "the National Enterprise Board".
1989 c. 43.	The Statute Law (Repeals) Act 1989.	In Schedule 2, paragraph 13.
1990 c. 42.	The Broadcasting Act 1990.	In Schedule 20, paragraph 22. In Schedule 22, paragraph 5(2)(a).

PART II

REPEALS ON DISSOLUTION OF CORPORATION

Chapter	Short title	Extent of repeal
1967 c. 32.	The Development of Inventions Act 1967.	Section 1. Section 15(1) and (2). The Schedule so far as unrepealed.
1975 c. 24.	The House of Commons Disqualification Act 1975.	In Part III of Schedule 1 the entries relating to the chairman and managing director of the National Research Development Corporation.
1975 c. 25.	The Northern Ireland Assembly Disqualification Act 1975.	In Part II of Schedule 1 the entry relating to members of the National Research Development Corporation.

PART III

REPEALS ON DISSOLUTION OF BOARD

Chapter	Short title	Extent of repeal
1975 c. 24.	The House of Commons Disqualification Act 1975.	In Part III of Schedule 1 the entries relating to the chairman and chief executive of the National Enterprise Board.
1975 c. 25.	The Northern Ireland Assembly Disqualification Act 1975.	In Part II of Schedule 1 the entry relating to the National Enterprise Board and in Part III of that Schedule the entry relating to the chief executive of the National Enterprise Board.
1975 c. 68.	The Industry Act 1975.	Section 1. Schedule 1 so far as unrepealed.
1980 c. 33.	The Industry Act 1980.	Section 7.

Section 17(3)   SCHEDULE 3

TRANSITIONAL PROVISIONS AND SAVINGS

Constitution of the Corporation and Board

1. During the transitional period section 1(2) of the Development of Inventions Act 1967 (constitution of the Corporation) shall have effect as if for "less than four" there were

substituted "less than three" and section 1(2) of the Industry Act 1975 (constitution of the Board) shall have effect as if for "not less than eight" there were substituted "not less than three".

Vesting of foreign property etc. in the successor company

2.—(1) It shall be the duty of the Corporation and the Board and of the successor company to take, as and when during the transitional period the successor company considers appropriate, all such steps as may be requisite to secure that the vesting in the successor company by virtue of section 1 of this Act or this paragraph of any foreign property, right or liability is effective under the relevant foreign law.

(2) Until the vesting in the successor company by virtue of section 1 of this Act or this paragraph of any foreign property, right or liability is effective under the relevant foreign law, it shall be the duty of the Corporation and the Board during the transitional period to hold that property or right for the benefit of, or to discharge that liability on behalf of, the successor company.

(3) Nothing in sub-paragraphs (1) and (2) above shall be taken as prejudicing the effect under the law of the United Kingdom, or of any part of the United Kingdom, of the vesting in the successor company by virtue of section 1 of this Act or this paragraph of any foreign property, right or liability.

(4) The Corporation and the Board shall have all such powers as may be requisite for the performance of its duties under this paragraph, but—

(a) it shall be the duty of the successor company during the transitional period to act on behalf of the Corporation and the Board (so far as possible) in performing the duties imposed on them by this paragraph; and

(b) any foreign property, rights and liabilities acquired or incurred by the Corporation or Board during that period shall immediately become property, rights and liabilities of the successor company.

(5) References in this paragraph to any foreign property, right or liability are references to any property, right or liability as respects which any issue arising in any proceedings would have been determined (in accordance with the rules of private international law) by reference to the law of a country or territory outside the United Kingdom.

(6) Any expenses incurred by the Corporation or Board under this paragraph shall be met by the successor company.

Application of enactments to certain continuing liabilities

3.—(1) Where any loan made to the Corporation under section 7 of the Development of Inventions Act 1967 or to the Board under paragraph 2 of Schedule 2 to the Industry Act 1975 (loans by Secretary of State) is in existence immediately before the appointed day, any terms which are then applicable to the loan shall continue to apply to it after it becomes a liability of the successor company by virtue of section 1 of this Act; and section 7(5) of the Act of 1967 and paragraph 2(2) of Schedule 2 to the Act of 1975 shall continue to have effect as respects sums received by virtue of this paragraph.

(2) Any sums received by the Secretary of State from the successor company in the discharge of any liability to make a payment under paragraph 5(3) or (3A) of Schedule 2 to the Industry Act 1975 (public dividend capital) which accrued before the appointed day (and accordingly has become a liability of the successor company by virtue of section 1 of this Act) shall be paid into the Consolidated Fund.

Treasury guarantees

4. Sub-paragraphs (2) to (5) of paragraph 4 of Schedule 2 to the Industry Act 1975 (Treasury guarantees) shall continue to apply in relation to any guarantee given by the Treasury under that paragraph with respect to a liability of the Board which becomes a liability of the successor company by virtue of section 1 of this Act, but as if the reference to the Board in sub-paragraph (4) were a reference to the successor company.

Final reports and accounts of the Corporation and the Board

5.—(1) Notwithstanding the repeal of section 13(2) of the Development of Inventions Act 1967 and paragraph 8 of Schedule 2 to the Industry Act 1975 (reports to the Secretary of State)—

(a) it shall continue to be the duty of the Corporation and the Board to make a report to the Secretary of State in accordance with those provisions in respect of each financial year of the Corporation and Board ending before the appointed day; and

(b) the Secretary of State shall lay a copy of any such report before each House of Parliament.

(2) Notwithstanding the repeal of section 12 of the Act of 1967 and paragraph 7 of Schedule 2 to the Act of 1975 (accounts and audit)—

(a) it shall continue to be the duty of the Corporation and Board to prepare such statements of accounts as are mentioned in those provisions in respect of each financial year of the Corporation or Board ending before the appointed day; and

(b) those provisions shall continue to apply during the transitional period in relation to those accounts and in relation also to the auditing of accounts kept in accordance with those provisions in respect of each such financial year.

(3) Any expenses incurred by the Corporation or Board under this paragraph shall be met by the successor company.

Accounts of the Secretary of State

6. Notwithstanding the repeal of section 7(6) of the Act of 1967 and paragraph 2(3) of Schedule 2 to the Act of 1975 (accounts of the Secretary of State), those provisions shall continue to apply in relation to—

(a) any financial year down to and including that in which the appointed day falls; and

(b) any subsequent financial year in which the Secretary of State receives any sum by virtue of paragraph 3 above.

Payment of dividend by successor company before laying or delivery of accounts

7.—(1) Where it is proposed to declare a distribution during the accounting reference period of the successor company which includes the appointed day, or before any accounts are laid or delivered to the registrar of companies in respect of that period, sections 270 to 276 of the Companies Act 1985 (relevant accounts) shall have effect as if—

(a) such accounts as are mentioned in sub-paragraph (2) below were accounts relevant under section 270, and

(b) references in section 273 to initial accounts included references to any such accounts,

and, if any direction has been given under section 8(2) of this Act which is relevant to the making of that distribution, shall accordingly have effect subject to that direction.

(2) The accounts referred to in sub-paragraph (1)(a) and (b) above are such accounts as, on the assumptions stated in sub-paragraph (3) below, would have been prepared under Part VII of the Companies Act 1985 in respect of the relevant year.

(3) Those assumptions are—

(a) that the relevant year had been a financial year of the successor company;

(b) that the vesting effected by section 1 of this Act had been a vesting of all the property, rights and liabilities to which the Corporation or Board was entitled or subject immediately before the beginning of the relevant year and had been effected immediately after the beginning of that year;

(c) that the value of any asset and the amount of any liability of the Corporation or Board vested in the successor company by virtue of that section had been the value or (as the case may be) the amount assigned to that asset or liability for the purposes of the statement of accounts prepared by the Corporation or Board in respect of its financial year immediately preceding the relevant year;

(d) that any securities of the successor company issued or allotted before the declaration of the distribution had been issued or allotted before the end of the relevant year; and

(e) such other assumptions (if any) as may appear to the directors of the successor company to be necessary or expedient for the purposes of this paragraph.

(4) For the purposes of such accounts as are mentioned in sub-paragraph (2) above the amount to be included in respect of any item shall be determined as if anything done by the Corporation or Board (whether by way of acquiring, revaluing or disposing of any asset, or incurring, revaluing or discharging any liability, or by carrying any amount to any provision or reserve, or otherwise) had been done by the successor company.

Accordingly (but without prejudice to the generality of the preceding provision) the amount to be included in any reserves of the successor company as representing its accumulated realised profits shall be determined as if any profits realised and retained by the Corporation or Board had been realised and retained by the company.

(5) Any such accounts shall not be regarded as statutory accounts for the purposes of section 8 of this Act.

(6) In this paragraph "the relevant year" means the last financial year of the Corporation or Board ending before the appointed day.

INDEX

References are to sections and Schedules

EXPORT AND INVESTMENT GUARANTEES ACT 1991

(1991 c. 67)

ARRANGEMENT OF SECTIONS

PART I

POWERS OF ECGD

An Act to make new provisions as to the functions exercisable by the Secretary of State through the Export Credits Guarantee Department; and make provisions as to the delegation of any such functions and the transfer of property, rights and liabilities attributable to the exercise of any such functions. 　　　　　　　　[22nd October 1991]

PARLIAMENTARY DEBATES
Hansard, H.C. Vol. 184, col. 1176; Vol. 189, col. 40; H.L. Vol. 529, col. 1008; Vol. 530, col. 1316; Vol. 531, cols. 113, 944, 967.
The Bill was debated in Standing Committee H from January 31 to March 7, 1991.

INTRODUCTION

This Act has two main functions: to re-enact the Export Guarantees and Overseas Investment Act 1978 and to clarify and update that legislation, in the main by way of increasing the Secretary of State's powers in relation to managing the assets and liabilities acquired by him, when acting through the Export Credit Guarantee Department and to facilitate the privatisation of the Insurance Service business of ECGD.

Part I bestows a range of powers upon the Secretary of State allowing him to provide the following: (1) financial facilities and assistance for the purposes of facilitating the supply abroad of goods and services by U.K. businesses and of rendering economic assistance to countries outside the U.K.; (2) insurance against the risk of losses in respect of investment overseas made by U.K. companies in certain circumstances; (3) arrangements to manage the portfolio of assets and liabilities arising from the activities mentioned in (1) and (2) in order to control or reduce the cost of these activities; (4) information and services related to credit insurance.

Part II empowers the Secretary of State to provide for the transfer of any property, rights and liabilities which are associated with the ECGD's Insurance Service business, and makes provisions in relation to the subsequent dealing with shares or securities in any transferee company or its holding company by the Secretary of State. Specific provision is made as to the application of the Transfer of Undertakings (Protection of Employment) Regulations 1981.

No change is envisaged in the financial arrangements applicable to ECGD's continuing trading operations as they exist as present, although the financial arrangements established under s.3 are intended to allow better management of assets and liabilities that are acquired in undertaking certain functions.

PART I

POWERS OF ECGD

Assistance in connection with exports of goods and services

1.—(1) The Secretary of State may make arrangements under this section with a view to facilitating, directly or indirectly, supplies by persons carrying on business in the United Kingdom of goods or services to persons carrying on business outside the United Kingdom.

(2) The Secretary of State may make arrangements under this section for the purpose of rendering economic assistance to countries outside the United Kingdom.

(3) The Secretary of State may make arrangements under this section with a view to facilitating—

(a) the performance of obligations created or arising, directly or indirectly, in connection with matters as to which he has exercised his powers under this section or section 2 of this Act or

(b) the reduction or avoidance of losses arising in connection with any failure to perform such obligations.

(4) The arrangements that may be made under this section are arrangements for providing financial facilities or assistance for, or for the benefit of, persons carrying on business; and the facilities or assistance may be provided in any form, including guarantees, insurance, grants or loans.

Insurance in connection with overseas investment

2.—(1) The Secretary of State may make arrangements for insuring any person carrying on business in the United Kingdom against risks of losses arising—

(a) in connection with any investment of resources by the insured in enterprises carried on outside the United Kingdom, or

(b) in connection with guarantees given by the insured in respect of any investment of resources by others in such enterprises, being enterprises in which the insured has any interest,

being losses resulting directly or indirectly from war, expropriation, restrictions on remittances and other similar events.

(2) The Secretary of State may make arrangements for insuring persons providing such insurance.

(3) References in subsection (1) above to a person carrying on business in the United Kingdom and to the insured include any company controlled directly or indirectly by him.

Financial management

3.—(1) The Secretary of State may make any arrangements which, in his opinion, are in the interests of the proper financial management of the ECGD portfolio, or any part of it.

(2) In pursuance of arrangements under this section the Secretary of State may enter into any form of transaction, including—

(a) lending, and

(b) providing and taking out insurance and guarantees.

(3) The Secretary of State may not, in pursuance of such arrangements, enter into any transaction for the purpose of borrowing money but, subject to that, he is not precluded from entering into any transaction by reason of its involving borrowing.

(4) In pursuance of such arrangements the Secretary of State may—

(a) alter any arrangements made under section 1 or 2 of this Act or the old law or make new arrangements in place of arrangements so made, or

(b) make further arrangements in connection with arrangements so made.

(5) Arrangements under this section may be made in anticipation of further rights being acquired or liabilities being incurred by the Secretary of State.

(6) In this section the "ECGD portfolio" means the rights and liabilities to which the Secretary of State is entitled or subject by virtue of the exercise of his powers under this Act or the old law or in consequence or arrangements made in the exercise of those powers.

(7) The Secretary of State may certify that any transaction he has entered into or is entering into has been or, as the case may be, is entered into in the exercise of the powers conferred by this section and such a certificate shall be conclusive evidence of the matters stated in it.

Provisions supplementary to sections 1 to 3

4.—(1) Transactions entered into in pursuance of arrangements made under sections 1 to 3 of this Act may be on such terms and conditions as the Secretary of State considers appropriate.

(2) The powers of the Secretary of State under those sections are exercisable only with the consent of the Treasury and such consent may be given in relation to particular cases or in relation to such descriptions of cases as may be specified in the consent.

(3) In those sections—

(a) "business" includes a profession,

(b) "guarantee" includes indemnity,

(c) references to persons carrying on business, in relation to things done outside the United Kingdom, include persons carrying on any other activities, and

(d) references to things done in or outside the United Kingdom are to things done wholly or partly in or, as the case may be, outside the United Kingdom.

(4) References in this and those sections to the United Kingdom include the Isle of Man and the Channel Islands.

Provision of services and information

5.—(1) The Secretary of State may provide to any person—

(a) information relating to credit or investment insurance,

(b) services ancillary to the provision by that person of credit or investment insurance, and

(c) such other goods or services as may be specified in an order under this section,

and may make such charges for doing so as he may determine.

(2) The power to make an order under this section is exercisable only with the consent of the Treasury.

Commitment limits

6.—(1) The aggregate amount of the Secretary of State's commitments at any time under arrangements relating to exports and insurance shall not exceed—

   (a) in the case of commitments in sterling, £35,000 million, and
   (b) in the case of commitments in foreign currency, 15,000 million special
      drawing rights.

(2) In subsection (1) above, "arrangements relating to exports and insurance" means—
   (a) arrangements under section 1 or 2 of this Act, other than arrangements for giving grants or arrangements under section 1(3), and
   (b) arrangements under the old law, other than arrangements for giving grants.

(3) The aggregate amount of the Secretary of State's commitments at any time under section 3 of this Act shall not exceed—
   (a) in the case of commitments in sterling, £15,000 million, and
   (b) in the case of commitments in foreign currency, 10,000 million special
      drawing rights.

(4) The Secretary of State may by order increase or further increase—
   (a) either of the limits in subsection (1) above by a sum specified in the order not exceeding £5,000 million or, as the case may be, 5,000 million special drawing rights,
   (b) either of the limits in subsection (3) above by a sum specified in the order not exceeding £3,000 million or, as the case may be, 2,000 million special drawing rights,

but the Secretary of State shall not in respect of any limit exercise the power on more than three occasions.

(5) For the purposes of this section and section 7 of this Act—
   (a) the commitments of the Secretary of State under any arrangements are his rights and liabilities relating to the arrangements,
   (b) the amount of any commitments shall be ascertained in accordance with principles determined from time to time by the Secretary of State with the consent of the Treasury,
   (c) "foreign currency" means any currency other than sterling, including special drawing rights and any other units of account defined by reference to more than one currency,
   (d) whether any commitments are in sterling or foreign currency is to be determined by reference to the currency in which the amount of the commitments is measured (rather than the currency of payment) but, if the commitments are expressed to be subject to a sterling or foreign currency limit, the commitments are to be taken to be in sterling or, as the case may be, foreign currency, and
   (e) the equivalent in special drawing rights of the amount of any commitments in foreign currency shall be ascertained at intervals determined from time to time by the Secretary of State with the consent of the Treasury and in accordance with principles so determined.

(6) A determination under subsection (5)(e) above may provide for leaving out of account for the purposes of the limit in subsection (1)(b) or (3)(b) above any amount by which the limit would otherwise be exceeded to the extent that the amount is attributable to—
   (a) a revaluation of commitments under subsection (5)(e) above, or
   (b) the fulfillment of an undertaking which, had it been fulfilled when given, would not have caused the limit to be exceeded.

(7) Any power to make an order under this section is exercisable only with the consent of the Treasury.

Reports and returns

7.—(1) The Secretary of State shall prepare an annual report on the discharge of his functions under sections 1 to 5 of this Act.

(2) The Secretary of State shall prepare, as soon as practicable after 31st March in each year, a return showing separately the aggregate amounts of

the commitments in sterling and in foreign currency on that date for the purposes of the limits in section 6(1) and (3) of this Act.

(3) Any return under this section may also give such further information as to the amounts of his commitments for the purposes of those limits as the Secretary of State may determine for that return.

(4) The first return under this section shall be prepared as soon as practicable after 31st March 1991.

(5) Reports and returns prepared under this section shall be laid before Parliament.

PART II

TRANSFER OR DELEGATION OF ECGD FUNCTIONS

Scheme of transfer

8.—(1) The Secretary of State may make a scheme or schemes for the transfer to any person or persons or such property, rights and liabilities as are specified in or determined in accordance with the scheme, being property, rights or liabilities—

(a) to which the Secretary of State (or, in the case of copyright, Her Majesty) is entitled or subject immediately before the day on which the scheme providing for the transfer comes into force, and

(b) which then subsisted for the purposes of or in connection with or are otherwise attributable (wholly or partly) to the exercise of functions under Part I of this Act or the old law.

(2) Without prejudice to the generality of subsection (1)(b) above, any property, rights or liabilities shall be taken to fall within that subsection if the Secretary of State issues a certificate to that effect.

(3) A scheme under this section may apply—

(a) to property wherever situated, and

(b) to property, rights and liabilities whether or not otherwise capable of being transferred or assigned by the Secretary of State or, as the case may be, Her Majesty.

(4) A scheme under this section shall come into force on such day as may be specified in, or determined in accordance with, the scheme; and on that day the property, rights and liabilities to which the scheme applies shall be transferred and vest in accordance with the scheme.

(5) A scheme under this section may contain such supplementary, incidental, consequential or transitional provisions as appear to the Secretary of State to be necessary or expedient.

(6) The Schedule to this Act (scheme of transfer: supplementary provisions) shall have effect.

(7) References below in this Act to a transferee are to any person to whom anything is transferred by virtue of a scheme under this section.

Transferred staff

9.—(1) No scheme under section 8 of this Act shall provide for the transfer of any rights or liabilities relating to a person's employment, but the Transfer of Undertakings (Protection of Employment) Regulations 1981 shall apply to the transfer of property, rights or liabilities by virtue of such a scheme whether or not the transfer would, apart from this subsection, be a relevant transfer for the purposes of those regulations.

(2) Where, by reason of the operation of those regulations in relation to a transfer of property, rights or liabilities by virtue of such a scheme, a person ceases to be employed in the civil service of the State and becomes employed by a transferee—

(a) he shall not, on so ceasing, be treated for the purposes of any scheme

67–5

under section 1 of the Superannuation Act 1972 as having retired on redundancy, and

(b) his ceasing to be employed in that service shall not be regarded as an occasion of redundancy for the purposes of the agreed redundancy procedures applicable to persons employed in that service.

Vehicle companies

10.—(1) In this section "vehicle company" means a company formed or acquired for the purpose of—

(a) becoming a transferee, or

(b) holding shares in a company formed or acquired for that purpose.

(2) Subject to subsections (3) and (4) below, the Secretary of State may—

(a) subscribe for or otherwise acquire shares in or securities of a vehicle company, or acquire rights to subscribe for such shares or securities,

(b) by a direction given to a company formed or acquired for the purpose of becoming a transferee require it, in consequence of the transfer by virtue of a scheme under section 8 of this Act of property, rights or liabilities, to issue to him, or to such other person as may be specified in the direction, such shares or securities as may be so specified,

(c) from time to time by a direction given to a vehicle company require it to issue to him, or to such other person as may be specified in the direction, such shares or securities as may be so specified, or

(d) make loans to a vehicle company on such terms and conditions as he may determine.

(3) A direction under subsection (2)(b) or (c) above may require any shares to which it relates to be issued as fully or partly paid up.

(4) The Secretary of State shall not—

(a) subscribe for or otherwise acquire shares in or securities of a vehicle company, or acquire rights to subscribe for such shares or securities, unless all the relevant shares are to be held by or on behalf of the Crown, or

(b) at any time give a direction or make a loan to a vehicle company unless all the relevant shares are then held by or on behalf of the Crown.

(5) For the purposes of subsection (4) above—

(a) shares are held by or on behalf of the Crown where the Crown or any person acting on behalf of the Crown has a legal interest in them; and

(b) "relevant shares", in relation to a vehicle company, means the issued shares of that company or, if it is a subsidiary of another vehicle company, the issued shares of that other company.

(6) A scheme under section 8 of this Act may, as between any vehicle companies or as between a vehicle company and the Secretary of State, confer or impose rights and liabilities in connection with any of the matters as to which the Secretary of State may exercise his powers under this Act.

(7) The Secretary of State shall not exercise any of the powers conferred by the preceding provisions of this section or dispose of any shares in or securities of a vehicle company without the consent of the Treasury.

Reinsurance

11.—(1) The Secretary of State may make arrangements with any transferee under which the transferee insures the Secretary of State against risks of losses arising in consequence of arrangements made, before the day on which any scheme under section 8 of this Act comes into force, under Part I of this Act or the old law.

(2) The Secretary of State shall from time to time determine, in relation to such classes of risk determined by him as might be insured by him under section 1 of this Act, whether it is expedient in the national interest for him

to exercise his powers under that section to make arrangements for reinsuring persons providing insurance for risks of that class.

(3) This section is without prejudice to any power of the Secretary of State under Part I of this Act.

Delegation of assistance function

12.—(1) The Secretary of State may make arrangements for any of the functions to which this section applies to be exercised on his behalf by any transferee or any other person, instead of through the Export Credits Guarantee Department, on such terms and conditions as he may determine.

(2) This section applies to the power of the Secretary of State to make arrangements under section 1 of this Act and to any functions of his under arrangements so made, or arrangements under the old law, including, so far as relating to any such arrangements, arrangements made by virtue of section 3(4) of this Act.

(3) This section does not affect any requirement for the consent of the Treasury.

PART III

GENERAL

The Export Credits Guarantee Department and the Export Guarantees Advisory Council

13.—(1) All the functions of the Secretary of State under Part I of this Act, except the power to make orders under section 5 or 6 of this Act, shall be exercised and performed through the Export Credits Guarantee Department, which shall continue to be a Department of the Secretary of State.

(2) There shall continue to be an Export Guarantees Advisory Council.

(3) The function of the Council shall be to give advice to the Secretary of State, at his request, in respect of any matter relating to the exercise of his functions under this Act.

(4) In exercising his duty under section 11(2) of this Act, the Secretary of State shall consult the Export Guarantees Advisory Council.

Expenses

14.—(1) Any sums required by the Secretary of State for making payments or for defraying his administrative expenses under this Act shall be paid out of money provided by Parliament and any sums received by the Secretary of State by virtue of this Act shall be paid into the Consolidated Fund.

(2) If any sum required by the Secretary of State for fulfilling his liabilities under this Act is not paid out of money provided by Parliament, it shall be charged on and paid out of the Consolidated Fund.

Short title, interpretation, commencement, etc.

15.—(1) This Act may be cited as the Export and Investment Guarantees Act 1991.

(2) In this Act "the old law" means the Export Guarantees and Overseas Investment Act 1978 and any earlier enactment from which any provision of that Act was derived.

(3) Any power to make an order under section 5 or 6 of this Act shall be exercisable by statutory instrument and no such order shall be made unless a draft of it has been laid before and approved by resolution of the House of Commons.

(4) The Export Guarantees and Overseas Investment Act 1978 is repealed.

(5) Subsection (4) above does not affect any power exercisable by the Secretary of State in respect of arrangements made under the old law.

(6) This Act shall come into force on such day as the Secretary of State may by order made by statutory instrument appoint and different days may be appointed for different provisions and for different purposes.

Section 8   SCHEDULE

SCHEME OF TRANSFER: SUPPLEMENTARY PROVISIONS

Certificate of vesting

1. A certificate by the Secretary of State that anything specified in the certificate has vested on any day in any person by virtue of a scheme under section 8 of this Act shall be conclusive evidence for all purposes of that fact.

Construction of agreements etc.

2.—(1) This paragraph applies to any agreement made, transaction effected or other thing (not contained in an enactment) which—
   (a) has been made, effected or done by, to or in relation to the Secretary of State,
   (b) relates to any property, right or liability transferred from the Secretary of State in accordance with the scheme, and
   (c) is in force or effective immediately before the day on which the scheme comes into force.

(2) The agreement, transaction or other thing shall have effect on and after that day as if made, effected or done by, to or in relation to the transferee.

(3) Accordingly, references to the Secretary of State which relate to or affect any property, right or liability of the Secretary of State vesting by virtue of the scheme in the transferee and which are contained—
   (a) in any agreement (whether or not in writing), deed, bond or instrument,
   (b) in any process or other document issued, prepared or employed for the purpose of any proceeding before a court or other tribunal or authority, or
   (c) in any other document whatever (other than an enactment) relating to or affecting any property, right or liability of the Secretary of State which vests by virtue of the scheme in the transferee,

shall be taken on and after that day to refer to the transferee.

INDEX

References are to section and Schedule numbers

CONSOLIDATED FUND (No. 3) ACT 1991

(1991 c. 68)

An Act to apply certain sums out of the Consolidated Fund to the service of the years ending on 31st March 1992 and 1993.   [19th December 1991]

Parliamentary Debates
Hansard, H.C. Vol. 200, col. 1046; H.L. Vol. 533, col. 1466.

Introduction
This Act provides for the issue of certain sums from the Consolidated Fund for the years ending March 31, 1992 and 1993.

Issue out of the Consolidated Fund for the year ending 31st March 1992

1. The Treasury may issue out of the Consolidated Fund of the United Kingdom and apply towards making good the supply granted to Her Majesty for the service of the year ending on 31st March 1992 the sum of £3,427,284,000.

Issue out of the Consolidated Fund for the year ending 31st March 1993

2. The Treasury may issue out of the Consolidated Fund of the United Kingdom and apply towards making good the supply granted to Her Majesty for the service of the year ending on 31st March 1993 the sum of £75,069,116,000.

Short title

3. This Act may be cited as the Consolidated Fund (No. 3) Act 1991.

INDEX

References are to section numbers

WELSH DEVELOPMENT AGENCY ACT 1991

(1991 c. 69)

An Act to increase the financial limit in section 18(3) of the Welsh Development Agency Act 1975.   [19th December 1991]

PARLIAMENTARY DEBATES
Hansard, H.C. Vol. 199, col. 1093; H.L. Vol. 533, cols. 590, 1194.

INTRODUCTION
This Act provides for the increase in the statutory financial limit of the Welsh Development Agency from £700 million under s.18(3) of the Welsh Development Agency Act 1975 to £950 million. The limit applies to the total cumulative amount of the sums granted to the agency by way of grant-in-aid and public dividend capital (less repayments made by the Agency and excluding sums paid in respect of administrative expenditure), the Agency's outstanding borrowings, third party loans guaranteed by the Agency and any sums issued by the Treasury in consequence of their guaranteeing Agency borrowings which had not been repaid to the Treasury.

Increase of financial limit

1. In section 18(3) of the Welsh Development Agency Act 1975 (financial limit for Agency) for the words "£700 million" there shall be substituted the words "£950 million".

Short title and repeals

2.—(1) This Act may be cited as the Welsh Development Agency Act 1991.

(2) Section 2(2) of the Industry Act 1981 and the Welsh Development Agency Act 1988 (which relate to the financial limit of the Agency and are now superseded) are hereby repealed.

INDEX

References are to section numbers

CARE OF CHURCHES AND ECCLESIASTICAL JURISDICTION MEASURE 1991

(1991 No. 1)

ARRANGEMENT OF SECTIONS

PART I

GENERAL PRINCIPLE

A Measure passed by the General Synod of the Church of England to make provision as to the care of churches and the lands and articles appertaining thereto and of documents of historic interest to the Church of England; to amend the law relating to the inspection of churches; to amend the law relating to ecclesiastical courts, commissions, judges and registrars; to make further provision as to the grant of faculties; to enable bishops to remove the legal effects of consecration; to repeal section 4 of the Parish Notices Act 1837; and for purposes connected therewith.

[25th July 1991]

PART I

GENERAL PRINCIPLE

Duty to have regard to church's purpose

1. Any person or body carrying out functions of care and conservation under this Measure or under any other enactment or rule relating to churches shall have due regard to the role of a church as a local centre of worship and mission.

PART II

CARE, INSPECTION AND ACCOUNTABILITY

Diocesan advisory committees

2.—(1) In every diocese there shall continue to be an advisory committee for the care of churches, to be known as "the Diocesan Advisory Committee".

(2) For each advisory committee there shall be a written constitution provided by the diocesan synod of the diocese concerned, containing the provisions set out in Schedule 1 to this Measure or provisions to the like effect.

(3) The written constitution required by subsection (2) above may include such further provisions consistent with those set out in Schedule 1 to this Measure as the diocesan synod considers appropriate—
(a) in connection with its procedure; or
(b) for the establishment of sub-committees and the delegation thereto of any of its functions.

(4) The written constitution required by subsection (2) above shall be provided as soon as practicable and in any event not later than the expiration of the period of three years immediately following the coming into operation of this section.

(5) The advisory committee shall have the functions specified in Schedule 2 to this Measure and such other functions as may be determined by the diocesan synod of the diocese concerned by resolution; and in carrying out its functions the committee and sub-committees (if any) shall have regard to the rites and ceremonies of the Church of England.

(6) Any expenses incurred for the purpose of giving the advisory committee a written constitution under this section and for enabling it to discharge

its functions properly and effectively shall be paid by the Diocesan Board of Finance for the diocese concerned:

Provided that a Diocesan Board of Finance shall not be liable for any expenses by virtue of this subsection unless the expenses were approved by the Board before they were incurred.

(7) As soon as practicable after the end of each year the advisory committee shall prepare a report of its work and proceedings during that year and cause it to be laid before the diocesan synod of the diocese concerned; and the secretary to the committee shall send a copy of the report to the Council for the Care of Churches.

(8) Section 13 of the 1964 Measure shall cease to have effect, but until such time as the advisory committee is given a written constitution under this section it shall continue to be formed and act in accordance with the provisions contained in that section.

Amendment of Inspection of Churches Measure 1955

3. The Inspection of Churches Measure 1955 shall have effect subject to the amendments specified in Schedule 3 to this Measure.

Duties of churchwardens as to recording of information about churches

4.—(1) In every parish it shall be the duty of the churchwardens—
(a) to compile and maintain—
    (i) a full terrier of all lands appertaining to the church;
    (ii) a full inventory of all articles appertaining to the church;
(b) to insert in a log-book maintained for the purpose a full note of all alterations, additions and repairs to, and other events affecting, the church and the lands and articles appertaining thereto and of the location of any other documents relating to such alterations, additions, repairs and events which are not kept with the log-book.

(2) In carrying out their duty under subsection (1) above the churchwardens shall act in consultation with the minister.

(3) The form of the terrier, inventory and log-book shall accord with such recommendations as the Council for the Care of Churches may make.

(4) The churchwardens shall send a copy of the inventory to such person as the bishop of the diocese concerned may designate from time to time for the purpose of this subsection as soon as practicable after it is compiled and shall notify that person of any alterations at such intervals as the bishop may direct from time to time.

(5) This section applies in relation to each church in a parish containing more than one church.

Duties of churchwardens as to fabric etc. of churches

5.—(1) In every parish it shall be the duty of the churchwardens—
(a) at least once in every year, to inspect or cause an inspection to be made of the fabric of the church and all articles appertaining to the church;
(b) in every year, to deliver to the parochial church council and on behalf of that council to the annual parochial church meeting a report (referred to below as "the annual fabric report") on the fabric of the church and all articles appertaining to the church, having regard to the inspection or inspections carried out under paragraph (a) above, including an account of all actions taken or proposed during the previous year for their protection and maintenance and, in particular, for the implementation of any recommendation contained in a report under a scheme made in pursuance of section 1 of the Inspection of Churches Measure 1955.

(2) In carrying out their duty under subsection (1) above the church-wardens shall act in consultation with the minister.

(3) The annual fabric report shall be delivered to the parochial church council at its meeting next before the annual parochial church meeting and, with such amendments as that council may make, to the ensuing annual parochial church meeting.

(4) The churchwardens shall, as soon as practicable after the beginning of each year, produce to the parochial church council the terrier, the inventory and the log-book relating to events occurring in the previous year and such other records as they consider likely to assist the council in discharging its functions in relation to the fabric of the church and articles appertaining to the church.

(5) Any terrier, inventory or log-book produced to the parochial church council in accordance with subsection (4) above shall be accompanied by a statement, signed by the churchwardens, to the effect that the contents thereof are accurate.

(6) This section applies in relation to each church in a parish containing more than one church.

(7) In this section "year" means calendar year.

Provisions relating to trees in churchyards

6.—(1) The powers, duties and liabilities of a parochial church council with respect to the care and maintenance of churchyards shall extend to trees therein, including those proposed to be planted.

(2) Where a tree in a churchyard maintainable by a parochial church council is felled, lopped or topped the council may sell or otherwise dispose of the timber and the net proceeds of any sale thereof shall be paid to the council and applied for the maintenance of any church or churchyard maintainable by the council.

(3) The chancellor of a diocese shall, after consultation with the advisory committee, give written guidance to all parochial church councils in the diocese as to the planting, felling, lopping and topping of trees in churchyards.

(4) The provisions of section 20 of the Repair of Benefice Buildings Measure 1972 (which relates to the felling etc. of trees) in so far as they relate to trees in churchyards shall cease to have effect.

(5) In this section "churchyard" includes a closed churchyard.

Payment of expenses in connection with ruins

7. Any expenses properly incurred by a parochial church council, with the prior approval in writing of the Diocesan Board of Finance for the diocese concerned, for the purpose of implementing a recommendation contained in a report made in respect of a ruin in pursuance of section 1A(b) of the Inspection of Churches Measure 1955 shall be paid by that Board.

PART III

ECCLESIASTICAL JURISDICTION

Amendment of Ecclesiastical Jurisdiction Measure 1963

8.—(1) The 1963 Measure shall have effect subject to the amendments specified in Schedule 4 to this Measure.

(2) The amendment made by paragraph 2(c)(ii) of that Schedule (which relates to the retirement age of chancellors) shall not have effect in relation to any appointment to the office of chancellor of a diocese made before the coming into operation of that amendment.

Amendment of Ecclesiastical Judges and Legal Officers Measure 1976

9. The Ecclesiastical Judges and Legal Officers Measure 1976 shall have effect subject to the amendments specified in Schedule 5 to this Measure.

Amendment of Ecclesiastical Fees Measure 1986

10. The Ecclesiastical Fees Measure 1986 shall have effect subject to the amendments specified in Schedule 6 to this Measure.

General provisions as to faculty jurisdiction

11.—(1) For the avoidance of doubt and without prejudice to the jurisdiction of consistory courts under any enactment or rule of law, it is hereby declared that the jurisdiction of the consistory court of a diocese applies to all parish churches in the diocese and the churchyards and articles appertaining thereto.

(2) Except as provided by subsection (3) below, a building licensed by the bishop of a diocese after the coming into operation of this section for public worship according to the rites and ceremonies of the Church of England and all articles appertaining thereto shall be subject to the jurisdiction of the consistory court of the diocese as though the building were a consecrated church.

(3) Where the bishop of a diocese, after consultation with the advisory committee, considers that any building in the diocese so licensed should not be subject to the faculty jurisdiction he may by order direct that subsection (2) above shall not apply to the building.

(4) Where the bishop of a diocese, after consultation with the advisory committee, considers that any article appertaining to a building in the diocese so licensed in respect of which an order under subsection (3) above is in force should be subject to the faculty jurisdiction by reason of its being—

    (a) of outstanding architectural, artistic, historical or archaeological value; or

    (b) of significant monetary value; or

    (c) at special risk of being stolen or damaged,

he may by order direct that the article shall be subject to the jurisdiction of the consistory court of the diocese during such period as may be specified in the order.

(5) Any article in respect of which an order under subsection (4) above is in force shall, during the period specified in the order, be subject to the jurisdiction of the court specified in the order as though it were an article appertaining to a consecrated church.

(6) An order under subsection (3) or (4) above may be varied or revoked by an order made by the bishop of the diocese concerned after consultation with the advisory committee.

(7) An order under this section which has the effect of subjecting an article to the faculty jurisdiction shall not render unlawful any act done before the making of the order nor shall require the issue of faculties confirming such acts.

(8) The chancellor of a diocese shall give written guidance to all parochial church councils, ministers and churchwardens in the diocese as to those matters within the jurisdiction of the consistory court which he for the time being considers, after consultation with the advisory committee, to be of such a minor nature that they may be undertaken without a faculty.

Grant of faculties, etc

12.—(1) In any proceedings for obtaining a faculty, the court may grant the faculty subject to conditions, including in particular—

    (a) a condition requiring the work authorised thereby or any part thereof

to be carried out under the supervision of the archdeacon concerned
or of any other person nominated by the court in that behalf;

(b) in the case of a faculty authorising the disposal of an article, a
condition requiring a specified period to elapse before the disposal
takes place.

(2) Where the court grants a faculty to a person other than an archdeacon
and considers that the work authorised thereby should be carried out
(whether or not by that person), it may also order that, in default of that
person carrying out the work, a faculty shall issue to the archdeacon concerned authorising him to carry out the work and, in that event, that the
expenses incurred by the archdeacon in carrying out the work be paid by that
person.

Orders against persons responsible for defaults

13.—(1) Subject to subsection (7) below, if in any proceedings by any
person for obtaining a faculty it appears to the court that any other person
being a party to the proceedings was responsible wholly or in part for any act
or default in consequence of which the proceedings were instituted the court
may order the whole or any part of the costs and expenses of the proceedings
or consequent thereon, including expenses incurred in carrying out any
work authorised by the faculty (so far as such costs and expenses have been
occasioned by that act or default), to be paid by the person responsible.

(2) Subject to subsection (7) below, in any such proceedings the court may
by way of special citation add as a further party to the proceedings any
person alleged to be so responsible or partly responsible and not already a
party and notwithstanding that such person resides outside the diocese
concerned.

(3) A special citation under subsection (2) above may require the person
to whom it is issued to attend the court concerned at such time and place as
may be specified in the citation.

(4) Where at any time (whether before or after faculty proceedings have
been instituted) it appears to the consistory court of a diocese that a person
intends to commit or continue to commit, or cause or permit the commission
or continuance of, any act in relation to a church or churchyard in the
diocese or any article appertaining to a church in the diocese, being an act
which would be unlawful under ecclesiastical law, the court may issue an
injunction restraining the first-mentioned person from committing or continuing to commit that act or from causing or permitting the commission or
continuance of that act, as the case may be.

(5) Where at any time (whether before or after faculty proceedings have
been instituted) it appears to the consistory court of a diocese that a person
has committed, or caused or permitted the commission of, any act in relation
to a church or churchyard in the diocese or any article appertaining to a
church in the diocese which was unlawful under ecclesiastical law, the court
may make an order (a "restoration order") requiring that person to take
such steps as the court may consider necessary, within such time as the court
may specify, for the purpose of restoring the position so far as possible to
that which existed immediately before the act was committed.

(6) An injunction under subsection (4) above may be issued and a restoration order under subsection (5) above may be made on an application made
by the archdeacon concerned or any other person appearing to the court to
have a sufficient interest in the matter or on its own motion.

(7) In any proceedings for obtaining a faculty the court shall not make an
order under subsection (1) above or issue a special citation under subsection
(2) above in respect of any act unless the court is satisfied that the proceedings were instituted less than six years after the act was committed.

(8) The court shall not make a restoration order under subsection (5)
above in respect of any act unless the court is satisfied that less than six years
have elapsed since the act was committed.

(9) Where proceedings for obtaining a faculty are instituted by an archdeacon or an application for a restoration order under subsection (5) above is made by an archdeacon and any fact relevant to the institution of such proceedings or the making of such an application has been deliberately concealed from him the period of six years mentioned in subsection (7) above or, as the case may be, subsection (8) above, shall not begin to run until the archdeacon has discovered the concealment or could with reasonable diligence have discovered it.

(10) For the purpose of subsection (9) above, deliberate commission of a breach of duty in circumstances in which it is unlikely to be discovered for some time amounts to deliberate concealment of the facts involved in that breach of duty.

(11) Failure to comply without reasonable excuse with any requirement of a special citation or injunction issued, or a restoration order made, under this section by any court shall be a contempt of the court.

Delegation to archdeacons of power to grant faculties

14.—(1) Subject to the following provisions of this section the chancellor of a diocese shall confer upon the archdeacon of every archdeaconry in the diocese the jurisdiction of the consistory court of the diocese in such faculty matters relating to the archdeaconry, to such extent and in such manner as may be prescribed.

(2) An archdeacon upon whom such jurisdiction is conferred shall have power to grant a faculty in any cause of faculty falling to be considered by him which is unopposed.

(3) Where, in any cause of faculty falling to be considered by an archdeacon—
   (a) he declines to grant a faculty; or
   (b) he considers that the matter should be dealt with as a matter of urgency without reference to the advisory committee for advice in accordance with section 15(2) below; or
   (c) the grant of a faculty is opposed by any person,
he shall cause the matter to be referred to the chancellor of the diocese concerned to be dealt with by him.

(4) A faculty granted by an archdeacon under subsection (2) above shall have effect as if it had been granted by the chancellor of the diocese concerned.

(5) Nothing in this section shall be construed as enabling an archdeacon to—
   (a) order any costs or expenses to be paid by any person; or
   (b) issue an injunction or make a restoration order against any person; or
   (c) grant an interim faculty pending the final determination of the matter;
and where an archdeacon considers that any question arises as to the payment of costs or expenses, the issue of an injunction, the making of a restoration order or the grant of an interim faculty, he shall cause the matter to be referred to the chancellor of the diocese concerned to be dealt with by him.

(6) A certificate issued by an archdeacon under section 12 of the 1964 Measure before the coming into operation of this section shall continue in force and have effect as if it were a faculty granted under subsection (2) above.

Consultation with diocesan advisory committees

15.—(1) The chancellor of a diocese shall seek the advice of the advisory committee before making a final determination in any cause of faculty or issuing a permanent injunction under section 13(4) above or making a restoration order under section 13(5) above, unless the action proposed relates exclusively to exhumation or the reservation of a grave space or he is satisfied that the matter is sufficiently urgent to justify the grant of a faculty or issue of an injunction without obtaining the committee's advice.

(2) An archdeacon shall seek the advice of the advisory committee before making a final determination in any cause of faculty, unless the action proposed relates exclusively to exhumation or the reservation of a grave space.

(3) In every diocese the secretary to the advisory committee shall compile and maintain a register of all petitions for a faculty referred to the committee for advice under this section, and shall ensure that the register is available for inspection by the public by prior appointment at such place in the diocese as the bishop of the diocese may designate for the purposes of this subsection.

Parties

16.—(1) Proceedings for obtaining a faculty may be instituted by—
(a) the archdeacon of the archdeaconry in which the parish concerned is situated; or
(b) the minister and churchwardens of the parish concerned; or
(c) any other person appearing to the court to have a sufficient interest in the matter.

(2) For the purposes of any proceedings for obtaining a faculty the archdeacon shall be deemed to have an interest as such, and any person whose name is entered on the church electoral roll of the parish concerned but who does not reside therein shall be deemed to have an interest as though he were a parishioner of that parish.

(3) If—
(a) the archdeaconry is vacant; or
(b) the archdeacon is incapacitated by absence or illness from acting; or
(c) in the opinion of the bishop—
(i) the archdeacon is for any other reason unable or unwilling to act; or
(ii) it would be inappropriate for the archdeacon to act,
such other person as the bishop shall appoint in that behalf in writing (either generally or in a particular case) shall have power to act in the place of the archdeacon for the purposes of this Measure or of any other enactment relating to the institution of, or participation in, proceedings in the court.

(4) If the archdeacon or such other person as may be appointed under subsection (3) above institutes or intervenes in any proceedings for obtaining a faculty all costs and expenses properly incurred by him or which he is ordered by the court to pay shall be paid by the Diocesan Board of Finance for the diocese concerned:

Provided that a Diocesan Board of Finance shall not be liable for any sum by virtue of this subsection unless the institution of proceedings or intervention is approved by the bishop of the diocese concerned in writing after consultation with the Board and, if such approval is duly given, any order in the proceedings that the costs or expenses of the archdeacon or other appointed person be paid by any other party may be enforced by the Board in the name of the archdeacon or other appointed person.

(5) Anything done under or for the purposes of section 9 of the 1964 Measure and having effect immediately before the coming into force of this section shall continue to have effect and be deemed to have been done under or for the purposes of this section.

Faculties for demolition of churches

17.—(1) A court shall not grant a faculty for the demolition or partial demolition of a church except on the grounds specified in this section.

(2) Subject to the following provisions of this section, a court may grant a faculty for the demolition of the whole or part of a church if it is satisfied that another church or part of a church will be erected on the site or curtilage of the church or part of a church in question or part thereof to take the place of that church or part of a church.

(3) Subject to the following provisions of this section, a court may grant a faculty for the demolition of part of a church if it is satisfied that—

(a) the part of the church left standing will be used for the public worship of the Church of England for a substantial period after such demolition; or

(b) such demolition is necessary for the purpose of the repair or alteration of the church or the reconstruction of the part to be demolished.

(4) The court shall not grant a faculty under subsection (2) or (3)(a) above unless—

(a) the person bringing proceedings for the faculty has—

(i) obtained the written consent of the bishop of the diocese concerned to the proceedings being brought; and

(ii) within the prescribed time, caused to be published in "The London Gazette" and in such other newspapers as the court may direct a notice stating the substance of the petition for the faculty;

(b) the registrar has given notice in writing to the Council for the Care of Churches and the advisory committee of the diocese concerned of the petition;

(c) the judge of the court has thereafter considered such advice as the advisory committee has tendered to the court; and

(d) the judge has heard evidence in open court, after application for the purpose has been made to the court in the prescribed manner, from—

(i) a member of the said Council or some person duly authorised by the Council; and

(ii) any other person, unless in the opinion of the judge his application or the evidence which he gives is frivolous or vexatious.

(5) Without prejudice to the requirements of subsection (4) above, the court shall not grant a faculty under subsection (2) or (3)(a) above in the case of a church which is a listed building or in a conservation area unless—

(a) the registrar has given notice in writing to—

(i) the Secretary of State;

(ii) the local planning authority concerned;

(iii) the Historic Buildings and Monuments Commission for England; and

(iv) the national amenity societies;

(b) the judge of the court has thereafter considered such advice as any of those bodies may have tendered to the court;

(c) the registrar has given notice in writing to the Royal Commission on the Historical Monuments of England and thereafter either—

(i) for a period of at least one month following the giving of the notice reasonable access to the church has been made available to members or officers of the said Royal Commission for the purpose of recording it; or

(ii) the said Royal Commission have, by their Secretary or other officer of theirs with authority to act on their behalf for the purposes of this section, stated in writing that they have completed their recording of the church or that they do not wish to record it.

(6) A court shall not grant a faculty under subsection (3)(b) above unless—

(a) the court is satisfied, after consultation with the advisory committee, that when the proposed repair, alteration or reconstruction is completed the demolition will not materially affect the external or internal appearance of the church or the architectural, archaeological, artistic or historic character of the church; or

(b) the requirements of subsection (4) above and also, in the case of a church which is a listed building or in a conservation area, the requirements of subsection (5) above have been complied with.

(7) Anything done under or for the purposes of section 2 of the 1964 Measure and having effect immediately before the coming into force of this section shall continue to have effect and be deemed to have been done under or for the purposes of this section.

Emergency demolition of churches

18.—(1) Without prejudice to the powers exercisable under any rule of law by diocesan chancellors at the coming into operation of this section, where the chancellor of a diocese is satisfied—
   (a) that the demolition of the whole or part of a church in the diocese is necessary in the interests of safety or health or for the preservation of the church and, having regard to the urgency of the matter, there is insufficient time to obtain a faculty in respect of it; and
   (b) in the case of a church which is a listed building or is in a conservation area—
         (i) that it is not practicable to secure safety or health or, as the case may be, the preservation of the building by works of repair or works for affording temporary support or shelter; and
         (ii) that the works to be carried out are limited to the minimum measures immediately necessary,
he may by an instrument under his hand authorise the carrying out of the demolition without a faculty.

(2) An instrument under subsection (1) above—
   (a) may require the person to whom it is issued (subject to his obtaining any necessary faculty) to carry out such works for the restoration of the church following its demolition or partial demolition as may be specified in the instrument;
   (b) in the case of partial demolition of a church which is a listed building or is in a conservation area, shall require the person to whom it is issued, as soon as practicable after the works have been carried out, to give to the local planning authority notice in writing describing the works carried out.

(3) Where the chancellor of a diocese issues an instrument under subsection (1) above he shall send a copy of the instrument to the Council for the Care of Churches and the local planning authority.

Meaning of "church"

19. In this Part, unless the context otherwise requires, "church" includes any building which is licensed for public worship according to the rites and ceremonies of the Church of England and is subject to the faculty jurisdiction.

PART IV

MISCELLANEOUS AND GENERAL

Discussion and reporting of defaults

20. If it appears to an archdeacon that—
   (a) anything has been done in a parish in his archdeaconry which ought not to have been done without a faculty; or
   (b) anything which ought to have been done in connection with the care of any church in his archdeaconry or any article appertaining to any such church has not been done,
he may convene an extraordinary meeting of the parochial church council, or an extraordinary parochial church meeting, of the parish concerned for

the purpose of discussing the matter, and shall either take the chair himself or shall appoint a chairman to preside. The chairman, not being otherwise entitled to attend such meeting, shall not be entitled to vote upon any resolution before the meeting.

Deposit of articles in places of safety

21.—(1) If it appears to an archdeacon that any article appertaining to a church in his archdeaconry, being an article which he considers to be of architectural, artistic, historical or archaeological value, is exposed to danger of loss or damage and ought to be removed to a place of safety, he may subject to subsection (2) below order that the article in question shall be removed from the church and deposited in such place of safety as may be specified in the order.

(2) Unless the archdeacon is of the opinion that the article in question should be removed to a place of safety immediately, he shall notify the churchwardens and any other person having custody of the article and the parochial church council and advisory committee of the facts as they appear to the archdeacon and inform them that he will consider any written representations made to him by any of them before a date specified in the notice being a date not less than twenty-eight days after service of the notice; and in that event the archdeacon shall not make an order under this section before that date and shall before making such an order consider any representations duly made to him under this subsection.

(3) Where the archdeacon makes an order under this section without giving the advisory committee an opportunity to make representations to him in connection with the making of the order, he shall, as soon as practicable after the removal of the article in question to a place of safety, notify the committee of the removal.

(4) An order under this section shall be in such form as may be prescribed and shall be directed to, and served on, the churchwardens and any other person having custody of the article in question.

(5) If any person on whom an order made by an archdeacon under this section is served refuses or fails to comply with the order, the archdeacon may apply to the consistory court of the diocese in which the article in question is for an order that that person shall deliver the article to the place of safety specified in the order made by the archdeacon, and the court, if satisfied that that order was made in accordance with the provisions of this section, may make an order accordingly.

(6) Where an order is made by an archdeacon under this section the archdeacon shall, within twenty-eight days after the removal of the article in question to a place of safety, apply to the consistory court of the diocese concerned for a faculty authorising the retention of the article in the place of safety.

(7) In this section "article" does not include a record or register to which section 10(1) of the Parochial Registers and Records Measure 1978 applies.

Power of bishop to remove legal effects of consecration

22.—(1) Where the bishop of a diocese, on the application of the archdeacon of an archdeaconry in the diocese in respect of any building or land in the archdeaconry which is subject to the legal effects of consecration, is satisfied that—
   (a) the building or land is not held or controlled by any ecclesiastical corporation (that is to say, any corporation in the Church of England, whether sole or aggregate, which is established for spiritual purposes) or by any Diocesan Board of Finance; and
   (b) no purpose will be served by its remaining subject to the legal effects of consecration,

he may by order direct that the building or land or part of the building or land shall not be subject to the legal effects of consecration.

(2) Subject to subsection (3) below, an order under subsection (1) above may impose such conditions and requirements as the bishop thinks fit as to—

(a) the preservation or disposal of any human remains believed to be buried in or beneath any building affected by the order or in any land so affected and of any tombstones, monuments or memorials commemorating the deceased persons; and

(b) the maintenance of orderly behaviour in or on the building or land so affected;

and for the purposes of paragraph (a) above such an order may apply to the building or land such provisions of section 65 of and Schedule 6 to the 1983 Measure as may be specified in the order subject to such modifications and adaptations as may be so specified.

(3) A condition or requirement as to a matter falling within paragraph (a) of subsection (2) above shall not be imposed by an order under subsection (1) above except with the consent of the Secretary of State.

(4) Where an order is made under subsection (1) above in respect of any building or land then—

(a) the building or land shall not be subject to the legal effects of consecration; and

(b) in particular, the jurisdiction of any court or person with respect to the granting of faculties shall cease to extend to the building or land.

(5) Any conditions or requirements imposed under subsection (2) above shall be enforceable as if the archdeacon of the archdeaconry in which the building or land affected is situated was the owner of adjacent land and the conditions or requirements were negative covenants expressed to be entered into for the benefit of that adjacent land.

(6) For the purposes of subsection (5) above the enforcement of a condition or requirement shall be deemed to be for the benefit of the archdeacon concerned.

(7) Section 84 (except subsection (2)) of the Law of Property Act 1925 (which enables the Lands Tribunal to discharge or modify restrictions affecting land) shall not apply in relation to conditions and requirements imposed under subsection (2) above.

(8) A condition or requirement imposed by an order under subsection (1) above shall be a local land charge, and for the purposes of the Local Land Charges Act 1975 the bishop by whom the order was made shall be treated as the originating authority as respects the charge constituted by the condition or requirement.

Application of section 22 in relation to Crown land

23.—(1) Subject to subsection (2) below, section 22 above shall apply in relation to Crown land and to buildings situated on Crown land as it applies to other land and buildings.

(2) A condition or requirement as to a matter falling within paragraph (b) of subsection (2) of section 22 above shall not be imposed by an order under subsection (1) of that section relating to Crown land or a building situated on Crown land except with the consent of the appropriate authority.

(3) For the purposes of subsection (2) above any land which is used for the purposes of the Church of England and which will become Crown land on ceasing to be so used or on the exercise of a right of re-entry shall be treated as Crown land.

(4) In this section "Crown land" and "the appropriate authority" have the same meanings as in section 293 of the Town and Country Planning Act 1990; and, if any question arises as to what authority is the appropriate

authority in relation to any land or building, that question shall be referred to the Treasury, whose decision shall be final.

Repeal of s.4 of Parish Notices Act 1837

24. Section 4 of the Parish Notices Act 1837 (decrees, etc. of ecclesiastical courts not to be read in churches) shall cease to have effect.

Rule Committee

25.—(1) There shall be a Rule Committee which shall consist of the following persons, namely—
  (a) a diocesan bishop nominated by the Archbishops of Canterbury and York;
  (b) the Dean of the Arches and Auditor;
  (c) one archdeacon nominated by the Archbishops of Canterbury and York;
  (d) two diocesan chancellors nominated by the Archbishops of Canterbury and York;
  (e) two diocesan registrars nominated by the Archbishops of Canterbury and York;
  (f) one person nominated by the Council for the Care of Churches;
  (g) two persons nominated by the Standing Committee of the House of Laity from among the members of that House,
together with six other persons nominated for particular purposes in accordance with subsection (2) below.

(2) The members of the committee to be nominated for particular purposes shall be as follows—
  (a) for the purpose of making rules relating to proceedings in the Court of Ecclesiastical Causes Reserved or a Commission of Review appointed under section 11 of the 1963 Measure, one person nominated by the Lord Chancellor, being a person who holds or has held high judicial office;
  (b) for the purpose of making rules relating to cathedral churches—
        (i) one person nominated by the Standing Committee of the General Synod, being a person who is a member of the administrative body of a cathedral church;
        (ii) one person nominated by the Cathedrals Fabric Commission from among the members of that Commission, being a person having special knowledge of the conservation of cathedrals;
  (c) for the purpose of making rules relating to proceedings in respect of offences cognisable under section 14 of the 1963 Measure—
        (i) a diocesan bishop nominated by the Archbishops of Canterbury and York (in addition to the bishop nominated under subsection (1)(a) above);
        (ii) the Prolocutor of the Lower House of the Convocation of Canterbury or a member of that House nominated by him;
        (iii) the Prolocutor of the Lower House of the Convocation of York or a member of that House nominated by him.

(3) The quorum of the committee shall be five members, but a member nominated for a particular purpose under subsection (2) above shall not be included in a quorum for any other purpose.

(4) The chairman of the committee shall be the Dean of the Arches and Auditor, unless he declines or is unable to act as such in which case the chairman shall be such other member of the committee as may be nominated by the Dean of the Arches and Auditor after consultation with the Archbishops of Canterbury and York.

(5) Subject to subsection (3) above, the committee may act notwithstanding any vacancy in its membership and may regulate its own procedure.

Functions of Rule Committee

26.—(1) The Rule Committee may make rules for carrying into effect the provisions of—
 (a) this Measure;
 (b) the 1963 Measure;
 (c) the 1964 Measure;
 (d) the Care of Cathedrals Measure 1990;
(hereafter referred to in this section as "the relevant provisions").
 (2) Rules made under subsection (1) above may in particular (so far as the same are not regulated by the relevant provisions or by rules made under section 4 of the Church of England (Legal Aid and Miscellaneous Provisions) Measure 1988) make provision for—
 (a) regulating the procedure and practice (including the mode and burden of proof and admissibility of evidence) of all courts, commissions, committees and examiners provided for in the 1963 Measure or the Care of Cathedrals Measure 1990, including courts of appellate jurisdiction (so far as rules made by the Judicial Committee of the Privy Council do not extend);
 (b) the procedure and practice where archdeacons have jurisdiction in faculty matters under section 14 above;
 (c) the appointment and duties of officers of the said courts, commissions and committees;
 (d) the time within which any act required or permitted to be performed by the relevant provisions is to be performed;
 (e) matters relating to the appointment of authorised complainants and prosecutors in connection with proceedings or contemplated proceedings under the relevant provisions;
 (f) the forms of complaint instituting proceedings under the relevant provisions and of any answers to be made thereto;
 (g) all other forms and notices required in connection with the relevant provisions;
 (h) the mode of effecting service of complaints, articles or other documents including provision for substituted service;
 (i) the fixing of the time and place of any hearing or trial and for notifying the parties thereof;
 (j) the passing of censures and the forms of certificates of findings;
 (k) matters relating to costs, fees and expenses in respect of any proceedings under the relevant provisions;
 (l) enabling evidence to be obtained of compliance with the relevant provisions; and
 (m) any matter which may be prescribed by virtue of the relevant provisions.
 (3) The Rule Committee may also make rules containing provision—
 (a) for enabling a parochial church council, after consultation with the advisory committee of the diocese concerned, to deposit (without a faculty) moveable articles appertaining to a church in the parish concerned for safekeeping in places approved for the purpose by such persons as may be specified in the rules, subject to such requirements, terms and conditions as may be so specified or as may be determined by persons so specified;
 (b) for requiring parochial church councils to keep records of the location of burials carried out in churchyards in their parish and of reserved grave-spaces in respect of which a faculty has been granted;
 (c) for the safe-keeping, care, inspection and preservation of books and other documents (not being register books or records within the meaning of section 25 of the Parochial Registers and Records Measure 1978) which, in the opinion of such person as may be specified in

the rules, are of historic interest to the Church of England, including provision for the appointment of persons with duties in that respect.

Supplementary provisions as to rules

27.—(1) Any rule made under—
(a) section 65 of the 1963 Measure; or
(b) section 14 of the 1964 Measure; or
(c) section 16 of the Care of Cathedrals Measure 1990,
being a rule in force immediately before the coming into force of this section, shall continue in force and be deemed to have been made under section 26 above.

(2) Any rules made under section 26 above shall be laid before the General Synod and shall not come into force until approved by the General Synod, whether with or without amendment.

(3) Where the Standing Committee determines that the rules do not need to be debated by the General Synod then, unless—
(a) notice is given by a member of the General Synod in accordance with its Standing Orders that he wishes the rules to be debated, or
(b) notice is so given by any such member that he wishes to move an amendment to the rules and at least twenty-five other members of the General Synod indicate when the amendment is called that they wish the amendment to be moved,
the rules shall for the purposes of subsection (2) above be deemed to have been approved by the General Synod without amendment.

(4) The Statutory Instruments Act 1946 shall apply to any rules approved by the General Synod under subsection (2) above as if they were statutory instruments and were made when so approved, and as if this Measure were an Act providing that any such rules should be subject to annulment in pursuance of a resolution of either House of Parliament.

General provisions as to orders by bishops

28. The bishop of a diocese shall send every order made by him under this Measure to the registrar of the diocese and the registrar shall register any order so made in the diocesan registry.

Diocesan registrars' fees

29. There shall be payable to a diocesan registrar for registering any order under section 28 above and for permitting searches for and inspection and furnishing copies of any such order such fees as may from time to time be authorised by an order made under Part II of the Ecclesiastical Fees Measure 1986.

Service of notices and orders

30.—(1) Any notice, order or other document required or authorised by this Measure to be served on or sent or given to any person may be served, sent or given by delivering it to him, or by leaving it at his proper address, or by post.

(2) For the purposes of this section and of section 7 of the Interpretation Act 1978 the proper address of the person on or to whom any such notice, order or other document is required or authorised to be served, sent or given shall be the last known address of that person.

Interpretation

31.—(1) In this Measure, unless the context otherwise requires—
"the 1963 Measure" means the Ecclesiastical Jurisdiction Measure 1963;

"the 1964 Measure" means the Faculty Jurisdiction Measure 1964;

"the 1983 Measure" means the Pastoral Measure 1983;

"administrative body"—

(a) in relation to a cathedral church in respect of which there is a corporate body known as the dean and chapter, means the body by which administrative functions in relation to the cathedral church are performed by virtue of paragraph (b) of section 7 of the Cathedrals Measure 1963;

(b) in relation to any other cathedral church, means the body by which administrative functions in relation to the cathedral church are performed by virtue of paragraph (b) of section 8 of that Measure;

"advisory committee" in relation to a diocese or archdeaconry means the Diocesan Advisory Committee of the diocese or of the diocese in which the archdeaconry is situated, as the case may be;

"article" includes part of an article and any thing affixed to land or a building;

"building" includes any structure or erection, and any part of a building as so defined;

"Cathedrals Fabric Commission" means the Cathedrals Fabric Commission for England;

"conservation area" has the same meaning as in the Planning (Listed Buildings and Conservation Areas) Act 1990;

"Council for the Care of Churches" means the body so named at the passing of this Measure or any body subsequently exercising the functions of that body under a different name or with a different constitution;

"Diocesan Board of Finance" has the same meaning as in the Endowments and Glebe Measure 1976;

"high judicial office" has the meaning assigned to it by section 25 of the Appellate Jurisdiction Act 1876;

"inventory" means the inventory maintained under section 4(1) above;

"land" includes buildings;

"listed building" has the same meaning as in the Planning (Listed Buildings and Conservation Areas) Act 1990;

"local planning authority" in relation to any area means the body exercising the functions of a local planning authority under section 8 of the Planning (Listed Buildings and Conservation Areas) Act 1990 in that area;

"log-book" means the log-book maintained under section 4(1) above;

"minister", in relation to a parish, means—

(a) in a case where a special cure of souls in respect of the parish has been assigned to a vicar in a team ministry by a scheme under the 1983 Measure or by his licence from the bishop, that vicar;

(b) in any other case—

(i) the incumbent of the benefice comprising the parish; or

(ii) a curate licensed to the charge of the parish or a minister acting as priest-in-charge of the parish, where rights of presentation are suspended;

"national amenity society" means any of the following, the Ancient Monuments Society, the Council for British Archaeology, the Georgian Group, the Society for the Protection of Ancient Buildings, the Victorian Society and such other body as may from time to time be designated by the Dean of the Arches and Auditor as a national amenity society for the purpose of this Measure;

"parish" means—

(a) an ecclesiastical parish; and

(b) a district which is constituted a "conventional district" for the cure of souls;

"parish church" does not include a parish church cathedral to which the Care of Cathedrals Measure 1990 applies;

"place of worship" includes the curtilage of a place of worship;

"prescribed" means prescribed by rules made under section 26 above;

"Rule Committee" means the Rule Committee established under section 25 above;

"terrier" means the terrier maintained under section 4(1) above.

(2) In Parts I, II and IV of this Measure "church" means—

(a) any parish church;

(b) any other church or chapel (not being a cathedral church to which the Care of Cathedrals Measure 1990 applies or chapel which is not subject to the jurisdiction of the bishop of a diocese or the Cathedral Church of Christ in Oxford) which has been consecrated for the purpose of public worship according to the rites and ceremonies of the Church of England; and

(c) any building licensed for public worship according to the rites and ceremonies of the Church of England other than—

(i) a building which is in a university, college, school, hospital or public or charitable institution but which has not been designated under section 29(2) of the 1983 Measure as a parish centre of worship;

(ii) a building which has been excluded from the provisions of Parts II and IV of this Measure by direction of the bishop of the diocese concerned with the approval of the advisory committee; and

(iii) a building used solely for the purpose of religious services relating to burial or cremation.

(3) In this Measure references to work authorised by a faculty shall be construed as including a reference to work ordered by a faculty.

(4) In this Measure references to the consistory court of a diocese and to the chancellor of a diocese shall, in their application to the diocese of Canterbury, be construed as references to the commissary court thereof and to the commissary general of such court respectively.

(5) Any reference in any enactment to an advisory committee for the care of churches appointed under section 13 of the 1964 Measure shall be construed as including a committee constituted under section 2 above.

(6) Nothing in this Measure shall be construed as prejudicing or affecting the provisions of the Ancient Monuments and Archaeological Areas Act 1979, the Town and Country Planning Act 1990 or the Planning (Listed Buildings and Conservation Areas) Act 1990 or any instrument made thereunder.

Amendments and repeals

32.—(1) The enactments specified in Schedule 7 to this Measure shall have effect subject to the amendments specified in that Schedule, being minor amendments or amendments of a consequential nature.

(2) The enactments specified in Schedule 8 to this Measure are hereby repealed to the extent specified in the third column of that Schedule.

Citation, commencement and extent

33.—(1) This Measure may be cited as the Care of Churches and Ecclesiastical Jurisdiction Measure 1991.

(2) This Measure shall come into operation on such date as the Archbishops of Canterbury and York may jointly appoint, and different dates may be appointed for different provisions.

(3) This Measure shall extend to the whole of the provinces of Canterbury and York except the Channel Islands and the Isle of Man, but the provisions thereof may be applied to the Channel Islands as defined in the Channel Islands (Church Legislation) Measures 1931 and 1957, or either of them, in accordance with those Measures and if an Act of Tynwald or an instrument made under an Act of Tynwald so provides, shall extend to the Isle of Man subject to such modifications, if any, as may be specified in such Act of Tynwald or other instrument.

SCHEDULES

Section 2(2)   SCHEDULE 1

PROVISIONS TO BE INCLUDED IN DIOCESAN ADVISORY COMMITTEE CONSTITUTIONS

Name

1. The committee shall be known as the [name of diocese concerned] Diocesan Advisory Committee.

Membership

2. The committee shall consist of a chairman, the archdeacons of the diocese and not less than twelve other members.

3. The chairman shall be appointed by the bishop of the diocese after consultation with the bishop's council, the chancellor and the Council for the Care of Churches.

4. The other members shall be—
(a) two persons appointed by the bishop's council of the diocese from among the elected members of the diocesan synod of the diocese;
(b) not less than ten other persons appointed by the bishop's council of the diocese, of whom one shall be appointed after consultation with the Historic Buildings and Monuments Commission for England, one shall be appointed after consultation with the relevant associations of local authorities and one shall be appointed after consultation with the national amenity societies;
(c) such other persons as may be co-opted under paragraph 12 below.

5. In making appointments under paragraph 4(b) above, the bishop's council shall ensure that the persons appointed have, between them,—
(a) knowledge of the history, development and use of church buildings;
(b) knowledge of Church of England liturgy and worship;
(c) knowledge of architecture, archaeology, art and history; and
(d) experience of the care of historic buildings and their contents.

6. The first appointment of the chairman and other members of the committee under paragraph 4(a) and (b) above shall take place as soon as practicable, and subsequent new appointments of the chairman and those members shall be made within the period of one year following the formation of the second new diocesan synod after the latest appointments.

7. The term of office of the chairman and any other member of the committee appointed under paragraph 4(a) or (b) above shall be the period from his appointment to the making of new appointments in accordance with paragraph 6 above.

8. A member of the committee who ceases to hold a qualification by virtue of which he became a member shall thereupon cease to be a member.

9. A member of the committee who ceases to hold office otherwise than by virtue of paragraph 8 above shall be eligible for re-appointment.

10. Where a casual vacancy occurs among the chairman and other members of the committee appointed under paragraph 4(a) or (b) above, the bishop shall appoint a person to fill the vacancy, and if the person whose place is to be filled was a member of the committee by virtue of his membership of the diocesan synod of the diocese the person so appointed shall also be a member of that diocesan synod.

11. Any person appointed to fill a casual vacancy shall hold office only for the unexpired portion of the term of office of the person in whose place he is appointed.

12. With the consent of the bishop of the diocese, the committee may from time to time co-opt such persons (of a number not exceeding one third of the total number of the other members) as it thinks fit to be additional members of the committee, but any person so co-opted shall cease to be a member of the committee on the making of new appointments of members in accordance with paragraph 6 above.

Miscellaneous

13. The bishop of the diocese may appoint suitably qualified persons to act as consultants to the committee if the committee request him to do so.

14. The secretary to the committee shall be appointed by the bishop of the diocese after consultation with the chairman of the committee and the chief administrative officer of the diocese.

15. In this constitution "national amenity society" has the same meaning as in the Care of Churches and Ecclesiastical Jurisdiction Measure 1991.

In paragraph 4(b) above "relevant associations of local authorities" means such associations as may from time to time be designated by the Dean of the Arches and Auditor as the relevant associations of local authorities for the purposes of this Schedule in relation to the diocese concerned.

Section 2(5)　　　　　　　　　　　SCHEDULE 2

FUNCTIONS OF DIOCESAN ADVISORY COMMITTEE

1. The functions of a Diocesan Advisory Committee shall be—
(a) to act as an advisory body on matters affecting places of worship in the diocese and, in particular, to give advice when requested by any of the persons specified in paragraph 2 below on matters relating to—
   (i) the grant of faculties;
   (ii) the architecture, archaeology, art and history of places of worship;
   (iii) the use, care, planning, design and redundancy of places of worship;
   (iv) the use and care of the contents of such places;
   (v) the use and care of churchyards and burial grounds;
(b) to review and assess the degree of risk to materials, or of loss to archaeological or historic remains or records, arising from any proposals relating to the conservation, repair or alteration of places of worship, churchyards and burial grounds and the contents of such places;
(c) to develop and maintain a repository of records relating to the conservation, repair and alteration of places of worship, churchyards and burial grounds and other material (including inspection reports, inventories, technical information and photographs) relating to the work of the committee;
(d) to issue guidance for the preparation and storage of such records;
(e) to make recommendations as to the circumstances when the preparation of such a record should be made a condition of a faculty;
(f) to take action to encourage the care and appreciation of places of worship, churchyards and burial grounds and the contents of such places, and for that purpose to publicise methods of conservation, repair, construction, adaptation and re-development;
(g) to perform such other functions as may be assigned to the committee by any enactment, by any Canon of the Church of England or by resolution of the diocesan synod or as the committee may be requested to perform by the bishop or chancellor of the diocese.

2. The persons referred to in paragraph 1(a) above are—
(a) the bishop of the diocese;
(b) the chancellor of the diocese;
(c) the archdeacons of the diocese;
(d) the parochial church councils in the diocese;
(e) intending applicants for faculties in the diocese;
(f) the pastoral committee of the diocese;
(g) persons engaged in the planning, design or building of new places of worship in the diocese, not being places within the jurisdiction of the consistory court;
(h) such other persons as the committee may consider appropriate.

Section 3　　　　　　　　　　　SCHEDULE 3

AMENDMENT OF INSPECTION OF CHURCHES MEASURE 1955

1. The Inspection of Churches Measure 1955 shall be amended as follows.

2. In subsection (2) of section 1 (which provides for the establishment of schemes for the inspection of churches)—
(a) in paragraph (c) for the words "an architect or architects" there shall be inserted the words "a qualified person or persons";
(b) in paragraph (d) for the words "and to the parochial church council of the parish" there shall be substituted the words ", to the parochial church council of the parish in which the

church is situate and to the incumbent of the benefice comprising that parish and to the secretary of the advisory committee of the diocese".

3. After section 1 there shall be inserted the following sections:—

"Inspections to extend to certain valuable articles, etc

1A. Where, in accordance with a scheme established under section 1 of this Measure, a person inspects a church the inspection shall extend to—

(a) any movable article in the church which he is directed by the archdeacon concerned, after consultation with the advisory committee, to treat as being, and such other articles as the person inspecting the church considers to be,—

(i) of outstanding architectural, artistic, historical or archaeological value; or

(ii) of significant monetary value; or

(iii) at special risk of being stolen or damaged;

(b) any ruin in the churchyard (open or closed) which is for the time being designated by the Council for British Archaeology and the Royal Commission on the Historical Monuments of England acting jointly as being of outstanding architectural, artistic, historical or archaeological value;

(c) any tree in the churchyard (open or closed) belonging to the church in respect of which a tree preservation order under the Town and Country Planning Act 1990 is for the time being in force,

and references in this Measure to the inspection of a church shall be construed accordingly.

Duty of bishops to establish schemes

1B.—(1) Where, for any diocese to which this Measure applies, a scheme has not been made in pursuance of section 1 of this Measure it shall be the duty of the bishop of the diocese to establish a scheme for the purpose specified in subsection (1) of that section complying with the provisions of subsection (2)(a) to (d) thereof and containing such other provisions not inconsistent with this Measure as the bishop shall think fit.

(2) Any scheme made in pursuance of this section shall, for the purposes of this Measure (except section 1(4)), be deemed to have been made in pursuance of section 1 of this Measure.".

4. In section 2 (which empowers the archdeacon to ensure the inspection of churches every five years)—

(a) in subsection (1) for the words "an architect" there shall be substituted the words "a qualified person";

(b) at the end there shall be inserted the following subsection:—

"(3) For the purposes of this section any reference to a church shall be construed as including a reference to any movable article in a church which the archdeacon concerned, after consultation with the advisory committee, considers to be—

(a) of outstanding architectural, artistic, historic or archaeological value; or

(b) of significant monetary value; or

(c) at special risk of being stolen or damaged."

5. In section 6 (interpretation)—

(a) after the definition of "the bishop" there shall be inserted the following definition:—

" "church" means—

(a) any parish church other than one to which the Care of Cathedrals Measure 1990 applies;

(b) any other church or chapel (not being a cathedral church to which the Care of Cathedrals Measure 1990 applies or a church or chapel which is not subject to the jurisdiction of the bishop of a diocese or the Cathedral Church of Christ in Oxford) which has been consecrated for the purpose of public worship according to the rites and ceremonies of the Church of England; and

(c) any building licensed for public worship according to the rites and ceremonies of the Church of England other than—

(i) a building which is in a university, college, school, hospital or public or charitable institution but which has not been designated under section 29(2) of the 1983 Measure as a parish centre of worship;

(ii) a building which has been excluded from the provisions of this Measure by direction of the bishop with the approval of the advisory committee; and

(iii) a building used solely for the purpose of religious services relating to burial or cremation;";

(b) at the end there shall be inserted the following definitions:—

" "qualified person" means a person registered under the Architects Registration Acts 1931 to 1969 or a member of the Royal Institution of Chartered Surveyors qualified as a chartered building surveyor;
"ruin" means any site comprising the remains of any building above the surface of the land, not being—
(a) a monument (within the meaning of section 3 of the Faculty Jurisdiction Measure 1964); or
(b) a site which is for the time being used for the purpose of public worship according to the rites and ceremonies of the Church of England".

Section 8   SCHEDULE 4

AMENDMENT OF ECCLESIASTICAL JURISDICTION MEASURE 1963

1. The Ecclesiastical Jurisdiction Measure 1963 shall be amended as follows.
2. In section 2 (judge of consistory court)—
(a) after subsection (1) there shall be inserted the following subsection—
"(1A) Before appointing a person to be chancellor of a diocese the bishop shall consult the Lord Chancellor and the Dean of the Arches and Auditor.";
(b) in subsection (2) after the words "barrister at law" there shall be inserted the words "or solicitor";
(c) in subsection (4)—
(i) for the words "the last foregoing subsection" there shall be substituted the words "subsections (3) and (4A) of this section";
(ii) for the words "of seventy-five years" in both places where they occur there shall be substituted the words "at which a Circuit judge is obliged to vacate that office";
(d) after subsection (4) there shall be inserted the following subsection—
"(4A) Where the bishop of a diocese considers it desirable in the interests of the diocese to retain the chancellor of the diocese in office after the time at which he would otherwise retire in accordance with subsection (4) above, he may from time to time authorise the continuance in office of the chancellor until such date, not being later than the date on which the chancellor attains the age at which a puisne judge of the High Court is obliged to vacate that office, as he thinks fit.".
3. In section 3 (judges of the Arches and Chancery Courts)—
(a) in subsection (1) for the words "five in number" there shall be substituted the words "as set out in subsection (2) of this section";
(b) in subsection (2) at the end there shall be inserted the following paragraph—
"(d) the others shall be all the diocesan chancellors appointed under section 2 of this Measure (in whichever province), except the chancellor of the diocese in Europe;";
in subsection (3) after the word "who" there shall be inserted the words "holds or"(c)
(d) in subsection (5) after the words "The appointment of any person" there shall be inserted the words "under paragraph (a), (b) or (c) of subsection (2) of this section";
(e) in subsection (6) for the words from the beginning to "his office" there shall be substituted the words "The Dean of the Arches and Auditor and every chancellor of a diocese shall, before he enters on the execution of his office as a judge of the said Courts";
(f) in subsection (7) for the words from the beginning to "appointed" there shall be substituted the words "A person appointed under paragraph (b) or (c) of subsection (2) of this section".
4. In section 4 (appointment of deputy judges)—
(a) in subsection (1)—
(i) for the words from the beginning to "any chancellor" there shall be inserted the words "Where the Dean of the Arches and Auditor or any chancellor is for any reason unable to act as such, or the office of the Dean or any chancellor is vacant";
(ii) for the words "such illness or incapacity" there shall be substituted the words "the period of inability or vacancy";
(iii) for the words "person for whom he is appointed to act" there shall be substituted the words "office in respect of which he is appointed to act as deputy";
(b) after subsection (1) there shall be inserted the following subsection—
"(1A) The Dean of the Arches and Auditor or any chancellor may, with the consent of the Archbishops of Canterbury and York in the former case, and the bishop of the diocese concerned in the latter, appoint a fit and proper person to act as deputy Dean of the Arches and Auditor or deputy chancellor of such diocese as the case may be for such period not exceeding twelve months or for such purpose as may be specified in the instrument of

appointment, and during that period or for that purpose every person so appointed shall have all the powers and perform all the duties of the office in respect of which he is appointed to act as deputy.";

(c) in subsection (2) for the word "subsection" there shall be substituted the word "subsections".

5. In section 6 (jurisdiction of the consistory court) in subsection (1) after paragraph (b) there shall be inserted the following paragraph—

"(bb) proceedings for an injunction or restoration order under section 13 of the Care of Churches and Ecclesiastical Jurisdiction Measure 1991;".

6. In section 7 (jurisdiction of Arches and Chancery Courts)—

(a) in subsection (1) at the end there shall be inserted the words—

"or (c) in proceedings for an injunction under section 13(4) of the Care of Churches and Ecclesiastical Jurisdiction Measure 1991 or for a restoration order under section 13(5) of that Measure,

and from interlocutory orders of those consistory courts in causes of faculty involving matter of doctrine, ritual or ceremonial;

(b) in subsection (2) at the end there shall be inserted the words "but in a civil suit only with the leave of the consistory court or, if leave is refused by that court, of the Dean of the Arches and Auditor".

7. In section 10 (jurisdiction of Court of Ecclesiastical Causes Reserved)—

(a) in subsection (3) the words "and such certificate shall be conclusive" shall be omitted;

(b) at the end there shall be inserted the following subsections—

"(4) In any proceedings in the Court of Ecclesiastical Causes Reserved on an appeal from a judgment, order or decree of a consistory court of a diocese given, made or pronounced in a cause of faculty, the court—

(a) if it considers that it has heard and determined the appeal in so far as it relates to matter involving doctrine, ritual or ceremonial but that the appeal relates also to other matter, may, if it considers it expedient to do so, deal with the other matter, but otherwise shall refer it, and

(b) if it considers that no matter of doctrine, ritual or ceremonial is involved, shall refer the appeal (notwithstanding any certificate to the contrary issued under subsection (3) of this section),

to the Arches Court of Canterbury or the Chancery Court of York, as appropriate, to be heard and determined by that court.

(5) In any proceedings in the Arches Court of Canterbury or the Chancery Court of York on an appeal from a judgment, order or decree of a consistory court of a diocese given, made or pronounced in a cause of faculty, the court may, if it considers that the appeal relates to matter involving doctrine, ritual or ceremonial, refer the appeal (notwithstanding any certificate to the contrary issued under subsection (3) of this section) to the Court of Ecclesiastical Causes Reserved to be heard and determined by that court.

(6) Subject to any rules made under section 26 of the Care of Churches and Ecclesiastical Jurisdiction Measure 1991, any reference of an appeal under subsection (4) or (5) of this section shall be in accordance with such practice directions as may be issued jointly by the Dean of the Arches and Auditor and the two judges of the Court of Ecclesiastical Causes Reserved appointed in accordance with section 5 of this Measure by virtue of their holding, or having held, high judicial office.".

8. In section 47 (proceedings in Arches and Chancery Courts) for subsection (1) there shall be substituted the following subsection—

"(1) Proceedings in the Arches Court of Canterbury or the Chancery Court of York shall be heard and disposed of—

(a) in the case of an appeal from a judgment of the consistory court of a diocese given in such proceedings as are mentioned in section 6(1)(a) of this Measure, by all the judges of the Court mentioned in paragraphs (a), (b) and (c) of section 3(2) of this Measure;

(b) in any other case, by the Dean of the Arches and Auditor and two diocesan chancellors designated by him for the purposes of the case.".

9. In section 60 (powers of courts and commissions in regard to costs) at the end there shall be inserted the following subsections—

"(5) Where an order for payment of taxed costs has been made under subsection (2) of this section any party to the proceedings may appeal to the chancellor of the diocese in which the proceedings took place against the registrar's taxation, and on any such appeal the chancellor may confirm or vary the registrar's taxation.

(6) An appeal under subsection (5) of this section shall be lodged and conducted in such manner as may be prescribed."

10. In section 66(1) (interpretation) in the definition of "prescribed" for the words "this Measure" there shall be substituted the words "section 26 of the Care of Churches and Ecclesiastical Jurisdiction Measure 1991".

11. In section 81 (evidence and general powers and rights of courts and commissions) for subsections (2) and (3) there shall be substituted the following subsections—

"(2) If any person does or omits to do anything in connection with proceedings before, or with an order made by, such court or commission which is in contempt of that court or commission by virtue of any enactment or which would, if the court or commission had been a court of law having power to commit for contempt, have been in contempt of that court, the judge or presiding judge of the court or the presiding member of the commission, as the case may be, may certify the act or omission under his hand to the High Court.

(3) On receiving a certificate under subsection (2) above the High Court may thereupon inquire into the alleged act or omission and after hearing any witnesses who may be produced against or on behalf of the person who is the subject of the allegation, and after hearing any statement that may be offered in defence, exercise the same jurisdiction and powers as if that person had been guilty of contempt of the High Court.

(4) In this section "order" includes a special citation under subsection (2) of section 13 of the Care of Churches and Ecclesiastical Jurisdiction Measure 1991 and an injunction under subsection (4) of that section.".

Section 9   SCHEDULE 5

AMENDMENT OF ECCLESIASTICAL JUDGES AND LEGAL OFFICERS MEASURE 1976

1. The Ecclesiastical Judges and Legal Officers Measure 1976 shall be amended as follows.
2. In section 3 (office of registrar of a province)—
(a) after subsection (4) there shall be inserted the following subsections—

"(4A) The registrar of a province may, with the consent of the archbishop of the province, appoint a fit and proper person to act as deputy registrar of the province for such period and for such purpose as may be specified in the instrument of appointment; and during that period and for that purpose a person so appointed shall have all the powers and duties of the registrar.

(4B) Where the registrar of a province ceases to hold that office, a person appointed to act as deputy registrar under subsection (4A) above shall cease to hold that office when a new registrar is appointed.

(4C) If, in the opinion of the archbishop of the province concerned, the registrar of the province is for any reason unable or unwilling to perform the duties of a registrar or it would be inappropriate for him to perform those duties and there is no person appointed to act as deputy registrar under subsection (4A) above able to perform those duties, the archbishop may request the registrar of the other province to appoint a fit and proper person to perform those duties for such period as the instrument of appointment may specify; and during that period a person so appointed shall have all the powers and duties of the registrar of the first-mentioned province.";
(b) in subsection (5) after the word "office" there shall be inserted the words "or to act as deputy registrar".

3. In section 4 (office of the registrar of a diocese) at the end there shall be inserted the following subsections—

"(5A) The registrar of a diocese may, with the consent of the bishop of the diocese, appoint a fit and proper person to act as deputy registrar of the diocese for such period and for such purpose as may be specified in the instrument of appointment; and during that period and for that purpose a person so appointed shall have all the powers and duties of the registrar.

(5B) Where the registrar of a diocese ceases to hold that office, a person appointed to act as deputy registrar under subsection (5A) above shall cease to hold that office when a new registrar is appointed.

(5C) If, in the opinion of the bishop of the diocese concerned, the registrar of the diocese is for any reason unable or unlikely to perform the duties of a registrar or it would be inappropriate for him to perform those duties and there is no person appointed to act as deputy registrar under subsection (5A) above able to perform those duties, the bishop may request the registrar of the province within which the diocese is situated to appoint a fit and proper person to perform those duties for such period as the instrument of appointment may specify; and during that period a person so appointed shall have all the powers and duties of the registrar of the diocese.

(5D) If the registrar of the diocese concerned is also the registrar of the province within which the diocese is situated the reference in subsection (5C) above to the registrar of the province within which the diocese is situated shall be construed as a reference to the registrar of the other province.".

Section 10   SCHEDULE 6

<small>AMENDMENT OF ECCLESIASTICAL FEES MEASURE 1986</small>

1. The Ecclesiastical Fees Measure 1986 shall be amended as follows.
2. In section 5 (Legal Officers (Annual Fees) Orders)—
(a) in subsection (1)—
> (i) after the words "paid to" there shall be inserted the words "ecclesiastical judges and";
> (ii) the words "(to be known as a "Legal Officers (Annual Fees) Order")" shall be omitted;
(b) in subsection (2) at the end there shall be inserted the words ", including provision for payments in respect of reasonable expenses incurred by ecclesiastical judges and legal officers on travel, subsistence, accommodation and the holding of court hearings";
(c) in subsections (4) and (5) for the words "a Legal Officers (Annual Fees) Order" in both places where they occur there shall be substituted the words "an order made under subsection (1) above".
3. In section 6 (Ecclesiastical Judges and Legal Officers (Fees) Orders)—
(a) in subsection (1) for the words from "(not, in the case of legal officers" to the end there shall be substituted the words "to such persons as are so specified, and the Commission may make an order to give effect to their recommendations";
(b) in subsection (2) at the end there shall be inserted the words ", including provision for payments to be made in respect of reasonable expenses incurred by ecclesiastical judges and legal officers on travel, subsistence, accommodation and the holding of court hearings".
4. In section 10 (interpretation)—
(a) in the definition of "ecclesiastical judges" at the end there shall be inserted the words ", and the deputies of any of them";
(b) in the definition of "legal officers" at the end there shall be inserted the words ", and the deputy provincial and diocesan registrars".

Section 32(1)   SCHEDULE 7

<small>MINOR AND CONSEQUENTIAL AMENDMENTS</small>

Faculty Jurisdiction Measure 1964

1. In section 4 of the Faculty Jurisdiction Measure 1964—
(a) in subsection (1) the words "appropriated to the use of any parish or place" shall be omitted;
(b) in subsection (2) the words "and is so appropriated" shall be omitted.
2. In section 6(1) of that Measure after the word "has" there shall be inserted the words ", before the coming into force of section 11 of the Care of Churches and Ecclesiastical Jurisdiction Measure 1991,".
3. In section 15 of that Measure—
(a) after the definition of "bishop" there shall be inserted the following definition—
> " 'church' includes any building or part of a building which is licensed for public worship according to the rites and ceremonies of the Church of England and is subject to the faculty jurisdiction;";
(b) in the definition of "prescribed" for the words "section fourteen of this Measure" there shall be substituted the words "section twenty-six of the Care of Churches and Ecclesiastical Jurisdiction Measure 1991".

Synodical Government Measure 1969

4. In Schedule 3 to the Synodical Government Measure 1969 (Church Representation Rules)—
(a) in rule 8(1) in sub-paragraph (f), at the end there shall be inserted the words ", under section 5 of the Care of Churches and Ecclesiastical Jurisdiction Measure 1991";
(b) in rule 24(2)(a)(vii) and (3)(a)(ii) after the word "finance" there shall be inserted in both places the words "and the chairman of the diocesan advisory committee".

Pastoral Measure 1983

5. In section 56(3) of the Pastoral Measure 1983 at the end there shall be inserted the following paragraph—

"(c) affect the power of the bishop of a diocese under section 22 of the Care of Churches and Ecclesiastical Jurisdiction Measure 1991 to make an order directing that a building or land shall not be subject to the legal effects of consecration".

Care of Cathedrals Measure 1990

6. In section 20(1) of the Care of Cathedrals Measure 1990 in the definition of "prescribed" for the words "section 16 of this Measure" there shall be substituted the words "section 26 of the Care of Churches and Ecclesiastical Jurisdiction Measure 1991".

Section 32(2)   SCHEDULE 8

ACT AND MEASURES REPEALED

Chapter	Short title	Extent of repeal
7 Will 4 & 1 Vict c.45.	Parish Notices Act 1837.	Section 4.
1963 No. 1	Ecclesiastical Jurisdiction Measure 1963.	Section 64. Section 65.
1964 No. 5	The Faculty Jurisdiction Measure 1964.	Section 2. In section 4, in subsection (1) the words "appropriated to the use of the minister of the parish or place" and in subsection (2) the words "and is so appropriated". Section 5. Section 9. Section 10. Section 12. Section 13. Section 14. Schedule
1972 No. 2	The Repair of Benefice Buildings Measure 1972.	In section 20, in subsection (1) the words from "and the timber growing" to "such consent", subsections (3) and (4) and in subsection (6) the words from ", in the case of timber in a churchyard" to "in other cases".
1978 No. 3	The Church of England (Miscellaneous Provisions) Measure 1978.	Section 9.
1990 No. 2	Care of Cathedrals Measure 1990.	Section 16.

DIOCESAN BOARDS OF EDUCATION MEASURE 1991

(1991 No. 2)

A Measure passed by the General Synod of the Church of England to make provision as to Diocesan Boards of Education.   [12th July 1991]

Diocesan Boards of Education

1.—(1) For every diocese there shall be a Diocesan Board of Education which shall have the functions assigned to it by this Measure and shall be responsible to the diocesan synod; and references in this Measure to "the Board" shall be construed as referring to the Diocesan Board of Education for the diocese concerned.

(2) The Board shall be constituted in accordance with the provisions of Part I of the Schedule to this Measure, except that if the diocesan synod resolve that instead of being so constituted the Board shall be constituted in accordance with provisions agreed by that synod, the diocesan synod may with the consent of the bishop request the Secretary of State to make an order for the Board to be constituted in accordance with that resolution, and the Secretary of State upon receiving such a request may if he thinks fit make an order accordingly.

(3) The Secretary of State may amend or revoke an order made under subsection (2) above only upon a request made by the diocesan synod with the consent of the bishop of the diocese, and the amendment or revocation shall be in accordance with the resolution of that synod.

(4) The bishop, after consultation with the Board, shall appoint a director of education for the diocese who shall act as secretary of the Board.

(5) The Board may be a body corporate or unincorporate.

(6) The provisions of Part II of the Schedule to this Measure shall have effect with respect to the proceedings of the Board, whether the Board is constituted in accordance with the provisions of Part I of that Schedule or an order made by the Secretary of State.

Functions of Board

2.—(1) The functions of the Board shall be—

(a) to promote or assist in the promotion of education in the diocese, being education which is consistent with the faith and practice of the Church of England;

(b) to promote or assist in the promotion of religious education and religious worship in schools in the diocese;

(c) to promote or assist in the promotion of church schools in the diocese and to advise the governors of such schools and trustees of church educational endowments and any other body or person concerned on any matter affecting church schools in the diocese;

(d) to promote cooperation between the Board and bodies or persons concerned in any respect with education in the diocese;

(e) the functions assigned to the Board by this Measure; and

(f) such other functions not contrary to this Measure as are assigned to the Board by the diocesan synod, other than functions relating to church schools or church educational endowments.

(2) The Board shall have power to do all such things as are incidental or conducive to the discharge of its functions.

(3) The Board shall make to the diocesan synod, as soon as may be after the end of each year, a report on the exercise of its functions since the last report or (in the case of the first) since the Board's establishment.

Transactions for which advice or consent of Board is required

3.—(1) The governing body of any church school, and the trustees of any church educational endowment held wholly or partly for or in connection with any church school, shall obtain the advice of the Board for the diocese in which the school is situated and shall have regard to that advice before making any application to or entering into any agreement or arrangement with any body or person for or in connection with the discontinuance of the school, any change in the status, size or character of the school, significant enlargement of its premises, any disposal (whether by sale or otherwise) of the premises of the school or any part thereof, or any amalgamation of that school with any other school.

(2) Subject to subsection (3) below, the governing body of any church school which is an aided or special agreement school shall not, unless it has obtained the consent in writing of the Board for the diocese in which the school is situated, enter into any agreement or arrangement with any body or person for or in connection with any alteration or repair of the premises of the school, being an alteration or repair in respect of which grant may be paid by the Secretary of State or of which the approval of the Secretary of State is required before it is carried out.

(3) Subsection (2) above shall not apply in relation to any alteration or repair of premises of which the estimated cost is less than such amount as may from time to time be determined by the Board for the diocese in which the school is situated.

(4) In the case of any Church of England voluntary school which is eligible for grant-maintained status, if the governing body decides by a resolution passed under paragraph (a) of section 60(1) of the 1988 Act to hold a ballot of parents on the question of whether grant-maintained status should be sought for the school it shall, not later than twenty-one days after the passing of the resolution, obtain the advice of the Board for the diocese in which the school is situated and have regard to that advice before confirming that decision by a further resolution under that paragraph.

(5) Without prejudice to subsection (2) of section 89 of the 1988 Act, no proposals shall be published under that section for the purpose of making a significant change in the religious character of a church school unless the Board for the diocese in which the school is situated has given its consent in writing to the change in question.

(6) Where the giving of advice under subsection (1) or (4) or consent under subsection (2) or (5) above is to be considered at any meeting of the Board, at least fourteen days' notice of the time and place at which the

meeting is to be held shall be given by the secretary of the Board to the secretary of the governing body of the school concerned, and the governors of that school shall be entitled to attend that meeting.

Advice of Board required for alteration of purposes of church educational endowments

4. The trustees of any church educational endowment held wholly or partly for or in connection with a church school shall obtain the advice of the Board for the diocese in which the school is situated and shall have regard to that advice before making or agreeing to the making of any alteration in the purposes for which the endowment may be applied.

Proposals for acquisition of grant-maintained status

5. The statement annexed under subsection (5) of section 62 of the 1988 Act to proposals for acquisition of grant-maintained status for a Church of England voluntary school shall include an account of the advice given by the Board under section 3(4) above and provide confirmation that the governing body of the school has had regard to that advice and, if it has departed from it, its reasons for so doing.

Board to be consulted in certain cases

6.—(1) Without prejudice to section 13(1) of the 1988 Act, a local education authority shall consult the Board for any diocese in which the authority exercises its functions before appointing a person to represent the Church of England as a member of a standing advisory council on religious education under section 11 of that Act.

(2) Before making any modifications of a trust deed or other instrument relating to a church school by order under section 102 of the 1988 Act the Secretary of State shall consult the Board for the diocese in which the school is situated, as well as the persons with whom consultation is required by subsection (1) of that section.

Powers of Board to give directions to governing bodies of aided church schools

7.—(1) Where the Board is satisfied that the governing body of any aided church school in the diocese is discharging its functions in relation to any matter affecting the status, continuance, size or character of the school or any significant enlargement of its premises in a manner which is not in the best interests of that school or of church schools generally or that the governing body of any such school has failed to discharge its functions in relation to any such matter, the Board shall have power to give directions to that governing body as to the exercise of those functions.

(2) Where the giving of directions under subsection (1) above is to be considered at any meeting of the Board, at least fourteen days' notice of the time and place at which the meeting is to be held shall be given by the secretary of the Board to the secretary of the governing body of the school concerned, and the governors of that school shall be entitled to attend that meeting; and no directions shall be given unless they have been approved by a two-thirds majority of the members of the Board present and voting at the meeting.

(3) It shall be the duty of a governing body to comply with any lawful directions given to it under subsection (1) above and if, before the expiration of the period of six months beginning on the date on which the directions are given, the governing body fails to comply with directions with respect to any of the following matters, that is to say—

    (a) an application under section 15(4) of the Education Act 1944 (revocation of order whereby school is an aided school); or

(b) the submission to the Secretary of State of proposals under section
13(1)(b) of the Education Act 1980 (change in character of school),
the Board may itself make that application or submit those proposals and the
provisions of the Education Acts 1944 to 1988 shall apply in relation to
anything done by the Board by virtue of this subsection as if it had been done
by the governing body of the school.

(4) Where the Board gives any directions under subsection (1) above it
shall cause a report thereon to be laid before the next meeting of the
diocesan synod.

(5) In this section any reference to the functions of a governing body shall
be construed as excluding functions in relation to the acquisition of grant-
maintained status.

Powers of Board to give directions to trustees of church educational endowments

8.—(1) Where the Board is satisfied that the trustees of any church
educational endowment held wholly for a church school in the diocese are
discharging their functions in relation to the endowment in such a manner
that the endowment is not being applied in the best interests of the school or
that the trustees of any such endowment have failed to discharge their
functions in relation to that endowment, the Board shall have power to give
directions to those trustees as to the exercise of those functions; and it shall
be the duty of the trustees to comply with those directions before the
expiration of the period of six months beginning with the date on which the
directions are given.

(2) Where the Board gives any directions under subsection (1) above it
shall as soon as practicable cause a report thereon to be laid before the
diocesan synod.

Attendance of diocesan director of education at aided school governing bodies' proceedings

9. Where, in the case of an aided church school, the chief education officer
of the local education authority concerned or officer of the authority nominated by him is entitled, by virtue of section 45(6) of the 1988 Act, to attend
any proceedings of the governing body of the school for the purpose of
giving advice to the governing body the diocesan director of education
concerned shall also be entitled to attend the proceedings for that purpose.

Interpretation

10.—(1) In this Measure—
   "the 1988 Act" means the Education Reform Act 1988;
   "church educational endowment" means an educational endowment
       which includes among the purposes for which it may be applied
       religious education according to the faith and practice of the
       Church of England;
   "Church of England voluntary school" means a voluntary school in
       respect of which any trust deed or other instrument requires provi-
       sion to be made at the school for religious education according to
       the faith and practice of the Church of England or in which, in the
       absence of any such instrument, such provision has been made by
       custom and practice;
   "church school" means a Church of England voluntary school or a
       grant-maintained school which was such a voluntary school imme-
       diately before it became a grant-maintained school;
   "educational endowment" means an endowment which, or the income
       of which, may be applied for the purposes of education;

"endowment" includes property not subject to any restriction on the expenditure of capital.

(2) Any reference in this Measure to a change in the character of a school means a change in the religious character of the school or a change in character resulting from education beginning or ceasing to be provided for pupils above or below a particular age, for boys as well as for girls, or for girls as well as for boys, or from the making or alteration of arrangements for the admission of pupils by reference to ability or aptitude; and any reference to a matter affecting the character of a school shall be construed accordingly.

(3) Expressions used in this Measure which are also used in the 1988 Act shall, unless the context otherwise requires, have the same meanings as in that Act.

Amendment and repeal

11.—(1) In section 5(5) of the Parochial Church Councils (Powers) Measure 1956—

(a) for the words "diocesan education committee of the diocese" there shall be substituted the words "diocesan board of education for the diocese"; and

(b) the words from "In this subsection" to the end of the section shall be omitted.

(2) The Diocesan Education Committees Measure 1955 is hereby repealed.

Transitional provisions

12.—(1) Any diocesan education committee constituted, or deemed to be constituted, in accordance with the Schedule to the Diocesan Education Committees Measure 1955 shall, if in existence on the date on which this Measure comes into force, be deemed to be a Diocesan Board of Education constituted in accordance with Part I of the Schedule to this Measure and shall continue in existence until the 1st January next after the first elections of elected members of the Board held under Part I of the Schedule to this Measure.

(2) Any diocesan education committee constituted in accordance with an order made by the Minister of Education or the Secretary of State under section 1 of the Diocesan Education Committees Measure 1955 shall, if that order is in force on the date on which this Measure comes into force, be deemed to be a Diocesan Board of Education constituted in accordance with an order made by the Secretary of State under section 1(2) of this Measure, and the order made under the said Measure of 1955 shall continue in force until—

(a) such time as a new Diocesan Board of Education is constituted in accordance with Part I of the Schedule to this Measure or with an order so made; or

(b) on the expiry of the period of three years following the coming into force of this Measure,

whichever first occurs.

(3) Any diocesan education committee which is deemed to be a Diocesan Board of Education by virtue of subsection (1) or (2) above shall not have power to give directions under section 7 or 8 of this Measure.

Short title, extent and commencement

13.—(1) This Measure may be cited as the Diocesan Boards of Education Measure 1991.

(2) This Measure shall extend to the whole of the provinces of Canterbury and York, except the Channel Islands and the Isle of Man, but may be applied to the Channel Islands, as defined in the Channel Islands (Church

Legislation) Measures 1931 and 1957, or either of them, in accordance with those Measures, and may be extended to the Isle of Man by or under Act of Tynwald.

(3) This Measure shall come into force on such date as the Archbishops of Canterbury and York may jointly appoint.

SCHEDULE

DIOCESAN BOARD OF EDUCATION

PART I

Membership

1. The Board shall consist of—
(a) the bishop;
(b) two persons nominated by the bishop, each person so nominated being either a suffragan bishop or a full-time assistant bishop in the diocese or an archdeacon of an archdeaconry in the diocese;
(c) not less than fourteen or more than eighteen members elected in accordance with the provisions of paragraph 2 below;
(d) not less than four or more than eight members co-opted by the Board of whom—
    (i) four members shall be persons with experience of church schools in the diocese, and
    (ii) the other members (if any) shall be persons with experience of other areas of work with which the Board is concerned;
and the bishop may nominate two additional persons (whether in Holy Orders or not) to be members of the Board.

2. Subject to paragraph 3 below, the diocesan synod shall by resolution determine whether sub-paragraph (a), (b) or (c) of this paragraph is to apply in relation to the elected members of the Board, that is to say—
(a) such number of members as the diocesan synod may determine, not being less than fourteen or more than eighteen, shall be elected by the diocesan synod, and of those members—
    (i) at least two shall be clerks in Holy Orders beneficed or licensed in the diocese, and
    (ii) at least six shall be lay persons, and
    (iii) at least six shall be members of the diocesan synod; or
(b) such number of members as the diocesan synod may determine, not being less than two, shall be elected by the diocesan synod in respect of each archdeaconry in the diocese, the number to be so elected being determined so as to ensure that the total number of elected members is not less than fourteen or more than eighteen, and of the members elected in respect of any archdeaconry—
    (i) at least one shall be a clerk in Holy Orders beneficed or licensed in the archdeaconry,
    (ii) at least one shall be a lay person, and
    (iii) at least one shall be a member of the diocesan synod; or
(c) the elected members shall consist of—
    (i) two members elected by the diocesan synod from among its own members, and of those two members one shall be a clerk in Holy Orders beneficed or licensed in the diocese and the other shall be a lay person, and
    (ii) one member, whether a clerk in Holy Orders or a lay person, elected by each deanery synod in the diocese from among its own members,
and upon such a resolution being carried, the number of elected members of the Board, the eligibility of candidates for election and the synod by which they are to be elected shall be determined accordingly.

3. Where the number of deaneries in a diocese is less than twelve or more than sixteen, paragraph 2 above shall have effect as if sub-paragraph (c) were omitted therefrom.

4. The bishop shall be chairman of the Board except that, if he does not desire to be chairman, the Board after consultation with the bishop, shall appoint some other person (whether or not a member of the Board) to be chairman, and the person so appointed shall be an ex officio member of the diocesan synod.

5. The election of the elected members of the Board shall take place every three years in the same year as, but after, the election of members of the diocesan synod, except that where the

diocesan synod determines that sub-paragraph (c) of paragraph 2 above is to apply to the Board the election of the elected members shall take place in the same year as, but after, the election of the deanery synods; and the elected members shall be elected in such manner as may be determined by the synod by which they are elected and shall begin to hold office on the 1st January next following their election.

6. Where an elected member of the Board ceases to be a member of a diocesan or deanery synod then, notwithstanding that he was elected by reason of his membership of that synod, he shall continue, unless he resigns, to be a member of the Board for the remainder of the period of office for which he was elected.

7. Any casual vacancy among the elected members of the Board shall be filled in such manner as may be determined by the diocesan synod.

8. All members of the Board other than the bishop of the diocese shall cease to hold office on the 1st January on which the newly elected members begin to hold office, except that a member of the Board shall be eligible for re-election or re-appointment on the termination of any period of office.

9. A person who is in receipt of any remuneration as an officer or member of the staff of the Board shall not be eligible for membership of the Board.

PART II

Proceedings

10. The quorum of the Board shall be eight of which four shall be elected members.

11. The Board shall meet on at least three occasions during a year, and an additional meeting shall be held if at any time eight or more members of the Board make a request in writing to the chairman for the holding of such a meeting.

12. The Board may establish committees to assist in the discharging of its functions, and the membership of any committee established under this paragraph may include persons who are not members of the Board.

13. Subject to paragraph 10 above, the validity of any proceedings of the Board shall not be affected by any vacancy among its members or by any defect in the appointment of any member.

14. Subject to the preceding provisions of this Schedule and to any directions as to procedure given by the diocesan synod, the Board shall have power to regulate its own procedure and the procedure and membership of its committees.

CURRENT LAW
STATUTE CITATOR 1991

This is the third part of the Current Law Statute Citator 1991 and is up to date to December 31, 1991. It comprises in a single table:

    (i) Statutes passed between January 1 and December 31, 1991;
    (ii) Statutes affected during this period by Statutory Instrument;
    (iii) Statutes judicially considered during this period;
    (iv) Statutes repealed and amended during this period.

    (S.) Amendments relating to Scotland only.

ACTS OF THE PARLIAMENT OF SCOTLAND

CAP.

6. Tutors Act 1474.
repealed: 1991, c. 50, sch. 2.

29. Lyon King of Arms Act 1592.
see *Procurator Fiscal in the Lyon Court v. P. Baird Construction, The Scotsman*, November 21, 1990.

2. Tutors and Curators Act 1672.
repealed: 1991, c. 50, sch.2.

47. Lyon King of Arms Act 1672.
see *Procurator Fiscal in the Lyon Court v. P. Baird Construction, The Scotsman*, November 21, 1990.

CAP.

85. Oaths of Minors Act 1681.
repealed: 1991, c. 50, sch. 1.

8. Tutors and Curators Act 1696.
repealed: 1991, c. 50, sch. 1.

25. Blank Bonds and Trusts Act 1696.
see *Sutman International Inc. v. Herbage, The Scotsman*, August 14, 1991.

7. Union with England Act 1706.
Art. IV, see *Pringle, Petr.*, 1991 S.L.T. 330.

ACTS OF THE PARLIAMENTS OF ENGLAND, GREAT BRITAIN AND THE UNITED KINGDOM

CAP.

26 Hen. 8 (1534)

3. repealed (Isle of Man): 1991, c. 61, sch. 2.
17. repealed (Isle of Man): 1991, c. 61, sch. 2.

27 Hen. 8 (1535)

8. repealed (Isle of Man): 1991, c. 61, sch. 2.

32 Hen. 8 (1540)

38. Marriage Act 1540.
repealed (Isle of Man): 1991, c. 61, sch. 2.

33 Hen. 8 (1541)

6. repealed (Isle of Man): 1991, c. 61, sch. 2.

5 Eliz. 1 (1562)

1. repealed (Isle of Man): 1991, c. 61, sch. 2.

23 Eliz. 1 (1580)

1. repealed (Isle of Man): 1991, c. 61, sch. 2.

CAP.

27 Eliz. 1 (1584)

2. repealed (Isle of Man): 1991, c. 61, sch. 2.

29 Eliz. 1 (1586)

6. repealed (Isle of Man): 1991, c. 61, sch. 2.

1 Jac. 1 (1603)

4. repealed (Isle of Man): 1991, c. 61, sch. 2.

3 Jac. 1 (1605)

1. repealed (Isle of Man): 1991, c. 61, sch. 2.

12 Car. 2 (1660)

14. repealed (Isle of Man): 1991, c. 61, sch. 2.

29 Car. 2 (1677)

3. Statute of Frauds 1677.
s. 4, see *Elpis Maritime Co.* v. *Marti Chartering Co; Maria D, The* [1991] 3 W.L.R. 330, H.L.; *A Debtor (No. 517 of 1991), Re, The Times*, November 25, 1991, Ferris J.

CAP.

1 Geo. 1, Stat. 2 (1714)

13. repealed (Isle of Man): 1991, c. 61, sch. 2.

3 Geo. 4 (1822)

60. repealed (Isle of Man): 1991, c. 61, sch. 2.

5 Geo. 4 (1824)

83. **Vagrancy Act 1824.**
   see *Hunt* v. *D.P.P.* [1990] Crim.L.R. 812, D.C.

2 & 3 Will. 4 (1832)

71. **Prescription Act 1832.**
   see *Dance* v. *Triplow, The Times,* December 4, 1991, C.A.

3 & 4 Will. 4 (1833)

41. **Judicial Committee Act 1833.**
   s. 24, order 90/2297.

4 & 5 Will. 4 (1834)

34. repealed (Isle of Man): 1991, c. 61, sch. 2.

7 Will. 4 & 1 Vict. (1837)

26. **Wills Act 1837.**
   ss. 15, 20, see *Finnemore (dec'd), Re* [1991] 1 W.L.R. 793, Micklem J.

1 & 2 Vict. (1837–38)

110. **Judgments Act 1838.**
   s. 17, see *Thomas* v. *Bunn* [1991] 2 W.L.R. 27, H.L.
   ss. 17, 18, see *Legal Aid Board* v. *Russell* [1991] 2 W.L.R. 1300, H.L.; *Westminster City Council* v. *Wingrove* [1991] 2 W.L.R. 708, D.C.

2 & 3 Vict. (1839)

47. **Metropolitan Police Act 1839.**
   s. 11, repealed: 1991, c. 53, sch. 13.

5 & 6 Vict. (1842)

14. repealed (Isle of Man): 1991, c. 61, sch. 2.
94. **Defence Act 1842.**
   s. 15, amended (S.): 1991, c. 50, sch. 1.

CAP.

7 & 8 Vict. (1844)

69. **Judicial Committee Act 1844.**
   s. 1, order 90/2297.

8 & 9 Vict. (1845)

19. **Lands Clauses Consolidation (Scotland) Act 1845.**
   s. 7, see *Jack's Exrx.* v. *Falkirk District Council, The Scotsman,* February 14, 1991.
   ss. 7, 67, 69, 70, amended: 1991, c. 50, sch. 1.
   s. 114, amended: 1991, c. 34, sch. 17.
109. **Gaming Act 1845.**
   s. 18, see *Lipkin Gorman* v. *Karpnale* [1991] 3 W.L.R. 10, H.L.
117. **Poor Removal Act 1845.**
   repealed (Isle of Man): 1991, c. 61, sch. 2.

10 & 11 Vict. (1847)

89. **Town Police Clauses Act 1847.**
   s. 28, see *Cheeseman* v. *D.P.P.* [1991] 2 W.L.R. 1105, D.C.

12 & 13 Vict. (1849)

51. **Judicial Factors Act 1849.**
   s. 1, repealed in pt. (S.): 1991, c. 50, sch. 2.
   s. 10, amended (S.): *ibid.*, sch. 1.
   ss. 25, 26, repealed in pt. (S.): *ibid.*, sch. 2.
   s. 27, amended (S.): *ibid.*, sch. 1.
   s. 30, repealed (S.): *ibid.*, sch. 2.
   s. 31, amended (S.): *ibid.*, sch. 1; repealed in pt. (S.): *ibid.*, sch. 2.
   ss. 32–34, amended (S.): *ibid.*, sch. 1.
   s. 34A, Acts of Sederunt 91/1413, 1915.
   ss. 36, 37, 40, amended (S.): 1991, c. 50, sch. 1.

18 & 19 Vict. (1855)

27. repealed (Isle of Man): 1991, c. 61, sch. 2.

22 Vict. (1859)

12. **Defence Act 1859.**
   s. 5, repealed: order 91/724.

22 & 23 Vict. (1859)

30. repealed (Isle of Man): 1991, c. 61, sch. 2.

24 & 25 Vict. (1861)

100. **Offences against the Person Act 1861.**
   ss. 18, 20, see *R.* v. *Rotherham Magistrates' Court, ex p. Brough* [1991] C.O.D. 89, D.C.

CAP.

24 & 25 Vict. (1861)—cont.

100. Offences against the Person Act 1861—cont.
s. 20, see *R.* v. *Norwood* (1989) 11 Cr.App.R.(S.) 479, C.A.
ss. 20, 47, see *R.* v. *Savage; D.P.P.* v. *Parmenter, The Times*, November 8, 1991, H.L.
s. 38, see *R.* v. *Brightling* [1991] Crim.L.R. 364, C.A.

27 & 28 Vict. (1864)

114. Improvement of Land Act 1864.
ss. 18, 24, 68, amended (S.): 1991, c. 50, sch. 1.

28 & 29 Vict. (1865)

73. Naval and Marine Pay and Pensions Act 1865.
ss. 4, 5, repealed: 1991, c. 62, s. 16, sch. 3.

29 & 30 Vict. (1866)

65. Colonial Branch Mint Act 1866.
repealed (Isle of Man): 1991, c. 61, sch. 2.

31 & 32 Vict. (1868)

64. Land Registers (Scotland) Act 1868.
s. 25, order 91/2093.
101. Titles to Land Consolidations (Scotland) Act 1868.
s. 3, repealed in pt.: 1991, c. 50, sch. 2.
ss. 24, 62, amended: *ibid.*, sch. 1.
s. 119, amended: *ibid.*, repealed in pt.: *ibid.*, sch. 2.
s. 121, repealed in pt.: *ibid.*, sch. 2.
s. 139, repealed: *ibid.*

32 & 33 Vict. (1869)

71. Bankruptcy Act 1869.
repealed (Isle of Man): 1991, c. 61, sch. 2.
115. Metropolitan Public Carriage Act 1869.
s. 9, order 91/1301.

33 & 34 Vict. (1870)

52. Extradition Act 1870.
see *R.* v. *D.P.P., ex p. Sinclair, The Times*, April 16, 1991, H.L.; *R.* v. *Immigration Appeal Tribunal, ex p. Hussain* [1990] Imm.A.R. 51, C.A.
ss. 2, 21, orders 91/997, 1699, 1701, 1702, 1720.
sch. 1, see *Nazir Chindy, Re* [1991] C.O.D. 105, D.C.

CAP.

37 & 38 Vict. (1874)

81. Great Seal (Offices) Act 1874.
s. 9, order 90/2319.

38 & 39 Vict. (1875)

17. Explosives Act 1875.
s. 23, see *Lord Advocate* v. *Aero Technologies (In Receivership)* (O.H.), 1991 S.L.T. 134.
ss. 33, 40 (in pt.), repealed: regs. 91/2097.
86. Conspiracy and Protection of Property Act 1875.
s. 7, see *D.P.P.* v. *Fidler, The Times*, August 27, 1991, D.C.
89. Public Works Loans Act 1875.
s. 41, regs. 91/1139.

39 & 40 Vict. (1876)

59. Appellate Jurisdiction Act 1876.
repealed (Isle of Man): 1991, c. 61, sch. 2.
s. 3, see *John G. McGregor (Contractors)* v. *Grampian Regional Council* (H.L.), 1991 S.L.T. 365.

40 & 41 Vict. (1877)

2. Treasury Bills Act 1877.
s. 9, regs. 91/1667.
59. Colonial Stock Act 1877.
s. 26, amended (S.): 1991, c. 50, sch. 1.

42 & 43 Vict. (1879)

11. Bankers' Books Evidence Act 1879.
see *R.* v. *Lewes Crown Court, ex p. Hill* [1991] Crim.L.R. 376, D.C.
s. 7, see *DB Deniz Nakliyati Tas* v. *Yugopetrol, The Independent*, February 15, 1991, C.A.
58. Public Offices Fees Act 1879.
ss. 2, 3, order 91/1948.

43 & 44 Vict. (1880)

4. Judicial Factors (Scotland) Act 1880.
s. 3, repealed in pt.: 1991, c. 50, sch. 2.

46 & 47 Vict. (1883)

3. Explosive Substances Act 1883.
s. 4, see *R.* v. *Whale; R.* v. *Lockton, The Times*, May 9, 1991, C.A.; *R.* v. *Berry* [1991] 1 W.L.R. 125, C.A.
38. Trial of Lunatics Act 1883.
see *R.* v. *Burgess* [1991] 2 W.L.R. 1206, C.A.

47 & 48 Vict. (1884)

44. Naval Pensions Act 1884.
s. 2, amended: 1991, c. 62, s. 16.

49 & 50 Vict. (1886)

29. Crofters Holdings (Scotland) Act 1886.
s. 33, see *Guthrie* v. *MacLean*, 1991 S.L.C.R. 47.

52 & 53 Vict. (1889)

39. Judicial Factors (Scotland) Act 1889.
s. 11, repealed: 1991, c. 50, sch. 2.

54 & 55 Vict. (1891)

21. Savings Bank Act 1891.
repealed (Isle of Man): 1991, c. 61, sch. 2.
69. Penal Servitude Act 1891.
repealed (Isle of Man): 1991, c. 61, sch. 2.

55 & 56 Vict. (1892)

4. Betting and Loans (Infants) Act 1892.
repealed (S.): 1991, c. 50, sch. 2.
23. Foreign Marriage Act 1892.
order 90/2592.
43. Military Lands Act 1892.
s. 14, see *D.P.P.* v. *Hutchinson; D.P.P.* v. *Smith, sub nom. D.P.P.* v. *Hutchinson; R.* v. *Secretary of State for Defence, ex p. Parker; R.* v. *Same, ex p. Hayman* [1990] 3 W.L.R. 196, H.L.

57 & 58 Vict. (1894)

44. Heritable Securities (Scotland) Act 1894.
s. 13, amended: 1991, c. 50, sch. 1.
60. Merchant Shipping Act 1894.
s. 55, amended (S.): 1991, c. 50, sch. 1.
s. 418, orders 91/768, 769.
s. 653, amended: 1991, c. 52, s. 31.
s. 738, order 90/2587; 91/768, 769, 2875.

58 & 59 Vict. (1895)

14. Courts of Law Fees (Scotland) Act 1895.
s. 2, orders 91/331–333.

59 & 60 Vict. (1896)

48. Light Railways Act 1896.
s. 3, orders 91/134, 933, 1965, 2136, 2194.
ss. 7, 9–12, orders 90/2350; 91/134, 933, 1111, 1162, 1619, 1965, 2136, 2194, 2210.
s. 24, orders 91/1965, 2136.

60 & 61 Vict. (1897)

38. Public Health (Scotland) Act 1897.
s. 16, see *City of Glasgow District Council* v. *Carroll*, 1991 S.L.T. (Sh.Ct.) 46.

61 & 62 Vict. (1898)

36. Criminal Evidence Act 1898.
s. 1, see *R.* v. *Lasseur* [1991] Crim.L.R. 53, C.A.
44. Merchant Shipping (Mercantile Marine Fund) Act 1898.
s. 5, regs. 91/487, 1797.

63 & 64 Vict. (1900)

56. Military Lands Act 1900.
repealed (Isle of Man): 1991, c. 61, sch. 2.

6 Edw. 7 (1906)

41. Marine Insurance Act 1906.
s. 33, see *Bank of Nova Scotia* v. *Hellenic Mutual War Risks Association (Bermuda); Good Luck, The* [1991] 2 W.L.R. 1279, H.L.

7 Edw. 7 (1907)

51. Sheriff Courts (Scotland) Act 1907.
s. 6, see *Lord Advocate* v. *West End Construction* (Sh.Ct.), 1990 S.C.L.R. 777.
s. 27, see *Black* v. *Black*, 1991 S.L.T. (Sh.Ct.) 5; *Fagan* v. *Fagan*, 1991 S.L.T. (Sh.Ct.) 2; *Richardson* v. *Richardson*, 1991 S.L.T. (Sh.Ct.) 7.
s. 40, Acts of Sederunt 91/290, 848, 1135.
sch. 1, see *Hoad* v. *Hoad*, 1991 S.L.T. (Sh.Ct.) 4; *Farley* v. *Farley*, 1991 S.L.T. 74; *Frank H. Dale* v. *Scotia Leyland Daf*, 1991 S.L.T. (Sh.Ct.) 21; *Gillespie & Gifford, W.S.* v. *Dunlop*, 1991 S.L.T. 160; *Jack* v. *Mackay* (Sh.Ct.), 1990 S.C.L.R. 816; *Alloa Brewery* v. *Parker* (I.H.), 1991 S.C.L.R. 70; *Johnston* v. *Dewart* (I.H.), 1991 S.C.L.R. 447; *Cosy Legs of Scotland* v. *Razno & Co.*, 1991 S.L.T.(Sh.Ct) 52; *Murray* v. *Murray*, 1991 S.L.T. (Sh.Ct.) 74; *McChristie* v. *Ems Promotions*, 1991 S.L.T. 934.
53. Public Health Acts Amendment Act 1907.
s. 81, see *Cheeseman* v. *D.P.P.* [1991] 2 W.L.R. 1105, D.C.
55. London Cab and Stage Carriage Act 1907.
s. 1, order 91/1301.

8 Edw. 7 (1908)

36. Small Holdings and Allotments Act 1908.
s. 29, amended: order 91/1730.

10 Edw. 7 & 1 Geo. 5 (1910)

8. Finance (1909–10) Act 1910.
s. 74, see *Kildrummy (Jersey)* v. *Inland Revenue*, 1991 S.C.L.R. 498.

1 & 2 Geo. 5 (1911)

57. Maritime Conventions Act 1911.
see *Asianic International Panama S.A. and Transocean Transport Co.* v. *Transocean Ro-Po Corp.; Seaspeed America, The* [1990] 1 Lloyd's Rep. 150, Sheen J.

4 & 5 Geo. 5 (1914)

14. Currency and Bank Notes Act 1914.
repealed (Isle of Man): 1991, c. 61, sch. 2.

50. Merchant Shipping (Convention) Act 1914.
repealed (Isle of Man): 1991, c. 61, sch. 2.

59. Bankruptcy Act 1914.
repealed (Isle of Man): 1991, c. 61, sch. 2.
s. 133, order 91/494.

5 & 6 Geo. 5 (1914–15)

18. Injuries in War Compensation Act 1914 (Session 2).
s. 1, scheme 91/911.

28. Naval Medical Compassionate Fund Act 1915.
s. 1, order 91/994.

90. Indictments Act 1915.
s. 5, see *R.* v. *Wells (Jeffrey)* [Note] (1991) 92 Cr.App.R. 24, C.A.; *R.* v. *Dixon* [Note] (1991) 92 Cr.App.R. 43, C.A.; *R.* v. *Cannan* (1991) 92 Cr.App.R. 16, C.A.; *R.* v. *Ismail, Ismail and Yassine* (1991) 92 Cr.App.R. 92, C.A.

6 & 7 Geo. 5 (1916)

64. Prevention of Corruption Act 1916.
s. 3, see *Carmichael* v. *Kennedy*, 1991 S.C.C.R. 145.

8 & 9 Geo. 5 (1918)

55. School Teachers (Superannuation) Act 1918.
repealed (Isle of Man): 1991, c. 61, sch. 2.

10 & 11 Geo. 5 (1920)

33. Maintenance Orders (Facilities for Enforcement) Act 1920.
ss. 4, 6, amended: 1991, c. 17, sch. 1.

10 & 11 Geo. 5 (1920)—cont.

41. Census Act 1920.
s. 3, regs. 91/796.
s. 8, amended: 1991, c. 6, s. 1.

72. Roads Act 1920.
s. 10, amended: 1991, c. 22, sch. 8.

81. Administration of Justice Act 1920.
see *Owens Bank* v. *Bracco (Nos. 1 and 2), The Times*, April 15, 1991, C.A.

11 & 12 Geo. 5 (1921)

58. Trusts (Scotland) Act 1921.
s. 2, amended: 1991, c. 50, sch. 1.

13 & 14 Geo. 5 (1923)

8. Industrial Assurance Act 1923.
s. 43, regs. 91/539.

14 & 15 Geo. 5 (1924)

27. Conveyancing (Scotland) Act 1924.
s. 4, amended: 1991, c. 50, sch. 1.

15 & 16 Geo. 5 (1924–25)

20. Law of Property Act 1925.
see *Westminster City Council* v. *Duke of Westminster* (1990) 23 H.L.R. 174, Harman J.
s. 3, amended: order 91/724.
s. 30, see *Citro, Domenico (A Bankrupt), Re; Citro, Carmine (A Bankrupt), Re* [1990] 3 W.L.R. 880, C.A.
s. 30, repealed in pt.: order 91/724.
s. 40, see *Toogood* v. *Farrell* [1988] 2 E.G.L.R. 233, C.A.
s. 49, amended: order 91/724.
s. 53, see *Crago* v. *Julian, The Independent*, November 22, 1991, C.A.
s. 66, amended: order 91/724.
s. 84, see *Holdom* v. *Kidd* [1991] 02 E.G. 163, C.A.
ss. 89–92, amended: order 91/724.
s. 109, see *Knight* v. *Lawrence* [1991] 1 E.G. 105, Browne-Wilkinson V.-C.
s. 136, see *Montedipe SpA* v. *JTP.-Ro Jugotanker; Jordan Nicolov, The* [1990] 2 Lloyd's Rep. 11, Hobhouse J.
s. 136, amended: order 91/724.
s. 140, see *Land* v. *Sykes* [1991] 16 E.G. 125, Mr. Timothy Lloyd, Q.C.
s. 146, see *Greenwich London Borough Council* v. *Discreet Selling Estates* [1990] 48 E.G. 113, C.A.; *Cardigan Properties* v. *Consolidated Property Investments* [1991] 7 E.G. 132, Mr. P. J. Cox, Q.C.; *Sood* v. *Barker* [1991] E.G.C.S. 13, C.A.; *Billson* v. *Residential Apartments* [1991] 3 All E.R. 265, C.A.
s. 146, repealed in pt.: order 91/724.
ss. 181, 188, sch. 1, amended: *ibid*.

CAP.
15 & 16 Geo. 5 (1924–25)—cont.

21. Land Registration Act 1925.
see *Behzadi* v. *Shaftesbury Hotels* [1991]
2 W.L.R. 1251, C.A.
s. 144, rules 90/2613.
s. 145, order 91/1948.

16 & 17 Geo. 5 (1926)

16. Execution of Diligence (Scotland) Act 1926.
s. 6, Acts of Sederunt 91/290, 291.
28. Mining Industry Act 1926.
s. 23, amended (prosp.): regs. 91/2531.

17 & 18 Geo. 5 (1927)

10. Finance Act 1927.
s. 55, see *Swithland Investments* v. *I.R.C.* [1990] S.T.C. 448, Ferris J.
36. Landlord and Tenant Act 1927.
s. 19, see *Vaux Group* v. *Lilley* [1991] 4 E.G. 136, Knox J.

18 & 19 Geo. 5 (1928)

43. Agricultural Credits Act 1928.
ss. 1, 2, 4, repealed: 1991, c. 33, sch.

19 & 20 Geo. 5 (1929)

13. Agricultural Credits (Scotland) Act 1929.
ss. 1, 2, 4, repealed: 1991, c. 33, sch.
34. Infant Life (Preservation) Act 1929.
s. 1, see *Rance* v. *Mid-Downs Health Authority* [1991] 2 W.L.R. 159, Brooke J.

20 & 21 Geo. 5 (1929–30)

25. Third Party (Rights against Insurers) Act 1930.
see *Lefevre* v. *White* [1990] 1 Lloyd's Rep. 569, Popplewell J.

22 & 23 Geo. 5 (1931–32)

35. Agricultural Credits Act 1932.
repealed: 1991, c. 33, sch.
39. Extradition Act 1932.
s. 1, see *Nazir Chinoy, Re* [1991] C.O.D. 105, D.C.
45. Rights of Way Act 1932.
s. 1, see *Att.-Gen. (ex rel. Yorkshire Derwent Trust)* v. *Brotherton, The Times*, December 10, 1991, H.L.
48. Town and Country Planning Act 1932.
s. 34, see *Att.-Gen. (ex rel. Scotland)* v. *Barratt (Manchester), The Times*, July 11, 1991, C.A.

23 & 24 Geo. 5 (1932–33)

12. Children and Young Persons Act 1933.
s. 1, see *R.* v. *Wills* [1990] Crim.L.R. 714, C.A.

CAP.
23 & 24 Geo. 5 (1932–33)—cont.

12. Children and Young Persons Act 1933—*cont.*
s. 7, amended: 1991, c. 23, s. 1; repealed in pt.: *ibid.*
s. 31, amended: 1991, c. 53, sch. 8.
s. 34, repealed in pt.: *ibid.*, sch. 13.
s. 34A, added: *ibid.*, s. 56.
s. 38, amended: *ibid.*, sch. 11; repealed in pt.: *ibid.*, sch. 13.
s. 39, see *R.* v. *Southwark Crown Court, ex p. Godwin; R.* v. *Same, ex p. The Daily Telegraph; R.* v. *Same, ex p. MGN; R.* v. *Same, ex p. Associated Newspapers; R.* v. *Same, ex p. Newspaper Publishing, The Times*, May 30, 1991, C.A.; *R.* v. *Leicester Crown Court, ex p. S.* [1991] Crim.L.R. 365, D.C.
s. 45, amended: 1991, c. 53, sch. 11.
s. 46, amended: *ibid.*, schs. 8, 11.
s. 47, amended: *ibid.*, sch. 11.
s. 48, amended: *ibid.*, schs. 8, 11.
s. 49, amended: *ibid.*, sch. 11.
s. 53, see *R.* v. *De Silva* (1988) 10 Cr.App.R.(S.) 479, C.A.; *R.* v. *Hartley and McCann* (1988) 10 Cr.App.R.(S.) 491, C.A.; *R.* v. *Georgeoulas* (1989) 11 Cr.App.R.(S.) 416, C.A.; *R.* v. *Bell* (1989) 11 Cr.App.R.(S.) 472, C.A.; *R.* v. *Donovan* (1990) 12 Cr.App.R.(S.) 156, C.A.
s. 55, amended: 1991, c. 53, s. 57.
s. 56, amended: *ibid.*, sch. 11.
ss. 99, 107, amended: *ibid.*, sch. 8.
s. 108, sch. 2, amended: *ibid.*, sch. 11.
13. Foreign Judgments (Reciprocal Enforcement) Act 1933.
s. 1, order 91/1724.
36. Administration of Justice (Miscellaneous Provisions) Act 1933.
s. 2, see *R.* v. *Manchester Crown Court, ex p. Williams and Simpson* [1990] Crim.L.R. 654, D.C.; *R.* v. *Stewart* (1990) 91 Cr.App.R. 301, C.A.; *R.* v. *Ismail, Ismail and Yassine* (1991) 92 Cr.App.R. 92, C.A.
s. 2, amended: 1991, c. 53, sch. 6.
41. Administration of Justice (Scotland) Act 1933.
s. 12, repealed: 1991, c. 50, sch. 2.
51. Local Government Act 1933.
s. 249, see *D.P.P.* v. *Jackson* (1990) 88 L.G.R. 876, D.C.

24 & 25 Geo. 5 (1933–34)

20. Water Supplies (Exceptional Shortage Orders) Act 1934.
repealed: 1991, c. 60, sch. 3.
36. Petroleum Production Act 1934.
s. 6, regs. 91/981.

CAP.

24 & 25 Geo. 5 (1933–34)—cont.

41. Law Reform (Miscellaneous Provisions) Act 1934.
see *Black* v. *Yates* [1991] 3 W.L.R. 90, Potter J.

49. Whaling Industry (Regulation) Act 1934.
ss. 6, 9, amended: 1991, c. 53, sch. 4.

26 Geo. 5 & 1 Edw. 8 (1935–36)

49. Public Health Act 1936.
ss. 17–19, 21, 22, 27, 30, 31, 34, 36, 42, repealed: 1991, c. 60, sch. 3.
s. 48, amended: *ibid.*, sch. 1; repealed in pt.: *ibid.*, sch. 3.
s. 90, repealed in pt.: *ibid.*
s. 94, see *Herbert* v. *Lambeth London Borough Council, The Times*, November 27, 1991, D.C.
ss. 94, 99, see *Sandwell Metropolitan Borough Council* v. *Bujok* [1990] 1 W.L.R. 1350, H.L.
s. 227, amended: 1991, c. 60, sch. 1.
ss. 278, 339, repealed in pt.: *ibid.*, sch. 3.
s. 343, amended: *ibid.*, sch. 1.

1 Edw. 8 & 1 Geo. 6 (1936–37)

34. Sheep Stocks Valuation (Scotland) Act 1937.
repealed: 1991, c. 55, sch. 13.

37. Children and Young Persons (Scotland) Act 1937.
s. 18, amended and repealed in pt.: 1991, c. 23, s. 2.

40. Public Health (Drainage of Trade Premises) Act 1937.
ss. 1–3, 4 (in pt.), 7, 7A, 9, 10, 13, 14, repealed: 1991, c. 60, sch. 3.

1 & 2 Geo. 6 (1937–38)

22. Trade Marks Act 1938.
ss. 4, 7, 8, 13, 21, 30, 68, see *Portakabin* v. *Powerblast* [1990] R.P.C. 471, Mummery J.
s. 9, see *Solid Fuel Advisory Service Mark* [1990] R.P.C. 535, Mr. B. F. Smith; *Laura Ashley Trade Mark* [1990] R.P.C. 539, Robin Jacob Q.C.
ss. 9, 10, 17, see *Au Printemps Trade Mark* [1990] R.P.C. 518, Mr. A. Hume.
ss. 9, 11, see *Guntrum Trade Mark, Re* [1990] R.P.C. 27, Trade Marks Registry.
ss. 9, 17, see *Colorcoat Trade Mark* [1990] R.P.C. 511, Robin Jacob, Q.C.
ss. 11, 12, see *Star Trade Mark* [1990] R.P.C. 522, Mr. J.M. Myall.
ss. 12, 23, see *Terbuline Trade Mark, Re* [1990] R.P.C. 21, Board of Trade.

CAP.

1 & 2 Geo. 6 (1937–38)—cont.

22. Trade Marks Act 1938—*cont.*
ss. 25, 32, 64, see *Tradam Trading Co. (Bahamas)'s Trade Mark* [1990] F.S.R. 200, Mummery J.
s. 39A, order 90/2593.
s. 40, rules 91/675, 1431, 1898.
s. 41, rules 91/1898.
s. 58C, amended: order 91/724.
s. 68, rules 91/1431, 1898.

34. Leasehold Property (Repairs) Act 1938.
s. 1, see *Greenwich London Borough Council* v. *Discreet Selling Estates* [1990] 48 E.G. 113, C.A.

73. Nursing Homes Registration (Scotland) Act 1938.
ss. 1A, 4, regs. 91/1320.

2 & 3 Geo. 6 (1938–39)

49. House of Commons Members' Fund Act 1939.
sch. 1, amended: resolution 91/992.

69. Import, Export and Customs Powers (Defence) Act 1939.
s. 1, order 91/1583.

82. Personal Injuries (Emergency Provisions) Act 1939.
ss. 1, 2, scheme 91/708.

4 & 5 Geo. 6 (1940–41)

50. Agriculture (Miscellaneous Provisions) Act 1941.
s. 15, amended: 1991, c. 60, sch. 1

6 & 7 Geo. 6 (1942–43)

39. Pensions Appeal Tribunals Act 1943.
s. 6, see *Rivett* v. *Secretary of State for Social Security* [1990] C.O.D. 479, Drake J.

7 & 8 Geo. 6 (1943–44)

26. Rural Water Supplies and Sewerage Act 1944.
repealed: 1991, c. 60, sch. 3.

28. Agriculture (Miscellaneous Provisions) Act 1944.
ss. 2, 8, (in pt.), repealed: 1991, c. 33, sch.

31. Education Act 1944.
ss. 7, 8, see *R.* v. *Kingston upon Thames Royal Borough Council, ex p. Kingwell, The Guardian*, May 30, 1991, D.C.
ss. 8, 99, see *R.* v. *Inner London Education Authority, ex p. Ali* [1990] C.O.D. 317, D.C.
s. 10, regs. 90/2351.
s. 14, see *R.* v. *Secretary of State for Education and Science, ex p. Inner London Education Authority* [1990] C.O.D. 412, C.A.
s. 40, amended: 1991, c. 53, sch. 11.

CAP.

7 & 8 Geo. 6 (1943–44)—cont.

31. Education Act 1944—*cont.*
s. 70, regs. 91/1034.
s. 76, see *R.* v. *Governors of the Buss Foundation Camden School for Girls, ex p. Lukasiewicz* [1991] C.O.D. 98, Otton J.
s. 80, regs. 91/1582.
s. 100, regs. 91/1831, 1975.
s. 111A, regs. 91/1975.
s. 114, regs. 91/1034.
sch. 1, see *R.* v. *Birmingham City Council and Secretary of State for Education, ex p. Kaur* [1991] C.O.D. 21, D.C.

43. Matrimonial Causes (War Marriages) Act 1944.
repealed (Isle of Man): 1991, c. 61, sch. 2.

8 & 9 Geo. 6 (1944–45)

18. Local Authorities Loans Act 1945.
s. 2, regs. 1140, 1539.

28. Law Reform (Contributory Negligence) Act 1945.
see *Youell* v. *Bland Welch; Superhulls Cover Case (No. 2), The* [1990] 2 Lloyd's Rep. 431, Phillips J.
s. 1, see *Pitts* v. *Hunt* [1990] 3 W.L.R. 542, C.A.

42. Water Act 1945.
ss. 7, 14 (in pt.), 15, 16, 21, 35 (in pt.), 41, 43, 45, 48, 53, 56, 59, repealed: 1991, c. 60, sch. 3.

9 & 10 Geo. 6 (1945–46)

73. Hill Farming Act 1946.
s. 9, amended: 1991, c. 55, sch. 11.
ss. 28–31, sch. 2, repealed (S.): *ibid.,* sch. 13.

10 & 11 Geo. 6 (1946–47)

24. Naval Forces (Enforcement of Maintenance Liabilities) Act 1947.
s. 1, amended: 1991, c. 62, s. 15; repealed in pt.: *ibid.,* s. 15, sch. 3.
s. 2, repealed: *ibid.,* sch. 3.

39. Statistics of Trade Act 1947.
s. 5, order 90/2597.

40. Industrial Organisation and Development Act 1947.
s. 7, amended: regs. 91/1997.

41. Fire Services Act 1947.
see *Thorn Securities* v. *Sackville, The Times,* January 15, 1991, D.C.
s. 3, amended: 1991, c. 22, sch. 8.
ss. 14, 15, amended: 1991, c. 60, sch. 1.
s. 18, regs. 91/343(S.), 369.
s. 26, order 91/1097.
s. 38, amended: 1991, c. 22, sch. 8.

CAP.

10 & 11 Geo. 6 (1946–47)—cont.

42. Acquisition of Land (Authorisation Procedure) (Scotland) Act 1947.
sch. 1, see *Thornbank Developments (Galashiels)* v. *Secretary of State for Scotland,* 1991 S.C.L.R. 532.
sch. 1, amended: 1991, c. 34, sch. 17.

43. Local Government (Scotland) Act 1947.
s. 247, Act of Sederunt 91/1920.

44. Crown Proceedings Act 1947.
see *R.* v. *H.M. Treasury, ex p. Petch* [1990] C.O.D. 19, Popplewell J.

11 & 12 Geo. 6 (1947–48)

10. Emergency Laws (Miscellaneous Provisions) Act 1947.
repealed (Isle of Man): 1991, c. 61, sch. 2.

17. Requisitioned Land and War Works Act 1948.
s. 15, amended: 1991, c. 60, sch. 1.

22. Water Act 1948.
ss. 5 (in pt.), 6, repealed: 1991, c. 60, sch. 3.

29. National Assistance Act 1948.
s. 22, regs. 91/437, 686(S.).
s. 26, amended and repealed in pt.: 1991, c. 20, s. 2.
s. 64, regs. 91/686.

36. House of Commons Members' Fund Act 1948.
s. 3, resolution 91/992.
s. 4, amended and repealed in pt.: 1991, c. 5, s. 7.

37. Radioactive Substances Act 1948.
ss. 5, 7, repealed in pt.: 1991, c. 27, sch.

38. Companies Act 1948.
s. 268, see *Esal Commodities (No. 2), Re* [1990] BCC 125, Millett J.
sch. 1, see *Parkstone* v. *Gulf Guarantee Bank* [1990] BCC 534, Warner J.

43. Children Act 1948.
see *F.* v. *Wirral Metropolitan Borough Council* [1991] 2 W.L.R. 1132, C.A.
s. 48, amended: 1991, c. 53, sch. 11.

44. Merchant Shipping 1948.
s. 5, regs. 91/784.

45. Agriculture (Scotland) Act 1948.
ss. 52, 54 (in pt.), repealed: 1991, c. 55, sch. 13.

56. British Nationality Act 1948.
see *Motala* v. *Att.-Gen., The Times,* November 8, 1991, H.L.
s. 12, see *R.* v. *Secretary of State for Foreign and Commonwealth Affairs, ex p. Ross-Clunis, The Times,* July 3, 1991, H.L.
s. 32, see *R.* v. *Secretary of State for the Home Department, ex p. Uddin (Shafique)* [1990] Imm.A.R. 104, C.A.

CAP.
11 & 12 Geo. 6 (1947–48)—cont.
63. Agricultural Holdings Act 1948.
s. 2, see *Padbury* v. *York* [1990] 41 E.G.
65, Evans-Lombe Q.C.; *Crawford* v.
Elliott [1991] 13 E.G. 163, C.A.; *Colchester Borough Council* v. *Smith*
[1991] 2 W.L.R. 540, Ferris J.

12, 13 & 14 Geo. 6 (1948–49)

42. Lands Tribunal Act 1949.
s. 1, see *British Home Stores* v. *Assessor for Strathclyde Region*, 1991 S.L.T.
(Lands Tr.) 68.
s. 3, rules 91/658(S.).
43. Merchant Shipping (Safety Convention) Act 1949.
s. 33, regs. 91/784, 1404.
47. Finance Act 1949.
s. 36, amended: 1991, c. 31, s. 114.
54. Wireless Telegraphy Act 1949.
s. 1, see *Mitchell* v. *McKenzie*, 1991
S.C.C.R. 745.
s. 1, regs. 91/436, 1523.
s. 2, regs. 91/436, 542.
s. 3, regs. 91/1523.
s. 5, see *McMeekin* v. *MacPhail*, 1991
S.C.C.R. 432.
67. Civil Aviation Act 1949.
ss. 8, 41, 57–59, 61, orders 91/189, 1697.
s. 62, order 91/1697.
s. 73, regs. 91/98.
74. Coast Protection Act 1949.
s. 20, amended: order 91/1730.
s. 49, amended: 1991, c. 60, sch. 1.
75. Agricultural Holdings (Scotland) Act 1949.
repealed: 1991, c. 55, sch. 13.
s. 28, see *Cambusmore Estate Trust* v.
Little, 1991 S.L.T. (Land Ct.) 33.
s. 84, repealed in pt.: 1990, c. 50,
sch. 2.
87. Patents Act 1949.
ss. 23, 41, see *Research Corp.'s Patent*
[1990] R.P.C. 663, Hoffmann J.
s. 41, see *American Cyanamid Co.'s*
(Fenbufen) Patent [1990] R.P.C. 309,
Aldous J.
s. 66, see *Mölnlycke A.B.* v. *Procter and*
Gamble [1990] R.P.C. 267, Morritt J.
88. Registered Designs Act 1949.
ss. 3, 43, see *Masterman's Application,*
Re, The Times, December 19, 1990,
Aldous J.
s. 36, rules 91/675, 1628.
ss. 40, 44, rules 91/1628.
97. National Parks and Access to the Countryside Act 1949.
ss. 15A, 16, amended: 1991, c. 28,
sch. 2.
s. 32, see *R.* v. *Devon County Council,*
ex p. Fowler [1990] C.O.D. 325, Kennedy J.
s. 103, amended: 1991, c. 28, sch. 2.
s. 114, amended: 1991, c. 60, sch. 1.

CAP.
14 Geo. 6 (1950)
12. Foreign Compensation Act 1950.
s. 7, order 91/190.
27. Arbitration Act 1950.
see *Craske* v. *Norfolk County Council*
[1991] E.G.C.S. 10, H.H. Judge Marder Q.C.
ss. 1, 25, see *Ulysses Compania Naviera*
S.A. v. *Huntingdon Petroleum*
Services; Ermoupolis, The [1990] 1
Lloyd's Rep. 160, Steyn J.
s. 12, see *Fal Bunkering of Sharjah* v.
Grecale of Panama [1990] 1 Lloyd's
Rep. 369, Saville J.
s. 22, see *King* v. *Thomas McKenna*
[1991] 1 All E.R. 653, C.A.
s. 23, see *Blexen* v. *G. Percy Trentham*
[1990] 42 E.G. 133, C.A.
s. 26, amended and repealed in pt.:
order 91/724.
s. 27, see *Navigazione Alta Italia SpA* v.
Comordia Maritime Chartering A.B.;
Stena Pacifica, The [1990] 2 Lloyd's
Rep. 234, Evans J.
28. Shops Act 1950.
s. 47, see *Kirklees Metropolitan*
Borough Council v. *Wickes Building*
Supplies [1990] 1 W.L.R. 1237, Mervyn Davies J.; *Stoke-on-Trent City*
Council v. *B. & Q.; Norwich City*
Council v. *B. & Q.* (1990) 88 L.G.R.
884, Hoffmann J.; *W.H. Smith Do-It-*
All and Payless DIY v. *Peterborough*
City Council [1990] 2 C.M.L.R. 577,
D.C.; *B. & Q.* v. *Shrewsbury and*
Atcham Borough Council [1990] 3
C.M.L.R. 535, Northcote J.
ss. 47, 50, see *Wellingborough Borough*
Council v. *Payless D.I.Y., Kettering*
Borough Council v. *W.H. Smith Do-*
It-All [1990] 1 C.M.L.R. 773, Northampton Crown Ct.
37. Maintenance Orders Act 1950.
ss. 18, 19, 22, 24, amended: 1991, c. 17,
sch. 1.
39. Public Utilities Street Works Act 1950.
repealed: 1991, c. 22, sch. 9.

14 & 15 Geo. 6 (1950–51)

18. Livestock Rearing Act 1951.
s. 1, repealed in pt. (S.): 1991, c. 55,
sch. 13.
35. Pet Animals Act 1951.
s. 2, see *White* v. *Kilmarnock &*
London District Council (Sh.Ct.),
1990 S.C.L.R. 771.
65. Reserve and Auxiliary Forces (Protection of Civil Interests) Act 1951.
ss. 21, 22, amended: 1991, c. 55,
sch. 11.
s. 24, repealed in pt. (S.): *ibid.*, sch. 3.
s. 38, amended: *ibid.*, sch. 11.

CAP.

14 & 15 Geo. 6 (1950–51)—cont.

66. Rivers (Prevention of Pollution) (Scotland) Act 1951.
s. 17, amended: 1991, c. 28, sch. 10.

15 & 16 Geo. 6 & 1 Eliz. 2 (1951–52)

39. Motor Vehicles (International Circulation) Act 1952.
s. 1, orders 91/771, 1727.
52. Prison Act 1952.
s. 3, see *R. v. Secretary of State for the Home Department, ex p. Allard* [1990] C.O.D. 261, C.A.
s. 8, see *McClaren v. The Home Office* [1990] I.C.R. 824, C.A.
s. 12, see *R. v. Deputy Governor of Parkhurst Prison, ex p. Hague* [1990] 3 All E.R. 687, C.A.
s. 25, repealed: 1991, c. 53, sch. 13.
s. 43, amended: *ibid.*, s. 68, sch. 8.
66. Defamation Act 1952.
s. 7, see *Kingshott v. Associated Kent Newspapers* [1990] 3 W.L.R. 675, C.A.
67. Visiting Forces Act 1952.
s. 1, amended: 1991, c. 4, sch.
s. 12, see *Cherwell District Council v. Oxfordshire Valuation and Community Charge Tribunal, The Independent*, November 13, 1991, Hodgson J.

1 & 2 Eliz. 2 (1952–53)

10. Agricultural Land (Removal of Surface Soil) Act 1953.
s. 2, amended: 1991, c. 34, sch. 7.
s. 4, amended (S.): *ibid.*, sch. 13.
20. Births and Deaths Registration Act 1953.
ss. 1, 9, 10, 10A, 39, 41, regs. 91/2275.

2 & 3 Eliz. 2 (1953–54)

56. Landlord and Tenant Act 1954.
see *City of London v. Fell, The Times*, August 7, 1991, Desmond Perrett, Q.C.
s. 10, see *Blatherwick (Services) v. King* [1991] 2 W.L.R. 848, C.A.; *Gurton v. Parrott* [1991] 18 E.G. 161, C.A.
s. 22, see *Grosvenor Estates Belgravia v. Cochran* [1991] E.G.C.S. 51, C.A.
s. 23, see *Wandsworth London Borough Council v. Singh, The Independent*, March 6, 1991, C.A.; *Kent Coast Property Investments v. Ward* [1990] 45 E.G. 107, C.A.; *Gurton v. Parrott* [1990] E.G.C.S. 159, C.A.
Pt. II (ss. 23–46), see *Hodge v. Clifford Cowling & Co.* [1990] 46 E.G. 120, C.A.

CAP.

2 & 3 Eliz. 2 (1953–54)—cont.

56. Landlord and Tenant Act 1954—*cont.*
s. 25, see *Smith v. Draper* (1990) 60 P. & C.R. 252, C.A.; *Bridgers v. Stanford, The Times*, April 30, 1991, C.A.
ss. 25, 30, see *Baglarbasi v. Deedmethod* [1990] E.G.C.S. 155, H.H. Judge Baker, Q.C.
s. 30, see *Teesside Indoor Bowls v. Stockton on Tees Borough Council* [1990] 46 E.G. 116, C.A.
ss. 30, 31A, see *Romulus Trading Co. v. Henry Smith's Charity Trustees (No. 2)* [1991] 11 E.G. 112, C.A.
s. 63, amended and repealed in pt.: order 91/724.
s. 65, see *Electricity Supply Nominees v. Thorn EMI Retail* [1991] E.G.C.S. 48, C.A.

3 & 4 Eliz. 2 (1954–55)

13. Rural Water Supplies and Sewerage Act 1955.
repealed: 1991, c. 60, sch. 3.
18. Army Act 1955.
continued in force: 1991, c. 62, s. 1; order 91/1696.
s. 71, amended: 1991, c. 62, s. 7.
s. 71A, amended: 1991, c. 53, sch. 9; c. 62, s. 2; repealed in pt.: *ibid.*, s. 2, sch. 3.
s. 71AA, amended: 1991, c. 53, sch. 9; c. 62, s. 3; repealed in pt.: 1991, c. 53, schs. 9, 13; c. 62, s. 3, schs. 2, 3.
s. 71AB, added: *ibid.*, s. 4.
s. 71B, amended: *ibid.*, sch. 2.
s. 79, amended: *ibid.*, sch. 2.
s. 93, amended: 1991, c. 53, sch. 9; c. 62, sch. 2; repealed in pt.: 1991, c. 53, sch. 13; c. 62, schs. 2, 3.
s. 99, amended: *ibid.*, sch. 2.
s. 122, repealed in pt.: *ibid.*, sch. 3.
ss. 122, 123, rules 91/826.
ss. 127, 131, repealed in pt.: 1991, c. 62, schs. 2, 3.
ss. 133, 134, amended: *ibid.*, sch. 2.
s. 145, amended: *ibid.*, repealed in pt.: *ibid.*, schs. 2, 3.
s. 150, amended: *ibid.*, s. 14; repealed in pt.: *ibid.*, s. 14, sch. 3.
s. 151, amended: *ibid.*, s. 14.
ss. 180, 181, see *R. v. Secretary of State for Health, ex p. Gandhi, The Times*, January 23, 1991, D.C.
s. 181, see *R. v. Army Board of the Defence Council, ex p. Anderson* [1991] 3 W.L.R. 42; [1991] 3 All E.R. 375, D.C.
s. 203, see *Happe v. Happe* [1990] 2 F.L.R. 212, C.A.; *Thomson v. Thomson* (Sh.Ct.), 1991 S.C.L.R. 655.

CAP.

3 & 4 Eliz. 2 (1954–55)—cont.

18. Army Act 1955—*cont.*
s. 204A, amended: 1991, c. 62, sch. 2.
s. 209, amended: *ibid.*, s. 11.
s. 216, amended: *ibid.*, s. 24; repealed in pt.: *ibid.*, s. 24, sch. 3.
s. 225, amended: 1991, c. 4, sch.; repealed in pt.: 1991, c. 62, s. 7, sch. 3.
sch. 5A, amended: 1991, c. 53, schs. 4, 9; c. 62, ss. 5, 9, 13; repealed in pt.: *ibid.*, ss. 5, 6, sch. 3.

19. Air Force Act 1955.
continued in force: 1991, c. 62, s. 1; order 91/1696.
s. 71, amended: 1991, c. 62, s. 7.
s. 71A, amended: 1991, c. 53, sch. 9; c. 62, s. 2; repealed in pt.: *ibid.*, s. 2, sch. 3.
s. 71AA, amended: 1991, c. 53, sch. 9; c. 62, s. 3; repealed in pt.: 1991, c. 53, schs. 9, 13; c. 62, s. 3, schs. 2, 3.
s. 71AB, added: *ibid.*, s. 4.
s. 71B, amended: *ibid.*, sch. 2.
s. 79, amended: *ibid.*, s. 11.
s. 93, amended: 1991, c. 53, sch. 9; c. 62, sch. 2; repealed in pt.: 1991, c. 53, sch. 13; c. 62, schs. 2, 3.
s. 99, amended: *ibid.*, sch. 2.
s. 122, repealed in pt.: *ibid.*, sch. 3.
ss. 122, 123, rules 91/825.
ss. 127, 131, repealed in pt.: 1991, c. 62, schs. 2, 3.
ss. 133, 134, amended: *ibid.*, sch. 2.
s. 145, amended: *ibid.*, repealed in pt.: *ibid.*, schs. 2, 3.
s. 150, amended: *ibid.*, s. 14; repealed in pt.: *ibid.*, s. 14, sch. 3.
s. 151, amended: *ibid.*, s. 14.
s. 204A, amended: *ibid.*, sch. 2.
s. 209, amended: *ibid.*, s. 11.
s. 214, amended: *ibid.*, s. 24; repealed in pt.: *ibid.*, s. 24, sch. 3.
s. 223, amended: 1991, c. 4, sch.; repealed in pt.: *ibid.*, s. 7, sch. 3.
sch. 5A, amended: 1991, c. 53, schs. 4, 9; c. 62, ss. 5, 9, 13; repealed in pt.: *ibid.*, ss. 5, 6, sch. 3.

21. Crofters (Scotland) Act 1955.
s. 5, see *Ward* v. *Shetland Islands Council*, 1990 S.L.C.R. 119.
s. 12, see *Fennell* v. *Paterson*, 1990 S.L.C.R. 42; *Trustees of the Tenth Duke of Argyll* v. *MacCormick*, 1991 S.L.T. 900.
s. 12, amended: 1991, c. 18, s. 2.
s. 13, see *Corbett* v. *MacLeod*, 1990 S.L.C.R. 25.
s. 14, amended: 1991, c. 55, sch. 11.
s. 16A, see *Fennell* v. *Paterson*, 1990 S.L.C.R. 42; *MacCormick* v. *Crofters Commission*, 1990 S.L.C.R. 79; *Sutherland* v. *Crofters Commission*, 1991 S.L.T. (Land Ct.) 81.

CAP.

3 & 4 Eliz. 2 (1954–55)—cont.

21. Crofters (Scotland) Act 1955—*cont.*
s. 25, amended: 1991, c. 18, ss. 1, 2.
s. 26, amended: *ibid.*, s. 2.
s. 26A, added: *ibid.*, s. 1.
s. 27, amended: 1991, c. 18, s. 2.
s. 37, amended: 1991, c. 55, sch. 11.
sch. 2, see *Corbett* v. *MacLeod*, 1990 S.L.C.R. 25; *Trustees of the Tenth Duke of Argyll* v. *MacCormick*, 1991 S.L.T. 900.
sch. 2, amended: 1991, c. 18, s. 2; c. 55, sch. 11; repealed in pt.: 1991, c. 18, s. 2.
sch. 5, amended: *ibid.*

4 & 5 Eliz. 2 (1955–56)

18. Aliens' Employment Act 1955.
s. 1, amended: order 91/1221.

30. Food and Drugs (Scotland) Act 1956.
s. 8, see *Guild* v. *Gateway Foodmarkets*, 1991 S.L.T. 578.

38. Agricultural Mortgage Corporation Act 1956.
ss. 1 (in pt.), 2–4, repealed: 1991, c. 33, sch.

49. Agriculture (Safety, Health and Welfare Provisions) Act 1956.
s. 25, amended: 1991, c. 55, sch. 11.

52. Clean Air Act 1956.
s. 11, orders 90/2457; 91/1282, 2892.
s. 34, order 91/1282.

54. Finance Act 1956.
s. 27, amended; 1991, c. 31, s. 76.

60. Valuation and Rating (Scotland) Act 1956.
s. 6, see *Forest Hills Trossachs Club* v. *Assessor for Central Region*, 1991 S.L.T. (Lands. Tr.) 42.

69. Sexual Offences Act 1956.
s. 32, see *R.* v. *Goddard* (1991) 92 Cr.App.R. 185, C.A.

74. Copyright Act 1956.
s. 21, see *Holmes* v. *D.P.P.* [1990] C.O.D. 150, D.C.
s. 48, see *Johnstone Safety* v. *Peter Cook (Int.)* [1990] F.S.R. 161, C.A.

5 & 6 Eliz. 2 (1957)

11. Homicide Act 1957.
s. 3, see *R.* v. *Clarke* [1991] Crim.L.R. 383, C.A.
s. 4, see *R.* v. *Wood* [1990] Crim.L.R. 264, C.A.

24. House of Commons Members Fund Act 1957.
s. 1, order 91/1685.

31. Occupiers' Liability Act 1957.
see *Cunningham* v. *Reading Football Club, The Independent*, March 20, 1991, Drake J.
s. 2, see *Murphy* v. *Bradford Metropolitan Council, The Times*, February 11, 1991, C.A.

CAP.

5 & 6 Eliz. 2 (1957)—cont.

53. Naval Discipline Act 1957.
continued in force: 1991, c. 62, s. 1; order 91/1696.
s. 43, amended: 1991, c. 62, s. 8.
s. 43A, amended: 1991, c. 53, sch. 9; c. 62, s. 2; repealed in pt.: *ibid.*, s. 2, sch. 3.
s. 43AA, amended: 1991, c. 53, sch. 9; c. 62, s. 3; repealed in pt.: 1991, c. 53, schs. 9, 13; c. 62, s. 3, sch. 3.
s. 43AB, added: *ibid.*, s. 4.
s. 43B, amended: *ibid.*, sch. 2.
s. 49, amended: *ibid.*, s. 8.
s. 60, amended: 1991, c. 53, sch. 9; c. 62, sch. 2; repealed in pt.: 1991, c. 53, sch. 13; c. 62, schs. 2, 3.
s. 90, amended: *ibid.*, s. 12.
s. 101, amended: *ibid.*, s. 15.
s. 125, amended: *ibid.*, s. 24; repealed in pt.: *ibid.*, sch. 3.
s. 128G, added: *ibid.*, s. 16.
s. 129, amended: *ibid.*, sch. 2; repealed in pt.: *ibid.*, sch. 3.
s. 135, amended: 1991, c. 4, sch.
sch. 3, amended: 1991, c. 62, sch. 2.
sch. 4A, amended: 1991, c. 53, sch. 9; c. 62, ss. 5, 9, 12, sch. 2; repealed in pt.: *ibid.*, ss. 5, 6, sch. 3.

59. Coal-Mining (Subsidence) Act 1957.
repealed: 1991, c. 45, sch. 8.
s. 5, amended: 1991, c. 60, sch. 1.
s. 10, amended: 1991, c. 55, sch. 11.

6 & 7 Eliz. 2 (1957–58)

17. Recreational Charities Act 1958.
s. 1, see *Russell's Exr.* v. *I.R.C.*, 1991 S.L.T. 855.

30. Land Powers (Defence) Act 1958.
s. 16, repealed in pt.: 1991, c. 22, sch. 9.
s. 18A, added: *ibid.*, sch. 8.

39. Maintenance Orders Act 1958.
ss. 2–4, amended: 1991, c. 17, sch. 1.
s. 4A, added: *ibid.*
s. 5, amended: *ibid.*

47. Agricultural Marketing Act 1958.
amended: regs. 91/1735(S.).

51. Public Records Act 1958.
sch. 1, amended: 1991, c. 40, sch. 5.

56. Finance Act 1958.
s. 34, amended: 1991, c. 31, s. 113.

61. Interest on Damages (Scotland) Act 1958.
s. 1, see *Boots the Chemist* v. *G. A. Estates, The Scotsman*, July 4, 1991.

69. Opencast Coal Act 1958.
s. 5, repealed in pt.: 1990, c. 60, sch. 3.
ss. 14A, 24–28, 52, schs. 6, 7, amended: 1991, c. 55, sch. 11.

71. Agriculture Act 1958.
s. 3, sch. 1, repealed (S.): 1991, c. 55, sch. 13.

CAP.

7 & 8 Eliz. 2 (1958–59)

5. Adoption Act 1958.
ss. 43, 47, 48, amended: 1991, c. 53, sch. 11.

24. Building (Scotland) Act 1959.
s. 2, regs. 91/159, 1528.
s. 4, regs. 91/158, 159.
s. 9, regs. 91/159.
s. 24, regs. 91/159, 160, 1528.
s. 29, regs. 91/159, 1528.
sch. 3, regs. 91/159.

40. Deer (Scotland) Act 1959.
s. 1, amended: 1991, c. 28, sch. 2.
s. 25C, amended: 1991, c. 54, s. 17.

72. Mental Health Act 1959.
s. 60, see *Knight* v. *Home Office* [1990] 3 All E.R. 237, Pill J.

8 & 9 Eliz. 2 (1959–60)

22. Horticulture Act 1960.
s. 1, amended: 1991, c. 55, sch. 11.
s. 14, amended: order 91/1997.

30. Occupiers' Liability (Scotland) Act 1960.
s. 2, see *McGuffie* v. *Forth Valley Health Board*, 1991 S.L.T. 231.

33. Indecency with Children Act 1960.
see *R.* v. *Clayton* [1990] Crim.L.R. 447, C.A.

34. Radioactive Substances Act 1960.
s. 2, orders 90/2512; 91/477, 563(S.).
ss. 6, 7, order 90/2512.
s. 11D, regs. 90/2504.
s. 15, orders 91/477, 563(S.).
sch. 1, amended: 1991, c. 60, sch. 1; repealed in pt.: *ibid.*, sch. 3.

58. Charities Act 1960.
s. 8, amended: order 91/1997.
s. 19, order 91/1141.

62. Caravan Sites and Control of Development Act 1960.
s. 24, see *R.* v. *Shropshire County Council, ex p. Bungay* [1990] C.O.D. 392, Otton J.

65. Administration of Justice Act 1960.
s. 12, see *Pickering* v. *Liverpool Daily Post,* [1991] 2 W.L.R. 513.
s. 13, see *Clarke* v. *Clarke* [1990] 2 F.L.R. 115, C.A.; *Att.-Gen.* v. *Hislop* [1991] 2 W.L.R. 219, C.A.

66. Professions Supplementary to Medicine Act 1960.
sch. 1, amended: regs. 91/1997.

67. Public Bodies (Admission to Meetings) Act 1960.
sch., amended: 1991, c. 60, sch. 1.

9 & 10 Eliz. 2 (1960–61)

33. Land Compensation Act 1961.
see *Fox* v. *Secretary of State for the Environment* (1991) 31 R.V.R. 171, Roch J.

CAP.
9 & 10 Eliz. 2 (1960–61)—cont.
33. Land Compensation Act 1961—*cont.*
s. 5, see *Hughes* v. *Doncaster Metropolitan Borough Council* [1991] 2 W.L.R. 16; [1991] 1 All E.R. 295, H.L.; *Hertfordshire County Council* v. *Ozanne* [1991] 1 W.L.R. 105, H.L.
s. 5, repealed in pt.: 1991, c. 34, schs. 15, 19.
s. 10A, added: *ibid.*, sch. 15.
s. 14, amended: *ibid.* s. 64, sch. 15.
s. 15, amended: *ibid.*, sch. 6; repealed in pt.: *ibid.*, schs. 6, 19.
s. 17, see *R.* v. *Secretary of State for the Environment, ex p. Fox, The Times*, June 25, 1991, Roch J.
s. 17, amended: 1991, c. 34, s. 65, sch. 15; repealed in pt.: *ibid.*, s. 65, schs. 15, 19.
s. 19, amended: *ibid.*, sch. 15.
s. 22, repealed in pt.: *ibid.*, schs. 15, 19.
ss. 23–29, sch. 3, added: *ibid.*, sch. 14.
34. Factories Act 1961.
see *Dexter* v. *Tenby Electrical Accessories, The Guardian*, February 22, 1991, D.C.
s. 29, see *Gitsham* v. *C. H. Pearce & Sons, The Times*, February 11, 1991, C.A.
s. 72, see *Fotheringham* v. *Dunfermline District Council* (O.H.), 1991 S.L.T. 610.
39. Criminal Justice Act 1961.
s. 29, see *R.* v. *Secretary of State for the Home Department, ex p. Wynne, The Times*, August 1, 1991, D.C.
49. Covent Garden Market Act 1961.
s. 46, amended: regs. 91/1997.
57. Trusts (Scotland) Act 1961.
s. 1, amended: 1991, c. 50, sch. 1; repealed in pt.: *ibid.*, sch. 2.
58. Crofters (Scotland) Act 1961.
s. 3, amended: 1991, c. 18, s. 2.
s. 4, see *Crofters Commission* v. *Gunn*, 1991 S.L.T. (Land Ct.) 53.
s. 13, amended: 1991, c. 55, sch. 11.
62. Trustee Investments Act 1961.
s. 12, order 91/999.
sch. 1, repealed in pt.: 1991, c. 33, sch.
64. Public Health Act 1961.
s. 1, repealed in pt.: 1991, c. 60, sch. 3.
s. 54, amended: *ibid.*, sch. 1.
ss. 59–64, 66–68, 69 (in pt.), repealed: *ibid.*, sch. 3.

10 & 11 Eliz. 2 (1961–62)

12. Education Act 1962.
s. 1, regs. 91/827, 1838.
s. 3, regs. 91/831, 1079.
s. 4, regs. 91/827, 831, 1079, 1838.
sch. 1, regs. 91/827, 1838.

CAP.
10 & 11 Eliz. 2 (1961–62)—cont.
19. West Indies Act 1962.
ss. 5, 7, order 91/988.
46. Transport Act 1962.
s. 24, amended: regs. 91/1997.
58. Pipeline Act 1962.
s. 15, amended: 1991, c. 22, sch. 8.
ss. 16, 17, substituted: *ibid.*
s. 31, amended: *ibid.*
s. 66, amended: *ibid.*; c. 60, sch. 1.

1963

2. Betting, Gaming and Lotteries Act 1963.
s. 55, amended: regs. 91/1997.
sch. 1, see *William Hill (Scotland)* v. *Kyle and Carrick District Licensing Board*, Second Division, December 7, 1990.
sch. 1, orders 91/2176, 2496(S.); amended: *ibid.*
schs. 2, 3, amended: order 91/2175.
sch. 5, order 91/2592.
11. Agriculture (Miscellaneous Provisions) Act 1963.
s. 21, repealed (S.): 1991, c. 55, sch. 13.
12. Local Government (Financial Provisions) Act 1963.
s. 15, see *Forest Hills Trossachs Club* v. *Assessor for Central Region*, 1991 S.L.T. (Lands Tr.) 42.
33. London Government Act 1963.
s. 1, see *Hazell* v. *Hammersmith and Fulham London Borough Council* [1991] 2 W.L.R. 372, H.L.
s. 19, repealed: 1991, c. 22, sch. 9.
sch. 9, repealed in pt.: *ibid.*, c. 60, sch. 3.
schs. 11, 14, repealed in pt.: *ibid.*
36. Deer Act 1963.
repealed: 1991, c. 54, sch. 4.
37. Children and Young Persons Act 1963.
ss. 3, 18, 23, 26, 28, amended: 1991, c. 53, sch. 11.
s. 29, amended: *ibid.*, schs. 8, 11.
s. 57, amended: *ibid.*, sch. 11.
38. Water Resources Act 1963.
s. 2, repealed: 1991, c. 60, sch. 3.
ss. 17, 19, 22–32, 36–55, 60, 63, 64, 71 (in pt.), 78, 79 (in pt.), 81, 82, 88, 91, 105, 106, 109, 114–118, 120, 123, 126 (in pt.), 128 (in pt.), 131, 132, 133 (in pt.), 134 (in pt.), 135 (in pt.), schs. 7, 10, repealed: 1991, c. 60, sch. 3.
s. 60, see *National Rivers Authority* v. *Newcastle and Gateshead Water Co.; Sunderland and South Shields Water Co. Intervening, sub nom. Northumbria Water Authority* v. *Newcastle and Gateshead Water Co.* (1991) 31 R.V.R. 48, H.L.

CAP.

1963—cont.

38. Water Resources Act 1963—*cont.*
ss. 131, 136, see *British Waterways Board* v. *Anglian Water Authority* [1991] E.G.C.S., Davies J.

41. Offices, Shops and Railway Premises Act 1963.
s. 84, amended: 1991, c. 4, sch.

51. Land Compensation (Scotland) Act 1963.
s. 8, see *The Royal Bank of Scotland* v. *Clydebank District Council* (O.H.), 1991 S.L.T. 635.
s. 12, see *M.B.E. Leisure* v. *Strathclyde Regional Council*, 1991 S.L.T. (Lands Tr.) 62; *Cameron* v. *Nature Conservancy Council*, 1991 S.L.T. (Lands Tr.) 85.
s. 12, repealed in pt.: 1991, c. 34, schs. 17, 19.
s. 17A, added: *ibid.*, sch. 17.
s. 22, amended: *ibid.*, s. 74, sch. 17.
s. 23, amended: *ibid.*, sch. 12, repealed in pt.: *ibid.*, schs. 12, 19.
ss. 23, 24, see *City of Aberdeen District Council* v. *Skean Dhu*, 1991 S.L.T. (Lands Tr.) 22.
s. 25, amended: 1991, c. 34, s. 75, sch. 17; repealed in pt.: *ibid.*, schs. 17, 19.
ss. 27, 28, amended: *ibid.*, sch. 17.
s. 30, repealed in pt.: *ibid.*, schs. 17, 19.
ss. 31–37, sch. 3, added: *ibid.*, sch. 16.

1964

14. Plant Varieties and Seeds Act 1964.
ss. 1, 3, 5, 7, scheme 90/2634.
s. 9, regs. 90/2633; 91/655.
s. 16, regs. 91/656, 657, 1537, 1601, 1602, 2206.
s. 36, regs. 90/2633; 91/655–657, 1601, 1602, 2206.
s. 38, regs. 90/2633; 91/2206; scheme 90/2634.

22. British Nationality Act 1964.
s. 1, see *R.* v. *Secretary of State for the Home Department, ex p. Patel (Pratimakumari); R.* v. *Secretary of State for the Home Department, ex p. Wahid (Abdul)* [1991] Imm.A.R. 25, Pill J.

24. Trade Union (Amalgamations, etc.) Act 1964.
s. 7, regs. 91/484.

26. Licensing Act 1964.
s. 20, see *R.* v. *Chelmsford Crown Court, ex p. Larkin* [1990] C.O.D. 447, Otton J.; *R.* v. *Liverpool Crown Court, ex p. Lennon and Hongkins* [1991] C.O.D. 127, Otton J.
ss. 59, 76, 77, see *Edwards* v. *D.P.P., The Times*, May 29, 1991, D.C.
s. 193B, see *R.* v. *Totnes Licensing JJ., ex p. Chief Constable of Devon and Cornwall* [1990] C.O.D. 404, Roch J.

CAP.

1964—cont.

40. Harbours Act 1964.
s. 14, orders; 90/2359(S.); 91/43(S.), 106–108, 237, 238, 540, 993, 1063, 1082(S.), 1106(S.), 1257, 1258, 1745(S.), 1852, 1853.
s. 27, amended: 1991, c. 60, sch. 1.
s. 31, see *Cowie, ex p., The Times*, May 10, 1991, Popplewell J.
s. 58, repealed in pt.: 1991, c. 60, sch. 3.

41. Succession (Scotland) Act 1964.
s. 2, see *Allan, Petitioners*, 1991 S.L.T. 202.
s. 16, amended: 1991, c. 55, sch. 11.
s. 28, repealed: 1991, c. 50, sch. 2.
s. 29, amended: 1991, c. 53, sch. 11.
sch. 2, repealed in pt.: *ibid.*, sch. 13.

42. Administration of Justice Act 1964.
s. 12, amended: 1991, c. 53, sch. 11.

48. Police Act 1964.
see *R.* v. *Secretary of State for the Environment, ex p. Avon County Council*, [1991] C.O.D. 137, D.C.
s. 14, see *R.* v. *Secretary of State for the Home Department, ex p. Lancashire Police Authority, The Times*, November 19, 1991, Webster J.
ss. 21, 22, order 91/209.
s. 33, regs. 90/2619; 91/1673, 1961.
s. 35, regs. 90/2618.
s. 51, see *R.* v. *Brightling* [1991] Crim.L.R. 364, C.A.

51. Universities and Colleges Estates Act 1964.
sch. 3, repealed in pt.: 1991, c. 45, sch. 8.

60. Emergency Laws (Re-enactments and Repeals) Act 1964.
ss. 2, 7, directions 91/629.

65. Zambia Independence Act 1964.
s. 3, see *Motala* v. *Att.-Gen., The Times*, November 8, 1991, H.L.

84. Criminal Procedure (Insanity) Act 1964.
s. 4, substituted: 1991, c. 25, s. 2.
s. 4A, added: *ibid.*
s. 5, substituted: *ibid.*, s. 3.
s. 8, amended: *ibid.*, sch. 3; repealed in pt.: *ibid.*, sch. 4.
sch. 1, repealed: *ibid.*

89. Hairdressers (Registration) Act 1964.
s. 13, amended: regs. 91/1997.

90. Spray Irrigation (Scotland) Act 1964.
repealed: 1991, c. 28, sch. 11.

1965

4. Science and Technology Act 1965.
sch. 2, repealed in pt.: 1991, c. 60, sch. 3.

12. Industrial and Provident Societies Act 1965.
ss. 70, 71, regs. 91/520, 521.

CAP.

1965—cont.

14. **Cereals Marketing Act 1965.**
s. 13, order 91/1303.
s. 16, order 91/1302.
s. 21, amended: regs. 91/1997.
ss. 23, 24, orders 91/1302, 1303.
19. **Teaching Council (Scotland) Act 1965.**
s. 6, regs. 91/1136.
sch. 1, amended: regs. 91/1997.
25. **Finance Act 1965.**
s. 24, see *Marshall (Inspector of Taxes)*
v. *Kerr, The Times*, November 13,
1991, Harman J.
s. 42, see *Jones (Inspector of Taxes)* v.
Lincoln-Lewis, The Times, May 21,
1991, Hoffmann J.
36. **Gas Act 1965.**
ss. 15, 23, amended: 1991, c. 60, sch. 1.
s. 28, repealed in pt.: *ibid.*, sch. 3.
sch. 3, repealed in pt.: 1991, c. 34,
schs. 6, 12(S.), 19, Pts. II, IV(S.).
sch. 4, amended: 1991, c. 60, sch. 1.
37. **Carriage of Goods by Road Act 1965.**
see *Microfine Materials & Chemicals* v.
Transferry Shipping Co., The Times,
July 24, 1991, Kershaw J.; *Texas
Instruments* v. *Nason (Europe)* [1991]
1 Lloyd's Rep. 146, Evans J.
45. **Backing of Warrants (Republic of Ireland) Act 1965.**
ss. 2A, 8, Act of Adjournal 91/19.
49. **Registration of Births, Deaths and Marriages (Scotland) Act 1965.**
s. 20, amended: 1991, c. 50, sch. 1;
repealed in pt.: *ibid.*, sch. 2.
ss. 28A, 37, 38, 40, regs. 90/2638.
s. 42, regs. 91/1260.
s. 43, regs. 90/2638.
s. 43, repealed in pt.: 1991, c. 50,
sch. 2.
s. 47, regs. 90/2638.
s. 54, regs. 90/2638; 91/1260.
s. 56, regs. 90/2638.
s. 56, repealed in pt.: 1991, c. 50,
sch. 2.
51. **National Insurance Act 1965.**
s. 36, amended: order 91/503.
56. **Compulsory Purchase Act 1965.**
s. 3, amended: 1991, c. 34, sch. 15.
s. 4, see *Westminster City Council* v.
Quereshi (1990) 60 P. & C.R. 380,
Aldous J.
s. 5, amended: 1991, c. 34, s. 67.
ss. 20, 31, amended: *ibid.*, sch. 15.
57. **Nuclear Installations Act 1965.**
s. 7, see *Merlin* v. *British Nuclear Fuels*
[1990] 3 W.L.R. 383; [1990] 3 All
E.R. 711, Gatehouse J.
63. **Public Works Loans Act 1965.**
sch. 1, amended: 1991, c. 60, sch. 1.
74. **Superannuation Act 1965.**
s. 13, amended: 1991, c. 28, sch. 10.
s. 39, repealed in pt.: *ibid.*, sch. 11.

CAP.

1966

13. **Universities (Scotland) Act 1966.**
s. 12, amended: regs. 91/1997.
34. **Industrial Development Act 1966.**
sch. 2, repealed in pt.: order 91/510.
36. **Veterinary Surgeons Act 1966.**
s. 5A, amended: order 91/1218.
s. 19, order 91/1412.
sch. 1A, repealed in pt.: order 91/1218.
sch. 3, amended: order 91/1412;
repealed in pt. (prosp.): *ibid.*
38. **Sea Fisheries Regulation Act 1966.**
s. 18, amended: 1991, c. 60, sch. 1.
42. **Local Government Act 1966.**
ss. 35, 40, sch. 3, order 91/2175.
45. **Armed Forces Act 1966.**
s. 2, regs. 90/2373.
51. **Local Government (Scotland) Act 1966.**
ss. 42, 45, sch. 4, order 91/2495.

1967

7. **Misrepresentation Act 1967.**
s. 2, see *Garden Neptune Shipping* v.
*Occidental Worldwide Investment
Corp. and Concord Petroleum Corp.*
[1990] 1 Lloyd's Rep. 330; *Royscot
Trust* v. *Rogerson* [1991] 3 W.L.R.
57; [1991] 3 All E.R. 294.
8. **Plant Health Act 1967.**
s. 1, orders 90/2398; 91/240, 1640, 1777,
1905(S.).
s. 2, orders 90/2398; 91/240.
s. 3, orders 90/2398; 91/240, 1777,
1905(S.).
s. 4, order 91/1905(S.).
s. 4A, order 91/1640.
9. **General Rate Act 1967.**
ss. 7, 17, 40, 53, sch. 1, see *Hummingbird Entertainments* v. *Birmingham
City Council* [1991] R.A. 165, D.C.
s. 103, see *R.* v. *Ealing Justices, ex p.
Cloves* (1991) 31 R.V.R. 169, D.C.
10. **Forestry Act 1967.**
s. 38, amended: 1991, c. 43, s. 1.
13. **Parliamentary Commissioner Act 1967.**
sch. 2, amended: 1991, c. 28, sch. 10;
c. 40, sch. 5; c. 60, sch. 1; repealed in
pt.: 1991, c. 28, sch. 11.
22. **Agriculture Act 1967.**
s. 19, amended: regs. 91/1997.
ss. 26–29, 48, amended: 1991, c. 55,
sch. 11.
s. 50, repealed in pt.: 1991, c. 60,
sch. 3.
ss. 63, 68, repealed in pt.: 1991, c. 33,
sch.
sch. 3, amended: 1991, c. 55, sch. 11.
24. **Slaughter of Poultry Act 1967.**
ss. 3, 6, regs. 91/1676.
27. **Merchant Shipping (Load Lines) Act
1967.**
see *Donald* v. *Roberts, The Times*, May
16, 1991, D.C.

(15)

CAP.
1967—cont.

27. **Merchant Shipping (Load Lines) Act 1967**—*cont.*
s. 18, order 91/1298.
s. 26, regs. 91/784; order 91/2543.

29. **Housing Subsidies Act 1967.**
s. 32, amended: regs. 91/2705.

32. **Development of Inventions Act 1967.**
s. 1, repealed: 1991, c. 66, sch. 2, Pt. II.
ss. 2–11, repealed: *ibid.*, Pt. I.
s. 12, amended: regs. 91/1997; repealed: 1991, c. 66, sch. 2, Pt. I.
s. 13, repealed in pt.: *ibid.*
s. 15, repealed in pt.: *ibid.*, Pts. I, II.
sch., repealed: *ibid.*, Pt. II; repealed in pt.: *ibid.*, Pt. I.

41. **Marine, Etc., Broadcasting (Offences) Act 1967.**
s. 2A, order 90/2503.
ss. 3, 5, see *R.* v. *Murray* [1990] 1 W.L.R. 1360, C.A.

43. **Legal Aid (Scotland) Act 1967.**
ss. 14A, 15, regs. 91/568.

48. **Industrial and Provident Societies Act 1967.**
s. 7, regs. 91/520, 521.

58. **Criminal Law Act 1967.**
s. 6, see *R.* v. *Mearns* [1990] 3 W.L.R. 569, C.A.; *R.* v. *Savage; D.P.P.* v. *Parmenter, The Times*, November 8, 1991, H.L.

64. **Anchors and Chain Cables Act 1967.**
s. 1, regs. 91/784.

65. **Antarctic Treaty Act 1967.**
ss. 7, 10, order 91/756.

66. **Welsh Language Act 1967.**
s. 2, regs. 91/118, 877, 974, 1403; order 91/1169.

68. **Fugitive Offenders Act 1967.**
see *R.* v. *Governor of Brixton Prison, ex p. Osman* [1991] C.O.D. 103, D.C.

77. **Police (Scotland) Act 1967.**
s. 41, see *Stocks* v. *Hamilton*, 1991 S.C.C.R. 190; *Brannon* v. *Carmichael*, 1991 S.C.C.R. 383; *Grant* v. *Lockhart*, 1991 S.C.C.R. 385.

80. **Criminal Justice Act 1967.**
s. 9, see *Paterson* v. *D.P.P.* [1990] R.T.R. 329, D.C.
ss. 9, 10, see *R. (A Minor) (Wardship: Witness in Criminal Proceedings), Re, The Times*, January 24, 1991, C.A.
s. 11, see *R.* v. *Fields and Adams* (1990) 154 J.P.N. 722, C.A.
s. 56, see *R.* v. *Isaacs* [1990] R.T.R. 240, C.A.
ss. 59–64, repealed: 1991, c. 53, sch. 13.
s. 67, amended: *ibid.*, sch. 11; repealed in pt.: *ibid.*, sch. 13.
s. 91, see *D.P.P.* v. *Kitching* [1990] Crim.L.R. 394, D.C.
sch. 2, repealed: 1991, c. 53, sch. 13.

84. **Sea Fish (Conservation) Act 1967.**
s. 3, order 91/1380.
s. 4, see *Wither* v. *Cowie; Wither* v. *Wood*, 1990 S.C.C.R. 741.

CAP.
1967—cont.

84. **Sea Fish (Conservation) Act 1967**—*cont.*
s. 4, order 91/2196.
s. 5, orders 90/2304, 2394, 2481, 2554; 91/1163, 1473, 2085.
s. 11, amended: 1991, c. 53, sch. 4.
s. 15, orders 90/2304, 2394, 2481, 2554; 91/1163, 1380, 1473, 2085, 2196.
s. 16, amended: 1991, c. 53, sch. 4.
s. 18, amended: 1991, c. 60, sch. 1.
s. 20, orders 91/1163, 2196.
s. 22, orders 90/2304, 2394, 2481, 2554; 91/1163, 1380, 1473, 2085, 2196.

86. **Countryside (Scotland) Act 1967.**
amended: 1991, c. 28, s. 14.
Pt. I (ss. 1–9), repealed: *ibid.*, sch. 11.
s. 10, amended: *ibid.*, sch. 3; repealed in pt.: *ibid.*, sch. 11.
s. 12, repealed in pt.: *ibid.*
s. 13, amended: *ibid.*, sch. 3; repealed in pt.: *ibid.*, schs. 10, 11.
s. 14, amended: *ibid.*, sch. 3; repealed in pt.: *ibid.*, sch. 11.
s. 15, amended: *ibid.*, sch. 3; repealed in pt.: *ibid.*, schs. 3, 11.
ss. 16–18, amended: *ibid.*, sch. 3.
s. 20, amended: *ibid.*, repealed in pt.: *ibid.*
ss. 22–24, 26–28, amended: *ibid.*
s. 29, amended: *ibid.*; repealed in pt.: *ibid.*
ss. 49A, 54, 60, 61, 66, 69, 70, amended: *ibid.*, sch. 10.
ss. 71, 75 (in pt.), 78 (in pt.), sch. 1, repealed: *ibid.*, sch. 11.
schs. 2–4, amended: *ibid.*, sch. 10.

87. **Abortion Act 1967.**
s. 1, see *G. (Mental Patient: Termination of Pregnancy), Re, The Times*, January 31, 1991, Sir Stephen Brown P.; *Rance* v. *Mid-Downs Health Authority* [1991] 2 W.L.R. 159, Brooke J.
s. 2, regs. 91/460(S.)., 499.

88. **Leasehold Reform Act 1967.**
see *Mayhew* v. *Free Grammar School of John Lyon, The Times*, June 11, 1991, C.A.
ss. 1, 23, see *Woodruff* v. *Hambro* [1991] 2 E.G. 63, C.A.

1968

4. **Erskine Bridge Tolls Act 1968.**
s. 4, order 91/1402.

7. **London Cab Act 1968.**
s. 1, order 91/1301.

13. **National Loans Acts 1968.**
s. 6, repealed in pt.: 1991, c. 60, sch. 3.
s. 14, amended (S.): 1991, c. 50, sch. 1.

14. **Public Expenditure and Receipts Act 1968.**
s. 5, sch. 3, orders 90/2515, 2637(S.); 91/274(S.), 2005.

1968—cont.

14. Public Expenditure and Receipts Act 1968—cont.
ss. 157, 158, amended: order 91/2005.
sch. 3, repealed in pt.: 1991, c. 34, schs. 6, 12(S.), 19, Pt. II, IV(S.).

16. New Towns (Scotland) Act 1968.
s. 8, amended: 1991, c. 22, sch. 8.
s. 39, amended: regs. 91/1997.

19. Criminal Appeal Act 1968.
see *R.* v. *Johnson* [1990] 3 W.L.R. 745, C.A.; *R.* v. *Registrar of Criminal Appeals, ex p. Ampaw* [1991] C.O.D. 45, D.C.
s. 1, see *R.* v. *Wharton* [1990] Crim.L.R. 877, C.A.
s. 2, see *R.* v. *Harper-Taylor; R.* v. *Bakker* (Note) [1991] R.T.R. 76, C.A.
s. 6, substituted: 1991, c. 25, s. 4.
s. 10, amended: 1991, c. 53, sch. 11.
s. 14, substituted: 1991, c. 25, s. 4.
s. 14A, added: *ibid.*
s. 15, amended: *ibid.*, sch. 3.
s. 16, amended: *ibid.*; repealed in pt.: *ibid.*, schs. 3, 4.
s. 17, see *R.* v. *Secretary of State for the Home Department, ex p. Garner* [1990] C.O.D. 457, C.A.; *R.* v. *Secretary of State for the Home Department, ex p. Pegg (Kenneth Stephen)* [1991] C.O.D. 46, D.C.
s. 17, amended: 1991, c. 25, sch. 3.
s. 50, repealed in pt.: 1991, c. 53, schs. 11, 13.
s. 51, amended: 1991, c. 25, sch. 3.
schs. 1, 5 (in pt.), repealed: *ibid.*, sch. 4.

20. Courts-Martial (Appeals) Act 1968.
s. 8, repealed in pt.: 1991, c. 62, sch. 3.
s. 19, repealed in pt.: *ibid.*, schs. 2, 3.

27. Firearms Act 1968.
s. 1, see *R.* v. *Stubbings* [1990] Crim.L.R. 811, C.A.; *R.* v. *Waller* [1991] Crim.L.R. 381, C.A.
s. 5, see *R.* v. *Formosa; R.* v. *Upton* [1990] 3 W.L.R. 1179, C.A.
s. 6, order 90/2621.
s. 16, see *R.* v. *East* [1990] Crim.L.R. 413, C.A.
s. 17, see *R.* v. *Guy, The Times*, February 21, 1991, C.A.

29. Trade Descriptions Act 1968.
see *Devlin* v. *Hall* [1990] R.T.R. 320, D.C.
s. 1, see *R.* v. *Nash* [1990] R.T.R. 343, C.A.; *May* v. *Vincent* (1991) 10 T.L.R. 1, D.C.
ss. 1, 4, see *Swithland Motors* v. *Peck* [1991] Crim.L.R. 386, D.C.

1968—cont.

29. Trade Descriptions Act 1968—cont.
s. 24, see *Lewin* v. *Fuell* [1990] Crim.L.R. 658, D.C.; *Hurley* v. *Martinez and Co.* [1990] T.L.R. 189, D.C.; *Denard* v. *Smith & Dixons* (1991) 10 T.L.R. 86, D.C.

34. Agriculture (Miscellaneous Provisions) Act 1968.
s. 2, regs. 91/1477.
Pt. II (ss. 9–17), schs. 4, 5, repealed (S.): 1991, c. 55, sch. 13.

35. Water Resources Act 1968.
repealed: 1991, c. 60, sch. 3.

41. Countryside Act 1968.
s. 15, amended: 1991, c. 28, sch. 2.
s. 37, repealed in pt.: *ibid.*, sch. 11.

47. Sewerage (Scotland) Act 1968.
ss. 12, 24, amended: 1991, c. 28, sch. 10.
s. 41, amended: 1991, c. 22, sch. 8.
s. 46, amended: 1991, c. 28, sch. 10.
s. 59, amended: 1991, c. 22, sch. 8.

48. International Organisations Act 1968.
s. 1, order 91/757.

49. Social Work (Scotland) Act 1968.
s. 5, regs. 91/536.
s. 5B, order 90/2519.
s. 15, see *M.* v. *Dumfries and Galloway Regional Council* (Sh.Ct.), 1991 S.C.L.R. 481.
ss. 16, 18, amended: 1991, c. 50, sch. 1.
ss. 30, 94, see *C.* v. *Kennedy, The Scotsman*, March 27, 1991.
ss. 35, 40, 42, 50, see *Sloan* v. *B.*, 1991 S.L.T. 530.
s. 37, see *L.* v. *Strathclyde Regional Council* (Sh.Ct.), 1991 S.C.L.R. 658.
s. 44, see *D.* v. *Strathclyde Regional Council* (Sh.Ct.), 1991 S.C.L.R. 185.
s. 72, amended: 1991, c. 53, sch. 3; repealed in pt.: *ibid.*, schs. 3, 13.
s. 94, repealed in pt.: 1991, c. 50, sch. 2.

50. Hearing Aid Council Act 1968.
s. 11, rules 91/1732.
s. 12, amended: regs. 91/1997.

52. Caravan Sites Act 1968.
s. 1, see *Stoke-on-Trent City Council* v. *Frost, The Times*, November 26, 1991, C.A.
s. 6, see *R.* v. *Essex County Council, ex p. Curtis, Barton and Barton* [1991] C.O.D. 9, Pill J.; *R.* v. *Shropshire County Council, ex p. Bungay* (1990) 23 H.L.R. 195, Otton J.
ss. 6, 16, see *R.* v. *Shropshire County Council, ex p. Bungay* [1990] C.O.D. 392, Otton J.
s. 12, see *R.* v. *Camden London Borough, ex p. Maughan & McDonagh* (1990) 23 H.L.R. 95, Otton J.
s. 12, orders 91/1125, 1326, 1951.

CAP.

1968—cont.

55. Friendly and Industrial and Provident Societies Act 1968.
s. 7, amended: regs. 91/1997.
s. 8, amended and repealed in pt.: *ibid*.

59. Hovercraft Act 1968.
s. 1, order 90/2594.
s. 1, amended: 1990, c. 43, sch. 15.

60. Theft Act 1968.
s. 1, see *R.* v. *Gomez* [1991] 3 All E.R. 394, C.A.
s. 3, see *R.* v. *Stringer and Banks; The Daily Telegraph*, April 11, 1991, C.A.; *R.* v. *Wheeler* (1991) 92 Cr.App.R. 279, C.A.
s. 5, see *R.* v. *Wills (Graham George)* (1991) 92 Cr.App.R. 297, C.A.
s. 7, amended: 1991, c. 53, s. 26.
s. 15, see *R.* v. *O'Connell, The Times*, June 11, 1991, C.A.
s. 17, see *R.* v. *Choraria and Golechha* [1990] Crim.L.R. 865, C.A.
s. 20, see *R.* v. *King, The Times*, June 26, 1991, C.A.; *R.* v. *Kassim* [1991] 3 W.L.R. 254, H.L.

64. Civil Evidence Act 1968.
see *Proetta* v. *Times Newspapers* [1991] 1 W.L.R. 337, C.A.
s. 11, amended: 1991, c. 53, sch. 11; repealed in pt.: *ibid.*, schs. 11, 13.

65. Gaming Act 1968.
s. 14, regs. 91/871, 987(S.).
s. 15, regs. 91/871.
s. 16, see *Crockfords Club* v. *Mehta, The Times*, March 20, 1991, Henry J.
s. 20, orders 91/870, 986(S.).
s. 20, amended: order 91/870.
s. 22, regs. 91/1892, 2047.
s. 34, sch. 9, see *Scotia Leisure* v. *City of Glasgow District Council* (I.H.), 1991 S.C.L.R. 232.
s. 48, orders 91/60, 273(S.), 2177, 2499(S.):
s. 48, amended: orders 91/60, 2177, 2499(S.).
s. 51, regs. 91/987(S.), 1892, 2047; orders 91/60, 870, 986(S.), 2177, 2499(S.).

67. Medicines Act 1968.
s. 1, order 91/962.
ss. 15, 35, order 91/633.
s. 57, order 90/2496.
s. 58, orders 91/962, 1392.
s. 59, order 91/1392.
s. 129, orders 90/2496; 91/962, 1392.
s. 132, order 91/962.

70. Law Reform (Miscellaneous Provisions) (Scotland) Act 1968.
s. 5, see *Allan, Petr.*, First Division, 1991 S.L.T. 203.

73. Transport Act 1968.
s. 6, see *D.P.P.* v. *Howard* (1991) 155 J.P.N. 27, D.C.
s. 14, amended: regs. 91/1997.

CAP.

1968—cont.

73. Transport Act 1968—*cont.*
ss. 24 (in pt.), 25, 27 (in pt.)–29 (in pt.), repealed: order 91/510.
s. 41, repealed in pt.: regs. 91/1997.
s. 42, amended: 1991, c. 63, s. 1.
ss. 44, 47, 50, repealed in pt.: order 91/510.
s. 60, see *D.P.P.* v. *Howard* [1991] R.T.R. 49, D.C.
ss. 60, 69E, 69G, regs. 91/2239.
s. 82, amended: 1991, c. 40, sch. 4.
ss. 85, 86, regs. 91/2239.
ss. 89, 91, regs. 91/1969, 2239.
s. 96, regs. 91/213, 299.
s. 97, see *Baron Meats* v. *Lockhart*, 1991 S.C.C.R. 537.
s. 97, regs. 91/381; amended: *ibid*.
s. 99, amended: 1991, c. 40, sch. 4.
s. 109, amended: 1991, c. 60, sch. 1.
s. 118, repealed in pt.: 1991, c. 22, sch. 9.
s. 121, orders 91/134, 933, 1162, 2194, 2210.
s. 159 (in pt.), schs. 1 (in pt.), 7, 16 (in pt.), repealed: order 91/510.
sch. 15, amended: regs. 91/1997.

77. Sea Fisheries Act 1968.
s. 5, amended: 1991, c. 53, sch. 4.

1969

10. Mines and Quarries (Tips) Act 1969.
s. 28, substituted: order 91/724.

46. Family Law Reform Act 1969.
s. 7, see *C. (A Minor), Re, The Times*, November 18, 1991, Sir Stephen Brown P.; *Calderdale Borough Council* v. *H. and P.* [1991] 1 F.L.R. 461, Hutchison J.
s. 22, regs. 91/12, 839.

48. Post Office Act 1969.
sch. 9, amended: 1991, c. 34, schs. 6, 12(S.).

54. Children and Young Persons Act 1969.
s. 1, amended: 1991, c. 53, sch. 11.
s. 2, see *R.* v. *B. County Council, ex p. P.* [1991] 1 W.L.R. 221, C.A.
s. 2, amended: 1991, c. 53, sch. 11.
s. 3, amended: *ibid.*; repealed in pt.: *ibid.*, sch. 13.
ss. 4, 5, repealed: *ibid.*, s. 72, sch. 13.
s. 7, amended: *ibid.*, sch. 11; repealed in pt.: *ibid.*, sch. 13.
ss. 7, 20A, see *R.* v. *Booth* (1989) 11 Cr.App.R.(S.) 258, C.A.
s. 8, repealed: 1991, c. 53, s. 72, sch. 13.
s. 10, amended: *ibid.*, sch. 11; repealed in pt.: *ibid.*, sch. 13.
s. 12AA, repealed in pt.: *ibid*.
s. 12D, amended: *ibid.*, sch. 11.
s. 15, substituted: *ibid.*, s. 66, sch. 7; amended: *ibid.*, sch. 11.
ss. 16, 16A, 20A–22, amended: *ibid*.

39. Rating Act 1971.
s. 2, see *Hardy* v. *Buxted P.C.C.*, 1991, C.A.

(20)

CAP.

1969—cont.

54. Children and Young Persons Act 1969—cont.
s. 23, substituted: *ibid.*, ss. 60, 62.
s. 25, amended and repealed in pt.: regs. 91/2032.
s. 26, order 91/2031.
s. 26, amended: regs. 91/2032.
s. 29, amended: 1991, c. 53, sch. 8.
s. 34, repealed in pt.: *ibid.*, sch. 13.
s. 69, order 91/2031.
s. 70, amended: 1991, c. 53, schs. 8, 11.
sch. 4, amended: *ibid.*, sch. 11; repealed in pt.: *ibid.*, sch. 13.

1970

9. Taxes Management Act 1970.
s. 18, amended: 1991, c. 31, sch. 11.
s. 20, see *R.* v. *I.R.C., ex p. T.C. Coombs & Co., The Times,* February 15, 1991, H.L.
s. 42, see *Gallic Leasing* v. *Coburn (Inspector of Taxes)* [1991] S.T.C. 151, C.A.
s. 54, see *I.R.C.* v. *Aken* [1990] 1 W.L.R. 1374; [1990] S.T.C. 497, C.A.
s. 56, see *Getty Oil Co.* v. *Steele (Inspector of Taxes)* [1990] S.T.C. 434, Vinelott J.; *Danquah* v. *Inland Revenue Commissioners* [1990] S.T.C. 672, Vinelott J.; *Billows* v. *Robinson (Inspector of Taxes)* [1991] S.T.C. 127, C.A.; *Gordon* v. *I.R.C., I.R.C.* v. *Gordon,* 1991 S.L.T. 730; *Fitzpatrick* v. *I.R.C.,* 1991 S.L.T. 841.
s. 63, Act of Sederunt 91/1920.
s. 65, order 91/1625; amended: *ibid.*
s. 66, amended and repealed in pt.: order 91/724.
s. 73, amended (S.): 1991, c. 50, sch. 1.
s. 78, see *R.* v. *I.R.C., ex p. Commerzbank AG* [1991] S.T.C. 271, D.C.
s. 78, amended: 1991, c. 31, s. 81; repealed in pt.: *ibid.*, s. 81, sch. 19.
s. 86, amended: *ibid.*, sch. 15; repealed in pt.: *ibid.*, sch. 19.
s. 87A, amended: *ibid.*, sch. 15.
s. 98, amended: *ibid.*, s. 33.
s. 99A, added: *ibid.*, s. 82.
s. 118, amended (S.): 1991, c. 50, sch. 1.

10. Income and Corporation Taxes Act 1970.
see *Shilton* v. *Wilmhurst (Inspector of Taxes)* [1991] 2 W.L.R. 530, H.L.
s. 8, see *Rignell (Inspector of Taxes)* v. *Andrews* [1990] S.T.C. 410, Ferris J.; *Holmes* v. *Mitchell (Inspector of Taxes), The Times,* December 6, 1990, Vinelott J.
s. 42, see *Holmes* v. *Mitchell (Inspector of Taxes), The Times,* December 6, 1990, Vinelott J.

CAP.

1970—cont.

10. Income and Corporation Taxes Act—cont.
s. 52, see *Moodie* v. *I.R.C.; Sotrick* v. *I.R.C.* [1990] 1 W.L.R. 1084, Hoffmann J.
s. 114, see *Peracha* v. *Miley (Inspector of Taxes)* [1990] S.T.C. 512, C.A.
ss. 135, 186, see *Ball (Inspector of Taxes)* v. *Phillips* [1990] S.T.C. 675, Hoffmann J.
s. 181, see *Shilton* v. *Wilmshurst (Inspector of Taxes)* [1991] 2 W.L.R. 530, H.L.; *McMenamin (Inspector of Taxes)* v. *Diggles, The Times,* June 19, 1991, Scott J.
s. 184, see *Leonard* v. *Blanchard (Inspector of Taxes), The Times,* November 29, 1991, Hoffmann J.
s. 189, see *Smith (Inspector of Taxes)* v. *Abbott; Same* v. *Holt; Same* v. *Scovell; Same* v. *Shuttleworth; Same* v. *Woodhouse, The Times,* October 23, 1991, Warner J.
s. 230, amended: 1991, c. 31, s. 76.
s. 258, see *Sainsbury (J.)* v. *O'Connor (Inspector of Taxes), The Times,* May 29, 1991, C.A.; *Gallic Leasing* v. *Coburn (Inspector of Taxes), The Times,* December 3, 1991, H.L.
s. 287, see *Collins* v. *Addies (Inspector of Taxes); Greenfield* v. *Bains (Inspector of Taxes), The Times,* July 16, 1991, Millett J.
ss. 342, 342A, amended: 1991, c. 31, ss. 95, 96; repealed in pt.: *ibid.*, s. 95, sch. 19.
s. 343, see *R.* v. *I.R.C., ex p. Woolwich Equitable Building Society* [1990] 1 W.L.R. 1400, H.L.

24. Finance Act 1970.
see *Mettoy Pension Trustees* v. *Evans* [1990] 1 W.L.R. 1587, Warner J.
s. 19, repealed in pt.: 1991, c. 31, s. 36.
s. 20A, added: *ibid.*

27. Fishing Vessels (Safety Provisions) Act 1970.
s. 6, regs. 91/784, 1404.
s. 7, rules 91/1342.

30. Conservation of Seals Act 1970.
s. 3, orders 90/2337(S.), 2338, 2500.
s. 10, amended: 1991, c. 28, sch. 2.
s. 14, order 90/2337(S.).

31. Administration of Justice Act 1970.
s. 36, see *First National Bank* v. *Syed* [1991] 2 All E.R. 250, C.A.
s. 41, see *R.* v. *Komsta; R.* v. *Murphy* (1990) 12 Cr.App.R.(S.) 63, C.A.
s. 41, repealed in pt.: order 91/724.

35. Conveyancing and Feudal Reform (Scotland) Act 1970.
s. 1, see *British Steel* v. *Kaye,* 1991 S.L.T. (Lands Tr.) 7; *Spafford* v. *Brydon,* 1991 S.L.T. (Lands Tr.) 49; *United Auctions (Scotland)* v. *British Railways Board,* 1991 S.L.T. (Lands Tr.) 71.

1970—cont.

35. Conveyancing and Feudal Reform (Scotland) Act 1970—*cont.*
s. 2, see *Watters* v. *Motherwell District Council*, 1991 S.L.T. (Lands Tr.) 2.
s. 25, see *Dick* v. *Clydesdale Bank*, 1991 S.L.T. 678.
s. 27, see *Alliance & Leicester Building Society* v. *Hecht* (Sh.Ct.), 1991 S.C.C.R. 562.
sch. 1, amended: 1991, c. 55, sch. 11.

36. Merchant Shipping Act 1970.
ss. 1–3, regs. 91/2144.
s. 68, regs. 91/2144, 2145.
s. 69, regs. 91/2144.
s. 84, regs. 91/784.
s. 92, regs. 91/1365, 1366.
s. 99, regs. 91/1819.

40. Agriculture Act 1970.
ss. 28, 29, schemes 91/2, 1338, 1339.
s. 66, regs. 91/973, 1475, 2197, 2840.
s. 67, regs. 91/973.
ss. 68–70, regs. 91/1475, 2197, 2840.
s. 73, regs. 91/1475.
s. 74, regs. 91/1475, 2197, 2840.
s. 74A, regs. 91/973, 1475, 2197, 2840.
ss. 75–79, regs. 91/973.
s. 84, regs. 91/973, 1475, 2197, 2840.

44. Chronically Sick and Disabled Persons Act 1970.
s. 20, amended: 1990, c. 40, sch. 4.
s. 21, amended: *ibid.*, s. 35; repealed in pt.: *ibid.*, s. 35, sch. 8.

1971

3. Guardianship of Minors Act 1971.
s. 1, see *G. (A Minor) (Child Abduction: Enforcement), Re* [1990] 2 F.L.R. 325, Booth J.
s. 9, see *W.* v. *B., The Times*, March 26, 1991, Ewbank J.
s. 11B, see *H. & O., The Times*, July 8, 1991, Ward J.

10. Vehicles (Excise) Act 1971.
s. 1, amended: 1991, c. 31, sch. 3.
s. 4, amended: *ibid.*, s. 8, sch. 3; repealed in pt.: *ibid.*, s. 8, sch. 19.
s. 5, amended: *ibid.*, sch. 3; c. 40, sch. 4.
s. 7, amended: 1991, c. 21, sch. 2; c. 31, sch. 3; repealed in pt.: *ibid.*, s. 8, schs. 3, 19, Pts. III, IV.
s. 9, amended: 1991, c. 31, sch. 3; c. 53, sch. 11; repealed in pt.: *ibid.*, schs. 11, 13.
s. 13, amended: 1991, c. 31, sch. 3.
s. 18, amended: *ibid.*; repealed in pt.: *ibid.*
s. 18A, amended: *ibid.*
s. 18B, added: *ibid.*, s. 9; amended: *ibid.*, sch. 3.
s. 22, amended: *ibid.*
s. 26, amended: *ibid.*, s. 9.
s. 27, amended: *ibid.*, sch. 3.

1971—cont.

10. Vehicles (Excise) Act 1971—*cont.*
s. 28A, substituted: *ibid.*
ss. 31, 32, 34, 35, amended: *ibid.*
s. 37, amended: *ibid.*, s. 9, sch. 3.
s. 38, repealed in pt.: *ibid.*, sch. 19.
s. 40, amended: *ibid.*, sch. 3.
sch. 1, amended: *ibid.*, s. 4, sch. 3.
sch. 2, amended: *ibid.*, sch. 3.
sch. 3, amended: *ibid.*, s. 4, sch. 3.
sch. 4, amended: *ibid.*, sch. 3.
sch. 4A, amended: *ibid.*, c. 40, sch. 4.
sch. 6, repealed: 1991, c. 31, sch. 19.

19. Carriage of Goods by Sea Act 1971.
sch., see *Cia Portorafti Commerciale S.A.* v. *Ultramar Panama Inc.; Captain Gregos, The* [1990] 1 Lloyd's Rep. 310, C.A.

22. Animals Act 1971.
s. 2, see *Hunt* v. *Wallis, The Times*, May 10, 1991, Pill J.

23. Courts Act 1971.
sch. 8, repealed in pt.: 1991, c. 53, sch. 13.

29. National Savings Bank Act 1971.
ss. 2, 8, regs. 91/72.

32. Attachment of Earnings Act 1971.
s. 3, amended: 1991, c. 17, sch. 2; repealed in pt.: *ibid.*, schs. 2, 3.
s. 7, order 91/356.
s. 23, amended: 1991, c. 53, sch. 4.

38. Misuse of Drugs Act 1971.
s. 2, order 90/2589.
s. 3, see *Nazir Chinoy, Re* [1991] C.O.D. 105, D.C.
s. 4, see *Clements* v. *H.M. Advocate*, 1991 S.L.T. 388.
ss. 4, 5, see *McDowall* v. *H.M. Advocate*, 1991 S.C.C.R. 197.
s. 5, see *Davidson* v. *H.M. Advocate*, 1990 S.C.C.R. 699; *McCreadie* v. *Walkingshaw*, 1990 S.C.C.R. 761; *Murray* v. *MacPhail*, 1991 S.C.C.R. 245; *Hodder* v. *D.P.P.; Matthews* v. *D.P.P.* [1990] Crim.L.R. 261, D.C.
s. 7, regs. 90/2360; order 90/2631; S.Rs. 1991 Nos. 1, 2.
s. 10, regs. 90/2360; S.R. 1991 No. 1.
s. 20, see *R.* v. *Ahmed* [1990] Crim.L.R. 648, C.A.
s. 23, see *Weir* v. *Jessop*, 1991 S.C.C.R. 242.
s. 28, see *R.* v. *McGowan* [1990] Crim.L.R. 399, C.A.
s. 30, regs. 91/339.
s. 31, regs. 90/2360; 91/339; S.R. 1991 No. 1.
s. 33, see *Nazir Chinoy, Re* [1991] C.O.D. 105, D.C.
s. 37, regs. 91/339.
sch. 2, see *Hodder* v. *D.P.P.; Matthews* v. *D.P.P.* [1990] Crim.L.R. 261, D.C.

39. Rating Act 1971.
s. 2, see *Hambleton District Council* v. *Buxted Poultry, The Times*, August 8, 1991, C.A.

1971—cont.

40. Fire Precautions Act 1971.
ss. 12, 40, regs. 91/259.

49. Rural Water Supplies and Sewerage Act 1971.
repealed: 1991, c. 60, sch. 3.

56. Pensions (Increase) Act 1971.
s. 5, regs. 91/786–788.
s. 13, regs. 91/2419.

58. Sheriff Courts (Scotland) Act 1971.
s. 32, Acts of Sederunt 91/24, 145, 821, 1920, 2205, 2214.
s. 37, see *Data Controls (Middlesbrough)* v. *British Railways Board*, 1991 S.L.T. 426.
s. 37, amended: 1991, c. 50, sch. 1.

59. Merchant Shipping (Oil Pollution) Act 1971.
s. 11, regs. 90/2345.

61. Mineral Workings (Offshore Installations) Act 1971.
ss. 2, 4, 5, regs. 91/679.
s. 6, regs. 91/308, 679.
s. 11, see *MacMillan* v. *Wimpey Offshore Engineers and Constructors*, 1991 S.L.T. 515.
s. 12, regs. 91/679.
sch. 1, regs. 91/308.

62. Tribunals and Inquiries Act 1971.
s. 7, amended: 1991, c. 21, sch. 2; c. 48, sch. 5.
s. 15, order 91/2699.
sch. 1, amended: 1991, c. 21, sch. 2; c. 40, sch. 7; c. 48, sch. 5.

68. Finance Act 1971.
s. 41, see *Ensign Tankers (Leasing)* v. *Stokes (Inspector of Taxes)* [1991] S.T.C. 136, C.A.
sch. 8, see *Barclays Mercantile Industrial Finance* v. *Melluish (Inspector of Taxes)* [1990] S.T.C. 314, Vinelott J.

69. Medicines Act 1971.
see *R.* v. *Secretary of State for Health, ex p. Natural Medicines Group* [1991] C.O.D. 60, Pill J.
regs. 90/2326.
s. 1, regs. 91/632, 1474, 2063.

77. Immigration Act 1971.
see *Vilvarajah (Nadarajah)* v. *Secretary of State for the Home Department; Skandarajah (Vaithlialingham)* v. *Same* [1990] Imm.A.R. 457, C.A.; *Grazales (Jorge)* v. *Secretary of State for the Home Department* [1990] Imm.A.R. 505, C.A.
s. 1, see *R.* v. *Secretary of State for the Home Department, ex p. Begum (Angur); Same* v. *Same, ex p. Begum (Rukhshanda)* [1990] Imm.A.R. 1, C.A.

1971—cont.

77. Immigration Act 1971—*cont.*
s. 3, see *R.* v. *Secretary of State for the Home Department, ex p. Oladehinde; R.* v. *Same, ex p. Alexander* [1990] 3 W.L.R. 797; [1990] 3 All E.R. 393, H.L.; *R.* v. *Secretary of State for the Home Department, ex p. Cheblak, The Times,* February 7, 1991, C.A.; *R.* v. *Secretary of State for the Home Department, ex p. Balogun (Bolanle)* [1989] Imm. A.R. 603, C.A.; *Bamgbose, Re* [1990] Imm.A.R. 135, C.A.; *R.* v. *Secretary of State for the Home Department, ex p. Rakesh Arora* [1990] Imm.A.R. 89, McCullough J.; *R.* v. *Secretary of State for the Home Department, ex p. Singh (Madanjit)* [1990] Imm.A.R. 124, C.A.; *R.* v. *Secretary of State for the Home Department, ex p. Kuku* [1990] Imm.A.R. 27, C.A.; *R.* v. *Secretary of State for the Home Department, ex p. Mowla* [1990] Imm.A.R. 244, Roch J.; *R.* v. *Secretary of State for the Home Department, ex p. Anderson* [1991] C.O.D. 38, C.A.; *R.* v. *Secretary of State for the Home Department, ex p. Islam* [1990] Imm.A.R. 220, Simon Brown J.; *Ayo (Bashiru Adebola)* v. *Immigration Appeal Tribunal* [1990] Imm.A.R. 461, C.A.; *R.* v. *Secretary of State for the Home Department, ex p. Sadiq* [1990] Imm.A.R. 364, Otton J.; *R.* v. *Secretary of State for the Home Department, ex p. Saffu-Mensah (Kwadwo)* [1991] Imm.A.R. 43, Webster J.; *Fawehinmi* v. *Secretary of State for the Home Department* [1991] Imm.A.R. 1, C.A.; *R.* v. *Secretary of State for the Home Department, ex p. Adebodun (Adedayo Williams)* [1991] Imm.A.R. 60, Pill J.
s. 3, orders 91/77, 980, 1083.
s. 4, orders 91/77, 980, 1083; regs. 91/965.
ss. 4, 8, see *R.* v. *Secretary of State for the Home Department, ex p. Bagga* [1990] 3 W.L.R. 1013, C.A.
s. 5, see *R.* v. *Secretary of State for the Home Department, ex p. Cheblak, The Times,* February 7, 1991, C.A.
s. 6, see *R.* v. *Omojudi, The Times,* October 28, 1991, C.A.
s. 8, see *R.* v. *Secretary of State for the Home Department, ex p. Man Keng Wilan* [1989] Imm. A.R. 501, Farquharson J.

CAP.

1971—cont.

77. Immigration Act 1971—*cont.*

s. 13, see *R.* v. *Immigration Appeal Tribunal, ex p. Secretary of State for the Home Department* [1990] 1 W.L.R. 1126; [1990] 3 All E.R. 652, C.A.; *R.* v. *Secretary of State for the Home Department, ex p. Balogun (Bolanle)* [1989] Imm. A.R. 603, C.A.; *Secretary of State for the Home Department* v. *Immigration Appeal Tribunal and an Adjudicator* [1990] Imm.A.R. 492, C.A.

s. 14, see *R.* v. *Secretary of State for the Home Department, ex p. Sadiq* [1990] C.O.D. 341, Otton J.; *R.* v. *Secretary of State for the Home Department, ex p. Selo Wa-Selo* [1990] Imm.A.R. 76, C.A.

ss. 15, 18, see *R.* v. *Secretary of State for the Home Department, ex p. Cheblak, The Times,* February 7, 1991, C.A.

s. 21, see *R.* v. *Secretary of State for the Home Department, ex p. Uddin (Noor)* [1990] Imm.A.R. 181, McCullough J.; *R.* v. *Immigration Appeal Tribunal, ex p. Ali (Jaifor)* [1990] Imm.A.R. 531, Kennedy J.

s. 22, rules 91/1545.

s. 26, see *R.* v. *Secretary of State for the Home Department, ex p. Saffu-Mensah (Kwadwo)* [1991] Imm.A.R. 43, Webster J.

s. 33, see *R.* v. *Secretary of State for the Home Department, ex p. Balogun (Bolanle)* [1989] Imm. A.R. 603, C.A.; *R.* v. *Secretary of State for the Home Department, ex p. Chomsuk (Saichon)* [1991] Imm.A.R. 29, Pill J.; *Fawehinmi* v. *Secretary of State for the Home Department* [1991] Imm.A.R. 1, C.A.

s. 36, order 91/2630.

sch. 2, see *R.* v. *Secretary of State for the Home Department, ex p. Bagga* [1990] 3 W.L.R. 1013, C.A; *R.* v. *Secretary of State for the Home Department, ex p. Labiche, The Times,* January 14, 1991, C.A.; *R.* v. *Secretary of State for the Home Department, ex p. Rehal (Tejpartap Singh)* [1989] Imm. A.R. 576, C.A.; *R.* v. *Secretary of State for the Home Department, ex p. Singh (Parshottam)* [1989] Imm. A.R. 469, C.A.; *R.* v. *Secretary of State for the Home Department, ex p. K. Alnafeesi* [1990] C.O.D. 262, C.A.; *R.* v. *Secretary of State for the Home Department, ex p. Minton* [1990] Imm.A.R. 199, C.A.; *R.* v. *Secretary of State for the Home Department, ex p. Nwauarue, The Independent,* August 29, 1991, Auld J.; *R.* v. *Secretary of State for the Home Department, ex p. Kumar*

CAP.

1971—cont.

77. Immigration Act 1971—*cont.*

[1990] Imm.A.R. 265, Hodgson J.; *Maybasan (Serif); Cobantay (Filit); Sultan Basanmay; Oral (Rifat); Bakgitar (Nugret); Taycur (Mehmet); Maybaskarn (Huseyan), Re* [1991] Imm.A.R. 89, Otton J.; *R.* v. *Secretary of State for the Home Department, ex p. Saffu-Mensah (Kwadwo)* [1991] Imm.A.R. 43, Webster J.; *R.* v. *Secretary of State for the Home Department, ex p. Yassine (Khalil)* [1990] Imm.A.R. 354, Schiemann J.

sch. 2, rules 91/1545.

78. Town and Country Planning Act 1971.

see *R.* v. *Razzell* (1990) 12 Cr.App.R. (S.) 142, C.A.

s. 22, see *Cambridge City Council* v. *Secretary of State for the Environment,* [1991] 09 E.G. 119, Widdicombe Q.C.; *Northumberland County Council* v. *Secretary of State for the Environment and British Coal Corporation* (1990) 59 P. & C.R. 468, D.C.

s. 23, see *South Ribble Borough Council* v. *Secretary of State for the Environment and Shires* (1991) 61 P. & C.R. 87, D.C.

ss. 23, 25, see *Westminster City Council* v. *Secretary of State for the Environment and Dukegrade* [1990] J.P.L. 277, D.C.

s. 29, see *Bath Society* v. *Secretary of State for the Environment* [1991] 2 P.L.R. 51, C.A.

ss. 29, 30, see *Proberun* v. *Secretary of State for the Environment, sub nom. Medina Borough Council* v. *Proberun* (1991) 61 P. & C.R. 77, C.A.

ss. 29, 41–43, see *R.* v. *Lewes District Council, ex p. Saunders* [1991] C.O.D. 75, McCullough J.

s. 43, see *Thayer* v. *Secretary of State for the Environment, The Independent,* August 15, 1991, C.A.; *Oakimber* v. *Elmbridge Borough Council* [1991] E.C.G.S. 33, C.A.

s. 51, see *R.* v. *East Hertfordshire District Council, ex p. Smith* (1991) 23 H.L.R. 23, C.A.

s. 52, see *Barclays Bank Application, Re* (1990) 60 P. & C.R. 354, Lands Tr.; *Att.-Gen. (ex rel. Scotland)* v. *Barratt (Manchester)* (1990) 60 P. & C.R. 475, Scott J.; *Secretary of State for the Environment and Rochester upon Medway City Council* v. *Hobday* (1990) 61 P. & C.R. 225, C.A.

s. 53, see *Hendricks (J.M.)* v. *Secretary of State for the Environment and Eastbourne Borough Council* (1990) 59 P. & C.R. 443, D.C.

1971—cont.

78. Town and Country Planning Act 1971—*cont.*

s. 60, see *R.* v. *Alath Construction; R.* v. *Brightman* [1990] 1 W.L.R. 1255, C.A.

ss. 64, 88, see *Westminster City Council* v. *Secretary of State for the Environment and Bally Group (U.K.)* [1990] 1 P.L.R. 30, Popplewell J.

ss. 65, 88, see *R.* v. *Oxford Crown Court, ex p. Smith* [1990] C.O.D. 211, Simon Brown J.

s. 87, see *Gregory* v. *Secretary of State for the Environment; Rawlins* v. *Same* (1990) 60 P. & C.R. 413, C.A.

s. 88, see *Barraclough* v. *Secretary of State for the Environment and Leeds City Council* [1990] J.P.L. 911, Mr. R. Vandermeer, Q.C.; *R.* v. *Wychavon District Council, ex p. Saunders, The Times,* November 15, Popplewell J.; *Kaur* v. *Secretary of State for the Environment* (1989) 61 P. & C.R. 249, D.C.

ss. 88, 88A, 88B, 92, see *Newbury District Council* v. *Secretary of State for the Environment* [1991] 6 E.G. 164, C.A.

s. 90, see *Arora* v. *Hackney London Borough Council; Motivation Display* v. *Same, The Times,* January 24, 1991, D.C.; *R.* v. *Pettigrove and Roberts* [1990] Crim.L.R. 747, C.A.; *East Hampshire District Council* v. *Davies* [1991] 10 E.G. 149, C.A.

s. 92, see *R.* v. *Chichester Justices, ex p. Chichester District Council* (1990) 60 P. & C.R. 342, D.C.

s. 102, see *R.* v. *Alath Construction; R.* v. *Brightman* [1990] 1 W.L.R. 1255, C.A.

s. 109, see *Kingsley* v. *Hammersmith and Fulham London Borough Council, The Times,* April 30, 1991, D.C.

s. 112, see *Sharkey* v. *Secretary of State for the Environment* [1990] 45 E.G. 113, Roch J.

ss. 172, 173, see *Ramsey* v. *Secretary of State for the Environment* (1991) 2 P.L.R. 112, Gerald Moriarty, Q.C.

ss. 180, 181, see *Gavaghan* v. *Secretary of State for the Environment and South Hams District Council* (1990) 60 P. & C.R. 515, C.A.

s. 209, see *Vasiliou* v. *Secretary of State for Transport* [1991] 2 All E.R. 77, C.A.

s. 244, see *South Western Regional Health Authority* v. *Avon County Council* [1990] J.P.L. 919, Mr. Malcolm Spence, Q.C.

1971—cont.

78. Town and Country Planning Act 1971—*cont.*

s. 245, see *Times Investment* v. *Secretary of State for the Environment and London Borough of Tower Hamlets* (1990) 3 P.L.R. 111, C.A.; *Westminster City Council* v. *Secretary of State for the Environment and Dukegrade* [1990] J.P.L. 277, D.C.; *Reading Borough Council* v. *Secretary of State for the Environment* [1990] C.O.D. 383, Schiemann J.; *Charnwood Borough Council* v. *Secretary of State for the Environment* (1990) 60 P. & C.R. 498, Lionel Read Q.C.; *Gavaghan* v. *Secretary of State for the Environment and South Hams District Council* (1990) 60 P. & C.R. 515, C.A.; *Save Britain's Heritage* v. *Secretary of State for the Environment and Number 1 Poultry and City Index Property* [1991] 1 W.L.R. 153, H.L.; *West Oxfordshire District Council* v. *Secretary of State for the Environment and Wates Built Homes* [1991] J.P.L. 58, Mr. L. Read, Q.C.; *Orchard* v. *Secretary of State for the Environment and Stroud District Council* [1991] J.P.L. 64, Mr. Gerald Moriarty, Q.C.; *Swishbrook* v. *Secretary of State for the Environment and Islington Borough Council* [1990] J.P.L. 824, C.A.; *James* v. *Secretary of State for the Environment and Chichester District Council* (1990) 61 P. & C.R. 234, D.C.

s. 246, see *R.* v. *Secretary of State for the Environment, ex p. Botton, The Times,* March 26, 1991, D.C.; *R.* v. *Secretary of State for the Environment, ex p. Davidson* (1990) 59 P. & C.R. 480, Nolan J.; *Secretary of State for the Environment and Rochester upon Medway City Council* v. *Hobday* (1990) 61 P. & C.R. 225, C.A.; *Blue Anchor Leisure* v. *Secretary of State for the Environment and East Lindsey District Council* [1990] J.P.L. 934, Mr. R. Vandermeer Q.C.

s. 277, see *Unex Dumpton* v. *Secretary of State for the Environment and Forest Heath District Council* [1990] 2 P.L.R. 1, Mr. Roy Vandermeer Q.C.; *Bath Society* v. *Secretary of State for the Environment* [1991] 2 P.L.R. 51, C.A.; *South Lakeland District Council* v. *Secretary of State for the Environment* (1991) 2 P.L.R. 97, C.A.

s. 290, see *Cambridge City Council* v. *Secretary of State for the Environment* [1991] 09 E.G. 119, Mr. David Widdicombe Q.C.

sch. 24, see *Oakimber* v. *Elmbridge Borough Council* [1991] E.C.G.S. 33, C.A.

CAP.
1972
11. Superannuation Act 1972.
see *R.* v. *H.M. Treasury, ex p. Petch* [1990] C.O.D. 19, Popplewell J.
s. 1, order 91/1166 (S.).
s. 7, regs. 90/2480; 91/78(S.), 1203.
s. 10, regs. 91/584.
s. 12, regs. 91/78(S.), 584, 1203.
s. 24, regs. 90/2380; 91/584.
sch. 3, regs. 91/584.
sch. 4, repealed in pt.: 1991, c. 66, sch. 2.

15. Transport (Grants) Act 1972.
s. 1, repealed in pt.: order 90/510.

18. Maintenance Orders (Reciprocal Enforcement) Act 1972.
ss. 7–9, amended: 1991, c. 17, sch. 1.
s. 27, amended: *ibid.*, repealed in pt.: *ibid.*, schs. 1, 3.
ss. 28, 28A, 33, 34, amended: *ibid.*, sch. 1.
s. 34A, added: *ibid.*
s. 35, amended: *ibid.*

20. Road Traffic Act 1972.
s. 5, see *Pelosi* v. *Jessop*, High Court of Justiciary, February 6, 1990; *Capell* v. *D.P.P.* (1991) 155 J.P.N. 139, D.C.
ss. 7, 8, see *Jones* v. *D.P.P.* [1990] Crim.L.R. 656, D.C.; *R.* v. *Thomas* [1990] Crim.L.R. 269, D.C.
s. 8, see *McIntosh* v. *Lowe*, 1991 S.C.C.R. 154; *D.P.P.* v. *Eddowes* [1991] R.T.R. 35, D.C.; *Young* v. *Carmichael*, 1991 S.C.C.R. 332; *D.P.P.* v. *Byrne* [1991] R.T.R. 119, D.C.
s. 10, see *Butler* v. *D.P.P.* [1990] R.T.R. 377, D.C.; *Millard* v. *D.P.P.* [1990] R.T.R. 201, D.C.
ss. 25, 166, see *R.* v. *Kingston upon Thames Crown Court, ex p. Scarll* [1990] Crim.L.R. 429, D.C.
s. 40, see *D.P.P.* v. *Marshall and Bell* [1990] R.T.R. 384, D.C.; *D.P.P.* v. *Young* [1991] R.T.R. 56, D.C.
s. 53, see *Mowbray* v. *Valentine*, 1991 S.C.C.R. 494.
s. 148, see *Pitts* v. *Hunt* [1990] 3 W.L.R. 542, C.A.
s. 179, see *D.P.P.* v. *Pidhajeckyi* [1991] R.T.R. 136, D.C.
s. 196, see *Price* v. *D.P.P.* [1990] R.T.R. 413, D.C.

27. Road Traffic (Foreign Vehicles) Act 1972.
ss. 1, 2, 7, amended: 1991, c. 40, sch. 4.
sch. 1, repealed in pt.: *ibid.*, sch. 8.
sch. 2, amended: *ibid.*, sch. 4.

35. Defective Premises Act 1972.
s. 1, see *Andrews* v. *Schooling* [1991] 1 W.L.R. 783, C.A.

41. Finance Act 1972.
s. 85, see *Procter & Gamble* v. *Taylerson (Inspector of Taxes)* [1990] S.T.C. 624, C.A.

CAP.
1972—cont.
41. Finance Act 1972—cont.
s. 134, repealed in pt.: 1991, c. 31, sch. 19.

48. Parliamentary and Other Pensions Act 1972.
ss. 3, 7, 9, 10, 13, 15, 16, 25, amended: regs. 91/609.
s. 26, amended: 1991, c. 5, s. 1.
s. 27, repealed in pt.: *ibid.*
s. 28, amended: *ibid.*
s. 29, repealed: *ibid.*
sch. 5, added: regs. 91/609.

52. Town and Country Planning (Scotland) Act 1972.
s. 5, amended: 1991, c. 34, sch. 13.
ss. 9–13, see *Falkirk District Council* v. *Secretary of State for Scotland* (I.H.), 1991 S.L.T. 553.
s. 18A, added: 1991, c. 34, s. 58.
s. 19, see *Anderson* v. *Secretary of State for Scotland*, 1991 S.C.L.R. 570.
s. 19, amended: 1991, c. 34, ss. 44, 45; repealed in pt.: *ibid.*, schs. 12, 19.
s. 21, order 91/147.
ss. 21, 23, amended: 1991, c. 34, sch. 13.
s. 24, substituted: *ibid.*, s. 46.
s. 26, see *North East Fife District Council* v. *Secretary of State for Scotland* (I.H.), 1990 S.C.L.R. 647; *Ladbroke Racing* v. *Secretary of State for Scotland*, 1990 S.C.L.R. 705; *City of Aberdeen District Council* v. *Skean Dhu*, 1991 S.L.T. (Lands Tr.) 22; *Clydesdale District Council* v. *Law Mining* (I.H.), 1991 S.C.L.R. 236.
s. 26, amended: 1991, c. 34, s. 46.
s. 26A, added: *ibid.*, s. 47.
s. 26B, added: *ibid.*, s. 48.
s. 27, see *North East Fife District Council* v. *Secretary of State for Scotland* (I.H.), 1990 S.C.L.R. 647.
s. 27A, amended: 1991, c. 34, sch. 8.
s. 28, amended: *ibid.*, sch. 13; repealed in pt.: *ibid.*, sch. 19.
s. 29, substituted: *ibid.*, sch. 13.
ss. 31, 32, amended: *ibid.*
s. 33, see *Clydesdale District Council* v. *Law Mining* (I.H.), 1991 S.C.L.R. 236.
s. 33, amended: 1991, c. 34, s. 50, sch. 13; repealed in pt.: *ibid.*, sch. 13.
s. 34, amended: *ibid.*, s. 47, sch. 13; repealed in pt.: *ibid.*, s. 47.
ss. 35, 36, repealed: *ibid.*, schs. 12, 19.
s. 37, amended: *ibid.*, sch. 12.
s. 38, amended: *ibid.*, schs. 8, 13.
s. 39, amended: *ibid.*, sch. 13.
s. 40, amended: *ibid.*, schs. 12, 13.
ss. 40, 41, see *North East Fife District Council* v. *Secretary of State for Scotland* (I.H.), 1990 S.C.L.R. 647.

CAP.

1972—cont.

52. Town and Country Planning (Scotland) Act 1972—cont.

s. 41A, amended: 1991, c. 34, sch. 8; repealed in pt.: *ibid.*, sch. 19.

s. 49, amended: *ibid.*, schs. 8, 13.

ss. 49A, 49B, 49F, amended: *ibid.*, sch. 8.

s. 49H, added: *ibid.*, s. 52.

s. 50, amended: *ibid.*, s. 49.

s. 51, repealed: *ibid.*, schs. 13, 19.

s. 53, amended: *ibid.*, sch. 10.

s. 55, amended: *ibid.*, sch. 13.

s. 56G, amended: *ibid.*, sch. 12.

s. 56L, amended: *ibid.*, sch. 10.

s. 58, repealed in pt.: *ibid.*, schs. 12, 19.

s. 60, see *Brown* v. *Michael B. Cooper* (Sh.Ct.), 1990 S.C.C.R. 675.

s. 61, repealed in pt.: 1991, c. 34, sch. 19.

ss. 83C, 83D, added: *ibid.*, s. 33.

s. 84A, amended: *ibid.*, sch. 13.

s. 85, see *Anderson* v. *Secretary of State for Scotland*, 1991 S.C.L.R. 570.

s. 85, amended: 1991, c. 34, s. 38, sch. 13; repealed in pt.: *ibid.*, schs. 13, 19.

s. 86, substituted: *ibid.*, s. 40.

s. 87, amended: *ibid.*, s. 41, sch. 13.

s. 87A, amended: *ibid.*, sch. 13.

s. 88, amended: *ibid.*, s. 39; repealed in pt.: *ibid.*, schs. 13, 19.

s. 89, amended: *ibid.*, sch. 13.

s. 89A, substituted: *ibid.*

s. 90, substituted: *ibid.*, s. 42.

ss. 90A–90C, added: *ibid.*

s. 91, amended: *ibid.*, sch. 13; repealed in pt.: *ibid.*, schs. 13, 19.

ss. 91A–91C, added: *ibid.*, s. 43.

s. 92, amended: *ibid.*, sch. 10; repealed in pt.: *ibid.*

s. 93, amended: *ibid.*, repealed in pt.: *ibid.*, schs. 10, 19.

s. 94, substituted: *ibid.*, sch. 10.

s. 95, amended: *ibid.*

ss. 97AB, 97AC, added: *ibid.*

s. 97B, amended: *ibid.*

ss. 97BA–97BC, added: *ibid.*

s. 98, see *Brown* v. *Michael B. Cooper* (Sh.Ct.), 1990 S.C.C.R. 675.

s. 98, amended: 1991, c. 34, s. 54; repealed in pt.: *ibid.*, s. 54, sch. 19.

s. 99, amended: *ibid.*, s. 54.

ss. 99A–99C, added: *ibid.*

s. 100, amended: *ibid.*, sch. 8.

s. 101, amended: *ibid.*, sch. 13; repealed in pt.: *ibid.*, sch. 19.

s. 101A, added: *ibid.*, s. 56.

s. 106, repealed in pt.: *ibid.*, schs. 12, 19.

Pt. VII (ss. 123–152), exc. s. 145, repealed: *ibid.*, s. 60, sch. 19.

CAP.

1972—cont.

52. Town and Country Planning (Scotland) Act 1972—cont.

s. 145, amended: *ibid.*, sch. 13; repealed in pt.: *ibid.*

s. 153, amended: *ibid.*, sch. 12.

s. 153A, repealed: *ibid.*, schs. 8, 19.

s. 154, amended: *ibid.*, s. 44.

s. 155, amended: *ibid.*, sch. 12; repealed in pt.: *ibid.*, schs. 12, 19.

s. 156, repealed: *ibid.*, schs. 12, 19.

ss. 156A, 156B, added: *ibid.*, sch. 12.

s. 157, amended: *ibid.*, repealed in pt.: *ibid.*, schs. 12, 19.

ss. 158, 160, repealed: *ibid.*, s. 60, sch. 19.

s. 166, amended: *ibid.*, s. 41, sch. 13; repealed in pt.: *ibid.*, schs. 13, 19.

s. 167A, substituted: *ibid.*, sch. 8.

ss. 167B, 167C, repealed: *ibid.*, schs. 8, 19.

ss. 169, amended: *ibid.*, sch. 8; repealed in pt.: *ibid.*, schs. 8, 19.

ss. 176, 179, amended: *ibid.*, sch. 12.

ss. 181, 182, 190, amended: *ibid.*, sch. 17.

s. 201, repealed in pt.: *ibid.*, schs. 13, 19.

s. 209, amended: 1991, c. 22, sch. 8.

s. 214, repealed in pt.: 1991, c. 34, schs. 13, 19.

s. 218, substituted: *ibid.*, sch. 17.

s. 231, amended: *ibid.*, sch. 13; repealed in pt.: *ibid.*, schs. 12, 19.

ss. 231–233, see *Anderson* v. *Secretary of State for Scotland*, 1991 S.C.L.R. 570.

ss. 231, 233, see *Clydesdale District Council* v. *Law Mining* (I.H.), 1991 S.C.L.R. 236.

s. 233, see *North East Fife District Council* v. *Secretary of State for Scotland* (I.H.), 1990 S.C.L.R. 647; *Ladbroke Racing* v. *Secretary of State for Scotland*, 1990 S.C.L.R. 705.

s. 234, repealed: 1991, c. 34, schs. 13, 19.

s. 242, repealed in pt.: *ibid.*, sch. 13.

s. 244, amended: *ibid.*, sch. 12; repealed in pt.: *ibid.*, schs. 12, 19.

ss. 245, 246 (in pt.), repealed: *ibid.*

s. 247, amended: *ibid.*, sch. 13; repealed in pt.: *ibid.*, sch. 12.

ss. 248, 249 (in pt.), repealed: *ibid.*, schs. 12, 19.

s. 251, amended: *ibid.*, sch. 8; repealed in pt.: *ibid.*, schs. 8, 19.

s. 251A, substituted: *ibid.*, sch. 8.

s. 253, amended: *ibid.*, sch. 13.

s. 254, amended: *ibid.*, s. 49.

s. 255, amended: *ibid.*, sch. 12.

s. 262C, amended: 1991, c. 28, s. 6; repealed in pt.: *ibid.*, sch. 11.

CAP.

1972—cont.

52. Town and Country Planning (Scotland) Act 1972—*cont.*

ss. 263, 264, repealed: 1991, c. 34, schs. 12, 19.

s. 265, amended: *ibid.*, schs. 10, 13; repealed in pt.: *ibid.*, schs. 13, 19.

s. 266, amended: *ibid.*, s. 43, sch. 13.

s. 273, order 91/147.

s. 273, amended: 1991, c. 34, sch. 17.

s. 275, amended: *ibid.*, s. 55, schs. 8, 13; repealed in pt.: *ibid.*, schs. 8, 12, 13, 19.

sch. 5, see *City of Aberdeen District Council* v. *Skean Dhu*, 1991 S.L.T. (Lands Tr.) 22.

sch. 6, amended: 1991, c. 34, sch. 12; repealed in pt.: *ibid.*, schs. 12, 19.

sch. 6A, amended: *ibid.*, sch. 11; repealed in pt.: *ibid.*, schs. 12, 19.

sch. 7, see *North East Fife District Council* v. *Secretary of State for Scotland* (I.H.), 1990 S.C.L.R. 647.

sch. 7, amended: 1991, c. 34, s. 50, sch. 13; repealed in pt.: *ibid.*, sch. 19.

sch. 10, amended: *ibid.*, sch. 13.

sch. 10A, added: *ibid.*, sch. 9.

sch. 12, repealed: *ibid.*, sch. 19.

schs. 13–15, repealed: *ibid.*, s. 60, sch. 19.

sch. 19, amended: *ibid.*, sch. 13; repealed in pt.: *ibid.*, schs. 12, 19.

sch. 24, see *The Royal Bank of Scotland* v. *Clydebank District Council* (O.H.), 1991 S.L.T. 635.

61. Land Charges Act 1972.

s. 1, amended and repealed in pt.: order 91/724.

sch. 2, amended: 1991, c. 60, sch. 1.

65. National Debt Act 1972.

s. 11, regs. 91/73–76, 1031, 1337, 1407.

68. European Communities Act 1972.

s. 1, order 91/758.

s. 2, see *R.* v. *Secretary of State for Transport, ex p. Factortame (No. 2)* [1990] 3 W.L.R. 818, H.L.

s. 2, regs. 90/2325, 2336, 2377, 2640, 2641, 2660; 91/3, 52, 139, 187, 214, 300, 335, 381, 392, 447, 486, 777, 780(S.), 820, 823, 824, 832, 1285, 1396, 1439, 1475, 1527, 1609(S.), 1620, 1630, 1735(S.), 1993, 2000, 2198, 2232, 2237, 2239, 2242, 2531, 2704, 2724, 2725, 2727, 2749, 2840; orders 91/755, 1218, 1221, 1847, 2289; S.Rs. 1990 Nos. 440, 444, 455; 1991 Nos. 5, 6, 14, 58, 141, 157, 187, 205, 257, 264, 286, 339, 376, 405.

ss. 2, 3, see *McKechnie* v. *UBM Building Supplies (Southern)* [1991] I.R.L.R. 283, E.A.T.

s. 3, see *Thomas* v. *Chief Adjudication Officer and Secretary of State for Social Security; Cooze* v. *Same; Beard* v. *Same; Murphy* v. *Same; Morley* v. *Same* [1990] I.R.L.R. 436, C.A.

CAP.

1972—cont.

70. Local Government Act 1972.

see *Sheffield City Council* v. *Yorkshire Water Services* [1991] 1 W.L.R. 58; [1991] 2 All E.R. 280, Browne-Wilkinson, V.-C.

ss. 51, 67, orders 91/264, 271, 281, 282, 284–287, 309–311, 2247.

s. 73, order 91/366.

s. 73, amended: 1991, c. 60, sch. 1.

s. 83, orders 90/2477; 91/1169.

s. 94, see *Readman* v. *D.P.P., The Times*, March 4, 1991, D.C.

s. 100A, see *R.* v. *Kensington and Chelsea London Borough Council, ex p. Stoop, The Times*, September 10, 1991, Otton J.

ss. 101, 111, see *Hazell* v. *Hammersmith and Fulham London Borough Council* [1991] 2 W.L.R. 372; [1991] 1 All E.R. 545, H.L.

s. 111, see *Runneymede Community Charge Registration Officer* v. *Data Protection Registrar; South Northamptonshire Community Charge Registration Officer* v. *Same; Harrow Community Charge Registration Officer* v. *Same* (1990) 30 R.V.R. 236, Data Protection Tribunal; *R.* v. *North Tyneside Metropolitan Borough Council, ex p. Allsop, The Independent*, October 17, 1991, D.C.

s. 148, order 91/1730.

ss. 173, 175, 177, 178, regs. 91/351.

s. 183, amended: 1991, c. 60, sch. 1.

s. 222, sch. 5, see *Kirklees Metropolitan Borough Council* v. *Wickes Building Supplies* [1990] 1 W.L.R. 1237.

s. 233, see *Lambeth London Borough Council* v. *Mullings* (1990) R.V.R. 259, D.C.

s. 265, orders 91/205, 446.

s. 270, regs. 91/351.

s. 272, see *D.P.P.* v. *Jackson* (1990) 88 L.G.R. 876, D.C.

sch. 12A, see *R.* v. *Kensington and Chelsea London Borough Council, ex p. Stoop, The Times*, September 10, 1991, Otton J.

sch. 12A, amended: 1991, c. 34, sch. 7.

sch. 13, see *Hazell* v. *Hammersmith and Fulham London Borough Council* [1991] 2 W.L.R. 372; [1991] 1 All E.R. 545.

sch. 13, repealed in pt.: 1991, c. 60, sch. 3.

sch. 17, amended: 1991, c. 34, sch. 4.

sch. 21, repealed in pt.: 1991, c. 22, sch. 9.

71. Criminal Justice Act 1972.

s. 24, repealed in pt.: 1991, c. 40, sch. 8.

s. 35, repealed: 1991, c. 53, sch. 13.

s. 51, amended: *ibid.*, sch. 11.

CAP.
1973

16. Education Act 1973.
s. 3, regs. 91/827, 1838.
18. Matrimonial Causes Act 1973.
s. 3, see *Happe* v. *Happe* [1990] 2 F.L.R. 212, C.A.
s. 10, see *Garcia* v. *Garcia, The Times*, May 29, 1991, C.A.
s. 23, see *Delaney* v. *Delaney* [1990] 2 F.L.R. 457, C.A.
ss. 24A, 37, see *Crittenden* v. *Crittenden* [1990] 2 F.L.R. 361, C.A.
s. 25, see *Schuller* v. *Schuller* [1990] 2 F.L.R. 193, C.A.; *S.* v. *X. & X. (Interveners)* [1990] 2 F.L.R. 187, Ward J.; *Happe* v. *Happe* [1990] 2 F.L.R. 212, C.A.; *K.* v. *K. (Ancillary Relief), Re* [1990] 2 F.L.R. 225, Scott-Baker J.; *E.* v. *E. (Financial Provision)* [1990] 2 F.L.R. 233, Ewbank J.
ss. 25, 25A, see *Hedges* v. *Hedges* [1991] 1 F.L.R. 196, C.A.
s. 31, see *Peacock* v. *Peacock* [1991] 1 F.L.R. 324, Thorpe J.; *Popat* v. *Popat* [1991] Fam.Law 100, C.A.
s. 37, see *Shipman* v. *Shipman* [1991] 1 F.L.R. 250, Lincoln J.; *Sherry* v. *Sherry* [1991] 1 F.L.R. 307, C.A.
s. 50, rules 91/530.
21. Overseas Pensions Act 1973.
s. 2, amended: 1991, c. 16, s. 1.
26. Land Compensation Act 1973.
see *Dhenin* v. *Department of Transport* (1990) 60 P. & C.R. 349, Lands Tr.
s. 5, amended: 1991, c. 34, schs. 6, 12; repealed in pt.: *ibid.*, schs. 6, 12, 19.
s. 13, amended: *ibid.*, sch. 15.
s. 20A, added: *ibid.*
s. 26, amended: *ibid.*, s. 62, sch. 15.
s. 29, amended: *ibid.*, s. 68, sch. 15; repealed in pt.: *ibid.*, s. 68, schs. 15, 19.
s. 29A, added: *ibid.*, s. 69.
s. 30, substituted: *ibid.*, s. 68.
s. 32, amended: *ibid.*, s. 68, sch. 15.
s. 33, amended: *ibid.*, s. 68.
s. 34, amended: *ibid.*, sch. 15; repealed in pt.: *ibid.*, schs. 15, 19.
s. 39, see *R.* v. *East Hertfordshire District Council, ex p. Smith* (1991) 23 H.L.R. 26, C.A.
s. 44, amended: 1991, c. 60, sch. 1.
s. 48, repealed in pt.: 1991, c. 34, sch. 19.
s. 52, amended: *ibid.*, s. 63, sch. 15; repealed in pt.: *ibid.*, schs. 15, 19.
s. 52A, added: *ibid.*, s. 63.
s. 58, amended: 1991, c. 60, sch. 1.
s. 59, amended: 1991, c. 34, sch. 15.
29. Guardianship Act 1973.
s. 13, repealed in pt.: 1991, c. 50, sch. 2.

CAP.
1973—*cont.*

33. Protection of Wrecks Act 1973.
s. 1, orders 90/2573; 91/1110.
36. Northern Ireland Constitution Act 1973.
s. 38, orders 91/1715, 2874.
sch. 2, amended: 1991, c. 48, sch. 5.
37. Water Act 1973.
ss. 10–12, 29–31, see *National Rivers Authority* v. *Newcastle and Gateshead Water Co.; Sunderland and South Shields Water Co. Intervening, sub nom. Northumbria Water Authority* v. *Newcastle and Gateshead Water Co.* (1991) 31 R.V.R. 48, H.L.
s. 14, sch. 8, repealed in pt.: 1991, c. 60, sch. 3.
38. Social Security Act 1973.
ss. 51, 64, 96, 99, sch. 16, regs. 91/167.
41. Fair Trading Act 1973.
s. 42, see *Director General of Fair Trading* v. *Stuart* [1990] 1 W.L.R. 1500, C.A.
s. 64, see *R.* v. *Monopolies and Mergers Commission, ex p. South Yorkshire Transport and South Yorkshire Transport Authority, Financial Times*, December 5, 1991, C.A.
ss. 89, 90, orders 91/750, 785.
s. 133, amended: 1991, c. 60, sch. 1.
43. Hallmarking Act 1973.
sch. 4, amended: regs. 91/1997.
50. Employment and Training Act 1973.
s. 26, order 91/1995.
51. Finance Act 1973.
s. 28, sch. 12, see *Sainsbury (J.)* v. *O'Connor (Inspector of Taxes)* [1990] S.T.C. 516, Millett J.
s. 29, see *Shepherd (Inspector of Taxes)* v. *Law Land* [1990] S.T.C. 795, Ferris J.
s. 56, regs. 90/2365; 91/457–459, 873, 1228, 1318, 2098; S.R. 1991 No. 102.
sch. 19, see *Swithlands Investments* v. *I.R.C.* [1990] S.T.C. 448, Ferris J.
52. Prescription and Limitation (Scotland) Act 1973.
s. 3, see *Cumbernauld and Kilsyth District Council* v. *Dollar Land (Cumbernauld)* (O.H.), 1991 S.L.T. 806.
ss. 4, 6, 9, see *John O'Connor (Plant Hire)* v. *Kier Construction* (O.H.), 1990 S.C.L.R. 761.
s. 6, see *Smithy's Place* v. *Blackadder and McMonagle* (O.H.), 1991 S.L.T. 790.
ss. 6, 11, see *Fergus* v. *MacLennan* (O.H.), May 24, 1990.
s. 6, sch. 1, see *Lord Advocate* v. *Butt* (O.H.), 1991 S.L.T. 248; *Lord Advocate* v. *Shipbreaking Industries* (O.H.), 1991 S.C.L.R. 88.
s. 17, see *Mackie* v. *Currie* (O.H.), 1991 S.L.T. 407.

CAP.

1973—cont.

52. Prescription and Limitation (Scotland) Act 1973—cont.
ss. 17, 19A, see *McLaren* v. *Harland and Wolff* (O.H.), 1991 S.L.T. 85; *Anderson* v. *John Cotton (Colne)* (O.H.), 1991 S.L.T. 696.
sch. 2, see *Bank of Scotland* v. *Laverock* (I.H.), 1991 S.C.L.R. 369.

54. Nature Conservancy Council Act 1973.
sch. 1, repealed in pt.: 1991, c. 54, sch. 4.

56. Land Compensation (Scotland) Act 1973.
s. 5, repealed in pt.: 1991, c. 34, sch. 19.
s. 18A, added: *ibid.*, sch. 17.
s. 24, amended: *ibid.*, s. 76, sch. 17.
s. 27, amended; *ibid.*, s. 71, sch. 17; repealed in pt.: *ibid.*, s. 17, schs. 17, 19.
s. 27A, added: *ibid.*, s. 72.
s. 28, substituted: *ibid.*, s. 71.
ss. 29, 30, amended: *ibid.*
s. 31, amended: *ibid.*, sch. 17; c. 55, sch. 11; repealed in pt.: 1991, c. 34, schs. 17, 19.
s. 44, amended: 1991, c. 55, sch. 11.
s. 48, amended: 1991, c. 34, s. 73, sch. 17; repealed in pt.: *ibid.*, schs. 17, 19.
s. 48A, added: *ibid.*, s. 73.
s. 52, amended: 1991, c. 55, sch. 11.
s. 55, amended: 1991, c. 34, sch. 17; c. 55, sch. 11.
s. 80, amended: *ibid.*
sch. 2, repealed in pt.: 1991, c. 34, sch. 19.

57. Badgers Act 1973.
s. 2, amended: 1991, c. 36, s. 1.
s. 8, amended: *ibid.*, ss. 2, 3.
s. 9, amended: 1991, c. 28, sch. 2; c. 36, s. 4; repealed in pt.: 1991, c. 28, sch. 11.
s. 10, amended: 1991, c. 53, s. 26.
s. 11, amended: 1991, c. 36, s. 5.

62. Powers of Criminal Courts Act 1973.
ss. 1A–1C, added: 1991, c. 53, s. 8, sch. 1.
s. 2, see *R.* v. *Hollywood* [1990] Crim.L.R. 817, C.A.
s. 2, substituted: 1991, c. 53, s. 8.
ss. 3–4B, substituted: *ibid.*, s. 9.
ss. 5, 6, repealed: *ibid.*, s. 14, sch. 13.
ss. 7–9, repealed: *ibid.*, s. 8, sch. 13.
s. 10, repealed: *ibid.*, sch. 13.
s. 11, amended: *ibid.*, s. 8, sch. 11.
s. 12, amended: *ibid.*, sch. 11.
s. 13, repealed: *ibid.*, s. 8, sch. 13.
s. 14, amended: *ibid.*, s. 10, sch. 11; repealed in pt.: *ibid.*, s. 10, sch. 13.
s. 15, amended: *ibid.*, s. 10, sch. 11.
ss. 16, 17, repealed: *ibid.*, s. 14, sch. 13.

CAP.

1973—cont.

62. Powers of Criminal Courts Act 1973—cont.
ss. 17A–17C, repealed: *ibid.*, sch. 13.
s. 20, see *R.* v. *Horney* (1990) 12 Cr.App.R.(S.) 20, C.A.
ss. 20, 20A, repealed: 1991, c. 53, sch. 13.
s. 22, amended: *ibid.*, s. 5.
ss. 28, 29, repealed: *ibid.*, s. 5, sch. 13.
s. 30, repealed in pt.: *ibid.*, sch. 13.
s. 31, see *R.* v. *Wood Green Crown Court, ex p. Howe, The Times*, March 8, 1991, D.C.
s. 31, amended: 1991, c. 53, s. 23, sch. 11.
s. 35, see *R.* v. *Vaughan* (1990) 12 Cr.App.R.(S.) 46, C.A.; *Herbert* v. *Lambeth London Borough Council, The Times*, November 27, 1991, D.C.
s. 38, amended: 1991, c. 62, sch. 2.
s. 42, repealed in pt.: 1991, c. 53, sch. 13.
s. 43, see *R.* v. *Highbury Corner Magistrates' Court, ex p. Di Matteo* (1991) 92 Cr.App.R. 263, D.C.; *R.* v. *Joyce* (1989) 11 Cr.App.R.(S.) 253, C.A.; *R.* v. *McDonald (John Leonard)* [1991] Crim.L.R. 144, C.A.
s. 43, amended: 1991, c. 40, s. 36.
ss. 43, 44, see *R.* v. *Devine* [1990] Crim.L.R. 753, C.A.
s. 44, amended: 1991, c. 40, s. 38; repealed in pt.: *ibid.*, sch. 8.
s. 45, repealed: 1991, c. 53, sch. 13.
s. 46, amended: *ibid.*, sch. 11.
s. 48, repealed: *ibid.*, sch. 13.
s. 51, amended: *ibid.*, ss. 94, 96.
s. 54, orders 90/2643; 91/57, 68, 69, 156, 791, 794, 1917.
s. 57, repealed in pt.: 1991, c. 53, sch. 13.
ss. 58, 59, amended: *ibid.*, sch. 11.
s. 97, amended: *ibid.*, sch. 4.
sch. 1, repealed: *ibid.*, s. 14, sch. 13.
sch. 1A, added: *ibid.*, s. 9, sch. 1.
sch. 3, orders 90/2643; 91/57, 68, 69, 156, 791, 794, 1917; rules 91/2035.
sch. 3, amended: 1991, c. 53, ss. 75, 94, 97, sch. 11; repealed in pt.: *ibid.*, schs. 11, 13.

63. Government Trading Funds Act 1973.
s. 1, orders 91/773, 857, 875, 876, 1795, 1796.
s. 2, orders 91/773, 857, 875, 1795, 1796.
s. 2, amended: 1991, c. 31, s. 119; repealed in pt.: *ibid.*, s. 119, sch. 19.
s. 2A, orders 91/773, 857, 875.
s. 2B, orders 91/773, 857, 875, 1795, 1796.
s. 4, order 91/1796.

65. Local Government (Scotland) Act 1973.
s. 17, order 91/398.
ss. 45, 47, 49A, 50, regs. 91/397.

CAP.

1973—cont.

65. Local Government (Scotland) Act 1973—*cont.*

s. 97, amended and repealed in pt.: regs. 91/1997.

ss. 110, 111, regs. 91/382.

s. 135A, added: 1991, c. 28, sch. 10.

ss. 173, 174, amended: 1991, c. 34, sch. 13.

s. 179, see *Strathclyde Regional Council* v. *Secretary of State for Scotland* (I.H.), 1991 S.C.L.R. 311.

s. 179, amended: 1991, c. 34, sch. 13.

s. 225, order 90/2370.

s. 228, repealed in pt.: 1991, c. 55, sch. 13.

s. 235, regs. 91/397.

sch. 14, repealed in pt.: 1991, c. 22, sch. 9.

sch. 27, repealed in pt.: 1991, c. 45, sch. 8.

1974

3. Slaughterhouses Act 1974.

s. 38, amended: 1991, c. 30, s. 1.

s. 40, amended: *ibid.*, s. 2.

s. 41, amended: *ibid.*, s. 4.

s. 41A, added: *ibid.*, s. 5.

4. Legal Aid Act 1974.

s. 9, see *Watkinson* v. *Legal Aid Board, The Independent*, December 12, 1990, C.A.

s. 20, see *R.* v. *Legal Aid Committee No. 10 (East Midlands), ex p. McKenna* [1990] C.O.D. 358, D.C.

7. Local Government Act 1974.

s. 25, amended: 1991, c. 60, sch. 1.

14. National Insurance Act 1974.

s. 6, regs. 91/167.

s. 6, amended: 1991, c. 3, s. 3.

23. Juries Act 1974.

s. 16, see *R.* v. *Hornsey* [1990] Crim.L.R. 731, C.A.

sch. 1, amended: 1991, c. 53, sch. 11.

24. Prices Act 1974.

s. 4, orders 91/206, 1382, 1690; S.R. 1991 No. 284.

28. Northern Ireland Act 1974.

sch. 1, order 91/2874.

37. Health and Safety at Work etc. Act 1974.

s. 1, regs. 91/562(S.).

s. 2, see *Cardle* v. *David Cardlaw Engineering (Glasgow)*, 1991 S.C.C.R. 807.

s. 6, see *McKay* v. *Unwin Pyrotechnics, The Times*, March 5, 1991, D.C.

s. 15, regs. 90/2325, 2605; 91/562(S.), 1531, 1913, 1914, 2097, 2431.

s. 43, regs. 91/1921.

s. 82, regs. 90/2325; 91/562(S.), 1531, 1921, 2097.

sch. 3, regs. 90/2325; 91/562(S.), 1531, 1914, 2097, 2431.

CAP.

1974—cont.

38. Land Tenure Reform (Scotland) Act 1974.

s. 8, amended: 1991, c. 55, sch. 11.

39. Consumer Credit Act 1974.

s. 16, orders 91/1393, 1949.

s. 22, regs. 91/817.

s. 44, see *First National Bank* v. *Secretary of State for Trade and Industry* [1990] T.L.R. 184, C.A.

s. 129, see *First National Bank* v. *Syed* [1991] 2 All E.R. 250, C.A.

s. 139, repealed in pt.: order 91/724.

s. 147, regs. 91/817.

s. 174, amended: 1991, c. 60, sch. 1.

s. 182, orders 91/1393, 1949.

s. 189, regs. 91/817.

s. 189, repealed in pt.: 1991, c. 50, sch. 2.

sch. 4, repealed in pt.: 1991, c. 31, sch. 19.

40. Control of Pollution Act 1974.

Commencement order: 91/1173.

s. 3, see *Leigh Land Reclamation* v. *Walsall Metropolitan Borough Council* [1991] Crim.L.R. 298, D.C.

ss. 3, 4, regs. 91/508.

ss. 3, 30, see *Kent County Council* v. *Queenborough Rolling Mill Co.* [1990] Crim.L.R. 813, D.C.

s. 30, regs. 91/2539(S.).

s. 30B, regs. 91/1609(S.).

s. 30D, amended (S.): 1991, c. 60, s. 4, sch. 1.

s. 31, amended: 1990, c. 55, sch. 11; (S.) 1991, c. 60, s. 4, sch. 1.

s. 31A, regs. 91/346(S.).

s. 33, order 91/1156.

ss. 43, 44 (in pt.), 45, repealed: 1991, c. 60, sch. 3.

s. 54, amended: 1991, c. 28, sch. 10.

s. 55A, added: *ibid.*

s. 58, see *Wellingborough Borough Council* v. *Gordon* [1991] C.O.D. 154, D.C.

ss. 93, 94, amended: 1991, c. 28, sch. 10.

s. 102, regs. 91/1609(S.).

ss. 104, 105, regs. 91/346(S.), 508, 1609(S.).

s. 105, amended: 1991, c. 22, sch. 8.

s. 109, order 91/1173.

schs. 2, 3, repealed in pt.: 1991, c. 60, sch. 3.

sch. 23, order 91/1156.

43. Merchant Shipping Act 1974.

s. 17, sch. 5, regs. 91/784.

44. Housing Act 1974.

sch. 8, see *Mayhew* v. *Free Grammar School of John Lyon, The Times*, June 11, 1991, C.A.

46. Friendly Societies Act 1974.

s. 36, amended: regs. 91/1997.

s. 37, repealed in pt.: *ibid.*

s. 104, regs. 91/519.

CAP.

1974—cont.

47. Solicitors Act 1974.
s. 43, amended: 1991, c. 53, sch. 11.
s. 69, amended and repealed in pt.:
order 91/724.

48. Railways Act 1974.
s. 3, amended: 1991, c. 63, s. 2.

52. Trade Union and Labour Relations Act 1974.
s. 8, regs. 91/484.
ss. 13, 17, see *Shell U.K.* v. *McGillivray* (O.H.), 1991 S.L.T. 667.
s. 18, see *Alexander* v. *Standard Telephones and Cables (No. 2); Wall* v. *Standard Telephones and Cables (No. 2)* [1991] I.R.L.R. 286, Hobhouse J.

53. Rehabilitation of Offenders Act 1974.
see *Galloway* v. *Mackenzie*, 1991 S.C.C.R. 548.
s. 1, amended: 1991, c. 53, sch. 11; repealed in pt.: *ibid.*, sch. 13.
s. 5, amended: *ibid.*, s. 68, sch. 8; repealed in pt.: 1991, c. 62, sch. 3.
s. 7, repealed in pt.: 1991, c. 50, sch. 2.

1975

3. Arbitration Act 1975.
s. 1, see *Hayter* v. *Nelson Home Insurance* [1990] 2 Lloyd's Rep. 265, Saville J.
ss. 3, 5, 7, see *Hiscox* v. *Outhwaite, The Times,* July 29, 1991, H.L.

7. Finance Act 1975.
ss. 19, 20, 38, see *Baird's Exrs.* v. *I.R.C.,* 1991 S.L.T. (Lands Tr.) 9.
s. 20, see *I.R.C.* v. *Spencer-Nairn,* First Division, December 14, 1990.
s. 58, repealed: 1991, c. 31, sch. 19.
sch. 6, see *Russell's Exr.* v. *I.R.C.,* 1991 S.L.T. 855.

14. Social Security Act 1975.
see *R.* v. *Secretary of State for Social Security, ex p. Smithson,* [1991] C.O.D. 70, D.C.
s. 1, amended: 1991, c. 3, s. 1; c. 42, ss. 1, 2.
s. 3, regs. 91/640.
s. 4, see *R.* v. *Department of Social Security, ex p. Overdrive Credit Card* [1991] 1 W.L.R. 635, C.A.
s. 4, amended: 1991, c. 21, s. 1; orders 91/505, 2909.
s. 4A, added: 1991, c. 21, s. 1.
ss. 7–9, amended: orders 91/505, 2909.
ss. 7A, 9, regs. 91/1935.
s. 9, amended: order 91/2909.
s. 13, regs. 91/1165.
s. 15, amended: 1991, c. 21, s. 9.
ss. 15, 45, 45A, see *Jones* v. *Chief Adjudication Officer* [1990] I.R.L.R. 533, C.A.
s. 17, regs. 91/545.
ss. 27, 36, 37, 37A, see *Thomas* v. *Chief Adjudication Officer and Secretary of State for Social Security; Cooze* v. *Same; Beard* v. *Same; Murphy* v. *Same; Morley* v. *Same* [1990] I.R.L.R. 436, C.A.

CAP.

1975—cont.

14. Social Security Act 1975—cont.
s. 33, regs. 90/2642.
s. 34, amended: 1991, c. 21, s. 1; repealed in pt.: *ibid.*, sch. 4.
s. 35, see *R.* v. *Attendance Allowance Board, ex p. Moran* [1990] C.O.D. 381, D.C.; *Social Security Decision No. R(A) 1/91; Devlin* v. *Secretary of State for Social Services,* 1991 S.L.T. 815.
s. 35, amended: 1991, c. 21, s. 2, sch. 2; repealed in pt.: *ibid.*, sch. 4.
s. 36, amended: *ibid.*, sch. 2.
ss. 36, 36A, regs. 91/1747.
s. 37, see *Invalid Care Allowance (No. G/29/1987), Re* [1989] 3 C.M.L.R. 205, Social Security Commissioner.
s. 37, regs. 91/307.
s. 37A, regs. 91/706.
s. 37A, repealed: 1991, c. 21, s. 2, sch. 4.
ss. 37ZA–37ZC, regs. 91/2890.
ss. 37ZA–37ZE, added: 1991, c. 21, s. 1.
s. 37ZD, regs. 91/2890, 2891.
s. 37ZE, regs. 91/2890.
s. 41, amended: order 91/503.
ss. 49, 58, regs. 91/545.
s. 64, order 91/546; amended: *ibid.*
ss. 76, 77, regs. 91/1938.
s. 85, regs. 91/547, 1617, 2890.
s. 93, amended: 1991, c. 42, s. 3.
ss. 93, 94, see *Scrivner* v. *Chief Adjudication Officer* [1990] 1 C.M.L.R. 637, C.A.
ss. 98–100, amended: 1991, c. 21, sch. 1.
ss. 100A–100D, added: *ibid.*
s. 101, amended: *ibid.*, repealed in pt.: *ibid.*, schs. 1, 4.
s. 102, amended: *ibid.*, sch. 1.
s. 104, regs. 91/2284.
s. 104, amended: 1991, c. 21, sch. 1.
s. 104A, added: *ibid.*
ss. 105, 106, repealed: *ibid.*, sch. 4.
s. 114, regs. 91/706, 2890.
s. 115, regs. 91/2284.
s. 115, 115A, 115B, amended: 1991, c. 21, sch. 1; repealed in pt.: *ibid.*, sch. 4.
ss. 115C, 115D, added: *ibid.*, sch. 1.
s. 119, see *Secretary of State for Social Security* v. *Tunnicliffe* [1991] 2 All E.R. 712, C.A.
s. 119, regs. 91/1878, 1950.
ss. 120, 121, orders 91/505, 2909.
s. 122, order 91/505.
s. 123A, order 91/505.
s. 128, regs. 91/639, 1747.
s. 129, regs. 91/504, 1747.
s. 131, regs. 91/545, 639, 1747.
s. 132, regs. 91/1747.

CAP.

1975—cont.

14. Social Security Act 1975—*cont.*
s. 134, amended: 1991, c. 42, s. 4.
s. 135, amended: 1991, c. 21, sch. 1;
repealed in pt.: *ibid.*, sch. 4.
s. 140, repealed: *ibid.*
s. 143, order 91/767.
s. 151, amended: 1991, c. 42, s. 2.
s. 165A, regs. 91/2284.
s. 165A, amended: 1991, c. 21, sch. 1.
s. 165D, amended: *ibid.*, sch. 2;
repealed in pt.: *ibid.*, sch. 4.
s. 166, regs. 90/2302, 2564, 2642; 91/4,
166–168, 234–236, 251, 441, 504, 544,
547, 588, 639, 706, 1520, 1559, 2890,
2891; orders 91/427, 506, 587, 849,
1033, 1175, 1599, 1617, 1656, 1747,
1878, 1935, 1950, 2238, 2273, 2284,
2334, 2606, 2888, 2911.
s. 168, regs. 91/166–168, 429, 588, 1165,
2273.
sch. 1, regs. 91/640, 1632.
sch. 4, amended: order 91/503;
repealed in pt.: 1991, c. 21, sch. 4.
sch. 5, amended: 1991, c. 42, s. 2.
sch. 10, amended: 1991, c. 21, sch. 1.
sch. 10A, added: *ibid.*
sch. 11, repealed: *ibid.*, sch. 4.
sch. 13, regs. 91/2284.
sch. 13, amended: 1991, c. 21, sch. 1.
sch. 16, repealed in pt.: *ibid.*, sch. 4.
sch. 20, regs. 90/2642; 91/166–168, 307,
429, 504, 545, 588, 639, 640, 706,
1165, 1617, 1632, 1747, 1878, 1938,
1966, 2273, 2890.
sch. 20, amended: 1991, c. 21, s. 9,
sch. 1.

**15. Social Security (Northern Ireland) Act
1975.**
s. 3, S.Rs. 1990 No. 398; 1991 No. 106.
ss. 7A, 9, S.R. 1991 No. 404.
s. 13, S.R. 1991 No. 202.
s. 17, S.R. 1991 No. 78.
s. 33, S.R. 1990 No. 445.
s. 35, S.R. 1990 No. 398.
ss. 36, 36A, S.R. 1991 No. 333.
s. 37, S.R. 1991 No. 56.
s. 37A, S.Rs. 1990 No. 398; 1991 No.
107.
ss. 49, 58, S.R. 1991 No. 78.
s. 64, S.R. 1991 No. 72.
ss. 76, 77, S.Rs. 1990 No. 398; 1991 No.
414.
s. 85, S.Rs. 1991 Nos. 88, 314.
s. 104, S.Rs. 1990 No. 398; 1991 Nos.
401, 406.
s. 114, S.Rs. 1990 No. 398; 1991 No.
107.
s. 119, S.Rs. 1991 Nos. 401, 406.
s. 120, S.R. 1991 No. 73.
s. 123, regs. 91/639.
s. 124, S.Rs. 1991 Nos. 68, 333.
s. 126, S.Rs. 1991 Nos. 78, 80, 333.
s. 134, S.R. 1991 No. 139.

CAP.

1975—cont.

**15. Social Security (Northern Ireland) Act
1975—*cont.***
s. 154A, S.R. 1990 No. 398.
sch. 1, S.Rs. 1990 No. 398; 1991 Nos.
106, 310.

**16. Industrial Injuries and Diseases (Old
Cases) Act 1975.**
ss. 2, 4, schemes 90/2538; 91/718.
ss. 2, 7, amended: order 91/503.
ss. 5, 8, scheme 90/2538.

**17. Industrial Injuries and Diseases (North-
ern Ireland Old Cases) Act 1975.**
ss. 2, 4, S.Rs. 1990 No. 445; 1991 No.
108.

**21. Criminal Procedure (Scotland) Act
1975.**
ss. 26, 35, see *Welsh, Petr.*, 1990
S.C.C.R. 763.
ss. 68, 160, 161, see *Russell* v. *H.M.
Advocate*, 1991 S.C.C.R. 785.
s. 101, see *R.* v. *H.M. Advocate*, 1991
S.C.C.R. 343; *Lyle* v. *H.M. Advocate*, 1991 S.C.C.R. 599; *Duffy* v.
H.M. Advocate, 1991 S.C.C.R. 685.
s. 102, see *McKnight* v. *H.M. Advocate*,
1991 S.C.C.R. 751.
ss. 140A, 141, see *Cordiner* v. *H.M.
Advocate*, 1991 S.C.C.R. 652.
s. 145, see *Livingston* v. *H.M. Advocate*, 1991 S.C.C.R. 350.
s. 160, see *McGroarty* v. *H.M. Advocate, The Scotsman*, May 29, 1991;
McAvoy v. *H.M. Advocate*, 1991
S.C.C.R. 123.
ss. 179, 219, see *McRobbie* v. *H.M.
Advocate*, 1990 S.C.C.R. 767; *H.M.
Advocate* v. *Clegg*, 1991 S.L.T. 192.
s. 183, amended: 1991, c. 53, sch. 3.
s. 188, amended: *ibid.*; repealed in pt.:
ibid.
s. 189, repealed: *ibid.*
ss. 205, 206, see *R.J.K.* v. *H.M. Advocate*, 1991 S.C.C.R. 703.
s. 206, see *Clayton, Petr.*, 1991
S.C.C.R. 261.
s. 218, see *Cannon* v. *H.M. Advocate*,
1991 S.L.T. 195; *Grummer* v. *H.M.
Advocate*, 1991 S.C.C.R. 194.
s. 223, amended: 1991, c. 40, s. 37.
s. 223A, added: *ibid.*, s. 39.
s. 228, see *Stillie* v. *H.M. Advocate*,
1990 S.C.C.R. 719.
ss. 228, 231, see *Evans, Petr.*, 1991
S.C.C.R. 160.
s. 229, see *Gilchrist, Petr.*, 1991 S.L.T.
919.
s. 231, see *McRobbie* v. *H.M. Advocate*, 1990 S.C.C.R. 767.
s. 233, see *Mitchell* v. *H.M. Advocate*,
1991 S.C.C.R. 216.

1975—cont.

21. Criminal Procedure (Scotland) Act 1975—*cont.*

s. 252, see *Perrie* v. *H.M. Advocate*, 1991 S.C.C.R. 255; *Perrie, Petr.*, 1991 S.C.C.R. 475.

s. 254, see *McGougan* v. *H.M. Advocate*, 1991 S.C.C.R. 49; *McGroarty* v. *H.M. Advocate, The Scotsman*, May 29, 1991.

s. 281, see *Perrie, Petr.*, 1991 S.C.C.R. 475.

s. 282, Acts of Adjournal 91/19, 847, 1916.

s. 289, amended: 1991, c. 53, s. 17.

s. 289D, order 91/810.

s. 289G, amended: 1991, c. 53, s. 17.

s. 311, see *Findlay* v. *McNaughtan*, 1991 S.C.C.R. 321; *Wilson* v. *Carmichael*, 1991 S.C.C.R. 587.

s. 312, see *Newlands* v. *McPhail*, 1991 S.C.C.R. 88; *Wimpey Homes Holdings* v. *Lees*, 1991 S.C.C.R. 447; *Larkin* v. *Docherty*, 1991 S.C.C.R. 377.

s. 331, see *Buchan* v. *McNaughton*, 1990 S.C.C.R. 688; *Carmichael* v. *Kennedy*, 1991 S.C.C.R 145; *Harvey* v. *Lockhart*, 1991 S.C.C.R. 83; *Young* v. *MacPhail, The Scotsman*, May 15, 1991; *Kennedy* v. *Carmichael*, 1991 S.C.C.R. 458; *Anderson* v. *Lowe*, 1991 S.C.C.R. 712; *McNellie* v. *Walkingshaw*, 1991 S.L.T. 892.

s. 334, see *Fletcher* v. *Webster*, High Court of Justiciary, January 9, 1991; *Harvey* v. *Lockhart*, 1991 S.C.C.R. 83.

s. 335, see *Hoyers (UK)* v. *Houston*, 1991 S.L.T. 934.

s. 337A, see *McDonald* v. *Knight* (Sh.Ct.), 1990 S.C.C.R. 641.

s. 344, see *Strang* v. *Annan*, 1991 S.L.T. 676.

s. 357, see *Kerr* v. *Jessop*, 1991 S.C.C.R. 27.

s. 359, see *Wilson* v. *Carmichael*, 1991 S.C.C.R. 587.

s. 384, amended: 1991, c. 53, sch. 1.

s. 389, amended: *ibid.*; repealed in pt.: *ibid.*

s. 390, repealed: *ibid.*

s. 396, see *Nash, Petr., The Scotsman*, October 17, 1991; *Paterson* v. *McGlennan*, 1991 S.L.T. 832.

s. 403, repealed in pt.: 1991, c. 53, sch. 13.

s. 407, amended: *ibid.*, s. 23.

s. 431, see *Tulloch* v. *Annan*, 1991 S.C.C.R. 24; *Brady* v. *MacNeill*, 1991 S.C.C.R. 234.

s. 436, see *McQueeney* v. *Carmichael*, 1991 S.C.C.R. 221; *Findlay* v. *McNaughtan*, 1991 S.C.C.R. 321.

s. 436, amended: 1991, c. 40, s. 37.

1975—cont.

21. Criminal Procedure (Scotland) Act 1975—*cont.*

s. 436A, added: *ibid.*, s. 39.

s. 439, see *Hepwood* v. *Stewart, The Scotsman*, October 30, 1991.

s. 442, see *Harvey* v. *Lockhart*, 1991 S.C.C.R. 83.

ss. 442–442B, see *Cowan* v. *Guild*, 1991 S.C.C.R. 424.

s. 444, see *Anderson* v. *McClory*, 1991 S.C.C.R. 571.

s. 452, see *Stein* v. *Lowe*, 1991 S.C.C.R. 692.

s. 452A, see *Kelly* v. *Docherty*, 1991 S.C.C.R. 312; *Millar* v. *Lees*, 1991 S.C.C.R. 799.

s. 453A, see *Harvey* v. *Lockhart*, 1991 S.C.C.R. 83.

s. 453B, see *Campbell* v. *MacDougal*, 1991 S.C.C.R. 218.

s. 457, Acts of Adjournal 91/19, 847, 1916.

s. 462, see *Wilson* v. *Carmichael*, 1991 S.C.C.R. 587.

sch. 9, repealed in pt.: 1991, c. 53, sch. 13.

22. Oil Taxation Act 1975.

ss. 3, 10, amended: 1991, c. 31, s. 103.

sch. 2, see *R.* v. *Special Commissioners, ex p. Fina Exploration, The Times*, December 11, 1991, Hodgson J.

sch. 2, amended: 1991, c. 31, s. 109.

sch. 5, amended: *ibid.*, s. 107.

24. House of Commons Disqualification Act 1975.

s. 1, order 90/2596.

s. 5, order 90/2585.

sch. 1, amended: 1991, c. 21, sch. 2; c. 28, sch. 10; c. 40, sch. 5; c. 48, sch. 5; c. 49, sch. 1; c. 60, sch. 1; c. 66, schs. 1, 2, Pts. II, III; repealed in pt.: order 91/510; 1991, c. 21, sch. 4; c. 28, sch. 11; c. 33, sch.

25. Northern Ireland Assembly Disqualification Act 1975.

sch. 1, amended: 1991, c. 21, sch. 2; c. 40, sch. 5; c. 48, sch. 5; c. 60, sch. 1; c. 66, schs. 1, 2, Pts. II, III.

26. Ministers of the Crown Act 1975.

s. 1, orders 90/2598; 91/188, 1728.

27. Ministerial and other Salaries Act 1975.

s. 1, order 91/2886.

s. 1, amended: 1991, c. 5, s. 3; order 91/2886.

schs. 1, 2, amended: order 91/2886.

30. Local Government (Scotland) Act 1975.

s. 6, orders 91/646–649, 914–917, 940–950, 1811, 1812.

s. 9A, order 91/1780.

s. 16, regs. 91/385.

s. 35, orders 91/646–649, 914–917, 940–950, 1811, 1812.

s. 37, orders 91/646–649, 914–917, 940–950, 1780, 1811, 1812.

sch. 3, regs. 91/385.

1975—cont.

35. Farriers (Registration) Act 1975.
sch. 1, amended and repealed in pt.:
regs. 91/1997.

45. Finance (No. 2) Act 1975.
s. 6, repealed: 1991, c. 31, sch. 19.
s. 73, repealed in pt.: 1991, c. 50,
sch. 2.

**46. International Road Haulage Permits Act
1975.**
s. 1, amended: 1991, c. 40, sch. 4;
repealed in pt.: *ibid.*, sch. 8.

**51. Salmon and Freshwater Fisheries Act
1975.**
s. 5, amended: 1991, c. 60, sch. 1.
ss. 6, 28, repealed in pt.: *ibid.*, sch. 3.
s. 32, see *Richardson* v. *North West
Water Authority* [1991] C.O.D. 77,
D.C.
s. 39, amended: 1991, c. 60, sch. 1.
s. 41, see *Gray* v. *Blamey* [1991] 1
W.L.R. 47; [1991] 1 All E.R. 1, D.C.
s. 41, amended: 1991, c. 60, sch. 1.
sch. 3, amended: *ibid.*, sch. 1; repealed
in pt.: *ibid.*, sch. 3.

56. Coal Industry Act 1975.
ss. 2, 7, sch. 1, repealed in pt.: 1991,
c. 45, sch. 8.

60. Social Security Pensions Act 1975.
s. 1, regs. 91/639.
s. 6, regs. 91/1165.
s. 6, amended: order 91/503.
s. 16A, added: 1991, c. 21, s. 9.
s. 21, order 91/1108.
s. 22, repealed: 1991, c. 21, sch. 4.
s. 35, regs. 91/1165.
s. 37A, orders 91/427, 2888.
s. 40, regs. 91/2273.
ss. 41B, 41C, 41E, regs. 91/166.
ss. 44, 44ZA, 44A, 45, regs. 91/429.
s. 52, regs. 91/2273.
s. 52A, order 91/2606.
s. 52C, regs. 91/167, 2273.
s. 52P, regs. 91/167.
s. 59, order 91/684.
s. 59C, regs. 91/588.
s. 62, regs. 91/167.
s. 66, regs. 91/166–168, 588.
sch. 1A, regs. 91/167, 168.
sch. 2, regs. 91/2273.
sch. 4, repealed in pt.: 1991, c. 21,
sch. 4.

61. Child Benefit Act 1975.
s. 3, regs. 91/2105.
s. 3, amended: order 91/1881.
s. 5, order 91/543; regs. 91/502, 1595.
s. 15, order 91/767.
s. 22, regs. 91/2105.
s. 24, regs. 91/502, 1595, 2105.
sch. 1, regs. 91/2105.

**63. Inheritance (Provision for Family and
Dependants) Act 1975.**
see *Andrew* v. *Andrew* [1990] 2 F.L.R.
376, Judge Fricker, Q.C.
s. 1, see *Bishop* v. *Plumley* [1991] 1 All
E.R. 236, C.A.
ss. 1–3, see *Moody* v. *Stevenson, The
Times,* July 30, 1991, C.A.

1975—cont.

**63. Inheritance (Provision for Family and
Dependants) Act 1975**—*cont.*
s. 9, see *Jessop* v. *Jessop, The Times,*
October 16, 1991, C.A.

65. Sex Discrimination Act 1975.
s. 1, see *Bullock* v. *Alice Otley School,
The Times,* July 10, 1991, E.A.T.
ss. 1, 2, 29, see *Bain* v. *Bowles* [1991]
I.R.L.R. 356, C.A.
ss. 1, 3, 5, see *Greater Manchester
Police Authority* v. *Lea* [1990]
I.R.L.R. 372, E.A.T.
ss. 1, 4, 5, see *Bullock* v. *Alice Ottley
School* [1991] I.R.L.R. 324, E.A.T.
ss. 1, 6, see *R.* v. *Hammersmith and
Fulham London Borough Council, ex
p. NALGO* [1991] I.R.L.R. 249,
D.C.; *Berrisford* v. *Woodard Schools
(Midland Division)* [1991] I.R.L.R.
247, E.A.T.
ss. 6, 65, 66, see *Marshall* v. *Southampton and South-West Hampshire Area
Health Authority (No. 2)* [1990]
I.R.L.R. 481, C.A.
s. 41, see *Enterprise Glass Co.* v. *Miles*
[1990] I.C.R. 787, E.A.T.

68. Industry Act 1975.
s. 1, repealed: 1991, c. 66, sch. 2, Pt. III.
Pt. I (ss. 1–10), exc. s. 1, repealed: *ibid.*,
Pt. I.
ss. 13, 14, 16, 19, 20, 26, 37 (in pt.),
repealed: *ibid.*
sch. 1, repealed in pt.: *ibid.*, Pt. III;
repealed: *ibid.*, Pt. I.
sch. 2, amended: regs. 91/1997;
repealed: 1991, c. 66, sch. 2, Pt. I.

70. Welsh Development Agency Act 1975.
s. 18, amended: 1991, c. 69, s. 1.

71. Employment Protection Act 1975.
s. 6, order 91/968.
s. 8, regs. 91/484.
s. 99, see *Hough* v. *Leyland DAF* [1991]
I.R.L.R. 194, E.A.T.
ss. 99, 101, 103, see *R.* v. *Hammersmith
and Fulham London Borough Council, ex p. NALGO* [1991] I.R.L.R.
249, D.C.
s. 123, order 91/968.

72. Children Act 1975.
s. 47, repealed in pt.: 1991, c. 50,
sch. 2.

**74. Petroleum and Submarine Pipe-lines Act
1975.**
ss. 26, 27, regs. 91/680.

75. Policyholders Protection Act 1975.
sch. 1, amended: regs. 91/1997.

76. Local Land Charges Act 1975.
s. 10, amended: order 91/724.

1976

13. Damages (Scotland) Act 1976.
s. 1, see *Morris* v. *Drysdale, The Scotsman,* February 27, 1991.

1976—cont.

13. Damages (Scotland) Act 1976—*cont.*
sch. 1, see *Cohen* v. *Shaw, The Scotsman*, July 17, 1991.

14. Fatal Accidents and Sudden Deaths Inquiry (Scotland) Act 1976.
s. 4, see *Lockhart, Petr.* (Sh.Ct.), 1991 S.C.L.R. 215.

15. Rating (Caravan Sites) Act 1976.
s. 3A, repealed: 1991, c. 2, s. 2.

21. Crofting Reform (Scotland) Act 1976.
ss. 1, 9, see *Trustees of the Tenth Duke of Argyll* v. *MacCormick*, 1991 S.L.T. 900.
ss. 4, 21, see *Livingstone* v. *Nelson* (Land Ct.), *The Scotsman*, January 16, 1991.
sch. 2, repealed in pt.: 1991, c. 55, sch. 13.

22. Freshwater and Salmon Fishing (Scotland) Act 1976.
s. 1, orders 91/215, 2234–2236.

26. Fair Employment (Northern Ireland) Act 1976.
s. 28, S.R. 1991 No. 325.

27. Theatres Trust Act 1976.
sch., amended: regs. 91/1997.

30. Fatal Accidents Act 1976.
see *Black* v. *Yates* [1991] 3 W.L.R. 90, Potter J.; *Cresswell* v. *Eaton* [1991] 1 All E.R. 484, Brown J.
s. 1A, order 90/2575.
s. 4, see *Stanley* v. *Sadique* [1991] 2 W.L.R. 459.
s. 11, amended: 1991, c. 31, sch. 3.
sch. 1, repealed in pt.: 1991, c. 45, sch. 8.

32. Lotteries and Amusements Act 1976.
ss. 18, 24, orders 91/61, 2174, 2178, 2497(S.), 2498(S.).
sch. 1, amended: order 91/2178.
sch. 3, amended: order 91/2174.

34. Restrictive Trade Practices Act 1976.
s. 4, amended: 1991, c. 60, sch. 1.
s. 9, order 91/1896.
s. 18, order 91/1897.
s. 35, see *Director General of Fair Trading* v. *Hulett, sub nom. Ready Mixed Concrete, Re* [1991] I.C.R. 52, R.P.C.

35. Police Pensions Act 1976.
s. 1, regs. 91/1304, 1517.
s. 2, regs. 91/1304.
ss. 3, 4, regs. 91/1304, 1507.
ss. 5–7, regs. 91/1304.

36. Adoption Act 1976.
see *L. (A Minor) (Adoption: Procedure), Re* [1991] 1 F.L.R. 171, C.A.
s. 9, regs. 91/2030.
s. 12, see *D. (A Minor) (Adoption Order: Validity), Re* [1991] 2 W.L.R. 1215, C.A.
ss. 34, 37, amended: 1991, c. 53, sch. 11.

1976—cont.

36. Adoption Act 1976—*cont.*
s. 51, see *R.* v. *Registrar-General, ex p. Smith* [1991] 2 W.L.R. 782, C.A.
s. 51, regs. 91/1981.
s. 51A, rules 91/952.
s. 57A, regs. 91/2030, 2130.
s. 65A, regs. 91/2051.
s. 66, rules 91/1880.
s. 67, regs. 91/1981; rules 91/1880.

39. Divorce (Scotland) Act 1976.
s. 1, see *Findlay* v. *Findlay* (O.H.), 1991 S.L.T. 457.

50. Domestic Violence and Matrimonial Proceedings Act 1976.
s. 2, see *Kendrick* v. *Kendrick* [1990] 2 F.L.R. 107, C.A.

52. Armed Forces Act 1976.
s. 8, amended: 1991, c. 53, sch. 4; c. 62, sch. 2.

55. Agriculture (Miscellaneous Provisions) Act 1976.
s. 2, repealed: 1991, c. 33, sch.
ss. 13, 14, repealed (S.): 1991, c. 53, sch. 13.
sch. 3, repealed in pt.: 1991, c. 60, sch. 3.

57. Local Government (Miscellaneous Provisions) Act 1976.
s. 7, repealed in pt.: 1991, c. 34, schs. 7, 19.
s. 15, amended: 1991, c. 22, sch. 8.
ss. 46, 80, see *Lovelady* v. *Taylor, The Times*, May 30, 1991, D.C.
ss. 51, 59, amended: 1991, c. 40, s. 47.

58. International Carriage of Perishable Foodstuffs Act 1976.
ss. 1–3, 20, regs. 91/425, 969.

63. Bail Act 1976.
see *R.* v. *Wirral District Magistrates' Court, ex p. Meikle* [1990] Crim.L.R. 801, D.C.
s. 4, amended: regs. 87/299; 1991, c. 53, sch. 11.
s. 7, see *R.* v. *Liverpool City Justices, ex p. D.P.P., The Times*, December 10, 1991, D.C.
sch. 1, see *R.* v. *Dover and East Kent Justices, ex p. Dean, The Times*, August 22, 1991, D.C.
sch. 1, amended: 1991, c. 53, sch. 11; repealed in pt.: *ibid.*, schs. 11, 13.
sch. 2, repealed in pt.: 1991, c. 25, sch. 4.

66. Licensing (Scotland) Act 1976.
s. 8, order 90/2458.
s. 17, sch. 1, see *Loosefoot Entertainment* v. *Glasgow District Licensing Board*, 1991 S.L.T. 843.
ss. 67, 99, sch. 5, see *Stainton* v. *McNaughtan*, 1991 S.C.C.R. 339.

1976—cont.
66. Licensing (Scotland) Act 1976—*cont.*
s. 99, see *Scotia Leisure* v. *City of Glasgow District Council* (I.H.), 1991 S.C.L.R. 232.
s. 135, order 90/2458.
70. Land Drainage Act 1976.
ss. 4–19, 21–61, 63, 64, repealed: 1991, c. 60, sch. 3.
ss. 65, 66, repealed: regs. 91/523.
s. 67, repealed: 1991, c. 60, sch. 3.
ss. 68, 69, repealed in pt.: regs. 91/523; repealed; 1991, c. 60, sch. 3.
s. 70, repealed: regs. 91/523.
s. 71, repealed: 1991, c. 60, sch. 3.
s. 72, repealed in pt.: regs. 91/523; repealed: 1991, c. 60, sch. 3.
s. 73, repealed: regs. 91/523.
s. 80, repealed in pt.: regs. 91/523; 1991, c. 60, sch. 3.
s. 81, repealed: regs. 91/523.
ss. 82–100, 102–104A, 106–115, 116 (in pt.)–118 (in pt.). sch. 1, repealed: 1991, c. 60, sch. 3.
sch. 2, repealed in pt.: regs. 91/523; repealed: 1991, c. 60, sch. 3.
schs. 3, 4, 6, 7 (in pt.), 8, repealed: *ibid.*
74. Race Relations Act 1976.
s. 1, see *Crown Suppliers (PSA)* v. *Dawkins, The Times*, April 29, 1991, E.A.T.
ss. 1, 4, see *British Gas* v. *Sharma* [1991] I.C.R. 19, E.A.T.; *R.* v. *Hammersmith and Fulham London Borough Council, ex p. NALGO* [1991] I.R.L.R. 249, D.C.
ss. 1, 18, see *R.* v. *Birmingham City Council and Secretary of State for Education, ex p. Kaur* [1991] C.O.D. 21, D.C.
s. 4, see *R.* v. *Army Board of the Defence Council, ex p. Anderson* [1991] 3 W.L.R. 42, D.C.; *Barclays Bank* v. *Kapur* [1991] 2 W.L.R. 401; [1991] 1 All E.R. 646, H.L.; *Qureshi* v. *Newham London Borough* [1991] I.R.L.R. 264, C.A.
ss. 12, 54, see *R.* v. *Secretary of State for Health, ex p. Gandhi, The Times*, January 23, 1991, D.C.
s. 47, order 91/227.
s. 56, see *British Gas* v. *Sharma* [1991] I.C.R. 19, E.A.T.
s. 65, see *Qureshi* v. *Newham London Borough* [1991] I.R.L.R. 264, C.A.
s. 68, see *Dimtsu* v. *Westminster City Council, The Times*, February 12, 1991, E.A.T.; *Clarke* v. *Hampshire Electroplating Co., The Times*, October 1, 1991, E.A.T.
ss. 68, 78, see *Barclays Bank* v. *Kapur* [1991] 2 W.L.R. 401; [1991] 1 All E.R. 646, H.L.

1976—cont.
74. Race Relations Act 1976—*cont.*
s. 71, see *R.* v. *Birmingham City Council and Secretary of State for Education, ex p. Kaur* [1991] C.O.D. 21, D.C.; *R.* v. *Hammersmith and Fulham London Borough Council, ex p. NALGO* [1991] I.R.L.R. 249, D.C.
s. 75, see *R.* v. *Army Board of the Defence Council, ex p. Anderson* [1991] 3 W.L.R. 42, D.C.
75. Development of Rural Wales Act 1976.
s. 12, amended: 1991, c. 1, s. 1.
sch. 3, amended: 1991, c. 22, sch. 8.
80. Rent (Agriculture) Act 1976.
ss. 2, 4, sch. 4, see *Burgoyne* v. *Griffiths* [1991] 13 E.G. 164, C.A.
s. 33, amended: 1991, c. 34, sch. 7.
82. Sexual Offences (Amendment) Act 1976.
s. 1, see *R.* v. *R. (Rape: Marital Exemption)* [1991] 2 W.L.R. 1065, C.A.
s. 2, see *R.* v. *Redguard* [1991] Crim.L.R. 213, C.A.
86. Fishery Limits Act 1976.
s. 3, see *Wither* v. *Cowie; Wither* v. *Wood*, 1990 S.C.C.R. 741.

1977
3. Aircraft and Shipbuilding Industries Act 1977.
s. 1, regs. 91/1560; amended: *ibid.*
s. 17, amended: regs. 91/1997.
4. Roe Deer (Close Seasons) Act 1977.
repealed: 1991, c. 54, sch. 4.
5. Social Security (Miscellaneous Provisions) Act 1977.
s. 2, order 91/766.
s. 13, regs. 91/2890.
s. 13, amended: 1991, c. 21, sch. 2.
15. Marriage (Scotland) Act 1977.
ss. 3, 19, 25, 26, regs. 90/2636.
30. Rentcharges Act 1977.
s. 10, amended and repealed in pt.: order 91/724.
32. Torts (Interference with Goods) Act 1977.
s. 3, see *IBL* v. *Coussens* [1991] 2 All E.R. 133, C.A.
s. 13, amended and repealed in pt.: order 91/724.
s. 14, repealed in pt.: *ibid.*
36. Finance Act 1977.
s. 6, repealed: 1991, c. 31, sch. 19.
sch. 7, see *Leonard* v. *Blanchard (Inspector of Taxes), The Times*, November 29, 1991, Hoffmann J.
37. Patents Act 1977.
s. 1, see *Gale's Patent Application, Re, Financial Times*, December 18, 1990, C.A.
ss. 1, 3, 14, see *Edwards* v. *Acme Signs and Displays* [1990] R.P.C. 621, Aldous J.

1977—cont.

37. Patents Act 1977—*cont.*

s. 2, see *Asahi Kasei Kogyo Kabushiki Kaisha, The Financial Times*, May 14, 1991, H.L.

ss. 2, 13, see *Pall Corp.* v. *Commercial Hydraulics (Bedford)* [1990] F.S.R. 329, Falconer J.

ss. 2, 14, 15, see *Asahi Kasei Kogyo KK's Application* [1990] F.S.R. 546, C.A.

s. 3, see *Mölnlycke* v. *Proctor & Gamble (No. 3)* [1990] R.P.C. 498, Mummery J.

ss. 5, 8, 12–21, 24, 25, rules 90/2384.

s. 27, see *Minister of Agriculture's Patent* [1990] R.P.C. 61, Aldous J.

s. 28, see *Sony Corporation's Patent* [1990] R.P.C. 152, Aldous J.

ss. 28, 32, 40, 47, rules 90/2384.

ss. 46, 48, 50, see *Research Corp.'s Patent* [1990] R.P.C. 663, Hoffmann J.

ss. 46, 50, 60, see *American Cyanamid Co.'s (Fenbufen) Patent* [1990] R.P.C. 309, Aldous J.

ss. 48, 50, 60, see *Kaken Pharmaceutical Co.'s Patent* [1990] R.P.C. 72, Patent Office.

s. 52, rules 90/2384.

s. 60, see *Southco Inc.* v. *Dzus Fastener Europe* [1990] R.P.C. 587, Patents Ct.

ss. 60, 72, 76, see *Edwards* v. *Acme Signs and Displays* [1990] R.P.C. 621, Aldous J.

ss. 61, 63, 71, 72, see *Ferro Corp.* v. *Escol Products* [1990] R.P.C. 651, Hoffmann J.

s. 70, see *Bowden Controls* v. *Acco Cable Controls* [1990] R.P.C. 427, Aldous J.

s. 71, see *Vax Appliances* v. *Hoover* [1990] R.P.C. 656, Mummery J.

ss. 71, 74, see *Mölnlycke A.B.* v. *Procter and Gamble* [1990] R.P.C. 267, Morritt J.

s. 72, see *Mölnlycke A.B.* v. *Proctor & Gamble (No. 3)* [1990] R.P.C. 498, Mummery J.

s. 73, see *Toyama Chemical Co.'s Application* [1990] R.P.C. 555, Pat.Ct.

ss. 77, 78, 80, 81, 89, 89A, 92, 97, 118, 120, rules 90/2384.

s. 123, rules 90/2384, 2517; 91/675, 1627.

s. 124, rules 90/2384.

ss. 125, 130, see *Edwards* v. *Acme Signs and Displays* [1990] R.P.C. 621, Aldous J.; *Southco Inc.* v. *Dzus Fastener Europe* [1990] R.P.C. 587, Patents Ct.

1977—cont.

37. Patents Act 1977—*cont.*

ss. 125, 139, see *Improver Corp.* v. *Remington Consumer Products* [1990] F.S.R. 181, Hoffmann J.

ss. 125A, 127, 130, sch. 1, rules 90/2384.

sch. 4, rules 90/2384, 2517; 91/675, 1627.

42. Rent Act 1977.

see *Kent Coast Property Investments* v. *Ward* [1990] 45 E.G. 107, C.A.

ss. 1, 137, see *Grosvenor Estates Belgravia* v. *Cochran* [1991] E.G.C.S. 51, C.A.

s. 4, see *Guestheath* v. *Mirza* (1990) 22 H.L.R. 399, Alliott J.

s. 8, regs. 91/233.

s. 22, see *Central YMCA Housing Association* v. *Saunders* [1990] 1 E.G.C.S. 154, C.A.

s. 120, see *Steele* v. *McMahon* [1990] 44 E.G. 65, C.A.

sch. 1, see *Hedgedale* v. *Hards, The Times*, January 11, 1991, C.A.

sch. 15, see *Theodotou* v. *Potsos, The Times*, April 3, 1991, C.A.; *Springfield Investments* v. *Bell* (1990) 22 H.L.R. 441, C.A.

43. Protection from Eviction Act 1977.

s. 3A, order 91/1943.

s. 5, see *Norris (T/A J. Davis & Son)* v. *Checksfield, The Times*, April 23, 1991, C.A.

45. Criminal Law Act 1977.

s. 1, see *R.* v. *Boyle; Same* v. *Mears, The Times*, July 22, 1991, C.A.; *Nazir Chinoy, Re* [1991] C.O.D. 105, D.C.

s. 2, see *R.* v. *Chrastny, The Times*, March 14, 1991, C.A.

s. 44, see *R.* v. *Harper-Taylor; R.* v. *Bakker* (Note) [1991] R.T.R. 76, C.A.

s. 47, repealed: 1991, c. 53, s. 5, sch. 13.

s. 51, amended: *ibid.*, s. 26.

schs. 1, 6, repealed in pt.: 1991, c. 60, sch. 3.

sch. 12, repealed in pt.: 1991, c. 53, sch. 13.

46. Insurance Brokers (Registration) Act 1977.

s. 11, amended and repealed in pt.: regs. 91/1997.

s. 25, amended: *ibid.*

ss. 27, 28, order 90/2461.

s. 29, repealed in pt.: regs. 91/1997.

49. National Health Service Act 1977.

ss. 1–3, 23, see *R.* v. *Secretary of State for Health, ex p. Keen* [1990] C.O.D. 371, D.C.

s. 5, amended: order 91/1236.

s. 8, orders 91/325, 326, 2039, 2040.

1977—cont.

49. National Health Service Act 1977—*cont.*
s. 11, regs. 90/2647; orders 91/226, 327, 389, 407, 1102, 2001.
s. 12, regs. 90/2583, 2647, 2648; 91/328, 1103; order 91/1102.
s. 13, regs. 91/275, 408, 553, 554, 1025, 1645.
ss. 14, 15, regs. 91/554.
ss. 16, 17, regs. 91/408, 553.
s. 18, regs. 91/275, 408, 553, 554, 1025, 1645.
s. 20, regs. 91/275.
s. 29, regs. 90/2513; 91/555, 2263.
s. 30, regs. 90/2513.
ss. 31, 32, regs. 91/406.
s. 33, see *R.* v. *Secretary of State for Health, ex p. Gandhi, The Times,* January 23, 1991, D.C.
ss. 33, 34, regs. 90/2513.
ss. 35, 36, regs. 90/2501; 91/581, 1348.
s. 37, regs. 91/581.
ss. 38, 39, regs. 91/583.
s. 41, regs. 91/2263.
s. 42, regs. 90/2513; 91/553, 555, 2263.
ss. 43, 45, regs. 91/555.
s. 77, regs. 91/579.
s. 78, regs. 91/581, 583.
ss. 79, 79A, regs. 91/581.
ss. 81, 82, regs. 91/583.
s. 83, regs. 91/581.
s. 83A, regs. 91/557, 579.
s. 103, orders 91/509, 580.
s. 121, regs. 91/438.
s. 126, regs. 90/2501, 2513, 2583, 2647, 2648; 91/275, 328, 408, 482, 553–557, 579–583, 725, 1103, 1347, 1348, 1680, 2263; orders 91/325–327, 389, 407, 509, 580, 1102, 1594, 2001, 2039, 2040.
s. 128, regs. 90/2583, 2648; 91/275, 329, 408, 482, 556, 582, 725, 1103, 1347, 1645, 2041.
sch. 5, regs. 90/2583, 2647, 2648; 91/328, 481, 553, 1103; orders 91/226, 407, 1102, 2001, 2002.
sch. 7, regs. 91/275.
sch. 12, regs. 91/579, 581, 583, 1680.
sch. 15, repealed in pt.: 1991, c. 21, sch. 4.

50. Unfair Contract Terms Act 1977.
s. 2, see *Johnstone* v. *Bloomsbury Health Authority* [1991] 2 All E.R. 293, C.A.
ss. 2, 3, 11, see *Flamar Interocean* v. *Denmac (Formerly Denholm Maclay Co.); Flamar Pride and Flamar Progress, The* [1990] 1 Lloyd's Rep. 434, Potter J.
s. 10, see *Tudor Grange Holdings* v. *Citibank N.A., The Times,* April 30, 1991, Browne-Wilkinson V.-C.

1977—cont.

50. Unfair Contract Terms Act 1977—*cont.*
s. 11, see *Garden Neptune Shipping* v. *Occidental Worldwide Investment Corp. and Concord Petroleum Corp.* [1990] 1 Lloyd's Rep. 330, C.A.
ss. 15, 21, 25, see *G.M. Shepherd* v. *North West Securities,* 1991 S.L.T. 499.
ss. 20, 24, sch. 2, see *Denholm Fishselling* v. *Anderson,* 1991 S.L.T. (Sh. Ct.) 24.

1978

3. Refuse Disposal (Amenity) Act 1978.
s. 2, see *Clacher* v. *McClory,* 1991 S.C.C.R. 561.
ss. 4, 5, 11, regs. 91/336.

5. Northern Ireland (Emergency Provisions) Act 1978.
repealed: 1991, c. 24, sch. 8.
continued in force (pt.): order 91/779.
s. 27, regs. 91/1759.
s. 28A, S.R. 1990 No. 441.
s. 33, order 91/779.

10. European Parliamentary Elections Act 1978.
sch. 1, regs. 91/1243, 1675.

18. Export Guarantees and Overseas Investment Act 1978.
repealed: 1991, c. 66, s. 15.

22. Domestic Proceedings and Magistrates' Courts Act 1978.
s. 20ZA, added: 1991, c. 17, s. 5.
ss. 23, 32, amended: *ibid.,* sch. 2.

23. Judicature (Northern Ireland) Act 1978.
s. 52, S.R. 1991 No. 327.
s. 55, S.Rs. 1991 Nos. 231, 232, 330, 334, 335.
s. 70, S.R. 1991 No. 230.
s. 116, S.Rs. 1991 Nos. 121–124, 291–293.
sch. 5, repealed in pt.: 1991, c. 24, sch. 8.

28. Adoption (Scotland) Act 1978.
ss. 6, 16, 18, see *Central Regional Council* v. *M.* (I.H.), 1991 S.C.L.R. 300.
s. 12, amended: 1991, c. 50, s. 2.; repealed in pt.: *ibid.,* sch. 2.
s. 18, amended: *ibid.,* s. 2.
ss. 18, 39, see *F.* v. *F.,* 1991 S.L.T. 357.
s. 65, amended: 1991, c. 50, sch. 1.
sch. 1, regs. 91/1261.

29. National Health Service (Scotland) Act 1978.
s. 2, orders 90/2639; 91/570; regs. 91/809.
s. 10, order 91/900; regs. 91/564.
s. 12A, regs. 91/358, 535.
s. 19, regs. 90/2509; 91/572, 574, 1188, 2241.
s. 22, regs. 91/576.

1978—cont.

29. National Health Service (Scotland) Act 1978—*cont.*
ss. 23, 24, regs. 91/572.
s. 25, regs. 90/2497; 91/569, 1188, 1349.
s. 26, regs. 91/534, 1188.
s. 27, regs. 90/2509; 91/572, 574, 1188, 2241.
s. 28, regs. 91/572.
s. 69, regs. 91/574.
s. 70, regs. 91/534, 569.
ss. 71, 71A, regs. 91/569.
s. 73, regs. 91/534.
s. 75, regs. 91/569, 574.
s. 75A, regs. 91/575.
s. 87A–87C, regs. 91/573.
s. 105, regs. 90/2497, 2509; 91/345, 358, 535, 537, 564, 569, 572–576, 809, 1188, 1349, 1751, 2487; orders 91/570, 900.
s. 106, regs. 90/2509; 91/573.
s. 108, regs. 90/2497, 2509; 91/345, 534, 535, 537, 564, 569, 572–576, 809, 1188, 1349, 1751, 2241, 2487.
sch. 1, regs. 91/537, 809.
sch. 5, regs. 91/345, 537, 564.
sch. 7A, regs. 91/535.
sch. 11, regs. 91/534, 569, 574, 1751, 2487.
sch. 16, repealed in pt.: 1991, c. 21, sch. 4.

30. Interpretation Act 1978.
s. 5, sch. 1, see *Hummingbird Entertainments* v. *Birmingham City Council* [1991] R.A. 165, D.C.
s. 20, see *R.* v. *Secretary of State for the Home Department, ex p. Patel (Pratimakumari); R.* v. *Secretary of State for the Home Department, ex p. Wahid (Abdul)* [1991] Imm.A.R. 25, Pill J.
sch. 1, see *R.* v. *Secretary of State for the Environment, ex p. Birmingham Friendship Housing Association* [1990] C.O.D. 334, Garland J.
sch. 1, amended: 1991, c. 60, sch. 1.

31. Theft Act 1978.
s. 2, see *R.* v. *Attewell-Hughes, The Times,* January 31, 1991, C.A.

35. Import of Live Fish (Scotland) Act 1978.
s. 1, amended: 1991, c. 28, sch. 2.

42. Finance Act 1978.
s. 9, repealed: 1991, c. 31, sch. 19.

44. Employment Protection (Consolidation) Act 1978.
see *R.* v. *Secretary of State for Employment, ex p. Equal Opportunities Commission, The Times,* October 11, 1991, D.C.
s. 1, see *Eagland* v. *British Telecommunications* [1990] I.R.L.R. 328, E.A.T.

1978—cont.

44. Employment Protection (Consolidation) Act 1978—*cont.*
ss. 1, 4, see *Alexander* v. *Standard Telephones and Cables (No. 2); Wall* v. *Standard Telephones and Cables (No. 2)* [1991] I.R.L.R. 286, Hobhouse J.
s. 15, order 91/464; amended: *ibid.*
s. 18, order 90/2330.
s. 28, see *Luce* v. *Bexley London Borough Council* (1990) 88 L.G.R. 909, E.A.T.
s. 53, see *Catharine Haigh Harlequin Hair Design* v. *Seed* [1990] I.R.L.R. 175, E.A.T.
s. 54, see *Telephone Information Services* v. *Wilkinson* [1991] I.R.L.R. 148, E.A.T.
s. 55, see *White* v. *Reflecting Roadstuds* [1991] I.R.L.R. 331, E.A.T.
s. 57, see *Stephenson & Co. (Oxford)* v. *Austin* [1990] I.C.R. 609, E.A.T.; *Morgan* v. *Electrolux* [1991] I.R.L.R. 89, C.A.; *Hough* v. *Leyland DAF* [1991] I.R.L.R. 194, E.A.T.; *British Gas* v. *McGarrick* [1991] I.R.L.R. 305, C.A.; *Fuller* v. *Lloyds Bank* [1991] I.R.L.R. 336, E.A.T.; *Post Office Counters* v. *Heavey* [1990] I.C.R. 1, E.A.T.
s. 58, see *Fitzpatrick* v. *British Railways Board* [1990] I.C.R. 674, E.A.T.
s. 59, see *Alexander* v. *Standard Telephones and Cables (No. 2); Wall* v. *Standard Telephones and Cables (No. 2)* [1991] I.R.L.R. 286, Hobhouse J.
s. 62, see *McKenzie* v. *Crosville Motor Services* [1990] I.C.R. 172, E.A.T.
s. 64, see *Harber* v. *North London Polytechnic* [1990] I.R.L.R. 198, C.A.; *Brook* v. *British Telecommunications, The Times,* December 5, 1991, C.A.
s. 67, see *James W. Cook and Co. (Wivenhoe)* v. *S. Tipper* [1990] I.R.L.R. 386, C.A.; *Jean Sorelle* v. *Rybak* [1991] I.C.R. 127, E.A.T.; *Telephone Information Services* v. *Wilkinson* [1991] I.R.L.R. 148, E.A.T.
ss. 69, 75, see *O'Laoire* v. *Jackel International* [1991] I.R.L.R. 170, C.A.
s. 73, order 91/467; amended: *ibid.*
s. 74, see *Slaughter* v. *C. Brewer & Sons* [1990] I.C.R. 730, E.A.T.; *James W. Cook and Co. (Wivenhoe)* v. *S. Tipper* [1990] I.R.L.R. 386, C.A.; *Tele-Trading* v. *Jenkins* [1990] I.R.L.R. 430, C.A.; *Lytlarch* v. *Reid* [1991] I.C.R. 216, E.A.T.
s. 75, order 91/466; amended: *ibid.*
s. 75A, order 91/467; amended: *ibid.*

1978—cont.

44. Employment Protection (Consolidation) Act 1978—cont.

s. 81, see *Alexander* v. *Standard Telephones and Cables (No. 2); Wall* v. *Standard Telephones and Cables (No. 2)* [1991] I.R.L.R. 286, Hobhouse J.; *Berwick Salmon Fisheries Co.* v. *Rutherford* [1991] I.R.L.R. 203, E.A.T.

s. 82, see *McKechnie* v. *UBM Building Supplies (Southern)* [1991] I.R.L.R. 283, E.A.T.

s. 122, order 91/464; amended: *ibid.*

s. 131, see *Bowater* v. *Charlwood* [1991] I.R.L.R. 340, E.A.T.

ss. 138, 146, see *R.* v. *Civil Service Appeal Board, ex p. Cunningham* [1991] I.R.L.R. 297, C.A.

s. 140, see *Telephone Information Services* v. *Wilkinson* [1991] I.R.L.R. 148.

s. 141, see *Wood* v. *Cunard Line* [1990] I.R.L.R. 281, C.A.

s. 148, order 91/464.

s. 149, order 91/818.

s. 153, see *Broaders* v. *Kalkare Property Maintenance* [1990] I.R.L.R. 421, E.A.T.

s. 154, orders 91/464, 466, 467, 818.

s. 154, amended: order 91/464.

s. 176, see *Parker Foundry* v. *Slack, The Times*, October 30, 1991, C.A.

sch. 11, see *Bowater* v. *Charlwood* [1991] I.R.L.R. 340, E.A.T.

sch. 13, see *Gibson* v. *Motortune* [1990] I.C.R. 740, E.A.T.; *Berwick Salmon Fisheries Co.* v. *Rutherford* [1991] I.R.L.R. 203, E.A.T.; *Harber* v. *North London Polytechnic* [1990] I.R.L.R. 198, C.A.

sch. 14, order 91/464; amended: *ibid.*

47. Civil Liability (Contribution) Act 1978.

sch. 1, repealed in pt.: 1991, c. 22, sch. 9.

49. Community Service by Offenders (Scotland) Act 1978.

s. 6, amended: 1991, c. 53, sch. 3; repealed in pt.: *ibid.*

1979

2. Customs and Excise Management Act 1979.

see *R.* v. *Customs and Excise Commissioners, ex p. Tsahl* [1990] C.O.D. 230, Nolan J.

s. 1, amended: 1991, c. 31, s. 11; regs. 91/2724, 2725, 2727; repealed in pt.: regs. 91/2725, 2727.

ss. 1, 6, 8, 170, see *Montes* v. *H.M. Advocate*, 1990 S.C.C.R. 645.

s. 20, substituted: regs. 91/2724.

s. 20A, added: *ibid.*

s. 21, amended: *ibid.*

s. 22, substituted: *ibid.*

s. 22A, added: *ibid.*

1979—cont.

2. Customs and Excise Management Act 1979—cont.

s. 25, substituted: *ibid.*

s. 25A, added: *ibid.*

s. 27, amended: regs. 91/2725.

ss. 37, 42, amended: regs. 91/2724.

ss. 92, 98, amended: regs. 91/2725.

s. 100A, orders 91/1737–1740.

s. 100B, repealed: regs. 91/1727.

s. 100C, amended and repealed in pt.: *ibid.*

ss. 100D, 100E, repealed: *ibid.*

Pt. VIIIB (ss. 100G, 100H, 100J), added: 1991, c. 31, sch. 4.

Pt. IXA (ss. 118A–118G), added: *ibid.*, sch. 5.

s. 129, amended: regs. 91/2724.

s. 141, see *Customs and Excise Commissioners* v. *Air Canada* [1991] 2 W.L.R. 344, C.A.

s. 167, see *R.* v. *Lomas* [1990] 1 C.M.L.R. 513, H.H. Judge Balston.

3. Customs and Excise Duties (General Reliefs) Act 1979.

ss. 1, 4, order 90/2645.

s. 11A, order 91/2089.

s. 13, orders 91/1286, 1287, 1293.

4. Alcoholic Liquor Duties Act 1979.

ss. 1, 2, amended: 1991, c. 31, sch. 2, repealed in pt.: *ibid.*, schs. 2, 19.

s. 3, repealed in pt.: *ibid.*

s. 4, amended: *ibid.*, sch. 2; repealed in pt.: *ibid.*, schs. 2, 19.

s. 5, amended: *ibid.*, s. 1.

s. 36, amended; *ibid.*; substituted: *ibid.*, s. 7.

ss. 37–40, repealed: *ibid.*, schs. 2, 19.

s. 41, substituted: *ibid.*, sch. 2.

s. 41A, added: *ibid.*, s. 7.

ss. 42–44, amended: *ibid.*, sch. 2.

s. 45, amended: *ibid.*, repealed in pt.: *ibid.*, schs. 2, 19.

s. 46, substituted: *ibid.*, sch. 2.

ss. 47, 48, substituted: *ibid.*, s. 7.

s. 49, substituted: *ibid.*, sch. 2.

s. 49A, amended: *ibid.*

s. 50, repealed: *ibid.*, schs. 2, 19.

s. 52, substituted: *ibid.*, sch. 2.

s. 53, repealed: *ibid.*, schs. 2, 19.

s. 62, amended: *ibid.*, s. 1.

ss. 71A, 72, repealed: *ibid.*, schs. 2, 19.

sch. 1, amended: *ibid.*, s. 1., sch. 1.

5. Hydrocarbon Oil Duties Act 1979.

ss. 6, 11, 13A, 14, amended: 1991, c. 31, s. 3.

sch. 1, repealed in pt.: *ibid.*, sch. 19.

7. Tobacco Products Duty Act 1979.

sch. 1, amended: 1991, c. 31, s. 2.

10. Public Lending Right Act 1979.

s. 2, order 91/858; amended: *ibid.*

s. 3, order 90/2360.

14. Capital Gains Tax Act 1979.

s. 5, order 91/736.

CAP.

1979—cont.

14. Capital Gains Tax Act 1979—*cont.*
s. 13, amended: 1991, c. 31, s. 97.
s. 54, see *Swires (Inspector of Taxes)* v. *Renton, The Times*, July 18, 1991, Hoffmann J.
s. 72, see *O'Rourke (Inspector of Taxes)* v. *Binks, The Times*, July 9, 1991, Vinelott J.
ss. 101, 102, amended: 1991, c. 31, s. 93.
s. 123, see *Gordon* v. *I.R.C.; I.R.C.* v. *Gordon*, 1991 S.L.T. 730.
s. 126C, repealed: 1991, c. 31, s. 92.
s. 142A, regs. 91/851.
s. 149B, amended: 1991, c. 31, s. 57.
sch. 1, amended: 1991, c. 21, sch. 2; order 91/2874.
sch. 2, order 91/2678.
sch. 5, see *Smith* v. *Schofield (Inspector of Taxes)* [1990] 1 W.L.R. 1447, Hoffmann J.

17. Vaccine Damage Payments Act 1979.
s. 1, order 91/939.

18. Social Security Act 1979.
ss. 2 (in pt.), 3, repealed: 1991, c. 21, sch. 4.

21. Forestry Act 1979.
s. 1, amended: 1991, c. 18, s. 3.

29. International Monetary Fund Act 1979.
s. 1, order 90/2352.

32. Industry Act 1979.
s. 1, sch., repealed in pt.: 1991, c. 66, sch. 2.

34. Credit Unions Act 1979.
s. 31, regs. 91/521.

36. Nurses, Midwives and Health Visitors Act 1979.
s. 20, amended and repealed in pt.: regs. 91/1997.
sch. 4, repealed, exc. N.I.: *ibid.*

38. Estate Agents Act 1979.
s. 3, orders 91/860, 861, 1032, 1091.
s. 10, amended: 1991, c. 60, sch. 1.
s. 14, amended: regs. 91/1997.
s. 18, see *Solicitors' Estate Agency (Glasgow)* v. *MacIver* (Sh.Ct.), 1990 S.C.L.R. 595.
s. 18, regs. 91/859.
s. 30, orders 91/859–861.

39. Merchant Shipping Act 1979.
s. 20, order 90/2595.
s. 21, regs. 90/2602, 2605; 91/65, 638, 784, 1300, 1341, 1404.
s. 22, regs. 90/2602, 2605; 91/65, 1300, 1341, 1404.
s. 34, order 91/347.
s. 47, order 91/763.
sch. 4, see *Bowbelle, The* [1990] 1 W.L.R. 1330, Sheen J.

41. Pneumoconiosis etc. (Workers' Compensation) Act 1979.
ss. 1, 7, regs. 91/899.

CAP.

1979—cont.

42. Arbitration Act 1979.
s. 1, see *Blexen* v. *G. Percy Trentham* [1990] 42 E.G. 133, C.A.; *National Westminster Bank* v. *Arthur Young McClelland Moores (No. 2)* [1990] 50 E.G. 45, Knox J.; *Geogas S.A.* v. *Trammo Gas, The Independent*, July 19, 1991, H.L.
s. 2, see *Taylor* v. *Vectapike* [1990] 44 E.G. 75, Morritt J.

43. Crown Agents Act 1979.
s. 22, amended: regs. 91/1997.

46. Ancient Monuments and Archaeological Areas Act 1979.
ss. 47, 60, 61, regs. 91/2512, 2647.
sch. 4, repealed in pt.: 1991, c. 45, sch. 8; c. 60, sch. 3.

54. Sale of Goods Act 1979.
s. 3, repealed in pt.: 1991, c. 50, sch. 2.
ss. 17, 19, see *Armour* v. *Thyssen Edelstahlwerke AG* [1990] 3 W.L.R. 810; [1990] 3 All E.R. 481, H.L.
s. 22, see *R.* v. *Wheeler* (1991) 92 Cr.App.R. 279, C.A.
s. 29, see *Saveheat Insulations* v. *McVean* (Sh.Ct.), 1991 S.C.L.R. 28.
s. 50, see *Shearson Lehman Hutton Inc.* v. *Maclaine Watson & Co. (No. 2)* [1990] 1 Lloyd's Rep. 441, Webster J.
s. 51, see *Sealace Shipping Co.* v. *Oceanvoice; Alecos, The* [1991] 1 Lloyd's Rep. 120, C.A.

55. Justices of the Peace Act 1979.
s. 18, rules 91/1966.
s. 23, orders 91/121, 412, 586, 1828, 2048, 2212, 2215.
s. 29, amended: 1991, c. 17, sch. 2.
ss. 35, 37, 38, amended: 1991, c. 53, sch. 11.
s. 55, amended: *ibid.*, ss. 79, 93.
s. 58, amended: *ibid.*, ss. 79, 93, sch. 11.
s. 59, substituted: *ibid.*, s. 93.
s. 70, amended: *ibid.*

1980

4. Bail etc. (Scotland) Act 1980.
s. 1, see *Gilchrist, Petr.*, 1991 S.L.T. 919.
s. 2, see *McMahon* v. *MacPhail*, 1991 S.C.C.R. 470.

5. Child Care Act 1980.
s. 2, see *R.* v. *Gwynedd County Council, ex p. B., The Independent*, April 5, 1991, C.A.
ss. 5–7, amended: 1991, c. 53, sch. 11.
s. 12, see *S.* v. *Newham London Borough Council, The Times*, May 24, 1991, Sir Stephen Brown P.
ss. 12C–12E, 21A, amended: 1991, c. 53, sch. 11.

CAP.

1980—cont.

5. Child Care Act 1980—cont.
ss. 12C, 12F, see *R. v. Pontlottlyn Juvenile Court, ex p. Reeves* [1991] C.O.D. 27, Waite J.
s. 22A, regs. 90/2399.
s. 45, amended: 1991, c. 21, sch. 3.
ss. 67, 79, amended: 1991, c. 53, sch. 11.
s. 85, regs. 90/2399.

6. Foster Children Act 1980.
ss. 11, 12, 14, amended: 1991, c. 53, sch. 11.

9. Reserve Forces Act 1980.
s. 59, amended: 1991, c. 62, s. 16.
sch. 6, repealed in pt.: *ibid.*, schs. 2, 3.

11. Protection of Trading Interests Act 1980.
s. 8, order 90/2291.

13. Slaughter of Animals (Scotland) Act 1980.
s. 9, amended: 1991, c. 30, s. 1.
s. 16, amended: *ibid.*, s. 3.
s. 19, amended: *ibid.*, s. 4.
s. 19A, added: *ibid.*, s. 5.

20. Education Act 1980.
s. 6, see *R. v. Kingston upon Thames Royal Borough Council, ex p. Kingwell, The Guardian*, May 30, 1991, D.C.; *R. v. Bromley London Borough Council, ex p. C., The Times*, June 6, 1991, D.C.
ss. 6–8, 15, 16, sch. 2, see *R. v. Dorset County Council, ex p. Greenwood* [1990] C.O.D. 235, Macpherson J.
ss. 6, 8, sch. 2, see *R. v. Governors of the Buss Foundation Camden School for Girls, ex p. Lukasiewicz* [1991] C.O.D. 98, Otton J.
s. 8, regs. 91/1265, 1582, 1658, 1813.
s. 12, see *R. v. Birmingham City Council and Secretary of State for Education, ex p. Kaur* [1991] C.O.D. 21, D.C.
s. 17, regs. 91/1767.
s. 18, regs. 91/1830.
s. 35, regs. 91/1767, 1830.

21. Competition Act 1980.
s. 19, amended: 1991, c. 60, sch. 1.

23. Consular Fees Act 1980.
s. 1, orders 90/2586; 91/996, 2291.

30. Social Security Act 1980.
ss. 9, 18, amended: 1991, c. 3, s. 3.
s. 17, sch. 3, amended: 1991, c. 21, sch. 2.

32. Licensed Premises (Exclusion of Certain Persons) Act 1980.
s. 1, amended: 1991, c. 53, sch. 11.

33. Industry Act 1980.
ss. 1, 2, 4–6, repealed in pt.: 1991, c. 66, sch. 2, Pt. I.
s. 7, repealed: *ibid.*, Pt. III.
ss. 8, 21, repealed in pt.: *ibid.*, Pt. I.

43. Magistrates' Courts Act 1980.
s. 1, see *R. v. Highbury Corner Magistrates' Court, ex p. Health and Safety Executive* [1991] C.O.D. 156, D.C.

CAP.

1980—cont.

43. Magistrates' Courts Act 1980—cont.
Pt. I (ss. 1–50), amended: 1991, c. 53, sch. 8.
s. 9, see *R. v. Dorchester Justices, ex p. D.P.P.* [1990] R.T.R. 369, D.C., *R. v. Watford Justices, ex p. D.P.P.* [1990] R.T.R. 374, D.C.; *R. v. Redbridge JJ., ex p. Ram, The Times*, August 16, 1991, D.C.
ss. 9, 10, see *R. v. Ripon Liberty Justices, ex p. Bugg* [1991] C.O.D. 57, D.C.
ss. 9, 11, see *R. v. Teesside Justices, ex p. Nilsson* [1991] C.O.D. 58, D.C.
s. 11, see *R. v. Nuneaton Justices, ex p. Bingham* [1991] C.O.D. 56, D.C.
s. 12, see *R. v. Coventry Magistrates' Court, ex p. D.P.P.* [1990] R.T.R. 193, D.C.
s. 12, amended: 1991, c. 53, s. 69, sch. 11.
s. 20, see *R. v. Brentwood Justices, ex p. Nicholls, The Times*, July 5, 1991, H.L.
s. 20, amended: 1991, c. 53, sch. 11.
s. 22, amended: *ibid.*, sch. 8.
s. 24, see *R. v. Rotherham Magistrates' Court, ex p. Brough* [1991] C.O.D. 89, D.C.
s. 24, amended: 1991, c. 53, s. 17; repealed in pt.: *ibid.*, sch. 13.
s. 29, amended: *ibid.*, sch. 11.
s. 32, amended: *ibid.*, s. 17.
ss. 33, 34, amended: *ibid.*, sch. 4.
s. 35, repealed: *ibid.*, sch. 13.
s. 37, amended: *ibid.*, s. 60; repealed in pt.: *ibid.*, sch. 13.
s. 38, see *R. v. Doncaster JJ., ex p. Goulding, The Independent*, October 30, 1991, D.C.
s. 38, substituted: 1991, c. 53, s. 25; amended: *ibid.*, sch. 8.
s. 40, amended: *ibid.*, sch. 4.
s. 44, see *Edwards v. D.P.P., The Times*, May 29, 1991, D.C.
s. 59, substituted: 1991, c. 17, s. 2.
ss. 59A, 59B, added: *ibid.*, s. 3.
s. 60, substituted: *ibid.*, s. 4.
s. 62, amended: *ibid.*, sch. 2.
s. 63, amended: 1991, c. 53, sch. 4.
s. 75, amended: 1991, c. 17, sch. 2.
s. 76, amended: *ibid.*, s. 7.
s. 81, amended: 1991, c. 53, schs. 8, 11.
s. 87, repealed in pt.: order 91/724.
s. 93, amended: 1991, c. 17, sch. 2.
s. 94A, added: *ibid.*, s. 7.
s. 95, substituted: *ibid.*, sch. 2.
s. 96A, amended: 1991, c. 53, sch. 8.
s. 97, see *P., Re, The Guardian*, January 23, 1991, C.A.; *R. v. B. County Council, ex p. P.*, [1991] 1 W.L.R. 221, C.A.
s. 97, amended: 1991, c. 53, sch. 4.

1980—cont.

43. Magistrates' Courts Act 1980—*cont.*
s. 103, amended: *ibid.*, s. 55; repealed in pt.: *ibid.*, s. 55, sch. 13.
s. 104, amended: *ibid.*, sch. 11.
s. 108, repealed in pt.: *ibid.*, sch. 13.
s. 111, see *R.* v. *Bideford JJ., ex p. South West Water Authority* [1990] C.O.D. 369, D.C.; *R.* v. *Chesterfield JJ., ex p. Kovacs* [1990] C.O.D. 367, Roch J.
s. 121, see *R.* v. *Ripon Liberty Justices, ex p. Bugg* [1991] C.O.D. 57, D.C.; *R.* v. *Liverpool City Justices, ex p. D.P.P., The Times*, December 10, 1991, D.C.
s. 122, see *R.* v. *Teesside Justices, ex p. Nilsson* [1991] C.O.D. 58, D.C.
s. 127, see *Torridge District Council* v. *Turner, The Times*, November 27, 1991, D.C.
s. 128A, order 91/2667.
ss. 128, 129, see *R.* v. *Liverpool City JJ., ex p. Grogan* [1991] C.O.D. 148, D.C.
s. 133, see *R.* v. *Isaacs* [1990] R.T.R. 240, C.A.
ss. 135, 136, amended: 1991, c. 53, sch. 8.
s. 142, see *R.* v. *Nuneaton Justices, ex p. Bingham* [1991] C.O.D. 56, D.C.
s. 143, amended: 1991, c. 17, sch. 2; c. 53, sch. 8; repealed in pt.: *ibid.*, sch. 13.
s. 144, rules 91/1074, 1395, 1405, 1426, 1923, 1991, 2096, 2099.
s. 146, amended: 1991, c. 53, sch. 11.
sch. 3, repealed in pt.: *ibid.*, sch. 13; repealed: *ibid.*, s. 25.
sch. 4, amended: *ibid.*, s. 23, sch. 11.
sch. 6A, substituted: *ibid.*, s. 17, sch. 4.
sch. 7, repealed in pt.: 1991, c. 17, sch. 3; c. 60, sch. 3.

44. Education (Scotland) Act 1980.
s. 2, regs. 91/1682.
s. 35, see *MacIntyre* v. *Annan*, 1991 S.C.C.R. 465.
s. 49, regs. 91/834.
ss. 73, 74, regs. 90/2551; 91/834, 1494, 1522.
ss. 75A, 75B, regs. 91/1495.
s. 77, regs. 90/2387.
s. 105, see *University Court of the University of Glasgow*, Petrs. (I.H.), 1991 S.C.L.R. 402.
s. 111, amended: regs. 91/1997.
s. 135, regs. 90/2386.

45. Water (Scotland) Act 1980.
ss. 10, 13, 23, amended: 1991, c. 22, sch. 8.
ss. 31, 33, amended: *ibid.*, sch. 10.
s. 72, order 91/2573.
ss. 76A, 76B, 76J, regs. 91/1333.
s. 76K, amended: 1991, c. 28, sch. 10; repealed in pt.: *ibid.*

1980—cont.

45. Water (Scotland) Act 1980—*cont.*
ss. 77–79, repealed: *ibid.*, sch. 11.
s. 101, regs. 91/1333.
s. 101, amended: 1991, c. 22, sch. 10.
s. 103, amended: *ibid.*, sch. 8.
s. 109, regs. 91/1333.
s. 109, amended: 1991, c. 22, schs. 8, 10.
schs. 3, 4, amended: *ibid.*, sch. 8.
schs. 5, 6, repealed: *ibid.*, sch. 11.
sch. 10, repealed in pt.: 1991, c. 55, sch. 13.

46. Solicitors (Scotland) Act 1980.
s. 42, see *Council of the Law Society of Scotland* v. *McKinnie, The Scotsman*, May 22, 1991.

47. Criminal Appeal (Northern Ireland) Act 1980.
sch. 4, repealed in pt.: 1991, c. 24, sch. 8.

48. Finance Act 1980.
s. 5, repealed: 1991, c. 31, sch. 19.
s. 64, see *Barclays Mercantile Industrial Finance* v. *Melluish (Inspector of Taxes)* [1990] S.T.C. 314, Vinelott J.
s. 80, amended: 1991, s. 31, s. 94.

49. Deer Act 1980.
repealed: 1991, c. 54, sch. 4.

51. Housing Act 1980.
s. 8, see *Alexander* v. *I.R.C.* (1991) 23 H.L.R. 236, C.A.

52. Tenants' Rights, Etc. (Scotland) Act 1980.
s. 15, see *Midlothian District Council* v. *Drummond*, 1991 S.L.T. (Sh.Ct.) 67.
s. 15, sch. 2, see *Gordon District Council* v. *Acutt*, 1991 S.L.T. (Sh.Ct.) 78.

58. Limitation Act 1980.
s. 11, see *Hendy* v. *Milton Keynes Health Authority, The Times*, March 8, 1991, Blofeld J.
ss. 11, 33, see *Hartley* v. *Birmingham City Council, The Independent*, August 16, 1991, C.A.
ss. 14, 33, see *Halford* v. *Brookes* [1991] 1 W.L.R. 428, C.A.

62. Criminal Justice (Scotland) Act 1980.
s. 3, see *H.M. Advocate* v. *B.* (Sh.Ct.), 1991 S.C.C.R. 533.
s. 26, see *Hamilton* v. *Ross*, 1991 S.C.C.R. 165.
s. 32, see *Lang, Petr.*, 1991 S.C.C.R. 138.
s. 67, amended: 1991, c. 62, sch. 2.

63. Overseas Development and Co-operation Act 1980.
s. 4, orders 91/150, 717, 1144.
s. 6, order 91/462.

65. Local Government, Planning and Land Act 1980.
see *R.* v. *Secretary of State for the Environment, ex p. Merton London Borough Council* (1991) 31 R.V.R. 78, C.A.

CAP.

1980—cont.

65. Local Government, Planning and Land Act 1980—*cont.*
ss. 7, 9, 23, regs. 91/243(S.).
s. 66, see *R.* v. *Secretary of State for the Environment, ex p. North Tyneside Borough Council* [1990] C.O.D. 195, D.C.
s. 87, regs. 90/2474(S.).
s. 87, amended (S.): 1991, c. 34, sch. 13.
s. 114, repealed in pt.: *ibid.*, sch. 19, Pts. III, IV(S.).
s. 141, amended: *ibid.*, schs. 15, 17(S.).
s. 149, order 90/1568.
s. 167, amended: 1991, c. 22, sch. 8.
s. 170, repealed in pt.: 1991, c. 66, sch. 2.
s. 181, repealed in pt.: 1991, c. 60, sch. 3.
s. 185, amended: *ibid.*, sch. 1.
sch. 29, amended: 1991, c. 34, schs. 3, 7.
sch. 30, amended: *ibid.*, schs. 10, 13(S.).
sch. 31, amended: regs. 91/1997.

66. Highways Act 1980.
see *R.* v. *Essex County Council, ex p. Curtis, Barton and Barton* [1991] C.O.D. 9, Pill J.
ss. 1, 2, amended: 1991, c. 22, s. 21.
s. 10, amended: *ibid.*, s. 22; repealed in pt.: *ibid.*
ss. 10, 41, see *R.* v. *Secretary of State for Transport, ex p. Esso Petroleum* [1991] C.O.D. 110, McCullough J.
s. 17, amended: 1991, c. 22, s. 20.
s. 19, amended: *ibid.*, s. 21.
ss. 20, 21 (in pt.), repealed: *ibid.*, sch. 9.
s. 38, amended: *ibid.*, s. 22.
s. 42, amended: 1990, c. 40, sch. 4.
ss. 58 (in pt.), 60, 64 (in pt.), repealed: 1991, c. 22, sch. 9.
ss. 90A, 90B, amended: 1991, c. 40, sch. 4.
s. 90E, repealed in pt.: 1991, c. 22, sch. 19.
s. 90F, amended: 1991, c. 40, sch. 4.
s. 95A, added: *ibid.*, s. 40.
s. 100, amended; 1991, c. 60, sch. 1.
s. 105A, amended: 1991, c. 22, s. 19.
s. 116, see *Ramblers Association* v. *Kent County Council* (1990) 60 P. &. C.R. 464, D.C.
s. 118, see *R.* v. *Secretary of State for the Environment, ex p. Cheshire County Council* [1990] C.O.D. 426, C.A.
s. 125, see *R.* v. *Secretary of State for Transport, ex p. Esso Petroleum* [1991] C.O.D. 110, McCullough J.
s. 137, see *Devon County Council* v. *Gateway Foodmarkets* [1990] C.O.D. 324, D.C.
s. 139, amended: 1991, c. 22, sch. 8.
s. 140A, added: *ibid.*
s. 144, amended: *ibid.*
ss. 156, 160, repealed: *ibid.*, sch. 9.

CAP.

1980—cont.

66. Highways Act 1980—*cont.*
ss. 169, 170, amended: *ibid.*, sch. 8.
s. 171A, added: *ibid.*
ss. 174, 179, amended: *ibid.*
ss. 181–183, repealed: *ibid.*, sch. 9.
s. 184, amended: *ibid.*, sch. 8; repealed in pt.: *ibid.*, schs. 8, 9.
Pt. X (ss. 186–202), repealed: 1991, c. 34, s. 81, sch. 19.
ss. 203, 232, repealed in pt.: *ibid.*, sch. 19.
s. 246, amended: *ibid.*, s. 62, sch. 15.
s. 278, see *R.* v. *Secretary of State for Transport, ex p. Esso Petroleum* [1991] C.O.D. 110, McCullough J.
s. 278, substituted: 1991, c. 22, s. 23.
ss. 285, 290, 292, amended: *ibid.*, sch. 8.
s. 307, repealed in pt.: 1991, c. 34, sch. 19.
s. 314, amended: 1991, c. 22, sch. 8.
s. 325, amended: *ibid.*, s. 20, sch. 8; repealed in pt.: *ibid.*, s. 20, sch. 9; c. 34, sch. 19.
s. 326, repealed in pt.: 1991, c. 22, sch. 9; c. 34, sch. 19.
s. 329, amended: 1991, c. 22, sch. 8.
s. 330, repealed in pt.: *ibid.*, sch. 9.
s. 334, amended: *ibid.*, sch. 8; repealed in pt.: *ibid.*, sch. 9.
s. 339, amended: 1991, c. 60, sch. 3.
s. 340, repealed in pt.: 1991, c. 22, sch. 9.
sch. 22, repealed in pt.: 1991, c. 34, sch. 19.
sch. 23, order 91/960.
sch. 23, repealed in pt.: 1991, c. 22, sch. 9; c. 34, sch. 19.
sch. 24, repealed in pt.: 1991, c. 22, sch. 9; c. 60, sch. 3.

67. Anguilla Act 1980.
s. 1, order 91/988.

1981

6. Industry Act 1981.
s. 1, repealed: 1991, c. 66, sch. 2.
s. 2, repealed in pt.: 1991, c. 1, s. 1; c. 69, s. 2.

7. House of Commons Members' Fund and Parliamentary Pensions Act 1981.
s. 2, resolution 91/992; amended: *ibid.*

12. Water Act 1981.
s. 6, amended: 1991, c. 22, sch. 8; repealed: 1991, c. 60, sch. 3.

13. English Industrial Estates Corporation Act 1981.
s. 7, amended: regs. 91/1997.

14. Public Passenger Vehicles Act 1981.
s. 3, orders 91/288, 634.
s. 6, amended: 1991, c. 40, sch. 4.
s. 7, repealed: *ibid.*, s. 9, sch. 8.
s. 8, repealed in pt.: *ibid.*, s. 11, sch. 8.
s. 9, repealed: *ibid.*, s. 12, sch. 8.
s. 9A, repealed in pt.: *ibid.*, sch. 8.
s. 10, regs. 91/456.
s. 10, amended: 1991, c. 40, sch. 4.
s. 20, repealed in pt.: *ibid.*, sch. 8.

CAP.
1981—cont.

14. Public Passenger Vehicles Act 1981—*cont.*
s. 51, amended: *ibid.*, sch. 4; repealed in pt.: *ibid.*, sch. 8.
s. 52, regs. 91/456.
s. 53, repealed in pt.: 1991, c. 40, sch. 8.
s. 60, regs. 90/2612; 91/456.
s. 61, regs. 90/2612.
ss. 65, 66A, 68, repealed in pt.: 1991, c. 40, sch. 8.
s. 80, orders 91/288, 634.
s. 82, sch. 7, repealed in pt.: 1991, c. 40, sch. 8.

20. Judicial Pensions Act 1981.
s. 21, order 91/862; amended: *ibid.*

22. Animal Health Act 1981.
s. 1, orders 90/2627, 2628; 91/404, 456, 631, 1030, 1155, 1251, 1381, 1770, 1879, 1992, 2246, 2814.
s. 7, orders 91/404, 631, 1155, 1381, 1770, 2246, 2814.
s. 8, orders 90/2627, 2628; 91/1155, 1251, 1381, 1879, 1992, 2246, 2814.
s. 11, order 91/58.
s. 14, order 91/1879.
s. 15, orders 91/1030, 1155, 1381, 1992, 2246, 2814.
s. 17, orders 91/1251, 1381, 1992, 2814.
ss. 21, 22, amended: 1991, c. 28, sch. 2.
s. 23, orders 91/404, 631, 1251, 1381, 1770, 1992, 2814.
s. 25, orders 91/1381, 1992, 2814.
s. 28, order 91/1155.
ss. 32, 35, 36, order 91/2246.
ss. 37, 38, orders 90/2627, 2628.
s. 72, see *R.* v. *Cheshire County Council Trading Standards Dept., ex p. Alan Helliwell* [1991] Crim.L.R. 210, D.C.
s. 72, orders 90/2627, 2628; 91/1155, 1251, 2246, 2814.
s. 83, orders 91/1030, 1155, 1251, 1381, 1992, 2246, 2814.
s. 84, orders 91/405, 1168.
s. 86, orders 90/2627, 2628; 91/58.
s. 87, orders 90/2627, 2628; 91/1155, 1251, 2246, 2814.
s. 88, orders 91/1155, 1251, 1381, 2246, 2814.

28. Licensing (Alcohol Education and Research) Act 1981.
s. 10, amended: regs. 91/1997.

29. Fisheries Act 1981.
ss. 4, 14, order 91/417.
s. 11, amended: regs. 91/1997.
s. 30, see *Olsen* v. *Thom*, 1991 S.L.T. 380.
s. 30, orders 90/2528; 91/138, 522.
sch. 4, amended: 1991, c. 60, sch. 1.

35. Finance Act 1981.
s. 8, repealed: 1991, c. 19, sch. 19.
s. 79, amended: 1991, c. 31, s. 92.
s. 80, amended: *ibid.*, s. 89, sch. 18.
s. 80A, added: *ibid.*, sch. 18.

CAP.
1981—cont.

35. Finance Act 1981—*cont.*
s. 81, amended: *ibid.*
s. 82A, added: *ibid.*
s. 83, amended: *ibid.*
s. 88, repealed: *ibid.*, s. 92.
sch. 9, see *Shaw (Inspector of Taxes)* v. *Samuel Montagu & Co.* [1990] S.T.C. 538, Scott J.

38. British Telecommunications Act 1981.
sch. 3, amended: 1991, c. 22, sch. 8; repealed in pt.: *ibid.*, sch. 9.

47. Criminal Attempts Act 1981.
s. 1, see *R.* v. *Williams (Kevin John)* (1991) 92 Cr.App.R. 158, C.A.; *R.* v. *Campbell* [1991] Crim.L.R. 269, C.A.
s. 9, see *R.* v. *Liverpool Stipendiary Magistrate, ex p. Ellison*, [1990] R.T.R. 220, D.C.

49. Contempt of Court Act 1981.
see *R.* v. *Hutton* [1990] Crim.L.R. 875, C.A.; *Pickering* v. *Liverpool Daily Post and Echo Newspaper* [1991] 2 W.L.R. 513, H.L.
ss. 1–3, see *Solicitor-General* v. *Henry and News Group Newspapers* [1990] C.O.D. 307, D.C.
s. 4, see *Central Independent Television, Re* [1991] 1 W.L.R. 4, C.A.
s. 12, see *R.* v. *Selby JJ., ex p. Frame* [1991] 2 W.L.R. 965, D.C.
s. 12, amended: 1991, c. 53, sch. 4, Pts. I, V, sch. 11.
s. 14, amended: *ibid.*, sch. 4, Pts. I, V.

54. Supreme Court Act 1981.
s. 18, see *R.* v. *Blandford Justices, ex p. Pamment* [1990] 1 W.L.R. 1490, C.A.; *Land and Property Trust Company, Re, The Times*, May 7, 1991, C.A.; *Atlas Maritime Co. SA* v. *Avalon Maritime, The Times*, May 21, 1991, C.A.; *R.* v. *Secretary of State for the Home Department, ex p. Garner* [1990] C.O.D. 457, C.A.
s. 20, see *Bain Clarkson* v. *Owners of Sea Friends, The Times*, April 18, 1991, C.A.
s. 28, see *R.* v. *Chesterfield JJ., ex p. Kovacs* [1990] C.O.D. 367, Roch J.; *Petrofina S.A.* v. *AOT; Mærsk Nimrod, The* [1991] 3 All E.R. 161, Phillips J.
s. 29, see *R.* v. *Leicester Crown Court, ex p. S.* [1991] Crim.L.R. 365, D.C.
s. 31, see *R.* v. *Haringey London Borough Council, ex p. Secretary of State for the Environment* (1990) R.V.R. 261, D.C.; *R.* v. *Football Association of Wales, ex p. Flint Town United Football Club* [1991] C.O.D. 44, D.C.; *R.* v. *Westminster City Council, ex p. Hilditch* [1990] C.O.D. 434, C.A.

1981—cont.

54. Supreme Court Act 1981—*cont.*

s. 32A, see *Willson* v. *Ministry of Defence* [1991] 1 All E.R. 638, Baker J.

s. 35A, see *Marshall* v. *Southampton and South-West Hampshire Area Health Authority (No. 2)* [1990] I.R.L.R. 481, C.A.

s. 37, see *Fresh Fruit Wales* v. *Halbert, The Times*, January 29, 1991, C.A.

s. 42, see *R.* v. *Highbury Corner Magistrates' Court, ex p. Ewing, sub nom. Ewing, ex p.* [1991] 3 All E.R. 192, C.A.

s. 43, see *R.* v. *Nuneaton Justices, ex p. Bingham* [1991] C.O.D. 56, D.C.

s. 47, see *R.* v. *Komsta; R.* v. *Murphy* (1990) 12 Cr.App.R.(S.) 63, C.A.; *R.* v. *Miller* (1991) 92 Cr.App.R. 191, C.A.; *R.* v. *Stillwell; R.* v. *Jewell, The Times*, August 22, 1991, C.A.; *R.* v. *Evans (Kelvin), The Times*, October 18, 1991, C.A.; *R.* v. *Crozier* (1990) 12 Cr.App.R.(S.) 206, C.A.

s. 61, see *A.P.A.C. Rowena* v. *Norpol Packaging, The Times*, July 16, 1991, Harman J.

s. 61, order 91/1210.

s. 69, see *H.* v. *Ministry of Defence* [1991] 2 W.L.R. 1192, C.A.

s. 81, amended: 1991, c. 25, sch. 3.

s. 84, rules 91/531, 1288.

s. 85, rules 90/2599; 91/531, 1329, 1884.

s. 86, rules 91/1288.

s. 127, rules 91/1876.

s. 133, rules 90/2471.

sch. 1, amended: order 91/1210.

sch. 5, repealed in pt.: 1991, c. 60, sch. 3.

55. Armed Forces Act 1981.

s. 14, repealed: 1991, c. 62, s. 19, sch. 3.

56. Transport Act 1981.

sch. 3, amended and repealed in pt.: order 91/510.

sch. 8, see *McIntosh* v. *Lowe*, 1991 S.C.C.R. 154.

59. Matrimonial Homes (Family Protection) (Scotland) Act 1981.

s. 2, see *Porter* v. *Porter* (Sh.Ct.), 1990 S.C.L.R. 752.

ss. 3, 4, see *Millar* v. *Millar* (Sh.Ct.), 1991 S.C.L.R. 649.

s. 7, amended: 1991, c. 50, sch. 1.

s. 13, amended: 1991, c. 51, sch. 11.

60. Education Act 1981.

s. 7, see *R.* v. *Secretary of State for Education and Science, ex p. E., The Times*, May 9, 1991, C.A.; *R.* v. *Newham London Borough Council, ex p. D, The Times*, May 27, 1991, Brooke J.

1981—cont.

60. Education Act 1981—*cont.*

s. 12, regs. 91/450.

s. 13, regs. 91/449.

s. 19, regs. 91/449, 450.

61. British Nationality Act 1981.

ss. 10, 52, see *R.* v. *Secretary of State for the Home Department, ex p. Patel (Pratimakumari); R.* v. *Secretary of State for the Home Department, ex p. Wahid (Abdul)* [1991] Imm.A.R. 25, Pill, J.

s. 37, order 90/1502.

s. 41, regs. 91/183.

s. 53, order 91/2630.

sch. 3, amended: order 90/1502.

63. Betting and Gaming Duties Act 1981.

s. 7, amended: 1991, c. 31, s. 5.

s. 14, amended: *ibid.*, s. 6; repealed in pt.: *ibid.*, s. 6, sch. 19.

s. 15, amended: *ibid.*, s. 6.

s. 16, sch. 2, regs. 91/1798.

sch. 2, amended: 1991, c. 31, s. 6; repealed in pt.: *ibid.*, s. 6, sch. 19.

64. New Towns Act 1981.

s. 11, amended: 1991, c. 22, sch. 8.

s. 41, order 91/1980.

s. 68, amended: regs. 91/1997.

66. Compulsory Purchase (Vesting Declarations) Act 1981.

ss. 3, 4, see *Westminster City Council* v. *Quereshi* (1990) 60 P. & C.R. 380, Aldous J.

67. Acquisition of Land Act 1981.

ss. 6, 7, 12, 16, 17, 19, amended: 1991, c. 34, sch. 15.

s. 20, repealed: *ibid.*, sch. 19.

s. 23, see *Bolton Metropolitan Borough Council* v. *Secretary of State for the Environment and Greater Manchester Waste Disposal Authority* (1990) 61 P. & C.R. 343, C.A.

ss. 23, 24, see *Sharkey* v. *Secretary of State for the Environment* [1990] 45 E.G. 113, Roch J.

s. 31, sch. 1, amended: 1991, c. 34, sch. 15.

sch. 3, amended: *ibid.*; repealed in pt.: *ibid.*, schs. 15, 19.

sch. 4, repealed in pt.: 1991, c. 60, sch. 3.

68. Broadcasting Act 1981.

s. 29, see *R.* v. *Secretary of State for the Home Department, ex p. Brind* [1991] 2 W.L.R. 588, H.L.

s. 42, amended: regs. 91/1997.

s. 65, sch. 3, repealed in pt.: 1991, c. 66, sch. 2.

69. Wildlife and Countryside Act 1981.

s. 5, amended: 1991, c. 39, s. 1; repealed in pt.: *ibid.*

s. 6, regs. 91/479.

s. 7, regs. 91/478.

CAP.
1981—cont.
69. Wildlife and Countryside Act 1981—cont.

s. 11, amended: 1991, c. 39, s. 1; repealed in pt.: *ibid.*

s. 22, order 91/367.

ss. 27, 27A, amended: 1991, c. 28, sch. 2.

s. 28, see *Southern Water Authority* v. *Nature Conservancy Council, The Times*, June 17, 1991, D.C.

s. 29, amended: 1991, c. 28, sch. 2.

s. 34, repealed in pt.: *ibid.*, sch. 11.

s. 42, order 91/616.

s. 50, see *Cameron* v. *Nature Conservancy Council*, 1991 S.L.T. (Lands Tr.) 85.

s. 52, order 91/616.

s. 52, amended: 1991, c. 28, sch. 2.

ss. 53, 56, see *R.* v. *Secretary of State for the Environment, ex p. Simms; R.* v. *Same, ex p. Burrows, sub nom. R.* v. *Secretary of State, ex p. Burrows* (1990) 60 P. & C.R. 105, C.A.

sch. 5, amended: order 91/367.

sch. 7, repealed in pt.: 1991, c. 54, sch. 4.

1982
6. Transport (Finance) Act 1982.

s. 1, repealed: 1991, c. 63, s. 1.

s. 4, repealed: order 91/510.

9. Agricultural Training Board Act 1982.

s. 8, amended: regs. 91/1997.

10. Industrial Training Act 1982.

s. 1, orders 90/2549; 91/28, 263, 334, 1305.

s. 4, orders 90/2549; 91/263, 334.

s. 8, amended: regs. 91/1997.

14. Reserve Forces Act 1982.

s. 2, repealed in pt.: 1991, c. 62, sch. 3.

16. Civil Aviation Act 1982.

see *R.* v. *Warburton-Pitt* (1991) 92 Cr.App.R. 136, C.A.

ss. 2, 7, 11, regs. 91/1672.

s. 15, amended: regs. 91/1997.

s. 53, repealed in pt.: 1991, c. 34, schs. 6, 12, 19, Pts. I, IV(S.).

ss. 60, 61, order 91/1726.

ss. 64–67, regs. 91/1672.

s. 73, regs. 90/2482, 2514; 91/470.

s. 74, regs. 91/470.

ss. 84, 85, regs. 91/1672.

s. 97, orders 91/768, 769.

s. 102, orders 91/1672, 1726.

sch. 1, regs. 91/1672.

19. Deer (Amendment) (Scotland) Act 1982.

sch. 2, repealed in pt.: 1991, c. 54, sch. 4.

24. Social Security and Housing Benefits Act 1982.

s. 7, orders 91/506, 2911; amended: orders 91/503, 506, 2911.

CAP.
1982—cont.
24. Social Security and Housing Benefits Act 1982—cont.

s. 9, regs. 91/428, 694.

s. 9, amended: 1991, c. 3, ss. 1, 2; repealed in pt.: *ibid.*, s. 1, sch.

s. 26, regs. 91/428, 589, 694.

s. 45, regs. 91/589; orders 91/506, 2911.

s. 47, regs. 91/428, 589, 694.

27. Civil Jurisdiction and Judgments Act 1982.

see *Owens Bank* v. *Bracco (Nos. 1 and 2), The Times*, April 15, 1991, C.A.; *Rank Film Distributors* v. *Lanterna Editrice SRL, Financial Times*, June 14, 1991, Saville J.; *Macaulay* v. *Macaulay* [1991] 1 All E.R. 865, D.C.; *Medway Packaging* v. *Meurer Maschinen GmbH and Co.* [1990] 2 Lloyd's Rep. 112, C.A.; *Kloeckner and Co. Ag (Formerly Kloeckner & Co. K.G. aA)* v. *Gatoil Overseas Inc.* [1990] 1 Lloyd's Rep. 177, Hirst J.; *Republic of Haiti* v. *Jean-Claude Duvalier* [1989] E.E.C. 449, C.A.; *New Hampshire Insurance Co.* v. *Strabag Bau AG* [1990] 2 Lloyd's Rep. 61, Potter J.; *Rewia, The* [1991] 1 Lloyd's Rep. 69, Sheen J.

s. 1, amended: 1991, c. 12, s. 2.

s. 2, see *Shevill* v. *Presse Alliance S.A., The Times*, March 13, 1991, C.A.; *Po, The* [1990] 1 Lloyd's Rep. 419, Sheen J.

ss. 2, 3, amended: 1991, c.12, sch. 2.

ss. 3A, 3B, added: *ibid.*, s.1

s. 4, amended: *ibid.*, sch. 2.

s. 5, amended: 1991, c. 17, sch. 1.

s. 6, amended: 1991, c. 12, sch. 2.

s. 9, amended: *ibid*, s.1, sch. 2.

ss. 10–13, amended: *ibid.*, sch. 2.

s. 14, order 90/2591.

ss. 14–16, amended: 1991, c.12, sch. 2.

s. 20, sch. 8, see *Lord Advocate* v. *West End Construction* (Sh.Ct.) 1990 S.C.L.R. 777.

ss. 25, 27, 28, 30, 32, 33, amended: 1991, c.12, sch. 2.

s. 34, see *Office Angels* v. *Rainer-Thomas* [1991] I.R.L.R. 214, C.A.; *Black* v. *Yates* [1991] 3 W.L.R. 90, Potter J.

ss. 41–49, amended: 1991, c. 12, sch. 2.

s. 50, amended and repealed in pt.: *ibid.*

sch. 3C, added: *ibid.*, s.1, sch. 1.

sch. 4, see *Davenport* v. *Corinthian Motor Policies at Lloyd's*, 1991 S.L.T. 774.

sch. 8, see *Bruckash* v. *Lonie (No. 2)* (Sh.Ct.), 1990 S.C.L.R. 780.

28. Taking of Hostages Act 1982.

s. 2, repealed in pt.: 1991, c. 24, sch. 8.

CAP.

1982—cont.

30. Local Government (Miscellaneous Provisions) Act 1982.

see *R. v. Manchester City Council, ex p. King, The Times*, April 3, 1991, D.C.; *Quietlynn* v. *Southend on Sea Borough Council* [1990] 3 All E.R. 207, European Ct.; *R. v. Liverpool Crown Court, ex p. Lennon and Hongkins* [1991] C.O.D. 127, Otton J.

s. 1, see *Lunn* v. *Colston-Hayter, The Times*, February 28, 1991, D.C.

s. 21, repealed in pt.: 1991, c.22, sch. 9.

32. Local Government Finance Act 1982.

s. 17, see *R. v. Westminster City Council, ex p. Hilditch* [1990] C.O.D. 434, C.A.

ss. 17, 20, see *Fleming* v. *Lees* [1991] C.O.D. 50, Rose J.

s. 18A, added: 1991, c. 15, s. 1.

s. 19, see *Hazell* v. *Hammersmith and Fulham London Borough Council* [1991] 2 W.L.R. 372, H.L.

ss. 19, 20, amended: order 91/724.

ss. 24, 31, amended: 1991, c. 15, s. 1.

s. 33, amended: 1991, c. 34, sch. 7.

sch. 5, repealed in pt.: 1991, c. 60, sch. 3.

34. Forfeiture Act 1982.

s. 4, amended: 1991, c. 3, s. 3.

36. Aviation Security Act 1982.

sch. 2, repealed in pt.: 1991, c. 24, sch. 8.

39. Finance Act 1982.

s. 5, repealed in pt.: 1991, c. 31, sch. 19.

s. 6, repealed in pt.: *ibid.*, sch. 19, Pt. III; repealed: *ibid.*, sch. 19, Pt. IV.

ss. 7, 9, repealed in pt.: *ibid.*, sch. 19.

s. 86, see *Smith* v. *Schofield (Inspector of Taxes)* [1990] 1 W.L.R. 1447, Hoffmann J.

schs. 4, 5 (in pt.), repealed: 1991, c. 39, sch. 19.

41. Stock Transfer Act 1982.

s. 1, regs. 90/2547; 91/1145.

s. 2, order 91/340.

sch. 1, amended: *ibid.*

45. Civic Government (Scotland) Act 1982.

s. 13, sch. 1, see *Ranachan* v. *Renfrew District Council*, 1991 S.L.T. 625.

s. 18, see *City of Glasgow District Council* v. *Traffic Commissioner for the Scottish Traffic Area*, (I.H.), 1990 S.C.L.R. 737.

s. 39, sch. 1; see *Hughes* v. *Hamilton District Council*, 1991 S.L.T. 628.

s. 44, order 91/1253.

s. 49, see *Black, Petr.*, 1991 S.C.C.R. 1.

s. 57, see *McBurnie* v. *McGlennan*, 1991 S.C.C.R. 756.

CAP.

1982—cont.

45. Civic Government (Scotland) Act 1982—cont.

s. 58, see *Newlands* v. *MacPhail*, 1991 S.C.C.R. 88.

s. 60, see *Davidson* v. *Brown*, High Court of Justiciary, March 15, 1990.

ss. 87, 105, see *Gardner* v. *City of Edinburgh District Council, The Scotsman*, July 31, 1991.

sch. 1, see *The Noble Organisation* v. *City of Glasgow District Council (No. 3)*, 1991 S.L.T. 213; *Jolly* v. *Hamilton District Council*, Extra Division, June 21, 1991.

47. Duchy of Cornwall Management Act 1982.

s. 9, amended: regs. 91/1997.

48. Criminal Justice Act 1982.

s. 1, see *R. v. Southwark Crown Court, ex p. Ager* (1990) 91 Cr.App.R. 322, D.C.; *R. v. Thompson* (1989) 11 Cr.App.R.(S.) 246, C.A.; *R. v. Mussell; R. v. Blackburn; R. v. Moore; R. v. Marshall* [1991] 1 W.L.R. 187, C.A.; *R. v. Harris* [1990] Crim.L.R. 816, C.A.; *R. v. Steed* [1990] Crim.L.R. 816, C.A.; *R. v. Howard* (1991) 92 Cr.App.R. 223, C.A.; *R. v. Horney* (1990) 12 Cr.App.R.(S.) 20, C.A.; *R. v. Rhoades* [1990] Crim.L.R. 274, C.A.; *R. v. Selby JJ., ex p. Frame* [1991] 2 W.L.R. 965, D.C.; *R. v. Parsley* [1991] Crim.L.R. 223, C.A.; *R. v. Martin (Kim Linda)* (1989) 11 Cr.App.R.(S.) 424, C.A.; *R. v. Hunter* [1991] Crim.L.R. 146, C.A.; *R. v. Beddoes (Phillip Arthur)* [1991] Crim.L.R. 146, C.A.; *R. v. Pike (Matthew Kenneth Ray)* [1991] Crim.L.R. 147, C.A.; *R. v. Smith; R. v. Gilhooley* (1990) 12 Cr.App.R.(S.) 172, C.A.

s. 1, amended: 1991, c. 53, sch. 11; repealed in pt.: *ibid.*, sch. 13.

s. 1A, amended: *ibid.*, s. 63, sch. 11; repealed in pt.: *ibid.*, sch. 13.

s. 1B, amended: *ibid.*, s. 63, sch. 11; repealed in pt.: *ibid.*, s.63, sch. 13.

s. 1C, amended: *ibid.*, s. 63.

ss. 1, 2, see *R. v. Camp* (1989) 11 Cr.App.R.(S.) 196, C.A.

ss. 1, 9, see *Mason* v. *Lawton*, [1991] 1 W.L.R. 322, C.A.

s. 2, repealed: 1991, c. 53, sch. 13.

s. 3, amended: *ibid.*, sch. 11.

ss. 8, 9, amended: *ibid.*, s. 63.

s. 13, amended: *ibid.*, sch. 11.

s. 15, repealed: *ibid.*, sch. 13.

s. 16, amended: *ibid.*, sch. 11.

s. 17, amended: *ibid.*, s. 67, sch. 11; repealed in pt.: *ibid.*, s. 67, sch. 13.

CAP.

1982—cont.

48. Criminal Justice Act 1982—cont.
s. 18, amended: *ibid.*, s. 67; repealed in
pt.: *ibid.*, s. 67, sch. 13.
s. 19, amended: *ibid.*, s. 67.
s. 33, repealed: *ibid.*, sch. 13.
s. 37, amended: *ibid.*, s. 17.
ss. 48 (in pt.), 62, repealed: *ibid.*,
sch. 13.
s. 81, order 91/2630.
sch. 1, amended: 1991, c. 40, sch. 4.
sch. 3, amended: 1991, c. 53, sch. 11.
schs. 5, 11 (in pt.), 13 (in pt.), 14 (in
pt.), repealed: *ibid.*, sch. 13.

49. Transport Act 1982.
s. 9, amended: 1991, c. 40, sch. 4;
repealed in pt.: *ibid.*, schs. 4, 8.
s. 10, amended: *ibid.*, sch. 4; repealed
in pt.: *ibid.*, sch. 8.
s. 19, repealed: *ibid.*
s. 20, substituted: *ibid.*, sch. 4.
s. 21, amended: *ibid.*; repealed in pt.:
ibid., schs. 4, 8.
s. 23, repealed in pt.: *ibid.*, sch. 8.
ss. 24, 26, amended: *ibid.*, sch. 4.
s. 70, amended: 1991, c. 21, schs. 2, 3;
repealed in pt.: *ibid.*, sch. 4.
sch. 5, amended: order 91/510;
repealed in pt.: *ibid.*, 1991, c. 40,
sch. 8.

50. Insurance Companies Act 1982.
s. 7, repealed in pt.: 1991, c. 50, sch. 2.
s. 21, amended: regs. 91/1997.
s. 31, repealed in pt.: 1991, c. 50, sch. 2.
s. 94A, regs. 91/621.
ss. 97, 98, regs. 91/1999.

51. Mental Health (Amendment) Act 1982.
sch. 3, repealed in pt.: 1991, c. 25,
sch. 4.

53. Administration of Justice Act 1982.
Commencement orders: 91/1245, 1786.
s. 9, see *Ingham* v. *John G. Russell
(Transport)*, 1991 S.L.T. 739.
s. 12, see *Robertson* v. *British Bakeries*
(O.H.), 1991 S.L.T. 434.
s. 20, see *Wordingham* v. *Royal
Exchange Trust Co., The Times*,
December 11, 1991, Evans-Lombe,
Q.C.
s. 38, rules 91/1227.
s. 42, scheme 91/1209.
s. 76, orders 91/1245, 1786.
sch. 3, repealed in pt.: order 91/724.

1983

2. Representation of the People Act 1983.
s. 28, order 91/152.
s. 29, orders 91/1687, 1688.
s. 29, amended: 1991, c. 11, s. 1; order
91/1728.
s. 36, amended: order 91/1730.
s. 47, amended: order 91/1728.
s. 53, regs. 91/1674.

CAP.

1983—cont.

**2. Representation of the People Act
1983—cont.**
s. 76, amended: order 91/951.
s. 76A, order 91/951.
s. 197, order 91/951; amended: *ibid.*
s. 201, regs. 91/1674; amended: order
91/1728.
sch. 1, amended: regs. 91/1674.
schs. 1, 2, regs. 91/1674.

3. Agricultural Marketing Act 1982.
s. 5, amended: regs. 91/1997.

13. Merchant Shipping Act 1983.
s. 5, sch., regs. 91/784.

18. Nuclear Materials (Offences) Act 1983.
Commencement order: 91/1716.
s. 4, repealed in pt.: 1991, c. 24, sch. 8.
s. 7, orders 91/1717–1719.
s. 8, order 91/1716.

19. Matrimonal Homes Act 1983.
see *Kalsi* v. *Kalsi, The Times*, November 25, 1991, C.A.

20. Mental Health Act 1983.
see *R.* v. *Secretary of State for the Home
Department, ex p. K.* [1990] 3
W.L.R. 755, C.A.; *R.* v. *Kirk* (1989)
10 Cr.App.R.(S.) 453, C.A.
s. 4, see *R.* v. *Birch* (1989) 11
Cr.App.R.(S.) 202, C.A.
s. 26, amended: order 91/1881.
ss. 37, 41, see *R.* v. *Crozier* (1990) 12
Cr.App.R.(S.) 206, C.A.
s. 39A, added: 1991, c. 53, s. 27.
s. 50, repealed in pt.: *ibid.*, sch. 13.
s. 54A, added: *ibid.*, s. 27.
s. 143, amended: *ibid.*
sch. 4, repealed in pt.: 1991, c. 25,
sch. 4.

23. Water Act 1983.
sch. 4, repealed in pt.: 1991, c. 60,
sch. 3.

28. Finance Act 1983.
s. 4, sch. 3, repealed in pt.: 1991, c. 31,
sch. 19.

**29. Miscellaneous Financial Provisions Act
1983.**
sch. 2, repealed in pt.: 1991, c. 66,
sch. 2.

40. Education (Fees and Awards) Act 1983.
ss. 1, 2, regs. 91/830, 834(S.), 1839.

**41. Health and Social Services and Social
Security Adjudications Act 1983.**
s. 10, regs. 91/1123.

44. National Audit Act 1983.
sch. 4, repealed in pt.: order 91/510.

**46. Agricultural Holdings (Amendment)
(Scotland) Act 1983.**
repealed: 1991, c. 55, sch. 13.

47. National Heritage Act 1983.
s. 33, amended: 1991, c. 34, s. 29.
s. 36, regs. 91/2512.
sch. 3, amended: regs. 91/1997.

CAP.

1983—cont.

53. Car Tax Act 1983.
s. 5A, amended: 1991, c. 31, s. 19.
s. 7, regs. 91/1755.
s. 7, amended: 1991, c. 31, s. 20.
sch. 1, regs. 91/1755; Act of Sederunt 91/1920.

54. Medical Act 1983.
s. 4, amended: 1991, c. 38, s. 1.
s. 32, order 91/53.
sch. 1, amended: regs. 91/1997.

55. Value Added Tax Act 1983.
see *George Kilpatrick Dodds* v. *Customs and Excise Commissioners* (1989) V.A.T.T.R. 98, VAT Tribunal; *The Lord Mayor of London and Citizens of the City of Westminster* v. *Customs and Excise Commissioners* [1989] V.A.T.T.R. 71, VAT Tribunal.
s. 2, see *Stormseal (UPVC) Window Co.* v. *Customs and Excise Commissioners* [1989] V.A.T.T.R. 303, VAT Tribunal, Manchester.
ss. 2, 3, see *Philips Exports* v. *Customs and Excise Comrs.* [1990] S.T.C. 508, Roch J.
ss. 2–4, see *Trustees for the Greater World Association Trust* v. *Customs and Excise Commissioners* [1989] V.A.T.T.R. 91, VAT Tribunal.
s. 3, see *Battersea Leisure* v. *Customs and Excise Commissioners* [1989] V.A.T.T.R. 265, VAT Tribunal, London.
s. 5, see *Securicor Granley Systems* v. *Customs and Excise Commissioners* [1990] V.A.T.T.R. 9, VAT Tribunal, London.
s. 9, amended: 1991, c. 31, s. 13.
ss. 9, 10, see *Music & Video Exchange* v. *Customs and Excise Commissioners* [1990] V.A.T.T.R. 26, VAT Tribunal, London.
s. 10, see *Boots* v. *Customs and Excise Commissioners (No. C–126/88)* [1990] S.T.C. 387, European Ct.
s. 14, see *Anholt (Anthony)* v. *Customs and Excise Commissioners* [1989] V.A.T.T.R. 297, VAT Tribunal, London.
s. 14, regs. 91/532; order 91/2306.
s. 14, amended: 1991, c. 31, s. 14.
s. 16, orders 90/2553; 91/737, 2534; regs. 91/1332.
s. 17, orders 90/2553; 91/737, 2534.
s. 19, order 90/2548.
s. 20, repealed in pt.: 1991, c. 60, sch. 3.
s. 21, see *Waterways Services* v. *Customs and Excise Commissioners* [1990] V.A.T.T.R. 37, VAT Tribunal, London.

CAP.

1983—cont.

55. Value Added Tax Act 1983—*cont.*
s. 29, amended: 1991, c. 31, s. 16.
s. 35A, order 91/2569.
s. 38A, orders 91/1754, 2282.
ss. 38A, 38B, added: 1991, c. 31, s. 17.
s. 40, see *Don Pasquale (A Firm)* v. *Customs and Excise Comrs.* [1990] S.T.C. 556, C.A.; *Lord Advocate* v. *Shanks* (Sh.Ct.), 1991 S.C.L.R. 82; *Trust Securities Holdings* v. *Customs and Excise Commissioners* [1990] V.A.T.T.R. 1, VAT Tribunal, London; *Moore (James K.)* v. *Customs and Excise Commissioners* (1989) V.A.T.T.R. 276, VAT Tribunal, London.
s. 40, amended: 1991, c. 31, s. 17.
s. 47, see *Gardner (James Jesse)* v. *Customs and Excise Commissioners* [1989] V.A.T.T.R. 132, VAT Tribunal.
s. 48, orders 90/2553; 91/2534, 2569; regs. 91/371, 532, 691, 737, 1332.
sch. 1, order 91/738; regs. 91/2312.
sch. 1, amended: order 91/738.
sch. 2, see *Philips Exports* v. *Customs and Excise Comrs.* [1990] S.T.C. 508, Roch J.
sch. 4, see *Gold Star Publications* v. *Customs and Excise Commissioners* [1989] V.A.T.T.R. 328, VAT Tribunal, London.
sch. 5, see *Customs and Excise Comrs.* v. *British Airways* [1990] S.T.C. 643, C.A.; *Norman Riding Poultry Farm* v. *Customs and Excise Commissioners* [1989] V.A.T.T.R. 124, VAT Tribunal.
sch. 5, amended: 1991, c. 21, sch. 2; orders 91/737, 2534, 2874; repealed in pt.: 1991, c. 21, sch. 4; orders 91/737, 2534, 2874.
sch. 6, see *Dogbreeders Associates* v. *Customs and Excise Commissioners* (1989) V.A.T.T.R. 317, VAT Tribunal, London; *North West Leicestershire Youth Training Scheme* v. *Customs and Excise Commissioners* [1989] V.A.T.T.R. 321, VAT Tribunal, Manchester; *Company Moves* v. *Customs and Excise Commissioners* [1990] V.A.T.T.R. 50, VAT Tribunal, London.
schs. 6, 6A, amended and repealed in pt.: order 91/2569.
sch. 7, see *Don Pasquale (A Firm)* v. *Customs and Excise Comrs.* [1990] S.T.C. 556, C.A.; *Lord Advocate* v. *Shanks* (Sh.Ct.), 1991 S.C.L.R. 82.
sch. 7, regs. 91/532, 691, 2312; Act of Sederunt 91/1920.
sch. 8, rules 91/186.

56. Oil Taxation Act 1983.
ss. 9, 12, orders 91/1982–1984.
s. 9, sch. 3, see *BP Oil Development* v. *I.R.C.* [1990] S.T.C. 632, C.A.

CAP.

1984

10. Town and Country Planning Act 1984.
s. 1, amended (S.): 1991, c. 34, s. 13.

11. Education (Grants and Awards) Act 1984.
ss. 1, 3, regs. 90/2518.

12. Telecommunications Act 1984.
s. 9, orders 90/2271, 2375, 2376, 2397, 2400, 2478, 2479, 2523, 2572, 2661; 91/32, 33(S.), 34, 54–56, 81, 82, 117, 172, 173, 202, 203, 279, 293–298, 372, 373, 374(S.), 422, 448, 483, 610, 676, 687, 688, 709, 778, 955, 1044, 1045, 1069, 1070, 1143, 1174, 1292, 1334, 1335(S.), 1336, 1350(S.), 1359, 1360(S.), 1361(S.), 1362, 1363, 1503, 1629, 1647–1649, 1691, 1734, 1778, 1779, 1833, 1977, 2141–2143.
s. 11, repealed in pt.: 1991, c. 22, sch. 9.
s. 84, orders 91/874, 1523.
ss. 98, 101, amended: 1991, c. 60, sch. 1.
sch. 2, amended: 1991, c. 22, sch. 8; repealed in pt.: *ibid.* schs. 8, 9.
sch. 4, repealed in pt.: *ibid.*, sch. 9; c. 60, sch. 3.

16. Foreign Limitation Periods Act 1984.
ss. 1, 2, see *Hellenic Steel Co.* v. *Svolmar Shipping Co.; Komninos S., The* [1990] 1 Lloyd's Rep. 541, Leggatt J.

22. Public Health (Control of Diseases) Act 1984.
ss. 2–4, order 91/1773.

23. Registered Homes Act 1984.
see *Coombs* v. *Hertfordshire County Council, The Times*, April 26, 1991, Kennedy J.
s. 1, amended: 1990, c. 20, s. 1.
ss. 2, 5, 12, 14, 15, see *Avon County Council* v. *Lang* [1990] C.O.D. 365, Rose J.
s. 4, substituted: 1990, c. 20, s. 1.
s. 5, see *Harrison* v. *Cornwall County Council, The Times*, August 1, 1991, C.A.
ss. 5, 8, amended: 1991, c. 20, s. 1.
s. 8A, added: *ibid.*.
ss. 9, 10, 20, amended: *ibid.*

24. Dentists Act 1984.
s. 45, regs. 91/1706.
s. 46, order 91/1705; repealed in pt.: *ibid.*

26. Inshore Fishing (Scotland) Act 1984.
ss. 2, 4, see *Walkingshaw* v. *Marshall*, 1991 S.C.C.R. 397.

27. Road Traffic Regulation Act 1984.
s. 1, amended: 1991, c. 22, sch. 8; repealed in pt.: *ibid.*, schs. 8, 9.
s. 2, amended: *ibid.*, sch. 8.
ss. 3, 5, repealed in pt.: *ibid.*, schs. 8, 9.
s. 6, order 91/1972.

CAP.

1984—cont.

27. Road Traffic Regulation Act 1984—cont.
s. 6, amended: 1991, c. 22, sch. 8; repealed in pt.: *ibid.*, schs. 8, 9.
s. 7, amended: 1991, c. 40, sch. 7.
s. 8, amended: *ibid.*, s. 65; repealed in pt.: 1991, c. 22, schs. 8, 9.
s. 9, amended: *ibid.*, sch. 8; c. 40, sch. 4.
ss. 10, 12, amended: 1991, c. 22, sch. 8.
s. 13A, added: 1991, c. 40, sch. 7.
s. 14, amended: 1991, c. 22, sch. 8; substituted: 1991, c. 26, s. 1, sch. 1.
s. 15, substituted: *ibid.*
s. 16, amended: *ibid.*, s. 1; repealed in pt.: 1991, c. 22, schs. 8, 9.
s. 17, see *McCrory* v. *D.P.P.* [1990] C.O.D. 386, D.C.
s. 17, amended: 1991, c. 22, sch. 8; c. 40, sch. 4; repealed in pt.: 1991, c. 22, schs. 8, 9; c. 40, sch. 8.
s. 17A, added: 1991, c. 22, sch. 8.
s. 18, amended: *ibid.*
s. 19, amended: *ibid.*; repealed in pt.: *ibid.*, schs. 8, 9.
ss. 20, 21, amended: *ibid.*, sch. 8.
s. 22, amended: *ibid.*; c. 28, sch. 10.
s. 23, amended: 1991, c. 22, sch. 8; repealed in pt.: *ibid.*, schs. 8, 9.
s. 24, amended: *ibid.*, sch. 8.
ss. 29, 30, substituted: *ibid.*
ss. 31, 32, amended: *ibid.*
s. 34, amended: *ibid.*; repealed in pt.: *ibid.*, sch. 9.
s. 35, repealed in pt.: 1991, c. 40, s. 44, sch. 8.
s. 35C, added: *ibid.*, s. 41.
ss. 37, 38, 43, 45, amended: 1991, c. 22, sch. 8.
s. 44, amended: 1991, c. 40, sch. 4.
s. 46, amended: *ibid.*, s. 64.
s. 46A, added: *ibid.*, s. 42.
s. 47, amended: *ibid.*, s. 65.
s. 49, amended: *ibid.*, sch. 4.
s. 49A, added: *ibid.*, s. 40.
s. 51, repealed in pt.: *ibid.*, schs. 4, 8.
s. 53, amended: 1991, c. 22, sch. 8.
s. 55, amended: *ibid.*; c. 40, sch. 7; repealed in pt.: 1991, c. 22, schs. 8, 9; c. 40, schs. 7, 8.
s. 63A, added: *ibid.*, s. 44.
s. 64, amended: *ibid.*, sch. 8.
s. 65, amended: 1991, c. 22, sch. 8; c. 40, sch. 4.
ss. 66, 67, amended: 1991, c. 22, sch. 8.
s. 68, amended: *ibid.*, c. 26, s. 1; repealed in pt.: 1991, c. 22, sch. 9.
ss. 69–71, 73, 77, 79, 80, 82, 83, amended: *ibid.*, sch. 8.
s. 84, amended: *ibid.*; c. 40, s. 45.
s. 85, amended: 1991, c. 22, sch. 8; repealed in pt.: *ibid.*, schs. 4, 8.

1984—cont.

27. Road Traffic Regulation Act 1984—cont.
s. 86, see *McCrory* v. *D.P.P.* [1990] C.O.D. 386, D.C.
s. 86, amended: 1991, c. 22, sch. 8; repealed in pt.: *ibid.*, sch. 9.
s. 91, repealed in pt.: *ibid.*, schs. 8, 9.
ss. 92–94, amended: *ibid.*, sch. 8.
s. 96, amended: 1991, c. 40, sch. 4.
s. 99, amended: *ibid.*; repealed in pt.: *ibid.*, sch. 8.
s. 100, amended: 1991, c. 22, sch. 8.
s. 101, regs. 91/336.
s. 101, amended: 1991, c. 40, s. 67.
s. 102, regs. 91/336.
s. 102, amended: 1991, c. 40, s. 68; repealed in pt.: *ibid.*, sch. 8.
s. 103, amended: *ibid.*, sch. 4.
s. 104, regs. 91/338.
s. 104, amended: 1991, c. 40, sch. 4; repealed in pt.: *ibid.*, sch. 8.
s. 105, amended: *ibid.*, schs. 4, 5; repealed in pt.: *ibid.*, sch. 5.
s. 106, amended: 1991, c. 22, sch. 8; repealed in pt.: *ibid.*, schs. 8, 9; c. 40, sch. 8.
s. 106A, added: 1991, c. 40, s. 75.
s. 117, amended: *ibid.*, s. 35; repealed in pt.: *ibid.*, sch. 8.
s. 121A, added: 1991, c. 22, sch. 8.
s. 122, amended: *ibid.*; c. 40, sch. 7.
s. 122A, added: *ibid.*; ss. 24, 44(S.).
ss. 124, 125, repealed in pt.: 1991, c. 22, schs. 8, 9.
ss. 130, 131, amended: *ibid.*, sch. 8.
s. 132, amended: *ibid.*; repealed in pt.: *ibid.*, schs. 8, 9.
s. 132A, repealed: *ibid.*, sch. 9.
s. 134, amended: *ibid.*, sch. 8.
s. 136, see *McCrory* v. *D.P.P.* [1990] C.O.D. 386, D.C.
ss. 136, 137, sch. 6, see *D.P.P.* v. *Holtham* [1991] R.T.R. 5, D.C.
s. 141, repealed: 1991, c. 40, sch. 8.
s. 141A, added: *ibid.*, s. 46.
s. 142, regs. 91/336, 338.
s. 142, amended: 1991, c. 22, sch. 8.
s. 193A, added: 1991, c. 40, s. 46.
sch. 3, amended: 1991, c. 22, sch. 8; repealed: 1991, c. 26, sch. 2.
sch. 9, see *R.* v. *Warwickshire City Council, ex p. Boyden; Boyden* v. *Warwickshire County Council* [1991] C.O.D. 31, Otton J.
sch. 9, amended: 1991, c. 22, sch. 8; c. 26, s. 1; c. 40, sch. 4; repealed in pt.: 1991, c. 22, schs. 8, 9.
sch. 13, repealed in pt.: 1991, c. 40, sch. 8.

28. County Courts Act 1984.
s. 2, order 91/2211.
ss. 15, 16, 21, repealed in pt.: order 91/724.

1984—cont.

28. County Courts Act 1984—cont.
s. 22, see *Newport Borough Council* v. *Khan (Sabz Ali)* [1990] 1 W.L.R. 1185, C.A.
ss. 24, 25, repealed in pt.: order 91/724.
s. 38, regs. 91/1222.
s. 40, see *Practice Direction (Queen's Bench Division: Transfer of Proceedings to County Court)* [1991] 1 W.L.R. 643; [1991] 3 All E.R. 349.
s. 45, see *Forey* v. *London Buses* [1991] 1 W.L.R. 327, C.A.
s. 55, amended: 1991, c. 53, sch. 4.
s. 73, regs. 91/1815.
s. 74, order 91/1184.
s. 75, rules 91/525, 526, 1126, 1132, 1328, 1340, 1882.
s. 77, order 91/1877.
s. 118, amended: 1991, c. 53, sch. 4.
ss. 139, 147, repealed in pt.: order 91/724.

30. Food Act 1984.
s. 8, see *Daventry District Council* v. *Olins* [1990] Crim.L.R. 414, D.C.
ss. 16, 17, see *Leeds City Council* v. *Dewhurst J.H.* [1990] Crim.L.R. 725, D.C.

31. Rating and Valuation (Amendment) (Scotland) Act 1984.
s. 15, repealed: 1991, c. 2, s. 2.

32. London Regional Transport Act 1984.
s. 23, amended: regs. 91/1997.
sch. 4, repealed in pt.: order 91/510.
sch. 6, repealed in pt.: 1991, c. 60, sch. 3.

35. Data Protection Act 1984.
ss. 6, 8, 40, 41, regs. 91/1160.
ss. 7, 10, 14, 36, see *Runneymede Community Charge Registration Officer* v. *Data Protection Registrar; South Northamptonshire Community Charge Registration Officer* v. *Same; Harrow Community Charge Registration Officer* v. *Same* [1990] 30 R.V.R. 236, Data Protection Tribunal.

36. Mental Health (Scotland) Act 1984.
ss. 17, 18, see *V.* v. *F.* (Sh.Ct.), 1991 S.C.L.R. 225.
ss. 18, 24, 26, see *J.* v. *C.* (Sh.Ct.), 1990 S.C.L.R. 783.
s. 21, amended: 1991, c. 47, s. 2.
ss. 24, 26, see *R., Petr.* (O.H.), 1990 S.C.L.R. 757.
s. 26, amended: 1991, c. 47, s. 3.
s. 26A, added: *ibid.*, s. 1.
ss. 28, 33, 35, 59, amended: *ibid.*, s. 3.
sch. 2, amended: *ibid.*; repealed in pt.: *ibid.*

37. Child Abduction Act 1984.
s. 6, repealed in pt.: 1991, c. 50, sch. 2.

42. Matrimonial and Family Proceedings Act 1984.
Commencement order: 91/1211.

CAP.

1984—cont.

42. Matrimonial and Family Proceedings Act 1984—*cont.*
s. 33, order 91/1809.
s. 40, rules 91/1247, 1832, 2113.
s. 41, order 91/2114.
s. 47, order 91/1211.

43. Finance Act 1984.
s. 5, repealed in pt.: 1991, c. 31, sch. 19.
s. 64, amended: *ibid.*, s. 98, sch. 10; repealed in pt.: *ibid.*, s. 98.
s. 126, order 91/1202.
sch. 23, see *Leonard* v. *Blanchard (Inspector of Taxes), The Times*, November 29, 1991, Hoffmann J.

46. Cable and Broadcasting Act 1984.
s. 13, order 91/1246.
s. 20, amended: regs. 91/1997.

47. Repatriation of Prisoners Act 1984.
ss. 2, 3, sch., amended: 1991, c. 53, sch. 11.

49. Trade Union Act 1984.
ss. 1, 2, 5, see *R.* v. *Certification Officer for Trade Unions and Employers' Associations, ex p. Electrical Power Engineers' Association* [1990] I.R.L.R. 398, H.L.
s. 5, see *Veness and Chalkley* v. *National Union of Public Employees* [1991] I.R.L.R. 76, D.C.
ss. 5, 6, see *Lenahan* v. *Union of Construction Allied Trades and Technicians* [1991] I.R.L.R. 78, Hoffmann J.
s. 10, see *Secretary of State for Scotland* v. *Scottish Prison Officers' Association* (O.H.), 1991 S.L.T. 658.

51. Inheritance Tax Act 1984.
ss. 5, 160, 162, 222, see *Alexander* v. *Inland Revenue Commissioners* [1991] S.T.C. 112, C.A.
s. 8, order 91/735.
ss. 74, 89, amended: 1991, c. 21, sch. 2; order 91/2874.
s. 256, regs. 91/1248, 1249(S.), 1250.
sch. 1, amended: order 91/735.
sch. 3, amended: 1991, c. 28, sch. 2.

52. Parliamentary Pensions etc. Act 1984.
s. 13, repealed: 1991, c. 5, s. 4.

54. Roads (Scotland) Act 1984.
s. 8, amended: 1991, c. 22, s. 45.
s. 10, amended: *ibid.*, s. 46.
s. 20A, amended: *ibid.*, s. 42; c. 28, sch. 10; repealed in pt.: *ibid.*, sch. 11.
s. 35, amended: 1991, c. 22, sch. 8.
s. 36, amended: 1991, c. 40, sch. 4.
ss. 37, 38, regs. 90/2623.
s. 39, amended: 1991, c. 22, sch. 8.
s. 40, amended: 1991, c. 40, sch. 4.
s. 55A, amended; 1991, c. 22, s. 42.
ss. 56, 57, 59, amended: *ibid.*, sch. 8.
s. 60, see *MacPhail* v. *Tayside Regional Council*, 1991 S.C.C.R. 370.

CAP.

1984—cont.

54. Roads (Scotland) Act 1984—*cont.*
s. 60, amended: 1991, c. 22, sch. 8; repealed: *ibid.*
s. 61, amended: *ibid.*
s. 61A, added: *ibid.*
s. 85, amended: *ibid.*
s. 98, amended: 1991, c. 28, sch. 10; repealed in pt.: *ibid.*, sch. 11.
s. 106, amended: 1991, c. 34, s. 76.
s. 121, amended: 1991, c. 22, sch. 8.
s. 127, repealed: *ibid.*, sch. 9.
s. 132, amended: *ibid.*, sch. 8.
ss. 133, 134 (in pt.), repealed: *ibid.*, sch. 9.
s. 135, amended: *ibid.*, sch. 8.
s. 143, regs. 90/2623.
s. 143, amended: 1991, c. 22, sch. 8; repealed in pt.: *ibid.*, schs. 8, 9.
s. 151, see *Young* v. *Carmichael*, 1991 S.C.C.R. 332; *Viewpoint Housing Association* v. *Lothian Regional Council (O.H.), The Scotsman*, November 6, 1991.
ss. 151, 155, schs. 1, 2, amended: 1991, c. 22, sch. 8.
sch. 7, repealed in pt.: *ibid.*, sch. 9.
sch. 9, see *Young* v. *Carmichael*, 1991 S.C.C.R. 332.
sch. 9, repealed in pt.: 1991, c. 22, sch. 9; c. 45, sch. 8.
sch. 10, repealed in pt.: 1991, c. 22, sch. 9.

55. Building Act 1984.
see *NHBC Building Control Services* v. *Sandwell Borough Council* (1990) 50 B.L.R. 101, D.C.
s. 1, 3, 16, regs. 90/2600.
ss. 18, 25, amended: 1991, c. 60, sch. 1.
s. 34, regs. 90/2600.
s. 35, see *Torridge District Council* v. *Turner, The Times*, November 27, 1991, D.C.
ss. 35, 50, regs. 90/2600.
s. 101, amended: 1991, c. 60, sch. 1.
s. 126, regs. 90/2600.
s. 126, amended: 1991, c. 60, sch. 1.
sch. 1, regs. 90/2600.

58. Rent (Scotland) Act 1984.
s. 25, amended: 1991, c. 55, sch. 11.
ss. 41, 53, 56, 80, 112, regs. 91/1521.

60. Police and Criminal Evidence Act 1984.
Commencement order: 91/2686.
see *R.* v. *Howden-Simpson* [1991] Crim.L.R. 49, C.A.; *R.* v. *Nagah* [1991] Crim.L.R. 55, C.A.; *Marcel* v. *Comr. of Police of the Metropolis, The Independent*, July 24, 1991, C.A.; *G., Re; R., Re (Note (Wards) (Police Interviews))* [1990] 2 F.L.R. 347, Sir Stephen Brown P.
s. 9, see *R.* v. *Lewes Crown Court, ex p. Hill* [1991] Crim.L.R. 376, D.C.
s. 24, amended: 1991, c. 19, s. 5.

1984—cont.

60. Police and Criminal Evidence Act 1984—*cont.*

ss. 24–26, see *R.* v. *Robson (Kenneth); R.* v. *Mitchell (Bernard); R.* v. *Richards (Alan)* [1991] Crim.L.R. 362, H.H. Judge Ord.

s. 26, see *D.P.P.* v. *Kitching* [1990] Crim.L.R. 394, D.C.

s. 32, see *R.* v. *Beckford, The Times,* June 12, 1991, C.A.

s. 37, repealed in pt.: 1991, c. 53, s. 72, sch. 13.

s. 38, see *R.* v. *Chief Constable of Cambridgeshire, ex p. Michel* (1990) 91 Cr.App.R. 325, D.C.

s. 38, amended: 1991, c. 53, s. 59.

s. 42, see *R.* v. *Taylor, The Times,* January 11, 1991, C.A.

s. 58, see *R.* v. *Keriwala, The Times,* January 4, 1991, C.A.; *R.* v. *McGovern* (1991) 92 Cr.App.R. 228, C.A.; *R.* v. *Chung* (1991) 92 Cr.App.R. 314, C.A.

s. 60, order 91/2687.

s. 66, see *D.P.P.* v. *D (A Juvenile); Same* v. *Rous, The Times,* July 11, 1991, D.C.

s. 67, see *R.* v. *Twaites; R.* v. *Brown* (1991) 92 Cr.App.R. 106, C.A.

s. 67, order 90/2580.

s. 68, see *R.* v. *Olisa* [1990] Crim.L.R. 721, C.A.

ss. 68, 69, see *R.* v. *Mather* [1991] Crim.L.R. 285, C.A.

s. 69, see *R.* v. *Neville* [1991] Crim.L.R. 288, C.A.; *R.* v. *Robson (Kenneth); R.* v. *Mitchell (Bernard); R.* v. *Richards (Alan)* [1991] Crim.L.R. 362, H.H. Judge Ord.

s. 74, see *R.* v. *Chapman* [1991] Crim.L.R. 44, C.A.; *R.* v. *Barnes* [1991] Crim.L.R. 132, C.A.; *R.* v. *Boyson* [1991] Crim.L.R. 274, C.A.

s. 76, see *Lam Chi-Ming* v. *The Queen, The Daily Telegraph,* April 18, 1991, P.C.; *R.* v. *McGovern* (1991) 92 Cr.App.R. 228, C.A.; *R.* v. *Morse* [1991] Crim.L.R. 195, Beezley J.; *R.* v. *Beales* [1991] Crim.L.R. 118, H.H. Judge Hyam; *R.* v. *Silcott; R.* v. *Braithwaite; R.* v. *Raghip, The Times,* December 6, 1991, C.A.; *R.* v. *Barry, The Times,* December 11, 1991, C.A.

ss. 76, 77, see *R.* v. *Moss* (1990) 91 Cr.App.R. 371, C.A.

ss. 76, 78, see *R.* v. *Chung* (1991) 92 Cr.App.R. 314, C.A.; *R.* v. *Crampton* (1991) 92 Cr.App.R. 369, C.A.; *R.* v. *Blake* [1991] Crim.L.R. 119, H.H. Judge Mendle; *R.* v. *Sparks* [1991] Crim.L.R. 128, C.A.

s. 78, see *D.P.P.* v. *Wilson, The Times,* February 12, 1991, D.C.; *R.* v. *Gillard; R.* v. *Barratt* (1991) 92

1984—cont.

60. Police and Criminal Evidence Act 1984—*cont.*

Cr.App.R. 61, C.A.; *R.* v. *Moss* (1990) 91 Cr.App.R. 371, C.A.; *R.* v. *Twaites; R.* v. *Brown* (1991) 92 Cr.App.R. 106, C.A.; *R.* v. *Scott* [1991] Crim.L.R. 56, C.A.; *Andrews* v. *D.P.P., The Times,* April 2, 1991, D.C.; *R.* v. *McGovern* (1991) 92 Cr.App.R. 228, C.A.; *R.* v. *Thomas* [1990] Crim.L.R. 269, D.C.; *R.* v. *Samms, Elliott and Bartley* [1991] Crim.L.R. 197, Inner London Crown Court; *Nazir Chinoy, Re* [1991] C.O.D. 105, D.C.; *R.* v. *McDonald* [1991] Crim.L.R. 122, C.A.

ss. 78, 82, see *R.* v. *Robson (Kenneth); R.* v. *Mitchell (Bernard); R.* v. *Richards (Alan)* [1991] Crim.L.R. 362, H.H. Judge Ord.

s. 80, see *R.* v. *Cruttenden,* [1991] 2 W.L.R. 921, C.A.

s. 89, see *R.* v. *Police Complaints Authority, ex p. Thompson; Same* v. *Same, ex p. Sullman* [1990] C.O.D. 205, D.C.

ss. 94, 103, see *R.* v. *Police Complaints Authority, ex p. Wells* [1991] C.O.D. 95, Popplewell J.

s. 101, regs. 91/1673.

s. 121, order 91/2686.

sch. 1, see *R.* v. *Northampton Magistrates' Court, ex p. D.P.P., The Times,* April 18, 1991, D.C.; *R.* v. *Liverpool Crown Court and Chief Constable of Merseyside Police, ex p. George Wimpey, The Independent,* April 11, 1991, D.C.; *R.* v. *Lewes Crown Court, ex p. Hill* [1991] Crim.L.R. 376, D.A.

sch. 5, amended: 1991, c. 40, sch. 4.

sch. 6, see *D.P.P.* v. *Kitching* [1990] Crim.L.R. 394, D.C.

sch. 6, repealed in pt.: 1991, c. 54, sch. 4.

62. Friendly Societies Act 1984.

s. 4, order 91/2293.

1985

6. Companies Act 1985.

see *R.* v. *Seelig; R.* v. *Lord Spens, The Independent,* May 3, 1991, C.A.; *Exeter Trust* v. *Screenways, The Times,* May 14, 1991, C.A.

s. 36, see *Cotronic (U.K.)* v. *Dezonie T/A Wendaland Builders; Osborne Third Party* [1991] BCC 200, C.A.

s. 60, amended: regs. 91/2000.

s. 88, see *Park Business Interiors* v. *Park* (O.H.), 1991 S.L.T. 818.

s. 103, see *Bradford Investments, Re* [1990] BCC 740, Hoffmann J.

s. 138, see *Anglo American Insurance Co.* [1991] BCC 208, Harman J.

CAP.

1985—cont.

6. Companies Act 1985—*cont.*
ss. 151, 152, see *Neilson* v. *Stewart* (H.L.), 1991 S.L.T. 523.
s. 190, regs. 91/879, 1259.
s. 191, regs. 91/1998.
s. 203, amended (S.): 1991, c. 50, sch. 1.
ss. 210, 216, amended: order 91/1646.
s. 219, regs. 91/1998.
s. 245, regs. 90/2570.
s. 245C, order 91/13.
s. 254, amended: regs. 91/2705.
ss. 255–255B, substituted: regs. 91/2705.
s. 255C, amended and repealed in pt.: *ibid.*
s. 257, regs. 91/2705.
ss. 260, 262A, amended: *ibid.*
s. 287, regs. 91/1259.
s. 288, regs. 91/1259, 1998.
s. 303, see *Currie* v. *Cowdenbeath Football Club, The Times*, October 31, 1991.
s. 325, regs. 91/1998.
ss. 327, 328, amended (S.): 1991, c. 50, sch. 1.
s. 330, see *Neilson* v. *Stewart* (H.L.), 1991 S.L.T. 523.
s. 349, see *Rafsanjan Pistachio Producers Co-operative* v. *S. Reiss* [1990] BCLC 352, Potter J.
s. 353, regs. 91/879, 1259.
s. 356, regs. 91/1998.
ss. 363, 364, regs. 91/1259.
s. 371, see *Downs Wine Bar, Re* [1990] BCLC 839, Harman J.
s. 383, regs. 91/1998.
s. 390B, regs. 91/2128.
s. 395, see *Weldtech Equipment, Re* [1991] BCC 16, Hoffmann J.
ss. 395, 401, see *Screenways, Re, The Independent*, June 15, 1991, C.A.
s. 404, see *Chantry House Developments, Re* [1990] BCC 646, Scott J.
ss. 445, 454–456, amended: order 91/1646.
s. 458, see *R.* v. *Director of the Serious Fraud Office, ex p. Smith, The Independent*, November 8, 1991, D.C.
s. 459, see *Company, A (No. 00789 of 1987), Re, ex p. Shooter; Company, A (No. 3017 of 1987), Re, ex p. Broadhurst* [1990] BCLC 384, Harman J.; *Swindon Town Football Club Co., Re* [1990] BCLC 467, Harman J.; *Hydrosan, Re* [1991] BCC 19, Harman J.; *Milgate Developments, Re* [1991] BCC 24, Edward Nugee, Q.C.; *Company, A (No. 002708 of 1989), Re, ex p. W.; Company, A (No. 004247 of 1989), ex p. BR* [1990] BCLC 795, Knox J.
s. 459, amended: 1991, c. 60, sch. 1.
s. 461, see *Nuneaton Borough Association Football Club (No. 2), Re* [1991] BCC 41, Harman J.
s. 651, see *Workvale, Re* (1991) BCC 109, Harman J.

CAP.

1985—cont.

6. Companies Act 1985—*cont.*
s. 663, order 91/494.
s. 685, amended: regs. 91/1997.
s. 708, regs. 91/1206.
ss. 716, 717, amended: regs. 91/1997.
s. 718, regs. 90/2571.
s. 723A, regs. 91/1998.
s. 726, see *Innovare Displays* v. *Corporate Booking Services*, [1991] BCC 174, C.A.
s. 727, see *Home Treat, Re* [1991] BCC 165, Harman J.; *Kirbys Coaches, Re* [1991] BCC 130, Hoffmann J.
s. 744, regs. 91/879, 1259.
sch. 9, renumbered (Pts. I, II) as sch. 9A, regs. 91/2705.
schs. 9, 9A, amended and repealed in pt.: *ibid.*
sch. 10, repealed in pt.: *ibid.*
sch. 11, amended and repealed in pt.: *ibid.*
sch. 13, regs. 91/1998.
sch. 22, regs. 90/2571.
sch. 22, amended: regs. 91/2705.
9. Companies Consolidation (Consequential Provisions) Act 1985.
sch. 2, repealed in pt.: 1991, c. 66, sch. 2.
14. Courts of Law Fees (Scotland) Act 1985.
s. 2, order 91/659.
19. Town and Country Planning (Compensation) Act 1985.
see *Camden London Borough Council* v. *ADC Estates* (1990) 3 P.L.R. 121, C.A.
21. Films Act 1985.
s. 6, sch. 1, order 91/1725.
23. Prosecution of Offences Act 1985.
see *R.* v. *Isleworth Crown Court, ex p. Montague and Co.* [1990] C.O.D. 86, D.C.
s. 3, see *R.* v. *Stafford Justices, ex p. Customs and Excise Comrs.* [1990] 3 W.L.R. 656, D.C.; *R.* v. *D.P.P., ex p. Langlands-Pearse* [1991] C.O.D. 92, Nolan J.
s. 16, see *Westminster City Council* v. *Wingrove* [1991] 2 W.L.R. 708, D.C.
s. 16, amended: 1991, c. 25, sch. 3.
s. 19, see *D.P.P.* v. *Denning* [1991] 3 All E.R. 439, D.C.
s. 19, amended: 1991, c. 25, sch. 3.
s. 19A, see *Practice Direction (C.A.) (Crime: Costs in Criminal Proceedings), The Times*, May 20, 1991.
s. 19A, regs. 91/789.
s. 19A, added: 1990, c. 41, s. 111.
s. 20, regs. 91/789.
s. 22, see *Roddie and Rose, Re* (1991) 155 J.P.N. 236, D.C.; *R.* v. *Sheffield Justices, ex p. Turner* [1991] 1 All E.R. 858, D.C.; *R.* v. *Birmingham Crown Court, ex p. Ricketts* [1991] R.T.R. 105, D.C.; *R.* v. *Governor of Winchester Prison, ex p. Roddie; R.* v. *Southampton Crown Court, ex p. Roddie* [1991] 1 W.L.R. 303, D.C.

1985—cont.

23. Prosecution of Offences Act 1985—*cont.*
s. 22, regs. 91/1515.
s. 22, amended: 1991, c. 53, sch. 11.
s. 29, regs. 91/1515.

30. Ports (Finance) Act 1985.
s. 4, amended: regs. 91/1997.

35. Gaming (Bingo) Act 1985.
s. 3, regs. 91/872.

37. Family Law (Scotland) Act 1985.
see *Thomson* v. *Thomson* (Sh.Ct.), 1991 S.C.L.R. 655.
ss. 1, 4, see *Forbes* v. *Forbes* (Sh.Ct.), 1991 S.C.C.R. 389.
s. 2, amended: 1991, c. 50, sch. 1; repealed in pt.: *ibid.*, sch. 2.
ss. 3–5, see *Walker* v. *Walker* (O.H.), 1991 S.C.L.R. 419; 1991 S.L.T. 649.
s. 4, amended: 1991, c. 48, sch. 5.
ss. 6, 7, 16, see *Ellerby* v. *Ellerby* (Sh.Ct.), 1991 S.C.L.R. 608.
s. 7, see *Hoad* v. *Hoad*, 1991 S.L.T. (Sh.Ct.) 4.
s. 8, see *Mackin* v. *Mackin* (Sh.Ct.), 1990 S.C.L.R. 728; *Farrell* v. *Farrell* (Sh.Ct.), 1990 S.C.L.R. 717; *Walker* v. *Walker* (I.H.), 1991 S.L.T. 157; *Demarco* v. *Demarco* (O.H.), 1990 S.C.L.R. 635.
ss. 8–10, see *Wallis* v. *Wallis* (Sh.Ct.), 1991 S.C.L.R. 192.
s. 9, see *Gray* v. *Gray* (Sh.Ct.), 1991 S.C.L.R. 422; *McGuire* v. *McGuire's Curator Bonis*, 1991 S.L.T. (Sh.Ct.) 76.
ss. 9, 10, see *Anderson* v. *Anderson*, 1991 S.L.T. (Sh.Ct.) 11; *Skarpaas* v. *Skarpaas*, 1991 S.L.T. (Sh.Ct.) 15; *Farrell* v. *Farrell* (Sh.Ct.) 1990 S.C.L.R. 717.
s. 10, see *George* v. *George*, 1991 S.L.T. (Sh.Ct.) 8; *Pryde* v. *Pryde*, 1991 S.L.T. (Sh.Ct.) 26.
s. 11, see *Farrell* v. *Farrell* (Sh.Ct.), 1990 S.C.L.R. 717.
ss. 12, 13, see *Mackin* v. *Mackin* (Sh.Ct.), 1990 S.C.L.R. 728.
s. 14, see *Demarco* v. *Demarco* (O.H.), 1990 S.C.L.R. 635; *Reynolds* v. *Reynolds* (Sh.Ct.), 1991 S.C.L.R. 175.
s. 16, see *Anderson* v. *Anderson*, 1991 S.L.T. (Sh.Ct.) 11; *McAfee* v. *McAfee* (O.H.), 1990 S.C.L.R. 805; *Young* v. *Young (No. 2)*, 1991 S.L.T. 869.
s. 19, see *Thom* v. *Thom* (O.H.), 1990 S.C.L.R. 800.
s. 27, see *Demarco* v. *Demarco* (O.H.), 1990 S.C.L.R. 635.
s. 28, see *Jenkins* v. *Jenkins* (O.H.), November 9, 1989; *Macleod* v. *Macleod* (O.H.), 1991 S.L.T. 633.

1985—cont.

43. Local Government (Access to Information) Act 1985.
s. 1, sch. 1, see *R.* v. *Kensington and Chelsea London Borough Council, ex p. Stoop, The Times*, September 10, 1991, Otton J.

44. Sexual Offences Act 1985.
s. 2, see *Darroch* v. *D.P.P.* (1990) 91 Cr.App.R. 378, D.C.

48. Food and Environment Protection Act 1985.
s. 1, order 91/1386(S.).
ss. 1, 24, orders 90/2582; 91/5, 6, 20(S.), 110, 498, 703, 1235, 1415, 1533(S.), 1608(S.), 1681(S.), 1800(S.), 1810(S.), 1848(S.), 1849(S.), 1863, 1944, 1958(S.), 2077(S.), 2078(S.), 2126(S.), 2482(S.); S.R. 1991 No. 8.

50. Representation of the People Act 1985.
s. 6, regs. 91/1198, 1226(S.), 1674.

51. Local Government Act 1985.
s. 48, order 91/606.
s. 67, orders 91/490, 497, 517, 710.
s. 77, orders 91/184, 439, 517.
s. 100, order 91/497.
s. 101, orders 91/439, 2296.
sch. 4, repealed in pt.: 1991, c. 22, sch. 9; c. 34, sch. 19; c. 60, sch. 3.
sch. 5, orders 91/516, 808.
sch. 5, amended: 1991, c. 22, sch. 8; c. 40, sch. 7; repealed in pt.: 1991, c. 22, sch. 9; c. 26, sch. 2.
sch. 7, repealed in pt.: 1991, c. 60, sch. 3.

53. Social Security Act 1985.
s. 5, amended: 1991, c. 3, s. 3.
s. 19, repealed: *ibid.*, sch.

54. Finance Act 1985.
s. 14, amended: 1991, c. 31, s. 18.
s. 18, orders 91/348, 1078, 1472, 2195.
s. 19, see *Barney & Freeman* v. *Customs and Excise Commissioners* [1990] V.A.T.T.R. 19, VAT Tribunal, London.
ss. 19, 32, see *Customs and Excise Comrs.* v. *Palco Industry Co.* [1990] S.T.C. 594, Hodgson J.
s. 20, see *Kitsfern* v. *Customs and Excise Commissioners* [1989] V.A.T.T.R. 312, VAT Tribunal, London; *W. Timms & Son* v. *Customs and Excise Commissioners* [1990] V.A.T.T.R. 45, VAT Tribunal, London.
s. 33, see *J.E. Scally* v. *Customs and Excise Commissioners* [1989] V.A.T.T.R. 245, VAT Tribunal, Manchester.
s. 68, amended: 1991, c. 31, ss. 78, 99; repealed in pt.: *ibid.*, s. 78, sch. 19.
ss. 69, 70, amended: *ibid.*, s. 100.
schs. 2, 3, repealed in pt.: *ibid.*, sch. 19.
sch. 19, amended: *ibid.*, s. 99.
sch. 20, amended: *ibid.*, s. 100.

1985—cont.

60. Child Abduction and Custody Act 1985.
see *A (Minors), Re, The Independent,* January 8, 1991, C.A.; *H. (Minors), Re; S. (Minors), Re, The Independent,* June 14, 1991, H.L.; *V.* v. *B. (A Minor) (Abduction)* [1991] F.L.R. 266, Sir Stephen Brown P.; *N. (Minors) (Abduction), Re* [1991] 1 F.L.R. 413, Bracewell J.
Pt. I (ss. 1–11), see *Dickson* v. *Dickson* (I.H.), 1990 S.C.L.R. 692.
s. 2, orders 91/995, 1461, 1698.
s. 2, sch. 1, see *H. (Minors) (Abduction: Custody Rights), Re; S (Minors) (Abduction: Custody Rights), Re* [1991] 3 W.L.R. 68, H.L.
Pt. II (ss. 12–24), see *G. (A Minor) (Child Abduction: Enforcement), Re* [1990] 2 F.L.R. 325, Booth J.
s. 13, order 91/1461.
sch. 1, see *F. (A Minor: Abduction: Jurisdiction), Re* [1990] 3 All E.R. 97, C.A.
61. Administration of Justice Act 1985.
Commencement order: 91/2683.
s. 9, order 91/2684.
s. 22, amended: regs. 91/1997.
s. 39, repealed in pt.: *ibid.*
s. 61, amended: 1991, c. 53, sch. 11.
s. 69, order 91/2683.
sch. 3, amended: regs. 91/1997.
62. Oil and Pipelines Act 1985.
sch. 3, amended: regs. 91/1997.
63. Water (Fluoridation) Act 1985.
repealed: 1991, c. 60, sch. 3.
s. 1, amended (S.): *ibid.*, s. 4, sch. 1.
65. Insolvency Act 1985.
sch. 8, repealed in pt.: 1991, c. 60, sch. 3.
66. Bankruptcy (Scotland) Act 1985.
ss. 6, 63, see *The Royal Bank of Scotland* v. *J. & J. Messenger* (O.H.), 1991 S.L.T. 492.
s. 12, see *Bank of Scotland* v. *Mackay* (O.H.), 1991 S.L.T. 163; *National Westminster Bank* v. *W.J. Elrick & Co.* (O.H.), 1991 S.L.T. 709; *Accountant in Bankruptcy* v. *Allans of Gillock; Allans of Gillock* v. *Accountant in Bankruptcy* (O.H.), 1991 S.L.T. 765.
ss. 12, 14, see *Campbell* v. *Sheriff*, 1991 S.L.T. (Sh.Ct.) 37.
ss. 12, 63, see *Accountant in Bankruptcy* v. *Allans of Gillock; Allans of Gillock* v. *Accountant in Bankruptcy* (O.H.), 1991 S.L.T. 765.
ss. 16, 17, see *Wright* v. *Tennent Caledonian Breweries*, 1991 S.L.T. 823.
s. 31, see *Alliance & Leicester Building Society* v. *Hecht* (Sh.Ct.), 1991 S.C.C.R. 562.
s. 32, amended: 1991, c. 48, sch. 5.

1985—cont.

66. Bankruptcy (Scotland) Act 1985—*cont.*
s. 33, see *Council of the Law Society of Scotland* v. *McKinnie, The Scotsman,* May 22, 1991.
s. 34, see *Short's Tr.* v. *Chung*, 1991 S.L.T. 472.
s. 37, amended: 1991, c. 48, sch. 5.
ss. 54, 63, see *Pattison* v. *Halliday* (O.H.), 1991 S.L.T. 645.
s. 55, amended: 1991, c. 48, sch. 5.
sch. 3, amended: 1991, c. 31, sch. 2.
67. Transport Act 1985.
s. 7, amended: 1991, c. 22, sch. 8.
s. 16, see *R.* v. *Middlesbrough District Council, ex p. I.J.H. Cameron (Holdings), The Times*, November 19, 1991, Popplewell J.
ss. 47–53, repealed: order 91/510.
s. 54, order 91/510.
ss. 76, 77, amended: regs. 91/1997.
s. 137, repealed in pt.: 1991, c. 22, schs. 8, 9.
schs. 2, 7, repealed in pt.: 1991, c. 40, sch. 8.
68. Housing Act 1985.
see *Waltham Forest London Borough Council* v. *Thomas, The Times,* February 18, 1991, C.A.
s. 51, amended: regs. 91/1997.
s. 59, see *R.* v. *Lambeth London Borough Council, ex p. Vagliviello* (1990) 22 H.L.R. 393, C.A.
s. 60, see *R.* v. *Tower Hamlets London Borough Council, ex p. Rouf, The Times*, May 21, 1991, C.A.; *R.* v. *Cardiff City Council, ex p. Barry* [1991] C.O.D. 112, Rose J.; *R.* v. *Hammersmith and Fulham London Borough Council, ex p. Luisa* (1991) 23 H.L.R. 260, Roch J.
s. 69, see *R.* v. *Brent London Borough Council, ex p. Omar, The Independent*, April 30, 1991, Henry J.
s. 79, see *Westminster City Council* v. *Clarke, The Times*, March 25, 1991, C.A.; *Central YMCA Housing Association* v. *Saunders* [1990] 1 E.G.C.S. 154, C.A.
s. 84, see *Haringey London Borough Council* v. *Stewart, The Times*, July 3, 1991, C.A.
s. 86, see *London City Corp.* v. *Brown* (1990) 60 P. & C.R. 42, C.A.
ss. 87, 88, see *Bassetlaw District Council* v. *Renshaw, The Times*, July 17, 1991, C.A.
Pt. V (ss. 118–188), see *Burrows and Burrows* v. *Sharp* (1989) 23 H.L.R. 82, C.A.
s. 156, orders 90/2390; 91/619, 2052.
s. 164, regs. 91/974.

CAP.

1985—cont.

68. Housing Act 1985—cont.
Pt. X (ss. 324–344), see *Nolan* v. *Leeds City Council* (1990) 23 H.L.R. 135, C.A.
ss. 365, 375, 377, see *Wandsworth London Borough Council* v. *Bowes* [1990] C.O.D. 167, Kennedy J.
s. 444, orders 90/2391; 91/2053.
s. 445, order 91/819.
Pt. XVI (ss. 527–577), see *R.* v. *Thurrock Borough Council, ex p. Wellham, The Times*, May 14, 1991, Kennedy J.
s. 582, repealed in pt.: order 91/724.
s. 609, see *Beech's Application, Re* (1990) 59 P. & C.R. 502, Lands Tribunal.
s. 614, regs. 91/974.
s. 622, repealed in pt.: 1991, c. 34, sch. 19.
sch. 1, see *Hyde Housing Association* v. *Harrison* (1990) 23 H.L.R. 57, C.A.

69. Housing Associations Act 1985.
ss. 42, 52, see *R.* v. *Secretary of State for the Environment, ex p. Birmingham Friendship Housing Association* [1990] C.O.D. 334, Garland J.
s. 97, amended: regs. 91/1997.
sch. 3, amended and repealed in pt.: *ibid.*

70. Landlord and Tenant Act 1985.
s. 11, see *Staves and Staves* v. *Leeds City Council* (1990) 23 H.L.R. 95, Hutton J.
s. 28, amended and repealed in pt.: regs. 91/1997.
s. 34, see *Orchid Lodge U.K.* v. *Extel Computing* [1991] EGCS 21, C.A.

71. Housing (Consequential Provisions) Act 1985.
sch. 2, repealed in pt.: 1991, c. 34, sch. 19; c. 45, sch. 8.

72. Weights and Measures Act 1985.
s. 4, regs. 90/2626.
s. 5, regs. 90/2626; 91/1775.
s. 15, regs. 91/2019.
s. 86, regs. 90/2626; 91/1775, 2019.
s. 94, regs. 90/2626.

73. Law Reform (Miscellaneous Provisions) (Scotland) Act 1985.
s. 4, see *C.I.N. Properties* v. *Dollar Land (Cumbernauld)* (O.H.), June 19, 1990.
s. 7, amended: 1991, c. 55, sch. 11.
s. 8, see *Bank of Scotland* v. *Graham* (O.H.), 1991 S.L.T. 879.
s. 14, see *Rae* v. *Rae*, (O.H.), 1991 S.L.T. 45; *Westcott* v. *James Dickie & Co.* (O.H.), 1991 S.L.T. 200.
s. 32, repealed: 1991, c. 55, sch. 13.

CAP.

1986

3. Atomic Energy Authority Act 1986.
s. 3, order 91/1736.

5. Agricultural Holdings Act 1986.
s. 1, see *E.W.P.* v. *Moore, The Times*, September 10, 1991, C.A.
ss. 2, 26, see *Crawford* v. *Elliott* [1991] 13 E.G. 163, C.A.
s. 26, sch. 3, see *Earl of Stradbroke* v. *Mitchell* [1991] 3 E.G. 128, 4 E.G. 132, C.A.
sch. 2, see *Mann* v. *Gardner* (1991) 61 P. & C.R. 1, C.A.
sch. 3, see *Land* v. *Sykes* [1991] 16 E.G. 125, Mr. Timothy Lloyd, Q.C.
sch. 3, amended: 1991, c. 60, sch. 1.
sch. 6, order 91/1888.
sch. 14, repealed in pt.: 1991, c. 45, sch. 8; c. 55, sch. 13 (S.).

9. Law Reform (Parent and Child) (Scotland) Act 1986.
s. 3, see *Armstrong* v. *Gibson*, 1991 S.L.T. 193; *F.* v. *F.*, 1991 S.L.T. 357.
s. 3, see *M.* v. *Dumfries and Galloway Regional Council* (Sh.Ct.), 1991 S.C.L.R. 481.
s. 3, repealed in pt.: 1991, c. 50, sch. 2.
s. 4, substituted: *ibid.*, sch. 1.
s. 6, amended: *ibid.*
s. 8, amended: *ibid.*; repealed in pt.: *ibid.*, sch. 2.
sch. 1, repealed in pt.: *ibid.*

14. Animals (Scientific Procedures) Act 1986.
s. 8, order 90/2459.
s. 25, see *R.* v. *Bolton Borough Council, ex p. Manchester City Council, The Independent*, April 17, 1991, Kennedy J.

21. Armed Forces Act 1986.
s. 1, order 91/1696.
ss. 1, 13, sch. 1 (in pt.), repealed: 1991, c. 62, sch. 3.

31. Airports Act 1986.
see *R.* v. *Bolton Borough Council, ex p. Manchester City Council, The Times*, October 7, 1991, C.A.
ss. 22, 23, amended: regs. 91/1997.
s. 61, repealed in pt.: 1991, c. 34, schs. 6, 12, 19, Pts. II, IV(S.).
s. 62, amended: 1991, c. 22, sch. 8.
s. 74, amended: 1991, c. 60, sch. 1.
sch. 2, repealed in pt.: *ibid.*, sch. 3.
sch. 5, amended: regs. 91/1997.

32. Drug Trafficking Offences Act 1986.
see *R.* v. *Saunders* (1991) 92 Cr.App.R. 6, C.A.; *R.* v. *Harrow Justices, ex p. D.P.P., The Times*, April 1, 1991, D.C.; *R.* v. *Johnson* [1990] 3 W.L.R. 745, C.A.; *M., Re, The Times*, May 20, 1991, Henry J.

CAP.

1986—cont.

32. Drug Trafficking Offences Act 1986—*cont.*

s. 1, see *R. v. Porter* [1990] 1 W.L.R. 1260, C.A.; *R. v. Miller* (1991) 92 Cr.App.R. 191, C.A.; *R. v. Richards, The Times*, December 11, 1991, C.A.

s. 2, see *R. v. Enwezor, The Times*, February 18, 1991, C.A.; *R. v. Harper (Terence)* (1989) 11 Cr.App.R. (S.) 240, C.A.

s. 4, see *R. v. Robson (Steven Kenneth)* (1991) 92 Cr.App.R. 1, C.A.; *R. v. Isemann* [1991] Crim.L.R. 141, C.A.

s. 5, see *R. v. Robson (Steven Kenneth)* (1991) 92 Cr.App.R. 1, C.A.; *R. v. Chrastny (No. 2), The Times*, March 14, 1991, C.A.; *R. v. Chapman, The Times*, November 18, 1991, C.A.

ss. 5, 8, see *D.P.P.* v. *P. and W.* [1990] C.O.D. 410, C.A.

s. 8, see *M., Re, The Times*, April 17, 1991, Otton J.

s. 13, see *Customs and Excise Comrs.* v. *Norris* [1991] 2 W.L.R. 962, C.A.

s. 24, see *R. v. Colle, The Times*, September 3, 1991, C.A.; *Nazir Chinoy, Re* [1991] C.O.D. 105, D.C.

s. 26, order 91/1465.

33. Disabled Persons (Services, Consultation and Representation) Act 1986.

s. 16, repealed in pt.: 1991, c. 50, sch. 2.

41. Finance Act 1986.

ss. 3, 4, 8, repealed in pt.: 1991, c. 31, sch. 19.

s. 58, repealed in pt.: *ibid.*, s. 92.

sch. 2, repealed in pt.: *ibid.*, sch. 19.

sch. 18, amended: *ibid.*, sch. 13.

44. Gas Act 1986.

s. 17, regs. 91/1471.

s. 42, amended: 1991, c. 60, sch. 1.

s. 48, regs. 91/1471.

sch. 4, amended: 1991, c. 22, sch. 8; repealed in pt.: *ibid.*, schs. 8, 9.

sch. 7, amended: *ibid.*, sch. 8; repealed in pt.: *ibid.*, sch. 9; c. 60, sch. 3.

45. Insolvency Act 1986.

s. 11, see *Atlantic Computer Systems, Re,* [1990] BCC 859, C.A.

s. 14, see *Griffiths* v. *Provincial & City Property Co., Financial Times,* December 19, 1990, Scott J.

s. 27, see *Charnley Davies, Re* [1990] BCC 605, Millett J.

s. 108, see *A.J. Adams (Builders), Re* [1991] BCC 62, Warner J.

s. 127, see *Company, A, Re (No. 00687 of 1991)* [1991] BCC 210, Harman J.; *Company, A (No. 004502 of 1988), Re, ex p. Johnson* [1991] BCC 234, Harman J.

CAP.

1986—cont.

45. Insolvency Act 1986—*cont.*

s. 133, see *Seagull Manufacturing Co. (In Liquidation), Re, The Times*, May 10, 1991, Mummery J.

s. 212, see *Welfab Engineers, Re* [1990] BCC 600, Hoffmann J.; *Gray* v. *Davidson*, 1991 S.L.T. (Sh.Ct.) 61.

ss. 212, 214, see *Purpoint, Re* [1991] BCC 121, Vinelott J.

ss. 212, 214, 239, see *DKG Contractors, Re* [1990] BCC 903, John Weeks, Q.C.

ss. 234, 436, see *Welsh Development Agency* v. *Export Finance Co., The Times*, November 28, 1991, C.A.

s. 236, see *Cloverbay (No. 3), Re* [1990] BCLC 471, Harman J.; *Cloverbay* v. *B.C.C.I.* [1990] 3 W.L.R. 574, C.A.; *British & Commonwealth Holdings, Re, Financial Times*, August 6, 1991, Hoffmann J.; *Jeffrey S. Levitt, Re, The Times*, November 6, 1991, Vinelott J.

s. 238, see *Paramount Airways, Re, The Times*, June 20, 1991, Mervyn Davies J.

s. 239, see *Beacon Leisure, Re* [1990] BCC 213, Robert Wright, Q.C.

s. 252, see *M., Re, The Times*, April 17, 1991, Otton J.

ss. 260, 271, see *Debtor, A (No. 2389 of 1989), Re, ex p. Travel General Insurance Co.* v. *Debtor* [1991] 2 W.L.R. 578, Vinelott J.

s. 281, amended: 1991, c. 48, sch. 5.

s. 282, see *Robertson (A Bankrupt), Re* [1989] 1 W.L.R. 1139, Warner J.

s. 306, see *London City Corp.* v. *Brown* (1990) 60 P. & C.R. 42, C.A.

ss. 411, 412, rules 91/495.

s. 413, amended: 1991, c. 60, sch. 1.

ss. 414, 415, order 91/496.

s. 423, see *Arbuthnot Leasing International* v. *Havelet Leasing (No. 2)* [1990] BCC 636, Scott J.; *Chohan* v. *Saggar, The Times*, October 16, 1991, Mr. Edward Evans-Lombe, Q.C.

sch. 6, amended: 1991, c. 31, sch. 2.

46. Company Directors Disqualification Act 1986.

see *T. & D. Services (Timber Preservation and Damp Proofing Contractors) Re* [1990] BCC 592, Vinelott J.; *Travel Mondial (U.K.), Re* [1991] BCC 224, Browne-Wilkinson, V.-C.; *Secretary of State for Trade and Industry* v. *Desai, The Times*, December 5, 1991, C.A.

s. 16, see *Secretary of State for Trade and Industry* v. *Langridge; Cedac, Re* [1991] 1 W.L.R. 1343; [1991] 3 All E.R. 591.

1986—cont.

47. Legal Aid (Scotland) Act 1986.
ss. 4, 10, 33, see *Drummond & Co.,
W.S.* v. *Scottish Legal Aid Board*
(Ex.Div.), *The Scotsman*, January
30, 1991.
s. 5, amended: regs. 91/1997.
s. 9, regs. 91/1096.
s. 11, regs. 91/1095.
s. 17, regs. 91/1904.
s. 19, see *MacDonald* v. *Galson Estate*,
1990 S.L.C.R. 128.
s. 33, regs. 91/565–567.
s. 36, regs. 91/745, 746, 1094–1096,
1904.
s. 37, regs. 91/745, 1094, 1095, 1904.
s. 42, regs. 91/745.

48. Wages Act 1986.
see *Home Office* v. *Ayres, The Times*,
October 22, 1991, E.A.T.; *McCree* v.
*Tower Hamlets London Borough
Council, The Times*, October 22,
1991, E.A.T.
ss. 1, 5, see *Reid* v. *Camphill Engravers*
[1990] I.C.R. 435, E.A.T.
ss. 1, 7, see *Foster Wheeler (London)* v.
Jackson [1990] I.C.R. 757, E.A.T.
ss. 1, 7, 8, see *Delaney* v. *Staples (T/A
De Montfort Recruitment)*, [1991] 2
W.L.R. 627, C.A.; *Janstorp International (U.K.)* v. *Allen* [1990] I.C.R.
779, E.A.T.

49. Agriculture Act 1986.
Commencement order: 91/2635.
ss. 14, 16, amended: 1991, c. 55,
sch. 11.
s. 18, amended: 1991, c. 28, sch. 10;
c. 55, sch. 11.
ss. 19, 23, amended: 1991, c. 53,
sch. 11.
s. 24, order 91/2635.
sch. 1, order 91/1994.
sch. 2, order 91/2309(S.).
sch. 2, amended: 1991, c. 53, sch. 11;
repealed in pt.(S.): *ibid.*, sch. 13.
sch. 3, repealed in pt.: 1991, c. 60,
sch. 3.

50. Social Security Act 1986.
ss. 5, 16, regs. 90/429.
s. 20, see *R.* v. *Penwith District Council,
ex p. Menear, The Times*, October 21,
1991, Kennedy J.
s. 20, regs. 90/2564; 91/234–236, 544,
849, 1175, 1520, 1559, 1599.
s. 20, amended: 1991, c. 21, ss. 6, 8.
s. 21, regs. 91/235, 849.
s. 21, amended: 1991, c. 21, s. 6.
s. 22, see *Chief Adjudication Officer
and Secretary of State for Social
Security* v. *Foster, The Guardian*,
February 27, 1991, C.A.
s. 22, regs. 91/234–236, 544, 1033, 1175,
1520, 1559, 1599, 1656, 2334.
s. 23, amended: order 91/503.

1986—cont.

50. Social Security Act 1986—*cont.*
s. 24A, amended: 1991, c. 17, s. 9.
s. 27B, added: 1991, c. 21, s. 7.
s. 29, regs. 91/235, 1599.
s. 30, regs. 91/235, 441; order 91/587.
s. 31A, regs. 91/234, 849.
ss. 31C, 31D, regs. 91/234, 849, 1599.
s. 31F, orders 91/441, 587.
s. 32, see *R.* v. *Social Fund Inspector,
ex p. Healey, The Times*, April 22,
1991, D.C.
s. 32, regs. 90/2302; 91/251, 2238.
ss. 32–34, see *R.* v. *Secretary of State for
Social Services, ex p. Stitt; R.* v. *Social
Security Fund Inspector, ex p. Sher-
win; R.* v. *Same, ex p. Roberts* [1991]
C.O.D. 68, C.A.
s. 49, regs. 91/590, 2284.
s. 50, regs. 91/590.
s. 51, regs. 91/235, 1175, 1599, 2284,
2891.
s. 51, amended: 1991, c. 21, sch. 3.
s. 51A, regs. 91/234, 849, 1033, 1175.
s. 52, amended: 1991, c. 21, schs. 2, 3.
s. 53, see *Page* v. *Chief Adjudication
Officer, The Times*, July 4, 1991,
C.A.; *R.* v. *Secretary of State for
Social Security, ex p. Britnell* [1991] 1
W.L.R. 198, H.L.; *Secretary of State
for Social Security* v. *Tunnicliffe*
[1991] 2 All E.R. 712, C.A.
s. 53, amended: 1991, c. 21, sch. 3.
s. 54, regs. 91/1935, 2284.
s. 63, order 91/503.
s. 63, amended: 1991, c. 21, schs. 2, 3.
s. 64, regs. 91/545.
s. 65, amended: 1991, c. 21, sch. 3.
ss. 71, 72, repealed: *ibid.*, sch. 4.
s. 79, amended: *ibid.*, sch. 3.
s. 84, regs. 90/2302, 2564; 91/234–236,
251, 429, 441, 544, 590, 641, 849,
1165, 1175, 1520, 1559, 1560, 1599,
1656, 2238, 2284, 2334.
s. 84, amended: 1991, c. 3, s. 3.
s. 85, amended: 1991, c. 21, sch. 3.
s. 89, see *R.* v. *Secretary of State for
Social Security, ex p. Britnell* [1991] 1
W.L.R. 198, H.L.
s. 89, regs. 91/1165, 1600.
sch. 4, regs. 91/590, 641, 2284.
sch. 5, amended: 1991, c. 3, s. 2;
repealed in pt.: *ibid.*, sch.; c. 21,
sch. 4.
schs. 6, 7, amended: *ibid.*, sch. 2.

51. Education (No. 2) Act 1986.
see *R.* v. *Birmingham City Council,
ex p. McKenna, The Times*, May 16,
1991, Kennedy J.

53. Building Societies Act 1986.
s. 2, regs. 91/277.
s. 7, order 90/2363; rules 90/2362.
s. 8, rules 90/2362.

CAP.

1986—cont.

53. Building Societies Act 1986—*cont.*
s. 18, orders 91/357, 1358, 2581.
s. 20, rules 90/2362.
s. 21, regs. 91/1785, 2580.
s. 23, order 91/2582.
s. 41, order 91/1518; continued in force: *ibid.*
s. 45, order 91/702.
Pt. VIII (ss. 71–82), amended: order 91/1729.
s. 72, repealed in pt.: *ibid.*
s. 73, regs. 90/2364; 91/2086.
s. 104, orders 91/1729, 2738.
s. 110, amended: order 91/2738.
s. 116, regs. 91/277.
s. 119, order 91/701; amended: order 91/1729.
schs. 5, 11, amended: regs. 91/1997.
55. Family Law Act 1986.
ss. 1, 2A, 3, 6, 10, 11, 13, amended: order 91/1723.
ss. 1, 16, 18, 35, amended (S.): 1991, c. 50, sch. 1.
s. 15, see *T.* v. *T., The Times*, August 2, 1991, Douglas Brown J.
ss. 15, 20, 21, 23, 25–28, amended: order 91/1723.
ss. 27, 28, Act of Sederunt 91/2205.
ss. 31–33, 35, amended: order 91/1723.
s. 36, amended and repealed in pt.: *ibid.*
ss. 38, 41, 42, amended: *ibid.*
s. 43, order 91/1723.
s. 64, rules 91/530.
60. Financial Services Act 1986.
see *R.* v. *Life Assurance Unit Trust Regulatory Organisation, ex p. Ross, The Times*, July 11, 1991, D.C.
s. 2, orders 90/1104, 1516.
s. 46, orders 91/493, 1516.
s. 54, see *Securities and Investments Board* v. *Financial Intermediaries, Managers and Brokers Regulatory Association, The Times*, July 9, 1991, Morritt J.
s. 62A, regs. 91/489.
s. 75, order 91/1516.
s. 114, orders 91/200, 1256.
s. 118, order 91/200.
s. 142, amended and repealed in pt.: regs. 91/2000.
s. 157, repealed: *ibid.*
sch. 1, amended: orders 91/1104, 1516.
sch. 11, regs. 91/538; S.R. 1991 No. 374.
sch. 16, repealed in pt.: 1991, c. 66, sch. 2.
61. Education (No. 2) Act 1986.
s. 43, see *R.* v. *University of Liverpool, ex p. Caesar-Gordon* [1990] 3 W.L.R. 667, D.C.
s. 49, regs. 91/1511.
s. 50, regs. 91/1768, 1804.
s. 63, regs. 91/1511, 1768, 1804.

CAP.

1986—cont.

62. Salmon Act 1986.
ss. 1, 2, order 91/2271(S.).
s. 6, order 91/2115(S.).
s. 8, regs. 91/116(S.), 2007(S.).
s. 33, repealed in pt.: 1991, c. 60, sch. 3.
sch. 1, regs. 91/116(S.).
63. Housing and Planning Act 1986.
s. 9, repealed in pt.: 1991, c. 34, sch. 19.
s. 42, repealed in pt.: 1991, c. 60, sch. 3.
64. Public Order Act 1986.
ss. 2, 4, 7, see *R.* v. *Carson* [1991] 92 Cr.App.R. 236; [1990] Crim.L.R. 729, C.A.
s. 4, see *R.* v. *Horseferry Road Magistrates' Court, ex p. Siadatan* [1990] 3 W.L.R. 1006, D.C.
ss. 5, 6, see *D.P.P.* v. *Clarke, The Times*, August 27, 1991, D.C.

1987

1. Teachers' Pay and Conditions Act 1987.
repealed: 1991, c. 49, sch. 2.
continued in force: order 90/2516.
s. 3, order 91/1459.
s. 6, order 90/2516.
3. Coal Industry Act 1987.
s. 1, order 91/1225; amended: *ibid.*
sch. 1, repealed in pt.: 1991, c. 45, sch. 8; c. 60, sch. 3.
12. Petroleum Act 1987.
s. 22, order 91/207.
s. 23, see *R.* v. *McNair and Master* (1989) 12 Cr.App.R.(S.) 465, C.A.
16. Finance Act 1987.
s. 2, repealed in pt.: 1991, c. 31, sch. 19.
s. 6, repealed: regs. 91/2724.
s. 61, reg. 90/2469.
sch. 1, repealed in pt.: 1991, c. 31, sch. 19.
sch. 10, regs. 90/2469.
18. Debtors (Scotland) Act 1987.
ss. 1, 15, amended: 1991, c. 48, sch. 5.
s. 46, see *Slater* v. *Grampian Regional Council* (Sh.Ct.), 1991 S.C.L.R. 344.
ss. 46, 47, see *Scobie* v. *Dumfries and Galloway Regional Council*, 1991 S.L.T. (Sh.Ct.) 33.
ss. 54, 72, 73, amended: 1991, c. 48, sch. 5.
s. 75, Act of Sederunt 91/1397.
s. 106, amended: 1991, c. 48, sch. 5; repealed in pt.: *ibid.*
sch. 5, see *Norris, Applicant* (Sh.Ct.), 1990 S.C.L.R. 628.
21. Pilotage Act 1987.
Commencement orders: 91/1028, 1029.
s. 1, order 91/1633.
s. 5, order/regulations 91/1959.

CAP.

1987—cont.

21. Pilotage Act 1987—*cont.*
s. 26, order 91/1028.
s. 32, order/regulations 91/1959.
s. 33, order 91/1029.

22. Banking Act 1987.
s. 4, regs. 91/29, 2168; orders 91/66, 2734.
s. 7, order 91/1776.
s. 22, see *Chancery, Re* [1991] BCC 171, Harman J.
s. 64, order 91/1684.
ss. 68, 69, order 91/66.
sch. 2, amended: orders 91/66, 2734.
sch. 4, amended: regs. 91/1997.

24. Immigration (Carriers' Liability) Act 1987.
s. 1, order 91/1497; amended: *ibid.*
s. 2, order 91/2630.

26. Housing (Scotland) Act 1987.
ss. 46, 52, 61, 64, 66, see *Cooper's Exrs.* v. *City of Edinburgh District Council* (H.L.), 1991 S.L.T. 518.
s. 48, see *Midlothian District Council* v. *Brown*, 1991 S.L.T. (Sh.Ct.) 80; *Gordon District Council* v. *Acutt*, 1991 S.L.T. (Sh.Ct.) 78; *Midlothian District Council* v. *Drummond*, 1991 S.L.T. (Sh.Ct.) 67; *Renfrew District Council* v. *Inglis*, 1991 S.L.T. (Sh.Ct.) 83.
s. 52, see *Roxburgh District Council* v. *Collins*, 1991 S.L.T.(Sh.Ct.) 49.
s. 61, see *Martin* v. *Motherwell District Council*, 1991 S.L.T. (Lands Tr.) 4.
s. 73, see *Jack's Exrx.* v. *Falkirk District Council, The Scotsman*, February 14, 1991.
ss. 191, 192, orders 91/244, 245.
s. 193, order 91/245.
s. 204, order 90/2550.
s. 222, order 91/819.
ss. 256, 338, sch. 8, amended: 1991, c. 55, sch. 11.
sch. 3, see *Gordon District Council* v. *Acutt*, 1991 S.L.T. (Sh.Ct.) 78.
sch. 8, amended: 1991, c. 55, sch. 11.
sch. 23, repealed in pt.: 1991, c. 45, sch. 8.

28. Deer Act 1987.
repealed: 1991, c. 54, sch. 4.

30. Northern Ireland (Emergency Provisions) Act 1987.
repealed: 1991, c. 24, sch. 8.
continued in force (pt.): order 91/779.
s. 26, order 91/779.

31. Landlord and Tenant Act 1987.
ss. 1, 12, see *Denetower* v. *Toop, The Times*, April 5, 1991, C.A.
s. 13, see *Gregory* v. *Saddiq (Y/LVT/0032)* [1991] 16 E.G. 141 and [1991] 17 E.G. 97, Lands Tribunal.
s. 24, see *Howard* v. *Midrome* [1990] 03 E.G. 135, Warner J.

CAP.

1987—cont.

37. Access to Personal Files Act 1987.
s. 3, regs. 91/1587.

38. Criminal Justice Act 1987.
s. 2, see *R.* v. *Director of the Serious Fraud Office, ex p. Smith, The Independent*, November 8, 1991, D.C.
s. 9, see *Tariq, Re* [1991] 1 W.L.R. 101, C.A.

41. Criminal Justice (Scotland) Act 1987.
s. 12, see *R.* v. *Boyle; Same* v. *Mears, The Times*, July 22, 1991, C.A.
s. 30, order 91/1467.
s. 48, see *Montes* v. *H.M. Advocate*, 1990 S.C.C.R. 645.

42. Family Law Reform Act 1987.
s. 4, see *H. (Minors) (Local Authority: Parental Rights) (No. 3), Re* [1991] 2 W.L.R. 763, C.A.; *D.* v. *Hereford and Worcester County Council* [1991] 2 W.L.R. 753, Ward J.; *C. (Minors) (Parental Rights), Re, The Times*, August 8, 1991, C.A.; *B. (A Minor) (Adoption), Re* [1991] Fam.Law 136, C.A.
s. 12, see *H.* v. *O., The Times*, July 8, 1991, Ward J.

43. Consumer Protection Act 1987.
see *McKay* v. *Unwin Pyrotechnics, The Times*, March 5, 1991, D.C.
s. 11, regs. 91/447, 1530.
s. 14, see *R.* v. *Birmingham City Council, ex p. Ferrero, The Independent*, May 24, 1991, C.A.; *The Times*, May 30, 1991, C.A.
s. 26, regs. 91/199.
ss. 28, 30, regs. 91/447.

45. Parliamentary and other Pensions Act 1987.
s. 2, regs. 91/609.
s. 2, amended: 1991, c. 5, s. 2.

47. Abolition of Domestic Rates Etc. (Scotland) Act 1987.
s. 2, regs. 90/1486.
s. 2, amended: 1991, c. 2, s. 2.
s. 3A, regs. 91/42, 114.
s. 8, see *Pringle, Petr.*, 1991 S.L.T. 330.
s. 9A, regs. 90/2539; 91/854, 855.
s. 10, see *Bank of Scotland* v. *Community Charges Registration Officer for Central Region* (Sh.Ct.), 1991 S.C.L.R. 394.
s. 10, regs. 91/41.
ss. 13–15, regs. 91/51.
s. 16, see *Malloch* v. *Community Charges Registration Officer for Central Region* (Sh.Ct.), 1990 S.C.L.R. 731.
s. 17, see *Wood* v. *Dumbarton District Council* (O.H.), 1991 S.L.T. 586.
ss. 17, 20, regs. 91/51.
ss. 17, 29, see *Fraser* v. *MacCorquodale*, First Division, July 24, 1990.

1987—cont.

47. Abolition of Domestic Rates Etc. (Scotland) Act 1987—*cont.*
s. 20B, regs. 91/224.
s. 20C, regs. 91/51.
s. 22, amended: 1991, c. 51, s. 2.
s. 26, regs. 90/1486, 2539; 91/41, 42, 51, 114, 224, 854–856.
s. 31, regs. 90/1486, 2539; 91/41, 51, 224, 854–856.
sch. 2, regs. 91/856; Act of Sederunt 91/1920.
sch. 3, amended: 1991, c. 51, s. 2.
sch. 4, orders 91/323, 971.

49. Territorial Sea Act 1987.
s. 4, order 91/1722.

51. Finance (No. 2) Act 1987.
s. 102, orders 91/811, 1142.

53. Channel Tunnel Act 1987.
s. 10, order 91/1212.
s. 11, orders 90/2371; 91/577, 1236.
s. 13, order 90/2371.

1988

1. Income and Corporation Taxes Act 1988.
s. 1, order 91/732; amended: *ibid.*
s. 13, amended: 1991, c. 31, s. 25.
s. 38, see *I.R.C.* v. *Eurocopy, The Times*, November 22, 1991, Davies J.
s. 74, see *Lawson (Inspector of Taxes)* v. *Johnson Matthey* [1991] S.T.C. 259, C.A.
s. 76, amended: 1991, c. 31, s. 47, sch. 7; repealed in pt. (prosp.): *ibid.*, schs. 7, 19.
s. 84, substituted: *ibid.*, s. 68.
s. 84A, added: *ibid.*, s. 42.
s. 85A, added: *ibid.*, s. 43.
s. 88B, regs. 90/2529.
s. 91A, amended: 1991, c. 34, s. 83.
s. 114, repealed in pt.: 1991, c. 31, schs. 15, 19.
s. 118, amended: *ibid.*, sch. 15.
s. 129, regs. 90/2552.
s. 129, amended: 1991, c. 31, s. 57.
s. 154, amended: *ibid.*, s. 30.
ss. 154, 156, see *Pepper (Inspector of Taxes)* v. *Hart, The Times*, November 15, 1990, C.A.
s. 159A, added: 1991, c. 31, s. 30.
s. 160, amended: *ibid.*, sch. 6.
s. 161, amended: *ibid.*, s. 31.
s. 167, amended: *ibid.*, sch. 6.
s. 171, amended: *ibid.*, s. 37.
s. 184, amended and repealed in pt.: regs. 91/1997.
s. 185, amended: 1991, c. 31, s. 39.
ss. 185, 187, see *I.R.C.* v. *Eurocopy, The Times*, November 22, 1991, Davies J.
s. 187, amended: 1991, c. 31, ss 38, 41.
s. 190, amended: 1991, c. 5, s. 4.

1988—cont.

1. Income and Corporation Taxes Act 1988—*cont.*
s. 201A, amended: 1991, c. 31, s. 69.
s. 203, regs. 91/435, 1080.
s. 242, amended: 1991, c. 31, sch. 15.
s. 243, repealed in pt.: *ibid.*, schs. 15, 19.
s. 257, amended: order 91/732.
s. 257A, amended: *ibid.*; 1991, c. 31, s. 22.
s. 257B, amended: 1991, c. 31, s. 33.
s. 257C, order 91/732.
ss. 257D, 265, amended: 1991, c. 31, s. 33.
s. 324, order 91/1202.
s. 326C, regs. 90/2361.
s. 333, regs. 91/733.
s. 333, amended: 1991, c. 31, s. 70.
s. 338, see *Minsham Properties* v. *Price (Inspector of Taxes); Lysville* v. *Same* [1990] S.T.C. 718, Vinelott J.
s. 338, amended: 1991, c. 31, s. 71.
s. 339A, amended: *ibid.*, s. 71; repealed: *ibid.*, s. 71, sch. 19.
s. 343, see *Falmer Jeans* v. *Rodin (Inspector of Taxes)* [1990] S.T.C. 270, Millett J.
s. 343, amended: 1991, c. 31, sch. 15; repealed in pt.: *ibid.*, schs. 15, 19.
s. 349, amended: *ibid.*, sch. 11; repealed in pt.: *ibid.*, schs. 11, 19.
s. 350, regs. 91/512.
s. 353, amended: 1991, c. 31, s. 27.
s. 354, repealed in pt.: *ibid.*, s. 28, sch. 19.
s. 367, repealed in pt.: *ibid.*, sch. 19.
s. 369, amended: *ibid.*, s. 27.
s. 370, see *R.* v. *Inspector of Taxes, ex p. Kelly, The Times*, July 26, 1991, C.A.
s. 376, see *Tither* v. *I.R.C.* [1990] S.T.C. 416, European Ct.
s. 376, orders 91/618, 2604.
s. 393, amended: 1991, c. 31, sch. 15; repealed in pt.: *ibid.*, s. 73, schs. 15, 19.
s. 393, added: *ibid.*, s. 73.
s. 394, repealed: *ibid.*, sch. 19.
ss. 395, 397, 399, 400, 403, 407, amended: *ibid.*, sch. 15.
s. 431, amended; *ibid.*, sch. 7.
s. 432A, amended: *ibid.*; repealed in pt. (prosp.): *ibid.*, schs. 7, 19.
ss. 432C, 432D, amended: *ibid.*, sch. 7.
s. 432E, order 90/2546.
s. 434, amended: 1991, c. 31, sch. 15.
ss. 436, 437, amended: *ibid..*, sch. 7; repealed in pt. (prosp.): *ibid.*, schs. 7, 19.
s. 438A, added: *ibid.*, s. 49.
ss. 440, 440A, amended: *ibid.*, sch. 7.
s. 446, repealed in pt. (prosp.): *ibid.*, schs. 7, 19.

1988—cont.

1. **Income and Corporation Taxes Act 1988**—*cont.*

s. 447, amended: *ibid.*, sch. 7; repealed in pt. (prosp.): *ibid.*, schs. 7, 19.

s. 448, repealed in pt. (prosp.): *ibid.*, schs. 7, 19.

s. 451, regs. 90/2524; 91/851.

s. 458, amended: 1991, c. 31, sch. 15.

s. 460, amended: *ibid.*, sch. 9.

s. 462A, added: *ibid.*

s. 464, amended: *ibid.*

s. 465, repealed in pt.: *ibid.*, sch. 19.

s. 467, amended: *ibid.*, s. 74.

s. 474, repealed in pt. (prosp.): *ibid.*, schs. 7, 19.

s. 477A, amended: *ibid.*, s. 52, sch. 11.

s. 477B, added: *ibid.*, sch. 10.

s. 482A, added: *ibid.*, s. 75.

s. 492, amended: *ibid.*, sch. 15.

s. 497, amended: *ibid.*, s. 66.

s. 503, amended: *ibid.*, sch. 15.

s. 518, amended: *ibid.*; repealed in pt.: *ibid.*, schs. 15, 19.

ss. 547, 549, amended: 1991, c. 31, sch. 7.

s. 566, regs. 91/1081.

s. 582A, order 91/1694.

s. 582A, added: 1991, c. 31, s. 118.

s. 587A, added: *ibid.*, sch. 12.

s. 590, amended: order 91/734; 1991, c. 31, s. 34; repealed in pt.: *ibid.*, s. 36, sch. 19.

s. 590C, order 91/734.

s. 591, regs. 91/1614.

s. 591A, added: 1991, c. 31, s. 35.

s. 591B, added: *ibid.*, s. 36.

s. 615, amended: 1991, c. 16, s. 2.

s. 617, amended: 1991, c. 21, schs. 2, 3; repealed in pt.: order 91/2874.

s. 656, added: 1991, c. 31, s. 76.

s. 663, amended (S.): 1991, c. 50, sch. 1.

s. 710, amended: 1991, c. 31, sch. 10.

s. 726, repealed: *ibid.*, sch. 19.

s. 726A, added: *ibid.*, sch. 12.

s. 731, amended: *ibid.*, s. 55.

s. 732, amended: *ibid.*, s. 56.

s. 736A, added: *ibid.*, s. 58.

s. 737, amended: *ibid.*, sch. 13; repealed in pt.: *ibid.*, sch. 19.

s. 738, amended: *ibid.*, sch. 13; repealed in pt.: *ibid.*, schs. 13, 19.

s. 768A, added: *ibid.*, sch. 15.

s. 769, amended: *ibid.*

s. 788, order 90/2590.

ss. 790, 797, see *Yates (Inspector of Taxes)* v. *GCA International; GCA International* v. *Yates (Inspector of Taxes)* [1991] S.T.C. 157, Scott J.

ss. 808, 825, 826, amended: 1991, c. 31, sch. 15.

s. 828, amended: *ibid.*, s. 118.

1988—cont.

1. **Income and Corporation Taxes Act 1988**—*cont.*

s. 843, repealed in pt.: *ibid.*, schs. 15, 19.

sch. 4, amended: *ibid.*, sch. 12.

sch. 5, amended: *ibid.*, sch. 15; repealed in pt.: *ibid.*, sch. 19.

sch. 6, amended: *ibid.*, s. 29.

sch. 7, amended: *ibid.*, sch. 6; repealed in pt.: *ibid.*, schs. 6, 19.

sch. 9, see *I.R.C.* v. *Eurocopy, The Times*, November 22, 1991, Davies J.

sch. 9, amended: 1991, c. 31, ss. 38–40.

sch. 10, amended: *ibid.*, ss. 38, 89.

sch. 12, amended: *ibid.*, s. 45.

sch. 15, repealed in pt.: *ibid.*, schs. 9, 19.

sch. 16, amended: *ibid.*, sch. 11.

sch. 18, amended: *ibid.*, s. 77.

sch. 19A, regs. 91/851.

sch. 19AB, added: 1991, c. 31, sch. 8.

sch. 23A, added: *ibid.*, sch. 13.

sch. 26, amended: *ibid.*, sch. 15.

sch. 28, repealed in pt. (prosp.): *ibid.*, schs. 7, 19.

sch. 29, repealed in pt.: *ibid.*, sch. 19.

sch. 30, amended: *ibid.*, sch. 15; repealed in pt.: *ibid.*, sch. 19.

2. **Arms Control and Disarmament (Privileges and Immunities) Act 1988.**

s. 1, order 91/1704.

4. **Norfolk and Suffolk Broads Act 1988.**

s. 25, amended: 1991, c. 60, sch. 1.

5. **Welsh Development Agency Act 1988.**

s. 2, repealed in pt.: 1991, c. 69, s. 2.

7. **Social Security Act 1988.**

s. 1, repealed in pt.: 1991, c. 21, sch. 4.

ss. 13, 15A, regs. 91/585.

9. **Local Government Act 1988.**

see *R.* v. *Lambeth Borough Council, ex p. Secretary of State for the Environment* [1991] C.O.D. 132, C.A.

s. 2, orders 91/262, 312, 2438.

s. 6, regs. 90/2498; 91/232, 2006.

s. 8, regs. 91/232.

s. 15, regs. 90/2498; 91/232, 2006; orders 91/262, 312, 2438.

s. 25, amended: 1991, c. 60, sch. 1.

12. **Merchant Shipping Act 1988.**

see *R.* v. *Secretary of State for Transport, ex p. Factortame, The Independent*, July 25, 1991, European Ct.

s. 11, orders 91/770, 1469.

s. 13, regs. 91/784.

s. 14, see *R.* v. *Secretary of State for Transport, ex p. Factortame (No. 2)* [1990] 3 W.L.R. 818, H.L.

s. 17, order 91/1808.

ss. 25, 26, 44, 46, regs. 91/1805.

s. 50, regs. 91/1367.

s. 56, orders 91/1703, 2875.

sch. 2, regs. 91/784.

1988—cont.

13. Coroners Act 1988.

s. 10, amended: 1991, c. 53, sch. 4.

s. 11, see *R.* v. *H.M. Coroner for Birmingham, ex p. Secretary of State for the Home Department* [1991] C.O.D. 82, D.C.

s. 13, see *R.* v. *West Berkshire Coroner, ex p. Thomas, The Times*, April 5, 1991, D.C.; *Att.-Gen.* v. *Coroner for the County of Hampshire* [1991] C.O.D. 11, D.C.; *R.* v. *South Powys Coroner's Court, ex p. Jones (Mark Stewart)* [1991] C.O.D. 14, D.C.; *Taylor* v. *Elgar* [1990] C.O.D. 400, D.C.

ss. 16, 17, amended: 1991, c. 40, sch. 4.

s. 21, amended: 1991, c. 53, sch. 4.

14. Immigration Act 1988.

Commencement order: 91/1001.

see *R.* v. *Secretary of State for the Home Department, ex p. K. Alnafeesi* [1990] C.O.D. 262, C.A.

s. 5, see *R.* v. *Secretary of State for the Home Department, ex p. Panchan, The Times*, May 7, 1991, Popplewell J.; *R.* v. *Secretary of State for the Home Department, ex p. Egbe, The Independent*, September 27, 1991, C.A.; *R.* v. *Secretary of State for the Home Department, ex p. Quakkouche (Mustafa)* [1991] Imm.A.R. 5, Kennedy J.

s. 12, orders 91/1001, 2630.

16. Farm Land and Rural Development Act 1988.

s. 1, scheme 91/1406.

s. 2, scheme 91/1631.

s. 2, amended: 1991, c. 18, s. 3.

19. Employment Act 1988.

s. 3, see *Transport and General Workers Union* v. *Webber* [1990] I.C.R. 711, E.A.T.

ss. 3, 4, see *Meldhurst* v. *NALGO* [1990] I.C.R. 387, E.A.T.; *National and Local Government Officers' Association* v. *Killorn and Sim* [1990] I.R.L.R. 464, E.A.T.

ss. 3–5, see *Bradley* v. *National and Local Government Officers' Association* [1991] I.R.L.R. 159, E.A.T.

s. 15, see *Veness and Chalkley* v. *National Union of Public Employees* [1991] I.R.L.R. 76, D.C.

ss. 15, 23, see *Lenahan* v. *Union of Construction Allied Trades and Technicians* [1991] I.R.L.R. 78, Hoffmann J.

s. 26, order 91/1995.

20. Dartford—Thurrock Crossing Act 1988.

s. 24, amended: 1991, c. 26, s. 2.

1988—cont.

26. Landlord and Tenant Act 1988.

s. 1, see *Midland Bank* v. *Chart Enterprises* [1990] 44 E.G. 68, Popplewell J.

32. Civil Evidence (Scotland) Act 1988.

s. 2, see *Gordon* v. *Grampian Health Board*, 1991 S.C.L.R. 213.

33. Criminal Justice Act 1988.

s. 23, see *R.* v. *Acton Justices, ex p. McMullen; R.* v. *Tower Bridge Magistrates' Court, ex p. Lawlor* (1991) 92 Cr.App.R. 98, C.A.; *R.* v. *Burke* [1990] Crim.L.R. 401, H.H. Judge Starforth Hill; *R.* v. *Case* [1991] Crim.L.R. 192, C.A.

s. 32, amended: 1991, c. 53, s. 55.

s. 32A, added: *ibid.*, s. 54.

s. 33A, added: *ibid.*, s. 52.

s. 34, see *R.* v. *Pryce* [1991] Crim.L.R. 379, C.A.

s. 34, amended: 1991, c. 53, sch. 11; repealed in pt.: *ibid.*, s. 55, sch. 13.

s. 34A, added: *ibid.*, s. 55.

s. 36, see *Att.-Gen.'s Reference (No. 15 of 1990)* (1991) 92 Cr.App.R. 194, C.A.; *Att.-Gen.'s Reference (No. 17 of 1990)* (1991) 92 Cr.App.R. 288, C.A.

s. 38, repealed in pt.: 1991, c. 53, s. 55.

s. 39, see *D.P.P.* v. *Taylor; Same* v. *Little, The Independent*, July 17, 1991, D.C.

ss. 39, 40, see *R.* v. *Savage* (1990) 91 Cr.App.R. 317, C.A.

s. 40, see *R.* v. *Mearns* [1990] 3 W.L.R. 569, C.A.; *R.* v. *Callaghan, The Independent*, August 14, 1991, C.A.

s. 41, see *R.* v. *Foote, The Times*, July 8, 1991, C.A.; *R.* v. *Miall, The Times*, August 27, 1991, C.A.

s. 69, see *R.* v. *Highbury Corner Magistrates' Court, ex p. Di Matteo* (1991) 92 Cr.App.R. 263, D.C.

s. 71, see *Randle and Pottle, Re, The Independent*, March 26, 1991, Webster J.

ss. 71–74, 76, 77, 102, see *K., Re* [1991] C.O.D. 18, McCullough J.

ss. 71–78, see *O., Re* [1991] 1 All E.R. 330, C.A.

s. 123, see *R.* v. *Mussell, The Times*, January 1, 1991, C.A.

ss. 123, 131, repealed in pt.: 1991, c. 53, sch. 13.

sch. 7, amended: 1991, c. 62, sch. 2.

schs. 8, 10, 15, repealed in pt.: 1991, c. 53, sch. 13.

sch. 16, repealed in pt.: *ibid.*, s. 23, sch. 13.

CAP.

1988—cont.

34. Legal Aid Act 1988.
Commencement order: 91/790.
s. 2, regs. 91/2038, 2112.
s. 3, amended: 1991, c. 53, sch. 11.
s. 6, regs. 91/524.
s. 7, amended: regs. 91/1977.
s. 9, regs. 91/636, 2305.
s. 15, regs. 91/635.
s. 15, amended: order 91/1924; regs. 91/2036.
s. 16, regs. 91/635, 2036.
ss. 16, 17, see *Lockley* v. *National Blood Transfusion Service, The Times,* November 11, 1991, C.A.
s. 19, amended: 1991, c. 53, sch. 11.
s. 20, amended: 1991, c. 13, s. 3; c. 53, sch. 6; repealed in pt.: 1991, c. 13, s. 3; c. 53, sch. 13.
ss. 21, 23, regs. 91/637.
s. 25, regs. 91/ 529, 837.
ss. 27, 28, amended: 1991, c. 53, sch. 11.
s. 30, regs. 91/837.
s. 30, amended: 1991, c. 53, sch. 11.
s. 31, regs. 91/524, 1753, 2036.
s. 34, regs. 91/524, 527–529, 635–637, 837, 838, 1753, 1925, 2036–2038, 2112, 2305.
s. 39, repealed in pt.: order 91/724.
s. 43, regs. 91/524, 527–529, 635–637, 837, 838, 1753, 1925, 2036–2038, 2112, 2305.
s. 47, order 91/790.
sch. 3, amended: 1991, c. 53, sch. 11; repealed in pt.: order 91/790.

36. Court of Session Act 1988.
s. 5, Acts of Sederunt 91/272, 291, 846, 1157, 1158, 1183, 1413, 1621, 1915, 2213, 2483.
s. 11, see *Morris* v. *Drysdale, The Scotsman,* February 27, 1991.
ss. 32, 33, see *F.* v. *F.*, 1991 S.L.T. 357.
s. 40, see *John G. McGregor (Contractors)* v. *Grampian Regional Council* (H.L.), 1991 S.L.T. 365.

39. Finance Act 1988.
s. 4, repealed in pt.: 1991, c. 31, sch. 19.
s. 64, amended: *ibid.*, s. 67.
ss. 68, 77, amended: *ibid.*, s. 44.
s. 102, amended: *ibid.*, sch. 6.
schs. 1, 2, repealed in pt.: *ibid.*, sch. 19.
sch. 8, amended: *ibid.*, s. 78; repealed in pt.: *ibid.*, s. 78, sch. 19.
sch. 9, amended: *ibid.*, s. 101; repealed in pt.: *ibid.*
sch. 12, amended: *ibid.*, s. 79.

40. Education Reform Act 1988.
Commencement order: 91/409.
see *R.* v. *Secretary of State for Education and Science, ex p. Newham London Borough Council, The Times,* January 11, 1991, D.C.

CAP.

1988—cont.

40. Education Reform Act 1988—*cont.*
s. 4, orders 91/751, 752, 678, 681, 1668, 1683, 1851, 1860, 2169, 2170, 2562, 2563, 2608.
s. 14, see *R.* v. *Governors of Bacon's School, ex p. Inner London Education Authority* [1990] C.O.D. 414, D.C.
s. 20, orders 91/678, 681.
s. 21, regs. 91/1657.
s. 22, regs. 91/1265, 1278, 1582, 1658, 1813.
s. 27, order 91/410.
s. 28, regs. 91/411.
s. 39, repealed in pt.: regs. 91/1890.
s. 41, regs. 91/1890.
s. 46, repealed in pt.: 1991, c. 49, sch. 2.
s. 51, repealed in pt.: order 91/1890.
ss. 79, 81, regs. 91/353.
s. 103, regs. 91/1278, 1582.
s. 105, see *R.* v. *Governors of Bacon's School, ex p. Inner London Education Authority* [1990] C.O.D. 414, D.C.
s. 103, regs. 91/1658, 1813.
ss. 105, 108, see *R.* v. *Secretary of State for Education and Science, ex p. Inner London Education Authority* [1990] C.O.D. 412, C.A.
s. 110, amended: 1991, c. 21, sch. 3.
ss. 122, 126, order 91/1976.
s. 128, orders 91/550, 2155.
s. 133, regs. 91/2307.
s. 134, see *R.* v. *Secretary of State for Education and Science, ex p. Association of Polytechnic and College Teachers, The Independent,* August 9, 1991, Simon Brown J.
s. 180, order 91/1457.
s. 185, orders 91/184, 439.
s. 187, orders 91/497, 964, 1787.
s. 206, see *Hines* v. *Birkbeck College (No. 2), The Times,* June 17, 1991, C.A.; *Pearce* v. *University of Aston in Birmingham (No. 1)* [1991] 2 All E.R. 461, C.A.
s. 210, regs. 91/131.
s. 216, orders 91/383, 384.
s. 218, regs. 91/1134, 1840, 2240.
s. 227, order 91/1391.
s. 231, orders 91/184, 497, 559, 1457, 1787.
s. 232, regs. 91/131, 353, 1134, 1265, 1658, 1813, 1890; orders 91/410, 497, 505, 751, 752, 964, 1668, 1683, 1787, 1840, 1851, 1860, 1976, 2155, 2169, 2170, 2240, 2562, 2608.
s. 236, order 91/409.
sch. 4, repealed in pt.: regs. 91/1890.
sch. 7, order 91/1976.
sch. 7, amended: regs. 91/1997.

1988—cont.

40. Education Reform Act 1988—*cont.*
sch. 11, order 91/1427.
sch. 12, repealed in pt.: 1991, c. 49,
sch. 2.

41. Local Government Finance Act 1988.
see *R. v. Bristol Magistrates' Court and Bristol City Council, ex p. Willsman* [1991] R.A. 106, D.C.; *Bradford City Metropolitan Council* v. *Anderton* [1991] R.A. 45, Hutchinson J.; *R. v. Secretary of State for the Environment, ex p. Avon County Council* [1991] C.O.D. 137, D.C.; *Cherwell District Council* v. *Hodges* (1991) 31 R.V.R. 163, Auld J.
s. 2, see *Cherwell District Council* v. *Oxfordshire Valuation and Community Charge Tribunal, The Independent*, November 13, 1991, Hodgson J.
s. 3, repealed in pt.: 1991, c. 2, s. 1.
s. 4, order 91/474.
s. 4, amended: *ibid.*; repealed in pt.: 1991, c. 2, s. 1.
ss. 6, 23, 26, 26A, 40, see *Runneymede Community Charge Registration Officer* v. *Data Protection Registrar; South Northamptonshire Community Charge Registration Officer* v. *Same; Harrow Community Charge Registration Officer* v. *Same* (1990) 30 R.V.R. 236, Data Protection Tribunal.
s. 8, regs. 90/2468.
s. 13A, regs. 91/212, 230, 352, 835, 844.
s. 15, regs. 90/2468.
s. 19, regs. 90/2475.
s. 19, repealed in pt.: 1991, c. 2, s. 1.
s. 22, see *Evans* v. *South Ribble Borough Council* [1991] R.A. 191, Simon Brown J.
s. 31, regs. 91/212.
ss. 31, 33, repealed in pt.: 1991, c. 2, s. 1.
ss. 32, 35, see *R. v. Lambeth Borough Council, ex p. Secretary of State for the Environment* [1991] C.O.D. 132, C.A.
ss. 32, 35, 89, 91, 95, 102, 107, 146, see *R. v. Haringey London Borough Council, ex p. Secretary of State for the Environment* (1990) R.V.R. 261, D.C.
s. 35, amended: 1991, c. 8, s. 1; repealed in pt.: *ibid.*, s. 1, sch.
s. 35A, added: *ibid.*, s. 2.
s. 35B, added: *ibid.*, s. 3.
s. 35C, added: *ibid.*, s. 4.
s. 36, amended: *ibid.*, s. 5.
s. 40, regs. 90/2475.
s. 40, repealed in pt.: 1991, c. 2, s. 1.
s. 50, regs. 91/148, 149.
s. 53, regs. 91/723.
s. 55, regs. 91/471, 723, 2111.
s. 60, repealed in pt.: 1991, c. 2, s. 1.

1988—cont.

41. Local Government Finance Act 1988—*cont.*
s. 64, regs. 91/471, 475.
s. 65, regs. 91/471.
s. 66, order 91/474; amended: *ibid.*
s. 73, regs. 91/979.
ss. 73, 74A, regs. 91/148, 149.
s. 75, regs. 91/523.
ss. 95, 107, see *R. v. Lambeth Borough Council, ex p. Secretary of State for the Environment* [1991] C.O.D. 132, C.A.
s. 100, see *R. v. Secretary of State for the Environment, ex p. Hammersmith and Fulham London Borough Council* [1990] 3 W.L.R. 898; [1990] 3 All E.R. 589, H.L.
ss. 101, 103 (in pt.), repealed: 1991, c. 51, s. 1.
s. 104, order 91/1230.
s. 107, repealed in pt.: 1991, c. 8, s. 5, sch.
s. 118, regs. 91/523.
s. 128, regs. 91/645.
s. 140, regs. 90/2472, 2499; 91/64, 118, 212, 230, 352, 434, 835, 844, 959, 2259, 2260.
s. 143, regs. 90/2329, 2472, 2475, 2499, 2656, 2657; 91/1, 64, 118, 140–142, 148, 149, 212, 223, 228, 230, 241, 242, 352, 434, 523, 835, 841–844, 979, 1127, 2111; order 91/959.
s. 143, repealed in pt.: 1991, c. 51, s. 1.
s. 146, regs. 90/2472, 2475, 2499, 2656, 2657; 91/1, 118, 140–142, 148, 149, 210, 212, 228, 230, 278, 352, 434, 471, 523, 723, 842–844, 877, 979, 1127, 1189; order 91/959.
s. 147, regs. 91/241; orders 91/185, 983, 1730.
sch. 1, see *Cherwell District Council* v. *Oxfordshire Valuation and Community Charge Tribunal, The Independent*, November 13, 1991, Hodgson J.
sch. 1, order 91/739; amended: *ibid.*
sch. 2, regs. 90/2656, 2657; 91/118, 140, 148, 149, 223, 230, 242, 352, 434, 837, 841–844, 877, 979, 1127.
sch. 3, regs. 91/148, 149, 842, 877, 979.
sch. 4, see *Evans* v. *South Ribble Borough Council* [1991] R.A. 191, Simon Brown J.
sch. 5, amended: 1991, c. 60, sch. 1.
sch. 6, regs. 91/278, 959.
sch. 7, order 91/182.
sch. 7A, regs. 90/2329.
sch. 8, regs. 90/2499.
sch. 9, regs. 91/118, 141, 148, 149, 228.
sch. 11, regs. 91/1, 210, 1189.
sch. 12A, regs. 91/64, 2260.

43. Housing (Scotland) Act 1988.
s. 70, order 91/533.
sch. 4, amended: 1991, c. 55, sch. 11.

CAP.

1988—cont.

45. Firearms (Amendment) Act 1988.
Commencement order: 90/2620.
s. 27, order 90/2620.

48. Copyright, Designs and Patents Act 1988.
see *BBC* v. *British Satellite Broadcasting, The Times*, January 22, 1991, Scott J.
s. 75, order 91/1116.
s. 99, see *Lagenes* v. *It's At (U.K.), The Times*, March 12, 1991, Ferris J.
s. 115, amended: order 91/724.
ss. 150, 152, rules 91/201.
ss. 205, 232, amended: order 91/724.
s. 250, rules 91/1626.
s. 298, see *BBC Enterprises* v. *Hi-Tech Xtravision* [1991] 1 W.L.R. 1, H.L.
sch. 1, rules 91/201.

50. Housing Act 1988.
Commencement order: 91/954.
ss. 27, 28, see *Tagro* v. *Cafane* [1991] 1 W.L.R. 378; [1991] 2 All E.R. 235, C.A.
s. 40, repealed in pt.: order 91/724.
ss. 60, 62, order 91/1641.
s. 67, amended: 1991, c. 34, schs. 3, 7.
ss. 104, 111, 112, 114, regs. 91/1899.
s. 121, order 91/426.
s. 141, order 91/954.
sch. 1, regs. 91/233.
sch. 8, amended and repealed in pt.: regs. 91/1997.
sch. 9, repealed in pt.: 1991, c. 66, sch. 2.

51. Rate Support Grants Act 1988.
see *R.* v. *Secretary of State for the Environment, ex p. Merton London Borough Council* (1991) 31 R.V.R. 78, C.A.

52. Road Traffic Act 1988.
s. 1, see *Att.-Gen.'s Reference (No. 15 of 1990)* (1991) 92 Cr.App.R. 194, C.A.; *Hamilton* v. *H.M. Advocate*, 1991 S.L.T. 555.
ss. 1, 2, substituted: 1991, c. 40, s. 1.
s. 2, see *Morrison* v. *Valentine*, 1990 S.C.C.R. 692.
s. 2A, added: 1991, c. 40, s. 1.
s. 3, see *Wilson* v. *MacPhail*, 1991 S.C.C.R. 170; *Hamilton* v. *H.M. Advocate*, 1991 S.L.T. 555.
s. 3, substituted: 1991, c. 40, s. 2.
s. 3A, added: *ibid.*, s. 3.
s. 4, amended: *ibid.*, s. 4.
s. 5, see *D.P.P.* v. *O'Connor; Same* v. *Allett; Same* v. *Connor; Same* v. *Chapman; R.* v. *Chichester Crown Court, ex p. Moss; D.P.P.* v. *Allen, The Times*, July 11, 1991, D.C.

CAP.

1988—cont.

52. Road Traffic Act 1988—*cont.*
s. 7, see *Holling* v. *D.P.P.* (1991) 155 J.P.N. 250, D.C.; *Jones* v. *D.P.P.* [1991] R.T.R. 41, D.C.; *D.P.P.* v. *Beech, The Times*, July 15, 1991, D.C.; *D.P.P.* v. *D (A Juvenile); Same* v. *Rous, The Times*, July 11, 1991, D.C.; *Hawthorn* v. *Jessop*, 1991 S.C.C.R. 674; *MacDougall* v. *MacPhail*, 1991 S.L.T. 801; *Walker* v. *Walkingshaw*, 1991 S.C.C.R. 695; *Simpson* v. *Lowe*, 1991 S.C.C.R. 728.
s. 7, amended: 1991, c. 40, sch. 4.
s. 8, see *D.P.P.* v. *Poole, The Times*, April 1, 1991, D.C.; *Jones* v. *D.P.P.* [1991] R.T.R. 41, D.C.; *D.P.P.* v. *D (A Juvenile); Same* v. *Rous, The Times*, July 11, 1991, D.C.
ss. 10–13, amended: 1991, c. 40, sch. 4.
s. 13A, added: *ibid.*, s. 5.
s. 14, regs. 91/1255.
s. 14, amended: 1991, c. 40, sch. 4.
ss. 15 (in pt.), 19A, repealed: *ibid.*, sch. 8.
s. 22, amended: *ibid.*, sch. 4.
s. 22A, added: *ibid.*, s. 6; amended: 1991, c. 22, sch. 8; repealed in pt.: *ibid.*, sch. 9.
s. 28, substituted: 1991, c. 40, s. 7.
ss. 29, 30, repealed in pt.: *ibid.*, sch. 8.
s. 31, amended: *ibid.*, sch. 4.
s. 39, amended: 1991, c. 22, sch. 8.
s. 40A, added: 1991, c. 40, s. 8.
s. 41, regs. 91/1526, 1527, 2003, 2125.
s. 41, amended: 1991, c. 40, sch. 4; repealed in pt.: *ibid.*, sch. 8.
ss. 41A, 41B, added: *ibid.*, s. 8.
s. 42, substituted: *ibid.*
s. 43, regs. 91/1526.
s. 44, amended: 1991, c. 40, sch. 4.
ss. 45, 46, regs. 91/253, 455, 1525, 2229.
ss. 45, 46, amended: 1991, c. 40, sch. 4.
s. 47, regs. 91/253.
s. 48, repealed in pt.: 1991, c. 40, sch. 8.
s. 49, regs. 91/252, 454.
s. 49, amended: 1991, c. 40, sch. 4.
s. 50, amended: *ibid.*; repealed in pt.: *ibid.*, schs. 4, 8.
s. 51, regs. 91/252, 454.
s. 51, repealed in pt.: 1991, c. 40, sch. 8.
s. 54, regs. 91/1021, 1022, 1970, 1971.
s. 61, regs. 91/1021, 1022, 1318, 1970, 1971.
s. 61, repealed in pt.: 1991, c. 40, sch. 8.
s. 66A, added: *ibid.*, s. 9.
s. 67, amended: *ibid.*, s. 10; repealed in pt.: *ibid.*, sch. 8.
s. 68, repealed in pt.: *ibid.*, s. 9; substituted: *ibid.*, s. 11.

1988—cont.

52. Road Traffic Act 1988—*cont.*
s. 69, substituted: *ibid.*, s. 12.
s. 69A, added: *ibid.*
s. 70, amended: *ibid.*, s. 13.
s. 71, substituted: *ibid.*, s. 14.
s. 72, substituted: *ibid.*, s. 15.
s. 72A, added: *ibid.*
s. 73, amended: *ibid.*, sch. 4; repealed in pt.: *ibid.*, sch. 8.
s. 74, amended: *ibid.*, sch. 4.
s. 75, see *R.* v. *Nash* [1990] R.T.R. 343, C.A.
s. 75, amended: 1991, c. 40, s. 16; repealed in pt.: *ibid.*, schs. 4, 8.
s. 76, amended: *ibid.*, sch. 4.
s. 79, amended: *ibid.*; repealed in pt.: *ibid.*, schs. 4, 8.
s. 80, regs. 91/1979.
ss. 84, 85, amended: 1991, c. 40, sch. 4.
s. 86, amended: *ibid.*; repealed in pt.: *ibid.*, sch. 8.
s. 87, amended: *ibid.*, s. 17.
s. 88, regs. 90/2612.
s. 89, regs. 90/2334, 2612; 91/485, 515, 1121, 1122, 1541.
s. 89, amended: 1991, c. 40, sch. 4.
ss. 89A, 91, 92, regs. 90/2612.
ss. 92, 94, amended: 1991, c. 40, s. 18.
s. 94A, added: *ibid.*
s. 97, regs. 90/2334, 2385, 2612; 91/515.
s. 97, repealed in pt.: 1991, c. 40, s. 17, sch. 8.
s. 98, regs. 90/2334, 2612.
s. 98, repealed in pt.: 1991, c. 40, sch. 8.
s. 99, regs. 90/2612.
s. 101, regs. 90/2612; 91/485.
s. 103, substituted: 1991, c. 40, s. 19.
s. 105, regs. 90/2334, 2385, 2612; 91/485, 515, 1121, 1122, 1541.
s. 105, repealed in pt.: 1991, c. 40, sch. 8.
s. 108, regs. 90/2334, 2385, 2612; 91/485, 515, 1121, 1122, 1541.
s. 114, regs. 90/2612; 91/515.
ss. 115, 117, regs. 90/2612.
ss. 115, 117, amended: 1991, c. 40, sch. 4.
s. 118, regs. 90/2612.
ss. 120, 121, regs. 90/2612; 91/515.
s. 122, regs. 90/2612.
ss. 125, 127, regs. 91/1129.
s. 128, amended: *ibid.*
ss. 132, 134, 141, regs. 91/1129.
s. 143, see *Gibb* v. *McGlennan*, 1990 S.C.C.R. 759.
s. 144, amended: 1991, c. 40, s. 20.
s. 151, repealed in pt.: *ibid.*, sch. 8.
ss. 152, 163, amended: *ibid.*, sch. 4.
ss. 164, 165, amended: *ibid.*, repealed in pt.: *ibid.*, sch. 8.

1988—cont.

52. Road Traffic Act 1988—*cont.*
ss. 166, 168, 170, amended: *ibid.*, sch. 4.
s. 172, substituted: *ibid.*, s. 21.
s. 173, amended: *ibid.*, sch. 4; repealed in pt.: *ibid.*, sch. 8.
ss. 176, 177, 181, amended: *ibid.*, sch. 4.
s. 183, regs. 90/2612.
s. 183, amended: 1991, c. 40, sch. 4; repealed in pt.: *ibid.*, sch. 8.
s. 192, regs. 90/2612; 91/515.
s. 192, amended: 1991, c. 22, sch. 8; c. 40, sch. 4; repealed in pt.: *ibid.*, schs. 4, 8.
s. 193, repealed: *ibid.*, sch. 8.
s. 195, regs. 90/2612.
sch. 1, amended: 1991, c. 14, s. 2.
sch. 4, amended: 1991, c. 40, sch. 4; repealed: *ibid.*, sch. 8.

53. Road Traffic Offenders Act 1988.
ss. 1, 2, amended: 1991, c. 40, sch. 4.
s. 4, amended: 1991, c. 14, s. 3.
ss. 5, 7, 11, 12, 14, amended: 1991, c. 40, sch. 4.
s. 15, see *D.P.P.* v. *Elstrob, The Times,* November 20, 1991, D.C.; *MacDougall* v. *MacPhail*, 1991 S.L.T. 801.
s. 15, amended: 1991, c. 40, sch. 4.
s. 17, amended: *ibid.*; repealed in pt.: *ibid.*, schs. 4, 8.
s. 20, substituted: *ibid.*, s. 23.
s. 21, amended: *ibid.*, sch. 4.
s. 23, amended: *ibid.*, repealed in pt.: *ibid.*, schs. 4, 8.
s. 24, substituted: *ibid.*, s. 24.
s. 26, substituted: *ibid.*, s. 25.
s. 27, amended: *ibid.*, sch. 4; repealed in pt.: *ibid.*, schs. 4, 8.
s. 28, substituted: *ibid.*, s. 27.
s. 29, see *Keenan* v. *Carmichael*, 1991 S.C.C.R. 680.
s. 29, substituted: 1991, c. 40, s. 28.
s. 30, amended: *ibid.*, sch. 4; repealed in pt.: *ibid.*, schs. 4, 8.
ss. 31, 32, amended: *ibid.*, sch. 4.
s. 34, see *D.P.P.* v. *Corcoran* (1991) 155 J.P.N. 268, D.C.; *Lowe* v. *Mulligan* (Sh.Ct.), 1991 S.C.C.R. 561.
s. 34, amended: 1991, c. 40, s. 29.
ss. 34A–34C, added: *ibid.*, s. 30.
s. 35, see *Clumpas* v. *Ingram*, 1991 S.C.C.R. 223; *Marshall* v. *MacDougall*, 1991 S.C.C.R. 231; *McLaughan* v. *Docherty*, 1991 S.C.C.R. 227; *Keenan* v. *Carmichael*, 1991 S.C.C.R. 680.
s. 35, amended: 1991, c. 40, sch. 4.
s. 36, substituted: *ibid.*, s. 32.
s. 37, amended: *ibid.*, s. 33, sch. 4.
s. 41A, added: *ibid.*, sch. 4.

CAP.

1988—cont.

53. Road Traffic Offenders Act 1988—*cont.*
ss. 42, 45, amended: *ibid.*
s. 46, amended: 1991, c. 53, sch. 11; repealed in pt.: *ibid.*, schs. 11, 13.
s. 47, amended: 1991, c. 40, sch. 4.
ss. 48, 53, substituted: *ibid.*
s. 54, amended: *ibid.*; repealed in pt.: *ibid.*, sch. 8.
ss. 59 (in pt.), 60, repealed: *ibid.*
ss. 61, 69, amended: *ibid.*, sch. 4.
ss. 75–77, substituted: *ibid.*, s. 34.
ss. 86, 89, 90, 92, 93, 98, amended: *ibid.*, sch. 4.
sch. 1, amended: *ibid.*, s. 22, sch. 1; repealed in pt.: *ibid.*, schs. 1, 8.
sch. 2, see *Lowe* v. *Mulligan* (Sh.Ct.), 1991 S.C.C.R. 561.
sch. 2, amended: 1991, c. 14, s. 3; repealed in pt.: 1991, c. 22, sch. 9; c. 40, schs. 2, 8.
sch. 3, amended: *ibid.*, sch. 4; repealed in pt.: 1991, c. 22, sch. 9; c. 40, sch. 8.
sch. 5, amended: *ibid.*, sch. 4.

54. Road Traffic (Consequential Provisions) Act 1988.
s. 6, repealed: 1991, c. 40, sch. 8.
s. 8, amended: *ibid.*, sch. 4.
sch. 2, repealed in pt.: *ibid.*, s. 49, sch. 8.
schs. 3 (in pt.), 5, repealed: *ibid.*, sch. 8.

55. Consolidated Fund (No. 2) Act 1988.
repealed: 1991, c. 32, sch. (C).

1989

2. Consolidated Fund Act 1989.
repealed: 1991, c. 31, sch. (C).

3. Elected Authorities (Northern Ireland) Act 1989.
s. 6, sch. 2, amended: 1991, c. 24, sch. 7.

4. Prevention of Terrorism (Temporary Provisions) Act 1989.
continued in force (pt.), orders 91/549, 779.
ss. 10, 17, amended: 1991, c. 24, sch. 7.
s. 16, order 91/2649.
ss. 21–24, repealed: 1991, c. 24, sch. 8.
s. 27, orders 91/549, 779.
s. 27, amended: 1991, c. 24, sch. 7; repealed in pt.: *ibid.*, sch. 8.
s. 28, repealed: *ibid.*
sch. 3, amended: *ibid.*, sch. 7.
sch. 4, Act of Sederunt 91/1183.
sch. 4, amended: 1991, c. 24, sch. 7.
sch. 6, repealed in pt.: order 91/2649.
sch. 8, repealed in pt.: 1991, c. 24, sch. 8.

6. Official Secrets Act 1989.
sch. 1, repealed in pt.: 1991, c. 24, sch. 8.

CAP.

1989—cont.

10. Disabled Persons (Northern Ireland) Act 1989.
Commencement order: S.R. 1990 No. 456.
s. 12, S.R. 1990 No. 456.

14. Control of Pollution (Amendment) Act 1989.
Commencement order: 91/1618.
ss. 1–6, 8, 9, regs. 91/1624.
s. 11, order 91/1618.

15. Water Act 1989.
see *Sheffield City Council* v. *Yorkshire Water Services* [1991] 1 W.L.R. 58, Sir Nicolas Browne-Wilkinson, V.-C.; *National Rivers Authority* v. *Newcastle and Gateshead Water Co.; Sunderland and South Shields Water Co. Intervening, sub nom. Northumbria Water Authority* v. *Newcastle and Gateshead Water Co.* (1991) 31 R.V.R. 48, H.L.
ss. 1 (in pt.), 2, 3, 5 (in pt.), 6 (in pt.), 7, 10, 11 (in pt.), 12–68, repealed: 1991, c. 60, sch. 3.
ss. 52, 53, 56, 65, regs. 91/1837.
ss. 70 (in pt.), 71–82, 97–136, repealed: 1991, c. 60, sch. 3.
s. 104, regs. 91/1597.
s. 110, regs. 91/324.
s. 116, order 91/2285.
s. 132, amended: 1991, c. 22, sch. 8.
ss. 137 (in pt.), 138, 139 (in pt.), 140, 141 (in pt.), 142 (in pt.), 143–167, repealed: 1991, c. 60, sch. 3.
s. 162, orders 90/2318, 2567; 91/368, 1294.
ss. 170–172, repealed: 1991, c. 60, sch. 3.
s. 171, regs. 91/1597.
s. 174, amended: 1991, c. 60, sch. 1.
s. 176, repealed: *ibid.*, sch. 3.
s. 178, see *Dwr Cymru Cyfyngedig* v. *Williams, The Times*, October 9, 1991, D.C.
ss. 178–182, 184 (in pt.), repealed: 1991, c. 60, sch. 3.
s. 185, regs. 91/324, 1409, 1597, 1837.
s. 185 (in pt.), 186, 188, repealed: 1991, c. 60, sch. 3.
s. 189, amended: 1991, c. 22, sch. 8; repealed in pt.: *ibid.*, sch. 9; c. 60, sch. 3.
s. 192, repealed in pt.: *ibid.*
s. 194, order 91/1172.
sch. 1, amended: regs. 91/1997; repealed in pt.: 1991, c. 60, sch. 3.
schs. 3 (in pt.), 4 (in pt.), 5–7, 8 (in pt.), 9–16, 17 (in pt.), 18, repealed: *ibid.*
sch. 19, amended: 1991, c. 22, sch. 8; repealed in pt.: *ibid.*, sch. 9; repealed: 1991, c. 60, sch. 3.
sch. 20, regs. 91/1409.

CAP.

1989—cont.

15. Water Act 1989—*cont.*
schs. 20, 21, 24, repealed: 1991, c. 60, sch. 3.
sch. 25, repealed in pt.: 1991, c. 22, sch. 9; c. 45, sch. 8; c. 60, sch. 3.
sch. 26, amended: *ibid.*, sch. 1; repealed in pt.: *ibid.*, sch. 3.

18. Common Land (Rectification of Registers) Act 1989.
s. 1, see *White Row Cottages (1–4), Bewerley, Re* [1991] 3 W.L.R. 229, Mummery J.

22. Road Traffic (Driving Licences and Information Systems) Act 1989.
Commencement orders: 90/2228, 2610.
s. 1, regs. 90/2611.
s. 12, repealed in pt.: 1991, c. 22, sch. 9.
s. 17, orders 90/2228, 2610.
sch. 1, regs. 90/2611.
sch. 3, repealed in pt.: 1991, c. 40, sch. 8.
sch. 4, repealed in pt.: 1991, c. 22, sch. 9.

23. Transport (Scotland) Act 1989.
ss. 1, 2, see *Henjac 171* v. *Secretary of State for Scotland, The Times,* October 10, 1991.

24. Social Security Act 1989.
s. 8, repealed: 1991, c. 21, sch. 4.
s. 22, regs. 91/694, 1175.
s. 22, amended: 1991, c. 3, s. 1.
s. 30, regs. 91/1175.
s. 162, order 91/461.
sch. 2, amended: 1991, c. 21, sch. 2; repealed in pt.: *ibid.*, sch. 4.
schs. 3, 7, repealed in pt.: *ibid.*

25. Appropriation Act 1989.
repealed: 1991, c. 31, sch. (C.)

26. Finance Act 1989.
ss. 3, 14 (in pt.), 62 (in pt.), 63, repealed: 1991, c. 31, sch. 19.
ss. 84–86, amended: *ibid.*, sch. 7.
s. 87, repealed in pt.: *ibid.*, sch. 19.
s. 92, regs. 91/851.
s. 178, regs. 91/889, 1120, 1377, 1695, 2070.
s. 178, amended: 1991, c. 52, s. 14.
sch. 11, amended: 1991, c. 31, sch. 12.

29. Electricity Act 1989.
s. 39, regs. 91/1344.
s. 57, amended: 1991, c. 60, sch. 1.
s. 60, regs. 91/1344.
s. 74, order 91/1199.
s. 80, orders 91/852(S.), 853(S.).
s. 100, orders 90/2348; 91/88.
sch. 4, amended: 1991, c. 22, sch. 8; c. 60, sch. 1.; repealed in pt.: 1991, c. 22, sch. 9.
sch. 9, amended: 1991, c. 28, sch. 10.
sch. 11, amended: 1991, c. 31, s. 80.
sch. 16, repealed in pt.: 1991, c. 22, sch. 9; c. 60, sch. 3.

CAP.

1989—cont.

31. Human Organ Transplants Act 1989.
s. 3, regs. 91/408, 1645.

32. Fair Employment (Northern Ireland) Act 1989.
ss. 25, 26, S.R. 1990 No. 453.
ss. 27–29, 47, regs. 91/324.

33. Extradition Act 1989.
s. 4, orders 91/1699, 1701, 1702, 1720.
s. 5, order 91/1700.
s. 6, see *Osman, Re, The Independent,* May 30, 1991, D.C.
s. 8, see *Farinha, Re, The Times,* November 13, 1991, D.C.
ss. 10, 14, Act of Adjournal 91/19.
s. 20, amended; 1991, c. 53, sch. 11.
s. 22, orders 91/1699, 1701, 1702, 1720.
s. 30, order 91/1702.
s. 37, orders 91/997, 1699, 1701, 1702, 1720.
sch. 1, Act of Adjournal 91/19.

34. Law of Property (Miscellaneous Provisions) Act 1989.
s. 2, see *Record* v. *Bell, The Times,* December 21, 1990, Baker Q.C.

37. Football Spectators Act 1989.
Commencement order: 91/1071.
s. 27, order 91/1071.
sch. 1, amended: 1990, c. 19, s. 5.

40. Companies Act 1989.
Commencement orders: 90/2569; 91/488, 878, 1452, 1996, 2173.
ss. 35, 36, regs. 91/1566.
s. 50, regs. 91/1997.
s. 135, regs. 91/1646.
s. 152, amended: 1991, c. 60, sch. 1.
s. 155, regs. 91/880; amended: *ibid.*
s. 158, regs. 91/880.
s. 159, amended: *ibid.*
s. 160, regs. 91/880; amended: *ibid.*
s. 162, amended: *ibid.*
s. 173, regs. 91/880; amended: *ibid.*
s. 174, regs. 91/880.
s. 175, amended: *ibid.*
ss. 185–187, regs. 91/880.
s. 215, orders 90/2569; 91/488, 878, 1452, 1996, 2173.
sch. 21, amended: regs. 91/880.

41. Children Act 1989.
Commencement orders: 91/828, 1990.
see *R.* v. *Cornwall County Council, ex p. Cornwall and Isles of Scilly Guardians ad Litem and Reporting Officers' Panel, The Times,* November 20, 1991, Sir Stephen Brown, P.
s. 4, regs. 91/1478.
s. 15, amended: 1991, c. 17, sch. 2.
s. 17, amended: 1991, c. 21, sch. 3.
s. 23, regs. 91/890, 893, 910, 2033.
s. 24, regs. 91/894, 895.
s. 25, regs. 91/1505, 2034.
s. 26, regs. 91/894, 895, 2033.
s. 29, amended: 1991, c. 21, sch. 3.

1989—cont.

41. Children Act 1989—cont.
s. 31, see *C (A Minor), Re, The Times*, November 18, 1991, Sir Stephen Brown P.
s. 34, regs. 91/891.
s. 41, regs. 91/2051.
s. 51, regs. 91/1507.
s. 52, regs. 91/1414.
s. 59, regs. 91/890, 894, 895, 910, 2033.
s. 60, amended: 1991, c. 20, s. 2.
s. 62, regs. 91/910, 1506.
s. 63, regs. 91/1506.
s. 63, amended: 1991, c. 20, s. 2.
s. 67, regs. 91/2050.
s. 68, regs. 91/2033.
s. 71, regs. 91/2076, 2129.
s. 87, regs. 91/975.
s. 87, amended: 1991, c. 20, s. 2.
s. 90, amended: 1991, c. 53, sch. 11.
s. 92, order 91/1677.
s. 94, order 91/1801.
s. 96, order 91/1115.
s. 99, order 91/1924.
s. 101, regs. 91/2032.
s. 104, regs. 91/890, 893–895, 975, 1478, 1505–1507, 2033, 2050, 2051, 2076, 2129; orders 91/1115, 1924.
s. 105, amended: 1991, c. 20, s. 2.
s. 108, orders 91/828, 1881, 1990.
sch. 1, amended: 1991, c. 17, s. 6; c. 48, s. 58.
sch. 2, regs. 91/890, 892, 893, 910, 2033.
sch. 2, amended: 1991, c. 21, sch. 3.
sch. 4, regs. 91/890, 1505, 1506, 2033.
sch. 5, regs. 91/890, 1505, 1506, 2033, 2094.
sch. 6, regs. 91/890, 894, 1505, 1506, 2033.
sch. 7, regs. 91/894, 2033.
sch. 8, regs. 91/2050.
sch. 8, amended: 1991, c. 20, s. 2.
sch. 9, regs. 91/1689, 2076, 2094, 2129.
sch. 11, order 91/1677.
sch. 12, repealed in pt.: 1991, c. 53, sch. 13; c. 62, sch. 3.
sch. 13, repealed in pt.: 1991, c. 17, sch. 3; c. 53, sch. 13.
sch. 14, order 91/1924.
sch. 14, amended: 1991, c. 53, sch. 11; c. 62, sch. 3; order 91/828.

42. Local Government and Housing Act 1989.
Commencement orders: 91/344, 953.
s. 6, regs. 91/445.
s. 9, regs. 91/1398; order 91/2150.
s. 13, regs. 90/2476; 91/1398.
ss. 15, 17, regs. 91/1398.
s. 18, regs. 91/397(S.).
s. 31, order 90/2477.
s. 34, regs. 91/473.
s. 39, order 91/423; 91/548.
s. 40, regs. 91/500, 548.

1989—cont.

42. Local Government and Housing Act 1989—cont.
s. 43, regs. 91/548, 551.
s. 48, regs. 91/500.
s. 49, regs. 91/97, 548.
s. 58, regs. 91/500.
s. 59, regs. 91/500, 548.
s. 61, regs. 91/500.
s. 66, regs. 91/501, 548.
s. 80, see *R. v. Secretary of State for the Environment, ex p. Greenwich London Borough Council* (1990) 22 H.L.R. 543, D.C.
s. 102, regs. 91/80, 898, 1403.
s. 109, regs. 91/897.
s. 114, amended and repealed in pt.: order 91/1881.
s. 137, regs. 91/897, 898, 1403.
s. 138, regs. 91/80, 1403.
ss. 150, 152, regs. 91/982.
s. 172, regs. 90/2366; 91/1281.
s. 189, repealed: 1991, c. 53, sch. 13.
s. 190, regs. 90/2366, 2476; 91/80, 397(S.), 473, 501, 548, 551, 897, 1281, 1398, 1403.
s. 191, regs. 91/80, 1403.
s. 195, regs. 90/2581; orders 91/344, 953.
sch. 1, regs. 91/1398.
sch. 3, regs. 91/500, 548.

43. Statute Law (Repeals) Act 1989.
sch. 2, repealed in pt.: 1991, c. 66, sch. 2.

44. Opticians Act 1989.
s. 10, order 91/79.
s. 32, amended: regs. 91/1997.

45. Prisons (Scotland) Act 1989.
ss. 25, 43, see *Clayton, Petr.*, 1991 S.C.C.R. 261.
ss. 39, 42, see *Leech v. Secretary of State for Scotland* (O.H.), 1991 S.L.T. 910.

1990

1. Capital Allowances Act 1990.
s. 1, amended: 1991, c. 31, sch. 14.
s. 2, amended: *ibid.*; repealed in pt.: *ibid.*, schs. 14, 19.
s. 3, amended: *ibid.*, sch. 14; repealed in pt.: *ibid.*, sch. 19.
ss. 4, 8, amended: *ibid.*, sch. 14.
s. 17, amended: *ibid.*, sch. 15.
s. 18, amended: *ibid.*, s. 60; c. 60, sch. 1.
ss. 20, 21, amended: *ibid.*, s. 60.
s. 22, amended: 1991, c. 21, sch. 2; c. 31, sch. 14.
s. 24, amended: 1991, c. 31, sch. 14.
s. 26, amended: *ibid.*; repealed in pt.: *ibid.*, sch. 19.
s. 35, amended: *ibid.*, s. 61.
s. 36, amended: 1991, c. 21, sch. 2.

CAP.

1990—cont.

1. Capital Allowances Act 1990—*cont.*
ss. 37, 54, 75, 76, 137, 138, amended: 1991, c. 31, sch. 14.
ss. 140, 144, amended: *ibid.*, s. 60.
s. 153, order 91/518.
s. 159, amended: 1991, c. 31, sch. 14.
s. 159A, added: *ibid.*
sch. 1, repealed in pt.: *ibid.*, sch. 19.

5. Criminal Justice (International Co-operation) Act 1990.
Commencement orders: 91/1072, 2108.
see *Nazir Chinoy, Re* [1991] C.O.D. 105, D.C.
s. 3, order 91/1224.
ss. 7, 8, order 91/1297.
s. 9, orders 91/1463, 1464, 1468(S.).
s. 10, rules 91/1074, 1288, 1468(S.), S.R. 1991 No. 244.
s. 13, regs. 91/1285.
s. 29, order 91/1816.
s. 32, orders 91/1072, 2108.

6. Education (Student Loans) Act 1990.
s. 1, regs. 91/829, 1299.
sch. 2, regs. 91/1299.

8. Town and Country Planning Act 1990.
s. 5, amended: 1991, c. 34, sch. 7.
s. 12, amended: *ibid.*, sch. 4; repealed in pt.: *ibid.*, schs. 4, 19.
s. 12A, added: *ibid.*, sch. 4.
s. 13, substituted: *ibid.*
s. 14, amended: *ibid.*, repealed in pt.: *ibid.*, schs. 4, 19.
ss. 16–20, amended: *ibid.*, sch. 4.
s. 21, amended: *ibid.*; repealed in pt.: *ibid.*, schs. 4, 19.
s. 22, repealed in pt.: *ibid.*
s. 23, amended: *ibid.*, sch. 4; repealed in pt.: *ibid.*, schs. 4, 19.
ss. 26, 31, amended: *ibid.*, sch. 4.
ss. 32–41, substituted: *ibid.*
s. 36, see *Att.-Gen. (ex rel. Scotland)* v. *Barratt (Manchester), The Times,* July 11, 1991, C.A.
ss. 42–45, amended: 1991, c. 34, sch. 4.
ss. 46–48, substituted: *ibid.*
s. 49, repealed in pt.: *ibid.*, schs. 4, 19.
s. 50, amended: *ibid.*, sch. 4; repealed in pt.: *ibid.*, schs. 4, 19.
s. 51, repealed in pt.: *ibid.*
s. 51A, added: *ibid.*, sch. 4.
ss. 52, 53, amended: *ibid.*; repealed in pt.: *ibid.*, schs. 4, 19.
s. 54, amended: *ibid*, sch. 4.
s. 54A, added: *ibid.*, s. 26.
s. 55, order 91/1567.
s. 55, amended: 1991, c. 34, ss. 13, 14; repealed in pt.: *ibid.*, schs. 6, 19, Pts. I, II.
s. 56, see *Oakimber* v. *Elmbridge Borough Council* [1991] E.C.G.S. 33, C.A.

CAP.

1990—cont.

8. Town and Country Planning Act 1990—*cont.*
s. 56, amended: 1991, c. 34, schs. 6, 7.
ss. 59, 60, orders 90/2032; 91/1536, 2268.
s. 61, orders 91/1536, 2268.
ss. 63, 64, repealed: 1991, c. 34, schs. 7, 19.
ss. 65–68, substituted: *ibid.*, s. 16.
s. 69, repealed in pt.: *ibid.*, schs. 7, 19.
s. 70, amended: *ibid.*, sch. 7.
s. 70A, added: *ibid.*, s. 17.
s. 71, amended: *ibid.*, s. 16, sch. 7.
s. 71A, added: *ibid.*, s. 15.
s. 72, amended: *ibid.*, sch. 1.
s. 73A, added: *ibid.*, sch. 7.
s. 74, amended: *ibid..*, s. 19; repealed in pt.: *ibid.*, schs. 7, 19.
s. 77, amended: *ibid.*, sch. 7.
s. 78, see *Uttlesford District Council* v. *Secretary of State for the Environment* [1991] E.G.C.S. 29, D.C.
s. 78, amended: 1991, c. 34, s. 17.
s. 79, amended: *ibid.*, s. 18, sch. 7.
ss. 80, 81, repealed: *ibid.*, schs. 6, 19.
s. 90, amended: *ibid.*, sch. 6.
s. 91, amended: *ibid.*, schs. 1, 7.
s. 97, amended: *ibid.*, sch. 1; repealed in pt.: *ibid.*, sch. 19.
s. 100, amended: *ibid.*, sch. 1.
s. 102, amended: *ibid.*, schs. 1, 7.
s. 105, substituted: *ibid.*, sch. 1.
s. 106, substituted: *ibid.*, s. 12.
ss. 106A, 106B, added: *ibid.*
s. 107, amended: *ibid.*, schs. 1, 6.
s. 108, amended: *ibid.*, s. 13.
s. 109, amended: *ibid.*, sch. 6.
s. 111, amended: *ibid.*; repealed in pt.: *ibid.*, schs. 6, 19.
ss. 112 (in pt.), 113, repealed: *ibid.*
s. 114, repealed: *ibid.*, s. 31, sch. 19.
s. 116, substituted: *ibid.*, sch. 1.
s. 117, amended: *ibid.*
Pt. V (ss. 119–136), repealed: *ibid.*, s. 31, sch. 19.
ss. 138, 144, amended: *ibid.*, sch. 6.
ss. 150, 161, 162, amended: *ibid.*, sch. 15.
ss. 171A, 171B, added: *ibid.*, s. 4.
ss. 171C, 171D, added: *ibid.*, s. 1.
ss. 172, 173, substituted: *ibid.*, s. 5.
s. 173A, added: *ibid.*
s. 174, see *Uttlesford District Council* v. *Secretary of State for the Environment* [1991] E.G.C.S. 29, D.C.
s. 174, amended: 1991, c. 34, s. 5, repealed in pt.: *ibid.*, sch. 7.
s. 175, amended: *ibid.*, sch. 6.
ss. 175, 183, see *Doncaster Borough Council* v. *Green, The Times,* November 21, 1991, C.A.

1990—cont.

8. **Town and Country Planning Act 1990**—*cont.*

s. 176, repealed in pt.: 1991, c. 34, sch. 19.

s. 177, amended: *ibid.*, schs. 6, 7.

s. 178, amended: *ibid.*, s. 7; repealed in pt.: *ibid.*, schs. 7, 19.

s. 179, substituted: *ibid.*, s. 8.

s. 180, substituted: *ibid.*, sch. 7.

s. 181, amended: *ibid.*

s. 183, see *East Hampshire District Council* v. *Davies* [1991] 10 E.G. 149, C.A.

s. 183, amended: 1991, c. 34, s. 9.

s. 184, amended: *ibid.*, s. 9, sch. 7.

s. 186, amended: *ibid.*; repealed in pt.: *ibid.*, schs. 7, 19.

s. 187, amended: *ibid.*, s. 9.

s. 187A, added: *ibid.*, s. 2.

s. 187B, added: *ibid.*, s. 3.

s. 188, amended: *ibid.*, sch. 7; repealed in pt.: *ibid.*, schs. 7, 19.

s. 189, amended: *ibid.*, sch. 1.

s. 190, repealed in pt.: *ibid.*, schs. 7, 19.

ss. 191–194, substituted: *ibid.*, s. 10.

s. 195, amended: *ibid.*, sch. 7.

s. 196, amended: *ibid.*; repealed in pt.: *ibid.*, schs. 7, 19.

ss. 196A–196C, added: *ibid.*, s. 11.

s. 198, repealed in pt.: *ibid.*, schs. 6, 7, 19, Pts. I, II.

ss. 207–209, amended: *ibid.*, s. 23.

s. 210, amended: *ibid.*, repealed in pt.: *ibid.*, s. 23, sch. 19.

ss. 214A–214D, added: *ibid.*, s. 23.

s. 216, amended and repealed in pt.: *ibid.*, sch. 7.

s. 219, repealed in pt.: *ibid.*, schs. 7, 19.

s. 220, repealed in pt.: *ibid.*, schs. 6, 7, 19, Pts. I, II.

s. 221, repealed in pt.: *ibid.*, sch. 19.

s. 224, amended: *ibid.*, sch. 7.

s. 231, repealed in pt.: *ibid.*, schs. 15, 19.

s. 250, repealed in pt.: *ibid.*, schs. 7, 19.

s. 256, amended: 1991, c. 22, sch. 8.

ss. 262, 263, repealed in pt.: 1991, c. 34, schs. 6, 19.

s. 264, amended: 1991, c. 60, sch. 1.

s. 266, repealed in pt.: 1991, c. 34, schs. 6, 19.

s. 284, amended: *ibid.*, sch. 4; repealed in pt.: *ibid.*, schs. 4, 6, 7, 19, Pts. I, II.

s. 285, repealed in pt.: *ibid.*, schs. 7, 19.

s. 286, amended: *ibid.*, sch. 7; repealed in pt.: *ibid.*, schs. 7, 19.

s. 287, amended: *ibid.*, sch. 4; repealed in pt.: *ibid.*, schs. 4, 19.

s. 289, amended: *ibid.*, s. 6.

s. 290, repealed: *ibid.*, schs. 7, 19.

s. 296, amended: *ibid.*, s. 12, sch. 7.

1990—cont.

8. **Town and Country Planning Act 1990**—*cont.*

s. 298, amended: *ibid.*, sch. 6.

s. 299, amended: *ibid.*, sch. 7.

s. 299A, added: *ibid.*, s. 12.

s. 303, regs. 90/2473.

s. 303, amended: 1991, c. 34, s. 6.

s. 306, amended: *ibid.*, schs. 4, 7; repealed in pt.: *ibid.*, schs. 4, 19.

ss. 308 (in pt.), 309, 310 (in pt.), 311 (in pt.), 312, 313 (in pt.), repealed: *ibid.*, schs. 6, 19.

s. 315, amended: *ibid.*, sch. 1; repealed in pt.: *ibid.*, schs. 6, 19.

s. 316, substituted: *ibid.*, s. 20.

s. 316A, added: *ibid.*, sch. 7.

s. 318, amended: *ibid.*, schs. 6, 15.

s. 319, substituted: *ibid.*, sch. 7.

s. 322A, added: *ibid.*, s. 30.

s. 324, amended: *ibid.*, s. 23, sch. 4; repealed in pt.: *ibid.*, ss. 11, 23, schs. 6, 19, Pts. I, II.

s. 325, amended: *ibid.*, s. 23, sch. 7.

ss. 326, 327, repealed: *ibid.*, schs. 6, 19.

s. 328, amended: *ibid.*, sch. 6.

s. 329, amended and repealed in pt.: *ibid.*, sch. 7.

s. 333, orders 90/2032; 91/1536, 1567, 2268.

s. 336, amended: 1991, c. 34, s. 24, schs. 1, 4; repealed in pt.: *ibid.*, schs. 6, 19, Pts. I, II.

sch. 1, amended: *ibid.*, s. 19, schs. 1, 4, 7; repealed in pt.: *ibid.*, s. 19, schs. 1, 5, 6, 19, Pts. I, II.

sch. 2, amended: *ibid.*, sch. 4; repealed in pt.: *ibid.*, schs. 4, 19.

sch. 3, amended: *ibid.*, sch. 6; repealed in pt.: *ibid.*, schs. 6, 19.

sch. 5, amended: *ibid.*, sch. 1; repealed in pt.: *ibid.*, schs. 1, 19.

sch. 6, amended: *ibid.*, sch. 7; repealed in pt.: *ibid.*, schs. 7, 19.

sch. 7, amended: *ibid.*, sch. 5; repealed in pt.: *ibid.*, schs. 5, 19.

sch. 8, amended: *ibid.*, sch. 7.

sch. 9, amended: *ibid.*, sch. 1.

sch. 11, repealed: *ibid.*, schs. 1, 19.

sch. 12, repealed: *ibid.*, s. 31, sch. 19.

sch. 13, amended: *ibid.*, schs. 4, 7, 15; repealed in pt.: *ibid.*, schs. 4, 19.

sch. 16, amended: *ibid.*, schs. 6, 7; repealed in pt.: *ibid.*, schs. 6, 7, 19, Pts. I, II.

sch. 17, repealed in pt.: *ibid.*, sch. 19.

9. **Planning (Listed Buildings and Conservation Areas) Act 1990.**

s. 9, amended: 1991, c. 34, sch. 3; repealed in pt.: *ibid.*, schs. 3, 19.

s. 27, repealed in pt.: *ibid.*, s. 31, sch. 19.

s. 30, repealed in pt.: *ibid.*, schs. 6, 19.

CAP.

CAP.

1990—cont.

9. Planning (Listed Buildings and Conservation Areas) Act 1990—cont.
ss. 31, 32, amended: *ibid.*, sch. 6.
ss. 38, 39, amended: *ibid.*, sch. 3; repealed in pt.: *ibid.*, schs. 3, 19.
s. 41, amended: *ibid.*, sch. 3.
s. 42, amended: *ibid.*; repealed in pt.: *ibid.*, schs. 3, 19.
s. 43, substituted: *ibid.*, sch. 3.
s. 44A, added: *ibid.*
s. 46, amended: *ibid.*
s. 49, repealed in pt.: *ibid.*, schs. 6, 19.
s. 55, repealed in pt.: *ibid.*, schs. 3, 19.
s. 59, amended: *ibid.*, sch. 7.
s. 65, amended: *ibid.*, sch. 3.
ss. 67, 73, amended: *ibid.*, sch. 7.
s. 82, amended: *ibid.*, sch. 3.
s. 86, amended: *ibid.*, sch. 15.
s. 88, amended: *ibid.*, sch. 3; repealed in pt.: *ibid.*, schs. 3, 6, 19, Pts. I, II.
ss. 88A, 88B, added: *ibid.*, sch. 3.
s. 89, amended: *ibid.*, ss. 29, 30.
s. 90, amended: *ibid.*, sch. 6; repealed in pt.: *ibid.*, schs. 6, 19.
ss. 91, 92, repealed in pt.: *ibid.*
sch. 3, amended: *ibid.*, sch. 3.
sch. 4, amended: *ibid.*, schs. 3, 7.

10. Planning (Hazardous Substances) Act 1990.
ss. 23, 24, amended: 1991, c. 34, sch. 3.
s. 24A, added: *ibid.*
s. 25, amended: *ibid.*; repealed in pt.: *ibid.*, schs. 3, 19.
s. 26, amended: *ibid.*, sch. 3.
s. 26AA, added: *ibid.*
s. 31, amended: *ibid.*
s. 34, amended: *ibid.*, sch. 15.
s. 36, amended: *ibid.*; repealed in pt.: *ibid.*, schs. 3, 19.
ss. 36A, 36B, added: *ibid.*, sch. 3.
s. 37, amended: *ibid.*, s. 30.

11. Planning (Consequential Provisions) Act 1990.
Commencement order: 91/2698.
sch. 2, repealed in pt.: 1991, c. 34, sch. 19, Pts. I, II, III; c. 60, sch. 3.
sch. 3, see *Oakimber* v. *Elmbridge Borough Council* [1991] E.C.G.S. 33, C.A.
sch. 4, order 91/2698.
sch. 4, repealed in pt.: 1991, c. 34, schs. 4, 19.

16. Food Safety Act 1990.
Commencement order: 90/2372.
s. 4, regs. 90/2392(S.), 2463, 2487–2490, 2492–2495, 2505(S.)–2508(S.), 2615, 2625(S.); 91/289(S.), 984, 1231, 1284, 1476, 1593, 2825; orders 90/2372, 2462, 2486, 2487.
s. 5, order 90/2462.
s. 6, regs. 90/2488–2490, 2492, 2495, 2507(S.), 2615; 91/370, 984, 1284, 1593.

1990—cont.

16. Food Safety Act 1990—*cont.*
s. 16, regs. 90/2392(S.), 2488–2490, 2492, 2495, 2505(S.)–2508(S.), 2615.; 91/289(S.), 984, 1231, 1284, 1476, 1593, 2825.
s. 17, regs. 90/2495, 2505(S.), 2506(S.), 2508(S.), 2615; 91/289(S.), 1476.
s. 18, regs. 90/2490, 2492; 91/370, 1231.
s. 19, regs. 90/2490, 2492, 2507(S.), 2825.
s. 26, regs. 90/2488–2490, 2492, 2495, 2505(S.)–2508(S.), 2615; 91/370, 984, 1284, 1476, 1593, 2825.
s. 27, regs. 90/2463.
ss. 30, 31, regs. 90/2463.
s. 45, regs. 90/2490, 2494; 91/1593, 2825.
s. 48, regs. 90/2392(S.), 2488–2490, 2492–2495, 2505(S.)–2508(S.), 2615; 91/370, 984, 1284, 1343, 1476, 1593, 2825.
s. 49, regs. 90/2463, 2614; 91/100, 2825.
s. 55, amended: 1991, c. 60, sch. 1; repealed in pt.: *ibid.*, sch. 3.
s. 57, order 90/2486.
s. 59, orders 90/2486, 2487, 2625(S.).
s. 60, order 90/2372.
s. 68, order 91/393.
sch. 1, regs. 90/2490, 2492–2495, 2507; 91/289(S.), 1476, 1593.

19. National Health Service and Community Care Act 1990.
Commencement orders: 90/2510(S.), 2511; 91/388, 607.
s. 4, regs. 91/725.
s. 5, trusts 90/2401–2456; orders 91/109, 1327, 1594, 2316–2333, 2335–2418, 2697.
ss. 14–17, regs. 91/582.
s. 15, amended: *ibid.*
s. 18, regs. 91/556.
s. 23, regs. 90/2513.
s. 39, regs. 91/572.
s. 62, regs. 91/578.
s. 67, orders 90/2510(S.), 2511; 91/388, 552, 607.
sch. 1, regs. 91/329.
sch. 2, trusts 90/2401–2456; orders 91/109, 2316–2333, 2335–2418, 2697; regs. 91/482, 1347.

23. Access to Health Records Act 1990.
ss. 8, 10, regs. 91/2295(S.).

26. Gaming (Amendment) Act 1990.
Commencement order: 91/59.
s. 2, order 91/59.

27. Social Security Act 1990.
Commencement order: 91/558.
s. 1, repealed in pt.: 1991, c. 21, sch. 4.
s. 21, regs. 91/4.
s. 23, order 91/558.

29. Finance Act 1990.
s. 5, repealed in pt.: 1991, c. 31, sch. 19.
s. 11, regs. 91/371.
s. 11, amended: 1991, c. 31, s. 15.
s. 25, repealed: *ibid.*, s. 71, sch. 19.

1990—cont.

29. Finance Act 1990—*cont.*
s. 27, repealed in pt.: *ibid.*, sch. 19.
s. 46, amended: *ibid.*, sch. 7.
s. 61, repealed: *ibid.*, sch. 19.
s. 128, regs. 91/1318, 1948.
s. 131, regs. 91/371.
sch. 2, repealed in pt.: 1991, c. 31, sch. 19.
schs. 6, 7, repealed in pt. (prosp.): *ibid.*
sch. 8, amended: *ibid.*, sch. 7.
sch. 14, repealed in pt.: *ibid.*, sch. 19.

30. Government Trading Act 1990.
Commencement order: 91/132.
s. 4, order 91/132.

31. Aviation and Maritime Security Act 1990.
sch. 3, repealed in pt.: 1991, c. 24, sch. 8.

32. Representation of the People Act 1990.
Commencement orders: 91/1244, 1618, 1634, 1686.
s. 2, orders 91/1244, 1618, 1686.
s. 3, order 91/1634.

35. Enterprise and New Towns (Scotland) Act 1990.
s. 22, order 91/283.
s. 38, order 91/387.

36. Contracts (Applicable Law) Act 1990.
Commencement order: 91/707.
s. 7, order 91/707.

37. Human Fertilisation and Embryology Act 1990.
Commencement orders: 91/480, 1400.
ss. 9, 10, regs. 91/1889.
s. 14, regs. 91/1540.
s. 30, see *W. (Minors) (Surrogacy), Re* [1991] 1 F.L.R. 385, Baker J.
s. 43, regs. 91/1588.
s. 45, regs. 91/1540, 1588, 1889.
s. 49, orders 91/480, 1400, 1781.

38. Employment Act 1990.
Commencement orders: 90/2378; 91/89.
s. 1, see *R.* v. *Certification Officer for Trade Unions and Employers' Associations, ex p. Electrical Power Engineers' Association* [1990] I.R.L.R. 398, H.L.
s. 1, regs. 90/2379.
s. 7, see *Tanks and Drums* v. *Transport and General Workers' Union, The Times*, July 10, 1991, C.A.
s. 12, orders 91/999, 1264.
s. 18, orders 90/2378; 91/89.

40. Law Reform (Miscellaneous Provisions) (Scotland) Act 1990.
Commencement orders: 90/2624; 91/330, 822, 850, 1252, 1903, 2151.
s. 75, orders 90/2624; 91/330, 822, 850, 1252, 1903, 2151.
sch. 1, amended: regs. 91/1997.

1990—cont.

41. Courts and Legal Services Act 1990.
Commencement orders: 90/2484; 91/608, 985, 1364, 1883.
s. 1, order 91/724.
s. 10, amended: 1991, c. 17, sch. 2.
s. 22, order 90/2485.
s. 89, order 91/2831.
s. 124, orders 90/2484; 91/608, 985, 1364, 1883.
schs. 1, 5, amended: regs. 91/1997.
sch. 11, amended: 1991, c. 21, sch. 2.

42. Broadcasting Act 1990.
Commencement orders: 90/2347, 2566.
s. 16, order 91/1408.
s. 43, order 91/1820.
s. 66, order 91/881.
s. 72, orders 90/2389; 91/2188.
s. 79, order 91/2124.
s. 97, order 90/2536.
s. 127, order 90/2540.
s. 143, order 90/2566.
s. 174, orders 91/1709, 1710.
s. 200, orders 90/2347, 2536, 2579; 91/1176.
s. 204, orders 90/2347; 91/191–193, 998, 1709, 1710.
sch. 1, amended: regs. 91/1997.
sch. 2, order 91/1176.
schs. 3, 6, 8, amended: regs. 91/1997.
sch. 12, order 90/2388.
schs. 13, 19, amended: regs. 91/1997.
schs. 20, 22, repealed in pt.: 1991, c. 66, sch. 2.
sch. 22, order 90/2579.

43. Environmental Protection Act 1990.
Commencement orders: 90/2565, 2635; 91/96, 685, 1042, 1319, 1577.
s. 1, amended: 1991, c. 60, sch. 1.
s. 2, regs. 91/472, 836.
s. 7, amended: 1991, c. 60, sch. 1.
s. 10, regs. 91/507.
s. 11, regs. 91/507, 836.
ss. 15, 20, regs. 91/507.
s. 20, amended: 1991, c. 60, sch. 1.
s. 22, regs. 91/507.
s. 28, amended: 1991, c. 60, sch. 1.
ss. 36, 54, amended: 1991, c. 28, sch. 2.
s. 86, orders 91/337, 476, 561, 961, 1043.
s. 88, order 91/111.
s. 89, amended: 1991, c. 26, s. 2.
s. 90, order 91/1325.
s. 94, order 91/1324.
s. 97, regs. 91/719.
s. 128, amended: 1991, c. 28, sch. 2; repealed in pt.: *ibid.*, sch. 11.
ss. 130, 131, order 91/685.
s. 132, amended: 1991, c. 28, sch. 2.
s. 138, order 91/2923.
s. 140, order 91/1487.
s. 145, repealed in pt.: 1991, c. 60, sch. 3.
s. 152, regs. 91/1399, 1590.
s. 153, orders 91/146(S.), 682, 1179.
s. 153, amended: order 91/682.

CAP.

1990—cont.

43. Environmental Protection Act 1990—cont.
s. 164, orders 90/2565, 2635; 91/96, 685, 1042, 1319, 1577.
sch. 1, regs. 91/507, 836; order 91/513.
sch. 3, regs. 90/2483.
sch. 6, repealed in pt.: 1991, c. 28, sch. 11.
sch. 8, repealed in pt.: 1991, c. 22, sch. 9; c. 60, sch. 3.
sch. 9, repealed in pt.: 1991, c. 28, sch. 11; c. 54, sch. 4; c. 60, sch. 3.
sch. 12, regs. 91/1488.
sch. 15, repealed in pt.: 1991, c. 26, sch. 2; c. 60, sch. 3.

1991

1. Development Board for Rural Wales Act 1991.
Royal Assent, February 12, 1991.
2. Caravans (Standard Community Charge and Rating) Act 1991.
Royal Assent, February 12, 1991.
s. 1, regs. 91/471.
3. Statutory Sick Pay Act 1991.
Royal Assent, February 12, 1991.
Commencement order: 91/260.
s. 2, regs. 91/428.
s. 3, regs. 91/694.
s. 4, order 91/260.
4. Namibia Act 1991.
Royal Assent, February 28, 1991.
s. 5, order 91/772.
5. Ministerial and other Pensions and Salaries Act 1991.
Royal Assent, February 28, 1991.
s. 5, order 91/772.
6. Census (Confidentiality) Act 1991.
Royal Assent, March 7, 1991.
7. Consolidated Fund Act 1991.
Royal Assent, March 21, 1991.
8. Community Charges (Substitute Setting) Act 1991.
Royal Assent, March 21, 1991.
9. Community Charges (General Reduction) Act 1991.
Royal Assent, March 28, 1991.
s. 1, regs. 91/842, 877.
s. 3, regs. 91/856.
10. Consolidated Fund (No. 2) Act 1991.
Royal Assent, May 9, 1991.
11. Representation of the People Act 1991.
Royal Assent, May 9, 1991.
Commencement order: 91/1634.
s. 3, order 91/1634.
12. Civil Jurisdiction and Judgments Act 1991.
Royal Assent, May 9, 1991.
13. War Crimes Act 1991.
Royal Assent, May 9, 1991.
14. Motor Vehicles (Safety Equipment for Children) Act 1991.
Royal Assent, June 27, 1991.

CAP.

1991—cont.

15. Local Government Finance (Publicity for Auditors' Reports) Act 1991.
Royal Assent, June 27, 1991.
16. Oversea Superannuation Act 1991.
Royal Assent, June 27, 1991.
17. Maintenance Enforcement Act 1991.
Royal Assent, June 27, 1991.
Commencement order: 91/2042.
s. 12, order 91/2042.
18. Crofter Forestry (Scotland) Act 1991.
Royal Assent, June 27, 1991.
19. Football (Offences) Act 1991.
Royal Assent, June 27, 1991.
Commencement order: 91/1564.
s. 1, order 91/1565.
s. 6, order 91/1564.
20. Registered Homes (Amendment) Act 1991.
Royal Assent, June 27, 1991.
21. Disability Living Allowance and Disability Working Allowance Act 1991.
Royal Assent, June 27, 1991.
Commencement orders: 91/1519, 2617.
s. 3, regs. 91/1746.
s. 5, regs. 91/2890, 2891.
s. 11, regs. 91/2891.
s. 15, orders 91/1519, 2617.
22. New Roads and Street Works Act 1991.
Royal Assent, June 27, 1991.
Commencement orders: 91/2286(S.), 2288.
s. 64, amended: 1991, c. 40, sch. 7.
s. 89, amended: 1991, c. 60, sch. 1.
s. 170, orders 91/2286(S.), 2288.
sch. 4, amended: 1991, c. 60, sch. 1.
sch. 8, repealed in pt.: 1991, c. 26, sch. 2.
23. Children and Young Persons (Protection from Tobacco) Act 1991.
Royal Assent, June 27, 1991.
Commencement order: 91/2500 (N.I.)
s. 8, order 91/2500.
24. Northern Ireland (Emergency Provisions) Act 1991.
Royal Assent, June 27, 1991.
25. Criminal Procedure (Insanity and Unfitness to Plead) Act 1991.
Royal Assent, June 27, 1991.
Commencement order: 91/2488.
s. 9, order 91/2488.
26. Road Traffic (Temporary Restrictions) Act 1991.
Royal Assent, June 27, 1991.
27. Radioactive Material (Road Transport) Act 1991.
Royal Assent, June 27, 1991.
28. Natural Heritage (Scotland) Act 1991.
Royal Assent, June 27, 1991.
sch. 7, amended: 1991, c. 22, sch. 8.
29. Property Misdescriptions Act 1991.
Royal Assent, June 27, 1991.
30. Welfare of Animals at Slaughter Act 1991.
Royal Assent, June 27, 1991.

1991—cont.

67. Export and Investment Guarantees Act 1991.
Royal Assent, October 22, 1991.
Commencement order: 91/2430.
s. 15, order 91/2430.

1991—cont.

68. Consolidated Fund (No. 3) Act 1991.
Royal Assent, December 19, 1991.
69. Welsh Development Agency Act 1991.
Royal Assent, December 19, 1991.

INDEX

This is the third part of the Current Law Statutes Index 1991 and is up to date to December 31, 1991. References, e.g. 3/1 are to the Statutes of 1991, Chapter 3, section 1

[1]

INDEX

INDEX

INDEX

INDEX

[8]

INDEX

INDEX

INDEX